THE KALEIDOSCOPE BRITISH CHRISTMAS TELEVISION GUIDE 1937-2013

EDITED BY
CHRIS PERRY
SIMON COWARD & RICHARD DOWN

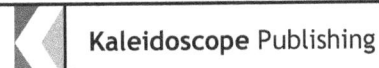

ISBN 978-1-900203-60-9

The Kaleidoscope British Christmas Television Guide 1937-2013

Edited by Chris Perry, Simon Coward and Richard Down

Copyright © 2013, 2014 Kaleidoscope Publishing

This publication is a revised and much expanded version of

A Kaleidoscope Christmas

Edited by Chris Perry

Copyright © 2013 Kaleidoscope Publishing

Original Kaleidoscope Publishing logo design by Clayton Hickman

Guide section generated by the Kaleidoscope Database, designed by Simon Coward

All Rights Reserved. No part of this publication may be reproduced, stored in a retrieval system or transmitted in any form or by any means: electronic, electrostatic, magnetic tape, magnetic disk, mechanical, photocopying, recording or otherwise without permission in writing from the copyright holders.

Kaleidoscope Publishing
42 Victoriana Way
Handsworth Wood
B20 2SZ
United Kingdom

www.kaleidoscopepublishing.co.uk
contact@kaleidoscopepublishing.co.uk

For Arlene and my son, Tristan,
who share Christmas with me

THE KALEIDOSCOPE BRITISH CHRISTMAS TELEVISION GUIDE FORMAT

The layout of the listings may seem a little daunting at first, but trying to pack this much information into a book does necessitate some compromises over instant readability. Each listing is split into up to four levels of information, though nearly all use three or fewer. The first of these levels reflects the information that relates to the programme as a whole. Now this "programme" might be a one-off special, a single six-part series, or a long-running programme with several hundred editions. Details which remain constant throughout the whole of the programme's run will be listed here. In most cases this means that the companies which commissioned and made the programme will be listed here, as would any writer, director or producer who fulfilled that role throughout. The duration, in minutes, will be generally found here too, as will the name of the company whose broadcast dates are used in the episode section. Here's a fictitious sample entry:

PACK MY BOX WITH FIVE DOZEN CHRISTMAS LIQUOR JUGS
Produced by BBC Birmingham for BBC1. Transmission details are for BBC1. Duration: 50 minutes.
Main regular credit(s):   Music by Carry Goffin; executive producer Gerald Roy.
Main regular cast: Carlton Simon (Quiz-Master); Jesamine Taylor (Hostess).

Where a programme is split into more than one series, the next entry will be for the first series. This may be no more than a simple entry saying just "SERIES 1", but it can contain the same types of information as found at programme level. For example:

SERIES 1
Main regular credit(s):   Produced by Di Vengram.

In this case, no single producer worked throughout the various series of **Pack My Box with Five Dozen Christmas Liquor Jugs** but Di Vengram fulfilled this role on the first series, so she gets credited here. Someone else will no doubt be credited for the second and third series. We'll come back to the third level in a moment, but in most cases, the next set of entries will be the episodes. Here's another fictional sample:

	Production No	VT Number	Holding / Source Format
24.12.1967	K22/456	T1029	R1N|n / 40

Programme associate Hedley McIlroy; directed by T. S. Wilson.
Gerry Knox, Frank Allaway.

23.12.1968 **Celebrity Special**			J / Live

Carlton Simon quizzes a group of celebrities in the special festive edition.
Programme associate Walter Hobday; directed by T. S. Wilson.
Winnie Wise, Stephen Harland, Audrey Godwin, Old Bill White*.

—.—.——	K22/459	T1033	R1 / 40

Alternative transmissions: BBC 2: 30.12.1968
Programme associate Hedley McIlroy; directed by Brian Hobday.
Fred Dunn, Doreen Rogers.

Each entry has a similar pattern. It starts with a transmission date and is followed by the episode title. Where a programme doesn't use episode titles, there will sometimes be a short description in its place and these will always be put in "speech marks" like this. Where the information is available, a production number and/or video tape recording number will be included. Finally, we list the current archive holding status of the episode and the original transmission format where we know it. See the end of the book for a list of archive and transmission format codes and other formatting symbols.

Lastly, the credits and cast for the particular episode are shown, excluding any regulars who have already been listed at programme or series level. Where a performer appears in multiple episodes in a particular named role, that role will be noted, otherwise just the name of the performer is listed. Sometimes, for quite long-running series, only those performers appearing most frequently will have their role recorded. If a performer appears in almost every episode of a long running series, he or she will sometimes be credited at programme level as though in every episode and the episodes they did not appear in will carry a note "So-and-so did not appear in this edition". Lastly, you may see some cast or credit information highlighted with an asterisk as in Old Bill White's credit in the second edition listed above. This shows that the apperance in question was uncredited and, while we believe the information to be correct, in many cases this is based upon unpublished information and so may not be separately verifiable.

The third level, between series and episode, can have more than one meaning. In most cases it's used where a dramatic programme or series is broken down into a number of shorter stories – *Doctor Who* is a good example of this – and where each story might have common cast or credits.

Each section may be complemented by a synopsis which, if present, will appear towards the top of the section and/or some brief (or in some cases, not so brief) notes, which follow the entry.

A list of the codes used in the Holding / Source Format column may be found at the end of the book.

OTHER CONVENTIONS USED

All dates are shown in standard UK format: day, then month, then year – e.g. 7th June 2005 is shown as 07.06.05 or 07.06.2005.

Where a transmission date is shown as —.—.—— then no transmission has been found for the particular standard channel or BBC region whose dates form the main listing for the programme. There are, however, alternative transmission details, for another channel or region – and these will be shown below.

Where a transmission date is shown as ##.##.#### then in most cases, the programme in question was either not made or was made but is known to have never been transmitted. In a few cases, the programme may have been shown but we will have been unable to trace a tx date. Usually, where this is unclear, an explanatory note will accompany the entry.

Sometimes while reading this Guide, under the actual entry for a series or play you might find an unusual note:

07/05/62 - PANORAMA (LCA6861D) - front: great big chunk of end of "This Is Your Life: Ellaline Terris"; 'UK' logo with announcement 'This is BBC Television' (as above). End: 'Circle' logo, no narration; in-vision announcer, start of verbal trail for play in the series "Suspense" after the news - recording speeds up; obscured bit of News presented by Michael Aspel, snatch of sound at start.

This footnote refers to a piece of continuity film held by the BBC archives on R1, R3 or D3 (for later post-1969 sequences.) It was standard practice in the earlier days of television for telerecordings to start early before the actual intended programme started, or finish late to ensure the whole show was kept. Many of these examples of trailers, BBC globes and in-vision announcers that survive, are kept on the starts or ends of programmes shown live.

To read the extract above: 07/05/62 - PANORAMA (LCA6861D) The date is the date that the trailer/continuity was recorded, the title in capital letters is the live show on the film reel and the number in brackets is the BBC accession number to find the sequence. What follows is then a shot by shot description of the actual footage. Most of these continuity trails are not formally catalogued on the BBC's system, and are included in this guide to help researchers examining programmes that suffered timeslot changes or other unforeseen circumstances not reflected in the Radio Times. It also shows that many clips exist from shows officially catalogued as wiped, which may help future broadcasters looking for the early work of Michael Caine or the first ever title sequence to Top of The Pops (which only survives in this format).

10 MINUTE TALES

Alternative/Working Title(s): 12 DAYS OF CHRISTMAS
An Endor production for Sky One. Transmission details are for Sky One. Duration: 9 minutes.
Script editor Tom Nash; executive producers Elaine Pyke, Huw Kennair-Jones and Ann Harrison-Baxter; line producer Rachel Salter.

	Holding / Source
21.12.2009 **Deep And Crisp And Even**	HD/DB / HDC

Written by Maggie Souter and Peter Souter; script supervisor Leigh Nicol; music by Peter Raeburn; director of photography Mark Patten; titles by Alice Tonge; art director Andrea Coathupe; designed by Candida Otton; production manager Nicky Earnshaw; produced by Hilary Bevan Jones and Timothy Bricknell; directed by Brett Foraker.

With Timothy Spall, Natascha McElhone, Amanda Lawrence, Henry Castle, Bradley Ford.

22.12.2009 The Walkers — HD/DB / HDC

Written by Lucy Gannon; script supervisor Julia Chiavetta; music by Mike Smith; director of photography Tony Miller; art director Matthew King; designed by Sarah Hauldren; production manager Nicky Earnshaw; produced by Hilary Bevan Jones and Tim Whitby; directed by Tim Whitby.

With Stephen Mangan (Tom), Liza Tarbuck (Katy), Celia Cruwys-Finnigan (Mo), Jack Whitby (George).

23.12.2009 Ding Dong — HD/DB / HDC

Written by Dawn Shadforth; script supervisor Leigh Nicol; music by Joby Talbot; director of photography Tat Radcliffe; titles by Alice Tonge; assistant director Richard Styles; designed by Nick Ellis; production manager Nicky Earnshaw; produced by Timothy Bricknell and Hilary Bevan Jones; directed by Dawn Shadforth.

With Mackenzie Crook (Joe), Lyndsey Marshal (Gemma), Karen Bryson (Second Midwife), Julia Davis (Overbearing Midwife), Dustin Demri Burns (Clumsy Medic), Kevin Harvey (Policeman), Mickey Morris (Small Boy), Lucian Msamati (Flirty Orderly), Daniel Tuite (Patient in Bed), Gemma Whelan (Pretty Nurse), Woody The Dog (Himself).

24.12.2009 Let It Snow — HD/DB / HDC

Written by Roy Williams; script supervisor Leigh Nicol; music by Samuel Sim; director of photography Ulf Brantås; assistant director Sacha Bowling; art director Hauke Richter; designed by Stevie Herbert; produced by Timothy Bricknell and Hilary Bevan Jones; directed by Sam Miller.

With Angela Griffin (Clare), Paterson Joseph (Paul), Ella Thompson (Faye), Kershaney Samuels (Young Paul), Maya Charley (Young Clare), Olivette Cole-Wilson (Mother), Simon Anthony Rhoden (Brother).

25.12.2009 Statuesque — HD/DB / HDC

Written by Neil Gaiman; script supervisor Julia Chiavetta; music by Sxip Shirey; director of photography Henry Braham; assistant director Peter Stenning; art director Andrea Coathupe; designed by Candida Otton; production manager Nicky Earnshaw; produced by Hilary Bevan Jones; directed by Neil Gaiman.

With Bill Nighy (Mr Jellaby), Amanda Palmer (Yvette), Emilie Bera (Galatea), Duncan Meadows (Barbarian), Damilola Odusote (Hip Hop Spaceman), Becca Rosenthal (Airman).

26.12.2009 Dog Alone — HD/DB / HDC

Written by Guy Hibbert; script supervisor Ruth Atkinson; music by Howard Goodall; director of photography Philipp Blaubach; assistant director Peter Stenning; designed by Donal Woods; production manager Nicky Earnshaw; produced by Dan McCulloch and Hilary Bevan Jones; directed by Lia Williams.

With Hunter the Dog (Himself), Milly the Dove (Herself), Lalor Roddy (Man for Life).

27.12.2009 The Three Kings — HD/DB / HDC

Written by William Boyd; script supervisor Karen Jones; music by Stephen Warbeck; director of photography Ben Smithard; assistant director Martin Harrison; art director Mark Kebby; designed by Donal Woods; production manager Nicky Earnshaw; produced by Hilary Bevan Jones; directed by Richard Eyre.

With Chuk Iwuji (Soldier 1), Daniel Kaluuya (Soldier 2), Andrew Simpson (Soldier 3), Riz Ahmed (Joseph), Michael Karim (Shepherd Boy), Sebastian Sharma (Baby), Elisa Terren (Mary).

28.12.2009 Through The Window — HD/DB / HDC

Written by Barry Skolnick; script supervisor Leigh Nicol; music by Jennie Muskett; director of photography Ulf Brantås; assistant director Anthony Wilcox; art director Andrea Coathupe; designed by Candida Otton; production manager Nicky Earnshaw; produced by Hilary Bevan Jones; directed by Barry Skolnick.

With Claire Foy (Woman), Lee Ingleby (Man), Sinead Michael (Child), Lauren Kelly (Toddler), Savannah Perkins (Baby).

29.12.2009 Syncing — HD/DB / HDC

Written by Tony Grisoni; script supervisor Sylvia Parker; music by James Bradell; director of photography Florian Hoffmeister; assistant director Anthony Wilcox; art director Nick Dent; designed by Cristina Casali; production manager Nicky Earnshaw; produced by Dan McCulloch and Hilary Bevan Jones; directed by Tony Grisoni.

With Peter Capaldi (The Man), Neve McIntosh (The Woman), Lucy Russell (Chicken Team Leader), Pip Carter (Doctor), Isabella Laughland (Hotel Check Out Girl), Olive Supple-Still (Girl on the Beach), Auriol Britton (Singer).

30.12.2009 Perfect Day — HD/DB / HDC

Written by Helen Greaves; script supervisor Ruth Atkinson; music by Nicholas Hooper; edited by Ian Davies; director of photography David Katznelson; assistant director Peter Stenning; art director Andrea Coathupe; production designer Candida Otton; production manager Nicky Earnshaw; produced by Helen Greaves and Hilary Bevan Jones; directed by Jeremy Brock.

With Katie Jarvis (Girl), Merveille Lukeba (Boy), Carter Gates (Baby), Charlotte Sinclaire (Baby), Alfie Cowie (Baby).

31.12.2009 The Running Of The Deer — HD/DB / HDC

Written by Lucy Gannon; script supervisor Julia Chiavetta; music by Mike Smith; edited by Trevor Waite; director of photography Tony Miller; assistant director Matt Carver; art director Lucy Spofforth; production designer Candida Otton; production manager Nicky Earnshaw; produced by Hilary Bevan Jones; directed by Tim Whitby.

With Ross Kemp (Liam), Sam Parham (Jono), Elizabeth McGovern (Ex Wife), Julian Wadham (New Boyfriend).

Pre-publicity mentioned a 12th edition written by Jez Butterworth and directed by Ian Rickson, but Kaleidoscope has no further details. Broadcast magazine says that 12 were commissioned.

10 SHARP

An LWT production. Transmission details are for the London Weekend Television region. Duration: 10 minutes.
Pat Sharp (Presenter).

SERIES 1

	Holding / Source
21.12.1997 **Christmas Special**	D2 / D2S

With New Kids On The Block, Jason Donovan, Dannii Minogue, Tony Blackburn, Timmy Mallett, Windsor Davies, June Brown, Ted Rogers.

1001 NIGHTS OF TELEVISION

An Illuminations production for Channel 4. Transmission details are for Channel 4. Duration: 180 minutes.

Main regular credit(s): Written by Dick Fiddy and Richard Curson-Smith; research Tony Mechele; music by Steve Beresford; art directors Michael Carter and Tanya Cochrane; associate producer Richard Curson-Smith; production manager Christine Keats; produced by John Wyver and Linda Zuck; directed by Steve Connelly.

Main regular performer(s): Alison Steadman (Presenter), Michael Palin (Presenter), Patrick Barlow (Presenter), Adam Faith (Presenter), Rory Bremner (Presenter), Gary Lineker (Presenter), Bobby Charlton (Presenter), John Hegley (Presenter), Alan Bennett (Presenter), Andy Kershaw (Presenter), Vic Reeves (Presenter), Biddy Baxter (Presenter), Ruby Wax (Presenter).

	Holding / Source
01.01.1991	B / 1"
##.##.#### **Rushes**	B / 1"

Held by Kaleidoscope.

THE 11 O'CLOCK SHOW

Alternative/Working Title(s): THE NEWS ALTERNATIVE
A Talkback production for Channel 4. Transmission details are for Channel 4.

SERIES 3

	Holding / Source
22.12.1999 **Christmas Special**	DB / DBS

Duration: 60 minutes.

2 POINT 4 CHILDREN

A BBC production for BBC 1. Transmission details are for BBC 1. Usual duration: 30 minutes.
Main regular credit(s): Written by Andrew Marshall; theme music by Howard Goodall.
Main regular cast: Gary Olsen (Ben Porter), Belinda Lang (Bill Porter), Julia Hills (Rona Harris), John Pickard (David Porter).

SERIES 2
Main regular credit(s): Production manager Nick Bye; produced and directed by Richard Boden.
Main regular cast: With Clare Woodgate (Jenny Porter).

	Holding / Source
22.12.1992 **Misery**	DB / D3S

The Porters agree reluctantly to spend Christmas with Bill's mother Bette.
Designed by David Buckingham and Richard Hogan.
With Liz Smith (Bette), Kim Benson (Christine).
The role of the genie was uncredited on-screen.

SERIES 3
Main regular credit(s): Designed by Gwen Evans; production manager Murray Peterson; produced and directed by Richard Boden.
Main regular cast: With Clare Buckfield (Jenny Porter).

	Holding / Source
20.12.1993 **Babes In The Wood**	DB / D3S

Lyrics by Al Stillman; music by Robert Allen.
With Liz Smith (Bette), Barbara Lott (Auntie Pearl), Kim Benson (Christine).

SERIES 4
Main regular credit(s): Produced and directed by Richard Boden.
Main regular cast: With Clare Buckfield (Jenny Porter).

	Holding / Source
26.12.1994 **Relax-Ay-Voo**	DB / D3S

Duration: 35 minutes.
Ben wants to go to France for the Christmas holiday, but after last year's mishaps, Bill is determined to stay at home, where nothing disastrous can happen.
Choreography by Nicky Hinkley; designed by Gwen Evans and Steve Wright; production managers Murray Peterson and Sharon Bradley.
With Liz Smith (Bette), Barbara Lott (Pearl), Kim Benson (Christine), Michael Zimmerman (US Marine), Jamie Leyser (Carol Singer).

SERIES 5

Main regular credit(s): Produced and directed by Richard Boden.
Main regular cast: With Clare Buckfield (Jenny Porter).

	Holding / Source
24.12.1995 **Porky's**	DB / D3S

With Kim Benson (Christine), Annette Kerr.

SERIES 6

Main regular credit(s): Produced by Andrew Marshall; directed by Nick Wood.
Main regular cast: With Clare Buckfield (Jenny Porter).

	Holding / Source
26.12.1996 **2.4 Christmas - Two Years Before The Mast**	DB / D3S

Duration: 40 minutes.
With Liz Smith (Bette), Barbara Lott (Pearl), Sandra Dickinson.

2009 UNWRAPPED WITH MIRANDA HART

A BBC Productions production for BBC 2. Transmission details are for BBC 2. Duration: 60 minutes.

Written by Mark Doherty, Simon Evans, Jason Hazeley, Jon Holmes, Joel Morris and Barry Murphy; additional material by Adam Buxton, Cassetteboy, Jonathan Harvey, Rx and Henry White; directors of photography Peter Edwards and Jeremy Hewson; art director Laura Marsh; designed by Simon Rogers; assistant producers Jackie Ramsamy and Newton Velji; production executive Eirwen Davies; executive producer Jack Cheshire; production manager Andy Bennions; produced and directed by Alex Walsh-Taylor.

Miranda Hart (Presenter), Chizzy Akudolu, Stephen K. Amos, Duncan Ballantyne, Ed Byrne, Adam Buxton, Sally Chattaway, Annette Crosbie, Simon Evans, Rich Fulcher, Jon Glover, Richard Glover, Richard Katz, James Holmes, Jon Holmes, Joan Linder, Harmonie London, Geoff McGivern, Barry Murphy, John O'Farrell, Jack Shalloo, Sally Phillips, Isy Suttie, Tony Way.

	Holding / Source
30.12.2009	DB / DBSWF

2010 UNWRAPPED WITH MIRANDA HART

A BBC Productions production for BBC 2. Transmission details are for BBC 2. Duration: 60 minutes.

Written by Carl Carter, Simon Evans, Bob Fletcher, Jason Hazeley, Jon Holmes, Joel Morris, Barry Murphy and Guy Venables; research David Sutheran; directors of photography Peter Edwards and Robin Fox; art director Lucy Gardetto; designed by Laura Marsh; assistant producers Eamonn Bownes and Newton Velji; production executive Eirwen Davies; executive producer Jack Cheshire; production manager Andy Bennions; produced and directed by Alex Walsh-Taylor.

Miranda Hart (Presenter), Jon Glover (Voice Over), Stuart Hall (Voice Over), Maggie Service (Voice Over), William Ely, Peter Barnes, Ben Bishop, John Fricker, Rich Fulcher, Jon Holmes, Miles Jupp, Shappi Khorsandi, Jason Lewis, Jonathan Linsley, Ray Macallan, Chris McCausland, Barry Murphy, Chris Packham, Vicki Pepperdine, Tim Preece, Isy Suttie, Kate Terence, John Voce, Claire Vousden, Joe Wilkinson, Francis Wheen.

	Holding / Source
28.12.2010	DB / DBSWF

2012: A FUNNY OLD YEAR

An ITV Studios production for ITV 1. Transmission details are for the Central region. Duration: 48 minutes.

Jason Manford is joined by a starry line-up of comedians to reflect on the stories that made the headlines over the year. We rejoiced in the Diamond Jubilee and thrilled to the Olympics and Paralympics, but will this year ultimately be remembered for unleashing the Gangnam Style dance craze?

Produced by Katharine Begg; directed by Toby Baker.

Jason Manford (Host)

	Holding / Source
31.12.2012	HD/DB / HDC

2013: A FUNNY OLD YEAR

Commissioned by ITV 1. Transmission details are for the Central region. Duration: 48 minutes.

A comedic celebration of the highs and lows of the past 12 months. The Mancunian funnyman offers his personal slant on the most memorable TV and sporting moments, as well as the gaffes, feuds and trends that made 2013 unforgettable.

Executive producer Nicholas Steinberg; produced by Chris Curley.

Jason Manford (Host).

	Holding / Source
31.12.2013	HD/DB / HDC

---

21 YEARS

A Southern Television production. Transmission details are for the Southern Television region. Duration varies - see below for details.

Main regular credit(s): Research James Montgomery and Alan Griffiths; executive producer Derek Heasman; produced and directed by Paul Smith.

	Holding / Source
28.12.1979 **Fact... And Fiction**	DB / 2"

Duration: 50 minutes.
Postponed from 30.08.1979.

28.12.1979 **Music, Music, Music**	DB / 2"

Duration: 50 minutes.
Postponed from 30.08.1979.

21 YEARS (continued)

It was to have been shown on 30/08/1979, which was actually the 21st birthday and was to have been called "21 Today" but the ITV strike of 1979 stopped that. So it was re-scheduled for Christmas week under the title "21 Years".

Held at the Wessex Archive. Wessex dubbed the two shows from the 2 inch masters. An engineer had an off air VHS from when they went out so he included the off air announcer intro etc from this VHS on the back end of the Digis. There are also adverts, a promo for part two, the Southern Weather and various idents.

24 CARROTT GOLD

A Celador production for BBC 1. Transmission details are for BBC 1. Duration: 50 minutes.

Written by Jasper Carrott; produced and directed by Paul Smith.

Jasper Carrott (Presenter).

	Holding / Source
28.12.1990	DB / 1"

2DTV

A 2D Productions production for ITV 1. made in association with Channel Television. Transmission details are for the Central region. Duration: 25 minutes.

Main regular credit(s): Produced by Giles Pilbrow; directed by Tim Searle.

Main regular cast: Jon Culshaw, Dave Lamb, Jan Ravens.

SERIES 1

Main regular credit(s): Executive producer Richard Bennett.

Main regular cast: With Mark Perry.

	Holding / Source
31.12.2001	DB / DBSW

Satirical animation show.

3 2 1

A Yorkshire Television production. Transmission details are for the ATV/Central region. Duration: 50 minutes.

Main regular credit(s): Theme music by Johnny Pearson.

Main regular performer(s): Ted Rogers (Host).

SERIES 1

Transmission details are for the ATV midlands region.

Main regular credit(s): Written by Brad Ashton and Mike Goddard; additional material by Wally Malston; music by Johnny Pearson; associate producer Mary David; produced by Derek Burrell-Davis; directed by David Millard.

Main regular performer(s): With Duggie Brown (Regular), Chris Emmett (Regular), Debbie Arnold (Regular), Holly Allen Smith (Gentle Sec), Mireille Allonville (Gentle Sec), Jenny Layland (Gentle Sec), Gail Playfair (Gentle Sec), Patsy Ann Scott (Gentle Sec), Tula (Gentle Sec).

		VT Number	Holding / Source
27.01.1979	Christmas Show	L124	1" / 2"

Postponed from 25.12.1978.

With Jack Douglas, Rusty Goffe, Annie St John, Honey Wheeler, Rachel Heyhoe Flint, Mike Channon, Clodagh Rodgers, Terry Wogan, Pat Coombs, Julian Orchard.

SERIES 2

Transmission details are for the ATV midlands region.

Main regular credit(s): Music directed by Laurie Holloway; music by Johnny Pearson and Richard Holmes; produced by Alan Tarrant; directed by Paddy Russell.

Main regular performer(s): With Chris Emmett (Comic), Felix Bowness (Comic), Jenny Layland (Hostess), Annie St John (Hostess), Patsy Ann Scott, Mireille Allonville, Karen Palmer.

		VT Number	Holding / Source
25.12.1979	Dickensian Xmas Show	L160	1" / 2"

Written by John Bartlett, Mike Goddard, Geoff Leack and Wally Malston; associate producer Mike Goddard.

With Mike Newman (Comic), Mireille Allonville (Hostess), Karen Palmer (Hostess), Patsy Ann Scott (Hostess), Wilfrid Brambell, The Ramblers, Terry Scott, Bill Maynard, Carmel McSharry, The Krankies, Black Dyke Mills Band.

SERIES 3

Transmission details are for the ATV midlands region.

Main regular credit(s): Additional material by Wally Malston; music directed by Laurie Holloway; designed by Gordon Livesey and Andrew Sanderson; executive producer Alan Tarrant; produced by Mike Goddard.

Main regular performer(s): With Fiona Curzon (Hostess), Karen Palmer (Hostess), Libby Roberts (Hostess), Alison Temple Savage (Hostess).

		VT Number	Holding / Source
25.12.1980	Christmas Pantomime	L257	1" / 2"

Written by John Bartlett; research Shirley E. Jones; directed by Ian Bolt.

With Jacqui Scott, Bill Maynard, Mike Newman, Mike Reid, Derek Batey, Nicholas Parsons, Paul Luty, Bob Carolgees, Sheila Steafel, Barbara Woodhouse, Doctor Magnus Pyke, Cyril Smith M.P., Chris Emmett.

Wally Malston wrote Ted Rogers' material.

British Christmas Television Guide　　　**3 2 1 (continued)**

SERIES 4
Transmission details are for the Central region.
Main regular credit(s):　　Music directed by Laurie Holloway; executive producer Alan Tarrant; produced by Ian Bolt.
Main regular performer(s):　With Chris Emmett, Mike Newman, Lipstick.

	VT Number	Holding / Source

25.12.1982　Christmas Special　　　　　　　　　　　　　　　　　　　　　　　　　L413　　　　　1" / 2"
Written by John Bartlett, Chris Emmett and Wally Malston; music by Laurie Holloway; designed by Gordon Livesey; directed by Ian Bolt.
With Karan David, Anna Dawson, Henry McGee, Patti Gold, Joan Sims, Bernie Winters, David Yip, The Brian Rogers Dancers [as The Brian Rogers Connection].

SERIES 6
Transmission details are for the Central region.
Main regular credit(s):　　Music directed by Laurie Holloway; associate producer John Bartlett; executive producer Alan Tarrant.
Main regular performer(s):　With Caroline Munro (Hostess), Chris Emmett.

　　Holding / Source

24.12.1983　Dick Whittington　　　　　　　　　　　　　　　　　　　　　　　　　　　　　　　　1" / 1"
Written by Chris Emmett, Graham Ripley, John Bartlett, Eric Davidson and Wally Malston; designed by Richard Jarvis; produced and directed by Don Clayton.
With Mike Newman (Comic), Alan Curtis, Dana, Kenneth Connor, Billy Dainty, Charlie Williams, Julie Rogers, Danny O'Dea, The Brian Rogers Connection.

SERIES 7
Transmission details are for the Central region.
Main regular credit(s):　　Written by John Bartlett and Eric Davidson; music directed by Robert Hartley; designed by Gordon Livesey; associate producer John Bartlett; executive producer Alan Tarrant; produced by Terry Henebery.

	VT Number	Holding / Source

22.12.1984　Pantomania　　　　　　　　　　　　　　　　　　　　　　　　　　L436/17　　　　1" / 1"
Additional material by Eric Davidson, Wally Malston and Chris Emmett; directed by Terry Henebery.
With Chris Emmett (Comic), Mike Newman (Comic), Caroline Munro (Hostess), Roy Hudd, June Whitfield, John Inman, Larry Noble, Bernie Clifton, Suzanne Dando, Anita Harris, Barbara Windsor, Bernie Winters, Billy Dainty, Arthur English, Fred Feast, Davy Kaye, Norman Vaughan, Carmen Munroe.

SERIES 9
Transmission details are for the Central region.
Main regular credit(s):　　Written by John Bartlett and Eric Davidson; additional material by Wally Malston.
Main regular performer(s):　With Caroline Munro (Hostess), Lynda Lee Lewis (Hostess), John Benson.

　　Holding / Source

21.12.1986　Xmas At Toad Hall　　　　　　　　　　　　　　　　　　　　　　　　　　　　　　　1" / 1"
Additional material by Chris Emmett and Graham Ripley; produced and directed by Don Clayton.
With Bill Pertwee, Kenneth Connor, Tony Selby, John Boulter, Anna Dawson, Lance Percival, Felix Bowness, Chris Emmett, Janet Lloyd.

SERIES 10
Transmission details are for the Central region.
Main regular credit(s):　　Written by Eric Davidson and Wally Malston; executive producer Alan Tarrant.
Main regular performer(s):　With Lynda Lee Lewis (Hostess), John Benson.

	VT Number	Holding / Source

19.12.1987　Christmas Special　　　　　　　　　　　　　　　　　　　　　　　L488/13　　　　1" / 1"
Produced and directed by Graham Wetherell.
With John Benson (Voice Over), Ricky Tomlinson, Bernie Winters, Gareth Hunt, Pat Coombs, Norman Collier, Henry Cooper, Ell Woods, The Brian Rogers Connection, Nina Myskow, Felix Bowness, Jan Leeming, Denis Law, Sharron Davies, Bob Champion, Elizabeth Dawn, William Tarmey, Sue Johnston, Jean Rogers, Freddie Pyne.

SERIES 11
Transmission details are for the Central region.
Main regular credit(s):　　Written by Eric Davidson; additional material by Garry Chambers; produced and directed by Terry Henebery.
Main regular performer(s):　With Lynda Lee Lewis (Hostess).

　　Holding / Source

24.12.1988　Christmas Special - Pantomania　　　　　　　　　　　　　　　　　　　　　　　　1" / 1"
Music directed by Robert Hartley; choreography by Brian Rogers; designed by Andrew Sanderson.
With Aiden J. Harvey, Allan Stewart, Hilary O'Neil, Bernie Clifton, Felix Bowness, Geoff Capes, Linda Nolan, Maria Whittaker, Suzanne Mizzi, Christopher Biggins, Adrian Moorhouse.

THE 39 STEPS

A BBC Productions production for BBC 1. Transmission details are for BBC 1. Duration: 89 minutes.

Adapted by Lizzie Mickery; based on a book by John Buchan; script supervisor Heather Storr; script editor Jeremy Swimer; music by Rob Lane; consultant Gordon Ronald; designed by Pat Campbell; executive producers Hilary Salmon and John Yorke; production manager Mark Devlin; produced by Lynn Horsford; directed by James Hawes.

Rupert Penry-Jones (Richard Hannay), Lydia Leonard (Victoria Sinclair), David Haig (Sir George Sinclair), Patrick Malahide (Professor Fisher), Patrick Kennedy (Hellory Sinclair), Eddie Marsan (Scudder), Alex Jennings (Captain Kell), Steven Elder (Vicar / Wakeham), Werner Daehn (Ackerman), Peter Stark (Engel), Del Synnott (London Constable), Roger de Courcey (Ventriloquist), David Gallacher (Professor's Butler), James Bryce (Concierge At Club), Stewart Preston (Waiter At Club), Sandy Neilson (Old Man At Club), Barbara Downie (Woman On Stairs), Anna Guthrie (Maid), George Docherty (Train Policeman), Sean Kane (Town Hall Policeman), Mitchell Fleming (Little Boy), Charlotte Fleming (Little Girl), Kathryn Howden (Landlady), Allan Sawers (Sergeant At Stirling Castle), David McDowell (Sentry At Stirling Castle), Michael Stokes (German Accomplice), Paul Comrie (German Accomplice), Johnny Meres (Station Attendant).

28.12.2008

Holding / Source
HD/DB / HDC

45

A Granada production. Transmission details are for the ATV midlands region.

Main regular credit(s): Music directed by Derek Hilton; choreography by Ken Martyne; designed by Derek Batley; produced by Muriel Young; directed by Peter Walker.

25.12.1974 **Christmas Rock With 45**

Production No: P815/26

Holding / Source: J / 2"

Duration: 40 minutes.

With David 'Kid' Jensen (Presenter), Rosko, The Bay City Rollers, Russ Ballard, Colin Blunstone, Ken Boothe, Dave Cousins, Rick Wakeman, Queen, Zig Zag.

THE 5:19 SHOW

A BBC Productions production for BBC Switch. Transmission details are for BBC 2. Duration: 14 minutes.

Main regular credit(s): Theme music by Tom Barber; art director Stefan Arif; designed by Chris Elphick, Kathryn Leach, Alan Klein and Tamory Elphick; executive producer Geoffrey Goodwin; series producers Beth Garrod, Anna Abenson and Simon Judge; produced by James Payne.

Main regular performer(s): Tom Deacon (Presenter), A. J. Odudu (Presenter).

02.01.2010 **New Year's Special**

Holding / Source
DB / DBSW

Directed by Thomas Orger.

With compilation of previous material.

New links and studio fun mixed with highlights of previous guests.

50/50

A BBC production for BBC 1. Transmission details are for BBC 1.

SERIES 2

27.12.1998 **Christmas Special**

Holding / Source
DB / D3S

THE 6 O'CLOCK SHOW

An LWT production. Transmission details are for the London Weekend Television region.

19.12.1986 **Christmas Special**

Holding / Source
D2 / 1"

Executive producer David Cox; directed by Sue McMahon, John Oven and Liddy Oldroyd.

THE 70S STOP HERE!

A BBC production for BBC 1. Transmission details are for BBC 1. Duration: 80 minutes.

Produced and directed by Frances Whitaker.

Penelope Keith (Presenter), John Cleese, Michael Parkinson, Rod Hull and Emu, The Goodies, Elton John, Angela Rippon, Richard Briers, Felicity Kendal, Paul Eddington, Michael Crawford, David Frost, Larry Grayson, Morecambe and Wise, Esther Rantzen, Arthur Lowe, John Le Mesurier, Keith Michell, Ian Holm, Tom Conti, Derek Jacobi, John Hurt, Alan Dobie, Alan Bates, Anne Stallybrass, Susan Littler, John Duttine, Joanna David, Jeremy Brett, Anna Massey, Christopher Timothy, Robert Hardy, Clare Francis, John Curry, Olga Korbut, Nadia Comaneel, Mary Peters, Virginia Wade, Monty Python, Alistair Cooke, Doctor Jacob Bronowski, Ronnie Barker, Ronnie Corbett, The Wilkins Family.

31.12.1979

Holding / Source
DB-D3 / 2"

Compilation of short extracts from some of the more notable BBC programmes of the 1970s.

8 OUT OF 10 CATS

A Zeppotron production for Channel 4. Transmission details are for Channel 4. Duration varies - see below for details.

Main regular credit(s): Theme music by Mat Osman.

Main regular performer(s): Jimmy Carr (Host), Sean Lock (Team Captain).

Holding / Source
DB / DBSW

23.12.2010 Christmas Special
Duration: 45 minutes.
Programme associates Jimmy Carr, Richard Cohen, Steve Edge, Dominic English, Lee Stuart Evans, Shaun Pye, Christine Rose, Aiden Spackman, Fraser Steele, Dan Swimer and Martin Trenaman; script supervisor Jemilah Findlay; script editor Charlie Skelton; designed by Patrick Doherty; assistant producers Christopher Barbour, Matt Nida and Kate Staples; executive producers Richard Osman and Ruth Phillips; head of production Debra Blenkinsop; production manager Charlotte Hopkinson; series producer Andrew Westwell; produced by Russell Balkind; directed by Richard Valentine.
With Jason Manford (Team Captain), John Pohlhammer (Voice Over), Christopher Biggins, Jack Dee, Lorraine Kelly, Josie Long.

Holding / Source
HD/DB / HDC

23.12.2011 Christmas Special
Duration: 48 minutes.
Produced by Karen Murdoch; directed by Geri Dowd.
With Jon Richardson (Team Captain), JEdward, Micky Flanagan, Liza Tarbuck, Greg Davies, Arlene Phillips, Keith Harris & Orville.

SERIES 14

Holding / Source
HD/DB / HDC

24.12.2012 Christmas Special
Duration: 48 minutes.
Programme associates Jimmy Carr, Dominic English, Shaun Pye, Christine Rose, Aidan Spackman, Martin Trenaman, Will Ing, Neil Webster, Fraser Steele, Lee Stuart Evans, Kevin Day, Andrew Bird and Giles Boden; script editor Charlie Skelton; designed by Patrick Doherty; executive producers Richard Osman and Ruth Phillips; produced by Richard Cohen, Adam Hutchinson and David Price; directed by Richard Valentine.
With Jon Richardson (Team Captain), Nick Helm (Santa Claus), Sarah Millican, Stephen Mangan, Joe Wilkinson, Bruno Tonioli.

SERIES 16

Holding / Source
HD/DB / HDC

29.12.2013 Christmas Special
Duration: 48 minutes.
Programme associates Jimmy Carr, Dominic English, Christine Rose, Aidan Spackman, Martin Trenaman, Will Ing, Neil Webster, Fraser Steele, Lee Stuart Evans, Kevin Day, Matt Forde, Andrew Bird and James Farmer; script editor Charlie Skelton; designed by Patrick Doherty; executive producers Richard Osman, Ruth Phillips and Andrew Westwell; series producer Richard Cohen; produced by Adam Hutchinson and Lisa Kirk; directed by Barbara Wiltshire.
With Jon Richardson (Team Captain), Holly Willoughby, Henning Wehn, Roisin Conaty, Alan Davies, Joe Wilkinson, Nick Helm.

81 TAKE 2

A BBC Scotland production for BBC 1. Transmission details are for BBC 1. Duration: 35 minutes.
Assistant producer Colin Gilbert; produced by Sean Hardie; directed by Rod Natkiel.
John Bett, Ron Bain, Robbie Coltrane, Celia Imrie, Rik Mayall, Chic Murray, The Hee Bee Gee Bees.

Holding / Source
DB-D3 / 2"

31.12.1981

84 CHARING CROSS ROAD (RADIO)

A BBC production for BBC Radio 4. Transmission details are for BBC Radio 4. Duration: 90 minutes.
Adapted by James Roose-Evans; based on a book by Helene Hanff; play production by Tracey Neale.
Gillian Anderson (Helene), Denis Lawson (Frank), Brid Brennan (Nora), Alison Pettitt (Cecily), Ella Smith (Megan), Simon Treves (William), Peter Marinker (George), Laurel Lefkow (Maxine), Marlene Sidaway (Mary).

Holding / Source
DA /

25.12.2007

99-1

A Zenith Films production for Carlton. Transmission details are for the Central region. Duration: 50 minutes.

Main regular credit(s):	Devised by Barbara Cox, Steve Clark-Hall and Terry Johnson; music by Michael Gibbs; executive producer Archie Tait; co-produced by Barbara Cox; produced by Steve Clark-Hall.
Main regular cast:	Leslie Grantham (Mick Raynor), Adie Allen (Detective Constable Liz Hulley), Niall Buggy (Elbow).

SERIES 1
Duration: 51 minutes.

Main regular credit(s):	Script supervisor Julie Robinson; costume Paul Minter; make-up Michelle Daniels; director of photography Barry McCann; art director Chris Townsend; designed by Max Gottlieb; production supervised by Laura Julian.
Main regular cast:	With Robert Stephens (Commander Oakwood).

Holding / Source

05.01.1994 **Doing The Business**   D2 / C1S

The day before Christmas Eve, and a gruesome dead body turns up in an office block. Simultaneously Mick Raynor learns he is going to be shafted by the Met....
Written by Terry Johnson; directed by Charles McDougall.
With Gwyneth Strong (Charlotte), Malcolm Storry (Detective Superintendent Travis), Andrew Tiernan (Billy Pink), Barbara Keogh, Robert Carlyle, Paul Barber, John Vine, Nick Hobbs, Oliver Parker, Peter McNamara, Colette Brown.

'ALLO 'ALLO!

A BBC production for BBC 1. Transmission details are for BBC 1. Duration varies - see below for details.

Main regular credit(s):	Created by Jeremy Lloyd and David Croft; theme music by David Croft and Roy Moore.
Main regular cast:	Gorden Kaye (René Artois), Carmen Silvera (Edith Melba Artois), Vicki Michelle (Yvette Carte-Blanche), Kirsten Cooke (Michelle Dubois), Richard Marner (Herr Colonel Kurt Von Strohm), Guy Siner (Lieutenant Hubert Gruber), Kim Hartman (Helga Geerhart).

SERIES 2

Main regular credit(s):	Written by Jeremy Lloyd and David Croft; designed by David Buckingham; production team Bernadette Darnell, Jackie Wright, Simon Spencer and Arch Dyson; production manager Martin Dennis; produced and directed by David Croft.
Main regular cast:	With Richard Gibson (Herr Otto Flick), Francesca Gonshaw (Maria), Jack Haig (M Leclerc), Sam Kelly (Captain Hans Geering), Rose Hill (Mother), John D. Collins (Flying Officer Fairfax), Nicholas Frankau (Flying Officer Carstairs).

Holding / Source

26.12.1985 "The gateaux from the chateau"   DB / 1"
Duration: 48 minutes.
With Hilary Minster (Von Klinkerhoffen), Phoebe Scholfield (Henriette), Philip Kendall ('London Calling'), Joy Allen, Julie-Christian Young.

SERIES 3

Main regular credit(s):	Written by Jeremy Lloyd and David Croft; designed by David Buckingham; production team Bernadette Darnell, Roy Gould and Charles Garland; produced by David Croft.
Main regular cast:	With Richard Gibson (Herr Otto Flick), Francesca Gonshaw (Maria), Jack Haig (M Roger Leclerc), Sam Kelly (Captain Hans Geering), Rose Hill (Mother), Arthur Bostrom (Crabtree), John D. Collins (Flying Officer Fairfax), Nicholas Frankau (Flying Officer Carstairs).

Holding / Source

26.12.1986 "The airmen plan to fly away, René becomes a roadworker"   DB / 1"
Alt.Title(s): *Flight of Fancy*
Duration: 45 minutes.
Production manager Martin Dennis; directed by David Croft and Robin Carr.
With Paul Cooper ('London Calling'), Sherry Louise Plant, Trevor T. Smith, Len Keyes, Robert Aldous, Philip McInnerny.

SERIES 8

Main regular credit(s):	Written by Jeremy Lloyd and Paul Adam; designed by John Stout; production manager Jez Nightingale; produced and directed by John B. Hobbs.
Main regular cast:	With Richard Gibson (Herr Otto Flick), Sue Hodge (Mimi Labonq), John Louis Mansi (Herr Engelbert Von Smallhausen), Kenneth Connor (Monsieur Alfonse), Rose Hill (Madame Fanny), Arthur Bostrom (Officer Crabtree), Robin Parkinson (Ernest Leclerc), Hilary Minster (Von Klinkerhoffen).

Holding / Source

24.12.1991 "Yvette is pregnant"   DB / D3
Alt.Title(s): *A Bun in the Oven*
Duration: 44 minutes.
With Paul Cooper (London Voice), Michael Cotterill.

'TIS CHRISTMAS NIGHT!

An ATV production. Transmission details are for the ATV midlands region. Duration: 25 minutes.
Produced by Donald Shingler; directed by Tony Parker.
David Lloyd (Host), Philip Harben, T. P. McKenna, Robert Spencer, Lyn and Graham McCarthy, Midland Boy Singers.

Holding / Source

25.12.1967   J /

From Aston Hall, Birmingham.

| British Christmas Television Guide | ABC AT LARGE |

ABC AT LARGE

An ABC production. Transmission details are for the ABC north region. Duration: 18 minutes.

Reports on events in the North and the Midlands that make the nation's news.

                      Holding / Source

23.12.1961 **Christmas Edition**   J /

Introduced by David Mahlowe; edited by Roy Bottomley and Tom Brennand; designed by Philip Harrison; directed by Pamela Lonsdale.

ABOLISH CHRISTMAS!

A Thames Television production. Transmission details are for the Thames Television region.

By Christmas eve, many people have had enough of the great Christian festival. One such person, who would abolish Christmas, is Bill Grundy. He feels it has become little more than an excuse for eating, drinking and excessive spending on presents. However, Dr John Rae, headmaster of Westminster School is among those who think there is still enough of value in the celebration of Christ's birth to retain Christmas. Both men put their case and debate the issue which is likely to arise in households all over the land.

Designed by Jim Nicholson; executive producer Diana Potter; produced and directed by Robert Fleming.

Bill Grundy (Presenter), John Rae (Presenter).

                      Holding / Source

24.12.1981   DB / 2"

ABOUT RELIGION

An ATV production. Transmission details are for the ATV London region. Duration: 25 minutes.

Religious documentray series featuring occasional dramatic plays.

SERIES 1

                      Holding / Source

09.12.1956 **Two Famous Journeys**   J /

The Reverend H. A. Hamilton will take viewers on one of the most exciting journeys man has ever made, and talk of the more famous journey we remember at Christmas.

With Michael Redington (Presenter), Reverend H. A. Hamilton.

23.12.1956 **The Christmas Story**   J /

A Nativity Play which is acted in the Church of St. Peter-upon-Cornhill in the City of London by their own Players.

With Michael Redington (Presenter).

25.12.1956 **Some Thoughts On Christmas Day**   J /

Prebendary Douglas Owen, with the use of films, shows the different ways that Christmas is celebrated all over the world.

With Michael Redington (Presenter), Douglas Owen.

SERIES 2

                      Holding / Source

21.12.1958 **Christmas Is Coming...**   J /

20.12.1959 **Christmas Night**   J /

Written by Emma Smith; designed by Anthony Waller; produced by Michael Redington.

With Gary Raymond, Lisa Madron, Norman Tyrrell, Frederick Peisley, Ralph Nossek, Gibb McLaughlin, Daniel Thorndike, Martin Spiers.

27.12.1959 **From Darkness To Light**   J /

03.01.1960 **Behind The Christmas Card**   J /

22.12.1963 **Something's Coming, Something Good**   J /

Produced by Emmeline Garnett; directed by Shaun O'Riordan.

26.12.1965   J /

ABSOLUTELY FABULOUS

Produced for BBC Variety by a variety of companies (see details below). Transmission details are for BBC. Usual duration: 30 minutes.

Main regular credit(s):   Written by Jennifer Saunders; based on an idea by Jennifer Saunders and Dawn French.

Main regular cast: Jennifer Saunders (Edina Monsoon), Joanna Lumley (Patsy Stone), Julia Sawalha (Saffron).

A Saunders & French production. made in association with Comedy Central. Transmission details are for BBC 1.

                      Holding / Source

27.12.2002 **Gay**   DB / DBSW

Duration: 54 minutes.

Script supervisor Katie Collins; script editor Ruby Wax; music by Simon Brint; director of photography Dick Quinlan; designed by Harry Banks; production executive Claire Bridgland; executive producer Jon Plowman; production managers Rebecca Rivo and Julia Weedon; produced by Jo Sargent; directed by Tristram Shapeero.

With Jane Horrocks (Bubble / Lola), Christopher Ryan, Mo Gaffney, Harriet Thorpe, Helen Lederer, Josh Hamilton, Danny Burstein, Nathan Lee Graham, Whoopi Goldberg, Debbie Harry, Graham Norton, Jared Gold, Rufus Wainwright.

ABSOLUTELY FABULOUS (continued)

SERIES 5
A Saunders & French production. made in association with Oh!. Transmission details are for BBC 1.

Main regular credit(s): Additional material by Sue Perkins; script supervisor Bernadette Darnell; script editor Ruby Wax; director of photography Peter Edwards; designed by Harry Banks; production executive Claire Bridgland; executive producer Jon Plowman; production manager Francis Gilson; produced by Jo Sargent; directed by Dewi Humphreys.

Main regular cast: With June Whitfield (Mother).

	Holding / Source
24.12.2003 **Cold Turkey**	DB / DBSW

Duration: 35 minutes.
Music by Simon Brint and Ben Lee-Delisle.
With Jane Horrocks (Bubble), Alex Lowe, Felix Dexter, Eleanor Bron, Kate O'Mara, Helen Lederer, Harriet Thorpe, Mo Gaffney, Christopher Malcolm, Chris Ryan, Amy Phillips, Simon Brodkin, Marion Pashley.

Made in association with Oh! Oxygen. Transmission details are for BBC 1.

	Holding / Source
25.12.2004 "Redecorating the kitchen"	DB / DBSW

Alt.Title(s): *White Box*
A Saunders & French production. Duration: 40 minutes.
Script supervisor Tessa Kimbell; script editor Ruby Wax; music by Simon Brint; director of photography John Sorapure; designed by Harry Banks; production team Kelley James, Samantha Waite and Abigail Wilson; production executive Jez Nightingale; executive producer Jon Plowman; production manager Jenny Penrose; produced by Jo Sargent; directed by Ed Bye.
With June Whitfield (Mother), Jane Horrocks (Bubble), Miranda Richardson, Patrick Barlow, Laurie Metcalf, Nathan Lane, Sir Terence Conran, Mo Gaffney, Christopher Ryan, Miranda Hart.

Transmission details are for BBC 1.

	Holding / Source
25.12.2011 **Identity**	HD/DB / HDC

Patsy is forced into trying to find out who she really is by a frightening visitor.

The series was inspired by a sketch from "French & Saunders" entitled "Modern Mother and Daughter" with Jennifer Saunders as the Mother and Dawn as the daughter.

ABSURD PERSON SINGULAR

A BBC production for BBC 1. Transmission details are for BBC 1. Duration: 115 minutes.
Written by Alan Ayckbourn; designed by Campbell Gordon; produced by Shaun Sutton; directed by Michael Simpson.
Cheryl Campbell (Eva), Michael Gambon (Geoffrey), Nicky Henson (Sidney), Maureen Lipman (Jane), Geoffrey Palmer (Ronald), Prunella Scales (Marion), John Baddeley (Dick), Lesley Joseph (Lottie).

	Holding / Source
01.01.1985	DB / 1"

ACCORDING TO DORA

A BBC production for BBC 1. Transmission details are for BBC 1. Duration: 25 minutes.

Main regular cast: Dora Bryan (Herself).

SERIES 1: A Bryan's-Eye View of the World

Main regular credit(s): Script editor David Climie; music directed by Geoff Love; produced and directed by Robin Nash.

	Holding / Source
31.12.1968 **Past, Present And Future**	J /

Written by Lew Schwarz, John Junkin, Ronald Wolfe and Ronald Chesney; music by Dennis Wilson; designed by Kenneth Sharp.
With Hugh Paddick, Aubrey Woods, Tim Barrett, Michael Stainton, Barbara New.

ACROSS THE YEARS

A BBC production for BBC 1. Transmission details are for BBC 1. Duration: 25 minutes.
Television presentation by Tim Marshall.
John Craven, Paul McDowell, Sir Ranulph Fiennes, Thora Hird, Patrick Moore, Sir Rex Hunt, Reverend David Cooper.

Old Father Time - a Nationwide English Celebration of New Year's Eve

	Holding / Source
31.12.1982	DB-D3-2" / 2"

AD LIB

A Yorkshire Television production. Transmission details are for the ATV midlands region. Duration: 25 minutes.

Main regular cast: Duncan Goodhew (Presenter), Tilly Vosburgh (Presenter).

SERIES 2

Main regular credit(s): Executive producer Joy Whitby; produced by Peter Murphy; directed by Alister Hallum.

Main regular cast: With Ian Bartholomew, Nicky Christian, Duncan Goodhew, Oona Kirsch, Liz Lewis, Craig Lynn, Nicky Margolis, Beverley Martin, David Nunn, Nick Rowan, Tilly Vosburgh.

	VT Number	Holding / Source
24.12.1981	C411	D3 / 2"

Designed by Agnes Hall.

AD LIB

ADE'S CHRISTMAS CRACKERS

Commissioned by ITV 1. Transmission details are for the Central region. Duration: 48 minutes.

A trip down memory lane in the company of Adrian Edmondson, who delves deep into the archives and picks out the best and worst of Christmas TV from the past 60 years. Among the gems are Eric Morecambe making an improvised live appearance in the World of Sport studio, a schedule being interrupted by a live broadcast of the first ever Moon orbit and Den serving Angie her divorce papers in EastEnders.

Executive producer Jeremy Phillips; directed by Caz Stuart.

Ade Edmondson (Presenter).

	Holding / Source
23.12.2012	HD/DB / HDC

THE ADVENTURES OF ALICE

A BBC production. Transmission details are for BBC. Duration: 55 minutes.

Adapted by Charles Lefeaux; based on a book by Lewis Carroll; music by Antony Hopkins; produced by Charles Lefeaux; directed by Gordon Murray.

Gillian Ferguson (Alice), Sonia Dresdel (Red Queen), Marian Spencer (White Queen), Ernest Milton (The Mad Hatter), Peter Sallis (Tweedledee), Gordon Davies (Lewis Carroll), Cyril Shaps (The March Hare), Carla Challoner (The Dormouse), Arthur Ridley (The Gryphon), Eric Shilling (The Mock Turtle), Erik Chitty (The Caterpillar), Barrie Cookson (Tweedledum), Frederick Treves (Red King), Vivienne Chatterton (The Sheep), David March (Humpty Dumpty), Philip Ray (White King), Arthur Ridley (The Unicorn), Erik Chitty (The Lion), Geoffrey Bayldon (White Knight), John Murray-Scott (The Creature With A Long Beak).

	Holding / Source
23.12.1960	R3 /

Puppet Sequences by Television Puppet Theatre.

THE ADVENTURES OF BOOTY MOLE

An Associated-Rediffusion production. Transmission details are for Associated-Rediffusion.

Main regular credit(s): Created by Joan Reed and Jane Johnson.

Main regular cast: Peter Hawkins (Voices), Ivan Owen (Voices), Edwina Coven (Voices).

SERIES 1

Main regular credit(s): Written by Joan Reed and Jane Johnson; animated by Elizabeth Shingler, Anne Newell and Hal Danby.

	Holding / Source
19.12.1960 **Booty Mole And The Christmassy Weasel**	NR / Live

With No guest cast.

THE ADVENTURES OF MOLE

A Martin Gates production for Channel 4. Transmission details are for Channel 4. Duration: 60 minutes.

Adapted by Sue Radley and Marion Edwards; based on a book by Kenneth Grahame; produced and directed by Martin Gates.

Peter Davison (Voices), Richard Briers (Voices), Hugh Laurie (Voices), Paul Eddington (Voices).

	Holding / Source
24.12.1995	D3 / D3S

THE ADVENTURES OF NODDY

A Dudley Productions production for ATV. Transmission details are for the ATV London region. Duration: 15 minutes.

Main regular credit(s): Based on stories by Enid Blyton; music played by Robin Richmond; music by Denis Arundell; puppetry by Peter Hayes; produced by A. D. Peters.

Main regular cast: Denise Bryer (Voices), Jasmine Bligh (Voices), Cyril Shaps (Voices), Tony Sympson (Voices).

SERIES 1

	Holding / Source
25.12.1955 **A Present For Noddy**	B1N / B1

Alternative transmissions: ATV Midlands: 25.05.1956.

Directed by Quentin Lawrence.

THE ADVENTURES OF ROBIN HOOD

A Sapphire Films production for ITP, made in association with ITC. Transmission details are for the ABC midlands region. Usual duration: 25 minutes.

Main regular credit(s): Theme music by Albert Elms.

Main regular cast: Richard Greene (Robin Hood).

SERIES 3

A Hannah Weinstein production for Sapphire Films. Transmission details are for the ABC midlands region.

Main regular credit(s): Script supervisor Albert G. Ruben; music by Albert Elms; associate producer Thelma Connell; produced by Sidney Cole.

	Holding / Source
04.01.1958 **The Christmas Goose**	DB / B3

Davey, an 11-year-old boy, has a pet goose named Matilda. One day she saves him from a flogging from Sir Leon's men, but is caught— and as a punishment is sentenced to become Sir Leon's Christmas dinner.

Written by Ring Lardner Jr and Ian McLellan Hunter [jointly credited as Oliver Skene]; directed by Don Chaffey.

With Alexander Gauge (Friar Tuck), Archie Duncan (Little John), Jon Whiteley (Davey), Jack Watling (Sir Leon), Paul Eddington (Bailiff), Jane Asher (Susan), John Baker (Quentin), Victor Woolf (Derwent), Anne Firth (Stella).

(Previously televised December 22, 1957) states the TV Times. Kaleidoscope assumes this date refers to ATV London.

The information detailing the real writers behind the on-screen pseudonyms was collated by Steve Neale and has previously been published in "Pseudonyms, Sapphire and Salt" (Historical Journal of Film, Radio and Television, Vol. 23, No. 3, 2003), "Swashbucklers and Sitcoms, Cowboys and Crime, Nurses, Just Men and

THE ADVENTURES OF ROBIN HOOD (continued)

Defenders: Blacklisted Writers and TV in the 1950s and 1960s" (Film Studies, Issue 7, Winter 2005) and "Un-American Hollywood: Politics and Film in the Blacklist Era" (Rutgers University Press, 2008).

THE ADVENTURES OF RUPERT BEAR

An ITC production for ATV. Transmission details are for the ATV midlands region. Duration: 14 minutes.

Main regular credit(s): Script editor Ruth Boswell; theme music by Peter Callendar [credited as Ron Roker], Len Beadle and Jackie Lee; produced by Mary Turner and John Read; directed by Mary Turner.

Main regular cast: Judy Bennett (Narrator).

SERIES 1

Date	Title	Holding / Source
23.12.1970	**Rupert And The Christmas Toffee**	C1 / C1

Written by Jill Fenson.

30.12.1970	**Rupert And The Snowman**	C1 / C1

Adapted by Jill Fenson.

SERIES 3

Date	Title	Holding / Source
19.12.1973	**Rupert And The Christmas Stocking**	J / C1
26.12.1973	**Rupert's Christmas Party**	J / C1

Written by Marcia Webb.

02.01.1974	**Rupert At The Pantomime**	J / C1

Written by Marcia Webb.

18.12.1974	**Rupert And The White Christmas**	J / C1

THE ADVENTURES OF SHERLOCK HOLMES (RADIO)

A BBC production for BBC Radio 4. Transmission details are for BBC Radio 4. Duration: 47 minutes.

Main regular credit(s): Based on stories by Sir Arthur Conan Doyle.

Main regular cast: Clive Merrison (Sherlock Holmes), Michael Williams (Doctor John Watson).

Date	Title	Holding / Source
02.01.1991	**The Blue Carbuncle**	DAS /

Dramatised by Bert Coules; music by Leonard Friedman; produced and directed by Patrick Rayner.

With Peter Blythe, Hugh Dickson, Vincent Brimble, Naomi Capron, Ben Onwukwe, Elaine Claxton, Christopher Good, David Goudge, Ian Lindsay.

THE ADVENTURES OF SHERLOCK HOLMES

A Granada production. Transmission details are for the Central region. Duration: 52 minutes.

Main regular credit(s): Based on the stories of Sir Arthur Conan Doyle; music by Patrick Gowers; developed by John Hawkesworth; associate producer Stuart Doughty; produced by Michael Cox.

Main regular cast: Jeremy Brett (Sherlock Holmes), David Burke (Doctor Watson).

SERIES 1

Date	Title	Production No	Holding / Source
05.06.1984	**The Blue Carbuncle**	P1125/7	DB / C1

Dramatised by Richard Harris and John Hawkesworth [jointly credited as Paul Finney]; directed by David Carson.

With Rosalie Williams (Mrs Hudson), Rosalind Knight, Ros Simmons, Ken Campbell, Desmond McNamara, Amelda Brown, Brian Miller, Frank Mills, Frank Middlemass, Don McCorkindale, Eric Allan, Maggie Jones, Ricki Scott, John Cannon, Eric Kent, Ted Beyer.

Paul Finney is a pseudonym, hiding the identity of the original writer who asked for his name to be taken off the episode as he disagreed with some changes made to his script by John Hawkesworth. Television Today (17.03.1983) contained an feature on the series more than a year before its first broadcast. It lists Richard Harris as the writer responsible for dramatising this episode. A month later (21.04.1983) it also noted that John Davies was originally contracted to direct this episode, and two others, but was unable to fulfil his commitments due to illness.

See also: (SIR ARTHUR CONAN DOYLE'S) SHERLOCK HOLMES (BBC)

THE ADVENTURES OF THE SCARLET PIMPERNEL

A Towers of London Productions production for ITP. made in association with Towers of London Productions. Transmission details are for the ATV midlands region. Duration: 25 minutes.

Main regular cast: Marius Goring (Sir Percy Blakeney).

Date	Title	Holding / Source
11.05.1956	**The Christmas Present**	B3 / B3

Alternative transmissions: Associated-Rediffusion: 20.12.1955.

Written by Ralph Gilbert Bettinson; produced by Dennis Vance and Marius Goring; directed by David MacDonald.

With Patrick Troughton (Sir Andrew Ffoulkes), Anthony Newlands (Sir Richard Hastings), Alexander Gauge (The Prince of Wales), Stanley van Beers (Chauvelin), Sybil Arundale, Arthur Young, Ann Padwick, Mark Lawton, Christopher Toyne, Lesley Dudley, Richard Rogers, Nicola Braithwaite, Amanda Coxell.

THE ADVENTURES OF THE SCARLET PIMPERNEL

ADVERTISING MAGAZINES

An ITV Various production. Duration varies - see below for details.

Viewers will need no introduction to adverts. They have been around since the first night of ITV, but in the early days of independent television, programmes often were adverts themselves.

'Shopper's Guides' and 'Advertising Documentaries / Magazines' were debated in the passing of the 1954 Television Act. According to the 1958 'Advertising Rules and Practices' an admag had to follow this criteria:

"Definition - An Advertising Magazine consists of a linked series of advertisements for different products and services. The advertisements may originate from one advertiser or from a number of different advertisers.

Content - The content of the programme as a whole must clearly and unmistakably reveal and serve its advertising purpose."

There were several types of these programmes:

The Posh Shop

Elizabeth Allan or Katie Boyle would swan about some expensive shop, such as Harrods or Marshall and Snelgrove being patronising. Unbelievably the BBC used to make this kind of programme for themselves, although they needed to disguise the shops and the prices! 'Going Shopping with Elizabeth Allan' was a pre-filmed ad-mag visiting Harrods: how to make Tetley's Tea Bags (1/6s for 18); using escalators; Martell's Brandy and Bex Housewares.

The Corner Shop

Various styles, set in a more recognisable shop environment. Examples were Shop on the Corner, Watson's Store (Jack Howarth) and In Store (Kenneth Horne, Richard Murdoch and Tommy Trinder).

Young Fun

Teenagers cooing over the latest fashions. Main programmes were Flair and Girl With a Date.

Jim's Inn

Over 300 episodes made of this programme set in a pub staring Jimmy Hanley.

Industry Bodies

Sometimes an industry, or supplier and shop would join together to make a presentation. Marks and Spencers made use of this style, including one telling their own story, 'Fashion in the Making'. This example used actresses to portray real people. Mary Ward as Mrs Scarsdale, Joan Henley as Mrs Exeter, Wendy Perschky as Ginny Scarsdale and Helena de Crespo as Barbara Lawson.

Many well-known start began their careers in admags. In 1956 'About Homes and Gardens' was presented by Noele Gordon and Raymond Bishop! Many directors also began their careers on admags including Ted Childs, Lloyd Shirley and Chris Hodson. Rex Firkin, an early director, remembers:

"The IBA had ruled that very distinctly that it was a sin beyond all other sins if a programme person – a producer or director – spoke to an advertiser. The result would have been not only dismissal for the person but removal of the contract of the company for whom they worked. It was fierce law. But after not very long they realized there was a hole in their theory. Companies who wanted to broadcast started to approach commercial companies to say could they do a live commercial – that seemed to be forbidden because it would mean contact between the companies making the programmes and the advertiser. The advertising side of all companies had started to agitate fiercely for something they called an advertising magazine – there should be a series of short programmes – Jim Inn's – set in a pub – was one. I ran Tea with Joyce Shelton – JS was a delightful middle-aged soprano of the Vera Lynn school and was very popular. Various guests would come to the studio and she would give them tea, would talk about a product – cut to a packed shot of product – and so on. There was also pressure from the companies for it to be possible for advertisers to speak to the people making the programmes which formed the autumn schedule so that they could know what the programmes coming up were. So the IBA had to change tack. They did it by making a designated section of each company that were permitted to talk to advertisers. They were not in theory supposed to talk to anyone else in the company. I was stuck being in that unit. In ATV we called it 'Advertising Production Unit'. It was a lonely place to be. We worked hard doing advertising magazines and live commercials and didn't speak to anybody because we weren't supposed to. It was extremely hard work but a marvellous way to learn how to direct programmes in studios with cameras – you very soon learnt that the cameras were virtually on the ends of your fingers. It was a marvellous way of technically directing the programme – it didn't have much to do with how you guided an artist – but it was something you could profit from, a great learning curve."

These admags that were shown 3-4 times weekly are now very hard to find. Few examples exist and Kaleidoscope are always keen to find examples if any readers have some on film. One surviving example 'Triang Toy Fair' must be aimed at adults, though how many adults buy toys is debatable! This 1961 outing had Jimmy and Jennifer Hanley as Presenters.

Set up in 1960, the Pilkington Committee under the Chairmanship of Sir Harry Pilkington was appointed to consider the future of broadcasting services in the UK. Around this time there was some disquiet about acquired programming, particularly US crime series and Westerns. The Pilkington Committee reported in 1962, blaming ITV for trivialising television. Admags were particularly criticsed for being bland, led by advertisers and misleading for viewers who thought they were watching unbiased comment.

Pilkington said, "Those who say they give the public what it wants begin by underestimating public taste, and end by debauching it". Having put the knife into this style of advertising, it was finally outlawed by the 1964 Television Act, although the Postmaster-General had already directed that they were to be discontinued from 31 March 1963.

Source: Dick Fiddy/Chris Perry.

Going Shopping With Elizabeth Allan

An Advertising Features Ltd production for ATV London. Transmission details are for the ATV London region.
Main regular performer(s): With Elizabeth Allan (Presenter).

Holding / Source

20.11.1955 **Christmas Market With Elizabeth Allen** J /
Directed by Alan Tarrant.

Jim's Inn

An Associated-Rediffusion production. Transmission details are for Associated-Rediffusion. Duration: 15 minutes.
Main regular performer(s): With Jimmy Hanley (Presenter).

Holding / Source

27.12.1962 **Jim's Christmas Spirit** J /
Written by Jimmy Hanley; designed by John Emery; produced and directed by Cyril Butcher.
With Maggie Hanley, Jack Edwardes, Roma Cresswell, John Sherlock, Diane Watts, Ken Haward, Denis Bowen.

Midweek Miscellany

An Advertising Features Ltd production for ATV Midlands. Transmission details are for the ATV midlands region.

Holding / Source

26.12.1956 J /

ADVERTISING MAGAZINES (continued)

Misc Rediffusion

An Associated-Rediffusion production. Transmission details are for Associated-Rediffusion.

Main regular credit(s):   Introduced by Margot Lovell.

	Holding / Source
22.11.1956 **Dear Santa**	J / Live

Duration: 14 minutes.

A fantasy in which we visit Santa in the midst of his yearly preparations. The solutions he finds to Christmas problems will certainly be more than welcome.

Written by Diana Noel; directed by Daphne Shadwell.

29.11.1956 **Dear Santa** — J / Live

Duration: 14 minutes.

As Christmas draws nearer Santa is getting overwhelmed with phone calls and is faced with his yearly problem of making sure everybody gets the present they want.

Written by Robert Evans; directed by Pat Baker.

07.12.1956 **Treat In Store** — J / Live

Duration: 14 minutes.

Francis Coudrill and his famous puppet Cassy set out to solve some of their Christmas present problems. They hope viewers will join them in this amusing visit to a famous London store as there's an opportunity to win a gold watch.

Presented by Francis Coudrill; written by Zita Dundas; directed by Joan Kemp-Welch.

10.12.1956 **Christmas Fare** — J / Live

Duration: 14 minutes.

With Margot Lovell who will be giving you some tips for the Christmas festivities. If you wish to know more about the products seen in this programme, write to: Margot Lovell, Associated-Rediffusion Ltd., Television House, London, W.C.2.

Presented by Margot Lovell; written by Mary Hill; directed by Pat Baker.

11.12.1956 **Sing Holly-Go-Whistle** — J / Live

Duration: 14 minutes.

With Kenneth Connor who is in the throes of creating a Christmas pantomime.

Presented by Kenneth Connor; written by Diana Noël; directed by Daphne Shadwell.

13.12.1956 **Christmas Party** — J / Live

Presented by Jack Warner; written by Bob Kellett; directed by Joan Kemp-Welch.

18.12.1956 **Last Minute Buys** — J / Live

Written by Zita Dundas; directed by Pat Baker.

21.11.1957 **Christmas Ahead** — J / Live

Written by David Edwards; directed by Ian Fordyce.

26.11.1957 **Christmas Ahead** — J /

03.12.1957 **Christmas Ahead** — J /

11.12.1957 **Christmas Fare** — J /

31.12.1957 **New Year Resolutions** — J / Live

Presented by Barry Cookson and Avril Conquest; written by David Edwards; directed by Marion Radclyffe.

With Hughie Green.

05.12.1958 **Christmas Ahead** — J / Live

09.12.1958 **Christmas Gifts** — J /

12.12.1958 **Christmas Party** — J / Live

16.12.1958 **Christmas Fare** — J /

23.12.1958 **Last Minute Buys** — J /

AFFINITY

A Box Television production for ITV 1. made in association with Cite-Aitierique / Movie Central / Showcase / The Movie Network. Transmission details are for the Central region. Duration: 100 minutes.

Adapted by Andrew Davies; based on a book by Sarah Waters; script executive Julian Stevens; script supervisor Alina Apostu; music by Frédéric Weber; designed by Alison Riva; executive producers Gub Neal, Vivianne Morin, Andrew Davies, Patrick Irwin and Justin Thomson-Glover; co-produced by Vlad Paunescu; produced by Adrian Bate and Greg Dummett; directed by Tim Fywell.

Zoe Tapper (Selina), Anna Madeley (Margaret), Domini Blythe (Mother), Amanda Plummer (Miss Ridley), Mary Jo Randle (Mrs Jelf), Caroline Loncq (Ruth Vigers), Vincent Leclerc (Theophilus), Anne Reid (Mrs Brink), Anna Massey (Miss Haxby), Ferelith Young (Helen), Sara Lloyd Gregory (Madeleine), Brett Watson (Stephen), Candis Nergaard (Black Eyed Sue), Kenneth Hadley (Prison Porter), Sarah Crowden (Ada), Sarah Bedi (Agnes D'Esterre), Jason Morell (Mr Shillitoe), Buffy Davis (Mrs Sylvester), Paul Clayton (Mr Vincy), Kate Rutter (Mrs Vincy), Nickolas Grace (Mr Hither), Jackie Fielding (Susan Pilling), Jayne Denny (Shop Lady), Simon Green (Mr Tredlicott), Simon Markey (Mr Dance).

	Holding / Source
28.12.2008	DB / DBSWF

AFTER HENRY

Produced for Thames Television by a variety of companies (see details below). Transmission details are for the Central region. Duration: 25 minutes.

One of the more literate sitcoms to grace the screens of ITV over any number of years was Simon Brett's After Henry. Unashamedly middle-class and wordy, the series started life as a radio programme made by the BBC who then turned down the suggestion of remaking the comedy for television, and so the rights were snapped up by Thames Television.

By the time the television version began broadcasting, the radio programme had already been running for three series and two Christmas specials, and would continue for another series in parallel with the television version.

The series was mostly about three women who shared the same house. Sarah France was a forty-two year-old widow whose husband, Henry, had died a couple of years earlier and she was still living in the house she had previously shared with her doctor husband and their daughter. Sarah was played in both the radio and television versions of the series by Prunella Scales who at this point – the late 1980s – was still very much associated with the role of Basil Fawlty's awful wife Sybil in Fawlty Towers, and After Henry gave her a good opportunity to be linked with a more sympathetic character in the mind of the public. Although appearing in numerous dramas over the years it was definitely in comedy that Scales made her most memorable small-screen appearances – another long-running role being that of Kate Starling opposite Richard Briers in numerous series of the BBC sitcom Marriage Lines in the mid-1960s.

Living in one self-contained flat in the same house was Sarah and Henry's daughter Clare, aged around eighteen when the series started. On radio, Clare was played by Gerry Cowper now most familiar as Rosie Miller in EastEnders. But Cowper would have been 30 years old later in the same year that the television series started, and it was felt that she was too old to play the teenage Clare on screen, so the role went to TV newcomer Janine Wood.

A second flat in the house was given over to Eleanor Prescott, Sarah's mother. Eleanor was played in both versions with great relish and her usual precision by the always reliable Joan Sanderson. Sanderson, who had been acting on television since the start of the 1950s was originally brought into the public consciousness as the formidable Doris Ewell in various series of Please Sir! in the late 1960s and early 1970s. By the late 1980s, though, I would imagine most people would recall her in a one-off role – that of Mrs Richards, the guest who was very hard of hearing in an episode of Fawlty Towers.

The final regular cast character, and the only male one, was Russell Bryant, the owner and manager of Bygone Books, the second-hand bookshop in which Sarah works. Russell acts as a confidant to Sarah, particularly when her daughter and her mother gang up on her and she needs someone outside the family to discuss things with. Benjamin Whitrow played the radio Russell, whereas on television Jonathan Newth took the role.

Much of the humour in the series stems from the similarities in the relationships between the two mothers and their daughters and sometimes Simon Brett would script the episodes with almost identical scenes for Sarah France - one with her as the mother complaining to or questioning her daughter about something; and then later a similar scene would be played out between Eleanor and Sarah with Sarah forced into the same position as she'd earlier placed her daughter.

Another long-running joke was Eleanor's "geriatric mafia" as Sarah called them. Despite apparently only rarely leaving the house, Eleanor gets to hear all that's going on through a tortuous chain of people involving the likes of "Valerie Brown on the pension counter's sister, Mary" and "Mrs Graham the receptionist at the surgery's brother-in-law's stepson, Colin".

In all, 34 radio episodes and 38 television episodes were made with the latter running from January 1988 until August 1992. The entire television series is available to buy on DVD, while the radio version was regularly re-run on BBC Radio 7, though whether that will continue with its rebranding as BBC Radio 4 Extra remains to be seen.

Main regular credit(s): Written by Simon Brett.

Main regular cast: Prunella Scales (Sarah France), Joan Sanderson (Eleanor Prescott), Janine Wood (Clare France), Jonathan Newth (Russell Bryant).

SERIES 2

A Thames Television production.

Main regular credit(s): Theme music by George Gershwin and Ray Cook; produced and directed by Peter Frazer-Jones.

	VT Number	Holding / Source
26.12.1988 **A Quiet Christmas**	46290	1" / 1"

Designed by Philip Blowers.

With Peggy Ann Wood (Vera Poling), Albert Welch, Mike O'Malley.

SERIES 3

A Thames Television production.

Main regular credit(s): Theme music by George Gershwin and Ray Cook; produced and directed by Peter Frazer-Jones.

	VT Number	Holding / Source
25.12.1989 **A Week Of Sundays**	48665	1" / 1"

Duration: 24 minutes.

Designed by Philip Blowers.

With Peggy Ann Wood (Vera Poling), John Yeates.

See also: AFTER HENRY (RADIO) (BBC)

AFTER HENRY (RADIO)

A BBC production for BBC Radio 4. Transmission details are for BBC Radio 4. Duration: 30 minutes.

Main regular credit(s): Written by Simon Brett; produced and directed by Pete Atkin.

Main regular cast: Prunella Scales (Sarah), Joan Sanderson (Eleanor), Benjamin Whitrow (Russell), Gerry Cowper (Clare).

	Holding / Source
22.12.1985 **A Week Of Sundays**	DA /

With Alan Thompson.

	Holding / Source
25.12.1987 **The Season Of Relative Good Will**	DA /

See also: AFTER HENRY

AFTER NOON

A Thames Television production. Transmission details are for the Thames Television region. Duration: 25 minutes.

	Holding / Source
22.12.1977	J / LivePAL

AFTER THEY WERE FAMOUS

Produced for ITV by a variety of companies (see details below). Transmission details are for the Central region. Duration: 25 minutes.

SERIES 4
A Tyne Tees Television production.
Main regular credit(s): Executive producer Judith Holder.

	Holding / Source
23.12.2002 **Z Cars**	DB / DBSW

SERIES 5
A Tyne Tees Television production.

	Holding / Source
27.12.2003 **Willy Wonka And The Chocolate Factory**	DB / DBSW

Produced and directed by Jason Beresford.
With Matthew Kelly (Narrator), Peter Ostrum, Julie Dawn Cole, Denise Nickerson, Michael Bollner, Paris Themmen.

31.12.2003 **Bugsy Malone**	DB / DBSW

With Jodie Foster, Scott Baio.

24.12.2004 **Chitty Chitty Bang Bang**	DB / DBSW

With Dick Van Dyke, Sally Anne Howes.

AFTER YOU'VE GONE

A BBC production for BBC 1. made in association with Rude Boy Productions. Transmission details are for BBC 1. Duration varies - see below for details.

Main regular credit(s): Created by Fred Barron; music by Jamie Cullum; production executive Sarah Hitchcock; produced by Rosemary McGowan.
Main regular cast: Nicholas Lyndhurst (Jimmy Venables), Celia Imrie (Diana Neal).

SERIES 2
Main regular credit(s): Script supervisor Tessa Kimbell; script editor Paula Hines; designed by Harry Banks; executive producers Kenton Allen, Ian Brown and James Hendrie; produced by Rosemary McGowan; directed by Ed Bye.
Main regular cast: With Dani Harmer (Molly Venables), Ryan Sampson (Alex Venables), Lee Oakes (Kev), Vincent Ebrahim (Bobby), Amanda Abbington (Siobhan).

	Holding / Source
23.12.2007 **And So This Is Christmas**	DB / HDC

Duration: 45 minutes.
Written by Andrea Solomons.
With Tom Goodman-Hill, Roxanne Ricketts, Catherine Shepherd, Robert Knox, Billy Roberts, Rupert Bates.

SERIES 3
A BBC Productions production.
Main regular credit(s): Script supervisor Tessa Kimbell; script editor Paula Hines; designed by Harry Banks; executive producers Kenton Allen, Ian Brown and James Hendrie; production manager Andy Bennions; directed by Ed Bye.
Main regular cast: With Dani Harmer (Molly Venables), Ryan Sampson (Alex Venables), Lee Oakes (Kev), Vincent Ebrahim (Bobby).

	Holding / Source
21.12.2008 **There Will Be Pud**	HD/DB / HDC

Duration: 40 minutes.
Written by Ian Brown and James Hendrie.
With Michael Brandon, Lorelei King, Lee Cornes, Philip Pope, Joe Prospero, Aedan Day, Dan Johnston, Amelia Bamford, Lizzie Roper, Jordan Long.

AGATHA CHRISTIE'S MARPLE

Alternative/Working Title(s): AGATHA CHRISTIE MARPLE
A Granada production for ITV 1. made in association with Agatha Christie Ltd / WGBH Boston. Transmission details are for the Central region. Duration: 100 minutes.

Main regular credit(s): Based on books by Agatha Christie.
Main regular cast: Geraldine McEwan (Miss Jane Marple).

SERIES 1
Main regular credit(s): Script editor Karen Thrussell; music by Dominik Scherrer; executive producers Rebecca Eaton, Phil Clymer, Michele Buck and Damien Timmer; produced by Matthew Read.

	Holding / Source
26.12.2004 **4.50 From Paddington**	DB / V1SW

Adapted by Stephen Churchett; script supervisor Mary Haddow; directed by Andy Wilson.
With Jenny Agutter, Niamh Cusack, Ben Daniels, John Hannah, Celia Imrie, Maritxell Lavanchy, Neve McIntosh, Ciaran McMenamin, Kurtis O'Brien, Pip Torrens, Griff Rhys Jones, David Warner, Charlie Creed-Miles, Pam Ferris, Tim Stern, Michael Landes, Toby Marlow, Rob Brydon, Rose Keegan, Amanda Holden, Tasha Bertham, Meritxell Lavanchy.

SERIES 3
An ITV Productions production.

Main regular credit(s): Script editor Jude Liknaitzky; music by Dominik Scherrer; designed by Michael Pickwood; production executive Jon Williams; executive producers Rebecca Eaton, Phil Clymer, Michele Buck and Damien Timmer; produced by Karen Thrussell.

Holding / Source

01.01.2009 Nemesis — DB / V1SW

Adapted by Stephen Churchett; script supervisor Lorely Farley; music by Richard Hammarton; directed by Nicolas Winding Refn.

With Laura Michelle Kelly, Dan Stevens, Graeme Garden, Richard E. Grant, Ruth Wilson, Johnny Briggs, George Cole, Ronni Ancona, Adrian Rawlins, Emily Woof, Will Mellor, Anne Reid, Amanda Burton, Lee Ingleby, Heidi Monsen.

The on-screen title for this show is gramatically incorrect.

AGATHA CHRISTIE'S MARPLE

An ITV Studios production for ITV 1. made in association with Agatha Christie Ltd / WGBH Boston. Transmission details are for the Central region. Duration: 100 minutes.

Main regular credit(s): Based on books by Agatha Christie.

Main regular cast: Julia McKenzie (Miss Jane Marple).

SERIES 1
Main regular credit(s): Produced by Karen Thrussell.

Holding / Source

01.01.2010 They Do It With Mirrors — HD/DB / HD/DB

Adapted by Paul Rutman; script supervisor Kim Armitage; music by Richard Hammarton and Dominik Scherrer; director of photography Peter Greenhalgh; art director Miranda Cull; directed by Andy Wilson.

With Elliot Cowan, Alexei Sayle, Tom Payne, Emma Griffiths Malin, Joan Collins, Penelope Wilton, Brian Cox, Jordan Long, Sarah Smart, Maxine Peake, Liam Garrigan, Nigel Terry, Ian Ogilvy, Alex Jennings, Sean Hughes.

AGATHA CHRISTIE'S MISS MARPLE

A BBC production for BBC 1. made in association with Arts & Entertainment Network / Network 7 / Seven Network, Australia. Transmission details are for BBC 1. Duration varies - see below for details.

Main regular credit(s): Based on novels by Agatha Christie; theme music by Ken Howard and Alan Blaikley.

Main regular cast: Joan Hickson (Miss Marple).

The Body In The Library
Duration: 55 minutes.

Main regular credit(s): Adapted by T. R. Bowen; music by Ken Howard and Alan Blaikley; produced by Guy Slater; directed by Silvio Narizzano.

Main regular cast: With David Horovitch (Detective Inspector Slack), Gwen Watford (Mrs Bantry), Moray Watson (Colonel Bantry), Valentine Dyall (Lorrimer), Frederick Jaeger (Colonel Melchett), Andrew Cruickshank (Conway Jefferson), Ciaran Madden (Adelaide Jefferson), Jess Conrad (Raymond Starr), Trudie Styler (Josie Turner), Anthony Smee (Basil Blake).

Holding / Source

26.12.1984 Episode 1 — DB / C1

Duration: 51 minutes.

With Karin Foley (Mary), Hugh Walters (Mr Prescott), Debbie Arnold (Dinah Lee), Colin Higgins (Malcolm), John Bardon (Police Constable Palk), Anne Rutter (Mrs Palk).

27.12.1984 Episode 2 — DB / C1

With Hugh Walters (Mr Prescott), Colin Higgins (Malcolm), John Bardon (Police Constable Palk), Raymond Francis (Sir Henry Clithering), Ian Brimble (Detective Constable Lake), John Moffatt (Edwards), Keith Drinkel (Mark Gaskell), Sally Jane Jackson (Ruby Keene), Martyn Read (Hugo McLean), Kathleen Breck (Bridget), Arthur Bostrom (George Bartlett), Andrew Downer (Peter Carmody), Sidney Livingstone (Mr Brogan), Stephen Churchett (Major Reeve).

28.12.1984 Episode 3 — DB / C1

With Raymond Francis (Sir Henry Clithering), Ian Brimble (Detective Constable Lake), John Moffatt (Edwards), Keith Drinkel (Mark Gaskell), Sally Jane Jackson (Ruby Keene), Martyn Read (Hugo McLean), Andrew Downer (Peter Carmody), Sarah Whitlock (W P C), Debbie Arnold (Dinah Lee), Astra Sheridan (Pamela Reeve), Karen Seacombe (Florrie Small).

Holding / Source

25.12.1986 The Murder At The Vicarage — DB / C1

Duration: 95 minutes.

Adapted by T. R. Bowen; music directed by John Altman; music by Ken Howard; designed by Raymond London; production associate Thea Murray; executive producer Guy Slater; produced by George Gallaccio; directed by Julian Amyes.

With Paul Eddington (Reverend Leonard Clement), Cheryl Campbell (Griselda Clement), Robert Lang (Colonel Lucius Protheroe), Polly Adams (Ann Protheroe), Tara MacGowran (Lettice Protheroe), James Hazeldine (Lawrence Redding), Christopher Good (Christopher Hawes), Norma West (Mrs Lestrange), Michael Browning (Doctor Haydock), David Horovitch (Detective Inspector Slack), Ian Brimble (Detective Sergeant Lake), Jack Galloway (Bill Archer), Rachel Weaver (Mary Wright), Rosalie Crutchley (Mrs Price-Ridley), Barbara Hicks (Miss Hartnell), Kathleen Bidmead (Miss Wetherby), Deddie Davies (Mrs Salisbury), Tony Brandon (Fred Abbot), Kenneth Keeling (Ned Abbot).

AGATHA CHRISTIE'S MISS MARPLE (continued)

Holding / Source

25.12.1987 4.50 From Paddington — DB / C1
Duration: 110 minutes.
Adapted by T. R. Bowen; music directed by John Altman; music by Ken Howard; designed by Raymond Cusick [credited as Ray Cusick]; production associate Anna Kalnars; production manager Peter Markham; produced by George Gallaccio; directed by Martyn Friend.

With Juliette Mole (Anna Stravinska), David Beames (Bryan Eastley), Mona Bruce (Mrs McGillicudy), Nicholas Blane (Paddington Porter), Katy Jarrett (Mary), Leslie Adams (Desk Sergeant), David Horovitch (Detective Inspector Slack), Ian Brimble (Detective Sergeant Lake), Rhoda Lewis (Mrs Brogan), Jill Meager (Lucy Eyelesbarrow), Joanna David (Emma Crackenthorpe), Maurice Denham (Luther Crackenthorpe), Andrew Burt (Doctor Quimper), Pamela Pitchford (Mrs Kidder), Christopher Haley (Alexander Eastley), Daniel Steel (James Stoddart-West), Bernard Brown (Harold Crackenthorpe), Robert East (Alfred Crackenthorpe), John Hallam (Cedric Crackenthorpe), Alan Penn (Patmore), David Waller (Chief Inspector Ducker), Will Tacey (Arthur Wimborne), Jean Boht (Madame Joliet), David Allen (Pianist), Naomi Sorkin (Dancer), Derek Dean (Dancer), Emma Hitching (Francoise), Richard Ashley (Detective Sergeant).

25.12.1989 A Caribbean Mystery — DB / C1
Duration: 110 minutes.
Adapted by T. R. Bowen; music directed by John Altman; music by Ken Howard; designed by Don Giles; production manager David Mason; produced by George Gallaccio; directed by Christopher Petit.

With Trevor Bowen (Raymond West), Donald Pleasence, Adrian Lukis, Sophie Ward, T. P. McKenna, Michael Feast, Sheila Ruskin, Frank Middlemass, Robert Swan, Sue Lloyd, Barbara Barnes, Stephen Bent, Joseph Mydell, Valerie Buchanan, Isabelle Lucas, Shaughan Seymour, Gregory Munroe, James Curran.

29.12.1991 They Do It With Mirrors — DB-D3 / C1S
Duration: 110 minutes.
Adapted by T. R. Bowen; music by Ken Howard; associate producer Ian R. Wallace; produced by George Gallaccio; directed by Norman Stone.

With David Horovitch (Chief Inspector Slack), Ian Brimble (Sergeant Lake), Jean Simmons, Joss Ackland, Faith Brook, Gillian Barge, Neal Swettenham, Christopher Villiers, Jay Villiers, Holly Aird, Todd Boyce, Saul Reichlin, Matthew Cottle, John Bott, Brenda Cowling, David Doyle, Jake Wood, Tom Kerridge, Anne Atkins, Stee Billingsley, Rachel Bond, Bryn Walters.

Seven Network had no involvement in this episode.

27.12.1992 The Mirror Crack'd From Side To Side — DB-D3 / C1S
Duration: 116 minutes.
Adapted by T. R. Bowen; music by Ken Howard; production associate Camilla Griffith-Jones; produced by George Gallaccio; directed by Norman Stone.

With David Horovitch (Superintendant Slack), John Castle (Inspector Craddock), Ian Brimble (Sergeant Lake), Gwen Watford (Dolly Bantry), Trevor Bowen (Raymond West), Claire Bloom, Barry Newman, Glynis Barber, Judy Cornwell, Margaret Courtenay, Norman Rodway, Elizabeth Garvie, John Cassady, Christopher Hancock, Anna Niland, Rose Keegan, Rhoda Lewis, Christopher Good, Barbara Hicks, Celia Ryder, Jon Croft, Vince Rayner, Constantine Gregory, Michael Stroud, Stuart Harrison, Amanda Elwes, Reggie Oliver.

Seven Network had no involvement in this episode.

AGATHA CHRISTIE'S POIROT

Alternative/Working Title(s): HERCULE POIROT'S CASEBOOK

Produced for LWT by a variety of companies (see details below). Transmission details are for the Central region. Duration varies - see below for details.

Main regular credit(s): Based on novels by Agatha Christie.

Main regular cast: David Suchet (Hercule Poirot).

SERIES 3
A Carnival Films production for LWT.

Main regular credit(s): Theme music by Christopher Gunning; titles by Pat Gavin; executive producer Nick Elliott; production supervised by Donald Toms; production manager Kieron Phipps; produced by Brian Eastman.

24.02.1991 The Theft Of The Royal Ruby — VT Number 12063 — DB / V1
Duration: 46 minutes.
Dramatised by Clive Exton and Anthony Horowitz; script supervisor Sheila Wilson; incidental music by Fiachra Trench; supervising editor Derek Bain; director of photography Chris O'Dell; assistant directors Simon Hinkly, Adam Goodman and Gilly Raddings; art director Peter Wenham; production designer Rob Harris; directed by Andrew Grieve.

With Frederick Treves (Colonel Lacey), Stephanie Cole (Mrs Lacey), David Howey (Jesmond), Tariq Alibai (Prince Farouk), Helena Michell (Sarah Lacey), John Vernon (David Welwyn), Nigel Le Vaillant (Desmond Lee-Wortley), Robyn Moore (Gloria), John Dunbar (Peverill), Alessia Gwyther (Bridget), Jonathan S. Bancroft (Colin), Edward Holmes (Michael), Siobhan Garahy (Annie Bates), Susan Field (Mrs Ross), Gordon Reid (Chocolate Shop Owner), Christopher Leaver (Parsloe), Peter Aldwyn (Durbridge), Iain Rattray (Head Waiter), James Taylor (Waiter).

SERIES 6
A Carnival Films production for LWT. Duration: 103 minutes.

Main regular credit(s): Music by Christopher Gunning; associate producer Christopher Hall; executive producer Sarah Wilson; produced by Brian Eastman.

01.01.1995 Hercule Poirot's Christmas — VT Number 12221 — DB / V1
Dramatised by Clive Exton; script supervisor Maggie Lewty; edited by Andrew McClelland; director of photography Simon Kossoff; assistant director Bill Kirk; art director Peter Wenham; production designer Rob Harris; directed by Edward Bennett.

With Philip Jackson (Chief Inspector Japp), Vernon Dobtcheff (Simeon Lee), Simon Roberts (Alfred), Catherine Rabett (Lydia), Eric Carte (George), Andrée Bernard (Magdalene), Brian Gwaspari (Harry), Sasha Behar (Pilar), Mark Tandy (Sugden), Olga Lowe (Stella), Ayub Khan Din (Horbury), John Horsley (Tressilian), Scott Handy (Young Simeon), Liese Benjamin (Young Stella), Oscar Pearce (Gerrit), Steve Delaney (Sergeant Combes), Colin Meredith (Shopkeeper), Peter Hughes (Mr Charlton), Joanna Dickens (Cook), Michael Keats (Constable), Christopher Webber (Train Steward).

AGATHA CHRISTIE'S POIROT

AGATHA CHRISTIE'S POIROT (continued)

The BBC Radio 4 dramatisation has Peter Sallis in the role of the famous Belgian detective, Hercule Poirot.

SERIES 9

An Agatha Christie Ltd production for ITV 1. made in association with Arts & Entertainment Network / Chorion plc. Duration: 98 minutes.

Main regular credit(s): Script executive Derek Wax; script supervisor Caroline O'Reilly; script editor Karen Thrussell; music by Christopher Gunning; associate producer David Suchet; executive producers Delia Fine, Phil Clymer, Michele Buck and Damien Timmer; produced by Margaret Mitchell.

	VT Number	Holding / Source
26.12.2003 **Sad Cypress**	13045	D5H-DB/DB / V1SW

Adapted by David Pirie; directed by David Moore.

With Elisabeth Dermot-Walsh, Rupert Penry-Jones, Kelly Reilly, Paul McGann, Phyllis Logan, Marion O'Dwyer, Diana Quick, Stuart Laing, Linda Spurrier, Alistair Findlay, Louise Callaghan, Geoffrey Beevers, Ian Taylor, Jack Galloway, Timothy Carlton.

SERIES 12

An ITV Studios production for ITV 1. made in association with Agatha Christie Ltd / WGBH Boston. Duration: 100 minutes.

Main regular credit(s): Theme music by Christopher Gunning; associate producer David Suchet; production executive Julie Burnell; line producer Matthew Hamilton; produced by Karen Thrussell.

	Production No	Holding / Source
25.12.2009 **Appointment Wth Death**	1/5274/0004	HD/DB / HD/DB

Adapted by Guy Andrews; script supervisor Sue Hills; script editor Ben Newman; music by Stephen McKeon; director of photography Peter Greenhalgh; art directors Nic Pallace and Miranda Cull; designed by Jeff Tessler; executive producers Rebecca Eaton, Phil Clymer, Michele Buck and Damien Timmer; co-produced by Gabriel Silver; directed by Ashley Pearce.

With Tim Curry, Cheryl Campbell, Jawad Elalami, Christina Cole, Tom Riley, Zoe Boyle, Emma Cunniffe, Angela Pleasence, Abdelkader Aizoun, Paul Freeman, Beth Goddard, Christian McKay, Mark Gatiss, Badri Mansour, John Hannah, Zakaria Atifi, Elizabeth McGovern.

Issued on DVD a long time before shown on TV.

		Holding / Source
25.12.2010 **Murder On The Orient Express**		HD/DB / HD/DB

Adapted by Stewart Harcourt; script executive Jennie Scanlon; script supervisor Sue Hills; script editor Meriel Baistow-Clare; music by Christian Henson; director of photography Alan Almond; titles by Title Film and Television; art director Miranda Cull; executive producers Rebecca Eaton, Mathew Prichard, Mary Durkan, Michele Buck and Damien Timmer; directed by Philip Martin.

With Toby Jones, Tristan Shepherd, Elena Satine, Sam Crane, Brian J. Smith, David Morrissey, Jessica Chastain, Stewart Scudamore, Serge Hazanavicius, Eileen Atkins, Susanne Lothar, Denis Menochet, Barbara Hershey, Hugh Bonneville, Marie-Josée Croze, Stanley Weber, Joseph Mawle, Samuel West.

AGATHA CHRISTIE'S THE PALE HORSE

An United Film & TV Productions production for Anglia Films. made in association with Arts & Entertainment Network. Transmission details are for the Central region. Duration: 102 minutes.

Adapted by Alma Cullen; based on the book by Agatha Christie; script supervisor Lorely Farley; script editor Vicky Featherstone; music by Colin Towns; assistant director Simon Hinkly; production designer Robin Tarsnane; associate producer Liz Bunton; executive producers Delia Fine and Simon Lewis; produced by Adrian Bate; directed by Charles Beeson.

Colin Buchanan (Mark Easterbrook), Jayne Ashbourne (Kate Mercer), Hermione Norris (Hermia Redcliffe), Leslie Phillips (Lincoln Bradley), Michael Byrne (Venables), Jean Marsh (Thyrza Grey), Ruth Madoc (Sybil Stamfordis), Andy Serkis (Sergeant Corrigan), Trevor Byfield (Inspector Lejeune), Tim Potter (Doctor Osborne), Louise Jameson (Florence Tuckerton), Catherine Holman (Poppy Tuckerton), Richard O'Callaghan (Donald), Emma Croft (Tilly), Anna Livia Ryan (Tilly Tuckerton), Maggie Shelvin (Bella), Brett Fancy (Ricky Flood), Geoffrey Beevers (Father Gorman), Wendy Nottingham (Eileen Brandon), Tricia Thorns (Jessie Davis), Johanna Kirby (Mrs Coppins), Kieran Cunningham (Barman), Martin Oldfield (Desk Sergeant), Martin Milman (Doctor Wylie), Sam Bond (Doctor), Steve Weston (Ned Thackeray), Martin Kennedy (Tate).

	Holding / Source
23.12.1997	DB / V1S

AGONY

An LWT production. Transmission details are for the ATV midlands region. Usual duration: 25 minutes.

Main regular credit(s): Devised by Len Richmond and Anna Raeburn; theme music by Graham Field; theme sung by Babs Fletcher; photographed by Clive Arrowsmith.

Main regular cast: Maureen Lipman (Jane Lucas), Simon Williams (Laurence Lucas), Maria Charles (Bea Fisher).

SERIES 3

Duration: 26 minutes.

Main regular credit(s): Written by Stan Hey and Andrew Nickolds; designed by Rae George; production manager Mike McLoughlin; produced and directed by John Reardon.

Main regular cast: With Jeremy Bulloch (Rob Illingworth).

	Production No	Holding / Source
01.03.1981 **Rings Off Their Fingers**	9L/90125	DB / 2"

Graphics by Tony Oldfield; costume Janey Evers; make-up Marella Shearer; lighting director Trevor Saunders; sound supervisor Mike Ayres; senior camera Dave Taylor.

With Peter Blake (Andy Evol), Robert Austin (Junior Truscome), Peter Denyer (Graham Simpson), Jan Holden (Diana), Diana Weston (Val Dunn), Peter Joyce (Phone-In Voice).

ALADDIN

The companies who commissioned and produced this production are not known. Never intended for transmission.

Choreography by Roger Hannah; produced and directed by Roger Hannah.

Jeremy Beadle (Wishee Washee), Gareth Hunt (Abanazar), Barry Howard (Window Twankey), Hilary O'Neil (Aladdin), Sophie Joyce (The Princess), Nicola Alexis (Genie Of The Ring), Kevin A. J. Ranson (The Emperor), The Acromaniacs (Chinese Policemen), Lynda Radford (The Empress).

	Holding / Source
##.##.####	DV /

Filmed at Bournemouth Pavilion Theatre between 14th December 2000 - 7th January 2001.

ALADDIN

The companies who commissioned and produced this production are not known. Never intended for transmission.

Music directed by Mark Stevens; produced and directed by Peter Duncan.

Jeremy Beadle (The Genie), Brian Hibbard (Abanazer), Rebecca Callard (The Princess).

	Holding / Source
##.##.####	DV /

Filmed at Lewisham Theatre, Catford, from 19th December 1994 - 15th January 1995.

ALADDIN

A B & M Video Productions production. Never intended for transmission.

Written by Mike Goddard; choreography by Lorinda King; produced and directed by Mike Goddard.

Jeremy Beadle (Wishee Washee), Paul Stead (Emperor Of China), Mystina (Genie Of The Lamp), Peter John (Widow Twankey), Peter Piper, Lorinda King, Paul Critchlow, Craig Deegan.

	Holding / Source
##.##.####	DV /

Filmed at City Varieties Music Hall, Leeds from Thursday 21st December 1989 - Saturdayt 27th January 1990.

ALADDIN

A BBC production. Transmission details are for BBC. Duration: 90 minutes.

Written by Peter Ling; music by Steve Race and Jack Jordan; orchestra directed by Jack Jordan; choreography by Peter Glover; settings by Stephen Taylor; produced by Michael Westmore and Gilchrist Calder; directed by Michael Westmore and Gilchrist Calder.

Peter Glover (Genie Of The Lamp), Pat Sinnott (Genie Of The Ring), Bill Shine (Emperor Of China), Pamela Galloway (Princess), Peter Hawkins (Lord High Chamberlain), Nesta Ross (Lady-In-Waiting), David Jacobs (Aladdin), Peter Butterworth (Widow Twankey), Humphrey Lestocq (Abanazar), David Nixon (Wisheee-Washee), Anthony Valentine (Boy), Edward Markillie (Fat Man), Alex Drew (Thin Man), Wilfred Johns (Policeman), Sam Williams (Puppeteer).

	Holding / Source
26.12.1951	NR / Live

ALADDIN

A BBC production. Transmission details are for BBC. Duration: 70 minutes.

Written by Rex Tucker; music by John Hotchkis and The Goldsbrough Orchestra; produced and directed by Rex Tucker.

David Cole (Aladdin), Hugh David (Abanazar), Douglas Wilmer (The Caliph), Mildred Mayne (Princess Badroulboudour), Bruno Barnabe (The Vizier), Steve Plytas (Eunuch-In-Chief), Nan Marriott Watson (Aladdin's Mother), Ewen Solon (Slave of the Lamp), Philip Locke (Slave of the Ring), Brenda Bennett (Yasmin), Chin Yu (Ming Yu), Patrick Troughton (Gambler), Philip Rose (Guard or Slave or Person of Baghdad), Rashidi Onikoyi (Guard or Slave or Person of Baghdad), Herbert Gomez (Guard or Slave or Person of Baghdad), Isola Oki (Guard or Slave or Person of Baghdad), K. A. Medas (Guard or Slave or Person of Baghdad), Edet Effiong (Guard or Slave or Person of Baghdad), Sam Mansaray (Guard or Slave or Person of Baghdad), Edna McKenzie (Guard or Slave or Person of Baghdad), Robert Norman (Guard or Slave or Person of Baghdad), Brian Sheehy (Guard or Slave or Person of Baghdad), Leslie Smith (Guard or Slave or Person of Baghdad), Frank Olegario (Guard or Slave or Person of Baghdad), Anthea Wyndam (Guard or Slave or Person of Baghdad), Claude Bonsor (Guard or Slave or Person of Baghdad).

	Holding / Source
26.12.1957	J /

ALADDIN

A Rediffusion Television production. Transmission details are for the ATV midlands region. Duration: 75 minutes.

Written by David Croft; additional material by Dick Vosburgh; lyrics by The Shadows; music directed by Norrie Paramour; music by The Shadows; designed by Frank Nerini; produced by Bill Hitchcock.

Cliff Richard (Aladdin), Arthur Askey (Widow Twankey), Alan Curtis (Abanazar), Katerina Holden (Genie), Bill Tasker (Town Crier), The Maljohns (Policemen), The Lynton Boys (Horse), Bruce Welch (Wishee), Hank Marvin (Washee), Brian Bennett (Noshee), John Rostill (Poshee), Wendy Padbury (So-Shy), Anna Perry (Tai-Ping), Vanessa Howard (Princess), Julian Orchard (Emperor), Michael Henry (Grand Vizier), David Davenport (Slave of The Lamp), The Mike Sammes Singers, The Pamela Devis Dancers.

	Production No	VT Number	Holding / Source
25.12.1967	LE/44/30-3	W4479/5240(HI)	J / 40

Recorded 31.10.1967 - 03.11.1967.

ALADDIN

ALADDIN

A Yorkshire Television production. Transmission details are for the ATV midlands region. Duration: 65 minutes.

Written by Bill Roberton; music directed by Gareth Davies; choreography by Malcolm Goddard; produced by Bill Roberton; directed by David Mallet.

Bernie Winters (Aladdin), Mike Winters (Abanazar), Jack Douglas (Genie of The Lamp), Jimmy Logan (Widow Twankey), Josef Locke (Emperor), Peter Vernon (Vizier), Maggie Vickers (Princess), The Malcolm Goddard Dancers, Bel Canto Singers.

	Holding / Source
25.12.1969	J / 2"

ALADDIN

A BBC production for BBC 1. Transmission details are for BBC 1. Duration: 90 minutes.

Written by Ronnie Taylor; based on a book by Phil Park and Albert J. Knight; choreography by Irving Davies; produced and directed by Michael Hurll.

Cilla Black (Aladdin), Alfred Marks (Abanazar), Roy Castle (Wishee Washee), Norman Vaughan (Widow Twankey), Derek Dene (Chief Of Police), Elaine Paige (Princess), Tom Chatto (Emperor), Bertie Hare (Vizier), Milton Reid (Slave), Sandra Michaels (Genie), Eric Coverdale (Pekin Police), Bill Herbert (Pekin Police), Laurie Johnson (Pekin Police), Isabell Hurll (Handmaiden), Bob Parvin (Town Crier), The Irving Davies Dancers, Ronnie Hazlehurst and his Orchestra, The Breakaways, The Fred Tomlinson Singers.

	Holding / Source
25.12.1971	J / 2"

ALADDIN

Alternative/Working Title(s): THE STORY OF ALADDIN

A BBC production for BBC 1. Transmission details are for BBC 1. Duration: 60 minutes.

Written by Bob Hedley and Tony Hare; choreography by Flick Colby; designed by Richard Morris; produced and directed by Robin Nash; film sequences directed by Alan Bell.

Michael Aspel, Jacqueline Clarke, Dana, Peter Glaze, The Goodies, Barrie Gosney, Derek Griffiths, Deryck Guyler, Jan Hunt, Don Maclean, Pan's People, Ed Stewart, Richard Wattis, Bert Hayes and his Orchestra.

	VT Number	Holding / Source
24.12.1974 [Crackerjack Pantomime]	VTC/6HT/96121B	DB-D3 / 2"

ALADDIN

An LWT production. Transmission details are for the Central region. Duration: 74 minutes.

Written by Simon Nye; music by Philip Pope; edited by Mykola Pawluk; production team Jo Dench, James Gibbons, Ben Russell and Mark Vella; executive producer Nigel Lythgoe; production manager Keith Lascelles; produced by Lisa Clark; directed by Geoff Posner.

Ed Byrne (Aladdin), Julian Clary (Genie of The Lamp), Martin Clunes (Abanazar), Patsy Kensit (Prncess), Ralf Little (Wishee Washee), Paul Merton (Spirit of The Ring), Billy Murray (Police Chief), Griff Rhys Jones (Emperor), Lisa Riley (Handmaiden), John Savident (Widow Twankey), Meera Syal (High Priestess), Leslie Phillips (Older Prince), Trisha Goddard (Trisha), S Club 7.

	Holding / Source
25.12.2000	DB / DBS

ALADDIN AND HIS WONDERFUL LAMP

A BBC production. Transmission details are for BBC. Duration: 75 minutes.

Devised by Bertram Montague; written by Barry Lupino and Arty Ash; lyrics by Barry Lupino and Arty Ash; choreography by Harriet James; produced by Rex London; directed by Bertram Montague.

Marjorie Sandford (Aladdin), Rex London (Widow Twankey), Philip Godfrey (Abanazar), Jack Anton (Wishee Washee), Ruth Miller (Princess Luvlee), Arthur Stanley (Grand Vizier), The Chikolas (Wun Hi And Wun Lung, Chinese Policemen), Clive Drummond (Emperor Wangchow), Paddy Johnson (Pekoe), Joyce Down (So-Koy), Nickie Hilliard (Osram Ben Mazda), Gillian Leach (Genie Of The Ring).

	Holding / Source
07.01.1951	NR / Live

Excerpts from Bertam Montague's pantomime.

ALADDIN AND HIS WONDERFUL LAMP

A BBC production for BBC 1. Transmission details are for BBC 1. Duration: 85 minutes.

Written by David Croft; music by Art Day and Harry Rabinowitz; orchestra directed by Harry Rabinowitz; choreography by Douglas Squires; produced by David Croft; directed by Peter Whitmore.

Arthur Askey (Widow Twankey), Roy Castle (Wishee Washee), Alan Curtis (Abanazar), Angela Richards (Aladdin), Ian Wallace (The Emperor), Mary Millar (The Princess), Peter Grant (The Vizier), Pat Goh (So Shy), Christine Child (Genie of the Ring), David Davenport (Slave of the Lamp), Charlie Cairoli, The Douglas Squires Dancers, George Mitchell Singers.

	Holding / Source
25.12.1966	DB-R1 /

ALADDIN AND THE FORTY THIEVES

A BBC Children's Department production for BBC 1. Transmission details are for BBC 1. Duration: 55 minutes.

Written by John Morley; drawings by Alison Darke; music directed by Roy Civil; choreography by Chris Power; designed by Marjorie Pratt; production manager David Lardner; produced and directed by Jeremy Swan.

Edward Brayshaw (Abanazar), Floella Benjamin (Genie of the Ring), Sarah Greene (Aladdin), Terry Nutkins (Wishee Washee), Johnny Morris (Widow Twankey), Jan Francis (Princess Balroubador), Sue Nicholls (Her Nurse), Brian Cant (Emperor of China), Ann Emery (Empress), Johnny Ball (Mr Wu), Todd Carty (Ali Baba), William Perrie (Ali Baba's Horse), John Asquith (Ali Baba's Horse), Carol Chell (Mrs Chow Mein), Hal Dyer (Mrs Sing Hi), Molly Weir (Mrs Ping Pong), Kenneth Connor (Abdul, The Chief Thief), Jeffrey Segal (Cassim), James Marcus (Achmoud), Paddie O'Neil (Handmaiden), Janet Ellis (Handmaiden), Christopher Biggins (Genie of the Lamp), John Craven (Palace Newsreader), Clive Dunn (Chamberlain), Kenneth Williams (Mustapha Drink), Peter Duncan (Suitor), Mike Read (Suitor), Keith Chegwin (Suitor), Mark Curry (Suitor), Ben Ellison (Suitor), Geoffrey Russell (Suitor), Tracey Childs (Pekinese Chorus), Matthew Devitt (Pekinese Chorus), Brian Jameson (Pekinese Chorus), Elizabeth Watts (Pekinese Chorus), Heather Williams (Pekinese Chorus), Keith Woodhams (Pekinese Chorus), George Armstrong (Thief), Jonathan Cohen (Thief), Adrian Hedley (Thief), Bill Homewood (Thief), Mat Irvine (Thief), Delia Morgan (Thief), Paul McCarthy (Thief), Jolyon McDowell (Thief), Stuart McGugan (Thief), Andrew Secombe (Thief), Howard Stableford (Thief), Barry Took (Thief), Brian Trueman (Thief), Gary Wilmot (Thief).

	Holding / Source
01.01.1984	DB / 1"

ALADDIN, THE CHINESE LAUNDRY BOY (RADIO)

A BBC production for BBC Radio 4. Transmission details are for BBC Radio 4. Duration: 60 minutes.

Written by Stewart Permutt, John Langdon and Bruce Hyman; music by Philip Pope, Nick Mason and Kevin Powell; produced and directed by Bruce Hyman.

Terry Jones (Abanazzar), Clive Anderson (Grand Vizier), Penelope Keith (Empress of China), Tony Robinson (Aladdin), Jennifer Ehle (Princess Mah-Jong), Tony Hawks (Wishee Washee), Robbie Coltrane (Widow Twankey), Lesley Joseph (Genie of The Ring), Jeremy Hardy (Genie of The Lamp), Cantate Youth Choir (Pekinese People).

	Holding / Source
25.12.1999	DA /

ALADIN AND HIS MAGIC LAMP

A BBC Wales production for BBC 2 Wales Digital. Transmission details are for BBC 2 Wales Digital.

Written by Alan Wightman; produced by Ailsa Jenkins; directed by Clive Harpwood.

Kelly Marie (Aladdin), Owen Money (Wishee Washee), Maureen Rees (Maureenie The Genie), Jayne Case, Ieuan Rhys, Roy Noble, Sara Edwards.

	Holding / Source
31.12.2001	DB / DBSW

Alternative transmissions: BBC 2: 01.01.2002.

ALAN CARR: CHATTY MAN

An Open Mike production for Channel 4. Transmission details are for Channel 4. Usual duration: 45 minutes.

Main regular performer(s): Alan Carr (Host).

SERIES 2

Main regular credit(s): Script supervisor Rebecca Havers; music by Dan McGrath and Josh Phillips; titles by Double G Studios; art director Lucy Fyfe; designed by Dennis De Groot; assistant producers Tasoulla Georgiou, John Greathead, Rose Hanson and Jon Holman; executive producers Andrew Beint and Addison Cresswell; production manager Louise Shepherd; series producer Richard Ackerman; produced by James Longman; directed by Steve Smith.

	Holding / Source
22.12.2009 **Christmas Special**	DB / DBSW

Duration: 65 minutes.
Written by Alan Carr, Giles Boden, Aiden Spackman, Les Keen and Stewart Williams.
With Cilla Black, David Walliams, Justin Lee Collins, The Saturdays, Christopher Biggins, Eoghan Quigg, Abbey Clancy.

29.12.2009 **New Year's Special**	DB / DBSW

Written by Alan Carr, Aiden Spackman, Giles Boden, Les Keen and Stewart Williams.
With David Tennant, Davina McCall, Spandau Ballet, Catherine Tate.

SERIES 5

Main regular credit(s): Script supervisor Rebecca Havers; music by Dan McGrath and John Phillips; titles by Jump; art director Lucy Fyfe; designed by Dennis De Groot; assistant producers Aoife Dunne, Kate Edmunds, Rose Hanson and Danny Julian; executive producers Richard Ackerman, Andrew Beint and Addison Cresswell; production manager Louisa Shepherd [credited as Louisa Shephard]; produced by Jon Holman; directed by Steve Smith.

	Holding / Source
26.12.2010 **Christmas Special**	DB / DBSW

Written by Alan Carr, Giles Boden, Les Keen, Aiden Spackman and Stewart Williams.
With The Wanted, Chris Evans, Catherine Tate, Mickey Rourke.

SERIES 7

Main regular credit(s): Music by Dan McGrath and Josh Phillips; titles by Jump; designed by Dennis De Groot; executive producers Andrew Beint, Addison Cresswell and Richard Ackerman; series producer Jon Holman.

	Holding / Source
25.12.2011	HD/DB / HDC

With Ruth Jones, David Walliams, JEdward, Steps.

| British Christmas Television Guide | ALAN CARR: CHATTY MAN (continued) |

31.12.2011 **Alan Carr's New Year Spectacular** HD/DB / HDC
Duration: 125 minutes.
Series producer Seamus Murphy-Mitchell.
With Jonathan Ross, Micky Flanagan, Rachel Riley, Melanie Sykes, Gok Wan, Kirstie Allsopp, Alesha Dixon, Bruno Tonioli, Heston Blumenthal, Olly Murs, Paddy McGuinness, Shelley Von Strunckel, JLS, The Ting Tings.

SERIES 9
Main regular credit(s): Executive producers Andrew Beint and Addison Cresswell.

                                     Holding / Source
25.12.2012 HD/DB / HDC
Series producer Jon Holman.
With JLS, David Walliams, Hilary Devey, McFly.

31.12.2012 **Alan Carr's New Year Spectacular** HD/DB / HDC
Duration: 100 minutes.
Series producer Russell Balkind.
With Gok Wan, Jack Whitehall, Rylan Clark, Jonathan Ross, Jimmy Carr, Melanie Sykes, Christine Bleakley, Bruno Mars.

Main regular credit(s): Executive producers Andrew Beint and Addison Cresswell.

                                     Holding / Source
25.12.2013 HD/DB / HDC
Duration: 48 minutes.
Series producer Jon Holman.
With Russell Brand, Davina McCall, David Dickinson, Little Mix.

31.12.2013 **Alan Carr's New Year Specstacular** HD/DB / HDC
Duration: 100 minutes.
Series producer Chris Little; produced by Tommy Panays.
With James Corden, Leigh Francis [as Keith Lemon], Ben Cohen, Abbey Clancy, Tinie Tempah, Katy B.

ALAN CARR'S CELEBRITY DING DONG
An Open Mike production for Channel 4. Transmission details are for Channel 4.
Main regular performer(s): Alan Carr (Host).
SERIES 2
Main regular credit(s): Written by Giles Boden and Alan Carr; script supervisor Helena Taylor; music by SNK Music; programme consultant Dean Nabarro; designed by Patrick Doherty; executive producers Andrew Beint and Addison Cresswell; production manager Louisa Shepherd; series producer Chris Curley; produced by Phil Harris and Paul McGettigan; directed by Chris Howe.
Main regular performer(s): With Peter Dickson (Voice Only).

                                     Holding / Source
23.12.2008 **Alan Carr's Christmas Ding Dong** DB / DBSW
Duration: 40 minutes.
Additional material by David Cadji-Newby, Les Keen, Aiden Spackman and Nico Tatarowicz.
With Adele Silva, Paul Daniels, Debra Stephenson, Barbara Windsor, Claire Sweeney, John Thomson, Michelle Collins, Joe Pasquale.

ALAN TITCHMARSH AT CHRISTMAS
A Spun Gold TV production for ITV 1. Transmission details are for the Central region. Duration: 48 minutes.
Script supervisor Silvana Job; theme music by Music 4; designed by Simon Kimmel; associate producer Stephanie McIntosh; executive producers Nick Bullen, Annie Sweetbaum and Matt Young; production manager Jim Boyers; produced by Nichola Hegarty; location sequences directed by Madeline Addy; directed by Peter Orton.
Alan Titchmarsh (Host), Mark Dolan (Voice Over), Julie Walters, Will Young, Andrea Bocelli, Emma Bunton.

                                     Holding / Source
21.12.2008 DB / DBSW

ALAS SMITH AND JONES
A BBC production for BBC 2. Transmission details are for BBC 2. Duration: 30 minutes.
Main regular cast: Mel Smith (Various roles), Griff Rhys Jones (Various roles).

                                     Holding / Source
23.12.1987 **The Home Made Xmas Video** DB / 1"
Written by Robin Driscoll; produced by John Kilby; directed by Jamie Rix.
With Diane Langton, Robin Driscoll, Dorothea Alexander, Brian Coburn, Frankie Cosgrave, Janice Cramer, Nigel Harman, Jenny Jay, Raymond Mason, Peter McCarthy, Walter Sparrow, Rebecca Stevens, Stan Young.

25.12.1988 **Alas Sage And Onion** DB / 1"
A Talkback production. Duration: 40 minutes.
Written by Clive Anderson, Moray Hunter, John Docherty, Robin Driscoll, Roger Planer, Abi Grant, Laurie Rowley, Griff Rhys Jones, Jamie Rix, Nick Wilton, Paul Smith, Terry Kyan and Jockeys of Norfolk; music by Peter Brewis; designed by Robin Tarsnane; produced by Jamie Rix; directed by John Kilby.
With Lindsay Duncan, Clive Mantle, Tony Slattery, Geoff McGivern, Foxes.

ALI G'S ALTERNATIVE CHRISTMAS MESSAGE

A Talkback production for Channel 4. Transmission details are for Channel 4. Duration: 15 minutes.

Written by Sacha Baron Cohen, Dan Mazer, Andrew Newman and Jamie Glassman; executive producer Peter Fincham; produced and directed by Dan Mazer.

Sacha Baron Cohen (Ali G).

	Holding / Source
25.12.1999	DB /

ALICE

A BBC production. Transmission details are for BBC. Duration: 40 minutes.

Dramatised by Clemence Dane; adapted by George More O'Ferrall; based on the book by Lewis Carroll; music by Richard Addinsell; play production by George More O'Ferrall.

Vivian Pickles (Alice), Erik Chitty (White Rabbit), Desmond Walter-Ellis (Mad Hatter), John Baker (March Hare), Gwyneth Lewis (Dormouse), Dorothy Stuart (Caterpillar), John Roderick (Dodo), Betty Potter (Mouse), Philip Stainton (Mock Turtle), Hilary Pritchard (Gryphon), Madge Brindley (The Ugly Duchess), Miriam Karlin (Cook), Josephine Gundry (First Rose), Nancy Harrison (Second Rose), D. A. Mehan [as D. A. Meehan] (King of Hearts), Kenneth Buckley (Queen of Hearts), Eric Lindsay (Knave of Hearts), Eric Stocker (Two of Spades), Kevin Sheldon (Five of Spades), Anthony Bridge (Seven of Spades).

		Holding / Source
21.12.1946	First Performance	NR / Live
24.12.1946	Second Performance	NR / Live

Subtitled: Some of her adventures in Wonderland.

ALICE THROUGH THE LOOKING BOX

An ABC production. Transmission details are for the ABC midlands region. Duration: 75 minutes.

Written by Sid Colin and Jimmy Grafton; dances staged by Tommy Linden; designed by Voytek; produced by Brian Tesler; directed by Michael Mills.

Jeannie Carson (Alice), Spike Milligan (The White Rabbit), Bernard Braden (Himself), Dora Bryan (The Red Queen), Bernard Bresslaw (The March Hare), Ronnie Corbett (The Dormouse), Fanny Cradock (The Duchess of Larkin), David Ensor (The Judge), Joe Henderson (Court Pianist), David Hughes (The King of Hearts), Barbara Kelly (Herself), Simon Kester (The Prosecuting Counsel), David Kossoff (The Duke of Larkin), Adele Leigh (The Queen of Hearts), Michael Medwin (The Knave of Hearts), Glenn Melvyn (The Walrus), Bob Monkhouse (The Cheshire Cat), Ron Moody (The Mad Hatter), Pete Murray (The Red King), Donald Pleasence (The Caterpillar), Danny Ross (The Carpenter), Harry Secombe (Humpty Dumpty), Joan Sims (Chambermaid), Mike Winters (Tweedledee), Bernie Winters (Tweedledum), John Bentley (Inspector Paul Derek), Donald Gray (Mark Saber), Ian Hendry (Doctor Geoffrey Brent), Conrad Phillips (William Tell), Jackie Rae, Janette Scott, Marty Wilde, The Vernon Girls, Bob Sharples and his Music.

	Holding / Source
25.12.1960	J / 40

Advance publicity suggested that Raymond Francis and Eric Lander would be taking part as Lockhart and Baxter but they are not listed in TV Times.

ALICE'S ADVENTURES IN WONDERLAND AND THROUGH THE LOOKING GLASS

A BBC production. Transmission details are for BBC. Duration: 105 minutes.

Adapted by John Glyn-Jones; based on books by Lewis Carroll; based on a play by Herbert M. Prentice; dances staged by Sheila Rawle; music composed by Alfred Reynolds; orchestra directed by Alfred Reynolds; settings by Barry Learoyd; play production by John Glyn-Jones.

James McKechnie (Lewis Carroll), Margaret Barton (Alice), Roddy Hughes (White Rabbit), Cameron Miller (Caterpillar), Walter Plinge (The Frog Footman), Beatrice Rowe (Cook), Olive Walter (Duchess), Morris Sweden (Cheshire Cat), Anthony Oliver (March Hare), Robert Webber (Mad Hatter), Charles Wade (Dormouse), Ray James (Two of Spades), Archie Angus (Five of Spades), Derek Ensor (Seven of Spades), Bruce Belfrage (King of Hearts), Sybil Arundale (Queen of Hearts), Victor Platt (Knave of Hearts), Stewart Vartan (Executioner / Walrus), Dennis Bowen (Gryphon), Gordon Bell (Mock Turtle), Louise Hampton (The Red Queen), Ian Wallace (Tweedledum), James Hayter (Tweedledee), Charles Rolfe (Carpenter), Ann Codrington (The White Queen), Jack Howarth (Humpty-Dumpty), Harold Scott (The White King), Anthony Sharp (The White Knight).

		Holding / Source
25.12.1948	First Performance	NR / Live

ALISTAIR MCGOWAN'S BIG IMPRESSION

A Vera production for BBC 1. Transmission details are for BBC 1. Usual duration: 30 minutes.

Main regular cast: Alistair McGowan (Various roles).

		Holding / Source
30.12.2000	Alistair McGowan's 2000 Impressions	DB / DBSW

Produced by Charlie Hanson; directed by Gareth Carrivick.

With Ronni Ancona.

SERIES 2

Main regular credit(s): Produced by Charlie Hanson.
Main regular cast: With Ronni Ancona.

		Holding / Source
25.12.2001	Christmas Special	DB / DBSW

Duration: 38 minutes.
Directed by Angela De Chastelai Smith.
With Jan Ravens, Roger Blake, Rory Bremner.

British Christmas Television Guide   ALISTAIR MCGOWAN'S BIG IMPRESSION (continued)

SERIES 3

Main regular credit(s): Written by Simon Blackwell, Laurence Howarth, Alan Francis and Daniel Maier; produced by Charlie Hanson; directed by Gareth Carrivick.

Main regular cast: With Ronni Ancona.

	Holding / Source
25.12.2002 **The Big Impression**	DB / DBSW

Duration: 35 minutes.

ALL CREATURES GREAT AND SMALL

A BBC Birmingham production for BBC 1. Transmission details are for BBC 1. Usual duration: 50 minutes.

Main regular credit(s): Based on novels by James Herriot; theme music by Johnny Pearson; produced by Bill Sellars.

Main regular cast: Christopher Timothy (James Herriot), Robert Hardy (Siegfried Farnon).

SERIES 2

Main regular credit(s): Script editor Ted Rhodes; production unit manager John Nathan-Turner.

Main regular cast: With Peter Davison (Tristan Farnon), Carol Drinkwater (Helen Herriot), Mary Hignett (Mrs Hall).

	Holding / Source
24.12.1978 **Merry Gentlemen**	DB-D3 / 2"

Duration: 51 minutes.

Tricki-Woo, overfed by Mrs Pumphrey again, feels ill and is nursed back to health by Helen — which provides the inevitable hamper — a welcome addition at any time, but especially at Christmas. But Christmas at Skeldale House, with carols, holly and mistletoe, can be a strange experience.

Written by Anthony Steven; designed by David Crozier; directed by Christopher Barry.

With Margaretta Scott (Mrs Pumphrey), Donald Nithsdale, Michael Holt, Robert Brown, Cynthia Etherington, Frank Birch.

SERIES 3

Main regular cast: With Peter Davison (Tristan Farnon), Carol Drinkwater (Helen Herriot), Mary Hignett (Mrs Hall).

	Holding / Source
25.12.1979 **Plenty to Grouse About**	DB-D3 / 2"

Written by Terence Dudley; directed by Christopher Barry.

With Andrew Robertson, John Ringham, Frank Birch, Stuart Golland, Jackie Shinn, Joyce Kennedy, Malcolm Raeburn, Julian Garlick, Jayne Lester, Catriona MacDonald.

The Lord God Made Them All

Duration: 90 minutes.

Main regular cast: With Peter Davison (Tristan Farnon), Carol Drinkwater (Helen Herriot).

	Holding / Source
25.12.1983 **Episode 1**	DB / C1

Written by Brian Finch; directed by Terence Dudley.

With Harry Brayne (Jimmy Herriot), John Sharp (Biggins), Margaretta Scott (Mrs Pumphrey), Teddy Turner (Hodgekins), John Collin, Marjorie Sudell, Tim Barker, Geoffrey Bayldon, Joseph Peters, Annie Lambert, Madeline Smith, Steve Halliwell, John Arthur, Graham Hamilton, Eddie Caswell, Wilfred Grove, Anna Turner, Sharon Cheyne, David Straun.

25.12.1985 **Episode 2**	DB / C1

Written by Johnny Byrne; directed by Peter Moffatt.

With Oliver Wilson (Jimmy Herriot), Rebecca Smith (Rosie Herriot), Irene Sutcliffe, John Woodvine, Paul Gee, Judy Wilson, Judi Maynard, Graham Rigby, Tony Capstick, Nigel Collins, James Tear, Fine Time Fontayne, George Little, Bobby Knutt, Bill Lund, Tommy Harper, Alan Hulse, D. J. Huckerby, Sean Glenn.

SERIES 7

Main regular cast: With Peter Davison (Tristan Farnon), Lynda Bellingham (Helen Herriot).

	Holding / Source
24.12.1990 **Brotherly Love**	1" / V1

Duration: 90 minutes.

Written by Christopher Penfold; directed by Michael Brayshaw.

With John Sharp (Biggins), Jean Heywood (Mrs Alton), Megs Jenkins, Sam Dale, David Ellison, Sidney Livingstone, Rio Fanning, Hugh Walters, Jack Watson, Dee Marston, Roger Brierley, Gemma Peers, Tim Barker, Steve Sangster, Jack Carr, Steve Halliwell, David Hershaw, Elaine Donnelly, Aubrey Phillips, Mike Kay, Ted Richards.

"The James Herriot Story", tx: 27.4.99 on Yorkshire Television talked to stars of the series. Produced and directed by Sheilagh Matheson. Presented by Andy Kluz. 24 mins 5 seconds.

ALL KINDS OF MUSIC

An ATV production. Transmission details are for the ATV midlands region. Duration: 60 minutes.

SERIES 1

Main regular credit(s): Produced by Francis Essex.

Main regular performer(s): With Jack Parnell and his Concert Orchestra.

	VT Number	Holding / Source
26.12.1961	TR4036	R1 /

Music associate Jack Chivers; designed by Henry Graveney.

With Cliff Richard, The Kaye Sisters, Max Jaffa, Ralph Downes, Boscoe Holder and his Caribbean Dancers, Susan Lane, Curtis Pierre and The Trinidad Steel Band, The London Orpheus Choir.

ALL KINDS OF MUSIC (continued)	British Christmas Television Guide

Holding / Source

25.12.1967   J /

Designed by Bill McPherson; produced and directed by Dicky Leeman.

With Roy Budd, Vince Hill, New Faces, Malcolm Roberts, Andee Silver, Elizabeth Vaughan, The Mike Sammes Singers, The Hendon Grammar School Choir, Jack Parnell and his Orchestra.

25.12.1968   J /

Designed by Anthony Waller; produced and directed by Dicky Leeman.

With Dusty Springfield, Malcolm Roberts, The Tremeloes, Kiki Dee, Trio Athenee, The Spinners, Roger Webb, David Snell, Des Ryan, The Mike Sammes Singers, The Breakaways, Jack Parnell and his Orchestra.

See also: VAL PARNELL'S STAR TIME

THE ALL NEW ALEXEI SAYLE SHOW

A BBC production for BBC 2. Transmission details are for BBC 2. Duration: 30 minutes.

Main regular credit(s):   Produced by Alan Nixon; directed by Metin Hüseyin.

Main regular cast: Alexei Sayle (Various roles / Presenter), Jean Marsh.

Holding / Source

27.01.1994   **Alexei's Extra Special Xmas Show**   DB-D3 / 1"

With Billy Bragg.

ALL RISE FOR JULIAN CLARY

A BBC production for BBC 2. Transmission details are for BBC 2.

Main regular credit(s):   Written by Julian Clary and John Irwin; executive producer Jon Plowman.

Main regular performer(s):   Julian Clary (Judge).

Holding / Source

22.12.1997   DB-D3 / D3S

With June Whitfield (Clerk).

ALL STAR COMEDY CARNIVAL

Produced for ATV by a variety of companies (see details below). Transmission details are for the ATV midlands region. Duration: 75 minutes.

Main regular credit(s):   Executive producer Bill Ward.

	VT Number	Holding / Source
25.12.1969 **[presentation]**	2499	J / 2"

An ATV production.

Written by Tony Hawes and Bryan Blackburn; produced and directed by Albert Locke.

With Des O'Connor (Host).

25.12.1969   **Doctor In The House**   2499   J / 2"

An LWT production.

Written by Graeme Garden and Bill Oddie; based on books by Richard Gordon; produced by Humphrey Barclay; directed by Mark Stuart.

With Geoffrey Davies, Barry Evans, George Layton, Robin Nedwell, Martin Shaw, Simon Cuff.

25.12.1969   **On The Buses**   2499   J / 2"

An LWT production.

Written by Ronald Wolfe and Ronald Chesney; designed by Roger Hall; produced and directed by Stuart Allen.

With Reg Varney, Bob Grant, Stephen Lewis, Anna Karen, Doris Hare, Michael Robbins.

25.12.1969   **Please Sir!**   2499   J / 2"

An LWT production.

Written by John Esmonde and Bob Larbey; designed by Barbara Bates; produced and directed by Mark Stuart.

With John Alderton, David Barry, Erik Chitty, Peter Cleall, Richard Davies, Peter Denyer, Liz Gebhardt, Deryck Guyler, Noel Howlett, Malcolm McFee, Penny Spencer, Joan Sanderson.

25.12.1969   **Mr Digby Darling**   2499   J / 2"

A Yorkshire Television production.

Written by Ken Hoare and Mike Sharland; lyrics by Herbert Kretzmer; music by Dave Lee; designed by Roger Cheveley; executive producer Sid Colin; produced and directed by Christopher Hodson.

With Sheila Hancock, Peter Jones.

25.12.1969   **Jokers Wild**   2499   J / 2"

A Yorkshire Television production.

With Les Dawson, Ted Ray, Ted Rogers.

25.12.1969   **The Dustbinmen**   2499   DB / 2"

A Granada production.

Written by Jack Rosenthal; designed by Peter Caldwell; produced and directed by Richard Everitt.

With Bryan Pringle, Trevor Bannister, Graham Haberfield, Tim Wylton.

25.12.1969   **Coronation Street**   2499   J / 2"

A Granada production.

Written by Ron McDonnell; produced by H. V. Kershaw; directed by June Howson.

With Alan Browning, Violet Carson, Peter Adamson, Jean Alexander, Margot Bryant, Eileen Derbyshire, Betty Driver, Patricia Fuller, Sandra Gough, Jack Howarth, Gorden Kaye, Arthur Leslie, William Moore, Patricia Phoenix, Anne Reid, William Roache, Doris Speed, Bernard Youens.

ALL STAR COMEDY CARNIVAL

	VT Number	Holding / Source
25.12.1969 Cribbins	2499	J / 2"

A Thames Television production.
Written by Brian Cooke and Johnnie Mortimer; designed by Bernard Spencer; produced and directed by Alan Tarrant.
With Bernard Cribbins, Carmel McSharry, Terence Brady, Bob Todd.

25.12.1969 Father, Dear Father — 2499 — J / 2"

A Thames Television production.
Written by Johnnie Mortimer and Brian Cooke; designed by Malcolm Goulding and Sylva Nadolny; produced and directed by William G. Stewart.
With Patrick Cargill, Natasha Pyne, Noël Dyson.

25.12.1969 Never Mind The Quality, Feel The Width — 2499 — J / 2"

A Thames Television production.
Written by Harry Driver and Vince Powell; incidental music by Ronnie Baxter; designed by Jim Nicolson; produced by Ronnie Baxter.
With John Bluthal, Joe Lynch.

25.12.1969 Dear Mother... Love Albert — 2499 — J / 2"

A Yorkshire Television production.
Written by Rodney Bewes and Derrick Goodwin; designed by Bernard Spencer and Roger Allan; produced by Rodney Bewes and Derrick Goodwin; directed by Derrick Goodwin.
With Rodney Bewes, Garfield Morgan.

25.12.1969 Two In Clover — 2499 — J / 2"

A Thames Television production.
Written by Vince Powell and Harry Driver; designed by Roger Allan; produced and directed by Alan Tarrant.
With Sidney James, Victor Spinetti.

25.12.1969 Mike Yarwood — 2499 — J / 2"

An ATV production.
Written by Tony Hawes and Bryan Blackburn; produced and directed by Albert Locke.
With Mike Yarwood.

25.12.1969 Other people taking part: — 2499 — J / 2"

With Hughie Green, Paddy Joyce, Patrick Newell, Siobhan Quinlan, Yutte Stensgaard, Joy Stewart.

Main regular credit(s):   Executive producer Philip Jones.

	VT Number	Holding / Source
25.12.1970 [presentation]	3390	J / 2"

A Thames Television production.
Written by Spike Mullins, Dick Vosburgh, Vince Powell and Harry Driver; music by Geoff Love; designed by Norman Garwood; production associate David Clark; produced and directed by Peter Frazer-Jones.
With Max Bygraves (Host), Cheadle Kingsway School Choir, The Hendon County Grammar School Choir.

25.12.1970 Girls About Town — 3390 — J / 2"

An ATV production.
Written by Adele Rose; designed by Ken Wheatley; produced by Shaun O'Riordan; directed by Paul Annett.
With Denise Coffey, Julie Stevens.

25.12.1970 The Worker — 3390 — J / 2"

An ATV production.
Written by Charles Drake; designed by Ken Wheatley; produced and directed by Shaun O'Riordan.
With Charlie Drake, Henry McGee.

25.12.1970 The Des O'Connor Show — 3390 — J / 2"

An ATV production.
Written by Tony Hawes; designed by Don Fisher; produced and directed by Albert Locke.
With Des O'Connor.

25.12.1970 Coronation Street — 3390 — J / 2"

A Granada production.
Written by Ron McDonnell; designed by Tim Farmer; executive producer H. V. Kershaw; directed by Eric Prytherch.
With Jean Alexander, Peter Baldwin, Alan Browning, Margot Bryant, Neville Buswell, Violet Carson, Eileen Derbyshire, Betty Driver, Kenneth Farrington, Julie Goodyear, Sandra Gough, Jack Howarth, David Jason, Steven King, Jennifer Moss, Joe Lynch, Patricia Phoenix, Anne Reid, Doris Speed, Bernard Youens.

25.12.1970 The Lovers — 3390 — J|a / 2"

A Granada production.
Written by Jack Rosenthal; designed by Colin Pocock; produced by Jack Rosenthal; directed by Michael Apted.
With Richard Beckinsale, Paula Wilcox.

25.12.1970 Hark At Barker — 3390 — J / 2"

An LWT production.
Written by Gerald Wiley; from an idea by Alun Owen; designed by Roger Hall; produced by Humphrey Barclay; directed by Maurice Murphy.
With Ronnie Barker, Moira Foot, Josephine Tewson.

25.12.1970 Doctor In The House — 3390 — J / 2"

An LWT production.
Written by Graham Chapman and Bernard McKenna; based on books by Richard Gordon; designed by Roger Hall; produced by Humphrey Barclay; directed by Maurice Murphy.
With Simon Cuff, Geoffrey Davies, George Layton, Robin Nedwell.

ALL STAR COMEDY CARNIVAL (continued)

25.12.1970 **Jokers Wild**	3390	J / 2"

A Yorkshire Television production.
Written by Barry Cryer and Ray Cameron; designed by Howard Dawson; produced and directed by David Mallet.
With Barry Cryer, Les Dawson, Ray Martine, Warren Mitchell, Ted Ray.

25.12.1970 **Dear Mother... Love Albert**	3390	J / 2"

A Yorkshire Television production.
Written by Rodney Bewes and Derrick Goodwin; designed by Richard Jarvis; produced and directed by David Mallet.
With Rodney Bewes.

25.12.1970 **Albert And Victoria**	3390	J / 2"

A Yorkshire Television production.
Written by Reuben Ship; designed by Howard Dawson; produced and directed by David Mallet.
With Alfred Marks, Zena Walker, John Ash, Miriam Mann.

25.12.1970 **For The Love Of Ada**	3390	J / 2"

A Thames Television production.
Written by Vince Powell and Harry Driver; designed by Harry Clark; produced and directed by Ronnie Baxter.
With Irene Handl, Wilfred Pickles.

25.12.1970 **Cribbins**	3390	J / 2"

A Thames Television production.
Written by Brian Cooke and Johnnie Mortimer; designed by Norman Garwood; produced and directed by Alan Tarrant.
With Bernard Cribbins, Bob Todd, Sheila Steafel.

25.12.1970 **Father, Dear Father**	3390	J / 2"

A Thames Television production.
Written by Brian Cooke and Johnnie Mortimer; produced and directed by William G. Stewart.
With Patrick Cargill, Natasha Pyne, Noël Dyson.

##.##.#### **Other people taking part:**		J / 2"

With Arthur Askey, Tim Barrett, Mary Baxter, Sally Bazely, Anthony Bygraves, Richard Caldicot, Melinda Churcher, Fred Evans, Bill Fraser, Hughie Green, Philippa Markham, Barbara Murray, David Nixon, Linda Oxer, Joan Scott, Harry Shacklock, Joy Stewart, Paul Stratford, Irene Sutcliffe, Frank Williams.

Main regular credit(s): Executive producer Philip Jones.

	Production No	VT Number	Holding / Source
25.12.1972 **[presentation]**	6558	6558	D3 / 2"

A Thames Television production.
Written by Tony Hawes, Eric Davidson, Mike Craig, Lawrie Kinsley and Ron McDonnell; music by Ronnie Aldrich; designed by Harry Clark; produced and directed by Terry Henebery.
With Jimmy Tarbuck (Host), Rod Hull and Emu, Wandsworth School Choir, David Nixon, Moira Anderson, Tony Jacklin.

25.12.1972 **Love Thy Neighbour**	6558	6558	D3 / 2"

A Thames Television production.
Written by Vince Powell and Harry Driver; designed by Frank Gillman; produced and directed by Stuart Allen.
With Nina Baden-Semper, Jack Smethurst, Rudolph Walker, Kate Williams, Keith Marsh, Tommy Godfrey.

25.12.1972 **On The Buses**	6558	6558	D3 / C1

An LWT production.
Written by Bob Grant and Stephen Lewis; designed by John Newton Clarke; produced and directed by Bryan Izzard.
With Reg Varney, Bob Grant, Stephen Lewis, Doris Hare, Anna Karen.

25.12.1972 **Christmas With Wogan**	6558	6558	D3 / 2"

An ATV production.
Written by Bryan Blackburn; music directed by Johnny Patrick; designed by Colin Andrews; produced and directed by Mike Lloyd.
With Terry Wogan (Host), Peggy Mount, Penny Lane, Carl Wayne.

25.12.1972 **Nearest And Dearest**	6558	6558	D3 / 2"

A Granada production.
Written by Tom Brennand and Roy Bottomley; designed by Eric Deakins; produced and directed by Bill Podmore.
With Jimmy Jewel, Hylda Baker, Madge Hindle, Edward Malin.

25.12.1972 **Thirty Minutes Worth**	6558	6558	D3 / 2"

A Thames Television production.
Written by Roy Tuvey and Maurice Sellar; designed by Bill Palmer; produced and directed by Les Chatfield.
With Harry Worth.

25.12.1972 **Sez Les**	6558	6558	D3 / 2"

A Yorkshire Television production.
Written by Brad Ashton and Peter Dulay; music by Syd Lawrence and his Orchestra; designed by Andrew Drummond; produced by Bill Hitchcock and Peter Dulay; directed by David Mallet.
With Les Dawson, Roy Barraclough.

25.12.1972 **The Fenn Street Gang**	6558	6558	D3 / 2"

An LWT production.
Written by John Esmonde and Bob Larbey; executive producer Mark Stuart; produced and directed by Philip Casson.
With Peter Cleall, Peter Denyer, Liz Gebhardt, Carol Hawkins, Malcolm McFee, David Barry.

ALL STAR COMEDY CARNIVAL

British Christmas Television Guide

ALL STAR COMEDY CARNIVAL (continued)

	VT Number	Holding / Source
25.12.1972 **Father Dear Father**	6558 6558	D3 / 2"

A Thames Television production.
Written by Johnnie Mortimer and Brian Cooke; designed by Roger Allan; produced and directed by William G. Stewart.
With Patrick Cargill, Noël Dyson, Ann Holloway, Natasha Pyne, H. G. Wells (The Dog).

##.##.#### **Other people taking part:** D3 / 2"
With Anne Aston, Lynda Bellingham, Judy Buxton, Jeremy Child, The Coffee Set, Leslie Crowther, Ann George, Noele Gordon, Larry Grayson, Damaris Hayman, Hugh Lloyd, William Mervyn, Sylvia Syms, Bob Todd, Mona Washbourne, Eli Woods, Jenny Lee-Wright.

Alternative/Working Title(s): All Star Christmas Spectacular
Main regular credit(s): Executive producer Philip Jones.
Main regular cast: With Jimmy Tarbuck (Host).

	VT Number	Holding / Source
25.12.1973 **[presentation]**	8177	D3 / 2"

A Thames Television production.
Introduced by David Hamilton; written by Dick Hills, Lawrie Kinsley, Mike Craig and Ron McDonnell; music directed by Ronnie Aldrich; designed by David Marshall; associate producer David Clark; produced and directed by Albert Locke.
With Jimmy Tarbuck (Host), Alan Ball*, Lynda Bellingham, Henry Cooper, Val Doonican, Neville King*, Kenny Lynch, Bobby Moore, Hugh Paddick, Fyfe Robertson, Josephine Tewson, Bob Todd, Frank Williams, Ronnie Aldrich Orchestra, Wandsworth School Choir.

| 25.12.1973 **Man About The House** | 8177 | D3 / 2" |

A Thames Television production.
Written by Johnnie Mortimer and Brian Cooke; designed by Alex Clarke; produced and directed by Peter Frazer-Jones.
With Yootha Joyce, Brian Murphy, Richard O'Sullivan, Sally Thomsett, Paula Wilcox.

| 25.12.1973 **Billy Liar** | 8177 | D3 / 2" |

An LWT production.
Written by Keith Waterhouse and Willis Hall; designed by Gordon Toms; produced and directed by Stuart Allen.
With George A. Cooper, Colin Jeavons, Jeff Rawle, Pamela Vezey, Sally Watts, May Warden.

| 25.12.1973 **Sez Les** | 8177 | D3 / 2" |

A Yorkshire Television production.
Designed by Robert Macgowan; produced by Bill Hitchcock; directed by David Mallet.
With Les Dawson, Roy Barraclough, The Syd Lawrence Orchestra, The Irving Davies Dancers.

| 25.12.1973 **My Good Woman** | 8177 | D3 / 2" |

An ATV production.
Written by Ronnie Taylor; designed by Paul Dean Fortune; produced and directed by William G. Stewart.
With Leslie Crowther, Sylvia Syms, Glyn Houston.

| 25.12.1973 **Spring And Autumn** | 8177 | D3 / 2" |

A Thames Television production.
Written by Vince Powell and Harry Driver; designed by David Richens; produced and directed by Ronnie Baxter.
With Jimmy Jewel, Charlie Hawkins.

| 25.12.1973 **Doctor In Charge** | 8177 | D3 / 2" |

An LWT production.
Written by Jonathan Lynn and George Layton; based on books by Richard Gordon; designed by Andrew Gardner; produced by Humphrey Barclay; directed by Bill Turner.
With Ernest Clark, Geoffrey Davies, George Layton, Reg Lye, Robin Nedwell, Richard O'Sullivan, Rachel Stuart.

See also: MIKE AND BERNIE WINTERS' ALL-STAR CHRISTMAS COMEDY CARNIVAL

ALL STAR DON'T FORGET THE LYRICS

Commissioned by Sky One. Transmission details are for Sky One. Duration: 48 minutes.
Shane Richie (Host), Gareth Gates, Cerys Matthews, David Gest.

	Holding / Source
22.12.2008	DB / DBSW

THE ALL STAR IMPRESSIONS SHOW

A Pett Television production for ITV 1. made in association with Baby Cow Productions. Transmission details are for the Central region. Duration: 48 minutes.
Written by Jane Lamacraft, Tony Way, Steve Burge, Matthew Leys, Martin Trenaman, Carl Carter, Tony Cooke, Marc Blakewill and James Harris; script supervisor Amanda Faulkner; music by Dan McGrath and Josh Phillips; art director Emily Straight; designed by David Ferris; assistant producer Alex Moody; executive producer Henry Normal; head of production Erika Leonard; produced by Lisa Clark; studio direction by John F. D. Northover; additional direction by Ben Wheatley.
Stephen Mulhern (Host), Peter Dickson (Voice Only), Diane Abbott MP, Tony Blackburn, Mackenzie Crook, Paul Daniels, Bobby Davro, Les Dennis, Vanessa Feltz, David Gest, Jerry Hall, Chesney Hawkes, Tim Healy, Harry Hill, Eamonn Holmes, Iain Lee, Sally Lindsay, Lisa Maxwell, Joe Pasquale, JLS, Stevie Riks, Liz Smith, Claire Sweeney, Nico Tatarowicz, Mark Wingett.

	Holding / Source
26.12.2009	DB / DBSW

ALL STAR MR AND MRS

A Celador production for ITV 1. Transmission details are for the Central region. Duration: 48 minutes.

Main regular credit(s): Format by 2Way Traffic International.

Main regular performer(s): Fern Britton (Host), Phillip Schofield (Host), Peter Dickson (Voice Only).

	Holding / Source
20.12.2008	DB / DBSW

Written by Les Keen, Bert Tyler-Moore and George Jeffrie; script supervisor Helena Taylor; theme music by Dan McGrath, Josh Phillips, Tony Hatch and Jackie Trent; music by Dan McGrath and Josh Phillips; designed by Dominic Tolfts; executive producers Victoria Ashbourne and Danielle Lux; series producer Kevin Mundye; produced by Kevin Mundye; directed by Steve Smith.

With Ronan Keating, Yvonne Keating, Terry Venables, Yvette Venables, Tamzin Outhwaite, Tom Ellis.

SERIES 3

A CPL (Celador) production.

Main regular credit(s): Written by Les Keen, The Dawson Brothers and Lee Stuart Evans; script supervisor Helena Taylor; theme music by Dan McGrath, Josh Phillips, Tony Hatch and Jackie Trent; music by Dan McGrath and Josh Phillips; titles by Huge Designs; art director Josh Grace; designed by Dominic Tolfts; associate producers Lawrie Jordan, Harriet Manby and Laura Price; executive producers Victoria Ashbourne and Danielle Lux; production manager Annie King; series producer Leon Wilson; produced by Tamara Gilder; directed by Steve Smith.

	Holding / Source
25.12.2009	DB / DBSW

With Joan Collins, Percy Gibson, Emma Bunton, Jade Jones, Andy Whyment, Nichola Whyment.

THE ALL STAR RECORD BREAKERS

A BBC production for BBC 1. Transmission details are for BBC 1. Duration varies - see below for details.

	Holding / Source
27.12.1974	DB-D3 / 2"

Duration: 30 minutes.

Music arranged by Johnny Pearson, Larry Ashmore and Derek Warne; choreography by Sally Gilpin; designed by Garry Freeman; produced and directed by Alan Russell.

With Roy Castle (Presenter), John Noakes, Brian Cant, John Craven, Bernard Cribbins, Tony Hart, Lesley Judd, Pat Keysall, Johnny Morris, Peter Purves, Michael Rodd, Valerie Singleton, Julie Stevens, Norris McWhirter, Ross McWhirter, Bob Armstrong, Bob Emmines, Tom Nichol, Jon Peggs.

30.12.1975	DB-D3 / 2"

Duration: 35 minutes.

Music directed by Johnny Pearson; music arranged by Larry Ashmore, Frank Barber and Derek Warne; choreography by Sally Gilpin; lighting by Derek Slee; sound Adrian Bishop-Laggett; designed by John Hurst; produced and directed by Alan Russell.

With Roy Castle (Presenter), Lesley Judd, Bernard Cribbins, John Noakes, John Craven, Derek Griffiths, Pat Keysall, Susan King, Johnny Morris, Peter Purves, Michael Rodd, Valerie Singleton, Julie Stevens.

24.12.1976	DB-D3 / 2"

Duration: 50 minutes.

Music directed by Johnny Pearson; music arranged by Larry Ashmore, Johnny Coleman, Johnny Pearson and Derek Warne; choreography by Sally Gilpin; lighting by Geoff Shaw; sound Adrian Stocks; designed by Ken Starkey; produced and directed by Alan Russell.

With Roy Castle (Presenter), Bernard Cribbins, Toni Arthur, David Wood, Keith Chegwin, John Craven, Maggie Henderson, Jan Hunt, Lesley Judd, Pat Keysall, Susan King, Johnny Morris, John Noakes, Peter Purves, Julie Stevens, Norris McWhirter.

28.12.1977	DB-D3 / 2"

Duration: 55 minutes.

Music directed by Johnny Pearson; music arranged by Larry Ashmore, Frank Barber, Johnny Pearson and Derek Warne; choreography by Sally Gilpin; lighting by Geoff Shaw; sound Adrian Stocks; designed by Ken Starkey; produced and directed by Alan Russell.

With Roy Castle (Presenter), Keith Chegwin, Maggie Henderson, John Craven, Noel Edmonds, Jan Hunt, Lesley Judd, Susan King, Lucy Mathen, Johnny Morris, John Noakes, Peter Purves, Julie Stevens, Kenneth Williams, David Wood.

27.12.1978	DB-D3 / 2"

Duration: 55 minutes.

Music hall entertainment.

Music directed by Johnny Pearson; music arranged by Frank Barber, Johnny Coleman, Johnny Pearson and Derek Warne; choreography by Sally Gilpin; lighting by Clive Thomas; sound Adrian Stocks; designed by Ken Starkey; produced and directed by Alan Russell.

With Roy Castle (Presenter), Keith Chegwin, Brian Cant, Maggie Philbin, Bernie Clifton, Jonathan Cohen, John Craven, Sam Dale, Simon Groom, Maggie Henderson, Jan Hunt, Lesley Judd, Susan King, Carol Leader, Lucy Mathen, Stuart McGugan, John Noakes, Peter Purves, Julie Stevens, Christopher Wenner, David Wood, Norris McWhirter.

27.12.1979	DB-D3 / 2"

Duration: 55 minutes.

Join Roy for the Fun of the Fair.

Music directed by Johnny Pearson; music arranged by Frank Barber, Johnny Coleman, Johnny Pearson and Derek Warne; choreography by Sally Gilpin; lighting by Clive Thomas; sound Adrian Stocks; designed by Roger Cann; produced and directed by Alan Russell.

With Roy Castle (Presenter), Simon Groom, Jonathan Cohen, Toni Arthur, Floella Benjamin, Brian Cant, Keith Chegwin, George Chisholm, John Craven, Sam Dale, Noel Edmonds, Tina Heath, Maggie Henderson, Jan Hunt, Su Ingle, Lesley Judd, Susan King, Carol Leader, Lucy Mathen, Stuart McGugan, Maggie Philbin, Peter Purves, Julie Stevens, Christopher Wenner, Norris McWhirter, Valerie Singleton.

British Christmas Television Guide **THE ALL STAR RECORD BREAKERS (continued)**

24.12.1980 DB-D3 / 2"

Duration: 55 minutes.

Down on the farm for a Record-Breaking Party. Laurel and Hardy stage a comeback.

Music directed by Johnny Pearson; music arranged by Frank Barber, Johnny Pearson and Alan Tew; choreography by Sally Gilpin; lighting by Duncan Thomas; sound Keith Gunn; designed by John Stout; produced and directed by Alan Russell.

With Roy Castle (Presenter), Maggie Philbin, Toni Arthur, Anita Dobson, Su Ingle, Jonathan Cohen, Johnny Ball, Floella Benjamin, Brian Cant, Keith Chegwin, John Craven, Peter Duncan, Noel Edmonds, Stu Francis, Kim Goody, Sarah Greene, Simon Groom, Tina Heath, Maggie Henderson, Jan Hunt, Lesley Judd, Susan King, Paul McDowell, Stuart McGugan, Jan Michelle, Peter Purves, Julie Stevens, Norris McWhirter.

27.12.1981 DB-D3 / 2"

Duration: 50 minutes.

Music directed by Johnny Pearson; music arranged by Peter Bye, Johnny Pearson, Alan Tew and Kenny Woodman; choreography by Sally Gilpin; designed by Stephen Scott; produced and directed by Alan Russell.

With Roy Castle (Presenter), Peter Powell, Johnny Ball, Keith Chegwin, Sarah Greene, Stu Francis, Mark Curry, Floella Benjamin, Colin Bennett, John Craven, Sam Dale, Peter Duncan, Janet Ellis, Sheelagh Gilbey, Kim Goody, Simon Groom, Tony Hart, Adrian Hedley, Su Ingle, Lesley Judd, Carol Leader, Paul McDowell, Stuart McGugan, Norris McWhirter, Leigh Miles, Maggie Philbin, Peter Purves, Lucie Skeaping, Sally Ann Triplett, Heather Williams, The Krankies.

26.12.1982 DB-D3 / 2"

Duration: 50 minutes.

Superstore holds a party for 'Star Customers'.

Music directed by Johnny Pearson; music arranged by Peter Bye, Frank Barber and Johnny Pearson; choreography by Sally Gilpin; lighting by Peter Wesson; sound Keith Gunn; designed by Valerie Warrender; produced and directed by Alan Russell.

With Roy Castle (Presenter), Keith Chegwin, Johnny Ball, Rosalind Wilson, Sarah Greene, Ben Bazell, Floella Benjamin, Colin Bennett, Brian Cant, Jonathan Cohen, John Craven, Mark Curry, Julie Dorne [as Julie Dorne Brown], Peter Duncan, Sally Gilpin, Kim Goody, Simon Groom, David Icke, Su Ingle, Dulice Liecier, Paul McDowell, Stuart McGugan, Leigh Miles, Delia Morgan, Liz Millbank, Maggie Philbin, Mike Read, Mark Savage, Lucie Skeaping, Ben Thomas, Norris McWhirter.

ALL THE BEST FOR CHRISTMAS

A BBC production for BBC 1. Transmission details are for BBC 1. Duration: 59 minutes.

Mike Yarwood introduces favourite moments from the archives of BBC Christmas comedy and links the clips with impressions. Famous names range from Tony Hancock to Lenny Henry and there are outings for such classic series as Till Death Us Do Part and One Foot in the Grave.

Produced by Tom Webber; directed by Richard Valentine.

Mike Yarwood (Host).

Holding / Source
23.12.1995 DB-D3 / D3S

ALL THE BEST FOR CHRISTMAS

A BBC production for BBC 1. Transmission details are for BBC 1. Duration: 56 minutes.

Highlights from some of the BBC Christmas shows over the years including clips from THE LIKELY LADS, SMITH AND JONES, BIRDS OF A FEATHER and MORECOMBE AND WISE.

Produced by Tom Webber; directed by John L. Spencer.

Brian Conley (Host).

Holding / Source
24.12.1996 DB-D3 / D3S

ALL THE BEST FOR CHRISTMAS

A BBC production for BBC 1. Transmission details are for BBC 1. Duration: 50 minutes.

Compilation programme of seasonal BBC comedy presented by Ronnie Corbett. Among the classic programmes featured are PORRIDGE, THE GOOD LIFE, MORECAMBE AND WISE, STEPTOE AND SON, THE GOOD LIFE and BOTTOM.

Programme associates Ian Davidson, Peter Robinson and Peter Vincent; designed by Gina Parr and Scot Todd; assistant producer Clare Ragsdale; produced by Tom Webber; directed by Gareth Carrivick.

Ronnie Corbett (Host), Laurie Holloway (Pianist).

Holding / Source
24.12.1997 DB / DBSW

ALL THE JOKERS - FULL HOUSE!

A Yorkshire Television production. Transmission details are for the ATV midlands region. Duration: 50 minutes.

Written by Barry Cryer and Brad Ashton; music by Syd Lawrence and his Orchestra; designed by Andrew Drummond; produced by Bill Hitchcock and Peter Dulay; directed by David Mallet.

Barry Cryer (Host), Norman Collier, Peter Goodwright, Thora Hird, Jenny Lee-Wright, Chic Murray, Clodagh Rodgers, Les Dawson, Billy Dainty, Keith Harris, Roy Hudd, Brian Marshall, David Nixon.

Holding / Source
26.12.1972 DB / 2"

ALL THIS - AND CHRISTMAS TOO!

A Yorkshire Television production. Transmission details are for the ATV midlands region. Duration: 50 minutes.

If you have finished all the preparations for The Big Day, now is the time to relax in the company of Sid James, Kenneth Connor and many other top showbiz personalities to see how they cope. For starters there's a baby due, neighbours are at loggerheads and aunty's long-delayed visit. But there's nothing that can't be solved during the time of goodwill. Is there?

Written by Sam Cree; designed by Gordon Livesey; executive producer John Duncan; produced and directed by Bill Hitchcock.

Sidney James (Sid Jones), Beryl Mason (Peggy Jones), Juliet Kempson (Linda Jones), Katie Allan (Sally Jones), Kenneth Connor (Willie Beattie), Nicolette Roeg (Emily Beattie), Rose Power (Mrs Hall), Joe Gladwin (Patrick Hall), Janet Webb (Aunt Maud), Brian Marshall (Dennis Hall), John Lawrence (Bus Conductor).

	VT Number	Holding / Source
24.12.1971	2395	1" / 2"

THE ALLAN STEWART SHOW

A Thames Television production. Transmission details are for the ATV midlands region. Duration: 25 minutes.

Written by John Junkin and Alex Shearer; music directed by Ronnie Aldrich; designed by David Richens; produced and directed by Stuart Hall.

Allan Stewart (Host), Terence Alexander, The Maggie Stredder Singers, Anna Dawson, Bob Todd.

	Holding / Source
29.12.1980	D3 / 2"

THE ALLEYN MYSTERIES

A BBC production for BBC 1. made in association with WGBH Boston. Transmission details are for BBC 1.

Main regular credit(s): Based on novels by Ngaio Marsh.

Made in association with WGBH Boston.

	Holding / Source
23.12.1990 **Artists In Crime**	DB / V1

Duration: 103 minutes.

When an exercise for artists ends with the death of the model, it's a case for Chief Inspector Alleyn.

Adapted by T. R. Bowen; executive producer Rebecca Eaton; produced by George Gallaccio; directed by Silvio Narizzano.

With Simon Williams (Chief Inspector Alleyn), Ursula Howells (Lady Alleyn), Belinda Lang (Agatha Troy), Leslee Udwin (Katti Bostock), Piers Gibbon (Julian Malmesley), William Simons (Inspector Fox), Pippa Hinchley (Phyllida Lee), Georgia Allen (Valmai Seacliff), Nick Reding (Basil Pilgrim), Edward Judd (Sir Norman Chapple), Reginald Marsh (Colonel Pascoe), Janet Henfrey (Mrs Hipkins), Tim Dutton (Sergeant Bailey), Andrew Baker (Wolf Garcia), Siri Neal (Sonia Gluck).

ALL-STAR FAMILY FORTUNES

A Talkback Thames production for ITV 1. Transmission details are for the Central region. Duration: 40 minutes.

Main regular performer(s): Vernon Kay (Presenter).

SERIES 2

Main regular credit(s): Written by Adam Bostock-Smith and Rob Colley; script supervisors Liz Minchin and Lisa Gettings; theme music by Simon Darlow and Ash Alexander; designed by Richard Plumb; associate producer Denise Kelly; executive producer Claire Horton; head of production Dean Jones; series producer Toby Gorman; directed by Jonathan Bullen.

Main regular performer(s): With Peter Dickson (Voice Over).

	Holding / Source
25.12.2007	DB / DBSW

With Nikki Sanderson, Greg Rusedski.

SERIES 5

Main regular credit(s): Written by Adam Bostock-Smith and Rob Colley; script supervisor Lisa Gettings; theme music by Simon Darlow and Ash Alexander; titles by Jump Design; art director Shaun Burley; designed by Richard Plumb; associate producer Denise Kelly; executive producer Suzy Lamb; head of production Dean Jones; production manager Shirley McIntyre; series producer Mel Balac; produced by Sean Hancock and Amanda Wood; directed by John L. Spencer; co-directed by Sean Hancock and Amanda Wood.

Main regular performer(s): With Peter Dickson (Voice Only).

	Holding / Source
26.12.2009 **The Websters v The Kings**	DB / DBSW

With Peter Armitage, Kelsey Beth Crossley, Helen Flanagan, Michael Le Vell, Tom Lister, Nick Miles, Lucy Pargeter, Nicola Wheeler, Sally Whittaker, Brooke Vincent.

SERIES 6

Main regular credit(s): Written by Adam Bostock-Smith and Rob Colley; script supervisor Liz Minchin; theme music by Simon Darlow and Ash Alexander; titles by Jump; art director Shaun Burley; designed by Richard Plumb; associate producers Denise Kelly and Cathy Byron-Grange; executive producer Suzy Lamb; production manager Shirley Kelly; series producer Andrew Cartmel [credited as Andrew Cartmell]; produced by Mike Maclaine, Jon Williams and Amanda Wood; directed by John L. Spencer, Mike Maclaine and Jon Williams.

Main regular performer(s): With Peter Dickson (Voice Over).

	Holding / Source
25.12.2010 **Emmerdale v This Morning**	HD/DB / HDC

With Ruth Langsford, Paul Ross, Alison Hammond, Jason Gardiner, Sharon Marshall, Christopher Chittell [as Chris Chittell], Charlie Hardwick, Matthew Wolfenden, Rokhsanah Ghawam-Shahidi, Natalie Anderson.

SERIES 7

Main regular credit(s): Executive producer Suzy Lamb; series producer Kate Middleditch.

	Holding / Source
25.12.2011 **The Only Way Is Essex V Benidorm**	HD/DB / HDC

ALL-STAR FAMILY FORTUNES

	Holding / Source
27.12.2012 **Emmerdale V Daybreak**	HD/DB / HDC

Duration: 48 minutes.
Executive producer Suzy Lamb; series producer Kate Middleditch.
With Lucy Pargeter, Aled Jones.

ALPHABET ZOO

A Granada production. Transmission details are for the Central region. Duration: 10 minutes.

SERIES 2
Main regular credit(s):   Produced by Stephen Leahy; directed by Lorne Magory.
Main regular cast: With Nerys Hughes (Host), Ralph McTell (Host).

	Production No	Holding / Source
19.12.1983 **Duster's Christmas**	P1160/53	DB / 2"

Written by Valerie Pye; designed by Paul Danson.

THE ALTERNATIVE CHRISTMAS MESSAGE

Produced for Channel 4 by a variety of companies (see details below). Transmission details are for Channel 4.

	Holding / Source
25.12.1996	D3 / D3S

A Vera production. Duration: 15 minutes.
Written by Rory Bremner and John Langdon; produced by Geoff Atkinson and Elaine Morris; directed by Steve Smith.
With Rory Bremner (Diana, Princess Of Wales).

AMAHL AND THE NIGHT VISITORS

A BBC production. Transmission details are for BBC. Duration: 50 minutes.
Written by Gian Carlo Menotti; music by Sinfonia of London; play production by Christian Simpson.
Malcolm Day (Amahl), Graham Saunders (Amahl), Gladys Whitred (Amahl's Mother), John Lewis (King Kaspar), John Cameron (King Melchior), Scott Joynt (King Balthazar), John Carvalho (Page), Josephine Gordon (Dancer).

	Holding / Source
20.12.1955	J /

AMAHL AND THE NIGHT VISITORS

A BBC production. Transmission details are for BBC. Duration: 45 minutes.
Written by Gian Carlo Menotti; play production by Christian Simpson.
Christopher Nicholls (Amahl, A Crippled Boy), Elsie Morison (Mother), John Kentish (King Kaspar), Hervey Alan (King Melchior), Forbes Robinson (King Balthazar), Thomas Baptiste (Page), Molly Kenny (Dancer), Glynebourne Festival Chorus, Royal Philharmonic Orchestra.

	Holding / Source
24.12.1959	R3|n /

AMAHL AND THE NIGHT VISITORS

A BBC production for BBC 2. Transmission details are for BBC 2. Duration: 50 minutes.
A Christmas opera about the three Kings.
Written by Gian Carlo Menotti; costume Odette Barrow; make-up Shirley Channing-Williams; orchestra conducted by Nicholas Braithwaite; choreography by Ronald Hynd; lighting by Peter Wesson; sound Raymund Angel; designed by Keith Cheetham; produced and directed by Brian Large.
Paul Maurel (Amahl), April Cantelo (His Mother), Michael Langdon (King Balthazar), Edward Byles (King Kaspar), Michael Maurel (King Melchior), John Tomlinson (The Page), Diana Vere (Dancer), Gary Sherwood (Dancer), The Ambrosian Opera Chorus, English Chamber Orchestra.

	Holding / Source
24.12.1974	DB / 2"

AMAZINGLY ENOUGH IT'S ROD HULL AND EMU

A Thames Television production. Transmission details are for the ATV midlands region. Duration: 14 minutes.
Main regular cast: Rod Hull and Emu (Presenters).

SERIES 1
Main regular credit(s):   Written by Rod Hull; designed by Peter Le Page; produced and directed by Stan Woodward.

	Holding / Source
18.12.1973 **Emu - Father Christmas**	J / 2"

SERIES 2
Main regular credit(s):   Produced and directed by Stan Woodward.

	Holding / Source
10.12.1974 **Take A Christmas Cruise**	J / 2"
24.12.1974 **Emu's Christmas Holiday**	J / 2"
31.12.1974 **New Year's Dinner At Emu's Palace**	J / 2"

AMDANI

Commissioned by S4C. Transmission details are for S4C. Duration: 47 minutes.

SERIES 1

		Holding / Source
10.10.1999	"It's the week before Christmas and everything seems to be happening at once. Llinos is persuaded to go to an aerobics course, and there's also the children's concert and the first home game"	DB /
17.10.1999	"The tension is rising as Christmas arrives. Els manages to buy the kids expensive presents despite his financial difficulties"	DB /

In Welsh.

AMNESTY INTERNATIONAL'S BIG 30

A Working Title Productions production for Central. Transmission details are for the Central region. Duration: 100 minutes.

Produced by Dave Morley and Graham K. Smith; directed by David G. Hillier.

Jonathan Ross (Host), Paula Yates (Host), Jools Holland (Host), Dave Stewart, Alexei Sayle, Cathy McGowan, Keith Chegwin, Steve Coogan, Phil Cornwell, Mark Little, Mike McShane, Steve Punt, Hugh Dennis, Rowland Rivron, Frank Skinner, Spinal Tap, Trev and Simon, Roseanne Barr*, John Cleese*, Angus Deayton*, Gregor Fisher*, Dawn French*, Gareth Hale*, Ian Hislop*, Griff Rhys Jones*, Paul Merton*, Bob Mortimer*, Norman Pace*, Vic Reeves*, Jennifer Saunders*, Mel Smith*, Spitting Image Puppets*, Tom Jones, EMF, Morrissey, Jason Donovan, Lisa Stansfield, Emo Philips, Julian Clary, Rick Astley, Roger Daltrey, Daryl Hall, Seal, Andrew Strong, Gerry Sadowitz, Rob Newman, David Baddiel.

	Holding / Source
28.12.1991	1" / 1"

AN ANGEL FOR MAY

A Barzo Productions production for ITV. Transmission details are for the Central region. Duration: 100 minutes.

Adapted by Peter Milligan; based on a book by Melvin Burgess; music by Carl Davis; designed by Michael Kane; associate producer Clive Waldron; executive producers Tim Buxton, Keith Evans, Emma Hayter, Anna Home and Alex Marshall; produced by Michael Cowan, Harley Cokeliss and Jason Piette; directed by Harley Cokeliss.

Charlotte Wakefield (May), Matthew Beard (Tom), Anna Massey (Rosie), Tom Wilkinson (Sam Wheeler), Geraldine James (Susan Higgins), Angeline Ball (Tom's Mother), Hugo Speer (Bob Harris), Julie Cox (Alison Wheeler), John Benfield (Police Constable Clegg), Richard Fleeshman (School Team Captain), Dora Bryan (Evelyn), James Joyce (Big Kid), Daniel Mason (Short Hair), Jonathan Bradd (Sir), Andrew Foxcroft (Number 2), Ashley Rhodes (Small Boy), Janine Birkett (Woman Police Constable), Nina Wadia (Science Teacher), Kate Anthony (Mrs Cranshaw), Carol McGuigan (Nurse), Andy Devine (Drunken Man), Rob Riley (Desk Sergeant), Terence Maynard (Reverend Campbell), John Skevington (Jim).

	Holding / Source
23.12.2002	DB /

AN ASTRONOMER'S CHRISTMAS

A BBC production for BBC 1. Transmission details are for BBC 1. Duration: 7 minutes.

Sir Bernard Lovell (Director of Jodrell Bank Experimental Station).

	Holding / Source
26.12.1967	B1 / B1

AND IT'S GOODBYE FROM US

A Southern Television production. Transmission details are for the Southern Television region. Duration: 50 minutes.

Christopher Robbie (Presenter), Roger Royle, Lillian Watson, Brian Nissen, Norman Goodland, Arnold Wilson, Preston Witts, Christopher Peacock, John Caine, Fred Dinenage, Steve Harris, David Bobin, Brian Shallcross, Veronica Charlwood, James Montgomery, Donald Dougal, Max Legrand, Malcolm Mitchell, Mike Fuller, Roger Livingston, Peter Clark, Mike Field, Pat Sloman, Ann Ladbury, Daphne Lee, Cherry Marshall, Lucy Morgan, Mary Morris, Mark Jenner, Jack Hargreaves, David Wilson, Trevor Baker, Derek Williamson, Jill Cochrane.

	Holding / Source
31.12.1981	DB / 2"

Final show of Southern TV including last-ever closedown. No end credits.

AND NOW THE GOOD NEWS

A BBC Manchester production for BBC 2. Transmission details are for BBC 2. Duration: 25 minutes.

Main regular credit(s): Written by Richard Stilgoe; produced by Ken Stephinson; directed by Tom Gutteridge.

Main regular performer(s): Richard Stilgoe (Host).

		Holding / Source
26.12.1978	Review Of The Year	DB-D3 / 2"
20.12.1979		DB-D3 / 2"

ANDRE PREVIN'S CHRISTMAS MUSIC NIGHT

A BBC production for BBC 1. Transmission details are for BBC 1. Duration varies - see below for details.

Main regular performer(s): André Previn.

	Holding / Source
24.12.1974	DB-D3 / 2"

Duration: 55 minutes.

Orchestra conducted by André Previn; lighting by Ken Macgregor; sound Raymund Angel; designed by John Hurst; produced and directed by John Culshaw.

With Janet Baker, London Symphony Orchestra.

ANDRE PREVIN'S CHRISTMAS MUSIC NIGHT (continued)

24.12.1975   DB-D3 / 2"
Duration: 50 minutes.
Designed by Anna Ridley; produced and directed by John Culshaw.
With Janet Baker, The London Symphony Orchestra.

24.12.1976   DB-D3 / 2"
Duration: 55 minutes.
Orchestra conducted by André Previn; lighting by Peter Wesson; sound Alan Edmonds; designed by Anna Ridley; produced by John Culshaw; directed by Ron Isted.
With Janet Baker, London Symphony Orchestra.

24.12.1977   DB-D3 / 2"
Duration: 65 minutes.
Designed by Jeremy Bear; produced and directed by Ian Engelmann.
With The London Symphony Orchestra, Lillian Watson, John Williams, The Philip Jones Brass Ensemble, Judi Dench, Choir of King's College, Cambridge, Osian Ellis.

30.12.1978   DB-D3 / 2"
Duration: 45 minutes.
Postponed from 23.12.1978.
Lighting by Peter Winn; sound Alan Edmonds; designed by Daphne Shortman; produced and directed by Ian Engelmann.
With London Symphony Orchestra, Benjamin Luxon, Robert Tear, Peter Lloyd, Osian Ellis, Judi Dench, Simon Carney.

ANDREW O'CONNOR'S JOKE MACHINE

A Border Television production. Transmission details are for the Central region.
Main regular credit(s):   Programme associate Tony Nicholson; produced and directed by Harry King.
Main regular cast: Andrew O'Connor.

Holding / Source
30.12.1987   1" / 1"
Duration: 14 minutes.
A Christmas pantomime.
Executive producer Paul Corley.

ANDY PANDY

A BBC production. Transmission details are for BBC. Duration: 15 minutes.

SERIES 2

Holding / Source
25.12.1951   **Andy Pandy's Christmas**   J /

SERIES 3

Commissioned by BBC. Transmission details are for BBC.
Main regular credit(s):   Written by Maria Bird; music by Maria Bird; produced and directed by Maria Bird.
Main regular cast: With Audrey Atterbury (Puppeteer), Molly Gibson (Puppeteer).

Holding / Source
25.12.1955   **Andy Pandy's Christmas**   B3 / B3

ANGELS

A BBC production for BBC 1. Transmission details are for BBC 1.
Main regular credit(s):   Theme music by Alan Parker.

SERIES 6

Duration: 25 minutes.
Main regular credit(s):   Script editor Tony Holland; produced by Julia Smith.

Holding / Source
23.12.1980   **Episode 34**   DB-D3 / 2"
Christmas at St Angela's. Old friends turn up for the show. And a child is born...
Written by Gilly Fraser; directed by Patrick Tucker.
With Kathryn Apanowicz (Rose Butchins), Martin Barrass (Ron Frost), Shirley Cheriton (Katy Smart), Susan Gilmore (Elizabeth Fitt), Fay Howard (Adrienne O'Shea), Judith Jacob (Beverley Slater), Joanna Monro (Anna Newcross), Sharon Rosita (Fleur Frost), Michael Howarth (Ken Hastings), Carol Holmes (Jean MacEwen), William Lindsay (Doctor Drew), Stephen Reynolds (Russell Potter), Shelley King (Jay Choudry), Debby Cumming, John Fowler, Gwen Cherrell, Christina Lohr, Deborah Manship.

ANGELS AT PARTRIDGE COTTAGE (RADIO)

A BBC Birmingham production for BBC Radio 4. Transmission details are for BBC Radio 4. Duration: 60 minutes.
Written by Lucy Gannon; produced and directed by Philip Martin.
Hedli Niklaus (Zoe), Ellie Haddington (Polly), Roger Hume (Charlie), John Dixon (Magnus), Ken Cumberlidge (Gary), Bernadette Windsor (Sophy).

Holding / Source
22.12.1988   DA /
In Stereo.

ANGELS IN THE ANNEXE

A BBC Birmingham production for BBC 1. Transmission details are for BBC 1. Duration: 53 minutes.

Mr Brittain is determined that this year the school will do a really different Christmas show. Unfortunately Miss Jarvis has always organised the nativity play, and this is her last year before retirement. She is unlikely to change her ways without a battle.

Written by Janey Preger; script editor Roger Gregory; designed by Stanley Morris; production associate Jenny Brewer; production manager William Hartley; produced by Robin Midgley; directed by Rob Walker.

Siobhan McKenna (Betty Jarvis), Alfred Molina (Mike Brittain), Lesley Manville (Jenny Bailey), Gilly Coman (Susanna), June Ellis (Mrs Hancock), Jacquie Crago (Mrs Elliott), Tim Potter (Mr Lomax), Sheila Chitnis (Mrs Dhani), Ladypool Primary School, Birmingham, Rakshanda, Lavina, Khuram, Richard, Mandeep, Julian, Malti, Jetinder, Neville, Umar, Paul, Ramtirath.

		Holding / Source
24.12.1984		DB / 1"

ANIMAL MAGIC

A BBC Bristol production for BBC 1. Transmission details are for BBC 1.

Main regular cast: Johnny Morris (Presenter).

SERIES 2
Transmission details are for BBC.

		Holding / Source
19.12.1962	Robin Feeding / Christmas Day At The Zoo / Big Red / Red Deer	B1SEQ /

SERIES 33
Duration: 25 minutes.
Main regular credit(s): Produced and directed by Mike Beynon.
Main regular cast: With Tony Soper (Presenter).

		Holding / Source
13.12.1977	Gift Ideas For Christmas / Looking After Tropical Fish	C1SEQ / 2"

With Bill Oddie.

Film sequences only.

SERIES 34
Duration: 25 minutes.
Main regular credit(s): Produced by Mike Beynon.
Main regular cast: With Tony Soper (Presenter).

		Holding / Source
13.12.1978	Gifts For Christmas	DB-D3 / 2"

ANITA IN JUMBLELAND

An ITV Various production. Transmission details are for the ATV midlands region.

Main regular cast: Anita Harris (Anita).

SERIES 1
A Thames Television production. Duration: 10 minutes.
Main regular credit(s): Written by Peter Cundall; designed by Tony Borer; produced and directed by Peter Frazer-Jones.
Main regular cast: With Joanne Gorman, Andrew Ashby, Marc Neighbour.

		VT Number	Holding / Source
25.12.1970	"Christmas Day in Jumbleland"	3372	J / 2"

It's Christmas Day in Jumbleland and among the junk Anita and the kids discover a Christmas tree, a sleigh and a present for Anita herself. Songs include Sleigh Ride, Rudolph the Red-nose Reindeer, White Christmas and Ave Maria.

| 28.12.1970 | "Seasonal songs" | | J / 2" |

SERIES 2
A Thames Television production. Duration: 14 minutes.
Main regular credit(s): Written by Peter Cundall; programme associate Mike Margolis; designed by Nevil Dickin; produced and directed by Peter Frazer-Jones.
Main regular cast: With David Arnold (Peter Jumble), Harry Stoneham ('Ard 'Earted 'Arry).

		Holding / Source
21.12.1971	"A festive show"	J / 2"
24.12.1971	"A Christmas Day party"	J / 2"

ANT AND DEC'S CHRISTMAS SHOW

A Gallowgate Production production for ITV 1. Transmission details are for the Central region. Duration: 65 minutes.

Written by Andrew Milligan, Mark Augustyn, Chris England, Paul Powell, Aiden Spackman and Lee Stuart Evans; script supervisor Amanda Faulkner; music directed by Steve Sidwell; choreography by Michele Thorne; titles by Jump Design; art director Charlotte Pearson; designed by Andrew Gates; assistant producers Sophie Cousens, Nina Clement and Gemma Nightingale; executive producer Ed Forsdick; production manager Phil Elwell; line producer Adrian Pegg; produced by Tom McKay, Anna Blue and Nick Symons; directed by Tom McKay and Chris Power.

Ant & Dec (Hosts), Noddy Holder (Voice Only), Robbie Williams, Amanda Holden, Santa, Peter André, Emma Bunton, Alexandra Burke, Simon Cowell, Gino D'Acampo, Judy Finnigan, Geri Halliwell, Gary Lineker [as Gary Lineker OBE], Richard Madeley, Colin McAllister, Piers Morgan, Sir Cliff Richard, Justin Ryan, The Saturdays, X Factor Finalists, Paul Allison, Joseph Claus, Robert Dowton, Newley Aucutt, Chris Theo Cook, Ben David Mann.

	Holding / Source
26.12.2009	DB / DBSW

ANT AND DEC'S GEORDIE CHRISTMAS

An Ant and Dec Production production for Channel 4. Transmission details are for Channel 4. Duration: 35 minutes.

Ant McPartlin and Declan Donnelly return home to Newcastle upon Tyne to host a festive entertainment show on board a boat.

Executive producer Peter Murphy; produced by Conor McAnally.

Ant & Dec (Presenters), Jayne Middlemiss, Peter André, Joanne Guest, Kenickie, Felix Dexter, Joe Pasquale, Aled Jones.

	Holding / Source
22.12.1997	DB / DBS

ANT AND DEC'S SATURDAY NIGHT TAKEAWAY

A Granada/ITV Productions production for ITV 1. Transmission details are for the Central region. Duration varies - see below for details.

Main regular credit(s): Theme music by Will Slater and Rumble Music; executive producers Anthony McPartlin and Declan Donnelly.

Main regular performer(s): Anthony McPartlin (Himself), Declan Donnelly (Himself).

SERIES 5

An ITV Productions production.

Main regular credit(s): Written by Giles Boden, Rob Colley and Andrew Milligan; script supervisors Amanda Faulkner and Lisa Harvey; assistant producers Emma Conway and Harriet Jaine; executive producer Ed Forsdick; head of production Leah Milton; series producer Georgie Hurford-Jones; produced by Mike Agnew, Sam Eastall, Chris Little, Ben Schafer and Adam Wimpenny; directed by Chris Power, Mike Agnew, Sam Eastall, Chris Little, Ben Schafer and Adam Wimpenny.

Main regular performer(s): With Kirsty Gallacher (Host), Lorraine Ashdown (Voice).

	Holding / Source
25.12.2005	DB / DBSW

Duration: 74 minutes.

With David Beckham, Lord Charles Brocket, Les Dennis, Andy Fordham, G4, Kirsty Gallacher, Ricky Gervais, Tony Green, Christine Hamilton, Neil Hamilton, Matt Lucas, Lulu, Carol Thatcher, David Walliams, Robbie Williams.

ANY DREAM WILL DO: THE WINNER'S STORY

A BBC production for BBC 1. Transmission details are for BBC 1. Duration: 60 minutes.

Executive producers Martin Scott and Chris Wilson; produced by Chris Wilson and Nic Patten; directed by Chris Wilson and Nic Patten.

Lee Mead (Host), Graham Norton (Narrator), Andrew Lloyd Webber, John Barrowman, Denise van Outen.

	Holding / Source
29.12.2007	DB / V1SW

ANYONE FOR DENIS?

A Thames Television production. Transmission details are for the Central region. Duration: 75 minutes.

Written by John Wells; designed by Martyn Hébert; executive producers Robert Fox and Julian Seymour; directed by Dick Clement.

John Cater (Maurice Picarda), Nicky Henson (Vouvrey), Mark Kingston (Hamilton Thisp), Roy Kinnear (Boris), Alfred Molina (Eric), John Nettleton (Jenkins), Terence Rigby (Major), Joan Sanderson (Rear-Admiral), Robert Stephens (Schubert), Angela Thorne (Maggie), John Wells (Denis).

	Holding / Source
28.12.1982	D3 / 2"

AQUARIUS

An LWT production. Transmission details are for the ATV midlands region. Usual duration: 40 minutes.

SERIES 2

	Production No	Holding / Source
26.12.1970	9A/01295	D2 / 2"

With John Betjeman, Peter Bull, Peter Blundel.

The Wandsworth School Choir / Sir John Betjemen / Lance Lagault / Peter Bull / Peter Blundel

AQUARIUS (continued)

SERIES 5

Main regular credit(s): Edited by Humphrey Burton.

	Production No	Holding / Source
24.12.1971 **The Other Belfast**	9A/01500	D2 / 2"

Duration: 34 minutes.

One of the leading film directors of the Aquarius production team left his home town of Belfast four years ago to work in London. This month, he has been back to make a film about his city as the traditional Christmas celebrations of peace and goodwill approach.

Designed by Bryan Bagge; associate producer Russell Harty; directed by Derek Bailey and Bruce Gowers.

With Nicol Williamson.

Derek Bailey's view of Belfast / Nicol Williamson reads Henry Williamson

SERIES 7

	Production No	Holding / Source
16.12.1972 **Down By The Greenwood Side - A Pantomime With A Difference**	1577	D2 / 2"

Duration: 40 minutes.

Composer Harrison Birtwistle has based this musical entertainment on the English mummers' plays which, since the Middle Ages, were traditionally performed on the village green at Christmas.

You meet St. George, the gallant knight who slew the dragon, and the Bold Slasher, a wicked infidel, who does battle with him. But help is at hand when Dr. Blood, a thoroughly professional man of medicine, and Jack Finney, a weird spirit who heals through sacred ritual, appear on the scene.

A more sombre tradition, the Ballad of the Cruel Mother, comes into the play in the person of the mysterious baby killer Mrs Green. The sanguine figure of Father Christmas, acting as compere and referee, presides over the proceedings and brings all to an amicable conclusion.

Written by Michael Nyman; music by Harrison Birtwistle; orchestra conducted by Elgar Howarth; edited by Humphrey Burton; designed by Barbara Bates; produced by Bryan Izzard; directed by Barrie Gavin.

With Jenny Hill (Mrs Green), Michael Kilgarriff (Father Christmas), Eric Allen (St George), Keith Washington (The Bold Slasher), Roger Delgado (Doctor Blood), Wayne Pritchard (Jack Finney), Keith Chegwin (Boy), Philip Baldwin (Boy), London Sinfonietta.

23.12.1972 **A Play In A Manger**	1578	D2 / 2"

Two weeks ago playwright Brian Clark gathered together a group of people for a weekend at a residential college in Debden, Essex. There they discussed the Christmas story in terms of today, 1,972 years on. They improvised, wrote and rehearsed it, then performed their new Nativity in a traditional setting in the local Anglican church on the Sunday evening. An Aquarius film unit stayed with the group throughout the weekend recording the play as it developed—and in the end the crew members, too, were caught up in the action!

Edited by Humphrey Burton; directed by Derek Bailey.

With Humphrey Burton (Presenter), Brian Clark.

SERIES 8

Main regular credit(s): Edited by Humphrey Burton.

	Holding / Source
23.12.1973 **Trouble In Tahiti**	D2 / 2"

Written by Leonard Bernstein; music by Leonard Bernstein; executive producers Humphrey Burton and Harry Kraut; produced by David Griffiths; directed by Bill Hays.

With Nancy Williams (Dinah), Julian Patrick (Sam), Antonia Butler (Chorus), Michael Clark (Chorus), Mark Brown (Chorus).

This is an opera.

22.12.1974 **Christmas Party: Peter And The Wolf**	D2 / 2"

Introduced by Humphrey Burton; written by Prokofiev; produced by Derek Bailey.

With Johnny Morris (Narrator), Harry Rabinowitz, The London Symphony Orchestra.

THE ARCHBISHOP OF CANTERBURY

An Associated-Rediffusion production. Transmission details are for the ATV midlands region. Duration: 8 minutes.

He talks to you about his thoughts at Christmas time. The programme comes from his home which is in the precincts of Canterbury Cathedral.

Produced and directed by Graham Watts.

Archbishop of Canterbury.

	Holding / Source
25.12.1963	J /

"ARE YOU BEING SERVED?"

A BBC production for BBC 1. Transmission details are for BBC 1. Usual duration: 30 minutes.

Main regular credit(s): Created by Jeremy Lloyd and David Croft; theme music by Ronnie Hazlehurst.

Main regular cast: Mollie Sugden (Mrs Betty Slocombe), Wendy Richard (Miss Shirley Brahms), Frank Thornton (Captain Stephen Peacock), John Inman (Mr Wilberforce Humphries), Nicholas Smith (Mr Cuthbert Rumbold).

SERIES 3

Main regular credit(s): Produced by David Croft.

Main regular cast: With Arthur Brough (Mr Ernest Grainger), Harold Bennett (Young Mr Grace), Trevor Bannister (Mr Dick Lucas).

	Holding / Source
22.12.1975 **Christmas Crackers**	DB-D3 / 2"

Written by Jeremy Lloyd and John Chapman; directed by David Croft.

| British Christmas Television Guide | "ARE YOU BEING SERVED?" (continued) |

SERIES 4

Main regular credit(s): Written by Jeremy Lloyd and David Croft; produced by David Croft.

Main regular cast: With Arthur Brough (Mr Ernest Grainger), Harold Bennett (Young Mr Grace), Trevor Bannister (Mr Dick Lucas).

                                                                         Holding / Source

24.12.1976 **The Father Christmas Affair**   DB-D3 / 2"

Directed by Ray Butt.

With Arthur English (Mr Harman), Jeanne Mockford, Dorothy Vernon, Penny Irving, Donald Waugh.

SERIES 6

Main regular credit(s): Written by Jeremy Lloyd and David Croft; produced by David Croft; directed by Bob Spiers.

Main regular cast: With Trevor Bannister (Mr Lucas), James Hayter (Mr Tebbs), Arthur English (Mr Harman), Harold Bennett (Young Mr Grace), Penny Irving (Miss Bakewell), Vivienne Johnson (Nurse).

                                                     Holding / Source

26.12.1978 **Happy Returns**   DB-D3 / 2"

With Michael Halsey, Doremy Vernon.

SERIES 7

Main regular credit(s): Written by Jeremy Lloyd and David Croft; produced by David Croft.

Main regular cast: With Trevor Bannister (Mr Lucas), Alfie Bass (Mr Harry Goldberg), Arthur English (Mr Harman), Harold Bennett (Young Mr Grace), Penny Irving (Miss Bakewell), Vivienne Johnson (Nurse).

                                                     Holding / Source

26.12.1979 **The Punch And Judy Affair**   DB-D3 / 2"

Directed by David Croft.

With Doremy Vernon, Hilda Fenemore.

SERIES 8

Main regular credit(s): Written by Jeremy Lloyd and David Croft; produced by David Croft; directed by John Kilby.

Main regular cast: With Mike Berry (Mr Spooner), Arthur English (Mr Harman), Milo Sperber (Mr Grossman), Kenneth Waller (Old Mr Grace), Vivienne Johnson (Nurse).

                                                     Holding / Source

24.12.1981 **Roots?**   DB-D3 / 2"

Music by Ronnie Hazlehurst.

With Benny Lee (Mr Klein), Harold Bennett (Young Mr Grace), Louise Burton, The Maggie Stredder Singers.

See also: THE STORY OF ARE YOU BEING SERVED? (BBC)

ARE YOU STONE COLD, SANTA CLAUS?

An ATV production. Transmission details are for the ATV midlands region. Duration: 30 minutes.

Fame, from Jamaica, is frightened by cold, unfriendly London. Can she be persuaded to leave her bedsitter and take her son to see Santa Claus?

Adapted by Roy Russell; based on a story by Rick Ferreira; designed by Michael Eve; produced and directed by Richard Bramall.

Cheryl Branker (Esme), Paul Newney (Sam), Nadia Cattouse (Auntie), Andrew Lane (Bus Conductor), Loftus Burton (Young Man), Kevin Mathurin (Clifton), Johanna Kirby (Mrs Henson), Terry Kinsella (Pete Henson).

	Production No	VT Number	Holding / Source
24.12.1977	2390	2390/77	J / 2"

ARENA

A BBC production for BBC 2. Transmission details are for BBC 2. Duration varies - see below for details.

SERIES 3

Transmission details are for BBC 2.

                                                     Holding / Source

15.12.1976 **Cinema: Christmas Special**   DB-D3 / 2"

Transmission details are for BBC 2.

                                                     Holding / Source

24.12.2008 **Paul Scofield**   DB / DBSW

Duration: 60 minutes.

Produced and directed by David Thompson.

With Paul Scofield (Subject of Documentary).

29.12.2010 **Rolf Harris Paints His Dream**   DB / DBSWF

Duration: 90 minutes.

Series editor Anthony Wall; directed by Vikram Jayanti.

With Rolf Harris, Alwen Harris, Lily Cole, Emer Kenny, Dervla Kirwan, Lizzy Jagger.

ARGUMENTAL

Alternative/Working Title(s): WHOSE SIDE ARE YOU ON?
A Tiger Aspect production for Dave. Transmission details are for Dave. Duration: 29 minutes.
Main regular credit(s): Based on an idea by Ricky Kelehar; music by Will Slater; executive producer Clive Tulloh.

SERIES 4

		Holding / Source
22.12.2011	**Christmas Special**	DB / DBSW

With Sean Lock (Host), Micky Flanagan, Robert Webb, Seann Walsh, Jason Manford.

THE ARMSTRONG & MILLER SHOW

An Absolutely production for Channel 4. Transmission details are for Channel 4.
Main regular cast: Alexander Armstrong, Ben Miller.

SERIES 3

Main regular credit(s): Written by Alexander Armstrong, Ben Miller, Bert Tyler-Moore, George Jeffrie, David Mitchell and Robert Webb; programme associate Morwenna Banks; script supervisor Christine Moses; music by Willie Dowling and Sugar Plum Fairies; art director Emily Straight; designed by Chrysoula Sofitsi; associate producers Alexander Armstrong and Ben Miller; production executive Tim Sealey; executive producer Miles Bullough; production manager Caroline Ward; produced by Phil Clarke; directed by Matt Lipsey.
Main regular cast: With Alexander Armstrong, Ben Miller, Sarah Alexander, Charlie Condou, Tony Gardner, Dave Lamb, Melissa Lloyd, Kim Wall.

		Holding / Source
22.12.1999	**Armstrong And Miller's Festive Highlights**	B / BS

Duration: 30 minutes.

THE ARMY GAME

A Granada production. Transmission details are for the ATV midlands region. Usual duration: 25 minutes.
Main regular credit(s): Created by Sid Colin; theme music by Pat Napier and Leslie Fyson.

SERIES 2
Main regular cast: With Alfie Bass (Private Montague 'Excused Boots' Bisley).

		Holding / Source
26.12.1958	**Ebeneezer Scrooge**	J / Live

SERIES 3
Duration: 26 minutes.
Main regular cast: With Alfie Bass (Private Montague 'Excused Boots' Bisley), Bill Fraser (Company Sergeant Major Claude Snudge), Ted Lune (Private Leonard Bone), Frank Williams (Captain T. R. Pocket), Harry Fowler (Corporal 'Flogger' Hoskins).

		Production No	Holding / Source
20.11.1959	**Miracle In Hut 29**	P156/8	DB-R1 / Live

Brought forward from 25.12.1959.
Written by Sid Colin, Lewis Schwarz and Maurice Wiltshire; designed by Stanley Mills; produced and directed by Max Morgan-Witts.
With Mario Fabrizi (Lance Corporal Ernest 'Moosh' Merryweather), Geoffrey Palmer.
The film print has no end credits.

01.01.1960	**Happy New Year**	P156/14	DB-R1 / Live

Written by Sid Colin, Lewis Schwarz and Maurice Wiltshire; designed by Stanley Mills; produced by Peter Eton; directed by Max Morgan-Witts.
With Mario Fabrizi (Ernest Merryweather).
The surviving film print has incomplete end credits.

07.01.1960	**'Bootserella' [Chelsea At Nine]**		DB-R1 / Live

Duration: 8 minutes.
Alternative transmissions: Granada: 06.07.1960.
Produced by Tim Hewat; directed by Gordon Flemyng.

SERIES 4
Main regular credit(s): Produced by Peter Eton.
Main regular cast: With William Hartnell (CSM Bullimore), Geoffrey Sumner (Major Upshot-Bagley), Ted Lune (Private Len Bone), Harry Fowler (Corporal 'Flogger' Hoskins), Dick Emery (Private 'Chubby' Catchpole), Mario Fabrizi (Lieutenant/Corporal Ernest 'Moosh' Merryweather).

		Production No	Holding / Source
27.12.1960	**Private Cinders**	P218/3	J / 40

ART ATTACK

Produced for ITV by a variety of companies (see details below). Transmission details are for the Central region. Duration: 25 minutes.
Main regular cast: Neil Buchanan (Presenter).

SERIES 6
A Meridian production.

		Holding / Source
13.12.1994	**Christmas Cracker**	1" / 1"

SERIES 7
A Meridian production.

	Holding / Source
12.12.1995 **Christmas Cracker**	1" / 1"

SERIES 9
A Meridian production.

	Holding / Source
18.12.1996 **Christmas Cracker**	D2 / D2S
17.12.1997 **Christmas Cracker**	D2 / D2S

ARTEMIS 81

A BBC Birmingham production for BBC 1. Transmission details are for BBC 1. Duration: 185 minutes.
Written by David Rudkin; script editor Roger Gregory; music by Dave Greenslade; designed by Gavin Davies; produced by David Rose; directed by Alastair Reid.
Hywel Bennett (Gideon Harlax), Dinah Stabb (Gwen Meredith), Dan O'Herlihy (Von Drachenfels), Sting (Helith), Anthony Steel (Trsitram Guise), Margaret Whiting (Laura Guise), Roland Curram (Asrael), Ingrid Pitt (Hitchcock Blonde), Ian Redford (Jed Thaxter), Sevilla Delofski (Magog), Mary Ellen Ray (Sonia), Cornelius Garrett (Pastor), Siv Borg (Pastor's Wife), Sylvia Coleridge (Gorgon Scholar), Daniel Day Lewis (Exhibitioner).

	Holding / Source
29.12.1981	B / C1

ARTHUR HAYNES MISCELLANEOUS

Commissioned and produced by a variety of companies (see details below). Duration varies - see below for details.

Pathé News items
An Associated British Pathe production.

	Holding / Source
##.##.#### **Xmas Time's Good Time**	B1 / B1
Duration: 6 minutes.	
##.##.#### **Show Biz Santa Claus**	B1 / B1
Duration: 1 minutes.	

ASPECTS OF MAX WALL

A Thames Television production. Transmission details are for the ATV midlands region. Duration: 75 minutes.
Music directed by William Blezard; produced and directed by Peter Frazer-Jones.
Max Wall (Host), Tony Parkinson (Percussion).

	VT Number	Holding / Source
22.12.1975	10904	DB / 2"

AT HOME WITH VIC AND BOB

A BBC production for BBC 2. Transmission details are for BBC 2. Duration varies - see below for details.
Main regular credit(s): Executive producer John Whiston; produced by David Housham; directed by John Birkin.
Main regular cast: Vic Reeves (Noddy Holder), Bob Mortimer (Dave Hill), Simon Le Bon, Neil Morrissey, Charlie Higson, Mark Williams, Paul Whitehouse.

	Holding / Source
27.12.1994 **Bob's New Hairstyle**	DB-D3 / D3S
Duration: 8 minutes.	
27.12.1994 **The Bra Men**	DB-D3 / D3S
Duration: 4 minutes.	
27.12.1994 **Shooting Stars**	DB-D3 / D3S
Duration: 25 minutes.	
27.12.1994 **Slade At Christmas**	DB-D3 / D3S
Duration: 8 minutes.	
27.12.1994 **Mulligan And O'Hare**	DB-D3 / D3S
Duration: 4 minutes.	
27.12.1994 **Vic And Bob Closedown**	DB-D3 / D3S
Duration: 4 minutes.	

AT LAST - IT'S 1984!

A BBC Birmingham production for BBC 1. Transmission details are for BBC 1. Duration: 55 minutes.
Designed by Sally Engelbach; produced by David Weir; directed by Tony Wolfe.
Michael Barrymore (Host), Anita Harris, The Shadows, Harvey and The Wallbangers, Stefan Bednarczyk, Syd Lawrence and his Orchestra.

	Holding / Source
01.01.1984	DB / 1"

AT LAST IT'S FRIDAY

A Granada production. Transmission details are for the Granada region.
Main regular credit(s):   Executive producer Michael Scott.
Main regular performer(s):   The Derek Hilton Bandsmen.

	Production No	Holding / Source
24.12.1968 **At Last It's Christmas**	P610/17	DB-R1 / 40

Duration: 19 minutes.
The cast of the studio show 'At last it's Friday' hold a party on a double decker bus. The bus - a brand-new red-and-white, sixpence-in-the-slot Mancunian model drives around Manchester picking up guest stars and passengers for a Christmas Eve party on wheels. Kenny Lynch has his finger on the bell as a musical bus conductor, and Manchester's Freddie Garritty is among the pop people on board. The Derek Hilton bandsmen are also on the bus, as well as some surprise guests.
Research David Duffy and Martin Lucas; produced by Chris Kelly [credited as Christopher Kelly]; directed by Bryan Shiner.
With Chris Kelly (Host), Kenny Lynch (Host), Ken Dodd, Keith Dewhurst, Freddie Garrity, Richard Stilgoe, Derek Hilton, Jean Hart, Jeremy Taylor, Ray Gosling, John McGregor, Mike Scott, Alan Towers, Bob Greaves.

Regional entertainment show from the north.

AT LAST IT'S HOGMANAY

A Dover Productions production for Channel 4. Transmission details are for Channel 4. Duration: 70 minutes.
Produced by Alistair Rae and Dave Cash; directed by Gordon Elsbury.
Billy Connolly, Midge Ure, Rab Noakes, Maggie Bell, Robbie Coltrane, Gallagher & Lyle, John Bett, The Communards, Tony Roper, Jim Diamond.

	Holding / Source
31.12.1985	1" / 1"

AT LAST THE 1973 SHOW

An LWT production. Transmission details are for the ATV midlands region. Duration: 100 minutes.
Music directed by Harry Rabinowitz; designed by Bill McPherson; produced by David Bell; directed by Bruce Gowers.
David Frost (Host), Ethel Merman, Eartha Kitt, Stubby Kaye, Harve Presnell, Jimmy Edwards, Stanley Baxter, Peter Cook, Dudley Moore, Maurice Woodruff.

	Holding / Source
31.12.1972	J / 2"

AT THE ELEVENTH HOUR

A BBC production for BBC 1. Transmission details are for BBC 1. Duration: 35 minutes.
Main regular credit(s):   Produced by Anthony Smith; directed by Peter Chafer.

	Holding / Source
30.12.1967	J /

Music directed by John Cameron; designed by Paul Allen.
With Jeannie Lambe, Miriam Margolyes, Roger McGough, Richard Neville, Alan Shallcross, The Scaffold.

AT THE TURN OF THE YEAR

A Southern Television production. Transmission details are for the Thames Television region. Duration: 45 minutes.
Music directed by Kennie Clayton; produced by Angus Wright; directed by Dave Heather.
Petula Clark (Host), Choir of Chichester Cathedral.

	VT Number	Holding / Source
31.12.1978	2829	DB / 2"

This was sold by Southern Star/ Endomol, with the other music and opera programmes, to EuroArts in Germany. However there was a protection copy with the tapes at Meridian and David King has since put this onto Digibeta and is at Wessex.

ATV CONTINUITY

An ATV production. Transmission details are for the ATV midlands region.

	Holding / Source
##.##.#### **Christmas Means ITV**	C1 / C1

ATV TODAY

An ATV production. Transmission details are for the ATV midlands region. Duration: 25 minutes.

	Holding / Source
29.12.1978 **ATV Review Of The Year**	DB|n / 2"

All material held by MACE or Kaleidoscope.

AN AUDIENCE WITH CHARLES DICKENS

An Independent Image production for BBC 2. Transmission details are for BBC 2. Duration: 29 minutes.
Main regular credit(s):   Based on a story by Charles Dickens; music by Carl Davis; series consultant Professor Philip Collins; assistant producer Hans Petch; executive producer Roger Thompson; produced and directed by Tom Kinninmont.
Main regular cast: Simon Callow (Charles Dickens).

	Holding / Source
23.12.1996 **Sikes And Nancy**	D3 / D3S
24.12.1996 **A Christmas Carol: Episode 1**	D3 / D3S

AN AUDIENCE WITH CHARLES DICKENS

25.12.1996	**A Christmas Carol: Episode 2**	D3 / D3S
26.12.1996	**The Trial From Pickwick**	D3 / D3S
30.12.1996	**Doctor Marigold**	D3 / D3S

AUDITION

A BBC Bristol production for BBC 2. Transmission details are for BBC 2. Duration: 4 minutes.

It was Matthew's chance to sing in the choir of St Mary's Church. The real conversation between him and the choirmaster became the sound-track for this animated film.

Animated by Bill Mather; produced by Colin Thomas; directed by Bill Mather.

Holding / Source

25.12.1976   C1 / C1

AUDITIONS

An ATV production. Transmission details are for the ATV midlands region. Duration: 52 minutes.

For dancers, the end of the summer season at Wellington Pier, Great Yarmouth, marks the start of another seemingly endless round of dole queues, dancing classes and auditions. This film follows three girl dancers- Penni, Janet and Karen through the good times and the bad to their next job... in pantomime.

Sound Bob Bentley; camera operated by Chris Menges; film editor Jonathon Morris; directed by Kenneth Loach.

Penni Dunlop, Janet Cooper, Karen Williams.

Holding / Source

23.12.1980   C1 / C1

AUF WIEDERSEHEN PET.

Produced for BBC 1 and Central Television by a variety of companies (see details below).

Main regular credit(s):   Based on an idea by Franc Roddam.

Main regular cast: Tim Healy (Dennis Patterson), Jimmy Nail (Oz Osborne), Kevin Whately (Neville Hope), Timothy Spall (Barry Taylor), Christopher Fairbank (Moxey).

SERIES 5

A ZIJI Productions production for BBC 1. Transmission details are for BBC 1. Duration: 60 minutes.

Main regular credit(s):   Written by Dick Clement and Ian La Frenais; script supervisor Lisa Mail; script editor Steven Williams; music by John Lunn and Jim Williams; executive producers Franc Roddam and Laura Mackie; produced by Joy Spink; directed by Sandy Johnson.

Main regular cast: With Noel Clarke (Wyman), Branka Katic (Tatiana), Alexander Hanson (Tarquin), Julia Tobin (Brenda), Rachael Blake (Naomi), Joanne Good (Elena), Pornchai Tipol (Two Dragons).

Holding / Source

28.12.2004   **Episode 1**   DB / V1SW

With Lucy Bayler, Patrick Toomey, Dominic Charles-Rouse, Philip Hayton, Elaine Tan, Apichat Choosakul, Jadej Maneenatr, Clyta Rainford, Rungnapa Kittivatkirn, Tanapol Suksrida.

29.12.2004   **Episode 2**   DB / V1SW

This final ever episode finished with the lads departing for work in Germany, accompanied by the original Joe Fagin theme tune, "Auf Wiedersehen, Pet".

With Sirakoop Madhanee, Junix Inocian, Manoon Thaiyanan, Daryl Kwan, Dominic Jephcott, Sandra James-Young, Simon Wilson, Sasha Scarlett Eastabrook, Criselda Cabitac, Pariwut Prachayanan.

This was made as a single TV-film, dedicated to the memory of Pat Roach 1937-2004.

AUNTIE'S BLOOMERS

A BBC production for BBC 1. Transmission details are for BBC 1. Duration varies - see below for details.

Holding / Source

29.12.1991   **[pilot]**   DB / 1"S

A Celador production.

Produced by Paul Smith; directed by Patricia Mordecai.

With Terry Wogan (Host).

Holding / Source

26.12.1994   **Auntie's New Bloomers**   DB / DBS

Duration: 40 minutes.

Produced by Tom Webber; directed by John L. Spencer.

With Terry Wogan (Host).

01.01.1995   **Auntie's New Bloomers**   DB / DBS

Duration: 40 minutes.

Produced by Tom Webber; directed by John L. Spencer.

With Terry Wogan (Host).

25.12.2001   **Dazzling Bloomers**   DB / DBSW

29.12.2001   **Glittering Bloomers**   DB / DBSW

Duration: 30 minutes.

With Terry Wogan (Presenter).

THE AVENGERS

Produced for ABC by a variety of companies (see details below). Duration: 50 minutes.

Main regular cast: Patrick Macnee (John Steed).

SERIES 3

An Iris production. Transmission details are for the ABC midlands region.

Main regular credit(s): Story editor Richard Bates; music by John Dankworth; produced by John Bryce.

Main regular cast: With Honor Blackman (Catherine Gale).

	Production No	Holding / Source
28.12.1963 **Dressed To Kill**	3617	HD-R1 / 40

Alternative transmissions: TWW: 28.12.1963.

Written by Brian Clemens; designed by David Marshall; directed by Bill Bain.

With Leonard Rossiter (Robin Hood aka William Cavendish), Alexander Davion (Napoleon aka Frederick Preston), Richard Leech (Policeman), John Junkin (Sheriff), Anneke Wills (Pussy Cat aka Jane Wentworth), Anthea Wyndam (Highwaywoman aka Dorothy Wilson), Leon Eagles (Newman), Frank Maher (Barman), Peter Fontaine (First Officer), Richard Pescud* (Radar Operator).

The characters billed as Policeman and Sheriff were named Jack Roberts and Kenneth Johnson but it isn't clear from the programme itself which is which.

SERIES 4

A Telemen production. Transmission details are for the ABC midlands region.

Main regular credit(s): Music by Laurie Johnson; associate producer Brian Clemens; produced by Julian Wintle.

Main regular cast: With Diana Rigg (Emma Peel).

	Production No	Holding / Source
25.12.1965 **Too Many Christmas Trees**	E.64.10.6	HD-B3 / B3

Alternative transmissions: Rediffusion Television: 23.12.1965; TWW: 25.12.1965.

Written by Tony Williamson; directed by Roy Baker.

With Mervyn Johns, Edwin Richfield, Jeannette Sterke, Alex Scott, Robert James, Barry Warren.

THE A-Z OF TV

An Illuminations production for Channel 4. Transmission details are for Channel 4. Duration: 150 minutes.

Programme of television archive footage, split into 26 alphabetically themed sections each introduced by a different celebrity.

Devised by Dick Fiddy; written by Dick Fiddy; produced by Linda Zuck; directed by Philip McDonald.

Michael Palin (Presenter), Valerie Singleton (Presenter), Rodney Bewes (Presenter), John Sessions (Presenter), Raymond Baxter (Presenter), Daniel Farson (Presenter), Michael Hordern (Presenter), Janice Nicholls (Presenter), Joan Bakewell (Presenter), Katie Boyle (Presenter), George Melly (Presenter), Beryl Reid (Presenter), Cyril Smith (Presenter), Shaw Taylor (Presenter), Duncan Campbell (Presenter), Johnny Morris (Presenter), Bob Danvers-Walker (Presenter), Stanley Unwin (Presenter), Mark Lawson (Presenter), John Peel (Presenter (Voice Only)), Sylvia Anderson (Presenter (Voice Only)).

	Holding / Source
01.01.1990	B / 1"

Kaleidoscope store the master tapes and studio tapes.

BABES IN THE WOOD

A Jack Hylton Productions production for Associated-Rediffusion. Transmission details are for Associated-Rediffusion. Duration: 50 minutes.

Music directed by Arnold Eagle; produced and directed by Richard Bird.

Arthur Askey (Nurse "Big-Hearted" Martha), Patricia Burke (Robin Hood), Bertram Dench (Baron Stonehart), Bonnie Downs (Maid Marion), Bobby Breen (Wicked Robber), Harry Moreny (Wicked Robber).

	Holding / Source
23.12.1955	J /

From the Streatham Hill Theatre.

BABES IN THE WOOD

A Yorkshire Television production. Transmission details are for the ATV midlands region. Duration: 50 minutes.

An old story with new jokes and songs; big stars like Peter Goodwrright, Susan Maughan, Little and Large, Norman Collier, and little stars like Showtime's own Bonnie Langford and Mark Curry; old favourites like Bobby Bennett and Old Mother Riley, and a host of new, sparkling, junior talent - that's the mixture for Junior Showtime's Christmas Panto. Babes in the Wood comes from the stage of the Alhambra Theatre, Bradford before a specially-invited audience.

Written by Denis Gifford; music directed by Tony Cervi; designed by Howard Dawson; production associates Peter Max-Wilson, Roger Cheveley, Jean Pearce and Minnie Thompson; executive producer Jess Yates; produced by Peter Sontar; directed by Pat Johns.

Bobby Bennett (Robin Hood), Peter Goodwright (Alan A'Dale), Susan Maughan (Maid Marian), Roy Rolland (Nanny Riley), John Gower (Sheriff of Nottingham), Little and Large (Private Little / Sergeant Large), Colin Prince (Little John), Norman Collier (Will Scarlett), Bonnie Langford (The Babe), Mark Curry (The Babe), Helen Watson (Ballerina), William Atherton (Court Entertainer), The Blaize Brothers (Court Entertainers), Gary Husband (Court Entertainer), Sandra Romanes (Court Entertainer), Marcia Annesley (Court Entertainer), Dominic Savage (Court Entertainer), Enrico Tomasoe (Court Entertainer), Junior Showtime Singers and Dancers.

	Holding / Source
24.12.1973	DB-DVSEQ|n / 2"

Ex-1500.
See also: JUNIOR SHOWTIME

BABES IN THE WOOD

A Lucky Dog production for Carlton. Transmission details are for the Central region.

Main regular credit(s):	Created by Geoff Deane.
Main regular cast:	Denise van Outen (Leigh Jackson), Natalie Walter (Carayln), Karl Howman (Charlie Lovall), Mark Hayford (Benito).

SERIES 1

Main regular credit(s):	Executive producers Mick Pilsworth and Mark Bussell; produced by Kenton Allen; directed by Andy De Emmony.
Main regular cast:	With Samantha Janus (Ruth).

	Holding / Source
30.12.1998 "New Year's Eve"	DB / DBSW

Duration: 45 minutes.

While Ruth, Leigh and Caralyn prepare for a New Year's Eve bash, Charlie has the surprise of his life.

Written by Geoff Deane.

With Felicity Montagu (Sasha), Tania Rodrigues (Midwife), Michael Brogan (Mickey), Eddie Allen, Dominic Taylor.

THE BABES IN THE WOOD

A BBC production. Transmission details are for BBC. Duration: 60 minutes.

Written by Brad Ashton, S. C. Green, R. M. Hills and Dick Vosburgh; orchestra conducted by George Clouston; choreography by Denny Bettis; designed by Malcolm Coulding; produced and directed by Graeme Muir.

Eamonn Andrews, Kenneth Connor, Isobel Barnett, The Beverley Sisters, Derek Bond, Sam Costa, Peter Dimmock, Charlie Drake, Peter Haigh, Tony Hancock, Derek Hart, Benny Hill, Sidney James, Lenny The Lion, Terry Hall, Alex Macintosh, Bill Maynard, Jean Metcalfe, Cliff Michelmore, Pete Murray, Jack Payne, Sylvia Peters, Ted Ray, Geoffrey Johnson Smith, Peter West, Huw Wheldon, Frankie Vaughan, The Dancers, The George Mitchell Singers.

	Holding / Source
25.12.1957	J /

BACKCHAT WITH JACK WHITEHALL AND HIS DAD

A BBC production for BBC 3. Transmission details are for BBC 3. Duration: 30 minutes.

Comedy and chat.

Main regular cast:	Jack Whitehall (Host), Michael Whitehall (Host).

	Holding / Source
24.12.2013	HD/DB / HDC

With Lee Mack, Cast, Bad Education.

BAD GIRLS

A Shed Productions production for Granada. Transmission details are for the Central region. Usual duration: 50 minutes.

Main regular credit(s): Devised by Maureen Chadwick, Eileen Gallagher and Ann McManus.

Main regular cast: Victoria Alcock (Julie Saunders), Kika Mirylees (Julie Johnston), Helen Fraser (Sylvia Hollamby).

Holding / Source
19.12.2005 Christmas Special — DB / DBSWF

Duration: 75 minutes.

Christmas Eve, a blizzard and a strange new inmate.

Written by Paul Mousley; script associate Suzi McIntosh; music by Michael Walton; executive producer Brian Park; head of production Rosalind Taylor; produced by Rachel Snell; directed by Martin Hutchings.

With Nicola Redmond (Miranda Miles), Gaynor Howe (Christy Mackay), Ellie Haddington (Joy Masterton), Orlessa Altass (Vicky Floyd), Jack Ellis (Ghost of Jim Fenner), Antonia Okonma (Darlene Cake), Nicola Stapleton (Janine Nebeski), Victoria Bush (Tina O'Kane), Rebecca Hazlewood (Arun Parmar), Dannielle Brent (Natalie Buxton), Andrew Scarborough (Kevin Spiers), Stephanie Beacham (Phyllida Oswyn), Amanda Barrie (Beverley Tull), Laura Rogers (Sheena Williams), Liz May Brice (Pat Kerrigan), James Gaddas (Neil Grayling), Tracey Wilkinson (Di Fenner), Michael Fish, Candida Gubbins.

SERIES 8

Main regular credit(s): Script associate Roxanne Harvey; series script editor Lucy Raffety; theme music by Walton and Gotts; music by Michael Walton; executive producer Brian Park; head of production Rosalind Taylor; produced by Sharon Houlihan.

Holding / Source
20.12.2006 Christmas Special — DB / DBSWF

Christmas Eve. Pregnant Janine goes into labour, a decomposing human hand floats out of an overflowing toilet and thr ghost of Natalie Buxton visits Wing Governor Sylvia Hollamby.

Written by Phil Ford; directed by Laurence Moody.

With Angela Bruce (Mandy Goodhue), Stephanie Beacham (Phyllida Oswyn), Amanda Barrie (Beverley Tull), Nicola Stapleton (Janine Nebeski), Sid Owen (Donny Kimber), Victoria Bush (Tina O'Kane), Liz May Brice (Pat Kerrigan), Dannielle Brent (Natalie Buxton), Steven Webb, Louis Waymouth, Paul Bridle, Gugu Mbatha-Raw.

BALAMORY

A CBBC Scotland production for CBeebies. Transmission details are for CBeebies. Duration: 20 minutes.

SERIES 1

Holding / Source
25.12.2002 Panto — DB / DBSW

SERIES 2

Holding / Source
24.12.2003 Winter Special: The Snowflake Fairy — DB / DBSW

BALLYKISSANGEL

A World production for BBC Northern Ireland. Transmission details are for BBC 1. Usual duration: 55 minutes.

Main regular credit(s): Created by Kieran Prendiville; theme music by Shaun Davey.

Main regular cast: Tony Doyle (Brian Quigley), Niall Toibin (Father MacAnally), Tina Kellegher (Niamh Egan), Gary Whelan (Brendan).

A Ballykea production for World.

Holding / Source
21.12.1997 As Happy As A Turkey On Boxing Day — D3 / V1S

Duration: 75 minutes.

Written by Barry Devlin; produced by Chris Griffin; directed by Dermot Boyd.

With Frankie McCafferty (Donal), Joe Savino (Liam), Peter Caffrey (Padraig), Birdy Sweeney (Eamon), Dervla Kirwan (Assumpta Fitzgerald), Stephen Tompkinson (Father Peter Clifford), Peter Hanly, Deirdre Donnelly, Bosco Hogan, Aine Ni Mhuiri, John Cleere, Niall O'Shea, Doreen Keogh, Jo Kellegher, Alan Barry, Gerard Walsh.

SERIES 5

A Ballykea production for World.

Main regular credit(s): Executive producers Sophie Balhetchet and Robert Cooper; produced by Chris Clough.

Main regular cast: With Lorcan Cranitch (Sean Dillon), Victoria Smurfit (Orla), Pauline McLynn (Bella Mooney), Don Wycherley (Father Aidan).

Holding / Source
28.12.1999 The Wedding — DB / V1S

Written by Ted Gannon; directed by Simon Massey.

With Owen Roe (Paul Dooley), Ciaran Owens (Dermot Dooley), Katie Cullen (Grainne Dooley), James Ellis (Uncle Minto), Jeff O'Toole, Deirdre Donnelly, Kate McEnery, Colin Farrell, Aine Ni Mhuiri, Marion O'Dwyer, Mark Benton, Maire Ni Ghrainne, Bill Hickey, Sam Farrar.

BARBARA

A Carlton production for ITV 1. Transmission details are for the Central region. Duration: 25 minutes.

Main regular credit(s):	Executive producer Nick Symons; produced by Mark Bussell and Justin Sbresni.
Main regular cast:	Gwen Taylor (Barbara Liversidge), Madge Hindle (Doreen), Sam Kelly (Ted Liversidge), Elizabeth Carling (Linda Liversidge Pond), Mark Benton (Martin Pond), Benedict Sandiford (Neil Liversidge), Sherrie Hewson (Jean).

SERIES 2

Main regular credit(s):	Written by Mark Bussell, Rob Clark, Ramsay Gilderdale, Graham Mark Walker and Justin Sbresni; executive producer Nick Symons; produced by Mark Bussell and Justin Sbresni; directed by Nic Phillips.

Holding / Source

24.12.2000 **Fox** — DB / DBSW

Ted becomes his football club's mascot. Barbara's plans to look after her grandson receive a setback.
With Lucy Moss (Baby George), John Arthur (Phil), Amy Moss (Baby George), Julie Driscoll (Clare), Frances Burns, Anil Desai, Luke Gell, Jack Curtis, Tobias Clayton, Gilly Tompkins.

BARNEY

A BBC production for BBC 1. Transmission details are for BBC 1. Duration: 4 minutes.

Main regular credit(s):	Produced by John Coates; directed by Bob Balser.
Main regular cast:	Tim Brooke-Taylor (Voices), Harry Enfield (Voices), Jan Ravens (Voices), Enn Reitel (Voices).

Holding / Source

27.12.1988 **Barney's Christmas Surprise** — DB / 1"

BARNEY'S CHOICE

A BBC Manchester production. Transmission details are for BBC 1. Duration: 45 minutes.

Introduced by Barney Colehan; music directed by Bernard Herrmann; designed by Dugald Findlay; produced by Barney Colehan; directed by Tony Harrison.
Robert White, Sheila Steafel, David Copperfield, Jackie and Norbert Deschant, Jan Lesley, Bright & Breeze, Neal Antin, Claire Lutter, Michelle Waugh.

Holding / Source

30.12.1981 — DB / 2"

THE BARRON KNIGHTS SHOW

A Barron Knights Ltd production for Channel 4. Transmission details are for Channel 4. Duration: 50 minutes.
Executive producer Tony Avern; produced by Butch Baker; directed by Tony Vanden-Ende.
The Barron Knights, Lois Lane, Captain Sensible.

Holding / Source

28.12.1984 — 1" / 1"

THE BARROW POETS' CHRISTMAS PARTY

A Thames Television production. Transmission details are for the Thames Television region. Duration: 25 minutes.
Produced and directed by Jim Pople.
Susan Baker, William Bealby-Wright, Heather Black, Gerard Benson, Jim Parker, Cicely Smith.

Holding / Source

15.12.1970 — J / 2"

BARRYMORE

An LWT production. Transmission details are for the Central region. Duration varies - see below for details.

Main regular performer(s): Michael Barrymore (Host).

SERIES 1

Main regular credit(s):	Written by Simon Greenall and Chris Lang; choreography by Don Hunt; associate producer Chris O'Dell; produced and directed by Ian Hamilton.

Holding / Source

21.12.1991 — D2 / 1"
Duration: 52 minutes.
Join Michael Barrymore in a special holiday edition of his new series in which anything can happen.
With Alan Harding, Pride of Murray Pipe Band, Stuart Anderson, The Rumbergers.

SERIES 2

Holding / Source

25.12.1992 — D2 / D2S
Duration: 52 minutes.

THE BASIL BRUSH SHOW   British Christmas Television Guide

THE BASIL BRUSH SHOW

A BBC production for BBC 1. Transmission details are for BBC 1. Duration varies - see below for details.

Main regular performer(s): Basil Brush (Himself).

SERIES 4
Duration: 30 minutes.
Main regular credit(s):   Written by George Martin; music by The Bert Hayes Sextet; designed by Pat Jackson; produced and directed by Johnny Downes.
Main regular performer(s): With Derek Fowlds (Mr Derek).

                        Holding / Source

25.12.1970 Basil's Christmas Morning   J / 2"

With Ken Brooke, The Idle Jacks.

SERIES 5
Duration: 30 minutes.
Main regular credit(s):   Written by George Martin; lyrics by George Martin; music by The Bert Hayes Sextet.
Main regular performer(s): With Derek Fowlds (Mr Derek), The Roger Stevenson Marionettes.

                        Holding / Source

25.12.1971 Basil In Pantoland   J / 2"

SERIES 7
Duration: 30 minutes.
Main regular credit(s):   Written by George Martin; music by The Bert Hayes Sextet; designed by Pamela Lambooy; produced and directed by Robin Nash.
Main regular performer(s): With Derek Fowlds (Mr Derek).

                        Holding / Source

23.12.1972 What The Dickens   DB-1" / 2"

With Maina Gielgud, Bob Hunter, Eric Bramall and his Puppets, Carey Wilson, Richard Day Lewis, Nigel Beavan, Alan Lynton, Dee Griffiths, Pat Stark, Liz Pearson, Ingrid Lynton, Richard Beaumont, Earl Rhodes, Debbie Thau, Candida Prior.

SERIES 8
Main regular credit(s):   Written by George Martin; music by The Bert Hayes Sextet; designed by Pamela Lambooy; produced by Robin Nash.
Main regular performer(s): With Roy North (Mr Roy).

                        Holding / Source

23.12.1973 Christmas Edition   DB-D3 / 2"

Duration: 30 minutes.
Directed by Bill Ersser.
With Pat Stark, Paul Whitford, Carey Wilson, Ronald Mayer, Jodi Sherwood, Carole Hill, Ian Sharrock, Maxine Gordon, Roy Pollard, Sally Lamb, Mark Brown, Alan Lynton, Ingrid Lynton, Peter O'Dell, Jackie Stillwell, Bob Hunter, The Eric Bramall Puppets.

SERIES 9
Main regular credit(s):   Written by George Martin; designed by Pamela Lambooy; produced by Robin Nash; directed by Brian Penders.
Main regular performer(s): With Roy North (Mr Roy), The Bert Hayes Orchestra, Paul and Peta Page, Steve Greenfield.

                        VT Number   Holding / Source

22.12.1974 Basil Brush's A Christmas Fantasy   VTC/6HT/96139   DB-1" / 2"

Duration: 32 minutes.
With Len Lowe, Carey Wilson, Mark Brown, Raymond Cooke, Richard Day Lewis, Leila Hart, Bob Hunter, Jane Marlow, Peter O'Dell, Michelle Scott, Julia Brill, Dennis Howes, Nigel Erskine, Annalia Mallor, Eric Holliday, Tony Page, Sara Ross, Ronald Emblen.
Trailer for Basil Brush's Christmas Fantasy, plus continuity announcement and weather forecast by Keith Best (transmitted approx. 12.11pm, 21.12.1974) exists on audio, held by Kaleidoscope.

SERIES 10
A BBC Birmingham production.
Main regular credit(s):   Written by George Martin; music by The Bert Hayes Sextet; produced by Robin Nash; directed by Brian Penders.
Main regular performer(s): With Roy North (Mr Roy).

                        Holding / Source

20.12.1975 Basil Brush's Christmas In Norway   DB-D3 / 2"

Duration: 30 minutes.
Designed by Gerry Scott.
With Larry Parker, Olaf Pooley, Susie Baker, Mark Brown, Michael Clarke, Raymond Cooke, Roger Green, Philip Haigh, Leila Hart, Chrissie Kendall, Jane Marlow, Jill Nicholson, Peter O'Dell, David L. Tate, Val Williams.
This edition was made in London, not at Pebble Mill in Birmingham.

SERIES 11
Duration: 30 minutes.
Main regular credit(s):   Written by George Martin; music by The Bert Hayes Orchestra; designed by Jeremy Bear; produced and directed by Brian Penders.
Main regular performer(s): With Roy North (Mr Roy).

                        Holding / Source

18.12.1976 Basil In Neverland   DB-D3 / 2"

With Brian Blessed, Boobsy, the Human Dog, Melinda Clancy, Jan Hunt, Johnny Wade, The Nigel Brooks Singers.

THE BASIL BRUSH SHOW

THE BASIL BRUSH SHOW (continued)

SERIES 12
A BBC Birmingham production. Duration: 30 minutes.
Main regular credit(s): Written by George Martin; music by The Bert Hayes Orchestra; choreography by Samantha Stevens; designed by Tim Dann; produced and directed by Brian Penders.
Main regular performer(s): With Howard Williams (Mr Howard).

	Holding / Source
25.12.1977 **Basil Through The Looking Glass**	DB-D3 / 2"

With Anna Quayle, Tommy Godfrey, Johnny Wade, Barrie Gosney, Brian Hayes, John Muirhead, The Cox Twins, The Nigel Brooks Singers.

SERIES 13
A BBC Birmingham production.
Main regular credit(s): Written by Colin Bostock-Smith, Tom Magee-Englefield, Ivan Owen and Peter Robinson; script editor Peter Robinson; music by The Bert Hayes Orchestra; produced by Jim Franklin.
Main regular performer(s): With Howard Williams (Mr Howard).

	Holding / Source
23.12.1978 **Basil Brush's Magical Christmas**	DB-D3 / 2"

Duration: 35 minutes.
Designed by Cynthia Kljuco; directed by Paul Ciani.
With David Nixon, Deryck Guyler, Richard Baker, Len Lowe, Fran Fullenwider, The Nigel Brooks Singers.

SERIES 14
A BBC Birmingham production.
Main regular credit(s): Music by The Bert Hayes Orchestra; produced and directed by Paul Ciani.
Main regular performer(s): With Billy Boyle (Mr Billy).

	Holding / Source
22.12.1979 **Basil's Christmas In The Country**	DB-D3 / 2"

Duration: 35 minutes.
Written by Peter Robinson, John Morley and Colin Bostock-Smith; designed by Peter Blacker.
With Sacha Distel, Percy Edwards.

SERIES 15
Main regular credit(s): Written by Peter Robinson, John Morley and Colin Bostock-Smith; music directed by Nigel Hess; produced and directed by Paul Ciani.
Main regular performer(s): With Billy Boyle (Mr Billy).

	Holding / Source
27.12.1980 **Basil's Christmas Cruise**	DB-D3 / 2"

Duration: 35 minutes.
Designed by Barbara Gosnold.
With Michael Hordern, Dilys Watling, The Pasadena Roof Orchestra, Legs & Co..

THE BAY CITY ROLLERS WITH GILBERT O'SULLIVAN

A Granada production. Transmission details are for the ATV midlands region. Duration: 50 minutes.

The Bay City Rollers feature in this Christmas Special. Elton John performs Step into Christmas and Gilbert O'Sullivan sings Who Knows Perhaps Maybe; Can't Get Enough of You; White Christmas and The Marriage Machine. Showaddywaddy perform Heavenly. Xmas Trail at start (partial); Ads during breaks are: Mr Quilp (film musical); Barker's sale; Smarties; Lassie dog food; Holiday brochures (Spanish dancers); Ronnie Barker advertising ?; Lucky Lady (film); Holiday brochures (different); Jones and Higgins sale v/o Philips Elsmore. Most ads have bits cut out of them for some reason... Partial Christmas trail at end (David Copperfield), followed by Bay City Rollers on BBC Vince Hill show singing "Shout" TX: 11/11/1975.

Research David Wason; graphics by Jim Quick; produced by Muriel Young; directed by Peter Walker.

The Bay City Rollers (Presenters), Gilbert O'Sullivan, The Drifters, Elton John, Showaddywaddy, Him and Us.

	Production No	Holding / Source
25.12.1975	P840/21	DB / 2"

BBC FOUR SESSIONS

A BBC production for BBC 4. Transmission details are for BBC 4. Duration varies - see below for details.

	Holding / Source
17.12.2009 **The Christmas Session**	DB / DBSW

Alt.Title(s): *Fire and Ice*
Duration: 60 minutes.
Script supervisor Lisa Seabrook; designed by Miranda Jones; production executive Stephania Minici; executive producer Mark Cooper; production managers Joanne Housden and Gesa Schlotfeldt; produced by Serena Cross; directed by Janet Fraser Crook.
With Paul Sartin (Chairman), Bellowhead, The Unthanks, Thea Gilmore, Lisa Knapp, Belshazzar's Feast, Jim Moray.

19.12.2010 **Soul Noel**	DB / DBSW

Duration: 60 minutes.
Script supervisor Claire Mathias; music directed by Ken Burton; orchestra conducted by Ken Burton; art director Laurence Archer; designed by Simon Rogers; production executive Stephania Minici; executive producer Mark Cooper; production manager Joanne Housden; produced by Stephanie McWhinnie; directed by Janet Fraser Crook.
With Beverley Knight, Bryn Christopher, Ola Onabule, Carleen Anderson, The Golden Gate Quartet, The Soul Noel Choir.

BBC NEWS BROADCASTS

A BBC News production for BBC. Transmission details are for BBC.
Transmission details are for BBC 1.

	Holding / Source
26.12.1952	DB / B1
24.12.1984 + Weather Forecast	DV / Live
25.12.1998	DV / Live

Kaleidoscope hold the VHS masters. BBC Archives retain the digibetas.

BBC NEWS FOOTAGE

A BBC production. Transmission details are for BBC.

	Holding / Source
25.12.1973 Christmas Day Bulletin	C1SEQ / 2"

Film inserts only.

THE BBC3 CHRISTMAS ROCK OPERA:AD/BC

A Baby Cow Productions production for BBC 3. Transmission details are for BBC 3. Duration: 28 minutes.

Written by Richard Ayoade and Matt Berry; lyrics by Richard Ayoade and Matt Berry; script supervisor Emma John; music by Matt Berry; choreography by Carol Fletcher; director of photography Nanu Segal; art director Mel Stenhouse; designed by Simon Rogers; executive producers Mark Freeland, Henry Normal and Steve Coogan; production manager Paula Munro; line producer Kerry Waddell; produced by Alison MacPhail; directed by Richard Ayoade.

Matt Berry (Innkeeper / Tim Wynde), Julia Davis (Ruth), Julian Barratt (Tony Iscariot), Richard Ayoade (Joseph), Matt Lucas (God), Noel Fielding (Shepherd), Tom Hillenbrand [as Tom Hillendbrand] (Shepherd), Karl Theobald (Shepherd), Lydia Fox (Wise Man), Lucy Montgomery (Wise Man), Sophie Winkleman (Wise Man), Marc Cieslak (Townsfolk), Sean Douglas (Townsfolk), Laurence Fox (Townsfolk), Rich Fulcher (Townsfolk), David Lambert (Townsfolk), Graham Linehan (Townsfolk), Richard Pitt (Townsfolk), Rob Tofield (Townsfolk), Dan Antopolski (King Herod), Djenba Aduayom (Dancer), Lene Godfrey (Dancer), Damien Hendricks (Dancer), K (Dancer), Suzanne Mole (Dancer), Senay Taormina (Dancer), Richard Pitt (Additional Vocals), University of Westminster Choir.

	Holding / Source
21.12.2004	DB / DBSWF

BEADLE'S ABOUT

An LWT production. Transmission details are for the Central region. Duration: 25 minutes.

Main regular cast: Jeremy Beadle (Presenter).

SERIES 2

	Holding / Source
23.12.1986	D2 / 1"

BEADLE'S DAREDEVILS

An LWT production. Transmission details are for the Central region. Duration: 50 minutes.
Produced and directed by Nigel Lythgoe.
Jeremy Beadle.

	Holding / Source
25.12.1993	D2 / D2S

A BEAR BEHIND

A BBC production for BBC 1. Transmission details are for BBC 1. Duration: 10 minutes.

Main regular cast: Lindsay Coulson (Presenter).

SERIES 3

Main regular credit(s): Produced by Angela Beeching; directed by Nel Romano.

	Holding / Source
17.12.1990 Christmas	DB-D3 / 1"

With Bill Wallis (Boz).

BEAT CITY

An Associated-Rediffusion production. Transmission details are for the ATV midlands region. Duration: 40 minutes.

Written by Daniel Farson; produced and directed by Charles Squires.

Daniel Farson (Host), Gerry and The Pacemakers, Rory Storm and The Hurricanes, Faron's Flamingoes, Earl Preston and The T.T.'s, The Chants, Chick Graham, The Coasters, The Spinners, Jacqueline McDonald, Birdie O'Donnell, Billy Kietly, Paul Cunningham.

	Holding / Source
24.12.1963	B1|n / B1

With Gerry and The Pacemakers, Rory Storm and The Hurricanes, Faron's Flamingoes, The Chants, The Spinners.

BEAT IN THE NEW!

A BBC production for BBC 2. Transmission details are for BBC 2. Duration: 75 minutes.

Lighting by Peter Smee; sound Bryan Forgham; designed by Judy Steele; produced and directed by Barry Langford.

Pat Campbell (Host), Billy J. Kramer and The Dakotas, The Kinks, The Merseybeats, Graham Bond Organisation, Christine Holmes, Ray Singer, Peter and The Headlines, David Jacobs, Davy Kaye, P. J. Proby, The Rockin' Berries, Julie Rogers, Les Beat Room Can-Can Ladies.

	Holding / Source
31.12.1964	J /

BEAUTY AND THE BEAST

A Thames Television production. Transmission details are for the Central region. Duration: 31 minutes.

Written by Ted Hughes; adapted by Michael Baldwin; story editor Zanna Beswick; music by Nick Bicat; designed by Alison Waugh; produced by Pamela Lonsdale; directed by John Woods.

Ian Richardson (Father), Ronald Lacey (Doctor), Dandy Nichols (Floor Sweeper), Matthew Solon (Son), Lysette Anthony (Floreat), David Rappaport (Bear Keeper), Andrew Forbes (Beast / Youth), David Valentine Webb (Footman), Anthony Valentine Webb (Footman).

	Holding / Source
22.12.1982	DB / 2"

BEDTIME

A Hat Trick production for BBC 1. Transmission details are for BBC 1. Duration: 29 minutes.

Main regular credit(s):	Written by Andy Hamilton; music by Matthew Scott; produced by Sue Howells; directed by Andy Hamilton.
Main regular cast:	Timothy West (Andrew Oldfield), Sheila Hancock (Alice Oldfield).

SERIES 3

Main regular credit(s):	Produced by Sue Howells.
Main regular cast:	With Fay Ripley (Jill), Neil Stuke (John), Vincent Ebrahim (Mohammad), Nicholas Farrell (Ray), Preeya Kalidas (Mumtaz), Therese Bradley (Woman Police Constable), Victoria Carling (Jools), Paul Clarkson (Nigel), Jeff Rawle (Simon), Paul Bhattacharjee (Ali), Nathaniel Gleed (Tommy).

		Holding / Source
15.12.2003	Christmas Eve	DB / V1SW
16.12.2003	Christmas Day	DB / V1SW
17.12.2003	Boxing Day	DB / V1SW

BEFORE THEY WERE FAMOUS

A BBC Light Entertainment production for BBC 1. Transmission details are for BBC 1. Duration varies - see below for details.

Clips of famous people in early roles.

	Holding / Source
25.12.1999	DB / DBSW

Duration: 40 minutes.
Executive producer Caroline Wright; produced by Samantha Peters.
With Angus Deayton (Presenter).

25.12.2000	DB / DBSW

Duration: 40 minutes.
Executive producer Caroline Wright; produced by Samantha Peters.
With Angus Deayton (Presenter).

25.12.2001	DB / DBSW

Duration: 35 minutes.
Executive producer Caroline Wright; produced by Samantha Peters.
With Angus Deayton (Presenter).

26.12.2002	DB / DBSW

Duration: 40 minutes.
Executive producer Caroline Wright; produced by Mike Parkinson and Samantha Peters.
With Angus Deayton (Presenter).

25.12.2004	DB / DBSW

Duration: 40 minutes.
Executive producer Caroline Wright; produced by Helen Tumbridge.
With Angus Deayton (Presenter).

BEFORE THEY WERE FAMOUS II

A Mentorn Films production for BBC Manchester. Transmission details are for BBC 1. Duration: 35 minutes.

Written by Danny Baker and Angus Deayton; research Christopher Perry*, Liam Carroll* and Robert Heading*; theme music by Dave Stewart; designed by John Asbridge; assistant producer Samantha Peters; executive producer Rosetta Bain; production manager Peter Hackett; produced by Caroline Wright; directed by Stuart McDonald.

Angus Deayton (Presenter).

	Holding / Source
26.12.1997	DB-D3 / D3S

BEFORE THEY WERE FAMOUS III

A Mentorn Films production for BBC Manchester. Transmission details are for BBC 1. Duration: 40 minutes.

Written by Danny Baker and Angus Deayton; theme music by Dave Stewart; designed by John Asbridge; assistant producer Will Bryant; executive producers Caroline Wright and Rosetta Bain; production manager Simon Ashdown; produced by Samantha Peters; directed by Geraldine Dowd.

Angus Deayton (Presenter).

	Holding / Source
25.12.1998	DB-D3 / D3S

BEING RONNIE CORBETT

Alternative/Working Title(s): ALL ABOUT RONNIE CORBETT

A Little Britain Productions production for BBC 2. made in association with BBC Productions. Transmission details are for BBC 2. Duration: 60 minutes.

A nostalgic look back at the comedian's long career, with contributions from a wide range of admirers.

Research Rory Sheehan; art director Frank Centurion; designed by Andrew Tye; production executive Stan Matthews; executive producers Caroline Wright and Geoff Posner; production manager Jill Hallowell; produced and directed by Andy Humphries.

Matt Lucas*, Rob Brydon*, Michael Palin*, Ronnie Corbett, Bruce Forsyth*, David Walliams*, Catherine Tate*, Bill Bailey*, Reece Shearsmith*, Stephen Merchant*, Miranda Hart*, Sue Perkins*, Jon Culshaw*, Ben Miller*, Stephen K. Amos*, Jessica Hynes*, Kevin Bishop*, Tamsin Greig*.

	Holding / Source
23.12.2010	DB / DBSW

BELLAMY'S BUGLE

A Yorkshire Television production. Transmission details are for the Central region. Duration: 14 minutes.

Main regular cast: David Bellamy (Presenter), Kate Lee (Smart Alice).

SERIES 4

		VT Number	Holding / Source
28.12.1987	Journey To The Centre Of The Earth	C041/25	1" / 1"

THE BELLS OF ASTERCOTE

A BBC production for BBC 1. Transmission details are for BBC 1. Duration: 55 minutes.

"'What is the secret of the wood?' Mair asked. "I've noticed none of the village people seem to want to talk about it." When Mair and her brother finally discover the secret the wood contains, the past comes eerily alive.

Adapted by Valerie Georgeson; based on a book by Penelope Lively; film camera Maurice Fisher; film editor Paul Carter; designed by John Bone; executive producer Anna Home; produced and directed by Marilyn Fox.

Siobhan Brooks (Mair), Ifor Williams (Peter), John Branwell (Goacher), Janis Winters (Evadne), Ivor Roberts (Mr Tranter), Kristine Howarth (Mrs Tranter), Alison Rolfe (Betsy Tranter), Davyd Harries (Mr Jenkins), John Malcolm (Tom Craddock), Lloyd Lamble (Major Pratt), Brenda Cowling (Mrs Fletcher), Richard Hunter (Luke Tranter), Pat Quayle (Mrs Fowler), Keith James (Frank Turner), Sarah Grazebrook (TV Reporter), Bill McGuirk (TV Cameraman), Val Lorraine (Village Woman), Penny Jones (Estate Girl).

	Holding / Source
23.12.1980	C1 / C1

BENEATH THE CHRISTMAS TREE

A HTV production. Transmission details are for the Scottish Television region. Duration: 45 minutes.

Songs and carols.

Music directed by Eric Wetherell; designed by Hywel Morris; associate producer Sir Geraint Evans; produced and directed by Terry Delacey.

Sir Geraint Evans, Stuart Burrows, Eirian James, Spike Milligan, Bristol Sinfonia, Cardiff Polyphonic.

	Holding / Source
25.12.1975	

BENIDORM

A Tiger Aspect production for ITV 1. Transmission details are for the Central region. Duration varies - see below for details.

Main regular credit(s): Music by Mark Thomas; executive producer Sophie Clarke-Jervoise; head of production Toby Ward.

	Holding / Source
26.12.2010 **Christmas Special**	DB / DBSWF

Duration: 48 minutes.

The Garveys are back to spend Christmas with Mel and Madge Harvey in their luxury hilltop villa.

Written by Derren Litten; script supervisor Sue Jones; script editor Simon Carlyle; music by Mark Thomas; director of photography Andy Hollis; titles by Jump Design; art director Margaret Spohrer; designed by Heather Gibson; associate producers Derren Litten and Sandy Johnson; executive producer Sophie Clarke-Jervoise; head of production Toby Ward; line producer Simon Bird; produced by Ben Cavey; directed by John Henderson.

With Jake Canuso (Mateo), Janine Duvitski (Jacqueline), Siobhan Finneran (Janice), Tim Healy (Les / Leslie), Kenny Ireland (Donald), Elsie Kelly (Noreen), Steve Pemberton (Mick), Sheila Reid (Madge), Crissy Rock (Janey), Oliver Stokes (Michael), Brian Murphy (Clive), Su Pollard (Herself), Louie Spence (Marvin), Roy Wood (Himself), Richard Morris, Fabio Tassone, Shaun Foster-Conley, Asa Elliott.

Dedicated to Geoffrey Hutchings 1939-2010.

BENNY HILL

A BBC production. Transmission details are for BBC.
Main regular cast: Benny Hill (Various Roles).

SERIES 2
A BBC production. Transmission details are for BBC. Duration: 25 minutes.
Main regular credit(s): Written by Dave Freeman; music by Ron Grainer; produced and directed by Duncan Wood.

	Holding / Source
21.12.1962 **Mervyn's Christmas Pudding**	J /

Written by Dave Freeman; designed by Tony Abbott.

With Graham Stark, Moyra Fraser, Priscilla Morgan, Patricia Hayes, Peter Vernon, Lala Lloyd, David Keir.

	Holding / Source
26.12.1962 **The Secret Of Planet Seven**	J /

Designed by Tony Abbott.

With Graham Stark, Penny Morrell, Colin Douglas, Arthur Mullard, Joe Gibbons, Coral Morphew, Valerie Cooney, Tricia Money, Gillian Watt, Caron Gardner, Valerie Stanton.

THE BENNY HILL SHOW

Produced for BBC/ITV by a variety of companies (see details below). Duration varies - see below for details.
Main regular cast: Benny Hill.

A BBC production. Transmission details are for BBC/BBC1.

	Holding / Source
26.12.1968	B3SEQ / 62

Duration: 45 minutes.

Written by Benny Hill; music directed by Burt Rhodes; designed by Brian Tregidden; produced and directed by Kenneth Carter.

With Tammy Jones, June Whitfield, Henry McGee, Jenny Lee-Wright, John Wright, Doris Rogers, Jim Tyson, Kedd Senton, Carolyn Moody, David G. March, Richard Mottau.

BBC hold film inserts and also hold a DV of complete show in poor quality.

An ATV production. Transmission details are for the ATV midlands region.

	Holding / Source
26.12.1967	DB-R1 / 40

Duration: 52 minutes.

Written by Benny Hill; music associate Derek Scott; choreography by Pamela Devis; designed by Vic Symonds; produced by Jon Scoffield; directed by Philip Casson.

With The Seekers, Vince Hill, Nicholas Parsons, Dorita y Pepe, Arthur Mullard, Rita Webb, Dave Freeman, Yvonne Antrobus, Bettine Le Beau, Peter Diamond, Gerry Wain, Jack Parnell and his Orchestra, The Pamela Devis Dancers, The Mike Sammes Singers.

The digibeta and film print are currently lost, so ITV only hold it on low-band Umatic.

A Thames Television production. Transmission details are for the ATV midlands region.

	VT Number	Holding / Source
25.12.1969	2308	D3 / 2"

Duration: 52 minutes.

Written by Benny Hill; songs by Benny Hill; music directed by Ronnie Aldrich; designed by Harry Clark; produced and directed by John Robins.

With Eira Heath, Nicholas Parsons, Robertson Hare, Rita Webb, Michael Sharvell-Martin, The Ladybirds, Tommy Mann, Yvonne Paul, Valerie Stanton, David Hamilton, Connie Georges, Lillian Padmore, Wally Goodman, Valeria St. John, Bill Straiton, Michael Moore.

23.12.1970	3455	D3 / 62

Duration: 51 minutes.

Written by Benny Hill; songs by Benny Hill; music directed by Ronnie Aldrich; designed by Tony Borer; produced and directed by John Robins.

With Nicholas Parsons, Trisha Noble, The Ladybirds, Liz Fraser, Jack Wright, Tommy Mann, Sue Bond, Jan Butlin, Kay Frazer, Charmaine Seal.

22.12.1971	4883	D3 / 2"

Duration: 52 minutes.

Written by Benny Hill; songs by Benny Hill; music directed by Ronnie Aldrich; designed by Tony Borer; produced and directed by David Bell.

With Nicholas Parsons, Bob Todd, Rita Webb, Clovissa Newcombe, Ronnie Brody, The Ladybirds, Bettine Le Beau, Carol Mills, Johnny Greenland, Kay Frazer, Mia Martin, John Trayhorn [as John Trayhorne].

27.12.1972	6617	D3 / 2"

Duration: 52 minutes.

Written by Benny Hill; songs by Benny Hill; music directed by Ronnie Aldrich; designed by Neville Green and Darrell Lass; produced and directed by Keith Beckett.

With Nicholas Parsons, Bob Todd, Jimmy Thompson, Diana King, Pat Ashton, Jenny Lee-Wright, The Ladybirds, Jack Wright, Walter Goodman, Anthony Kenyon, Bella Emberg, Sue Bond, Lillian Padmore, Cherry Gillam, Dennie Bayliss.

27.12.1973	8373	D3 / 2"

Duration: 52 minutes.

Written by Benny Hill; songs by Benny Hill; music directed by Albert Elms; designed by Tony Borer; associate producer William Cartlidge; produced and directed by John Robins.

With Anne Shelton, Henry McGee, Andrée Melly, Bob Todd, Lesley Goldie, The Ladybirds, Jack Wright, Bella Emberg, Carole Ball, Malou Cartwright, John John Keefe, Judy Gridley, Marilyn Harrison, Ian Kaye, David Wright, George May, Claire Russell, Earl Stephenson.

| THE BENNY HILL SHOW (continued) | | British Christmas Television Guide |

26.12.1978 "Wheelchair Rally / Friday Night Fever" 20043 D3 / 2"
Duration: 50 minutes.
Written by Benny Hill; songs by Benny Hill; music directed by Ronnie Aldrich; choreography by Samantha Stevens; titles by Bernard Allum; designed by Michael Minas; produced and directed by Ronald Fouracre.

With Henry McGee, Jenny Lee-Wright, Felicity Buirski, Roger Finch, Johnny Vyvyan, John Quayle, Cyril Cross, Eddie Connor, Len Keyes, Sharon Bond, Tina Bond, Louise English, Erica Ludlow, Stephanie Lawrence, Mandy Perryment, Victoria Shellard, Sue Upton.

BERGERAC

A BBC production for BBC 1. made in association with Seven Network, Australia. Transmission details are for BBC 1. Duration varies - see below for details.

Main regular credit(s):   Created by Robert Banks Stewart; theme music by George Fenton.
Main regular cast: John Nettles (Jim Bergerac), Terence Alexander (Charles Hungerford), Sean Arnold (Barney Crozier (Series 1-8 only)).

SERIES 5
Main regular credit(s):   Music by Ray Russell; produced by Jonathan Alwyn.
Main regular cast: With Louise Jameson (Susan Young), Nancy Mansfield (Peggy Masters).

Holding / Source
26.12.1986 **Fires In The Fall**   DB / C1
Duration: 90 minutes.
Written by Chris Boucher; script editor John Chapman; production associate Peter Norris; directed by Tom Clegg.

With Deborah Grant (Deborah), Mela White (Diamante Lil), Lindsay Heath (Kim Bergerac), Geoffrey Leesley (Detective Constable Wilson), Jolyon Baker (Detective Constable Goddard), Barrie Ingham, Amanda Redman, Margaretta Scott, Donald Churchill, Paul Brooke, Ron Pember, Jim McManus, Tony Westrope, Nicholas McArdle, Guy Standeven.

26.12.1987 **Treasure Hunt**   DB / C1
Duration: 90 minutes.
Written by Rod Beacham; script editor John Chapman; designed by Phil Roberson; production associate Dave Edwards; production manager Steve Goldie; directed by Robert Tronson.

With Liza Goddard (Philippa Vale), Geoffrey Leesley (Detective Constable Wilson), Jolyon Baker (Detective Constable Goddard), Peter Jeffrey, James Maxwell, David Horovitch, Carole Harrison, John Grillo, Lynette Davies, Greg Hicks, Michael Melia, Steve Paget, Rosemary Frankau, Stuart Saunders, John Cassady, David Beckett, Christopher Donat, John Crocker, Marilyn Le Conte, Chris Dunne, Penny Smith, Theresa Fresson, Dorothea Alexander, Gareth Milne.

SERIES 6
Main regular credit(s):   Script editor David Crane; music by Ray Russell; production associate Jeremy Gwilt; produced by George Gallaccio.
Main regular cast: With Louise Jameson (Susan Young), Nancy Mansfield (Peggy Masters), John Telfer (Detective Constable Willy Pettit), David Kershaw (Detective Constable Ben Lomas).

Holding / Source
27.12.1988 **Retirement Plan**   DB / C1
Duration: 95 minutes.
Written by Edmund Ward; directed by Edward Bennett.

With Nicholas Ball, Sue Lloyd, James Laurenson, Sylvester Morand, Constantine Gregory, Carmen Du Sautoy, Anthony Calf, Micha Bergese, Barrie Houghton, Bill Stewart, Hilary Mason, Robert McBain, Catherine Livesey, Daniel Webb, Dave Atkins, Matyelok Gibbs, Paul Angelis, Jonathan Oliver.

SERIES 8
Main regular credit(s):   Script editor David Crane; music by Ray Russell and Kevin Townend; production associate Mike Hudson; produced by George Gallaccio.
Main regular cast: With John Telfer (Detective Constable Willy Pettit), David Kershaw (Detective Constable Ben Lomas).

Holding / Source
26.12.1989 **Second Time Around**   DB / C1
Duration: 97 minutes.
Written by Ian Kennedy Martin; designed by Martin Methven; production manager David Mason; directed by Peter Ellis.

With Lisa Climie (Wendy), David Schofield, Andrew Sachs, Donald Sumpter, Jennifer Landor, Elizabeth Bradley, Rupert Frazer, Derrick Branche, Clare Byam Shaw, Sarah Neville, Pavel Douglas, Prentis Hancock, Richard Hawley, Chris Langham.

26.12.1990 **There For The Picking**   DB / C1
Duration: 95 minutes.
Written by Desmond Lowden; designed by Bob Cove; production manager David Harvey; directed by Gordon Flemyng.

With Thérèse Liotard (Danielle Aubry), Michael Mellinger (Albert Leufroid), Wayne Morris, Warren Saire, Melanie Thaw, Kenneth Cranham, Simon Chandler, Lawrence Davidson, Altay Lawrence, Julian Freeman, David Hargreaves, Paula Topham, Rupert Holliday Evans, Tim Meats, Graham Fletcher-Cook, Grant Oatley, Luke Hanson, Leslie Clack, David Keys, Bill Moody.

SERIES 9
Main regular credit(s):   Script editor David Crane; music by Ray Russell and Kevin Townend; production associate Mike Hudson; produced by George Gallaccio.
Main regular cast: With David Kershaw (Detective Constable Ben Lomas), John Telfer (Detective Constable Willy Pettit).

Holding / Source
26.12.1991 **All For Love**   DB / C1S
Duration: 107 minutes.
Written by John Milne; music by Ray Russell; designed by Stephen Sharratt [credited as Steve Sharratt] and Merle Downie; production manager Johnathan Young; directed by Terry Marcel.

With Deborah Grant (Deborah), Roger Sloman (Inspector Deffand), Charmaine Parsons (Ellie), Suzan Crowley, Simon Williams, Bill Nighy, Al Ashton, Philip Glenister, Catherine Rabett, Gordon Salkilld, Jane Downs, Peter Watts, Bruno Madinier, Iain Rattray, Malcolm Gerrard.

See also: THE DETECTIVES (BBC)

BERNARD AND THE GENIE

An Atta Boy production for BBC 1. made in association with Talkback. Transmission details are for BBC 1. Duration: 67 minutes.

Written by Richard Curtis; script editor Emma Freud; music by Howard Goodall; director of photography Roger Pratt; designed by John Beard and Rod McLean; associate producer Andy McClean; executive producers Peter Fincham and Mary Francis; produced by Jacinta Peel; directed by Paul Weiland.

Lenny Henry (Genie), Alan Cumming (Bernard Bottle), Rowan Atkinson (Charles Pinkworth), Dennis Lill (Kepple), Kevin Allen (Kevin), Andrée Bernard (Judy), Angie Clarke (Carrie), John Gabriel (Wizard), Bealyn Bryant (Nurse), Janet Henfrey (Miss Purse), Marcia Ashton (Miss Temple), Sheila Latimer (Bernard's Mother), Sally Geoghegan (Waitress), Gary Whelan (Officer), Trevor Laird (Police Constabke Parker), Stacy Davies (Desk Sergeant), Lee Sheward (Third Police Constable), David Forman (Ninja Turtle), Trevor McDonald (Newscaster), Vincent Hanna (Reporter), Daniel Daniels (Child In Santa's Grotto), Carly Langridge (Child In Santa's Grotto), Scott Argyle (Child In Santa's Grotto), Ben Rennis (Child In Santa's Grotto), Stephen Monroe (Child In Santa's Grotto), Max Weiland (Child In Santa's Grotto), Liatt Joseph-Mitchell (Child In Santa's Grotto), Bob Geldof, Melvyn Bragg, Gary Lineker.

Date	Holding / Source
23.12.1991	1" / C1S

BERNARD DELFONT PRESENTS... TALK OF THE TOWN

An ATV production. Transmission details are for the ATV midlands region. Duration: 50 minutes.

Date	Holding / Source
31.12.1959 **Gala New Year's Eve Edition**	J /

Dances staged by Lionel Blair; music directed by Jack Parnell; designed by Anthony Waller; produced by Brian Tesler.

With Sidney Simone and his Orchestra, The Hermanos Deniz Cuban Rhythm Band, The Talk of the Town Dancers.

BEST FRIENDS - CLEO LAINE AND JOHN WILLIAMS

A Yorkshire Television production. Transmission details are for the Central region. Duration: 50 minutes.

Designed by Colin Pigott; produced and directed by Vernon Lawrence.

Cleo Laine, John Williams, Nigel Kennedy, Emma Johnson, Edward Moore, Johnny Dankworth and his Orchestra.

Date	Holding / Source
23.12.1984	1" / 1"

THE BFG

A Cosgrove Hall production for Thames Television. Transmission details are for the Central region.

Adapted by John Hambley; based on a book by Roald Dahl; music by Keith Hopgood and Malcolm Rowe; executive producer John Hambley; produced by Mark Hall and Brian Cosgrove; directed by Brian Cosgrove.

David Jason (Voice of B.F.G.), Amanda Root (Voice of Sophia), Angela Thorne (Voice of the Queen), Ballard Berkeley (Voice of Head of Army), Michael Knowles (Voice of Head of Air Force), Don Henderson (Voice of Sergeant & Giants), Mollie Sugden (Voice of Mary), Jimmy Hibbert (Other Voices), Frank Thornton (Other Voices), Myfanwy Talog (Other Voices).

Date	Holding / Source
25.12.1991	1" / 1"

BIG BAD MOUSE

A Thames Television production. Transmission details are for the ATV midlands region. Duration: 75 minutes.

Written by Philip King and Falkland Cary; based on an idea by Ivan Butler; television presentation by John Robins and Robert Gillette; produced for the stage by John Downing.

Eric Sykes (Mr Bloome), Jimmy Edwards (Mr Price-Hargreaves), Joan Young (Lady Chesapeake), Diane Holland (Miss Spencer), Wendy Lovelock (Doris Povey), Iain Smith (Harold Hopkins), Joyce Irving (Fiona Jones).

Date	VT Number	Holding / Source
26.12.1972	5600	D3 / 2"

By arrangement with Bernard Delfont, Paul Elliott and Duncan C. Weldon.

BIG BREAK - A CELEBRITY CHRISTMAS SPECIAL

A BBC production for BBC 1. Transmission details are for BBC 1. Usual duration: 30 minutes.

Main regular performer(s): Jim Davidson (Presenter), John Virgo (Referee).

Date	Holding / Source
##.##.#### [untransmitted pilot]	DB / 1"

With Mike Reid (Presenter).

24.12.1991	DB / 1"S

Produced by John Burrowes; directed by Nick Hurran.

With Stephen Hendry, Steve Davis, Jimmy White, Linda Lusardi, Jean Alexander, Charlie Drake.

26.12.1992	DB / 1"

Duration: 40 minutes.

Produced by John Burrowes; directed by Charles Garland.

With Patrick Moore, Ruth Madoc, Anthea Turner, Dennis Taylor, Allison Fisher, Willie Thorne.

27.12.1994 **Big Break In Wonderland**	DB-D3 / D3S

Duration: 40 minutes.

Produced by John Burrowes; directed by Charles Garland.

With Zoe Ball, John Parrott, Marti Caine, Terry Griffiths, Craig Charles, Steve Davis.

BIG BREAK - A CELEBRITY CHRISTMAS SPECIAL (continued)

28.12.1995 **Panto Edition**   DB-D3 / D3S
Produced by John Burrowes; directed by Babara Jones.
With Wendy Richard, Frank Carson, Diane-Louise Jordan, Ray Reardon, Jimmy White, Peter Ebdon.

27.12.1996   DB-D3 / D3S
Produced by John Burrowes; directed by Phil Chilvers.
With Patsy Palmer, Bella Emberg, Floella Benjamin, Steve Davis, John Parrott, Dennis Taylor.

28.12.1998   DB / DBS
Produced by David Taylor; directed by Duncan Cooper.
With Isla Fisher, Little and Large, Barbara Windsor, Jimmy White, John Higgins, John Parrott.

THE BIG FAT QUIZ OF THE YEAR

A Hotsauce TV production for Channel 4. Transmission details are for Channel 4. Duration: 100 minutes.

Holding / Source

28.12.2004   DB / DBSW
Written by Jimmy Carr, Jim Pullin, Shaun Pye and Fraser Steele; additional material by Lee Stuart Evans, Neil Southgate and Nick Wealthall; script supervisor Sue Davies; music by Pete Baikie; associate producers Neil Calow and Matt Cox; executive producers Debbie Cox and Jonathan Ross; production manager Peter Hackett; produced by Anthony Caveney and Jane Goldman; directed by Mick Thomas.
With Jimmy Carr (Host), Rob Brydon, Simon Pegg, Jonathan Ross, June Sarpong, Liza Tarbuck, David Walliams, Nadia Almada, Leigh Francis [as The Bear], Bono, Derren Brown, Kelly Holmes, Richard Madeley [as Richard & Judy], Judy Finnigan [as Richard & Judy], Louis Walsh, Children from Mitchell Brook Primary School*.

26.12.2005   DB / DBSW
Written by Jimmy Carr, Jim Pullin, Shaun Pye and Fraser Steele; research Matt Nida and Barnaby Slater; script supervisor Sue Davies; edited by Steve Andrews; art director Tayyaba Irtizaali; assistant producers Mike Maclaine and Luke Shiach; executive producer Jonathan Ross; produced by Jane Goldman and Emily Dean; directed by Mick Thomas.
With Jimmy Carr (Host), Rob Brydon, David Mitchell, Sharon Osbourne, Gordon Ramsay, Jonathan Ross, Denise van Outen, Jordan, Peter André, David Tennant, Walter Wolfgang, Susie Doku, Richard Madeley*, Judy Finnigan*, Charlotte Church*, Jon Snow*, Cameron Diaz*, Toni Collette*, Kevin Pietersen*, Children from Mitchell Brook Primary School*.

27.12.2006   DB / DBSW
Written by Jimmy Carr, Jim Pullen, Shaun Pye and Fraser Steele; additional material by Dominic English and Frankie Boyle; research Daniel-Konrad Cooper and Ben Knappett; art director Tayyaba Irtizaali; assistant producers Matt Nida and Luis Pulido; executive producer Jonathan Ross; head of production Peter Hackett; production manager Polly Mann; produced by Jane Goldman and Emily Dean; directed by Mick Thomas.
With Jimmy Carr (Host), Russell Brand, Rob Brydon, Cat Deeley, Noel Fielding, Jonathan Ross, David Walliams, Myleene Klass, Matt Willis, Guy Goma, Boy George, Lily Allen*, Girls Aloud*, Ian McKellen*, Jon Snow*, Carol Vorderman*, Sacha Baron Cohen*, Courtney Love*, Children from Mitchell Brook Primary School*.
In his insert, Sacha Baron Cohen appeared in character as Borat Sagdiyev.

30.12.2007   DB / DBSW
Written by Jimmy Carr, Jim Pullin, Shaun Pye, Fraser Steele and Will Dixon; script supervisor Sue Davies; music by Peter Baikie; designed by Richard Drew; associate producers Barney Slater, Simon Crewdson, Ben Knappett and Matt Nida; executive producer Jonathan Ross; head of production Adam Hayes; produced by Emily Dean and Jane Goldman; directed by Mick Thomas.
With Jimmy Carr (Host), Jonathan Ross, Russell Brand, Rob Brydon, Noel Fielding, David Mitchell, Lily Allen, Christopher Biggins, Cerys Matthews, Paul Croft, John Smeaton.

28.12.2008   DB / DBSW
Written by Jimmy Carr, Shaun Pye, Jim Pullin and Fraser Steele; additional material by Christine Rose, Martin Trenaman and Lee Stuart Evans; script supervisor Sue Davies; music by Peter Baikie; designed by Richard Drew; associate producers Marko Gowan, Matt Nida and Ben Knappett; executive producers Emily Dean and Jane Goldman; head of production Adam Hayes; produced by Seamus Murphy-Mitchell; directed by Mick Thomas.
With Jimmy Carr (Host), James Corden, Michael McIntyre, Sean Lock, Dara Ó Briain, Davina McCall, Claudia Winkleman, Alan Carr, James Degale, Christina Ohuruogu, Mark Foster, Katy Perry, John Hurt, Sarah Silverman, Jodie Kidd, Jon Snow, Kayvan Novak, Sir Alan Sugar.

01.01.2010   DB / DBSW
Written by Jimmy Carr, Fraser Steele, Shaun Pye and Jez Stevenson; additional material by Honey Ross; script supervisor Sue Davies; music by Peter Baikie; titles by Jump Design; art directors Helen Mooney, Luke Whitelock and Paul Richardson; designed by Richard Drew; associate producer Matt Nida; executive producer Jonathan Ross; head of production Adam Hayes; line producer Carla McGilchrist; produced by Jane Goldman and Emily Dean; directed by Mick Thomas.
With Jimmy Carr (Host), Russell Brand, Charlie Brooker, Rob Brydon, David Mitchell, Jonathan Ross, Claudia Winkleman, Peter André, Daniel 'Lionheart' Lerwell*, James 'Lights Out' Lilley*, Jon Snow*, 50 Cent*, Tim Minchin*, Stuart Broad*, David Attenborough*, David Tennant*, Doctor David Starkey*, Children from Mitchell Brook Primary School*.

03.01.2011   HD/DB / HDC
Written by Jimmy Carr, Dominic English, Jim Pullen, Shaun Pye and Fraser Steele; script supervisor Sue Davies; music by Pete Baikie; titles by Jump Design; art directors Helen Mooney and Mark Sutherland; associate producer Kate Staples; executive producers Jane Goldman and Jonathan Ross; head of production Adam Hayes; line producer Carla McGilchrist; produced by Ben Knappett and Matt Nida; directed by Mick Thomas.
With Jimmy Carr (Host), Richard Ayoade, Alan Carr, Noel Fielding, Ruth Jones, Michael McIntyre, Jonathan Ross, Will Ferrell*, Nicole Scherzinger*, Jack Black*, Simon Pegg*, Darryl Mann, Lola the Cat, Russell Brand*, Jamie Oliver*, Louie Spence, Jon Snow*, Seth Rogan*, Nathan Stewart-Jarrett*, Lauren Socha*, Iwan Rheon*, Antonia Thomas*, Robert Sheehan*, Children from Mitchell Brook Primary School.

27.12.2011   HD/DB / HDC
Written by Jimmy Carr, Jim Pullin, Shaun Pye, Fraser Steele, Jez Stevenson, Charlie Skelton, Aidan Spackman and Dan Swimer; produced by Ben Knappett and Matt Nida; directed by Mick Thomas.
With Jimmy Carr (Host), Jonathan Ross, Jamie Oliver, David Mitchell, Jon Snow, David Walliams, Miranda Hart, Eddie Izzard.

30.12.2012   HD/DB / HDC
Written by Jimmy Carr, Shaun Pye, Dominic English, Jez Stevenson, Charlie Skelton, Aidan Spackman and Keith Leaf; executive producers Jane Goldman and Jonathan Ross; produced by Ben Knappett and Matt Nida; directed by Mick Thomas.
With Jimmy Carr (Host), Jonathan Ross, Russell Howard, James Corden, Jack Whitehall, Jon Snow, Richard Ayoade, Gabby Logan.

| British Christmas Television Guide | THE BIG FAT QUIZ OF THE YEAR (continued) |

26.12.2013   HD/DB / HDC
Series producer Matt Nida; produced by Aoife Dunne.
With Jimmy Carr (Host), Jack Whitehall, Jonathan Ross, Dara Ó Briain, Kristen Schaal, Noel Fielding, Richard Ayoade.

Cast entries marked as 'uncredited' generally relate to people who asked questions in pre-recorded inserts. Unlike the studio guests who posed questions, these people were not usually credited at the end of the programmes (2004 was an exception).

THE BIG H

A BBC production for BBC 2. Transmission details are for BBC 2. Duration: 45 minutes.
Written by Tony Harrison and Dominic Muldowney; music by Tony Harrison and Dominic Muldowney; designed by Stuart Walker; produced by Andrée Molyneux; directed by Bill Hays.
Barrie Rutter (Maths Teacher, Herod 1), June Watson (History Teacher, Herod 2), Jim Carter (Geography Teacher, Herod 3).

Holding / Source
26.12.1984   DB-D3 / 2"

BIG HUG: THE STORY OF TELETUBBIES

A BBC production for BBC 2. Transmission details are for BBC 2. Duration: 40 minutes.
Research Karen Keith; consultant Judy Whitfield; designed by Candida Otton; executive producer Sue Nott; production manager Paulette Gardiner; produced and directed by Patrick Reams.
Victoria Carling (Narrator), Anne Wood*, Andy Davenport*.

Holding / Source
25.12.1998   DB / DBS

Documentary about the pre-school children's television series TELETUBBIES, looking at how children's television has evolved over the years, featuring interviews with programme makers.
See also: TELETUBBIES (BBC)

BIG LITTLE PICTURES

A HTV Wales production. Transmission details are for the HTV Wales region. Duration: 25 minutes.

Holding / Source
15.12.2000   **Oh Little Town Of Bethlehem**   DB / V1S
Written by Melvyn Williams; produced by Maurice Hunter; directed by Darren Ripley.

BIG NIGHT OUT

An ABC production. Transmission details are for the ABC midlands region. Duration: 52 minutes.

Holding / Source
26.12.1964   **Boxing Night Out**   J / 40
Written by John Morley and Brad Ashton; music directed by Bob Sharples; designed by Brian Eatwell; produced and directed by Pat Johns.
With Mike and Bernie Winters (Hosts), David Nixon, Gerry and The Pacemakers, Ray Alan and Lord Charles, Peter Gordeno and his Dancers, Lionel Blair and his Dancers, Bob Sharples and his ABC Television Showband.
From the ABC Theatre, Blackpool.

THE BIG STAGE

An LWT production for Channel 5. Transmission details are for Channel 5. Duration: 48 minutes.
Main regular performer(s): Bradley Walsh (Host).

Holding / Source
29.12.2000   **Magic And Illusion Special**   DB / DBS
Script editor Colin Edmonds; executive producer Lisa Clark; produced by Chris O'Dell; directed by Mick Thomas.
With Steve Best, Richard Cadell, Ian Keable, Malte Knappe, Shahid Malik, Mostafa The Wazyr, Mandy Muden, Brett Sherwood, Russ Stevens, Trois Fois L'ete, Paul Zenon.

THE BIG TOP

A Thames Television production. Transmission details are for the ATV midlands region. Duration: 35 minutes.
Music directed by Bernard Weller; music associate Clarry Sampson; produced and directed by Christopher Palmer.
David Hamilton (Ringmaster), William Vos, The Astoris, The Nicolodis, Mary Chipperfield.

Holding / Source
25.12.1972   DB / 2"

BILI A'R DOWCAR HUD

A BBC Wales production for BBC 1 Wales. Transmission details are for BBC 1 Wales. Duration: 30 minutes.
Written by Dyfed Glyn Jones; designed by Ted Boyce; play production by Brynmor Wiliams.
Hywel Gwynfryn (Storyteller), Dyfed Thomas (Mrs Rwdlan), Elliw Haf (Bili), Dafydd Hywel (Meri Marjarin), Geraint Jarman (Sion Hir Arian).

Holding / Source
25.12.1975   J / 2"
Pantomime in Welsh!

BILL BAILEY: TINSELWORM

A glassbox production for Channel 4. Transmission details are for Channel 4. Duration: 50 minutes.

Written by Bill Bailey; choreography by Katie Prince; executive producers Bill Bailey and Kris Bailey; produced by Ben Swaffer; directed by Russell Thomas.

Bill Bailey.

	Holding / Source
30.12.2010	DB / DBSW

THE BILL

A Thames Television production. Transmission details are for the Central region. Duration varies - see below for details.

Main regular credit(s): Devised by Geoff McQueen.

SERIES 4

A Thames Television production for Thames/Yorkshire/Carlton/ITV1. Duration: 25 minutes.

Main regular credit(s): Theme music by Andy Pask and Charlie Morgan.

Main regular cast: With Eric Richard (Sergeant Bob Cryer (until 24.4.01)), Nula Conwell (Viv Martella (until 26.3.93)), Jeff Stewart (Police Constable Reg Hollis), Christopher Ellison (Detective Inspector Jack Burnside (16.08.88-07.09.93)), Peter Ellis (Chief Superintendent Brownlow (until 03.11.00)), Jon Iles (Detective Constable Mike Dashwood (until 02.07.1992)), Tony Scannell (Detective Sergeant Ted Roach (until 15.05.93)), Graham Cole (Police Constable Tony Stamp), Ben Roberts (Chief Inspector Conway (until 28.03.2002)), Kevin Lloyd (Detective Constable Tosh Lines (27.10.88-09.06.98)), Andrew Mackintosh (Detective Superintendent Greig (3.01.89-28.07.98)), Huw Higginson (Police Constable Garfield (9.5.89-16.12.99)), Lynne Miller (Woman Police Constable Cathy Marshall (20.6.89-19.11.1996)), Seeta Indrani (Woman Police Constable Norika Datta (19.9.89-25.8.98)), Stephen Bent (Police Constable Martin (21.11.89-?), Andrew Paul (Police Constable David Quinnan (21.12.89-), Colin Tarrant (Inspector Monroe (11.1.90-11.4.2002)), Tom Butcher (Police Constable Loxton (7.8.90-14.11.1997)), Nick Stringer (Police Constable Ron Smollett (21.8.90-), Natasha Williams (Woman Police Constable Delia French (2.10.90-26.3.92)), Carolyn Pickles (Detective Chief Inspector Kim Reid (20.12.90-13.02.92)), Sam Miller (Sergeant Maitland (26.12.90-27.5.93?)), Steve Morley (Sergeant Lamont (1.1.91-3.10.97)), Tony O'Callaghan (Sergeant Matthew Boyden (7.11.91-), Jonathan Dow (Police Constable Stringer (7.1.92-?)), Simon Rouse (Detective Chief Inspector Jack Meadows (24.03.92-), Louise Harrison (Woman Police Constable Donna Harris (24.3.92-), Mary Jo Randle (Woman Detective Sergeant Jo Morgan (9.3.93-12.10.95)), Mark Wingett (Jim Carver), Larry Dann (Sergeant Peters (until 11.2.92)), Tom Cotcher (Detective Constable Alan Woods (14.07.92-), Lisa Geoghan (Woman Police Constable Polly Page (15.10.92-), Clive Wedderburn (Police Constable McCann (10.12.92-99?)), Philip Whitchurch (Chief Inspector Philip Cato (26.01.93-3.03.95)), Liz Crowther (Sergeant Kendall (23.2.93-May 93?)), Kerry Peers (Woman Police Constable Croft (11.2.93-?)), Martin Marquez (Detective Sergeant Danny Pearce (22.05.93-?)), Jaye Griffiths (Woman Detective Sergeant Johnson (21.8.93-27.1.95)), Gary Whelan (Detective Inspector Haines (11.09.93-31.12.1993)), Robert Perkins (Sergeant Ray Steele (4.12.93-11.4.96)), Stephen Beckett (Police Constable Jarvis (18.1.94-7.5.98)), Carl Brincat (Police Constable Bostock (7.1.94-1995?)), Iain Fletcher (Skase (11.2.94-1999)), Gail Abbott (Woman Police Constable Hughes (26.6.93-28.12.95)), Shaun Scott (Detective Sergeant Chris Deakin (02.08.94-), Billy Murray (Detective Sergeant Don Beech (3.2.95-), Andrea Mason (Womand Police Constable Debbie Keane (7.3.95-15.9.98)), Alan Westaway (Police Constable Nick Slater (7.3.95-Nov 97)), Mark Spalding (Chief Inspector Stritch (28.03.95-12.10.95?)), Ray Ashcroft (Detective Sergeant Daly (04.06.96-26.01.1999)), Russell Boulter (Detective Sergeant John Boulton (02.11.1995--20.10.00)), Libby Davison (Woman Detective Constable Liz Rawton (10.9.96-), Lolita Chakrabarti (Woman Police Constable Jamila Blake (31.12.1996-5.6.98)), Gregory Donaldson (Detective Constable Tom Proctor (01.08.97-), Scott Neal (Police Constable Luke Ashton (9.12.97-22.7.1999)), Trudie Goodwin (Woman Police Constable June Ackland).

	Holding / Source
24.12.1991 **Vital Statistics**	D3 / MII

Duration: 50 minutes.

A dramatic disappearance on the Sun Hill patch threatens Stamp's attempt to defend the honour of the relief.

Written by Christopher Russell; executive producer Michael Chapman; produced by Brenda Ennis; directed by Jeremy Summers.

With Josephine Blake (Jan Jarvis), Annette Badland (Stella King), Matt Bardock (Ray Jarvis), John Cater, Jenny Jay, Chris Gascoyne, Val McLane.

31.12.1991 **Breakout**	D3 / MII

Duration: 50 minutes.

Hopes for a peaceful New Year's Eve are shattered when a dangerous criminal escapes from custody.

Written by Carolyn Sally Jones; executive producer Michael Chapman; produced by Brenda Ennis; directed by Frank W. Smith.

With Robert Hudson (Yorkie Smith), Margot Leicester, Russell Milton, Glyn Grimstead, Caroline Quentin, Daniel Hill, Lisa Geoghan, Sarah Lancashire, Miranda Forbes, Buddug Morgan.

23.12.1994 **Stuffed**	D3 / D3

Ackland and Quinnan are led on a wild goose chase by two juveniles. Meanwhile, Stamp thinks he's going to strike it lucky and get a date at the Sun Hill Christmas party.

Written by Mark Holloway; executive producer Michael Chapman; produced by Richard Handford; directed by Christopher Hodson.

With Annette Ekblom (Danielle Sherstone), Ray Ashcroft (Police Constable Leach), Emily Aston (Jodie Sherstone), Thomas Aston (Alex Sherstone), Susie Ann Watkins (Eloise Parkes), Ewan Bailey (Carl Wickes), Helena Little (Lucy Newsom).

24.12.1996 **Merrily On High**	D3 / D3S

It's Christmas at Sun Hill, but Assistant Commissioner Hicks has banned the traditional seasonal tipple. In retaliation Skase and Beech decide to run a drinks scam.

Written by Robert Jones; executive producer Michael Chapman; produced by Chris Clough; directed by Michael Cocker.

With Mike Burnside (District Assistant Commissioner Hicks), Frank Mills (Kenny Chalker), Belinda Sinclair (Pat Robson), Charlotte Fryer (Shelly Kendall), Lizzie Clough (Scarlett Kendall), Mark Kempner (Publican).

22.12.1997 **Twanky**	D3 / D3S

Duration: 50 minutes.

Directing the Christmas pantomime and dealing with police prima donnas seems to be the toughest case of the year for WPC Page, while DI Deakin is tracked by the brother of a man charged with assault.

Written by Mark Holloway; executive producer Michael Chapman; produced by Chris Clough; directed by Mike Cocker.

With Adam Magnani (Kieran Harper), Siobhan Fogarty (Jo Miller), Christopher Beaumont (Terry Poole), Siân Liquorish (Kelly Poole), J. J. Beckford (Darren Poole), Leah Fitzgerald (Lauren Poole).

THE BILL (continued)

A Thames Television production for Carlton/ITV1.

Main regular credit(s):	Theme music by Andy Pask and Charlie Morgan.
Main regular cast:	With Trudie Goodwin (Woman Police Constable June Ackland), Caroline Catz (Woman Police Constable Fox (25.8.1998-22.6.1999)), Joy Brook (Woman Detective Constable Kerry Holmes (20.10.1998-2001)), Aden Gillett (Detective Sergeant Lockyer (10.11.1998-2001)), George Rossi (Detective Constable Duncan Lennox (27.11.1998.-2001), Jane Wall (Woman Police Constable Worrell (11.5.1999-11.4.2002)), Mickey Ambrose (Police Constable Tate (11.5.1999-), Suzanne Maddock (Police Constable Cass Rickman (29.6.1999-12.12.2002)), Karl Collins (Detective Constable Glaze (29.6.1999-), Alex Walkinshaw (Police Constable, Later Sergeant, Dale Smith (20.7.1999-ongoing), Rene Zagger (Police Constable Nick Klein (16.9.1999-25.3.2004)), Clara Salaman (Detective Sergeant Claire Stanton (23.09.1999-), Chris Simmons (Detective Constable Mickey Webb (13.04.2000-), Holly Davidson (Police Constable Clarke (19.9.2000-), Ben Peyton (Police Constable Hayward (19.9.2000-), Ged Simmons (Detective Inspector Cullen (03.11.2000-), Steven Hartley (Superintendent Tom Chandler (3.11.2000-16.10.2002)), Raji James (Detective Sergeant Singh (3.11.2000-), Natalie Roles (Detective Sergeant Debbie McAllister (03.11.2000-10.11.2004)), Tania Emery (Detective Constable Spears (03.11.2000-11.04.2002)), Gary Grant (Detective Constable Riley (03.11.2000-11.04.2002)).

Holding / Source

24.12.1998 Christmas Star DB / DBS

Duration: 50 minutes.

Emmanuel Petit visits a little girl in hospital who's been knocked down by a hit-and-run driver.

Written by Terry Hodgkinson; executive producer Richard Handford; produced by Pat Sandys; directed by Tom Cotter.

With Emmanuel Petit (Himself), Peter Blake (Greg Beattie), Lynne Pearson (Angie Beattie), Niven Boyd (Alex Forbes), Jenny Bolt (Maggie Forbes), Neil Conrich (Gerry Duff), Laura Kennington (Sophie), Bobby Knutt (Santa), Ajay Chhabra (Mr Wadia).

24.12.1999 When The Snow Lay Round About DB / DBSW

Duration: 50 minutes.

Ballet star Irek Mukhamedov makes his acting debut in this festive edition. A group of Russian singers arrive at Sun Hill claiming a member of their group has stolen their clothes and money.

Written by Chris Ould; executive producer Richard Handford; produced by Michael Simpson; directed by Albert Barber.

With Brian Murphy (Danny the Elf), Irek Mukhamedov (Sergei), Scott Charles (Glen Massey), Nick Von Schlippe (Braslav Petrovitch), Yuri Stepanov (Vladimir), Alexei Jawdokimov (Ivan), Victor Lindegrin (Boris), Godfrey Jackman (Mr Stansfield), Julie Teal (Ms Boal), Ben Cartwright (Simms).

31.12.1999 All Change DB / DBSW

Duration: 50 minutes.

The CID officers have to change back into uniform as they are sent out on to the Sun Hill beat to police the biggest and busiest night of the century.

Written by Mark Holloway; executive producer Richard Handford; directed by Michael Cocker.

With Robert McCulley (Eddie Cochlin), Pippa Hinchley (Rosie Goddard), Michael Wilson (Ronald MacDonald), Peter Gordon (Harry Marsh), Tony Wadham (Charlie Ward), William Beck (Adam Thwaite), Belinda Chapman (Valerie Overton), Bryan Matheson (Harold Owen), Kyle Stewart (Junior), Bronson Webb (Ricky).

22.12.2000 1: The Night Before DB / DBSW

Duration: 50 minutes.

Webb and Lennox investigate a shoplifting case with more to it than meets the eye, while it's make or break for Page and Quinnan.

Written by Richard Stoneman; executive producer Richard Handford; directed by Christopher Lovett.

With Lesley McGuire (Mrs Quinnan).

At some point during 2003 Carson Black became a shortlived Series Producer. Due to poor listings magazines we cannot be more specific in some details. Where on-screen credits are available we have noted the relevant Executive Producer.

A Thames Television (Talkback Thames) production for ITV 1. Duration: 48 minutes.

Main regular credit(s):	Story consultant Jackie Malton; story producer Kevin Rundle; theme music by Andy Pask and Charlie Morgan; executive producer Johnathan Young; head of production Nigel Taylor; senior producer Tim Key.

Holding / Source

17.12.2008 Santa's Little Helper DB / DBSW

Detective Sergeant Turner and Detective Constable Moss set up a sting aimed at burglars using a Santa's grotto competition to get people's addresses.

Written by Sally Tatchell; senior story editor Kara Manley; script supervisor Jenny Bowman; series editor James Hall; story editor Noemi Spanos; script editor Claire Miller; designed by Ian Russell and Adam Marshall; production manager Amanda Black; produced by Andrea Sapsford; directed by Diana Patrick.

With Gary Lucy (Police Constable Will Fletcher), Lucy Speed (Detective Constable Stevie Moss), Doug Rao (Detective Sergeant Stuart Turner), Ben Richards (Police Constable Nate Roberts), Micah Balfour (Police Constable Benjamin Gayle), Claire Goose (Sergeant Rachel Weston), Abhin Galeya (Police Constable Arun Ghir), Simon Rouse (Detective Chief Inspector Jack Meadows), Francis Magee, Steve Gibbs, Abigail Hood, Jordan Clarke, James Greene, Peter Lindford, Bill Ward, Michael Nardone.

BILLY BUNTER OF GREYFRIARS SCHOOL

A BBC production. Transmission details are for BBC. Duration: 25 minutes.

Main regular credit(s):	Written by Frank Richards.
Main regular cast:	Gerald Campion (Billy Bunter).

SERIES 1

Holding / Source

04.03.1952 Bunter's Christmas Party NR / Live

Produced and directed by Joy Harington.

With John Charlesworth (Harry Wharton), Barry MacGregor (Johhny Bull), Keith Faulkner (Bob Cherry), David Spenser (Hurree Jamset Ram Singh), Michael Danvers-Walker (Frank Nugent), Hamlyn Benson (Mr Carter), John Benson (Hubert Tankerton), Frederick Piper (Brown).

BILLY BUNTER OF GREYFRIARS SCHOOL (continued)

SERIES 3

Main regular credit(s): Produced and directed by Shaun Sutton.

Main regular cast: With Brian Roper (Bob Cherry), Anthony Valentine (Harry Wharton), Lawrence Harrington (Frank Nugent), David Coote (Johnny Bull), Kynaston Reeves (Mr Quelch), Barry Barnett (Hurree Singh).

Holding / Source

14.10.1956 Bunter's Christmas Box R3 /

Designed by Eileen Diss.

With Glyn Dearman (Lord Mauleverer), Christopher Hodge (Gosling), Douglas Blackwell (The Man), Sidney Monckton (Wells), Roger Maxwell (Colonel Wharton).

THE BILLY COTTON BAND SHOW

A BBC production. Transmission details are for BBC. Duration varies - see below for details.

Main regular performer(s): Billy Cotton (Host).

Holding / Source

26.12.1957 A Boxing Day Party J /

Duration: 60 minutes.

Choreography by Leslie Roberts; designed by Richard Henry; associate producer Leslie Roberts; produced by Albert Stevenson and Bill Cotton Jnr; directed by Albert Stevenson and Bill Cotton Jnr.

With Kathie Kay, Vera Lynn, George Formby, Eric Robinson, Alan Breeze, Rodolpho, The Leslie Roberts Silhouettes.

Duration: 60 minutes.

Main regular credit(s): Written by Jimmy Grafton; choreography by Leslie Roberts; associate producer Leslie Roberts; produced and directed by Bill Cotton Jnr.

Holding / Source

27.12.1958 The Wakey Wakey Circus J /

Designed by Douglas Smith.

With The Leslie Roberts Silhouettes, Alan Breeze, The High-Lights.

Duration: 45 minutes.

Main regular credit(s): Written by Jimmy Grafton; choreography by Leslie Roberts; associate producer Leslie Roberts; produced and directed by Bill Cotton Jnr.

Holding / Source

25.12.1959 Billy Cotton's Christmas Party J /

Designed by Malcolm Goulding.

With Kathie Kay, Russ Conway, Alan Breeze, Harry Corbett, Sooty, Percy Press.

Duration: 50 minutes.

Main regular credit(s): Written by Jimmy Grafton; choreography by Leslie Roberts; associate producer Leslie Roberts.

Holding / Source

24.12.1960 The Wakey Wakey Tavern J /

Orchestra conducted by Harry Rabinowitz; produced and directed by Bill Cotton Jnr.

With Billy Fury, Kathie Kay, Alan Breeze, The High-Lights, The Leslie Roberts Silhouettes, Russ Conway, Harry Worth, Jeremy Lloyd.

Duration: 45 minutes.

Main regular credit(s): Written by Jimmy Grafton; orchestra conducted by Harry Rabinowitz; choreography by Leslie Roberts; designed by Lionel Radford; associate producer Leslie Roberts; produced and directed by Bill Cotton Jnr.

Holding / Source

24.12.1961 R1 /

With Alan Breeze, Kathie Kay, Eric Sykes, Hattie Jacques, Jeremy Lloyd, The High-Lights, John Williams, Mrs Mills, The Leslie Roberts Silhouettes.

BILLY ELLIOT

Alternative/Working Title(s): DANCER

A Tiger Aspect production for BBC Films. Transmission details are for BBC 1. Duration: 110 minutes.

Written by Lee Hall; executive producers Charles Brand, Tessa Ross, David M. Thompson and Natascha Wharton; produced by Greg Brenman and Jonathan Finn; directed by Stephen Daldry.

Jamie Bell (Billy Elliot), Julie Walters (Mrs Wilkinson), Gary Lewis (Dad), Jamie Draven (Tony), Jean Heywood (Grandmother), Stuart Wells (Michael), Mike Elliott (George Watson), Barbara Leigh-Hunt (Vice-Principal), Patrick Malahide (Principal).

Holding / Source

28.12.2003 C3 / C3SW

BILLY LIAR

An LWT production. Transmission details are for the ATV midlands region. Usual duration: 25 minutes.

Main regular credit(s): Written by Keith Waterhouse and Willis Hall; produced by Stuart Allen.

Main regular cast: Jeff Rawle (Billy Fisher), George A. Cooper (Geoffrey Fisher), Pamela Vezey (Alice Fisher), May Warden (Grandma, Florence Boothroyd).

SERIES 1

Date	Title	Production No	Holding / Source
21.12.1973	Billy And The Gift Of The Magi	9L/09270	D2 / 2"

Designed by Gordon Toms; directed by Stuart Allen.

With Colin Jeavons (Mr Shadrack), Sally Watts (Barbara), Mary Ashton.

BILLY SMART'S CHRISTMAS CIRCUS

A Thames Television production. Transmission details are for the ATV midlands region. Duration: 55 minutes.

Music directed by Gordon Rose; designed by Robin Parker; produced and directed by Christopher Palmer.

Yasmine Smart (Ring Mistress), Hagenbeck Horses, The Yong Brothers, The Christianis, The Kovatchevi, The Espanas, The Castros, Rex Grey Showgirls.

	Holding / Source
25.12.1978	DB / 2"

BILLY SMART'S CHRISTMAS CIRCUS

A Thames Television production. Transmission details are for the Tyne Tees region.

Script associate Howard Imber; music directed by Alan Braden; designed by Bill Palmer; produced and directed by Christopher Palmer.

Bernie Winters (Ringmaster), The Kozjaks, Angela Revelle, Di Lello, The Flying Oslers, The Ciuca Comedy Taxi, Mary Chipperfield, Clarrison's Sealions, Leigh Marsh, Rex Grey Showgirls.

	Holding / Source
26.12.1979	DB / 2"

BILLY SMART'S CHRISTMAS CIRCUS

A Thames Television production. Transmission details are for the Tyne Tees region. Duration: 65 minutes.

Europe's largest Big Top, at Winkfield, near Windsor in Berkshire.

Music directed by Alan Braden; designed by Graham Probst; produced and directed by Christopher Palmer.

Keith Harris (Ringmaster), The Flying Ramos, The Rodogells, Fritz Mullen's Comedy Mules, Roberto Gasser, The Hsiung Family, The Ashtons, Anna Smart, Noe Noe and Gary, The Rex Grey Showgirls.

	Holding / Source
25.12.1980	D3 / 2"

BILLY'S CHRISTMAS ANGELS

A BBC Children's Department production for BBC 1. Transmission details are for BBC 1. Duration: 35 minutes.

Written by Sheila Fox; music by Mint Juleps, Griff Fender and Rita Ray; choreography by Charles Augins; executive producer Paul Stone; produced by Brenda Ennis; directed by Christopher Baker.

Jeremy Stuart (Billy), Mint Juleps (Billy's Angels), Deborah Manship (Mum), Christopher Quinn (Dad), John Shackley (Dave), Daniel Peacock (Mr Big), Victor Romero Evans (Faith), Fay Masterson (Hope), Nabil Shaban (Charlie), Stephen Johnson (Henchman).

	Holding / Source
23.12.1988	DB / 1"

BING CROSBY'S MERRIE OLDE CHRISTMAS

An ATV production. Transmission details are for the ATV midlands region. Duration: 52 minutes.

A Christmas celebration with Bing Crosby, his family and a host of famous stars including David Bowie, Ron Moody, Stanley Baxter and Twiggy. Includes a performance of the hit single 'Peace On Earth - Little Drummer Boy' with David Bowie, plus 'White Christmas' and many more. The show was recorded in London in September 1977. Bing Crosby died one month later and the programme was broadcast later that year.

Written by Buz Kohan; additional material by Ken Hoare; music directed by Ian Fraser; choreography by Norman Maen; designed by Henry Graveney; executive producer Franklin Konigsberg; production manager Harry Bell; produced by Gary Smith and Dwight Hemion; directed by Dwight Hemion.

Bing Crosby (Host), Stanley Baxter, Twiggy, David Bowie, Ron Moody, Trinity Boys Choir, Kathryn Crosby, Harry Crosby, Mary Crosby, Frances Crosby, Nathaniel Crosby, Royce Mills.

Date	VT Number	Holding / Source
24.12.1977	2351/77	DB / 2"

BING CROSBY'S WHITE CHRISTMAS

An ATV production. Transmission details are for the ATV midlands region. Duration: 52 minutes.

Written by Herbert Baker; music directed by Peter Knight; music associate Colin Keyes; choreography by Norman Maen; designed by Ken Wheatley; executive producer Franklin Konigsberg; produced and directed by Norman Campbell.

Bing Crosby (Host), Jackie Gleason, Bernadette Peters, Kathryn Crosby, Mary Frances Crosby, Harry Crosby, Nathaniel Crosby.

	Holding / Source
24.12.1976	DB / 2"

BIRDS OF A FEATHER

An Alomo production for BBC 1. Transmission details are for BBC 1. Usual duration: 30 minutes.

Main regular credit(s): Created by Laurence Marks and Maurice Gran.

Main regular cast: Pauline Quirke (Sharon), Linda Robson (Tracey), Lesley Joseph (Dorien).

Holding / Source
26.12.1989 **Sailing** — D3 / 1"

Written by Laurence Marks and Maurice Gran; series producer Esta Charkham; produced by Tony Charles; directed by Geoffrey Sax.

With Alun Lewis (Darryl), Alan Ford.

SERIES 2

Main regular credit(s): Series producer Nic Phillips.

Holding / Source
25.12.1990 **Falling In Love Again** — D3 / 1"

Duration: 75 minutes.

Written by Laurence Marks and Maurice Gran; directed by Nic Phillips.

With Alun Lewis (Darryl), Peter Polycarpou (Chris), Al Ashton, Marcus Eyre, Stephen Greif, Lila Kaye, Linda Henry, Jennifer Guy, Simon Slater, Peter Tilbury, Elizabeth Downes, Thomas Englert, Benedick Blythe, Ruth Goring, Romana Azzaro, Rolf Marnitz, Christopher Lamb, Leslie Crowther.

SERIES 3

Main regular credit(s): Produced by Nic Phillips.

Holding / Source
25.12.1991 **We'll Always Have Majorca** — D3 / 1"

Duration: 50 minutes.

Written by Peter Tilbury; directed by Nic Phillips.

With Ray Winstone, Alun Lewis, Peter Polycarpou, Matthew Savage, Brian Hibbard, John Bluthal, John Ringham, Georgia Mitchell, Stephen Mackenna, Victoria Scarborough, Russell Gold, Alison McGuire, Linda Regan, Helen Martin.

SERIES 4

Main regular credit(s): Series producer Candida Julian-Jones; directed by Terry Kinane.

Holding / Source
25.12.1992 **The Chigwell Connection** — D3 / D3S

Duration: 50 minutes.

Written by Laurence Marks and Maurice Gran.

With Alun Lewis (Darryl), Peter Polycarpou (Chris), Matthew Savage (Garth), Robert Kilroy-Silk, Nigel Humphreys, Jan Goodman, Michael Feast, Daniel Peacock, Barbara Keogh, Jon Cartwright, Paul Keown, Alex Hardy, Jane Van Hool, Colin Mace, Scott Ransome, Michael Stainton, Jacey Salles.

SERIES 5

Main regular credit(s): Script editor Micheal Jacob; executive producers Allan McKeown and Michael Pilsworth; supervising producers Laurence Marks and Maurice Gran; produced by Charlie Hanson.

Holding / Source
25.12.1993 **It Happened In Hollywood** — D3 / D3S

Duration: 60 minutes.

Written by Geoffrey Deane; directed by Terry Kinane.

With Alun Lewis (Darryl), Peter Polycarpou (Chris), Amma Asante, Charles Grant, George Hamilton, George Wendt, Richard Branson, Lionel Blair, Miguel Sandoval, Bill Brochtrup, Lorelei King, Geoffrey Drew, Roy Heather.

SERIES 6

Main regular credit(s): Script editor Micheal Jacob; designed by Helen Scott; executive producer Allan McKeown; production manager Chris Miles; produced by Charlie Hanson.

Holding / Source
24.12.1994 **Christmas In Dreamland** — D3 / D3S

Duration: 50 minutes.

Written by Maurice Gran and Laurence Marks; script supervisor Diane Taylor; music directed by John Collins; art director Bill Crutcher; directed by Charlie Hanson.

With Alun Lewis (Darryl), Peter Polycarpou (Chris), Matthew Savage (Garth), David Emanuel, Lisa Jacobs, Nick Stringer, Alison Lomas, Michael Winner, Mary Reynolds, Hazel Galloway.

SERIES 8

Main regular credit(s): Script supervisor Diane Taylor; script editor Micheal Jacob; music by Graham Jarvis; art director Richard Drew; designed by David Ferris; executive producer Claire Hinson; production manager Juliet Dowling; produced by Tony Charles; directed by Hugh Thomas.

Holding / Source
27.12.1997 **Reservoir Birds** — D3 / D3S

Duration: 50 minutes.

Written by Gary Lawson and John Phelps.

With Christopher Ellison, David Roper, Terence Hillyer, Aden Gillett, Luisa Bradshaw-White, Robin Lermitte, Raymond Trickitt, Darren Saul, Sacha Pitimson, Richard Trahair, Andrew Harrison, Paul Viragh, Joan Oliver, Anna Skye, Richard Christopher, Jason Griffiths.

BIRDS OF A FEATHER (continued)

SERIES 9

Main regular credit(s): Produced by Tony Charles; directed by Terry Kinane.

		Holding / Source
24.12.1998	**Holy Ground**	DB / DBS

Duration: 40 minutes.
Written by Geoff Rowley.
With John Cormack, John Paul Connolly, James Ellis, Ciaran McIntyre, Connor Byrne.

BIRD'S-EYE VIEW

A BBC production for BBC 2. Transmission details are for BBC 2. Duration: 50 minutes.

Main regular credit(s): Series editor Edward Mirzoeff.

		Holding / Source
24.12.1967	**Birds-Eye View Of Great Britain** [pilot]	C1 / C1
25.12.1969	**Beside The Seaside**	C1 / C1
25.12.1970	**From Bishop Rock To Muckle**	DB / C1
26.12.1971	**Switzerland**	C1 / C1

A land flowing with milk and money... A country of mountain spectacle and peaceful neutrality... That's the cliché view of the tourist. But Switzerland is much more than that. A proud but violent history and a multitude of modern problems are revealed by the helicopter's perspective and the views of a Swiss writer, Herbert Meier.
Produced by Paul Bonner.
With Vladek Sheybal (Commentator).
A BBC/SRG/RAI/BR co-production.

THE BIRTH OF CHRIST

A Yorkshire Television production. Transmission details are for the Yorkshire Television region. Duration: 13 minutes.

A look at the hidden meaning behind some of the paintings most often used to illustrate Christmas cards. Presenter Oliver Hunkin discusses the birth of Christ as seen by the Old Masters.
Produced and directed by Len Lurcuck.
Oliver Hunkin (Presenter), Bill Croasdale (Bible Readings).

	Holding / Source
24.12.1984	1" / 1"

BIRTHDAY

A HED Production production for Channel 4. Transmission details are for Channel 4. Duration: 14 minutes.

Poetry of The Rev Alan Ecclestone, whose message is that the greatest birthday of all is really the birthday of us all.
Written by Alan Ecclestone; produced by Tim Cooper and Alison Porteous; directed by Tim Cooper and Alison Porteous.
Alan Ecclestone (Presenter), Judi Dench.

	Holding / Source
25.12.1989	1" / 1"

BIRTHDAY GIRL

Alternative/Working Title(s): BEATING JESUS / THE LUCKY ONES

A Yorkshire Television production for ITV 1. Transmission details are for the Central region. Duration: 100 minutes.

Written by Jonathan Harvey; executive producer Carolyn Reynolds; produced and directed by Morag Fullarton.

Sarah Lancashire (Rachel Jones), Emma Fielding (Tracey Jones), Mina Anwar (Nina Kapoor), Julia Ford (Karen), Ciaran McMenamin (Donal), Peter Gunn (Charlie Boyd), Paul Higgins (Drew), Jenny Metcalfe (Keeley), Siobhan Dunn (Elizabeth), Adil Hussain (Daljit), Michael McNulty (Justin), Rico Henshion (Bashir), Beatrice Kelley (Dulcie), Jean Stevens (Maureen), Christine Mackie (Doctor Kate Morris), Ruth Holden (Doreen Jones), Scott Taylor (Peter), Michael J. Jackson (Noddy).

	VT Number	Holding / Source
22.12.2002	D718	DB / V1SW

A BIT OF A DO

A Yorkshire Television production. Transmission details are for the Central region. Usual duration: 50 minutes.

Main regular credit(s): Written by David Nobbs; theme music by Ray Russell; executive producer Vernon Lawrence; produced by David Reynolds.

Main regular cast: David Jason (Ted Simcock), Gwen Taylor (Rita Simcock), Nicola Pagett (Liz Rodenhurst), Michael Jayston (Neville Badger), Stephanie Cole (Betty Sillitoe), Tim Wylton (Rodney Sillitoe), David Thewlis (Paul Simcock), Sarah-Jane Holm (Jenny Simcock), Wayne Foskett (Elvis Simcock), Nigel Hastings (Simon Roderhurst).

SERIES 1

Main regular cast: With Paul Chapman (Laurence Rodenhurst (until 10.02.1989)).

		VT Number	Holding / Source
27.01.1989	**The Angling Club Christmas Party**	L514/03	DB / 1"

Directed by David Reynolds.
With David Roper, Peter Martin, Richard Beale, Ruth Holden, Mike Timoney.

A BIT OF DISCRETION

A Yorkshire Television production. Transmission details are for the ATV midlands region. Duration: 52 minutes.

Written by John Whitewood; executive producer Peter Willes; directed by Marc Miller.

Paul Jones (Colin Dixon), Julia Foster (Sally Mainwaring), Gerald Sim (George Dixon), Noël Dyson (Clara Dixon), Griffith Davies (Gypsy), John Rees (Man), Frank Mills (Barman).

	Production No	VT Number	Holding / Source
28.12.1968	Y/0156/0001	1004	DB / 62

Alternative transmissions: Yorkshire Television: 12.12.1968.

The tape is damaged.

A BIT OF FRY AND LAURIE

A BBC production for BBC 2. Transmission details are for BBC 2. Duration varies - see below for details.

Main regular credit(s): Written by Stephen Fry and Hugh Laurie.

Main regular cast: Stephen Fry, Hugh Laurie.

	Holding / Source
26.12.1987	DB / 1"

Duration: 36 minutes.

Additional material by William Wegman; theme music by Harry Stoneham; designed by Derek Evans; production manager Matt Dickinson; produced and directed by Roger Ordish.

With James Ottaway.

THE BLACK AND WHITE MINSTREL SHOW

A BBC production for BBC Various. Transmission details are for BBC Various. Duration varies - see below for details.

Main regular credit(s): Devised by George Inns.

Main regular performer(s): The George Mitchell Singers [as The Mitchell Minstrels].

SERIES 1

Commissioned by BBC. Transmission details are for BBC. Duration: 60 minutes.

Main regular credit(s): Produced by George Inns.

	Holding / Source
20.12.1958	J / Live

Conducted by George Mitchell and Eric Robinson; dance direction by Larry Gordon; designed by Douglas Smith.

With Kenneth Connor (Master of Ceremonies), Benny Lee, Rosemary Squires, Glen Mason, Lew Carlson, Norrie Paramor and his Big Ben Banjo Band, The Television Toppers, The Minstrel Orchestra.

SERIES 3

Commissioned by BBC. Transmission details are for BBC.

Main regular credit(s): Vocal arrangements by George Mitchell; music arranged by Alan Bristow and Ray Terry; conducted by Eric Robinson and George Mitchell; dance direction by Larry Gordon; settings by Stanley Dorfman; produced by George Inns.

Main regular performer(s): With Stan Stennett, Leslie Crowther, The Television Toppers, The Jackpots, Dai Francis, Tony Mercer, John Boulter, Valerie Brooks, Benny Garcia, The Minstrel Orchestra.

	Holding / Source
23.12.1960	R1 / 40

Duration: 60 minutes.

With George Chisholm's Jazzers.

SERIES 4

Commissioned by BBC. Transmission details are for BBC.

Main regular credit(s): Vocal arrangements by George Mitchell; music arranged by Alan Bristow and Ray Terry; conducted by Eric Robinson and George Mitchell; dance direction by Larry Gordon; settings by Stanley Dorfman; produced by George Inns.

Main regular performer(s): With Leslie Crowther, Semprini, Penny Nicholls, John Boulter, Dai Francis, Tony Mercer, Benny Garcia, The Jackpots, The Television Toppers.

	Holding / Source
25.12.1961	R1SEQ / 40

Duration: 55 minutes.

Puppetry by Paul and Peta Page.

With George Chisholm.

16mm telerecording (incomplete recording – 20 minutes only)

THE BLACK AND WHITE MINSTREL SHOW (continued)

SERIES 5
Commissioned by BBC. Transmission details are for BBC.
Main regular credit(s): Vocal arrangements by George Mitchell; conducted by Eric Robinson and George Mitchell; dance direction by Larry Gordon; settings by Stanley Dorfman; produced by George Inns.
Main regular performer(s): With Stan Stennett, George Chisholm, John Boulter, Dai Francis, Tony Mercer, Benny Garcia, Valerie Brooks, The Jackpots, The Television Toppers.

Holding / Source
23.12.1962 J / 40
Duration: 55 minutes.
Orchestrations by Alan Bristow and Ray Terry.
With Jeannie Lambe, Leslie Crowther.

SERIES 6
Commissioned by BBC. Transmission details are for BBC. Duration: 45 minutes.

Holding / Source
22.12.1963 R1 / 40
Additional material by George Chisholm; vocal arrangements by George Mitchell; orchestrations by Alan Bristow and Ray Terry; conducted by George Mitchell and Eric Robinson; dance direction by Larry Gordon; settings by Roger Andrews; produced by George Inns.
With Leslie Crowther, George Chisholm, John Boulter, Dai Francis, Tony Mercer, Benny Garcia, The Jackpots, The Television Toppers, Margaret Savage.

SERIES 8
Commissioned by BBC 1. Transmission details are for BBC 1.

Holding / Source
25.12.1965 **Max Bygraves Meets The Black And White Minstrels** J / 40
Duration: 60 minutes.
Additional material by Verdini and Spike Mullins; vocal arrangements by George Mitchell; orchestrations by Alan Bristow and Ray Terry; orchestra conducted by George Mitchell and Eric Robinson; dance direction by Roy Gunson; settings by Brian Tregidden; produced by George Inns.
With Max Bygraves, John Boulter, Dai Francis, Tony Mercer, Margaret Savage, Bob Clayton, The Television Toppers, Delia Wicks, Penny Jewkes.

Commissioned by BBC 1. Transmission details are for BBC 1.

Holding / Source
25.12.1966 J / 40
Duration: 35 minutes.
Vocal arrangements by George Mitchell; orchestrations by Alan Bristow; orchestra conducted by George Mitchell and Eric Robinson; dance direction by Roy Gunson; settings by Brian Tregidden; produced by George Inns.
With John Boulter, Dai Francis, Tony Mercer, Don Arrol, Margaret Savage, Don Cleaver, The Television Toppers, Delia Wicks, Penny Jewkes, Lew Rawlings, Wilf Todd and His Trio, Stretch and Della.

SERIES 10
Commissioned by BBC 2. Transmission details are for BBC 2. Duration: 45 minutes.
Main regular credit(s): Vocal arrangements by George Mitchell; orchestra conducted by George Mitchell and Eric Robinson; dance direction by Roy Gunson; produced by George Inns.
Main regular performer(s): With Leslie Crowther (Compere), John Boulter, Dai Francis, Tony Mercer, Margaret Savage, The Television Toppers, Delia Wicks, Don Cleaver, Penny Jewkes, Les Rawlings.

Holding / Source
25.12.1967 DB-D3 / 2"
Orchestrations by Alan Bristow; settings by Lionel Radford.
With Semprini, Sheila Bernette, Peter Glaze.

Transmission details are for BBC 1.

Holding / Source
25.12.1968 **The Black And White Minstrel Christmas Show** J / 40
Duration: 50 minutes.
Vocal arrangements by George Mitchell; orchestrations by Alan Bristow; orchestra conducted by George Mitchell and Eric Robinson; choreography by Roy Gunson; settings by Lionel Radford; produced by George Inns.
With John Boulter, Dai Francis, Tony Mercer, Semprini, Margaret Savage, The Television Toppers, Delia Wicks, Don Cleaver, Penny Jewkes, Les Rawlings, Sheila Bernette, Peter Glaze.

Commissioned by BBC 1. Transmission details are for BBC 1.

Holding / Source
26.12.1970 **The Black And White Minstrel Show Christmas Special** R1 / 2"
Duration: 45 minutes.
Vocal arrangements by George Mitchell; orchestra conducted by George Mitchell and Alan Bristow; choreography by Roy Gunson; designed by Martin Collins; produced by Ernest Maxin.
With The Monarchs: Eric and Cedric, Jimmy Marshall, Leslie Crowther, Jimmy Jewel, George Chisholm, John Boulter, Dai Francis, Margaret Savage, Andy Cole, The Television Toppers, Les Rawlings, Jan Austen, Penny Jewkes, Delia Wicks.

THE BLACK AND WHITE MINSTREL SHOW (continued)

SERIES 13
Commissioned by BBC 1. Transmission details are for BBC 1. Duration: 45 minutes.

Main regular credit(s): Vocal arrangements by George Mitchell; orchestrations by Alan Bristow; conducted by George Mitchell and Alan Bristow; choreography by Roy Gunson; designed by Martin Collins; produced by Ernest Maxin.

Main regular performer(s): With John Boulter, Dai Francis, Margaret Savage, The Television Toppers, The Monarchs: Eric and Cedric, Andy Cole, Les Rawlings, Penny Jewkes, Delia Wicks.

	Holding / Source
25.12.1971	DB-D3 / 2"

Orchestrations by Alan Bristow; designed by Martin Collins.

With No guest cast.

SERIES 15
Commissioned by BBC 1. Transmission details are for BBC 1.

	Holding / Source
25.12.1973	DB-D3 / 2"

Duration: 45 minutes.

Vocal arrangements by George Mitchell; conducted by George Mitchell and Alan Bristow; choreography by Fred Peters; designed by Peter Brachacki; produced by Ernest Maxin.

With Ted Darling, Les Rawlings, Les Want, Karl Scott, Jane Marlow, Elspeth Hands, Dorothy Ogden, The Monarchs: Eric and Cedric, The Television Toppers.

Commissioned by BBC 1. Transmission details are for BBC 1.

	Holding / Source
20.12.1975	DB-D3 / 2"

Duration: 45 minutes.

Written by Howard Imber and Lenny Henry; vocal arrangements by George Mitchell; orchestrations by Alan Bristow; orchestra conducted by George Mitchell; choreography by Roy Gunson; designed by David Myerscough-Jones; produced by Brian Whitehouse.

With Don Maclean, Margaret Savage, Ted Darling, Les Rawlings, Les Want, Karl Scott, Elspeth Hands, Jane Marlow, Dorothy Ogden, Lenny Henry, Jan Hunt, The Television Toppers.

Commissioned by BBC 1. Transmission details are for BBC 1.

	Holding / Source
18.12.1976	DB-D3 / 2"

Duration: 45 minutes.

Vocal arrangements by George Mitchell; orchestrations by Alan Bristow; orchestra conducted by George Mitchell; choreography by Flick Colby; designed by John O'Hara; produced by Brian Whitehouse.

With Margaret Savage, Ted Darling, Les Rawlings, Les Want, Bob Hunter, Jane Marlow, Rita Morris, Dorothy Ogden, Pam Ayres, Keith Harris, Les Brian, Brooks Aehron, The Television Toppers.

BLACK CHRISTMAS

A BBC Birmingham production for BBC 2. Transmission details are for BBC 2. Duration: 50 minutes.

As Christmas approaches, Gertrude gathers her family. A perfect Christmas seems destined for disaster...

Written by Michael Abbensetts; script editor Peter Ansorge; designed by Sally Williams; produced by Tara Prem; directed by Stephen Frears.

Carmen Munroe (Gertrude), Norman Beaton (Bertie), Shope Shodeinde (Renee), Janet Bartley (Dolly), Stefan Kalipha (Herman), Linda Goddard (Lily).

	Holding / Source
20.12.1977	C1 / C1

BLACK VELVET BAND

A Yorkshire Television production. Transmission details are for the Central region. Duration: 102 minutes.

Created by Chris McHallem; written by Jonathan Critchley; executive producer Keith Richardson; produced by Peter Waller; directed by Robert Knights.

Nick Berry (Martin Tusco), Todd Carty (Pentecost), Chris McHallem (Shut-Eye), Stephen Marcus (Nudge), Ian Roberts (Dwyer), Michael Atkinson (Lord George Grey), Nick Borrain (Private Secretary), Aldo Brincat (First Sailor), Michael Brunner (Piet), John Carson (Colonel Rowan), Gabrielle Cirillo (Louisa), Jackie Davids (Mrs Rex), Frantz Dobrowsky (Leach), Ralph Draper (Magistrate), Desmond Dube (Undertaker's Assistant), Alex Ferns (Major Watson), Ronald France (Sir Harry Smith), Nicole Franco (Maria Rex), Ken Gampu (Witch Doctor), Zukile Gqobofe (Watson's Corporal), Jonathan Griffin (Hannah), Thomas Hall (Duthie), Stephen Jennings (Edward Rex), Kyle Jones (Thomas), David Lee (Sergeant Howe), Emily McArthur (Rose Tusco), Ken Marshall (Cart Driver), Amy Marston (Half-Pint), Victor Mellaney (Lord Chief Justice), Greg Melvill-Smith (P. E. Bartender), Eric Nobbs (Fruit Farmer), Michael Richard (Bar Owner), Robin Smith (Vermeer), Lee Sparrowhawk (Walker), Adrian Steed (Sir John Jervis), Chris Steyn (Bus Driver), Ashley Taylor (Surgeon Lieutenant Fenwick), Jonathan Taylor (Second Sailor), Iain Winter Smith (Captain Moore), James White (Magistrate's Clerk), Ian Yule (Yeoman Warder).

	Holding / Source
24.12.1997	DB / V1SW

BLACKADDER RIDES AGAIN

A Tiger Aspect production for BBC 1. made in association with 2 Entertain. Transmission details are for BBC 1. Duration: 65 minutes.

Archive producer Aileen McAllister; assistant producer Adam McLean; production executive Caroline Bourne; executive producers Katie Taylor and Ricky Kelehar; production manager Tina D'Arcy; produced and directed by Matt O'Casey.

John Sergeant (Narrator), Rowan Atkinson, John Lloyd, Stephen Fry, Ben Elton, Griff Rhys Jones, Hugh Laurie, Tony Robinson, Rik Mayall, Richard Curtis, Chris Wadsworth, Miranda Richardson, Tim McInnerny, Miriam Margolyes.

	Holding / Source
25.12.2008	DB / DBSWF

BLACKADDER RIDES AGAIN

BLACKPOOL: BIG NIGHT OUT

A BBC production for BBC 2. Transmission details are for BBC 2. Duration: 60 minutes.

The seaside resort in the north west of England was once the beating heart of the entertainment industry, launching the career of Morecambe and Wise and attracting stars such as Frank Sinatra. This is a look at the town through the eyes of some of those who have graced its stages.

Executive producer Caroline Wright; produced and directed by Andy Humphries.

	Holding / Source
26.12.2012	HD/DB / HDC

BLANKETY BLANK

A BBC production for BBC 1. made in association with Mark Goodson / Talbot TV Ltd. Transmission details are for BBC 1. Duration varies - see below for details.

Main regular credit(s): Theme music by Ronnie Hazlehurst.

SERIES 2
Duration: 35 minutes.
Main regular credit(s): Programme associate Tony Hawes; designed by Bob Cove; produced by Alan Boyd; directed by Marcus Plantin.
Main regular performer(s): With Terry Wogan (Host).

	Production No	Holding / Source
25.12.1979	LLVB222Y	DB-D3 / 2"

With Lennie Bennett, Lorraine Chase, Wendy Craig, Sandra Dickinson, Shirley Anne Field, Kenny Everett, Liza Goddard, David Hamilton, David Jason, Roy Kinnear, Patrick Moore, Beryl Reid, John Vyvyan.

SERIES 3
Main regular credit(s): Programme associate Tony Hawes; designed by Bob Cove and Malcolm Thornton; produced by Alan Boyd; directed by Stanley Appel.
Main regular performer(s): With Terry Wogan (Host).

	Holding / Source
26.12.1980	DB-D3 / 2"

Duration: 34 minutes.
With Katie Boyle, Windsor Davies, Les Dawson, Sandra Dickinson, Shirley Anne Field, David Hamilton, Roy Hudd, The Krankies, Rula Lenska, Patrick Moore, Beryl Reid, Madeline Smith, Jimmy Tarbuck, Kenny Everett*.

SERIES 4
Duration: 35 minutes.
Main regular credit(s): Programme associate Tony Hawes; designed by Tim Gleeson; produced by Marcus Plantin; directed by Geoff Posner.
Main regular performer(s): With Terry Wogan (Host).

	Holding / Source
26.12.1981 **Christmas**	DB-D3 / 2"

With Lorraine Chase, Liza Goddard, Larry Grayson, Lenny Henry, Beryl Reid, Jimmy Tarbuck.

SERIES 5
Main regular credit(s): Programme associate Tony Hawes; music by Ronnie Hazlehurst; produced by Marcus Plantin.
Main regular performer(s): With Terry Wogan (Host).

	Holding / Source
27.12.1982	DB-D3 / 2"

Duration: 05 minutes.
With Lorraine Chase, Dana, Diana Dors, Jimmy Edwards, Larry Grayson, Roy Hudd.

SERIES 6
Duration: 35 minutes.
Main regular credit(s): Produced and directed by Marcus Plantin.
Main regular performer(s): With Terry Wogan (Host).

	Holding / Source
25.12.1983	DB-D3 / 2"

With Sabina Franklyn, Roy Kinnear, Ruth Madoc, Patrick Moore, Beryl Reid, Freddie Starr.

SERIES 7
Main regular credit(s): Designed by Stephan Paczai; executive producer John Bishop; produced and directed by David Taylor.
Main regular performer(s): With Les Dawson (Host).

	Holding / Source
25.12.1984 **Christmas**	DB / 1"

Duration: 33 minutes.
Written by Neville Gurnhill, Mike Radford and Catherine Maunsell.
With Big Mick (Little Santa), Lorraine Chase, Suzanne Danielle, Ken Dodd, Russell Harty, Ruth Madoc, Derek Nimmo.

| BLANKETY BLANK (continued) | British Christmas Television Guide |

SERIES 13
Duration: 30 minutes.
Main regular credit(s): Produced by Stanley Appel; directed by John Burrowes.
Main regular performer(s): With Les Dawson.

	Holding / Source
27.12.1989 **Christmas**	DB / 1"

With Floella Benjamin, Anne Charleston, Linda Lusardi, Danny La Rue, Ian Smith, Peter Woods.

THE BLEAK OLD SHOP OF STUFF

A BBC production for BBC 2. Transmission details are for BBC 2. Duration: 60 minutes.

It's no use trying to hold out in the face of this daft Dickens spoof. Better to abandon yourself to its rich figgy pudding of rampant silliness. The idea is a loose relation of Radio 4's Bleak Expectations, with added visuals of London's brick alleyways, street urchins and wind-up top hats. Robert Webb plays our shopkeeper hero, Jedrington Secret-Past, whose emporium (selling treats such as hot and spicy dodo wings) and perfect family— including wife Conceptiva — are hauled off by the wicked Skulkingworm to meet an unpaid debt. What follows involves a lot of twiddly wordplay ("Oh, fiddlesticks and violin twigs!"), sight gags, pratfalls, treacle dependency, peals of wicked laughter and a man with a goose for a hat.

Written by Mark Evans; produced by Gareth Edwards; directed by Ben Gosling Fuller.

Robert Webb (Jedrington Secret-Past), Stephen Fry (Malifax Skullingworm), Finlay Christie (Victor), Katherine Parkinson (Conceptiva Secret-Past), Ambra Lily Keegan (Victoria), Una Stubbs (Aunt Good Spelling), Jude Wright (Archie), David Mitchell (Jolliforth), Celia Imrie (Miss Christmasham), Pauline McLynn (Maggotty), Johnny Vegas (Artful Codger), Judy Parfitt (Aunt Chastity), Phyllida Law (Aunt Sobriety), Terrence Hardiman (Fruitcake / Mr Christmasham).

	Holding / Source
19.12.2011	HD/DB / HDC

BLESS ME, FATHER

An LWT production. Transmission details are for the ATV midlands region. Duration: 25 minutes.

Main regular credit(s): Adapted by Peter De Rosa; based on books by Neil Boyd [credited as Peter De Rosa]; theme music by Philip Jones Brass Ensemble; produced and directed by David Askey.

Main regular cast: Arthur Lowe (Father Charles Duddleswell), Daniel Abineri (Friar Neil Boyd), Gabrielle Daye (Mrs Pring).

SERIES 2
Main regular credit(s): Designed by Quentin Chases.

	Production No	Holding / Source
23.12.1979 **The Season Of Goodwill**	9L/99383	DB / 2"

Designed by Quentin Chases.

With David Ryall (Billy Buzzle), Patrick McAlinney (Doctor Daley), Charles Lamb.

THE BLOOD-LETTING

A BBC Scotland production for BBC 1 Scotland. Transmission details are for BBC 1 Scotland. Usual duration: 50 minutes.

Main regular credit(s): Written by Tom Wright; designed by Archie Clark; produced by Pharic Maclaren; directed by Bob McIntosh.

Main regular cast: Donald Burton (Steven Marshall), Caroline Mortimer (Joan Henderson), Ian McCulloch (Henry MacNaughton), Bernard Horsfall (Inspector Macreadie).

	Holding / Source
31.12.1977 **Episode 1**	DB / 2"

With Anna Pitt (Marjorie Marshall), Prentis Hancock (Garry Walsh), David Gallacher, Wilma Duncan, Jake D'Arcy, Bill Paterson, Julie Agnew, Ian Halliburton, Peter Finlay, Shenah Douglas.

01.01.1978 **Episode 2**	DB / 2"

Duration: 46 minutes.

With Prentis Hancock (Garry Walsh), Frank Wylie (Newsvendor), Alec Heggie (Bagpiper Macnab), Ken Henderson, Martin Cochrane, Joan Fitzpatrick, James Kennedy, E. J. P. Mace, Shenah Douglas.

02.01.1978 **Episode 3**	DB / 2"

Duration: 52 minutes.

With Anna Pitt (Marjorie Marshall), Frank Wylie (Newsvendor), Alec Heggie (Bagpiper Macnab), Anne Kristen.

Recorded 15-16th November 1976.

BLUE PETER

A BBC production. Transmission details are for BBC/BBC1. Usual duration: 25 minutes.

The Fifties and Sixties
Credits: Production secretary Gillian Reilly.

Main regular credit(s): Presented by Christopher Trace and Leila Williams.

	Holding / Source
23.12.1958 **Programme 11**	NR / Live

Produced and directed by John Hunter Blair.

With Fred Barton, Derek Jones.

(TUESDAY TX) / A HAPPY CHRISTMAS FOR PETS WITH SENIOR INSPECTOR SPENSER OF THE RSPCA / SPARKY'S MAGIC ECHO-2 (Written by Alan Livingston / 9 captions by Tony Hart) / FRED BARTON PA / BLUE PETER LAYOUT: MODEL OF DIESEL BOBO LOCO + QUICK HELLO TO DEREK JONES WHO WORKS TRAINS AS CHRIS TALKS.

NB: This programme was Floor Managed by Edward Barnes, later to become a key member of the Blue Peter team.

BLUE PETER

| British Christmas Television Guide | BLUE PETER (continued) |

Main regular credit(s):   Presented by Christopher Trace and Valerie Singleton.

Holding / Source

17.12.1962 Programme 209   B3SEQ /
Produced by Biddy Baxter; directed by Edward Barnes.
DIEGO AND SPUGGY - BILLY SMARTS' CIRCUS CLOWNS / CHRISTMAS BOOKS REVIEW / DECORATING THE TREE / PREPARING THE CRIB / WHILE SHEPHERDS WATCHED THEIR FLOCKS AT NIGHT TK / OWEN REED (HEAD OF CHILDREN'S PROGRAMMES) PRESENTS BLUE PETER WITH A SUPRISE PARCEL - A PUPPY FOR THE PROGRAMME / PUPPY'S NAME COMP. LAUNCHED

NB: SHORTLY AFTER TRANSMISSION, THE ORIGINAL PETRA PUPPY DIED AND HAD TO BE REPLACED WITH AN ALMOST IDENTICAL DOG. VIEWERS WERE NOT TOLD!

23.12.1963 Programme 258   R1 /
Produced by Biddy Baxter; film sequences directed by Edward Barnes; directed by Edward Barnes.
CHRISTMAS CARDS SENT TO PROGRAMME / PETRA FLASHBACK TK / SWORD IN THE STONE TK CLIP / WILD BIRDS TK / BIRD'S CHRISTMAS TREE MAKE / WHILST SHEPHERDS WATCHED THEIR FLOCKS AT NIGHT TK / FINISHING THE CRIB MAKE / TOY DISTRIBUTION TK (Chris and Val) / STORY COMPETITION LAUNCHED
Original film sequences exist on B3 and B1.

21.12.1964 Programme 318   J /
Produced by Biddy Baxter; directed by Edward Barnes.
(RX'D 18.12.64) / FOURTH CANDLE LIT / LONDON TO BRIGHTON PHOTO COMP. RESULTS / THE STORY OF THE CHRISTMAS CRIB (Written by Dorothy Smith / 6 captions by Bob Broomfield / Told by Val) / BLUE PETER CRIB / THE CHRISTMAS OF THE WHITE RHINOCEROS TK (Written and Directed by Dorothea Brooking with Christine Tyrer (Christine) / Susan Beckwith (Susan) / Alan Sayers (Harry) / Colin Sayers (George) / Nicholas Facer (Paul) / Anna Harvey (Cody) / Adrian Harvey (Matt) / PRESENTS

1965 - 1966
Main regular credit(s):   Presented by Christopher Trace, Valerie Singleton and John Noakes; edited by Biddy Baxter; production team Gillian Reilly, Iris Furlong, Malcolm Walker, Tony Arnold, Britt Allcroft and Alan Russell; produced by Edward Barnes and Rosemary Gill; pets: Petra, Freda, Jason, Patch and Joey.

Holding / Source

23.12.1965 Programme 28   R1 /
Film sequences directed by Edward Barnes; directed by Alan Russell.
With Derek Freeman.
(405) FOURTH CANDLE LIT / CARDS AND DECORATIONS / HONEY'S RETURN (with Derek Freeman) / VT PRE-REC: THE STORY OF THE FLYING ENTERPRISE (Told by Chris) / KRISTKINDLESMARKT TK (Chris and Val) / THE STORY OF SILENT NIGHT (Written by Dorothy Smith / 20 captions by G. Galsworthy / Told by Val) / RIDGEWAY PRIMARY SCHOOL 'SILENT NIGHT' PA / OPENING PRESENTS / LAST VERSE OF CAROL

NB - THE SILENT NIGHT INSERT EXISTS ON D3 DUBBED FROM 2"

1966 - 1967
Main regular credit(s):   Presented by Christopher Trace, Valerie Singleton and John Noakes; edited by Biddy Baxter; production team Gillian Reilly, Alan Russell, Britt Allcroft, Tim Byford and John Adcock; produced by Edward Barnes and Rosemary Gill; pets: Petra, Freda, Jason, Patch and Joey.

Holding / Source

22.12.1966 Programme 28   R1 /
Film sequences directed by Edward Barnes (both); directed by Alan Russell.
With John Nettleton (Narrator).
(492) FOURTH CANDLE LIT / CRIB / TOTALISER + APPEAL NEWS / OXFORD STREET LIGHTS TK (John) / VT PRE-REC: THE STORY OF THE CHRISTMAS MAIL (50 captions by Bob Broomfield / Written by Rosemary Gill / Told by John Nettleton) / OPENING PRESENTS ROUND TREE / CAROLS ROUND THE TREE TK (All Three)

Original film sequences exist on B1.

22.12.66 – BLUE PETER (LCH5333D) – front: mute glimpse of start of "Jackanory" including first shot (location – big house); globe, plug for tomorrow's "Jackanory" with Susannah York (recording restarts during this), "Christmas at Green Knowe", announcement 'This is BBC1'. End: globe, announcement of last part of "Rumplestiltskin" in "Tales from Europe".

1967 - 1968
Main regular credit(s):   Presented by Valerie Singleton, John Noakes and Peter Purves; edited by Biddy Baxter; production team Alan Russell, Tim Byford, Gillian Reilly, John Adcock and Britt Allcroft; produced by Edward Barnes and Rosemary Gill; pets: Petra, Freda, Jason, Patch and Joey.

Holding / Source

21.12.1967 Programme 26   B1SEQ /
Film sequences directed by Edward Barnes; directed by Alan Russell.
(576) FOURTH CANDLE LIT / CARDS AND NUREMBERG CRIB / APPEAL NEWS + TOTALISER / AUSTRIAN SKIING TRIP TK (All Three) / VT PRE-REC: THE BEST CHRISTMAS TREE OF ALL (Written by Dorothy Smith) / PRESENTS ROUND THE TREE / HARK! THE HERALD ANGELS SING

1968 - 1969
Main regular credit(s):   Presented by Valerie Singleton, John Noakes and Peter Purves; edited by Biddy Baxter; production team Alan Russell, Tim Byford, Gillian Reilly, John Adcock, Sandra Swetman and Paul Stone; produced by Edward Barnes and Rosemary Gill; pets: Petra, Freda, Jason, Patch and Barney.

Holding / Source

23.12.1968 Programme 27   R1 /
Film sequences directed by Edward Barnes; directed by Alan Russell.
With Gary Watson (Narrator).

BLUE PETER (continued)

(661) FOURTH CANDLE LIT / CARDS + CRIB / TOTALISER + APPEAL NEWS / NORWAY TREE TK (All Three) / VT PRE-REC: THE STORY OF THE FIRST PICTURE (Adapted by Dorothy Smith/ 43 Captions by Bob Broomfield / Told by Gary Watson) / PRESENTS ROUND THE TREE / O COME ALL YE FAITHFUL
Original film sequences exist on B1.

1969 - 1970
Main regular credit(s): Presented by Valerie Singleton, John Noakes and Peter Purves; edited by Biddy Baxter; production team Alan Russell, Tim Byford, Gillian Reilly, John Adcock, Michael Cook, David Brown, Bill Craske, Geoff Wilson and Andrew Naylor; produced by Edward Barnes and Rosemary Gill; pets: Petra, Jason, Freda and Patch.

	VT Number	Holding / Source
22.12.1969 **Programme 29**	BRD271365	B-R1 /

Designed by Gerry Scott; film sequences directed by Edward Barnes; directed by Alan Russell.
(741) FOURTH CANDLE LIT / CARDS, TOTALISER + CRIB / BETHLEHEM TK (Val) / LAST MINUTE HANGING DECORATION MAKE / PRESENTS ROUND THE TREE / GOD REST YOU MERRY GENTLEMEN
Film Shot: 10-13.12.69
Original film sequences exist on B1.

1970 - 1971
Main regular credit(s): Presented by Valerie Singleton, John Noakes and Peter Purves; edited by Biddy Baxter; production team Geoffrey Wilson, Michael Cook, David Brown, David Langford and Mike Beynon; assistant producers Alan Russell and John Adcock; produced by Rosemary Gill; pets: Petra, Jason, Freda and Patch.

	VT Number	Holding / Source
24.12.1970 **Programme 30**	DC50871	DB-D3-2" /

Directed by Alan Russell.
(823)* TOTALISER + APPEAL NEWS / CARDS / CRIB / BETHLEMEN: THE CHRISTMAS STORY TK RPT ex-22.12.69 (Val) / FATHER CHRISTMAS ROOF CLIMBING SHOES DEMO'D / PRESENTS / O COME ALL YE FAITHFUL

1971 - 1972
Main regular credit(s): Presented by Valerie Singleton, John Noakes, Peter Purves and Lesley Judd; edited by Biddy Baxter; production team Michael Cook, David Langford, Geoffrey Wilson, Harry Cowdy, Ian 'Olly' Oliver, Daniel Wolf, Mike Harrison, Sarah Hellings, Robert Leacroft, Bill Nicholson and Richard Smith; assistant producers John Adcock and Alan Russell; produced by Rosemary Gill; pets: Petra, Jason, Freda and Shep.

	Holding / Source
23.12.1971 **Programme 30**	DB-D3-2" /

Film sequences directed by John Adcock; directed by Alan Russell.
With Katherine Ettlinger.
(904)* CARDS + CRIB / KATHERINE ETTLINGER INTERVIEW / NUTCRACKER BALLET VT ex-04.03.71 / NUREMBERG CHRISTMAS MARKET TK (John and Peter) / PRESENTS / HARK THE HERALD ANGELS
Film Shot: 09-12.12.71

1972 - 1973
Main regular credit(s): Presented by Valerie Singleton, John Noakes, Peter Purves and Lesley Judd; edited by Biddy Baxter; assistant editor Rosemary Gill; production team Geoffrey Wilson, Michael Cook, Sarah Hellings, Ian 'Olly' Oliver, David Langford, Harry Cowdy, Mike Harrison and Daniel Wolf; produced by Alan Russell and John Adcock; pets: Petra, Jason, Freda and Shep.

	VT Number	Holding / Source
21.12.1972 **Programme 29**	DR16754	DB-D3-2" /

Film sequences directed by Mike Harrison; directed by David Langford.
(985)* (VAL IN STUDIO) CHRISTMAS CARDS / CRIB / PANTO HORSE ROUTINE / RETURN TO EDDYSTONE TK (Val and Lesley) / APPEAL NEWS / PRESENTS / O COME ALL YE FAITHFUL
Film Shot: 13.12.72

21.12.72 – BLUE PETER (LCH9249A)/JOHN CRAVEN'S NEWSROUND (LCH9250T) – front: caption trails for "Jackanory Playhouse" and "John Craven's Newsround"; globe with announcement (NB most of this is covered up by clock on D3 dubs – details from older VHS transfer). Middle: caption trail for "Jackanory Playhouse" (inc. photos & details); globe with announcement. End: caption trail for "The Record Breakers"; globe with announcement; start of "Yogi Bear" (to be followed by "Pixie and Dixie" according to announcement).

1973 - 1974
Main regular credit(s): Presented by Valerie Singleton, John Noakes, Peter Purves and Lesley Judd; edited by Biddy Baxter; assistant editor Rosemary Gill; production team Michael Cook, Ian 'Olly' Oliver, David Langford, Sarah Hellings, Crispin Evans, Daniel Wolf, Harry Cowdy and Ron Jones; produced by John Adcock; pets: Petra, Jason and Shep.

	VT Number	Holding / Source
24.12.1973 **Programme 31**	DR7826	DB-D3-2" /

Directed by Ian Oliver.
With Lesley Judd (Prince Charming), Valerie Singleton (Cinderella), Arthur Askey, Tony Hall, Chalk Farm Branch of the Salvation Army.
(1066)* (VAL IN STUDIO) CHRISTMAS CARDS AND CRIB / VT PRE-REC: CINDERELLA PANTO WITH ARTHUR ASKEY / TONY HALL MESSAGE ETHIOPIA TK / BETHLEHEM TK FLASHBACK ex-23.12.69 / PRESENTS / HARK THE HERALD ANGELS

25.12.1973 **A Stocking Full Of Stars Insert**		C1 / C1

Directed by Harry Cowdy.
BLUE PETER: COTSWOLD FARM PARK TK (John, Peter and Lesley) Dur: 5'29"
Film Shot: 21.11.73

BLUE PETER

| British Christmas Television Guide | BLUE PETER (continued) |

1974 - 1975

Main regular credit(s): Presented by Valerie Singleton, John Noakes, Peter Purves and Lesley Judd; edited by Biddy Baxter; assistant editor Rosemary Gill; production team Michael Cook, Harry Cowdy, David Langford, Sarah Hellings, Crispin Evans, Ian 'Olly' Oliver, Mike Ward, Adam Kempton, Daniel Wolf and Ron Jones; produced by Alan Russell and John Adcock; pets: Petra, Jason, Freda and Shep.

	VT Number	Holding / Source
23.12.1974 **Programme 31**	DC125323	DB-D3-2" /

Film sequences directed by Crispin Evans; directed by Ian Oliver.

With Derek Freeman.

(1147)* (VAL'S LAST STUDIO APPEARANCE AS ONE OF THE TEAM) CHRISTMAS CARDS / CRIB / WOKINGHAM GUIDE DOG CENTRE TK-1 (Peter with Derek Freeman) / FLYING DEMO / VT PRE-REC 19.12.74: BLUE PETER CHRISTMAS FLYING BALLET VT (All Four) / O COME ALL YE FAITHFUL
Film Shot: 17.12.74

1975 - 1976

Main regular credit(s): Presented by John Noakes, Peter Purves and Lesley Judd; edited by Biddy Baxter; assistant editor Rosemary Gill; production team Michael Cook, Ian Oliver, David Langford, Sarah Hellings, Mike Ward, Crispin Evans and Alex Leger; produced by John Adcock; pets: Petra, Jason, Freda, Shep, Jack and Jill.

	VT Number	Holding / Source
22.12.1975 **Programme 31**	DC55281	DB-D3-2" /

Film sequences directed by Sarah Hellings (Message); directed by Ian Oliver.

(1226)* (NO LESLEY) FOURTH CANDLE LIT / CHRISTMAS CARDS / CRIB / TOTALISER / ALICE IN BLUE PETER LAND VT (All Three) / PRESENTS / LESLEY'S CHRISTMAS PRESENT + MESSAGE TK (Lesley) / HARK THE HERALD ANGELS
Film Shot: 19.12.75 (Message)

1976 - 1977

Main regular credit(s): Presented by John Noakes, Peter Purves and Lesley Judd; edited by Biddy Baxter; assistant editor John Adcock; produced by Alan Russell; pets: Petra, Freda, Shep, Jack and Jill.

	VT Number	Holding / Source
20.12.1976 **Programme 29**	DC47472	DB-D3-2" /

Directed by Mike Ward.

(1307)* BIRD CARVINGS / CINDERELLA PANTO VT RPT ex-23.12.73 / APPEAL NEWS / THE STORY OF THE FLYING ENTERPRISE + TK / CHRISTMAS TABLE DECORATION MAKE (by Margaret Parnell).

20.12.76 – BLUE PETER (LCH2088L)/JOHN CRAVEN'S NEWSROUND (LCH9448J) – front: [PPGD clock?], end of (caption?) trail for "Jackanory" (?) with Alec McCowen tomorrow; globe with ident and announcement. End: globe, plug for "Three Gifts for Cinderella", announcement; incomplete PasB of "John Craven's Newsround" (logged on Infax anyway).

	VT Number	Holding / Source
23.12.1976 **Programme 30**	DC47407	DB-D3-2" /

Directed by Mike Ward.

With Chris Drake.

(1308)* CHRISTMAS CARDS / CRIB / APPEAL TK-4 (Chris Drake) / PRE-REC AM 16.12.76 LONDON FESTIVAL BALLET - NUTCRACKER KIDS INTERVIEWED + PA (D: David Langford) / PRESENTS ROUND THE TREE / O COME ALL YE FAITHFUL

1977 - 1978

Main regular credit(s): Presented by John Noakes, Peter Purves, Lesley Judd and Simon Groom; edited by Biddy Baxter; assistant editor John Adcock; production team Sarah Hellings, Michael Cook, Alex Leger, Mike Ward, Renny Rye, Joanna Gollings and Christopher Rowlands; pets: Freda, Shep, Jack, Jill and Goldie.

	VT Number	Holding / Source
22.12.1977 **Programme 30**	DC131662	DB-D3-2" /

Directed by Mike Ward and John Adcock (Panto).

With Percy Thrower, Sally Gilpin.

(1388)* FOURTH CANDLE LIT / CARDS + CRIB / APPEAL NEWS + LINCOLNSHIRE POLICE DONATION OF 600 KEYS / JACK AND THE COFFEEBEANSTALK VT (with Percy Thrower and Sally Gilpin (Cow)) / PRESENTS / HARK THE HERALD ANGELS

22.12.77 – BLUE PETER (LCH2312N) – front: menu caption with end of voice-over announcement – 'Holiday Programmes: 9.45 The Wombles, 9.50 Jackanory, 10.05 Boris the Bold, 10.10 The King of Argos, 10.35 Flash Gordon Conquers the Universe, 10.55 Elvis in King Creole: Tomorrow on BBC1'; globe with announcement. End: menu caption 'Children's Programmes: 3.55 Play School, 4.20 Deputy Dawg, 4.40 Plum's Plots and Plans, 5.05 Countdown to the Festival, 5.35 Ivor the Engine: Tomorrow on BBC1', with part of voice-over narration…

1978 - 1979

Main regular credit(s): Presented by Lesley Judd, Simon Groom, Christopher Wenner and Tina Heath; edited by Biddy Baxter; assistant editor John Adcock; production team David Langford, Alex Leger, Michael Cook, Pat Mordecai, Sylvia Bone, Patrick Turley, Kate Harris, Roger Gale and Hazel Gill; produced by Renny Rye; pets: Freda, Jack, Jill, Goldie, Maggie and Jim.

	VT Number	Holding / Source
18.12.1978 **Programme 29**	DC84241	DB-D3-2" /

Film sequences directed by Renny Rye; directed by David Langford.

(1466)* THIRD CANDLE LIT / ROYAL NAVY GUN CARRIAGE AND LIMBER PLUS GIANT PUDDING / CHRISTMAS FLOWER DECORATION MAKE (by Margaret Parnell) / TRAFALGAR SQUARE NEWS - LESLEY'S SWITCH ON BLACKED OUT BY INDUSTRIAL ACTION / TRAFALGAR SQUARE CHRISTMAS TREE FELLING TK (Simon and Chris) / CHRISTMAS FLOWER DECORATIONS MAKE (by Margaret Parnell) / TOTALISER AND DEPOT FINDS
Film Shot: 22.11+ 28.11 + 14.12.78

BLUE PETER (continued)	British Christmas Television Guide

1979 - 1980

Main regular credit(s): Presented by Simon Groom, Christopher Wenner, Tina Heath and Sarah Greene; edited by Biddy Baxter; assistant editor John Adcock; production team Frances Gifford, Hazel Gill, Bill Nicol, Roger Gale, Alex Leger, Michael Cook, Kate Harris, Sylvia Bone, Peter Dale, Mike Burgess, Mig Harper and Paul Pierrot; produced by Renny Rye; pets: Jack, Jill, Goldie, Maggie and Jim.

	VT Number	Holding / Source
24.12.1979 Programme 31	DR7822	DB-D3-2" /

Film sequences directed by Alex Leger; directed by Renny Rye.

With Hedwyn Taylor.

(1547)* CARDS / CRIB / MAP / HEDWYN TAYLOR - MAN WITH HALF A BEARD FOR APPEAL FINALLY HAS SHAVE IN BLUE PETER BARBER SET / CHRISTMAS APPEAL AUCTION TK (All Three) / TOTALISER - TARGET REACHED - WHAT MONEY WILL BUY / ALL STAR RECORD BREAKERS: GNOMES VT CLIP / PRESENTS / O COME ALL YE FAITHFUL

Film Shot: 21.12.79

1980 - 1981

Main regular credit(s): Presented by Simon Groom, Sarah Greene and Peter Duncan; edited by Biddy Baxter; production team David Langford, Michael Cook, Frances Gifford, Sylvia Bone, George Auckland, Rob Benfield, Clare Elstow, Michael Forte, Hazel Gill and Anne Dixon; produced by Alex Leger and Michael Turner; pets: Jack, Jill, Goldie, Maggie and Jim.

	VT Number	Holding / Source
22.12.1980 Programme 31	N/K ex-H3300	DB-1" /

Music directed by Dave Cooke; film sequences directed by Alex Leger (B and B), David Langford (B and B) and Renny Rye; directed by David Langford.

(1625)* CARDS - INC. TWELVE DAYS OF CHRISTMAS COLLAGE / CRIB / BLUE PETER VICTORIAN MUSIC HALL (Musical Director: Dave Cooke) / TOTALISER + APPEAL DONATIONS / KESWICK BRING AND BUY TK (Peter) / RECORD BREAKERS COSTUMES + VT CLIP / PRESENTS ROUND THE TREE / HARK THE HERALD ANGELS SING .

Film Shot: 13.12.80

BB: Good prog

1981 - 1982

Main regular credit(s): Presented by Simon Groom, Sarah Greene and Peter Duncan; edited by Biddy Baxter; assistant editors Ian Oliver and Renny Rye; production team Sylvia Bone, Gillian Reilly, Michael Cook, Michael Forte, Sue Beardsmore, Hazel Gill, Rob Benfield and Anne Dixon; produced by Alex Leger and Michael Turner; pets: Jack, Jill, Goldie, Maggie and Jim.

	VT Number	Holding / Source
24.12.1981 Programme 30	N/K ex-H7778	DB-1" /

Music directed by Dave Cooke; directed by Michael Turner and Renny Rye.

With Tina Heath.

(1708)* CARDS / CRIB / CINDERELLA VT PRE-REC 11.12 (with Tina Heath. Director: Renny Rye / Musical Director: Dave Cooke) / JAVA DEPOT TK / TOTALISER / ALL STAR RECORD BREAKERS VT CLIP / PRESENTS / O COME ALL YE FAITHFUL.

BB: Good prog

1982 - 1983

Main regular credit(s): Presented by Simon Groom, Sarah Greene, Peter Duncan and Janet Ellis; edited by Biddy Baxter; production team Michael Cook, Andrew Whitman, Jack King, Sally Fraser, Rob Benfield, Greg Childs and Nick Heathcote; produced by Alex Leger, Michael Turner and Lewis Bronze; pets: Jack, Jill, Goldie and George.

	VT Number	Holding / Source
23.12.1982 Programme 30	DC190875	DB-D3 / 1"

Music directed by Dave Cooke; film sequences directed by Renny Rye; directed by Michael Turner.

(1787)* CARDS / 12FT TEDDY / CRIB / PANTO PARADE VT PRE-REC'D 10.12.82 (Musical Director: Dave Cooke / Choreographer: Sally Gilpin) / APPEAL: AMBULANCE-2 TK (Sarah) / TOTALISER / ALL STAR RECORD BREAKERS VT CLIP / PRESENTS / HARK THE HERALD ANGELS SING.

Film Shot: 17.12.82

1983 - 1984

Main regular credit(s): Presented by Simon Groom, Peter Duncan and Janet Ellis; edited by Biddy Baxter; assistant editor Lewis Bronze; production team Michael Cook, Sylvia Rutter, Andrew Whitman, David Langford, Sally Fraser, David Crichton, David Blount and Nick Heathcote; produced by Alex Leger, Michael Turner and Angela Sharp; pets: Jack, Goldie and George.

	VT Number	Holding / Source
22.12.1983 Programme 30	CU439224 ex-H78410	DB / 1"

Film sequences directed by Rob Benfield (Noggin) and Alex Leger (Peru); directed by Michael Turner.

(1866)* FOURTH CANDLE LIT / CARDS + CRIB / NOGGIN THE NOG TK (Peter) / APPEAL NEWS / PERU TK: CHILDREN (Simon) / APPEAL NEWS / FLASH GORDON TK CLIP (with Peter) / PRESENTS / O COME ALL YE FAITHFUL.

Film Shot: 06 + 09.12.83 (Noggin)

BB: Good prog

1984 - 1985

Main regular credit(s): Presented by Simon Groom, Janet Ellis and Michael Sundin; edited by Biddy Baxter; assistant editor Lewis Bronze; production team Michael Cook, Peter Brown, Ben Robinson, Barbara Kindred, Rob Benfield, Sally Fraser and Richard Kelly; produced by Alex Leger and Michael Turner; pets: Jack, Goldie and George.

	VT Number	Holding / Source
24.12.1984 Programme 31	N/K ex-H83613	DB / 1"

Film sequences directed by Alex Leger; directed by Michael Turner.

BLUE PETER

| British Christmas Television Guide | BLUE PETER (continued) |

(1944)* FOURTH CANDLE LIT / TINY FELT CHRISTMAS TREE / CARDS + CRIB / TOTALISERS / ETHIOPIA TK-2 (Simon) / VT PRE-REC AT TV THEATRE 18.12.84: THE STORY OF THE NUTCRACKER / INTERVIEW WITH CHILDREN DANCING IT / LONDON FESTIVAL BALLET NUTCRACKER PA / PRESENTS / HARK THE HERALD ANGELS SING.

1985 - 1986
Main regular credit(s): Presented by Simon Groom, Janet Ellis and Peter Duncan; edited by Biddy Baxter; assistant editor Lewis Bronze; production team David Langford, Michael Cook, Richard Kelly, Martyn Suker, Ben Robinson, Alison Payne and Anne Dixon; produced by Alex Leger and Andrew Whitman; pets: Jack, Goldie, George and Bonnie.

	VT Number	Holding / Source
23.12.1985 **Programme 31**	N/K ex-H31448	DB / 1"

Film sequences directed by Lewis Bronze (Appeal); directed by David Langford.
(2023)* CARDS / CRIB / TOTALISER / DEPOT DELIVERY TK (No Presenter) / APPEAL BOY TK (Peter) / PETER PIPER'S PANTOMIME PUZZLE VT (Written and directed by Andrew Whitman) / PRESENTS / O COME ALL YE FAITHFUL.
Film Shot: 10.12.85 (CLIP FROM FILM TX'ING 06.01.86)

BB: Good prog – vt ran late @ end.

1986 - 1987
Main regular credit(s): Presented by Janet Ellis, Peter Duncan, Mark Curry and Caron Keating; edited by Biddy Baxter; assistant editor Lewis Bronze; production team Michael Cook, Rob Benfield, Peter Brown, Richard Kelly, Steven Andrew, Alison Payne and Ben Robinson; produced by Alex Leger, Andrew Whitman and Nick Heathcote; pets: George, Bonnie and Willow.

	VT Number	Holding / Source
22.12.1986 **Programme 31**	:U377653 ex-H10344	DB / 1"

Music directed by Dave Cooke; film sequences directed by Alex Leger; directed by Alex Leger.
(2107)* GREAT YARMOUTH PRIMARY SCHOOL CHRISTMAS COLLAGE / CARDS + CRIB / TOTALISER + MALAWI TK-3 (Mark) / VINTAGE POLYPHON DEMO / VT PRE-REC 05.12.86: BLUE PETER CHRISTMAS VARIET SHOW INC THAT'S ENTERTAINMENT! (All Four)/O'RAFFERTY'S MOTOR CAR (Caron)/A YORKSHIRE LIFE FOR ME (Mark)/BOILED BEEF AND CARROTS (Peter)/YOU ARE MY LUCKY STAR (Janet)/SANTA CLAUS IS COMING TO TOWN (All Four / Musical Director: Dave Cooke, Choreographer: Cherry Gillespie D: Andrew Whitman) / PRESENTS / HARK THE HERALD ANGELS SING.

1987 - 1988
Main regular credit(s): Presented by Mark Curry, Caron Keating and Yvette Fielding; edited by Biddy Baxter; assistant editor Lewis Bronze; production team Michael Cook, John Comerford, Oliver Macfarlane, Steven Andrew, Gabby Ballantine, Cathy Derrick, Peter Brown, Lorna Squires and Lak Singh; produced by Alex Leger, Nick Heathcote and Andrew Whitman; pets: George, Bonnie and Willow.

	VT Number	Holding / Source
24.12.1987 **Programme 30**	:U378458 ex-H11589	DB / 1"

Music directed by Dave Cooke; film sequences directed by Alex Leger; directed by Andrew Whitman.
(2185)* LAST CANDLE LIT / CARDS, CRIB AND TOTALISER / APPEAL TK-5: BRADFORD RIDING CLASS (Mark) / CULDROSE AIRLIFT TK (No Presenter) / VT PRE-REC 17.12 PM + 18.12: HOORAY FOR HOLLYWOOD VT inc HOORAY FOR HOLLYWOOD (All Three), PUTTIN' ON THE RITZ (Mark and Yvette), THE DEADWOOD STAGE (Yvette), HAVE YOURSELF A VERY MERRY CHRISTMAS (Mark and Caron) and SLEIGH RIDE (All Three) (Choreographer: Cherry Gillespie. Musical Director: Dave Cooke) / PRESENTS / O COME ALL YE FAITHFUL.
Film Shot: 15-16.12.87

1988 - 1989
Main regular credit(s): Presented by Mark Curry, Caron Keating, Yvette Fielding and John Leslie; edited by Lewis Bronze; production team Michael Cook, John Comerford, Cathy Derrick, Mick Evans, Steven Andrew, Penny Ewing, David Coyle, Anne Gilchrist, Kelsey Geekie, Linda Arkinstall, Richard Kelly, Anne Dixon and Gabby Ballantine; produced by Alex Leger, Andrew Whitman, Nick Heathcote, Roy Milani, Oliver Macfarlane and Peter Charlton; pets: George, Bonnie and Willow.

	VT Number	Holding / Source
22.12.1988 **Programme 30**	N/K ex-H109128	DB / 1"

Music directed by Dave Cooke; directed by Andrew Whitman.
(2264)* LAST CANDLE LIT / CARDS AND PRESENTS FOR ANIMALS / CRIB / TOTALISER AND APPEAL RECAP / LAST MINUTE CHRISTMAS DECORATIONS MAKE / AROUND THE WORLD IN EIGHT MINUTES VT inc THE OLD BAZAAR IN CAIRO (All Three) A MILLION KINDS OF COFFEE IN BRAZIL (All Three) O LITTLE TOWN OF BETHLEHEM (All Three) WINTER WONDERLAND (All Three) (Choreographer: Cherry Gillespie. Musical Director: Dave Cooke, D: Andrew Whitman) / HARK THE HERALD ANGELS SING.

1989 - 1990
Main regular credit(s): Presented by Caron Keating, Yvette Fielding, John Leslie and Diane-Louise Jordan; theme music by Simon Brint; edited by Lewis Bronze; production team Michael Cook, Anne Gilchrist, David Coyle, Peter Brown, Penny Ewing, Anne Dixon, Steven Andrew, Sally Ashman, Pamela Hossick, Andrew Chater, Nick Gardner, Kimberley Jenkins, Berry-Anne Billingsley, Bill Locke, Christine Owen, David Heels and Gillian Shearing; produced by Alex Leger, Oliver Macfarlane, Richard Simkin, John Comerford and Roy Milani; pets: George, Bonnie and Willow.

	VT Number	Holding / Source
21.12.1989 **Programme 30**	N/K ex-H44112	DB / 1"

Film sequences directed by Bill Locke (Hanukkah), Alex Leger (Xmas Tree) and Peter Brown (Appeal); directed by Andrew Whitman.
(2341)* CHRISTMAS CARDS AND TREE / HANUKKAH JEWISH CHRISTMAS VT (No Presenter) / TOTALISER / APPEAL VT-8: LEEDS BABY UNIT (John) / CRIB / CHRISTMAS SLEDGE MAKE / GIANT CHRISTMAS TREE VT (Caron) / ANIMALS PRESENTS / O COME ALL YE FAITHFUL.
Film Shot: 19.12.89 (Hanukkah) 02-03 + 09.12.89 (Tree) 01-02.12.89 (Appeal)

BLUE PETER

| BLUE PETER (continued) | British Christmas Television Guide |

1990 - 1991

Main regular credit(s): Presented by Yvette Fielding, John Leslie and Diane-Louise Jordan; theme music by Simon Brint; edited by Lewis Bronze; production team Anne Gilchrist, Bill Locke, Anne Dixon, David Coyle, Christine Wilson, Peter Brown, Helena Appio, Andrew Adamyk, Sukai Eccleston, Mary Saunders, Val Fraser and Bridget Caldwell; produced by Alex Leger, Oliver Macfarlane, John Comerford, Richard Simkin and Cathy Derrick; pets: George, Bonnie, Willow and Honey.

	VT Number	Holding / Source
24.12.1990 **Programme 31**	N/K ex-H113094	DB / 1"

Music directed by Dave Cooke; choreography by Cherry Gillespie; designed by Roz Johnston and Christine Castle; film sequences directed by Alex Leger; directed by Oliver Macfarlane and Anne Gilchrist (Christmas Wish).

With Mark Curry, Caron Keating.

(2419)* FOURTH CANDLE LIT / CARDS + TOTALISER / APPEAL VT-7: CHRISTMAS IN ROMANIA (Yvette) / CRIB / CHRISTMAS ONCE ONLY TABLE MATS MAKE / A CHRISTMAS WISH VT PRE-REC 29-30.11.90 inc YOU CAN DO MAGIC (Diane) CHRISTMAS RAPPING (John) I FEEL GOOD (Yvette) and SANTA CLAUS IS COMING TO TOWN (All Five) (Musical Director: Dave Cooke / Choreographer: Cherry Gillespie) / PET'S PRESENTS / HARK THE HERALD ANGELS SING.

1991 - 1992

Main regular credit(s): Presented by Yvette Fielding, John Leslie and Diane-Louise Jordan; edited by Lewis Bronze; production team Cathy Derrick, Anne Dixon, Anne Gilchrist, Bridget Caldwell, Caroline Bacon, Pat Baker, Reem Nouss, Jeff Bannis, Catrina McLean, Gabrielle Osrin and Rosalyn Walsh; produced by Alex Leger, Oliver Macfarlane and John Comerford; pets: George, Bonnie, Kari and Oke.

	VT Number	Holding / Source
23.12.1991 **Programme 31**	N/K ex-H213342	DB / 1"

Music directed by Steve Brown; film sequences directed by Bill Locke (Choristers) and Anne Gilchrist (Panto); directed by Oliver Macfarlane.

With Clare Bradley.

(2498)* LAST CANDLE LIT / CARDS + CRIB / TOTALISER / KINGS COLLEGE CHORISTERS VT (No Presenter) / PUDDING PLANNER GAME MAKE / TWELVE DAYS OF CHRISTMAS CHALLENGE VT (All Three / Musical Director: Steve Brown) / 532 BLUE PETER NEWS / ANIMALS'PRESENTS / CLARE BRADLEY JOINS / O COME ALL YE FAITHFUL.

Film Shot: 13-14.12.91 (Choristers) 04 + 06.12.91 (Panto)

1992 - 1993

Main regular credit(s): Presented by John Leslie, Diane-Louise Jordan and Anthea Turner; theme music by Simon Brint; edited by Lewis Bronze; production team Anne Dixon, Peter Brown, Bridget Caldwell, Caroline Bacon, Bill Locke, Penny Ewing, Mary Saunders, Catherine Whelton, Joanne Kay and Sharon Parker; produced by Alex Leger, Oliver Macfarlane, John Comerford, Cathy Derrick and Susie Staples; pets: George, Bonnie, Kari and Oke.

	VT Number	Holding / Source
24.12.1992 **Programme 30**	D397304	DB-D3 /

Written by Jeremy Swan; music directed by Dave Cooke; choreography by Chris Power; directed by Cathy Derrick and Jeremy Swan.

With Clare Bradley.

(2573)* VT PRE-REC 26 / 27.11.92: PRESENTERS ENTER STUDIO ON SLEIGH / CARDS / APPEAL NEWS + CRIB / LAST MINUTE CHRISTMAS DECORATION MAKE / VT PRE-REC 26 + 27.11.92: A CHRISTMAS CAROL inc SANTA CLAUS IS COMING TO TOWN, ME AND MY SHADOW and WE NEED A LITTLE CHRISTMAS (All Three / Musical Director: Dave Cooke / Choreographer: Chris Power / Written and Directed by Jeremy Swan) / ANIMALS PRESENTS - CLARE JOINS / HARK THE HERALD ANGELS SING.

1993 - 1994

Main regular credit(s): Presented by John Leslie, Diane-Louise Jordan, Anthea Turner and Tim Vincent; edited by Lewis Bronze; production team Anne Dixon, Bill Locke, Bridget Caldwell, Mary Saunders, Caroline Bacon, Penny Ewing, Marc Goodchild, Joanne Kay, Deborah Hinnigan, Paul Murphy and Richard Nash; produced by Alex Leger, Oliver Macfarlane, John Comerford, Cathy Derrick and Susie Staples; pets: George, Bonnie, Kari and Oke.

	VT Number	Holding / Source
23.12.1993 **Programme 30**	DR20928	DB / D3S

Written by Jeremy Swan; music by Jonathan Cohen; choreography by Jeff Thacker; film sequences directed by Bridget Caldwell; directed by Cathy Derrick and Jeremy Swan.

With Clare Bradley.

(2652)* FOURTH CANDLE LIT / CARDS / APPEAL VT-9: APPEAL HUNT (Diane) / TOTALISER / CRIB / MOTORISED NATIVITY SCENE / VT PRE-REC 13-14.12.93 - ALADDIN AND THE BLUE PETER LAMP incl Abadabbadabba and Sleigh Ride (All Four. Music: Jonathan Cohen / Choreographer: Jeff Thacker / Written and Directed by Jeremy Swan) / ANIMALS' PRESENTS + CLARE BRADLEY JOINS / O COME ALL YE FAITHFUL.

Film Shot: 03.12.93

1994 - 1995

Main regular credit(s): Presented by Diane-Louise Jordan, Tim Vincent and Stuart Miles; edited by Lewis Bronze; designed by Louise Jackson; production team Anne Dixon, Bill Locke, Mary Saunders, Bridget Caldwell, Sarah Hudson, Tony King, Caroline Bacon, Tim Dunn, Catrina McClean, Angela Ferreira, Sarah Colclough and Marc Goodchild; produced by Alex Leger, Oliver Macfarlane, Cathy Derrick, Susie Staples, Joe Godwin and Steve Hocking; pets: George, Bonnie, Kari and Oke.

	VT Number	Holding / Source
22.12.1994 **Programme 30**	D489503	DB-D3 /

Music by Michael Omer; choreography by Jenny Arnold; film sequences directed by Bill Locke; directed by Oliver Macfarlane.

With Diane-Louise Jordan (Cinderella), Tim Vincent (Prince Charming), Stuart Miles (Ugly Sister), Tim Vincent (Ugly Sister), Clare Bradley (Fairy Godmother), Stuart Miles (Giant).

(2727)* FOURTH CANDLE LIT / CARDS / MAP + APPEAL VT-6: WELL ARRIVAL (Diane) / TOTALISER + CRIB / CINDERELLA VT – WITH SONGS - SISTERS (All Three)/OH! WHAT A BEAUTY (Diane and Clare)/ROCKING AROUND THE CHRISTMAS TREE (All) / ANIMALS PRESENTS + CLARE / HARK THE HERALD ANGELS SING.

Film Shot: 29-30.11.94

| British Christmas Television Guide | BLUE PETER (continued) |

1995 - 1996

Main regular credit(s): Presented by Diane-Louise Jordan, Tim Vincent, Stuart Miles, Katy Hill and Romana d'Annunzio; theme music by Yes/No People; edited by Lewis Bronze; assistant editor Oliver Macfarlane; production team Anne Dixon, Bridget Caldwell, Caroline Bacon, Mary Saunders, Reema Mongia, Marc Goodchild, Tracey Penfold, Min Clough, Angela Ferreira, Nadia Miller, Sarah Downing, Benjamin Perks, Piers Hanmer and Sion Taylor; produced by Alex Leger, Susie Staples, Cathy Derrick, Joe Godwin and Steve Hocking; pets: George, Bonnie, Kari, Oke and Mabel.

	VT Number	Holding / Source
22.12.1995 **Programme 45**	DGN588401	DB-D3 /

Film sequences directed by Susie Staples; directed by Caroline Bacon.
With John Leslie (Father Christmas).
(2831)* CARDS / ROYAL BALLET PA 'LES PATINEURS' / TOTALISER (with John Leslie as Father Christmas) / MINI CHRISTMAS TREE AND BOTTLE BAUBLES MAKE / CRIB / BETHLEHEM VT (Diane) / ANIMALS PRESENTS / BEST OF BLUE PETER TRAIL / O COME ALL YE FAITHFUL.
Film Shot: 08-11.12.95

1996 - 1997

Main regular credit(s): Presented by Tim Vincent, Stuart Miles, Katy Hill, Romana d'Annunzio and Richard Bacon; edited by Oliver Macfarlane; deputy editor John Comerford; production team Anne Dixon, Caroline Bacon, Sarah Hudson, Marc Goodchild, Sarah Downing, Piers Hanmer, Sarah Colclough, Kez Margrie, Stuart Maisner, Tanya Motie, Scott Ross, Juliet Dwek, Shaminder Sandu, Linda Ross and Gilly Longton; produced by Alex Leger, Steve Hocking, Joe Godwin, Amanda Gabbitas and Bridget Caldwell; pets: George, Bonnie, Kari, Oke and Mabel.

	VT Number	Holding / Source
23.12.1996 **Programme 46**	DR55914	DB-D3 /

Film sequences directed by Bill Locke; directed by Bridget Caldwell.
With Clare Bradley.
(2949)* LAST CANDLE LIT / CARDS / TOTALISER, MAP AND APPEAL VT STING / LAST MINUTE DECORATION MAKE / CRIB / ETHIOPIAN CHRISTMAS: FRANKINCENSE AND THE THREE KINGS VT (Katy) / ANIMALS' PRESENTS (with Clare Bradley) / HARK! THE HERALD ANGELS SING.
Film Shot: 16-18.11.96

1997 - 1998

Main regular credit(s): Presented by Stuart Miles, Katy Hill, Romana d'Annunzio, Richard Bacon and Konnie Huq; edited by Oliver Macfarlane; deputy editor John Comerford; production team Anne Dixon, Caroline Bacon, Sarah Hudson, Reema Mongia, Kez Margrie, Tanya Motie, Sham Sandu, Sarah Colclough, Gilly Longton, Linda Ross, Vanessa Cobb, Nadia Miller, Paul Tyler, Helen Church, Alison Cresswell, James Van Der Pool and Alison Hagger; produced by Alex Leger, Cathy Derrick, Steve Hocking, Amanda Gabbitas, Bridget Caldwell, Marc Goodchild, Richard Marson and Anne Gilchrist; pets: George, Bonnie, Kari, Oke and Mabel.

	VT Number	Holding / Source
24.12.1997 **Programme 47**	DGN89507	DB-D3 /

Film sequences directed by Sham Sandhu; directed by Bridget Caldwell.
(3065)* (NO ROMANA - PRE RX'D 21.12.97) / PRE-TITLES: PRESENTERS REVEAL CHRISTMAS STUDIO / FOURTH CANDLE LIT / CARDS / TALES OF BEATRIX POTTER VT ex-30.11.92 / TOTALISER + MAP / APPEAL VT REPRISE / CHRISTMAS ANGELS MAKE / THE STORY OF SILENT NIGHT VT (Stuart) / ANIMALS' PRESENTS / O COME ALL YE FAITHFUL.
Film Shot: 10-12.12.97

1998 - 1999

Credits: Presented by Stuart Miles, Katy Hill, Richard Bacon, Konnie Huq and Simon Thomas; edited by Oliver Macfarlane; deputy editor John Comerford; designed by Ross Dempster; production team Anne Dixon, Caroline Bacon, Kez Margrie, Tanya Motie, Sham Shamdu, Linda Ross, David Coyle, Gilly Longton, Reema Lorford, Joanna Robinson, Toby Smith, Jeanette Goulbourn, Paul Tyler, Emily Gale, Dominic McDonald and Viccy Harrison; pets: George, Bonnie, Mabel, Kari and Oke.

	VT Number	Holding / Source
23.12.1998 **Programme 46**	DGN256202	DB-D3 /

Film sequences directed by Paul Tyler; directed by Caroline Bacon.
With Simon Thomas (Father Christmas), Charlotte Church.
(3182)* PRE-TITLES TEASE: DARK STUDIO - 4TH CANDLE LIT / CARDS / ADVENT SWEET WREATH MAKE / APPEAL NEWS + TOTALISER (with Simon Thomas as Father Christmas) / CAN DASH VT (Stuart) / CHARLOTTE CHURCH PA 'AVE MARIA' / CRIB / ANIMALS' PRESENTS / O LITTLE TOWN OF BETHLEHEM.
Film Shot: 17.12.98

1999 - 2000

Main regular credit(s): Presented by Katy Hill, Konnie Huq, Simon Thomas and Matt Baker; theme music by David Arnold; edited by Steve Hocking; production team Anne Dixon, Caroline Bacon, Kez Margrie, Gilly Longton, Sarah Colclough, Amanda Gabbitas, Viccy Harrison, Joanna Robinson, Emma Clark, Jeanette Goulbourn, Paul Tyler, Jessica Wilson, Dermot Canterbury, Paul Shuttleworth, Moray London, Carolyn Wilshire and Sarah Rowlands; series producer Bridget Caldwell; produced by Alex Leger, Cathy Derrick, Richard Marson, Kelsey Geekie, Gillie Scothern and Tanya Motie; pets: George, Mabel, Kari, Oke and Lucy Pargeter.

	VT Number	Holding / Source
24.12.1999 **Programme 44**	BRD38195	DB / DBSW

Film sequences directed by Richard Marson; directed by Bridget Caldwell.
(3297)* (PRE RX'D 19.12.99) / PRESENTERS DRIVE INTO STUDIO ON MOTORISED BED / FOURTH CANDLE LIT / CARDS / THE NUTCRACKER VT RPT ex-03.12.97 / APPEAL NEWS + VT / LAST MINUTE MAKE - CHRISTMAS TIN CAN CONTAINER / CRIB / BETHLEHEM: THE CHRISTMAS STORY VT (Simon) / PETS' PRESENTS / REVIEW OF THE YEAR TRAIL / HARK! THE HERALD ANGELS SING.
Film Shot: 23.10.99

| BLUE PETER (continued) | British Christmas Television Guide |

25.12.1999 **Programme 45** BRD29460 DB / DBSW
Directed by Kez Margrie.
(NO NUMBER)* A CHRISTMAS BOX OF DELIGHTS: ALL FOUR INTRO: CAIRNGORM REINDEERS PART RPT ex-15.12.95 (Katy) / THE STORY OF SILENT NIGHT PART RPT ex-24.12.97 (Stuart) / TRAFALGAR SQUARE TREE VT PART RPT ex-06.12.96 (Tim Vincent) / FRANKINCENSE VT PART RPT ex-23.12.96 (Katy) / WELSH BETHLEHEM VT PART RPT ex-10.12.97 (Stuart) / THE CHRISTMAS STORY VT PART RPT ex-24.12.99 (Simon) / REVIEW OF THE YEAR TRAIL.

2000 - 2001

Main regular credit(s): Presented by Konnie Huq, Simon Thomas, Matt Baker and Liz Barker; theme music by David Arnold; edited by Steve Hocking; production team Viccy Harrison, Joanna Robinson, Emma Clark, Jeanette Goulbourn, Julian Smith and Dermot Canterbury; series producer Bridget Caldwell; produced by Alex Leger, Richard Marson, Kelsey Geekie, Tanya Motie, Kez Margrie, Sarah Colclough, Anne Dixon and Amanda Gabbitas; pets: George, Mabel, Kari, Oke and Lucy Pargeter.

	VT Number	Holding / Source
22.12.2000 **Programme 45**	BRD76474	DB / DBSW

Film sequences directed by Richard Marson; directed by Richard Marson.
(3413)* FOURTH CANDLE LIT / VIEWERS' CARDS / TOTALISER GOES UP + APPEAL NEWS + VT / LAST MINUTE MAKE - BUBBLE TREES (by Margaret Parnell) / CRIB / THE STORY OF ST FRANCIS OF ASSISI VT (Simon) / PETS' PRESENTS / O COME ALL YE FAITHFUL.
Film Shot: 01-03.10.00

SERIES 44: 2001 - 2002

Main regular credit(s): Presented by Konnie Huq, Simon Thomas, Matt Baker and Liz Barker; theme music by David Arnold; edited by Steve Hocking; production team Julian Smith, Steve Vickerstaff, Carolyn Wilshire, Michael Towner, Beverley Josling, Helen Scott, Adrian Johnson, Moray London, Kalpna Patel, Emma Clark, Dermot Canterbury, Jo Robinson, Archie Kalyana, Jeanette Goulbourn and Martin Williams; produced by Alex Leger, Richard Marson, Tanya Motie, Kez Margrie, Sarah Colclough, Amanda Gabbitas and Anne Dixon; pets: Mabel, Lucy Pargeter, Meg, Kari, Oke and George.

	VT Number	Holding / Source
24.12.2001 **Programme 75**	BRD119992	DB / DBSW

Series producer Richard Marson; film sequences directed by Richard Marson; directed by Richard Marson.
(3529)* (PRE-RX 21.12.01) FOURTH CANDLE LIT / VIEWERS' CARDS / VT PRE-REC 11.12.01: THE NUTCRACKER PA / APPEAL NEWS + VT + TOTALISER GOES UP / LAST MINUTE MAKE - SPARKLING SPUTNIK DECORATIONS / CRIB / HARVINGTON HALL - THE HOUSE OF SECRETS VT (Simon) / PANTO CLIP: UPTOWN GIRL VT ex-21.12.01 / PETS PRESENTS / HARK! THE HERALD ANGELS SING.
Film Shot: 30.10.01

SERIES 45: 2002 - 2003

Main regular credit(s): Presented by Konnie Huq, Simon Thomas, Matt Baker and Liz Barker; theme music by David Arnold; edited by Steve Hocking; production team Martin Williams, Lisa Madden, Cathy Wigley, Emma Clark, Paul Nash, Angela Young, Sarah Barnes, Anuj Goyal, Catherine Gildea, Dermot Canterbury, Chris Godwin, Steve Vickerstaff, Julian Smith, Debbie Martin, Lucie Abson, Sam Lockett, Helen Scott, James Morgan, Veronica Iacono and Catherine Ross; series producer Richard Marson; produced by Anne Dixon, Alex Leger, Kez Margrie, Melony Smith, Paul Shuttleworth, Andrea Christodoulou, Rob Unsworth and Richard Simkin; pets: George, Kari, Oke, Mabel, Lucy Pargeter and Meg.

	VT Number	Holding / Source
23.12.2002 **Programme 80: Christmas At The Club Blue Peter**	BRD177078	DB / DBSW

A CBBC production. Duration: 59 minutes.
Alternative transmissions: CBBC: 22.12.2002.
Written by Richard Marson; music directed by Dave Cooke; choreography by Gary Lloyd; designed by Alison Jeffery; production executive Caroline Morgan-Fletcher; executive producer Nigel Pickard; produced and directed by Richard Marson.
With Konnie Huq (Minnie McVee), Simon Thomas (J J (Jesse Josiah) Vanderfella III), Matt Baker (Junior / Big Daddy Baker), Liz Barker (Miss Venus Chartreuse), Sidney Sloane (Toothpick), Janet Ellis (Enchillada Chartreuse), S Club Juniors (Carol Singers), Richard Marson (Policeman), Carrie Grant (Additional Vocals), Jemma Cooke (Additional Vocals), Angellica Bell (Chorus Girl), Lisa Brockwell (Chorus Girl), Sophie McDonnell (Chorus Girl), Anna Kumble (Chorus Girl), Adrian Dickson (Toothpick's Henchman), Michael Absolon [as Abs] (Toothpick's Henchman), Anton Vamplew (Toothpick's Henchman), Becky Jago (Angry Date), Barney Harwood (Boyfriend), Ortis, Mark Speight (Detective), Joe Challands (Radio Announcer), Kirsten O'Brien, Tony Craig, Simon Grant, Steve Wilson, Jez Edwards, Ade Adepitan, Adam Fleming, Pineapple Performing Arts School.
(3644)* CHRISTMAS AT THE CLUB BLUE PETER.
INC SONGS: 'More, More, More', 'Venus', 'My Generation', 'Eat It', 'That Don't Impress Me Much', 'I Should Be So Lucky', 'Here Comes Santa Claus', 'Santa Baby', 'Those Boots Are Made For Walkin'', 'I'm Still Standing', 'Marshmallow World', 'Merry Christmas Everyone', 'Evergreen'.
Film Shot: 06-07.11 + 12-14.11 + 19-21.11 + 27-28.11 + 30.11 + 03-05.12 + 09.12.02 (Am Rec)

24.12.2002 **Programme 81** BRD173413 DB / DBSW
Film sequences directed by Richard Marson; directed by Richard Marson.
(3645)* (PRE RX'D 20.12.02) FOURTH CANDLE LIT / CARDS / SCHOOL BRING AND BUY VT (No Presenter) / APPEAL NEWS + TOTALISER / LAST MINUTE MAKE - SPARKLY STARS MAKE (by Gillian Shearing) / CRIB / THE STORY OF THE CHRISTMAS TRUCE VT (Simon and Matt) / CHRISTMAS NEWS + REVIEW OF THE YEAR VT TRAIL / PETS' PRESENTS / O COME ALL YE FAITHFUL.
Film Shot: 27-28.02.02

SERIES 46: 2003 - 2004

Main regular credit(s): Presented by Konnie Huq, Simon Thomas, Matt Baker and Liz Barker; theme music by David Arnold; edited by Steve Hocking; production team Sarah Barnes, Emma Clark, Dermot Canterbury, Debbie Martin, Catherine Gildea, Helen Scott, Martin Williams, Angela Young, Chris Godwin and Lucie Abson; series producer Richard Marson; produced by Anne Dixon, Alex Leger, Kez Margrie, Melony Smith, Rob Unsworth and Melissa Hardinge; pets: George, Kari, Oke, Mabel, Lucy Pargeter and Meg.

	Holding / Source
23.12.2003 **Programme 81**	DB / DBSW

Studio sequences directed by Martin Williams (Songbook Studio); film sequences directed by Catherine Gildea (Last Christmas); directed by Richard Marson.

BLUE PETER

| British Christmas Television Guide | BLUE PETER (continued) |

(3763)* FOURTH CANDLE LIT / CARDS / BLUE PETER CHRISTMAS SONGBOOK VT PRE-REC 08.12.03: MARY'S BOY CHILD / FROSTY THE SNOWMAN / I WISH IT COULD BE CHRISTMAS EVERY DAY / LAST CHRISTMAS / HAPPY CHRISTMAS (WAR IS OVER) / WHITE CHRISTMAS (Musical Director: Dave Cooke / Choreographer: Gary Lloyd) / APPEAL NEWS + TOTALISER AND MAP + VT / LAST MINUTE HANGING UMBRELLAS MAKE (by Gillian Shearing) / CRIB / PETS' PRESENTS / HARK! THE HERALD ANGELS SING.
Film Shot: 26.11.03 (Last Christmas)

SERIES 47: 2004 - 2005

Credits: Designed by Miranda Jones.

Main regular credit(s): Presented by Konnie Huq, Simon Thomas, Matt Baker, Liz Barker and Zöe Salmon; theme music by Nial Brown; edited by Richard Marson; production team Angela Young, Anna Davies, Becky Asprey, Chris Godwin, Debbie Martin, Ed Willson, Gillian Shearing, Hugo Ullberger, Jeanette Goulbourn, Jon Hancock, Kalpna Patel, Katie Oliver, Lotte Elwell, Matt Day, Matt Peacock, Natalie Barb, Nick Harris, Ros Sewell, Yvonne Stevenson, Carolyn Wilshire and Olga Drooglever; series producer Kez Margrie; produced by Annie Dixon, Alex Leger, Bridget Caldwell, Melissa Hardinge, Matt Gyves, Hugh Lawton and Karen Ackerman; pets: Mabel, Lucy Pargeter, Meg and Shelley and Smudge.

		Holding / Source
23.12.2004 **Programme 88**		DB / DBSW

Music directed by Dave Cooke; directed by Bridget Caldwell.
(3888)* FOURTH CANDLE LIT / GIANT PRESENT UNDER TREE UNWRAPPED TO REVEAL NEW PRESENTER ZOE SALMON / QUICK CHAT WITH ZOE / VT PRE-REC 06.12: THE MAGIC OF CHRISTMAS: GOOD MORNING, RUDOLPH THE RED NOSED REINDEER, MERRY CHRISTMAS EVERYONE, HAVE YOURSELF A VERY MERRY CHRISTMAS, SHAKE A TAIL FEATHER (Musical D: Dave Cooke, Choreography: Gary Lloyd) / VIEWER'S CARDS / APPEAL NEWS – FATHER CHRISTMAS (played by Gethin Jones) THROUGH TOTALISER / APPEAL VT RECAP / CRIB / CHRISTMAS NEWS + COMING SOON / PET'S PRESENTS / O COME ALL YE FAITHFUL.

NB - ZOE'S FIRST APPEARANCE – PRE RX'D 21.12

RM: Good programme

| 24.12.2004 | **A ROCK N'ROLL CHRISTMAS PSC RPT** | DB / DBSW |
| 28.12.2004 | **AN EASTEND CHRISTMAS PSC REVERSIONED RPT** | DB / DBSW |

SERIES 48: 2005 - 2006

Main regular credit(s): Presented by Konnie Huq, Simon Thomas, Matt Baker, Zöe Salmon and Liz Barker; edited by Richard Marson; production team Becky Asprey, Catherine Patterson, Diggy Hicks-Little, Ed Willson, Emma Cashmore, Helen Riddell, Hugo Ullberger, Lotte Elwell, Katie Oliver, Leo Morgan, Debbie Martin, Mignon Aylen, Lucy Tullet, Olga Drooglever, Kara Miller, Adrian Johnson, Brendan McCaul, Kalpna Patel, Matt Day, Ros Sewell, Tim Fransham, Nick Harris, Kieron Schiff, Charlotte Child and Traci Burns; series producer Kez Margrie; produced by Alex Leger, Melissa Hardinge, Matt Gyves, Bridget Caldwell, Karen Ackerman, Hugh Lawton, Anne Dixon, Sid Cole, Ife Okwudili and Wendy Stewart.

	VT Number	Holding / Source
23.12.2005 **Programme 82**	BRD309153	DB / DBSW

Directed by Bridget Caldwell.
(4108)* KONNIE LIGHTS FOURTH CANDLE / VIEWER'S CARDS / VT PRE-REC 12.12.05: MARY POPPINS PA 'STEP IN TIME' / APPEAL NEWS / APPEAL RECAP VT / CRIB / HANGING CANDLE DECORATION MAKE (by Gillian Shearing) / COMING SOON / PET'S CHRISTMAS PRESENTS / HARK! THE HERALD.

RM: Good programme

| 25.12.2005 **Programme 83** | BRD309194 | DB / DBSW |

Directed by Matt Gyves (Sri Lanka), Chris Godwin (Kenya), Ed Willson (Lifesaver) and Hugo Ullberger (Ryan and Frankie + Star for a Night).
With Rachel Maskell, Tommy Steele, Jennifer Ellison, Girls Aloud, Jonny Wilkinson, David Beckham, Chris Martin.
(4109)* (ALL PRESENTERS – STUDIO LINKS RX'D AM 15.12) BLUE PETER CHRISTMAS PRESENTS: RACHEL MASKELL - STAR FOR A NIGHT VT (Gethin with Tommy Steele and Jennifer Ellison) / DARREN SWAMPILLAI - SRI LANKA TSUNAMI VISIT VT (Zoe) / GEMMA FRASER - LIFESAVER VT (Matt with Girls Aloud) / RYAN AND FRANKIE GIBBONS - A TALE OF TWO BROTHERS VT (Liz with Jonny Wilkinson and David Beckham) / ELLIOT INGLIS - YOUNG CAMPAIGNER TO KENYA VT (Konnie with Chris Martin) / ALL GOLD BADGE WINNING KIDS IN STUDIO.
Film Shot: 18.11 + 01.12 (Rachel) 30.11 + 06-11.12.05 (Darren) 26.11 + 28.11 (Becks) + 09 (Jonny) + 14.12 (Two Brothers) 24-29.11 + 01.12 (Elliot) 05 + 08.12.05 (Gemma)

| 26.12.2005 | **ROCK N ROLL CHRISTMAS PSC RPT** | BRD119969 | DB / DBSW |

SERIES 50

Main regular credit(s): Presented by Konnie Huq, Zöe Salmon, Gethin Jones and Andy Akinwolere; edited by Tim Levell; deputy editor Jack Lundie; designed by Kathy Atty; production team Andy Clarke, Lucie Harvey, Becky Asprey, Tim Fransham, Debbie Martin, Richard Turley, Kara Miller, Jamie Wilson, Beckie Cooper, Rebecca McVeigh, Mark Reynaud, Shane Lindley, Iona Walters, Isabel Buxton, Oli Jones, Mary Albion and Leo Morgan; series producer Audrey Neil (to 04.08); produced by Alex Leger, Melissa Hardinge (till 12.07), Sid Cole, Ewan Vinnicombe, Dan Tucker and Catherine Gildea; pets: Mabel, Lucy Pargeter, The Shelley, Socks and Cookie.

	Holding / Source
19.12.2007 **Programme 26**	DB / DBSW

Film sequences directed by Richard Turley (Robin Hood) and Debbie Martin (Lapland); directed by Jason Garbett.
With Camilla Dallerup, All Angels, Aldo Zilli, Lucy Griffiths, Gordon Kennedy, Charlie Clements, David Tennant.

BLUE PETER (continued)

(4343)* PRE TITLES: PRESENTERS' TEXT STING / ALL FOUR ENTER TC1 PARTY STUDIO WITH AUDIENCE OF BARNARDOS YOUNG CARERS / BIG BROTHER'S SAM AND AMANDA HANDING OUT TINSEL IN CROWD / STRICTLY STUDIO DE-RIG TIME LAPSE VT + GETH THANKS VIEWERS FOR SUPPORT (with Camilla Dallerup) / KATIE'S STORY AND SURPRISE - KATIE CO-PRESENTS WITH GETH AND CHATS TO ALL ANGELS / ALL ANGELS PA 'SILENT NIGHT' WITH THE INTERNATIONAL HARP ENSEMBLE / ROBERT'S STORY AND SURPRISE - ITALIAN CHRISTMAS CAKE (with chef Aldo Zilli) / METIN AND KEALAN - THEIR STORY / ROBIN HOOD BEHIND THE SCENES VT (Konnie) / ARCHERY QUIZ COMPETITION (with Lucy Griffiths and Gordon Kennedy) - METIN IS THE WINNER / GOLD BADGE HIT VT: SERAN'S LAPLAND SURPRISE (Andy with Charlie Clements) / GUINNESS WORLD RECORD CRACKER PULLING ATTEMPT SET UP + STORY OF CRACKER VT FACT FILE / GETH AND ANDY VERSUS KONNIE AND ZOE - BOYS SET RECORD OF 34 IN A MINUTE / DISC DRIVE VT STING: DAVID TENNANT / BOOTY LOVE PA 'SANTA CLAUS IS COMING TO TOWN' / POST SHOW STING: FATHER CHRISTMAS TEXTS 'WELL DONE' TO PRESENTERS.

BLUE PETER RELATED RADIO MATERIAL

Commissioned and produced by a variety of companies (see details below). Duration varies - see below for details.

Transmission details are for BBC Radio 2.

	Holding / Source
28.12.1991 **Are You Sitting Comfortably: Christmas Special**	DA /

Duration: 27 minutes.

Written by Phil Swern and Shaun Greenfield; produced and directed by Andy Aliffe.

With Leslie Crowther (Reporter), Tommy Boyd, Patricia Driscoll, Christopher Trace.

BLUE PETER RELATED TELEVISION MATERIAL

Commissioned and produced by a variety of companies (see details below). Duration varies - see below for details.

Transmission details are for BBC 1.

	Holding / Source
28.12.1994 **The Movie Game Christmas Special**	DB / D3S

Presented by John Barrowman; produced by Chris Tandy; directed by Richard Marson.

With Diane-Louise Jordan, Tim Vincent.

Transmission details are for UK Horizons.

	VT Number	Holding / Source
24.12.1997 **A Blue Peter Christmas**	MRS144913	DB / DBSW

Commissioned by UK Horizons.

Assistant producer Sarah Downing; produced and directed by Lewis Bronze.

With Valerie Singleton (Presenter), Margaret Parnell, Diane-Louise Jordan.

This programme was made for an early satellite station that closed in 2004. The master tape was returned to the 'Blue Peter' production office who sent it to the BBC Archives. Master tape MRS144913 is accessioned and stored at TV Centre (in an overspill range there).

BLUESTONE 42

Commissioned by BBC 3. Transmission details are for BBC 3. Duration: 30 minutes.

Oliver Chris (Nick), Kelly Adams (Mary), Tony Gardner (Lieutenant Colonel), Katie Lyons (Bird), Stephen Wight (Simon).

	Holding / Source
26.12.2013	HD/DB / HDC

Postponed from 23.12.2013.

In this festive special, new team member Corporal House joins the bomb disposal detachment, but his attitude quickly gets him on the wrong side of Nick.

Written by James Cary and Richard Hurst; additional material by Nick Doody and Mark Evans; script editors Hannah Mackay and Emma Nisbet; music by Vince Pope; designed by Harry Banks; executive producer Stephen McCrum; produced by Michelle Farr; directed by Iain B. MacDonald.

With Matthew Lewis (Corporal Gordon House aka Towerblock), Scott Hoatson (Rocket), Jamie Quinn (Mac), Keeno Lee Hector (Faruq), Pierre Van Heerden (Pieter The Medic).

Originally scheduled to premiere on Monday 23rd December 2013 at 10pm, this episode was postponed due to the death of a soldier on the same day.

BO! SELECTA!

Produced for Channel 4 by a variety of companies (see details below). Transmission details are for Channel 4. Duration: 24 minutes.

Main regular credit(s): Created by Leigh Francis; developed by Leigh Francis and Ben Palmer.

Main regular cast: Leigh Francis (Avid Merrion).

SERIES 2

A Talkback Thames production.

	Holding / Source
23.12.2003 **Ho Ho Ho Selecta!**	DB / DBSW

Written by Leigh Francis and Spencer Millman; additional material by Paul Garner and Ben Palmer; music by Earshot Music [credited as Earshot]; art director Neil Barnes; designed by Richard Drew; associate producer Debi McGrath; production executive Beatrice Gay; executive producer Phil Clarke; production manager Will Cross; produced by Spencer Millman; title sequence directed by Lipsync Post; directed by Ben Palmer.

SERIES 3

	Holding / Source
28.12.2004 **A Bear Christmas Tail**	DB / DBSW

BOB AND MARGARET

A Snowden Fine Animation production for Channel 4. made in association with Global / National Film Board of Canada / Nelvana. Transmission details are for Channel 4. Duration: 25 minutes.

Main regular credit(s):	Created by Alison Snowden and David Fine; written by Alison Snowden and David Fine; executive producers Michael Hirsh, Patrick Loubert and Clive Smith; produced by Alison Snowden and David Fine; directed by Alison Snowden, David Fine and Jamie Whitney.
Main regular cast:	Andy Hamilton (Bob), Alison Snowden (Margaret).

SERIES 3

		Holding / Source
20.12.1999	The Burglary	DB /
21.12.1999	Shopping	DB /
22.12.1999	Love's Labour Lost	DB /
23.12.1999	Neighbours	DB /

Animated series.

THE BOB DOWNE SPECIAL!

A Watchmaker Productions production for Yorkshire Television. Transmission details are for the Central region. Duration: 50 minutes.

Written by Mark Trevorrow; music directed by Laurie Holloway; choreography by Brian Rogers; designed by Andy Walmsley; assistant producer Charlotte Wyatt; associate producer Vivienne Clore; executive producer Elaine Bedell; production manager Zoe Norman; produced by Martin Cunning; directed by Brian Klein.

Mark Trevorrow (Bob Downe), Ant & Dec, Anthony Newley, Martine McCutcheon, Kimberley Davies, Diana Moran, Lisa Kelly.

	Holding / Source
31.12.1996	D3 / D3S

THE BOB MONKHOUSE SHOW

A BBC production. Transmission details are for Various BBC Channels.

Main regular credit(s):	Produced by John Fisher.
Main regular cast:	Bob Monkhouse (Host).

SERIES 1

Alternative/Working Title(s): Bob Monkhouse Tonight
Commissioned by BBC 2. Transmission details are for BBC 2. Duration: 54 minutes.

Main regular credit(s):	Programme associate Neil Shand; script associates Dennis Berson and Spike Mullins; music directed by Harry Stoneham; designed by Paul Trerise.
Main regular cast:	With The Harry Stoneham Band.

	Holding / Source
25.12.1983	DB / 1"

Production manager Sue Bysh; directed by Geoff Miles.
With Norman Wisdom, Yakov Smirnoff, Bertice Reading.

BOB SAYS OPPORTUNITY KNOCKS

A BBC production for BBC 1. Transmission details are for BBC 1. Usual duration: 50 minutes.

Main regular performer(s): Bob Monkhouse (Host).

SERIES 3

Main regular credit(s):	Programme associates Colin Edmonds and John Junkin; additional material by Paul Alexander and Gavin Osbon; music directed by John Coleman; choreography by Di Cooke; programme consultant Hughie Green; designed by Garry Freeman; produced by Stewart Morris and Gavin Osbon; directed by Stewart Morris.

		Holding / Source
##.##.####	Christmas Tape	DV / 1"

BOB THE BUILDER

A Hit Entertainment production for BBC 1. Transmission details are for BBC 1.

Main regular cast: Neil Morrissey (Narrator).

SERIES 1

		Holding / Source
27.12.1999	Bob's White Christmas	DB / DB

SERIES 5

		Holding / Source
23.12.2002	A Christmas To Remember	DB / DB

SERIES 8

		Holding / Source
20.12.2004	Mr Bentley's Winter Fare	DB / DB

SERIES 10: Project Build It!

		Holding / Source
24.12.2006	Snowed Under	DB / DB

BOBBY DAVRO'S TV WEEKLY

A TVS production. Transmission details are for the Central region. Duration varies - see below for details.

Main regular cast: Bobby Davro, Jessica Martin, Alyn Ainsworth and his Orchestra.

Holding / Source
27.12.1986 Bobby Davro's TV Annual 1" / 1"
Duration: 40 minutes.
Written by Geoff Atkinson, Charlie Adams, Eric Davidson, Russel Lane, Paul Minett and Brian Leveson; designed by Quentin Chases; associate producer Alan Nixon; produced by John Kaye Cooper; directed by Nigel Lythgoe.
With No guest cast.

Holding / Source
26.12.1987 Bobby Davro's TV Annual '88 1" / 1"
Duration: 35 minutes.
Written by Paul Minett, Brian Leveson, Russel Lane and Charlie Adams; music directed by Alyn Ainsworth; choreography by Jeff Richer; produced and directed by Nigel Lythgoe.
With No guest cast.

BOB'S FULL HOUSE

A BBC production for BBC 1. Transmission details are for BBC 1. Usual duration: 35 minutes.

Main regular credit(s): Devised by Terry Mardell and David Moore; theme music by John Mealing.
Main regular performer(s): Bob Monkhouse (Host).

SERIES 1
Main regular credit(s): Programme associates Colin Edmonds and Neil Shand; designed by Paul Trerise; production manager Robert Randell; series producer Marcus Plantin; produced by John Bishop; directed by David Taylor and Tony Newman.

Production No | Holding / Source
26.12.1984 Bob's Christmas Full House | LLVG409A | DB / 1"
Duration: 35 minutes.
With John Inman, Bonnie Langford.

SERIES 2
Duration: 32 minutes.
Main regular credit(s): Programme associates Colin Edmonds and Neil Shand; production manager Andy Smith; produced by John Bishop.

Holding / Source
26.12.1985 Bob's Christmas Full House DB / 1"
Designed by John Stout; directed by David Taylor.

SERIES 3
Main regular credit(s): Programme associate Colin Edmonds; produced by Brian Whitehouse; directed by Geoff Miles.

Holding / Source
27.12.1986 Bob's Christmas Full House DB / 1"
Duration: 35 minutes.
Designed by Andrée Welstead Hornby.

SERIES 5
Main regular credit(s): Programme associates Colin Edmonds and John Junkin; additional material by Gavin Osbon and Paul Alexander; designed by Dacre Punt; production team Kathleen Reid and Jane Griffiths; production manager Simon Spencer; produced by Geoff Miles; directed by Bill Morton.

Holding / Source
24.12.1988 Bob's Christmas Full House: "Hong Kong" DB / 1"
The on-screen title omits the apostrophe in the opening credits but often includes it during the end titles.

BODGER AND BADGER

A BBC production for BBC 1. Transmission details are for BBC 1. Duration: 15 minutes.
SERIES 7

Holding / Source
16.12.1996 Mashy Christmas Everyone! DB / D3S

BOMBARDIER SECOMBE BACK AMONG THE BOYS

A BBC production for BBC 1. Transmission details are for BBC 1. Duration: 30 minutes.
Produced and directed by Kenneth Carter.
Harry Secombe, Karen Young, Johnny Ball, John Bouchier, Billy Burdon [as Billy Burden], Arthur Dakin, Tom Gilhooly, The Karlins.

Holding / Source
23.12.1969 C1 / C1

BON VIVEUR'S TELEVISION CHRISTMAS

An Associated-Rediffusion production. Transmission details are for Associated-Rediffusion. Duration: 25 minutes.

The last of three programmes in which Fanny Cradock shows how to deal with Roast Turkey and Plum Pudding without tears. She is joined by Johnny, and together they put the finishing touches and dish up the Christmas dinner.

Main regular credit(s): Produced by Rosemary Horstmann; directed by Alan Morris.

Main regular cast: Fanny Cradock (Cook), Johnny Cradock (Cook).

	Holding / Source
06.12.1956	J /
13.12.1956	J /
20.12.1956	J /

BOOBS IN THE WOOD

A BBC production. Transmission details are for BBC. Duration: 90 minutes.

Written by Ray Cooney and Tony Hilton; lyrics by Ray Cooney and Tony Hilton; music by Tommy Watt; produced by Mary Evans; directed by Wallace Douglas.

John Chapman (Sir Percival), Charles Cameron (Sir Trustworthy), Gerald Anderson (Sir Dukesbury), Peter Allenby (Baron De Colville), Basil Lord (Prince John), Peter Mercier (Baron Villiers), Moray Watson (First Player), Carole Shelley (Gwenny), Brian Rix (Oswald Irving), Leo Franklyn (Algernon Capone), Andrew Sachs (An Auld Scots Prisoner), Tony Hilton (Montgomery), Ray Cooney (Alexander), John Slater (Sergeant), Sheila Mercier (Nanny), Larry Noble (Woodman), Garth Adams (King Richard), Judie Mant (Dancer), Doreen Crann (Dancer), David Spurling (Dancer), Keith Galloway (Dancer).

	Holding / Source
26.12.1960	J /

THE BOOK PROGRAMME

A BBC production for BBC 2. Transmission details are for BBC 2. Duration: 30 minutes.

Main regular cast: Robert Robinson (Presenter).

	Holding / Source
23.12.1976 **Christmas Books 1876**	DB / 2"

Robert Robinson introduces a special edition looking back to the books published 100 years ago – the new Lewis Carroll, George Eliot's latest, new verse from the Poet Laureate Alfred, Lord Tennyson, and a collection of hit songs Boudoir Ballads.

Executive producer Will Wyatt; produced by Philip Speight; studio sequences directed by Martin L. Bell.

With David Bellamy, Margaret Powell.

20.12.1977 **Christmas Quiz**	DB-D3 / 2"

Literary quiz.

Produced by Philip Speight; studio sequences directed by Tony Tyley.

BOOKMARK

A BBC production for BBC 2. Transmission details are for BBC 2. Duration varies - see below for details.

	Holding / Source
25.12.1993 **Selected Exits**	DB / C1S

A BBC Wales production for BBC 1 Wales. Duration: 70 minutes.

Alternative transmissions: BBC 1 Wales: 25.12.1993.

Written by Alan Plater; produced by Geraint Morris; directed by Tristram Powell.

With Anthony Hopkins (Gwyn Thomas), Sue Roderick (Lyn Thomas), Robert Pugh (Gwyn's Father), Brendan O'Hea (Gwyn At 18), Gavin Rhys Ashcroft (Gwyn At 13), Bernard Lloyd (Walt Thomas Sr), Richard Lynch (Walt Thomas Jr), Abigail Harrison (Nana Thomas), John Grillo (Doctor Bronowski), Alan David (Headmaster), Rowena Cooper (Mrs Morris), Ian McDiarmid (George Devine).

25.12.1996 **Saint-Ex**	DB-D3 / V1S

A BBC Films production. Duration: 80 minutes.

Written by Frank Cottrell Boyce; produced and directed by Anand Tucker.

With Bruno Ganz (Antoine de Saint-Exupery), Miranda Richardson (Consuelo), Janet McTeer (Genevieve de Ville-Franche), Ken Stott (Prevot), Eleanor Bron (Marie), Katrin Cartlidge (Gabrielle), Brid Brennan (Simone), Karl Johnson (Didier), Daniel Craig (Guillaumet), Dominic Rowan (Aeropostale Clerk), Anna Calder-Marshall (Moisy), Aidan Cottrell Boyce (Young Antoine), Joe Cottrell Boyce (François), Alex Kingston (Chic Party Guest), Lucy Abigale Kent (Young Simone), Hannah Taylor Gordon (Young Gabrielle).

BOON

Alternative/Working Title(s): ANYTHING LEGAL CONSIDERED / BOX 13

A Central production. Transmission details are for the Central region. Duration varies - see below for details.

Main regular credit(s): Created by Jim Hill and Bill Stair; theme music by Jim Diamond and Chris Parren.

Main regular cast: Michael Elphick (Ken Boon), David Daker (Harry Crawford).

SERIES 7

Main regular credit(s): Script editors Julian Murphy and Vicky Featherstone; music by Dean Friedman and David Mackay; executive producer Ted Childs; produced by Simon Lewis.

Main regular cast: With Neil Morrissey (Rocky Cassidy), Elizabeth Carling (Laura Marsh).

	VT Number	Holding / Source
24.12.1991 **The Night Before Christmas**	6253/91	1" / 1"

Duration: 78 minutes.

Written by Peter Palliser; directed by John Woods.

With Jill Gascoine, Peter Vaughan, Alfred Molina, Clarke Peters, Dave Hill, Marcia Warren, P. P. Arnold, Geff Francis, Christina Greatrex, Garry Cooper, Maggie McCarthy.

BOON (continued)

THE BOOZE CRUISE II: THE TREASURE HUNT

A Granada Yorkshire production for ITV 1. made in association with Water Lane Productions. Transmission details are for the Central region. Duration: 92 minutes.

Written by Paul Minett and Brian Leveson; script supervisor Sam Warner; music by Jim Parker; designed by Sue Booth; executive producers Tim Hancock and David Reynolds; produced by Roy Gould; directed by Paul Seed.

Neil Pearson (Rob), Mark Benton (Dave), Brian Murphy (Maurice), Anne Reid (Grace), Karen Henthorn (Cath), Amanda Abbington (Leone), Ian Richardson (Marcus), Suzy Cooper (Jackie), Irene Sutcliffe (Elsie), Tom Bennett (Daniel), Jason Watkins (Laurence), Louise Callaghan (Chloe), Phoebe Thomas (Sally), Jalaal Hartley (Dominic), Emily Wachter (Clare), Alison Kahn (Alison), David Semark (Police Inspector), Larissa Murray (Tess), Stefan Welclawek (Carl), Ricky Nixon (Kev), Scott Worsfold (Detective), Vikky Evans-Hubbard (Hotel Receptionist), John Banfield (Night Porter), Sophie Wright (Barmaid), Maria Gough (Hospital Receptionist).

	Holding / Source
25.12.2005	DB / V1SW

BORGE PRESENTS BORGE

A Thames Television production. Transmission details are for the Thames Television region. Duration: 50 minutes.

Devised by Victor Borge; written by Victor Borge; music associate Syd Dale; orchestra conducted by Ronnie Aldrich; designed by Harry Clark; produced and directed by Peter Frazer-Jones.

Victor Borge (Host).

	Holding / Source
24.12.1968	R1SEQ / 62

BORN AND BRED

Alternative/Working Title(s): HEART OF THE VALLEY
A BBC production for BBC 1. Transmission details are for BBC 1.

Main regular credit(s): Created by Chris Chibnall and Nigel McCrery.

Main regular cast: Jenna Russell (Deborah Gilder), Maggie Steed (Phyllis Woolf), Clive Swift (Reverend Brewer), Donald Gee (Mr Boynton), John Henshaw (Wilf Bradshaw), Tracey Childs (Linda Cosgrove), Peter Gunn (Len Cosgrove), Naomi Radcliffe (Jean Bradshaw).

SERIES 2
Duration: 60 minutes.
Main regular credit(s): Executive producers Simon Lewis and Susan Hogg; produced by Chris Clough.
Main regular cast: With James Bolam (Arthur Gilder), Michael French (Tom Gilder), Charlotte Salt (Helen Gilder), Samuel Hudson (Eddie Mills), Polly Thompson (Catherine Gilder), Ross Little (Michael Gilder), Jenna Russell (Deborah Gilder).

	Holding / Source
21.12.2003 **A Very Ormston Christmas**	DB / V1SW

Written by Chris Chibnall; directed by Simon Massey.

With Stephanie Cole, Una Stubbs, John Forgeham, George Yiasoumi, Joan Worswick, Shirley White, Danielle da Costa, Nicola Jane Reading, Evan Fortescue.

THE BORROWERS

Commissioned by BBC 1. Transmission details are for BBC 1. Duration: 90 minutes.

Adapted by Ben Vanstone; based on a book by Mary Norton; produced by Radford Neville; directed by Tom Harper.

Christopher Eccleston (Pod), Sharon Horgan (Homily Clock), Aisling Loftus (Arrietty Clock), Robert Sheehan (Spiller), Victoria Wood (Granny Driver), Stephen Fry (Professor Mildeye), Shaun Dooley (Robert Millman), Charlie Hiscock (James), Anne Hirsch (Jenny), Warona Seane (Dean Karen Richards).

	Holding / Source
26.12.2011	HD/DB / HDC

BOTTOM

A BBC production for BBC 2. Transmission details are for BBC 2. Duration: 30 minutes.
Main regular credit(s): Written by Rik Mayall and Adrian Edmondson; theme music by Chips Moman.
Main regular cast: Rik Mayall (Richie Richard), Adrian Edmondson (Eddie Hitler).
SERIES 2
Main regular credit(s): Produced and directed by Ed Bye.

	Holding / Source
29.10.1992 **Holy**	DB-D3 / D3S

THE BOX OF DELIGHTS (RADIO)

A BBC production for BBC Home Service. Transmission details are for BBC Home Service. Duration: 90 minutes.

Adapted by John Keir Cross; based on a book by John Masefield; play production by David Davis.

Harman Grisewood (Kay Harker As A Man), Patricia Hayes (Kay Harker As A Boy), Cyril Shaps (Cole Hawlings), Henry Stamper (Foxy-Faced Man), Wilfred Babbage (Chubby Man), Carol Marsh (Miss Caroline Louisa), Noël Hood (Lady of the Ring), Jo Manning Wilson (Maria Jones), Sian Davies (Susan Jones), Eva Haddon (Peter Jones), Preston Lockwood (The Bishop), Felix Felton (Abner Brown), Norman Shelley (Rat), Stanley Unwin (Alf Rat), Hector Ross (Police Inspector), Joan Matheson (Sylvia Daisy Pouncer).

	Holding / Source
24.12.1966	J /

THE BOX OF DELIGHTS (RADIO)

A BBC production for BBC Radio 4. Transmission details are for BBC Radio 4. Duration: 90 minutes.

Main regular credit(s): Adapted by John Peacock; based on a book by John Masefield; music by Neil Brand; produced and directed by David Blount.

Main regular cast: Alastair Sooke (Kay Harker), Donald Sinden (Abner Brown), Lionel Jeffries (Cole Hawlings), Benjamin Guy (Peter), Kimberley Staines (Maria), Elisa Mason (Jemima), Holly Vote (Susan), Celia Imrie (Sylvia Daisy Pouncer), Simon Treves, David Holt, Geoffrey Matthews, David March, Chris Emmett, Gavin Muir, Richard Tate, Sandra James-Young, Jane Whittenshaw, Jill Graham, David Collings, Jonathan Keeble, Paul Jenkins, John Hartley, Zulema Dene, Roger May.

	Holding / Source
26.12.1995 **Part One**	DA /
27.12.1995 **Part Two**	DA /

With Spike Milligan (Arnold of Todi).

THE BOX OF DELIGHTS

A BBC production for BBC 1. made in association with Lella Productions plc. Transmission details are for BBC 1. Duration: 30 minutes.

Main regular credit(s): Adapted by Alan Seymour; based on a book by John Masefield; music by Roger Limb; designed by Bruce Macadie and David Buckingham; associate producer John Bird; production manager Tony Guyan; produced by Paul Stone; directed by Renny Rye.

Main regular cast: Devin Stanfield (Kay Harker), Robert Stephens (Abner Brown), Geoffrey Larder (Foxy Faced Charles), Jonathan Stephens (Chubby Joe), Flora Page (Susan), Joanna Dukes (Maria).

Holding / Source

19.11.1984 **When The Wolves Were Running** — DB / 1"
With Patrick Troughton (Cole Hawlings), Carol Frazer (Caroline Louisa), Bill Wallis (Rat), Crispin Mair (Peter), Glyn Baker (Herne The Hunter), Anne Dyson (The Old Lady), Heidi Burton (Jemima), John Horsley (The Bishop of Tatchester), Helen Fraser (Ellen), Johnny Cassino (Old Jim), Len Edwards, Stephen Lurcock.

26.11.1984 **Where Shall The 'nighted Showman Go?** — DB / 1"
With Patrick Troughton (Cole Hawlings), James Grout (Inspector), Glyn Baker (Herne The Hunter), Crispin Mair (Peter), Heidi Burton (Jemima), Helen Fraser (Ellen), Simon Barry (Mouse), Stewart Harwood (Pirate Rat), Nick Berry (Pirate Rat).

03.12.1984 **In Darkest Cellars Underneath** — DB / 1"
With Patricia Quinn (Sylvia Daisy Pouncer), James Grout (Inspector), Bill Wallis (Rat), Carol Frazer (Caroline Louisa), Anne Dyson (The Old Lady), John Horsley (The Bishop of Tatchester), Glyn Baker (Herne The Hunter), Crispin Mair (Peter), Heidi Burton (Jemima), Helen Fraser (Ellen), Simon Barry (Mouse), Paul Wilce (Alf), Nick Berry (Pirate Rat), Stewart Harwood (Pirate Rat), Joyce Latham, Bryan Matheson.

10.12.1984 **The Spider In The Web** — DB / 1"
With Patricia Quinn (Sylvia Daisy Pouncer), James Grout (Inspector), Carol Frazer (Caroline Louisa), Crispin Mair (Peter), Helen Fraser (Ellen), Johnny Cassino (Old Jim), Gordon Coulson.

17.12.1984 **Beware Of Yesterday** — DB / 1"
With Patricia Quinn (Sylvia Daisy Pouncer), James Grout (Inspector), Charles Pemberton (Chief Constable), Glyn Baker (Herne The Hunter), John Horsley (The Bishop of Tatchester), Carol Frazer (Caroline Louisa), Heidi Burton (Jemima), Jason Kemp (Waterfall Boy), Philip Locke, Bruce White, Julian Sands, Angus Kennedy.

24.12.1984 **Leave Us Not Little, Nor Yet Dark** — DB / 1"
With Patrick Troughton (Cole Hawlings), Patricia Quinn (Sylvia Daisy Pouncer), John Horsley (The Bishop of Tatchester), Carol Frazer (Caroline Louisa), James Grout (Inspector), Crispin Mair (Peter), Heidi Burton (Jemima), Jason Kemp (Waterfall Boy), Charles Pemberton (Chief Constable), Glyn Baker (Herne The Hunter), Anne Dyson (The Old Lady), Nicholas Chagrin, Dave Mitty, Michael Lewis, Ben Gallagher, Ben Leak, Hereford Cathedral Choir.

BOXPOPS

A BBC production for BBC 2. Transmission details are for BBC 2.

SERIES 2

Holding / Source

24.12.1989 **Christmas** — DB / 1"

THE BOY AND THE THRUSH

An Associated-Rediffusion production. Transmission details are for Associated-Rediffusion.

Holding / Source

24.12.1959 — NR / Live

BOY MEETS GIRLS

An ABC production. Transmission details are for the ABC midlands region. Duration: 25 minutes.

Main regular credit(s): Written by Trevor Peacock; music directed by Bill Shepherd; dance direction by Leslie Cooper; produced by Jack Good.

Main regular performer(s): Marty Wilde (Host), Cherry Warner, Don Storer, The Vernon Girls, Red Price, Jack Good's Firing Squad.

Holding / Source

26.12.1959 — J /
Designed by Voytek; directed by Ben Churchill.
With Gene Vincent, Little Tony, Janet Richmond.

BRACE YOURSELF SYDNEY

A Wonderdog Productions production for Channel 4. Transmission details are for Channel 4. Duration: 40 minutes.
Written by Julian Clary; produced by Elaine Morris; directed by John Henderson.
Julian Clary (Host), Warren Mitchell, Danny La Rue, Craig McLachlan.

Holding / Source

28.12.1993 — D3 / D3S

BRAMBLY HEDGE

A BBC production for BBC 1. Transmission details are for BBC 1. Duration: 23 minutes.

Main regular cast: Robert Lindsay (Narrator), Jim Broadbent (Voices), Charlotte Coleman (Voices), Noreen Kershaw (Voices), Rosemary Leach (Voices), Alun Lewis (Voices), Neil Morrissey (Voices), June Whitfield (Voices), Michael Williams (Voices).

		Holding / Source
25.12.1996	Winter Story	DB-D3 / C1

BREAD

A BBC production for BBC 1. Transmission details are for BBC 1. Duration varies - see below for details.

Main regular credit(s): Written by Carla Lane; theme music by David Mackay and Carla Lane.

Main regular cast: Jean Boht (Mrs Nellie Boswell).

SERIES 4

Main regular credit(s): Designed by Paul Trerise; produced and directed by Robin Nash.

Main regular cast: With Nick Conway (Billy Boswell), Peter Howitt (Joey Boswell), Jonathon Morris (Adrian), Bryan Murray (Shifty), Gilly Coman (Aveline Boswell), Kenneth Waller (Grandad), Ronald Forfar (Freddie Boswell).

		Holding / Source
25.12.1988	"Off to Rome on holiday"	DB / 1"

Duration: 65 minutes.
With Pamela Power (Martina), Hilary Crowson (Julie), Rita Tushingham (Celia Higgins), Eileen Pollock (Lilo Lill), Giles Watling (Oswald), Joanna Phillips-Lane (Roxy), James Culshaw, Patricia Martinelli, Nick Maloney, David Monico, Lia Williams.

SERIES 5

Main regular credit(s): Designed by Richard Dupré; produced and directed by Robin Nash.

Main regular cast: With Jonathon Morris (Adrian Boswell), Nick Conway (Billy Boswell), Graham Bickley (Joey Boswell), Melanie Hill (Aveline Boswell), Ronald Forfar (Mr Boswell), Kenneth Waller (Grandad).

		Holding / Source
25.12.1989	"A Quiet Ecological Christmas"	DB / 1"

Duration: 50 minutes.
With Victor McGuire (Jack), Hilary Crowson (Julie), Giles Watling (Oswald), Bryan Murray (Shifty), Joanna Phillips-Lane (Roxy), Eileen Pollock (Lilo Lill), Pamela Power (Martina), Peter Byrne, Bernard Merrick, David Williams, Jennifer Moss.

SERIES 6

Main regular credit(s): Produced and directed by John B. Hobbs.

Main regular cast: With Jonathon Morris (Adrian Boswell), Melanie Hill (Aveline), Nick Conway (Billy Boswell), Ronald Forfar (Mr Boswell), Graham Bickley (Joey Boswell), Victor McGuire (Jack Boswell), Kenneth Waller (Grandad).

	Holding / Source
25.12.1990	DB / 1"

Duration: 50 minutes.
With Bryan Murray (Shifty), Deborah Grant (Leonora Campbell), Eileen Pollock (Lilo Lill), Giles Watling (Oswald), Peter Byrne, Sharon Byatt, Pamela Powers, Sylvia Gatrill, Lesley-Anne Sharpe, Carl Griffiths, Andrew Hilton, Peter Colligan, Gary McKenna, Guy Bradley, Susanna Page, Jonathan Deverell.

BREAK IN FESTIVITIES

A BBC production. Transmission details are for BBC. Duration: 45 minutes.
Written by A. C. Thomas; play production by Terence Dudley.
Elizabeth Orion (Dorothy Mullins), Corinne Skinner (Susie), Harry Baird (Bill), Meriel Hobson (Mrs Killick), Joseph Wise (Charlie Townsend), Rita Webb (Mrs Wells), Daphne Cave (Gwen Stephens), Raymond Mason (George Mullins), Bart Allison (Harris), Gordon Harris (Roy Elliott), Julie Paul (Shirley Elliott), Arthur Goullet (Lister), John Barcroft (Clerk).

	Holding / Source
29.12.1959	J /

BREAKFAST TIME

A BBC production for BBC 1. Transmission details are for BBC 1.

	Holding / Source
20.12.1983	DB-1" / Live

With Rod Hull and Emu.

| 20.12.1984 | DB-1" / Live |

With Rod Hull and Emu.

BREMNER, BIRD AND FORTUNE

A Vera production for Channel 4. Transmission details are for Channel 4. Usual duration: 50 minutes.

Main regular cast: Rory Bremner (Various Roles), John Bird (Various Roles), John Fortune (Various Roles).

SERIES 3

		Holding / Source
31.12.2001	Geoffrey Malet A Hero Of Our Time	DB / DBSW

THE BRETTS

A Central production. Transmission details are for the Central region. Usual duration: 50 minutes.

Main regular credit(s):	Created by Rosemary Anne Sisson and Frank Marshall.
Main regular cast:	Norman Rodway (Charles Brett), Barbara Murray (Lydia Brett), David Yelland (Edwin Brett), Belinda Lang (Martha Brett), George Winter (Thomas Brett).

SERIES 1

Main regular credit(s):	Executive producers Ted Childs, Colin Callender and Frank Marshall; produced by Tony Charles.
Main regular cast:	With Tim Wylton (Sutton), Rhoda Lewis (Flora).

Holding / Source

27.12.1987 **Grand Finale**   1" / 1"

Faced with the disastrous fire at the Princess, the Bretts pull together to keep the show on the road — and what could be more appealing at Christmas than the Brett family pantomime?

Written by Rosemary Anne Sisson; directed by John Bruce.

With Frank Middlemass (George Brett), Billy Boyle (Hegarty), Rebecca Lacey (Emily), Sally Cookson (Perdita), Charles Collingwood (John Caldwell), Victoria Burton (Nell Caldwell), Jane Downs, Helena McCarthy, Daniel Hill, Colin Jeavons, Kate Dorning, Juliette Fleming, Simon Snellings, Aidan Hamilton, Paul Valler.

THE BRIAN CONLEY SHOW

An LWT production. Transmission details are for the Central region.

Main regular credit(s):	Executive producer John Kaye Cooper.
Main regular performer(s):	Brian Conley.

SERIES 4

Duration: 37 minutes.

Main regular credit(s):	Produced by Nigel Lythgoe; directed by Ian Hamilton.

	Production No	Holding / Source
22.07.1995 **Christmas Special**	3112	D2 / D2S

With Gerry Marsden, Mike Pender, Shania Twain, Domino, John Sachs.

... shown in July!

See also: BRIAN CONLEY'S CRAZY CHRISTMAS

BRIAN CONLEY'S CRAZY CHRISTMAS

A Talent TV Production production for Carlton. Transmission details are for the Central region. Duration: 50 minutes.

Written by Paul Minett, Brian Leveson, Mike Pugh and Brian Conley; additional material by Paul Tibby, Mark Simms and Adam Bostock-Smith; executive producer John Bishop; produced by John Kaye Cooper; directed by Pati Marr.

Brian Conley, Gareth Marks, Suzy Aitchison, Eternal, Ken Andrew.

Holding / Source

23.12.1997   DB / DBS

See also: THE BRIAN CONLEY SHOW

BRING IN THE NEW

A TVS production. Transmission details are for the TVS region. Duration: 25 minutes.

Executive producer Beverley Smith; directed by John Gorman.

Chris Pollard, Vyvyan Mackeson, Pestalozzi School Choir, John Doyle, Fred Dinenage, Trevor Baker.

Holding / Source

01.01.1982   DB / 1"

The end part of the 1" tape also includes an "ITN News" off air during the day, with Trevor McDonald with reports of the new ITV stations. There is also some of the raw inserts to "Bring in the New". This 1" tape was archived to Digibeta and is held by the Wessex Archives on Tape TVS214. The tape must be titled "Bring in the New" which doesn't give much clue that it also includes the station's first start-up.

BRING ME SUNSHINE - A TRIBUTE TO ERIC MORECAMBE, OBE

A Thames Television production. Transmission details are for the Central region. Duration: 125 minutes.

Introduced by Ernie Wise; written by Barry Cryer and Sid Colin; consultant Billy Marsh; designed by Peter Le Page; executive producers Philip Jones and Louis Benjamin; produced for the stage by Robert Nesbitt; directed by Mark Stuart.

Michael Aspel, Lionel Blair, Leslie Crowther, Dickie Davies, Bertice Reading, Wayne Sleep, Kenny Ball, Alison Bell, Max Bygraves, Cannon and Ball, James Casey, Roy Castle, Petula Clark, Barry Cryer, Suzanne Danielle, Jim Davidson, Frank Finlay, Bruce Forsyth, Jill Gascoine, Cherry Gillespie, Hannah Gordon, The Half Wits, Susan Hampshire, Dickie Henderson, Benny Hill, Diane Keen, Bonnie Langford, Lulu, Francis Matthews, Fulton Mackay, Nanette Newman, Des O'Connor, Mick Oliver, Elaine Paige, Michael Parkinson, Angela Rippon, Jimmy Tarbuck, John Thaw, The Tiller Girls, Arthur Tolcher, Bryn Williams, Eli Woods, Mike Yarwood, The Irving Davies Dancers, The Stephen Hill Singers.

Holding / Source

25.12.1984   1" / 1"

BRITAIN SINGS CHRISTMAS

An Initial Film & TV production for ITV 1. Transmission details are for the Central region. Duration varies - see below for details.

Main regular credit(s): Script supervisor Suzanne Baron; theme music by Cliff Masterson; music by David Grant and Carrie Grant; designed by Chris Webster; assistant producer Marcus English; production executive Jo Boylan; executive producer Anouk Fontaine; series producer Sophie Wainwright; produced and directed by Sam Eastall; studio sequences directed by Simon Staffurth.

Main regular performer(s): Kate Thornton (Host), Royal Philharmonic Orchestra.

Holding / Source

10.12.2007 **1**   DB / DBSW
Duration: 24 minutes.

22.12.2007 **2**   DB / DBSW
Duration: 48 minutes.
With Gaby Roslin, Jo Brand, Craig Doyle, Claire Goose, Kim Wilde.

BRITAIN'S FAVOURITE CHRISTMAS SONGS

A North One Television production for Channel 5. Transmission details are for Channel 5. Duration: 150 minutes.

Even those who dismiss seasonal songs as festive cheese are bound to find something to hum along to as some of the best known tunes are recalled, from the Jackson 5's Santa Claus Is Coming to Town and Mud's Lonely This Christmas to Jona Lewie's Stop the Cavalry, Greg Lake's I Believe in Father Christmas, the Pogues and Kirsty MacColl's Fairytale of New York and the Waitresses' Christmas Wrapping. Plus there's a look at how the songs and their accompanying videos were created.

Archive producer Andy Rossiter; consultants Kaleidoscope and Christopher Perry; executive producer John Quinn.

Holding / Source

25.12.2011   DB / DBSW

THE BRITTAS EMPIRE

A BBC production for BBC 1. Transmission details are for BBC 1. Duration: 30 minutes.

Main regular credit(s): Created by Richard Fegen and Andrew Norriss; theme music by Frank Renton; produced by Mike Stephens.

Main regular cast: Chris Barrie (Gordon Brittas), Tim Marriott (Gavin), Russell Porter (Tim), Pippa Haywood (Helen), Jill Greenacre (Linda), Mike Burns (Colin), Harriet Thorpe (Carole Parkinson).

SERIES 5

Main regular credit(s): Written by Richard Fegen and Andrew Norriss; directed by Mike Stephens.

Main regular cast: With Julia St. John (Laura), Judy Flynn (Julie).

Holding / Source

27.12.1994 **In The Beginning...**   DB-D3 / 1"S
Designed by John Bristow; production manager Garrie Mallen.
With Mark Gillis, Eddy Lemare, Walter Hepworth-Lewis.

SERIES 6

Main regular credit(s): Directed by Mike Stephens.

Main regular cast: With Judy Flynn (Julie).

Holding / Source

24.12.1996 **Surviving Christmas**   DB / D3S
Duration: 29 minutes.
Written by Tony Millan and Mike Walling; designed by John Bristow.
With Jeffery Dench, Mark Arden, Matthew Morgan.

BROOKSIDE

A Mersey TV production for Channel 4. Transmission details are for Channel 4. Usual duration: 25 minutes.

Main regular credit(s): Devised by Phil Redmond.

Holding / Source

21.12.1982 "Christmas Eve parties spell trouble for Lucy and Karen"   1"|n / 1"
Written by Andy Lynch; designed by Leigh Malone; executive producer Phil Redmond; produced by Nicholas Prosser; directed by Chris Lovett.

With Sue Johnston (Sheila Grant), Paul Usher (Barry Grant), Simon O'Brien (Damon Grant), Shelagh O'Hara (Karen Grant), Rob Spendlove (Roger Huntingdon), Amanda Burton (Heather Huntingdon), Jim Wiggins (Paul Collins), Doreen Sloane (Annabelle Collins), Nigel Rowley (Gordon Collins), Katrin Cartlidge (Lucy Collins), Christopher Wild (Jeff Bacon), Paul Green (Terry Rawlings), Mark Birch (Ducksie Brown), Robert T. Cullen (Gizzmo Hawkins), Ian Donnelly (Tim), Christopher Lord (Tony), Jeffrey Hooson (Joey), Dean Williams (George), Tom Branch (Jonah Jones), Asia Dualey (Janet Carver), Deanna Brown (Marie McGovern), Norman Gregory (Derek Hobbs), Elizabeth Mickery (Angela Hobbs), Tony Newbury (Jack Turner), Ronald Leak (Managemant Man), David Williams (Alan Torrenson), David Miller (Stan Broadbent), Beti Lloyd-Jones (Julia Broadbent).

22.12.1982 "Christmas Day"   1"|n / 1"
Written by Allan Swift; designed by Leigh Malone; executive producer Phil Redmond; produced by Nicholas Prosser; directed by Chris Lovett.

With Sue Johnston (Sheila Grant), Paul Usher (Barry Grant), Simon O'Brien (Damon Grant), Shelagh O'Hara (Karen Grant), Rob Spendlove (Roger Huntingdon), Amanda Burton (Heather Huntingdon), Jim Wiggins (Paul Collins), Doreen Sloane (Annabelle Collins), Nigel Rowley (Gordon Collins), Katrin Cartlidge (Lucy Collins), Christopher Wild (Jeff Bacon), Paul Green (Terry Rawlings), Mark Birch (Ducksie Brown), Robert T. Cullen (Gizzmo Hawkins), Ian Donnelly (Tim), Christopher Lord (Tony), Jeffrey Hooson (Joey), Dean Williams (George), Tom Branch (Jonah Jones), Asia Dualey (Janet Carver), Deanna Brown (Marie McGovern), Norman Gregory (Derek Hobbs), Elizabeth Mickery (Angela Hobbs), Tony Newbury (Jack Turner), Ronald Leak (Managemant Man), David Williams (Alan Torrenson), David Miller (Stan Broadbent), Beti Lloyd-Jones (Julia Broadbent).

| British Christmas Television Guide | BROOKSIDE (continued) |

20.12.1983 "Marie meets Father Christmas in the casualty ward" 1"|n / 1"
Written by Andrew Lynch; designed by Carol Sheeran; executive producer Phil Redmond; produced by Nicholas Prosser; directed by Peter Boisseau.
With Ricky Tomlinson (Bobby Grant), Sue Johnston (Sheila Grant), Paul Usher (Barry Grant), Amanda Burton (Heather Huntington), Anna Keaveney (Marie Jackson), Cliff Howells (George Jackson), Janet Rawson (Polly), Brian Regan (Terry), David Ross (Father Christmas), Simon Molloy (Mr Hulme), Bert Gaunt (Sid Huntington), Tim Barker (Trevor Johnson), Tony Scoggo (Matty Nolan).

24.12.1984 "Christmas Eve. Annabelle's catering is hijacked. Sheila is rushed to hospital" 1"|n / 1"
Written by Andy Lynch; designed by Carol Sheeran; directed by Bob Carlton.
With Doreen Sloane (Annabelle Collins), Jim Wiggins (Paul Collins), Betty Alberge (Edna Cross), Bill Dean (Harold Cross), Ricky Tomlinson (Bobby Grant), Sue Johnston (Sheila Grant), Paul Usher (Barry Grant), Simon O'Brien (Damon Grant), Shelagh O'Hara (Karen Grant), Anna Keaveney (Marie Jackson), Allan Patterson (Gary Jackson), Steven Patterson (Little George Jackson), Tracey Jay (Michelle Jones), Paul Beringer (Andrew), Stuart Organ (Kevin Cross), Ray Dunbobbin (Ralph Hardwick), Tony Scoggo (Matty Nolan), Ann Haydn Edwards (Teresa Nolan), Brian Regan (Terry Sullivan).

22.12.1986 "Billy gets an unexpected Christmas present. Harry is worried by Santa Claus" 1"|n / 1"
Written by John Oakden; executive producer Phil Redmond; produced by Stuart Doughty; directed by Peter Boisseau.
With Doreen Sloane (Annabelle Collins), Jim Wiggins (Paul Collins), John McArdle (Billy Corkhill), Kate Fitzgerald (Doreen Corkhill), Jason Hope (Rod Corkhill), Justine Kerrigan (Tracy Corkhill), Bill Dean (Harry Cross), Ray Dunbobbin (Ralph Hardwick), Ricky Tomlinson (Bobby Grant), Sue Johnston (Sheila Grant), Simon O'Brien (Damon Grant), David Easter (Pat Hancock), Brian Regan (Terry Sullivan), Mark Burgess (Gordon Collins), Dean Sullivan (Jimmy Corkhill), Valerie Blake (Gail), Paul Usher (Barry Grant), Shelagh O'Hara (Karen Grant), Joanne Black (Kirsty), Tony Scoggo (Matty Nolan), Shirley Stelfox (Madge Richmond), William Maxwell (Jack Sullivan).

23.12.1994 "Is Barry Grant coming back for Christmas?" 1"|n / 1"
In the early months production was credited to Brookside Productions Ltd. Kaleidoscope is not sure when that ceased and the name Mersey TV was adopted.

THE BROTHERS

A BBC production for BBC 1. Transmission details are for BBC 1. Duration: 50 minutes.

Main regular credit(s): Devised by Gerard Glaister and N. J. Crisp.

SERIES 7
Main regular credit(s): Script editor Cicely Cawthorne; produced by Bill Sellars.
Main regular cast: With Jean Anderson (Mary Hammond), Richard Easton (Brian Hammond), Robin Chadwick (David Hammond), Jennifer Wilson (Jennifer Hammond), Colin Baker (Paul Merroney), Liza Goddard (April Merroney), Norah Fulton (Mrs Merroney), Margaret Ashcroft (Gwen Riley), Derek Benfield (Bill Riley), Kate O'Mara (Jane Maxwell).

Holding / Source
19.12.1976 The Christmas Party DB-D3 / 2"
Written by N. J. Crisp; directed by Mary Ridge.
With Penelope Horner, Robin Langford, Julia Goodman.

BRUCE AND RONNIE

A BBC production for BBC 1. Transmission details are for BBC 1. Duration: 45 minutes.
Written by Barry Cryer, Ian Davidson, Spike Mullins, Laurie Rowley, Peter Vincent and Dick Vosburgh; script associates Barry Cryer and Peter Vincent; music directed by Don Hunt; choreography by Jeff Richer; designed by Donal Woods; production manager Sylvie Boden; produced and directed by Marcus Mortimer.
Bruce Forsyth (Host), Ronnie Corbett (Host), Fiona Fullerton, Mitch Dalton, Fiona Hendley, Jon Iles, Andre Messeder, Barry Morgan, Bobby Valentino, Jeff Richer Dancers.

Holding / Source
26.12.1988 DB / 1"

THE BRUCE FORSYTH SHOW

An ABC production. Transmission details are for the ABC midlands region. Duration: 50 minutes.
Main regular performer(s): Bruce Forsyth (Host).

| | VT Number | Holding / Source |
25.12.1965 TR5216 R1N / 40
Written by S. C. Green and R. M. Hills; designed by Neville Green; produced and directed by Philip Jones.
With Cilla Black, The Morgan James Duo, Miriam Karlin, Jack Douglas, Francis Matthews, Ann Hamilton, Josephine Blake, Aleta Morrison, Johnny Shack, Bob Sharples and his ABC Television Showband.

BRUCE FORSYTH'S BIG NIGHT

An LWT production. Transmission details are for the ATV midlands region. Duration varies - see below for details.
Main regular credit(s): Programme associates Barry Cryer, Garry Chambers, Colin Bostock-Smith, David Renwick and Andrew Marshall; research Charles Brand and Pamela Portugall; music associates Don Hunt and Trevor Brown; choreography by Brian Rogers and Ken Warwick; designed by Bill McPherson, Michael Oxley and Quentin Chases; executive producer David Bell; produced by Richard Drewett.
Main regular performer(s): Bruce Forsyth (Host), Anthea Redfern (Hostess), Alyn Ainsworth and his Orchestra, The Thirty Two Feet [as Thirty-Two Feet], The Third Kind.

| | Production No | Holding / Source |
24.12.1978 Bruce Forsyth's Christmas Eve 9L/99465 D2 / 2"
Duration: 104 minutes.
Programme associates Garry Chambers, David Renwick, Colin Bostock-Smith, Dennis Berson and Andrew Marshall; graphics by Peter Johnson and Ron Pearce; costume Brenda Fox and Barbara Painter; make-up Rosemary Field; lighting by John Fyfe; sound Vic Finch and Graham Hix; camera supervisor Tony Maynard; production manager Myra Hersh; directed by John Kaye Cooper, David Crossman and David Bell.
With Kenny Everett, Pat Jennings, John Conteh, Rod Hull and Emu, Diana Dors, Kenny Lynch, Cannon and Ball, The Carpenters.

Beat the Goalie devised by Hannes Schmidt.

Alan Ravenscroft produced the Pam Ayres sequences. Part way through the run, some ITV regions took THE WORKER segments as a separate programme earlier

BRUCE FORSYTH'S BIG NIGHT (continued)

in the evening. Others continued to bill it as part of BIG NIGHT. How this worked is presently unfathomable.
See also: CANNON AND BALL / THE GLUMS

BRUCE FORSYTH'S PLAY YOUR CARDS RIGHT

An LWT production. made in association with Goodson Todman Productions / Talbot TV Ltd. Transmission details are for the Central region. Duration: 25 minutes.
Main regular performer(s): Bruce Forsyth (Presenter).

Holding / Source

25.12.1982 — D2 / 1"
Duration: 30 minutes.
Designed by Richard Dunn; associate producer Dennis Berson; produced and directed by Alasdair MacMillan.
With Camilla Blair (Hostess), Gillian Duxbury (Hostess), Denni Kemp (Hostess), Natalie Shaw (Hostess), John Melainey (Host).

19.12.1986 — D2 / 1"
Designed by Rae George; associate producer Dennis Berson; produced and directed by Alasdair MacMillan.
With Alison Bell (Hostess), Carol Dean (Hostess), Denni Kemp (Hostess), Natalie Van De Braam (Hostess), Jane Melainey (Hostess), Dickie Davies, Liz Davies, Claire Rayner, Des Rayner.

Specials only listed.

BRUM

A BBC production for BBC 1. Transmission details are for BBC 1.

SERIES 4
Transmission details are for BBC 2.

Holding / Source

##.##.#### Brum And The Snow Thieves — DB / D3S

A BUCKET O' FRENCH AND SAUNDERS

A Saunders & French production for BBC 1. Transmission details are for BBC 1.
Main regular credit(s): Written by Dawn French and Jennifer Saunders; script supervisor Wendy Poon; music by Simon Brint; designed by Harry Banks; associate producer Abigail Wilson; production executive Jez Nightingale; executive producer Jo Sargent; produced by Nerys Evans; directed by Ben Fuller.
Main regular cast: French & Saunders.

Holding / Source

24.12.2007 A Christmas Bucket O' French & Saunders — DB / DBSW
Duration: 35 minutes.
With Kate Moss, Darcey Bussell, Richard Madeley, Judy Finnigan.

BULLSEYE

An ATV/Central production. made in association with Chatsworth Television. Transmission details are for the ATV/Central region. Usual duration: 35 minutes.
Main regular credit(s): Devised by Andrew Wood and Norman Vaughan; theme music by Johnny Patrick [credited as John Patrick].
Main regular performer(s): Jim Bowen (Presenter).

SERIES 2
Transmission details are for the Central region.
Main regular credit(s): Research Mickey Brennan; produced by Peter Holmans; directed by Peter Harris.
Main regular performer(s): With Tony Green (Out Of Vision Scorer).

Holding / Source

26.12.1982 Christmas Special — J / 1"
With Eric Bristow, Margo McDonald, Cliff Lazarenko, Katharine Whitehorn, Maureen Flowers, Nigel Mansell.

SERIES 4
Made in association with Chatsworth Television. Transmission details are for the Central region.
Main regular credit(s): Script associate Howard Imber; designed by Giovanni Guarino; produced and directed by Bob Cousins.
Main regular performer(s): With Tony Green (Scorer).

Holding / Source

23.12.1984 Christmas Special — J / 1"
Duration: 40 minutes.

SERIES 6
Transmission details are for the Central region.
Main regular credit(s): Script associate Howard Imber; designed by Su Chases; produced and directed by Bob Cousins.
Main regular performer(s): With Tony Green (Scorer).

Production No | Holding / Source

28.12.1986 Christmas Special — 867506 — 1" / 1"
With Stanley Unwin, Ray Alan and Lord Charles, Bob Anderson, Eric Bristow, Frank Carson, Tony Green, Sarah Greene, John Lowe, Fatima Whitbread, Jeanette Charles, Jerry Thomas.

BULLSEYE (continued)

SERIES 11

Transmission details are for the Central region. Duration: 23 minutes.

Main regular credit(s): Produced by Bob Cousins; directed by Dennis Liddington.

Main regular performer(s): With Tony Green (Scorer).

	Production No	Holding / Source
22.12.1991 **Christmas Special**	916338	1" / 1"

A Christmas edition of the game show hosted by Jim Bowen, in which three pairs of contestants, an amateur dart player and a non-dart player, compete in three rounds. With celebrity guests including Frank Bruno, Linda Lusardi, John McCririck and The Grumbleweeds. The darts players are Phil Taylor, Bob Anderson and Dennis Priestley, Warrant Officer Keith Angus (Royal Engineers) leads on representatives of the Armed Services, Army Steve Hutchins (Royal Signals), Royal Navy John Reid (Regulating Petty Officer) and RAF Kevin Turnbull (Senior Aircraftsman), who throw three darts each and raise two hundred pounds for charity (Soldiers, Sailors and Airforce Association) - which Jim doubled up to four hundred pounds. Jim was also handed a cheque for one thousand and twenty six pounds seventy five pence that had been collected by servicemen in Gibraltar. John and Dennis double their winnings to one thousand, six hundred and four pounds which was donated to their nominated charity The Sue Ryder Foundation.

With Frank Bruno, Linda Lusardi, John McCririck, The Grumbleweeds, Phil Taylor, Bob Anderson, Dennis Priestley.

BUMP

A BBC production for BBC 1. Transmission details are for BBC 1. Duration: 14 minutes.

Main regular cast: Simon Cadell (Narrator).

SERIES 2

Holding / Source

26.12.1994 **Bump's Christmas Story** — DB / D3S

BUSKER'S CHRISTMAS STORY

A BBC Manchester production for BBC 1. Transmission details are for BBC 1. Duration: 14 minutes.

Main regular credit(s): Script editor Noel Vincent; executive producer David Brown; produced by Alan Russell.

Main regular cast: Christopher Lillicrap (Narrator).

Holding / Source

24.12.1984 — DB / 1"

'I told you we should have booked.' Christopher Lillicrap tells how Mary and Joseph get some great news, but are shown the door by the inn-keepers of Bethlehem.

25.12.1984 — DB / 1"

'We've come to see the baby Missus.' Christopher Lillicrap to how Bert, Sid and Arthur bring a birthday present, and King Herod hears he's got a bit of competition.

26.12.1984 — DB / 1"

'There are three men without, Sire'. Christopher Lillicrap tells how Herod sends the Kings on an undercover mission, but Mary and Joseph get a tip-off in time.

BUT SERIOUSLY...

A BBC production for BBC 1. Transmission details are for BBC 1. Duration: 10 minutes.

Produced and directed by R. T. Brooks.

Joyce Grenfell, Cyril Fletcher, Ernie Wise.

Holding / Source

25.12.1970 — J / 2"

BUTTERFLIES

A BBC production for BBC 2. Transmission details are for BBC 2. Duration: 30 minutes.

Main regular credit(s): Written by Carla Lane; theme music by Ronnie Hazlehurst.

Main regular cast: Geoffrey Palmer (Ben), Wendy Craig (Ria), Nicholas Lyndhurst (Adam), Andrew Hall (Russell), Bruce Montague (Leonard).

Transmission details are for BBC 1.

Holding / Source

22.12.1979 — DB-D3 / 2"

Designed by Colin Green; produced by Gareth Gwenlan; directed by John B. Hobbs.

With Michael Ripper (Thomas), Joyce Windsor (Ruby), James Jebbia, David Cole.

See also: THE FUNNY SIDE OF CHRISTMAS (BBC)

BY JEORGE

A Thames Television production. Transmission details are for the ATV midlands region. Duration: 24 minutes.

Written by Larry Parker; designed by Jim Nicholson; produced and directed by Anthony Parker.

Jack O'Reilly (Himself), Frank Thornton (Mr Gorridge), Harold Goodwin (Dan), Lane Meddick (Johnson), Brian Dee (Pianist), Ali Bongo (Himself), George The Dog.

Holding / Source

27.12.1972 — J / 2"

BYDD YN WROL

Commissioned by S4C. Transmission details are for S4C. Duration: 75 minutes.

Menna Trussler, Matthew Rhys, Daniel Evans.

Holding / Source

25.12.1996 — D3 / V1S

BYS PRIODAHOL

Commissioned by S4C. Transmission details are for S4C. Duration: 15 minutes.

Holding / Source

27.12.2002

DB / V1SW

C.B.T.V.

A Thames Television production. Transmission details are for the Central region. Duration: 25 minutes.

SERIES 2: Channel 14

Main regular credit(s):	Produced by Dale Le Vack; directed by Stuart Hall.
Main regular cast:	With Mike Smith (Presenter Until 31.5.1983), Paul Henley (Presenter), Stephanie Laslett (Presenter), Steve Steen (Presenter), Jim Sweeney (Presenter), Anneke Rice (Presenter).

Holding / Source

21.12.1982 **Jim And Steve Review The Year**   D3 / 2"

THE CABALLE FAMILY CHRISTMAS WITH CHER

Commissioned by Meridian. Transmission details are for the London Weekend Television region. Duration: 75 minutes.

Produced by Judy Chesterman and Chris Hunt; directed by Robin Lough.

Trevor McDonald (Host), Montserrat Caballé, Montserrat Marti, Cher.

Holding / Source

24.12.1995   D3 / D3

CABBAGES AND KINGS

A Granada production. Transmission details are for the Central region. Duration: 25 minutes.

Main regular credit(s):	Devised by Nigel Rees.

SERIES 5

Transmission details are for the Central region.

Main regular credit(s):	Designed by Geoff Bentley; produced by Mike Murphy; directed by Peter Mullings.
Main regular performer(s):	With Robin Ray (Chairman), Gerry Cowan (Voices), Barbara Greenhalgh (Voices), David Mahlowe (Voices), Alan Coren, Benny Green, Bill Tidy.

Production No   Holding / Source

02.01.1983 **Christmas Edition**   P991/55   DB / 2"

With Richard Ingrams.

CADFAEL

A Central->Carlton UK production. Transmission details are for the Central region. Duration: 75 minutes.

Main regular credit(s):	Based on novels by Ellis Peters; executive producer Ted Childs; produced by Stephen Smallwood.
Main regular cast:	Derek Jacobi (Brother Cadfael), Michael Culver (Prior Robert).
Cast:	With Eoin McCarthy (Hugh Beringar), Terrence Hardiman (Abbot Radulfus).

Holding / Source

26.12.1995 **The Virgin In The Ice**   DB / V1S

Adapted by Russell Lewis; directed by Malcolm Mowbray.

With Julian Firth (Brother Jerome), Mark Charnock, Valentine Pelka, Robert Cavanah, Ronan Vibert, Amelia Curtis, Albie Woodington, William Mannering, Guy Oliver-Watts, Tim Barker, Eve Madarasz, Istvan Szilagy.

SERIES 4

Main regular cast:	With Anthony Green (Hugh Beringar), Terrence Hardiman (Abbot Radulfus).

Holding / Source

23.12.1998 **The Potter's Field**   DB / V1S

Adapted by Christopher Russell; directed by Mary McMurray.

With Julian Firth (Brother Jerome), Gregor Truter, Mel Martin, Jack Klaff, Sioned Jones, Robin Laing, Peter Baldwin, Anthony Green, John Bowler, Peter Aubrey, Philip Herbert, Shane Hickmott, Natalie Jones.

28.12.1998 **The Pilgrim Of Hate**   DB / V1S

Adapted by Richard Stoneman; directed by Ken Grieve.

With Julian Firth (Brother Jerome), Matt Patresi, Barney Craig, Anthony Green, Lee Ingleby, Natasha Little, Terence Beesley, Shane Hickmott.

CAFE CONTINENTAL

A BBC production. Transmission details are for BBC. Usual duration: 60 minutes.

Holding / Source

27.12.1947 **Christmas Masked Ball**   J / Live
27.12.1949 **Grand Gala de Noël**   J / Live
29.12.1951 **A Masked Ball**   J / Live

CALENDAR (INSERTS)

A Yorkshire Television production. Transmission details are for the Yorkshire Television region.

Holding / Source

24.12.1992   B / 1"

Duration: 1 minutes.

With Rotherham Schools Youth Brass Band.

Insert only.

CALL ME KIRI

A BBC production for BBC 1. Transmission details are for BBC 1. Duration: 60 minutes.

Choreography by Bill Drysdale and David Toguri; designed by Derek Dodd; produced and directed by Humphrey Burton.

Kiri Te Kanawa, Placido Domingo, Doreen Wells, Norma Burrowes, Harry Secombe, The Maori Rugby Team, Ursula Connors, Glenys Groves, Hilly Marshall, BBC Concert Orchestra.

	Holding / Source
26.12.1982	DB / 1"

CALL MY BLUFF

A BBC production for BBC 2. Transmission details are for BBC 2. Usual duration: 30 minutes.

Main regular credit(s): Devised by Mark Goodson and Bill Todman.

SERIES 4

Main regular credit(s): Produced by T. Leslie Jackson.

Main regular performer(s): With Robert Robinson (Referee).

	Holding / Source
25.12.1969 **Christmas Edition**	J / 2"

Directed by Michael Goodwin.

With Cliff Michelmore, Kenneth More, Lance Percival, Jean Metcalfe, Eleanor Summerfield, Hilary Pritchard.

SERIES 9

Duration: 25 minutes.

Main regular credit(s): Produced by Johnny Downes; directed by Michael Goodwin.

Main regular performer(s): With Robert Robinson (Referee).

	Holding / Source
30.12.1974	DB-D3 / 2"

With Frank Muir (Team Captain), The Marchioness of Tavistock, Edward Fox, Patrick Campbell (Team Captain), Pauline Collins, Antony Hopkins.

CALL OXBRIDGE 2000

An ATV production. Transmission details are for the ABC midlands region.

SERIES 2

Main regular credit(s): Produced by Philip Dale.

	Holding / Source
23.12.1962 "The show must go on at the Oxbridge Repertory Theatre"	J /

Christmas is just as busy a time for the doctors as any other. 'The show must go on' at Oxbridge Rep. Theatre, and Dr. Bennett is the guest of honour at Mrs. Connor's Party.

Written by Diana Morgan; settings by Alan Pickford; directed by Vivian Matalon.

With Godfrey Quigley (Doctor Henry Bennett), Jessie Evans (Miss Davies), Geoffrey Frederick (Doctor Bob Hamilton), Aileen Britton (Mrs Bennett), Jennifer Kennedy (Alison Graham), Nigel Arkwright (Mr Bassett), Mary Merrall, Eva Whishaw, Prunella Scales, Peter Bathurst, Ann Tirard, Betty Henderson.

See also: EMERGENCY - WARD 10

CALL THE MIDWIFE

Commissioned by BBC 1. Transmission details are for BBC 1. Duration varies - see below for details.

Main regular credit(s): Written by Heidi Thomas.

Main regular cast: Jessica Raine (Jenny Lee).

SERIES 1

	Holding / Source
25.12.2012 **Christmas Special**	HD/DB / HDC

Duration: 75 minutes.

As Christmas approaches, a baby is abandoned on the steps of the convent, an event which rallies the Poplar community.

With Jenny Agutter (Sister Julienne), Pam Ferris (Sister Evangelina), Miranda Hart (Chummy Noakes), Judy Parfitt (Sister Monica Joan), Helen George (Trixie Franklin), Bryony Hannah (Cynthia Miller), Laura Main (Sister Bernadette), Ben Caplan (Police Constable Peter Noakes), Stephen McGann (Doctor Turner).

SERIES 2

Credits: Produced by Hugh Warren.

	Holding / Source
25.12.2013	HD/DB / HDC

Duration: 75 minutes.

The Christmas festivities in Poplar are thrown into chaos by the discovery of an unexploded bomb. Jenny and Trixie break all the rules for a young couple expecting their first child.

Directed by Thea Sharrock.

With Jenny Agutter (Sister Julienne), Pam Ferris (Sister Evangelina), Miranda Hart (Chummy Noakes), Judy Parfitt (Sister Monica Joan), Helen George (Trixie Franklin), Bryony Hannah (Cynthia Miller), Laura Main (Sister Bernadette), Ben Caplan (Police Constable Peter Noakes), Stephen McGann (Doctor Patrick Turner), Cliff Parisi (Fred Buckle), Max Macmillan (Timothy Turner), Leo Staar (Alec Jesmond), Victoria Bewick (Yvonne Bridges), Sam Swainsbury (Alan Bridges), Lucy Kilpatrick (Maggie), Raymond Coulthard (Captain Goodacre), Jake Bailey (Jack Smith), Simon Armstrong (Major Fawcett), Nancy Carroll (Linda Buck), Sandi Toksvig (Sister Gibbs), Vanessa Redgrave (Voice Of Mature Jenny).

CAMELEON

An Elidir production for S4C. Transmission details are for S4C. Duration: 105 minutes.

Delme Davies deserts the army following the British evacuation of Dunkirk in World War II. He returns to his widowed mother in Wales who hides him in the loft. As the loft is connected to six other homes Delme finds that he his able to spy on all the families in the houses.

Written by Juliet Ace; music by Mark Thomas; designed by Pauline Harrison; executive producer Emlyn Davies; produced by Shan Davies and Ceri Sherlock; directed by Ceri Sherlock.

Aneirin Hughes (Delme Davies), Sue Jones-Davies (Iwanna Davies), Daniel Evans (Elfed Davies), Phylip Hughes (David George), Iris Jones (Hannah-Jane George), Sara McGaughey (Rita Thomas), Dilys Price (Marged-Ann Lewis), Simon Fisher (Howell Thomas).

	Holding / Source
25.12.1998	DB / V1SW

Period drama.

CANNON AND BALL

An LWT production. Transmission details are for the ATV/Central region. Duration varies - see below for details.

Main regular cast: Cannon and Ball (Hosts).

Transmission details are for the ATV midlands region.

	Production No	Holding / Source
20.12.1980 Cannon And Ball For Christmas	9L/90247	D2 / 2"

Duration: 39 minutes.

Designed by Bill McPherson; produced by Sid Green; directed by David Bell.

With Faith Brown, The Char-Lettes, Bertice Reading, Micquel Brown, Ena Cabayo, Jumoke Debayo, Peggy Phango, The Brian Rogers Dancers, Alyn Ainsworth and his Orchestra.

	Holding / Source
21.12.1985 Christmas Cannon And Ball	1" / 1"

Duration: 50 minutes.

Written by Sid Green; designed by Alison Humphries; associate producer Sid Green; produced and directed by Marcus Plantin.

With Ruth Madoc, Paul Nicholas, Pestalozzi Village Children, Natasha Bonnicci, Johnny Cashman, Terina Holloway, The Brian Rogers Dancers, Laurie Holloway and his Orchestra.

SERIES 7

Transmission details are for the Central region.

Main regular credit(s): Associate producer Bryan Blackburn; produced and directed by Marcus Plantin.

	Holding / Source
27.12.1986 The Cannon And Ball Special	D2 / 1"

Duration: 51 minutes.

Written by Bryan Blackburn; choreography by Brian Rogers; designed by Mike Oxley.

With Little Richard, Kate O'Mara, Kim Wilde, The Brian Rogers Dancers, Ray Monk and his Orchestra.

See also: BRUCE FORSYTH'S BIG NIGHT

THE CANNON AND BALL SHOW

A Yorkshire Television production. Transmission details are for the Central region. Duration: 50 minutes.

Written by Barry Cryer, Eddie Braben, Paul Vincent, Brian Leveson, Paul Minett and Bryan Blackburn; script editor Barry Cryer; music directed by Robert Hartley; designed by Alan Davis; produced and directed by Graham Wetherell.

Cannon and Ball (Hosts), Dennis Waterman, Kim Wilde, Linda Lusardi, Chris De Burgh, Brother Beyond, Nosher Powell, The Brian Rogers Dancers.

	Holding / Source
24.12.1988	1" / 1"

THE CANTERBURY TALES

A S4C production. made in association with a.k.a. Pizazz / BBC Wales / Beryl Productions / Christmas Films / Man and Time Studio / Picasso Pictures / Right Angle Productions / Varga Studio. Transmission details are for BBC 2. Duration: 30 minutes.

Animated version of Geoffrey Chaucer's poem.

Main regular credit(s): Adapted by Jonathan Myerson; based on stories by Geoffrey Chaucer; series editors Martin Lamb and Penelope Middelboe; executive in charge of production Jonathan Myerson; executive producer Christopher Grace.

Main regular cast: Bob Peck (Voices), Sean Bean (Voices), John Wood (Voices), Billie Whitelaw (Voices), Bill Nighy (Voices), Tim McInnerny (Voices), Richard Griffiths (Voices), Imelda Staunton (Voices), Robert Lindsay (Voices).

	Holding / Source
21.12.1998 Leaving London	DB / DBS

Directed by Aida Zyablikova.

21.12.1998 The Nun's Priest's Tale	DB / DBS

Directed by Dave Antrobus and Ashley Potter.

21.12.1998 The Knight's Tale	DB / DBS

Directed by Dave Antrobus and Mic Graves.

21.12.1998 The Wife Of Bath's Tale	DB / DBS

Directed by Joanna Quinn.

THE CANTERBURY TALES (continued)

British Christmas Television Guide

22.12.1998 **Arriving At Canterbury** DB / DBS
Directed by Aida Zyablikova.

22.12.1998 **The Merchant's Tale** DB / DBS
Directed by Valeri Ugarov.

22.12.1998 **The Pardoner's Tale** DB / DBS
Directed by Sergei Oilfirenko.

22.12.1998 **The Franklin's Tale** DB / DBS
Directed by Damian Gascoigne.

THE CANTERVILLE GHOST

A HTV production. Transmission details are for the ATV midlands region. Duration: 50 minutes.

An American family take over an English stately home, and also its resident spectre. But the ghost has a hard time with his haunting when he is plagued by the family's two sons, although their beautiful daughter proves his salvation.

Adapted by Robin Miller; based on a story by Oscar Wilde; designed by Voytek; associate producer Mike Towers; executive producer Patrick Dromgoole; produced by Timothy Burrill; directed by Walter Miller.

David Niven (Ghost), James Whitmore (Hyram B. Otis), Lynne Frederick (Virginia), Flora Robson (Mrs Umney), Audra Lindley (Mrs Otis), Maurice Evans (Lord Canterville), Bobby Doran (Stars), Christopher Morris (Stripes), Nicholas Jones (Duke of Cheshire), Elizabeth Tyrrell (Lady Canterville), Ronald Russell (Rector), Isla Blair (Lady Strutfield).

Holding / Source
31.12.1974 B|n / 2"

THE CANTERVILLE GHOST

A Tetra Films production for Carlton. Transmission details are for the Central region. Duration: 77 minutes.

Adapted by Olivia Hetreed; based on a book by Oscar Wilde; associate producers Melanie Stokes and David Mercer; executive producer Michael Forte; produced by Alan Horrox; directed by Crispin Reece.

Ian Richardson (Sir Simon de Canterville Baronet), Celia Imrie (Lucretia Otis), Rolf Saxon (Hiramotis), Sarah-Jane Potts (Virginia Otis), Pauline Quirke (Madame Murielle), Rik Mayall (Dampier), Donald Sinden (Lord Dumbleton), James D'Arcy (Lord Cheshire), Ian McNeice (Davenport), Tom Bowles (Tom Carter), Edna Doré (Mrs Umney).

Holding / Source
26.12.1997 DB / V1SW

CAPTAIN BEAKY'S WORLD OF WORDS AND MUSIC

A BBC production for BBC 2. Transmission details are for BBC 2. Duration: 45 minutes.

Main regular credit(s): Written by Jeremy Lloyd; drawings by Keith Michell; music by Jim Parker; conducted by Jim Parker; designed by Paul Trerise; produced and directed by Yvonne Littlewood.

Holding / Source
29.12.1980 **Volume II** DB-D3 / 2"
With Peter Skellern, Petula Clark, Penelope Keith, Keith Michell, Jeremy Lloyd, Noel Edmonds, Nash Chamber Orchestra, St Paul's Cathedral Boys' Choir.

CAPTAIN NOAH AND HIS FLOATING ZOO

A Granada production. Transmission details are for the ATV midlands region. Duration: 26 minutes.

A Christmas cartoon that sets out to prove a parallel with the Biblical story of Noah and our own world today.

Lyrics by Michael Flanders; music by Joseph Horovitz; produced by Douglas Terry; directed by Brian Cosgrove.

Michael Flanders (Storyteller).

Holding / Source
26.12.1974 DB / 2"

A CARD FOR CHRISTMAS

A Westward Television production. Transmission details are for the Thames Television region. Duration: 8 minutes.

Duirng the past few months viewers have been invited to design their own Christmas card, including a personal message or verse which they consider to reflect the spirit of Christmas '76. It was an enormous response, all over the country and this evening Sheila Kennedy presents a selection of words and greetings.

Designed by David Drewery; produced and directed by John Bartlett.

Sheila Kennedy (Presenter).

Holding / Source
26.12.1976 J / 2"

CARDIGANS AT CHRISTMAS

A BBC production for BBC 2. Transmission details are for BBC 2. Duration: 50 minutes.

This one-off programme examines the rise and demise of the festive light entertainment spectacular. The programme features classic rocking-chair crooners, choral fantasies and winter wonderlands. From CHRISTMAS NIGHT WITH THE STARS to Val Doonican and CHRISTMAS SNOWTIME SPECIAL, the show revisits a world of snow made from soapflakes, chorus lines sweating in winter woolies and recycled sleighs.

Edited by Gaynor Vaughan Jones; produced by Gabrielle Osrin.

Holding / Source
25.12.1997 DB / DBS

CARDIGANS AT CHRISTMAS

A CARLTON NEW YEAR

A Carlton production. Transmission details are for the Carlton region. Duration: 75 minutes.

Produced by Geoff Posner and Michael Hurll; directed by Geoff Posner and Michael Hurll.

Chris Tarrant (Host), Paul McCartney, Squeeze, London Insirational Choir, Paul McKenna, Frank Skinner, Marty Putz.

	Holding / Source
01.01.1993	D2 / D2S

CARMEN

A BBC Manchester production for BBC. Transmission details are for BBC. Duration: 100 minutes.

Written by Meilhac and Halévy; translated by Christopher Hassall; adapted by Rudolph Cartier; music by Georges Bizet; designed by Clifford Hatts; play production by Rudolph Cartier.

Rosalind Elias (Carmen), Raymond Nilsson (Don Jose), John Shirley-Quirk (Escamillo), Rita Hunter (Frasquita), Carole Rosen (Mercedes), Edward Byles (Remendalo), Dennis Brandt (Dancairo), Don Garrard (Zuniga), Desmond Cullum-Jones (Lillas Pastia), Tutte Lemkow (Dancer), Sara Luzita (Dancer), Maria Rosa (Gypsy Dancer), Teresa Moreno (Gypsy Dancer), Hazel Clarkson (Gypsy Dancer), Glynebourne Festival Chorus, Ealing Boys' Grammar School Choir, Philharmonia Orchestra.

	Holding / Source
20.12.1962	R3 /

Opera.

CAROLE KING AND FRIENDS AT CHRISTMAS

A BBC production for BBC 4. Transmission details are for BBC 4. Duration: 60 minutes.

Peel yourself a chestnut, here's the mellow concert of the season. Join Carole King, who has a new album out that's stuffed with Christmas songs.

Carole King, Richard Hawley, The Puppini Sisters, The Mummers, Gregory Porter.

	Holding / Source
22.12.2011	HD/DB / HDC

CAROLS FOR CHRISTMAS

A Granada production. Transmission details are for the Granada region. Duration: 21 minutes.

Executive producer Susan Woodward; produced by Kristin Hadland and Charisse Holder; directed by Tracy Henderson.

Dorothy Marsden, Mary Chadwick, Emma Edge, Bruce Jones, Steven Arnold, Noddy Holder, Peter Mitchell, Geoff Lloyd, Roy Wood, Michael Crawford, Terry Christian, Geoff Turner, Lucy Meacock, Kim Hughes, Fred Talbot, Liverpool Metropolitan Cathedral Choir, Lindow Primary School.

	Production No	Holding / Source
24.12.1998	P3044/1	DB / DBS

CAROLS FROM BUCKLEBURY

Commissioned by ITV. Transmission details are for the Central region. Duration: 48 minutes.

At a candlelit service in rural Berkshire, villagers come together in a rustic barn to celebrate the story of the Nativity and sing favourite carols including Silent Night! Holy Night!, In the Bleak Midwinter and O Come, All Ye Faithful. Kate Garraway also meets members of this pastoral community as they prepare for Christmas

Executive producer Ray Bruce; directed by John Kirby.

Kate Garraway (Presenter).

	Holding / Source
24.12.2011	HD/DB / HDC

CAROLS FROM CANTERBURY

A Meridian production. Transmission details are for the London Weekend Television region. Duration: 50 minutes.

Executive producer Peter Williams; produced by Sue Jerrard.

Archbishop of Canterbury, The Cathedral Choir.

	Holding / Source
24.12.1994	D2 / D2S

CAROLS FROM CHRIST CHURCH

A Central production for Channel 4. Transmission details are for Channel 4. Duration: 55 minutes.

Music directed by Francis Grier; associate producer Richard Holloway; produced and directed by Jon Scoffield.

The Christ Church Cathedral Choir, Alec McCowen, Ian Charleson, Warwick University Chamber Choir.

	Holding / Source
23.12.1984	1" / 1"

CAROLS IN KIRKGATE

A Yorkshire Television production. Transmission details are for the Thames Television region. Duration varies - see below for details.

	Holding / Source
25.12.1971	DB / 2"

Duration: 40 minutes.
Kirkgate is a reconstructed Victorian cobbled street of shops in the Castle Museum which sets the scene for this morning's traditional and colourful programme of carols. Both choirs are in period dress, and appear by permission d the Curator, R. Patterson.
Produced and directed by Graham Watts.
With York Philharmonic Male Voice Choir, Beckfield Secondary School Choir.
From The Castle Museum, York.

24.12.1975	DB / 2"

Duration: 25 minutes.
The York Philharmonic Male Voice Choir and the Beckfield Secondary School Choir are in period dress for this carol service which comes from Kirkgate, a reconstructed Victorian cobbled street in the Castle Museum, York.
Music directed by Richard B. Lister; produced and directed by Graham Watts.
With Alan Bloomfield (Organist).

CAROLS, COFFEE AND CRACKERS

An ATV production. Transmission details are for the ATV midlands region. Duration: 25 minutes.
A light-hearted carol sing-song for Christmas evening from the Youth Club of Yardley Parish Church, Birmingham.
Introduced by Shaw Taylor; produced and directed by Raymond Joss.
The Applejacks.

	Holding / Source
25.12.1963	J /

THE CARROLL LEVIS SHOW

An ATV production. Transmission details are for the ATV midlands region. Duration: 25 minutes.

SERIES 1

	Holding / Source
25.12.1957 **The Carroll Levis Christmas Show**	J /

Carroll Levis introduces discoveries who are guests at his Christmas party.
Settings by Jon Scoffield; produced and directed by Fred Wilby.
With Jerry Allen and his Trio.

CARROTT'S COMMERCIAL BREAKDOWN

A Celador production for BBC 1. Transmission details are for BBC 1. Duration varies - see below for details.
Main regular cast: Jasper Carrott.

	Holding / Source
29.12.1989	DB-D3 / 1"

Duration: 50 minutes.
Written by Steve Knight, Mike Whitehill, Paul Alexander and Jasper Carrott; produced and directed by Paul Smith.

27.12.1991	DB / 1"

Duration: 50 minutes.
Produced and directed by Paul Smith.
With Carrott's Commercial Breakdown (II).

28.12.1993	DB-D3 / D3S

Duration: 50 minutes.
Produced by Sue Fox; directed by Ian Hamilton.

CARROTT'S LIB

A BBC production for BBC 1. Transmission details are for BBC 1. Duration varies - see below for details.
Main regular cast: Jasper Carrott, Mark Arden, Debbie Bishop, Nick Wilton, Peter Brewis.

	Holding / Source
30.12.1983	DB-1" / Live

Duration: 45 minutes.
Written by Jasper Carrott, Kim Fuller, Rob Grant, Doug Naylor, James Hendrie, Tony Sarchet, Bob Sinfield and Andrea Solomons; script associate Neil Shand; music by Peter Brewis; designed by Jane Clement and Graeme Story; produced and directed by Geoff Posner.
With Nick Wilton, Chris Barrie [as Christopher Barrie], Nick Maloney, Jan Ravens.

CARROTT-U-LIKE

A Celador production for BBC 1. Transmission details are for BBC 1. Duration: 50 minutes.

Written by Jasper Carrott, Steve Knight and Mike Whitehill; additional material by Paul Alexander and Hattie Hayridge; music by Keith Strachan; designed by Andy Hamilton; executive producer Nic Phillips; production manager Barry Read; produced and directed by Ed Bye.

Jasper Carrott, Enn Reitel (Voice Only), Sara Crowe, Ann Bryson, Jonathan Cake, Julie Graham*.

	Holding / Source
27.12.1994	DB-D3 / D3S

CARRY ON LAUGHING'S CHRISTMAS CLASSICS

A Thames Television production. Transmission details are for the Central region. Duration: 25 minutes.

Created by Peter Rogers and Gerald Thomas; produced by Gerald Thomas; directed by David Clark.

Kenneth Williams (Host), Barbara Windsor (Host).

	VT Number	Holding / Source
22.12.1983	30215	DB / 2"

See also: CARRY ON...

CARRY ON...

A Thames Television production. Transmission details are for the ATV midlands region. Duration: 50 minutes.

The Carry On films need no introduction. They are classic, iconic slices of British life that no longer exist. Indeed, they probably never existed in the first place, but they are how people would like to remember the past. The first film was intended as a one-off but Carry On Sergeant proved so successful that it started a genre that continued until 1992 when Carry On Columbus closed the series.

By the advent of colour film the production schedule of films was well-established: two per year opening at the cinema every six months. So it is somewhat surprising to find that Thames Television persuaded Peter Rogers and Gerald Thomas to consider making a one-off Christmas pantomime for 1969. They were lured by the opportunity to work with the new colour technology on offer at Teddington Studios.

The 1969 special was based on Charles Dickens' 'A Christmas Carol'. The ensemble cast reflected the films with a single exception – Kenneth Williams was under contract to the BBC making his own show so he could not appear. Frankie Howerd, who had recently made Carry On Up The Jungle, replaced him as the Fairy Godmother. Sid James played Scrooge, supported by Terry Scott, Charles Hawtrey, Hattie Jacques, Barbara Windsor, Bernard Bresslaw and Peter Butterworth. It proved to be the number one rated show of the entire festive season, and a sequel was commissioned for 1970.

Christmas Eve 1970 saw Carry On Long John unveiled to the viewing public. Due to a technicians strike about using colour technology it was made in monochrome which restricted its future repeat. This time Sid James was Long John Silver with the same supporting cast as before except Frankie Howerd had returned to making his own material for the BBC. Charles Hawtrey as Old Pew caused numerous problems behind the scenes insisting on star billing and the best dressing room and he was dropped for future specials.

Thames Television commissioned two more specials for 1972 and 1973, but the cast were increasingly in demand for other TV work and some cast changes were made. In 1972 Sid James was doing Bless This House, so Kenneth Connor, Hattie Jacques and Barbara Windsor carried the piece; Sid returned in 1973 alongside Windsor, Joan Sims, Peter Butterworth and others. These latter specials abandoned the pantomime theme in favour of a series of sketches. The 1972 episode doesn't really gel as a unit, but by 1973 the sketches are risqué and sharp. Sid James as a naughty Santa Claus sums up the bawdy, unsubtle feel of the Carry On genre.

The best editions are 1969 and 1973, unsurprising to learn that they are written by Mr Carry On himself: Talbot Rothwell. The other specials were written by Dave Freeman and Sid Colin. Rogers and Thomas rated Dave Freeman so highly he went on to write for the cinema films including Carry On Behind.

Alan Tarrant who made the second special took the concept of Carry On TV series to the planners at ATV and Thames Television lost the rights. ATV went on to make Carry On Laughing and broadcast a version of the stage play Carry On London as a one-off special called What a Carry On. This 1973 staging does not exist – did any readers of this TV Memories record it??

Thames Television made one final outing into Carry On territory. The films were recut into a series of 25-minute TV compilations called Carry On Laughing. In 1983 Thames shot some new linking material with Kenneth Williams and Barbara Windsor. They introduced clips from the films. Carry On Laughing's Christmas Classics is best remembered for Williams dressed as a fairy, but is not repeated due to copyright problems, so viewers will never see his tutu again!

	VT Number	Holding / Source
24.12.1969 **Carry On Christmas**	2500	D3 / 2"

Even the ghosts of Christmas past, present and future take on a new significance when played by the Carry On team. Everyone knows just how mean old Scrooge was. But not even Dickens could have anticipated what happened when Ebenezer kept Frank N. Stein and Dracula short of development money... refused to lend Robert Browning the fare to take Elizabeth Barrett to Venice... and evicted Cinderella from her basement kitchen.

Written by Talbot Rothwell; designed by Roger Allan; produced by Peter Eton; directed by Ronnie Baxter.

With Sidney James (Scrooge), Terry Scott (Doctor Frank N. Stein), Charles Hawtrey (Spirit of Christmas Past), Hattie Jacques (Elizabeth Barrett), Barbara Windsor (Cinderella), Bernard Bresslaw (Cissie), Peter Butterworth (Dracula), Frankie Howerd (Robert Browning / The Fairy Godmother).

24.12.1970 **Carry On Long John**	3735	D3 / 62

Alt.Title(s): *Carry On Again Christmas*

When Robert Louis Stevenson penned his classic tale of piracy and plunder, Treasure Island, morality rather than mirth seems to have been uppermost in his mind. He can hardly have reckoned upon having his theme being re-worked for Peter Rogers' - producer of 23 Carry On films to date - team. Still less could he have visualised the petite blonde Barbara Windsor in the role of his cabin boy hero, Jim Hawkins. However, last year's Carry on Christmas was the most popular programme of Christmas week, and Carry On again Christmas bids fair - as Long John might have said - to do the same in 1970.

Written by Sid Collin and Dave Freeman; designed by Roger Allan; executive producer Peter Eton; produced and directed by Alan Tarrant.

With Sidney James (Long John Silver), Terry Scott (Squire Treyhornay), Charles Hawtrey (Old Pew / Nightwatchman), Kenneth Connor (Doctor Livershake), Barbara Windsor (Jim Hawkins), Bernard Bresslaw (Rollicky Bill), Bob Todd (Ben Gunn), Wendy Richard (Kate).

20.12.1972 **Carry On Christmas**	6818	D3 / 2"

Alt.Title(s): *Carry On Stuffing*

Written by Dave Freeman and Talbot Rothwell; designed by Tony Borer; executive producer Peter Rogers; produced by Gerald Thomas; directed by Ronnie Baxter.

With Hattie Jacques, Joan Sims, Barbara Windsor, Kenneth Connor, Peter Butterworth, Norman Rossington, Jack Douglas, Brian Oulton.

CARRY ON... (continued)

24.12.1973 Carry On Christmas   8600   D3 / 2"

What would the festive season be without the almost traditional buffoonery of the Carry On team, back for their fourth ITV Christmas special. In this year's brand-new show, their celebrations centre around how our ancestors have enjoyed Christmas down the centuries. But first a visit to Father Christmas in the fairy grotto of a department store. The cloak, hood and whiskers cannot disguise the moon-cratered features of Sidney James, borrowing a little of Santa's time to reminisce about the good old days.

Written by Talbot Rothwell; designed by Allan Cameron; executive producer Peter Rogers; produced by Gerald Thomas; directed by Ronald Fouracre.

With Sidney James, Joan Sims, Barbara Windsor, Kenneth Connor, Bernard Bresslaw, Jack Douglas, Peter Butterworth, Julian Holloway, Laraine Humphreys.

See also: CARRY ON LAUGHING'S CHRISTMAS CLASSICS

THE CASE OF THE FRIGHTENED LADY

A BBC production for BBC 2. Transmission details are for BBC 2. Duration: 74 minutes.

Adapted by Victor Pemberton; based on a story by Edgar Wallace; music by Marc Wilkinson; designed by Raymond Cusick; production associate Geoffrey Paget; production manager Elinor Carruthers; produced by Cedric Messina; directed by Chris Menaul.

Virginia McKenna (Lady Lebanon), Warren Clarke (Detective Chief Superintendent Tanner), Tim Woodward (Lord Lebanon), Elizabeth Garvie (Aisla Crane), William Maxwell (Sergeant Totty), Jeffrey Hardy (Detective Sergeant Ferraby), Edward Wiley (Gilder), James Berwick (Brooks), Derek Francis (Kelver), Dean Harris (Thomas Henry Briggs), Edward Hibbert (Studd), Bill McGuirk (Scots Police Sergeant), Stephen Jacobs (First Police Cadet), Peter McNamara (Second Police Cadet), Matthew Roberton (Warder), Thirzie Robinson (Partygoer), Rupert Baker (Partygoer), Peter Searles (Partygoer), Anthony Powell (Doctor Amersham), Cyril Cross (Village Constable).

Holding / Source
28.12.1983   DB-D3 / 2"

CASTLE HAVEN

A Yorkshire Television production. Transmission details are for the Yorkshire Television region. Duration: 25 minutes.

Main regular credit(s):   Created by Kevin B. Laffan; theme music by Bob Leaper.

Holding / Source
23.12.1969   J / 2"

Jo Mercer decides to offer Phil a choice of Christmas dinner. Tobias Angell makes a confession. Sarah Meek and Lorna Everitt put their heads together.

Written by Ron McDonnell; story editor David Crane; designed by Richard Jarvis; produced by Ray Mansell; directed by Hugh Munro.

With Roy Barraclough (Harry Everitt), Kathy Staff (Lorna Everitt), Gretchen Franklin (Sarah Meek), George Waring (Tom Meek), Sally James (Jo Mercer), Peter Schofield (Matthew Bennet), Colin Rix (Ivor Davies), Sidonie Bond (Fiona Morris), Robin Ford (Eric Waters), Lala Lloyd (Mabel Waters), Arthur Hewlett (Tobias Angell), Keith James (Jimmy Thorn), Ray Gatenby (Edward Pack), Raewyn Blade (Darlene).

24.12.1969   J / 2"

Meg Thorn looks forward to going to Australia. Sylvia Everitt walks out on her job. Sarah Meek makes a sale. The Pospichals come to a crucial decision.

With Ernst Walder (Josip Pospichal), Anna Korwin (Vlasta Popsichal), Jack Carr (Phil Mercer), Sharon Campbell (Sylvia Everitt), Alan Guy (Dickie Everitt), Keith James (Jimmy Thorn), Natalie Kent (Meg Thorn), Gretchen Franklin (Sarah Meek), Peter Schofield (Matthew Bennet), Sally James (Jo Mercer), Roy Barraclough (Harry Everitt), Kathy Staff (Lorna Everitt), George Waring (Tom Meek).

CASUALTY

Alternative/Working Title(s): A AND E / CITY HOSPITAL / FRONT LINE / ON THE NIONES

A BBC Bristol production for BBC 1. Transmission details are for BBC 1. Usual duration: 50 minutes.

Main regular credit(s):   Created by Jeremy Brock and Paul Unwin; theme music by Ken Freeman.

Main regular cast: Derek Thompson (Charlie Fairhead).

SERIES 7

Main regular credit(s):   Script editors Sally Haynes and Laura Mackie; produced by Geraint Morris.

Main regular cast: With Cathy Shipton (Lisa Duffin), Nigel Le Vaillant (Julian Chapman (until 14.12.1992)), Patrick Robinson (Martin Ashford), Maureen Beattie (Sandra Nicholl), Anne Kristen (Norma Sullivan), Jason Riddington (Robert Khalefa), Ian Bleasdale (Josh), Caroline Webster (Jane), Emma Bird (Maxine Price).

Holding / Source
24.12.1992 Silent Night   DB-D3 / 1"

Written by Ginnie Hole; directed by Michael Brayshaw.

With Toni-Sue Burley (Claire Fuller), Michael Jenner (Ozzy), Chris Tranchell (Orthopaedic Registrar), Sandra James-Young, Dorothy Tutin, T. P. McKenna, Jeff Rawle, Erica Hoffman, Rebecca Callard, Michael Melia, James Blackwell, Stafford Gordon, Judy Monahan, John Hudson, Jo Unwin.

SERIES 8

Main regular credit(s):   Produced by Michael Ferguson.

Main regular cast: With Patrick Robinson (Martin Ashford), Dona Croll (Adele Beckford), Ian Bleasdale (Josn Griffiths), Caroline Webster (Jane Scott).

Holding / Source
26.12.1993 Comfort And Joy   DB / D3S

Written by Barbara Machin; script editors Nicholas Palmer and Sarah Ward; directed by Richard Bramall.

With Clive Mantle (Mike Barratt), Martin Ball (Dave Masters), Tara Moran (Mary Skillett), Jo Unwin (Lucy Cooper), Naoko Mori (Mie Nishi-Kawa), Steven O'Donnell (Frankie Drummer), Suzanna Hamilton (Karen Goodliffe), Oliver Parker (Mark Calder), Robbie Medlock, Stuart Lang, Mark Williams, Billy Hartman, Paul Butterworth, Vernon Thompson, Annette Ekblom, Alex Scott, Mark Aiken, Grace Mattaka, Joseph Charles, Corinne Skinner-Carter, James Smith, David Auker, Suzy Aitchison.

CASUALTY (continued)

SERIES 9

Main regular credit(s): Associate producer Daphne Spink; produced by Corinne Hollingworth.

Main regular cast: With Clive Mantle (Mike Barratt), Patrick Robinson (Martin Ashford), Ian Bleasdale (Josh Griffiths), Jane Gurnett (Rachel Longworth), Sorcha Cusack (Kate Wilson), Joan Oliver (Eddie Gordon), Steven Brand (Adam Cooke), Jason Merrells (Matt Hawley), Lisa Coleman (Jude Kocarnik).

Holding / Source

24.12.1994 Talking Turkey — DB / D3S

Written by Lilie Ferrari; script editor Alison Davis; directed by Sallie Aprahamian.

With Sue Devaney (Liz Harker), Maggie Lynskey (Vicki, Paramedic), Melvyn Bedford, Isobel Middleton, Heather Baskerville, Dominic Rickhards, Simon Binns, Syan Blake, Claudette Williams, Burt Caesar, Chris Gilbert, Leona Wallace, Brian Knight, Tracy Whitwell, Matthew Delamere, Ken Hutchison, Joanne Allen, Luke Pursey, Sarah Eldin, Sarah Caplan.

SERIES 10

Main regular credit(s): Series script editor Ian Aldwinckle; associate producer Daphne Spink; produced by Corinne Hollingworth.

Main regular cast: With Clive Mantle (Mike Barratt), Patrick Robinson (Martin Ashford), Ian Bleasdale (Josh Griffiths), Jane Gurnett (Rachel Longworth), Sorcha Cusack (Kate Wilson), Lisa Coleman (Jude Kocarnik), Jason Merrells (Matt Hawley), Sue Devaney (Liz Harker), Julia Watson (Barbara 'Baz' Hayes), Craig Kelly (Daniel Perryman), Lizzy McInnerny (Laura Milburn).

Holding / Source

23.12.1995 Lost Boys — DB / D3S

An office party leads to tragedy and a priest's faith is put to the test.

Written by Ashley Pharoah; directed by Robert Gabriel.

With Michael N. Harbour (Trevor Wilson), Frank Grimes (Brian Hawley), Robert Duncan (Peter Hayes), Gary Bakewell (Tim Greenway), David Robb (Henry Reeve-Jones), Neil McCaul, John McAndrew, Bruce Alexander, Iain Grant, Andrew Hollingbury, Clifton College Prep School, Harriet Harrison, Gary Raymond, Delena Kidd, Jonathan Guy Lewis, Philip White, Stafford Gordon, Adrian Hammond, Danny Worters, Danny Davies, Ann Robertshaw.

SERIES 11

Main regular credit(s): Series script editor Karen Rigby; executive producer Adrian Bate; produced by Rosalind Anderson.

Main regular cast: With Sorcha Cusack (Kate Wilson), Ian Bleasdale (Josh Griffiths), Gray O'Brien (Richard McCaig), Ganiat Kasumu (Gloria Hammond), Sue Devaney (Liz Harker), Julia Watson (Barbara 'Baz' Hayes), Jason Merrells (Matt Hawley), Lisa Coleman (Staff Nurse Jude Kocarnik).

Holding / Source

14.12.1996 Do You Believe In Fairies? — DB / D3S

In the run-up to Christmas, the Casualty scriptwriters have produced a suitably sobering story about the consequences of drink driving. Equally traumatic is the storyline about a seven year-old who arrives at Holby City hospital after falling into a greenhouse. Meanwhile, Jude still hasn't shared her news with Matt, who is considering setting up a business abroad: "Give me one good reason why I shouldn't just pack my bags and move to Crete!" he exclaims. Will she give him a reason or won't she?

Written by Deborah Cook [credited as Debbie Cook]; script editor Christine Harmar-Brown; associate producer Diana Brookes; directed by Johnathan Young.

With Jonathan Kerrigan (Sam Colloby), Peter Birch (Jack Hathaway), Soo Drouet (Monica), Sheila Ruskin, Dale Rapley, Elizabeth Richmond, Eva Pope, Kate Steed, Brett Fancy, Patrick Drury, Lee Oakes, Paul Popplewell, Simon Bright, Michael Price, Daniel O'Brien, Roger Blake, Alastair Cumming.

21.12.1996 The Dying Of The Light — DB / D3S

Four days before Christmas and it's time for the hospital's fancy dress bash. The theme is James Bond which seems to give all the men the opportunity to impersonate Sean Connery. Matt is so busy organising the party that Jude still hasn't found time to tell him that she is pregnant. When she finally does, it's in an ill-timed outburst. For the rest of the team, work goes on as usual with the paramedics.

Written by Christopher Reason; script editor Kathleen Hutchison; associate producer Katrine Dudley; directed by Indra Bhose.

With Jonathan Kerrigan (Sam Colloby), Peter Birch (Jack Hathaway), Jerome Willis, Michael Thomas, Clare Kelly, Jim McManus, Robert Hands, Siobhan Flynn, Elizabeth Mansfield, Robert Woodall, Laura Kelman, Joanne Bruton, Sakuntala Ramanee, John Abbott, Jenny Forsyth, Anthony Beselle, John Summerfield, Peggy Mason, Natasha Bain.

SERIES 12

Main regular credit(s): Script executive John Yorke; produced by Sally Haynes.

Main regular cast: With Peter Guinness (Elliot Matthews), Rebecca Wheatley (Amy Howard), Rebecca Lacey (Doctor 'George' Woodman), Paterson Joseph (Staff Nurse Mark Grace), Claire Goose (Staff Nurse Tina Seabrook), Vincenzo Pellegrino (Derek 'Sunny' Sunderland), Julia Watson (Doctor Barbara 'Baz' Hayes), Ian Bleasdale (Josh Griffiths), Gray O'Brien (Doctor Richard McCaig), Barbara Marten (Eve Montgomery (29.11.1997 onwards)), Jonathan Kerrigan (Sam Colloby).

Holding / Source

27.12.1997 The Golden Hour — DB / D3S

Duration: 75 minutes.

Written by Barbara Machin; executive producer Laura Mackie; directed by Nigel Douglas.

With Donna Alexander (Penny Hutchens), Joseph May (Paul), Keeley Forsyth, Glynis Brooks, David Mallinson, Connor McIntyre, Moya Brady, Rhys Moore, Nina Warhurst, Colum Convey, Sabra Williams, Siobhan Burke, Mark Moraghan, Shaun Dooley, Biddy Wells.

CASUALTY (continued)

SERIES 13

Main regular credit(s): Series editor Alexei de Keyser; executive producer Mal Young; series producer Johnathan Young.

Main regular cast: With Robert Gwilym (Mr Max Gallagher), Rebecca Wheatley (Amy Howard), Rebecca Lacey (Doctor 'George' Woodman), Paterson Joseph (Staff Nurse Mark Grace), Claire Goose (Staff Nurse Tina Seabrook), Vincenzo Pellegrino (Derek 'Sunny' Sunderland), Ian Bleasdale (Josh Griffiths), Jonathan Kerrigan (Sam Colloby), Barbara Marten (Eve Montgomery), Pal Aron (Adam Osman), Cathy Shipton (Lisa 'Duffy' Duffin (19.9.1998 onwards)), Jan Anderson (Staff Nurse Chloe Hill), Gerald Kyd (Senior House Officer Doctor Sean Maddox), Donna Alexander (Penny Hutchens), Michelle Butterly (Mel Dyson (9.11.1998 onwards)).

Holding / Source

19.12.1998 Miracle On Casualty — DB / D3S

The first of two episodes over the Christmas period (the second is on next Saturday) finds Holby A&E in a party mood - at least they will be, if Sonny manages to book a band and sort out a certain Mr B Alloon, who's floating around one of the cubicles. There are plenty of seasonal malady storylines - including the Christmas pub quiz that, far from spreading peace and goodwill to all men, ends in a huge punch-up. However, the centrepiece is the hospital's annual party, where the usual seasonal smooching (and drinking) is taking place. Josh is certainly the worse for wear, Sam is drowning his sorrows over Lee, and Mark has a grin more suited to a Cheshire cat. But why are Christmas babies never born in a hospital bed?

Written by Tony McHale; directed by Michael Owen Morris.

With Michael French (Nick Jordan), Nicola Stephenson (Julie Fitzjohn), Ian Kershaw (Pat Garrett), Stephen Moore, Ram John Holder, Emma Tate, Desmond McNamara, Sandra James-Young, Katy Secombe, Emma Cunningham, Richard Huw, Judith Davis, Giles Ward, Stephen Ullathorne, Eleanor Ogbourne.

26.12.1998 New Year And All That — DB / D3S

Duration: 70 minutes.

Written by Tony McHale; produced by Alexei de Keyser; directed by Paul Wroblewski.

With Michael French (Nick Jordan), Nicola Stephenson (Julie Fitzjohn), Tobias Menzies (Frank Gallagher), Patrick Romer (Marius Lupescu), Ian Kershaw (Pat Garrett), Ian Sharrock, Amelia Lowdell, Louis Morgan, Clare Northover, Graham McTavish, Ralph Riach, Cira Leigh Brannigan, Richard Burke, Prue Clarke, Ian Glover, Simon Nicholls, Guy Normas, Carey Whitley, Simon Armstrong, Kate Redshaw.

SERIES 14

Main regular credit(s): Series editor Bronagh Taggart; executive producer Mal Young; series producer Alexei de Keyser.

Main regular cast: With Kwame Kwei Armah (Finlay Newton), Ian Kelsey (Doctor Patrick Spiller), Sandra Huggett (Holly Miles), Ronnie McCann (Barney Wolfe (20.11.99 onwards)), Ian Bleasdale (Josh Griffiths), Robert Gwilym (Mr Max Gallagher), Claire Goose (Staff Nurse Tina Seabrook), Vincenzo Pellegrino (Derek 'Sunny' Sunderland (until October 1999)), Barbara Marten (Eve Montgomery (until 30.10.1999)), Pal Aron (Adam Osman), Catherine Shipton (Lisa 'Duffy' Duffin), Jan Anderson (Staff Nurse Chloe Hill).

Holding / Source

26.12.1999 Christmas Casualty:: Peace On Earth — DB / D3S

Duration: 60 minutes.

Written by Tony McHale; assistant script editor Christopher Aird; art director Paul Cowell; designed by Lenny Birchenall; associate producer Mark Williams; produced by Tim Bradley; directed by Gill Wilkinson.

With Martina Laird (Darleen Devern), Gerald Kyd (Sean Maddox), Donna Alexander (Penny Hutchens), Rebecca Wheatley (Amy Howard), Michelle Butterfly (Mel Dyson), Damien Goodwin, Louise Breckon-Richards, Jean Grover, George Waring, Nicola Stephenson, Steve Toussaint, Jordan Maxwell, Jerome Holder, Shani Edwards, Ariyon Bakare, Lorenzo Camporese, James Bryce, Penny Stuttaford, Phil Holden, Mark Sealey, Sally Humphreys, Phillip Gates.

01.01.2000 New Year's Casualty:: The Morning After — DB / D3S

Duration: 60 minutes.

Written by Christopher Reason; script editor Jyoti Patel; art director Amelia Shankland; designed by Tim Luke; associate producer Alison Law; produced by Rachel Wright; directed by Tim Leandro.

With Gerald Kyd (Sean Maddox), Donna Alexander (Penny Hutchens), Rebecca Wheatley (Amy Howard), Harriet Thorpe, Simon Kunz, Andrew Scarborough, Tobias Menzies, Cordelia Bugeja, Sam Barriscale, Elizabeth Thomas, Ben Keaton, Geoffrey Hutchings, Joanne Good, Carol Harvey.

SERIES 15

Main regular credit(s): Executive producer Mal Young; series producer Rachel Wright.

Main regular cast: With Zita Sattar (Anna Paul (03.03.2001 onwards)), Will Mellor (Jack Vincent (24.3.2001 onwards)), Ben Keaton (Spencer), Adjoa Andoh (Colette Kierney), Grant Masters (Dan Robinson), Ian Bleasdale (Josh Griffiths), Robert Gwilym (Mr Max Gallagher), Cathy Shipton (Lisa 'Duffy' Duffin), Jan Anderson (Chloe Hill), Rebecca Wheatley (Amy Howard), Ian Kelsey (Patrick Spiller), Donna Alexander (Penny Hutchens), Ronnie McCann (Barney Wolfe), Michelle Butterly (Mel Dyson).

Holding / Source

23.12.2000 Merry Christmas Dr Spiller — DB / DBS

Duration: 60 minutes.

Written by Jeff Povey; produced by Bronagh Taggart; directed by Michael Owen Morris.

With Philip Bretherton (Doctor Andrew Boyer), Windsor Davies, Alexander Hanson, Philip Whitchurch.

30.12.2000 Epiphany — DB / DBS

Written by Suzie Smith; directed by Dominic Lees.

With Kieron Forsyth, Nicholas Lane, Eliza McClelland, Janet Dibley, Ian Embleton.

CASUALTY (continued)

SERIES 16

Main regular credit(s): Executive producer Mal Young; series producer Mervyn Watson.

Main regular cast: With Kwame Kwei Armah (Finlay Newton), Kelly Harrison (Nikki Marshall), Dan Rymer (Dillon Cahill), Martina Laird (Comfort Jones), Will Mellor (Jack Vincent), Zita Sattar (Anna Paul), Ian Kelsey (Patrick Spiller), Ben Keaton (Spencer), Bob Mason (Jeff McGuire), Judy Loe (Jan Goddard (29.9.01 onwards, sem-regular)), Adjoa Andoh (Colette Kierney), Christine Stephen-Daly (Lara Stone (29.9.01-onwards)), Ian Bleasdale (Josh Griffiths), Cathy Shipton (Lisa 'Duffy' Duffin (17.11.01 onwards)), Lee Warburton (Tony Vincent (24.11.2001-onwards)), Christopher Colquhoun (Simon Kaminski (23.3.2002-onwards)), Robert Gwilym (Mr Max Gallagher (until 18.5.2002)), Loo Brealey (Roxanne Bird (13.4.2002-onwards)), Simon MacCorkindale (Mr Harry Harper (8.6.2002-onwards)), Emily Dormer (Gilly (until 30.03.2002)).

Holding / Source

22.12.2001 Life And Soul — DB / DBSW

Duration: 60 minutes.

Written by Andrew Rattenbury and Katharine Way; produced by David Crean; directed by Jim O'Hanlon.

With Amy Robbins (Rachel James), Charis Thomas, Scott Cowan, Danny McCall, Sylvester McCoy, Lloyd Martin.

26.12.2001 Consequences — DB / DBSW

Duration: 60 minutes.

Written by Stuart Morris; produced by Tim Holloway; directed by Adrian Bean.

With Philip Wright, Ashley Miller, James Smith, Anthony Jackson, Thomas Fisher, Michael Sharvell-Martin, Linda George.

SERIES 17

Main regular credit(s): Executive producers Mal Young and Mervyn Watson; series producer Richard Handford.

Main regular cast: With Simon MacCorkindale (Harry Harper), Kelly Harrison (Nikki Marshall), Ian Bleasdale (Josh Griffiths), Cathy Shipton (Lisa Duffin (until 12.4.2003)), Christine Stephen-Daly (Lara Stone), Kwame Kwei Armah (Finlay Newton), Martina Laird (Comfort Jones), Will Mellor (Jack Vincent (until 1.2.2003, 22.3.2003-onwards)), Dan Rymer (Dillon Cahill), Lee Warburton (Tony Vincent), Zita Sattar (Anna Paul), Christopher Colquhoun (Simon Kaminski), Adjoa Andoh (Colette Grffiths (until 07.06.2003)), Loo Brealey (Roxanne Bird), Nicole Faraday (Heather Lincoln (21.9.2002-16.11.2002)), Russell Boulter (Ryan Johnson (28.9.2002-1.2.2003, 5.4.2003-12.4.2003)), N'Deaye Baa-Clements (Jane Winter (28.12.2002-3.5.2003)), Orlando Seale (Merlin Jameson (4.1.2003-10.5.2003)), Sarah Manners (Bex Reynolds (08.02.2003-onwards)), Matthew Wait (Luke Warren (19.4.2003-onwards)).

Holding / Source

21.12.2002 Some Comfort, No Joy And A Bit Too Much Love — DB / DBSW

Written by David Joss Buckley; produced by Foz Allan; directed by Jim O'Hanlon.

With Seeta Indrani (Paramedic Emma), Des McAleer, Lynda Rooke, Dominic Power, Rosie Alvarez, Simeon Andrews, Rosie Ede, Richard Rycroft, Sidney Kean, Miriam Brown, Roger Heathcott, Clare Boland, Burt Caesar, Liam Noble.

SERIES 18

Main regular credit(s): Series editor Jane Hudson; script editor Loretta Preece; associate producer Fiona Francombe; executive producers Mervyn Watson and Mal Young; series producer Foz Allan.

Main regular cast: With Kelly Harrison (Nikki Marshall (until 17.7.2004)), Maxwell Caulfield (Jim Brodie), Sarah Manners (Bex Reynolds), Matthew Wait (Luke Warren), Ian Bleasdale (Josh Griffiths), Simon MacCorkindale (Harry Harper), Christine Stephen-Daly (Lara Stone), Christopher Colquhoun (Simon Kaminski), Loo Brealey (Roxanne Bird), Suzanne Packer (Tess Bateman), James Redmond (Abs), Leanne Wilson (Claire Guildford), Kwame Kwei Armah (Finlay Newton), Martina Laird (Comfort Jones), Holly Davidson (Tally Harper).

Holding / Source

06.12.2003 Christmas Spirit — DB / DBSW

Written by Emma Frost; produced by Lowri Glain; directed by S. J. Clarkson.

With Julia Watson (Baz), Nigel Whitmey, Liam Hess, Kristian Lee Wilkin, Kim Oliver, Angela McHale, Samuel Clemens, Malcolm Scates, Julie Teal.

20.12.2003 Eat, Drink And Be Merry — DB / DBSW

Written by Jason Sutton; produced by Pippa Brill; directed by Ian White.

With Julia Watson (Baz), Nigel Whitmey, Liam Hess, Frank Windsor, Rebecca Blake, Tim Dantay, Tyra McKenzie-Gray, John Blakey, John-Paul Macleod, Chris Geere, Roland John-Leopoldie, Jed Staton, Surinder Duhra.

SERIES 20

Main regular credit(s): Series editor Loretta Preece; executive producer Mervyn Watson; series producer Jane Dauncey.

Main regular cast: With Susan Cookson (Maggie Coldwell).

Holding / Source

17.12.2005 Do They Know It's Christmas? — DB / DBSW

Written by Ann Marie Di Mambro; script supervisor Nicki Coles; script editor Samantha Davey; associate producer David Harvey; produced by Alex Perrin; directed by Declan O'Dwyer.

With Elyes Gabel (Gurpreet 'Guppy' Sandhu), Simon MacCorkindale (Harry Harper), Ben Price (Nathan Spencer), Suzanne Packer (Tess Bateman), James Redmond (John 'Abs' Denham), Rebekah Gibbs (Nina Farr), Mark Bonnar (Bruno Jenkins), Georgina Bouzova (Ellen Zitek), Janine Mellor (Kelsey Phillips), Will Thorp (Woody Joyner), Ian Bleasdale (Josh Griffiths), Martina Laird (Comfort Newton), Matthew Wait (Luke Warren), Luke Bailey (Sam Bateman), Elizabeth Carling, Madhav Sharma, Ben Roberts, Steven Cartait, Nicola Franklin, Rick Bacon, Shannon Murray, Luke Hamill, Maggie Tagney, Leona Walker, Glen Wallace, Michelle Boucher.

31.12.2005 Out Of Your Depth — DB / DBSW

Written by Catherine Tregenna; script supervisor Elaine Matthews; series editor Ellen Taylor; script editor Lindsay Alford; associate producer Fiona Black; produced by Jane Steventon; directed by Joss Agnew.

With James Redmond (John 'Abs' Denham), Elyes Gabel (Gurpreet 'Guppy' Sandhu), Rebekah Gibbs (Nina Farr), Simon MacCorkindale (Harry Harper), Ben Price (Nathan Spencer), Ian Bleasdale (Josh Griffiths), Georgina Bouzova (Ellen Zitek), Suzanne Packer (Tess Bateman), Matthew Wait (Luke Warren), Janine Mellor (Kelsey Phillips), Luke Bailey (Sam Bateman), Mark Bonnar (Bruno Jenkins), Derek Thompson, Madhav Sharma, Amy Shiels, Katy Allen, Neil Newbon, Nazim Kourgli, Tryphena Dawn, Gary Whitaker, Kate Sissons, Harry Taylor, Corinne Skinner-Carter, Phillip Browne, Donald Anderson, Roy Lorenzo, Carlos Hobday, Desmond Eaves.

CASUALTY (continued)

SERIES 21

Holding / Source

23.12.2006 Killing Me Softly — DB / DBSW

Duration: 60 minutes.

Written by Barbara Machin; script supervisor Nicki Coles; series editor Ellen Taylor; script editors Lindsey Alford and Jenny Van Der Lande; associate producer Vaughan Watkins; executive producer Mervyn Watson; series associate producer Michael Darbon; series producer Jane Dauncey; produced by Jane Steventon; directed by Diarmuid Lawrence.

With Ian Bleasdale (Josh Griffiths), Georgina Bouzova (Ellen Zitek), Derek Thompson (Charlie Fairhead), Simon MacCorkindale (Harry Harper), Susan Cookson (Maggie Coldwell), Elizabeth Carling (Selena Donovan), Suzanne Packer (Tess Bateman), Ben Price (Nathan Spencer), Janine Mellor (Kelsey Philips), Elyes Gabel (Gurpreet 'Guppy' Sandhu), James Redmond (John 'Abs' Denham), Jane Hazlegrove (Kathleen 'Dixie' Dixon), Luke Bailey (Sam Bateman), Sam Grey (Alice Chantrey), Jack Dedman, Holly Aird, Romy Irving, Maggie Lloyd-Williams, Fraser Ayres, Bradley Goff, Jeff Barnett, Frances Cuka, Carole Nimmons.

24.12.2006 Silent Night — DB / DBSW

Duration: 60 minutes.

Written by Barbara Machin; script supervisor Nicki Coles; series editor Ellen Taylor; script editors Lindsey Alford and Jenny Van Der Lande; associate producer Vaughan Watkins; executive producer Mervyn Watson; series associate producer Michael Darbon; series producer Jane Dauncey; produced by Jane Steventon; directed by Diarmuid Lawrence.

With Ian Bleasdale (Josh Griffiths), Georgina Bouzova (Ellen Zitek), Derek Thompson (Charlie Fairhead), Simon MacCorkindale (Harry Harper), Susan Cookson (Maggie Coldwell), Elizabeth Carling (Selena Donovan), Suzanne Packer (Tess Bateman), Ben Price (Nathan Spencer), Janine Mellor (Kelsey Philips), Elyes Gabel (Gurpreet 'Guppy' Sandhu), James Redmond (John 'Abs' Denham), Jane Hazlegrove (Kathleen 'Dixie' Dixon), Luke Bailey (Sam Bateman), Sam Grey (Alice Chantrey), Kip Gamblin (Greg Fallon), Joanne King (Cynthia 'Cyd' Pyke), Jack Dedman, Holly Aird, Romy Irving, Gary Kemp, Maggie Lloyd-Williams, Fraser Ayres, Julia St. John, Sian Webber, Grahame Fox, Bradley Goff, Richard Sutton, Jeff Barnett, Frances Cuka, Carole Nimmons, Nicholas Brown, Lidia Baker.

SERIES 22

A BBC Productions production for BBC Bristol.

Main regular credit(s): Series consultant Barbara Machin; series producer Oliver Kent.

Holding / Source

29.12.2007 Take A Cup Of Kindness Yet — DB / DBSWF

Written by Sasha Hails; script supervisor Lesley Pinder; series script editor Henry R. Swindell; script producer Bianca Rodway; script editor Rachel Knight; designed by Gary Brown; associate producer Hoe Yeoh; executive producers Belinda Campbell and Alison Davis; series associate producer Michael Darbon; produced by Ellen Taylor; directed by Paul Murphy.

With Sunetra Sarker (Zoe Hanna), James Redmond (John 'Abs' Denham), Janine Mellor (Kelsey Phillips), Suzanne Packer (Tess Bateman), Daphne Alexander (Nadia Talianos), Georgia Taylor (Ruth Winters), Tristan Gemmill (Adam Trueman), Sam Grey (Alice Chantrey), Charles Dale (Big Mac), Simon MacCorkindale (Harry Harper), Susan Cookson (Maggie Coldwell), Jane Hazlegrove (Kathleen 'Dixie' Dixon), Matt Bardock (Jeff Collier), Lindsay Coulson, James Anthony Pearson, Ian Kirkby, Myla Morris, Kacey Barnfield, Melissa Hamilton, Bryanie Parsons, Hazel Ellerby, Ian Ricketts, Sasha Pick, Chike Okonkwo, Frances Williams, Michael Skyers.

30.12.2007 For Auld Lang Syne — DB / DBSWF

Duration: 55 minutes.

Written by Sasha Hails; script supervisor Lesley Pinder; series script editor Henry R. Swindell; story producer Bianca Rodway; script editor Rachel Knight; designed by Gary Brown; associate producer Hoe Yeoh; executive producers Belinda Campbell and Alison Davis; series associate producer Michael Darbon; produced by Ellen Taylor; directed by Paul Murphy.

With James Redmond (John 'Abs' Denham), Janine Mellor (Kelsey Phillips), Suzanne Packer (Tess Bateman), Daphne Alexander (Nadia Talianos), Georgia Taylor (Ruth Winters), Tristan Gemmill (Adam Trueman), Sam Grey (Alice Chantrey), Charles Dale (Big Mac), Simon MacCorkindale (Harry Harper), Susan Cookson (Maggie Coldwell), Jane Hazlegrove (Kathleen 'Dixie' Dixon), Matt Bardock (Jeff Collier), Sunetra Sarker (Zoe Hanna), Frances Williams, Lindsey Coulson, James Anthony Pearson, Ian Kirkby, Myla Morris, Melissa Hamilton, Bryanie Parsons, Hazel Ellerby, Ian Ricketts, Sasha Pick, Chike Okonkwo, Sian Webber.

SERIES 23

A BBC Productions Bristol production for BBC Bristol.

Main regular credit(s): Titles by Hello Charlie; series consultant Mark Catley; executive producer Belinda Campbell; series producer Oliver Kent.

Main regular cast: With Tristan Gemmill (Adam Trueman), Sunetra Sarker (Zoe Hanna).

Holding / Source

21.12.2008 Took A Long Time To Come — DB / DBSWF

Duration: 60 minutes.

Written by Paul Logue; script supervisor Sandy McKellar; series script editor Ali Hope; script producer Bianca Rodway; story producer Anne Edyvean; story editor Sarah Beeson; script editor Hamish Wright; designed by Henry Jaworski and Gary Brown; production manager Jeff Golding; produced by Lucy Raffety; directed by Roberto Bangura.

With Gillian Kearney (Jessica Harrison), Ben Turner (Jay Faldren), Michael French (Nick Jordan), Georgia Taylor (Ruth Winters), Matthew Needham (Toby De Silva), Matt Bardock (Jeff Collier), Jane Hazlegrove (Kathleen 'Dixie' Dixon), Suzanne Packer (Tess Bateman), Charles Dale (Big Mac), Janine Mellor (Kelsey Phillips), Ivana Basic (Snezana Lalovic), Richard Dillane, Joe Absolom, Luke Hamill, Nick Williams, Andrew Sachs, Doraly Rosa, Frances Barber, Lee Williams, Jamie Foreman, Hannah Barrie, Stephen Scott.

SERIES 24

A BBC Productions Bristol production for BBC Bristol.

Main regular credit(s): Titles by Hello Charlie; executive producer Belinda Campbell; series producer Oliver Kent.

Holding / Source

19.12.2009 All I Want For Christmas — DB / DBSWF

Written by Martin Jameson; script supervisor Sandy McKellar; assistant script editor David Roden; script producer Bianca Rodway; story producer Anne Edyvean; story editor Sarah Beeson; script editor Kelly Jones; director of photography Jaz Castleton; series consultant Mark Catley; art director Tim Overson; designed by Neil Pollard and Gary Brown; production manager Hoe Yeoh; line producer Win Mensah-Larbie; produced by Hamish Wright; directed by Alan Grint.

With Georgia Taylor (Ruth Winters), Suzanne Packer (Tess Bateman), Ben Turner (Jay Faldren), Tristan Gemmill (Adam Trueman), Sunetra Sarker (Zoe Hanna), Laura Aikman (May Phelps), Steven Miller (Lenny Lyons), Gillian Kearney (Jessica Harrison), Matt Bardock (Jeff Collier), Sophia di Martino (Polly Emmerson), Will Sharpe (Yuki Reid), Charles Dale (Big Mac), Tony Marshall (Noel Garcia), Michael French (Nick Jordan), Sam Grey (Alice Chantrey), Tom Chadbon (Henry Williams), David Mallinson, Keith Barron, Hugh Lee, Anthony Grundy, Emma Stansfield, Charlotte Lucas, Chris Garner.

| British Christmas Television Guide | CASUALTY (continued) |

27.12.2009 Tidings Of Comfort And Joy DB / DBSWF
Duration: 59 minutes.
Written by Sasha Hails; script supervisor Sandy McKellar; assistant script editor David Roden; script producer Bianca Rodway; story editor Sarah Beeson; script editor Kelly Jones; director of photography Jaz Castleton; series consultant Mark Catley; art director Tim Overson; designed by Neil Pollard and Gary Brown; production manager Hoe Yeoh; line producer Win Mensah-Larbie; produced by Hamish Wright; directed by Alan Grint.

With Laura Aikman (May Phelps), Will Sharpe (Yuki Reid), Steven Miller (Lenny Lyons), Gillian Kearney (Jessica Harrison), Sunetra Sarker (Zoe Hanna), Charles Dale (Big Mac), Tony Marshall (Noel Garcia), Georgia Taylor (Ruth Winters), Ben Turner (Jay Faldren), Tristan Gemmill (Adam Trueman), Jane Hazlegrove (Kathleen 'Dixie' Dixon), Matt Bardock (Jeff Collier), Suzanne Packer (Tess Bateman), Sophia di Martino (Polly Emmerson), Sam Grey (Alice Chantrey), Tom Chadbon (Henry Williams), Richard Dillane, Sean Hughes, Miffy Englefield, Danny Emes, David Mallinson, Kate Edney, Derek Barr, Conleth Kane, Ram John Holder, John Benfield, Eleanor Dodson, Jack Burbidge, Molly Hardwick, Georgia Reece, Toby Dale, Amanda Horlock, Clare Welch, Michael Arrowsmith.

SERIES 25
A BBC Productions Bristol production.
Main regular credit(s): Executive producer Belinda Campbell; consultant producer Mark Catley; series producer Oliver Kent.

Holding / Source

18.12.2010 Season Of Goodwill DB / DBSWF
Storylines by Paul Logue; written by Dana Fainaru; script supervisor Juley Harding; assistant script editor Jackie Okwera; series script editor Roxanne Harvey; script producer Nicola Larder; script editor Kelly Jones; director of photography Peter Chapman; art director Mitch Silcott; designed by Phil Roberson and Steve Keogh; production manager Fiona Black; line producer Win Mensah-Larbie; produced by Anne Edyvean; directed by Reza Moradi.

With Ben Turner (Jay Faldren), Tristan Gemmill (Adam Trueman), Steven Miller (Lenny Lyons), Lucy Gaskell (Kirsty Clements), Georgia Taylor (Ruth Winters), Sunetra Sarker (Zoe Hanna), Charles Dale (Big Mac), Tony Marshall (Noel Garcia), Jane Hazlegrove (Kathleen 'Dixie' Dixon), Will Sharpe (Yuki Reid), Michael French (Nick Jordan), Suzanne Packer (Tess Bateman), Matt Bardock (Jeff Collier), Tom Chadbon (Henry Williams), Nicola Jo Cully, Stephen Lord, Holly Earl, Gavin Bell, Pippa Duffy, Tyler Roach, Stuart Wilkinson.

27.12.2010 Winter Wonderland DB / DBSWF
Storylines by Paul Logue; written by Daisy Coulam; script supervisor Caryn Langrick; series script editor Roxanne Harvey; script producer Nicola Larder; script editor Jackie Okwera; director of photography Simon Butcher; art director Alex Merchant; designed by Lenny Birchenall and Steve Keogh; production manager Hoe Yeoh; line producer Win Mensah-Larbie; produced by Anne-Louise Russell and Henry R. Swindell; directed by Declan O'Dwyer.

With Georgia Taylor (Ruth Winters), Ben Turner (Jay Faldren), Lucy Gaskell (Kirsty Clements), Tristan Gemmill (Adam Trueman), Hasina Haque (Madiha 'Mads' Durrani), Tony Marshall (Noel Garcia), Michael French (Nick Jordan), Suzanne Packer (Tess Bateman), Charles Dale (Big Mac), Sunetra Sarker (Zoe Hanna), Steven Miller (Lenny Lyons), Sophia di Martino (Polly Emmerson), Jane Hazlegrove (Kathleen 'Dixie' Dixon), Stephen Billington (Edward Thurlow), Travis Oliver, Stephen Lord, Holly Earl, Jody Latham, Hollie Jay Bowes, Lucy-Jo Hudson, James Midgley, Molly Jones, Jean Trend, Sian Breckin.

Since we like to be pedantic, the title of the series is now CASUAL+Y, - given that we take the on-screen title as "gospel". Same applies to HOLBY CI+Y too :-)
See also: CASUALTY AT HOLBY CITY (BBC) / CASUALTY AT HOLBY CITY (BBC) / HOLBY CITY (BBC)

CASUALTY AT HOLBY CITY
A BBC production for BBC 1. Transmission details are for BBC 1. Duration: 55 minutes.
Main regular credit(s): Written by Johanne McAndrew; script supervisor Jane Barton; script editor Pamela Hansson; theme music by Ken Freeman; associate producer Debbi Slater; executive producers Mervyn Watson, Kathleen Hutchison and Mal Young; produced by Belinda Campbell; directed by Michael Offer.
Main regular cast: Simon MacCorkindale (Harry Harper), Amanda Mealing (Connie Beauchamp), Matthew Wait (Luke Warren), Kim Vithana (Rosie Sattar), Ian Bleasdale (Josh Griffiths), Maxwell Caulfield (Jim Brodie), Hugh Quarshie (Ric Griffin), Jaye Jacobs (Donna Jackson), Suzanne Packer (Tess Bateman), Sarah Manners (Bex Reynolds), Ian Aspinall (Mubbs Hussein).

Holding / Source

26.12.2004 Episode 1 DB / DBSW
With Daniella Wilson, John McArdle, Dominic Jephcott, Rene Zagger, Nicola Stapleton, Freema Agyeman, Liam Noble, Tony Arunah Abbey, John Kirk, David Semark, Jay Simon, Michael Brown, Kerry Peers, Keith-Lee Castle.
There was no writer credited for episode one.

28.12.2004 Episode 2 DB / DBSW
With Liam Noble, Daniella Wilson, John McArdle, Kerry Peers, Dominic Jephcott, Keith-Lee Castle, Michael Brown, Ben Borowiecki, Nicola Stapleton, John Kirk, Tony Arunah Abbey, Jay Simon.

See also: HOLBY CITY (BBC)

CASUALTY AT HOLBY CITY
A BBC Bristol production for BBC 1. Transmission details are for BBC 1. Duration: 30 minutes.
Main regular credit(s): Theme music by Ken Freeman.
Main regular cast: Ian Bleasdale (Josh Griffiths), Martina Laird (Comfort Newton), James Gaddas (Carl O'Leary), James Anthony Pearson (Adrian Lucas), Jason Maza (Kris Burrows), Kate Scott (Emma Blakely), Anthony Shuster (Nick Bond).

Deny Thy Father
Main regular credit(s): Devised by Jeremy Brock and Paul Unwin; script supervisor Pam Humphries; script editor Katy Harmer; associate producer Katrine Dudley; executive producers Mervyn Watson and Richard Stokes; produced by Diana Kyle; directed by Paul Harrison.
Main regular cast: With Fiona Glascott (Tara Doyle), Jim Webster-Stewart (Lee Campbell), Jamie Belton (Sean Doyle), Judith Sweeney (Pamela Campbell), Gary Whelan (Bernie Doyle), Max Gold (David Parker), William MacBain (Mitch Campbell), Sarah Winman (Helen Davies), Michael French (Nick Jordan), Hugh Quarshie (Ric Griffin), Simon MacCorkindale (Harry Harper), Charlie Dickinson (Derek Ashton), Iain Fletcher (Iain Bain), Will Thorp (Woody Joyner), Mark Arends (Alan Ashton), Suzanne Packer (Tess Bateman), Derek Thompson (Charlie Fairhead), Susan Cookson (Maggie Coldwell), Elizabeth Carling (Selena Donovan), Amanda Mealing (Connie Beauchamp), Jaye Jacobs (Donna Jackson), Luke Bailey (Sam Bateman), Janine Mellor (Kelsey Phillips), Matthew Wait (Luke Warren), Kelly Adams (Nickie Hendrie), Julia Hills (Caroline Joyner), Ian Bleasdale (Josh Griffiths), Jack Dedman (Louis Fairhead), Sharon D. Clarke (Lola Griffin).

Holding / Source

24.12.2005 Episode One DB / DBSW
Written by Alun Nipper and Pete Hambly.

CASUALTY AT HOLBY CITY (continued)

27.12.2005 **Episode Two** DB / DBSW
Written by Gaby Chiappe.
With Gabriella Gabbitas [as Gabriella Gabitas], Ben Tinniswood, Gary Fordham, Lara Hazell.

See also: HOLBY CITY (BBC)

THE CATHERINE TATE SHOW

A Tiger Aspect production for BBC 2. Transmission details are for BBC 2. Duration varies - see below for details.

Main regular cast: Catherine Tate (Various Roles).

Credits: Produced by Geoffrey Perkins.

Holding / Source

20.12.2005 **Christmas Show** DB / DBSWF
Duration: 40 minutes.
Additional material by Jenny Lecoat, Niky Wardley and Mathew Horne; script supervisor Pamela Wylde; music by Philip Pope; executive producer Lucy Lumsden; directed by Christine Gernon.

With Aschlin Ditta, Mathew Horne, Derren Litten, Lee Ross, Niky Wardley, Joan Campion, Rosie Cavaliero, Jonathan McGuiness, Angela McHale, Nastasya Rush, Hugh Sachs, Una Stubbs, Callum Waller, Charlotte Church, Chas & Dave, Richard Park.

Holding / Source

25.12.2007 **The Catherine Tate Christmas Show** DB / DBSWF
Duration: 40 minutes.
Written by Catherine Tate, Aschlin Ditta and Gordon Anderson; script supervisor Suzanne Baron; theme music by Howard Goodall; music by Philip Pope; designed by Jo Sutherland; assistant producer Martina Klich; executive producer Lucy Lumsden; head of production Toby Ward; produced by Sophie Clarke-Jervoise; directed by Gordon Anderson.

With Adam Best, Nigel Betts, Kellie Bright, Gary Connery, Liam Cunningham, Aschlin Ditta, Tom Ellis, Nitin Ganatra, Philip Glenister, Mathew Horne, Valerie Lilley, Richard Lumsden, Colin Morgan, Tamzin Outhwaite, Lee Ross, Hugh Sachs, Una Stubbs, Niky Wardley, Simon Wolfe, Kathy Burke, George Michael.

Made in association with Bovvered Productions? / Pozzitive Television.

Holding / Source

25.12.2009 **Nan's Christmas Carol** HD/DB / HD/DB
Duration: 50 minutes.
Written by Catherine Tate, Aschlin Ditta and Gordon Anderson; script supervisor Katie Collins; music by Simon Brint; choreography by Nicky Hinkley; director of photography Rob Kitzmann; titles by Component Graphics; art directors Caroline Harper and Madelaine Leech; designed by Jo Sutherland; executive producers Simon Lupton, Sophie Clarke-Jervoise and Catherine Tate; head of production Toby Ward; line producer Pamela Wylde; produced by Geoff Posner; directed by Gordon Anderson.

With Catherine Tate (Nan), Flo ('Tiny Tim'), Roger Lloyd Pack, Ben Miller, David Tennant, Lorna Brown, Rosie Cavaliero, Dominic Coleman, Deddie Davies, Aschlin Ditta, Mathew Horne, Alana Knowles, Richard Lumsden, Owen Salthouse, Niky Wardley, Lorna Watson, Megan Winnard, Madness, James Martin.

CBBC PANTOMIME

A BBC Children's Department production for BBC 1. Transmission details are for BBC 1.

Holding / Source

22.12.1989 **Little Edd Riding Hood** DB / 1"
Duration: 9 minutes.
Produced by Christina Mackay-Robinson; directed by Jane Fletcher.
With Andy Crane, Andi Peters, Simon Parkin, Roy Castle, Jeannette Charles, Helen Rollason, Bill Giles, Phillip Schofield.

THE CBEEBIES CHRISTMAS PANTOMIME

A BBC production for CBeebies. Transmission details are for CBeebies. Duration: 30 minutes.

Holding / Source

18.12.2009 **Jack And Jill** HD/DB / HDC
Written by Chris Jarvis; designed by Sarah Milton; executive producer Tim Lowe; produced by Andrew Garland; directed by Jon Emmanuel and David Rees.
With Chris Evans (Narrator), Katy Ashworth, Andy Day, Justin Fletcher, Sidney Sloane, Alex Winters, Cerrie Burnell, Phil Gallagher, Jacob Scipio, Katrina Bryan, Chris Jarvis, Daisy (The Cow), Daisy The Cow, Dancers from the Joanna School of Dance.

17.12.2010 **Aladdin** HD/DB / HDC
Alternative transmissions: BBC 1: 26.10.2010.
Written by Iain Lauchlan; script supervisor Michelle Parr; music by Liz Kitchen; choreography by Carl Parris; designed by John Alston; assistant producer Claire Taylor; executive producers Alison Stewart and Ewan Vinnicombe; produced by Paul Shuttleworth; directed by Jeanette Goulbourn.
With Justin Fletcher (Nana Knickerbocker Twankey), Andy Day, Phil Gallagher, Katy Ashworth, Nisha Anil, Alex Winters, Neil Sterenberg, Dave Chapman, Chris Jarvis, Pui Fan Lee, Cerrie Burnell, Katrina Bryan, Sidney Sloane, Jacob Scipio, Barbara Speake Stage School.

19.12.2011 **Strictly Cinderella** HD/DB / HDC
With Katrina Bryan (Cinders), Phil Gallagher (Ugly Sister), Justin Fletcher (Ugly Sister), Artem Chigvintsev, Len Goodman, Bruno Tonioli, Craig Revel Horwood, Darcey Bussell.

THE CEDAR TREE

An ATV production. Transmission details are for the ATV midlands region. Duration varies - see below for details.

Main regular credit(s): Devised by Alfred Shaughnessy; theme music by Stephen Francis.

Main regular cast: Susan Engel (Helen Bourne (until 28.12.76)), Sally Osborn (Elizabeth Bourne), Susan Skipper (Victoria Bourne), Joyce Carey (Alice Bourne), Jennifer Lonsdale (Anne Bourne (until 28.12.76)), Kate Coleridge (Phyllis Bourne), Jean Taylor Smith (Nanny).

SERIES 1

Duration: 25 minutes.
Credits: Script editor Alfred Shaughnessy.
Cast: With Philip Latham (Arthur Bourne).

A Quiet Christmas

Duration: 25 minutes.
Main regular credit(s): Written by John Burton; produced by Ian Fordyce; directed by Robert Tronson.
Main regular cast: With Lillias Walker (Rosemary Cartland), John Oxley (Peter Cartland), Cyril Luckham (Charles Ashley), Shaun Scott, Alan Browning, Anthony Sharp.

		Production No	VT Number	Holding / Source
06.01.1977	Episode 1	2059	2059/76	DB / 2"
07.01.1977	Episode 2	2060	2060/76	DB / 2"

CELEBRATE CHRISTMAS

A BBC production for BBC 1. Transmission details are for BBC 1. Duration: 60 minutes.

Edited by Hugh Faupel; produced by Diane Reid.

Deborah McAndrew (Presenter), Charlotte Church, Lesley Garrett, Ladysmith Black Mambazo.

Holding / Source
25.12.1998 — DB / DBS

CELEBRATION

A HTV production. Transmission details are for the ATV midlands region. Duration: 50 minutes.

Singing at the romantic chambers of Castell Coch, near Cardiff.

Orchestra conducted by Owain Arwel Hughes; choreography by Clive Hicks Jenkins; designed by Doug James; produced and directed by Terry Delacey.

Sir Geraint Evans, Petula Clark, Ray Smith, Angharad Rees, Y Diliau, Ardwyn Singers, Llandaff Cathedral Boys Choristers, The Olive Guppy Juvenile Olivettes, The Welsh Philharmonia, Orchestra of the Welsh National Opera.

Holding / Source
25.12.1976

CELEBRATION

A BBC Scotland production for BBC 1. Transmission details are for BBC 1. Duration: 44 minutes.

Designed by Helen Rae; produced by Iain MacFadyen; directed by Anne Somers.

Peter Morrison, Alastair McDonald, Josephine McQueen, Allan Stewart, Norman McLean, The Jim Johnstone Scottish Country Dance Band, The Brian Sievwright Dancers, Brian Fahey and The Scottish Radio Orchestra, The British Caledonian Airways (Renfrew) Pipe Band.

Holding / Source
01.01.1977 — J / 2"

CELEBRATION

A HTV production. Transmission details are for the Thames Television region. Duration: 50 minutes.

Music directed by Norman Kay; associate producer Sir Geraint Evans; executive producer Aled Vaughan; produced and directed by Michael Hayes.

Sir Geraint Evans, Isla Blair, Ryland Davies, Lillian Watson, Ann Martin, Treorchy Male Choir, Cardiff Polyphonic, Aros Mae.

The Joys of Christmas in Words and Music

Holding / Source
25.12.1977

CELEBRATION

A Granada production. Transmission details are for the Granada region. Duration: 25 minutes.

		Production No	Holding / Source
04.12.1980	**Nativity Play**	P1013/35	DB / 2"
18.12.1980	**A Christmas Celebration**	P1013/34	DB / 2"

CELEBRATION

A BBC Scotland production for BBC 1. Transmission details are for BBC 1. Duration: 54 minutes.

Designed by Helen Rae; executive producer Iain MacFadyen; produced and directed by Anne Somers.

Peter Morrison, Alastair McDonald, The Krankies, Helen McArthur, Allan Stewart, Andy Cameron, Norman McLean, The Brian Sievwright Dancers, The Jim Johnstone Scottish Country Dance Band, British Caledonian Airways Pipe Band, Brian Fahey, Scottish Radio Orchestra.

Holding / Source
01.01.1980 — J / 2"

CELEBRITY FIFTEEN-TO-ONE

A Regent Productions production for Channel 4. Transmission details are for Channel 4.
Format by John M. Lewis; produced by William G. Stewart.
William G. Stewart (Host).

	Holding / Source
27.12.1990	1" / 1"

Duration: 35 minutes.
Directed by Simon Pearce.
With Richard Whiteley, Nicholas Parsons, Barry Cryer, Jayne Irving, Claire Rayner, Jan Leeming, David Hamilton, Anna Raeburn, Carol Vorderman, Bob Holness, Nigel Rees, Sally Jones, Rory McGrath, Matthew Parris, Nicholas Owen.

CELEBRITY JUICE

A Talkback Thames production for ITV 2. Transmission details are for ITV 2. Usual duration: 25 minutes.

Main regular credit(s): Format by Leigh Francis.
Main regular performer(s): Keith Lemon (Keith Lemon, Host), Holly Willoughby (Team Captain).
Duration: 40 minutes.
Main regular credit(s): Script supervisor Hayley Collett; music by Earshot Music; titles by Duke & Earl; art director Lucy Fyfe; designed by Dominic Tolfts; associate producers Laura Price and Ed Sleeman; executive producer Dan Baldwin; head of production Beatrice Gay; production manager Gemma Whitford; series producer Leon Wilson; directed by Toby Baker.
Main regular performer(s): With Fearne Cotton (Team Captain), Rufus Hound.

	Holding / Source
23.12.2010 **Christmas Special**	DB / DBSW

Programme associates Marc Haynes and Navelgazing.
With Lionel Blair*, Kian Egan, Mark Feehily, Russell Kane, JEdward.

SERIES 6

Main regular credit(s): Designed by Dominic Tolfts; executive producer Dan Baldwin; produced by Leon Wilson; directed by Toby Baker and Iain Titterington.
Main regular performer(s): With Fearne Cotton (Team Captain).

	Holding / Source
22.12.2011 **Christmas Special**	DB / DBSW

With Rufus Hound, Amy Childs, Paddy McGuinness, Michelle Keegan.

SERIES 7

Main regular performer(s): With Fearne Cotton (Team Captain).

	Holding / Source
13.12.2012 **A Juicemas Carol: Chapter One**	HD/DB / HDC

Duration: 48 minutes.
Highlights from series seven.
Designed by Dominic Tolfts; executive producers Dan Baldwin and Leon Wilson; produced by Ed Sleeman; directed by Toby Baker.
With Nitin Kundra (Indian Keith), Mark Wright (Ghosts Of Chhristmas), Emma Bunton (Team Captain), Jonathan Ross (Team Captain), JEdward.

| 24.12.2012 **A Juicemas Carol: Chapter Two** | HD/DB / HDC |

Duration: 48 minutes.
Christmas edition featuring highlights from the current series.
Designed by Dominic Tolfts; executive producers Dan Baldwin and Leon Wilson; produced by Ed Sleeman and Aaron Morgan; directed by Toby Baker and Benjamin Turner.
With Mark Wright (Ghosts of Christmas), Nitin Kundra (Indian Keith), JEdward.

| 27.12.2012 **Text Santa Christmas Special** | HD/DB / HDC |

Duration: 40 minutes.
Designed by Dominic Tolfts; executive producers Dan Baldwin and Leon Wilson; produced by Ed Sleeman; directed by Toby Baker.
With Aston Merrygold, Davina McCall, Stacey Solomon, Louis Smith, The Chuckle Brothers, Simon Gregson.

SERIES 10

	Holding / Source
12.12.2013 **Christmas Special**	HD/DB / HDC

Duration: 48 minutes.
Designed by Dominic Tolfts; executive producers Leon Wilson and Dan Baldwin; series producer Ed Thomas; produced by Arron Ferster; directed by Toby Baker and Jamie Deekes.
With Fearne Cotton (Team Captain), Kelly Brook (Team Captain), Olly Murs, Peter André, Vanessa White, Jason Byrne, Kim Wilde, James Blunt.

CELEBRITY PLAY YOUR CARDS RIGHT

An LWT production. Transmission details are for the Central region. Duration: 25 minutes.
Bruce Forsyth (Presenter).

	Holding / Source
19.12.1986	1" / 1"

Produced by Alasdair MacMillan.
With Dickie Davies, Liz Davies, Des Rayner, Claire Rayner.

CELEBRITY READY, STEADY, COOK

A BBC production for BBC 1. Transmission details are for BBC 1. Duration: 29 minutes.

SERIES 1
Main regular credit(s): Produced by Mary Ramsay; directed by Chris Fox.
Main regular performer(s): With Fern Britton (Host).

	Holding / Source
24.12.1997	DB / DBSW

With Ainsley Harriott (Chef), Antony Worrall Thompson (Chef), Gareth Hale, Norman Pace.

SERIES 3
Main regular credit(s): Produced by Mary Ramsay; directed by Chris Fox.
Main regular performer(s): With Fern Britton (Host).

	Holding / Source
24.12.1998	DB / DBSW

With Barbara Windsor, Lily Savage.

CELEBRITY SQUARES

Alternative/Working Title(s): BOB AND THE BIG BOX GAME! / BOB'S GALAXY GAME / BOB'S SUPERSQUARES / THE ATV SUNDAY QUIZ / THE BIG NAME GAME!

An ATV production. Transmission details are for the ATV midlands region. Duration: 39 minutes.

Bob himself named this quiz show which was based on the U.S. show Hollywood Squares.

Have you ever seen Bob's Supersquares, The ATV Sunday Quiz or Bob and the Big Box Game? No, because they were all Bob's own titles for a gameshow that began life in the USA as Hollywood Squares.

Devised by Merrill Heatter and Bob Quigley, Lew Grade acquired the rights to Hollywood Squares. The concept involving celebrities sitting in noughts or crosses boxes. Contestants would be asked a question, hear a plausible answer from the star and decide if their answer was true or false. A correct guess and you could try to form three noughts or crosses in a row and win the game.

ATV keen to keep Bob Monkhouse after his work on The Golden Shot gave the task of creating the new show to Francis Essex and Paul Stewart Laing. Essex wanted a wide variety format with musical acts so two pilots were made with musical contributions from Showaddywaddy and Sweet Sensation. Both acts had become famous on New Faces, directed by Paul Stewart Laing. Laing thought the music acts were poor, Essex agreed and they were dropped in favour of a charity quiz game called Bob's Full House.

From the outset ratings were high with many critics praising the witty quips from the guest stars, who included Willy Rushton, Diana Dors, Harry H. Corbett and Alfred Marks. Choosing a voice over artist was tricky, Laing insisted they use an ex-Radio 1 DJ who had fallen out with the BBC and was now unemployable. At the readthrough for Francis Essex the DJ was very straight-laced, but once he got the part, the real madcap Kenny Everett came to the fore, and his career was relaunched.

The witty jokes from the guest stars were not actually ab-libs, they were carefully scripted by Dennis Berson who wrote the jokes uncredited. Laing would brief contestants and never give them the answers. Only once did Diana Dors ask for an answer and she told the audience, much to Laing's anger. Anthea Redfern also insisted on the correct answers, but Laing told her the wrong answers, much to the amusement of her husband Bruce Forsyth who was watching the show.

Many of the answers were based on unusual trivia facts compiled by Jeremy Beadle. When the first series began to be transmitted, letters began to arrive complaining that the answers were factually wrong. Laing summoned Jeremy Beadle to his office and asked, "How do you get your answers?" Beadle replied he often made up the answers if they sounded "close enough"! After that, the answers had to be checked by an outside body.

Hollywood Squares finished with the winner being given the keys to a car. The IBA, the regulatory body that ran ITV, objected and said winners must earn their prize so Laing and Berson devised an endgame involving the winner answering nine questions on a theme to win the prize. The question one week was "Name nine types of bread?" One of the answers was bread rolls. ATV received complaints that bread rolls were not a type of bread. Laing replied by asking the irate complainers if they had the courage to contact the winner and ask for the prize back.

Eventually Laing left to become a freelance director working on This Is Your Life and London Night Out. Bob left to become the host of Family Fortunes. He returned in 1993 to remake the show for Central Television in association with Grundy Television. The concept remained similar, but the charity round was dropped. Guest start included John Inman, Wendy Richard, the Chippendales and new comedians such as Shane Richie and Joe Pasquale. The gags this time were created by Bob and Colin Edmonds, again uncredited. Bob Monkhouse died in 2003 and did not take part in a third remake from So! Television who made a pilot for Channel 5.

Main regular credit(s): Devised by Merrill Heatter and Bob Quigley; music by Jack Parnell.
Main regular performer(s): Bob Monkhouse (Presenter).

SERIES 1
Main regular credit(s): Written by Dennis Berson; produced and directed by Paul Stewart Laing.
Main regular performer(s): With Kenny Everett (Voice Only).

		VT Number	Holding / Source
25.12.1975	**Christmas Celebrity Squares**	1738/75	J|a / 2"

Additional material by Peter Vincent; designed by Ray White.

With Charlie Drake, Des O'Connor, Noele Gordon, John Inman, Keith Harris & Cuddles, Diana Dors, Alfred Marks, Arthur Mullard, Pat Coombs, Joy Dyer, Police Constable Mike Eckles.

CELEBRITY WHO WANTS TO BE A MILLIONAIRE?

Produced for ITV 1 by a variety of companies (see details below). Transmission details are for the Central region. Usual duration: 48 minutes.

Main regular credit(s): Devised by David Briggs, Steve Knight and Mike Whitehill.
Main regular performer(s): Chris Tarrant (Host).

A Celador production.

	Holding / Source
24.12.2002	DB / DBSW
25.12.2002	DB / DBSW
23.12.2006	DB / DBSW

With Nick Ross, Fiona Bruce, Kim Woodburn, Aggie MacKenzie.

CELEBRITY WHO WANTS TO BE A MILLIONAIRE? (continued)

26.12.2006 — DB / DBSW
With Melinda Messenger, Alastair Stewart, Jane Moore, Charles Kennedy M.P..

30.12.2006 — DB / DBSW
With Charles Kennedy M.P., Jane Moore, Bonnie Langford, Anton Du Beke.

A 2waytraffic production.
Main regular credit(s): Programme associate Tony Nicholson; music by Keith Strachan, Matthew Strachan and Ramon Covalo; designed by A1 Set.

Holding / Source

01.01.2008 — DB / DBSW
Script supervisor Carolyn Davey; executive producer Colman Hutchinson.
With Penny Lancaster Stewart, Ian Waite, Christopher Biggins.

23.12.2008 — DB / DBSW
Script supervisor Carolyn Davey; executive producer Colman Hutchinson; produced by David Briggs; directed by Patricia Mordecai.
With Antony Cotton, Suranne Jones, Gary Lineker, Austin Healey.

29.12.2008 — DB / DBSW
Script supervisor Carolyn Davey; executive producer Colman Hutchinson; produced by David Briggs; directed by Patricia Mordecai.
With Zac Purchase, Sarah Webb, Darren Kenny, Liz Johnson, Steve Williams, Christine Ohuruogu.

20.12.2009 — DB / DBSW
Programme associate Tony Nicholson; script supervisor Carolyn Davey; music by Keith Strachan, Matthew Strachan and Ramon Covalo; designed by A1 Set; associate producer Amanda Morris; executive producer Colman Hutchinson; production manager Steve Springford; produced by David Briggs; directed by Ian Hamilton.
With Terry Wogan, Chris Evans, Coleen Nolan, Maureen Nolan, Mike Read, Robin Gibb.

03.01.2012 **New Year Special** — DB / DBSW
Produced by Kim Ross; directed by Richard Vant Riet.

01.01.2013 **New Year Special** — HD/DB / HDC
Series producer Tamara Gilder; directed by Richard Vant Riet.

CENTRE PLAY

A BBC production for BBC 2. Transmission details are for BBC 2. Duration: 30 minutes.

SERIES 1
Main regular credit(s): Produced by Anne Head.

Holding / Source

31.12.1973 **The Illumination Of Mr Shannon** — J / 2"
Written by Don Haworth; produced and directed by Brian McDuffie.
With Patrick McAlinney (James Blakey), Frank Grimes (Michael Shannon), Gito Santana (Waiter).

See also: CENTRE PLAY FOR CHRISTMAS (BBC)

CENTRE PLAY FOR CHRISTMAS

A BBC production for BBC 2. Transmission details are for BBC 2.

Holding / Source

20.12.1975 **The Imp Of The Perverse** — DB-D3 / 2"
Duration: 31 minutes.
Adapted by Andrew Davies; based on a story by Edgar Allan Poe; script editor Alan Seymour; designed by Peter Kindred; produced by Louis Marks; directed by James Ormerod.
With Michael Kitchen (The Student), Philip Stone (The Philosopher), Lalla Ward (The Daughter), Milton Johns (The Servant), Gerald Cross (The Beggar).

See also: CENTRE PLAY (BBC)

CHAIN LETTERS

A Tyne Tees Television production. made in association with Action Time / Barry & Enright Productions. Transmission details are for the Central region. Duration: 25 minutes.
Main regular credit(s): Produced by Christine Williams.
Main regular performer(s): Jeremy Beadle (Presenter).

Holding / Source

22.12.1988 **Christmas Special** — 1" / 1"
Research Simon Ross and Amanda Stevens; designed by Peter Bingeman; produced by Christine Williams; directed by Michael Metcalf.
With Andrew O'Connor (Presenter).

CHALKFACE

A BBC Birmingham production for BBC 2. Transmission details are for BBC 2. Duration: 30 minutes.

Main regular credit(s):   Devised by John Godber; produced by Chris Parr.

Main regular cast: Michael Higgs (Paul Moon), Michael Simkins (Stephen Parker), Andrew Livingston (John Harrison).

	Holding / Source
25.06.1991 **Christmas Cheer**	DB / 1"

Written by Garry Lyons and Jane Thornton; directed by Tim Fywell.

With Jillie Meers (Joan), Jane Wymark (Claire Griffiths), Rosemary Martin (Barbara Kent), Terry Molloy (George Mellor), Niamh Cusack (Melanie Clough), Tony Armatrading (Des Bedford), John Rowe (Bob Silver), Eileen Kenning (Joyce Cox), Joanne Campbell (Betty Lee), Deborah Farrington (Lizzie Bowen), John Forgeham, Alison Hammond, Simone Rhone, Nicola Jones, Adrian Anderson, Kelly Whitehouse.

CHALLENGE ANNEKA

Produced for BBC/ITV by a variety of companies (see details below). made in association with Run Riot. Transmission details are for BBC 1.

Main regular performer(s):   Anneka Rice (Presenter).

	Holding / Source
01.01.1988	DB / 1"

CHANGING ROOMS

A BBC production for BBC 1. Transmission details are for BBC 1.

	Holding / Source
25.12.1998 **Changing Rooms At Christmas**	DB / DBSW

Duration: 30 minutes.

A special yuletide edition of the interior-design challenge show. Carol Smillie is on the isle of Arran, where two neighbours try to give each other's living rooms a special festive feel, with the help of design experts Linda Barker and Laurence Llewelyn-Bowen, DIY expert Andy Kane, and a budget of £500.

Produced by Caspar Peacock; directed by Clare Bradley and Lynda Maher.

With Carol Smillie (Presenter), Linda Barker, Laurence Llewellyn-Bowen, Andy Kane.

CHARLEY'S AUNT

A Yorkshire Television production. Transmission details are for the ATV midlands region. Duration: 66 minutes.

Charley's Aunt first opened in London in 1892 and set a record for the number of performances last century. The fun starts when Donna Lucie D'Alvadorez fails to arrive to act as chaperone, and Jack and Charley have to find a substitute in a hurry.

Adapted by Eric Sykes; based on a play by Brandon Thomas; music by Dennis Wilson; designed by Colin Pigott; produced and directed by Graeme Muir.

Eric Sykes (Brassett), Barbara Murray (Donna Lucia D'Alvadorez), Jimmy Edwards (Mr Spettigue), Gerald Flood (Sir Francis Chesney), Alun Lewis (Charley Wykeham), Osmund Bullock (Jack Chesney), Louise Hall-Taylor (Kitty Verdun), Judi Maynard (Amy Spettigue), Yvonne Nicholson (Ela Delahay).

	Holding / Source
29.12.1977	1" / 2"

CHARLIE BROOKER'S 2010 WIPE

A Zeppotron production for BBC 2. Transmission details are for BBC 2.

Presented by Charlie Brooker; archive producer Ben Jessop; written by Charlie Brooker; programme associates Jason Hazeley and Joel Morris; series editor Nick Vaughan Smith; assistant producers Anna Coane, Gemma Martin and Sam Terroni; executive producer Annabel Jones; head of production Debra Blenkinsop; production manager Sonia Coppi; produced by Jodie Krstic and Christian Watt; directed by Al Campbell.

Doug Stanhope, Grace Dent.

	Holding / Source
27.12.2010	HD/DB / HDC

CHARLIE BROOKER'S 2013 WIPE

A Zeppotron production for BBC 2. Transmission details are for BBC 2. Duration: 60 minutes.

A glance back at a year chock full of surprises, including meteors, cyclists on steroids, fake space monkeys, the Pope resigning, a new Pope, the death of Margaret Thatcher, Miley Cyrus, twerking, a royal baby, Russell Brand on Newsnight and a US government shutdown. Charlie will be discussing these and much more with a selection of guests.

Executive producer Charlie Brooker.

Charlie Brooker (Presenter).

	Holding / Source
28.12.2003	HD/DB / HDC

THE CHARLIE DRAKE SHOW

A BBC production. Transmission details are for BBC. Duration varies - see below for details.

Main regular cast: Charlie Drake (Himself).

SERIES 1

A BBC production. Transmission details are for BBC. Duration: 30 minutes.

Main regular credit(s):   Written by Charlie Drake and Richard Waring; produced and directed by Ronald Marsh.

	Holding / Source
23.12.1960 **A Christmas Carol**	J /

THE CHARLIE DRAKE SHOW (continued)

SERIES 4
A BBC production for BBC 2. Transmission details are for BBC 2. Duration: 45 minutes.
Main regular credit(s): Written by Charlie Drake; produced and directed by Ernest Maxin.
Main regular cast: With The George Mitchell Singers, The Show Dancers.

Holding / Source

24.12.1967 — J / 2"
Music directed by Harry Rabinowitz; choreography by Peter Gordeno.
With The Three Bells, Flight Four, Leslie Dwyer, Doremy Vernon, Dorothy Darke, Henry McGee.

THE CHARLOTTE CHURCH SHOW

A Monkey Films production for Channel 4. made in association with Chick Flicks. Transmission details are for Channel 4. Duration: 40 minutes.
Main regular performer(s): Charlotte Church (Host).

SERIES 1
Main regular credit(s): Additional material by Rob Colley, Simon Dean and Aiden Spackman [credited as Aiden Spacman]; associate producers Helen Albon, Leah Bull, Ben Cooper, Will Innes and Erika Kundig; executive producers Nick Fiveash, Mark Melton, David Granger and Will Macdonald; head of production Karen Morton; series producer Greg Bower; produced by Chris Jones and Kevin Mundye; directed by John F. D. Northover.

Holding / Source

22.12.2006 **Christmas Special** — DB / DBSW
With Paul O'Grady, Ben Elton, Sugababes.

SERIES 3
Main regular credit(s): Script supervisor Manique Ratner; associate producers Dan Louw, Simone Tai and Stephen Yemoh; executive producers Fi Cotter Craig, David Granger, Will Macdonald, Nick Fiveash and Mark Melton; head of production Karen Morton; series producer Clyde Holcroft; directed by Julia Knowles.
Main regular performer(s): With Simon Greenall (Studio Voiceover).

Holding / Source

21.12.2008 **The Charlotte Church Nutcracking Christmas Special** — DB / DBSW
Duration: 60 minutes.
Written by Phil Kerr, George Poles, Steve Parry and Laurence Rickard; designed by James Zafar; production manager Helena Parkhill.
With Ronnie Corbett, Jo Brand, James Corden, Ruth Jones, Jeremy Edwards, Rhydian Roberts, Bobby Fame and The Allstars, Tim Vincent, Claire Young, Michael Sophocles.

THE CHART SHOW

A Video Visuals production for Channel 4. Transmission details are for Channel 4. Usual duration: 40 minutes.

Holding / Source

30.12.1986 **The Chart Show Christmas Special** — 1"|n / 1"
Duration: 85 minutes.

27.12.1987 **The Chart Show Christmas Special** — 1"|n / 1"
Duration: 75 minutes.
All those who thought Christmas was over, stand by for this special seasonal edition of The Chart Show, featuring the Top 10 singles of the year and a selection of the best sellers of 1987 from the Dance, Heavy Metal, Album and Indies charts. Plus sneak previews of new video releases of 1988. Plus the best new band of 1987, the best foreign video and the best and worst videos of the year.
Executive producer Keith MacMillan; produced by Philip Davey.

02.01.1989 **The Chart Show Christmas Special** — 1"|n / 1"
Executive producer Keith MacMillan; produced by Philip Davey.

All NFTVA holdings are off-air recordings.

CHAS & DAVE'S KNEES-UP

An LWT production. Transmission details are for the Central region.
Main regular performer(s): Chas & Dave (Hosts).

Holding / Source

25.12.1982 **Chas & Dave's Christmas Knees-Up** — D2 / 1"
Duration: 50 minutes.
Designed by Michael Minas; produced by David Bell; directed by Alasdair MacMillan.
With Jim Davidson, Eric Clapton, Lenny Peters, Jimmy Cricket, Albert Lee, Cosmotheka, Alyn Ainsworth and his Orchestra.

CHEF!

Produced for BBC 1 by a variety of companies (see details below). Transmission details are for BBC 1. Duration: 30 minutes.

Main regular credit(s): Created by Peter Tilbury; based on an idea by Lenny Henry; theme music by Omar.

Main regular cast: Lenny Henry (Gareth Blackstock), Caroline Lee Johnson (Janice Blackstock), Roger Griffiths (Everton).

SERIES 1
An APC Production production. made in association with Crucial Films.

Main regular credit(s): Written by Peter Tilbury; music by Jakko M. Jakszyk; designed by Andrew Howe Davies; executive producer Polly McDonald; production manager Christopher Miles; produced by Charlie Hanson; directed by John Birkin.

Main regular cast: With Claire Skinner (Lucinda), Gary Parker (Piers), Erkan Mustafa (Otto).

Holding / Source

24.12.1993 **A Bird In The Hand** DB-D3 / V1SW

Script supervisor Sam Donovan; director of photography Frank Gell; art directors Chris Thompson and Philip Robinson. With Vivian Pickles.

CHEGGERS PLAYS POP

A BBC Manchester production for BBC 1. Transmission details are for BBC 1.

Main regular performer(s): Keith Chegwin (Presenter).

SERIES 3
Duration: 25 minutes.

	Production No	VT Number	Holding / Source
22.12.1980 **Christmas Special**	D2740/1188	NMR/S024X	DB-D3 / 2"

Designed by Barry Roach; assistant producer Martin Hughes; executive producer Peter Ridsdale Scott; produced and directed by Mike Stephens.

With Gordon Astley (Team Leader), Vivienne Mckone (Team Leader), Darts, Shakin' Stevens, Showaddywaddy, Jona Lewie, Peter Powell, Barbara Dickson, Dollar, B. A. Robertson.

SERIES 4

Holding / Source

30.12.1981 DB-D3 / 2"

SERIES 5
Duration: 25 minutes.

Holding / Source

26.12.1982 **Christmas Special** DB-D3 / 2"

Designed by Mel Bibby; executive producer Peter Ridsdale Scott; produced by Mike Stephens; directed by Martin Hughes.

With Vivienne Mckone (Team Leader), Jon Eden (Team Leader), Modern Romance, Dexy's Midnight Runners, Madness.

SERIES 6

Holding / Source

30.12.1983 DB / 1"

With Bucks Fizz, The Thompson Twins.

CHELSEA AT NINE

A Granada production. Transmission details are for the Granada region. Duration varies - see below for details.

SERIES 2
Main regular performer(s): With Bernard Braden (Host), Peter Knight and his Orchestra.

	Production No	Holding / Source
07.01.1960	P154/4	DB-4W / 40

Duration: 45 minutes.

Designed by Dan Snyder; produced by Tim Hewat; directed by Gordon Flemyng.

With Johnny Haymer, Los Machombos, Beryl Grey, Brian Ashbridge, The Hilltoppers, Frank Williams, Marjorie Rhodes, Alfie Bass, Harry Fowler, George Moon, Ann Taylor, Marion Breen, Ted Hare, Jackie Rae, Bill Fraser, Mario Fabrizi.

Including The Army Game: Bootserella

THE CHELSEA MURDERS

A Thames Television production. Transmission details are for the ATV midlands region. Duration: 104 minutes.

Devised by Andrew Brown; adapted by Jonathan Hales; based on a book by Lionel Davidson; story editor Robert Holmes; theme music by Andy Mackay; music by Anthony Isaac; choreography by Alan Harding; designed by Allan Cameron; executive producer Joan Rodker; produced by Brenda Ennis; directed by Derek Bennett.

Dave King (Warton), Antony Carrick (Summers), Christopher Bramwell (Mason), Michael Feast (Steve), Guy Gregory (Artie), Miranda Bell (Mary), David Gant (Frank), Darien Angadi (Abo), David Yip (Denny), Fiona Mathieson (Librarian), Douglas Sheldon (Otto), Anthony Barnett (Len), Richard Hampton (Editor), Penny Leatherbarrow (Barmaid), Lucy Griffiths (Mrs Bulstrode), Gavin Campbell (Chef), Toria Fuller (Wilhelmina), Derek Broome (Police Constable Nutter), Ishaq Bux (Arab Servant), Maryann Turner (Landlady), Robin Parkinson (Landlord), Chris Gannon (Publican), Susie Jenkinson (Girl), Harold Reese (Neighbour), James Charles (Policeman), Ian Liston (Policeman), Timothy Earle (Dancer), Philip Compton (Dancer), Caroline Funnell (Dancer), Vyvian Hall (Dancer), Andrew Johns (Dancer), Christopher Lawrence (Dancer), Vernon Nurse (Dancer), Georgina Provan (Dancer).

Holding / Source

30.12.1981 DB / 2"

Edited version of an untransmitted six-part ARMCHAIR THRILLER serial. If the title sequences and recaps are ignored, this version condenses approximately 134 minutes of material in the original serial down to 104 with the material removed being fairly evenly spread across the six episodes. The edited version was made at a

THE CHELSEA MURDERS (continued)   British Christmas Television Guide

time when the original recordings (i.e. before post-production) were still available as material which cross-faded to break- or end-titles in the episodic version appears here without the fades. Aside from this, it contains no VT material other than that in the six-parter although a very small amount of location film footage unused by the longer version appears here.

CHEWIN' THE FAT

A the Comedy Unit production for BBC Scotland. Transmission details are for BBC 1 Scotland. Duration: 30 minutes.

Main regular credit(s):   Executive producer Ewan Angus; produced by Colin Gilbert.

Main regular cast: Ford Kiernan, Greg Hemphill, Karen Dunbar.

Date	Title	Holding / Source
31.12.2000	**Hogmanay Special**	DB / DBSW
31.12.2001	**Hogmanay Special**	DB / DBSW
31.12.2002		DB / DBSW
31.12.2003		DB / DBSW
31.12.2004		DB / DBSW
31.12.2005		DB / DBSW

CHICKEN SHED

An LWT production. Transmission details are for the Central region. Duration: 48 minutes.

Produced and directed by Bryan Izzard.

Bob Hoskins (Presenter), The Chicken Shed Theatre Company (Players).

Holding / Source

25.12.1998   **Christmas Special**   DB / DBS

With Judi Dench (Narrator).

A CHILD IS BORN

A Southern Television production. Transmission details are for the ATV midlands region. Duration: 40 minutes.

A musical celebration of the Nativity, including For Unto Us A Child is Born, from Handel's Messiah, Vaughan Williams' Fantasia on Christmas Carols with baritone Richard Stilwell, and soprano Sheila Armstrong singing Rejoice Greatly.

    Young David Hurley, a chorister from Winchester Cathedral, sings Silent Night, while Ward Swingle has provided three arrangements of carols for his new jazz vocal group Swingle II. Kenneth Montgomery conducts the Bournemouth Symphony Orchestra, and Martin Neary the Winchester Cathedral Choir.

Orchestra conducted by Kenneth Montgomery; sound Cyril Vine; designed by John Dilly; associate producer Humphrey Burton; produced and directed by Dave Heather.

Sheila Armstrong, Richard Stilwell, Swingle II, Winchester Cathedral Choir, Bournemouth Symphony Orchestra, David Hurley.

Holding / Source

22.12.1974   DB / 2"

Held by Euroarts.

A CHILD OF THE SIXTIES

An LWT production. Transmission details are for the Anglia region. Duration: 70 minutes.

The 1960s seen through the eyes of a young man, Gyles Brandreth, President of the Oxford Union, whose knowledge and understanding of the world was shaped, almost exclusively, by television. He discusses the decade with Lady Langford, Fred W. Friendly, Iain Macleod and Michael Foot MP.

Research Sue Huskission; film editor John Lodge; designed by Bryan Bagge; produced and directed by Peter Morley.

Gyles Brandreth, Lady Longford, Fred Friendly, Iain McLeod M.P., Michael Foot M.P..

Holding / Source

27.12.1969   D2 /

THE CHILDREN OF GREEN KNOWE

A BBC Children's Department production for BBC 1. Transmission details are for BBC 1. Duration: 25 minutes.

Main regular credit(s):   Adapted by John Stadelman; based on a book by Lucy M. Boston; music by Peter Howell and BBC Radiophonic Workshop; designed by Alan Spalding; executive producer Paul Stone; production managers Tony Guyan and Gillian Harris; directed by Colin Cant.

Main regular cast: Alec Christie (Tolly), Daphne Oxenford (Mrs Oldknow).

Holding / Source

26.11.1986   **Episode 1**   DB / 1"

With Yvette Byrne (Miss Spud), Virginia Courtney (First Woman on Train), Meg Ritchie (Second Woman on Train), Brian Osborne (Taxi Driver), George Malpas (Boggis).

03.12.1986   **Episode 2**   DB / 1"

With George Malpas (Boggis), Heather Ramsay (Mother Oldknow), Joan Ogden (Granny Oldknow), Graham McGrath (Toby), Polly Maberly (Linnet), Peter Hughes (Doctor), James Trevelyan (Alexander).

10.12.1986   **Episode 3**   DB / 1"

With Polly Maberly (Linnet), James Trevelyan (Alexander), Gordon Kane (Ferdie), Ann Tirard (Petronella), Graham McGrath (Toby), Heather Ramsay (Mother Oldknow), Bev Willis (Captain Oldknow), Danny Schiller (Gabrielli), Iain Rattray (King Charles II).

THE CHILDREN OF GREEN KNOWE

17.12.1986 Episode 4 DB / 1"
Duration: 29 minutes.
With Brian Osborne (Taxi Driver), George Malpas (Boggis), Heather Ramsay (Mother Oldknow), Graham McGrath (Toby), James Trevelyan (Alexander), Polly Maberly (Linnet), Peter Poll (St Christopher), Mark Vella (Stone Child).

CHILDREN SING CHRISTMAS

A TVS production. Transmission details are for the Central region. Duration: 50 minutes.

Drawings by John Ryder; music by John Rutter; designed by Brian Motte; produced by Angus Wright and Dave Heather; directed by Angus Wright and Dave Heather.

Nanette Newman (Presenter), Choir of Salisbury Cathedral, The Cambridge Singers, Richard Seal, City of London Sinfonia.

	Holding / Source
26.12.1982	1" / 1"

CHILDREN SING CHRISTMAS AT CANTERBURY

A TVS production. Transmission details are for the Central region. Duration: 50 minutes.

A concert of favourite Christmas music from Canterbury Cathedral. During the singing a mysterious stranger leads two little children away from the pomp and brilliance of the high altar, as that they may discover Christmas again in the secret of the crypt.

Music directed by John Rutter; choreography by Karen Rabinowitz; designed by Christine Ruscoe; produced by Angus Wright and Dave Heather; directed by Angus Wright and Dave Heather.

Simon Ainley (The Clown), John Gage (The Boy), Louise Cox (The Girl), Barry Wilkinson (Shepherd / King), Barry Grantham (Shepherd / King), Robert Hopkins (Shepherd / King), Anthony Wellington (Shepherd / King), James Tillitt (Shepherd / King), Peter St James (Shepherd / King), Scott St Martyn (Shepherd / King), Stephen Varcoe (Baritone), The Pestalozzi Children's Village Choir, Holy Trinity C of E Primary School, Ramsgate, The Cambridge Singers, Choir of Canterbury Cathedral, London Gabrieli Brass Ensemble.

	Holding / Source
23.12.1984	1" / 1"

CHILDRENS ITV AWARDS

Produced for Various ITV Companies by a variety of companies (see details below). Transmission details are for the Central region. Duration varies - see below for details.

	Holding / Source
19.12.1997	DB / DBS

A Granada production. Duration: 70 minutes.

Written by Nigel Crowle; produced by Nigel Hall; directed by John Morgan.

With Neil Buchanan (Narrator), Shane Ritchie (Rockafella), Timmy Mallett (Dame Trott), Elliot Henderson Boyle (Reg), Isla Fisher (Dandini), Paul Leyshon (Buttons), Lisa Riley (Princess Jean), Jez Edwards (Mirror), Mark Speight (Jack), Jane Danson (Anthea), Georgia Taylor (Ulrika), Ace (Gladiator) (Robin Hood), Rhino (Will Scarlett), Tim Whitnall (Aladdin), Boyzone, Eternal, Peter André, Melisa Joan Hart, Alan Shearer, Louise, The Spice Girls.

CHILDREN'S WARD

A Granada production. Transmission details are for the Central region. Duration: 25 minutes.

Main regular credit(s):   Created by Paul Abbott and Kay Mellor.

SERIES 4
Main regular credit(s):   Script editor Russell T. Davies; designed by Stephen Graham; executive producer Ed Pugh; produced by Sita Williams.

		Production No	Holding / Source
25.12.1991	Christmas On Children's Ward	1/1519/50	1" / 1"

A special Christmas episode in which we meet up again with the Jordan family who have featured in the previous series. Barbra Jordan has to leave her kids to their own resources while she keeps an appointment with a money lender - trying to make Christmas special for the family. But Sally Jordan has a near fatal accident which brings home to everyone the fact that Christmas isn't a fun time in every household. Kieran and Diane make up their differences for the festive season and a new patient, Joey, is the cause of peace and harmony in his family.

Written by Paul Abbott; directed by Richard Signy.

With Ken Parry, Tom Higgins, Clinton Blake, Emily Oldfield, Jenny Luckraft, Janette Beverley, Jonathan Sassen, Gwenda Hughes, Martin Corrigan, Emily Aston, Natalie Wiblin, Susan Brown, Matthew Marsh, Eamon Riley, Kathy Jamieson, Emma Johnston, Phil Atkinson, Nasser Memarzia, Rita May, Judy Holt, Kiran Hocking, Jonathan Tristram, Vilma Hollingbery, Meg Johnson.

See also: THE WARD

A CHILD'S CHRISTMAS IN WALES

An Atlantis production for HTV. made in association with Atlantis Films. Transmission details are for the Central region. Duration: 50 minutes.

Adapted by Peter Kreutzer; based on a story by Dylan Thomas; executive producers Patrick Dromgoole, Michael MacMillan and Joseph Pierson; produced by Gillian Richardson and Seaton McLean; directed by Don McBrearty.

Denholm Elliott (Grandad Geraint), Mathonwy Reeves (Thomas), Jesse M. Brearty (Young Geraint), Calum McGeachie (Jim).

	Holding / Source
24.12.1987	1" / 1"

A CHILD'S CHRISTMAS IN WALES

Alternative/Working Title(s): NADOLIG PLENTYN YNG NGHYMRU
A Cwmni Da production for S4C. made in association with Brave New World. Transmission details are for S4C. Duration: 25 minutes.
Music by Michael Jeffrey; produced by Michael Jeffrey and Neville Hughes; directed by Dave Unwin.
Matthew Rhys (Narrator).

	Holding / Source
25.12.2008	DB / DBSW

Animated film, broadcast in Welsh.

A CHILD'S CHRISTMAS

A BBC Wales production for BBC. Transmission details are for BBC. Duration: 15 minutes.
Written by Dylan Thomas; produced and directed by Dafydd Gruffydd.
Emlyn Williams (Storyteller).

	Holding / Source
24.12.1958	B3 / B3

A CHILD'S CHRISTMASES IN WALES

A Boomerang production for BBC Wales. made in association with Tidy Productions Ltd. Transmission details are for BBC 4. Duration: 60 minutes.
Adapted by Mark Watson; based on a story by Dylan Thomas; script supervisor Pam Humphreys; music by Paul Clark; director of photography Ray Orton; art directors Tom Pearce and Dewi Thomas; designed by Cerwyn Lloyd; executive producers Gareth Rees and David Peet; head of production Carys Beynon-Williams; line producer Dic Jones; produced by Steve Doherty and Juliet Charlesworth; directed by Christine Gernon.
Ruth Jones (Mum), Mark Lewis Jones (Dad), Steve Speirs (Uncle Huw), Paul Kaye (Uncle Gorwel), Michael Sheen (Narrator), Oliver Bunyan (Young Owen), Jamie Burch (Young Maurice), Mark Charles Williams (Older Owen), Rhys McLellan (Older Maurice), Alex Beckett (Carol Singer).

	Holding / Source
17.12.2009	HD/DB / HD/DB

Alternative transmissions: BBC 2: 30.12.2009.

CHILD'S PLAY

An LWT production. Transmission details are for the Central region. Duration varies - see below for details.

SERIES 3
Main regular credit(s):   Associate producer Dave Morley; series producer Brian Wesley; produced by Richard Hearsey; directed by John Gorman.
Main regular performer(s): With Michael Aspel (Presenter).

	Holding / Source
22.12.1985	D2 / 1"

Duration: 35 minutes.
With Roy Castle, Janet Brown, Bobby Davro, Sandra Dickinson.

CHIPPERFIELD'S CHRISTMAS CIRCUS

A Thames Television production. Transmission details are for the ATV midlands region. Duration: 50 minutes.
Ringmaster Ed "Stewpot" Stewart meets the famous Chipperfield family under the big top at Clapham Common.
Music directed by Alan Braden; music associate Bobby Heath; designed by David Marshall; produced and directed by Christopher Palmer.
Ed Stewart (Ringmaster), The Tonitos, The Brizios, Phil Enos.

	Holding / Source
25.12.1973	DB / 2"

CHIPPERFIELD'S CHRISTMAS CIRCUS

A Thames Television production. Transmission details are for the ATV midlands region. Duration: 50 minutes.
Sensational acts from around the world.
Music directed by Alan Braden; music associate Bobby Heath; designed by Frank Gillman; produced and directed by Christopher Palmer.
Ed Stewart (Ringmaster), The Flying Palacios, Yuri and Tonya, The Mohawks, Leigh Marsh, Jacko Fossett, Little Billy and Company, The Chipperfield Elephants, Dick Chipperfield.

	Holding / Source
26.12.1974	DB / 2"

CHIPPERFIELD'S CHRISTMAS CIRCUS

A Thames Television production. Transmission details are for the ATV midlands region. Duration: 50 minutes.
Music directed by Alan Braden; designed by Robin Parker; produced and directed by Christopher Palmer.
Roy Hudd (Ringmaster), Les Ballan, The Hermans, The Laner Brothers, Dick Chipperfield, Mary Chipperfield, Charlie Cairoli, Rex Grey Showgirls.

	Holding / Source
25.12.1975	DB / 2"

CHIPPERFIELD'S CHRISTMAS CIRCUS

A Thames Television production. Transmission details are for the ATV midlands region. Duration: 50 minutes.

Music directed by Alan Braden; music associate Sam Harding; designed by Robin Parker; produced and directed by Christopher Palmer.

David Hamilton (Ringmaster), Mary Chipperfield, Sally Chipperfield, Jimmy Chipperfield, Dick Chipperfield, The Bruksons, The Leotaris, Los Alamos, Bubo Ernesto, Johnny Hutch, The Herculeans, Rex Grey Showgirls, Alan Braden Showband.

	VT Number	Holding / Source
27.12.1976	15537	DB / 2"

CHIPPERFIELD'S CHRISTMAS CIRCUS

A Thames Television production. Transmission details are for the ATV midlands region. Duration: 50 minutes.

Music directed by Alan Braden; music associate Bobby Heath; designed by Frank Gillman; produced and directed by Christopher Palmer.

David Hamilton (Ringmaster), Tommy Chipperfield, Dick Chipperfield, Lee Pee Ville, Cata Polen, Bocky, Randel and Co, James Clubb, Rogana, Rex Grey Showgirls, Alan Braden Circus Showband.

	Holding / Source
27.12.1977	J / 2"

CHIPS' COMIC

A Verronmead Productions production for Channel 4. made in association with Primetime. Transmission details are for Channel 4. Duration: 25 minutes.

Main regular credit(s): Written by David Wood; produced by Maureen Harter.

SERIES 2

Main regular credit(s): Music by Peter Hope and Juliet Lawson.

	Holding / Source
22.12.1984 **Party**	1" / 1"

Elsa, Inky and Rover get ready for their Christmas party to celebrate finishing the Chips' Comic Book.

Directed by Terence Dudley.

CHOIR PRACTICE

A BBC production for BBC 2. Transmission details are for BBC 2. Duration: 60 minutes.

Adapted by Elwyn Jones and John Lloyd; based on a play by Cliff Gordon; music directed by Peter Knight; designed by Stuart Walker; produced and directed by James Gilbert.

Glyn Houston (Geraint), Richard Davies (Cliff), Stuart Burrows (Saunders The Tenor), Jessie Evans (Bessie The Milk), Talfryn Thomas (Mr Lloyd), Dorothea Phillips (Mrs Lloyd), Nicholas Jones (Hywel), Hubert Rees (Dai), Islwyn Morris (Mr Davies), Margaret John (Mrs Davies), Beth Morris (Bronwen), Jack Walters (Owen), Charles Williams (William), John Garvin (Brychan Powell), Brychan Powell (Trumpeter).

	Holding / Source
24.12.1970	DB-R1 / 2"

CHOOSE CHOICE

A BBC production for BBC Choice. Transmission details are for BBC Choice. Duration: 22 minutes.

Written by John O'Farrell and Mark Burton; executive producer Beatrice Ballard; produced by Pollyana Worsley; directed by Daryl Goodrich.

Clive Anderson (Host), Lucy Fields.

	Holding / Source
23.12.1998	DB / D3S

Launch programme of BBC Choice.

CHORLTON AND THE WHEELIES

A Cosgrove Hall production for Thames Television. Transmission details are for the ATV midlands region.

Main regular credit(s): Created by Brian Cosgrove and Mark Hall; written by Brian Trueman and Joe Kemp; theme music by Joe Griffiths; produced by Brian Cosgrove and Mike Hall.

Main regular cast: Joe Lynch (Voices).

SERIES 2

	VT Number	Holding / Source
26.12.1977 **Chorlton In The Ice World**	37794	C1 / C1

Duration: 25 minutes.

It is Christmas in Wheelyworld, and Chorlton, the Happiness Dragon, the Wheelies and Pablo, the dancing duck, are preparing themselves for the Fancy Dress Ball. But Fenella uses her evil magic to lead Chorlton and the Wheelies off into a very strange world where they are confronted by some very peculiar creatures, including the wicked Snow King.

See also: COSGROVE HALL'S BOX OF CRACKERS

CHRIS MOYLES QUIZ NIGHT

A Magnum Media production for Channel 4. Transmission details are for Channel 4. Duration: 45 minutes.

Main regular performer(s): Chris Moyles (Host).

SERIES 3

Main regular credit(s): VT directors Adam Jarmaine and Sam Eastall; script supervisor Hayley Ayers; theme music by Music Four; music by Steve Sidwell and Pete Murray; art director Catherine Land; designed by Patrick Doherty; executive producers Andy Auerbach and Dean Nabarro; production manager Gemma McDonnell; series producer Michael Livingstone; produced by Kate Edmundson and Rose Hanson; studio sequences directed by Steve Smith; directed by Steve Smith.

Main regular performer(s): With Peter Dickson (Voice Only).

Holding / Source

22.12.2010 DB / DBSW

With Pamela Anderson, Kelly Osbourne, Paddy McGuinness, David Tennant, Jason Donovan.

SERIES 5

Main regular credit(s): Programme associate Michael Livingstone; theme music by Music Four; music by Steve Sidwell; designed by Patrick Doherty; executive producers Andy Auerbach and Dean Nabarro; produced by Rose Hanson and Kate Edmunds; studio direction by Steve Smith; directed by Julia Knowles.

Holding / Source

26.12.2011 **Christmas Quiz Night** HD/DB / HDC

With Olly Murs, James Corden, Louie Spence.

CHRISTMAS AND A MOUSE

A BBC production. Transmission details are for BBC. Duration: 20 minutes.

Produced and directed by Kevin Billington.

Alan Whicker (Storyteller).

Holding / Source

24.12.1963 J / B1

A Tonight Presentation.

CHRISTMAS AT THE RIVIERA

A Carnival Films production for ITV 1. Transmission details are for the Central region. Duration: 100 minutes.

Written by Mark Bussell and Justin Sbresni; script supervisor Suzanne Baron; script editor Clova McCallum; music by Nina Humphreys; designed by James Merifield; executive producers Simon Curtis and Sally Woodward Gentle; produced by Mark Bussell and Justin Sbresni; directed by Mark Bussell and Justin Sbresni.

Reece Shearsmith (Ashley Dodds), Alexander Armstrong (Reverend Miles Rogers), Darren Boyd (Tim Dunn), Anna Chancellor (Diane Rogers), Sam Kelly (Dennis Dunn), Warren Clarke (Maurice Hunt), Barbara Flynn (Rita Hunt), Pam Ferris (Avril Weston), Peter Vaughan (Glen), James Greene (Hugh Hodges), Lorna Watson (Svetlana), Katherine Parkinson (Vanessa Blyth), Ryan Watson (Edwin Hodges), Paul Raffield (Alan Hodges), Rasmus Hardiker (Luke), Cordelia Bugeja (Samantha), Alex Macqueen (Barry), Tim Key (Gary), William Travis (Christopher Hunt), Geoffrey Whitehead (Godfrey), Angus Barnett (Ellis), Marc Small (Policeman), Martin Trenaman (Photographer).

Holding / Source

24.12.2007 DB / V1SW

CHRISTMAS BOX

A BBC production. Transmission details are for BBC. Duration: 45 minutes.

Produced by Ronnie Taylor, Nicholas Crocker, Douglas Fleming and Bryan Sears; directed by Ronnie Taylor, Nicholas Crocker, Douglas Fleming and Bryan Sears.

McDonald Hobley (Host), Peter Haigh (Host), Cliff Michelmore (Host), Shirley Abicair, Eve Boswell, Carl Brisson, Charlie Chester, Sooty, Harry Corbett, Bill Maynard, Jimmy James, Bob Monkhouse, Edna Savage, Shani Wallis.

Holding / Source

25.12.1955 J /

A CHRISTMAS BOX FROM JOSEPH COOPER

A BBC production for BBC 2. Transmission details are for BBC 2. Duration: 60 minutes.

In a programme of melody (sometimes Hidden) and monologue The music includes Granados (The Maiden and the Nightingale), Tchaikovsky (Humoresque), Schumann (Traumerei), Satie (Gymnopedie) and a Rossini String Sonata movement: the monologues, The Artists' Room and The Choir Committee Meeting.

Produced and directed by Walter Todds.

Joseph Cooper, Joyce Grenfell, Neville Marriner, Academy of St. Martin-In-The-Fields.

Holding / Source

26.12.1974 J / 2"

CHRISTMAS CALL

A BBC Wales production for BBC 1 Wales. Transmission details are for BBC 1 Wales. Duration: 50 minutes.

Produced and directed by Derek Trimby.

Henry Jacobs (Host), Linda Lee, Brian Hoey, Max Boyce, Ivor Emmanuel, Patti Flynn, Nerys Hughes, Alex Munro, Tessie O'Shea, Brian Rix, Ryan and Ronnie, Harry Secombe, Stan Stennett, Johnny Stewart, Robert Young, Tom Jones.

Holding / Source

26.12.1973 C1SEQ / 2"

Film sequences featuring Nerys Hughes, Harry Secombe, Brian Rix, Tom Jones and an item called 'Belfast' exist.

CHRISTMAS CALL

A CHRISTMAS CARD FROM WALES

A BBC Wales production for BBC 1 Scotland. Transmission details are for BBC 1 Scotland. Duration: 30 minutes.
Music directed by Benny Litchfield; choreography by Clive Hicks Jenkins; designed by Julian Williams; produced and directed by Hywel Williams.
Ryan Davies, Gillian Humphreys, The Richard Williams Singers, Junior Salvation Army Band.

Holding / Source
15.12.1974   DB / 2"

A CHRISTMAS CAROL (RADIO)

A BBC production for BBC Radio 4. Transmission details are for BBC Radio 4. Duration: 90 minutes.
Adapted by Christopher Denys; based on a story by Charles Dickens; music by Elizabeth Parker; produced and directed by Janet Whitaker.
Michael Gough (Ebenezer Scrooge), Freddie Jones (Narrator), Robert Eddison (Ghost of Marley), Douglas Hodge (Scrooge's Nephew), Anna Wing (Mrs Dilbur), Elizabeth Lindsay (Ghost of Christmas Past), Peter Woodthorpe (Ghost of Christmas Present), Danny Schiller (Bob Cratchit), Vivian Pickles (Mrs Cratchit), Timothy Bateson (Mr Fezziwig), Maxine Audley (Mrs Fezziwig), Andrew Wincott (Young Scrooge), Terence Edmond (Dick Wilkins), Joanna Myers (Belle), Ronald Herdman (Old Joe), Petra Markham (Scrooge's Niece), Emma Gregory (Sister), Timothy Carlton (Topper), Ian Lindsay (Schoolmaster), Danielle Allan (Martha), Hugo Mendez (Tiny Tim).

Holding / Source
22.12.1990   DA /

CHRISTMAS CAROL CONCERT

A HTV production. Transmission details are for the ATV midlands region. Duration: 55 minutes.
Music directed by Michael Stocks; produced and directed by Terry Harding.
Somerset Youth Ochestra.

Holding / Source
25.12.1977   2" / 2"
From Wells Cathedral.

A CHRISTMAS CAROL CONCERT

A Granada production. Transmission details are for the Central region. Duration: 25 minutes.
Produced by Peter Heinze; directed by David Warwick.
Charles Farncombe (Conductor), Simon Lindley (Organist).

Holding / Source
23.12.1982   1" / 1"

CHRISTMAS CAROLS

A BBC production for BBC 2. Transmission details are for BBC 2. Duration: 25 minutes.
Introduced by Michael Flanders; designed by Roger Liminton; produced and directed by Patricia Foy.
Wandsworth School Choir.

Holding / Source
24.12.1969   R1 / 2"

CHRISTMAS CAROLS FROM CAMBRIDGE

A Thames Television production. Transmission details are for the Thames Television region.

Holding / Source
24.12.1978   J / 2"

CHRISTMAS CAROLS ON ITV

An ITV Studios production for ITV 1. Transmission details are for the Central region. Duration: 48 minutes.

Holding / Source
24.12.2012   HD/DB / HDC
Aled Jones is joined by Coronation Street cast members at the soap's local church for a retelling of the Nativity story, with music from Russell Watson, Jonathan and Charlotte and singing Army trio the Soldiers. Corrie stars Julie Hesmondhalgh and Sarnia Ghadie also reveal how they'll be spending Christmas.
Produced by Patrick Talbot; directed by Bridget Caldwell.
With Aled Jones (Presenter), Russell Watson, Samia Ghadie, Jonathan and Charlotte, Julie Hesmondhalgh.

24.12.2013   HD/DB / HDC
Aled Jones is joined by tenor Russell Watson, Britain's Got Talent finalists Richard and Adam, choirboy Jack Topping and Emmerdale's Natalie Anderson for performance of popular carols from St Michael the Archangel Church in the village of Kirkby Malham, North Yorkshire.
Produced by Simon Paintin; directed by Bridget Caldwell.
With Aled Jones (Presenter), Russell Watson, Richard and Adam, Jack Topping, Natalie Anderson.

CHRISTMAS CAROUSEL

A BBC Birmingham production for BBC 1. Transmission details are for BBC 1. Duration: 35 minutes.
Designed by Charles Carroll; produced and directed by Brian Hulme.
Ian Wallace (Presenter), Stephanie Voss (Presenter), Laurie Payne (Presenter), Tom Conti (Presenter), BBC Midland Light Orchestra.

Holding / Source
23.12.1969   J / 2"

| CHRISTMAS CARYL | British Christmas Television Guide |

CHRISTMAS CARYL
A HTV Wales production. Transmission details are for the HTV Wales region. Duration: 50 minutes.
Designed by Phil Williams; executive producer Peter Elias Jones; produced and directed by Ronw Protheroe.
Caryl Parry Jones, Caryl Thomas, Max Boyce, Gareth Lewis, Myfanwy Talog, Catrin Beard.

	Holding / Source
24.12.1987	1" / 1"

A CHRISTMAS CELEBRATION
A BBC production for BBC 1. Transmission details are for BBC 1. Duration: 45 minutes.
Written by Brian Sibley and Philip Glassborow; additional material by Murray Watts; music directed by Noel Tredinnick; edited by Stephen Whittle; designed by Eric Walmsley; production team Fiona Breslin, Adam Tandy and Chris Loughlin; associate producer Helen Morton; produced and directed by Christopher Mann.
Cliff Richard (Host), Sally Magnusson (Host), Michael Williams, Thora Hird, Wendy Craig, Kathleen McKellar Ferguson, Paul Freeman, Peter Goodwright, Graham Kendrick, Ian McCaskill, St Philip's Choir, John Wells, Precious Wilson, The All Souls Orchestra and Choir, Russell Boulter, Paul Burbridge, Alison Draper, Polly March.

	Holding / Source
25.12.1988 [Songs Of Praise]	DB / 1"

CHRISTMAS CELEBRITY BLIND DATE
An LWT production. Transmission details are for the Central region. Duration: 40 minutes.
Main regular credit(s): Executive producer Chris O'Dell; produced by Lee Connolly.
Main regular performer(s): Cilla Black (Host), Tara Palmer-Tomkinson, Alex Sibley.

	Holding / Source
25.12.2002	DB /
25.12.2002 Update Show	DB /

THE CHRISTMAS CHERRIES
A BBC production for BBC 1. Transmission details are for BBC 1. Duration: 25 minutes.
Written by Veronica Cecil; translated by John Hampden; based on a story by Chretien De Troyes; designed by Jeremy Bear; executive producer Anna Home; produced and directed by Marilyn Fox.
Martin Jarvis (Sir Cleges), Marilyn Taylerson (Dame Clarice), Kenneth Watson (King Uther), Hilary Minster (Steward), Milton Johns (Porter), Anthony Daniels (Usher), Paul Blake (Minstrel).

	Holding / Source
23.12.1975	J / 2"

A CHRISTMAS COLLECTION
A BBC North West production for BBC 1. Transmission details are for BBC 1. Duration: 30 minutes.
Written by George Sims; produced by Ray Colley; directed by Michael Healey.
Trevor Peacock (Role), Zoë Wanamaker (Role), Choristers From St Catherine's Church, Heald Green, Cheshire.

	Holding / Source
18.12.1972	J / 2"

CHRISTMAS COMES TO TOWN
A Granada production. Transmission details are for Associated-Rediffusion. Duration: 52 minutes.
THE TRAVELLING EYE visits a big Northern store to watch the busy crowd of Christmas shoppers and to meet some of the people who are part of the store's life.
Directed by Herbert Wise.

	Holding / Source
19.12.1956 [The Travelling Eye]	J /

CHRISTMAS COMPANY
An ATV production. Transmission details are for the ATV midlands region. Duration: 40 minutes.
Six talented teenagers first met on the ITV pop series Cool for Cats some 15 years ago. Since then, four have found fame as dramatic artists. But their talent for singing and dancing has not been forgotten. This versatile foursome meet again with dancers Roy Allen and Denys Palmer to give voice and verve to today's non-stop revue.
Music associates Derek Scott and Jack Chivers; music by Carl Davis; choreography by Denys Palmer; designed by Ray White; produced and directed by Joan Kemp-Welch.
Tony Bateman, Barbara Ferris, David Kernan, Anton Rodgers, Patsy Rowlands, Stephanie Voss, Lieutenant Pigeon, The Mike Sammes Singers, Jack Parnell and his Orchestra, Roy Allen, Denys Palmer, Mo Willsher, Domini Winter.

	Holding / Source
24.12.1972	R1 / 2"

A CHRISTMAS CONVERSATION

A BBC production for BBC 1. Transmission details are for BBC 1. Duration: 45 minutes.
Produced by John Drummond; directed by Darrol Blake.
Peter Ustinov, Judi Dench, Patrick Campbell, Kenneth Allsop.

	Holding / Source
26.12.1967	R1 /

CHRISTMAS COOKING PARTY

A Thames Television production. Transmission details are for the Yorkshire Television region. Duration: 50 minutes.
Join TVTimes cookery editor Kathie Webber, Shaw Taylor and an invited audience at Kathie's Kitchen.
Produced by Steve Minchin.
Kathie Webber (Presenter), Shaw Taylor (Presenter).

	Holding / Source
23.12.1970	J / 2"

CHRISTMAS CRACKER

A BBC production. Transmission details are for BBC. Duration: 60 minutes.
Devised by George Inns; produced and directed by George Inns.
Tessie O'Shea, Spike Milligan, Alfred Marks, Charlie Drake, George Martin.

	Holding / Source
22.12.1956	J /

CHRISTMAS DAY IN THE MORNING

A BBC production for BBC 1. Transmission details are for BBC 1. Duration: 55 minutes.
Don Maclean (Host), Ruth Madoc, Lord Montagu of Beaulieu, Clive Mantle, Harry Secombe, Tabitha Watling.

	Holding / Source
25.12.1995	DB-D3 / D3S

CHRISTMAS DAY PASSED QUIETLY

A BBC production for BBC 1. Transmission details are for BBC 1. Duration: 25 minutes.
Produced and directed by Vernon Sproxton.
John Snagge (Narrator), Colonel Scott Shepherd, Josef Sewald, Colonel Johannes Niemann, John Wilkins, Mme Robinson-Peulmeule.
The Story of the 1914 Truce

	Holding / Source
22.12.1968	DB / B1

A CHRISTMAS DICKENS

A BBC production for BBC 2. Transmission details are for BBC 2. Duration: 30 minutes.
Main regular credit(s):   Based on material by Charles Dickens; executive producer Roger Thompson; directed by Tom Kinninmont.
Main regular cast: Simon Callow (Charles Dickens).

		Holding / Source
21.12.1997	The Boy At Mugby	DB / D3S
22.12.1997	Mrs Gamp	DB / D3S
23.12.1997	Mr Chops The Dwarf	DB / D3S
25.12.1997	Bob Sawyer's Party	DB / D3S
26.12.1997	Mrs Lirriper's Lodgings	DB / D3S

CHRISTMAS EVE AT THE GOLDEN GARTER

A Granada production. Transmission details are for the ATV midlands region. Duration: 50 minutes.
A Christmas Eve party at one of Britain's top nightspots, with Peter Noone of Herman's Hermits hosting an all star gathering.
Music directed by Derek Hilton; designed by Colin Rees; produced by John Hamp; directed by Eric Prytherch.
Peter Noone (Host), Elaine Delmar, Johnny Hackett, Edmund Hockridge, Joe Henderson, Johnny Gray, Susan Maughan, Josef Locke, Frank Ifield, Ken Goodwin, Sheps Banjo Boys, Joan Turner, The Derek Hilton Band, Jerry Harris, Ayshea Brough, Jenny Logan, Jack Douglas.

	Holding / Source
24.12.1970	DB / 62

THE CHRISTMAS EVE SHOW

An Associated-Rediffusion production. Transmission details are for Associated-Rediffusion. Duration: 60 minutes.

Script by Ker Robertson; choreography by Douglas Squires; produced and directed by Joan Kemp-Welch.

Paul Anka, Petula Clark, Hughie Green, Michael Holliday, Dick Henderson Sr, Elizabeth Larner, Dennis Lotis, Ben Lyon, Laurie Payne, Tommy Steele, Sabrina, Anne Shelton, Sister Rosetta Tharpe, Dickie Valentine, Frankie Vaughan, Jerry Verno, Marcia Ashton, Tony Bateman, Jean Bayless, Hermene French, Linda Gray, John Gower, Robin Hunter, Robert James, Jean McDonald, Barbara Miller, Peter Moffat, Peter Reeves, Pat Rowlands, Hazel Sutton, Mavis Traill, Steve Race and his Orchestra, Norrie Paramor and his Big Ben Banjo Band, Ted Heath and his Music, Johnny Duncan and his Blue Grass Boys, Humphrey Lyttelton and his Band, The Douglas Squires Dancers, Cool for Cats Team, The Boys of the London Choir School.

	Holding / Source
24.12.1957	J / B1

CHRISTMAS EVE WITH PAM AYRES AND FIVEPENNY PIECE

A BBC Manchester production for BBC 2. Transmission details are for BBC 2. Duration: 30 minutes.

Produced and directed by Barry Bevins.

Pam Ayres (Host), Fivepenny Piece (Band).

	Holding / Source
24.12.1981	DB-D3 / 2"

CHRISTMAS EVE WITH VAL DOONICAN

A BBC production for BBC 1. Transmission details are for BBC 1. Duration: 45 minutes.

Written by Chris Miller and Val Doonican; music directed by Ronnie Hazlehurst; designed by John Anderson; produced and directed by Yvonne Littlewood.

Val Doonican (Host), Dennis Taylor, Evelyn Glennie.

	Holding / Source
24.12.1986	DB / 1"

CHRISTMAS EVE WITH VAL DOONICAN

A BBC production for BBC 1. Transmission details are for BBC 1. Duration: 50 minutes.

Written by Val Doonican and Chris Miller; costume Linda Woodfield; music directed by Ronnie Hazlehurst; music associate Roger Richards; lighting by Bill Millar; sound Mike Felton; designed by John Asbridge; produced and directed by Yvonne Littlewood.

Val Doonican (Host), Sky, Michala Petri, St Philip's Choir.

	Holding / Source
24.12.1987	DB / 1"

CHRISTMAS EVE WITH VAL DOONICAN

A BBC production for BBC 1. Transmission details are for BBC 1. Duration: 40 minutes.

Produced and directed by Yvonne Littlewood.

Val Doonican (Host), Elaine Paige, Gorden Kaye, Brian Kay.

	Holding / Source
24.12.1988	DB / 1"

CHRISTMAS FARE

An ATV production. Transmission details are for the ATV London region. Duration: 52 minutes.

Designed by Peter Roden; produced and directed by Dicky Leeman.

Cliff Richard and The Shadows, Sergio Franchi, The Mike Cotton Jazzmen, Sheila Southern, Susan Lane, The Mike Sammes Singers, Jack Parnell and his Orchestra.

	Holding / Source
25.12.1962	J /

CHRISTMAS FOLK

A HTV production. Transmission details are for the Tyne Tees region. Duration: 25 minutes.

A group of folk musicians and singers get together to bring you their musical version of a happy Christmas, Traditional modern, serious and funny, the folk songs span the whole range of emotions at this special time of year.

Designed by Ken Jones; produced and directed by Derek Clark.

Fred Wedlock, The Yetties, Sun, Mechanical Horsetrough, Strange Fruit, Joanna Carlin, Brenda Wootton.

	Holding / Source
21.12.1975	

CHRISTMAS GLORY

A Carlton production. made in association with SVC. Transmission details are for the Carlton region. Duration: 48 minutes.

	Holding / Source
24.12.1997	DB / DBS

Introduced by Prince Charles, The Prince of Wales; executive producers John Bishop and Andrew Bell.

With Harry Secombe, Richard Griffiths, Patricia Routledge, Kevin Whately, Kiri Te Kanawa.

24.12.1998	DB / DBS

Introduced by Princess Anne; produced by Timothy Woolford; directed by Humphrey Burton.

With José Carreras, Maggie Smith.

24.12.1999	DB / DBS

Introduced by Prince Philip, The Duke of Edinburgh; produced by Timothy Woolford; directed by Derek Bailey.

With Andrea Bocelli, Trevor McDonald, Thora Hird, Joan Plowright, Bryn Terfel, The Archbishop of Canterbury.

24.12.2000	DB / DBS

Introduced by Prince Andrew, The Duke of York; produced by Timothy Woolford; directed by John Michael Phillips.

With Robin Gibb, Monserrat Caballe, Derek Jacobi, Jenny Agutter, Richard Griffiths, Simon Callow.

24.12.2001 **Christmas Glory From New York**	DB / DBSW

Duration: 75 minutes.

Executive producers Andrew Bell and Rupert Dilnott-Cooper; produced by Timothy Woolford; directed by John Michael Phillips.

With Charlotte Church, Jessye Norman, James Galway, David Frost.

THE CHRISTMAS HOUR

An Associated-Rediffusion production. Transmission details are for Associated-Rediffusion. Duration: 52 minutes.

Written by Jimmy Coghill, Bill Smith and Vic Hallums; special material by Abbe Gail and Martin Slavin; music by Steve Race and his Orchestra; orchestrations by Alan Braden and Martin Slavin; choreography by Malcolm Goddard; settings by Henry Federer; produced and directed by Eric Croall.

Hughie Green (Host), Joan Rhodes, Winifred Atwell, David Blair, Allen Bruce, Fred Borders, Jean Clarke, Tommy Cooper, Plantagenent Somerset Fry, Ray Ellington, Lind Joyce, Dickie Henderson, Anthony Kerr, Rex North, Brian Reece, Ken Wilson, Ray Bennett, Joyce Blair, Harry Brunning, Jill Browne, Alma Cogan, Julie Demarco, Malcolm Goddard, McDonald Hobley, Marion Keene, Nadina Nerina, Veronica Page, Georgie Wood, The Malcolm Goddard Dancers, Band of H.M. Irish Guards, The Barney Gilbraith Singers.

	Holding / Source
25.12.1959	J /

CHRISTMAS IN CALLIOPE

A Tyne Tees Television production. Transmission details are for the Anglia region. Duration: 40 minutes.

A Christmas morning service with carols from H.M.S. Calliope, a shorebased naval training establishment on the Gateshead bank of the Tyne. Opened two years ago, H.M.S. Calliope was named after a I6-gun cruiser which, after distinguished active service, had served since 1901 as a training ship further up river.

The carols arc sung by a choir of officers, men and WRENS, and joining in arc other members of the ship's company together with relatives and friends. The lessons, unfolding the Christmas story, are read by the C.O., Captain J. S. Metcalfe, O.B.E., V.R.D., as well as sailors and WRENS.

Executive producer Maxwell Deas; directed by Roy Lomas.

Captain J. S. Metcalfe (Reader).

	Holding / Source
25.12.1969	J /

CHRISTMAS IS COMING - THIS IS A GOVERNMENT HEALTH WARNING

A Yorkshire Television production. Transmission details are for the Central region. Duration: 50 minutes.

Written by Barry Took, Alan Coren, Andrew Marshall, Raymond Briggs, Ken Hoare and Simon Welfare; music directed by Robert Hartley; designed by Alan Davis; produced by Simon Welfare; directed by Graham Wetherell.

Miriam Stoppard (Presenter), Alun Armstrong (Teacher / Father), Colin Douglas (Santa / Publican), Kenneth Waller (Grandad / Father Christmas), David Kelly (Waiter), Lisa York (Tessa), Simon Osborne (Trevor), Gwen Taylor (Mother / Patient), Joanna Van Gyseghem (Donna / Maternity Sketch), Richard Wilson (Foskett / Doctor), Liz Smith (Ethel Dogett), Vince Hill (Singer), Richard Digance (Singer), Anton Darby (Party Guest), Molly Kelly (Turkey Carver), Robert Hartley (Pianist).

	Holding / Source
23.12.1987	1" / 1"

CHRISTMAS IS COMING...

A Thames Television production. Transmission details are for the Thames Television region. Duration: 50 minutes.

Research Diana Wallis; designed by Tim Nicholson; executive producer Andy Allan; directed by Stuart Hall.

Margaret Powell (Dinner Party Host), Allan Hargreaves (Dinner Party Host), Pauline Collins, Lord Vic Feather, Virginia Wade, Gerald Harper, Lady Isobel Barnet, Alfred Marks.

	Holding / Source
19.12.1974	J / 2"

CHRISTMAS JOURNEY

A BBC production. Transmission details are for BBC. Duration: 40 minutes.

Adapted by Eric Crozier; based on a story by William Canton; music by Elizabeth Poston; play production by Joy Harington.

Jack MacGowran (The Stranger), John Southworth (Stephen), Christopher Hodge (Farmer), Maureen Beck (Mary), Wilfrid Brambell (Old Shepherd), Christopher Cooke (Boy Shepherd), Edward Hardwicke (Young Shepherd), David Watkins (Harpist), Ealing Boys' Grammar School Choir.

	Holding / Source
22.12.1959	J /

A CHRISTMAS LANTERN

A Central production. Transmission details are for the Central region. Duration: 50 minutes.

This magical Christmas tale shows how one family celebrates Christmas over 80 years... and without a sign of ageing. Incorporated within the play is a hilarious Charlie Chaplin ballet.

Devised by Jon Scoffield; written by Ronnie Cass and Nigel Lythgoe; music by Laurie Holloway; designed by Richard Plumb; associate producer Nigel Lythgoe; produced and directed by Jon Scoffield.

Cliff Richard, Wayne Sleep, Una Stubbs, Mike Reid, Robert Hardy, Daniel Kipling, Simon Nash, Christopher Timothy, Tom Yang, Sandy Strallen, Claud Paul Henry, The Ambrosian Singers, Desborough School Choir, Finola Hughes, Fred Evans, Peter Salmon, Karen Berry, Bryan Burdon, Ken Warwick, Peter Challis, Kim Gavin, Jeff Unkovich.

Date	Holding / Source
24.12.1982	1" / 1"

CHRISTMAS LIGHTS

A Granada production for ITV 1. Transmission details are for the Central region. Duration: 75 minutes.

Written by Bob Mills and Jeff Pope; script supervisor Dorothy Friend; script editor Roxy Spencer; music by Martin Phipps; executive producers Jeff Pope, Bob Mills and Andy Harries; co-produced by David Meddick; produced by Spencer Campbell; directed by Paul Seed.

Robson Green (Colin), Nicola Stephenson (Jackie), Mark Benton (Howie), Maxine Peake (Pauline), Keith Clifford (Eric), Nicola Headley (Brooke), Lee Worswick (Liam), Finlay Lowry (Leyton, As A Baby), Mason Walker (Leyton, At 18 Months), Ben Bradley (Leyton, Aged 3 Years), Denice Hope (June), Steve Edge (Gibbo), Russell Dixon (Guthrie), Ian Kershaw (Buchanan), David Fleeshman (Margolis), Stuart Wolfenden (Tony), Steve Royle (Wanking Santa), Jenni Howarth Williams (Bernie), Margaret Henshaw (Stall Holder), Eric Potts (David Draper), Helen Moon (Nurse).

Date	Holding / Source
20.12.2004	DB / V1SW

CHRISTMAS MANIA

A Granada production for ITV 1. Transmission details are for the Central region. Duration: 49 minutes.

Written by Richard Easter; designed by Simon Kimmel; associate producer Rob Walker; executive producer Jeff Thacker; head of production Leah Milton; production manager Keith Lascelles; produced by Simon Marsh; directed by Simon Staffurth.

Donny Osmond (Host), Peter Dickson (Voice Only), Jamie Cullum, Il Divo, Ronan Keating, Katie Melua, Janet Ramus, Clare Teal, Hayley Westenra, Westlife, Roy Wood, Cliff Richard*, Sharon Osbourne*, Danny Young*, Aled Jones*, Eamonn Holmes*, The Cheeky Girls*, Christine Hamilton*, Neil Hamilton*, Jane Danson*, Lucy-Jo Hudson*.

Date	Production No	Holding / Source
11.12.2004	9L50731/A	DB / DBSW

CHRISTMAS MANIA

A Granada production for ITV 1. Transmission details are for the Central region. Duration: 47 minutes.

VT director Stuart Locke; written by David Spicer; choreography by Leigh Miles; VT Producer Stuart Locke; executive producer Mark Wells; produced by John Ireland; directed by Janet Fraser Crook.

Girls Aloud (Host), Roger Hammond (Voice Over), Lee Ryan, Freefaller, Il Divo, The Choirboys, GMTV Presenters, Liz McClarnon, Aled Jones, Kate Garraway, Andrew Castle, Richard Arnold, Andrea McLean.

Date	Holding / Source
17.12.2005	DB / DBSW

A CHRISTMAS MESSIAH

A Granada production. Transmission details are for the ATV midlands region. Duration: 50 minutes.

Since its first performance in 1742 Handel's Messiah has become a Christmas institution, particularly in the North of England where in chapel, church or cathedral the music rings out every year. Tonight's performance captures the unique quality of the work as a living celebration of Christmas. The score is presented in a variety of settings sung by a variety of voices: the Halle Orchestra and Chorus, an amateur choir in the heart of the Yorkshire valleys, a black Gospel group and the rock voices of Kiki Dee and Paul Jones. The programme is prefaced by an introduction from the conductor Owain Arwel Hughes.

Introduced by Owain Arwel Hughes; music directed by Bill Connor; produced by Steve Hawes; directed by David Liddiment.

Sheila Armstrong, Kiki Dee, Alfreda Hodgson, Gwynne Howell, Paul Jones, Richard Morton, The Halle Orchestra, Ronald Frost, Earlene Bentley, Miquel Brown, Celena Duncan, Alastair Haigh, Richard Hill, Judi Kent, Richie Pitts, Holmfirth Choral Society.

Date	Holding / Source
27.12.1981	DB / 2"

CHRISTMAS MORNING WITH NOEL

A BBC production for BBC 1. Transmission details are for BBC 1. Duration varies - see below for details.

Main regular credit(s): Produced and directed by Michael Hurll.

Main regular performer(s): Noel Edmonds (Host).

Date	Holding / Source
25.12.1986	DB / 1"

Duration: 115 minutes.

Designed by Brian Sykes; production managers Neil Banks and David Nicolson.

With Bob Geldof, Paul McCartney, Mike Smith, Elton John, Cliff Richard, Dame Edna Everage, Feargal Sharkey, A-Ha, Tony Hadley, Holly Johnson, Leslie Ash, Pamela Stephenson, Rowan Atkinson, Go West, Danny La Rue, Billy Ocean, Dennis Waterman, Rula Lenska, Su Pollard, Robin Askwith.

In association with Network Ten Australia.

25.12.1987   DB / 1"
Duration: 89 minutes.
With Gorden Kaye, Kuan Lee, Margaret Thatcher, Danny La Rue, David Steel, Kylie Minogue, Neil Kinnock, Harry Gration, John Leslie, Elton John, Paul McCartney, Spike Milligan, Warren Mitchell, Anita Dobson, Paul Eddington, John Inman, Robert Hawke, Linda McCartney, Paul Clark, Viv Creegor, David Lange, Lisa Foden.

CHRISTMAS MUSIC FROM HAMPTON COURT

A BBC production for BBC 2. Transmission details are for BBC 2. Duration: 35 minutes.

Written by Michael Kerr; lighting by Bert Oaten; sound Vic Godrich; produced and directed by Ken Griffin.

Moray Watson (Compere), Gordon Reynolds (Organist / Choirmaster), Reverend Felix Boyce.

	Holding / Source
23.12.1974	DB / 2"

CHRISTMAS NATIVITY

A Thames Television production. Transmission details are for the ATV midlands region. Duration: 25 minutes.

Manorfield School, Poplar, Presents the Greatest Story Ever Told. The children of Manorfield School, Poplar, in the East End of London, present their version of the Nativity.

Arranged by John Forrest; music by Peter Bye; produced by Adrian Cooper.

Manorfield School, Poplar.

	VT Number	Holding / Source
24.12.1980	23807	DB / 2"

A CHRISTMAS NIGHT OF ONE HUNDRED STARS

An LWT production. Transmission details are for the Central region. Duration: 130 minutes.

Designed by Bill McPherson; produced by David Bell; directed by Alan Boyd.

Janet Dibley (Cinderella), Gordon Jay (Ugly Sister), Bunny Jay (Ugly Sister), Stu Francis (Buttons), Anita Harris (Aladdin), Gordon Honeycombe (Abanazar), Christopher Biggins (Mother Goose), Jenny Logan (Jack And The Beanstalk), Michael Kilgarriff (The Giant), Sarah Payne (Goldilocks), Paddie O'Neil (Three Bears), Gareth Marks (Three Bears), Graham Fletcher (Three Bears), Tony Adams (Dick Whittington), Derek Holt (His Cat), Dana (Snow White), Barbara Cook, The Royal Choral Society, Lazsey Endres, Roger de Courcey & Nookie Bear, George Hearn, Dennis Quilley, La Cage Au Folles, Allan Stewart, Aiden J. Harvey, Andrew O'Connor, Mike Osman, Hilary O'Neil, Cheryl Taylor, Richard Clayderman, Norman Collier, Tim Flavin, Marti Webb, Marti Caine, Lorna Dallas, Su Pollard, Sacha Distel, Gary Wilmot, Grace Kennedy, Clarke Peters, Sinitta, Lon Satton, Pearly Gates, Helen Gelzer, Miquel Brown, Patti Boulaye, The Inspirational Choir, Joe Longthorne, Roy Walker, Elaine Stritch, Johnny Mathis, Henry Mancini, James Rainbird, Moira Anderson, Boys Choir, Christchurch Cathedral, Oxford, Paddie O'Neil.

	Holding / Source
26.12.1986	1" / 1"

CHRISTMAS NIGHT WITH THE STARS

A BBC production. Transmission details are for BBC.

1958 edition

Duration: 75 minutes.

	Holding / Source
25.12.1958 [presentation]	R3 /

Written by David Whitaker; associate producer John Street; produced and directed by Graeme Muir.
With David Nixon (Host).

25.12.1958 **Charlie Chester**	R3 /

Written by Charlie Chester.
With Charlie Chester, Eric Grier, The George Mitchell Choir, The Television Toppers.

25.12.1958 **The Beverley Sisters**	R3 /

With The Beverley Sisters.

25.12.1958 **Charlie Drake**	R3 /

Written by Charlie Drake.
With Charlie Drake, Dave Freeman.

25.12.1958 **Perry Como**	R3 /

With Perry Como.

25.12.1958 **Ted Ray**	R3 /

With Ted Ray, Kenneth Connor.

25.12.1958 **David Nixon**	R3 /

With David Nixon, Sheila Holt.

25.12.1958 **Tony Hancock**	R3 /

Written by Ray Galton and Alan Simpson; produced and directed by Duncan Wood.
With Tony Hancock, Totti Truman Taylor, Alec Bregonzi, Percy Edwards.

25.12.1958 **Vera Lynn**	R3 /

With Vera Lynn, The Lynnettes.

25.12.1958 **Jimmy Edwards**	R3 /

Written by Frank Muir and Denis Norden.
With Jimmy Edwards, Arthur Howard, John Stirling, David Langford, Jeremy Roughton.

CHRISTMAS NIGHT WITH THE STARS (continued)   British Christmas Television Guide

25.12.1958 **Billy Cotton**   R3 /
Written by George Wadmore.
With Billy Cotton and his Band, Alan Breeze, The Leslie Roberts Silhouettes.

25.12.1958 **Dixon Of Dock Green**   R3 /
Written by Ted Willis.
With Jack Warner, Arthur Rigby, Jeanette Hutchinson, Peter Byrne, Anthony Parker, Moira Mannion, Graham Ashley.

1959 edition:
Duration: 75 minutes.

    Holding / Source

25.12.1959 **[presentation]**   J /
Written by David Whitaker; produced and directed by Graeme Muir.
With David Nixon (Host).

25.12.1959 **Ken Mackintosh And His Orchestra**   J /
Directed by Stewart Morris.
With Ken Mackintosh and his Orchestra.

25.12.1959 **Jimmy Logan**   J /
Written by Terry Nation and John Junkin; directed by Richard Francis.
With Jimmy Logan, Ron Moody.

25.12.1959 **David Hughes**   J /
Directed by John Street.
With David Hughes, The George Mitchell Choir.

25.12.1959 **Charlie Drake**   J /
Written by Charlie Drake; directed by Ernest Maxin.
With Charlie Drake, Mark Singleton.

25.12.1959 **Jack Warner**   J /
Written by Ted Willis; directed by Douglas Moodie.
With Arthur Rigby, Anthony Oliver, Moira Mannion, Harold Scott, Geoffrey Adams, Graham Ashley, David Webster, Dorothy Casey, Michael Brennan, Peter Byrne, Jeannette Hutchinson, The George Mitchell Choir.

25.12.1959 **Joan Regan**   J /
Directed by Francis Essex.
With Joan Regan.

25.12.1959 **Jimmy Edwards**   J /
Written by Frank Muir and Denis Norden; directed by Douglas Moodie.
With Jimmy Edwards, Arthur Howard, Jimmy Ray, Paul Norman, Sherree Winton, Katie Cashfield.

25.12.1959 **The Black And White Minstrels**   J /
Directed by George Inns.
With The Mitchell Minstrels, The Television Toppers, George Mitchell.

1960 edition:
Duration: 75 minutes.

    Holding / Source

25.12.1960 **[presentation]**   J /
Written by David Climie and David Whitaker; produced and directed by Graeme Muir.
With David Nixon (Host), The Showtime Dancers, The George Mitchell Singers.

25.12.1960 **The Black And White Minstrels**   J /
Directed by George Inns.
With The Mitchell Minstrels, The Television Toppers.

25.12.1960 **Sid James**   J /
Written by Ray Galton and Alan Simpson; directed by Philip Barker.
With Sidney James, Bill Kerr, Liz Fraser, Sydney Tafler.

25.12.1960 **Nina And Frederick**   J /
Directed by Bryan Sears.
With Nina and Frederick.

25.12.1960 **Harry Worth**   J /
Written by Lew Schwarz; directed by Dennis Main Wilson.
With Harry Worth, Deryck Guyler, Hugh Lloyd, George Roderick.

25.12.1960 **Kenneth McKellar**   J /
Directed by Graeme Muir.
With Kenneth McKellar, The Showtime Dancers.

25.12.1960 **David Nixon And Robert Harbin**   J /
Directed by Graeme Muir.
With David Nixon, Robert Harbin.

CHRISTMAS NIGHT WITH THE STARS

| British Christmas Television Guide | CHRISTMAS NIGHT WITH THE STARS (continued) |

25.12.1960 **Stanley Baxter And Betty Marsden** J /
Written by Richard Waring; directed by James Gilbert.
With Stanley Baxter, Betty Marsden.

25.12.1960 **Joan Regan** J /
Directed by John Street.
With Joan Regan.

25.12.1960 **Jimmy Edwards** J /
Written by Frank Muir and Denis Norden; directed by Eric Fawcett.
With Jimmy Edwards, Arthur Howard, Cyril Fletcher, Pip Hinton, Eric Robinson, John Vyvyan, Chan Canasta, David Nixon.

1962 edition:
Duration: 95 minutes.

Holding / Source

25.12.1962 **[presentation]** J /
Written by John Law and Eamonn Andrews; produced by Graeme Muir and Ronald Marsh; directed by Graeme Muir and Ronald Marsh.
With Eamonn Andrews (Host).

25.12.1962 **The Billy Cotton Band Show** J /
Directed by Johnnie Stewart.
With Billy Cotton and his Band, Alan Breeze, Kathie Kay, The High-Lights.

25.12.1962 **The Rag Trade** J /
Written by Ronald Wolfe and Ronald Chesney; produced and directed by Dennis Main Wilson.
With Peter Jones, Miriam Karlin, Reg Varney, Esma Cannon, Barbara Windsor, Sheena Marshe, Patricia Denys, Claire Davenport.

25.12.1962 **A Song For Everyone** J /
Music by Harry Rabinowitz; directed by Yvonne Littlewood.
With Kenneth McKellar, Tom McCall.

25.12.1962 **Sykes And His Sister** J /
Written by Eric Sykes; produced and directed by Sydney Lotterby.
With Eric Sykes, Hattie Jacques.

25.12.1962 **Adam Faith** J /
Music by Harry Rabinowitz; produced and directed by Graeme Muir.
With Adam Faith, Susan George.

25.12.1962 **Raise Your Glasses** J /
Written by Alan Melville; produced and directed by Bryan Sears.
With Arthur Askey, Alan Melville, Mary Hignett, Alec Bregonzi, Ken Grief.

25.12.1962 **Juke Box Jury: Hugh And I Versus Citizen James** J /
Written by John Chapman; produced and directed by David Croft.
With David Jacobs, Sidney James, Sydney Tafler, Terry Scott, Hugh Lloyd, Jill Curzon.

25.12.1962 **It's A Square World** J /
Written by Michael Bentine; produced and directed by John Street.
With Michael Bentine.

25.12.1962 **Russ's Requests** J /
Directed by Johnnie Stewart.
With Russ Conway, The Billy Cotton Band.

25.12.1962 **The Christmas Face Of Jim** J /
Written by Frank Muir and Denis Norden; produced and directed by James Gilbert.
With Jimmy Edwards, June Whitfield, Ronnie Barker, Michael Brennan, Eunice Black.

25.12.1962 **The White Heather Club** J /
Directed by Iain MacFadyen.
With Andy Stewart, The White Heather Dancers, Ian Powrie and his Band.

25.12.1962 **Steptoe And Son** J /
Written by Alan Simpson and Ray Galton; produced and directed by Duncan Wood.
With Harry H. Corbett, Wilfrid Brambell.
Extract exists in Looking at Television tx: 15/05/1963.

25.12.1962 **The Black And White Minstrels** J /
Music by George Mitchell and Eric Robinson; directed by George Inns.
With The Mitchell Minstrels, The Television Toppers.

25.12.1962 **Dixon Of Dock Green** J /
Written by Ted Willis; produced and directed by Douglas Moodie.
With Jack Warner, Arthur Rigby, Peter Byrne, Jeannette Hutchinson, Geoffrey Adams, Anne Ridler, John Hughes, Christopher Gilmore, Jocelyne Rhodes.

CHRISTMAS NIGHT WITH THE STARS (continued)

British Christmas Television Guide

1963 edition:
Duration: 80 minutes.

	Holding / Source
	J /

25.12.1963 [presentation]
Written by John Law and Eamonn Andrews; orchestra directed by Harry Rabinowitz; produced and directed by Graeme Muir.
With Eamonn Andrews (Host).

25.12.1963 The Black And White Minstrels   J /
Choreography by Larry Gordon; directed by George Inns.
With The Mitchell Minstrels, The Television Toppers, John Boulter, Dai Francis, Tony Mercer, Benny Garcia, Margaret Savage.

25.12.1963 Russ Conway   J /
Directed by Michael Hurll.
With Russ Conway.

25.12.1963 Billy Cotton And His Band   J /
Directed by Michael Hurll.
With Billy Cotton and his Band.

25.12.1963 Dixon Of Dock Green   J /
Written by Ted Willis; directed by Robin Nash.
With Jack Warner (George Dixon), Arthur Rigby, Peter Byrne, Jeannette Hutchinson, Larry Martyn, Laura Graham, Jean Marlow.

25.12.1963 Dick Emery And Joan Sims   J /
Written by John Warren and John Singer; directed by John Street.
With Dick Emery, Joan Sims, Michael Balfour.

25.12.1963 Hugh And I   J /
Written by John Chapman; directed by David Croft.
With Terry Scott, Patricia Hayes, Hugh Lloyd, Vi Stevens, Jack Haig.

25.12.1963 It's A Square World   J /
Devised by Michael Bentine and John Law; written by Michael Bentine and John Law; directed by Joe McGrath.
With Michael Bentine.

25.12.1963 Juke Box Jury   J /
Written by Ken Hoare; lyrics by Ken Hoare; music by Dennis Wilson; directed by James Gilbert.
With Stanley Baxter, David Jacobs.

25.12.1963 The Marriage Lines   J /
Written by Richard Waring; directed by Graeme Muir.
With Richard Briers, Prunella Scales.

25.12.1963 Kenneth McKellar   J /
Directed by Yvonne Littlewood.
With Kenneth McKellar.

25.12.1963 Nina And Frederik   J /
Orchestra conducted by John Barry; directed by Nick Burrell-Davis.
With Nina and Frederick.

25.12.1963 Andy Stewart   J /
Directed by Iain MacFadyen.
With Andy Stewart, Ian Powrie and his Band.

1964 edition:
Commissioned by BBC 1. Transmission details are for BBC 1. Duration: 90 minutes.

	Holding / Source

25.12.1964 [presentation]   R3 /
Written by Robert Gray and Jack Warner; orchestra directed by Harry Rabinowitz; produced and directed by Graeme Muir.
With Jack Warner (Host).

25.12.1964 The Black And White Minstrels   R3 /
Choreography by Larry Gordon; directed by George Inns.
With The Mitchell Minstrels, John Boulter, Dai Francis, Tony Mercer, Benny Garcia, Margaret Savage, The Television Toppers.

25.12.1964 Roy Castle   R3 /
Orchestra conducted by Harry Rabinowitz; directed by Dennis Main Wilson.
With Roy Castle.

25.12.1964 The Billy Cotton Band Show   R3 /
Choreography by Malcolm Goddard; directed by Terence Hughes.
With Billy Cotton and his Band, Ralph Reader, Boy Scout Gang Show, Kathie Kay, Alan Breeze, The Cotton Singers, The Cotton Dancers.

25.12.1964 Dick Emery   R3 /
Written by David Cumming; directed by David Croft.
With Dick Emery, Glen Mason.

British Christmas Television Guide   CHRISTMAS NIGHT WITH THE STARS (continued)

25.12.1964 **Benny Hill**   R3 /
Written by Benny Hill; directed by Kenneth Carter.
With Benny Hill, Alex Macintosh.

25.12.1964 **Hugh And I**   R3 /
Written by John Chapman; directed by David Croft.
With Terry Scott, Hugh Lloyd, Patricia Hayes, Charles Dyer, Jack Haig, Vi Stevens, Mollie Sugden, Jill Curzon, Maurice Podbrey.

25.12.1964 **Kathy Kirby**   R3 /
Orchestra conducted by Eric Robinson; directed by Ernest Maxin.
With Kathy Kirby.

25.12.1964 **The Likely Lads**   R3 /
Written by Dick Clement and Ian La Frenais; directed by Dick Clement.
With James Bolam (Terry), Rodney Bewes (Bob), Sheila Fearn (Audrey).

25.12.1964 **Marriage Lines**   R3 /
Written by Richard Waring; directed by Robin Nash.
With Richard Briers, Prunella Scales, Denzil Ellis.

25.12.1964 **Meet The Wife**   R3 /
Written by Ronald Wolfe and Ronald Chesney; directed by Graeme Muir.
With Thora Hird, Darryl Read, Freddie Frinton.

25.12.1964 **Andy Stewart**   R3 /
Directed by Iain MacFadyen.
With Andy Stewart, Ian Powrie and his Band.

25.12.1964 **Top Of The Pops**   R3 /
Directed by Johnnie Stewart.
With The Barron Knights.

1967 edition:
Commissioned by BBC 1. Transmission details are for BBC 1. Duration: 120 minutes.

                                             Holding / Source

25.12.1967 **[presentation]**   J /
Written by David Cumming, Alan Melville, John Law and Kenneth Williams; designed by Victor Meredith; produced and directed by Stewart Morris.
With Rolf Harris (Host), Cilla Black, Billy Cotton, Val Doonican, Lulu, David Nixon, Beryl Reid, Avril Elgar, Sandie Shaw, Kenneth Williams.

25.12.1967 **Till Death Us Do Part**   J|a /
Written by Johnny Speight; produced and directed by Dennis Main Wilson.
With Warren Mitchell, Dandy Nichols, Anthony Booth, Una Stubbs, Billy Milton.

25.12.1967 **Beggar My Neighour**   J /
Written by Ken Hoare and Mike Sharland; produced and directed by Eric Fawcett.
With Pat Coombs, Reg Varney, Desmond Walter-Ellis, June Whitfield, Rosemary Faith, Julian Orchard.

25.12.1967 **The Illustrated Weekly Hudd**   J /
Written by Eric Davidson; produced and directed by Michael Hurll.
With Roy Hudd, Doug Fisher, Marcia Ashton.

25.12.1967 **Harry Worth**   J /
Written by Ronnie Taylor; produced and directed by Duncan Wood.
With Harry Worth, Derek Francis.

25.12.1967 **Steptoe And Son**   B1SEQ /
Written by Ray Galton and Alan Simpson; produced and directed by Duncan Wood.
With Wilfrid Brambell, Harry H. Corbett, Annabelle Lee, George Tovey, Heidi Lane.
Steptoe and son stagger out of the pub and get onto cart, ringing a bell. A policeman breathalyses them and takes them off in a police car. No dialogue.

1968 edition:
Commissioned by BBC 1. Transmission details are for BBC 1. Duration: 125 minutes.

                                             Holding / Source

25.12.1968 **[presentation]**   J /
Written by Sid Green and Dick Hills; music directed by Alyn Ainsworth; choreography by Douglas Squires; designed by Roger Murray Leach; produced and directed by Stewart Morris.
With Morecambe and Wise (Hosts), Louis Armstrong, Nana Mouskouri, Petula Clark, Rolf Harris, Jimmy Logan, Lulu, Kenneth McKellar, Cliff Richard, The Seekers, The Young Generation.

25.12.1968 **Not In Front Of The Children**   J /
Written by Richard Waring; produced and directed by Graeme Muir.
With Wendy Craig (Jennifer), Ronald Hines (Henry), Frances Rowe (Mother), Roberta Tovey (Trudi), Hugo Keith-Johnston (Robin), Jill Riddick (Amanda).

25.12.1968 **Dad's Army**   J|a /
Written by Jimmy Perry and David Croft; produced and directed by David Croft.
With Arthur Lowe, John Le Mesurier, Clive Dunn, John Laurie, James Beck, Arnold Ridley, Ian Lavender, Edward Sinclair.

CHRISTMAS NIGHT WITH THE STARS (continued)

25.12.1968 Harry Worth J /
Written by Ronnie Taylor; produced and directed by Duncan Wood.
With Harry Worth, Derek Francis.

25.12.1968 Ice Cabaret J /
Music directed by Malcolm Lockyer; television presentation by Tom Arnold and Gerald Palmer; directed by Ernest Maxin.
With Ray Alan (Host), Reg Park, Michel and Carol, Sally Ross, Janet Mahoney, The Ice Cabaret Dancers, The Fred Tomlinson Singers.

25.12.1968 Marty Feldman Sings A Song Of Christmas J /
With Ealing Boys' Grammar School Choir.

25.12.1968 Oh Brother! All Gas And Gaiters J /
Written by David Climie, Austin Steele, Pauline Devaney and Edwin Apps; produced and directed by John Howard Davies.
With Derek Nimmo, Geoffrey Hibbert, Felix Aylmer, Robertson Hare, Colin Gordon, William Mervyn, Ernest Clark, Patrick McAlinney.

1969 edition:
Commissioned by BBC 1. Transmission details are for BBC 1. Duration: 90 minutes.

Holding / Source

25.12.1969 [presentation] J / 2"
Written by Austin Steele, David Climie and Val Doonican; music directed by Ken Thorne; choreography by Douglas Squires; designed by Brian Tregidden; associate producer Colin Charman; produced and directed by Terry Hughes.
With The Young Generation, Kenneth Williams, Cilla Black, Roy Castle, Wendy Craig, Rolf Harris, Mary Hopkin, Lulu, The Cliff Adams Singers.

25.12.1969 Dad's Army DB-D3-2" / 2"
Written by Jimmy Perry and David Croft; produced and directed by David Croft.
With Arthur Lowe, John Le Mesurier, Clive Dunn, John Laurie, James Beck, Arnold Ridley, Ian Lavender, Bill Pertwee, Robert Aldous.

25.12.1969 Dick Emery C3 / C3
Written by Peter Robinson; produced and directed by Ernest Maxin.
With Dick Emery, Peter Elliott.
plus 'snow effect' mute film insert.

25.12.1969 Marty J / 2"
Written by Marty Feldman and Barry Took; produced and directed by Roger Race.
With Tim Brooke-Taylor, Marty Feldman, John Junkin, Roland Macleod.

25.12.1969 Kenneth McKellar And Moira Anderson J / 2"
Music directed by Peter Knight; produced and directed by Yvonne Littlewood.
With Kenneth McKellar, Moira Anderson.

25.12.1969 Not In Front Of The Children J / 2"
Written by Richard Waring; produced and directed by Graeme Muir.
With Hugo Keith-Johnston, Wendy Craig, Ronald Hines, Verena Greenlaw, Jill Riddick, Reginald Marsh.

25.12.1969 Monty Python's Flying Circus DB-D3 / 2"
Written by John Cleese, Graham Chapman, Michael Palin, Terry Jones and Eric Idle; drawings by Terry Gilliam; produced and directed by Ian McNaughton.
With Carol Cleveland, John Cleese, Graham Chapman, Michael Palin, Terry Jones, Eric Idle.
NB this isn't new material, just a copy of the 'dirty fork' sketch.

1970 edition:
Commissioned by BBC 1. Transmission details are for BBC 1. Duration: 90 minutes.

Holding / Source

25.12.1970 [presentation] J / 2"
Introduced by Cilla Black; written by Ronnie Taylor; music directed by Ronnie Hazlehurst; choreography by Irving Davies; designed by Vic Meredith; associate producer James Moir; produced and directed by Michael Hurll.
With Bob Hope, Mary Hopkin, Graham Kerr, Jerry Lewis, Nana Mouskouri, Clodagh Rodgers, Frank Sinatra Jr, Jack Warner, The Breakaways.

25.12.1970 Dad's Army J / 2"
Written by Jimmy Perry and David Croft; produced and directed by David Croft.
With Arthur Lowe, John Le Mesurier, Clive Dunn, John Laurie, James Beck, Arnold Ridley, Ian Lavender, Bill Pertwee.

25.12.1970 Stanley Baxter J / 2"
Written by Ken Hoare; produced and directed by Roger Race.
With Stanley Baxter.

25.12.1970 Dick Emery J / 2"
Written by John Warren and John Singer; produced and directed by Colin Charman.
With Dick Emery.

25.12.1970 Bachelor Father J / 2"
Written by Richard Waring; produced and directed by Graeme Muir.
With Ian Carmichael, Pauline Yates, Ian Johnson, Briony McRoberts, Beverley Simons, Roland Pickering.

25.12.1970 Terry Scott And June Whitfield J / 2"
Written by Dave Freeman; produced and directed by Peter Whitmore.
With June Whitfield, Terry Scott.

CHRISTMAS NIGHT WITH THE STARS

| British Christmas Television Guide | CHRISTMAS NIGHT WITH THE STARS (continued) |

1971 edition:
Duration: 80 minutes.

	Holding / Source
25.12.1971 **[presentation]**	J|a / 2"

Introduced by Ronnie Barker and Ronnie Corbett; orchestra directed by Dennis Wilson; designed by Paul Joel; produced and directed by Terry Hughes.
With Engelbert Humperdinck, Lulu, Vera Lynn, Harry Secombe, The New Seekers.

25.12.1971 **Till Death Us Do Part** J|a / 2"
Written by Johnny Speight; produced and directed by Duncan Wood.
With Warren Mitchell, Dandy Nichols.

25.12.1971 **Bachelor Father** J / 2"
Written by Richard Waring; produced and directed by Graeme Muir.
With Ian Carmichael, Diana King, Ian Johnson, Briony McRoberts, Gaynor Jones, Geraldine Cowper, Jacqueline Cowper, Kevin Moran, Andrew Bowen, Peter Thornton.

25.12.1971 **Dick Emery** J / 2"
Written by John Warren and John Singer; produced and directed by Colin Charman.
With Gordon Clyde (Interviewer), Dick Emery.

25.12.1971 **A Policeman's Lot** J|a / 2"
Written by Eric Sykes; produced and directed by Roger Race.
With Eric Sykes, Hattie Jacques, Tony Melody, Leslie Noyes.

25.12.1971 **Look Mike Yarwood** J|a / 2"
Written by Eric Davidson; produced and directed by Stewart Morris.
With Mike Yarwood, Adrienne Posta.

25.12.1971 **The Young Generation** J / 2"
Choreography by Don Lurio; produced and directed by Stewart Morris.
With The Young Generation, Alyn Ainsworth and his Orchestra.

1972 edition:
Transmission details are for BBC 1. Duration: 80 minutes.

	Holding / Source
25.12.1972 **[presentation]**	DB-D3 / 2"

Introduced by Ronnie Barker and Ronnie Corbett; written by Garry Chambers, Barry Cryer, Tony Hawes, Ronnie King, Wally Malston, David McKellar, Spike Mullins, David Nobbs, Michael Palin, Terry Jones, Neil Shand, Joe Steeples, Peter Vincent, Dick Vosburgh and Ronnie Taylor; orchestra directed by Ronnie Hazlehurst; designed by Martin Collins; produced by Terry Hughes and Michael Hurll; directed by Michael Hurll and Terry Hughes.
With Cilla Black, The Young Generation, Lulu, The Breakaways.

25.12.1972 **Dad's Army** DB-D3 / 2"
Written by Jimmy Perry and David Croft; produced and directed by David Croft.
With Arthur Lowe, John Le Mesurier, Clive Dunn, John Laurie, James Beck, Arnold Ridley, Ian Lavender.

25.12.1972 **Look - Mike Yarwood!** DB-D3 / 2"
Written by Eric Davidson; produced and directed by Sydney Lotterby.
With Mike Yarwood, Adrienne Posta.

25.12.1972 **The Liver Birds** DB-D3 / 2"
Written by Carla Lane; produced and directed by Sydney Lotterby.
With Polly James, Nerys Hughes, Mollie Sugden, Sheila Fay.

25.12.1972 **The Goodies** DB-D3 / 2"
Written by Graeme Garden, Bill Oddie and Tim Brooke-Taylor; produced and directed by Jim Franklin.
With Tim Brooke-Taylor, Graeme Garden, Bill Oddie, Denise Distel, Paul Ellison.

25.12.1972 **The Young Generation** DB-D3 / 2"
Choreography by Nigel Lythgoe.
With The Young Generation, Alyn Ainsworth and his Orchestra, St Richard's with St Andrew's School Choir, Ham, Surrey.

Transmission details are for BBC 2.

	Holding / Source
27.12.1994	DB-D3 / D3S

Duration: 75 minutes.
Produced by Claudia Lloyd; directed by Geoff Posner.
With Hugh Laurie (Host), Stephen Fry (Host), Steve Coogan (Alan Partridge), Gregor Fisher (Rab C. Nesbitt), Reeves and Mortimer, The Real McCoy, Alexei Sayle, Ronnie Corbett, Sandie Shaw.

CHRISTMAS NIGHT WITH THE STARS

A BBC production for BBC 1. Transmission details are for BBC 1. Duration: 80 minutes.
Produced by Barrie Kelly; directed by Stuart McDonald.
Michael Parkinson (Host), Ozzy Osbourne, Kelly Osbourne, Victoria Beckham, Emma Bunton, Will Young, Busted, Jon Culshaw, The Kumars, Ricky Tomlinson.

	Holding / Source
25.12.2003	DB / DBSW

CHRISTMAS PANTOMIME

A BBC production. Transmission details are for BBC. Duration: 160 minutes.

	Holding / Source
02.01.1950 **Red Riding-Hood**	NR / Live

Introduced by Brian Johnston.

With Dick Tubb Jnr (Dame Trott), Vicky Gail (Robin Hood), Pat Trevor (Maid Marion), Derek Dohn (Simple Simon), Norman Clyne (Sheriff Hardhart), Nick Franks (Bad Bob), Billy Eugene (Ben Barmy), Betty Baxter (Red Riding-Hood), Frank Hughes (Wolf), Adah Le Cren (Fairy), The Three Spots, The Flying Renoes, Pat Van Den Brock's Shaftesbury Girls.

CHRISTMAS PARTY

An Associated-Rediffusion production. Transmission details are for Associated-Rediffusion.

	Holding / Source
22.12.1955	NR / Live
23.12.1955	NR / Live

CHRISTMAS PAST

A BBC production for BBC 2. Transmission details are for BBC 2. Duration: 30 minutes.

Introduced by James Cameron; executive producer David Collison; produced by Paul Jordan.

	Holding / Source
25.12.1977	C1 / C1

CHRISTMAS ROBBINS

A Granada production. Transmission details are for the Central region. Duration: 40 minutes.

Written by Geoff Atkinson, Jim Cass, Barnes Daniel, Richard Jones, Masters Griffiths, Steve Sheridan, Paul Simpkin and Peter Tonkinson; script editor Geoff Atkinson; music directed by Ray Monk; music by Kate Robbins; choreography by Chris Power; designed by Chris George; executive producer David Liddiment; produced by Trish Kinane; directed by Mike Adams.

Kate Robbins, Ted Robbins, Ainslie Foster, Michael Fenton Stevens, The Chris Power Dancers.

	Holding / Source
26.12.1987	1" / 1"

THE CHRISTMAS SHOW

A Carlton production for ITV 1. Transmission details are for the Carlton region.

Main regular credit(s):   Executive producers Maureen Goldthorpe and Nick Bullen; series producer Rachel Rosen.

Main regular performer(s):   Eamonn Holmes (Presenter), Tess Daly (Presenter).

	Holding / Source
01.12.2003	DB / DBSW
05.12.2003	DB / DBSW
09.12.2003	DB / DBSW
18.12.2003	DB / DBSW

CHRISTMAS SINGALONG WITH

An ATV production. Transmission details are for the ATV midlands region. Duration: 50 minutes.

They may not be the three wisest men, but they do have a lot of stars to follow; The Bachelors present their version of Christmas for the kids, Christmas around the world, and Christmas of comfort and love. Christmas for the kids with the whole cast piled into a vintage Bentley and singing "Chitty, Chitty, Bang, Bang"; Christmas round the world with festive songs from Scotland, England, Ireland and A:nerica; Christmas goodwill with songs like "What the World Needs Now".

Written by Bryan Blackburn; music associate Kenny Powell; designed by Bryan Holgate; produced by Les Cocks; directed by John Scholz-Conway.

The Bachelors, Moira Anderson, Sacha Distel, Howard Keel, Andee Silver, Jack Parnell and his Orchestra.

	Holding / Source
25.12.1971	J / 2"

CHRISTMAS SNOWTIME (SPECIAL)

A BBC production for BBC 1. Transmission details are for BBC 1. Duration varies - see below for details.

	Holding / Source
18.12.1978	DB-D3 / 2"

Duration: 50 minutes.

Choreography by Geoffrey Richer; assistant producer Bob Spiers; produced and directed by Michael Hurll.

With Demis Roussos (Host), Manhattan Transfer, Andy Williams, Petula Clark, Boney M, Sacha Distel, Charles Aznavour, The Three Degrees, Sheila B. Devotion, Jacqueline Harbord, Geoff Richer's First Edition, Maggie Stredder, Ronnie Hazlehurst and his Orchestra.

22.12.1979	DB-D3 / 2"

Duration: 47 minutes.

Written by Ian Davidson; choreography by Geoff Richer [credited as Geoffey Richer]; designed by Anna Ridley; produced by Michael Hurll; film sequences directed by Phil Bishop; outside broadcast director Michael Hurll.

With Barry Humphries [as Dame Edva Everage] (Host), Leo Sayer, Kate Bush, Abba, The Jacksons, Bonnie Tyler, Boney M, Geoff Richer's First Edition, Ronnie Hazlehurst and his Orchestra, The Maggie Stredder Singers [as Maggie Stredder and Her Singers].

CHRISTMAS SNOWTIME (SPECIAL)

CHRISTMAS SPIRITS

A Granada production. Transmission details are for the ATV midlands region. Duration: 35 minutes.

Written by Willis Hall; designed by Steven Fineren; executive producer Michael Cox [credited as Mike Cox]; produced and directed by June Wyndham-Davies.

Elaine Stritch (Julia Myerson), Norma West (Angela Antrey), Ben Aris (Charles Antrey), Stephanie Cole (Mrs Purvis).

	Production No	Holding / Source
01.01.1981	P800/13ED	DB / 2"

CHRISTMAS STAR GAMES

A Thames Television production. made in association with Trans World International. Transmission details are for the Thames Television region. Duration: 50 minutes.

Executive producer Brian Venner; produced and directed by Dave Rogers.

Michael Aspel (Host), Gerald Sinstadt (Football Commentary), Alan Pascoe, Pam Rhodes, Lynsey De Paul, Frazer Hines, Tony Osoba, Ray Lonnen, Tom O'Connor.

	Holding / Source
26.12.1980	DB / 2"

CHRISTMAS STARTIME

An ATV production. Transmission details are for the ATV midlands region. Duration: 45 minutes.

Theme music by Jack Parnell; designed by Peter Roden; produced and directed by Francis Essex.

Richard Hearne, Bruce Forsyth, David Nixon, Charlie Cairoli & Company, Bernard Braden, Barbara Kelly, Pearl Carr and Teddy Johnson, Acker Bilk and his Paramount Jazz Band, The Pirellis, Sheila Pugh, Christina Davies, Elizabeth Edmiston.

	Holding / Source
25.12.1963	J /

CHRISTMAS STORY

An Associated-Rediffusion production. Transmission details are for Associated-Rediffusion.

	Holding / Source
24.12.1962	NR / Live

THE CHRISTMAS STORY

An Associated-Rediffusion production. Transmission details are for Associated-Rediffusion. Duration: 12 minutes.

Illustrated by Alfred Wurmser; produced by Pat Baker.

Jean Ford (Storyteller).

	Holding / Source
20.12.1955	NR / Live

THE CHRISTMAS STORY

A Yorkshire Television production. Transmission details are for the ATV midlands region. Duration: 13 minutes.

Drawings by Alan Parry; based on a book by Jenny Robertson; produced by Peter Scroggs; directed by Len Lurcuck.

Paul Copley (Narrator).

	Holding / Source
25.12.1978	1" / 2"

CHRISTMAS SUNSHINE

A Scottish Television production. Transmission details are for the London Weekend Television region. Duration: 25 minutes.

Vocal group Sunshine provides happy Christmas music, including tunes from Disney and other children's films plus some Winter songs. The Scottish National Orchestra junior chorus joins in for a selection of carols. Members of Sunshine are: David Balfe, Alyson McInnes, Alisdair MacBean, Sandy Rogers and Drew Ross.

Music directed by Arthur Blake; designed by Jack Robinson; produced and directed by Archie McArthur.

Sunshine, The Scottish National Orchestra Junior Chorus.

	Holding / Source
26.12.1981	J / 2"

CHRISTMAS SWEET

A HTV production. Transmission details are for the Thames Television region. Duration: 25 minutes.

Written by Alan Dell; designed by John Biggs; produced and directed by Derek Clark.

Sweet Substitute.

	Holding / Source
23.12.1978	J / 2"

CHRISTMAS SWINGTIME

An ATV production. Transmission details are for the ATV midlands region. Duration: 50 minutes.

Settings by Anthony Waller; produced and directed by Francis Essex.

The King Brothers, Cliff Richard, The Shadows, Edmund Hockridge, Joan Regan, Kenny Baker, Tommy Whittle, Don Lusher, Boys Of The Scola Polyphonica, Jack Parnell and his Concert Orchestra.

	Holding / Source
25.12.1963	J /

A CHRISTMAS TREAT: THE DAZZLE

A Granada production. Transmission details are for the Granada region. Duration: 25 minutes.

Author Edna O'Brien reads her own story about Timothy and Matty the Mouse who fly off in 'The Dazzle' to visit a department store and play with the toys.

Written by Edna O'Brien; drawings by Murray Cook; music by Derek Hilton; designed by Chris Wilkinson; produced and directed by June Wyndham-Davies.

Edna O'Brien (Reading her short story).

	Production No	Holding / Source
25.12.1981	P1142/1	DB / 2"

THE CHRISTMAS TREE

An Associated-Rediffusion production. Transmission details are for the Southern Television region. Duration: 25 minutes.

Holding / Source

20.12.1960 The Christmas Story J /

Introduced by Geoffrey Frederick; compiled by Peter Ling; choreography by Harry Naughton; designed by Bernard Goodwin; produced and directed by Jim Pople.

With Lawrence Archer (Shepherd), Guy Gordon (Shepherd), Nicholas Evans (Shepherd), William Lyon Brown (Casper), Ronald Giffen (Melchior), Ayton Medas (Belthazar), Denis Cleary (Joseph), June Speight (Mary), Cleo Laine, Howard Williams, Wally Whyton, The Orpington Junior Singers.

27.12.1960 The Mummers / A Christmas Carol J /

Introduced by Geoffrey Frederick; compiled by Peter Ling; designed by Bernard Goodwin; produced and directed by Jim Pople.

With John Gabriel (Father Christmas), John Pike (Jerry Dout), Malcolm Webster (St George), Graham Crowden (The Turkish Knight), Roy Adams (The Doctor), Donald Hewlett (The Dragon), John Gabriel (Scrooge), John Pike (The Boy), Muriel Young, Redvers Kyle, Orpington Junior Singers.

03.01.1961 The Pantomime J /

Introduced by Geoffrey Frederick; compiled by Peter Ling; choreography by Harry Naughton; designed by Bernard Goodwin; directed by Jim Pople.

With Steve Race, Bert Weedon, Janet Nicolls, The Orpington Junior Singers, Diana Beevers (Cinderella), Richard Palmer (Buttons), June Monkhouse (Fairy Godmother), Elaine Carr (Spirit), Greta Hamby (Spirit), Valerie La Serve (Spirit), Ann Edgar (Spirit).

THE CHRISTMAS TREE

An Associated-Rediffusion production. Transmission details are for the ATV midlands region. Duration: 25 minutes.

Settings by Ken Jones; produced and directed by Eric Croall.

Ivan Owen, Janice Nicholls, Muriel Young, Wally Whyton, Anne Newell, Pan Wade, Peter Firmin, Howard Williams.

	Holding / Source
25.12.1963	J /

THE CHRISTMAS TREE

A BBC production for BBC 1. Transmission details are for BBC 1. Duration: 30 minutes.

Based on a story by Hans Christian Andersen; music by Patrick Harvey and Frederick; designed by Paul Allen; directed by Peter Ridsdale Scott.

Nina and Frederick.

	Holding / Source
25.12.1967	J /

THE CHRISTMAS TREE

A Yorkshire Television production. Transmission details are for the Central region. Duration: 80 minutes.

Adapted by William Corlett; based on a book by Jennifer Johnston; designed by Roger Andrews; associate producer Carol Williams; produced by David Cunliffe; directed by Herbert Wise.

Anna Massey (Constance Keating), Simon Callow (Jacob Weinberg), Maeve Germaine (Bridie May), T. P. McKenna (Doctor Bill Prendergast), Fiona Walker (Bibi Barry), Helen Ryan (Mrs Keating), Bernard Brown (Mr Keating), Morris Perry (Gynaecologist), Paul Rattigan (Young Man At Dance), Jayne Tottman (Young Constanc), Joan Beveridge (Young Bib), Gillian Kerrod (Nurse).

	Holding / Source
21.12.1986	1" / 1"

CHRISTMAS UNDER FIRE

A BBC production for BBC 2. Transmission details are for BBC 2. Duration: 90 minutes.

Hopefully we will all enjoy a merry and peaceful Christmas this year, but in 1939 the seasonal message of peace and goodwill toward men seemed an impossible dream. This documentary, narrated by Alan Bennett, features poignant personal recollections of the festive seasons during the Second World War, from both the battlefront and the home front. Food shortages and rationing were among the challenges for most families, and there are stomach-churning tales of what some creative mothers served up for Christmas dinner.

Executive producer Laurence Rees; produced by Jamie Muir.

Alan Bennett (Narrator).

	Holding / Source
24.12.2002	DB / DBSW

CHRISTMAS UNDER FIRE

CHRISTMAS WITH CLIFF

A BBC production for BBC 1. Transmission details are for BBC 1. Duration: 40 minutes.
Edited by Helen Alexander; produced by Bart Gavigan.
Sally Magnusson (Interviewer), Cliff Richard.

	Holding / Source
24.12.1995	DB-D3 / D3S

CHRISTMAS WITH THE APPLEYARDS

A BBC production. Transmission details are for BBC. Duration: 25 minutes.
Written by Kevin Sheldon; play production by Kevin Sheldon.
Constance Fraser (Mum), Douglas Muir (Dad), Derek Rowe (Tommy), Patricia Fryer (Margaret), David Edwards (John), Robert Dickens (Ronnie Grant), C. B. Poultney (Mr Spiller), Beatrix Mackey (Customer), Hazel Gardner (Customer), Eileen Draycott (Customer), John Brooking (Manager), Terry Baker (Milkman).

	Holding / Source
24.12.1960	J /

CHUCKLEVISION

A BBC production for BBC 1. Transmission details are for BBC 1.
Main regular cast: Paul Elliott (Chuckle Brother), Barry Elliott (Chuckle Brother).

SERIES 1
A BBC North West production. Duration: 20 minutes.
Main regular credit(s):   Produced by Martin Hughes.
Main regular cast: With Simon Lovell, Billy Butler.

	Holding / Source
19.12.1987 **Christmas**	DB / 1"

SERIES 2
Main regular cast: With Billy Butler.

	Holding / Source
24.12.1988 **Christmas Special**	DB / 1"

SERIES 15

	Holding / Source
24.12.2002 **Messy Christmas**	DB / DBSWF
27.12.2002 **A Christmas Chuckle**	DB / DBSWF

Postponed from 24.12.2002.
Not shown due to a technical error, Messy Christmas was repeated.

SERIES 20
Transmission details are for CBBC.

	Holding / Source
25.12.2008 **The Mystery of Little-Under-Standing**	DB / DBSWF

Written by Martin Hughes.

CHWARAE'N TROI'N CHWERW

Commissioned by S4C. Transmission details are for S4C. Duration: 75 minutes.

	Holding / Source
31.12.1995	D3 / V1S

CILLA

A BBC production for BBC 1. Transmission details are for BBC 1. Usual duration: 50 minutes.
Main regular performer(s):   Cilla Black (Host).

SERIES 3
Main regular credit(s):   Written by Ronnie Taylor; music directed by Ronnie Hazlehurst; choreography by Nita Howard; produced and directed by Michael Hurll.
Main regular performer(s): With The Breakaways.

	Holding / Source
24.12.1969	J / 2"

With Cliff Richard, Dusty Springfield, Kenny Everett.

	Holding / Source
26.12.1974	DB-D3 / 2"

Written by Ronnie Taylor; music directed by Jeff Wayne and Ronnie Hazlehurst; choreography by Irving Davies; designed by Robin Tarsnane; produced and directed by Michael Hurll; film sequences directed by Bob Spiers.
With Gerald Harper, The Wombles, David Essex, The Breakaways, The Irving Davies Dancers.

CILLA BLACK AND THE SEVEN TALL DWARFS

Commissioned by Associated-Rediffusion. Not made.
Cilla Black.

Holding / Source

##.##.#### NR /

Agreement dated 28.09.1965. Some paperwork also survives among the paperwork of Roger McGough held at the University of Liverpool.

CILLA BLACK'S CHRISTMAS

Alternative/Working Title(s): CILLA BLACK'S CHRISTMAS EVE
An LWT production. Transmission details are for the Central region. Duration: 50 minutes.
Written by Vince Powell; choreography by Tudor Davies; designed by Alison Humphries; produced by David Bell; directed by Noel D. Greene.
Cilla Black (Host), Frankie Howerd, Graham Fletcher, The Bee Gees, Julio Iglesias, George Benson, Alyn Ainsworth Orchestra and Singers, Wendy Padbury, Wincey Willis, Lennie Bennett, Melvyn Hayes.

Holding / Source

24.12.1983 D2 / 1"

CILLA SAYS GOODBYE TO THE 80'S

An LWT production. Transmission details are for the Central region. Duration: 81 minutes.
Written by Vince Powell; designed by Bill McPherson; associate producer Maurice Gallagher; executive producer Michael Hurll; produced by Lorna Dickinson; directed by Michael Hurll.
Cilla Black (Host), Ronnie Corbett, Deborah Harry, Michael Aspel, Hale and Pace, Tracey Ullman, Denis Norden, Alexei Sayle, Mark Austin, Barry McGuigan, Don King, John Suchet, Chay Blyth, Lawrence McGinty, Pamela Stephenson, Trevor McDonald, Jonathan Ross, Sir John Mills, President Bush, Leonid Zanyatin, Jason Donovan, Mick Hucknall, Duran Duran, Warren Cuccurullo, Sterling Campbell, Kingsmead School, Sylvia Young Theatre School, Cliff Richard, Dusty Springfield, Christian Solari.

	Production No	Holding / Source
31.12.1989	9L/92158	D2 / 1"

CINDERELLA

A BBC production. Transmission details are for BBC.
Presented by Ronald Adams; written by Margaret Carter; play production by Stephen Thomas.
Joan French (Cinderella), John Gattrell (Prince), Joan Luxton (Ugly Sister), Margaret Carter (Ugly Sister), W. S. Percy (Baron), Brember Wills (Chancellor), Patrick Gover (Dandini), Elfrida Burgiss (Lady Penelope), Roy Heeath (Choddles), Jack Williams (Servant), Maude Joliffe (Fairy Godmother), Betty Wych (Serving Maid), Mary Rame (Gieta), Veronica Cook (Piano), Gwyneth Trotter (Violin), Marie Dare (Cello).

Holding / Source

19.01.1937 NR / Live

Performed by members of Joan Luxton's Children's Theatre Company.

CINDERELLA

A BBC production. Transmission details are for BBC. Duration: 90 minutes.
Adapted by Archie Harradine and Eric Fawcett; based on a play by H. J. Byron; play production by Eric Fawcett; produced for the stage by Don Gemmell.
Joyce Cummings (Cinders), Elma Soiron (Prince Charming), Joan Sterndale Bennett (Dandini), Don Gemmell (Ugly Sister), May Hallatt [as May Hallett] (Ugly Sister), Phillada Sewell (Fairy Queen), Therese Langfield (First Fairy / Columbine), Marguerite Stewart (Second Fairy / Harlequin), Owen Holder (Buttons), Bill Shine (The Baron), Peggy Attfield (Page), John Hewer (Pantaloon), David Keir (Clown), June Gripper, Diana Rimer.

Holding / Source

02.01.1947 **First Performance** NR / Live
03.01.1947 **Second Performance** NR / Live

CINDERELLA

A BBC production. Transmission details are for BBC. Duration: 90 minutes.
Devised by Jack Hulbert and Walton Anderson; book by Max Kester; orchestra directed by Eric Robinson; settings by Richard Greenough; production assistant Stephen McCormack; play production by Jack Hulbert and Walton Anderson.
Jack Hulbert (Buttons), Joy Nichols (Prince Charming), Eunice Crowther (Dandini), Lois Green (Cinderella), Bill Fraser (The Baron), Diana Morrison (Ugly Sister), Doris Rogers (Ugly Sister), Harold Berens (The Broker's Men), Tony Arpino (The Broker's Men), The George Mitchell Choir.

Holding / Source

27.12.1948 **First Performance** NR / Live
04.01.1949 **Second Performance** NR / Live

CINDERELLA

A BBC production. Transmission details are for BBC. Duration: 120 minutes.

Written by Gordon Crier; music by Stanley Andrews; orchestra directed by Eric Robinson; choreography by Eunice Crowther and Irving Davies; settings by Richard Greenough; play production by Jack Hulbert and Walton Anderson.

Sally Ann Howes (Cinderella), Jack Hulbert (Baron De Stitute), Brenda Ralston (Fairy Godmother), John Stevens (Old Mean Time), Diana Morrison (Tabitha), Doris Rogers (Abigail), Marten Tiffen (Buttons), The Borstal Boys (Twist And Bust), Dennis Castle (Herald), Eunice Crowther (Dandini), Kathleen Moody (Prince Charming), Kamala Amesur, Patricia Brooks, June Charlier, Riccy Chisholm, Joan Chorlton, Marion Crawford, Eleanor Fazan, Diane Holland, Deirdre de Peyer, Anita Phillips, Mary Reynolds, Eugenie Sivyer, The George Mitchell Choir.

	Holding / Source
26.12.1950	NR / Live

CINDERELLA

A BBC production. Transmission details are for BBC. Duration: 90 minutes.

Orchestra directed by Edmund Welch; choreography by Lisa Brionda; television presentation by Richard Afton; produced by Jack Phillips.

Chuck O'Neill, George Moon, Billy Matchett, The Cox Twins, Audrey Jeans, Joan Burden, Billy Nelson, Roy Jefferies, Viki Emra, Billy Morris.

	Holding / Source
22.12.1951	NR / Live

Presented by S.H. Newsome at the Hippodrome Theatre, Dudley.

CINDERELLA

A BBC production. Transmission details are for BBC. Duration: 65 minutes.

Written by C. E. Webber; music by John Hotchkis and The Goldsbrough Orchestra; produced and directed by Shaun Sutton.

June Thorburn (Cinderella), John Fabian (Prince Florizel), Peter Sallis (Baron Aristide De Pennilac), Joan Benham (Araminta), Edna Petrie (Arabella), Kynaston Reeves (Grand Chamberlain), Frazer Hines (Buttons), Patrick Cargill (First Broker's Man), Colin Douglas (Second Broker's Man), Mary Mackenzie (Godmother), James Sharkey (Dandini), Dennis Ramsden (Major Domo), John Barrard (Count Grumblekin), Bernard Horsfall (Signor Benvenuto), Balbina (Mademoiselle Jojo).

	Holding / Source
26.12.1958	R1|n /

CINDERELLA

A Granada production. Transmission details are for the Granada region. Duration: 69 minutes.

Music directed by Hugo Rignold; music by Sergei Prokofiev; orchestra conducted by Hugo Rignold; choreography by Frederick Ashton; associate director Frederick Ashton; designed by Darrell Lass; produced and directed by Mark Stuart.

Margot Fonteyn (Cinderella), Michael Somes (Prince Charming), Alexander Grant (Jester), Gerd Larsen (Ugly Sister), Rosemary Lindsay (Ugly Sister), Franklin White (Cinderella's Father), Annette Page (Fairy Godmother), Merle Park (Spring Fairy), Georgina Parkinson (Summer Fairy), Shirley Grahame (Autumn Fairy), Christine Beckley (Winter Fairy), Pirmin Trecu (Dancing Master), Richard Farley (Cavalier), Bryan Lawrence (Cavalier), Christopher Newton (Cavalier), Keith Rosson (Cavalier).

	Holding / Source
13.04.1960	DB-4W / 40

The Royal Ballet Company from the Royal Opera House, Covent Garden appeared in a special 75-minute television production. The first performance in a television studio and the first time a full-length ballet on television had been danced exclusively by members of the Royal Ballet Company.

CINDERELLA

A BBC production for BBC 1. Transmission details are for BBC 1. Duration: 90 minutes.

Written by Michael Young; additional dialogue by Bryan Blackburn and Ron McDonnell; music directed by Harry Rabinowitz; choreography by Norman Maen; designed by Michael Young; produced by Freddie Carpenter; directed by Peter Whitmore.

Jimmy Tarbuck (Buttons), Terry Scott (Ugly Sister), Hugh Lloyd (Ugly Sister), Sally Smith (Cinderella), David Kernan (Prince Charming), Neville Jason (Dandini), Louida Vaughan (Fairy Godmother), Graham Squire (Baron), The Keefe Brothers (Buttons' Horse), Leigh Foster (Principal Dancer), Vreni Zullic (Principal Dancer), The Norman Maen Dancers, George Mitchell Singers.

	Holding / Source
25.12.1967	DVSEQ / 40

39 mins of footage exist on DV ex-CV2000.

CINDERELLA

A BBC production for BBC 1. Transmission details are for BBC 1. Duration: 90 minutes.

Additional material by Eddie Braben, George Evans and George Martin; music directed by Burt Rhodes; choreography by Denise Shaune; designed by Berkeley Sutcliffe; produced by Freddie Carpenter; directed by Peter Whitmore.

Jimmy Tarbuck (Buttons), Anita Harris (Cinderella), Beryl Reid (Ugly Sister Marlene), Jack Tripp (Ugly Sister Florence), Ursula Howells (Fairy Godmother), Ian Paterson (Prince Charming), Allen Christie (Dandini), Graham Squire (Baron), Basil Brush, The Denise Shaune Dancers, The Bowles Bevan Singers.

	Holding / Source
25.12.1969	DVSEQ / 2"

58 mins of footage exists on DV, ex-CV2000.

CINDERELLA

A Yorkshire Television production. Transmission details are for the ATV midlands region. Duration: 55 minutes.

Here's Cinderella with a difference. It's back to the good old days. Traditional pantomime without the modern idea of introducing pop groups and the like. Staged at the City Varieties Theatre, Leeds, it stars Dickie Henderson. And Dickie, like his father before him, has always been a traditionalist on the Christmas scene, with Buttons as his "speciality".

Adapted by Bert Gaunt and Jess Yates; based on a book by Derek Salberg; music directed by Charles Smitton; designed by Ian McCrow; executive producer Jess Yates; produced and directed by Bill Hitchcock.

Susan George (Cinders), Vince Hill (Prince Charming), Lionel Blair (Dandini), Dickie Henderson (Buttons), John Inman (Ugly Sister), Barry Howard (Ugly Sister), Jack Douglas (Baron Stoneybroke), The Lionel Blair Dancers, The Mike Sammes Singers, Jean Pearce Sunbeams, The Tiddleywinks.

Holding / Source
25.12.1970　　J / 2"

With Clive James, Susan George, Lionel Blair.

CINDERELLA

A Yorkshire Television production. Transmission details are for the ATV midlands region. Duration: 40 minutes.

Script editor Bob Block; designed by Chris George; executive producer Jess Yates; directed by David Millard.

Caroline Turner (Cinderella), Kathryn Apanowicz (Prince), Bobby Bennett (Baron Stoneybroke), Sharon Banks (Ugly Sister), Julie Shipley (Ugly Sister), Moira Phillips (Fairy), Janice Colley (Dandini), Mark Curry (Buttons), Janet Rees, The Muir Brothers, Arthur Smithurst, Scottish Drum Majorettes, Hammond Sauce Works Junior Band, Thompson School of Ballet.

Holding / Source
26.12.1972　　J / 2"

See also: JUNIOR SHOWTIME

CINDERELLA

A Thames Television production. Transmission details are for the ATV midlands region. Duration: 40 minutes.

Music by David Rohl and Stuart J. Wolstenholme; executive producer John Hambley; produced by Mark Hall and Brian Cosgrove; directed by Mark Hall.

Holding / Source
26.12.1979　　C1 / C1

Animated puppet film.

CINDERELLA

A Wishbone production for LWT. Transmission details are for the Central region. Duration: 74 minutes.

Written by Simon Nye; script supervisor Judy Packman-Reynolds; music by Philip Pope; choreography by Di Cooke; art director Sophie Geliot; executive producer Humphrey Barclay; production manager Melissa Daley; produced by Helen Pitcher; directed by Liddy Oldroyd.

Frank Skinner (Buttons), Sam Janus (Cinderella), Siân Phillips (The Baroness), Ronnie Corbett (Griselda), Paul Merton (Lucretia), Ben Miller (Dandini), Julian Clary (The Good Fairy), Alexander Armstrong (Prince Charming), Harry Hill (Master of Ceremonies), Edward Hayes-Neary, Lisa Stevens, Tamara Wall, Bryn Walters, Steven Wynn, Rachel Woolrich.

Holding / Source
02.01.2000　　DB / DBSW

CINDERELLA - THE SHOE MUST GO ON

A Central production. Transmission details are for the Central region. Duration: 78 minutes.

Written by Barry Cryer and Dick Vosburgh; music directed by Laurie Holloway; music by Laurie Holloway and Keith Strachan; choreography by Nigel Lythgoe; designed by Richard Plumb; associate producer Nigel Crowle; produced and directed by Jon Scoffield.

Les Dennis (Brokers Man), Bob Carolgees (Himself), Danny La Rue (Stepmother), Jimmy Cricket (Buttons), Brian Murphy (Amnesia), Faith Brown (Fairy Godmother), John Wells (Denis Thatcher), Roy Walker (Brokers Man), Steve Nallon (Maggie Thatcher), Basil Brush (Himself), Roy Hudd (Magnesia), Michael Howe (Prince Charming), Roy Kinnear (Baron Hardup), Cheryl Baker (Cinderella), Ross Davidson (Himself), Mike Reid (Major D'Omo), Judith Chalmers (Herself), Shaw Taylor (Himself), Jim Bowen (Game Show Host), Caroline Munro (Game Show Hostess), William Rushton (Narrator).

Holding / Source
25.12.1986　　1" / 1"

CINEMA

A Granada production. Duration varies - see below for details.

Transmission details are for the Granada region.

Holding / Source

26.12.1968　**Cinema Says It With Music**　　　　　　　　　　　　　　　　　　　　　　　　　　　　　　　　J / C1
Duration: 45 minutes.
The film musical is examined.
Research Peter Matthews; executive producer James Butler; directed by Eric Prytherch.
With Mark Shivas (Presenter).

CIRCLES OF DECEIT

A Yorkshire Television production. Transmission details are for the Central region. Duration varies - see below for details.

Main regular credit(s): Based on novels by Jill Arbon.
Main regular cast: Dennis Waterman (John Neil).

	Production No	VT Number	Holding / Source
27.12.1995 **Dark Secret**	Y/0360/0002	L617/03	DB / V1S

Duration: 100 minutes.
Adapted by Barry Appleton; executive producer Andrew Benson; produced by Simon Lewis; directed by Nick Laughland.

With Susan Jameson (Controller), Dave Hill (Andy), Corin Redgrave, Kate Buffery, Pippa Guard, Melanie Hill, Holly Aird, Sean McGinley, Adjoa Andoh, Joe Montana, Peter Birch, David Dixon, David Horovitch, Ann Aris, Romy Baskerville, Carolina Giammetta, Kenneth Alan Taylor, Christine Cox, David Bond, Chris Brailsford, Molly Bean, Roger Walker, Jim Millea, Ravin J. Ganatra, Vincent Davies, Peter Ivatts.

	Production No	VT Number	Holding / Source
23.12.1996 **Sleeping Dogs**	Y/0360/0004	L617/01	DB / V1S

Duration: 98 minutes.
Adapted by John Brown; executive producer Andrew Benson; produced by Simon Lewis; directed by Alan Grint.

With Susan Jameson (Controller), Dave Hill (Andy), Frances Barber, Paul Freeman, Nicholas Jones, William Armstrong, Leo McKern, Lalor Roddy, Ian Fitzgibbon, James Aubrey, Peter Armitage, Diane Bull, James Duggan, Emer Gillespie, Richard Sinnott, Norman Wan, Andy Tomlinson, Chris Bisson, Josh Moran.

THE CIRCUS COMES TO TOWN

An ITV Various production. Transmission details are for ITV. Duration varies - see below for details.

	Holding / Source
24.12.1965	J /

Duration: 45 minutes.
Produced by John Hamp; directed by Eric Harrison.
With Dubsky's Dogs, Chief Grey Arrow, Gentleman Jack, The Trio Wallys, The Four Failas, The Austins.

	Holding / Source
25.12.1965	J /
26.12.1965	J /
30.12.1966	J /
31.12.1966	J /

CIRCUSES

Produced for BBC 1 & some ITV stations by a variety of companies (see details below). Transmission details are for BBC 1. Duration varies - see below for details.

	Holding / Source
25.12.1962 **Billy Smart's Circus**	R3 / 40
25.12.1963 **Billy Smart's Children's Circus**	R3 / 40
25.12.1970 **Kelvin Hall Circus**	J / 2"

A Scottish Television production. Duration: 50 minutes.
Music directed by Bernard Weller; directed by Russell Galbraith.

With Alfred Delbosq (Ringmaster), Barbara Morris, Californian Sea Lions, Miss Wendy and Her Doves, Duo Dobritch, Les Dougalls, The Biasini Family, Los Platos, Phyllis Allen and her Poodles, Mary Fossett's Welsh Ponies, The Four Salvadors, Carl Pinder and The Circus Clowns, Sir Robert Fossett's Elephants, Mimi, Jukius Haeni, The Louis Freeman Orchestra.

	Holding / Source
25.12.1970 **Billy Smart's Circus**	DB-D3 / 62

Digibeta (ex b/w VT – originally colour).

	Holding / Source
25.12.1971 **Kelvin Hall Circus**	J / 2"

A Scottish Television production. Duration: 50 minutes.
Orchestra conducted by Bernard Weller; directed by Russell Galbraith.

With Alfred Delbosq (Ringmaster), Glen Michael, Enrico Caroli Family, The Five Hunors, The Castors, Phil Enos, The Veterans, The Circus Clowns, Robert Brothers' Elephants and Horses, Louis Freeman Orchestra.

	Holding / Source
25.12.1971 **Billy Smart's Christmas Circus**	DB-D3 / 2"
26.12.1971 **Queen's Hall Circus**	DB / 2"

A Yorkshire Television production. Duration: 52 minutes.
Introduced by Keith Macklin; directed by Geoff Hall.
With Captain Howes (Presenter), Professor Grimble, Gerone, Gina In The Moon, Bobby Roberts' Pigs.

	Holding / Source
25.12.1972 **Billy Smart's Circus**	DB-D3 / 2"
25.12.1973 **Billy Smart's Christmas Circus**	DB-D3 / 2"
25.12.1974 **Billy Smart's Christmas Circus**	DB-D3 / 2"

Duration: 60 minutes.
Music directed by Ken Griffin; television presentation by Ian Smith; designed by Andrew Davies.

With Yasmine Smart (Ringmistress), Ray Moore (Commentator), Tito Reyes, Hoffmann's Lions, Josephina, The Lavrenovis, Bario and Bario, The White Devils, Roberts Brothers' Elephants [as Roberts' Elephants], The Pendakovis.

	Holding / Source
25.12.1975 **Billy Smart's Circus**	DB-D3 / 2"
25.12.1976 **Billy Smart's Circus**	DB-D3 / 2"

CIRCUSES (continued)

25.12.1977 Billy Smart's Christmas Circus — DB-D3 / 2"
Duration: 60 minutes.
Introduced by Yasmine Smart; music directed by Ken Griffin; television presentation by Ian Smith; designed by Allan Anson.
With Ray Moore (Commentator), The Nicolodis, The Bauers, The Jonides, The Di Lellos, The Circus Elephants, Billy Wilson Smart, Miss Lisa, Willy Hagenbeck's Horses, Robert Brothers' Tigers, Carl Fischer, The Flying Ramos.

25.12.1978 Billy Smart's Christmas Circus — DB / 2"
A Thames Television production.

25.12.1980 Billy Smart's Christmas Circus — DB-D3 / 2"
A Thames Television production.

28.12.1981 Billy Smart's Christmas Circus — DB-D3 / 2"
A Thames Television production.

28.12.1982 Billy Smart's Christmas Circus — DB-D3 / 2"
A Thames Television production.

CITIZEN KHAN

A BBC production for BBC 1. Transmission details are for BBC 1. Duration: 30 minutes.
Written by Anil Gupta, Adil Ray and Richard Pinto.
Adil Ray (Mr Khan), Shobu Kapoor (Mrs Khan), Bhavna Limbachia (Alia), Maya Sondhi (Shazia), Abdullah Afzal (Amjad).

SERIES 2
Credits: Associate producer Paul Schlesinger; executive producer Mark Freeland; produced by Catherine Gosling Fuller, Adil Ray, Richard Pinto and Anil Gupta; directed by Ben Gosling Fuller.
Cast: With Matthew Cottle (Dave), Felix Dexter (Omar).

Holding / Source
20.12.2013 A Khan Christmas — HD/DB / HDC
Mrs Khan has decided to have a traditional family Christmas, their first one ever.
Directed by Ben Gosling Fuller.
With Harvey Virdi (Mrs Malik), Nish Nathwani (Riaz), Adlyn Ross (Naani), Phil Nice (Keith), Neil Edmond (Reverend Green), Delroy Brown (Christmas Tree Customer), Iziah Williams (Bradley), Adam Fray (Christmas Tree Vendor).

CITIZEN SMITH

A BBC production for BBC 1. Transmission details are for BBC 1. Duration varies - see below for details.
Main regular credit(s): Written by John Sullivan; lyrics by John Sullivan; theme music by John Sullivan and Ronnie Hazlehurst.
Main regular cast: Robert Lindsay (Wolfie Smith), Mike Grady (Ken), Hilda Braid (Mum).

SERIES 1
Main regular credit(s): Designed by Paul Allen; produced and directed by Dennis Main Wilson.
Main regular cast: With Peter Vaughan (Dad), Cheryl Hall (Shirley).

Holding / Source
22.12.1977 A Story For Christmas — DB-D3 / 2"
Duration: 29 minutes.
Lighting by Don Babbage; sound Malcolm Johnson; film camera Max Samett; designed by Paul Allen.
With Stephen Greif (Harry Fenning), George Tovey.

SERIES 4
Main regular credit(s): Designed by Tony Snoaden; produced and directed by Ray Butt.
Main regular cast: With Tony Steedman (Dad), Anthony Millan (Tucker), George Sweeney (Speed).

Holding / Source
31.12.1980 Buôn Natale — DB-D3 / 2"
Duration: 29 minutes.
As Wolfie's girlfriend Shirley cannot get home from Italy for Christmas, our intrepid TPF leader decides to visit her. What a surprise!
Designed by Marjorie Pratt.
With David Garfield (Ronnie Lynch), Susie Baker (Mandy Lynch), Anthony Morton (Police captain), Anthony Jackson (Italian barman), Julia Gaye (Girl on beach), Tex Fuller.

CITV CONTINUITY

A Central production for Carlton UK. Transmission details are for the Central region.

Holding / Source
25.12.2002 — DB / DBSW
26.12.2002 — DB / DBSW

THE CLAMPERS AT CHRISTMAS

A BBC production for BBC 1. Transmission details are for BBC 1. Duration: 30 minutes.
A seasonal edition of the documentary series following Britain's parking law enforcers, which was filmed over last Christmas.
   It's one of the busiest times of the year for the team, and damper Ray Brown gets into the holiday spirit by decorating his van. Meanwhile, an irate driver makes confetti of the ticket warden Sandy Macleod has issued him, and parking attendant Mike Greenidge discovers a load of illegally parked Christmas trees.
Series producer Kim Duke; produced by Jennie Cosgrove.
Ray Brown, Sandy Macleod, Mike Greenidge.

	Holding / Source
21.12.1998	DB / DBS

A CLAN FOR ALL SEASONS

A Scottish Television production. Transmission details are for the Scottish Television region.
Produced by Russell Galbraith; directed by David Dunn.
Dame Flora MacLeod.

	Holding / Source
01.01.1973	1" / 2"

CLAPPERBOARD

A Granada production. Transmission details are for the ATV midlands region. Usual duration: 23 minutes.
Main regular credit(s):   Produced by Muriel Young.
Main regular performer(s):   Chris Kelly (Presenter).

SERIES 1
Main regular credit(s):   Designed by Roy Graham.

	Holding / Source
25.12.1972 **Clapperboard's Christmas Cracker**	J / C1

Duration: 35 minutes.
Directed by David Warwick.

24.12.1973 **Magic And Music**	J / C1

Research by Graham Murray; designed by Roy Graham; directed by David Warwick.

SERIES 2

	Production No	Holding / Source
16.12.1974 **Christmas Holiday Films**		J / C1
26.12.1974 **Christmas Clapperboard**		J / C1

"The second star to the right and keep right on till morning", that's the way to Never Never Land according to Peter Pan. But in this special Christmas edition of Clapperboard Chris takes you the easy way to the incredible places that exist only in the imagination, when he shows clips from the new Disney film Island at the top of the World, and the re-released classic Peter Pan.

15.12.1975 **Christmas Holiday Films**		J / C1
22.12.1975 **Christmas Films**		J / C1
29.12.1975 **Christmas Holiday Films**		J / C1
19.12.1977 **Christmas Releases**		J / C1

Directed by Dave Warwick.

18.12.1978 **Films for Christmas**	P729/336	C1 / C1

Directed by Dave Warwick.

25.12.1978 **Christmas Clapperboard: Flying**	P729/337	C1 / C1

Duration: 27 minutes.
Directed by David Warwick and Dave Warwick.
With Christopher Lee.

17.12.1979 **Christmas Releases**	P729/378	C1 / C1

Duration: 26 minutes.
Directed by Mike Becker.
With Peter Ellenshaw.

24.12.1981 **Camera Magic**	P729/482	C1 / C1

Duration: 30 minutes.
Chris Kelly talks to Derek Meddings about special effects and shows clips from the following films: Robert Paul film, Aces High, Thunderbirds, Fear is the Key, The Land That Time Forgot, For Your Eyes Only, Superman (Movie), Superman II.
Directed by Richard Guinea.
With Derek Meddings.

08.12.1980 **Christmas Releases**	P729/428	C1 / C1

Duration: 26 minutes.
Directed by Eugene Ferguson.

CLAPPERBOARD (continued)   British Christmas Television Guide

19.12.1981 **Christmas Releases**   P729/481   C1 / C1

Duration: 26 minutes.

A preview of Christmas cinema fare. This includes the much-acclaimed Australian war film Gallipoli, the thriller Eye of the Needle and the new treatment of an old story, Zorro, The Gay Blade. Also Chris Kelly looks at the full-length animated Disney offering The Fox and the Hound and the re-issued classic Sleeping Beauty. You can see another edition of Clapperboard on Thursday. For the special Christmas Eve programme, Chris Kelly visits Pinewood Studios.

Research Nora Watts; produced by Muriel Young; directed by Richard Guinea.

CLARE IN THE COMMUNITY (RADIO)

Produced for BBC Radio 4 by a variety of companies (see details below). Transmission details are for BBC Radio 4.

Main regular credit(s):   Written by Harry Venning and David Ramsden; based on material by Harry Venning.

Main regular cast: Sally Phillips (Clare), Nina Conti (Megan), Gemma Craven (Helen), Alex Lowe (Brian), Richard Lumsden (Ray), Ellen Thomas (Irene), Andrew Wincott (Simon).

SERIES 3

A BBC production.

Main regular credit(s):   Produced and directed by Kate Tyrrell.

                                                                                                                                     Holding / Source

25.12.2006 **Merry Christmas Mrs Lawrence**   DA /

With Gerard McDermott (Grandad), Phil Davis (Malcolm), Brigit Forsyth (Celia), Christine Kavanagh (Emma).

Clare in the Community is a British comic strip in The Guardian newspaper, written by Harry Venning. The title is a pun on care in the community. Clare is a social worker who likes to sort out other people's problems while ignoring her own. She is white, middle class and heterosexual - but doesn't like to be reminded of it. She is a control freak but both her personal and professional lives are out of control.

CLASH OF THE SANTAS

An ITV Productions production for ITV 1. Transmission details are for the Central region. Duration: 100 minutes.

Bickering best friends Colin and Howie in a comedy adventure which sees the duo travel to Lithuania to compete in the World Santa championships. Howie represents England and Colin goes as his Elf helper. But then a chance presents itself for him to go head to head with his friend.

Written by Jeff Pope; additional material by Lewis McLeod; based on characters created by Jeff Pope and Bob Mills; script supervisor Val White; music by Daniel Pemberton; designed by Margaret Coombes; production executive Gail Kennett; executive producers Saurabh Kakkar and Jeff Pope; produced by Chris Carey; directed by Paul Seed.

Robson Green (Colin), Mark Benton (Howie), Nicola Stephenson (Jackie), Abbi Gray (Victoria), Sian Reeves (Pauline), Anthony Debaeck (Jean Luc), Emma Cunniffe (Alice), Lee Worswick (Liam), Alex Rimmer (Leyton), Alex Liang (Japanese Santa), Stuart Wade (Aussie Santa), Ian Puleston-Davies (Beryl), Edward Petherbridge (Village Elder), Carolin Stoltz (Tilda), Ralph Gassmann (Florian), Bibi Nerheim (Virgin Mary), Richard Sinnott (TV Presenter), Linzey Cocker (Brooke), St Peter's South Weald Choir.

                                                                                            Holding / Source

21.12.2008   DB / DBSWF

See also: CHRISTMAS LIGHTS

CLEO AND JOHN

A Yorkshire Television production. Transmission details are for the Central region. Duration: 50 minutes.

Written by Benny Green; designed by Colin Pigott; produced and directed by Vernon Lawrence.

Cleo Laine (Host), John Dankworth (Host), Rowan Atkinson, Julian Lloyd Webber, Linda Gibbs, The Mastersingers.

                                                                                          Holding / Source

25.12.1982   1" / 1"

CLEO AT WINCHESTER

A Southern Television production. Transmission details are for the ATV midlands region. Duration: 40 minutes.

Produced by Angus Wright; directed by Dave Heather.

Cleo Laine, Andrew Cruickshank (Introduced by), John Dankworth, Choir of Winchester Cathedral.

                                                                                          Holding / Source

01.01.1978   DB / 2"

CLEO'S CHRISTMAS SPECIAL

An ATV production. Transmission details are for the ATV midlands region. Duration: 50 minutes.

Written by Ronnie Cass; music by Derek Scott; designed by Richard Lake; produced and directed by Colin Clews.

Cleo Laine (Host), John Dankworth, Karen Winkermann, Scott Madden, Modesty, Brompton Oratory Junior Choir, Bevington School, West Green Primary School, Jack Parnell and his Orchestra.

                                                                                          Holding / Source

25.12.1979   DB / 2"

THE CLERKES OF OXENFORD

A BBC production for BBC 2. Transmission details are for BBC 2. Duration: 25 minutes.

Music directed by David Wulstan; produced and directed by David Buckton.

                                                                                          Holding / Source

24.12.1968   R1 / 2"

CLIFF FROM THE HIP

A Gordon Elsbury Production production for Channel 4. Transmission details are for Channel 4. Duration: 50 minutes.
Concert at London Hippodrome.
Music directed by Mike Moran; produced by Jill Sinclair and Gordon Elsbury; directed by Gordon Elsbury.
Cliff Richard, Elton John, Billy Ocean, Five Star, The Shadows, Marti Webb.

	Holding / Source
27.12.1986	1" / 1"

A CLIP ROUND THE YEAR

A BBC Scotland production for BBC 2. Transmission details are for BBC 2. Duration: 30 minutes.
Script editor Laurie Rowley; designed by Peter Deuling; assistant producer Philip Differ; produced and directed by Colin Gilbert.
John Sessions.

	Holding / Source
30.12.1983	DB-D3 / 2"

CLIVE JAMES ON 1990

A BBC production for BBC 1. Transmission details are for BBC 1. Duration: 60 minutes.
Edited by Richard Drewett; produced by Elaine Bedell.
Clive James (Presenter).

	Holding / Source
31.12.1990	DB / 1"

CLIVE JAMES ON 1991

A BBC production for BBC 1. Transmission details are for BBC 1. Duration: 95 minutes.
Executive producer Richard Drewett; produced by Elaine Bedell.
Clive James (Presenter), Alexandra Kazan.

	Holding / Source
31.12.1991	DB-D3 / D3S

CLIVE JAMES ON 1992

A BBC production for BBC 1. Transmission details are for BBC 1. Duration: 105 minutes.
Executive producer Richard Drewett; produced by Elaine Bedell.
Clive James (Presenter).

	Holding / Source
31.12.1992	DB-D3 / D3S

CLIVE JAMES ON 1993

A BBC production for BBC 1. Transmission details are for BBC 1. Duration: 89 minutes.
Executive producer Richard Drewett; produced by Carolyn Longton.
Clive James (Presenter), Louise Lombard, Diana Ross.

	Holding / Source
31.12.1993	DB-D3 / D3S

CLIVE JAMES ON 1994

A BBC production for BBC 1. Transmission details are for BBC 1. Duration: 95 minutes.
Executive producer Richard Drewett; produced by Carolyn Longton.
Clive James (Presenter), Caroline Langrishe, Vera Lynn.

	Holding / Source
31.12.1994	DB-D3 / D3S

CLIVE JAMES ON TELEVISION

An LWT production. Transmission details are for the Central region. Duration varies - see below for details.
Main regular performer(s): Clive James (Presenter).
Main regular credit(s): Executive producer Richard Drewett.

	VT Number	Holding / Source
28.12.1986	91497	D2 / 1"

Duration: 51 minutes.
Produced by Nicholas Barrett; directed by Nick Vaughan-Barratt.

CLIVE JAMES ON THE 80'S

A BBC production for BBC 1. Transmission details are for BBC 1. Duration: 120 minutes.

Script consultant Colin Bostock-Smith; edited by Richard Drewett; produced by Elaine Bedell; directed by Dominic Brigstocke.

Clive James (Presenter), Jerry Hall.

	Holding / Source
31.12.1989	DB / 1"

CLOSE (THAMES CLOSEDOWN SEQUENCES)

A Thames Television production. Transmission details are for the Thames Television region.

		Holding / Source
##.##.####	1979 Christmas Close 1 X 5 Mins	J / 2"
##.##.####	1981 Christmas Week Close 6 X 5 Mins	J / 2"

CLOSE ENCOUNTERS OF THE HERD KIND

An Absolute Digital production for BBC 1. made in association with Comic Relief. Transmission details are for BBC 1. Duration: 30 minutes.

Written by Mark Huckerby and Nick Ostler; theme music by Sophie Ellis Bextor; music by Rick Wentworth, Andrew McKenna, Carlton Studios, Robert McGinlay, Guy Fletcher, Mark Knopfler and Jody Talbot; executive producers Kevin Cahill, Cheryl Taylor, Helen Nabarro, Pete Thornton and Andy Russell; production manager Jill Wallace; produced and directed by Donnie Anderson.

Ardal O'Hanlon (Voice of Robbie The Reindeer), Jane Horrocks (Voice of Donner), Gillian Anderson (Voice of Vorkana), Keira Knightley (Voice of Em), Ozzy Osbourne (Voice of Vicar), Michael Palin (Voice of Gariiiiiii), Paul Whitehouse (Voice of Prancer), Sean Hughes (Voice of Tapir), Harry Enfield (Voice of Old Jingle), Graham Norton (Voice of Computer), Russell Brand (Voice of Earth Guardian), Shane Richie (Voice of Trooper 1), Ross Kemp (Voice of Trooper 2).

	Holding / Source
25.12.2007	DB / DBSW

Animated film.
See also: LEGEND OF THE LOST TRIBE (BBC)

CLOSEDOWN

A BBC production for BBC 2. Transmission details are for BBC 2. Duration: 5 minutes.

Main regular cast: Gabriel Woolf (Reader).

		Holding / Source
22.12.1974	The Journey Of The Magi	J / 2"

Written by T. S. Eliot.

23.12.1974	The Christmas Tree	J / 2"

Written by C. Day Lewis.

CLUEDO

A Granada production. Transmission details are for the Central region. Duration varies - see below for details.

		Production No	Holding / Source
26.12.1990	Christmas Past, Christmas Present	1/1718/7	1" / 1"S

Duration: 38 minutes.

Produced and directed by Mary McMurray.

With Trudie Goodwin (Detective), Leslie Grantham (Detective), Tony Scannell (Detective), Fiona Spence (Detective), Ian Lavender, Derek Nimmo, Kate O'Mara, David Robb, Joan Sims, Toyah Willcox.

Produced in association with Waddington's Games and Action Time.

A CLYDESIDE CAROL

A Scorpio Films production for BBC 1 Scotland. Transmission details are for BBC 1 Scotland. Duration: 22 minutes.

Based on a story by Charles Dickens; produced by Tom Busby; directed by Kees Ryninks.

Chic Murray (Smellie Broon), Jeff Rawle (Plywood), Alan Tull (Clydeside Spirit), Scott Johnson (Christmas Past), John Kerr (Christmas Present), Ian McNicol (Christmas Future), Stella Forge (Party Guest), Ranald MacColl (Man On Bench).

	Production No	VT Number	Holding / Source
24.12.1989	1/PSX/X/121P/01	HS7354	DB / 1"

COCKLESHELL BAY

A Thames Television production. Transmission details are for the ATV/Central region. Duration: 8 minutes.

SERIES 3

Transmission details are for the ATV midlands region.

Main regular credit(s): Written by Brian Trueman; music by David Rohl and Stuart J. Wolstenholme; produced by Mark Hall and Brian Cosgrove; directed by Jackie Cockle.

		Holding / Source
21.12.1981	A Cockleshell Christmas	1" / C1

COLD FEET

A Granada production. Transmission details are for the Central region. Usual duration: 50 minutes.

Main regular cast: James Nesbitt (Adam Williams), Helen Baxendale (Rachel Bradley), John Thomson (Pete Gifford), Fay Ripley (Jenny Gifford), Robert Bathurst (David Marsden), Hermione Norris (Karen Marsden), Jacey Salles (Ramona Ramirez).

SERIES 3

Main regular credit(s): Script editor Camilla Campbell; music by Mark Russell; executive producers Mike Bullen, Andy Harries and Christine Langan; co-produced by David Meddick; produced by Spencer Campbell.

Holding / Source

26.12.2000 **"The Best Man's Speech"** — DB / V1SSW

Written by Mike Bullen; script supervisor Eileen Wood; directed by Tim Whitby.

With Pooky Quesnel (Emma), Ben Miles (Robert), Paul Ridley, Sue Holderness, Norman Mills, Mike Bullen.

Bullen and Harries are listed as "Co-executive producer".

COLONEL MARCH OF SCOTLAND YARD

A Fountain Films production. made in association with Panda Productions. Transmission details are for the ATV London region. Duration: 25 minutes.

Colonel March, Head of the Department of Queer Complaints, in a new series of mystery stories.

Main regular credit(s): Based on stories by John Dickson Carr [credited as Carter Dickson].

Main regular cast: Boris Karloff (Colonel March).

Holding / Source

24.12.1955 **The Deadly Gift** — B1 / B3

Alternative transmissions: ATV Midlands: 14.08.1956.

A girl is left a legacy of a musical box which plays "The Twelve Days of Christmas". Colonel March sets out to solve a riddle.

Written by Paul Monash; music by Philip Green; edited by Geoffrey Foot; director of photography Lionel Banes; assistant director George Mills; art director Cedric Dawe; production supervised by Leslie Gilliat; directed by Bernard Knowles.

With Ewan Roberts (Inspector Ames), Sandra Dorne, George Coulouris, Tommy Duggan, John Gabriel, Maxwell Foster*.

COME DANCING WITH JOOLS HOLLAND

A Tyne Tees Television production for Channel 4. Transmission details are for Channel 4. Duration: 105 minutes.

Assistant producer Alastair Pirrie; executive producer Royston Mayoh; produced by Peter McHugh; directed by Royston Mayoh.

Jools Holland (Host), Rik Mayall, Adrian Edmondson, Philip Pope, Rory McGrath, Ruby Wax, Nigel Planer, Raw Sex, Buddy Curtis & The Grasshoppers, Who Dares Wins, Inspirational Gospel Choir, Julia Hills, Jimmy Mulville, Tony Robinson.

Holding / Source

31.12.1986 — 1" / 1"

See also: WHO DARES, WINS...

COME OUT ALAN BROWNING WE KNOW YOU'RE IN THERE

A Tyne Tees Television production. Transmission details are for the Tyne Tees region. Duration: 25 minutes.

Alan Browning, the Coronation Street star who died recently, was from Sunderland. In this documentary, he returned to the area to search for his roots.

Written by Andrea Masefield; executive producer Les Barrett; directed by Jeremy Lack.

Alan Browning (Presenter).

Holding / Source

28.12.1979 — DB / 2"

COME RAIN COME SHINE

An ITV Studios production for ITV 1. Transmission details are for the Central region. Duration: 100 minutes.

Written by Jeff Pope; script supervisor Angie Pontefract; music by Edmund Butt; director of photography Tony Coldwell; art director Dave Bowes; designed by Gillian Slight; associate producer Menzies Kennedy; executive producers David Reynolds, David Jason and Jeff Pope; head of production Gail Kennett; produced by David Reynolds; directed by David Drury.

David Jason (Don Mitchell), Alison Steadman (Dora Mitchell), Shaun Evans (David Mitchell), Anna Wilson-Jones (Christina Mitchell), Kellie Bright (Joanne Mitchell), Drew Blackall (Cameron Mitchell), Sally Oliver (Kerry), Kate Miles (Angela), Freddie Annobil-Dodoo (Dwayne), Christine Ellerbeck (Bet Perrett), Brian Croucher (Alfie Perrett), Simon Dutton (Andy), Celia Henebury (Diane), Jon Foster (Gary Perrett), Mark Longhurst (Dean), Miles Richardson (Consultant), Antonio Walker (Tauren), Jada Wallace-Mitchell (Jade), Adam Alfrey (Car Salesman), David Sigston (Garage Sales Assistant), Mark Morrell (Store Manager), Geoff Holman (Resident), Brian Phillips (Bootsie).

Holding / Source

20.12.2010 — HD/DB / HD/DB

COME SUNDAY

A Southern Television production. Transmission details are for the Southern Television region. Duration: 25 minutes.

Holding / Source

19.12.1976 — 2" / 2"

"Come Sunday", a Sunday evening network show of religious and semi-religious themes from churches around the region, frequently introduced by Andrew Cruickshank. The master copies of these went to EuroArts.

COMEDIANS DO IT ON STAGE

A Celador production for Channel 4. Transmission details are for Channel 4. Duration: 75 minutes.

Designed by Pip Gardner; produced by Paul Smith; directed by David MacMahon.

Dawn French, Jennifer Saunders, Gareth Hale, Norman Pace, Neil Innes, Terry Jones, Rory McGrath, Jimmy Mulville, Michael Palin, Mel Smith, Griff Rhys Jones, Richard Stilgoe, Victoria Wood, Rob Buckman, Chris Langham, The Trinity College Swing Band, Labi Siffre.

		Holding / Source
23.12.1986		1" / 1"

THE COMEDIANS

A Granada production. Transmission details are for the ATV midlands region. Usual duration: 25 minutes.

SERIES 2

Main regular credit(s):   Produced by John Hamp.
Main regular cast: With Shep's Banjo Boys.

	Holding / Source
24.12.1971 **The Comedians' Christmas Party**	D2 / 2"

Duration: 40 minutes.

Music directed by Derek Hilton; designed by Peter Caldwell; directed by Baz Taylor.

With George Roper, Ken Goodwin, Bernard Manning, Charlie Williams, Bryn Phillips, Tom O'Connor, Jos White, Frank Carson, Duggie Brown, Dave Butler.

	Holding / Source
31.12.1971 **Happy Auld Year**	DB / 2"

Duration: 31 minutes.

A studio audience watches a variety of stand up, impressions and sketches by some of the best known and most popular comics of the time, before welcoming in the New Year of 1972.

Directed by Walter Butler.

With Ken Goodwin, George Roper, Bernard Manning, Frank Carson, Charlie Williams, Shep's Banjo Boys.

SERIES 4

Main regular credit(s):   Produced by John Hamp; directed by Wally Butler.

	Production No	Holding / Source
25.12.1972	P731/2	D2 / 2"

With Bernard Manning, Charlie Williams, Frank Carson, Ken Goodwin, Duggie Brown, Jim Bowen, Shep's Banjo Boys.

SERIES 5

Granada Transmissions

	Production No	Holding / Source
29.12.1972	P712/35	D2 / 2"

With Dave Butler, Ken Goodwin, Jerry Harris, George Roper, Colin Crompton, Pat Mooney, Eddie Flanagan, Frank Carson, Duggie Brown, Shep's Banjo Boys.

ATV Transmissions

	Holding / Source
22.12.1973 **Christmas Comedians Music Hall**	D2 / 2"

Duration: 50 minutes.

Comedians Music Hall - Comedians involved in different sketches, dancers, Sheps Chairman Frank Carson. Frank Carson, George Roper, Colin Crompton, Duggie Brown, Bernard Manning, Mike Burton, Pat Mooney, Jimmy Marshall, Jim Bowen, Sammy Thomas, Jerry Harris, Bel Canto Singers, Pamela Devis Dancers, Sheps Banjo Boys, Derek Hilton Band

Music directed by Derek Hilton; designed by Mike Grimes; produced by John Hamp; directed by David Warwick.

With Frank Carson (Chairman), Mike Burton, Jerry Harris, George Roper, Duggie Brown, Jimmy Marshall, Jim Bowen, Colin Crompton, Russ Abbot, Sammy Thomas, Bernard Manning, Pat Mooney, Shep's Banjo Boys, The Pamela Devis Dancers, Bel Canto Singers, The Derek Hilton Band.

SERIES 11

Transmission details are for the Central region.

	Production No	Holding / Source
28.12.1993 **The Comedians Christmas Cracker**	1/1925/7	D2 / 1"

Duration: 51 minutes.

Produced by Jane Macnaught; directed by Jonathan Glazier.

With Frank Carson, Mick Miller, Stan Boardman, Ken Goodwin, Roy Walker, Jim Bowen, Duggie Brown, Johnnie Casson, Eddie Colinton, Les Dennis, Charlie Williams, Bernard Manning, George Roper.

THE COMEDY ANNUAL 2010

An ITV Studios production for ITV 1. made in association with Cineflix. Transmission details are for the Central region. Duration: 48 minutes.

Archive producer Geoff Walton; written by Kevin Day, Lee Stuart Evans, Judith Holder, Paul Powell and Colin Swash; programme associate Paul McGettigan; script supervisor Liz Hodges; art directors Tim Putnam and Candice White; designed by Peter Bingemann; assistant producer Andy Rowan; production executive Wendy Hutchinson; executive producers Guy Freeman, Lee Connolly and Saurabh Kakkar; production manager Emma Lyons; produced by Sue Andrew; directed by John L. Spencer.

Phillip Schofield (Host), Dave Lamb (Voice Over), John Bishop, Jenny Eclair, Keith Lemon, Jason Manford, Mark Watson.

	Holding / Source
22.12.2010	DB / DBSW

THE COMEDY ANNUAL 2011

An ITV Studios production for ITV 1. Transmission details are for the Central region. Duration: 48 minutes.

Produced by Paul McGettigan; directed by Richard Valentine.

Phillip Schofield (Host), Jason Manford, Alistair McGowan, Jason Byrne, Patrick Monahan, Alfie Boe.

	Holding / Source
20.12.2011	HD/DB / HDC

COMEDY BANDBOX

An ABC production. Transmission details are for the ABC midlands region.

SERIES 1

	Holding / Source
22.12.1962	J /

With Ted Ray, Charlie Cairoli, Paul King, Sandy Powell, Don Arroll, Saveen & Daisy May, Dottie Wayne, Johnny Lackwood.

COMEDY CHRISTMAS BOX

A Thames Television production. Transmission details are for the Central region. Duration: 75 minutes.

Join "Jim at home" on Christmas Day, when he presents a special compilation of clips from his favourite shows and performers.

Written by Neil Shand; research Lyn McConnell; associate producer Colin Fay; produced and directed by David Clark.

Jim Davidson (Presenter).

	Holding / Source
25.12.1989	1" / 1"

THE COMEDY CHRISTMAS

An Objective North production for BBC Manchester. Transmission details are for BBC 2. Duration: 70 minutes.

Written by Toby Hadoke, Stephen McGinn and Cybèle Rowbottom; assistant producer Sue Longmire; production executive Jan Morton; executive producers Katie Taylor, Stephen McGinn and Andrew O'Connor; head of production Debi Roach; produced and directed by Cybèle Rowbottom.

Melissa Sinden (Narrator), Paul Brown (Narrator), Russ Abbot, Ricky Tomlinson, Penelope Keith, David Jason, Ricky Gervais, John Sullivan, John Thomson, John Challis, James King, David Schneider, Mark Dolan, Peter Bowles, Debbie Chazen, Jon Plowman, Paul Mayhew-Archer, Charlie Catchpole, Stanley Baxter, David Renwick, Doreen Mantle, Joel Beckett, Stephen Merchant, Ashley Jensen.

	Holding / Source
24.12.2007	DB / DBSW

This documentary was linked with old Christmas BBC idents, some provided by Kaleidoscope.

THE COMEDY STORE

An Open Mike production for Channel 5. made in association with Paramount Comedy Channel. Transmission details are for Channel 5.

SERIES 3

Main regular credit(s):   Produced by John Tiffney.

	Holding / Source
24.12.1999 **Peter Kay Special**	DB / DBS

Directed by Tom Poole.

With Peter Kay.

THE COMIC STRIP PRESENTS

Produced for Channel 4 by a variety of companies (see details below). Transmission details are for Channel 4. Duration varies - see below for details.

A Comic Strip/Great Western Features production for Channel 4. Transmission details are for Channel 4.

	Holding / Source
28.12.2005 **sexactually**	DB / V1SW

Duration: 46 minutes.

Written by Peter Richardson and Peter Richens; music by Rod Melvin and Andre Jacquemin; director of photography Mike Robinson; assistant director James Blackwell; art director Mo Holden; production designer Kit Line; executive producers Cleo Rocos and Nick Smith; production manager Rebecca Carrigan; produced by Ben Swaffer; directed by Peter Richardson.

With Robert Bathurst (Charles), Phil Cornwell (Roy), Rebecca Front (Carol), Tamer Hassan (Luccio), Doon Mackichan (Diana), Rik Mayall (Bilbo), Nigel Planer (Graham), Glenna Scacchi Morrison (Jane), Sheridan Smith (Angie), Steven O'Donnell (Brian), Allan Hern (Ron), Elizabeth Beale-Stephens (Helen), Kate Langdon (Maid), Bryan Jacobs (Scientist), Dragos Florescu (Seb), Aleksandar Mikic (Mick), Sandra Beck (Carol Singer), Jeff Beck (Carol Singer), Chickpea (Carol Singer), Joy Maxwell-Davies (Carol Singer), David Styles (Carol Singer), Marion Styles (Carol Singer), Kit Line (Carol Singer), Charles Styles (Carol Singer), Sarah Styles (Carol Singer).

COMPACT

A BBC production. Transmission details are for BBC. Usual duration: 30 minutes.

In 1962 the BBC decided to challenge ITV's monopoly on soap operas and then commissioned Compact. Scheduled for Tuesday and Thursday nights to avoid Coronation Street it was the brainchild of Hazel Adair and Peter Ling who eventually finished the soap in 1965 and went on to create Crossroads for ATV.

Set in the editorial office of a women's magazine, the drama surrounded the lives of the photographers, editors, designers, writers and art directors. For many years people have wondered who the cover girl on the first issue was; records reveal it was Sylvia Steele who was photographed for the cover of 'Compact' on 1st December 1961.

James Cellan Jones was one of the staff directors who made episodes on a rota basis: "Eventually I had a message from Donald Wilson, Head of Serials: 'I want you to start on Compact next month,' he said. Compact was the worst sort of twice weekly romantically rubbishy serial about a woman's magazine. The writers were reputed to get £250 per half hour script which very often they would farm out to be ghosted by a hack for £100. I hated the idea.
I rang Donald and I said, 'It's not that I am too good for it. I think everybody is too good for it and it's meretricious rubbish.'
There was a pause. He said, 'You will either do this, or you will do nothing and I will personally see that you direct nothing for the rest of your life.'
'Well,' I said, 'If you put it that way…'

Compact was broadcast live on Tuesdays and recorded as live on Wednesdays for transmission on Thursdays. There was no time or money for editing, so unless one of the cast said 'f**k' (and it did happen) the show went out as recorded. I was due to start rehearsing my first two episodes on Boxing Day. I went to the rehearsal room in Putney. As was the custom then, I had worked out every move, every camera position and every lens. When I walked in they said, 'Change of plan, Bill Kerr's been run over and we have to re-write everything.'

I threw the camera script away and started from scratch. It was the best thing that could have happened. Robert Flemyng played the Editor. He was a superbly composed actor who took his position as leading man very seriously. He supported me gently without making it obvious. The rest of the cast were very supportive; when I decided to stage a scene in a gents' lavatory, (very daring in those days) Bobby Desmond said, 'You want to be known as the Alain Resnais of Putney Bridge South.'

Somehow we got through the rehearsals and after three and a half days we moved into the studio. It was all going to be all right. Somehow, I had got a couple of shows together and I knew they would work. Then disaster struck. Gretchen Franklin button-holed me. 'What time do we go out tonight dear?' She said.
'7.30 on the dot.'
'You do know I am in the theatre in Gentle Jack, and we go up at 7.30?'

I was dumb struck. Booking a tape machine to play in a scene was a very long wearisome business. Because of the seriousness of the occasion, we got the machine in the next half hour and pre-recorded Gretchen's scene, let her go and continued with the rehearsal. When 7.15 came around we were sitting in the gallery and the network was on the monitor. I wished they would turn it off, I wanted to concentrate. Suddenly I remembered that at 7.29 someone would say 'One minute' and at 7.29 and 45 seconds someone would say 'Stand by' and at 7.29 and 52 seconds I would say 'Run Telecine' and at 7.30 precisely we would be on the air.

It all happened, we seemed to be going well; and then I remembered Gretchen's scene. I croaked 'Stand by VT.' It needed 10 seconds to run up and giving a wild guess I cued it, 'Run VT.' It turned out more or less right and we played the scene and we finished the show. When Sydney Newman saw the episode, he said, 'This is brilliant,' which pleased me, though I thought it a bit over the top for a soap opera.

The next night went smoothly, I seemed to get on with the cast and I started a run of 18 episodes over several months. On the night BBC2 started, we had rehearsed and were ready to go. Suddenly all the lights went out, there had been a power failure. I was called up to Planning and agreed to record the first episode in the morning and spend the rest of the day rehearsing the second and record it at night. Nothing on Compact was ever quite the same again."

Extract from 'Forsyte and Hindsight – The Memoirs of James Cellan Jones" courtesy of Kaleidoscope Publishing

Main regular credit(s): Created by Peter Ling and Hazel Adair; theme music by Trevor Duncan.

Holding / Source

20.12.1962 Christmas Spirit   J / 40
Written by Hazel Adair and Peter Ling; designed by Jane Martin; produced by Douglas Allen; directed by Hugh Munro.
With Ronald Allen (Ian Harmon), Christine Pollon (Janet Ellis), Robert Desmond (Adrian Coombe), Frances Bennett (Gussie Brown), Louise Dunn (Iris), Betty Ellis (Chloe), Donald Morley (Mr Babbage), Pamela Pitchford (Mrs Aston), Monica Evans (Sally Harmon), Gareth Davies (Mark Viccars), Janet Hargreaves (Clare Farrell), Johnny Wade (Stan Millet), Mandy Miller (Carol 'Copper' Beach), Keith Buckley (Bryan Marchant), Betty Cooper (Alison Morley), Scot Finch (Tim Gray), Moray Watson (Richard Lowe), Ann Morrish (Clancey), Blake Butler (Mr Kipling), Marcia Ashton (Lily).

24.12.1963 Dress Rehearsal   J / 40
Written by Hazel Adair and Peter Ling; produced by Morris Barry; directed by Gerald Blake.
With Basil Moss (Alan Drew), Gareth Davies (Mark Viccars), Frances Bennett (Gussie), Robin Hawdon (Barry Southern), Robert Flemyng (Edmund Bruce), Vincent Ball (David Rome), Diana Beevers (Michele 'Mitch' Donnelly), Betty Cooper (Alison Morley), Robert Desmond (Adrian Coombe), Louise Dunn (Iris), Lawrence James (Doug), Carmen Silvera (Camilla Hope), Johnny Wade (Stan), Pauline Munro (Jenny Simms), Christine Pollon (Janet Ellis), Bill Kerr (Ben Bishop), Shane Rimmer (Russell Corrigan), Patricia Haines (Vivien Ames), David Langton (Marmot James), Scot Finch (Tim Gray).

26.12.1963 On Stage   J / 40
Written by Hazel Adair and Peter Ling; produced by Morris Barry; directed by Gerald Blake.
With Basil Moss (Alan Drew), Gareth Davies (Mark Viccars), Frances Bennett (Gussie), Robert Flemyng (Edmund Bruce), Vincent Ball (David Rome), Diana Beevers (Michele 'Mitch' Donnelly), Robert Desmond (Adrian Coombe), Louise Dunn (Iris), Lawrence James (Doug), Carmen Silvera (Camilla Hope), Ronald Allen (Ian Harmon), Johnny Wade (Stan), Pauline Munro (Jenny Simms), Bill Kerr (Ben Bishop).

31.12.1963 Happy New Year   J / Live
Written by Bob Stuart; produced by Morris Barry; directed by James Cellan Jones.
With Robert Flemyng (Edmund Bruce), Beryl Cooke (Mrs Chater), Ronald Allen (Ian Harmon), David Langton (Marmot James), Basil Moss (Alan Drew), Louise Dunn (Iris), Pauline Munro (Jenny Simms), Carmen Silvera (Camilla Hope), Bill Kerr (Ben Bishop), Frances Bennett (Gussie), Patricia Haines (Vivien Ames), Betty Cooper (Alison Morley), Scot Finch (Tim Gray), Diana Beevers (Michele 'Mitch' Donnelly), Vincent Ball (David Rome), Shane Rimmer (Russell Corrigan), Douglas Blackwell (Gym Instructor), Gretchen Franklin (Ella Bedford).

25.12.1964 A Surprise For Christmas   J / 40
Written by Rosemary Anne Sisson; produced by Morris Barry; directed by Michael Ferguson.

29.12.1964 A Partridge In A Pear Tree   J / Live
Written by Hazel Adair and Peter Ling; produced by Morris Barry; directed by Gerald Blake.

THE COMPLETE DRAMATIC WORKS OF WILLIAM SHAKESPEARE

Alternative/Working Title(s): THE SHAKESPEARE PLAYS
A BBC production for BBC 2. made in association with Time-Life Television. Transmission details are for BBC 2. Duration varies - see below for details.
Written by William Shakespeare.

	Holding / Source
06.01.1980 **Twelfth Night**	DB-D3 / 2"

Alt.Title(s): *What You Will*
Duration: 128 minutes.
Produced by Cedric Messina; directed by John Gorrie.
With Alec McCowen (Malvolio), Robert Hardy (Sir Toby Belch), Felicity Kendal (Viola), Annette Crosbie (Maria), Sinéad Cusack (Olivia), Trevor Peacock (Feste), Clive Arrindell (Orsino), Ronnie Stevens (Sir Andrew Aguecheek), Robert Lindsay (Fabian), Maurice Roëves (Antonio), Daniel Webb (Servant), Roderick Skeaping (Musician), Mark Caudle (Musician), Ian Gammie (Musician), Keith Thompson (Musician), Robert Spencer (Musician), Ryan Michael (Curio), Malcolm Reynolds (Valentine), Ric Morgan (Sea Captain), Jean Channon (Waiting Woman), Michael Thomas (Sebastian), Andrew Maclachlan (First Officer), Peter Holt (Second Officer), Arthur Hewlett (Priest).

A CONCERT FOR CHRISTMAS

A Thames Television production. Transmission details are for the Thames Television region. Duration: 40 minutes.
Carols - some old, some new, mostly traditional, sung by the Massed Hospital Choirs. This concert comes from The Royal Festival Hall, London, and is in aid of the Malcolm Sargent Cancer Fund for Children.
Orchestra conducted by Charles Farncombe; produced and directed by Steve Minchin.
John Birch (Organist), Jack Brymer (Solo Clarinet), Silver Trumpeters of the Royal Marines.

	VT Number	Holding / Source
24.12.1971	5379	DB / 2"

CONTACT

A BBC Birmingham production for BBC 1 Midlands. Transmission details are for BBC 1 Midlands. Duration: 30 minutes.

	Holding / Source
22.12.1970 **... But Once A Year**	J / 2"

A collection of music, pictures, poetry and prose for the Christmas season.
Introduced by Anthony Everitt; illustrated by Paul Winter; produced by Edmund Marshall; directed by John Clarke.
With John Baddeley, John Rowe, Joanna Tope, Ken Rattenbury and his Band, Boys of Worcester Cathedral Choir.

19.12.1972 **A Worcester Carol**	J / 2"

With Choir of Worcester Cathedral.

18.12.1973 **Not To Be Opened Till Christmas!**	J / 2"

Associate producer John Kingdon; produced by John Clarke; directed by Roger Casstles.
With The Midland Radio Orchestra, Keeley Ford, Nottingham Festival, Tom Coyne.

17.12.1974 **Here We Come A-Wassailing**
Music associate Paul Vaughan; produced by Edmund Marshall and John Clarke; directed by Roger Casstles.
With Band of The Coventry School of Music, The Willenhall Girl Pipers, Handbell Ringers of King Edward's School Birmingham, The Choir of Market Harborough Upper School, The Choir of Wolverhampton High School, The Choir of St Mary's Church, Warwick, The Choir of Wrekin College, The Choir of Quinton Junior School.

CONTINUITY

Commissioned and produced by a variety of companies (see details below).
A BBC production for BBC 1. Transmission details are for BBC 1.

	Holding / Source
20.12.1960 **Christmas Children's Trailer**	DB-R1 / Live

With Tony Hart (Presenter).

15.12.1976 **Christmas Radio Times Trailer**	DB / 2"

SPORTS REVIEW OF THE YEAR (NMR1134T) – front: sign off and end titles of 9 O'Clock News; stills trailer for "Tonight"; weather chart with v/o forecast; Christmas Radio Times trailer; globe with announcement.

30.12.1982 **New Year's Honours List**	DB-DV / Live
12.12.2008 **Christmas Trailer**	DB / DBSW

Kaleidoscope hold the VHS masters of news material. BBC Archives retain the digibetas.

A BBC production for BBC 2. Transmission details are for BBC 2.

	Holding / Source
25.12.1980 **Test Card F With Seasonal Music And Graphics**	DV / Live

Held by Kaleidoscope.
Kaleidoscope hold the VHS masters. BBC Archives retain the digibetas.

A Thames Television production. Transmission details are for the Thames Television region.

	Holding / Source
25.12.1981 **Harry and Walter/39 Steps /Dudley Moore/ Game for a Laugh Trailers**	DV / Live
16.12.1984 **The Great Muppet Caper Trailer**	DV / Live
##.##.#### **TVAM Trailer**	DV / Live

| CONTINUITY (continued) | British Christmas Television Guide |

An ATV production. Transmission details are for the ATV midlands region.

	Holding / Source
31.12.1981 **Closedown Of ATV**	DV / Live

With Mike Prince (Continuity Announcer), Shaw Taylor.

COPING WITH...

A Carlton UK production for Channel 4. Transmission details are for Channel 4. Duration: 25 minutes.

Main regular credit(s): Written by Peter Corey; executive producer Lewis Rudd; produced by Sue Nott.
Main regular cast: Greg Chisholm (Danny), Sara Cragg (Sprog), Shauna Shim (Mel).

	Holding / Source
25.12.1995 **Coping With Christmas**	D2 / D2S

Directed by Dan Zeff.
With Andrew Robinson, Rosalie Sears, Kerry Stacey.

CORNERS

A BBC Children's Department production for BBC 1. Transmission details are for BBC 1.

SERIES 2
Duration: 10 minutes.
Main regular credit(s): Assistant producer Roger Dacier; produced and directed by Anne Gobey.
Main regular cast: With Sophie Aldred (Host), Simon Davies (Host).

	Holding / Source
18.12.1987 **How Are Crackers Made?**	DB / 1"

SERIES 3
Main regular cast: With Sophie Aldred (Host), Stephen Johnson (Host).

	Holding / Source
23.12.1988	DB / 1"

SERIES 4
Main regular cast: With Diane-Louise Jordan (Host).

	Holding / Source
22.12.1989 **How Do They Make Snow On TV?**	DB / 1"

SERIES 5
Duration: 10 minutes.
Main regular credit(s): Series producer Jane Tarleton; produced by Alison Stewart.
Main regular cast: With Sophie Aldred (Host).

	Holding / Source
21.12.1990 **Why Do We Put Money In Christmas Puddings?**	DB / 1"

THE CORNET LESSON

A BBC production for BBC 2. Transmission details are for BBC 2. Duration: 30 minutes.
Written by Roy Kendall; script editor Robert Buckler; designed by Valerie Warrender; produced by Anne Head; directed by John Bruce.
Gerald James (Bandmaster), Sandy Ratcliff (Girl).

	Holding / Source
24.12.1973	DB-D3 / 2"

Made for 'Centre Play'.

THE CORNET PLAYER

An Associated-Rediffusion production. Transmission details are for Associated-Rediffusion. Duration: 25 minutes.
Written by S. L. Hastings; designed by Bernard Goodwin; produced and directed by Rollo Gamble.
Edward Jewesbury (Mr Knight), Barbara Ogilvie (Mrs Knight), Michael Caridia (Graham), Sylvia Davies (Susie), Anthony Valentine (The Cornet Player).

	Holding / Source
22.12.1959	J /

CORONATION STREET

Alternative/Working Title(s): FLORIZEL STREET
A Granada/Granada Manchester Television production for Granada. Duration varies - see below for details.
Main regular credit(s):   Created by Tony Warren; theme music by Eric Spear.

A Granada production. Transmission details are for the ATV midlands region. Duration: 25 minutes.

	Production No	Holding / Source
25.12.1961 "The men go to a sports outing and the wives prepare the dinner"	P228/108	R1 / 40

Christmas Day in Coronation Street— the men go off on a special sports outing while their wives have a long morning getting the dinner ready. Harry gives Concepta another present. Minnie entertains Ena and Martha, Kenneth and Frank Barlow have their first Christmas without Ida. Elsie cooks up a last-minute treat for Dennis. Annie and Jack ask some friends in for the Queen's broadcast— and greetings flow in from far and near.
Written by Tony Warren; story by Vince Powell and Harry Driver; designed by Denis Parkin; produced by Derek Granger; directed by John Moxey.
With Doris Speed (Annie Walker), Ivan Beavis (Harry Hewitt), Doreen Keogh (Concepta Hewitt), Betty Alberge (Florrie Lindley), Peter Adamson (Len Fairclough), William Roache (Ken Barlow), Frank Pemberton (Frank Barlow), Jack Howarth (Albert Tatlock), Violet Carson (Ena Sharples), Margot Bryant (Minnie Caldwell), Lynne Carol (Martha Longhurst), Patricia Phoenix (Elsie Tanner), Arthur Leslie (Jack Walker), Philip Lowrie (Dennis Tanner).

| 24.12.1962 "The Christmas play" | P228/212 | R1 / 40 |

'Lady Lawson Loses' is the Christmas play.
Written by Tony Warren; designed by Denis Parkin; produced by H. V. Kershaw; directed by Pauline Shaw.
With Doris Speed (Annie Walker), Arthur Lowe (Mr Swindley), Eileen Derbyshire (Miss Nugent), Jack Howarth (Albert Tatlock), Anne Reid (Valerie Barlow), William Roache (Kenneth Barlow), Christine Hargreaves (Christine Appleby), Pat Phoenix (Elsie Tanner), Anne Cunningham (Linda Cheveski), Ernst Walder (Ivan Cheveski), Violet Carson (Ena Sharples), Margot Bryant (Minnie Caldwell), Lynne Carol (Martha Longhurst), Kenneth Cope (Jed Stone), Graham Haberfield (Jerry Booth), Peter Adamson (Len Fairclough), Ivan Beavis (Harry Hewitt), Doreen Keogh (Concepta Hewitt), Betty Alberge (Florrie Lindley), Frank Pemberton (Frank Barlow).

| 25.12.1963 "Some old faces return to the Street" | P228/317 | R1 / 40 |

Written by H. V. Kershaw; designed by Peter Caldwell; produced by Margaret Morris; directed by Michael Beckham.
With Doris Speed (Annie Walker), Eileen Derbyshire (Miss Nugent), Jennifer Moss (Lucille Hewitt), Betty Alberge (Florrie Lindley), Anne Reid (Valerie Barlow), William Roache (Ken Barlow), Frank Pemberton (Frank Barlow), Jack Howarth (Albert Tatlock), Violet Carson (Ena Sharples), Margot Bryant (Minnie Caldwell), Philip Lowrie (Dennis Tanner), Christopher Sandford (Walter Potts), Patricia Phoenix (Elsie Tanner), Peter Adamson (Len Fairclough), Graham Haberfield (Jerry Booth), Arthur Leslie (Jack Walker), Lynne Carol (Martha Longhurst), Susan Jameson (Myra Booth), Doreen Keogh (Concepta Hewitt), Ivan Beavis (Harry Hewitt), Daphne Oxenford (Esther Hayes), Jon Rollason (David Robbins).

| 23.12.1964 "The show must go on.............but why ?" | P228/421 | R1 / 40 |

Cinderella hits a few snags.
Written by Tony Warren; story by Harry Driver and George Reed; designed by Peter Caldwell; produced by H. V. Kershaw; directed by Douglas Hurn.
With Doris Speed (Annie Walker), Arthur Leslie (Jack Walker), Jack Howarth (Albert Tatlock), Violet Carson (Ena Sharples), Margot Bryant (Minnie Caldwell), Jennifer Moss (Lucille Hewitt), Anne Reid (Valerie Barlow), William Roache (Kenneth Barlow), Patricia Phoenix (Elsie Tanner), Betty Alberge (Florrie Lindley), Peter Adamson (Len Fairclough), Philip Lowrie (Dennis Tanner), Arthur Lowe (Mr Swindley), Gordon Rollings (Charlie Moffit), Jean Alexander (Hilda Ogden), Bernard Youens (Stan Ogden), Sandra Gough (Irma Ogden), Alan Rothwell (David Barlow), Eileen Derbyshire (Miss Nugent), Eddie King (Alf Chadwick).

| 22.12.1965 | P228/525 | R1 / 40 |

The avenger is unmasked, and the newly-weds take a hard knock.
Written by Jack Rosenthal; story by George Reed and Susan Pleat; designed by Denis Parkin; executive producer H. V. Kershaw; produced by Howard Baker; directed by Walter Butler.
With Edward Evans (Lionel Petty), Jack Howarth (Albert Tatlock), Jean Alexander (Hilda Ogden), Bernard Youens (Stan Ogden), Peter Adamson (Len Fairclough), Doris Speed (Annie Walker), Margot Bryant (Minnie Caldwell), Violet Carson (Ena Sharples), William Roache (Kenneth Barlow), Alan Rothwell (David Barlow), Sandra Gough (Irma Barlow), Graham Haberfield (Jerry Booth), Mollie Sugden (Nellie Harvey), Aleksander Browne (Doctor).

| 05.12.1966 "Plans for Christmas and signs of an unhappy New Year" | P228/624 | R1 / 40 |

Written by John Finch; produced by H. V. Kershaw; directed by Bob Hird.
With Jennifer Moss (Lucille Hewitt), Patricia Phoenix (Elsie Tanner), Peter Adamson (Len Fairclough), Graham Haberfield (Jerry Booth), Eileen Mayers (Sheila Birtles), Sandra Gough (Irma Barlow), Bernard Youens (Stan Ogden), Violet Carson (Ena Sharples), Arthur Leslie (Jack Walker), Doris Speed (Annie Walker), Geoffrey Matthews (Neil Crossley), Anne Reid (Valerie Barlow), William Roache (Ken Barlow), Martha Bryant (Minnie Caldwell).

| 26.12.1966 "Fancy dress in the mission and the plain truth for Ena" | P228/630 | R1 / 40 |

Written by Jack Rosenthal; designed by Michael Grimes; produced by H. V. Kershaw; directed by Michael Apted.
With Jennifer Moss (Lucille Hewitt), Patricia Phoenix (Elsie Tanner), Peter Adamson (Len Fairclough), Graham Haberfield (Jerry Booth), Sandra Gough (Irma Barlow), Bernard Youens (Stan Ogden), Violet Carson (Ena Sharples), Arthur Leslie (Jack Walker), Doris Speed (Annie Walker), Anne Reid (Valerie Barlow), William Roache (Ken Barlow), Martha Bryant (Minnie Caldwell), Jean Alexander (Hilda Ogden), Jack Howarth (Albert Tatlock), Alan Rothwell (David Barlow), Philip Lowrie (Dennis Tanner), Ruth Holden (Vera Lomax), Joan Francis (Dorothy Greenhalgh).

| 25.12.1967 "The tug of war" | P228/733 | R1 / 40 |

Will this be Elsie's last Christmas in the UK?
Written by Geoffrey Lancashire; designed by Knowles Bentley; executive producer Richard Everitt; produced by Michael Cox; directed by Bill Podmore.
With Jennifer Moss (Lucille Hewitt), Graham Haberfield (Jerry Booth), Sandra Gough (Irma Barlow), Violet Carson (Ena Sharples), Arthur Leslie (Jack Walker), Doris Speed (Annie Walker), Anne Reid (Valerie Barlow), William Roache (Ken Barlow), Alan Rothwell (David Barlow), Philip Lowrie (Dennis Tanner), Peter Adamson (Len Fairclough), Margot Bryant (Minnie Caldwell), Jean Alexander (Hilda Ogden), Jack Howarth (Albert Tatlock), Patricia Phoenix (Elsie Tanner), Paul Maxwell (Steve Tanner), Bernard Youens (Stan Ogden), Eileen Derbyshire (Miss Nugent), Anne Cunningham (Linda Cheveski), Ernst Walder (Ivan Cheveski), Linda Cook (Jill Morris), Bud Ralston (Flying Horse Team Captain).

| 23.12.1968 "Aladdin" | P228/835 | R1 / 40 |

Written by Geoffrey Lancashire; story by Harry Driver, Esther Rose and Bruce Norman; designed by Roy Graham; executive producer H. V. Kershaw; produced by John Finch; directed by Tim Jones.
With Pat Phoenix (Elsie Tanner), Peter Adamson (Len Fairclough), Arthur Leslie (Jack Walker), Doris Speed (Annie Walker), Violet Carson (Ena Sharples), William Roache (Ken Barlow), Anne Reid (Valerie Barlow), Eileen Derbyshire (Miss Nugent), Jennifer Moss (Lucille Hewitt), Bill Kenwright (Gordon Clegg), Irene Sutcliffe (Maggie Clegg), Neville Buswell (Ray Langton), Gillian McCann (Audrey Fleming), Nigel Humphreys (Dickie Fleming), Jack Howarth (Albert Tatlock), Margot Bryant (Minnie Caldwell), Anne Dyson (Mrs Spicer), Jean Alexander (Hilda Ogden), Bernard Youens (Stan Ogden), Eric Dodson (Reverend Reginald James), Marjie Lawrence (Marji Griffin), Eddie King (Alf Chadwick).

CORONATION STREET (continued)   *British Christmas Television Guide*

25.12.1968   "A sing song is held in the Rovers and Ken is at home with Valerie"   P228/836   R1 / 40

Brought forward from 26.12.1968.

Written by Susan Pleat; story by Harry Driver, Esther Rose and Bruce Norman; executive producer H. V. Kershaw; produced by John Finch; directed by Tim Jones.

With Neville Buswell (Ray Langton), Arthur Leslie (Jack Walker), Bernard Youens (Stan Ogden), Peter Adamson (Len Fairclough), William Roache (Ken Barlow), Anne Reid (Valerie Barlow), Jack Howarth (Albert Tatlock), Nigel Humphreys (Dickie Fleming), Bill Kenwright (Gordon Clegg), Eric Dodson (Reverend James), Violet Carson (Ena Sharples), Doris Speed (Annie Walker), Marjie Lawrence (Marjorie Griffin), Anne Dyson (Effie Spicer), Jean Alexander (Hilda Ogden), Margot Bryant (Minnie Caldwell), Eileen Derbyshire (Miss Nugent), Jennifer Moss (Lucille Hewitt), Gillian McCann (Audrey Fleming), Patricia Phoenix (Elsie Tanner), Irene Sutcliffe (Maggie Clegg).

28.12.1968   **CHRISTMAS IN CORONATION STREET**   P620/1   DB-R1 / 40

Alt.Title(s):   *Christmas in the Street*

Duration: 44 minutes.

Pub licensees Jack and Annie Walker reminisce as they prepare for festivities in The Rovers Return, with flashbacks to bygone years including 1960, the first Christmas in Coronation Street, when Ena Sharples had to spend time in hospital.

Written by H. V. Kershaw, Geoffrey Lancashire, Jack Rosenthal and Tony Warren; produced by John Finch; directed by Tim Jones.

With Arthur Leslie (Jack Walker), Doris Speed (Annie Walker).

24.12.1969   "The talent contest"   P228/939   DB / 2"

The Rovers Return stage a talent show in the snug. Ernest is on piano with Len on drums. The acts are; Emily & Ernest reciting a song with a religious flavour, Minnie reciting The Owl & the Pussycat, Ken on trumpet, Irma as Hilda Baker, Ena & Emily singing Cockles and Mussels and Albert reciting a love poem (as the credits rolled).

     Hilda & Betty agree to stay Working to Rule as Annie sticks to her guns about the missing necklace being down to them. Then Mrs Heppelwhite appears in The Rovers with it on saying she collected it herself the other day. Jack tells Annie she has egg on her face and Annie makes amends by giving Hilda & Betty some Nylons which Jack asks them to accept 'for his sake'. Alan & Elsie are moving closer together. Albert's Santa Claus beard is stuck on fast but Stan manages to tear it off. Priceless.

Written by Leslie Duxbury; story by Harry Driver, Esther Rose and Anthea Ingham; designed by Tim Farmer; executive producer H. V. Kershaw; directed by Eric Prytherch.

With Arthur Leslie (Jack Walker), Doris Speed (Annie Walker), William Roache (Kenneth Barlow), Peter Adamson (Len Fairclough), Sandra Gough (Irma Ogden), Patricia Fuller (Sandra Butler), William Moore (Cyril Turpin), Alan Browning (Alan Howard), Neville Buswell (Ray Langton), Betty Driver (Betty Turpin), Eileen Derbyshire (Emily Nugent), Stephen Hancock (Ernest Bishop), Anne Reid (Valerie Barlow), Patricia Phoenix (Elsie Tanner), Gorden Kaye (Bernard Butler), Jack Howarth (Albert Tatlock), Violet Carson (Ena Sharples), Bernard Youens (Stan Ogden), Margot Bryant (Minnie Caldwell), Jean Alexander (Hilda Ogden), Betty England (Mrs Hepplewhite).

25.12.1969   **ALL STAR COMEDY CARNIVAL Insert**   J / 2"

Duration: 5 minutes.

Written by Ron McDonnell; produced by H. V. Kershaw; directed by Eric Prytherch and June Howson.

With Jean Alexander (Hilda Ogden), Arthur Leslie (Jack Walker), Bernard Youens (Stan Ogden), William Roache (Ken Barlow), Anne Reid (Valerie Barlow), Doris Speed (Annie Walker), Patricia Phoenix (Elsie Tanner), Alan Browning (Alan Howard), Gorden Kaye (Bernard Butler), Betty Driver (Betty Turpin), Peter Adamson (Len Fairclough), Margot Bryant (Minnie Caldwell), Violet Carson (Ena Sharples), Eileen Derbyshire (Miss Nugent), Sandra Gough (Irma Barlow), Graham Haberfield (Jerry Booth), William Moore (Police Constable Turpin).

23.12.1970   "Life must go on, it's Christmas"   P694/37   DB / 62

Duration: 26 minutes.

Everyone except Albert cancels the panto because of Joe's death and the tickets are given to underpriveleged children. They turn out to be completely wild and Albert has to look after them. Emily realises he won't be able to cope and goes with him. Elsie tells Alan she always thought Len had killed Steve. Greg and Gary decide to throw a farewell party in the Rovers. Det Chief Insp Castle interviews Irma, Stan, Minnie and Elsie. Albert handles the children but Emily disapears. Emily tells the residents Albert was a bigger handful than the children. Maggie is sad that Greg is leaving for Germany. Minnie doesn't like living with Albert.

Written by Leslie Duxbury; story by Harry Driver, Esther Rose and John Temple; designed by Eugene Ferguson; executive producer H. V. Kershaw; directed by Les Chatfield.

With Doris Speed (Annie Walker), Violet Carson (Ena Sharples), Pat Phoenix (Elsie Tanner), Peter Adamson (Len Fairclough), Bernard Youens (Stan Ogden), Jean Alexander (Hilda Ogden), Sandra Gough (Irma Barlow), Alan Browning (Alan Howard), Kenneth Farringdon (Billy Walker), Margot Bryant (Minnie Caldwell), Jack Howarth (Albert Tatlock), Eileen Derbyshire (Emily Nugent), Irene Sutcliffe (Maggie Clegg), Julie Goodyear (Bet Lynch), Bill Nagy (Greg Flint), Callen Angelo (Gary Strauss), Hugh Cross (Chief Inspector Castle).

25.12.1970   **ALL STAR COMEDY CARNIVAL Insert**   J / 2"

Duration: 5 minutes.

Written by Ron McDonnell; executive producer H. V. Kershaw; directed by Eric Prytherch.

With Bernard Youens (Stan Ogden), Anne Reid (Valerie Barlow), Jean Alexander (Hilda Ogden), Betty Driver (Betty Turpin), Patricia Phoenix (Elsie Tanner), Alan Browning (Alan Howard), Neville Buswell (Ray Langton), Jennifer Moss (Lucille Hewitt), Julie Goodyear (Bet Lynch), Kenneth Farrington (Billy Walker), Margot Bryant (Minnie Caldwell), Violet Carson (Ena Sharples), Eileen Derbyshire (Emily Nugent), Sandra Gough (Irma Barlow), Jack Howarth (Albert Tatlock), Irene Sutcliffe (Maggie Clegg).

22.12.1971   "All the Rovers staff want Boxing Night off"   P694/141   DB / 2"

Bet is asked by Annie to work till 1 am Boxing Day night but she intends to go to a party with Eddie. Betty is at the police ball that night so Annie tells Nellie & Kitty she cannot make the Ball until she finds out that a retired Naval Lieutenant ("he's a batchelor") will be guest of honour which sets Annie thinking. Stan is still mad with Hilda that they have a cocktail cabinet but no money for booze. Stan takes it on himself to sell it and immediately buys lots of take outs from The Rovers. Hilda is mad then glad when she sees the booze. Albert tells Ena & Minnie he is to spend Christmas with Ken then finds out Ken has left for Glasgow and his twins. Albert then tells them he is to be with Beattie but they take the hint and invite him for Christmas but he plays it cool. Elsie is telling nobody about her and Alan's row. He works all day at the garage, is called to The Rovers by Dave Smith for a 'proposition' then goes to see Elsie who slams the door in his face. He walks off as the Salvation Army play out the end credits.

Written by Barry Hill; designed by Eugene Ferguson; produced by Brian Armstrong; directed by Colin Cant.

With Violet Carson (Ena Sharples), Doris Speed (Annie Walker), Julie Goodyear (Bet Lynch), Jennifer Moss (Lucille Hewitt), Jack Howarth (Uncle Albert), Betty Driver (Betty Turpin), Bernard Youens (Stan Ogden), Jean Alexander (hilda Ogden), Irene Sutcliffe (Maggie Clegg), Margot Bryant (Minnie Caldwell), Patricia Phoenix (Elsie Howard), Reginald Marsh (Dave Smith), Del Henney (Eddie Duncan), Mollie Sugden (Nelly Harvey), Stella Moray (Kitty Stonely), George Malpas.

CORONATION STREET

| British Christmas Television Guide | CORONATION STREET (continued) |

26.12.1971 "Annie does go to the ball" P694/142 DB / 2"

Ena invites Betty & Bet over for a mince pie then tells them both to see to it that Annie goes to the Boxing Day Ball. Dave Smith offers to drive her as there are no taxis available. Annie emerges from The Rovers resplendent. At the ball, much to the disgust of Nellie & Kitty, the guest of honour immediately asks Annie to dance. Eddie Duncan's football team win the day's match and a pleased Dave Smith tells Bet she has been good for Eddie and there is some news for him from the club Directors. Ken goes off to see the Headmaster of Bessy St School for a Boxing Day interview and he gets the job. Ena is suspicious that Elsie and Alan are never together. He calls round his house for some things and softening, Elsie offers him her card but he tells her to put it with the others and walks out.

Written by Malcolm Lynch; story by Esther Rose, John Temple and Harry Driver; designed by Eugene Ferguson; produced by Brian Armstrong; directed by Roger Tucker.

With Betty Driver (Betty Turpin), Julie Goodyear (Bet Lynch), Violet Carson (Ena Sharples), Doris Speed (Annie Walker), Patricia Phoenix (Elsie Howard), Alan Browning (Alan Howard), Reginald Marsh (Dave Smith), William Roache (Ken Barlow), Irene Sutcliffe (Maggie Clegg), Graham Haberfield (Jerry Booth), Del Henney (Eddie Duncan), Jack Howarth (Albert Tatlock), Bernard Manning (Himself), Mollie Sugden [as Molly Sugden] (Nelly Harvey), Stella Moray (Kitty Stonely), David Davies, George Malpas, Alan O'Keefe, Jimmy Coleman, Ken Frith.

25.12.1972 "Elsie realises Alan is becoming an alcoholic at the 1940s show" P694/246 DB / 2"

Written by Brian Finch; story by Harry Driver, Esther Rose and Tony Perrin; designed by Ed Buziak; executive producer H. V. Kershaw; produced by Eric Prytherch; directed by Colin Cant.

With Betty Driver (Betty Turpin), Patricia Phoenix (Elsie Howard), Alan Browning (Alan Howard), Neville Buswell (Ray Langton), Eileen Derbyshire (Emily Bishop), Irene Sutcliffe (Maggie Clegg), Stephen Hancock (Ernest Bishop), Doris Speed (Annie Walker), Julie Goodyear (Bet Lynch), Jack Howarth (Albert Tatlock), Bernard Youens (Stan Ogden), Margot Bryant (Minnie Caldwell), Graham Haberfield (Jerry Booth), Bryan Mosley (Alf Roberts), Kenneth Farrington (Billy Walker), Barbara Mullaney (Rita Littlewood), Diana Davies (Norma Ford), Frances Tomelty (Christine Peters).

24.12.1973 "Jerry is made a partner" P694/350 DB / 2"

Ray turns up and Diedre makes an impassioned plea for him to become a partner of Fairclough & Langton which Len & Ray agree to. Ena moves in with Minnie not telling anyone that she did not have to move out on Christmas Eve. Minnie storms into The Rovers while they are all having a sing song and has a go at Emily & Ernest for chucking Ena out. Bet finds out that Annie plans to give her a box of chocolates as a thank you and trumps Annie in front of the regulars by giving her a box twice as big.

Written by H. V. Kershaw; story by Esther Rose, Peter Tonkinson and Harry Driver; edited by Ed Buziak; produced by Eric Prytherch; directed by Stephen Butcher.

With Doris Speed (Annie Walker), Peter Adamson (Len Fairclough), Violet Carson (Ena Sharples), Stephen Hancock (Ernest Bishop), Eileen Derbyshire (Emily Bishop), Bernard Youens (Stan Ogden), Jean Alexander (Hilda Ogden), Margot Bryant (Minnie Caldwell), Barbara Mullaney (Rita Littlewood), Anne Kirkbride (Deirdre Hunt), Julie Goodyear (Bet Lynch), Graham Haberfield (Jerry Booth), Thelma Barlow (Miss Riley), Neville Buswell (Ray Langton).

26.12.1973 "Everyone hates Ernest" P694/351 DB / 2"

Ernest is blamed by everyone for Ena being out of her job and Flat. Annie gives him strong words. Emily locks herself in the bathroom. He sees Ena and says he will try and get it all back for her but Ena has had another offer. Len, Ray & Jerry hold a bit of a do at the yard. Ray kisses Deirdre under the mistletoe. Rita tells Mavis she will one day marry Len.

Written by Julian Roach; story by Esther Rose, Peter Tonkinson and Harry Driver; edited by Ed Buziak; produced by Eric Prytherch; directed by Stephen Butcher.

With Doris Speed (Annie Walker), Peter Adamson (Len Fairclough), Violet Carson (Ena Sharples), Stephen Hancock (Ernest Bishop), Eileen Derbyshire (Emily Bishop), Bernard Youens (Stan Ogden), Jean Alexander (Hilda Ogden), Margot Bryant (Minnie Caldwell), Barbara Mullaney (Rita Littlewood), Anne Kirkbride (Deirdre Hunt), Julie Goodyear (Bet Lynch), Graham Haberfield (Jerry Booth), Thelma Barlow (Miss Riley), Neville Buswell (Ray Langton), Paula Tilbrook.

31.12.1973 "New Years' Eve at The Rovers" P694/352 DB / 2"

The Committee meet and decide to give Ena her job and flat back but she is off to stay in St Annes. Emily & Ernest see the postmark on Ena's letter and see that Ena had the offer well before Christmas. Nellie Harvey's husband Arthur turns up and tells Annie he has left Nellie. A New years Eve do is held at The Rovers. Jerry and Mavis touch. Ray & Deidre are getting on, Alf gets drunk and one of The Rovers extras keeps winking at Bet. #Unintentional camera glimpse over top of Rovers set.

Written by Kay McManus; story by Harry Driver, Esther Rose and Peter Tonkinson; edited by Ed Buziak; produced by Eric Prytherch; directed by Bill Gilmour.

With Violet Carson (Ena Sharples), Doris Speed (Annie Walker), Peter Adamson (Len Fairclough), Stephen Hancock (Ernest Bishop), Eileen Derbyshire (Emily Bishop), Margot Bryant (Minnie Caldwell), Barbara Mullaney (Rita Littlewood), Graham Haberfield (Jerry Booth), Thelma Barlow (Miss Riley), Neville Buswell (Ray Langton), Jack Howarth (Albert Tatlock), Betty Driver (Betty Turpin), Julie Goodyear (Bet Lynch), Bryan Mosley (Alf Roberts), Anne Kirkbride (Deirdre Hunt), Henry Moxon (Arthur Harvey), Wendy Marshall (Renee Delafonte).

23.12.1974 "Eddie Yeats arrives" P694/454 DB / 2"

Eddie Yeats turns up at Minnies' saying her original guest could not make it. He worms his way into her affections and persuades her to let him stay with her and Ena. He, meanwhile is planning to rob a supermarket with a fellow con. Things are still awkward between Jerry and Mavis. He plans to spend Christmas in a hotel. Deidre's mum, Blanche visits Annie and they come to a mutual agreement about Christmas Day. Stan buys a Christmas tree for Hilda for 50p but sells it to Eddie for £2 disappointing Hilda.

Written by Julian Roach; designed by NOT CREDITED; produced by Susi Hush; directed by Ken Grieve.

With Violet Carson (Ena Sharples), Ken Farrington (Kenneth Farrington), Doris Speed (Annie Walker), Julie Goodyear (Bet Lynch), Jack Howarth (Uncle Albert), Eileen Derbyshire (Emily Bishop), Betty Driver (Betty Turpin), Bernard Youens (Stan Ogden), Jean Alexander (Hilda Ogden), Neville Buswell (Ray Langton), Irene Sutcliffe (Maggie Cooke), Barbara Mullaney (Rita Littlewood), Peter Adamson (Len Fairclough), Stephen Hancock (Ernest Bishop), Margot Bryant (Minnie Caldwell), Graham Haberfield (Jerry Booth), Anne Kirkbride (Deirdre Hunt), Thelma Barlow (Mavis Riley), Geoffrey Hughes (Eddie Yeats), Jessie Evans (Granny Hopkins), Richard Davies (Idris Hopkins), Maggie Jones (Maggie Monks), Donald Webster.

25.12.1974 "Christmas Day At The Rovers" P694/455 DB / 2"

The Rovers is buzzing and everyone is having a sing song. Stan buys Bet a drink. Bet virtually asks Eddie Yeats for a date. The father of the children Emily & Ernest are looking after turns up. Jerry is feeling sorry for himself as Mavis is with Carlos and gives his hotel tickets to Len & Ray. Annie, Billy, Deidre and Blanche go back to Annie's after a meal at Blanche's but cannot eat a thing that Annie has provided. Eddie spends Christmas with Minnie & Ena. His friend in crime blacks out the Weatherfield lights in order to rob a supermarket and everyone continues to enjoy themselves in candlelight.

Written by Harry Kershaw; story by Esther Rose and Peter Tonkinson; script editor Leslie Duxbury; designed by NOT CREDITED; produced by Susi Hush; directed by Ken Grieve.

With Margot Bryant (Minnie Caldwell), Violet Carson (Ena Sharples), Irene Sutcliffe (Maggie Cooke), Betty Driver (Betty Turpin), Jack Howarth (Albert Tatlock), Jean Alexander (Hilda Ogden), Bernard Youens (Stan Ogden), Geoffrey Hughes (Eddie Yeats), Doris Speed (Annie Walker), Kenneth Farrington (Billy Walker), Neville Buswell (Ray Langton), Peter Adamson (Len Fairclough), Barbara Mullaney (Rita Littlewood), Thelma Barlow (Mavis Riley), Graham Haberfield (Jerry Booth), Stephen Hancock (Ernest Bishop), Eileen Derbyshire (Emily Bishop), Anne Kirkbride (Deirdre Hunt), Maggie Jones (Maggie Monks), Jessie Evans (Granny Hopkins), Richard Davies (Idris Hopkins), Duke Ozzie, Donald Webster, Thomas Sloane, Malcolm Hebden, Paul Blidgeon, Andrea Blidgeon.

CORONATION STREET (continued)		British Christmas Television Guide

22.12.1975 ANNIE AND BETTY'S CORONATION STREET MEMORIES P827/1 DB / 2"

Duration: 24 minutes.

Written by H. V. Kershaw; produced by Susi Hush; directed by Derek Lister.

With Doris Speed (Annie Walker), Betty Driver (Betty Turpin), Peter Adamson (Len Fairclough), Jean Alexander (Hilda Ogden), Betty Alberge (Florrie Lindley), Margot Bryant (Minnie Caldwell), Neville Buswell (Ray Langton), Violet Carson (Ena Sharples), Lynne Carol (Martha Longhurst), Eileen Derbyshire (Miss Nugent), Kenneth Farrington (Billy Walker), Julie Goodyear (Bet Lynch), Graham Haberfield (Jerry Booth), Stephen Hancock (Mr Spinks), Jack Howarth (Albert Tatlock), Christine Hargreaves (Christine Hardman), Ruth Holden (Vera Lomax), Doreen Keogh (Concepta Riley), Arthur Lowe (Mr Swindley), Arthur Leslie (Jack Walker), Paul Maxwell (Steve Tanner), Henry Moxon (Arthur Harvey), Jonathan Newth (Reverend Bryan Hesketh), Bill Nagy (Gregg Flint), Frank Pemberton (Frank Barlow), Anne Reid (Valerie Tatlock), William Roache (Kenneth Barlow), Gordon Rollings (Charlie Moffitt), Mollie Sugden (Nelly Harvey), Pat Phoenix (Elsie Tanner), Louise Jervis.

24.12.1975 "Cinderella" P694/559 DB / 2"

Written by Julian Roach; story by Esther Rose and Peter Tonkinson; designed by Knowles Bentley; produced by Susi Hush; directed by Derek Lister.

With Neville Buswell (Ray Langton), Peter Adamson (Len Fairclough), Violet Carson (Ena Sharples), Jean Alexander (Hidla Ogden), Kathy Jones (Tricia Hopkins), Barbara Mullaney (Rita Littlewood), Julie Goodyear (Bet Lynch), Bryan Mosley (Alf Roberts), Betty Driver (Betty Turpin), Anne Kirkbride (Deirdre Langton), Stephen Hancock (Ernest Bishop), Thelma Barlow (Mavis Riley), William Roache (Ken Barlow), Maggie Jones (Blanche Hunt), Jack Howarth (Albert Tatlock), Don Hawkins (Trevor Ogden).

22.12.1976 P694/663 DB / 2"

The girls continue to undress Ernie. Vera pulls his shirt off. He runs off in his vest and pants. Gail gets drunk and kisses Terry, he reads more into it, especially when she tells him she doesn't want him to leave the area. Annie refuses to lend glasses for the party as they got the drink from Renee. Terry asks Gail to go out with him; he'd like to settle down. She laughs at him and says she's only with him as there's noone else. He calls her a tart and slaps her face. Len is angry when Marie dumps him for Mike. Ernie's clothes can't be found so he has to wear denims. Annie test drives the Rover 2000. Terry leaves for Lancaster, planning to join up. Renee is upset at being on her own. Bet goes to the party fearing Vera has her claws in Mike but finds him on his own. He gives her the key to No.5 as a Christmas present.

Written by David Crane; story by Peter Tonkinson and Esther Rose; designed by Geoff Bentley; produced by Bill Podmore; directed by John Black.

With Madge Hindle (Renee Bradshaw), Eileen Derbyshire (Emily Bishop), Johnny Briggs (Mike Baldwin), Stephen Hancock (Ernest Bishop), Lynne Perrie (Ivy Tilsley), Elizabeth Dawn (Vera Duckworth), Pat Phoenix (Elsie Howard), Bob Mason (Terry Bradshaw), Helen Worth (Gail Potter), Roger Brierley (Lanky Potts), Julie Goodyear (Bet Lynch), Fred Feast (Fred Gee), Geoffrey Hughes (Eddie Yeats), Bryan Mosley (Alf Roberts), Doris Speed (Annie Walker), Lois Baxter (Marie Stanton), Peter Adamson (Len Fairclough), Robert Bettinson (Tom Pickup), Wenda Brown (Teresa Meakin).

26.12.1977 "Rita invites Elsie to Xmas Dinner at the Faircloughs', but what are her motives?" P694/768 DB / 2"

Written by H. V. Kershaw; story by Esther Rose and Peter Tonkinson; designed by Eric Deakins; produced by Bill Podmore; directed by Roger Cheveley.

With Betty Driver (Betty Turpin), Jack Howarth (Albert Tatlock), Jean Alexander (Hilda Ogden), Bernard Youens (Stan Ogden), Geoffrey Hughes (Eddie Yeats), Doris Speed (Annie Walker), Neville Buswell (Ray Langton), Peter Adamson (Len Fairclough), Barbara Knox (Rita Fairclough), Stephen Hancock (Ernest Bishop), Eileen Derbyshire (Emily Bishop), Anne Kirkbride (Deirdre Langton), Fred Feast (Fred Gee), Patricia Phoenix (Elsie Tanner), Bryan Mosley (Alf Roberts), Christabel Finch (Tracy Langton), Freddie Rayner (Sam Turner), Madge Hindle (Renee Bradshaw).

27.12.1978 P694/872 DB / 2"

Albert goes down with flu and spends Christmas in bed. Ron has enough of driving people to parties and throws one himself at No.11. Karen tells Ken that Dave is out of Risley and thinks she's been having an affair with Ken. Tim Gibbs hears about Ron's party and decides to gatecrash it with mate Brian Tilsley. Gail takes a fancy to Brian. Tim is annoyed that Suzie is not about but makes a play for Deirdre instead. Emily gets drunk on Eddie's home made wine. Brian gets drunk and asks Gail for a date. She agrees to meet him at the cinema. Tim takes Deirdre home and intends to stay the night. She is amused at his shock finding Ena babysitting. Deirdre gets him to walk Ena home instead. Dave warns Ken off Karen.

Written by John Stevenson; story by Esther Rose and Peter Tonkinson; designed by Eric Deakins; produced by Bill Podmore; directed by Jeremy Summers.

With Jack Howarth (Albert Tatlock), Doris Speed (Annie Walker), Pat Phoenix (Elsie Tanner), Peter Adamson (Len Fairclough), Jean Alexander (Hilda Ogden), William Roache (Ken Barlow), Bernard Youens (Stan Ogden), Violet Carson (Ena Sharples), Anne Kirkbride (Deirdre Langton), Betty Driver (Betty Turpin), Christabel Finch (Tracy Langton), Helen Worth (Gail Potter), Julie Goodyear (Bet Lynch), Geoffrey Hughes (Eddie Yeats), Eileen Derbyshire (Emily Bishop), Joe Lynch (Ron Mather), Catherine Neilson (Karen Barnes), Chris Quinten (Brian Tilsley), Ray Ashcroft (Tim Gibbs), Russell Dixon (Dave Barnes), William Tarmey (Jack Rowe).

24.12.1979 "Christmas Eve, a vanishing lady turns up out of the blue" P694/954 DB / 2"

Written by Leslie Duxbury; story by Peter Tonkinson and Barry Hill; designed by Eric Deakins; produced by Bill Podmore; directed by Malcolm Taylor.

With Betty Driver (Betty Turpin), Violet Carson (Ena Sharples), Barbara Knox (Rita Fairclough), Peter Adamson (Len Fairclough), Peter Dudley (Bert Tilsley), Lynne Perrie (Ivy Tilsley), Christopher Quinten (Brian Tilsley), Helen Worth (Gail Tilsley), Bernard Youens (Stan Ogden), Jean Alexander (Hilda Ogden), Patricia Phoenix (Elsie Tanner), Julie Goodyear (Bet Lynch), Bryan Mosley (Alf Roberts), Madge Hindle (Renee Roberts), Geoffrey Hughes (Eddie Yeats), Jack Howarth (Albert Tatlock), Sue Nicholls (Audrey Potter), Joe Lynch (Ron Mather).

26.12.1979 "Boxing Day menus" P694/955 DB / 2"

Written by John Stevenson; story by Peter Tonkinson and Barry Hill; designed by Eric Deakins; produced by Bill Podmore; directed by Malcolm Taylor.

With Betty Driver (Betty Turpin), Violet Carson (Ena Sharples), Barbara Knox (Rita Fairclough), Peter Adamson (Len Fairclough), Peter Dudley (Bert Tilsley), Lynne Perrie (Ivy Tilsley), Christopher Quinten (Brian Tilsley), Helen Worth (Gail Tilsley), Bernard Youens (Stan Ogden), Jean Alexander (Hilda Ogden), Patricia Phoenix (Elsie Tanner), Julie Goodyear (Bet Lynch), Bryan Mosley (Alf Roberts), Madge Hindle (Renee Roberts), Geoffrey Hughes (Eddie Yeats), Jack Howarth (Albert Tatlock), Sue Nicholls (Audrey Potter), Joe Lynch (Ron Mather).

22.12.1980 "Martin's dilemma" P694/1058 DB / 2"

Elsie Tanner's grandson Martin Cheveski faces a dilemma—should he spend Christmas with sweetheart Karen or go home to his parents?

Written by Tony Perrin; story by Peter Tonkinson and Esther Rose; designed by Eric Deakins; produced by Bill Podmore; directed by Stephen Butcher.

With Fred Feast (Fred Gee), Pat Phoenix (Elsie Tanner), Doris Speed (Annie Walker), Peter Adamson (Len Fairclough), Eileen Derbyshire (Emily Bishop), Bernard Youens (Stan Ogden), Jean Alexander (Hilda Ogden), Geoffrey Hughes (Eddie Yeats), Thelma Barlow (Mavis Riley), Julie Goodyear (Bet Lynch), Anne Kirkbride (Deirdre Langton), Chris Quentin (Brian Tilsley), Helen Worth (Gail Tilsley), Jonathan Caplan (Martin Cheveski), Barbara Knox (Rita Fairclough), Sally Jane Jackson (Karen Oldfield), Sue Nicholls (Audrey Potter), Jack Smethurst (Johnny Webb), Sandra Voe (Brenda Palin), Steve Dixon (Paul Siddall), David Bradles (Detective Sergeant Simms).

24.12.1980 "Christmas Eve party at the Ogdens" P694/1059 DB / 2"

Written by Julian Roach; story by Peter Tonkinson and Esther Rose; designed by Eric Deakins; produced by Bill Podmore; directed by Stephen Butcher.

With Fred Feast (Fred Gee), Pat Phoenix (Elsie Tanner), Doris Speed (Annie Walker), Peter Adamson (Len Fairclough), Eileen Derbyshire (Emily Bishop), Bernard Youens (Stan Ogden), Jean Alexander (Hilda Ogden), Geoffrey Hughes (Eddie Yeats), Thelma Barlow (Mavis Riley), Julie Goodyear (Bet Lynch), Anne Kirkbride (Deirdre Langton), Chris Quentin (Brian Tilsley), Helen Worth (Gail Tilsley), Jonathan Caplan (Martin Cheveski), Barbara Knox (Rita Fairclough), Sally Jane Jackson (Karen Oldfield), Sue Nicholls (Audrey Potter), Jack Smethurst (Johnny Webb), Sandra Voe (Brenda Palin), Steve Dixon (Paul Siddall), David Bradles (Detective Sergeant Simms).

CORONATION STREET

British Christmas Television Guide | **CORONATION STREET (continued)**

23.12.1981　　　　　　　　　　　　　　　　　　　　　　P694/1163　　　　　　　　　　　　　　　　　　　　　DB / 2"

Deirdre invites Emily for Christmas, she is delighted to accept. Fred goes to the hotel and tells Eunice he loves her and pleads with her to make a new start together. She tells him she's tired of struggling. He goes for Critchley, accusing him of taking his wife off him. Eunice tells Fred she likes Critchley more than him. Mavis goes to the wholesalers to see Bobby and is upset when he isn't interested in her. Rita tells Mavis that Bet took her place on the date. Fred realises his marriage is over. He is grateful when Annie offers him his old room back. Albert feels unwelcome in his own home. Fred moves back into the Rovers. Hilda is upset when Stan gives her an airfreshener as a Christmas present. Deirdre feels sorry for lonely Alf and invites him for Christmas, pleasing Albert. Mavis gets drunk and tells Bet what she thinks of her. Emily receives a letter from Arnold's solicitor asking to see her.

Written by Cliff Jerrard; story by Peter Tonkinson and Esther Rose; designed by Eric Deakins; produced by Bill Podmore; directed by Charles Kitchen.

With Doris Speed (Annie Walker), Pat Phoenix (Elsie Tanner), Peter Adamson (Len Fairclough), Fred Feast (Fred Gee), Thelma Barlow (Mavis Riley), Jean Alexander (Hilda Ogden), Bernard Youens (Stan Ogden), Geoffrey Hughes (Eddie Yeats), Barbara Knox (Rita Fairclough), Julie Goodyear (Bet Lynch), Bryan Mosley (Alf Roberts), William Roache (Ken Barlow), Betty Driver (Betty Turpin), Jack Howarth (Albert Tatlock), Anne Kirkbride (Deirdre Barlow), Eileen Derbyshire (Emily Bishop), Meg Johnson (Eunice Gee), Christabel Finch (Tracy Barlow), Joel David (Taxi Driver), Allan Surtees (Councillor Critchley), Rita Howard (Customer), Johnny Briggs (Mike Baldwin), Elizabeth Dawn (Vera Duckworth), Helene Palmer (Ida Clough), Lynne Perrie (Ivy Tilsley), Debbie Arnold (Sylvie Hicks), Terence Longdon (Wilf Stockwell), Sam Kydd (Frankie Baldwin), Peter Dudley (Bert Tilsley).

A Granada production. Transmission details are for the Central region. Duration: 25 minutes.

　　　Holding / Source

20.12.1982　"Eddie tries to sell stolen Christmas trees"　　　　　　　　　　　　　　　　　　　　　　　　DB / 2"

Written by Barry Hill; story by Peter Tonkinson and Esther Rose; designed by Eric Deakins; produced by Bill Podmore and Mervyn Watson; directed by John Michael Phillips.

With Doris Speed (Annie Walker), Peter Adamson (Len Fairclough), Patricia Phoenix (Elsie Tanner), Jean Alexander (Hilda Ogden), Bernard Youens (Stan Ogden), Anne Kirkbride (Deirdre Barlow), William Roache (Ken Barlow), Geoffrey Hughes (Eddie Yeats), Johnny Briggs (Mike Baldwin), Fred Feast (Fred Gee), Eileen Derbyshire (Emily Bishop), Lynne Perrie (Ivy Tilsley), Barbara Knox (Rita Fairclough), Thelma Barlow (Mavis Riley), Julie Goodyear (Bet Lynch), Peter Dudley (Bert Tilsley), Elizabeth Dawn (Vera Duckworth), William Tarmey (Jack Duckworth), Christopher Coll (Victor Pendelbury), Teddy Turner (Chalkie Whitely), Veronica Doran (Marion Willis).

22.12.1982　"The Christmas dance"　　　　　　　　　　　　　　　　　　　　　　　　　　　　　　　　DB / 2"

Written by Barry Hill; story by Peter Tonkinson and Esther Rose; designed by Eric Deakins; produced by Bill Podmore and Mervyn Watson; directed by John Michael Phillips.

With Doris Speed (Annie Walker), Peter Adamson (Len Fairclough), Patricia Phoenix (Elsie Tanner), Jean Alexander (Hilda Ogden), Bernard Youens (Stan Ogden), Anne Kirkbride (Deirdre Barlow), William Roache (Ken Barlow), Geoffrey Hughes (Eddie Yeats), Johnny Briggs (Mike Baldwin), Fred Feast (Fred Gee), Eileen Derbyshire (Emily Bishop), Lynne Perrie (Ivy Tilsley), Barbara Knox (Rita Fairclough), Thelma Barlow (Mavis Riley), Julie Goodyear (Bet Lynch), Peter Dudley (Bert Tilsley), Elizabeth Dawn (Vera Duckworth), William Tarmey (Jack Duckworth), Christopher Coll (Victor Pendelbury), Teddy Turner (Chalkie Whitely), Veronica Doran (Marion Willis).

26.12.1983　"Rita Visits The Woman Involved With Len's Death"　　　　　　　　　　　　　　　　　　DB / 2"

Written by Peter Whalley; based on stories by Esther Rose and Tom Elliott; executive producer Bill Podmore; produced by Mervyn Watson; directed by Stephen Butcher.

With Eileen O'Brien (Marjorie Proctor), Patricia Phoenix (Elsie Tanner), Barbara Knox (Rita Fairclough), Thelma Barlow (Mavis Wilton), Julie Goodyear (Bet Lynch), Eileen Derbyshire (Emily Bishop), Bryan Mosley (Alf Roberts), Jean Alexander (Hilda Ogden), Elizabeth Dawn (Vera Duckworth), William Roache (Ken Barlow), Anne Kirkbride (Deirdre Barlow), Betty Driver (Betty Williams), Kevin Kennedy (Curly Watts), Tracie Bennett (Sharon Gaskell), Jack Watson (Bill Gregory).

24.12.1984　"Christmas Eve. Vera gets a tree. Rita gets an unexpected visitor"　　　　　　　　　　　1" / 2"

Written by Leslie Duxbury; story by Tom Elliott and Peter Tonkinson; designed by Eric Deakins; executive producer Bill Podmore; produced by Mervyn Watson; directed by Patrick Lau.

With Peter Armitage (Bill Webster), Michael Le Vell (Kevin Webster), Sue Devaney (Debbie Webster), Julie Goodyear (Bet Lynch), David Daker (Gordon Lewis), Betty Driver (Betty Williams), Barbara Knox (Rita Fairclough), Lynne Perrie (Ivy Tilsley), Helen Worth (Gail Tilsley), Christopher Quinten (Brian Tilsley), William Tarmey (Jack Duckworth), Elizabeth Dawn (Vera Duckworth), Nigel Pivaro (Terry Duckworth), Bill Waddington (Percy Sugden), Jean Alexander (Hilda Ogden), Bryan Mosley (Alf Roberts), Kevin Kennedy (Curly Watts), Jack Carr (Tony Cunliffe), Margi Campi (Dulcie Froggatt), Ted Beyer (Tommy Markham).

26.12.1984　"Boxing Day. Rita mourns Len and learns something about herself"　　　　　　　　　　1" / 2"

Written by Peter Whalley; story by Tom Elliott and Peter Tonkinson; designed by Eric Deakins; executive producer Bill Podmore; produced by Mervyn Watson; directed by Patrick Lau.

With Peter Armitage (Bill Webster), Michael Le Vell (Kevin Webster), Sue Devaney (Debbie Webster), Julie Goodyear (Bet Lynch), David Daker (Gordon Lewis), Betty Driver (Betty Williams), Barbara Knox (Rita Fairclough), Lynne Perrie (Ivy Tilsley), Helen Worth (Gail Tilsley), Christopher Quinten (Brian Tilsley), William Tarmey (Jack Duckworth), Elizabeth Dawn (Vera Duckworth), Nigel Pivaro (Terry Duckworth), Bill Waddington (Percy Sugden), Jean Alexander (Hilda Ogden), Bryan Mosley (Alf Roberts), Kevin Kennedy (Curly Watts), Jack Carr (Tony Cunliffe), Margi Campi (Dulcie Froggatt), Ted Beyer (Tommy Markham).

25.12.1985　　　1" / 1"

Written by Julian Roach; executive producer Bill Podmore; produced by John G. Temple; directed by Gareth Morgan.

25.12.1987　"Hilda waves goodbye to the Street"　　　　　　　　　　　　　　　　　　　　　　　1" / 1"

Written by Leslie Duxbury; story associates Tom Elliott and Paul Abbott; designed by Ann Swarbrick and Chris Bradshaw; produced by Bill Podmore; directed by Ric Mellis.

With Colin Kerrigan (Gary Grimshaw), Jean Alexander (Hilda Ogden), Julie Goodyear (Bet Gilroy), Barbara Knox (Rita Fairclough), Mark Eden (Alan Bradley), Thelma Barlow (Mavis Wilton), Roy Barraclough (Alec Gilroy), Sue Nicholls (Audrey Roberts), Johnny Briggs (Mike Baldwin), William Roache (Ken Barlow), Christopher Quinten (Brian Tilsley), Helen Worth (Gail Tilsley), Lynne Perrie (Ivy Tilsley), Elizabeth Dawn (Vera Duckworth), William Tarmey (Jack Duckworth), Bryan Mosley (Alf Roberts), Anne Kirkbride (Deirdre Barlow), Michael Le Vell (Kevin Webster), Sue Jenkins (Gloria Todd), Eileen Derbyshire (Emily Bishop), Sally Whittaker (Sally Webster), Fanny Carby (Amy Burton), Geoff Hinsliff (Don Brennan), Bill Waddington (Percy Sugden), Kevin Kennedy (Curly Watts), Ruth Whitehead (Lisa Woods), Tom Mennard (Sam Tindall), Jill Summers (Phyllis Pearce), Warren Jackson (Nicky Tilsley), Lindsay King (Sarah Louise Tilsley), Robert Maxfield (Piano Player).

David Scase as Doctor Lowther did not appear despite being billed.

CORONATION STREET (continued)

25.12.1988 "Percy takes charge of Christmas at Emily's. Deirdre is held captive" 1" / 1"
Written by John Stevenson; story associates Tom Elliott and Diane Culverhouse; designed by Stephen Graham; produced by Bill Podmore; directed by Ian White.

With Rob Dixon (Brian Roscoe), William Roache (Ken Barlow), Anne Kirkbride (Deirdre Barlow), Dawn Acton (Tracy Barlow), Roy Barraclough (Alec Gilroy), Julie Goodyear (Bet Gilroy), Barbara Knox (Rita Fairclough), Mark Eden (Alan Bradley), Thelma Barlow (Mavis Wilton), Peter Baldwin (Derek Wilton), Eileen Derbyshire (Emily Bishop), Bill Waddington (Percy Sugden), William Tarmey (Jack Duckworth), Elizabeth Dawn (Vera Duckworth), Johnny Briggs (Mike Baldwin), Jill Summers (Phyllis Pearce), Alan Meadows (Police Sergeant), Maria Gough (Policewoman), Angela Marie Freear (Teenager), Mark Jordan (Police Constable), George Malpas [as George Malpass] (Tramp), Robert Maxfield (Pianist).

22.12.1989 "Derek gets locked in at work and leaves dressed as Santa Claus. On Christmas Eve, Deirdre tells Ken she knows about his affair with Wendy" 1" / 1"
Written by Stephen Mallatratt; story associates Paul Abbott and Trevor Suthers; story editor Tom Elliott; executive producer David Liddiment; produced by Mervyn Watson; directed by Ian White.

With Ken Morgan (Mr Holdsworth), Zall Anthony (Sid Cooper), Greta Mikaelsen (Student), Sean Wilson (Martin Platt), Sally Ann Matthews (Jenny Bradley), Helen Worth (Gail Tilsley), Warren Jackson (Nicky Tilsley), Geoff Hinsliff (Don Brennan), William Tarmey (Jack Duckworth), Kevin Kennedy (Curly Watts), Elizabeth Dawn (Vera Duckworth), Barbara Knox (Rita Fairclough), Thelma Barlow (Mavis Wilton), Eileen Derbyshire (Emily Bishop), Lynne Perrie (Ivy Tilsley), Sue Nicholls (Audrey Roberts), Bryan Mosley (Alf Roberts), Sally Whittaker (Sally Webster), Bill Waddington (Percy Sugden), Amanda Barrie (Alma Sedgwick), William Roache (Ken Barlow), Dawn Acton (Tracy Barlow), Roberta Kerr (Wendy Crozier), Anne Kirkbride (Deirdre Barlow), Johnny Briggs (Mike Baldwin), Julie Goodyear (Bet Lynch), Roy Barraclough (Alec Gilroy), Peter Baldwin (Derek Wilton), Michelle Holmes (Tina Fowler), Michael Le Vell (Kevin Webster), Suzanne Hall (Kimberley Taylor), Tracy Brabin (Tricia Armstrong).

25.12.1989 "Ken Barlow has a lot of explaining to do" 1" / 1"
Written by Peter Whalley; story by Diane Culverhouse and Trevor Suthers; story editor Tom Elliott; designed by Stephen Graham; produced by Mervyn Watson; directed by Spencer Campbell.

With Ling Tai (Chinese Student), William Roache (Ken Barlow), Anne Kirkbride (Deirdre Barlow), Helen Worth (Gail Tilsley), Sean Wilson (Martin Platt), Elizabeth Dawn (Vera Duckworth), William Tarmey (Jack Duckworth), Julie Goodyear (Bet Lynch), Roy Barraclough (Alec Gilroy), Kevin Kennedy (Curly Watts), Thelma Barlow (Mavis Wilton), Peter Baldwin (Derek Wilton), Eileen Derbyshire (Emily Bishop), Bill Waddington (Percy Sugden), Johnny Briggs (Mike Baldwin), Amanda Barrie (Alma Sedgwick), Sue Nicholls (Audrey Roberts), Bryan Mosley (Alf Roberts), Lynne Perrie (Ivy Tilsley), Geoff Hinsliff (Don Brennan), Barbara Knox (Rita Fairclough), Sally Ann Matthews (Jenny Bradley), Michael Le Vell (Kevin Webster), Sally Whittaker (Sally Webster), Betty Driver (Betty Williams), Warren Jackson (Nicky Tilsley), Lynsay King (Sarah-Louise Platt), Dawn Acton (Tracy Barlow), Stuart Wolfenden (Mark Casey), Nicholas Cochrane (Andy Watts), Simon Gregson (Steve McDonald), Beverley Callard (Liz McDonald), Charles Lawson (Jim McDonald), Michelle Holmes (Tina Fowler), Roberta Kerr (Wendy Crozier), William Ivory (Eddie Ramsden), Suzanne Hall (Kimberley Taylor), Ted Beyer (Tommy Markham).

24.12.1990 1" / 1"
Written by John Stevenson; produced by Mervyn Watson; directed by Oliver Horsbrugh.

25.12.1990 "Alec bites off more than he can chew" 1" / 1"
Written by John Stevenson; produced by Mervyn Watson; directed by Oliver Horsbrugh.

With Mel Fredericks (Chauffeur), Hilary Trott (Sister), Susie Hawthorne (Nurse), John Jardine (Mr Taylor), Dave Dutton (Photographer), Jill Summers (Phyllis Pearce), Barbara Knox (Rita Fairclough), Thelma Barlow (Mavis Wilton), Charles Lawson (Jim McDonald), William Roache (Ken Barlow), Sally Ann Matthews (Jenny Bradley), Deborah McAndrew (Angie Freeman), Dawn Acton (Tracy Barlow), Bryan Mosley (Alf Roberts), Sue Nicholls (Audrey Roberts), Julie Goodyear (Bet Lynch), Peter Baldwin (Derek Wilton), Roy Barraclough (Alec Gilroy), Beverley Callard (Liz McDonald), Bill Waddington (Percy Sugden), Anne Kirkbride (Deirdre Barlow), Sally Whittaker (Sally Webster), Stuart Wolfenden (Mark Casey), Michael Le Vell (Kevin Webster), Sarah Nixon (Amanda Worley), Johnny Briggs (Mike Baldwin), Lynne Perrie (Ivy Tilsley), Shirin Taylor (Jackie Ingram), Amanda Barrie (Alma Sedgwick), Christopher Coll (Victor Pendlebury), Philip Middlemiss (Des Barnes), Amelia Bullmore (Steph Barnes), Tommy Boyle (Phil Jennings), Eileen Derbyshire (Emily Bishop), Geoff Hinsliff (Don Brennan), Ken Morley (Reg Holdsworth), Suzanne Hall (Kimberley Taylor), Alexander Graham (Jamie Ramsden), Joy Blakeman (Marie Ramsden), Sean Wilson (Martin Platt), Nicholas Cochrane (Andy Watts), Helen Worth (Gail Tilsley), Warren Jackson (Nicky Tilsley), Lynsay King (Sarah-Louise Platt).

26.12.1990 1" / 1"
Written by Stephen Mallatratt; produced by Mervyn Watson; directed by Richard Signy.

25.12.1991 1" / 1"
Written by John Stevenson; directed by Ian White.

25.12.1991 1" / 1"
Written by John Stevenson; directed by Ian White.

25.12.1992 1" / 1"
Written by Julian Roach; directed by Dave Richards.

24.12.1993 1" / 1"
Written by Paul Abbott; directed by Romey Allison.

25.12.1994 "Samir has plans for the future, Jacks brother Clifford wants to make amends for the past" 1" / 1"
Written by John Stevenson; produced by Sue Pritchard; directed by Michael Kerrigan.

With Al Nedjari (Samir Rachid), David King (Clifford Duckworth), William Roache (Ken Barlow), Johnny Briggs (Mike Baldwin), Amanda Barrie (Alma Sedgwick), Simon Gregson (Steve McDonald), Angela Griffin (Fiona Middleton), Elizabeth Dawn (Vera Duckworth), William Tarmey (Jack Duckworth), Charles Lawson (Jim McDonald), Beverley Callard (Liz McDonald), Nicholas Cochrane (Andy Watts), Sarah Lancashire (Raquel Wolstenhulme), Sally Whittaker (Sally Webster), Michael Le Vell (Kevin Webster), Helen Worth (Gail Platt), Sean Wilson (Martin Platt), Kevin Kennedy (Curly Watts), Ken Morley (Reg Holdsworth), Elizabeth Bradley (Maud Grimes), Sherrie Hewson (Maureen Holdsworth), Anne Kirkbride (Deirdre Rachid).

26.12.1994 1" / 1"
Written by Peter Whalley; produced by Sue Pritchard; directed by Tim Dowd.

25.12.1995 "The police question Steve McDonald about stolen whisky" 1" / 1"
Duration: 48 minutes.
Written by Julian Roach; produced by Sue Pritchard; directed by John Michael Phillips.

With Georgine Anderson (Eunice Watts), John Pickles (Arthur Watts), Jennifer Piercey (Eileen Wolstenhulme), Peter Geddis (Larry Wolstenhulme), Kevin Kennedy (Curly Watts), Sarah Lancashire (Raquel Wolstenhulme), Philip Middlemiss (Des Barnes), Beverley Callard (Liz McDonald), Charles Lawson (Jim McDonald), Chloe Newsome (Victoria Arden), Simon Gregson (Steve McDonald), Sean Wilson (Martin Platt), Peter Armitage (Bill Webster), Peter Baldwin (Derek Wilton), Eileen Derbyshire (Emily Bishop), Denise Black (Denise Osbourne), Angela Griffin (Fiona Middleton), William Roache (Ken Barlow), Elizabeth Bradley (Maud Grimes), Elizabeth Dawn (Vera Duckworth), Sherrie Hewson (Maureen Holdsworth), Barbara Knox (Rita Sullivan), Thelma Barlow (Mavis Wilton), Betty Driver (Betty Williams), Geoff Hinsliff (Don Brennan), Malcolm Hebden (Norris Cole).

| British Christmas Television Guide | CORONATION STREET (continued) |

25.12.1996 "Don is consumed by despair, while Curly helps Maureen recover from her domestic boredom"   D3 / D3
Written by John Stevenson; produced by Sue Pritchard; directed by Brian Mills.

With Emily Iggulden (Lauren Hickson), John Henshaw (Mick Murphy), Emily Aston (Becky Palmer), Beverley Callard (Liz McDonald), Bill Waddington (Percy Sugden), Keith Woodason (Gerry Turner), Michael Le Vell (Kevin Webster), Anita Carey (Joyce Smedley), William Tarmey (Jack Duckworth), Geoff Hinsliff (Don Brennan), Terence Hillyer (Terry Goodwin), Bryan Mosley (Alf Roberts), Sue Nicholls (Audrey Roberts), Sally Whittaker (Sally Webster), Elizabeth Bradley (Maud Grimes), Joseph Gilgun (Jamie Armstrong), Tracy Shaw (Maxine Peacock), Glyn Grain (Fraser Henderson), Sean Wilson (Martin Platt), Kevin Kennedy (Curly Watts), Lynsay King (Sarah-Louise Platt), Roy Barraclough (Alec Gilroy), Sherrie Hewson (Maureen Holdsworth), Peter Armitage (Bill Webster), Ian Mercer (Pete Jackson), Helen Worth (Gail Platt), Gaynor Faye (Judy Mallett), Steven Arnold (Ashley Peacock), Betty Driver (Betty Williams), Tracy Brabin (Tricia Armstrong), Elizabeth Dawn (Vera Duckworth), Charles Lawson (Jim McDonald), Nicholas Cochrane (Andy Watts), Eve Steele (Anne Malone), Johnny Briggs (Mike Baldwin), Amanda Barrie (Alma Sedgwick), Tina Hobley (Samantha Failsworth), Angela Griffin (Fiona Middleton), Malcolm Hebden (Norris Cole).

25.12.1997 "Jon has some bad news for Deirdre"   D3 / D3
Written by Peter Whalley; produced by Brian Park; directed by Laurence Moody.

With Joanne Froggatt (Zoe Tattersall), Andrew Knott (Liam Shepherd), Niven Boyd (Paul Fisher), Margo Gunn (Linda Lindsay), Ian Mercer (Pete Jackson), Steven Arnold (Ashley Peacock), Sally Whittaker (Sally Webster), Denise Welch (Natalie Horrocks), Michael Le Vell (Kevin Webster), Bruce Jones (Les Battersby), Helen Worth (Gail Platt), Martin Hancock (Spider Nugent), Georgia Taylor (Toyah Battersby), Barbara Knox (Rita Sullivan), Elizabeth Dawn (Vera Duckworth), Anne Kirkbride (Deirdre Rachid), Owen Aaronovitch (Jon Lindsay), William Roache (Ken Barlow), William Tarmey (Jack Duckworth), Betty Driver (Betty Williams).

25.12.1998 "Jack And Vera Stage A Sit-In. Judy Mallett Gives Birth To Twins"   DB / DBS
Duration: 50 minutes.
Written by John Stevenson; produced by David Hanson; directed by Tim Dowd.

With Christine Brennan (Doctor Neville), Roy Barraclough (Alec Gilroy), Bryan Mosley (Alf Roberts), Amanda Barrie (Alma Sedgwick), Steven Arnold (Ashley Peacock), Sue Nicholls (Audrey Roberts), Betty Driver (Betty Williams), Maggie Jones (Blanche Hunt), Keith Clifford (Charlie West), Anne Kirkbride (Deirdre Rachid), Eileen Derbyshire (Emily Bishop), John Savident (Fred Elliott), Ian Mercer (Pete Jackson), Stephen Billington (Greg Kelly), Julie Hesmondhalgh (Hayley Patterson), Bill Tarmey (Jack Duckworth), Margi Clarke (Jackie Dobbs), Vicky Entwistle (Janice Battersby), Gaynor Faye (Judy Mallett), Michael Le Vell (Kevin Webster), William Roache (Ken Barlow), Jane Danson (Leanne Tilsley), Bruce Jones (Les Battersby), Joseph Jacobs (Marcus Wrigley), Sean Wilson (Martin Platt), Elizabeth Bradley (Maud Grimes), Tracey Shaw (Maxine Peacock), Johnny Briggs (Mike Baldwin), Adam Rickitt (Nick Tilsley), Barbara Knox (Rita Sullivan), Liz Dawn (Vera Duckworth), Chloe Newsome (Victoria Arden).

25.12.1999 "Martin and Rebecca have a night of passion. Natalie and Vinny get frisky. The Duckworths receive a surprise visitor"   DB / DBS
Duration: 50 minutes.
Written by Phil Ford; produced by Jane Macnaught; directed by David Kester.

With Lee Boardman (Jez Quigley), George Jackos (Sergei Kasparov), Tom Wisdom (Tom Ferguson), Naomi Radcliffe (Alison Wakefield), Amanda Barrie (Alma Sedgwick), Sue Nicholls (Audrey Roberts), Steven Arnold (Ashley Peacock), Betty Driver (Betty Williams), Kevin Kennedy (Curly Watts), Thomas Ormson (David Tilsley), Anne Kirkbride (Deirdre Rachid), John Bowe (Duggie Ferguson), Eileen Derbyshire (Emily Bishop), John Savident (Fred Elliott), Helen Worth (Gail Platt), Bill Tarmey (Jack Duckworth), Vicky Entwistle (Janice Battersby), Charles Lawson (Jim McDonald), William Roache (Ken Barlow), Michael Le Vell (Kevin Webster), Jane Danson (Leanne Tilsley), Bruce Jones (Les Battersby), Jacqueline Pirie (Linda Sykes), Paul Fox (Mark Redman), Sean Wilson (Martin Platt), Tracy Shaw (Maxine Peacock), Johnny Briggs (Mike Baldwin), Denise Welch (Natalie Horrocks), Rebecca Sarker (Nita Desai), Malcolm Hebden (Norris Cole), Jill Halfpenny (Rebecca Hopkins), Barbara Knox (Rita Sullivan), David Neilson (Roy Cropper), Sally Whittaker (Sally Webster), Tina O'Brien (Sarah-Lousie Platt), Emma Woodward (Sophie Webster), Martin Hancock (Spider Nugent), Simon Gregson (Steve McDonald), Nigel Pivaro (Terry Duckworth), Georgia Taylor (Toyah Battersby), Alan Halsall (Tyronne Dobbs), Liz Dawn (Vera Duckworth), Chris Bisson (Vikram Dessai), James Gaddas (Vinny Sorrell).

25.12.2000 "Natalie is stunned by Kevin's revelation. The Platts gather for Christmas"   DB / DBS
Duration: 52 minutes.
Written by Julie Gearey; executive producer Jane Macnaught; directed by John Anderson.

With Debbie Howard (Shirley Stewart), Tara Pendergast (Kerry Irving), Caroline O'Neill (Andrea Clayton), Lee Booth (Paul Clayton), Annabelle Tarrant (Alice Watts), Joe Simpson (Alex Swinton), John Bowe (Duggie Ferguson), Beverley Callard (Liz McDonald), Julie Hesmondhalgh (Hayley Patterson), Helen Worth (Gail Platt), Alan Halsall (Tyronne Dobbs), Bruce Jones (Les Battersby), Johnny Briggs (Mike Baldwin), David Neilson (Roy Cropper), Anne Kirkbride (Deirdre Rachid), John Savident (Fred Elliott), Georgia Taylor (Toyah Battersby), Barbara Knox (Rita Sullivan), Bill Tarmey (Jack Duckworth), Sue Nicholls (Audrey Roberts), Jill Halfpenny (Rebecca Hopkins), Niamh Daly (Nurse Carol Delaney), Ryan Thomas (JasonGrimshaw), Maggie Jones (Blanche Hunt), Angela Lonsdale (Emma Watts), Gary Damer (Wayne Hayes), Jack P. Shepherd (David Platt), Tina O'Brien (Sarah-Lousie Platt), Richard Standing (Danny Hargreaves), Suranne Jones (Mandy Phillips).

25.12.2001 "Is Jack having a heart attack? Deirdre and Dev sleep together"   DB / DBS
Duration: 51 minutes.
Written by David Lane; executive producer Jane Macnaught; directed by John Anderson.

With Geoffrey Banks (Wally), Daniel Poyser (Police Constable Watson), Michelle Newell (Gill Gregory), John O'Neill (Luke Ashton), Marcus Romer (DS Wilson), Bruce Jones (Les Battersby), Vicky Entwistle (Janice Battersby), Charles Dale (Dennis Stringer), Sean Wilson (Martin Platt), Sally Whittaker (Sally Webster), Georgia Taylor (Toyah Battersby), John Savident (Fred Elliott), Jack P. Shepherd (David Platt), Clare McGlinn (Charlie Ramsden), Stephen Beckett (Matt Ramsden), Melanie Kilburn (Evelyn Sykes), Scott Wright (Sam Kingston), Sue Nicholls (Audrey Roberts), Emma Woodward (Sophie Webster), Helen Flanagan (Rosie Webster), Tina O'Brien (Sarah-Lousie Platt), Bruno Langley (Todd Grimshaw), Julie Hesmondhalgh (Hayley Patterson), Malcolm Hebden (Norris Cole), David Neilson (Roy Cropper), Chris Gascoyne (Peter Barlow), Sally Lindsay (Shelly Unwin), Simon Gregson (Steve McDonald), Sue Cleaver (Elieen Grimshaw), Suranne Jones (Mandy Phillips), William Tarmey (Jack Duckworth), Elizabeth Dawn (Vera Duckworth), Alan Halsall (Tyronne Dobbs), Anne Kirkbride (Deirdre Rachid), William Roache (Ken Barlow), Maggie Jones (Blanche Hunt), Jimmi Harkishin (Dev Alahan), Jennifer James (Geena Gregory), Shobna Gulati (Sunita Parekh), Jennie McAlpine (Fiz Brown), Steven Arnold (Ashley Peacock), Tracy Shaw (Maxine Peacock), Nigel Pivaro (Terry Duckworth).

26.12.2001   DB / DBSW
Duration: 50 minutes.
Written by Mark Wadlow; executive producer Jane Macnaught; directed by John Anderson.

25.12.2002 "Richard nearly smothers Emily with a pillow"   DB / DBSW
Duration: 52 minutes.
Written by Peter Whalley; executive producer Carolyn Reynolds; produced by Kieran Roberts; directed by Tim Dowd.

With Tina O'Brien (Sarah-Lousie Platt), Helen Worth (Gail Hillman), Brian Capron (Richard Hillman), Jack P. Shepherd (David Platt), Sue Nicholls (Audrey Roberts), Roy Hudd (Archie Shuttleworth), Eileen Derbyshire (Emily Bishop), Malcolm Hebden (Norris Cole), Chris Gascoyne (Peter Barlow), Sally Lindsay (Shelly Unwin), Anne Kirkbride (Deirdre Rachid), William Roache (Ken Barlow), Maggie Jones (Blanche Hunt), Kathyrn Hunt (Angela Nelson), Richard Fleeshman (Craig Nelson), Thomas Craig (Tommy Nelson), Lucy-Jo Hudson (Katy Harris), Georgia Taylor (Toyah Battersby), Samia Ghadie (Maria Sutherland), Jennie McAlpine (Fiz Brown), Simon Gregson (Steve McDonald), Sue Cleaver (Elieen Grimshaw), Shobna Gulati (Sunita Parekh), Julie Hesmondhalgh (Hayley Patterson), William Tarmey (Jack Duckworth), Alan Halsall (Tyronne Dobbs), Steven Arnold (Ashley Peacock), John Savident (Fred Elliott), Bruce Jones (Les Battersby), Andrew Whyment (Kirk Sutherland), Paul Warriner (John Arnley), Elizabeth Dawn (Vera Duckworth), Barbara Knox (Rita Sullivan), Kate Ford (Tracy Preston), Jimmi Harkishin (Dev Alahan), Suranne Jones (Mandy Phillips), Prunella Gee (Doreen Heavey), Tracy Shaw (Maxine Peacock).

CORONATION STREET (continued)

25.12.2003 "Roy buys a virtual baby off the internet. Blanche buys Tracy a house" DB / DBSW
Duration: 50 minutes.

Written by Stephen Lowe; executive producer Carolyn Reynolds; produced by Kieran Roberts; directed by Charles Lauder.

With Julia Deakin (Brenda Fearns), Julie Hesmondhalgh (Hayley Patterson), David Neilson (Roy Cropper), Simon Gregson (Steve McDonald), Suranne Jones (Mandy Phillips), Anne Kirkbride (Deirdre Rachid), William Roache (Ken Barlow), Maggie Jones (Blanche Hunt), Lucy-Jo Hudson (Katy Harris), Sean Wilson (Martin Platt), Sally Lindsay (Shelly Unwin), Eileen Derbyshire (Emily Bishop), Barbara Knox (Rita Sullivan), Betty Driver (Betty Williams), Susie Blake (Bev Unwin), Thomas Craig (Tommy Nelson), Kathyrn Hunt (Angela Nelson), Richard Fleeshman (Craig Nelson), Tina O'Brien (Sarah-Lousie Platt), Bruno Langley (Todd Grimshaw), Malcolm Hebden (Norris Cole), Andrew Whyment (Kirk Sutherland), Jennie McAlpine (Fiz Brown), Alan Halsall (Tyronne Dobbs), Kate Ford (Tracy Barlow), Sue Cleaver (Elieen Grimshaw), Shobna Gulati (Sunita Parekh), Keith Duffy (Ciaran McCarthy), Helen Worth (Gail Platt), Sue Nicholls (Audrey Roberts), Jack P. Shepherd (David Platt), Adam Rickitt (Nick Tilsley).

25.12.2004 "Tracy and Steve race to find Karen" DB / DBSW
Duration: 48 minutes.

Written by John Fay; script supervisor Helen Moran; story associates Jane Pearson, Lyn Papadopoulos, Cathianne Hall, Jane Marlow and Lesley Westhead; series editor Gareth Philips; story editor Mark Bickerton; script editors Bryan Kirkwood and Jenny White; executive producer Carolyn Reynolds; produced by Tony Wood; directed by Terry Dyddgen-Jones.

With Andy Whyment (Kirk Sutherland), Yvonne O'Grady (Yvonne Casey), Anny Tobin (Beryl Peacock), Simon Gregson (Steve McDonald), Kate Ford (Tracy Barlow), Bruce Jones (Les Battersby), Suranne Jones (Mandy Phillips), Sue Cleaver (Elieen Grimshaw), Julia Haworth (Claire Peacock), Steven Arnold (Ashley Peacock), Johnny Briggs (Mike Baldwin), John Savident (Fred Elliott), Julie Hesmondhalgh (Hayley Patterson), David Neilson (Roy Cropper), Alan Halsall (Tyronne Dobbs), William Roache (Ken Barlow), Bradley Walsh (Danny Baldwin), Beverley Callard (Liz McDonald), Anne Kirkbride (Deirdre Rachid), Jennie McAlpine (Fiz Brown), Wendi Peters (Cilla Brown), Sam Aston (Chesney Brown), William Tarmey (Jack Duckworth), Elizabeth Dawn (Vera Duckworth), Ryan Thomas (JasonGrimshaw), Antony Cotton (Sean Tully), Jenny Platt (Violet Wilson), Sean Wilson (Martin Platt), Nikki Sanderson (Candice Stowe), Samia Ghadie (Maria Sutherland), Debra Stephenson (Frankie Baldwin), Eileen Derbyshire (Emily Bishop), Sue Nicholls (Audrey Roberts), Barbara Knox (Rita Sullivan), Benjamin Beresford (Joshua Peacock), Bill Ward (Charlie Stubbs), Malcolm Hebden (Norris Cole), Mark Hallett (Boris Weaver), Sally Lindsay (Shelly Unwin), Keith Duffy (Ciaran McCarthy), Lucy-Jo Hudson (Katy Harris), Gerry Hinks (Vicar), Maggie Jones (Blanche Hunt), Rupert Hill (Jamie Baldwin), Danny Young (Warren Baldwin).

―――――――――――――――――――――――――――――――――――――

A Granada Manchester production. Transmission details are for the Central region. Duration: 22 minutes.

	Production No	Holding / Source
25.12.2005 "Claire reveals she is pregnant"		DB / DBSW

Duration: 48 minutes.

Written by Joe Turner; script supervisor Joyce Kitchen; series editor Gareth Philips; story editor Bryan Kirkwood; script editors Jenny White and Anita Turner; head of production Trina Fraser; produced by Tony Wood; directed by John Anderson.

With Patricia Brake (Viv Baldwin), Rupert Hill (Jamie Baldwin), Sally Whittaker (Sally Webster), Kate Ford (Tracy Preston Nee Barlow), Steven Arnold (Ashley Peacock), Ian Reddington (Vernon Tomlin), Wendi Peters (Cilla Brown), Bradley Walsh (Danny Baldwin), Maggie Jones (Blanche Hunt), Julia Haworth (Claire Peacock), John Savident (Fred Elliott), Johnny Briggs (Mike Baldwin), Pauline Fleming (Penny King), Sam Robertson (Adam Barlow), Jane Danson (Leanne Tilsley), Jennie McAlpine (Fiz Brown), Andrew Whyment (Kirk Sutherland), Bruce Jones (Les Battersby-Brown), Jayne Tunnicliffe (Yana Lumb), Sam Aston (Chesney Brown), Lynne Pearson (Carol Baldwin), Elizabeth Dawn (Vera Duckworth), Debra Stephenson (Frankie Baldwin), Richard Fleeshman (Craig Nelson), Ian Redford (Phil Nail), Simon Gregson (Steve McDonald), Beverley Callard (Liz McDonald), Emma Stansfield (Ronnie Clayton), William Roache (Ken Barlow), Anne Kirkbride (Deirdre Rachid / Barlow), William Tarmey (Jack Duckworth), Sally Lindsay (Shelley Unwin), Susie Blake (Bev Unwin), Bill Ward (Charlie Stubbs), Tony Slattery (Eric), Sue Nicholls (Audrey Roberts), Michael Le Vell (Kevin Webster), Brooke Vincent (Sophie Webster), Helen Flanagan (Rosie Webster), Edward Applewhite.

26.12.2005 **CORONATION STREET PANTO: Cinderella** DB / DBSW
Duration: 48 minutes.

Written by John Stevenson; script associate Karl Lucas; script supervisor Nicky Gillham; music by Dorothy Fields, Jimmy McHugh and Mark Hinton Stewart; executive producer Tony Wood; head of production Trina Fraser; produced by Gareth Philips; directed by Tony Prescott.

With Brooke Vincent (Sophie Webster), Sam Aston (Chesney Battersby-Brown), Sally Lindsay (Shelley Unwin), William Tarmey (Jack Duckworth), Bradley Walsh (Danny Baldwin), Debra Stephenson (Frankie Baldwin), Antony Cotton (Sean Tully), Maggie Jones (Blanche Hunt), Jennie McAlpine (Fiz Brown), John Savident (Fred Elliott), Tina O'Brien (Sarah Platt), Andrew Whyment (Kirk Sutherland), Roy Hudd (Archie Shuttleworth), David Neilson (Roy Cropper), Malcolm Hebden (Norris Cole), Rupert Hill (Jamie Baldwin), Bruce Jones (Les Battersby-Brown), Sally Whittaker (Sally Webster), Susie Blake (Bev Unwin), Amy Walton (Bethany Platt), Emily Walton (Bethany Platt), Wendi Peters (Cilla Battersby-Brown), Danny Young (Warren Baldwin), Nikki Sanderson (Candice Stowe), Thomas Craig (Tommy Harris), Jimmi Harkishin (Dev Alahan), Peter Schmeichel (Himself).

26.12.2005 "An unwanted Christmas present awaits Ronnie. Mike refuses to accept help" - a DB / DBSW

Written by Jonathan Harvey; script supervisor Brenda Bentham; series editor Gareth Philips; story editor Bryan Kirkwood; script editors Jenny White and Anita Turner; head of production Trina Fraser; produced by Tony Wood; directed by Alan Wareing.

With Ian Reddington (Vernon Tomlin), Brooke Vincent (Sophie Webster), Steven Arnold (Ashley Peacock), Michael Le Vell (Kevin Webster), Johnny Briggs (Mike Baldwin), Bradley Walsh (Danny Baldwin), John Savident (Fred Elliott), Elizabeth Dawn (Vera Duckworth), Pauline Fleming (Penny King), Patricia Brake (Viv Baldwin), Sam Robertson (Adam Barlow), Simon Gregson (Steve McDonald), Emma Stansfield (Ronnie Clayton), Jane Danson (Leanne Tilsley), Sally Whittaker (Sally Webster), Helen Flanagan (Rosie Webster), Debra Stephenson (Frankie Baldwin), Rupert Hill (Jamie Baldwin), Vicky Entwistle (Janice Battersby), Daryl Kwan (Mr Wong), Wendi Peters (Cilla Brown), Bruce Jones (Les Battersby-Brown), Beverley Callard (Liz McDonald), Susie Blake (Bev Unwin), Julia Haworth (Claire Peacock), William Tarmey (Jack Duckworth), Antony Cotton (Sean Tully), Ian Redford (Phil Nail), David Crellin (Jimmy Clayton), Lynne Pearson (Carol Baldwin), Richard Fleeshman (Craig Nelson), Maggie McCarthy.

25.12.2006 "David unveils Ivy's secret diary. Emma brings a baby to the Grimshaw household...." DB / DBSW
Duration: 48 minutes.

Written by Stephen Russell; script supervisor Brenda Bentham; script editors Sarah Mann and Angela Sinden; assistant producer Gavin Blyth; executive producer Kieran Roberts; head of production Clare Winnick; produced by Steve Frost; directed by Tim O'Mara.

With Sherrie Hewson (Maureen Webster), Helen Worth (Gail Platt), Amy Walton (Bethany Platt), Anne Kirkbride (Deirdre Rachid / Barlow), Michael Le Vell (Kevin Webster), Eileen Derbyshire (Emily Bishop), Simon Gregson (Steve McDonald), Betty Driver (Betty Williams), Antony Cotton (Sean Tully), Alan Halsall (Tyrone Dobbs), Jack P. Shepherd (David Platt), Emily Walton (Bethany Platt), Tina O'Brien (Sarah-Lousie Platt), Steven Arnold (Ashley Peacock), Julia Haworth (Claire Peacock), Benjamin Beresford (Joshua Peacock), William Roache (Ken Barlow), Maggie Jones (Blanche Hunt), Sally Whittaker (Sally Webster), Brooke Vincent (Sophie Webster), Helen Flanagan (Rosie Webster), Barbara Knox (Rita Sullivan), William Tarmey (Jack Duckworth), Malcolm Hebden (Norris Cole), Vicky Binns (Molly Compton), Beverley Callard (Liz McDonald), Ian Reddington (Vernon Tomlin), Sue Nicholls (Audrey Roberts), Peter Armitage (Bill Webster), Sue Cleaver (Elieen Grimshaw), Ryan Thomas (Jason Grimshaw), Jenny Platt (Violet Wilson), Elizabeth Dawn (Vera Duckworth), Wendi Peters (Cilla Brown), Bruce Jones (Les Battersby-Brown).

| 24.12.2007 | 1/0694/6714 | DB / DBSW |
| 24.12.2007 | 1/0694/6715 | DB / DBSW |

CORONATION STREET

25.12.2007	1/0694/6716	DB / DBSW
26.12.2007	1/0694/6717	DB / DBSW
25.12.2008	1/0694/6975	DB / DBSW
26.12.2008	1/0694/6976	DB / DBSW
26.12.2008	1/0694/6977	DB / DBSW
25.12.2009	1/0694/7237	DB / DBSW
25.12.2009	1/0694/7238	DB / DBSW

See also: PARDON THE EXPRESSION

THE CORONATION STREET PANTOMIME

A Granada Manchester production for ITV 1. Transmission details are for the Central region. Duration: 48 minutes.

Written by John Stevenson; executive producer Tony Wood; produced by Gareth Philips; directed by Tony Prescott.

Debra Stephenson (Cinderella), Bradley Walsh (Prince Charming), Rupert Hill (Bttons), Malcolm Hebden (Ugly Sister), David Neilson (Ugly Sister), William Tarmey (Baron Hardup), Maggie Jones (Widow Twankey), Susie Blake (Fairy Godmother), Bruce Jones (Demon King), Antony Cotton (Aladdin).

Holding / Source

26.12.2005   DB / DBSW

See also: CORONATION STREET

THE CORRIE YEARS

A Shiver production for ITV 1. Transmission details are for the Central region. Duration: 23 minutes.

Series producer Kerry Allison.

Holding / Source

28.12.2012 **At Christmas**   HD/DB / HDC

A look back at some of the most memorable Christmas storylines on Coronation Street, from the departure of Alf Roberts to the wedding of Claire and Ashley Peacock.

Directed by Becky Sawle.

THE CORRIES ON THE ROAD

A BBC Scotland production for BBC 1 Scotland. Transmission details are for BBC 1 Scotland. Duration: 25 minutes.

The Corries.

Holding / Source

27.12.1977   J / 2"

COSGROVE HALL'S BOX OF CRACKERS

A Cosgrove Hall production for Thames Television. Transmission details are for the Central region. Duration varies - see below for details.

Main regular credit(s):   Produced by Mark Hall and Brian Cosgrove.

Holding / Source

30.12.1991 **The Talking Parcel**   C1 / C1

Duration: 35 minutes.

Alternative transmissions: ATV: 26.12.1978.

Adapted by Rosemary Anne Sisson; based on a story by Gerald Durrell; music by David Rohl and Stuart J. Wolstenholme; directed by Brian Cosgrove.

With Lisa Norris (Voice), Freddie Jones (Voice), Mollie Sugden (Voice), Roy Kinnear (Voice), Windsor Davies (Voice), Michael Hordern (Voice), Peter Woodthorpe (Voice), Harvey Ashby (Voice), Raymond Mason (Voice), Daphne Oxenford (Voice).

31.12.1991 **The Pied Piper Of Hamelin**   C1 / C1

Duration: 30 minutes.

Alternative transmissions: ATV: 01.01.1981.

Written by Robert Browning; music by David Rohl and Stuart J. Wolstenholme; directed by Mark Hall.

With Robert Hardy (Narrator).

This won a 1981 BAFTA award, so this date is clearly a repeat!

01.01.1992 **The Fool Of The World And The Flying Ship**   C1 / C1

Written by John Hambley.

02.01.1992 **Cinderella**   C1 / C1

Duration: 40 minutes.

Alternative transmissions: ATV: 28.12.1981.

Music by David Rohl and Stuart J. Wolstenholme; executive producer John Hambley; directed by Mark Hall.

See also: CHORLTON AND THE WHEELIES

COUNT ARTHUR STRONG'S CHRISTMAS SPECIAL (RADIO)

A BBC production for BBC Radio 4. Transmission details are for BBC Radio 4. Duration: 30 minutes.

Written by Steve Delaney; produced by Mark Radcliffe and John Leonard; directed by Mark Radcliffe and John Leonard.

Steve Delaney (Count Arthur Strong), Sue Perkins, Alastair Kerr, David Mounfield.

Holding / Source

26.12.2006   DA /

COUNT DUCKULA

A Cosgrove Hall production for Thames Television. Transmission details are for the Central region. Duration: 25 minutes.

Main regular credit(s): Created by Mike Harding and Brian Trueman; theme music by Mike Harding and Doreen Edwards; produced by Brian Cosgrove and Mark Hall.

Main regular cast: David Jason (Voice of Count Duckula), Jack May (Voice of Igor), Brian Trueman (Voice of Nanny), Barry Clayton (Narrator), Jimmy Hibbert (Voice of Von Goosewing), Ruby Wax (Voices).

SERIES 3

	Holding / Source
26.12.1990 **A Christmas Quacker**	1" / C1

See also: DANGER MOUSE

COUNTDOWN CHRISTMAS SPECIAL

A Yorkshire Television production. Transmission details are for Channel 4. Duration: 25 minutes.

Devised by Armand Jammot; written by Rick Vanes; theme music by Alan Hawkshaw; executive producer Arch Dyson; series producer Chantal Rutherford Browne; produced by Mark Nyman and Michael Wylie; directed by Brenda Wilson.

Richard Whiteley (Challenger), Carol Vorderman (Challenger), William G. Stewart (Host), Magnus Magnusson (Guest), Susie Dent (Mathematician).

	Holding / Source
25.12.1997	D3 / D3S

COUNTDOWN TO MIDNIGHT: TAKE THAT AND GUESTS LIVE AT THE O2 ARENA

A WhizzKid Television production for ITV 1. Transmission details are for the Central region. Duration: 75 minutes.

Script supervisors Cecilia Savage and Silvana Job; assistant producer Caroline Gale; associate producer Alex Muchamore; executive producers Lisa Chapman, Jessica Koravos, David Campbell, Sally Atkins and Malcolm Gerrie; head of production Philippe Luzy; produced by James O'Brien; directed by Simon Staffurth.

Kate Thornton (Host), Take That (Hosts), Sugababes.

	Holding / Source
31.12.2007	DB / DBSW

THE COUNTRY GAME

A BBC Bristol production for BBC 2. Transmission details are for BBC 2. Duration: 40 minutes.

	Holding / Source
20.12.1976 **Christmas Special**	DB-D3 / 2"

Produced and directed by Peter Crawford.

With Julian Pettifer (Captain), Phil Drabble, Elizabeth Eyden, Bernard Price, Richard Mabey, Gordon Beningfield.

COUNTRY HOLIDAY

A BBC production for BBC 2. Transmission details are for BBC 2. Duration: 45 minutes.

	Holding / Source
25.12.1977	DB-D3 / 2"

Produced by Douglas Hespe; directed by Rick Gardner.

With Crystal Gayle, Larry Gatlin, George Hamilton IV, Pete Sayers, Peace And Quiet, Family and Friends, The Bill Clarke 5.

23.12.1978	DB-D3 / 2"
23.12.1980	DB-D3 / 2"

Duration: 40 minutes.

25.12.1981	DB-D3 / 2"

COUNTRY HOLIDAY

A BBC production for BBC 2. Transmission details are for BBC 2. Duration: 40 minutes.

Music directed by Bill Clarke; produced by Douglas Hespe; directed by Rick Gardner.

Pete Sayers, Ginny Brown, Raymond Froggatt, Philomena Begley, The Minting Sisters, George Hamilton IV.

	Holding / Source
23.12.1980	DB-D3 / 2"

THE COUNTRYMAN AT CHRISTMAS

A BBC Bristol production for BBC 1. Transmission details are for BBC 1. Duration: 30 minutes.

	Holding / Source
24.12.1973	J / 2"

Produced and directed by Peter Crawford.

With Duncan Carse (Presenter), Michael Canney, Coach and Four.

22.12.1974 **The Week Before Christmas / Midwinter In Orkney / A Christmas Childhood**	DB / 2"

Produced and directed by Peter Crawford.

With Duncan Carse (Presenter).

Reversioned repeat of 24.12.1973.

THE COVENTRY NATIVITY PLAY

A BBC production. Transmission details are for BBC. Duration: 45 minutes.

Adapted by Douglas Allen; settings by Barry Learoyd; play production by Douglas Allen.

Joseph O'Conor (Gabriel), Joanna Horder (Mary), John Boxer (Joseph), James Viccars (First Shepherd), Julian Somers (Second Shepherd), Geoffrey Wilkinson (Third Shepherd), Robert Rietty (Herod's Herald), Alan Wheatley (Herod), George Howe (Jaspar, King of Taurus), Oliver Burt (Balthasar, King of Araby), Richard Pearson (Melchior, King of Aginara), Lalage Lewis (First Woman), Anne Stapleton (Second Woman), Rosamund Greenwood (Third Woman), Victor Adams (First Soldier), Anthony Viccars (Second Soldier).

	Holding / Source
24.12.1947	NR / Live

THE COVENTRY NATIVITY PLAY

A BBC production. Transmission details are for BBC. Duration: 45 minutes.

Adapted by Douglas Allen; play production by Douglas Allen.

Joseph O'Conor (Gabriel), Thea Holme (Mary), John Boxer (Joseph), James Viccars (First Shepherd), Julian Somers (Second Shepherd), Andrew Leigh (Third Shepherd), Robert Rietty (Herod's Herald), Alan Wheatley (Herod), George Howe (Jaspar, King of Taurus), Oliver Burt (Balthasar, King of Araby), Noel Howlett (Melchior, King of Aginara), Petra Davies (First Woman), Felicity Barrington (Second Woman), Rosamund Greenwood (Third Woman), Robert Brown (First Soldier), Anthony Viccars (Second Soldier), Peter Doughty (Angel), Richard Sherren (Angel), David Stoll (Angel), Robert Weeden (Angel), Kenneth Osbourne (Monk).

		Holding / Source
24.12.1949	First Performance	NR / Live
29.12.1949	Second Performance	NR / Live

THE COWARD REVUE

A BBC production for BBC 2. Transmission details are for BBC 2. Duration: 55 minutes.

Lyrics by Noël Coward; music by Noël Coward; designed by Stuart Walker; associate producer Freddie Carpenter; produced and directed by James Gilbert.

Georgia Brown, Ian Carmichael, Ray Davis, Nicky Henson, Cheryl Kennedy, Ronnie Barker, Dora Bryan, Ronnie Corbett, Clive Dunn, Danny La Rue, John Le Mesurier, Arthur Lowe, Kenneth More, Vanessa Redgrave.

	Holding / Source
26.12.1969	DB-D3 / 2"

The videotape is damaged.
See also: DAD'S ARMY (BBC)

CRACKERJACK

A BBC production for BBC 1. Transmission details are for BBC 1. Duration varies - see below for details.

SERIES 1

Transmission details are for BBC. Duration: 30 minutes.

Main regular credit(s):   Devised by Eamonn Andrews; written by Bill Douglas; produced and directed by Johnny Downes.

Main regular performer(s): With Eamonn Andrews (Presenter), Joe Baker, Jack Douglas, Trevor Little.

		Holding / Source
21.12.1955	Christmas Crackerjack	J /

With Tommy Elliott, Terry Hall, Bernard Riley, Eddie Mendoza and his Band.

SERIES 2

Transmission details are for BBC.

Main regular credit(s):   Written by Bill Douglas; produced and directed by Johnny Downes.

Main regular performer(s): With Eamonn Andrews (Presenter), Joe Baker, Jack Douglas, Eddie Mendoza and his Band.

		Holding / Source
19.12.1956	Christmas Crackerjack	J /

Duration: 55 minutes.

With Larry Parker, Shirley Abicair, Lenny The Lion with Terry Hall, David Berglas.

SERIES 3

Transmission details are for BBC. Duration: 45 minutes.

Main regular credit(s):   Written by Ronnie Corbett and Michael Darbyshire; designed by Marilyn Roberts; produced and directed by Johnny Downes.

Main regular performer(s): With Eamonn Andrews (Presenter), Ronnie Corbett, Michael Darbyshire, Bert Hayes and his Sextet.

		Holding / Source
18.12.1957	Christmas Crackerjack	J /

With Petula Clark, Lenny The Lion with Terry Hall, Larry Parker, Max Bygraves, Vicky Hammond.

An extract from the edition transmitted 18.12.57 exists on R3.

SERIES 4

Duration: 50 minutes.

Main regular credit(s):   Written by Jeremy Lloyd; produced and directed by Johnny Downes.

Main regular performer(s): With Eamonn Andrews (Presenter), Ronnie Corbett, Eddie Leslie, Pearl Carr, Teddy Johnson, Bert Hayes and his Sextet.

		Holding / Source
17.12.1958	Christmas Crackerjack	J /

Additional material by Alan Fell.

With Lenny The Lion with Terry Hall, David Berglas, Larry Parker and Nick Nissen.

CRACKERJACK (continued)

SERIES 5
Main regular credit(s): Written by Frank Roscoe; designed by Stanley Dorfman; produced and directed by Johnny Downes.
Main regular performer(s): With Eamonn Andrews (Presenter), Ronnie Corbett, Raymond Rollett, Pearl Carr, Teddy Johnson, Bert Hayes and his Sextet.

Holding / Source
24.12.1959 Christmas Crackerjack   J /
Duration: 55 minutes.
With Lenny The Lion with Terry Hall, Jerry Bergmann and Mimi, Ronnie Boyer and Jeanne Ravel.

SERIES 6
Duration: 50 minutes.
Main regular credit(s): Written by Stan Mars; designed by Charles Lawrence; produced and directed by Johnny Downes.
Main regular performer(s): With Eamonn Andrews (Presenter), Peter Glaze, Vivienne Martin, Leslie Crowther, The Bert Hayes Octet.

Holding / Source
22.12.1960   J /
With Shirley Abicair, Larry Parker.

SERIES 8
Duration: 50 minutes.
Main regular credit(s): Written by Eddie Maguire; produced and directed by Johnny Downes.
Main regular performer(s): With Eamonn Andrews (Presenter), Leslie Crowther, Peter Glaze, Jillian Comber, Pip Hinton, The Bert Hayes Octet.

Holding / Source
20.12.1962 Christmas Crackjack   J /
With David Nixon, Mark Wynter, Larry Parker.

SERIES 9
Duration: 45 minutes.
Main regular credit(s): Designed by Peter Brachacki; produced and directed by Johnny Downes.
Main regular performer(s): With Eamonn Andrews (Presenter), Leslie Crowther, Peter Glaze, Jillian Comber, Pip Hinton, The Bert Hayes Octet.

Holding / Source
19.12.1963 Christmas Crackerjack   J /
With David Nixon, Joe Brown and his Bruvvers, Daniel Rémy.

SERIES 10
Duration: 45 minutes.
Main regular credit(s): Produced by Johnny Downes.
Main regular performer(s): With Leslie Crowther (Presenter), Peter Glaze, Jillian Comber, Pip Hinton, Bert Hayes and his Octet.

Holding / Source
18.12.1964 Christmas Crackerjack   J /
Directed by Peter Whitmore.
With Harold Taylor.

SERIES 11
Duration: 45 minutes.
Main regular credit(s): Designed by Ken Jones; produced and directed by Peter Whitmore.
Main regular performer(s): With Leslie Crowther (Presenter), Peter Glaze, Jillian Comber, Valerie Walsh, Jig Jak, Bert Hayes and his Octet.

Holding / Source
24.12.1965 Christmas Crackerjack   J /
With The King Brothers, Joe Brown.

SERIES 13
Duration: 45 minutes.
Main regular credit(s): Written by Bob Block; music by Bert Hayes and his Band; designed by Jean Campbell; produced and directed by Peter Whitmore.
Main regular performer(s): With Leslie Crowther (Presenter), Peter Glaze, Christine Holmes, Jillian Comber.

Holding / Source
22.12.1967 Christmas Crackerjack   J /
With Dave Dee, Dozy, Beaky, Mick & Titch, Rolf Harris.

SERIES 14
Duration: 45 minutes.
Main regular credit(s): Music by Bert Hayes and his Orchestra; designed by Christine Ruscoe; produced by Peter Whitmore.
Main regular performer(s): With Michael Aspel (Presenter), Peter Glaze, Rod McLennan, Christine Holmes, Jillian Comber.

Holding / Source
20.12.1968 Christmas Crackerjack   J /
Written by Bob Block; music by Bert Hayes and his Orchestra; designed by Christine Ruscoe.
With Freddie Davis, The Scaffold.

CRACKERJACK

CRACKERJACK (continued)

SERIES 15
Duration: 45 minutes.
Main regular credit(s): Written by Bob Block and Tony Hare; produced by Peter Whitmore.
Main regular performer(s): With Michael Aspel (Presenter), Peter Glaze, Rod McLennan, Frances Barlow, Jillian Comber, Bert Hayes and his Orchestra.

Holding / Source
19.12.1969 **Christmas Crackerjack** — J / 2"
Directed by Peter Whitmore.
With Rolf Harris, The Scaffold.

SERIES 20
Main regular credit(s): Written by Bob Hedley, Tony Hare and Peter Robinson; music by Bert Hayes and his Orchestra; assistant producer Brian Penders.
Main regular performer(s): With Ed Stewart (Presenter), Peter Glaze, Don Maclean, Jan Hunt.

Holding / Source
24.12.1975 **Christmas Panto: Robinson Crusoe** — DB-D3 / 2"
Duration: 65 minutes.
Choreography by Jackie Jensen and Geoff Richer; designed by Christine Ruscoe; produced and directed by Robin Nash.
With Alan Curtis, Hilary Hutchins, New Edition, Keefe and Annette, Windsor Davies, Don Estelle, John Inman, John Laurie, Burt Rhodes and his Orchestra.

SERIES 23
Duration: 45 minutes.
Main regular credit(s): Written by Bob Hedley; music by Bert Hayes and his Orchestra; designed by Jim Clay; produced by Johnny Downes; directed by Alan Bell.
Main regular performer(s): With Ed Stewart (Presenter), Peter Glaze, Bernie Clifton, Jan Hunt, Val Mitchell.

Holding / Source
##.##.#### — DB / 2"
With Gene Cotton.
This edition recorded using strike breakers.

SERIES 27
Main regular credit(s): Written by George Martin and Mike Radford; music directed by Nigel Hess; designed by Graeme Thompson; produced by Paul Ciani; directed by John Bishop.
Main regular performer(s): With Stu Francis (Presenter), Leigh Miles, Julie Dorne Brown.

Holding / Source
24.12.1982 — DB-D3 / 2"
Duration: 41 minutes.
Production manager Valerie Wilson.
With Keith Harris & Orville, Shakatak, The Rockolas with Mike Read, Los Martinos, Larry Grayson, Su Pollard.

SERIES 28
Duration: 30 minutes.
Main regular credit(s): Written by Peter Robinson and Graham Deykin; music directed by Nigel Hess; designed by Carol Golder; produced by Paul Ciani; directed by David Taylor.
Main regular performer(s): With Stu Francis (Presenter), Leigh Miles, Julie Dorne Brown.

Holding / Source
23.12.1983 — DB / 1"
With The Great Soprendo, Chas and Dave.

SERIES 29
Duration: 45 minutes.
Main regular credit(s): Written by Graham Deykin and Peter Robinson; music directed by Barry Francis; designed by Rochelle Selwyn; produced by Paul Ciani; directed by Tony Newman.
Main regular performer(s): With Stu Francis (Presenter), Ling Tai, Sara Hollamby.

Holding / Source
21.12.1984 — DB / 1"
With Keith Harris, The Great Soprendo, Chas & Dave, Ralph McTell.

CRANFORD

A Thames Television production. Transmission details are for the ATV midlands region. Duration: 67 minutes.

Adapted by John Wells; based on a book by Mrs Elizabeth Gaskell; lyrics by John Wells; music by Carl Davis; magical adviser Ali Bongo; designed by David Marshall and Norman Garwood; executive producer Sue Turner; produced and directed by Pamela Lonsdale.

Judy Cornwell (Miss Matty), Colin Douglas (Thomas Holbrook), Ann Beach (Miss Betty Barker), Joyce Grant (Miss Pole), Pamela Charles (Mrs Forrester), Eleanor McCready (Mrs Jamieson), Jon Laurimore (Captain Brown), Barrie Gosney (Mr Hoggins), Janine Duvitski (Peggy), Kim Goody (Martha), Nigel Williams (Jem Hearn), Clifford Rose (Mr Johnson), David Kitchen (Mr Johnson's Assistant), Sandra Freeman (Deborah), Antony Brown (Peter), Martin Read (Young Thomas Holbrook), Robert Putt (Mulliner), Jean Boht (Lady Glenmire), Aubrey Woods (Signor Brunoni), Karan David (Fatimah), Stephen Whittaker (Mr Dobson), Paul Frowde (Fiddler), Charlotte Crow (First Child), Alison Portes (Second Child).

	VT Number	Holding / Source
28.12.1976	14270	D3 / 2"

From the original stage musical by Joan Littlewood and John Wells.

CRANFORD

Alternative/Working Title(s): MR HARRISON'S CONFESSIONS / MY LADY LUDLOW

A BBC production for BBC 1. made in association with Chestermead Ltd / WGBH Boston. Transmission details are for BBC 1.

SERIES 2

A BBC Productions production. Duration: 90 minutes.

Main regular credit(s): Written by Heidi Thomas; based on characters created by Mrs Elizabeth Gaskell; script executive Susie Conklin; script supervisor Vicki Howe; script editor Elizabeth Kilgarriff; music by Carl Davis; choreography by Jane Gibson; director of photography Ben Smithard; titles by Posy Simmonds; magical adviser Paul Kieve; consultant Gordon Ronald; art director Mark Kebby; designed by Donal Woods; executive producers Rebecca Eaton and Kate Harwood; co-produced by Rupert Ryle-Hodges; produced by Sue Birtwistle; directed by Simon Curtis.

Main regular cast: With Judi Dench (Miss Matty), Imelda Staunton (Miss Octavia Pole), Julia McKenzie (Mrs Forrester), Jonathan Pryce (Mr Buxton), Lesley Sharp (Mrs Bell), Jodie Whittaker (Peggy Bell), Tom Hiddleston (William Buxton), Matthew McNulty (Edward Bell), Bessie Carter (Margaret Gidman), Emma Fielding (Miss Galindo), Barbara Flynn (Mrs Jamieson), Lisa Dillon (Mary Smith), Michelle Dockery (Erminia Whyte), Adrian Scarborough (Mr Johnson), Deborah Findlay (Miss Tomkinson), Debra Gillett (Mrs Johnson), Jim Carter (Captain Brown), Celia Imrie (Lady Glenmire), Alex Jennings (The Reverend Hulton), Hannah Hobley (Bertha), Finty Williams (Mrs Clara Smith), Emma Lowndes (Bella Gregson), Roddy Maude-Roxby (Mulliner), Nicholas Le Prevost (Mr Peter Jenkyns), Alex Etel (Harry Gregson), Greg Wise (Sir Charles Maulver), Tim Curry (Signor Brunoni), Andrew Buchan (Jem Hearne).

		Holding / Source
20.12.2009	**August 1844**	HD/DB / HD/DB
27.12.2009	**October To December 1844**	HD/DB / HD/DB

THE CRAZY GANG - A CELEBRATION

A BBC Manchester production for BBC 1. Transmission details are for BBC 1. Duration: 60 minutes.

Documentary about the famous British comedy team, the Crazy Gang, comprising Flanagan and Allen, Nervo and Knox, Naughton and Gold and 'Monsewer' Eddie Gray. With contributions from Tommy Trinder, Charlie Chester, Richard Murdoch, Arthur English, Pat Kirkwood, Val Guest, Brian Johnston, Anne Hart, Danny Gray (Eddie Gray's brother) and George Holloway (Jimmy Nervo's brother).

Devised by Denis Gifford; assistant producer Paul Loosley; produced and directed by John Buttery.

Tommy Trinder, Charlie Chester, Richard Murdoch, Arthur English, Pat Kirkwood, Val Guest, Brian Johnston, Anne Hart, Danny Gray.

	Holding / Source
22.12.1983	C1 / C1

THE CRAZY GANG'S PARTY

A Jack Hylton TV Productions production for Associated-Rediffusion. Transmission details are for Associated-Rediffusion. Duration: 25 minutes.

Devised by Bud Flanagan; written by Bud Flanagan; music directed by Billy Ternent; produced and directed by Michael Westmore.

Arthur Askey, Bud Flanagan, Jimmy Nervo, Teddy Knox, Charlie Naughton, Jimmy Gold, Eddie Gray [as 'Monsewer' Eddie Gray], Peter Glaze, Alfred Marks, Chesney Allen, Sir Robert Boothby M.P., Donald Campbell, Jack Solomons, Jimmy Wheeler, Harry Green.

	Holding / Source
23.12.1957	R3N|n / R3

THE CRAZY WORLD OF JOE PASQUALE

An LWT production. Transmission details are for the Central region. Duration: 24 minutes.

Main regular credit(s): Written by Colin Edmonds, Rob Colley, John Junkin, Hughie O'Neill, Ray Tizzard and Brian Sykes; executive producer Nigel Lythgoe; produced by Mark Wells; directed by Ian Hamilton.

Main regular cast: Joe Pasquale (Host).

	Holding / Source
27.12.1998	DB / DBS

With Richard Whiteley, Maureen Rees, Leslie Grantham, Boyzone, Lisa Riley, Terry Ashe, Melinda Messenger.

CREATURE COMFORTS

An Aardman Animations production for ITV 1. Transmission details are for the Central region. Usual duration: 8 minutes.

Main regular credit(s): Created by Nick Park.

SERIES 2

Main regular credit(s): Script editor Toby Farrow; theme music by Rory McLeod; music by Mcasso; associate producers Claire Jennings and Abbie Ross; executive producers Peter Lord, David Sproxton and Nick Park; production manager Gareth Owen; produced by Julie Lockhart; directed by Richard Goleszowski.

		Holding / Source
25.12.2003	**Merry Christmas**	DB /

SERIES 3

Main regular credit(s): Script editors Toby Farrow and Paddy Makin; theme music by Rory McLeod; executive producers Miles Bullough, Peter Lord, Nick Park and David Sproxton; series producer Julie Lockhart; produced by Gareth Owen; directed by Richard Goleszowski.

		Holding / Source
25.12.2005	**Happy Christmas Everybody!**	DB /

Duration: 25 minutes.

Animated series using voices of the public.
See also: WALLACE AND GROMIT

CREATURE COMFORTS

CRIBBINS AT CHRISTMAS (RADIO)

A BBC production for BBC Radio 4. Transmission details are for BBC Radio 4. Duration: 15 minutes.

Main regular credit(s): Produced and directed by Martin Jenkins.
Main regular cast: Bernard Cribbins (Reader).

	Holding / Source
25.12.2007 **A Walk In The Park With Hodges**	DA /

Written by Alan Plater.

26.12.2007 **Ho! Ho! Ho!**	DA /

Written by Stephen Wyatt.

27.12.2007 **The Happy Prince**	DA /

Written by Oscar Wilde.

28.12.2007 **Mr Bromley's Folly**	DA /

Written by Roy Apps.

CROOKED HOUSE

A Tiger Aspect production for BBC 4. Transmission details are for BBC 4. Duration: 30 minutes.

Written by Mark Gatiss; script supervisor Karen Jones; music by David Arnold and Michael Price; designed by Sabina Sattar; executive producer Richard Fell; head of production Frith Tiplady; produced by Mark Gatiss and Paul Frift; directed by Damon Thomas.

	Holding / Source
22.12.2008 **The Wainscoting**	DB / DBSWF

With Lee Ingleby (Ben), Mark Gatiss (Curator), Beth Goddard (Mrs Glanville), Philip Jackson (Bloxham), Andy Nyman (Duncalfe), Julian Rhind-Tutt (Noakes), John Arthur (Coil), Cal Jaggers (Lucy).

23.12.2008 **Something Old**	DB / DBSWF

With Lee Ingleby (Ben), Mark Gatiss (Curator), Ian Hallard (Felix), Jennifer Higham (Ruth), Samuel Barnett (Billy), Rufus Jones (Niggs), Jayne Dickinson (Gracie), Jean Marsh (Lady Constance), Barbara Kirby (Miss Adams), Anna Madeley (Katherine), Lauren Jones (The Bride).

24.12.2008 **The Knocker**	DB / DBSWF

With Lee Ingleby (Ben), Mark Gatiss (Curator), Julia Dalkin (Jess), Daniela Denby-Ashe (Hannah), Derren Brown (Sir Roger Widdowson), Vanessa Havell (Lady Widdowson), David Ryall (Mr Paget), John Lebar (The Abomination).

CROSSROADS

Alternative/Working Title(s): THE MIDLAND ROAD

An ATV production. Transmission details are for the ATV/Central region. Duration: 25 minutes.

Main regular credit(s): Devised by Hazel Adair and Peter Ling; theme music by Tony Hatch.

Transmission details are for the ATV midlands region.

Main regular cast: With Noele Gordon (Meg Richardson), Roger Tonge (Sandy Richardson).

	Production No	VT Number	Holding / Source
24.12.1974 **Episode 2246**	9681	9681/74	J / 2"

Written by Peter Ling and Michala Crees; produced by Jack Barton; directed by Kenneth Carter.

With Noele Gordon (Meg Richardson), David Lawton (Mr Booth), Angus Lennie (Shughie McFee), Ann George (Amy Turtle), Jennifer Hill (Dot Smith), Zeph Gladstone (Vera Downend), Ronald Allen (David Hunter), Susan Hanson (Diane Parker), John Bentley (Hugh Mortimer), Morris Parsons (Wilf Harvey), Richard Frost (Roy Mollison), Penelope Shaw (Florrie Harvey), Sonia Fox (Sheila Mollison), Jack Woolgar (Sam Carne), Roger Tonge (Sandy Richardson), Jane Rossington (Jill Harvey), Edward Clayton (Stan Harvey), Trevor Bannister (Keith Willett).

31.12.1974 **Episode 2248**	9732	9732/74	DB / 2"

Meg and Hugh reminisce about 1974. Mr.Booth challenges Shughie to pipe in the new year with a rendition on the bagpipes.

Written by Peter Ling; produced by Jack Barton; directed by Michael Hart.

With Noele Gordon (Meg Richardson), David Lawton (Mr Booth), Angus Lennie (Shughie McFee), Ann George (Amy Turtle), Roger Tonge (Sandy Richardson), Trevor Bannister (Keith Willett), Jennifer Hill (Dot Smith), Caroline Dowdeswell (Anne Powell), Zeph Gladstone (Vera Downend), John Bentley (Hugh Mortimer), David Fennell (Brian Jarvis), Ronald Allen (David Hunter), Sonia Fox (Sheila Mollison), Penelope Shaw (Florrie Harvey), Morris Parsons (Wilf Harvey), Jack Woolgar (Sam Carne), Edward Clayton (Stan Harvey), Jane Rossington (Jill Harvey).

24.12.1975 **Episode 2450**	2973	2973/75	DB / 2"

Simon buys something very special.

Written by Michala Crees; script editor Ivor Jay; music by Tony Hatch; designed by Jay Clements; produced by Jack Barton; directed by Kenneth Carter.

With Noele Gordon (Meg Mortimer), John Bentley (Hugh Mortimer), Ronald Allen (David Hunter), Edward Clayton (Stan Harvey), Jane Rossington (Jill Harvey), Susan Hanson (Diane Parker), Zeph Gladstone (Vera Downend), Elizabeth Morgan (Rachel Fisher), David Henry (Bart Fisher), Barry Evans (Trevor Woods), Rosie Collins (Tina Webb), David Lawton (Mr Booth), Mark Colleano (Simon Whitaker), Ann George (Amy Turtle), Jo Richardson (Mrs Witton), Joy Andrews (Mrs Hope).

25.12.1975 **Episode 2451 Christmas Special**	2974	2974/75	DB / 2"

David Hunter extends an invitation.

Written by Arthur Schmidt; script editor Ivor Jay; designed by Jill Oxley; produced by Jack Barton; directed by Sid Kilbey.

With Noele Gordon (Meg Mortimer), Ronald Allen (David Hunter), John Bentley (Hugh Mortimer), Jo Richardson (Mrs Witton), Ann George (Amy Turtle), Jane Rossington (Jill Harvey), Edward Clayton (Stan Harvey), Susan Hanson (Diane Parker), Joy Andrews (Mrs Hope), Fiona Curzon (Faye Mansfield), Charles Stapley (Ted Hope), Gerald Case (Vicar), Sorrel Dunger (Sarah Jane Harvey), David Lawton (Mr Booth).

CROSSROADS (continued)

24.12.1980 Episode 3396 "Christmas Eve"   8486   8486/80   DB / 2"

Meg Mortimer is very surprised by news concerning David Hunter. Iris' Scott brags shamelessly.

Written by William Emms, Arthur Schmidt and David Garfield; story by Peter Ling; produced by Jack Barton; directed by Keith Farthing.

With Noele Gordon (Meg Mortimer), Lynette McMorrough (Glenda Brownlow), Pamela Vezey (Kath Brownlow), Peter Hill (Arthur Brownlow), Venetia Maxwell (Sister Celestine), Penelope Shaw (Mother Mary-Peter), Carina Wyeth (Alison Cotterill), Jane Rossington (Jill Harvey), Lynn Dalby (Rita Hughes), Kathy Staff (Doris Luke), Roger Tonge (Sandy Richardson), Tony Adams (Adam Chance), Philip Voss (Walter Fallon), Margaret John (Marian Owen), Graham Rees (Tom Peterson), Angela Webb (Iris Scott), Jack Haig (Archie Gibbs), Jean Munroe-Martyn (Disco Dancer), Samantha Hughes (Disco Dancer), Hilary O'Neil (Disco Dancer).

This tape includes a Christmas Message.

25.12.1980 Episode 3397 : Christmas Crossroads   8487   8487/80   DB / 2"

Reg Cotterill has a traumatic experience. Meg Mortimer learns something about Jill.

Written by Ivor Jay; produced by Jack Barton; directed by Geoff Husson.

With Noele Gordon (Meg Mortimer), Lynette McMorrough (Glenda Brownlow), Pamela Vezey (Kath Brownlow), Peter Hill (Arthur Brownlow), Venetia Maxwell (Sister Celestine), Penelope Shaw (Mother Mary-Peter), Carina Wyeth (Alison Cotterill), Jane Rossington (Jill Harvey), Lynn Dalby (Rita Hughes), Kathy Staff (Doris Luke), Roger Tonge (Sandy Richardson), Tony Adams (Adam Chance), Philip Voss (Walter Fallon), Margaret John (Marian Owen), Graham Rees (Tom Peterson), Angela Webb (Iris Scott), Jack Haig (Archie Gibbs), Jean Munroe-Martyn (Disco Dancer), Samantha Hughes (Disco Dancer), Hilary O'Neil (Disco Dancer).

31.12.1981 Episode 3554   9878   9878/81   DB / 2"

Produced by Jack Barton.

CROSSROADS

A Central->Carlton UK production. Transmission details are for the Central region. Duration: 25 minutes.

Main regular credit(s):   Theme music by Tony Hatch; executive producer Sharon Bloom.

Main regular cast: Jane Rossington (Jill Harvey (until 23.5.2001)), Jane Gurnett (Kate Russell), Kathy Staff (Doris Luke (until 6.3.2002)), Neil McCaul (Patrick Russell (until 12.12.2001)), Cindy Marshall-Day (Tracey Booth), Rhea Bailey (Chloe Simms), Colin Wells (Jake Booth), Joanne Farrell (Sarah-Jane Harvey), Sherrie Hewson (Virginia Raven), Julia Burchell (Nicola Russell/Berry), Luke Walker (Bradley Clarke (until 11.03.2002)), Jack Curtis (Daniel Curtis), Rebecca Hazlewood (Beena Shah), Peter Dalton (Minty Sutton), Gilly Gilchrist (Billy Taylor), Neil Grainger (Phil Berry), Keiran Hardcastle (Scott Booth), Marc Jordan (Des White), Natasha Marquiss (Mandy (until 12.3.2002)), Sarah Nerwal (Kully Gill), Roger Sloman (Rocky Wesson), Tony Adams (Adam Chance), James McKenzie Robinson (Ray Dobbs), Max Brown (Mark Russell (until 8.8.2002)), Rebecca Clarke (Joanne Gibson (until 21.3.2002, 13.5.2002-onwards)), Di Sherlock (Oona (7.6.2001-onwards)), Jeremy Bulloch (David Wheeler (13.06.2001 - seems to vanish from listings!)), Gary Webster (Richard (4.7.2001 - ?)), Carol Royle (Diane (28.06.2001 -?)), Jason Hetherington (Colin (25.07.2001- ?)), Geraldine Fitzgerald (Sylvia (17.8.2001-?)), Jim Dunk (Dave Stocks (24.10.2001-onwards)), Holly Newman (Sarah Harvey (13.12.2001-onwards)), Ray Lonnen (Vic Barnes (13.12.2001-onwards)), Jenny Jay (Anita (20.12.2001-?)), Sarah Joseph (Helen Stephanides (20.12.2001-?)), Danny J. Burns (Steve (2.1.2002-onwards)), Donna Leigh Bailey (Jenny (10.1.2002-onwards)), Olivia Hallinan (Hilary Barnes (30.1.2002-onwards)), Belinda Everett (Jazz Williams (4.4.2002-onwards)), Ramon Tikaram (Eddie Weaver (4.4.2002-onwards)), Doyne Byrd (Richard Baxter (2.5.2002-onwards)), Raine Davison (Abbie Baker (08.05.2002-onwards)), Jonathan Wrather (Sam Delaney (8.5.2002-onwards)), Sam Hudson-Thomas (Nicholas Hughes (9.5.2002-onwards)), Joyce Gibbs (Gay Owen (16.5.2002-onwards)), Lucy Pargeter (Helen Raven (15.7.2002-onwards)), Colin Maclachlan (Brian Noakes (until 16.07.2002)).

SERIES 1

Holding / Source

20.12.2001 "The Visitor To The Christmas Party"   DB / DBSW

Written by Helen Brandom; produced by Kay Patrick.

CROWN COURT

A Granada production. Transmission details are for the ATV midlands region. Duration varies - see below for details.

Main regular cast: Peter Wheeler (Court Reporter).

SERIES 1

Transmission details are for the ATV midlands region. Duration: 50 minutes.

Cast: With Peter Wheeler (Court Reporter).

	Production No	Holding / Source
27.12.1973 Murder Most Foul	P743/187	DB / 2"

Written by Pat Hooker; script editor Susi Hush; designed by Knowles Bentley; produced and directed by Quentin Lawrence.

With William Mervyn (Mr Justice Campbell), Terrence Hardiman (Stephen Harvesty), John Alkin (Barry Deeley), Arthur English (Mr Sampson), Liz Fraser (Lady Marjorie Esham), Betty Hardy (Miss Webster), John Le Mesurier (Reginald Standish), Gerald Flood (Sir Nicholas Esham), James Ottaway (Mr Prendergast), Tony Doyle (Bob Hammond), Richard Colson (Clerk of Court), Robert Putt (Jury Foreman), Joseph Berry (Court Usher), Peter Wheeler (Court Reporter).

Ring In The New Year

Duration: 25 minutes.

Main regular credit(s):   Written by Peter King; executive producer Michael Cox; produced by Kerry Crabbe; directed by Laurence Moody.

	Production No	Holding / Source
02.01.1975 **Episode 1**	P743/353	DB / 2"
03.01.1975 **Episode 2**	P743/354	DB / 2"

CROWN COURT (continued)

SERIES 4
Duration: 25 minutes.
Auld Lang Syne
Duration: 25 minutes.
Main regular credit(s): Written by Edward Boyd; produced by Dennis Woolf; directed by Bob Hird.
Main regular cast: With Peter Graves, Richard Wilson, Robert Flemyng, Virginia Starke, Miriam Margolyes, Joseph Brady, Gerald Slavin, Annie Ross, David McKail.

	Production No	Holding / Source
29.12.1976 **Episode 1**	P743/532	DB / 2"
30.12.1976 **Episode 2**	P743/533	DB / 2"
31.12.1976 **Episode 3**	P743/534	DB / 2"

CRUSH A GRAPE

A Border Television production. Transmission details are for the Central region.
Main regular credit(s): Designed by Ian Reed; associate producer Tony Nicholson; executive producer Paul Corley; produced and directed by Harry King.
Main regular cast: Stu Francis (Presenter), Charlie Cairoli, Linda Nolan, Nikki Ellen.

Holding / Source
30.12.1987 **(pilot)**   1" / 1"
Duration: 30 minutes.
Join Stu for a great Christmas party.
With Keith Harris & Orville, Pepe and Friends.

THE CRYSTAL MAZE

A Chatsworth Television production for Channel 4. Transmission details are for Channel 4.

Holding / Source
24.12.1994 **Children's Christmas Special**   D2 / D2S
Duration: 50 minutes.
Produced by Malcolm Heyworth; directed by David G. Croft.
With Edward Tudor-Pole (Presenter).

THE CUBE: CELEBRITY SPECIAL

An Objective Productions production for ITV 1. Transmission details are for the Central region. Duration: 48 minutes.
Main regular credit(s): Created by Adam Adler.
Main regular performer(s): Phillip Schofield (Presenter), The Body (The Body), Colin McFarlane (Voice of the Cube).

Holding / Source
24.12.2011   HD/DB / HDC
Executive producers Adam Adler, Andrew Newman and Nathan Eastwood.
With Ryan Thomas, Julie Hesmondhalgh.

23.12.2012   HD/DB / HDC
Executive producers Andrew Newman and Adam Adler; series producer Nathan Eastwood.
With Melanie Sykes, Ashley Banjo.

CUCUMBER CASTLE

A Robert Stigwood Organisation production for BBC 2. Transmission details are for BBC 2. Duration: 55 minutes.
Devised by Barry Gibb and Maurice Gibb; written by Barry Gibb and Maurice Gibb; music directed by Bill Shepherd; executive producer Robert Stigwood; produced by Mike Mansfield; directed by Hugh Gladwish.
The Bee Gees, Eleanor Bron, Pat Coombs, Julian Orchard, Blind Faith, Frankie Howerd, Lulu, Spike Milligan, Vincent Price.

Holding / Source
26.12.1970   C1|n / C1
Not a BBC show.

CUE GARY!

A Central production. Transmission details are for the Central region.
Main regular cast: Gary Wilmot, Martin Beaumont, Nikki Boughton.

Holding / Source
27.12.1987 **Cue Gary's Christmas!**   1" / 1"
Duration: 40 minutes.
Designed by Tony Ferris; produced by Tony Wolfe; directed by Dennis Liddington.
With Nikki Boughton, Janet Brown, Bill Oddie, Jim Bowen, Linda Lusardi, David 'Kid' Jensen, St Philip's Choir, The Kenny Warwick Dancers, Martin Beaumont.

THE CURIOUS CASE OF DR HERTZ VAN RENTAL

A BBC production for BBC 2. Transmission details are for BBC 2. Duration: 20 minutes.
A comic gothic horror story featuring the puppet stars of Dizzy Heights and House of Gristle.

Holding / Source
31.12.1995   DB-D3 / D3S

THE CURIOUS CASE OF SANTA CLAUS

An Edinburgh Films production for Channel 4. made in association with ABC Owned TV Stations / ABC Video Enterprises. Transmission details are for Channel 4. Duration: 51 minutes.

Santa Claus has an identity crisis. Is he really Santa Claus? Why do people call him Father Christmas? Wasn't he born St Nicholas? He goes to see a psychiatrist. In a hilarious travelogue, consultant psychiatrist Doctor Merryweather takes Santa from his birth in Turkey to our hearth in 1982.

Adapted by Bob Larbey; based on an idea by Robin Crichton; camera operated by Peter Warrilow; produced and directed by Robin Crichton.

James Coco (Santa Claus), Jon Pertwee (Doctor Merryweather), Sabina Franklyn (Barbara Jaeger), William Raymond (Professor Clement C. Moore).

Holding / Source
24.12.1982   1" / 1"

CYRIL STAPLETON AND HIS ORCHESTRA

An ATV production. Transmission details are for Associated-Rediffusion. Duration: 52 minutes.

Decor by Anthony Waller; produced and directed by Dicky Leeman.

Cyril Stapleton and His Orchestra, Eileen Joyce, Lynn Seymour, Desmond Doyle, Adele Leigh, John Hauxvell, Dennis Lotis, Jimmy Lloyd, Hendon County Grammar School Choir.

Holding / Source
25.12.1959   J /

THE CYRIL STAPLETON SHOW

An ATV production. Transmission details are for the ATV midlands region. Duration: 50 minutes.

Designed by Vic Symonds; produced by Dicky Leeman.

Cyril Stapleton and His Orchestra, Roberto Cardinali, Ronnie Carroll, The King Brothers, Cleo Laine, Janie Marden, The Hendon County Grammar School Choir.

Holding / Source
25.12.1961   J /

DAD

A BBC production for BBC 1. Transmission details are for BBC 1. Duration: 30 minutes.

Main regular credit(s): Written by Andrew Marshall.

Main regular cast: George Cole (Brian Hook), Kevin McNally (Alan Hook), Julia Hills (Beryl Hook), Toby Ross Bryant (Vincent Hook).

	Holding / Source
19.12.2000 **Christmas With Dad: Nemesis**	DB / DBSW

Postponed from 21.12.1999.
Executive producer Andrew Marshall; produced by Rosemary McGowan; directed by Angela De Chastelai Smith.
With Stephen Tompkinson.

DAD, YOU'RE A SQUARE

An ATV production. Transmission details are for the Southern Television region. Duration: 25 minutes.

	Holding / Source
25.12.1963	J /

DAD'S ARMY

A BBC production for BBC 1. Transmission details are for BBC 1. Usual duration: 30 minutes.

Main regular credit(s): Written by Jimmy Perry and David Croft; based on an idea by Jimmy Perry; theme music by Jimmy Perry and Derek Taverner; opening theme sung by Bud Flanagan; closing theme by Band of The Coldstream Guards; produced by David Croft.

Main regular cast: Arthur Lowe (Captain George Mainwaring), John Le Mesurier (Sergeant Arthur Wilson), Clive Dunn (Lance Corporal Jack Jones), John Laurie (Private James Frazer), Arnold Ridley (Private Charles Godfrey), Ian Lavender (Private Frank Pike).

SERIES 4

Main regular credit(s): Designed by Paul Joel.

Main regular cast: With James Beck (Private Joe Walker), Bill Pertwee (Chief Warden Hodges, The ARP Warden).

	Holding / Source
27.12.1971 **Battle Of The Giants!**	DB-D3 / 2"

Duration: 60 minutes.
Lighting by Howard King; directed by David Croft.
With Frank Williams (Vicar), Edward Sinclair (Verger), Colin Bean (Private Sponge), Geoffrey Lumsden (Captain Square), Robert Raglan (Captain Pritchard), Rosemary Faith (Ivy Samways), Charles Hill.

SERIES 7

Main regular credit(s): Directed by David Croft.

Main regular cast: With Bill Pertwee (Chief Warden Hodges), Edward Sinclair (Verger).

	Holding / Source
23.12.1974 **Turkey Dinner**	DB-D3 / 2"

When Jones accidentally kills a turkey, Mainwaring decides that Walmington on Sea should share a Christmas dinner.
With Talfryn Thomas (Private Cheeseman), Frank Williams (Vicar), Janet Davies (Mrs Pike), Harold Bennett (Mr Bluett), Pamela Cundell (Mrs Fox), Olive Mercer, Dave Butler.

SERIES 8

Main regular credit(s): Directed by David Croft.

	Holding / Source
26.12.1975 **My Brother And I**	DB-D3 / 2"

Duration: 39 minutes.
Designed by Robert Berk.
With Arthur Lowe (Barry Mainwaring), Bill Pertwee (Chief Warden Hodges), Frank Williams (Vicar), Edward Sinclair (Verger), Colin Bean (Private Sponge), Penny Irving, Arnold Diamond.

26.12.1976 **The Love Of Three Oranges**	DB-D3 / 2"

Designed by Barry Newbery.
With Pamela Cundell (Mrs Fox), Edward Sinclair (Verger), Bill Pertwee (Chief Warden Hodges), Colin Bean (Private Sponge), Frank Williams (Vicar), Janet Davies (Mrs Pike), Eric Longworth, Joan Cooper, Olive Mercer.

See also: THE COWARD REVUE (BBC) / DAD'S ARMY (RADIO) (BBC) / DAD'S ARMY: MISSING PRESUMED WIPED (BBC)

DAD'S ARMY (RADIO)

A BBC production for BBC Radio 4. Transmission details are for BBC Radio 4.

Main regular credit(s): Adapted by Harold Snoad and Michael Knowles; produced and directed by John Dyas.

Main regular cast: Arthur Lowe (Captain George Mainwaring), John Le Mesurier (Sergeant Arthur Wilson), Clive Dunn (Lance Corporal Jack Jones), John Laurie (Private James Frazer), Arnold Ridley (Private Charles Godfrey), Ian Lavender (Private Frank Pike).

	Holding / Source
25.12.1974 **Present Arms**	DA /

Duration: 60 minutes.
A VIP needs guarding, will Eastgate Platoon get the job?
Music by Jack Emblow and Len Johnson.
With Bill Pertwee (Hodges), Pearl Hackney, Jack Watson, Larry Martyn, Geoffrey Lumsden, Norman Bird, John Snagge.

See also: DAD'S ARMY (BBC)

DAD'S ARMY: MISSING PRESUMED WIPED

A BBC production for BBC 2. Transmission details are for BBC 2. Duration: 29 minutes.

TV documentary following the story of how two missing episodes of DAD'S ARMY were found and restored.

Script consultant Tim Niel; designed by Rudi Thackray; assistant producer Chloe Homewood; executive producer May Miller; produced and directed by Kathryn Ross.

Terry Wogan (Narrator), David Croft, Jimmy Perry, Dick Fiddy, Christine Slattery, Michael Billington, Graham McCann, Norman Langstone, Greg Dyke, Tony Benn, M.P., Paul Fox, Bill Pertwee, Ian Lavender, Clive Dunn, Sheelagh Storey, Andy Pawliszyn.

	Holding / Source
28.12.2001	DB / DBSW

See also: DAD'S ARMY (BBC)

DALZIEL AND PASCOE

Produced for BBC Birmingham by a variety of companies (see details below). Transmission details are for BBC 1. Duration: 90 minutes.

Main regular credit(s):   Based on the character created by Reginald Hill.

Main regular cast: Warren Clarke (Detective Superintendent Andy Dalziel), Colin Buchanan (Detective Sergeant Peter Pascoe).

SERIES 9: Dialogues Of The Dead

A BBC Birmingham production. Duration: 60 minutes.

Main regular credit(s):   Executive producer Mal Young; produced by Ann Tricklebank.

Main regular cast: With David Royle (Detective Sergeant Edgar Wield), John Light (Detective Constable Hat Bowler), James Quinn (Detective Constable George Headingly).

	Holding / Source
21.12.2002 **Episode 1**	DB / V1SW

Written by Hugh Stoddart; directed by Patrick Lau.

With Dervla Kirwan, Jack Dee, John Sessions, Dominic Mafham, Tim Plester.

22.12.2002 **Episode 2**	DB / V1SW

Written by Hugh Stoddart; directed by Patrick Lau.

With Lucy Davis, Andrew Woodall, Buffy Davis, Bill Maynard, Pauline McLynn, Francis Johnson, Debra Gillett, Pascal Langdale, Lorraine Bruce, James Puddephatt, Marc Bolton, Matthew Barry.

THE DAME EDNA EXPERIENCE

An LWT production. Transmission details are for the Central region. Duration varies - see below for details.

Main regular performer(s):   Barry Humphries (Dame Edna Everage).

SERIES 1

Main regular credit(s):   Research Claudia Rosencrantz; music directed by Laurie Holloway; theme music by Nic Rowley; choreography by Chris Power; programme consultants Iain Davidson and David Mitchell; production manager Myra Hersh; series producer Richard Drewett; produced by Judith Holder; directed by Ian Hamilton.

Main regular performer(s):   With Emily Perry (Madge).

	VT Number	Holding / Source
26.12.1987 The Dame Edna Christmas Experience	91595	D2 / 1"

Duration: 54 minutes.

Choreography by Chris Power; designed by Colin Monk and David Reekie; associate producers Lorna Dickinson and Sarah Williams.

With Lulu, Denis Healey [as Rt Hon Denis Healy M.P.], Roger Moore, Sir Les Patterson, Debbie Linden, Choristers of Wells Cathedral and Wells Cathedral School.

SERIES 2

Main regular credit(s):   Music directed by Laurie Holloway; theme music by Nic Rowley; programme consultants Ian Davidson and David Mitchell; designed by Margaret Howat; production manager Julia Weedon; series producer Nicholas Barrett; produced by Claudia Rosencrantz; directed by Alasdair MacMillan.

Main regular performer(s):   With Emily Perry (Madge), Robin Houston (Voice Only).

	VT Number	Holding / Source
22.12.1989 The Dame Edna Satellite Experience	92055	DB / 1"

Duration: 51 minutes.

With Ursula Andress, Robert Kilroy-Silk, Yehudi Menuhin [as Sir Yehudi Menuhin], Sir Les Patterson.

DAME EDNA IN HOLLYWOOD

A Together Again Productions production for LWT. Transmission details are for the Central region. Duration: 49 minutes.

Main regular credit(s):   Written by Barry Humphries and Ian Davidson; executive producer Barry Humphries; produced by Claudia Rosencrantz; directed by Bruce Gowers.

Main regular performer(s):   Barry Humphries (Dame Edna Everage).

	VT Number	Holding / Source
21.12.1991	92433	B / D2S

With Cher, Larry Hagman, Jack Palance, Mel Gibson, Bea Arthur.

26.12.1993	92744	B / D2S

With Ringo Starr, Burgess Meredith, Kim Basinger, George Hamilton IV, Chevy Chase, Rue McClanahan, Robin Williams.

24.12.1994 **Dame Edna's Hollywood Christmas**	92745	B / D2S

With Sean Young, Cesar Romero, Barry Manilow, Burt Reynolds.

DAME EDNA KISSES IT BETTER

An LWT production. Transmission details are for the Central region. Duration: 50 minutes.

Written by Barry Humphries, Ian Davidson and Jez Stevenson; executive producer Nigel Lythgoe; produced by Patricia McGowan; directed by John Birkin.

Barry Humphries (Dame Edna Everage / Sir Les Patterson), James Dreyfus (Doctor James Dreyfus), Rolf Harris, Cliff Richard, David Seaman, Melinda Messenger, Elle MacPherson, Jeffrey Archer [as Lord Archer], Kevin Lloyd, Seeta Indrani.

	Holding / Source
26.12.1997	DB / DBS

DAME EDNA LIVE AT THE PALACE!

A BBC production for BBC 1. Transmission details are for BBC 1. Duration: 60 minutes.

Executive producer Clive Tulloh; produced by Alex Hardcastle.

Barry Humphries (Dame Edna Everage), Jeremy Irons, Michael Gough, Ronnie Wood, Lulu, Lesley Garrett, Jerry Hall, Tamzin Outhwaite, Mel C.

	Holding / Source
30.12.2003	DB / DBSW

DANCE IN THE NEW YEAR

An Associated-Rediffusion production. Transmission details are for the ATV midlands region. Duration: 30 minutes.

Arranged by Eric Morley; produced and directed by Grahame Turner.

Kenneth MacLeod, Diane Hart, Eric Morley, Ken Barry, Tina Vaughan, The Sunnysiders, Lou Preager and his Orchestra.

	Production No	Holding / Source
31.12.1959	REM/1/31	J / 40

DANCE LEXIE DANCE

A Raw Nerve Productions production for BBC Northern Ireland. Transmission details are for BBC 2.

Lexie's awkward attempts to help his daughterto become a professional dancer bring them closer together.

Written by Dave Duggan; executive producer Robert Cooper; produced by Pearse Moore and Tim Loane; directed by Tim Loane.

Kimberley McConkey (Laura), Majel McLaughlin (Woman in Shop), Seamus Ball (Workmate), B. J. Hogg (Lexie).

	Holding / Source
25.12.1998	DB-D3 / V1SW
Duration: 15 minutes.	

DANCING ON ICE AT CHRISTMAS

An ITV Productions production for ITV 1. Transmission details are for the Central region. Duration: 48 minutes.

Written by Lee Stuart Evans; script supervisors Helen Dobson and Carolyn Davey; theme music by Paul Farrer; music by Paul Cartledge and Philip Jewson; designed by Markus Blee; associate producer Iain Peckham; executive producer Katie Rawcliffe; head of production Roz Pound; senior producer Cat Lawson; production manager Clare Nichols; series producers Jane Beacon and Glenn Coomber; produced by Heidi Shepherd and David Smyth; directed by Paul Kirrage.

Phillip Schofield (Host), Holly Willoughby (Host), Jayne Torvill (Coach), Christopher Dean (Coach), Robin Cousins (Judge), Ruthie Henshall (Judge), Jason Gardiner (Judge), Nicky Slater (Judge), Karen Barber (Judge), Tony Gubba (Commentator), John Sachs (Voice Only), Clare Buckfield, Zaraah Abrahams, Suzanne Shaw, Chris Fountain, Shakin' Stevens, Duncan James, Kyran Bracken.

	Holding / Source
25.12.2008	DB / DBSW

THE DANCING YEARS

An ATV production. Transmission details are for the ATV midlands region. Duration: 76 minutes.

Ivor Novello's romantic musical play, set in and around Vienna between 1911 and 1938. The story tells of three people bound together by love but whose lives are dramatically shaped by a promise made to a young girl.

Devised by Cecil Clarke; written by Christopher Hassall; based on a play by Ivor Novello; lyrics by Ivor Novello; music directed by Cyril Ornadel; choreography by Geraldine Stephenson; designed by Henry Graveney; associate producer Lorna Mason; produced by Cecil Clarke; directed by Richard Bramall.

Celia Gregory (Maria), Anthony Valentine (Rudi), Jeffrey Hardy (Officer), Neville Jason (Charles), Susan Skipper (Grete), Vera Jakob (Hattie), Tim Brierley (Franzel), Kate Coleridge (Lotte), Joyce Grant (Cacille Kurt), Corinna Seddon (Lilli), Jane Morant (Elizabeth), Marilyn Finlay (Wanda), Penelope Beaumont (Hilde), Belinda Sinclair (Emmy), Nina Thomas (Sonia), Judi Maynard (Sari), Jane Paton (Mitzi), Philip York (Officer), John Oxley (Officer), Richard Cornish (Officer), Geoffrey Leesley (Officer), Andrew Seear (Officer), James Murray (Officer), William Humbert (Officer), Terry Mitchell (Ceruti), Bruno Barnabe (Brietkopf), Joyce Graeme (Ballet Mistress), Stephen O'Shea (Carl), Michael Sheard (Captain Goetzer), Felicity Harrison (Lady Guest), Kevin Sullivan (Otto), Keith Jayne (Boy), Michael Hall (Oscar), David Rolfe (Manservant), Alan Collins (Nightwatchman), Roger Ostime (Footman), The Ambrosian Singers.

	Production No	VT Number	Holding / Source
30.12.1979	5181	5181/79	D2 / 2"
Postponed from 27.08.1979.			

DANGER MOUSE

A Cosgrove Hall production for Thames Television. Transmission details are for the ATV/Central region. Duration varies - see below for details.

Main regular credit(s): Created by Brian Cosgrove, Mark Hall, Mike Harding and Brian Trueman; theme music by Mike Harding.

Main regular cast: David Jason (Danger Mouse and numerous other voices), Terry Scott (Ernest Penfold and occasional other voices), Edward Kelsey (Colonel K / Baron Greenback (most episodes) and various other voices), Brian Trueman (Stiletto Mafiosa (most episodes) and various other voices).

SERIES 6

Transmission details are for the Central region.

Main regular credit(s): Written by Brian Trueman; produced by Brian Cosgrove and Mark Hall; directed by Brian Cosgrove.

		Production No	Holding / Source
25.12.1984	Once Upon A Time Slip	61374	1" / C1

Transmission details are for the Central region.

			Holding / Source
25.12.1985	Journey To The Earth's... Cor!		1" / C1

See also: COUNT DUCKULA

DANI'S HOUSE

A The Foundation production for CBBC. Transmission details are for BBC 1. Duration: 25 minutes.

Main regular cast: Dani Harmer (Dani).

SERIES 2

Transmission details are for CBBC.

		Holding / Source
21.12.2009	Scrooge Tube	DB / DBSWF

THE DARLING BUDS OF MAY

An Excelsior Films production for Yorkshire Television. made in association with Excelsior Films. Transmission details are for the Central region. Duration: 52 minutes.

Main regular credit(s): Based on novels by H. E. Bates; theme music by Philip Burley; music by Barrie Guard; executive producers Richard Bates, Vernon Lawrence and Philip Burley.

Main regular cast: David Jason (Pop Larkin), Pam Ferris (Ma Larkin), Philip Franks (Charley), Catherine Zeta Jones (Mariette Larkin), Christina Giles (Petunia Larkin), Katherine Giles (Zinnia Larkin), Stephanie Ralph (Victoria Larkin).

		Holding / Source
22.12.1991	Christmas Is Coming	DB / C1

Adapted by Richard Harris; produced by Peter Norris; directed by David Giles.

With Moray Watson (The Brigadier), Rachel Bell (Edith Pilchester), Abigail Rokison (Primrose Larkin), Ian Tucker (Montgomery Larkin), Ian Bartholomew, Tilly Vosburgh, Heather Canning, John Ringham, John Carlin, Murray Bryant, Aimee Bryant, Robert Gates, Max Mason.

SERIES 2

Main regular credit(s): Produced by Peter Norris.

		VT Number	Holding / Source
26.12.1992	Le Grand Weekend	L597/07	DB / C1S

Written by Stephen Bill; directed by Gareth Davies.

With Isla Blair, John Harding, Andy Serkis, Helen Pearson, Gabrielle Lloyd, Charmian May, Amanda Mealing, Danny McGrath, John Cater, Betty Marsden.

A DATE WITH MUSIC

An ITV Various production for ATV. Transmission details are for the ATV London region. Duration: 25 minutes.

Main regular credit(s): Produced by Bill Allenby.

SERIES 1

		Production No	VT Number	Holding / Source
19.12.1965	"Music from the Christmas Oratorio by J. S. Bach"	8829	8121	J / 40

An ATV production.

Introduced by Steve Race; devised by Wilhelmina Hoedeman; organist Clement McWilliam; conducted by Brian Brockless; directed by Fred Wilby.

With The New English Singers, The English Chamber Orchestra.

26.12.1965	Strike Sound			J /

A Westward Television production. Duration: 20 minutes.

Carols Of Thomas Merritt.

Introduced by Malcolm Arnold; directed by John Bartlett.

With Treverva Male Voice Choir, The Padstow Carol Choir.

		Production No	VT Number	Holding / Source
02.01.1966	"Unusual Christmas carols"	8887	8122	J / 40

An ATV production.

Introduced by Steve Race; devised by Wilhelmina Hoedeman; organist Clement McWilliam; directed by Fred Wilby.

With The New English Singers.

DAVE ALLEN

A BBC/Carlton production for BBC/ITV. Duration varies - see below for details.

Main regular cast: Dave Allen.

A Noel Gay Television production for Carlton. Transmission details are for the Central region.

Main regular credit(s):   Written by Dave Allen; script editors Ian Davidson and Peter Vincent; executive producer Bill Cotton; produced by Nick Symons; directed by Tom Poole.

	Holding / Source
26.12.1994	D2 / D2S

Duration: 37 minutes.

DAVE ALLEN AT LARGE

A BBC production for BBC 2. Transmission details are for BBC 2. Duration varies - see below for details.

Main regular cast: Dave Allen.

	Holding / Source
26.12.1979	DB-D3 / 2"

Duration: 45 minutes.
Written by Dave Allen, Peter Vincent and Ian Davidson; designed by Richard Morris; produced and directed by Peter Whitmore.
With Peter Bland, Kirsten Cooke, Robert East, Paul McDowell, Michael Sharvell-Martin.

See also: THE DAVE ALLEN SHOW (BBC)

DAVE ALLEN IN THE MELTING POT

An ATV production. Transmission details are for the ATV midlands region. Duration: 50 minutes.

Presented by Dave Allen; produced and directed by David Rea.

No guest cast.

	VT Number	Holding / Source
23.12.1969	9655	DB / 2"-C1

THE DAVE ALLEN SHOW

A BBC production for BBC 1. Transmission details are for BBC 1. Duration varies - see below for details.

Main regular cast: Dave Allen.

	Holding / Source
26.12.1984	DB / 1"

Duration: 50 minutes.
Written by Dave Allen and Peter Vincent; designed by Gloria Clayton and Raymond Cusick; production manager Bruce Millar; produced by Peter Whitmore and Bill Wilson; directed by Peter Whitmore and Bill Wilson.
With Susan Jameson, Michael Sharvell-Martin, Robert East, Paul McDowell, Sam Kelly, Roger Martin, Lisa Bloor.

31.12.1986	DB / 1"

Duration: 50 minutes.
Written by Dave Allen and Peter Vincent; produced by Peter Whitmore and Bill Wilson; directed by Peter Whitmore and Bill Wilson.
With Susan Jameson, Michael Sharvell-Martin, Robert East, Paul McDowell, Sam Kelly, Roger Martin, Lisa Bloor.

See also: DAVE ALLEN AT LARGE (BBC)

DAVID AND THE DONKEY

A Tyne Tees Television production. Transmission details are for the ATV midlands region. Duration: 25 minutes.

Designed by Eric Briers; produced and directed by Penny Wootton.

Edward McMurray (David), Derek Sydney (Esdras), Malcolm Taylor (Aaron), John Nightingale (Innkeeper), Jessie Evans (Wife), Ben Aris (Joseph), Cy Grant (Balthasar), Suresh Ashur (Caspar), John Slavid (Melchior), Elizabeth Fox (The Voice), Lisa Tait (Mary), Mokey The Donkey.

	Holding / Source
25.12.1967	J /

DAVID BOWIE - LIVE BY REQUEST

An Automatic Productions Inc production for ITV 1. Transmission details are for the Central region. Duration: 70 minutes.

Live concert recorded in New York June 2002, where David Bowie took song requests via a telephone link.

David Bowie.

	Holding / Source
26.12.2002	DB / DBSW

DAVID FROST'S END OF THE YEAR SHOW

A David Paradine Productions Ltd production for Channel 4. Transmission details are for Channel 4. Duration varies - see below for details.

Main regular cast: David Frost (Host).

	Holding / Source
31.12.1982	1" / 1"

Duration: 75 minutes.

Written by Tom Magee-Englefield, Mike Radford, Laurie Rowley, Peter Vincent and David McKellar; executive producer David Frost; produced by Derek Bailey; directed by Bruce Gowers.

With David Frost (Host), Alan Coren, Nigel Dempster, Jonathan Dimbleby, Peter Fiddick, Anthony Howard, Bernard Levin, Andrew Lloyd Webber, Joanna Lumley, Esther Rantzen, John Wells.

31.12.1983	1" / 1"

Duration: 75 minutes.

Written by Laurie Rowley, Tom Magee-Englefield, David McKellar, Graham Deakin, Peter Hickey, Spike Mullins and Wally Malston; script editor Fred Metcalf; designed by Bryce Walmsley; executive producer David Frost; produced and directed by William G. Stewart.

With Simon Cadell, John Wells, Alan Coren, Diana Dors, Clive James, Ken Livingstone, Denis Norden, Instant Sunshine.

DAVID FROST'S NEW YEAR SPECIAL

A Yorkshire Television production. Transmission details are for the ATV midlands region. Duration: 65 minutes.

Executive producers Michael Deakin and Frank Smith; produced by Hilary Lawson; directed by Peter Jones.

David Frost (Host).

	Holding / Source
01.01.1980	1" / 2"

THE DAVID NIXON SHOW

A Thames Television production. Transmission details are for the ATV midlands region. Duration varies - see below for details.

Main regular performer(s): David Nixon (Host).

	VT Number	Holding / Source
25.12.1974 **David Nixon's Christmas Magic**	10300	D3 / 2"

Duration: 40 minutes.

Written by David Nixon; music directed by Ronnie Aldrich; magical adviser Ali Bongo; designed by Peter Elliott; production associate George Martin; produced and directed by Royston Mayoh.

With Aimi MacDonald, Robert Harbin, Lynsey De Paul, Fred Kaps, Shari Lewis & Lamb Chop.

	VT Number	Holding / Source
23.12.1975 **David Nixon's Magic Hour**	12319	D3 / 2"

Duration: 50 minutes.

Written by David Nixon and George Martin; music directed by Ronnie Aldrich; magical adviser Ali Bongo; designed by Philip Blowers; production associate George Martin; produced and directed by Peter Frazer-Jones.

With Rolf Harris, Champagne, George Carl, Dash's Chimpanzees, Caterina Valente.

See also: GEORGE & MILDRED

THE DAWSON WATCH

A BBC production for BBC 1. Transmission details are for BBC 1. Duration: 30 minutes.

Main regular cast: Les Dawson (Host / Various roles).

SERIES 3

Main regular credit(s): Written by Andy Hamilton, Terry Ravenscroft and Les Dawson; produced and directed by Peter Whitmore.

	Holding / Source
23.12.1980 "Christmas"	DB-D3 / 2"

Designed by Bruce Macadie; production manager David Taylor.

With Lindy Benson (Dawson Control Girl), Ruth Burnett (Dawson Control Girl), Monica Teama (Dawson Control Girl), Roy Barraclough, Bella Emberg, Roger Avon, Neville Barber, Daphne Oxenford, Robin Parkinson, Gordon Peters, Michael Sharvell-Martin, April Walker.

DAY BY YESTERDAY

A Southern Television production. Transmission details are for the Southern Television region.

Contains Day by Day news reports from the past ten years, including behind the scenes footage of Carry On Girls.

	Holding / Source
31.12.1981	DB-DV / 2"

DAY TO REMEMBER

A Theatre of Comedy production for TVS. Transmission details are for Channel 4. Duration: 50 minutes.

Written by Jack Rosenthal; executive producers John Kaye Cooper and Martin C. Shute; produced by Humphrey Barclay; directed by Pedr James.

George Cole (Wally), Rosemary Leach (Hilda), Barbara Flynn (Judy), Ron Cook (Graham).

	Holding / Source
21.12.1986	1" / 1"

DEAD RINGERS

A BBC production for BBC 2. Transmission details are for BBC 2. Duration: 30 minutes.

Main regular credit(s): Music by John Whitehall.

SERIES 1

Main regular credit(s): Script supervisors Naomi Keenlyside and Katie Wilkinson; theme music by John Whitehall; director of photography Mike Radford; art director Liz Lander; designed by Graeme Story; production executive Claire Bridgland; executive producer Jon Plowman; line producer Ali Bryer Carron; produced by Bill Dare.

Main regular cast: With Phil Cornwell, Jon Culshaw, Jan Ravens, Kevin Connelly, Mark Perry.

	Holding / Source
26.12.2002	DB / DBSW

Written by Tom Jamieson, Nev Fountain, Laurence Howarth, Jon Holmes and Jon Culshaw; additional material by Simon Blackwell; directed by Jonathan Gershfield and Pati Marr.

With Catherine Marmier (Blob), Dominic Burdess (Blob), Colin Carmichael (Blob).

	Holding / Source
22.12.2003 **Christmas Special**	DB / DBSW

A look back at 2003.

Produced by Victoria Payne; directed by Geraldine Dowd.

02.01.2004 **New Year Special**	DB / DBSW

Produced by Victoria Payne; directed by Geraldine Dowd.

SERIES 4

Main regular credit(s): Executive producer Jon Plowman; produced by Gareth Edwards; directed by Ben Fuller and Pati Marr.

Main regular cast: With Jan Ravens, Phil Cornwell, Jon Culshaw.

	Holding / Source
26.12.2004 **Christmas Special**	DB / DBSW

With Peter Chong, Sam Hall, India Fisher, Paul Buchanan, Brian Hammond, Bill Olive, John Dartnell, Geoff Loynes, Daniel Elkan, Kieran Raja.

	Holding / Source
23.12.2005	DB / DBSWF

Written by Tom Jamieson, Nev Fountain, John Finnemore, Colin Birch, Richard Ward, Laurence Howarth, Steve Punt, Jon Culshaw and Jan Ravens; script supervisor Katie Wilkinson; music by John Whitehall and Richard Webb; production executive Jez Nightingale; executive producer Jon Plowman; series producer Bill Dare; produced by Caroline Norris; directed by Pati Marr and Ben Fuller.

With Jon Culshaw, Jan Ravens, Phil Cornwell.

DEATH AND THE DANCING FOOTMAN (RADIO)

A BBC production for BBC Radio 4. Transmission details are for BBC Radio 4. Duration: 90 minutes.

Jonathan Royal is a man rich enough to indulge his somewhat extravagant sense of the theatrical. But when he hits on the bizarre idea of throwing a weekend party with guests who have good reasons to loathe one another, his malicious comedy quickly turns to tragedy.

Adapted by Alan Downer; based on a book by Ngaio Marsh; play production by David Johnston.

Nigel Graham (Chief Detective Insector Roderick Alleyn), Laurence Payne (Jonathan Royal), Steven Pacey (Audrey Mandrake), Avril Clark (Sandra Compline), Stuart Organ (William Compline), Stephen Hattersley (Nicholas Compline), Jane Leonard (Chloris Wynne), Alan Downer (Doctor Francis Hart), Natasha Pyne (Mme Elise Lisse), Margaret Ward (Lady Hersey Amblington), Elaine Claxton (Troy Alleyn), Peter Tuddenham (James Bewling), Shaun Prendergast (The Reverend Copeland/Caper), Brian Hewlett (Detective Inspector Fox/Thomas).

	Holding / Source
27.12.1986 [Murder For Christmas]	DA /

DEATH COMES TO PEMBERLEY

A BBC production for BBC 1. Transmission details are for BBC 1. Duration varies - see below for details.

Mystery drama. On the eve of the Darcys' annual ball at their magnificent Pemberley home, Elizabeth and Fitzwilliam are entertaining their guests after supper when an unexpected visitor brings news of a murder in the woods.

Main regular credit(s): Written by Juliette Towhidi; based on a book by P. D. James; based on characters created by Jane Austen; produced by David M. Thompson and Eliza Mellor; directed by Daniel Percival.

Main regular cast: Matthew Rhys (Fitzwilliam Darcy), Anna Maxwell-Martin (Elizabeth Darcy), Rebecca Front (Mrs Bennet), James Fleet (Mr Bennet), Matthew Goode (George Wickham), Jenna Coleman (Lydia Wickham), Trevor Eve (Sir Selwyn Hardcastle), Penelope Keith (Lady Catherine De Burgh), Tom Ward (Colonel Fitzwilliam), Eleanor Tomlinson (Georgiana Darcy), James Norton (Henry Alveston), Nichola Burley (Louisa Bidwell), Philip Martin Brown (Mr Bidwell), Jennifer Hennesey (Mrs Bidwell), Joanna Scanlan (Mrs Reynolds), Lewis Rainer (Will Bidwell), Tom Canton (Captain Denny), Mariah Gale (Mrs Younge), Stephen Casey (Reverend Oliphant), Teresa Churcher (Mrs Piggott), Louisa Mal-Parker (Mrs Donovan), Alexander Bradshaw (Young Darcy), Royston Mayoh (Stoughton), Oliver Rix (Cartwright), Mike Burnes (Judge Moberley), Rachel Finnegan (Joan), Charlie May Clark (Betsy), Francis Paul King (Headborough Brownrigg), Kevin Eldon (Doctor McFee), Oliver Maltman (George Pratt), Tom Raven (Con Mason), Alexandra Moen (Jane Bingley), Christopher Wright (Frank Stirling), Ian Curley (John Simpson), Robin Bowerman (Buckle), Simon Hirst (Harried Farmer).

	Holding / Source
26.12.2013 **Episode 1**	HD/DB / HDC

Duration: 65 minutes.

27.12.2013 **Episode 2**	HD/DB / HDC

Duration: 60 minutes.

DEATH COMES TO PEMBERLEY (continued) British Christmas Television Guide

28.12.2013 **Episode 3** HD/DB / HDC
Duration: 60 minutes.

DECEMBER FLOWER

A Granada production. Transmission details are for the Central region. Duration: 75 minutes.

Newly-widowed Etta Marsh goes to stay with her elderly Aunt M, whom she has never met. She meets hostility and resentment from all the people who are close to the old lady. Etta is convinced that her aunt deserves — and will respond to — better treatment. Despite rows and a dramatic revelation by the family, she is determined to succeed.

Written by Judy Allen; music by Richard Hartley; camera operated by Ray Goode; designed by Chris Wilkinson; produced by Roy Roberts; directed by Stephen Frears.

Bryan Forbes (Harry Grey), Jean Simmons (Etta Marsh), Mona Washbourne (Aunt M), June Ritchie (Margaret Grey), Pat Heywood (Mrs Cullen), Ann-Marie Gwatkin (Jill Grey), Richard Warner (Doctor Waters), Richard Hope (Doctor Mere), Christopher Fulford (Engineer), Alan David (Cemetery Superintendent), James Carter (Dentist), Cyril Varley (Taxi Driver), Olive Pendleton (Wool Shop Lady), Judith Davis (Dress Shop Lady), Ann Aris (Receptionist).

	Production No	Holding / Source
23.12.1984	P775/15	1" / C1

Bryan Forbes' first acting appearance for seventeen years.

DECEMBER'S CHILD

An Associated-Rediffusion production. Transmission details are for the ATV midlands region. Duration: 25 minutes.

A little girl gets a donkey for Christmas when she complains her birthday presents are never separate from her Christmas presents.

Written by Mary Plumbly; produced and directed by Bimbi Harris.

Stephanie Voss (Gemma), Michael Goodman (Donald Seel), Susan George (Jenny Warren), Terence Woodfield (Martin Cooper), Grace Arnold (Hilda Vickers), Richard Owens (Jim), Joe Ritchie (Mr Price), Bobby Scott-Webber (Ned).

	Holding / Source
24.12.1963	J /

DEF II'S CHRISTMAS COMEDY CLUB

A BBC production for BBC 2. Transmission details are for BBC 2. Duration: 30 minutes.

Series editor Janet Street-Porter; produced by William Campbell; directed by Karen Skayfe.

Harry Enfield, Hale and Pace, Rory Bremner.

	Holding / Source
19.12.1988	DB / 1"

DENIS NORDEN'S WORLD OF TELEVISION

An LWT production. Transmission details are for the ATV midlands region. Duration: 50 minutes.

The Mexican glass muncher and the South African brick biter are two of the odder items that Denis Norden has picked from more than 500 hours of television programmes that he has watched around the world before making this personal selection of the funny, intriguing or simply unbelievable things that find their way onto the small screens in some countries.

Research Charles Brand and Stephen Smallwood; executive producer Richard Drewett; produced by Nicholas Barrett; directed by Ken O'Neill.

Denis Norden (Presenter).

	Holding / Source
28.12.1980	D2 / 2"

DES O'CONNOR ENTERTAINS

An ATV production. Transmission details are for the ATV midlands region.

Main regular performer(s): Des O'Connor (Host), Peters and Lee, Johnny Vyvyan, Jack Parnell and his Orchestra.

	Holding / Source
27.12.1974	J / 2"

Duration: 52 minutes.

Des 'Dimples' O'Connor returns to television with his unique brand of marvellous entertainment. It's all here - songs, jokes and sketches. Among his songs are Tie A Yellow Ribbon and Smile, Smile, Smile. And helping with the smiles in this bumper Christmas show is Colin Crompton, fresh from the Wheeltappers and Shunters Social Club, and Barbara Mitchell, star of Beryl's Lot.

Written by Michael Craig, Lawrie Kinsley, Ron McDonnell and Des O'Connor; music associate Colin Keyes; designed by Gerry Roberts; produced and directed by Colin Clews.

With Charlie Drake, Barbara Mitchell, The Mike Sammes Singers, Colin Crompton, Judy Buxton, Trevor Chance, Pat Carroll, Johnny Vyvyan, Eli Woods, Jack Parnell and his Orchestra.

THE DES O'CONNOR SHOW

An ATV production. Transmission details are for the ATV midlands region.

Main regular performer(s): Des O'Connor (Host).

	VT Number	Holding / Source
28.12.1973	8057/73	J / 2"

Duration: 52 minutes.

Written by Bryan Blackburn, Mike Craig, Lawrie Kinsley and Ron McDonnell; designed by Paul Dean Fortune; produced and directed by Colin Clews.

With Rod Hull, Bernie Winters, Patricia Carroll, Mike Winters, Jim Couton and Rex, Jack Parnell and his Orchestra.

THE DES O'CONNOR SHOW

DES O'CONNOR TONIGHT

A Thames Television production. Transmission details are for the Central region. Usual duration: 50 minutes.

Main regular performer(s): Des O'Connor (Host).

SERIES 1
Main regular credit(s): Programme associate Eric Davidson; music directed by Colin Keyes; designed by Philip Blowers; produced and directed by Brian Penders.

Holding / Source

27.12.1983 Christmas Show — 1" / 1"
Duration: 55 minutes.
With Jimmy Tarbuck, Marti Caine, Charlie Callas.

SERIES 2
Main regular credit(s): Programme associate John Graham; script associates Eric Davidson and Roy Tuvey; music directed by Colin Keyes; designed by Philip Blowers; produced and directed by Brian Penders.

Holding / Source

25.12.1984 Christmas Show — 1" / 1"
Duration: 55 minutes.
With Joan Collins, Dudley Moore, Alan King, Willie Tyler and Lester.

SERIES 3
Main regular credit(s): Programme associate Chris Greenwood; script associates Eric Davidson and Roy Tuvey; music directed by Colin Keyes; designed by Harry Clark and Philip Blowers; associate producer John Graham; produced and directed by Brian Penders.

Holding / Source

25.12.1985 — 1" / 1"
With Dudley Moore, Alan King, Joan Collins, Willie Tyler.

SERIES 4: Des O'Connor Tonight Live
Main regular credit(s): Additional material by Spike Mullins; script associates Eric Davidson, Wally Malston and Roy Tuvey; research Len Whitcher; programme consultant Chris Greenwood; designed by Harry Clark; associate producer John Graham; produced and directed by Brian Penders.
Main regular performer(s): With The Colin Keyes Orchestra, The Maggie Stredder Singers.

Holding / Source

23.12.1986 — 1" / Live
With Tom Jones, Shirley Bassey, Freddie Starr.

SERIES 5
Main regular credit(s): Script associates Bryan Blackburn, Eric Davidson, Wally Malston and Roy Tuvey; music directed by Colin Keyes; associate producer John Graham; produced and directed by Brian Penders.

Holding / Source

23.12.1987 Christmas Special — 1" / 1"
With Engelbert Humperdinck, Paul Nicholas, Gloria Gaynor.

SERIES 8
Main regular credit(s): Music directed by Colin Keyes; designed by Alex Clarke; produced and directed by Brian Penders.

Holding / Source

24.12.1990 — 1" / 1"
With Bob Monkhouse, Robin Day, Susan Hampshire, Jethro, Bananarama, Bernie Clifton.

SERIES 9
Main regular credit(s): Produced and directed by Brian Penders.

Holding / Source

23.12.1991 — 1" / 1"S
With Barry Manilow, Bernard Manning, Torvill & Dean, Vic Reeves, Cathy Dennis.

SERIES 10
Main regular credit(s): Produced and directed by Brian Penders.

Holding / Source

23.12.1992 — 1" / 1"
With Paul Anka, Sharon Gless, Brian Conley, Frank Bruno, Michael Bolton.

SERIES 11: 1
A Thames Television production for Central.
Main regular credit(s): Produced by Colin Fay; directed by Brian Penders.

Holding / Source

22.12.1993 — D2 / D2S
With Take That, Dinah Caroll, Ken Dodd, Michael Caine, The Nicholas Brothers.

DES O'CONNOR TONIGHT

A Thames Television production for Central. Transmission details are for the Central region. Usual duration: 50 minutes.

Main regular performer(s): Des O'Connor (Host).

SERIES 3
Main regular credit(s): Executive producer John Fisher; produced by Colin Fay; directed by Ian Hamilton.

Holding / Source

25.12.1996 **Christmas With The Stars**   D3 / D3S

With Julio Igelisias, Diana Ross, Lily Savage, Jennifer Paterson, Clarissa Dickson Wright, Julio Iglesias, Eric Sykes, Spike Milligan, Joe Pasquale, Vanessa Mae, The Back Street, The Woolpackers, Jennifer Patterson.

SERIES 4
Commissioned by Central->Carlton UK.

Main regular credit(s): Produced by Colin Fay; directed by Ian Hamilton.

Holding / Source

24.12.1997   DB / DBS

With Nick Berry, Todd Carty.

SERIES 5
Main regular credit(s): Script supervisor Ellie Gleave; music directed by Ray Monk; theme music by Colin Keyes; programme consultant Neil Shand; designed by Richard Morris; associate producer David N. Mason; executive producer John Fisher; production manager Mandy Lee; produced by Colin Fay; directed by Paul Kirrage.

Holding / Source

23.12.1998   DB / DBS

With The Spice Girls, Jackie Mason, Norman Wisdom, Barry Manilow, Joe Pasquale.

Commissioned by ITV.

Holding / Source

27.12.1999 **Christmas Special**   DB / DBS

Executive producer John Fisher; produced by Colin Fay.

With Pierce Brosnan, Robson Green, Charlotte Church, Celine Dion, Frank Skinner, Cast of 'Mamma Mia'.

24.12.2001 **At Christmas**   DB / DBS

Executive producer Richard Holloway; produced by Colin Fay; directed by Paul Kirrage.

With Victoria Beckham, Will Smith, Elton John, Anastacia.

31.12.2001 **At New Year**   DB / DBS

Executive producer Richard Holloway; produced by Colin Fay; directed by Paul Kirrage.

24.12.2002 **Christmas Special**   DB / DBS

Executive producer John Fisher; produced by Colin Fay.

With Barbara Windsor, Lionel Blair, Lee Evans, Joe Pasquale, Alan Davies, Darius Danesh, Declan Galbraith, Melanie Sykes.

DESMOND CAMPBELL FILM FOOTAGE

A BBC production. Transmission details are for BBC. Duration: 20 minutes.

Holding / Source

27.12.1938 **Dick Whittington And His Cat**   DB / C1

Written by Arthur Askey.

With Pamela Randall (Fairy Bow Belle), Cyril Fletcher (Emperor Of Morocco).

Television's first grand Christmas pantomime, written by Arthur Askey. This sequence opens with Pamela Randall as Fairy Bow Belle, and ends with Cyril Fletcher as the Emperor of Morocco.

23.12.1950 **Gala Variety**   DB / C1

With Tommy Cooper.

In 1949 the BBC purchased the old Gainsborough film studios in Lime Grove, Shepherds Bush. This was the first variety programme to be produced in the newly converted studios, in December 1950. It features Tommy Cooper in his first television appearance.

Footage recovered by the Alexandra Palace Television Society, filmed by Desmond Campbell.

DESMOND'S

A Humphrey Barclay Productions production for LWT. Transmission details are for Channel 4.

Main regular credit(s): Created by Trix Worrell.

Main regular cast: Norman Beaton (Desmond Ambrose), Carmen Munroe (Shirley Ambrose), Ram John Holder (Augustus 'Porkpie' Grant).

SERIES 6
Main regular credit(s): Produced by Paulette Randall.

Main regular cast: With Gyearbuor Asante (Matthew).

Holding / Source

19.12.1994 **O Little Town Of Peckham**   1" / 1"S

Duration: 50 minutes.

Written by Carol Williams; directed by Iain McLean.

With Geff Francis (Michael), Kim Walker (Gloria), Robbie Gee (Lee), Justin Pickett (Sean), Dean Gatiss (Ricky), Matilda Thorpe, Count Prince Miller.

THE DETECTIVES

A Celador production for BBC 1. Transmission details are for BBC 1. Usual duration: 30 minutes.

Main regular cast: Jasper Carrott (Bob Louis), Robert Powell (Dave Briggs), George Sewell (Superintendent Cottam).

SERIES 4

Main regular credit(s): Written by Steve Knight and Mike Whitehill; music by Matthew Strachan and Keith Strachan; designed by Andy Hamilton; produced by Nic Phillips.

Holding / Source

21.12.1995 **Thicker Than Water** D3 / V1S

While others may be celebrating the season, Bob and Dave can think of only one thing: avoiding Christmas Day duty.

Directed by Graeme Harper.

With Philip Whitchurch (Kelvin), Richard Clews (Santa), Freddie Stuart (Santa), Gordon Salkilld (Santa), Hilary Mason, Tony Purnell, Sakuntala Ramanee, Barbara Keogh.

SERIES 5

Main regular credit(s): Written by Steve Knight and Mike Whitehill; music by Matthew Strachan and Keith Strachan; designed by Andy Hamilton; associate producer Barry Read; produced by Nic Phillips.

Holding / Source

28.12.1997 **Go West Old Man** D3 / V1S

Duration: 48 minutes.

When ageing superintendent Frank Cottam goes missing in the Canadian Rocky Mountains, ace detectives Louis and Briggs are sent to track him down.

Line producer Barry Read; directed by Steve Knight.

With Rory McGrath (Tom Reid), John Ratzenberger (Edsel), Elizabeth Kelly (Mrs Connors), Brian Martell (Rattlesnake Jack), Jocelyne Loewen (Maisie), James Duggan (Priest), John Wright (Guard).

Barry Read was billed as Line Producer on this special, presumably he had to stay in Surrey and didn't go to Canada with the rest of the crew! :-)

See also: BERGERAC (BBC)

DIAL RIX

A BBC production. Transmission details are for BBC. Usual duration: 50 minutes.

Holding / Source

26.12.1962 **No Plums In The Pudding** J /

Written by Christopher Bond; music by Tommy Watt; produced and directed by Wallace Douglas.

With Brian Rix (Boy Rix), Basil Lord (Telephone Engineer), Colin Douglas (Fat Furniture Man), Andrew Sachs (Thin Furniture Man), William Kendall (Mr Bellenger), Elspet Gray (Penelope Rix), Gilbert Harrison (Postman), Hubert Cross (Small Dustman), Peter Mercier (Large Dustman), Larry Noble (Mr Jolliboy), Joan Sanderson (Mrs Hathaway), Terry Scott (Toby Murgatroyd), Helen Jessup (Norma Flatly), Patrick Cargill (Gunga Din), Hugh McDermott (Henry J. Hannenbocker), Hazel Douglas (Wilma Bloomer), John Chapman (Teddy Gibbons), Leo Franklyn (Jack Robinson), Linda Dixon (Reveller), Mary Mitchell (Reveller), Gerald Dawson (Reveller), Pearson Dodd (Reveller).

THE DIANE SOLOMON SHOW

A BBC Bristol production for BBC 1. Transmission details are for BBC 1. Duration varies - see below for details.

Main regular performer(s): Diane Solomon.

Holding / Source

24.12.1974 DB / 2"

Duration: 40 minutes.

Music directed by Ed Welch; designed by Desmond Chinn; produced and directed by John King.

With Spike Milligan, Demis Roussos, Arthur Negus, Three's A Crowd.

Holding / Source

26.12.1975 DB-D3 / 2"

Duration: 40 minutes.

Music directed by Ed Welch; designed by John Bone; produced by John King; directed by Colin Rose.

With Johnny Nash, George Melly, The Pontypridd Male Choir, Clare Torry, Laura Lee, Jill Mackintosh.

THE DICK EMERY SHOW

A BBC production for BBC 1. Transmission details are for BBC 1. Duration varies - see below for details.

Main regular cast: Dick Emery (Various Roles).

SERIES 2

Transmission details are for BBC. Duration: 45 minutes.

Main regular credit(s): Orchestra conducted by Harry Rabinowitz; choreography by Dougie Squires.

Holding / Source

29.12.1963 J /

Written by John Singer and John Warren; designed by Melvyn Cornish; produced and directed by John Street.

With Joan Sims, Mary Millar, Len Lowe, The Cliff Adams Singers, Miller and Archer.

THE DICK EMERY SHOW (continued)
British Christmas Television Guide

SERIES 12
Main regular credit(s): Written by John Warren and John Singer.
Main regular cast: With Gordon Clyde (Interviewer), Pat Coombs.

	Production No	VT Number	Holding / Source
26.12.1973	1243/1517	VTR/6HT/89108	DB-D3 / 2"

Duration: 30 minutes.
Designed by Lesley Joan Bremness; produced and directed by Colin Charman.
With Bill Treacher, June Jago, Reg Lye, Polly Adams, Annabelle Lanyon, Joan Scott, Scheherezade, Dora Vassilou, Eva Vassilou.

	Holding / Source
24.12.1974 **The Dick Emery Christmas Show**	DB-D3 / 2"

Duration: 35 minutes.
Written by John Warren and John Singer; designed by Robin Tarsnane; executive producer John Ammonds; produced and directed by Harold Snoad.
With Pat Coombs, Michael Napier Brown, Reg Lye, Gordon Clyde, Geoffrey Chater, Robert Dorning, Helen Fraser, Ella Milne, Victor Maddern.

SERIES 14
Duration: 30 minutes.
Main regular credit(s): Written by John Warren and John Singer; executive producer John Ammonds; produced and directed by Harold Snoad.

	Holding / Source
24.12.1975 **Christmas Special**	DB-D3 / 2"

Designed by Bryan Ellis.
With Ballard Berkeley, Madoline Thomas, Gordon Clyde, John Quayle, Josephine Tewson, Victor Maddern, Helen Fraser, Claire Nielson, Jamila Massey, Patricia Mason, George Moon, Pauline Peters, Patsy Smart.

SERIES 16
Main regular credit(s): Produced and directed by Harold Snoad.

	Holding / Source
24.12.1977 **The Texan Connection**	DB-D3 / 2"-C1

Alt.Title(s): *The Duchess and Luke Street*
Duration: 50 minutes.
Written by John Singer; music by Jack Point; designed by Peter Brachacki.
With Judy Cornwell (Stella), Robert Mill (Kincaide), Patrick Troughton (Potter), John Hamill (George), Roy Kinnear (Bovver Boy's Dad), Peter Carlisle (Luke Street), Helen Horton (Shirley Street), Jennifer Granville (Laverne Street), Dominic Ford (Chuck Street), June Whitfield (Jacqueline Clayton), Bella Emberg (Cook).

SERIES 18
Main regular credit(s): Produced by Harold Snoad.

	Holding / Source
27.12.1980 **For Whom The Jingle Bells Toll**	DB-D3 / 2"-C1

Duration: 47 minutes.
Written by John Singer and Steven Singer; music by Jack Point; designed by Tony Snoaden; directed by Harold Snoad.
With Dick Emery (Various Guises), Glynn Edwards (Bunce), Colin Fay (Georgie), Harry H. Corbett (Nico), Iain Cuthbertson (Jock, The Razor), Nick Brimble (Jimmy 1), Steve Kelly (Jimmy 2), Annie Ross (Maggie), Lee Montague (Charlie Coffin), John Kane (Eric), Bill Treacher (Dudley), Denis Bond (Charlie's Mum), Roy Kinnear (Bovver Boy's Dad), June Whitfield (Collette).

THE DICK EMERY SPECIAL

A Thames Television production. Transmission details are for the ATV midlands region. Duration: 50 minutes.
Written by Eric Merriman, John Singer and David Renwick; music by Peter Knight and Eric Merriman; designed by Tony Borer; associate producer Eric Merriman; produced and directed by Keith Beckett.
Dick Emery (Various roles), Anna Dawson, Tim Barrett, Ronald Leigh-Hunt, Robert Dorning, David Rayner, John Rutland, Frank Coda, Gemma Craven, The Three Degrees, Annabel, John Raven, Louise Beckett, Marie-Elise Grepne, Dawn Macdonald, Helen Thomas, Cathy Cordez, Sandra Easby, Lisabeth Greene, Penny Stevenson, Clare Smalley, Margaret Ede.

	Holding / Source
26.12.1979	D3 / 2"

With Ronald Leigh-Hunt, David Rayner, Gemma Craven, The Three Degrees.

THE DICK LESTER SHOW

An Associated-Rediffusion production. Transmission details are for Associated-Rediffusion. Duration: 25 minutes.
Devised by Dick Lester and Philip Saville; produced and directed by Douglas Hurn.
Dick Lester, Alun Owen, The Reg Owen Orchestra.

	Holding / Source
23.12.1955	NR / Live

DICK WHITTINGTON

A BBC production. Transmission details are for BBC. Duration: 90 minutes.

Written by Max Kester; music by Stanley Andrews; produced by Jack Hulbert; play production by Kenneth M. Buckley.

Jack Hulbert (Cook), Patricia Russell (Dick), Tom Linden (Cat), Arthur Hambling (Fitzwarren), Wallas Eaton (Idle Jack), Eunice Gayson (Alice), Philip Harben (Chef), Eunice Crowther (Ship's Captain), Abraham Sofaer (Sultan), Clive Stock (Pasha), Neal Arden (King Rat), Dennis Castle (Second Rat), Cecil Brock (Sultan's Bodyguard), John Milburn (Sultan's Bodyguard), Doreen Arden (Dancer), Lee Barrett (Dancer), Patricia Brooks (Dancer), Tanya Duray (Dancer), Cynthia Hayden (Dancer), Tamara Kirova (Dancer), Flora Stuart (Dancer), Manya Zarina (Dancer).

		Holding / Source
26.12.1949	First Performance	NR / Live
07.01.1950	Second Performance	NR / Live

DICK WHITTINGTON

A BBC production. Transmission details are for BBC. Duration: 45 minutes.

Written by Barbara Gordon and Basil Thomas; choreography by Pauline Grant; television presentation by Alan Chilvers; designed by Charles Reading; produced by Val Parnell.

Brian Johnston (Commentator), Frankie Howerd (Idle Jack), Mr Pastry (Mate), Sonnie Hale (Cook), Vanessa Lee (Dick Whittington), Lois Green (Alice Fitzwarren), Herbert Hare (Fitzwarren), David Dale (Captain), Bobby Vernon (Cat), Alan Bailey (King Rat), Rob Murray, Eliane and Rodolph, The Seven Volants, Knie's Chimpanzees, The George Mitchell Singers, The Aida Foster Children [as Aida Foster Babe's], Jimmy Currie's Water Scene.

	Holding / Source
28.12.1952	NR / Live

Excerpt from the London Palladium pantomime.

DICK WHITTINGTON

A BBC production. Transmission details are for BBC. Duration: 45 minutes.

Written by Emile Littler; lyrics by Hastings Mann; music by Hastings Mann; produced and directed by Alan Chivers; produced for the stage by Emile Littler.

George Formby (Idle Jack), Jeanne Craig (Tommy, The Immortal Cat), Don Murray (Town Crier), Joyce Mandre (Alice Fitzwarren), Ernest Arnley (Sarah, The Cook), Humphrey Heathcote (Alderman Fitzwarren), Beryl Stevens (Dick Whittington), Roy Pannell (King Rat), The Two Pirates (Captain Nelson / Half Nelson, His Mate), June Clare (Titania), Margaret Thackray (Principal Dancer), Martin Lawrence (Emperor of Morocco), The Palace Girls, The Terry Children, The Tudor Singers.

	Holding / Source
13.01.1957	J /

An excerpt from the pantomime televised from the Palace Theatre, London.

DICK WHITTINGTON

A BBC production. Transmission details are for BBC.

Adapted by John Law and Harry Carlisle; based on a book by John Law; music by Gordon Franks; orchestra conducted by Eric Robinson; choreography by Tommy Shaw and David Harding; produced by Harry Carlisle; directed by Peter Whitmore.

Terry Scott (Daphne), Hugh Lloyd (Jack), Reg Varney (Captain Reginald Fitzwarren), Barbara Von Der Hyde (Fairy), Patricia Lambert (Alice), David Davenport (Ebenezer Fitzwarren), Gerry Lee (Tommy), Yvonne Marsh (Dick Whittington), Alec Bregonzi (Selby), Norman Mitchell (J. Farthingale-Singleton), Ken Parry (The Sultan), Norman Mitchell (The Vizier), Leon Ward, Maggie Lee, The Tommy Shaw Dancers, Dawn Hughes, Doreen Hermitage, Jean Cragg, Ann Berreclough, Sandra Blair, Ann Bullen, Pat Cassy, Val Denester, Wendy Holland, Nicky Springfield, Barbara Staveley, Neil Fitzwilliam, Louis Godfrey, Peter Gordeno, John Gordon, Bernard Jamison, The George Mitchell Singers, The Eric Robinson Orchestra.

	Holding / Source
25.12.1963	J /

DICK WHITTINGTON

A BBC production for BBC 1. Transmission details are for BBC 1. Duration: 95 minutes.

Adapted by John Warren and John Singer; based on a book by Phil Park; music directed by Ronnie Hazlehurst and his Orchestra; choreography by Pamela Devis and Fred Peters; designed by Andy Dimond; production manager Colin Farnell; produced and directed by Colin Charman.

Dick Emery (Sarah The Cook), Peter Noone (Dick Whittington), Stratford Johns (The Sultan of Morocco), Michael Aspel (The Vizier), Gordon Peters (Idle Jack), David Healy (Captain Barnacle), Gemma Craven (Alice), Robert Dorning (Alderman Fitzwarren), Peter Elliott (Billy), Alan Curtis (King Rat), Mervyn Webb (Timmy The Cat), Trudi Van Doorn (Spirit of The Bells), The Fred Tomlinson Singers, The Pamela Devis Dancers, Peggy O'Farrell Children.

	Holding / Source
25.12.1972	DB-D3 / 2"

DICK WHITTINGTON

A Pozzitive Television production for LWT. made in association with Rockwood Edge Ltd. Transmission details are for the Central region. Duration: 74 minutes.

Written by Simon Nye; script supervisor Maggi Hilliard; music by Philip Pope; choreography by Gerry Zuccarello; edited by Mykola Pawluk; titles by Andy Carroll and Soho 601; art director John McHugh; production team Fran Branson, Caz Brill, Gazmond Doco, Christine Hagon, Ben Jerrit and Caroline Vent; associate producer Jed Leventhall; production manager Murray Peterson; produced by David Tyler and Geoff Posner; directed by Geoff Posner.

Amanda Barrie (The Queen of Tonga), Sanjeev Bhaskar (The Mayor), Kevin Bishop (Dick), Julian Clary (The Cat), Vanessa Feltz (Mrs Fitzwarren), James Fleet (Alderman Fitzwarren), Harry Hill (The Painter), Lee Mack (Idle Jack), Paul Merton (The Captain), Tina O'Brien (The Maid of Tonga), Debra Stephenson (Alice Fitzwarren), Jessica Stevenson (The Good Fairy), Mark Williams (King Rat), Richard Wilson (Sally The Cook), Hear'Say.

	Holding / Source
01.01.2002	DB / DBSW

DICK WHITTINGTON AND HIS CAT

A BBC production. Transmission details are for BBC. Duration: 36 minutes.

Additional dialogue by William Stephens; based on a book by Arthur Askey; music by Carrie Graham; play production by Reginald Smith.

Queenie Leonard (Dick Whittington), Brenda Perry (Tiddles), George Benson (Alderman Fitzwarren), Olive Delmar (Alice), William Stephens (Idle Jack), Cyril Fletcher (Emperor of Morocco), Pamela Randall (Fairy Bow Belle).

	Holding / Source
27.12.1937	NR / Live
01.01.1938	NR / Live

DICK WHITTINGTON AND HIS CAT

A BBC production. Transmission details are for BBC. Duration: 90 minutes.

Written by Barry Lupino Snr; music by Eric Robinson; play production by Richard Afton and Bertram Montague.

Max Miller (Idle Jack), Jean Kent (Dick Whittington), Jon Pertwee (Alderman Fitzwarren), Nat Mills (Sarah The Cook), Lester Ferguson (Emperor of Morocco), Jill Westlake (Alice Fitzwarren), Raymond (Coiffeur To Fitzwarren), Vic Wise (Captain), Kenneth Connor (Mate), Jack Brennan (The Cat), Bill Pertwee (King Rat), Audrey Craft (Fairy Queen), Pamela Young (Pan), Noberti, The George Mitchell Choir, The Television Toppers.

	Holding / Source
31.12.1958	J /

A DICKENS OF A CHRISTMAS

A Scottish Television production. Transmission details are for the Tyne Tees region. Duration: 55 minutes.

Written by Philip Parsons; music directed by Harry Rabinowitz; choreography by Norman Maen; designed by John Reid; directed by Paul Kimberley.

Bonnie Langford, Andrew Cruickshank, Marie Gordon Price, Danny Street, Molly Weir, Juniper Green, David Hillman, The Harry Rabinowitz Orchestra, The Tony Mansell Singers.

	Holding / Source
24.12.1978	J / 2"

THE DICKIE HENDERSON SHOW

A Harry Foster TV Productions production for Associated-Rediffusion. Transmission details are for the ATV midlands region. Duration: 25 minutes.

Main regular cast:	Dickie Henderson (Dickie).

SERIES 4

Main regular credit(s):	Executive writer Jimmy Grafton; music directed by Steve Race; orchestrations by Alan Braden; settings by David Catley; produced and directed by Bill Hitchcock.
Main regular cast:	With June Laverick (June), John Parsons (Richard), Lionel Murton (Jack).

	Production No	Holding / Source
25.12.1962 The Dickie Henderson Christmas Show	LE/52/25	J /

Written by Jimmy Grafton and Jeremy Lloyd.

With John Parsons (Richard), Lionel Murton (Jack), Bernard Bresslaw, Hughie Green, Alfred Marks, Richard Wattis, Leslie Sarony, Joe Ritchie, William Douglas, Harry Littlewood, Helen Ford, Lindsay Scott Patton, Susan George, David Palmer, The Ivor Raymonde Singers, The Pamela Devis Dancers.

Recorded in two parts, on 27.10.62 and 19.10.62.

A DIFFERENT WAY HOME

A Granada production. Transmission details are for the Granada region. Duration: 25 minutes.

Roy Barraclough stars in Jimmie Chin's story of family divisions. A fussy old bachelor tries to settle his differences with his sister as he reminisces about the recent death of his mother.

Written by Jimmie Chinn; designed by Chris George; executive producer Andy Harries; produced by Christine Langham; directed by Mervyn Cumming.

Roy Barraclough (Leslie).

	Production No	Holding / Source
23.12.1994	P2105	1" / 1"

dinnerladies

A Pozzitive Television / Good Fun production for BBC 1. Transmission details are for BBC 1. Duration varies - see below for details.

Main regular credit(s):	Written by Victoria Wood; music by Victoria Wood and David Firman; executive producers Phil McIntyre [credited as Philip McIntyre] and David Tyler; produced by Geoff Posner and Victoria Wood; directed by Geoff Posner.
Main regular cast:	Victoria Wood (Bren), Thelma Barlow (Dolly), Andrew Dunn (Tony), Shobna Gulati (Anita), Celia Imrie (Philippa), Maxine Peake (Twinkle), Duncan Preston (Stan), Anne Reid (Jean).

SERIES 2

Main regular credit(s):	Script supervisor Hayley Boyd; art director Nick Somerville; designed by Ken Starkey; production manager Murray Peterson.

	Holding / Source
24.12.1999 christmas	DB / DBSW

Duration: 30 minutes.

With Julie Walters (Petula), Sue Devaney (Jane), Christopher Greet (Mr Michaels), Bernard Wrigley [as Bernard Wrightley] (Bob), Rachel Gleaves, Janet Tough, Black Dyke Mills Band [as Black Dyke Band].

The standard closing theme music was replaced by a brass band version of the same melody.

	Holding / Source
30.12.1999 minnellium	DB / DBSW

Duration: 34 minutes.

With Kaleem Janjua (Reg), Peter Lorenzelli, Tej Patel.

The standard closing theme music was replaced by a version of the same melody, with lyrics, sung by Victoria Wood.

The programme title and all episode titles were always written completely in lower-case.

THE DINOSAURS HUNTERS

A Granada production for Channel 4. Transmission details are for Channel 4. Duration: 55 minutes.

Main regular credit(s): Dramatised by Steven Clarke, Andrew Piddington and John Wilsher; based on a book by Deborah Cadbury; executive producers Robert Maciver and Bill Jones; produced by Steven Clarke; directed by Andrew Piddington.

Main regular cast: Henry Ian Cusick (Gideon Mantell), Michael Pennington (William Buckland), Alan Cox (Richard Owen), Rachel Shelley (Mary Mantell), Robert Morgan (Charles Lyell), Paul Brightwell (Leney), Pascal Laurent (George Cutler), Hugh Sachs (Loddidge), Martin Neville (William Clift), Michele Bunyan (Caroline Clift), Patricia Villa (Mary Buckland), Derek Jacobi (Narrator), Rebecca Smith.

		Holding / Source
30.12.2002	**Episode 1**	DB / DBSW
31.12.2002	**Episode 2**	DB / DBSW

DISC A DAWN

A BBC Wales production for BBC 1 Wales. Transmission details are for BBC 1 Wales.

SERIES 1

	Holding / Source
24.12.1966	J / 40

In Welsh.

DISNEY TIME

A BBC production for BBC 1. Transmission details are for BBC 1. Duration varies - see below for details.

Main regular credit(s): Produced and directed by Richard Evans.

	Holding / Source
27.12.1971	J / 2"

Duration: 45 minutes.
Television presentation by Richard Evans.
With Valerie Singleton, John Noakes, Peter Purves.

	Holding / Source
26.12.1973	R1 / 2"

With Paul McCartney, Linda McCartney.

	Holding / Source
26.12.1975	C1NSEQ / 2"

With Bing Crosby, Natasha Pyne, Joan Sims, Robert Stevenson, Michael Stringer.

	Holding / Source
27.12.1976	DB-D3 / 2"

With The Goodies.

		Holding / Source
27.12.1977	**50th Programme**	R1 / 2"

Duration: 60 minutes.
Television presentation by Richard Evans.
With David Jacobs (Presenter), Sean Connery, Karen Dotrice, Jodie Foster, Susan Hampshire, Dean Jones, John Mills, Hayley Mills, Peter Ustinov.

	Holding / Source
26.12.1978	DB-D3 / 2"

With Paul Daniels.

	Holding / Source
26.12.1979	2"|n / 2"

With Rod Hull and Emu.

	Holding / Source
26.12.1980	DB / 2"

With Marti Caine.

	Holding / Source
27.12.1981	DB-D3 / 2"

With Windsor Davies.

	Holding / Source
26.12.1982	DB / 2"

Duration: 45 minutes.
Produced and directed by Richard Evans.
With Rolf Harris.

	Holding / Source
27.12.1983	DB / 1"

With Mike Read, Sarah Greene.

DISPATCHES

Produced for Channel 4 by a variety of companies (see details below). Transmission details are for Channel 4. Duration: 40 minutes.

SERIES 5

		Holding / Source
18.12.1991	**Christmas In Kurdistan**	1"|n / 1"

SERIES 21

		Holding / Source
10.12.2007	**Christmas Credit Crisis**	DB /
17.12.2007	**How Safe Are Your Christmas Toys?**	DB /

| DISPATCHES (continued) | British Christmas Television Guide |

SERIES 23

	Holding / Source
07.12.2009 **Christmas On Credit**	DB /

THE DISTRACTED PREACHER

A BBC South West production for BBC 2. Transmission details are for BBC 2. Duration: 50 minutes.

Adapted by John Hale; based on a story by Thomas Hardy; music by Tom McCall; designed by Desmond Chinn; produced and directed by Brandon Acton-Bond.

Stephanie Beacham (Lizzie Newbury), Christopher Gable (Robert Stockdale), Jerold Wells (George, The Carrier), Michael Goldie (Hardman, The Smith), Norman Jones (Owlett, The Miller), Susan Broadhurst (Martha), Ruby Luscombe (Mrs Simpkins), Ewan Hooper (Latimer, The Excise Officer), David Jackson (Jeremy, His Assistant).

	Holding / Source
26.12.1969	C1 / C1

DIXON OF DOCK GREEN

A BBC Light Entertainment production for BBC. Transmission details are for BBC. Duration varies - see below for details.

Police drama set in and around Dock Green police station.

Main regular credit(s):	Devised by Ted Willis.
Main regular cast:	Jack Warner (George Dixon), Peter Byrne (Andy Crawford).

SERIES 4

Transmission details are for BBC. Duration: 30 minutes.

Main regular credit(s):	Written by Ted Willis; produced and directed by Douglas Moodie.
Main regular cast:	With Arthur Rigby (Sergeant Flint), Moira Mannion (Sergeant Grace Millard), Jeanette Hutchinson (Mary Dixon), Anthony Parker (Police Constable Bob Penney).

	Holding / Source
21.12.1957 **Peace On Earth**	J / Live

Script associate Rex Edwards.

With Wilfrid Carter, Dorothy Casey, Fay Bura, Harry Brunning, Elaise Wyndham, Jane Hilary, Maurice Hedley, Rose Hill, William Sherwood, Beckett Bould, Duncan McIntyre.

George Dixon was a Police Constable still, but Andy Crawford had been promoted to C.I.D. in this series.

SERIES 5

Transmission details are for BBC. Duration: 30 minutes.

Main regular credit(s):	Written by Ted Willis; produced and directed by Douglas Moodie.
Main regular cast:	With Arthur Rigby (Flint), Moira Mannion (Grace Millard), Jeanette Hutchinson (Mary Dixon), Anthony Parker (Bob Penney).

	Holding / Source
20.12.1958 **The Old Christmas Spirit**	J / Live

With Graham Ashley (Police Constable Hughes), Geoffrey Adams (Lauderdale), Keith Buckley, Anthea Holloway, Max Latimer, Jack Newmark, Catherine Willmer, Barbara Couper, Michael Cleveland, Dorothy Casey, Fay Bura, William Patenall, Bill Horsley, Sydney Keith, Gladys Dawson.

31/07/59 – PRESS CONFERENCE (LCA7413J) – front: incomplete Public Information Film (recording stops and starts briefly during it) with Jack Warner in 'Dixon' uniform, about road manners; black screen for a few seconds, then programme starts.

SERIES 6

Transmission details are for BBC. Duration: 30 minutes.

Main regular credit(s):	Written by Ted Willis; produced and directed by Douglas Moodie.
Main regular cast:	With Arthur Rigby (Sergeant Fling), Moira Mannion (Sergeant Millard), Jeanette Hutchinson (Mary Dixon), Geoffrey Adams (Police Constable Lauderdale), Graham Ashley (Police Constable(later Detective Constable) Hughes), David Webster (Cadet Jamie MacPherson).

	Holding / Source
12.12.1959 **Send For Santa Claus**	J / Live

With Derek Tansley, Tony Sympson, Anthea Holloway, Dorothy Casey, George Betton, Philip Howard, Frederic Wheldon, Elizabeth Broom, Barry Raymond.

George Dixon was a Police Constable still, but Andy Crawford had been promoted to Detective Sergeant in this series.

SERIES 7

Transmission details are for BBC. Duration: 30 minutes.

Main regular credit(s):	Written by Ted Willis; script associate Fiona McConnell; produced and directed by Douglas Moodie.
Main regular cast:	With Arthur Rigby (Sergeant Flint), Moira Mannion (Grace Millard), Jeannette Hutchinson (Mary Dixon), Geoffrey Adams (Lauderdale), Graham Ashley (Hughes), David Webster (Jamie).

	Holding / Source
24.12.1960 **Christmas Eve At The Nick**	J / 40

With Robert Cawdron (Detective Inspector Cherry), Jocelyne Rhodes (Kay), Hilda Fenemore (Jennie Wren), Dorothy Casey, Gwen Lewis, Ronald Mayer, Robert Weeden, Roger May, Kenneth Cope, Geoffrey Wincott, Hilda Barry, Robert Raglan, Kristin Magnus, Eva Whishaw, Betty Cardno, Brian Dent, Mollie Maureen, Owen Berry.

DIXON OF DOCK GREEN

DIXON OF DOCK GREEN (continued)

SERIES 10
Transmission details are for BBC. Duration: 45 minutes.
Main regular credit(s): Produced by Ronald Marsh.
Main regular cast: With Arthur Rigby (Sergeant Flint), Jeannette Hutchinson (Mary Crawford, formerly Dixon), Anne Ridler (Woman Police Sergeant Freeman), Jan Miller (Woman Police Constable Johns), Geoffrey Adams (Detective Police Constable Lauderdale), John Hughes (Police Constable Jones).

	Holding / Source
21.12.1963 **Christmas Dip**	J / 40

Written by Eric Paice; directed by David Askey.

With Paul Elliott (Cadet Michael Bonnet), Hilda Fenemore (Jennie Wren), Dorothea Phillips, Hilda Barry, Harry Fowler, Desmond Cullum-Jones, Sally Lahee, Barbara Keogh, Paul Curran, Pamela Withers, Novel Johnson.

SERIES 18
Commissioned by BBC 1. Transmission details are for BBC 1. Duration: 45 minutes.
Main regular credit(s): Script consultant Derek Ingrey; produced by Joe Waters.
Main regular cast: With Geoffrey Adams (Detective Constable Lauderdale), Nicholas Donnelly (Sergeant Wills), Michael Osborne (Police Constable Newton).

	Holding / Source
27.12.1971 **Wingy**	J / 2"

Wingy takes home an unexpected Christmas present, an abandoned baby. But when the mother of the child decides that she wants it back, it leads to a busy day for Sgt Dixon and the Dock Green Police.

Written by N. J. Crisp; designed by Antony Thorpe; directed by Joe Waters.

With Ronald Gough (Police Constable Dowling), Joy Hope (Secretary), Jack Watson (Wingy), Rose Hill (Amy Wing), Harry Landis (Lodger), Connie Merigold (Housekeeper), Jeremy Wimble (Little Mark), Catherine Kessler (Clare Hayter), David Drummond (Vicar), Robin Askwith (Young Man), Brian Hayes (Car Owner), Leslie Weeks*.

DIZZY FEET
An ATV production. Transmission details are for the ATV midlands region. Duration: 50 minutes.

A musical in the world of dancing: tap, Latin American, comic jazz, the blues and classical ballet.

Devised by Jon Scoffield; choreography by Nigel Lythgoe and Norman Maen; designed by David Chandler; associate producer Nigel Lythgoe; produced and directed by Jon Scoffield.

Honi Coles, Sammy and Shirley Stopford, Wayne Sleep, Bomber Graham, Gymnastic Dance Theatre Company, Peter Newton, Jane Darling, Lesley Collier, David Wall, Helen Jenkins, Bobby Kingley, Chrissy Monk, Wanda Rokicki, Jenny Turnock, Mo Willsher, Kim Gavin, Alan Harding, Nicky Lloyd, Vince Logan, Steve St Klonis, Peter Salmon, Lorraine Meacher, Jack Parnell and his Orchestra.

	Holding / Source
30.12.1981	1" / 1"

DIZZY IN CONCERT
A Thames Television production. Transmission details are for the Thames Television region. Duration: 50 minutes.

Introduced by Benny Green; produced and directed by Christopher Palmer.

Dizzy Gillespie, Marian Montgomery, Laurie Holloway, Bud Shank, Royal Philharmonic Orchestra.

	Holding / Source
26.12.1985	1" / 1"

DO NOT ADJUST YOUR SET
Produced for ITV by a variety of companies (see details below). Transmission details are for the ATV midlands region. Duration: 25 minutes.
Main regular credit(s): Written by Eric Idle, Terry Jones and Michael Palin.
Main regular cast: Denise Coffey, Eric Idle, David Jason, Terry Jones, Michael Palin, The Bonzo Dog Doo-Dah Band.

Special
A Rediffusion Television production. Transmission details are for the Rediffusion Television region.

	Production No	Holding / Source
##.##.#### **A Happy Boxing Day And A Preposterous New Year**	CHI/45/6	J / 40

Additional material by Doug Fisher and Denise Coffey; theme music by Dave Lee; designed by Bryan Bagge; produced by Humphrey Barclay; directed by Daphne Shadwell.

Recorded 06.11.67. The Bonzos perform "Jollity Farm" and a Boxing Day song. Instead of the special going out on 26/12/1967, the first episode of series one was mistakenly transmitted. (See, From Fringe to Flying Circus/Wilmut, R.)

Special
A Thames Television production.

	VT Number	Holding / Source
25.12.1968 **Do Not Adjust Your Stocking**	1505	DB-R1 / 40

Duration: 40 minutes.

Captain Fantastic produced by Daphne Shadwell; additional material by Denise Coffey, David Jason and Terry Gilliam; script editor Ian Davidson; designed by Harry Clark; executive producer Lewis Rudd; directed by Adrian Cooper.

Bonzos perform "By a Waterfall" and "I'm the Urban Spaceman".

DO THEY KNOW IT'S CHRISTMAS?

A Polygram Filmed Entertainment production for UK Gold. Transmission details are for UK Gold. Duration: 30 minutes.
Directed by Dave Bridges and Rob Wright.
Bob Geldof.

Holding / Source
24.12.1994 | C1 / C1

Original Polygram promotional film from 1984.

DO YOU TRUST YOUR WIFE?

An ATV production. Transmission details are for the ATV midlands region. Duration: 25 minutes.
Game show with members of the public.
Main regular credit(s): Designed by Tom Lingwood; produced by John Irwin; directed by Colin Clews.
Main regular performer(s): Bob Monkhouse (Host), Denis Goodwin.

Holding / Source
25.12.1956 **Christmas Special** | J / Live

With Cyril Fletcher, Betty Astell, Leslie Randall, Joan Reynolds, Peter Sellers, Pat Coombs.

Produced in association with Don Fedderson and Don-Monya Inc.

DOC MARTIN

A Buffalo Pictures production for ITV 1. made in association with Homerun Productions. Transmission details are for the Central region.
Main regular credit(s): Created by Dominic Minghella; music by Colin Towns; associate producer Sandy Poustie; executive producer Mark Crowdy; produced by Philippa Brathwaite.
Main regular cast: Martin Clunes (Doctor Martin Ellingham), Caroline Catz (Louisa Glasson), Ian McNeice (Bert Large), Joe Absolom (Al Large), Stephanie Cole (Joan Norton).

Holding / Source
25.12.2006 **On The Edge** | DB / V1SW

Duration: 100 minutes.
Written by Jack Lothian; script supervisor Linda Gibson; script editor Evie Bergson; directed by Ben Bolt.
With Selina Cadell, Katherine Parkinson, Richard Johnson, Paul Ryder, Kenneth Cranham, Chris O'Dowd, Jonathan Aris, Paul Rider, Nicholas Pegg, Adam Bareham.

This series was based on the film , "Saving Grace", created by Craig Ferguson and Mark Crowdy. Sponsored by Lindemans.

DOCTOR FINLAY

A Scottish Television production. Transmission details are for the Central region. Duration: 50 minutes.
Main regular credit(s): Created by A. J. Cronin; theme music by The Scottish Chamber Orchestra and Richard Harvey; executive producer Robert Love.
Main regular cast: David Rintoul (Doctor John Finlay), Ian Bannen (Doctor Alexander Cameron), Annette Crosbie (Janet MacPherson / Livingstone).

SERIES 4
Main regular credit(s): Produced by Bernard Krichefski.
Main regular cast: With Jessica Turner (Doctor Napier).

Holding / Source
20.12.1996 **Snowblind** | 1" / V1SSW

It's the night before Hogmanay and Doctors Cameron, Finlay and Napier are dining together, attended on by Janet. In an unguarded and somewhat drunken moment Doctor Cameron insults Janet. Then, upon realising how deeply he has hurt her, Cameron suffers a heart attack. The weather worsens and Arden House is snowed in, setting the scene for an intense and sometimes very funny night of reckoning for all four leading characters.
Written by Carey Harrison; directed by Rodney Bennett.
With Jackie Morrison (Rhona Swanson), Gordon Reid (Angus Livingstone).

DOCTOR IN THE HOUSE (RADIO)

A BBC production for BBC Radio 4. Transmission details are for BBC Radio 4. Duration: 30 minutes.
Main regular credit(s): Adapted by Ray Cooney; based on a book by Richard Gordon; produced and directed by David Hatch.
Main regular cast: Richard Briers (Simon Sparrow), Ray Cooney (Tony Benskin).

Holding / Source
13.08.1968 **Happy Christmas** | J /

With Edward Cast (Taffy Evans), Dennis Ramsden, Norma Ronald.

DOCTOR WHO

A BBC Drama Serials production for BBC. Transmission details are for BBC 1. Duration varies - see below for details.

Main regular credit(s):   Theme music by Ron Grainer.

SERIES 3
Duration: 25 minutes.
Cast: With William Hartnell (The Doctor).

The Daleks' Master Plan

Alternative/Working Title(s): The Daleks (Part IV)
Duration: 25 minutes.
Main regular credit(s):   Story editor Donald Tosh; music by Tristram Cary; designed by Raymond Cusick; produced by John Wiles; directed by Douglas Camfield.
Main regular cast: With Peter Purves (Steven Taylor).

Holding / Source
25.12.1965 **The Feast Of Steven**   J SO|a / 40
Written by Terry Nation.

With Jean Marsh (Sara Kingdom), Clifford Earl, Norman Mitchell, Malcolm Rogers, Keneth Thornett, Reg Pritchard, Sheila Dunn, Leonard Grahame, Royston Tickner, Mark Ross, Conrad Monk, Steve Machin, Buddy Windrush, David James, Paula Topham, Robert Jewell [as Robert G. Jewell], Albert Barrington.

The Movie

A BBC/MCA Television Ltd production. Duration: 85 minutes.
Credits: Written by Matthew Jacobs; music by John Debney, John Sponsler and Louis Febre; executive producers Philip David Segal, Alex Beaton and Jo Wright; co-produced by Matthew Jacobs; produced by Peter V. Ware; directed by Geoffrey Sax.
Cast: With Paul McGann (The Doctor), Eric Roberts (The Master / Bruce), Daphne Ashbrook (Doctor Grace Holloway), Sylvester McCoy (The Doctor), Yee Jee Tso (Chang Lee), John Novak (Salinger), Michael David Simms (Doctor Swift), Catherine Lough (Wheeler), Delores Drake (Curtis), William Sasko (Pete), Jeremy Radick (Gareth), Eliza Roberts (Miranda), Bill Croft (Motorcycle Policeman), Dave Hurtubise (Professor Wagg), Joel Wirkkunen (Ted), Dee Jay Jackson (Security Guard), Gordon Tipple (The Old Master), Mi-Jung Lee (News Anchor), Joanna Piros (News Anchor).

Holding / Source
27.05.1996   DB / V1S
Set around New Year's Eve.

The movie was shot on 35mm film, transferred to 525i60 Digital Betacam and edited. The finished master is 525i60 Digital Betacam. The BBC owns a 625i50 upconversion of this on Digital Betacam and on D3.

A BBC Wales production.
Main regular credit(s):   Music by Murray Gold; executive producers Russell T. Davies and Julie Gardner.
Main regular cast: With David Tennant (The Doctor), Billie Piper (Rose Tyler).

Holding / Source
25.12.2005 **The Christmas Invasion**   DB / DBSWF
Duration: 59 minutes.
Written by Russell T. Davies; script editor Helen Raynor; associate producer Helen Vallis; produced by Phil Collinson; directed by James Hawes.

With Camille Coduri (Jackie Tyler), Noel Clarke (Mickey Smith), Penelope Wilton (Harriet Jones), Daniel Evans (Danny Llewelyn), Adam Garcia (Alex), Sean Gilder (Sycorax Leader), Chu Omambala (Major Blake), Anita Briem (Sally), Sian McDowall (Sandra), Paul Anderson (Jason), Cathy Murphy (Mum), Sean Carlsen (Policeman), Jason Mohammad [as Jason Mohammed] (Newsreader 1), Sagar Arya (Newsreader 2), Lachele Carl (Newsreader 3).

A BBC Wales production.
Credits: Executive producers Julie Gardner and Russell T. Davies; produced by Phil Collinson.
Cast: With David Tennant (The Tenth Doctor).

Holding / Source
25.12.2006 **The Runaway Bride**   DB / DBSWF
Duration: 60 minutes.
Written by Russell T. Davies; script editor Simon Winstone; designed by Edward Thomas; production executive Julie Scott; directed by Euros Lyn.

With Catherine Tate (The Bride, Donna Noble), Sarah Parish (Empress of Racnoss), Don Gilet (Lance Bennett), Howard Attfield (Geoff Noble), Jacqueline King (Sylvia Noble), Trevor Georges (Vicar), Glen Wilson (Taxi Driver), Krystal Archer (Nerys), Rhodri Meilir (Rhodri), Zafirah Boateng (Little Girl), Paul Kasey (Robot Santa).

SERIES 30

A BBC Wales production.
Main regular credit(s):   Music by Murray Gold; designed by Edward Thomas; production executive Julie Scott.
Main regular cast: With David Tennant (The Doctor).

Holding / Source
25.12.2007 **Voyage Of The Damned**   DB / DBSWF
Duration: 71 minutes.
Written by Russell T. Davies; script editor Brian Minchin; associate designer James North; executive producers Russell T. Davies and Julie Gardner; produced by Phil Collinson; directed by James Strong.

With Kylie Minogue (Astrid Peth), Geoffrey Palmer (Captain Hardaker), Russell Tovey (Midshipman Frame), George Costigan (Max Capricorn), Gray O'Brien (Rickston Slade), Andrew Havill (Chief Steward), Bruce Lawrence (Engineer), Debbie Chazen (Foon Van Hoff), Clive Rowe (Morvin Van Hoff), Clive Swift (Mr Copper), Jimmy Vee (Bannakaffalatta), Bernard Cribbins (Wilfred Mott), Nicholas Witchell (Himself), Paul Kasey (The Host), Stefan Davis (Kitchen Hand), Jason Mohammad (Newsreader), Colin McFarlane (Alien Voice), Ewan Bailey (Alien Voice), Jessica Martin (Voice of the Queen).

DOCTOR WHO (continued)

25.12.2008 **The Next Doctor** DB / DBSWF
Duration: 60 minutes.
Written by Russell T. Davies; script editor Lindsey Alford; associate producer Catrin Lewis Defis; executive producers Russell T. Davies and Julie Gardner; produced by Susie Liggat; directed by Andy Goddard.

With David Morrissey (Jackson Lake), Dervla Kirwan (Miss Mercy Hartigan), Vellie Tshabalala (Rosita), Ruari Mears (Cybershade), Paul Kasey (Cyberleader), Edmund Kente (Mr Scoones), Michael Bertenshaw (Mr Cole), Jason Morell (Vicar), Neil McDermott (Jed), Ashley Horne (Lad), Tom Langford (Frederic), Jordan Southwell (Urchin), Matthew Allick (Docker), Nicholas Briggs (Cyber Voices).

Cybermen originally created by Kit Pedler and Gerry Davis.

SERIES 31
A BBC Wales production.
Main regular credit(s): Music by Murray Gold; designed by Edward Thomas; production executive Julie Scott; executive producers Russell T. Davies and Julie Gardner; production manager Steffan Morris.
Main regular cast: With David Tennant (The Doctor).

Holding / Source

25.12.2009 **The End of Time - Part One** HD/DB / HD/DB
Duration: 60 minutes.
Written by Russell T. Davies; script editor Gary Russell; choreography by Ailsa Berk; director of photography Rory Taylor; designed by James North; associate producer Catrin Lewis Defis; produced by Tracie Simpson; directed by Euros Lyn.

With John Simm (The Master), Bernard Cribbins (Wilfred Mott), Timothy Dalton (The Narrator), Catherine Tate (Donna Noble), Jacqueline King (Sylvia Noble), Claire Bloom (The Woman), June Whitfield (Minnie Hooper), David Harewood (Joshua Naismith), Tracy Feachor (Abigail Naismith), Sinéad Keenan (Addams), Lawry Lewin (Rossiter), Alexandra Moen (Lucy Saxon), Karl Collins (Shaun Temple), Teresa Banham (Governor), Barry Howard (Oliver Barnes), Allister Bain (Winston Katusi), Simon Thomas (Mr Danes), Sylvia Seymour (Miss Trefusis), Pete Lee-Wilson (Tommo), Dwayne Scantlebury (Ginger), Lacey Bond (Serving Woman), Lachele Carl (Trinity Wells), Paul Kasey (Ood Sigma), Ruari Mears (Elder Ood), Max Benjamin (Teenager), Silas Carson (Voice of Ood Sigma), Brian Cox (Voice of Elder Ood).

No Production Manager credited.

01.01.2010 **The End of Time - Part Two** HD/DB / HD/DB
Duration: 75 minutes.
Written by Russell T. Davies; script editor Gary Russell; choreography by Ailsa Berk; director of photography Rory Taylor; designed by James North; associate producer Catrin Lewis Defis; produced by Tracie Simpson; directed by Euros Lyn.

With Matt Smith (The Doctor), John Simm (The Master), Bernard Cribbins (Wilfred Mott), Timothy Dalton (Lord President), Catherine Tate (Donna Noble), Jacqueline King (Sylvia Noble), Billie Piper (Rose Tyler), Camille Coduri (Jackie Tyler), John Barrowman (Captain Jack Harkness), Freema Agyeman (Martha Smith-Jones), Noel Clarke (Mickey Smith), Elisabeth Sladen (Sarah Jane Smith), Jessica Hynes (Verity Newman), June Whitfield (Minnie Hooper), Claire Bloom (The Woman), Thomas Knight (Luke Smith), Russell Tovey (Midshipman Frame), David Harewood (Joshua Naismith), Tracy Feachor (Abigail Naismith), Lawry Lewin (Rossiter), Sinéad Keenan (Addams), Joe Dixon (The Chancellor), Julie Legrand (The Partisan), Brid Brennan (The Visionary), Karl Collins (Shaun Temple), Krystal Archer (Nerys), Lachele Carl (Trinity Wells), Paul Kasey (Ood Sigma), Ruari Mears (Elder Ood), Silas Carson (Voice of Ood Sigma), Nicholas Briggs (Voice of Judoon), Dan Starkey (Sontaran).

No Production Manager credited.

Credits: Music by Murray Gold and BBC National Orchestra of Wales; production executive Julie Scott; executive producers Piers Wenger, Beth Willis and Steven Moffat.
Cast: With Matt Smith (The Doctor), Karen Gillan (Amy Pond), Arthur Darvill (Rory).

Holding / Source

25.12.2010 **A Christmas Carol** HD/DB / HD/DB
A BBC Wales production. Duration: 60 minutes.
Written by Steven Moffat; script executive Lindsey Alford; script supervisor Phillip Trow; director of photography Stephan Pehrsson; art director Stephen Nicholas; designed by Michael Pickwood; production manager Steffan Morris; line producer Diana Barton; produced by Sanne Wohlenberg; directed by Toby Haynes.

With Michael Gambon (Kazran/Elliot Sardick), Katherine Jenkins (Abigail), Laurence Belcher (Young Kazran), Danny Horn (Adult Kazran), Leo Bill (Pilot), Pooky Quesnel (Captain), Micah Balfour (Co-Pilot), Steve North (Old Benjamin), Bailey Pepper (Boy / Benjamin), Tim Plester (Servant), Nick Malinowski (Eric), Laura Rogers (Isabella), Meg Wynn Owen (Old Isabella).

A BBC Wales production.

Holding / Source

25.12.2011 **The Doctor, The Widow And The Wardrobe** HD/DB / HD/DB
A BBC Wales production. Duration: 60 minutes.
It's Christmas Eve 1938, and Madge Arwell helps an injured spaceman-angel. He promises to repay her kindness. Three years later, Madge escapes war-torn London with her children for a house in Dorset. The Arwells are greeted by a caretaker whose Christmas gift leads them into a magical wintry world.
Written by Steven Moffat; produced by Marcus Wilson; directed by Farren Blackburn.

With Matt Smith (The Doctor), Claire Skinner (Madge Arwell), Arabella Weir (Billis), Alexander Armstrong (Reg Arwell), Holly Earl (Lily Arwell), Maurice Cole (Cyril Arwell), Paul Bazely (Ven-Garr).

Holding / Source

25.12.2012 **The Snowmen** HD/DB / HDC
A BBC Wales production.
1892: snowfall is making for a picture postcard Christmas Eve, but a chilling menace threatens Earth as an unorthodox young governess, Clara, calls on the Doctor for help. He, however, is in mourning, reclusive and intent on ignoring the problems of the universe.
Written by Steven Moffat; produced by Marcus Wilson; directed by Saul Metzstein.

With Matt Smith (The Doctor), Jenna-Louise Coleman (Clara), Richard E. Grant (Doctor Simeon), Dan Starkey (Strax), Catrin Stewart (Jenny), Neve McIntosh (Vastra), Tom Ward (Captain Latimer), Liz White (Alice), Joseph Darcey-Alden (Digby).

| British Christmas Television Guide | DOCTOR WHO (continued) |

	Holding / Source
25.12.2013 **The Time Of The Doctor**	HD/DB / HDC

A BBC Wales production. Duration: 60 minutes.
The massed forces of the universe's deadliest alien species are drawn to a quiet planet by a mysterious message echoing out to the stars.
Written by Steven Moffat; produced by Marcus Wilson; directed by Jamie Payne.
With Matt Smith (The Doctor), Peter Capaldi (The Doctor), Jenna Coleman (Clara), Rob Jarvis (Abramal), Tessa Peake-Jones (Marta), Jack Hollington (Barnable), Sonita Henry (Colonel Merne), Kayvan Novak (Handles' Voice), Tom Gibbins (Young Man), Aidan Cook (Cyberman), Nicholas Briggs (Voice Of The Daleks), Barnaby Edwards (Dalek), Nicholas Pegg (Dalek), Ross Mullan (Silent).

See also: DOCTOR WHO CONFIDENTIAL (BBC) / K.9 AND COMPANY (BBC) / THE SARAH JANE ADVENTURES (BBC)

DOCTOR WHO AT THE PROMS

A BBC Wales production for BBC 1. Transmission details are for BBC 1. Duration: 60 minutes.
Main regular credit(s): Music by Murray Gold; designed by Eryl Ellis; production executive Julie Scott; executive producers Julie Gardner and Russell T. Davies.

	Holding / Source
01.01.2009	HD/DB / HDC

Produced by Paul Bullock; directed by Rhodri Huw.
With Freema Agyeman (Presenter), Melanie Pappenheim (Soloist), Ben Foster (Conductor And Arranger), Julian Bleach (Davros), Nicholas Briggs (Voice of the Dalek), Barnaby Edwards (Dalek Operator), Jimmy Vee (The Graske), Paul Kasey (Hero Monsters), Dan Starkey (Commander Skorr), Scott Baker (Other Monster), Alain Gilet (Other Monster), Ian Hilditch (Other Monster), Ken Hosking (Other Monster), Andy Jones (Other Monster), Ruari Mears (Other Monster), Adam Sweet (Other Monster), Joe White (Other Monster), Catherine Tate, BBC Philharmonic Orchestra, London Philharmonic Choir.

	Holding / Source
01.01.2009 **Music Of The Spheres**	HD/DB / HD/DB

Written by Russell T. Davies; produced by Catrin Defis; directed by Euros Lyn.
With David Tennant (The Doctor).

DOCTOR WHO CONFIDENTIAL

A BBC Wales production for BBC 3. Transmission details are for BBC 3. Duration varies - see below for details.
Main regular credit(s): Series producer Gilliane Seaborne.

SERIES 2

	Holding / Source
25.12.2006 **Music And Monsters**	HD/DB / HD/DB

Directed by Adam Page.
With David Tennant, Phil Collinson, Julie Gardner, Nicholas Briggs, Ben Foster, Paul Bullock, Murray Gold, Russell T. Davies, Paul Kasey, Catherine Tate.

SERIES 4

	Holding / Source
25.12.2007 **Doctor Who Confidential At Christmas**	DB / DBSW

Duration: 60 minutes.
With Kylie Minogue.

SERIES 5

	Holding / Source
25.12.2008 **Confidential Christmas 2008**	DB / DBSW

Duration: 60 minutes.
Assistant producers Ian Hay and Hannah Williams; production executive Stan Matthews; executive producers Mark Cossey, Russell T. Davies and Julie Gardner; production managers Katy Cartwright and Kirsty Reid; produced by Zoe Rushton.
With Anthony Head (Narrator), Susie Liggat, Russell T. Davies, David Tennant, David Morrissey, Andy Goddard, Ruari Mears, Paul Kasey, Dervla Kirwan, Tom Lucy, Danny Hargreaves, Richard Harris, Tom Langford, Vellie Tshabalala.

	Holding / Source
25.12.2009 **Lords And Masters**	HD/DB / HD/DB

Duration: 60 minutes.

SERIES 7

Credits: Theme music by Slam and Saw Productions; executive producer Mark Cossey; senior producer Zoe Rushton; series producer Gilliane Seaborne.

	Holding / Source
25.12.2010	HD/DB / HD/DB

Duration: 60 minutes.
Research Matthew Andrews and Robert Wootton; assistant producers Ian Hay and Donovan Keogh; production executive Stan Matthews; production manager Katy Cartwright.
With Russell Tovey (Narrator), Steven Moffat*, Matt Smith*, Sanne Wohlenberg*, Beth Willis*, Michael Gambon*, Toby Haynes*, Piers Wenger*, Laurence Belcher*, Katherine Jenkins*, Danny Horn*, Michael Pickwood*, Julian Luxton*, Tim Barter*, Murray Gold*, Ben Foster*.

See also: DOCTOR WHO (BBC)

DOCTORS

A BBC Birmingham production for BBC 1. Transmission details are for BBC 1. Usual duration: 30 minutes.

Main regular credit(s):	Theme music by Mike Badger and Paul Hemmings.
Main regular cast:	Christopher Timothy (Doctor Brendan 'Mac' McGuire (until 26.05.2006)), Corrinne Wicks (Doctor Helen Thompson (until 16.12.2005)), Maggie Cronin (Kate McGuire (until 7.5.2004)).

SERIES 2

Main regular credit(s):	Series script editor Peter Eryl Lloyd; script editors Faith Penhale and Myar Craig; executive producer Mal Young; series producer Carson Black; produced by Will Trotter.
Main regular cast:	With Mark Frost (Doctor Steve Rawlings), Akbar Kurtha (Doctor Rana Mistry), Jacqueline Leonard (Doctor Caroline Powers), Sarah Manners (Joanna Helm).

Holding / Source

15.12.2000 **I Saw Mommy Kissing Santa Claus**　　　　　　　　　　　　　　　　DB / DBSWF

Written by David Howard.

With Steven Brand (Chris Rawlings), Mark Adams (Phil Thompson), Stephanie Jacob, Paul Brightwell, Tara Coleman-Starr, Joshua Prime.

SERIES 9

Main regular credit(s):	Executive producer Mal Young; series producer Beverley Dartnall.
Main regular cast:	With Tom Butcher (Doctor Marc Eliot), Ariyon Bakare (Doctor Benjamin Kwarme), Natalie J. Robb (Doctor Jude Carlyle), Stirling Gallacher (Doctor Georgina Woodson), Eva Fontaine (Faith Walker), Diane Keen (Julia McGuire).

Holding / Source

18.12.2003 **All I Want For Christmas**　　　　　　　　　　　　　　　　　　　　DB / DBSWF

Written by Colin Brake; produced by Christiana Ebohon; directed by Trudy Coleman.

With Emma Fildes (Debbie McQueen), Sean Gleeson (Ronnie Woodson), Ivy Omere, Clive Wedderburn, Nadiyah Davis.

SERIES 15

Main regular credit(s):	Designed by Francis Boyle and Nick Turner; executive producer Will Trotter; senior producers Mike Hobson and Peter Eryl Lloyd.
Main regular cast:	With Stephen Boxer (Doctor Joe Fenton), Stirling Gallacher (Doctor Georgina Woodson), Adrian Lewis Morgan (Doctor Jimmi Clay), Michael McKell (Doctor Nick West), Donnaleigh Bailey (Michelle Corrigan), Diane Keen (Julia McGuire), Sean Gleeson (Ronnie Woodson), Anita Carey (Vivien March).

		Production No	Holding / Source
07.12.2007	Home For Christmas	LDXO317W	DB / DBSWF
15.12.2009	O Christmas Tree	DRAB393D	DB / DBSWF
16.12.2009	Mistletoe, Sushi And Wine	DRAB394X	DB / DBSWF

THE DOCTORS

A BBC Birmingham production for BBC 1. Transmission details are for BBC 1. Usual duration: 25 minutes.

Main regular credit(s):　　Format by Donald Bull; theme music by Tony Hatch.

Holding / Source

31.12.1969　　　　　　　　　　　　　　　　　　　　　　　　　　　　　　　　　　　J / 2"

John's heart trouble has caused Liz to have second thoughts about going home to spend Hogmanay in Edinburgh.

Written by Dick Sharples; story by Donald Bull; script editor Maggie Allen; produced by Colin Morris; directed by Gerald Blake.

With Pamela Duncan (Mrs Groom), Justine Lord (Liz McNeal), Lynda Marchal (Molly), Richard Leech (Roger Hayman), Frank Sieman (Deaf Patient), John Barrie (John Somers), Antony Stamboulieh (Andreas Joanides), Olga Lowe (Betty Hamilton), Alexandra Dane (Nella Somers), William Fisher (Malingerer), Angela Galbraith (Practice Nurse), Irene Hamilton (Louise Hayman), Jane Walker (Agnes), John Robinson (Sir Robert McNeal).

DODDY FOR CHRISTMAS

A BBC production for BBC 1. Transmission details are for BBC 1. Duration: 60 minutes.

Written by Eddie Braben and Ken Dodd; music directed by Ken Jones; designed by John Burrowes; produced and directed by Michael Hurll.

Ken Dodd, Graham Stark, Patricia Hayes, Dermot Kelly, Senor Wences, The New Faces, Judith Chalmers, Norman Caley, Jennifer Lowe, Doddy's Diddymen, Ryebank School, Children.

Holding / Source

25.12.1968　　　　　　　　　　　　　　　　　　　　　　　　　　　　　　　　　　　DV /

37 mins of footage held by Kaleidoscope.

DODDY'S CHRISTMAS BIZARRE

An LWT production. Transmission details are for the ATV midlands region. Duration: 53 minutes.

Script editor Barry Cryer; choreography by Bruce McClure; designed by Robert Macgowan; produced and directed by David Bell.

Ken Dodd (Host), Billy Eckstine, David Hamilton, Rudy Cardenas, Talfryn Thomas, The Diddymen.

Holding / Source

26.12.1969　　　　　　　　　　　　　　　　　　　　　　　　　　　　　　　　　　　J / 2"

DODDY'S CHRISTMAS FORCES SHOW

A BBC production for BBC 1. Transmission details are for BBC 1. Duration: 60 minutes.

A film made entirely on location in the Indian Ocean, Cyprus, Gibraltar and Ulster.

Choreography by Nigel Lythgoe; produced and directed by Michael Hurll.

Ken Dodd (Host), Neville King, Jan Hunt, Mark Raffles, Wendy Baldock, Alison Basham, Marie Betts, Marilyn Brown, Suzanne Danielle, Tricia Doran, Lynn Hayworth, Alison Minto, Lamona Snow, Suzie Toogood, The Stan Clarke Seven.

	Holding / Source
24.12.1973	DB-D3 / 2"

DODGER, BONZO AND THE REST

A Thames Television production. Transmission details are for the Central region. Duration: 25 minutes.

Main regular credit(s): Written by Geoffrey Case; produced by Sheila Kinany.

Main regular cast: Lee Ross (Dodger), Sophy McCallum (Bonzo).

	Holding / Source
22.12.1986 "The Christmas Job"	1" / 1"

See also: DRAMARAMA

THE DOG IT WAS THAT DIED

A Granada production for Channel 4. Transmission details are for Channel 4. Duration: 70 minutes.

Written by Tom Stoppard; music by Nigel Hess; produced by Roy Roberts; directed by Peter Wood.

Alan Bates (Blair), Alan Howard (Purvis), Simon Cadell (Hogbin), Michael Hordern (George), Ciaran Madden (Pamela), Maurice Denham (Vicar), Geoffrey Chater (Wren), Zoë Wanamaker (Matron), Sylvestra Le Touzel (Suleika), John Woodvine (Seddon), Robert Lang (Arlon), Steven Law (Suleika's Escort), Stephen Jenn (Boris), Andy Bradford (The Follower).

	Holding / Source
01.01.1989	1" / 1"

DONKEYS' YEARS

An ATV production. Transmission details are for the ATV midlands region. Duration: 75 minutes.

Television adaptation by Michael Frayn of his hit stage play about university life.

  Back they come to their old college - the junior minister, the successful surgeon, the man no one could ever remember, and all the rest-to relive for a nostalgic weekend the friendships and rivalries of their youth, the college port flows freely. Into the resulting beergarden stumbles the Master's wife, searching discreetly but short-sightedly for her lost love.

Written by Michael Frayn; designed by Richard Lake; produced by Joan Brown; directed by Kenneth Ives.

Penelope Keith (Lady Driver), Colin Blakely (Christopher Headingley), Denholm Elliott (Alan Quine), Robert Lang (David Buckle), Timothy Bateson (Dicky Sainsbury), Joe Melia (Kenneth Snell), Christopher Benjamin (Norman Tate), Cyril Luckham (Sidney Birkett), Kenneth Cranham (Bill Taylor).

	Production No	VT Number	Holding / Source
01.01.1980	5410	5410/79	DB / 2"

DON'T ASK ME

A Yorkshire Television production. Transmission details are for the ATV midlands region. Duration: 25 minutes.

	Holding / Source
26.12.1975	DB / 2"

Why do crackers crack, why do stars twinkle and why do candles flicker? Not the sort of festive puzzles that fall out of your Christmas crackers. On the afternoon after the morning after the night before, Don't Ask Me's trio of effervescent experts go into action to relieve your Boxing Day indigestion.

Executive producer Duncan Dallas; produced by Simon Welfare and David Taylor; directed by David Millard.

With Miriam Stoppard (Presenter), Doctor Magnus Pyke (Presenter), David Bellamy (Presenter).

DON'T SAY A WORD

Alternative/Working Title(s): ACTIONS SPEAK LOUDER / STUMP THE STARS

An Associated-Rediffusion production. Transmission details are for the ATV midlands region. Duration: 25 minutes.

Charades on TV, rather like GIVE US A CLUE.

Main regular credit(s): Devised by Mike Stokey.

SERIES 1

Main regular credit(s): Produced and directed by Robert Fleming.

Main regular performer(s): With Ronan O'Casey (Host), Jill Browne, Harry Fowler, Libby Morris, Kenneth Connor, Glen Mason, Una Stubbs.

	Production No	Holding / Source
25.12.1963	LE/25/52	J / Live

With Amanda Barrie, Miriam Karlin, Tony Tanner.

Recorded 25.11.1963. Libby Morris did not appear in this edition.

The game was played with two teams of four each comprising three regulars plus one of the guests. Apart from the Christmas edition, the teams comprised Browne, Morris and Fowler on the one hand and Connor, Mason and Stubbs on the other. For the Christmas show the teams were Browne, Connor, Barrie and Karlin against Fowler, Mason, Tanner and Stubbs.

DON'T SAY A WORD (continued)

Transmission details are for the Rediffusion Television region.

	Production No	Holding / Source
25.12.1964	LE/51/18	J / Live

Directed by John P. Hamilton.

With Jill Browne, Tony Tanner, Libby Morris, Harry Fowler, Diana Dors, Glen Mason, The Patients of Wembley Hospital.

Recorded 18.12.1964.

DOORS OPEN

A Sprout Pictures production for ITV 1. Transmission details are for the Central region. Duration: 100 minutes.

Businessman Mike Mackenzie is incensed by wealthy patrons keeping works of art hidden away. As he and two friends devise a plan to rip off a high-profile Edinburgh gallery, Mike aims to save the paintings and also win back the woman who broke his heart.

Adapted by James Mavor, Sandi Toksvig and Mike Walden; based on a book by Ian Rankin; produced by Jon Finn; directed by Marc Evans.

Douglas Henshall (Mike Mackenzie), Stephen Fry (Professor Robert Gissing), Kenneth Collard (Allan Cruickshank), Lenora Crichlow (Laura Stanton), Brian McCardie (Calloway), Elliot Cowan (Bruce Cameron), Rab Affleck (Hate), Paul McCole (Glenno), Jordan Young (Jonno), Raymond Mearns (Wee Martin), Niall Greig Fulton (Westie).

	Holding / Source
26.12.2012	HD/DB / HDC

DOUBLE YOUR MONEY

An Arlington Television and Radio production for Associated Rediffusion/Rediffusion Television. Transmission details are for Associated Rediffusion/Rediffusion Television. Duration: 25 minutes.

Main regular credit(s): Devised by John B. Beard.

Main regular performer(s): Hughie Green (Presenter).

SERIES 2

Transmission details are for Associated-Rediffusion.

Main regular credit(s): Designed by John Clements; directed by Audrey Starrett.

Main regular performer(s): With Sheila Pockett (Hostess‡), Shirley Deane (Hostess‡), Valerie Drew (Hostess‡), Lalita Rudra (Hostess‡), Maya Guba (Hostess‡), Pat Goddard (Hostess‡), Sheena Marshe (Hostess‡), Verna (Hostess‡), Jean Nunneley (Hostess‡).

	Holding / Source
19.12.1956	J / R1

Hughie brings another selection of contestants from all over the country and puts them through their paces in his own special way. There will be some extra money for Christmas for some of these lucky people.

SERIES 9

Transmission details are for Associated-Rediffusion.

Main regular credit(s): Organist Jackie Brown.

	Holding / Source
26.12.1963 **Christmas Special**	J / FNK

Directed by Don Gale.

With Julie De Marco (Hostess), Barbara Roscoe (Hostess).

When it started, the programmes were generally recorded in sessions of an hour or more and the finished programmes then assembled from material shot in one or more of these sessions. We are not sure when, if ever, the programme started to use videotape. Although 2" tape would have been available at the end of the 1950s, it wouldn't have allowed the flexibility of editing which that system required and so unless or until the programmes were shot live - in which case they may not have been recorded at all - or shot as live, the programme would have had to remain on film until well into the 1960s.

THE DOUG ANTHONY ALL-STARS

A Pozzitive Television production for BBC 2. Transmission details are for BBC 2. Duration: 30 minutes.

Produced and directed by Geoff Posner.

The Doug Anthony Allstars, Paul Livingston (Flacco).

	Holding / Source
31.12.1992	DB-D3 / D3S

DOUGLAS FAIRBANKS JR PRESENTS

A Dougfair Corporation production for ITV. Transmission details are for Associated-Rediffusion. Duration: 25 minutes.

Executive producer Douglas Fairbanks Jr.

	Holding / Source
13.08.1956 **One Way Ticket**	J / B3

Alternative transmissions: ATV Midlands: 17.08.1956.

It is Christmas Day in the sweltering tropics. Dolly Wagner, driven to desperation by home-sickness, makes a secret bargain with a stranger.

Written by Paul Bauman; produced by Lance Comfort; directed by Lawrence Huntington.

With Eunice Gayson (Dolly Wagner), Robert Ayres (Gregg), Lionel Ngakane (Robert), Sylvia Casimir (Primrose), Douglas Fairbanks Jr (Ricky).

Some episodes may have been made under the title "Douglas Fairbanks' Saturday Playhouse" or "Saturday Playhouse". In various regions, some were billed as "Crown Theatre", "Fireside Theatre", "Play Gems" and "Summer Theatre". As late as 1969 these were being shown by Granada under the title "The Short Story".

DOWN AT THE OLD BULL AND BUSH

A Rediffusion Television production. Transmission details are for the Anglia region. Duration: 50 minutes.

Music directed by Peter Knight; designed by Andrew Drummond; produced by Barry Cawtheray; directed by Nicholas Ferguson.

Johnny Ball (Host), The Bachelors, Bud Flanagan, Kenneth McKellar, Scott Walker, Kim Cordell, Kiki Dee, Tommy Bruce, Dixie Lee, Bruce Calder, Celia Hunt, Melville James, Tommy Pudding, Aimi MacDonald.

	Holding / Source
26.12.1967	R1N|n / 40

DOWNTON ABBEY

A Carnival Films production for ITV 1. made in association with Masterpiece. Transmission details are for the Central region. Duration varies - see below for details.

Main regular credit(s):   Created by Julian Fellowes.

SERIES 2

Credits: Written by Julian Fellowes; produced by Liz Trubridge.

	Holding / Source
25.12.2011 **Christmas At Downton Abbey**	HD/DB / HDC

Duration: 100 minutes.

Charge your glasses with the best sherry, find a wing-backed chair and a smoking jacket and prepare to luxuriate in a proper Christmas treat — two hours in the best-known country house in Britain. As the doors open again at Downton Abbey, the magnificent Christmas tree is lit and masters are giving servants their gifts. But there's a shadow across the celebrations as decent, wronged John Bates languishes alone and quietly despairing as he awaits trial for murder. And such is the weight of evidence, it seems that the hangman beckons... It's a terrific episode that crackles with life and rings with emotion. There's Bates's wife Anna, mourning the married life she may never see and Lady Mary trapped in a loveless and purely pragmatic engagement to cold, controlling press baron Carlisle. Her beloved Matthew hovers in her life but both are only too aware of their duty. Honestly, it has absolutely everything you could want for Christmas Night. Even snow.

Directed by Brian Percival.

With Hugh Bonneville (Robert, Earl Of Grantham), Laura Carmichael (Lady Edith Crawley), Jim Carter (Mr Carson), Brendan Coyle (John Bates), Michelle Dockery (Lady Mary Crawley), Maggie Smith (Violet, Dowager Countess Of Grantham), Siobhan Finneran (O'Brien), Joanne Froggatt (Anna), Rob James-Collier (Thomas), Phyllis Logan (Mrs Hughes), Elizabeth McGovern (Cora, Countess Of Grantham), Sophie McShera (Daisy), Lesley Nicol (Mrs Patmore), Dan Stevens (Matthew Crawley), Penelope Wilton (Isobel Crawley), Robert Bathurst (Sir Anthony Strallan), Samantha Bond (Lady Rosamund Painswick), Paul Copley (Mr Mason), Jonathan Coy (George Murray), Iain Glen (Sir Richard Carlisle), Nigel Havers (Lord Hepworth), Sharon Small (Marigold Shore), Timothy Carlton (Judge), Dominic Kemp (Jury Foreman), Simon Poland (Defence Barrister), Tony Pritchard (Prison Officer), Nick Sampson (Prosecuting Barrister).

SERIES 3

Credits: Written by Julian Fellowes; produced by Liz Trubridge.

	Holding / Source
25.12.2012 **A Journey To The Highlands**	HD/DB / HDC

Duration: 100 minutes.

The family are warmly welcomed on a summer break at Duneagle Castle in the Highlands, but there is no disguising the tension between their hosts, Rose's parents.

Directed by Andy Goddard.

With Hugh Bonneville (Robert, Earl Of Grantham), Laura Carmichael (Lady Edith Crawley), Jim Carter (Mr Carson), Brendan Coyle (John Bates), Michelle Dockery (Lady Mary Crawley), Maggie Smith (Violet, Dowager Countess Of Grantham), Siobhan Finneran (O'Brien), Joanne Froggatt (Anna), Rob James-Collier (Thomas), Phyllis Logan (Mrs Hughes), Elizabeth McGovern (Cora, Countess Of Granthan), Sophie McShera (Daisy), Lesley Nicol (Mrs Patmore), Dan Stevens (Matthew Crawley), Penelope Wilton (Isobel Crawley), Kevin Doyle (Molesley), Allen Leech (Tom Branson), Matt Milne (Alfred), Ed Speleers (Jimmy), Kenneth Bryans (Nield), MyAnna Buring (Edna), Ron Donachie (Mr McCree), Charles Edwards (Gregson), Peter Egan (Shrimpie Flintshire), Lily James (Lady Rose MacClare), Simone Lahbib (Wilkins), Phoebe Nicholls (Susan Flintshire), David Robb (Doctor Clarkson), Cara Theobald (Ivy), Shaun Hennessey (Tug-Of-War Judge), John Henshaw (Joss Tufton).

SERIES 4

Credits: Produced by Rupert Ryle-Hodges.

	Holding / Source
25.12.2013 **The London Season**	HD/DB / HDC

Duration: 100 minutes.

When the Crawleys arrive in London for the presentation of debutante Rose, the family becomes implicated in a scandal threatening the monarchy. Robert has to go to great lengths to protect the royal family - and his own.

Written by Julian Fellowes; directed by Jon East.

With Hugh Bonneville (Robert, Earl Of Grantham), Laura Carmichael (Lady Edith Crawley), Jim Carter (Mr Carson), Brendan Coyle (John Bates), Michelle Dockery (Lady Mary Crawley), Maggie Smith (Violet, Dowager Countess Of Grantham), Joanne Froggatt (Anna), Rob James-Collier (Thomas), Phyllis Logan (Mrs Hughes), Elizabeth McGovern (Cora, Countess Of Granthan), Sophie McShera (Daisy), Lesley Nicol (Mrs Patmore), Penelope Wilton (Isobel Crawley), Kevin Doyle (Molesley), Allen Leech (Tom Branson), Ed Speleers (Jimmy), Lily James (Lady Rose MacClare), Cara Theobald (Ivy), Shirley MacLaine (Martha Levinson), Paul Giamatti (Harold Levinson), Douglas Reith (Lord Merton), Poppy Drayton (Madeleine Allsopp), James Fox (Lord Aysgarth), Oliver Dimsdale (Prince Of Wales), Janet Montgomery (Freda Dudley Ward), Julian Ovenden (Charles Blake), Michael Benz (Ethan Slade), Raquel Cassidy (Baxter), Tom Cullen (Anthony Gillingham), Daisy Lewis (Sarah Bunting), Samantha Bond (Lady Rosamund Painswick), Patrick Kennedy (Terence Sampson), Alastair Bruce (Lord Chamberlain), Guy Williams (King George V), Adrian Scarborough (Tim Drewe), Pete Lee-Wilson (Porter).

DR WATSON AND THE DARKWATER HALL MYSTERY

A BBC production for BBC 1. Transmission details are for BBC 1. Duration: 73 minutes.

Written by Kingsley Amis; script editor Richard Broke; music by Tom McCall; designed by Spencer Chapman; produced by Mark Shivas; directed by James Cellan Jones.

Edward Fox (Doctor Watson), Christopher Cazenove (Sir Harry), Jeremy Clyde (Miles), Terence Bayler (Carlos), Elaine Taylor (Emily), John Westbrook (Bradshaw), Carmen Gomez (Dolores), Anthony Langdon (Black Paul), Anne Cunningham (Black Paul's Woman), Marguerite Young (Mrs Hudson), Derek Deadman (Maddocks).

	Production No	VT Number	Holding / Source
27.12.1974	2144/2274	VTC/6HT/95212/A	DB-D3 / 2"

DR. FINLAY'S CASEBOOK

A BBC production for BBC 1. Transmission details are for BBC 1. Usual duration: 50 minutes.

Main regular credit(s): Created by A. J. Cronin; by arrangement with Graham Stewart.

Main regular cast: Andrew Cruickshank (Doctor Cameron), Bill Simpson (Doctor Alan Finlay), Barbara Mullen (Janet).

SERIES 5
Main regular credit(s): Produced by Douglas Allen.

	Holding / Source
25.12.1966 **The Gifts Of The Magi**	DB-R1 /

Written by Harry Green; story editor John Maynard; directed by Joan Craft.

With Eric Woodburn (Doctor Snoddie), Helen Christie, Lynette Meredith, Elizabeth Kentish, Molly Urquhart, Brian Park, Robert Langley, Douglas Cameron, Edmund Bailey, Gaynor Jones, Mandy Mitchell, Lesley Roach, Robert Bartlett, John Walker, Doris Lang.

DRAKE'S VENTURE

A Westward Television production. made in association with Bayerische Rundfunk. Transmission details are for the ATV midlands region. Duration: 99 minutes.

Four hundred years ago Francis Drake set out on a secret mission. As the crew learned of the hazardous nature of the enterprise, Drake faced the rise of mutiny.

Written by John Nelson Burton; music by Stephen Joliffe; camera operated by David Howarth; designed by Jane Martin; executive producer Terry Fleet; produced and directed by Lawrence Gordon Clark.

John Thaw (Sir Francis Drake), Charlotte Cornwell (Queen Elizabeth I), Paul Darrow (Thomas Doughty), Michael Turner (Lord Burghley), David Ryall (Sir Francis Walsingham), Peter Cellier (Sir Christopher Hatton), Esmond Knight (John Dee), Terence Budd (John Drake), Michael Stroud (Admiral Winter), Alan Downer (Nuno Da Silva), Michael Irving (Vicary), Roger Adamson (Fletcher, The Chaplain), Paul Alexander (Ned Bright), John Curless (Pascoe), Philip Trewinnard (Tresillian), Michael Goldie (John Brewer), David Shaw (De Machaumont), Alan Penn (Royal Messenger), Doel Luscombe (First Fisherman), Martin Bax (Second Fisherman).

	Holding / Source
28.12.1980	1" / C1

DRAMARAMA

Produced for Various ITV Companies by a variety of companies (see details below). Transmission details are for the Central region. Usual duration: 25 minutes.

SERIES 5

	VT Number	Holding / Source
30.12.1986 **Frankie's Hat**	37162	1" / 1"

A Thames Television production.

When Sonia visits her married sister, she's looking forward to a grown-up outing. But Frankie has other ideas. She just wants to be a child again. Everywhere they go she manages to embarrass Sonia — and to top it all, she buys a stupid hat.

Based on a story by Jan Mark; music by Barbara Thompson and Jon Hiseman; designed by Peter Elliott; executive producer Alan Horrox; produced and directed by Peter Tabern.

With Zoe Nathenson (Frankie), Vicky Murdock (Sonia), Sharon Bower (Bridget), Paul Beringer (Duncan), Jake Wood (Footballer), Jon Sloane (Biker).

See also: DODGER, BONZO AND THE REST

THE DREAM FACTORY

A Meridian production. Transmission details are for the Meridian region. Duration: 23 minutes.

Fred Dinenage (Presenter), Jill Cochrane (Presenter), Chris Packham, Debbie Thrower, Greg Dyke, Jean Orba, Martin Muncaster, Nathan Colburn, Nigel Lythgoe, Phyllis West, Shaw Taylor, Trevor Baker.

	Holding / Source
30.12.2004	DB / D2S

No end credits.

DREAM TEAM

A Hewland International production for Sky One. Transmission details are for Sky One. Duration varies - see below for details.

SERIES 1
Duration: 25 minutes.

Main regular cast: With Michael Legge (Connor McCarthy), Darren Morfitt (Dean Hocknell), Bill Fellows (Des Baker), John Salthouse (Frank Patcham), Clemency Burton-Hill (Georgina Jacobs), Francis Johnson (Ian Coates), Terry Kiely (Karl Fletcher), Kate Farrah (Lucy Patcham), Katie Newell (Lynette Baker), David Hunt (Michael Jacobs), Helen Latham (Natalie Hocknell), Daymon Britton (Sean Hocknell), Eva Pope (Stephanie Jacobs), Michael Price (Vincent Osamabiku), Clinton Kenyon (Warren Masters), Sam Loggin (Zoe Baker).

	Holding / Source
24.12.1997 "It's Christmas Day. Whose offer should Mandy and Warren accept?"	DB /
31.12.1997 "The New Year's Party gives Sean and Zoe something to think about."	DB /

SERIES 2
Duration: 25 minutes.

Main regular cast: With Craig Robert Young (Alex Wilkinson), Phil Barantini (Billy O'Neil), John Salthouse (Frank Patcham), Kate Magowan (Helen Jenson), Francis Johnson (Ian Coates), Michael Melia (Jerry Block), Gary McDonald (John Black), Julie Smith (Julie Alexander), Terry Kiely (Karl Fletcher), Emma Gilmour (Kelly James), Nathan Constance (Leon Richards), Martin Crewes (Luis Amor Rodriguez), Alison King (Lynda Block), Katie Newell (Lynette Baker), Katisha Kenyon (Mica Hocknell), Helen Latham (Natalie Hocknell), Daymon Britton (Sean Hocknell), Clinton Kenyon (Warren Masters).

	Holding / Source
24.12.1998 "Des loses the ultimate Christmas present."	DB /

DREAM TEAM (continued)

SERIES 6
Duration: 50 minutes.
Main regular cast: With Andy Ansah (Assistant Manager / Manager Number 3), Andy Gray (Himself), Angela Saunders (Tash Parker), Chucky Venice (Curtis Alexander), Dannielle Brent (Jennifer Taylor (30.3.2003 onwards)), David Griffith (FA Committee Chairman (Ep 27)), David Schaal (Detective Inspector Hughes (Ep 13)), Dhafer L'Abidine (Marcel Sabatier), Dystin Johnson (Psychiatric Care Worker (Ep 17)), Emma Gill (Linzie Ferguson), Glen Murphy (Alan Rothman (30.03.2003 onwards)), Jane Campbell (Jacqui Wallis), Jim Alexander (Jamie Parker (until 4.5.2003)), Kevin Keatings (Sky Sports Commentator), Leigh Cranston (Paul Hankin), Ricky Whittle (Ryan Naysmith (27.10.2002 Onwards)), Tim Smith (Clyde Connelly (05.01.2003 Onwards)), Mirem Hernandez (Pilar Hernandez (16.3.2003 Onwards)), Rachel Brady (Abi Fletcher), Ray MacAllen (Jeff Stein), Terry Kiely (Karl Fletcher), Emma Harding (Tara Keane (3.11.2002-9.3.2003)), Scott Mean (Robbie Walsh (Until 23.2.2003)), Shaun Scott (Patrick Doyle), Neil Jackson (Phil Wallis), Lisa Burstow (Sandra Greene), Terence Maynard (Stuart Naysmith).

Holding / Source

22.12.2002 **Deep And Crisp And Getting Even** DB /
Written by Leon Coole.

SERIES 7
Duration: 50 minutes.
Main regular cast: With Terence Maynard (Stuart Naysmith), Mirem Hernandez (Pilar Hernandez), Angela Saunders (Tash Parker), Rachel Brady (Abi Fletcher), Michael Ryan (Dean Boyle), Ray MacAllen (Jeff Stein), Keeley Mills (Alison Hill), Suzanne Church (Anita Johnson), Karen Ferarri (Chelsea Wright (11.01.2004 onwards)), Jacob Lloyd (Christopher Hill), Claire Tomlinson (Herself), Tim Smith (Clyde Connelly), Chucky Venice (Curtis Alexander), Richard Derrington (David Douglas), David Jones (Sky Sports Reporter), Jo Goldie (Donna Connelly (Nee Gibb)), Nicholas Gecks (Doctor Solley), Gregory Donaldson (Detective Sergeant Bailey), Daniel M. Jackson (Elvis Minister), Tuff Sessions (Gospel Singers), Louise Rose (Grace Ikema), Jason Griffiths (Hypnotherapist), Sarah Berger (Jenny Davenport), Brett O'Brien (Joyc), David Larder (Judge), Cheryl Mackie (Karen Boyle (until 4.1.2004)), Kevin Keatings (Match Commentator), Kirsty Gallagher (Interviewer), James Watts (Lee Presley (16.11.2003 onwards)), Neil Newbon (Luke Davenport), Alison King (Lynda Block), Dhafer L'Abidine (Marcel Sabatier (until 9.5.2004)), James Daffern (Matt Webster (until 14.12.2003)), Crystal Yu (Mei Lee), Gordon Case (Minister), Simon Coates (Mr Conraught), Paul Clarkson (Mr Kirk), Stuart Ong (Mr Lau), Richard Woo (Mr Lee), Martine Brown (Mrs Connelly), Neil Warnock (Himself), Nina Muschalik (Nikki Peggs), David Cochran (OC Officer 1), Paul Johnston (OC Officer 2), Leigh Cranston (Paul Hankin), Phil Edwards (Himself), Neil Jackson (Phil Wallis), Ricky Whittle (Ryan Naysmith), Lisa Burstow (Sandra Greene), Daniel Green (Steve), Alan Stocks (Tony Boyle (until 21.12.2003)), Philip Brodie (Vivan 'Jaws' Wright (11.1.2004 onwards)), Jon Yang (Zhao 'Bruce' Qiang 19.10.2003-onwards)).

Holding / Source

21.12.2003 **Oh Come All Ye Faithful** DB /
Written by Harry Hewland and Ellen Taylor.

04.01.2004 **New Years Resolution** DB /
Written by Rachel Flowerday.

DRIVE-IN
A Thames Television production. Transmission details are for the Thames Television region. Duration: 25 minutes.
Main regular cast: Shaw Taylor (Presenter).

SERIES 1
Main regular credit(s): Produced by Jim Pople; directed by Bob Service.

Holding / Source

21.12.1971
Christmas drink driving campaign and snow chains on cars in the Winter.
With John Anthony, Richard Hudson-Evans.

DROP THE DEAD DONKEY
Alternative/Working Title(s): DEAD BELGIANS DON'T COUNT / DEAD KUWAITIS DON'T COUNT
A Hat Trick production for Channel 4. Transmission details are for Channel 4. Duration: 25 minutes.
Main regular credits(s): Created by Andy Hamilton and Guy Jenkin; theme music by Matthew Scott.
Main regular cast: Robert Duncan (Gus Hedges), Neil Pearson (Dave Charnley), Jeff Rawle (George Dent), David Swift (Henry Davenport), Stephen Tompkinson (Damien Day), Victoria Wicks (Sally Smedley).

SERIES 2
Main regular credit(s): Written by Andy Hamilton and Guy Jenkin; executive producer Denise O'Donoghue; produced by Andy Hamilton and Guy Jenkin; directed by Liddy Oldroyd.
Main regular cast: With Haydn Gwynne (Alex Pates), Susannah Doyle (Joy Merryweather).

Holding / Source

19.12.1991 **The Office Party** DB / 1"S
Alt.Title(s): *Xmas Party*
Tuesday 17th December. The Christmas Party. George gets drunk and can't remember anything. Why has he a signed photograph of Frankie Howerd? Alex wakes up in bed with Dave... will it stay a secret or will the office find out?
Additional material by Elly Brewer; costume Jo Thompson and Clodagh Scott; make-up Marella Shearer, Sue Ayling and Jenny Binsted; lighting director John Watt; sound supervisor Keith Mayes; camera supervisor Martin Hawkins; designed by Graeme Story and Wallace Heim; production manager Avon Harpley.
With Penelope Nice (Nurse), James Bowers (Photocopier Man).

DUNRULIN'

A Jon Blair Film Company production for BBC 1. Transmission details are for BBC 1. Duration: 30 minutes.

Dulwich: the distant future. Some people never really retire.

	Production No	Holding / Source
##.##.#### **[untransmitted 1990 pilot]**	LLCB050P	DB / 1"

Written by Alistair Beaton and John Wells; from an idea by Jon Blair; produced by Jon Blair; directed by Richard Boden.

With Angela Thorne (Mrs Thatcher), John Wells (Mr Thatcher), Larry Lamb (Chainsaw Smith), Owen Brenman (Master Thatcher), Hilary Gish (Miss Thatcher), John Cater (Mr Mickey), Jilly Johnson (Mandy), Jestyn Phillips (Registrar), Richenda Carey (1st Nurse), John Dougall [as John Dougal] (Junior Doctor), Janet Palmer (2nd Nurse), Malcolm Rogers (Man In Bed).

23.12.1990 **An Active Citizen Is A Healthy Citizen** DB / 1"

Written by Alistair Beaton and John Wells; produced by Jon Blair; directed by Richard Boden.

With Angela Thorne (Mrs Margaret Thatcher), John Wells (Mr Denis Thatcher), Hilary Gish (Ms Carol Thatcher), Owen Brenman (Master Mark Thatcher), Kenneth Cranham (Mr Kneecap Smith), Liz Smith (Mrs Trodd), John Cater (The Vicar), Eiji Kusuhara (Mr Kishimoto), Jilly Johnson (Mandy), Richenda Carey (Sister), Colin Starkey (Senior Doctor), John Dougall (Junior Doctor), Jan Ravens (BBC Announcer).

DUTY FREE

A Yorkshire Television production. Transmission details are for the Central region.

Main regular credit(s): Written by Eric Chappell and Jean Warr; music by Robert Hartley, Peter Knight and Alan Parker; produced by Vernon Lawrence.

Main regular cast: Keith Barron (David Pearce), Gwen Taylor (Amy Pearce), Joanna Van Gyseghem (Linda Cochran), Neil Stacy (Robert Cochran), Carlos Douglas (Carlos).

SERIES 3

Main regular credit(s): Designed by Colin Pigott; directed by Les Chatfield.

Holding / Source

25.12.1986 **A Duty Free Christmas** 1" / 1"

Duration: 53 minutes.

With John Barron, Damaris Hayman, Bobby Heath.

THE EAMONN ANDREWS SHOW

An ABC/Thames production.

Main regular performer(s): Eamonn Andrews (Host).

SERIES 5

A Thames Television production. Transmission details are for the ATV midlands region. Duration: 40 minutes.

Main regular credit(s): Produced by Bryan Izzard.

Holding / Source

26.12.1968 **Boxing Day Special** J / 40
With Kenny Ball, Danny La Rue, Roy Hudd, Don Henderson.

EARL 'FATHA' HINES

An ATV production. Transmission details are for the Scottish Television region. Duration: 50 minutes.

A celebration of the 70th birthday of the man the New York Times described as America's greatest musician, Earl "Fatha" Hines - a jazz-pianist who was playing professional piano before the word jazz was invented. The tribute to Earl Hines and his music begins in the roaring Twenties when "Fatha" Hines and Louis Armstrong were transforming the popular concept of jazz. After half a century of brilliant music-making, the London Times described Hines as "The Muhammad Ali of jazz piano."

Camera operated by Chris Menges and Jimmy Dibling; film editor Roger James; produced and directed by Charlie Nairn.

Earl Hines.

Holding / Source

30.12.1975 DB / C1

EASTENDERS

Alternative/Working Title(s): EAST 8

A BBC production for BBC 1. Transmission details are for BBC 1. Usual duration: 30 minutes.

Main regular credit(s): Created by Julia Smith and Tony Holland; theme music by Simon May and Leslie Osborne.

Main regular credit(s): Script editor Tony Holland; production associates Nicholas Orchard and Corinne Hollingworth; produced by Julia Smith.

Holding / Source

24.12.1985 "Right. All together on 'Good King Wencelas', and anybody not singing gets chucked out of the boozer and forced to watch Walford play on Boxing Day" DB / 1"

Written by Jim Hawkins; directed by Chris Clough.

With Anthony Short (John), Anna Wing (Lou Beale), Peter Dean (Pete Beale), Gillian Taylforth (Kathy Beale), Adam Woodyatt (Ian Beale), Wendy Richard (Pauline Fowler), Bill Treacher (Arthur Fowler), Susan Tully (Michelle Fowler), Leslie Grantham (Den Watts), Anita Dobson (Angie Watts), Letitia Dean (Sharon Watts), Tom Watt (Lofty Holloway), Gretchen Franklin (Ethel Skinner), June Brown (Dot Cotton), Nick Berry (Simon Wicks), Oscar James (Tony Carpenter), Paul J. Medford (Kelvin Carpenter), Delanie Forbes (Cassie Carpenter), Shirley Cheriton (Debbie Wilkins), Ross Davidson (Andy O'Brien), Andrew Johnson (Saeed Jeffery), Shreela Ghosh (Naima Jeffery), Sandy Ratcliff (Sue Osman), Nejdet Salih (Ali Osman), Linda Davidson (Mary Smith), Allan O'Keefe (Mary's Father), Douglas Fielding (Detective Sergeant Quick), Elaine Donnelly (Woman Police Constable), Sally Sagoe (Hannah Carpenter), Leonard Fenton (Doctor Legg).

26.12.1985 "I bet ours was the only Christmas where everyone sat round in woolly hats instead of paper ones" DB / 1"

Written by Tony McHale; directed by Chris Clough.

With Anthony Short (John), Anna Wing (Lou Beale), Peter Dean (Pete Beale), Gillian Taylforth (Kathy Beale), Adam Woodyatt (Ian Beale), Wendy Richard (Pauline Fowler), Bill Treacher (Arthur Fowler), Susan Tully (Michelle Fowler), Leslie Grantham (Den Watts), Anita Dobson (Angie Watts), Letitia Dean (Sharon Watts), Tom Watt (Lofty Holloway), Gretchen Franklin (Ethel Skinner), June Brown (Dot Cotton), Nick Berry (Simon Wicks), Oscar James (Tony Carpenter), Paul J. Medford (Kelvin Carpenter), Delanie Forbes (Cassie Carpenter), Shirley Cheriton (Debbie Wilkins), Ross Davidson (Andy O'Brien), Andrew Johnson (Saeed Jeffery), Shreela Ghosh (Naima Jeffery), Sandy Ratcliff (Sue Osman), Nejdet Salih (Ali Osman), Linda Davidson (Mary Smith), Allan O'Keefe (Mary's Father), Douglas Fielding (Detective Sergeant Quick), Elaine Donnelly (Woman Police Constable), Sally Sagoe (Hannah Carpenter), Leonard Fenton (Doctor Legg).

Holding / Source

23.12.1986 "Well I hope you show them more of the spirit of Christmas than you've shown me, Pete" DB / 1"

Written by Bill Lyons; series script editor Tony Holland; produced by Julia Smith; directed by Nicholas Prosser.

With Anita Dobson (Angie), Leslie Grantham (Den), Letitia Dean (Sharon), Jane How (Jan), Bill Treacher (Arthur), Wendy Richard (Pauline), Susan Tully (Michelle), Tom Watt (Lofty), Anna Wing (Lou), Peter Dean (Pete), Gillian Taylforth (Kathy), Adam Woodyatt (Ian), Nick Berry (Wicksy), Pam St. Clement (Pat), Linda Davidson (Mary), Shreela Ghosh (Naima), Shirley Cheriton (Debs), William Boyde (Willmott-Brown), June Brown (Dot Cotton), Christopher Hancock (Charlie Cotton), Gretchen Franklin (Ethel), Sally Sagoe (Hannah), Oscar James (Tony), Judith Jacob (Carmel), Paul J. Medford (Kelvin), Delanie Forbes (Cassie), Gary Hailes (Barry), Michael Cashman (Colin), Sandy Ratcliff (Sue), Nejdet Salih (Ali), Haluk Bilginer (Mehmet), Donald Tandy (Tom).

25.12.1986 "Den tells Angie he wants a divorce" DB / 1"

Written by Tony Holland; series script editor Tony Holland; script editor Estelle Daniel; production associates Corinne Hollingworth and Mike Hudson; produced and directed by Julia Smith.

With Jane How (Jan), Leslie Grantham (Den), Anita Dobson (Angie), Anna Wing (Lou), Wendy Richard (Pauline), Bill Treacher (Arthur), Adam Woodyatt (Ian), Gillian Taylforth (Kathy), Peter Dean (Pete), Pam St. Clement (Pat), Nick Berry (Wicksy), Susan Tully (Michelle), Tom Watt (Lofty), June Brown (Dot Cotton), Gretchen Franklin (Ethel), Letitia Dean (Sharon), Judith Jacob (Carmel), Linda Davidson (Mary), Donald Tandy (Tom), William Boyde (Willmott-Brown), Shirley Cheriton (Debs), Michael Cashman (Colin), Gary Hailes (Barry), Oscar James (Tony), Sally Sagoe (Hannah), Delanie Forbes (Cassie), Paul J. Medford (Kelvin), Sandy Ratcliff (Sue), Nejdet Salih (Ali).

25.12.1986 "They should bring back hanging for people like Den Watts" DB / 1"

Written by Tony Holland; series script editor Tony Holland; script editor Estelle Daniel; production associates Corinne Hollingworth and Mike Hudson; produced and directed by Julia Smith.

With Jane How (Jan), Leslie Grantham (Den), Anita Dobson (Angie), Anna Wing (Lou), Wendy Richard (Pauline), Bill Treacher (Arthur), Adam Woodyatt (Ian), Gillian Taylforth (Kathy), Peter Dean (Pete), Pam St. Clement (Pat), Nick Berry (Wicksy), Susan Tully (Michelle), Tom Watt (Lofty), June Brown (Dot Cotton), Gretchen Franklin (Ethel), Letitia Dean (Sharon), Judith Jacob (Carmel), Linda Davidson (Mary), Donald Tandy (Tom), William Boyde (Willmott-Brown), Shirley Cheriton (Debs), Michael Cashman (Colin), Gary Hailes (Barry), Oscar James (Tony), Sally Sagoe (Hannah), Delanie Forbes (Cassie), Paul J. Medford (Kelvin), Sandy Ratcliff (Sue), Nejdet Salih (Ali), Shreela Ghosh (Naima).

EASTENDERS (continued)   British Christmas Television Guide

                                                                       Holding / Source

24.12.1987 "I've never wanted anything else, Charlie. I couldn't be happier even if the Archangel Gabriel walked through that door"   DB / 1"

Written by Charlie Humphreys; script editor John Maynard; designed by Keith Harris, John Stout and Richard Dupré; production associates Corinne Hollingworth and Mike Hudson; production managers Gary Downie and Rob Evans; series producer Julia Smith; produced by Tony Virgo; directed by Tom Kingdon and Matthew Robinson.

With Bill Treacher (Arthur), William Boyde (James Willmott-Brown), Wendy Richard (Pauline), Anna Wing (Lou), Peter Dean (Pete), Gillian Taylforth (Kathy), Tom Watt (Lofty), Susan Tully (Michelle), Gary Hailes (Barry), Michael Cashman (Colin), June Brown (Dot Cotton), Christopher Hancock (Charlie Cotton), Gretchen Franklin (Ethel), Linda Davidson (Mary), Allan O'Keefe (Chris Smith), Leslie Grantham (Den), Nejdet Salih (Ali), Sandy Ratcliff (Sue), Pip Miller (McIntyre), Gary McDonald (Darren), Aaron Carrington (Junior), Anita Dobson (Angie), Letitia Dean (Sharon), Judith Jacob (Carmel), David Gillespie (Duncan), Maggie Ford (Joan), Jamie Lehane (Boy Reader), Kathryn Ludlow (Girl Reader), Adam Woodyatt (Ian).

25.12.1987 "Hello Mum, back again like a bad penny"   DB / 1"

Written by Jane Hollowood; script editor John Maynard; series producer Julia Smith; directed by Matthew Robinson.

With Bill Treacher (Arthur), William Boyde (James Willmott-Brown), Wendy Richard (Pauline), David Scarboro (Mark), Anna Wing (Lou), Peter Dean (Pete), Gillian Taylforth (Kathy), Tom Watt (Lofty), Susan Tully (Michelle), Gary Hailes (Barry), Michael Cashman (Colin), Leon Greene (Mr Clark), Gary Webster (Graham), June Brown (Dot Cotton), Christopher Hancock (Charlie Cotton), Gretchen Franklin (Ethel), Linda Davidson (Mary), Christopher McHallem (Rod), Allan O'Keefe (Chris Smith), Eileen O'Brien (Mrs Smith), Leslie Grantham (Den), Pam St. Clement (Pat), Matilda Ziegler (Donna), Adam Woodyatt (Ian), Nejdet Salih (Ali), Sandy Ratcliff (Sue), Pip Miller (McIntyre), Gary McDonald (Darren), Aaron Carrington (Junior), Anita Dobson (Angie), Letitia Dean (Sharon), Kathryn Apanowicz (Mags), Nick Berry (Wicksy), Jason Watkins (Gerry), Leonard Maguire (Uncle), Donald Tandy (Tom).

                                                                       Holding / Source

25.12.1990 "Diane gets a Christmas delivery"   DB / 1"

Written by Michael Russell; produced by Corinne Hollingworth; directed by Alan Wareing.

With Bryen Lawrence (Police Constable), Paddy Navin (Mrs Warren), Ellam Hull (Wayne Harris), Stewart Harwood (Father Christmas), Peter Dean (Pete), Sophie Lawrence (Diane), Todd Carty (Mark), Susan Tully (Michelle), Mark Bannister (Doctor), Michelle Collins (Cindy), Nick Berry (Wicksy), Adam Woodyatt (Ian), Pam St. Clement (Pat), Mike Reid (Frank), Rebecca Michael (Janine), Sid Owen (Ricky), Wendy Richard (Pauline), Bill Treacher (Arthur), June Brown (Dot Cotton), Gretchen Franklin (Ethel), Steve McFadden (Phil), Ross Kemp (Grant), Letitia Dean (Sharon), Jacqui Gordon-Lawrence (Etta), Leroy Golding (Celestine), Jill Brassington (Mrs George), Leonard Fenton (Doctor Legg), Gillian Taylforth (Kathy), Michael Melia (Eddie), Abigail Bond (Woman Police Constable), Danniella Westbrook (Sam), George Russo (Jason), Glyn Grimstead (Mr Warren), Steven Woodcock (Clyde), Tommy Eytle (Jules), Garey Bridges (Lloyd), Michelle Gayle (Hattie), Adjoa Andoh (Karen).

                                                                       Holding / Source

24.12.1991 "Ian wants some drama in the festive season"   DB / 1"S

Written by Tony McHale; produced by Corinne Hollingworth; directed by David Innes Edwards.

With Bill Treacher (Arthur Fowler), Peter Dean (Pete Beale), Wendy Richard (Pauline Fowler), Susan Tully (Michelle), Todd Carty (Mark Fowler), Jacquetta May (Rachel), Pam St. Clement (Pat), Mike Reid (Frank Butcher), Gillian Taylforth (Kathy), Adam Woodyatt (Ian Beale), Letitia Dean (Sharon), Ross Kemp (Grant Mitchell), Danniella Westbrook (Sam), Steve McFadden (Phil Mitchell), Steven Woodcock (Clyde), Michelle Gayle (Hattie), Mark Monero (Steve), June Brown (Dot Cotton), Peter Stockbridge (Jack), Sid Owen (Ricky Butcher), Gretchen Franklin (Ethel).

26.12.1991 "Grant's Boxing Day surprise"   DB / 1"S

Written by Tony McHale; produced by Corinne Hollingworth; directed by David Innes Edwards.

With Bill Treacher (Arthur Fowler), Peter Dean (Pete Beale), Wendy Richard (Pauline Fowler), Susan Tully (Michelle), Todd Carty (Mark Fowler), Jacquetta May (Rachel), Pam St. Clement (Pat), Mike Reid (Frank Butcher), Gillian Taylforth (Kathy), Adam Woodyatt (Ian Beale), Letitia Dean (Sharon), Ross Kemp (Grant Mitchell), Danniella Westbrook (Sam), Steve McFadden (Phil Mitchell), Steven Woodcock (Clyde), Michelle Gayle (Hattie), Mark Monero (Steve), June Brown (Dot Cotton), Peter Stockbridge (Jack), Sid Owen (Ricky Butcher), Gretchen Franklin (Ethel).

                                                                       Holding / Source

24.12.1992   DB / 1"S

Written by Tony McHale; directed by Bill Hays.

25.12.1992   DB / 1"S

Written by Tony McHale; directed by Leonard Lewis.

                                                                       Holding / Source

25.12.1993   DB / 1"S

Written by Tony McHale.

                                                                       Holding / Source

25.12.1994   DB / D3S

Written by Tony Jordan; directed by Jo Johnson.

26.12.1994   DB / D3S

Written by Tony Jordan; directed by Jo Johnson.

                                                                       Holding / Source

25.12.1995 "Pat's perfect Christmas is surprising" - a   DB / D3S

Written by David Richard-Fox; produced by Josephine Ward; directed by Pip Short.

With Bill Treacher (Arthur Fowler), Wendy Richard (Pauline Fowler), Michael Tudor Barnes (Willy Roper), Todd Carty (Mark Fowler), Caroline Paterson (Ruth Fowler), Pam St. Clement (Pat Butcher), Tony Caunter (Roy Evans), Sid Owen (Ricky Butcher), Michelle Collins (Cindy Beale), Adam Woodyatt (Ian Beale), Michael French (David Wicks), Shaun Williamson (Barry Evans), Shobu Kapoor (Gita Kapoor), Lyndham Gregory (Guppy Sharma), Mark Monero (Steve Elliott), Marlaine Gordon (Lydia), Harry Landis (Felix Kawalski), Barbara Windsor (Peggy Mitchell), Paul Bradley (Nigel Bates), Howard Antony (Alan Jackson), Lindsey Coulson (Carol Jackson), Mona Hammond (Blossom Jackson), Dean Gaffney (Robbie Jackson), John Pickard (Kevin), Debbie Arnold (April Branning), Gemma Bissix (Clare Tyler), Steve McFadden (Phil Mitchell), Gillian Taylforth (Kathy Mitchell), Ross Kemp (Grant Mitchell), Patsy Palmer (Bianca Jackson), Martine McCutcheon (Tiffany Raymond), Daniela Denby-Ashe (Sarah Hills), Mike Reid (Frank Butcher).

EASTENDERS

British Christmas Television Guide	EASTENDERS (continued)

25.12.1995 "The mystery visitor" - b DB / D3S
Written by David Richard-Fox; produced by Josephine Ward; directed by Pip Short.

With Bill Treacher (Arthur Fowler), Wendy Richard (Pauline Fowler), Michael Tudor Barnes (Willy Roper), Todd Carty (Mark Fowler), Caroline Paterson (Ruth Fowler), Pam St. Clement (Pat Butcher), Tony Caunter (Roy Evans), Sid Owen (Ricky Butcher), Michelle Collins (Cindy Beale), Adam Woodyatt (Ian Beale), Michael French (David Wicks), Shaun Williamson (Barry Evans), Shobu Kapoor (Gita Kapoor), Lyndham Gregory (Guppy Sharma), Mark Monero (Steve Elliott), Marlaine Gordon (Lydia), Harry Landis (Felix Kawalski), Barbara Windsor (Peggy Mitchell), Paul Bradley (Nigel Bates), Howard Antony (Alan Jackson), Lindsey Coulson (Carol Jackson), Mona Hammond (Blossom Jackson), Dean Gaffney (Robbie Jackson), John Pickard (Kevin), Debbie Arnold (April Branning), Gemma Bissix (Clare Tyler), Steve McFadden (Phil Mitchell), Gillian Taylforth (Kathy Mitchell), Ross Kemp (Grant Mitchell), Patsy Palmer (Bianca Jackson), Martine McCutcheon (Tiffany Raymond), Daniela Denby-Ashe (Sarah Hills), Mike Reid (Frank Butcher).

Holding / Source
26.12.1996 DB / D3S

Holding / Source
24.12.1998 DB / DBS

25.12.1998 DB / DBS

With Patsy Palmer (Bianca Butcher), Sid Owen (Ricky Butcher), Nadia Sawalha (Annie Palmer), Marc Bannerman (Gianni Di Marco), Andrew Lynford (Simon Raymond), Desune Coleman (Lenny Wallace), Leila Birch (Teresa Di Marco), Richard Driscoll (Alex Healy), Barbara Keogh (Lilly Mattock), Melanie Clark Pullen (Mary Flaherty), Martine McCutcheon (Tiffany Mitchell), Ross Kemp (Grant Mitchell), Steve McFadden (Phil Mitchell), Jack Ryder (Jamie Mitchell), Barbara Windsor (Peggy Mitchell), Mike Reid (Frank Butcher), Pam St. Clement (Pat Evans), Tony Caunter (Roy Evans), Shaun Williamson (Barry Evans), Dean Gaffney (Robbie Jackson), Louise Jameson (Rosa Di Marco), Michael Greco (Beppe Di Marco), Tamzin Outhwaite (Melanie), Leslie Schofield (Jeff Healy), June Brown (Dot), Todd Carty (Mark Fowler).

25.12.1999 "Grant's Christmas present helps Phil make things up with his mum" - a DB / DBSW
Written by Rob Gittins; executive producer Matthew Robinson.

With Roberta Taylor (Irene), Martine McCutcheon (Tiffany Mitchell), Ross Kemp (Grant Mitchell), Steve McFadden (Phil Mitchell), Mike Reid (Frank Butcher), Louise Jameson (Rosa Di Marco), Tamzin Outhwaite (Melanie), Leslie Schofield (Jeff Healy), June Brown (Dot), Martin Kemp (Steve Mitchell), Barbara Windsor (Peggy Mitchell), Gillian Taylforth (Kathy), Tamzin Outhwaite (Melanie Healy), Adam Woodyatt (Ian Beale), Lucy Benjamin (Lisa Shaw), Sid Owen (Ricky Butcher), Danniella Westbrook (Sam Mitchell), Charlie Brooks (Janine Butcher), Jack Ryder (Jamie Mitchell), Shaun Williamson (Barry Evans), Lucy Speed (Natalie Price), Cindy O'Callaghan (Andrea Price), Pam St. Clement (Pat Evans), Tony Caunter (Roy Evans), Michael Greco (Beppe Di Marco), Marc Bannerman (Gianni Di Marco), Race Davies (Jackie), Leila Birch (Teresa Di Marco), Gavin Richards (Terry), Jamie Jarvis (Troy Harvey), Todd Carty (Mark Fowler), Martin Kemp (Steve Owen), Wendy Richard (Pauline Fowler), June Brown (Dot Cotton), Dean Gaffney (Robbie Jackson), John Bardon (Jim), Troy Titus-Adams (Nina Harris), Joan Hooley (Josie McFarlane), Natalie Cassidy (Sonia Jackson), Krystle Williams (Kim McFarlane), James Alexandrou (Martin Fowler), Jake Kyprianou (Joe), Casey Anne Rothery (Lucy Beale), Carly Hillman (Nicky), Joe Absolom (Matthew Rose), Sylvester Williams (Mick McFarlane).

25.12.1999 "Barry tries to win back Natalie" DB / DBSW
Written by Rob Gittins; executive producer Matthew Robinson.

With Steve McFadden (Phil Mitchell), Barbara Windsor (Peggy Mitchell), Gillian Taylforth (Kathy), Tamzin Outhwaite (Melanie Healy), Adam Woodyatt (Ian Beale), Lucy Benjamin (Lisa Shaw), Mike Reid (Frank Butcher), Sid Owen (Ricky Butcher), Danniella Westbrook (Sam Mitchell), Charlie Brooks (Janine Butcher), Jack Ryder (Jamie Mitchell), Shaun Williamson (Barry Evans), Lucy Speed (Natalie Price), Cindy O'Callaghan (Andrea Price), Pam St. Clement (Pat Evans), Tony Caunter (Roy Evans), Louise Jameson (Rosa Di Marco), Michael Greco (Beppe Di Marco), Marc Bannerman (Gianni Di Marco), Race Davies (Jackie), Leila Birch (Teresa Di Marco), Roberta Taylor (Irene), Gavin Richards (Terry), Jamie Jarvis (Troy Harvey), Todd Carty (Mark Fowler), Martin Kemp (Steve Owen), Leslie Schofield (Jeff Healy), Wendy Richard (Pauline Fowler), June Brown (Dot Cotton), Dean Gaffney (Robbie Jackson), John Bardon (Jim), Troy Titus-Adams (Nina Harris), Joan Hooley (Josie McFarlane), Natalie Cassidy (Sonia Jackson), Krystle Williams (Kim McFarlane), James Alexandrou (Martin Fowler), Jake Kyprianou (Joe), Casey Anne Rothery (Lucy Beale), Carly Hillman (Nicky), Joe Absolom (Matthew Rose), Sylvester Williams (Mick McFarlane).

25.12.2000 DB / DBSW
Story consultant Tony Jordan; executive producer John Yorke.

25.12.2000 DB / DBSW
Story consultant Tony Jordan; executive producer John Yorke.

With John Altman (Nick), Jessie Wallace (Kat Slater), Elaine Lordan (Lynne Slater), Martin Kemp (Steve Mitchell), Michelle Ryan (Zoe Slater), Ricky Groves (Gary Hobbs), Todd Carty (Mark Fowler), Natalie Cassidy (Sonia), June Brown (Dot), Pam St. Clement (Pat Evans), James Alexandrou (Martin Fowler), Dean Gaffney (Robbie Jackson), Jack Ryder (Jamie Mitchell).

24.12.2001 DB / DBSW
Story consultant Tony Jordan; series producer Lorraine Newman.

25.12.2001 DB / DBSW
Story consultant Tony Jordan; series producer Lorraine Newman.

With Lucy Benjamin (Lisa), Alex Ferns (Trevor), Steve McFadden (Phil Mitchell), Letitia Dean (Sharon), Dean Gaffney (Robbie Jackson), Tamzin Outhwaite (Melanie), Perry Fenwick (Billy Mitchell), Kacey Ainsworth (Little Mo), Jack Ryder (Jamie Mitchell), Michelle Ryan (Zoe Slater), Tony Caunter (Roy Evans), Barbara Windsor (Peggy Mitchell), June Brown (Dot), John Bardon (Jim), Martin Kemp (Steve Mitchell).

24.12.2002 DB / DBSW
Story consultant Tony Jordan; series producer Lorraine Newman.

25.12.2002 DB / DBSW
Story consultant Tony Jordan; series producer Lorraine Newman.

With Nicholas R. Bailey (Anthony), Lucy Speed (Natalie), Jill Halfpenny (Kate), Jack Ryder (Jamie Mitchell), Michelle Ryan (Zoe Slater), Steve McFadden (Phil Mitchell), Hannah Waterman (Laura), Perry Fenwick (Billy Mitchell), Kacey Ainsworth (Little Mo), Shaun Williamson (Barry Evans), Natalie Cassidy (Sonia), Jessie Wallace (Kat Slater), Barbara Windsor (Peggy Mitchell), Laila Morse (Mo Slater), James Alexandrou (Martin Fowler), John Bardon (Jim), Ricky Groves (Gary Hobbs).

EASTENDERS (continued)

25.12.2003 "Alfie tries to arrange his wedding" - a — DB / DBSW
Duration: 40 minutes.
Written by Tony Jordan; story consultant Tony Jordan; series producer Lorraine Newman; produced by Jo Johnson; directed by Colin Wratten.
With David Walliams (Ray), Gary Beadle (Paul), Mary Woodvine (Mary), Shane Richie (Alfie Moon), Jessie Wallace (Kat Slater), Kacey Ainsworth (Little Mo), Michelle Ryan (Zoe Slater), Nabil Elouahabi (Tariq), Ray Panthaki (Ronny), Steve McFadden (Phil Mitchell), Leslie Grantham (Den Watts), Nigel Harman (Dennis Rickman), Jill Halfpenny (Kate), Letitia Dean (Sharon), Kim Medcalf (Sam), Shaun Williamson (Barry Evans), Charlie Brooks (Janine Butcher), Elaine Lordan (Lynne Slater), Ricky Groves (Gary Hobbs), Hannah Waterman (Laura), Ian Lavender (Derek).

25.12.2003 "Phil and Den have a showdown at the club. Alfie marries Kat" - b — DB / DBSW
Duration: 40 minutes.
Written by Tony Jordan; story consultant Tony Jordan; series producer Lorraine Newman; produced by Jo Johnson; directed by Colin Wratten.

24.12.2004 — DB / DBSW
Story consultant Tony Jordan; series producer Peter Rose.

25.12.2004 "Sharon leaves... alone" — DB / DBSW
Duration: 60 minutes.
Written by Deborah Cook and Simon Ashdown; script supervisor Sally Brocklehurst; story consultant Tony Jordan; series story editor Simon Winstone; series script editor Natasha Phillips; story producer Huw Kennair-Jones; story editor Laura Watson; script editor Madeleine Brookman; series consultant Tony Jordan; associate producer Michael Darbon; executive producer Kathleen Hutchison; series producer Sharon Hughff; produced by Colin Wratten; directed by Clive Arnold.
With Scarlett Johnson (Vicki), Christopher Parker (Spencer Moon), Michael Higgs (Andy Hunter), Simon Daye (Cabbie), Dan Milne (David), Desmond McNamara (Bob), James Kavaz (Terry), Angharad Parry (Sian), Raji James (Ash), Joe Swash (Mickey), Leslie Grantham (Den Watts), Letitia Dean (Sharon), Michelle Ryan (Zoe Slater), Nigel Harman (Dennis Rickman), Shane Richie (Alfie Moon), Hilda Braid (Nana Moon), Tracy-Ann Oberman (Chrissie Watts), Laurie Brett (Jane), Adam Woodyatt (Ian Beale), James Martin (Peter Beale), Melissa Suffield (Lucy Beale), Derek Martin (Charlie Slater), Pam St. Clement (Pat Evans), Laila Morse (Mo Slater), Ricky Groves (Gary Hobbs), Lacey Turner (Stacey Slater), Gerry Cowper (Rosie), David Spinx (Keith), Charlie G. Hawkins (Darren), Shana Swash (Demie), Wendy Richard (Pauline Fowler), Ian Lavender (Derek), June Brown (Dot), John Bardon (Jim), Kacey Ainsworth (Little Mo), Perry Fenwick (Billy Mitchell), Rudolph Walker (Patrick), Angela Wynter (Yolande), Kim Medcalf (Sam), Cliff Parisi (Minty), Pooja Shah (Kareena), Ameet Chana (Adi), Jemma Walker (Sasha), Ray Panthaki (Ronny), Nabil Elouahabi (Tariq), Mohammed George (Gus), Joseph Kpobie (Juley).

	Production No	Holding / Source

19.12.2005 "Kat consoles Alfie. Billy becomes Father Christmas. Juley's condom splits open causing Ruby to panic" — DB / DBSW
Written by David Lloyd; series story editor Kevin Rundle; script producer Tom Mullens; script editor Martina Lloyd; series consultant Tony Jordan; executive producer Kate Harwood; head of production Nigel Taylor; series producer Lorraine Newman; produced by Jyoti Fernandes; directed by Graeme Hattrick.
With Ricky Groves (Gary Hobbs), Jessie Wallace (Kat Slater), Cliff Parisi (Minty), Billy Murray (Johnny Allan), Shane Richie (Alfie Moon), James Alexandrou (Martin Fowler), Natalie Cassidy (Sonia), Wendy Richard (Pauline Fowler), Ray Brooks (Joe), Louisa Lytton (Ruby), Joseph Kpobie (Juley), Mohammed George (Gus), Perry Fenwick (Billy Mitchell), Emma Barton (Honey), Petra Letang (Naomi), Gerry Cowper (Rosie), David Spinx (Keith), Kara Tointon (Dawn), Charlie G. Hawkins (Darren), Shana Swash (Demie), Barbara Windsor (Peggy), Steve McFadden (Phil Mitchell), Lacey Turner (Stacey Slater), Daniel Ainsleigh, Davina Hemlall.

23.12.2005 "Carol singing for Wellard. Sonia leaves Martin, then Rebecca arrives for Christmas" — DB / DBSW
Written by Richard Davidson; series story editor Kevin Rundle; script producer Tom Mullens; script editor Martina Lloyd; series consultant Tony Jordan; executive producer Kate Harwood; head of production Nigel Taylor; series producer Lorraine Newman; produced by Jyoti Fernandes; directed by Graeme Hattrick.
With Kacey Ainsworth (Little Mo), Charlie G. Hawkins (Darren), Steve McFadden (Phil Mitchell), Natalie Cassidy (Sonia), James Alexandrou (Martin Fowler), Wendy Richard (Pauline Fowler), Ray Brooks (Joe), Jade Sharif (Rebecca), Shane Richie (Alfie Moon), Jessie Wallace (Kat Slater), Perry Fenwick (Billy Mitchell), Emma Barton (Honey), Louisa Lytton (Ruby), Billy Murray (Johnny Allan), Joseph Kpobie (Juley), Letitia Dean (Sharon), Nigel Harman (Dennis Rickman), Lacey Turner (Stacey Slater), Derek Martin (Charlie Slater), Barbara Windsor (Peggy), Ricky Groves (Gary Hobbs), Cliff Parisi (Minty), Mohammed George (Gus), Laurie Brett (Jane), Joel Beckett (Jake Moon), Kara Tointon (Dawn), Shana Swash (Demie).

25.12.2005 "Sharon tells Dennis she is pregnant. Alfie leaves for America with Kat" — DB / DBSW
Duration: 60 minutes.
Written by Sarah Phelps and Tony Jordan; series story editor Kevin Rundle; script producer Tom Mullens; script editor Neil Duncan; series consultant Tony Jordan; executive producer Kate Harwood; head of production Nigel Taylor; series producer Lorraine Newman; produced by Martha Cossey; directed by John Greening.
With David Spinx (Keith), Rudolph Walker (Patrick), Mohammed George (Gus), Charlie G. Hawkins (Darren), Jade Sharif (Rebecca), Jessie Wallace (Kat Slater), Shane Richie (Alfie Moon), James Alexandrou (Martin Fowler), Natalie Cassidy (Sonia), Letitia Dean (Sharon), Nigel Harman (Dennis Rickman), Barbara Windsor (Peggy), Steve McFadden (Phil Mitchell), Wendy Richard (Pauline Fowler), Ray Brooks (Joe), June Brown (Dot), John Bardon (Jim), Gerry Cowper (Rosie), Kara Tointon (Dawn), Shana Swash (Demie), Lacey Turner (Stacey Slater), Derek Martin (Charlie Slater), Laila Morse (Mo Slater), Kacey Ainsworth (Little Mo), Perry Fenwick (Billy Mitchell), Billy Murray (Johnny Allan), Louisa Lytton (Ruby), Joseph Kpobie (Juley), Adam Woodyatt (Ian Beale), Laurie Brett (Jane), James Martin (Peter Beale), Melissa Suffield (Lucy Beale), Cliff Parisi (Minty), Ricky Groves (Gary Hobbs), Emma Barton (Honey), Joel Beckett (Jake Moon), Mark Wingett (Mike), Michael Burgess, Blake Sporne, Carolyn Bazely.

25.12.2006 "Max gives in and beds Stacey" - a — DB / DBSW
Written by Simon Ashdown; script supervisor Juley Harding; series story producer Brigie De Courcy; series story editor Dominic Treadwell-Collins; series script editor Kay Sherwood; script producer Vicki Delow; story editors Alexander Lamb and Daisy Coulam; series consultant Tony Jordan; associate producer Simon Bird; executive producer Kate Harwood; series producer Lorraine Newman; produced by Julie Press; directed by Peter Rose.
With Lacey Turner (Stacey Slater), Charlie Jones (Ben), Diane Parish (Denise), Jake Wood (Max Branning), Wendy Richard (Pauline Fowler), Natalie Cassidy (Sonia), James Alexandrou (Martin Fowler), Charlie Clements (Bradley Branning), Gillian Wright (Jean Slater), Derek Martin (Charlie Slater), Laila Morse (Mo Slater), June Brown (Dot), John Bardon (Jim), Adam Woodyatt (Ian Beale), Laurie Brett (Jane), Barbara Windsor (Peggy), Steve McFadden (Phil Mitchell), Sophie Thompson (Stella), Cliff Parisi (Minty), Ricky Groves (Gary Hobbs), Perry Fenwick (Billy Mitchell), Emma Barton (Honey), Kara Tointon (Dawn), Phil Daniels (Kevin), David Spinx (Keith), Jo Joyner (Tanya), Madeline Duggan (Lauren), Lorna Fitzgerald (Abi), Jade Sharif (Rebecca), Rudolph Walker (Patrick), Angela Wynter (Yolande), Kellie Shirley (Carly), Joe Swash (Mickey), Thomas Law (Peter Beale), Melissa Suffield (Lucy Beale), Charlie G. Hawkins (Darren), Ann Akin.

EASTENDERS (continued)

25.12.2006 "Pauline decides to stay in Albert Square, but dies of a brain haemorrage" - b   DB / DBSW

Written by Simon Ashdown; script supervisor Juley Harding; series story producer Brigie De Courcy; series story editor Dominic Treadwell-Collins; series script editor Kay Sherwood; script producer Vicki Delow; story editors Alexander Lamb and Daisy Coulam; series consultant Tony Jordan; associate producer Simon Bird; executive producer Kate Harwood; series producer Lorraine Newman; produced by Julie Press; directed by Peter Rose.

With Wendy Richard (Pauline Fowler), Charlie Clements (Bradley Branning), Charlie Jones (Ben), Cliff Parisi (Minty), James Alexandrou (Martin Fowler), Natalie Cassidy (Sonia), June Brown (Dot), John Bardon (Jim), Jake Wood (Max Branning), Lacey Turner (Stacey Slater), Gillian Wright (Jean Slater), Jo Joyner (Tanya), Steve McFadden (Phil Mitchell), Barbara Windsor (Peggy), Sophie Thompson (Stella), Perry Fenwick (Billy Mitchell), Emma Barton (Honey), Ricky Groves (Gary Hobbs), Derek Martin (Charlie Slater), Laila Morse (Mo Slater), Adam Woodyatt (Ian Beale), Laurie Brett (Jane), Kara Tointon (Dawn), Madeline Duggan (Lauren), Lorna Fitzgerald (Abi), Jade Sharif (Rebecca), Kellie Shirley (Carly), Phil Daniels (Kevin), Diane Parish (Denise), Rudolph Walker (Patrick), Angela Wynter (Yolande), David Spinx (Keith), Joe Swash (Mickey), Charlie G. Hawkins (Darren), Thomas Law (Peter Beale), Melissa Suffield (Lucy Beale).

Date	Code	Holding / Source
25.12.2007	LDXO571F	DB / DBSW
25.12.2007	LDXO572A	DB / DBSW
25.12.2007	DRAA551Y	DB / DBSW
25.12.2008	DRAA854K	DB / DBSW
25.12.2008	DRAA388D	DB / DBSW
25.12.2008	DRAA389X	DB / DBSW
25.12.2009	DRAA225X	DB / DBSW
25.12.2010	DRAA458F	HD/DB / HDC

After 1991 credits in the 'Radio Times' became very sporadic and once the series went three times per week the credits would be mixed up together. Consequently, writer/director credits for episodes between 1994 and 2002 sometimes contain two writers/two directors and it is likely that only one writer and one director actually made the episodes. The other credit is superflous. Unfortunately, Kaleidoscope has no access to check this information for such a long-running series at this present time.

"Eastenders Revealed" on BBC3 goes behind the scenes.

EASTENDERS CHRISTMAS FALL OUTS

A BBC production for BBC 3. Transmission details are for BBC 3. Duration: 60 minutes.

Production executive Paul Williams; executive producers Diederick Santer and Mark Cossey; series producer Adam Page; produced by Darren New; directed by Mark Dandridge.

Shane Richie (Host), Jake Wood, Jo Joyner, Charlie Clements, Hannah Waterman, Lucy Benjamin.

Holding / Source
26.12.2007   DB / DBSWF

See also: EASTENDERS (BBC)

EASTENDERS CHRISTMAS PARTY

A BBC production for BBC 1. Transmission details are for BBC 1. Duration: 65 minutes.

Executive producer Beatrice Ballard; directed by Simon Staffurth.

Shane Richie (Host), Suggs, Richard E. Grant, Jo Brand, Greg Rusedski, Lulu, Liberty X, Mike Reid, Clarissa Dickson Wright, Michelle Gayle, Kim Medcalf, Jill Halfpenny.

Holding / Source
24.12.2003   DB / DBSW

EASTENDERS CHRISTMAS PARTY

A BBC production for BBC 1. Transmission details are for BBC 1.

Shane Richie (Host), McFly, Kelly Holmes, Mike Reid, Kim Woodburn, Lemar, John Sergeant, Linda Robson, Arlene Phillips, Eamonn Holmes, David Grant, Carrie Grant, Charles Kennedy, Aggie MacKenzie, Shreela Ghosh, Jan Graveson, Jill Halfpenny, Pam St. Clement, Laurie Brett, Rudolph Walker, Angela Wynter, Adam Woodyatt, Natalie Cassidy, Sylvia Young Stage School.

Holding / Source
23.12.2004   DB / DBSW

THE EDDIE FISHER SHOW

A BBC production. Transmission details are for BBC.

Holding / Source
27.12.1959   J /

Written by Denis Goodwin.

EDGE OF THE WIND

A BBC production for BBC 2. Transmission details are for BBC 2. Duration: 65 minutes.

'In the winter if I build a fire and the wind blows off the sea you could imagine you were back in the hills again.'

Written by Don Webb; script editor David Snodin; music by Kenyon Emrys-Roberts; designed by Bryan Ellis; produced by Brenda Reid; directed by Kenneth Ives.

John Mills (Blair), Omar Sharif (McCorquodale), Lucy Gutteridge (Miss Benton).

Holding / Source
25.12.1985   DB / 1"

EDUCATING ARCHIE

An Associated-Rediffusion production. Transmission details are for the ATV midlands region. Duration: 25 minutes.

Main regular cast: Peter Brough (Ventriloquist), Archie Andrews (Dummy).

SERIES 1

Main regular credit(s): Directed by Christopher Hodson.
Main regular cast: With Irene Handl, Dick Emery, Freddie Sales.

	Holding / Source
19.12.1958 "The Christmas party"	J /

Written by Marty Feldman and Ronald Chesney; settings by Sylva Nadolny.
With Bernard Bresslaw.

SERIES 2

	Holding / Source
25.12.1959 Archie's Christmas Party	J /

Written by Ronald Chesney; designed by John Emery; directed by Bill Turner.
With Ossie Noble (The Clown Prince), Harold Taylor (The Wizard of Magic), Ronald Chesney.
Was pre-recorded according to a launch article in the TV Times - though it doesn't make clear whether direct film or telerecording.

EDUCATING MARMALADE

A Thames Television production. Transmission details are for the Central region. Duration: 25 minutes.

Main regular credit(s): Written by Andrew Davies; theme music by Bad Manners; music by Andy Roberts; executive producer Pamela Lonsdale; produced by Sue Birtwistle.
Main regular cast: Charlotte Coleman (Marmalade Atkins), John Bird (Mr Atkins), Lynda Marchal (Mrs Atkins), Gillian Raine (Mrs Allgood).

Transmission details are for the Central region.

	VT Number	Holding / Source
20.12.1982 The Nativity Play	26830	D3 / 2"

Designed by Anthony Cartledge; directed by John Stroud.
With Tina Foley (Good Girl), Brian Glover (Sister Conception), Matthew Scurfield (Sister Purification), Sandra Osborn (Cherith Ponsonby), Lisa Hopton (Good Girl), Claire Callaghan (Good Girl), Donna Aspinall (Good Girl), Julia Sawalha (Good Girl), Gioia Izquierdo (Good Girl), Sarah Bryett.

THE EDWARD WOODWARD HOUR

A Thames Television production. Transmission details are for the ATV midlands region. Duration: 49 minutes.

Main regular performer(s): Edward Woodward (Host).

	VT Number	Holding / Source
27.12.1971 Another Edward Woodward Hour	5281	J / 2"

Written by Eric Merriman; music directed by Geoff Love; music associate Sid Lucas; designed by Norman Garwood; executive producer Philip Jones; produced by Reginald Collin; directed by Peter Frazer-Jones.
With Margaret Lockwood, Peter Jones, Julia Lockwood, Russell Hunter, Geoff Love and his Orchestra.

ELDORADO

Alternative/Working Title(s): LITTLE ENGLAND

A Cinema Verity/J. Dark y J. Todesco Production production for BBC 1. made in association with J DY T. Transmission details are for BBC 1. Duration: 30 minutes.

Main regular credit(s): Created by Tony Holland; from an idea by John Dark and Verity Lambert; theme music by Simon May; produced by Julia Smith.
Main regular cast: Patricia Brake (Gwen Lockhead), Campbell Morrison (Drew Lockhead), Josh Nathan (Blair Lockhead), Julie Fernandez (Nessa Lockhead), Polly Perkins (Trish Valentine), Kal Maurer (Dieter Schultz), Leslee Udwin (Joy Slater), Patch Connolly (Snowy White), Franco Rey (Roberto Fernandez), Stella Maris (Rosario Fernandez), Maria Sanchez (Maria Fernandez), Maria Vega (Abuela), Iker Ibanez (Javier Fernandez), Bo Corre (Ingrid), Jesse Birdsall (Marcus Tandy), Sandra Sandri (Pilar Moreno), Faith Kent (Olive King), Framboise Gommendy (Isabelle Leduc), Daniel Lombart (Philippe Leduc), Mikael Philippe (Arnaud Leduc), Nanna Moller (Lene Svendsen), Kim Romer (Per Svendsen), Marchell Betak (Trine Svendsen (early episodes only)), Darren Newton (Gavin Hindle), Jon Morrey (Allan Hindle), Buki Armstrong (Gerry), Roger Clarkson (Bunny Charlson), Roland Curram (Freddie), Kathy Pitkin (Fizz), William Lucas (Stanley Webb), Hilary Crane (Rosemary Webb), Hayley Bromley (Tracy), Jose Antonio Navarro (Antonio), Barry Mitchell (Phillip Wentworth), Keith Bookman (Roger Noble), Eric Flynn (Lars Olsson), Tusse Silberg (Monika Olsson), Clare Wilkie (Trine Svendsen (later episodes only)), Charlie Condou (Clive (19.10.1992 onwards)), Gareth Armstrong (Hugh Simmonds (19.10.1992 onwards)), Amerjit Deu (Ranjit Singh (2.11.1992 onwards)), Ravi Aujla (Jaskaran Singh (2.11.1992 onwards)), Tessa Wojtczak (Natalie Jackson (2.11.1992 onwards)), Robert Jolley (Adam (2.11.1992 onwards)), Chris Turner (Johnson (2.11.1992 onwards)), John Moreno (Doctor Garcia (9.11.1992 onwards)), Stephen Hattersley (Stephen Law (16.11.1992 onwards)), Jeannie Crowther (Kitty Hindle (16.11.1992 onwards)), James Mansfield (James Moore (14.12.1992 onwards)), Ben Murphy (Terry Flynn (21.12.1992 onwards)), Derek Martin (Alex Morris (18.01.1993 onwards)), Fiona Walker (Susan Wilkinson (5.4.1993 onwards)), Nicholas Amer (Ramon Colorado (14.5.1992 onwards)).

	Holding / Source
25.12.1992 "Christmas Disillusions Freddie"	DB-D3 / D3S

Written by Tony McHale; series producer Corinne Hollingworth; directed by Philip Casson.

ELTON'S NEW YEAR'S EVE PARTY: LIVE FROM THE O2 ARENA

A WhizzKid Television production for ITV 1. Transmission details are for the Central region. Duration: 80 minutes.

Script supervisors Cecilia Savage and Silvana Job; production executive Fiona Friel; executive producers David Campbell, Sally Atkins, Malcolm Gerrie and Lisa Chapman; production manager Gemma Ragg; produced by James O'Brien; directed by Simon Staffurth.

Elton John, Kate Thornton (Presenter), Alexandra Burke, Will Young, Elton John Band.

Holding / Source
31.12.2008   DB / Live

EMERGENCY - WARD 10

Alternative/Working Title(s): CALLING NURSE ROBERTS

An ATV production. Transmission details are for the ATV midlands region.

Main regular credit(s): Created by Tessa Diamond; from an idea by Bill Ward.

SERIES 1
Duration: 25 minutes.

Main regular cast: With Rosemary Miller (Nurse Pat Roberts), Jill Browne (Nurse Carole Young), Iris Russell (Nurse Stevenson), Glyn Owen (Patrick O'Meara), Charles Tingwell (Alan Dawson), Frederick Bartman (Simon Forrester (until 3.10.1958)), John Paul (R.S.O. Hughes (31.1.1958-28.7.1958)), Peter Howell (Doctor Peter Harrison (11.3.1958-)), Norah Gorsen (Nurse Ann Guthridge (1.7.1958-26.12.1958)), Barbara Clegg (Nurse Jo Buckley (8.7.1958-)), Yvette Wyatt (Staff Nurse Philles (22.7.1958-2.1.1959)), Kenneth Watson (Senior House Officer Graham (29.7.1958-26.12.1958))).

Holding / Source

24.12.1963 **Episode 665**   J /

Christmas Eve: and television comes to the Oxbridge!

Written by David Butler; produced by Cecil Petty; directed by Gordon Reece.

With Jill Browne (Nurse Carole Young), Desmond Carrington (Chris Anderson), Paula Byrne (Frances Whitney), John Carlisle (Mr Large), Michael McKevitt (James Gordon), Pamela Duncan (Sister Doughty), John Arnatt (Doctor Fitzgerald), John Line (Andrew Shaw), Frazer Hines (Tim Birch), Ilona Rodgers (Nurse Smith), Jane Rossington (Kate Ford), Peter Welch (Gunner Clark), Robert Lang (Doctor Griffiths), Charles Carson (George Ryder), Jean Kent (Gillian Blaine), John Abineri (Mario), Douglas Ives (Potter), Jean Trend (Nurse Webb), Elisabeth Murray (Jean Twillow), Enid Lindsey (Matron), Anne Brooks (Nurse Craig), David Butler (Nick Williams), Geoffrey Colville (Doctor Beckett), Peter Howell (Peter Harrison), Anne Lloyd (Nurse Jones), Noël Hood, Patricia Heneghan, Peter Reeves, Derek Royle, Reg Lye.

24.12.1965 **Episode 874**   J /

Christmas Eve - and carols.

Written by Basil Dawson; designed by Stanley Mills; produced by Josephine Douglas; directed by Jim Hodgetts.

With John Laurie (Professor Corliss), Gerald Campion (Himself), Geoffrey Colville (Doctor Beckett), David King (Mr Bailey), John Carlisle (Mr Large), Paul Darrow (Mr Verity), William Wilde (Doctor Brook), Pamela Duncan (Sister Doughty), Zulema Dene (Sister Wright), Anne Lloyd (Nurse Jones), Pik Sen Lim (Nurse Kwei Kim-Yen), Lockwood West.

31.12.1965 **Episode 876**   J /

New Year's Eve at Oxbridge- and Mr Verity misses his midnight kiss.

Written by Don Houghton; designed by Gerald Roberts; produced by Josephine Douglas; directed by Philip Dale.

With Larry Noble (Barney Chubb), William Wilde (Doctor Brook), Christopher Bidmead (Doctor Lomax), Paul Darrow (Mr Verity), Walter Horsbrugh (Superintendent), David King (Mr Bailey), John Carlisle (Mr Large), Geoffrey Colville (Doctor Beckett), Beatrice Kane (Sister Mills), Pamela Duncan (Sister Doughty), Zulema Dene (Sister Wright), Anne Lloyd (Nurse Jones), Pik Sen Lim (Nurse Kwei Kim-Yen), Gerald Campion (Himself), Arthur Haynes (Himself).

See also: CALL OXBRIDGE 2000

EMMA THOMPSON: UP FOR GRABS

A Limehouse production for Channel 4. Transmission details are for Channel 4. Duration: 40 minutes.

Written by Emma Thompson; designed by Pip Gardner; executive producer Jeremy Wallington; produced by Humphrey Barclay; directed by John Kaye Cooper.

Emma Thompson, Mark Kingston, Stephen Moore, Chris Jury, Matthew Kelly, Daniel Massey, Phyllida Law.

Holding / Source
28.12.1985   1" / 1"

EMMERDALE FARM

A Yorkshire Television production. Transmission details are for Various ITV Companies. Usual duration: 25 minutes.

Main regular credit(s): Created by Kevin Laffan; theme music by Tony Hatch.

SERIES 12
Transmission details are for the Central region.

Holding / Source

17.12.1987 "Joe Carries On With The Beckindale Panto Despite Getting Bad News"   1" / 1"

Written by James Robson; executive producer Keith Richardson; produced by Michael Russell; directed by Richard Holthouse.

With Sheila Mercier (Annie Sugden), Frederick Pyne (Matt Skilbeck), Ronald Magill (Amos Brearly), Arthur Pentelow (Henry Wilks), Clive Hornby (Jack Sugden), Frazer Hines (Joe Sugden), Jean Rogers (Dolly Skilbeck), Hugh Manning (Reverend Donald Hinton), Stan Richards (Seth Armstrong), Richard Thorp (Alan Turner), Diana Davies (Mrs Bates), Ian Sharrock (Jackie Merrick), Jane Hutcheson (Sandie Merrick), Malandra Burrows (Kathy Bates), Peter Alexander (Phil Pearce), Julia Chambers (Ruth Pennington), Christopher Chittell (Eric Pollard), Cy Chadwick (Nick Bates), Tony Pitts (Archie), Drew Dawson (Jock McDonald), Johnny Caesar (Bill Middleton), Benjamin Whitehead (Sam Skilbeck), Richard Smith (Robert Sugden).

22.12.1988   1" / 1"

Christmas Eve in Beckindale; the villagers sing carols, there's a break-in at Home Farm and Joe gets the best Christmas present possible.

Written by Harry Duffin; executive producer Keith Richardson; produced by Stuart Doughty; directed by Henry Foster.

EMMERDALE FARM (continued)

28.12.1988 "Boxing Day Festivities" 1" / 1"
Written by Peter J. Hammond; executive producer Keith Richardson; produced by Stuart Doughty; directed by Henry Foster.
With Sheila Mercier (Annie Sugden), Frederick Pyne (Matt Skilebck), Ronald Magill (Amos Brearly), Arthur Pentelow (Henry Wilks), Frazer Hines (Joe Sugden), Jean Rogers (Dolly Skilbeck), Ian Sharrock (Jackie Merrick), Malandra Burrows (Kathy Merrick), Jane Hutcheson (Sandie Merrick), Richard Thorp (Alan Turner), Diana Davies (Mrs Bates), Tony Pitts (Archie), Cy Chadwick (Nick Bates), Sally Knyvette (Kate Hughes), Peter Alexander (Phil Pearce), Christopher Chittell (Eric Pollard), Martin Dale (Sergeant MacArthur), Benjamin Whitehead (Sam Skilbeck).

EMMET OTTER'S JUG-BAND CHRISTMAS

An ATV production. Transmission details are for the ATV midlands region. Duration: 50 minutes.

Jim Henson, creator of the world-famous Muppets, presents a one-hour Christmas special with Emmet Otter and his friends... It tells how young Emmet one day passes a shop window and sees a guitar... just what he needs to join a hillbilly band. This story highlights a whole new dimension of the Muppets' antics.

Presented by Jim Henson.
Kermit The Frog (Narrator).

Holding / Source
24.12.1978 NT / 2"
Held in the US and released on DVD.
See also: THE MUPPET SHOW

EMO PHILIPS: COMEDIAN AND MAMMAL

A Consolidated Productions production for Channel 4. Transmission details are for Channel 4. Duration: 40 minutes.

Eccentric American comedian Emo Philips holds court at London's Playhouse Theatre. His performance spans his childhood, family and his warped view of the world.
Written by Emo Philips; produced by Juliet Blake and Trevor Hopkins; directed by Juliet Blake and Trevor Hopkins.
Emo Philips.

Holding / Source
29.12.1990 1" / 1"

EMU'S ALL-LIVE WINDMILL SHOW

A Central production. Transmission details are for the Central region.
Main regular credit(s): Devised by Rod Hull.
Main regular cast: Rod Hull and Emu.

SERIES 1
Main regular credit(s): Written by Rod Hull; music directed by Colin Campbell; designed by Norman Smith; produced and directed by Colin Clews.
Main regular cast: With Carol Lee Scott (Witch Grotbags), Corona Stage School.

Holding / Source
25.12.1984 **Emu At Christmas** 1" / 1"
Duration: 35 minutes.
Choreography by Alan Harding.
With Susan Maughan, Carl Wayne, Freddie Stevens.

See also: EMU'S PINK WINDMILL SHOW

EMU'S BROADCASTING CORPORATION (EBC 1)

A BBC Manchester production for BBC 1. Transmission details are for BBC 1. Usual duration: 25 minutes.
Main regular credit(s): Devised by Rod Hull.
Main regular cast: Rod Hull and Emu.

SERIES 3
Main regular credit(s): Written by Rod Hull; designed by Ray Langhorn; produced by Peter Ridsdale Scott; directed by Hazel Lewthwaite.

Holding / Source
24.12.1977 DB-D3 / 2"
With Billy Dainty, Barbara New.

SERIES 4
Main regular credit(s): Written by Rod Hull; production team Richard Greening, George Clarke and Anne Comer; produced by Peter Ridsdale Scott.
Main regular cast: With Billy Dainty, Barbara New.

	Production No	VT Number	Holding / Source
##.##.#### **Christmas Special**	02748/1116	NMR/S809X	DB-D3 / 2"

Duration: 37 minutes.
Designed by Ray Langhorn; location sequences directed by Peter Ridsdale Scott; studio direction by Mike Stephens.
With Tom Chatto, Michael Parkinson, Don Estelle, Stuart Hall, Patrick Moore, Alvin Stardust.
Recorded 30.11.1978. Made using strike breakers ths edition could not be shown once the strike was resolved.

SERIES 5

Holding / Source
23.12.1979 DB-D3 / 2"
With Michael Parkinson.

EMU'S CHRISTMAS ADVENTURE

An LWT production. Transmission details are for the ATV midlands region. Duration: 53 minutes.

Emu wreaks havoc in a Christmas story set in Toyland.

Written by David Wood; music directed by Harry Rabinowitz; designed by Bill McPherson; produced and directed by David Bell.

Rod Hull and Emu (Themselves), Arthur Lowe (Old King Cole), George A. Cooper (Santa), Jack Douglas ('Wicked' Jasper), Lesley Duff (Bo-Beep), Carl Wayne (Tom-Tom The Piper's Son), Henry McGee (Santa's Foreman), Tom Chatto (Lord Chamberlain), Lynda Bainbridge, Marilyn Brown, Wendy Gotelee, Kay Korda, Jane Warby, Lynne Jolly, Georgina Allen, Helen Thomas, Michael Lander, Jerry Manley, Ken Warwick, Ludovico Romano, Spencer Shires, Chris Power, John Melainey, Harry Higham.

	Production No	Holding / Source
25.12.1977	99096	D2 / 2"

EMU'S MAGICAL...

A BBC Manchester production for BBC 1. Transmission details are for BBC 1. Duration: 35 minutes.

Main regular performer(s): Rod Hull and Emu.

		Holding / Source
27.12.1980	**Music Show**	DB-D3 / 2"

Designed by Malcolm Thornton; executive producer Peter Ridsdale Scott; produced by Mike Stephens.

With The Corona Kids, Larry Parker, The Brother Lees, Showaddywaddy.

27.12.1981	**Xmas Music Show**	DB-1" / 2"

Executive producer Peter Ridsdale Scott; produced and directed by Mike Stephens.

With The Corona Children, The Cambridge Buskers, Alan Shaxon, The Grumbleweeds.

EMU'S PINK WINDMILL SHOW

A Central production. Transmission details are for the Central region. Duration: 45 minutes.

Main regular credit(s):   Devised by Rod Hull; written by Rod Hull; music directed by Colin Campbell; choreography by Alan Harding; designed by Tony Ferris; produced and directed by Colin Clews.

Main regular cast: Rod Hull and Emu, Carol Lee Scott (Grotbags), Corona Stage School.

		Holding / Source
26.12.1986	**Emu At Christmas**	1" / 1"

See also: EMU'S ALL-LIVE WINDMILL SHOW

EMU'S WORLD

A Central production. Transmission details are for the Central region.

Main regular credit(s):   Devised by Rod Hull.

Main regular cast: Rod Hull and Emu, Carol Lee Scott (Grot Bags).

SERIES 4

Main regular credit(s):   Written by Rod Hull; music directed by Colin Campbell; choreography by Alan Harding; designed by Norman Smith; produced and directed by Colin Clews.

		Holding / Source
21.12.1983	**Emu's World At Christmas**	D2 / 1"

Duration: 35 minutes.

With Freddie Stevens, Susan Maughan, Carl Wayne, Corona Stage School.

THE END OF THE YEAR SHOW

A Thames Television production. Transmission details are for the Thames Television region. Duration: 60 minutes.

Clips compilation of favourite moments.

Produced by Colin Fay.

	Holding / Source
31.12.1992	DB / D2S

Final programme of Thames TV.

THE END OF THE YEAR SHOW

A BBC Scotland production for BBC 1. Transmission details are for BBC 1. Duration: 63 minutes.

Produced by David Tyler; directed by David G. Hillier.

Angus Deayton (Host), Richard Wilson, Jack Dee, Maureen Lipman, Nick Hancock, Lily Savage, Alexei Sayle, Stomp.

	Holding / Source
31.12.1995	DB / D3S

THE END OF THE YEAR SHOW

A BBC production for BBC 1. Transmission details are for BBC 1. Duration: 65 minutes.

Executive producer Tony Moss; produced by Vincent Beasley.

Angus Deayton (Host), Julian Clary, David Baddiel, Lee Hurst, The Spice Girls, Anneka Rice, Alan Davies, Clarissa Dickson Wright, Eddie Izzard, Jennifer Paterson.

	Holding / Source
31.12.1996	DB-D3 / D3S

THE END OF THE YEAR SHOW

A BBC production for BBC 1. Transmission details are for BBC 1. Duration: 64 minutes.

Executive producer Caroline Wright; produced by Vincent Beasley; directed by Geraldine Dowd, Dominic Brigstocke and Christine Gernon.

Angus Deayton (Host), Patrick Moore, Zoe Ball, Dale Winton, Mark Lamarr, Mariella Frostrup, Maureen Lipman, James Greene, Lesley Garrett, Louise, Errol Brown, Jack Docherty.

	Holding / Source
31.12.1997	DB / D3S

THE END OF THE YEAR SHOW

A BBC production for BBC 1. Transmission details are for BBC 1. Duration: 55 minutes.

Executive producer Caroline Wright; produced by Patricia McGowan.

Angus Deayton (Host), Steve Coogan (Paul Calf / Tony Ferrino), Robbie Coltrane, Julie Walters.

	Holding / Source
31.12.1998	DB / DBS

THE ENGELBERT HUMPERDINCK SHOW

An ATV production. Transmission details are for the ATV midlands region.

Main regular performer(s): Engelbert Humperdinck.

	VT Number	Holding / Source
26.12.1969	648/69	DB-NT / 2"

Duration: 52 minutes.

Written by Sheldon Keller, Bryan Blackburn and Tony Hawes; music associates Derek Scott and Jack Chivers; choreography by Paddy Stone; designed by Henry Graveney; executive producer Gordon Mills; produced and directed by Colin Clews.

With José Feliciano, Barbara Eden, Tom Jones, Dionne Warwick, The Paddy Stone Dancers, The Mike Sammes Singers, Jack Parnell and his Orchestra.

ENGLAND, MY ENGLAND

A Ladbroke Productions production for Channel 4. Transmission details are for Channel 4. Duration: 100 minutes.

Written by John Osborne and Charles Wood; music by Henry Purcell; produced by Mike Bluett and Simon Flind; directed by Tony Palmer.

Michael Ball (Henry Purcell), Simon Callow (Charles), Lucy Speed (Nell Gwyn), Letitia Dean (Barbara), Robert Stephens (John Dryden), John Shrapnel (Samuel Pepys), Nina Young, Terence Rigby, Bill Kenwright, Murray Melvin, Corin Redgrave, John Fortune.

	Holding / Source
25.12.1995	D3 / C1SW

THE ENTERTAINERS

A BBC Factual and Learning production for BBC 2. Transmission details are for BBC 2. Duration: 30 minutes.

Main regular credit(s): Executive producers David Mortimer and Louis Theroux; series producer Stuart Cabb.

Main regular cast: Leo Sayer, Tony Blackburn, Nicholas Parsons, Bernie Clifton, Frank Carson, Bernard Manning.

	Holding / Source
31.12.2002 **Christmas Special**	DB / DBSW

This Christmas special follows Tony Blackburn turning on Oxford's lights, Bernard Manning shopping for a Christmas tree, Nicholas Parsons lighting his annula bonfire, Bernie Clifton and his ostrich appearing in panto and Frank Carson taking his grandchildren to Santa'a grotto.

ERIC AND ERNIE

A BBC Wales production for BBC 2. made in association with Blue Door Adventures Ltd. Transmission details are for BBC 2. Duration: 90 minutes.

You can warm your hands on the waves of affection that waft from writer Peter Bowker's funny, sweetnatured, BAFTA-winning look at the early years of our most beloved comic partnership, Eric Morecambe and Ernie Wise. We follow the duo before they really hit the big time, from the first meeting when they were both child stars, through the days touring clubs and music halls, up to their first, disastrous TV appearance. The evolution of the surreally brilliant act that was to make them adored is nicely done, thanks to Bowker's light touch and to a great cast, particularly comedian Daniel Rigby as the genial, uncomplaining but sharp-witted Morecambe.

Written by Peter Bowker; based on an idea by Victoria Wood; script executive Anna Ferguson; script supervisor Jane Burrows; music by Ilan Eshkeri; choreography by Sammy Brown; director of photography Tony Slater-Ling; art director Frederic Evard; designed by Pat Campbell; production executives Llyr Morus and Julie Scott; executive producers Piers Wenger, Beth Willis and Victoria Wood; production manager Dominique Molloy; line producer Chris Thompson; produced by Timothy Bricknell; directed by Jonny Campbell.

Jonah Lees (Young Eric), Reece Shearsmith (Harry Wiseman), Josh Benson (Little Ernie), Thomas Atkinson (Little Eric), Victoria Wood (Sadie Bartholomew), Thomas Aldersley (MC), Jim Moir (George Bartholomew), Ted Robbins (Jack Hytlon), Harry McEntire (Young Ernie), Ria Jones (Landlady), Pam Shaw (Lily), Daniel Rigby (Eric Morecambe), Bryan Dick (Ernie Wise), Hannah Steele (Doreen), Esme Bianco (Showgirl), Andrew Greenough (Gordon Noval), Marcus Taylor (Stage Door Keeper 1), Lee Oakes (Stage Door Keeper 2), Fine Time Fontayne (Stage Door Keeper 3), Robert Willox (Doug), Ian Ross-Henderson (Heckler), Emer Kenny (Joan), Julian Wadham (Ronnie Waldman), Alex Price (Nigel), Stephen Aintree (Vernon), Martin Walsh (Fishmonger), Angela Curran (Edna), Peter Gunn (Billy Crackers), Carolynne Good (Girl From Vasaria), Clara Darcy (Usherette).

	Holding / Source
01.01.2011	HD/DB / HD/DB

THE ERROL FLYNN THEATRE

Alternative/Working Title(s): ERROL FLYNN THEATRE

Produced for ITV by a variety of companies (see details below). Transmission details are for the ABC midlands region. Duration: 25 minutes.

Executive producer Marcel Le Duc; produced by Norman Williams.

	Holding / Source
30.03.1957 **The Evil Thoughts**	J / B3

Alt.Title(s):   *The Mirror And Markheim*

Alternative transmissions: ATV London: 22.12.1956.

Markheim is waiting in Mr. Henry's old antique shop to be shown some valuable jewellery. He sees a mirror on the wall. And staring back is not his face but a stranger's.

Adapted by John Lemont; based on a story by Robert Louis Stevenson; directed by John Lemont.

With Philip Saville, Christopher Lee, Arthur Lowe.

AN EVENING WITH KIRE TE KANAWA

A BBC production for BBC 2. Transmission details are for BBC 2. Duration varies - see below for details.

Main regular credit(s):   Conducted by John Mauceri; television presentation by Yvonne Littlewood.

Main regular performer(s):   Kiri Te Kanawa, The London Symphony Orchestra.

	Holding / Source
28.12.1987	DB / 1"

Duration: 55 minutes.

	Holding / Source
29.12.1987 **Songs From 'My Fair Lady'**	DB / 1"

Duration: 60 minutes.

Music composed by Frederick Loewe and Alan Jay Lerner.

With Jeremy Irons, Warren Mitchell, London Voices Choir.

AN EVENING WITH LEE EVANS

An Open Mike production for Channel 4. Transmission details are for Channel 4. Duration: 25 minutes.

Recorded at London's Duke of York Theatre.

Written by Lee Evans; executive producer Pete Ward; produced by Dave Morley; directed by David G. Hillier.

Lee Evans (Performer), Jack Dee, Bruce Forsyth.

	Holding / Source
30.12.1993	D3 / D3S

AN EVENING WITH LEE EVANS

Commissioned by Channel 4. Transmission details are for Channel 4. Duration: 25 minutes.

Recorded at the Duke of York's Theatre.

Produced by Dave Morley; directed by David G. Hillier.

Lee Evans, Bruce Forsyth, Jack Dee.

	Holding / Source
30.12.2011	DB / DBSW

EVER DECREASING CIRCLES

A BBC production for BBC 1. Transmission details are for BBC 1. Duration: 30 minutes.

Main regular credit(s):   Written by John Esmonde and Bob Larbey.

Main regular cast: Richard Briers (Martin Bryce), Peter Egan (Paul Ryman), Penelope Wilton (Ann Bryce), Stanley Lebor (Howard Hughes), Geraldine Newman (Hilda Hughes).

SERIES 2

Main regular credit(s):   Designed by Tom Yardley-Jones; production manager Sue Bysh; produced and directed by Sydney Lotterby.

	Holding / Source
23.12.1984	DB / 1"

With Harriet Reynolds, Leon Lissek.

SERIES 4

Main regular credit(s):   Designed by Eric Walmsley; produced and directed by Harold Snoad.

	Holding / Source
24.12.1989 **New Horizons**	DB / 1"

Duration: 81 minutes.

Music by Nick Ingman.

With Les Clack, Ann Davies, Simon Merrick, Frank Coda, David Janson, Vanessa Knox-Mawer, Brian Cant, Carmel Cryan, Alexander Scott, Noel Slattery, Sussex Army Cadet Force Band, Band of The Royal Marines.

THE EVERLY BROTHERS REUNION CONCERT

A BBC production for BBC 2. Transmission details are for BBC 2. Duration: 75 minutes.

Last September at the Royal Albert Hall Don and Phil Everly performed together for the first time in ten years. The concert was the popular music event of the year. With a fine band, including lead guitarist Albert Lee and Pete Wingfield on keyboards, the Everlys faithfully re-created the sound of their huge repertoire of hits. 'Cathy's clown', All I have to do is dream', 'When will I be loved', 'Wake up, little Susie' and the rest stirred the memories and emotions of a rapturous audience. The Everlys' harmonies are among the most special sounds in rock 'n' roll-and they sound as good as ever.

Lighting by John Mason; sound Barrie Hawes; associate producer Anthony Wall; produced by Alan Yentob and Stephanie Bennett; directed by Rick Gardner.

The Everly Brothers.

	Holding / Source
23.12.1983	DB / 1"

EVERY SECOND COUNTS

A BBC production for BBC 1. made in association with Group W Productions / Talbot TV Ltd. Transmission details are for BBC 1. Duration: 30 minutes.

Main regular credit(s): Theme music by John Mealing.

Main regular performer(s): Paul Daniels (Quizmaster), Philip Talbot (Voice Over).

SERIES 2

	Holding / Source
25.12.1986	DB / 1"

SERIES 7

	Holding / Source
30.12.1991	DB / 1"S

EVERYONE A SPECIAL KIND OF ARTIST: A WEE BIT CHEEKY

A Riverfront Pictures production for Channel 4. Transmission details are for Channel 4. Duration: 25 minutes.

Documentary about the life of Arnold Taylor, creator of the 'naughty' seaside postcard.

Edited by Andy Attenburrow; camera operated by Bryan MacDermott; produced and directed by Jeff Perks.

Ken Sprague (Presenter), Arnold Taylor (Subject of Documentary).

	Holding / Source
24.12.1983	1" / 1"

EXCEPT FOR VIEWERS IN ENGLAND

A BBC Wales production for BBC 1 Wales. Transmission details are for BBC 1 Wales.

Rob Brydon, Ruth Jones.

	Holding / Source
31.12.1992	DB / D3S

EXIT - IT'S THE WAY OUT SHOW!

Alternative/Working Title(s): EXIT - IT'S WAY OUT

A Rediffusion Television production. Transmission details are for the Rediffusion Television region. Duration: 25 minutes.

Main regular credit(s): Devised by Barry Langford.

Main regular performer(s): Pat Campbell (The Major (Voice Only)), Jane Bates [as Jane], Lesley Judd [as Leslie].

Main regular credit(s): Produced by Bill Costello.

Main regular performer(s): With Ed Stewart (Compere).

	Holding / Source
28.12.1967 "Christmas special"	J / 40

Directed by Barry Langford.

With Long John Baldry, Monica Rose, Lynn Redgrave, Tim Brooke-Taylor.

EXTRAORDINARY

A Yorkshire Television production. Transmission details are for the ATV midlands region. Duration: 25 minutes.

Main regular credit(s): Executive producer Joy Whitby.

	Holding / Source
24.12.1980 **Frank Muir's Christmas Extraordinary**	1" / 2"

Frank Muir takes a trip down memory lane when he talks to Valerie Pitts about his Christmas childhood memories.

Research Jane Natrac; designed by David McDermott; produced by Peter Murphy; directed by Doug Wilcox.

With Frank Muir (Presenter), Valerie Pitts (Presenter), Frank Muir.

EXTRAS

A BBC production for BBC 2. made in association with HBO. Transmission details are for BBC 2.

Main regular credit(s): Written by Ricky Gervais and Stephen Merchant; music by Glyn Hughes; production executive Jez Nightingale; executive producer Jon Plowman; produced by Charlie Hanson; directed by Ricky Gervais and Stephen Merchant.

Main regular cast: Ricky Gervais (Andy Millman), Ashley Jensen (Maggie Jacobs).

Transmission details are for BBC 1.

Holding / Source

27.12.2007   DB / DBSWF

Duration: 85 minutes.

Script supervisor Elise Mytton.

With Stephen Merchant (Agent), Shaun Williamson (Barry), Shaun Pye, Guy Henry, Liza Tarbuck, Sarah Moyle, Jamie Chapman, Andrew Buckley, Gerard Kelly, Adam James, Clive Owen, George Michael, Gordon Ramsay, David Tennant, Gareth Hale, Norman Pace, Lionel Blair, Dean Gaffney, June Sarpong, Lisa Scott-Lee, Chico, Jonathan Ross, Vernon Kay, Nicola Redmond, Steve Brody, Ben Willbond, Frog Stone, Susy Kane, Toby Foster, Claudia Sermbezis, Lolita Chakrabarti, Stuart McQuarrie, Scott Baker, Kerry Godliman, Jason Barnett, Fergus Craig, Dan Tetsell, Karl Pilkington, Liam Barham.

THE FABULOUS SINGLETTES

A BBC production for BBC 2. Transmission details are for BBC 2. Duration: 35 minutes.

It is 1962, and in a dingy flat in London's Earls Court three Australian girls pine for home.

Written by Andrew Nickolds; produced and directed by Geoff Posner.

Naomi Eyers (Fabulous Singlette), Alison Jiear (Fabulous Singlette), Simone Dee (Fabulous Singlette), Albert Welling (Reverend Truscott), Holly Aird (Susan), Ben Daniels (Brian), Anthony Jackson (Toni), Jerome Willis (Mr Higgins), Bernard Kay (Talent Scout), Adam Wood (Gilbert Johnson).

	Holding / Source
24.12.1990	DB / 1"

FACE THE MUSIC

A BBC production for BBC Various. Transmission details are for BBC Various. Duration varies - see below for details.

SERIES 1
Commissioned by BBC 2. Transmission details are for BBC 2. Duration: 30 minutes.
Main regular credit(s):   Produced by Walter Todds.
Main regular performer(s): With Joseph Cooper (Chairman).

	Holding / Source
26.12.1967	J / R3

With Juliet Mills, Richard Baker, Robin Ray, Geraint Evans (Guest Musician).

Commissioned by BBC 2. Transmission details are for BBC 2.

	Holding / Source
24.12.1972	J / 2"

Produced by Walter Todds; directed by Denis Moriarty.
With Joseph Cooper (Chairman), Joyce Grenfell, Bernard Levin, Robin Ray, Clifford Curzon (Guest).

Commissioned by BBC 2. Transmission details are for BBC 2.

	Holding / Source
25.12.1973	J / 2"

Duration: 40 minutes.
Produced by Walter Todds; directed by Denis Moriarty.
With Joseph Cooper (Questionmaster), Joyce Grenfell, Richard Baker, Robin Ray, Eileen Joyce (Guest).

Commissioned by BBC 2. Transmission details are for BBC 2.

	Holding / Source
25.12.1974	J / 2"

Duration: 45 minutes.
Produced by Walter Todds; directed by Denis Moriarty.
With Joseph Cooper (Questionmaster), Joyce Grenfell, Robin Ray, Bernard Levin, Sir Georg Solti (Guest).

SERIES 7
Commissioned by BBC 2. Transmission details are for BBC 2.
Main regular credit(s):   Produced by Walter Todds; directed by Robin Lough.
Main regular performer(s): With Joseph Cooper (Question-Master).

	Holding / Source
20.12.1975	DB-D3 / 2"

Duration: 40 minutes.
With Joyce Grenfell, Richard Baker, Robin Ray, André Previn (Guest Musician).

SERIES 8
Commissioned by BBC 2. Transmission details are for BBC 2. Duration: 30 minutes.
Main regular credit(s):   Produced by Walter Todds; directed by Peter Butler.
Main regular performer(s): With Joseph Cooper (Questionmaster).

	Holding / Source
26.12.1976	DB-D3 / 2"

Designed by Paul Montague.
With Patricia Owen, David Attenborough, John Julius Norwich, David Willcocks (Guest Musician).

Commissioned by BBC 2. Transmission details are for BBC 2.

	Holding / Source
25.12.1979	DB-D3 / 2"

Duration: 40 minutes.
Designed by Pamela Lambooy; produced by Walter Todds; directed by Helen Morton.
With Joseph Cooper (Questionmaster), Joyce Grenfell, David Attenborough, Robin Ray, Sir Robert Mayer (Special Guest).

THE FAME GAME

A BBC production for BBC 1. Transmission details are for BBC 1.

		Holding / Source
31.12.1998	**New Year Special 1**	DB / D3S
01.01.1999	**New Year Special 2**	DB / D3S

A FAMILY AT WAR

A Granada production. Transmission details are for the ATV midlands region. Duration: 50 minutes.

Main regular credit(s): Created by John Finch.

SERIES 2
Main regular credit(s): Executive producer Richard Doubleday.

		Production No	Holding / Source
11.11.1970	**The Other Side Of The Hill**	P636/14	DB / 2"

The episode begins with the Ashton family celebrating Christmas 1940 and then the New Year. Edwin is offered a manager's job with one of Sefton's business competitors, Dennis Pringle and Sefton realise how much they need to keep Edwin at the works. David is chatting up a girl near his RAF camp while Sheila waits for his phone call at home. Robert comes home on leave unexpectedly and almost misses seeing his mother who has been called away to see her sick mother.

Written by James Brabazon and John Finch; produced by Michael Cox; directed by Gerry Mill.

With Colin Douglas (Edwin Ashton), Shelagh Fraser (Jean Ashton), Lesley Nunnerley (Margaret Porter), Barbara Flynn (Freda Ashton), Coral Atkins (Sheila Ashton), Colin Campbell (David Ashton), David Dixon (Robert Ashton), Mark Dignam, Rowena Cooper, Peter Macann, Alan O'Keefe, Bill Dean.

SERIES 3
Main regular credit(s): Associate producer Michael Dunlop; executive producer Richard Doubleday; produced by Michael Cox.

		Production No	Holding / Source
16.02.1972	**... Yielding Place To New**	P636/53	DB / 2"

It is December 1945, and the first post-war Christmas. In this last episode of the series, the Briggs and Ashton families are together on Christmas Day, looking forward to the promise of a world at peace and remembering what that world had cost to win.

Written by John Finch; designed by Knowles Bentley; directed by Richard Doubleday.

With Colin Douglas (Edwin Ashton), Colin Campbell (David Ashton), Coral Atkins (Sheila Ashton), Lesley Nunnerley (Margaret Porter), Ian Thompson (John Porter), Barbara Flynn (Freda Ashton), John Nettles (Ian Mackenzie), John McKelvey (Sefton Briggs), Trevor Bowen (Tony Briggs), Georgine Anderson (Helen Hughes), Diana Davies (Doris), Patrick Troughton (Harry Porter), Michael Condon (Peter Ashton), Jane Hutcheson (Janet Ashton), Paul Brett (John George Porter).

FAMILY FORTUNES

An ATV/Central production. made in association with Goodson Todman Productions / Talbot TV Ltd. Transmission details are for the ATV/Central region. Usual duration: 24 minutes.

SERIES 3
An ATV production. Transmission details are for the ATV/Central region.

Main regular credit(s): Music by Jack Parnell and Dave Lindup; programme consultants Spike Mullins and Philip Parsons; designed by Richard Plumb; produced by William G. Stewart; directed by Graham C. Williams.

Main regular performer(s): With Bob Monkhouse (Host).

		VT Number	Holding / Source
26.12.1981	**Give Us A Clue v It Ain't Half Hot Mum**	9133/81	DV / 2"

Duration: 40 minutes.

With Michael Aspel, Lionel Blair, Una Stubbs, Roy Kinnear, Anna Dawson, Windsor Davies, Melvyn Hayes, Donald Hewlett, John Clegg, Michael Knowles.

SERIES 5
A Central production. Transmission details are for the Central region.

Main regular credit(s): Produced by William G. Stewart.

Main regular performer(s): With Max Bygraves (Host), Andrew Lodge (Voice Over).

		VT Number	Holding / Source
23.12.1983	**Christmas**	3159	1" / 1"

Directed by David Millard.

With Wincey Willis, Anne Diamond, Nick Owen, John Stapleton, Lizzie Webb, Katie Boyle, Virginia Ironside, Marjorie Proops, Deirdre Sanders, Claire Rayner.

SERIES 9
A Central production. Transmission details are for the Central region. Duration: 23 minutes.

Main regular credit(s): Produced by Mike Holgate.

Main regular performer(s): With Les Dennis (Host), Stephen Rhodes (Voice Over).

		VT Number	Holding / Source
22.12.1989	**Christmas Special: The Hardup Family v The Twanky Family**	4235	1" / 1"

In this Christmas show the Hardup Family from Cinderella meet the Twanky family from Aladdin. There are some boistrous battles as all the prizes are goiing to charity, but it's all good clean fun.

With Peter Howitt, Windsor Davies, Paul Shane, John Inman, Christopher Biggins, Lisa Maxwell, Cheryl Baker, Jessica Martin, Bella Emberg.

FAMILY FORTUNES (continued)

SERIES 10
A Central production. Transmission details are for the Central region.
Main regular credit(s): Produced by Dennis Liddington; directed by Jenny Dodd.
Main regular performer(s): With Les Dennis (Host), Stephen Rhodes (Voice Over).

	VT Number	Holding / Source
21.12.1990 **The Family Fortunes Christmas Show**	5505	1" / 1"

Duration: 23 minutes.
This charity Programme is hosted by Les Dennis, alias Buttons, the Yuletide Special turns into a real panto when the Whittington family - Marti Caine, Floella Benjamin, Barry Cryer and Linda Lusardi take on the Trot family - Brian Conley, Russell Grant, Bernadette Nolan, Barry McGuigan and Barbara Windsor.
With Les Dennis (Buttons), Wayne Dobson (The Genie), Floella Benjamin, Marti Caine, Barry Cryer, Windsor Davies, Linda Lusardi, Brian Conley, Russell Grant, Bernadette Nolan, Barry McGuigan, Barbara Windsor.

SERIES 12
A Central production. Transmission details are for the Central region.
Main regular credit(s): Executive producer Richard Holloway; produced by Dennis Liddington.
Main regular performer(s): With Les Dennis (Host), Stephen Rhodes (Voice Over).

	VT Number	Holding / Source
01.01.1993	912135	1" / 1"

SERIES 14
A Central production. Transmission details are for the Central region. Duration: 23 minutes.
Main regular credit(s): Produced by Dennis Liddington.
Main regular performer(s): With Les Dennis (Host), Stephen Rhodes (Voice Over).

	Holding / Source
24.12.1994 **Guys v Dolls Christmas Special**	D2 / D2S

With Mike Smith, Sarah Greene, Shane Ritchie, Jim Bowen, Dale Winton, John Stapleton, Judi Spiers, Valerie Singleton, Floella Benjamin, Michaela Strachan.

A FAMOUS JOURNEY

A Thames Television production. Transmission details are for the ATV midlands region. Duration: 50 minutes.
Sound Trefor Hunter; film camera Grenville Middleton; executive producer Diana Potter; produced by Margery Baker.
Kenneth Griffith (Host).

	Holding / Source
20.12.1979	C1 / C1

FANFARE FOR YOUNG MUSICIANS

A Thames Television production. Transmission details are for the ATV midlands region.

SERIES 5
Transmission details are for the Central region.
Main regular credit(s): Produced by Helen Best.
Main regular cast: With Melvyn Tan (Host).

	Holding / Source
30.12.1982 **Christmas Concert**	D3 / 2"

Duration: 50 minutes.
Directed by Stan Woodward.
With Alan Hacker, Fiona Hibbert, William Pleeth.

FARMHOUSE KITCHEN

A Yorkshire Television production. Transmission details are for the ATV midlands region. Duration: 25 minutes.
Credits: Designed by Gordon Livesey and Roger Tomlinson; produced by Graham Watts and Mary Watts; directed by Graham Watts and Mary Watts.
Cast: With Dorothy Sleightholme (Resident Cook).

	Holding / Source
22.12.1980 **After Christmas**	1" / 2"

Ideas for tasty dishes from Christmas leftovers.
With Grace Mulligan.

FAST AND LOOSE!

A BBC production. Transmission details are for BBC.

Main regular credit(s): Written by Bob Monkhouse and Denis Goodwin; music directed by Eric Robinson.

Main regular performer(s): Bob Monkhouse (Host), Denis Goodwin (Host).

SERIES 1
Duration: 45 minutes.

Main regular credit(s): Produced and directed by Kenneth Carter.

	Holding / Source
22.12.1954	NR|a|c / Live

Designed by John Clements.

With Irene Handl, Alexander Gauge, June Whitfield, The Tanner Sisters, Alma Cogan, Pat Coombs, Howard Greene, Bill Pertwee, Patti Carol, Lane Meddick, Eddie Le Roy, Jean Hart, Kit Terrington, Keith Davis, Diana Day, Laurence Payne, Arthur Askey.

FAST FREDDIE, THE WIDOW AND ME

Commissioned by ITV 1. Transmission details are for the Central region.

Jonathan is an obnoxious millionaire car dealer who is ordered to do community service with disadvantaged teens after he admits a drink-driving charge. One of the teens is an orphan, Freddie, who is in the final stages of a terminal illness and who wants his last Christmas to be perfect. (You're groaning, I can tell.) Of course, Jonathan discovers that, underneath the bluster, he's a decent bloke, as he sets about making Freddie's wishes come true.

Written by Chris Dunlop; produced by Madonna Baptiste; directed by David Richards.

Laurence Fox (Jonathan Donald), Sarah Smart (Laura Cooper), Jack McMullen (Freddie), Tamzin Outhwaite (Patsy Morgan), Marian McLoughlin (Julia), David Westhead (Charlie Archer), Larissa Toussaint-Grant (Kare), Vahid Gold (Mark), Faye Daveney (Natasha), Calvin Demba (Terry), Davood Ghadami (Alex), Judy Flynn (Cathy), Bill Paterson (Judge Underwood), Debra Baker (Susie Copeland), James Weber Brown (Max Greene), Nyasha Hatendi (Doctor David), Ann Beach (Freddie's Grandma), Reece Beaumont (Peter).

	Holding / Source
27.12.2011	HD/DB / HDC

THE FAST SHOW

Alternative/Working Title(s): BRILLIANT

A BBC production for BBC 2. Transmission details are for BBC 2. Usual duration: 30 minutes.

Main regular credit(s): Created by Charlie Higson and Paul Whitehouse; theme music by Philip Pope; executive producer Geoffrey Perkins.

Main regular cast: Paul Whitehouse, Charlie Higson.

SERIES 2
Main regular credit(s): Produced by Charlie Higson and Paul Whitehouse; directed by Sid Roberson and Mark Mylod.

Main regular cast: With Caroline Hook, John Thomson.

	Holding / Source
27.12.1996	DB-D3 / D3S

Duration: 45 minutes.

SERIES 4
Duration: 40 minutes.

Main regular credit(s): Produced by Charlie Higson and Paul Whitehouse; directed by Mark Mylod.

	Holding / Source
26.12.2000	DB / DBS
27.12.2000	DB / DBS
28.12.2000	DB / DBS

See also: TED AND RALPH (BBC)

FAT FRIENDS

A Tiger Aspect production for Yorkshire Television. made in association with Rollem Productions. Transmission details are for the Central region. Duration varies - see below for details.

Main regular credit(s): Created by Kay Mellor; theme music by The Beautiful South; executive producers Kay Mellor, David Reynolds and Greg Brenman.

Main regular cast: Alison Steadman (Betty Simpson), Gaynor Faye (Lauren Harris), Ruth Jones (Kelly Simpson), James Corden (Jamie Rymer), Janet Dibley (Carol McGary), Barrie Rutter (Douglas Simpson), Eleanor Bron (Marilyn Harris).

SERIES 3
Commissioned by Yorkshire Television. made in association with Rollem Productions.

Main regular credit(s): Produced by Josh Dynevor.

Main regular cast: With David Harewood (Max Robertson), Paul Warriner (Paul Thompson), Oliver Pickering (Russell Simpson), Andrew Lee-Potts (Jonathan Chadwick), Lynda Baron (Norma Patterson), Lisa Riley (Rebecca Patterson), Ruth Jones (Kelly Chadwick), Jonathan Ryland (Kevin Chadwick), Richard Ridings (Alan Ashburn), Kathryn Hunt (Val Lorrimer), Josie Lawrence (Julia Fleshman), Caroline Pegg (Pippa).

	Holding / Source
01.01.2004 "The Television Chat Show About Dieting"	DB / V1SW

Duration: 70 minutes.

Written by Kay Mellor; directed by John Deery.

With Trisha Goddard, Ian Kershaw, Bill Rodgers, Christine Mackie, Jacqueline Pilton, Jennifer Hennessy, Laurel Gibb, Nicola Bolton, Liam Barr.

FATHER CHRISTMAS

A Blooming Productions production for Channel 4. made in association with GaGa Communications / Palace Video. Transmission details are for the Central region.

Adapted by Dianne Jackson; based on books by Raymond Briggs; lyrics by Ian Llande; music by Mike Hewer and Phoenix Chamber Orchestra; executive producers Iain Harvey and Gower Frost; produced by John Coates; directed by Dave Unwin.

Mel Smith (Voice of Father Christmas).

	Holding / Source
24.12.1991	1" / C1

FATHER TED

A Hat Trick production for Channel 4. Transmission details are for Channel 4.

Main regular credit(s):	Written by Graham Linehan and Arthur Mathews; theme music by The Divine Comedy.
Main regular cast:	Dermot Morgan (Father Ted Crilly), Ardal O'Hanlon (Father Dougal McGuire), Frank Kelly (Father Jack Hackett), Pauline McLynn (Mrs Doyle).

SERIES 2

Main regular credit(s):	Assistant director Tony Aherne; art director Bill Crutcher; designed by Andrew Howe Davies; production team Christine Hagon, Sue Howells, Margaret Molnar and Paula Wilson; executive producer Mary Bell; production manager Peter Thornton; produced by Lissa Evans; directed by Declan Lowney.

	Holding / Source
24.12.1996 **A Christmassy Ted**	DB / DBS

Duration: 60 minutes.

Associate producers Graham Linehan, Arthur Mathews and Peter Thornton.

With Dervla Kirwan (Assumpta), Stephen Tompkinson (Father Clifford), Tony Guilfoyle (Fathwer Larry Duff), Gerard McSorley, Anne Gildea, Caoilinn McCormack, Barry Murphy, Sean Barrett, Donncha Crowley, Colum Gallivan, Neil McCaul, Kevin McKidd, Joe Taylor, Andrew McCulloch, Billy Boyle, John O'Mahony, Ed Byrne, Tom Farrelly, Tony Rohr, John Delaney, Brendan F. Dempsey, Aine O'Connor, Clive Geraghty, Brenoan Burke, Miche Doherty, Stephen Kennedy, Conor Mullen, Pat O'Mahony, Paul Tylak, John Quinn.

FATHER'S DAY

A Picture Partnership production for Channel 4. Transmission details are for Channel 4. Duration: 25 minutes.

Main regular credit(s):	Written by Peter Spence; produced by Brian Eastman; directed by Leszek Burzynski.
Main regular cast:	John Alderton (Lyall Jarvis), Dominique Barnes (Gemma), Zac Nicholson (Toby), Katie Alderton (Tasha).

SERIES 1

Transmission details are for Channel 4.

Main regular cast:	With Paul Angelis (Lyall's Father).

	Holding / Source
25.12.1983 **Guess Who's Coming To Christmas Dinner?**	DB / 2"

With Karen Archer (Dee), Ray Smith.

THE FATTEST MAN IN BRITAIN

An ITV Studios production for ITV 1. Transmission details are for the Central region. Duration: 100 minutes.

Written by Jeff Pope and Caroline Aherne; script supervisor Jane Houston; music by Stephen Hilton; art director Frederic Evard; designed by Luana Hanson; production executive Grace Boylan; executive producer Saurabh Kakkar; production manager Dominique Molloy; line producer Susan Dunn; produced by Jeff Pope; directed by David Blair.

Timothy Spall (Georgie), Bobby Ball (Morris), Akira Koeyama (Japanese Man), Yurri Naka (Japaenese Woman), Frances Barber (Janice), Jeremy Kyle (Himself), David Williams (Mad Bob), Archie Lal (Raj), Reba Dutta (Nana), Aisling Loftus (Amy), Richard Riddell (Joe), Brendan O'Carroll (Father O'Flaherty), Alice Barry (Joyce), Tim Woodward (Morley Raisin), Mark Chatterton (Richard Barter), Claire Ashforth (Newsreader), Julian Walsh (Clive), Barry Austin (Big Brian), Liz Hume-Dawson (Woman), Muhra Main (Joan Cropper), Max Pope (Boy), Milo Pope (Boy), Tony Walker (Heavy), Manchester Diamonds (Dance Troupe).

	Holding / Source
20.12.2009	DB / DBSWF

FAVOURITE CHRISTMAS CAROLS

A BBC production for BBC 1. Transmission details are for BBC 1. Duration: 30 minutes.

Programmes looking at the stories behind popular Christmas carols.

Main regular credit(s):	Produced by Helen Mansfield; directed by Suzy Klein.
Main regular performer(s):	Eamonn Holmes (Presenter).

	Holding / Source
19.12.2001	DB / DBSW

With Michael Ball, Josie Lawrence, Thelma Barlow, Becky Taylor, Finchley Children's Music Group, BBC Singers.

21.12.2001	DB / DBSW

With Charlie Dimmock, Linda Gray, Antony Worrall Thompson.

FELIX AND MURDO

Commissioned by Channel 4. Transmission details are for Channel 4. Duration: 25 minutes.

Written by Simon Nye; produced by Ben Farrell and Saskia Schuster; directed by Christine Gernon.

Ben Miller (Felix), Alexander Armstrong (Murdo), Georgia King (Winnie), Katy Wix (Fanny), Marek Larwood (Archie), Jonathan Coy (Father Of The Family), Pippa Haywood (Mother Of The Family), Lizzie Roper (Mrs Snivel).

	Holding / Source
28.12.2011	HD/DB / HDC

THE FENN STREET GANG

An LWT production. Transmission details are for the ATV midlands region. Duration: 25 minutes.

Main regular credit(s): Created by John Esmonde and Bob Larbey.

SERIES 1

Main regular credit(s): Executive producer Mark Stuart.

	Production No	Holding / Source
24.12.1971 **When Did You Last See Your Father?**	9L/00854	D2 / 2"

Written by David Barry; designed by John Emery; directed by Alan Wallis.

With David Barry (Frankie Abbott), Léon Vitali (Peter Craven), Peter Cleall (Eric Duffy), Peter Denyer (Dennis Dunstable), Barbara Mitchell, Ruth Holden, John J. Carney, Robert James, Michael Greatorex, Reginald Stewart, Meadows White.

See also: PLEASE SIR!

FERGUS FISH

A Rediffusion Television production. Transmission details are for the Rediffusion Television region. Duration: 12 minutes.

Main regular credit(s): Written by Harold Rottesman; produced and directed by Diana Potter.

	Holding / Source
22.12.1967 **Fergus Fish's Christmas**	J /

Recorded 23.08.1967.

THE FIFTIES

A Granada production. Transmission details are for the ATV midlands region. Duration: 45 minutes.

Introduced by Ian Carmichael; programme editor Alan Brien; produced and directed by Mike Wooller.

	Holding / Source
30.12.1959	DB-4W / 40

THE FIGHTING COCK

A BBC production for BBC 1. Transmission details are for BBC 1. Duration: 50 minutes.

Adapted by Lucienne Hill; based on a book by Jean Anouilh; by arrangement with John Clements and Martin Landau; television presentation by John Vernon; designed by Alan Tagg; directed by Norman Marshall.

John Clements (The General), Arthur Skinner (The Doctor), Margot Taylor (Marie-Christine), Rufus Frampton (Toto), Michael Howe (Milkman's Son), Barry Shawzin (Milkman), David Bird (Father Dominic), Philippa Gail (Sophie), John Standing (André Philippe Mendigales), Viola Lyel (Bise), Zena Walker (Aglae), Edward Burnham (Lebelluc), Brian Hayes (Michepain), Michael Aldridge (Baron Henri Belazor).

	Holding / Source
23.12.1966	J /

Scenes from the Chichester Festival Theatre Production.

THE FILE ON VORONOV

An Associated-Rediffusion production. Transmission details are for the ATV midlands region.

When Russian military attaché Maxim Voronov left his Embassy to attend a hush-hush international conference, he did not suspect that a network of high-level intrigue was about to ensnare him. Thanks to three small boys, it all began as a practical joke—but the end Scotland Yard, M.I.5, and the Security forces of a nation were all involved before "the File on Voronov" could be finally closed.

Written by Sheilah Ward and Peter Ling; produced and directed by David Eady.

George Murcell (Voronov), Gerald Anderson (Mr Croft), Richard Marner (Borganev), Peter Rosser (Hotel Manager), Ann Smith (Girl), Frank Sieman (Humbold), Glyn Dearman (Joe), Anthony Green (Charlie), Ian Hobbs (Steven).

	Holding / Source
25.12.1956	R3N|n / Live

FILM FUN

A Granada production. Transmission details are for the Central region.

Main regular cast: Derek Griffiths (Presenter).

	Production No	Holding / Source
25.12.1982 **Film Fun At Christmas**	P1154/21	DB / 2"

Duration: 50 minutes.

The Roxy cartoon cinema is open for business as usual as Doreen, Reg and the rest of the staff rehearse for their annual concert. But a mysterious handsome stranger arrives — could it be Doreen's heart throb, Julio Manilow? Also on the show are cartoons featuring Porky Pig, Snow White and Father Christmas.

Produced by Martyn Day; directed by Lorne Magory.

FILM ON FOUR

Produced for Channel 4 by a variety of companies (see details below). Transmission details are for Channel 4. Duration varies - see below for details.

SERIES 4

Holding / Source

20.12.1984 **Winter Flight**   C1 / C1

An Enigma/Goldcrest production. Duration: 100 minutes.

Written by Alan Janes; executive producer David Puttnam; produced by Robin Douet and Susan Richards; directed by Roy Battersby.

With Reece Dinsdale (Mal), Nicola Cowper (Angie), Gary Olsen (Dave), Sean Bean (Hooker), Beverly Hewitt (Lara), Shelagh Stephenson (Kel), Michael Percival (Doctor), Anthony Trent (Sergeant Bowyer), Tim Bentinck (Jack), Michael Hughes (Los), Mark Penfold (Flight Lieutenant Maynard), Annette Ekblom (Jill), Martin Gower (Murph), Robert Pugh (Military Policeman).

Holding / Source

19.12.1985 **Christmas Present**   C1 / C1

A Telekation Int. production. Duration: 70 minutes.

Written by Tony Bicât; produced by Barry Hanson; directed by Tony Bicât.

With Peter Chelsom (Nigel Playfayre), Bill Fraser (Sir Percy Hammond), Danny Wooder (Viv), Clive Parker (Gos), Karen Meagher (Anne), Mark Harvey (Stickey), Lesley Manville (Judy Tall), Richard Ireson (Ned), Janet Steel (Mary), Nadim Sawalha (Joseph), Hetty Baynes (Pamela), Elizabeth Bradley (Granny Harris), Badi Uzzaman (Mr Amir Mehrban), Jamila Massey (Mrs Mehrban), Sohan Maharaj (Talvar), Simmi Salimi (Younger Sister Munni), Maiser Asghar (Older Sister Tunnu), Abraham Osuagwu (Nigerian Tourist), Harry Jones (Placard Man), Nick Brimble (Tom), Amelda Brown (ITN Reporter), Philip Herbert (Santa Claus), Michael Melia (Hammonds Security Guard), Christopher Birch (Police Inspector), Jonathon Stratt (Police Constable), Pamela Abbott (Pamela's Mother), John Hart Dyke (Pamela's Father), Jackie D. Broad (Street Theatre Barker), Debbie Mullins (Street Theatre Actor), Les Sharp (Street Theatre Actor).

SERIES 13

Holding / Source

25.12.1992 **The Fool**   C1 / C1S

A Hobo/Sands Films production. Duration: 140 minutes.

Written by Christina Edzard and Olivier Stockman; directed by Christina Edzard.

With Derek Jacobi (Sir John / Mr Frederick), Cyril Cusack (Ballad Seller), Ruth Mitchell (Girl), Maria Aitken (Lady Amelia), Irina Brook (Georgiana Shillibeer), Paul Brooke (Lord Paramount), Joan Sims (Lady Daphne), Don Henderson (Bob), Michael Hordern (Mr Tatham).

Only predominantly British films have been included. "A Splice of Life - 15 Years of Film On Four" was shown on Channel 4, tx:25.12.97. 40mins.

THE FINAL QUEST

A Granada Yorkshire production for Yorkshire Television. made in association with Isle of Man Film Commission. Transmission details are for the Central region. Duration: 75 minutes.

Written by Douglas Livingstone; script supervisor Karen Wright; music by Ray Russell; executive producers David Reynolds and Steve Christian; produced by David Reynolds; directed by David Jason.

David Jason (Dave), Hywel Bennett (Ronno), Roy Hudd (Charlie), Greg Faulkner (Young Dave), Max Wrottesley (Young Ronno), Jim Sturgess (Young Charlie), Rachael Stirling (Young Annabelle), Stephen Moyer (Young Danny Duke), Jan Harvey (Annabelle), Andy Mulligan (Danny Duke), Paul Chapman (Lord Westcott), Joanna Van Gyseghem (Lady Westcott), Amy Marston (Agnes), Dolly Wells (Anthea), Peter Cellier (Hawkins), Jonathan Kydd (George), Amelda Brown (Rose), Diane Langton (Marian Snr), Stefanie Moore (Marian Jnr), Bobby Bragg (Compere 1961), Lorenzo Camporese (Windscreen Washer), Andrew Westfield (Lorry Driver), John Elkington (Waiter), Eddie Booth (M.C. 2004).

Holding / Source

27.12.2004   DB / V1SW

FINDING OUT

A Rediffusion Television production. Transmission details are for the ATV midlands region. Duration: 15 minutes.

Holding / Source

29.11.1965 **Christmas Programme**   J / 40

Introduced by Penny Whittam; written by Peter Pickering; directed by Angela Holder.

With Jonathan Collins (Squirrel), David Craig (Hedgehog), Clive Marshall (Reindeer), Jonathan Elsom (Tree / Musician / Arab / Eskimo).

THE FINDING

A Thames Television production. Transmission details are for the Central region. Duration: 50 minutes.

A baby boy is 'found' on the banks of the Thames and adopted by a loving, caring family. But questions about Alex's real parentage suddenly re-emerge when he turns 11. An extraordinary gift, instead of bringing happiness, creates immense family tensions and drives Alex into a series of adventures in a strange and frightening world. Will his own family ever 'find' him again?

Adapted by Stephen Wakelam; based on a book by Nina Bawden; music by Jim Parker; director of photography Simon Kossoff; designed by David Ferris; executive producer Alan Horrox; produced and directed by Carol Wiseman.

Alison Steadman (Mum), Roger Rees (Dad), Moira Lister (Gran), Miriam Margolyes (Poll), James Older (Alex), Mia Fothergill (Laura), Roger Lloyd Pack (Fowles), Aimée Delamain (Mrs Angel), Nicky Taylor (Willy), Claire Hunt (Carla), Jeffrey Gear (Photographer), Ross Boatman (Policeman), Sylvester Williams (Jake), Cheryl Miller (Petal), Sean Gascoine (Samson), Mark Heath (Preacher), Peggy Phango (Holy Roller Mother), Simon Snellings (Boy At Fair), Jason Savage (Boy At Burger Bar), Evelyn Duah (Boy At Burger Bar), Lisa O'Connor (Boy At Burger Bar), Bruce Savage (Boy At Burger Bar), Sammy Saddique (Boy At Burger Bar).

Holding / Source

23.12.1987   1" / 1"

FIRE AND ICE

An LWT production. Transmission details are for the Central region. Duration: 50 minutes.

The world's most exciting and acclaimed ice dancers, star in a fantasy love story conceived especially for television. They play two people from opposite worlds who meet and fall into a deep and forbidden love which threatens to destroy them.

Costume Stephen Adnitt; make-up Janis Gould; music by Carl Davis; choreography by Graeme Murphy; lighting by John Fyfe; designed by Michael Seymour; produced by Nick Elliott and Michael Linnit; directed by Tom Gutteridge.

Jayne Torvill (Princess), Christopher Dean (Prince), Claudie Algeranova (Queen), Stephen Beagley (Keeper Of The Flame), Stewart Avon Arnold (Courtier), Claire Bayliss (Courtier), Salome Brunner (Courtier), Leslie Bryant (Courtier), Tammy Crowson (Courtier), Linda Gibbs (Courtier), Liz Gilbert (Courtier), Barry Hagan (Courtier), Robin James (Courtier), Kelly Johnson (Courtier), Nicola Keen (Courtier), Shaun McGill (Courtier), Lea Ann Miller (Courtier), Tim Spain (Courtier), Edmund Strike (Courtier), Barry Hagan (King), Shaun McGill (Magician), Salome Brunner (Messenger), Karen Barber (Courtier), Gary Beacom (Courtier), Wayne Deweyert (Courtier), Billy Fauver (Courtier), Gia Guddat (Courtier), Kristan Lowery (Courtier), Stephen Pickavance (Courtier), Rainer Schonborn (Courtier), Marianne Van Bommel (Courtier), London Philharmonic Orchestra.

	Holding / Source
26.12.1986	D2 / 1"

FIREMAN SAM

Alternative/Working Title(s): SAM TAN

A Bumper Films / Siriol Productions production for BBC 1. Transmission details are for BBC 1. Duration: 10 minutes.

Main regular credit(s):   Created by Rob Lee.

SERIES 2

Main regular cast: With John Alderton (Narrator).

	Holding / Source
22.12.1988 **Snow Business**	1" / 1"

First tx'd on S4C in Welsh. All tx dates above are those of BBC 1.

THE FIRST CHRISTMAS

A Thames Television production. Transmission details are for the Thames Television region. Duration: 40 minutes.

A modern re-telling of the oldest Christmas story.

Produced and directed by John Michael Phillips.

Andrew Robertson, Shay Gorman, Coral Fairweather, Gordon Case, Jacob Witkin, John Ruddock, Katherine Levy.

	Holding / Source
22.12.1978	DB / 2"

THE FIRST COMMUNION OF CHRISTMAS

A BBC production for BBC 1. Transmission details are for BBC 1. Duration: 30 minutes.

Candlelit Communion service from Moreton Methodist Church on the Wirral, Merseyside.

Music directed by Helen Sheppard; television presentation by Noel Vincent.

Reverend Doctor John Newton (Preacher), Reverend Wesley Rooney, David Houlder (Organist), Arthur Lewis (Accompanist).

	Holding / Source
24.12.1987	DB / Live

THE FIRST DAY OF THE YEAR SHOW

A Scottish Television production. Transmission details are for the ATV midlands region. Duration: 25 minutes.

Executive producer Bryan Izzard; directed by Jim McCann.

Stanley Baxter, Steve Jones, Fulton Mackay, Rikki Fulton, Jack Milroy, The Krankies, Allan Stewart, Anne Lorne Gillies, Peter Morrison, Roger Hannah Dancers, The Harry Rabinowitz Orchestra.

	Holding / Source
01.01.1980	DVSEQ / 2"

The final 20m 52s of this is held on DVCam by Kaleidoscope, found on a Philips tape.

FIRST EDITION

An LWT production. Transmission details are for the ATV midlands region. Duration: 52 minutes.

	Production No	Holding / Source
23.12.1972 **Just In Time For Christmas**	9L/01420	D2 / 2"

Marriage for Professor Nottage and his wife has been remarkably quiet during their 20 years together. Then one day the tranquillity is shattered. Mrs. Nottage makes an announcement: she is pregnant. The Professor isn't pleased.

Written by Harold Lang; designed by David Catley; executive producer Rex Firkin; produced by Paul Knight; directed by Bill Hays.

With Alfred Burke (Leonard Nottage), Gwen Watford (Janet Nottage), Joan Hickson (Mrs Hope-Rising), Fanny Carby (Mrs Davis), Geoffrey Bayldon (Mr Nottage), Jane Wood (Young Mother), Meg Davies (Antigone), Clive Cazes (Waiter), Verne Morgan (Gallery Attendant), Mary Ann Severne (Nurse White), Angela Rooks (Sister Denny), Jumoke Debayo (Sister Viola).

Recorded 17th December 1971.

THE FIRST NIGHT OF PYGMALION

A BBC production for BBC 2. Transmission details are for BBC 2. Duration: 70 minutes.

Three monstrous — but brilliantly witty — egoists came together when Beerbohm Tree agreed to stage Shaw's new play Pygmalion at His Majesty's Theatre in April 1914. The star was the outrageous Mrs Patrick Campbell.

Written by Richard Huggett; costume Catriona Tomalin; make-up Tina Clare; lighting by Jim Richards; sound Derek Miller-Timmins; designed by Fanny Taylor; produced and directed by Hal Burton.

Max Adrian (Bernard Shaw), Miriam Karlin (Mrs Patrick Campbell), John Osborne (Sir Herbert Beerbohm Tree), John Graham (Stanley Bell), Olwen Brooks (Dame Edith Lyttleton), Richard Huggett (Henry Dana), Naomi Campbell (Carlotta Addison), Pamela Roland (Margaret Busse), Lynne White (Irene Delisse), Stuart Eames (Algernon Greig), Ernest Jennings (Edmund Gurney), Michael Behr (Philip Merivale), Winifred Hill (Rosamund Mayne-Young), Alexander John (Alexander Sarner), Ernest Claydon, Richard Hallifax, Verne Morgan, David Sparks.

	Holding / Source
23.12.1969	J / 2"

THE FIRST SILENT NIGHT

A BBC production for BBC 2. Transmission details are for BBC 2. Duration: 30 minutes.

This musical detective story uncovers the origin of the world's most famous Christmas carol. Using new evidence from the discovery in Austria of the song's oldest known version. it tells of Austrian priest Joseph Mohr and teacher Franz Gruber, who composed the work against a backdrop of war in the Salzburg region nearly 200 years ago.

A full performance of the carol re-creates the way in which it was probably heard forthe very first time on Christmas Eve 1818.

Produced and directed by Frederick Baker.

Gabriel Wolf (Narrator).

	Holding / Source
24.12.1997	DB-D3 / D3S

FIRSTIMERS

A Granada production. Transmission details are for the Granada region. Duration varies - see below for details.

	Holding / Source
26.12.1967 **Awards Edition**	J /

Duration: 10 minutes.
With The Summers, Mike Styan, Donna Jo, The Kentuckians, Tom and Smilie, Cuppa Tea, Frank Barry Duo.

THE FLAT - 1974

A BBC production for BBC 2. Transmission details are for BBC 2. Duration: 40 minutes.

Highlights of the 1974 Flat Racing season.

Edited by Alan Hart; film editor Brian Tomkins; produced by Jeff Goddard.

Julian Wilson (Presenter), Peter Walwyn, Pat Eddery, Lester Piggott, Jimmy Lindley, Yves St Martin, Peter O'Sullevan.

	Holding / Source
24.12.1974	R1 / 2"

FLICKS

A Thames Television production. Transmission details are for the Central region.

Main regular cast: Christopher Lillicrap (Host).

SERIES 3

	Holding / Source
17.12.1985 **The Twelve Days Of Christmas**	1" / 1"

FO A FE

Alternative/Working Title(s): THIS ONE AND THAT ONE

A BBC Wales production for BBC 1 Wales. Transmission details are for BBC Wales. Duration: 30 minutes.

Main regular credit(s): Written by Gwenlyn Parry and Rhydderch Jones; produced and directed by Jack Williams.

Main regular cast: Ryan Davies (Twm Twm), Gaynor Morgan Rees (Diana), Clive Roberts (George), Guto Roberts (Ephraim), Ieuan Rhys Williams (Sioni), Dilys Davies (Mrs Cadwaladr).

SERIES 3

	Holding / Source
25.12.1975 **Dydd O Ewyllys Da**	DB / 2"

With Dillwyn Owen.

SERIES 4

	Holding / Source
25.12.1976 **Ar Fore Dydd Nadolig**	DB / 2"

Situation comedy.

FOLLOW THE STAR

A BBC production for BBC 2. Transmission details are for BBC 2. Duration: 80 minutes.

The hit musical Nativity Play first produced by WENDY TOYE and designed by PETER WHITEMAN for the Chichester Festival Theatre.

Devised by Wendy Toye; written by Wally K. Daly; script editor Brenda Reid; music by Jim Parker; lighting by Clive Thomas; designed by Ken Sharp; produced by Innes Lloyd; directed by Wendy Toye.

Robert Dorning (Olly), Christopher Lillicrap (Gabby), Ian Bartholomew (Lofty), Cheryl Branker (Angy), Annie Wensack (Jelly), Tony Robinson (Chicago), Lewis Fiander (Herod), Sue Jones-Davies (Mary), Martin Smith (Joseph), Norman Warwick (Wise Man), Johnny Worthy (Wise Man), Michael Boothe (Wise Man), Allan Corduner (Shepherd), Desmond Barrit (Shepherd), Stephen Simmonds (Shepherd), Maurice Lane (Oxey), David Machin (Assy), Peter Olsen (Angel / Villager), Reginald Tsiboe (Angel / Villager), Nigel Hughes (Angel / Villager), Julia Deakin (Angel / Villager), Susan Coates (Angel / Villager), Maynard Williams (Angel / Soldier), Mark Caven (Angel / Soldier / Innkeeper), David Lester (Angel / Soldier / Innkeeper), Mike Finesilver (Angel / Soldier / Innkeeper), Tracey Perry (Angel Girl / Villager), Vincent Osborne (Angel Boy / Villager).

	Holding / Source
24.12.1979	DB-D3 / 2"

FOR "BETHLEHEM" READ "LITTLE THRAVES"

A BBC Manchester production for BBC Children's Department. Transmission details are for BBC 1. Duration: 30 minutes.

Maggie Tanner is pretty sure that she will get the part of Mary in the Nativity Play, but Sarah and Wendy have other ideas.

Written by Helen Cresswell; sound Dennis Cartwright; film camera David Jackson; film editor Peter Mayhew; executive producer Anna Home; produced and directed by John Prowse.

Melanie Bennett (Maggie), Catherine Taylor (Sarah), Karen Bache (Wendy), Claire Sandry (Kate), Merelina Kendall (Mrs Robinson), Reg Lye (Ben), Sonia Fox (Dora Tanner), Geoffrey Greenhill (Ted Tanner), Stephanie Turner (Mrs Garton), Emma Douglas (Narrator), Madelaine Williams (The Angel), June Ross (Organist), Guiting Power Parochial Primary School.

	Holding / Source
20.12.1977	C1 / C1

FOR AULD LANG SYNE

A BBC Scotland production for BBC 1 Scotland. Transmission details are for BBC 1 Scotland. Duration: 85 minutes.

	Holding / Source
31.12.1971	J / 2"

FOR AULD LANG SYNE

A BBC Scotland production for BBC 1 Scotland. Transmission details are for BBC 1 Scotland. Duration: 80 minutes.

	Holding / Source
31.12.1972	J / 2"

FOR AULD LANG SYNE

A BBC Scotland production for BBC 1 Scotland. Transmission details are for BBC 1 Scotland. Duration: 44 minutes.

Choreography by Brian Seivwright; designed by Alex Gourlay; produced and directed by Iain MacFadyen.

Peter Morrison, Alastair McDonald, Anne Lorne Gillies, Rolf Harris, Aimi MacDonald, Ronald Fraser, The Brian Sievwright Dancers, The Jim Johnstone Scottish Country Dance Band, Brian Fahey and The Scottish Radio Orchestra, Shotts and Dykehead, Caledonia Pipe Band.

	Holding / Source
31.12.1974	J / 2"

FOR AULD LANG SYNE

A BBC Scotland production for BBC 1. Transmission details are for BBC 1. Duration: 70 minutes.

Introduced by Tom Fleming; written by Edward Boyd [credited as Eddie Boyd]; music associate Bernard Sumner; choreography by Brian Seivwright; designed by Guthrie Hutton; executive producer Iain MacFadyen; produced by Terry Henebery, Anne Somers, Brian Hulme and Ian Christie.

Moira Anderson, Peter Morrison, The Corries, Larry Parker, Aly Bain, Roddy McMillan, John Grieve, Walter Carr, Alex McAvoy, The Toad Choir, The Brian Sievwright Dancers, Shotts and Dykehead, Caledonia Pipe Band, Brian Fahey and The Scottish Radio Orchestra, Alastair MacDonald, Jimmy Savile, Max Boyce.

	Holding / Source
31.12.1975	DB-D3 / 2"

FOR LOVING

A BBC Bristol production for BBC 2. Transmission details are for BBC 2. Duration: 45 minutes.

The story of a young and unmarried pregnant girl, who comes home for Christmas, and of her developing relationship with a young man she meets.

Written by John King; film camera Bernard Hedges; film editor Charles Aldridge; play production by John King.

Angela Scoular (Girl), Aileen Mills (Mother), Norman Tyrrell (Father), Rex Holdsworth (Father's Friend), Alfred Lynch (Man), Andrew Simpson (Driver), Hugh Smith-Marriott (Police Inspector), James Snell (Police Constable No 1), Peter Leabourne (Police Constable No 2), Peter Arne (Country Policeman).

	Holding / Source
24.12.1972	DB-D3 / 2"

FOR THE LOVE OF ADA

A Thames Television production. Transmission details are for the ATV midlands region.

Main regular credit(s):	Written by Vince Powell and Harry Driver; theme music by Ron Grainer; produced and directed by Ronnie Baxter.
Main regular cast:	Irene Handl (Ada Cresswell/Bingley), Wilfred Pickles (Walter Bingley).

SERIES 4

Main regular credit(s):	Designed by Bill Palmer.
Main regular cast:	With Barbara Mitchell (Ruth Pollitt), Jack Smethurst (Leslie Pollitt).

	VT Number	Holding / Source
27.12.1971	5087	D3 / 2"

Duration: 40 minutes.

How do the Bingleys and the Pollitts spend the festive season? Let's look-in at Cemetery Lodge... Peace on earth and goodwill to all men is the message of Christmas, but for Ma and Ruth this Boxing Day, there is very little peace, and for Walter and Leslie there is definitely no goodwill!

With Larry Martyn (Brian), Joanna Cooper (Liz).

There was also a feature film made.

FOR THIS CHRISTMAS ONLY

A HTV production. Transmission details are for the ATV midlands region. Duration: 55 minutes.

Christmas celebration in which Sir Geraint Evans sings "Silent Night", "Nazareth" and "Hark the Herald Angels Sing". With contributions from Tonyrefail Childrens Choir, Cory Silver Band, Pontypridd Male Voice Choir, Nigel Brooks Singers and Nancy Gotchard. The programme concludes with Sir Geraint Evans singing The Lord's Prayer with the Cardiff Polyphonic Choir. The programme with his Christmas reminiscences is introduced by Barry John.

Written by Neil Shand; music directed by Eric Wetherell; associate producer Michael Bakewell; executive producer Aled Vaughan; produced and directed by Terry Delacey.

Sir Geraint Evans (Presenter), Spike Milligan, Dame Flora Robson, Rachel Roberts, Kiri Te Kanawa, Ryland Davies, Wynford Vaughan Thomas, The Scholars.

	Holding / Source
25.12.1974	B / 2"

THE FOSTERS

An LWT production. Transmission details are for the ATV midlands region. Usual duration: 25 minutes.

Main regular credit(s):	Written by Jon Watkins; produced and directed by Stuart Allen.
Main regular cast:	Norman Beaton (Samuel Foster), Isabelle Lucas (Pearl Foster), Carmen Munroe (Wilma), Lenny Henry (Sonny Foster), Sharon Rosita (Shirley Foster), Laurie Mark (Benjamin Foster).

SERIES 1

Main regular credit(s):	Music by Denis Farnon and Denis King; series consultant Lawrence Innis; designed by Michael Oxley.

	Production No	Holding / Source
01.01.1977 New Year With The Fosters	9L/09801	D2 / 2"

With Irene Handl.

Based upon Tandem Productions 'Good Times'.

THE FOX

A BBC South West production for BBC 2. Transmission details are for BBC 2. Duration: 60 minutes.

Written by John Elliot and John King; designed by John Bone; produced and directed by John King.

Adrienne Corri (Mother), Peter Arne (Father), Simon King (Son), Ruby Luscombe (Midwife), Joe Pengelly (Priest), Juliet Ace (Lady of the Manor).

	Holding / Source
24.12.1973	DB-D3 / C1

FRAGGLE ROCK

A TVS production. Transmission details are for the Central region. Duration: 25 minutes.

Main regular credit(s):	Devised by Jim Henson.

SERIES 2

Main regular credit(s):	Written by Victor Pemberton; executive producers Anna Home and Jim Henson; produced by Duncan Kenworthy and Lawrence S. Mirkin.
Main regular cast:	With Fulton Mackay (The Captain), David Barclay, Mike Quinn, Kevin Bradshaw.

	VT Number	Holding / Source
22.12.1984 The Bells Of Fraggle Rock	4175	DV / 1"

It's Christmas Eve at the lighthouse and snowing heavily. The Captain and Sprocket are worried that the weather is too bad for the mailboat to get through with their Christmas dinner.

Directed by Jeremy Swan and Douglas Williams.

FRANK AND SELINA'S CHRISTMAS TIME

A BBC production for BBC 1. Transmission details are for BBC 1. Duration: 37 minutes.

Designed by Anthea West; assistant producers Nigel Crowle and Christopher Hutchins; produced by Jane Lush; directed by Bruce Thompson.

Frank Bough (Presenter), Selina Scott (Presenter), Mike Smith, Paul Daniels, Barry Norman, Noel Edmonds, Maureen Lipman, Jan Francis, Paul Nicholas.

	Holding / Source
23.12.1984	DB / 1"

THE FRANK SKINNER SHOW

A BBC production for BBC 1. Transmission details are for BBC 1.

Main regular performer(s): Frank Skinner (Host).

SERIES 3

Main regular credit(s): Produced by John McHugh; directed by Peter Orton.

	Holding / Source
24.12.1998	DB / DBSW

Duration: 38 minutes.

With Aled Jones, Gennifer Flowers, Mel C.

THE FRANK SKINNER SHOW

An Avalon Productions production for ITV 1. Transmission details are for the Central region.

Main regular performer(s): Frank Skinner (Host).

SERIES 1

Commissioned by LWT. Duration: 35 minutes.

Main regular credit(s): Series producer John McHugh; produced by Robyn O'Brien; directed by Peter Orton.

	Holding / Source
26.12.2000	DB / DBSW

SERIES 2

Duration: 40 minutes.

Main regular credit(s): Series producer John McHugh; produced by Robyn O'Brien; directed by Peter Orton.

	Holding / Source
26.12.2001	DB / DBSW

With Vinnie Jones, Nicky Byrne, Bryan McFadden, Brian Bennett.

SERIES 5

Duration: 50 minutes.

Main regular credit(s): Series producer Robyn O'Brien; directed by John F. D. Northover.

	Holding / Source
28.12.2004	DB / DBSW

With David Coulthard, Patrick Stewart, David Baddiel, Embrace.

This edition was shown as single 50-minute edition, the others were split into two parts with ITV News in between.

FRANKENSTEIN

A Western World Television production for Yorkshire Television. Transmission details are for the Central region. Duration: 80 minutes.

Adapted by Victor Gialanella; based on a book by Mary Shelley; music by Alan Parker; designed by Jeremy Bear; executive producers Lou Moore and Bob Rubin; produced by Bill Siegler; directed by James Ormerod.

Robert Powell (Victor Frankenstein), David Warner (Creature), Susan Wooldridge (Justine), Jon Rumney (Herr Mueller), Carrie Fisher (Elizabeth), Roberta Taylor (Gerta), Terence Alexander (Alphonse Frankenstein), John Gielgud (De Lacey), James Coyle (Scholz), Edward Judd (Metz), Graham McGrath (William Frankenstein), Michael Cochrane (Henry Clerval), Arnold Peters (Busch).

	VT Number	Holding / Source
27.12.1984	D038	1" / C1

FRANKENSTEIN

A David Wickes Television production for Thames Television. made in association with Turner Pictures. Transmission details are for the Central region. Duration: 115 minutes.

Adapted by David Wickes; based on a book by Mary Shelley; script supervisor Cheryl Leigh; music by John Cameron; executive producer David Wickes; directed by David Wickes.

Patrick Bergin (DoctorVictor Frankenstein), Randy Quaid (The Monster), John Mills (De Lacey), Lambert Wilson (Clerval), Fiona Gillies (Elizabeth), Jacinta Mulcahy (Justine), Ronald Leigh-Hunt (Alphonse), Timothy Stark (William), Vernon Dobtcheff (Chancellor), Roger Bizley (Captain), Michael Gothard (Bosun), Marcus Eyre (Zorkin), John Scarborough (Priest), Jon Laurimore (Sailor), Amanda Quaid (Amy), Maciek Czapski (Hunter 1), Piotr Szyma (Hunter 2), Wojciech Dabrowski (Officer), Teresa Musialek (Landlady), Ferdynand Matysik (Magistrate), Andrzej Galla (Innkeeper), Boleslaw Abart (Stonemason).

	Holding / Source
29.12.1992	1" / C1S

FRANKIE AND BRUCE'S CHRISTMAS SHOW

An ABC production. Transmission details are for the ABC midlands region. Duration: 75 minutes.

Written by Dick Hills and Sid Green; choreography by Malcolm Goddard; designed by Neville Green; executive producer Philip Jones; produced by Peter Dulay; directed by Peter Frazer-Jones.

Frankie Howerd (Host), Bruce Forsyth (Host), Cilla Black, Tommy Cooper, Tom Jones, The Kaye Sisters, Aleta Morrison, The Malcolm Goddard Dancers, Bob Sharples and his ABC Television Showband.

	Holding / Source
24.12.1966	J / 40

FRANKIE AND BRUCE'S CHRISTMAS SHOW

An ABC production. Transmission details are for the ABC midlands region. Duration: 75 minutes.

Written by Sid Green and Dick Hills; dances staged by Lionel Blair; music associate Colin Keyes; designed by Brian Eatwell; produced and directed by Peter Frazer-Jones.

Frankie Howerd (Host), Bruce Forsyth (Host), Tommy Cooper, Anita Harris, The Rockin' Berries, Lionel Blair, Aleta Morrison, Corin Redgrave, Frankie Vaughan, The Lionel Blair Dancers, The Mike Sammes Singers, Ted Brennan and his Orchestra.

	Holding / Source
23.12.1967	DVSEQ / 40

13 minutes of footage, ex-CV2000.

FRANKIE LAINE

A BBC Manchester production for BBC 1. Transmission details are for BBC 1. Duration: 35 minutes.

Produced by Peter Ridsdale Scott; directed by Tony Harrison.

Frankie Laine.

	Holding / Source
01.01.1976	DB-D3 / 2"

FRANKIE'S AND BRUCE'S CHRISTMAS SHOW

An ABC production. Transmission details are for the ABC midlands region.

Frankie Howerd (Host), Bruce Forsyth (Host).

	Holding / Source
24.12.1966	J / 40

FREDDIE STARR AT THE ROYALTY

A Thames Television production. Transmission details are for the Central region. Duration: 40 minutes.

Music directed by Alan Braden; designed by Rod Stratfold; produced and directed by Keith Beckett.

Freddie Starr (Host), Shirley Bassey, Lon Satton, Wayne Dobson, The Austen Brothers, Ken Wilson.

	Holding / Source
31.12.1984	1" / 1"

THE FREDDIE STARR COMEDY EXPRESS

A Thames Television production. Transmission details are for the Central region. Duration: 50 minutes.

Written by Sid Green, Eric Merriman, Keith Leonard, Len Marten and Freddie Starr; music directed by Alan Braden; choreography by Graham Fletcher, George May and Deirdra Lovell; designed by Alex Clarke; produced and directed by Keith Beckett.

Freddie Starr, Tim Barrett, Vee Brooks, Frank Coda, Anna Dawson, Glynn Edwards, Burt Kwouk, Susan Tagg, Jane West, Frank Bruno, Graham Fletcher, Terry Lawless, Lon Satton, Maggie Scott.

	Holding / Source
31.12.1985	1" / 1"

FREDDIE STARR ON THE ROAD

A Thames Television production. Transmission details are for the ATV midlands region. Duration: 65 minutes.

Produced and directed by Frank Cvitanovich.

Freddie Starr.

	Holding / Source
28.12.1981	DB / 2"

THE FREDDIE STARR SHOW

A BBC production for BBC 1. Transmission details are for BBC 1. Duration: 45 minutes.

Main regular credit(s):   Produced and directed by Terry Hughes.

Main regular performer(s): Freddie Starr.

	Holding / Source
31.12.1976	DB-D3 / 2"

Written by Freddie Starr; music directed by Arthur Greenslade; choreography by Nigel Lythgoe; designed by Martin Collins.
With Guys & Dolls [as Guys 'N' Dolls], The Nigel Lythgoe Dancers.

THE FREDDIE STAR SHOW

THE FREDDIE STARR SHOW

A Central production for Central->Carlton UK. Transmission details are for the Central region. Duration varies - see below for details.

Main regular credit(s): Executive producer Richard Holloway; produced by David G. Hillier and Paula Burdon; directed by David G. Hillier.
Main regular cast: Freddie Starr (Host).

Holding / Source
29.12.1997 D2 / D2S
Duration: 51 minutes.
The unpredictable Freddie Starr is joined by celebrity chef Antony Worrall Thompson for a hilarious demonstration of the art of stuffing a turkey in this special Christmas edition. There's madness and mayhem, comic guises, sketches and songs with a host of guest stars who dare to join him. The audience are also in for a few surprises as Freddie roams the aisle and clambers amongst the audience looking for volunteers. Freddie takes his own brand of comedy to the pitch at Notts County Football Ground where he is introduced as Ron Atkinson's replacement when Ron announces that he is leaving football management. Dressed in his crazy Hitler outfit, Freddie is interviewed by ITV sports presenter Gary Newbon. There's also a memorable rendition of the seasonal favourite, "White Christmas" by Freddie.
With Wayne Dobson, Leo Sayer, Status Quo, Gary Newbon, Antony Worrall Thompson.

Holding / Source
31.12.1998 D2 / D2S
Duration: 45 minutes.
With The Woolpackers, APU, The Grants, Boot Scoot, Wayne Dobson.

FREETIME

A Thames Television production. Transmission details are for the ATV/Central region. Duration: 25 minutes.

SERIES 6
Transmission details are for the Central region.
Main regular credit(s): Designed by John Plant; associate producer Cathy Parnall; produced by Kate Marlow; directed by Richard Handford and Peter Walker.
Main regular cast: With Trudi Dance (Presenter).

Holding / Source
23.12.1982 **The Freetime Christmas Show** D3 / 1"

SERIES 9
Transmission details are for the Central region.
Main regular credit(s): Presented by Mick Robertson.
Main regular cast: With Kim Goody (Presenter).

Holding / Source
24.12.1984 **Christmas Special** D3 / 1"
Join Mick and Kim for the Freetime Christmas extravaganza Play the game, meet the stars and can the Reindeer Rebels beat the Snowball Screamers?
Associate producer Kate Cargin; produced by Kate Marlow; directed by Jill Fullerton-Smith, Graeme Matthews and Andrew Thomas.

SERIES 12
Transmission details are for the Central region.
Main regular credit(s): Associate producer Kate Cargin; series producer Kate Marlow; produced by Brian Simmons; directed by Martin Head and Brian Simmons.
Main regular cast: With Andi Peters (Presenter).

Holding / Source
23.12.1988 D3 / 1"
Join Andi for Christmas celebrations in England and France. The Radford family from Birmingham take a day trip to Boulogne and join in the festivities as St Nicholas arrives in the town. At home, Andi meets some children taking part in a special Christmas panto.
Research Jayana Austin.

FRENCH AND SAUNDERS

A BBC Variety production for BBC 2. Transmission details are for BBC 2. Duration varies - see below for details.
Main regular cast: Jennifer Saunders (Various roles), Dawn French (Various roles).

SERIES 2
Main regular credit(s): Written by Dawn French and Jennifer Saunders; produced by Geoff Posner.
Main regular cast: With Raw Sex.

Holding / Source
28.12.1988 DB / 1"
Duration: 40 minutes.
Music by Simon Brint and Rowland Rivron; choreography by Nicky Hinkley; designed by Harry Banks and Graeme Story; directed by Geoff Posner.
With Alison Moyet, Harriet Thorpe, Raw Sex, George Avory, Ed Bishop, Max Gold, Eileen Page, Ellen Thomas, Simon Brint, Kathy Burke, Kevin Godley, Paula Yates.

Transmission details are for BBC 1.

Holding / Source
30.12.1994 DB-D3 / D3S
A Saunders & French production for BBC Variety. Duration: 40 minutes.
Written by Dawn French and Jennifer Saunders; produced by Jon Plowman; directed by Bob Spiers.
With Adrian Edmondson, Chris Ryan, Harriet Thorpe, Richard Briers.

A Saunders & French production for BBC Variety. Transmission details are for BBC 1.

	Holding / Source
26.12.1998 **Christmas Special**	DB / DBSW

Duration: 49 minutes.

Written by Dawn French and Jennifer Saunders; executive producer Jon Plowman; produced by Janice Thomas; directed by Gareth Carrivick and Edgar Wright.

With Adrian Edmondson, Joanna Lumley, Maggie Steed, Darryl Worbey, Helen Lederer, Geraldine McNulty, Riverdance, The Spice Girls, Pickettywitch, Gary Waldhorn, Rebecca Nagan, Donald Austen, Harriet Thorpe.

28.12.1999 **The French And Saunders Special**	DB / DBSW

Duration: 29 minutes.

Written by Dawn French and Jennifer Saunders; music by Simon Brint; executive producer Jon Plowman; produced by Jo Sargent; directed by Dominic Brigstocke.

With Martine McCutcheon, Melanie C, John Inman, Stephen Frost, Janette Tough, Matthew Francis, Andreas Petrides.

25.12.2002 **French And Saunders Celebrity Christmas Puddings**	DB / DBSW

Duration: 42 minutes.

Written by Dawn French and Jennifer Saunders; executive producer Jon Plowman; produced by Jon Rolph; directed by Tristram Shapeero.

With Trude Mostue, Patrick Barlow, Rosie Cavaliero, Jan Anderson, Richard Madeley, Judy Finnigan, Anthony Warren, Alistair Mackenzie, Craig Rogan, Sam Mackenzie, Fraser Hamilton.

26.12.2003 **French And Saunders Actually**	DB / DBSW

Duration: 41 minutes.

Written by Dawn French and Jennifer Saunders; executive producer Jon Plowman; produced by Jo Sargent; directed by Nick Wood.

With Alan Yentob, John Nettles, Felicity Kendal, Pam Ferris, Patrick Barlow, Harriet Thorpe, Suzy Aitchison, Lesley Vickerage, Marie Sutherland, Daniel Casey, Jacqueline Charlesworth.

See also: FRENCH AND SAUNDERS CHRISTMAS CELEBRITY SPECIAL (BBC)

FRENCH AND SAUNDERS CHRISTMAS CELEBRITY SPECIAL

A Saunders & French production for BBC Variety. Transmission details are for BBC 1. Duration: 40 minutes.

Written by Dawn French and Jennifer Saunders; script supervisor Marilyn Kirby; music by Simon Brint; production executive Jez Nightingale; executive producer Jon Plowman; produced by Jo Sargent; directed by Ed Bye.

Dawn French (Various Roles), Jennifer Saunders (Various Roles), John Humphrys, Kacey Ainsworth, Shane Richie, Jessie Wallace, Doctor Tanya Byron, Sally Phillips, Rufus Wainwright, Jeanette Krankie [as Janette Tough].

	Holding / Source
27.12.2005	DB / DBSW

See also: FRENCH AND SAUNDERS (BBC)

FRENCH FIELDS

A Thames Television production. Transmission details are for the Central region.

Main regular credit(s):	Written by John Chapman and Ian Davidson.
Main regular cast:	Julia McKenzie (Hester Fields), Anton Rodgers (William Fields).

SERIES 2

Main regular credit(s):	Produced by James Gilbert; directed by Mark Stuart.
Main regular cast:	With Liz Crowther (Jill Trendle), Robin Kermode (Hugh Trendle), Valerie Lush (Madame Remoleux), Olivier Pierre (Monsieur Dax), Pamela Salem (Chantal Moriac).

	Holding / Source
25.12.1990 **Noel, Noel**	1" / 1"S

Duration: 35 minutes.

Written by John Chapman and Ian Davidson; produced by James Gilbert; directed by Mark Stuart.

With Karen Ascoe (Emma), Philip Bird (Peter), Bridget McConnel, Frank Lazarus, John Moreno, John Melainey, Fernand Monast, Philippe Giraudeau, Victoria Baker, Daniel Gregory.

See also: FRESH FIELDS

FRENCHMAN'S CREEK

A Carlton production. made in association with WGBH Boston. Transmission details are for the Central region. Duration: 102 minutes.

Adapted by Patrick Harbinson; based on a novel by Daphne Du Maurier; script supervisor Heather Storr; script editors Damien Timmer and Liza Marshall; music by Graham Preskett and The Irish Film Orchestra; executive producers Jonathan Powell and Rebecca Eaton; produced by Hilary Heath; directed by Ferdinand Fairfax.

Tara Fitzgerald (Lady Dona St. Columb), Anthony Delon (Jean Aubery), Tim Dutton (Lord Rockingham), James Fleet (Sir Harry), Rupert Vansittart (Lord Godolphin), Jeremy Child (Lord Feversham), Richard Bonehill (Guillaume), Christian Cloarec (Labouret), Constantine Gregory (Killigrew), Thierry Harcourt (Jean-Jacques), Michael Jenn (Rashleigh), Emma Niven (Lucy), Patrick Romer (Masterson), Anna Popplewell (Henrietta), Mika Simmons (Prudence), Jack Snell (Charles), Yorick Van Wageningen (Van Basten), Danny Webb (William), Michelle Wesson (Lady Jane Godolphin), Steve Jarman (Coach Driver).

	Production No	Holding / Source
20.12.1998	CAR/2567ZZ/01/A	DB / V1SW

FRESH FIELDS

Alternative/Working Title(s): FRESH START
A Thames Television production. Transmission details are for the Central region.

Main regular credit(s):	Written by John Chapman; produced and directed by Peter Frazer-Jones.
Main regular cast:	Julia McKenzie (Hester Fields), Anton Rodgers (William Fields).

SERIES 3

Main regular cast: With Ann Beach (Sonia Barratt), Fanny Rowe (Nancy Penrose).

Holding / Source

25.12.1985 **A Dickens Of A Christmas**   1" / 1"
Duration: 40 minutes.
Designed by Stuart McCarthy.
With Ballard Berkeley (Guy), John Arthur (John Barratt), Debby Cumming (Emma), Daphne Oxenford, Zulema Dene.

See also: FRENCH FIELDS

THE FRIDAY NIGHT ARMISTICE

A BBC production for BBC 2. Transmission details are for BBC 2. Duration varies - see below for details.

Main regular credit(s): Theme music by Jonathan Whitehead; produced by Sarah Smith.
Main regular cast: Armando Iannucci (Presenter), Peter Baynham (Presenter), David Schneider (Presenter).
Main regular credit(s): Presented by Armando Iannucci, Peter Baynham and David Schneider; written by Armando Iannucci, Peter Baynham, Kevin Cecil, Dominic English, Andy Riley, David Schneider and Sarah Smith; designed by Dennis De Groot; production team Sarah Gibbs, Lucia Grounds, Zoë Parker, Angela Wallis and Grainne Jordan; assistant producer Tom Blakeson; production managers Jemma Rodgers and Hettie Hope; directed by Steve Bendelack.

Holding / Source

29.12.1997 **The Christmas Armistice**   DB-D3 / D3S
Duration: 44 minutes.
With Ian Ashpitel, Fiona Baker, Tom Binns, Eric Bristow, Daniel Bruce, Derek Draper, Dominic English, Ian Ralph, Tim Razzle, Harvey Thomas, Albert Welling, Simon Weybridge, Clara Schneider.

This was a compilation wrapped around with new material.

Main regular credit(s): Written by Armando Iannucci, Peter Baynham, David Schneider, Sarah Smith, Andy Riley and Kevin Cecil; art director Jo Sutherland; designed by Dennis De Groot; assistant producer Mike Montgomery; associate producer Adam Tandy; series director Steve Bendelack; directed by Sarah Smith.

Holding / Source

29.12.1998 **The Christmas Armistice**   DB / DBS
Duration: 30 minutes.
With Simon Pegg, Dominic Coleman, Penny Mosley.

01.01.1999 **The New Year Armistice**   DB / DBS
Duration: 31 minutes.
With Steve Pemberton, Arthur Kelly, Vicki Pepperdine, Patience Tomlinson, Sofia Phillips, Omid Djalili, Robert Meah, Tom Binns, Tony Haase, Melanie Hudson, Christopher & Mary Penfold.

These two editions were compilations wrapped around with new material.
See also: THE SATURDAY NIGHT ARMISTICE (BBC)

FRIDAY NIGHT PROJECT

A Princess Productions production for Channel 4. Transmission details are for Channel 4. Duration: 50 minutes.

Specials

Main regular performer(s): With Alan Carr (Host), Justin Lee Collins (Host).

Holding / Source

21.12.2007 **The Friday Night Christmas Project**   DB / DBSW
With Girls Aloud (Guest Hosts), Alex Zane, Christopher Biggins.

28.12.2007 **The Friday Night New Year Project**   DB / DBSW
With Davina McCall (Guest Host), Stereophonics, Chris Moyles, Fearne Cotton, Brian Belo.

FRIDAY NIGHT WITH DOUGIE DONNELLY

A BBC Scotland production for BBC 1 Scotland. Transmission details are for BBC 1 Scotland.
Main regular performer(s): Dougie Donnelly (Presenter).

SERIES 1

Holding / Source

31.12.1983 **Dougie Donnelly Revisited**   DB / 1"
Duration: 40 minutes.
Compilation of series 1.

FRIDAY NIGHT'S ALL WRIGHT

An LWT production. Transmission details are for the London Weekend Television region. Duration varies - see below for details.

Main regular credit(s): Produced by Ric Blaxill.
Main regular performer(s): Ian Wright (Host).

SERIES 1
Main regular credit(s): Executive producer Bob Massie; produced by Ric Blaxill; directed by John L. Spencer.
Main regular performer(s): With Caprice (Doorwoman).

	Holding / Source
26.12.1998	DB / DBSW

Duration: 45 minutes.
With Lighthouse Family, Dale Winton, Billie, The London Gospel Community Choir, Meat Loaf, Pete Tong, Alistair Macgowan, Jo Guest.

SERIES 2
Main regular credit(s): Written by Nigel Crowle; executive producer Bob Massie; produced by Ric Blaxill; directed by John Morgan.

	Holding / Source
24.12.1999	DB / DBSW

Duration: 25 minutes.
With Nell McAndrew, Julian Clary, Paula Yates, All Saints, Pete Tong, Lynden David Hall, Moloko, John Gregory.

FROM ALL OF US

An ATV production. Transmission details are for the ATV midlands region. Duration: 33 minutes.

Personalities who appear regularly in many of the programmes originating from the Midlands will be entertaining you with lighthearted entertainment from: Up And Doing, Lunch Box, Midland Profile, The Tingha and Tucker Club, Midland Farming, Midland Montage. Police Five, Post Bag, Midlands News and For Teenagers Only.
Produced and directed by Reg Watson.
Pat Astley (Presenter).

	Holding / Source
25.12.1963	J /

FROM GRANGE HILL TO ALBERT SQUARE - AND BEYOND

A BBC production for BBC 1. Transmission details are for BBC 1. Duration: 39 minutes.

Documentary celebrating the 21st anniversary of GRANGE HILL, the children's drama set in a comprehensive school. In this programme, cast members past and present reveal the backstage dramas behind the scenes.
Todd Carty, Susan Tully, Michelle Gayle, Sean Maguire.

	Holding / Source
01.01.1998	DB / DBS

See also: EASTENDERS (BBC) / GRANGE HILL (BBC)

FROM THE NORTH

A Granada production for Channel 4. Transmission details are for Channel 4.

	Holding / Source
30.12.1985 **Granada In The Sixties]**	DB / 1"

THE FROST INTERVIEW

A BBC production for BBC 2. Transmission details are for BBC 2. Duration: 30 minutes.
Main regular credit(s): Assistant producer Barbara Maxwell; produced by Iain Johnstone; directed by Mike Catherwood.
Main regular performer(s): David Frost (Interviewer).

	Holding / Source
18.12.1974 **Review of 1974**	DB-D3 / 2"

THE FROST REPORT

A BBC production for BBC 1. Transmission details are for BBC 1. Duration varies - see below for details.
Main regular cast: David Frost (Host).

SERIES 2
Main regular credit(s): Produced and directed by James Gilbert.
Main regular cast: With Ronnie Barker, John Cleese, Ronnie Corbett, Sheila Steafel, Julie Felix.

	Holding / Source
26.12.1967 **Frost Over Christmas**	J|a /

Duration: 40 minutes.
Designed by Robert McGowan.
With No guest cast.

THE FUNNY SIDE OF CHRISTMAS

A BBC production for BBC 2. Transmission details are for BBC 2. Duration: 80 minutes.
Produced by Robin Nash.

	Production No	Holding / Source

27.12.1982 **Presentation** — DB-D3 / 2"
Directed by Robin Nash.
With Frank Muir (Host).

27.12.1982 **The Fall And Rise Of Reginald Perrin** — LLCE231S/71 — DB / 2"
Written by David Nobbs.
With Leonard Rossiter (Reggie Perrin), John Barron (CJ), Michael Ripper (Tramp), Sue Nicholls [as Sue Nichols] (Joan), Geoffrey Palmer (Jimmy), Pauline Yates (Elizabeth), John Horsley (Doc Morrissey).

27.12.1982 **The Les Dawson Show** — DB-D3 / 2"
With Les Dawson (Cissie), Roy Barraclough (Ada).

27.12.1982 **Yes Minister** — DB-D3 / 2"
Written by Jonathan Lynn and Anthony Jay; directed by Sydney Lotterby.
With Paul Eddington (Jim Hacker, MP), Nigel Hawthorne (Humphrey Appleby), Derek Fowlds (Bernard).

27.12.1982 **Only Fools And Horses** — DB-D3 / C1
Written by John Sullivan; produced and directed by Ray Butt.
With David Jason (Derek Trotter), Nicholas Lyndhurst (Rodney Trotter), Lennard Pearce (Grandad), Roy Heather (Sid), John Pennington (Vicar).

27.12.1982 **Three Of A Kind** — DB-D3 / 2"
With Tracey Ullmann, Lenny Henry, David Copperfield.

27.12.1982 **Last Of The Summer Wine** — DB-D3 / 2"
Written by Roy Clarke; directed by Alan J. W. Bell.
With Brian Wilde (Compo), Peter Sallis (Clegg), Bill Owen (Foggy).

27.12.1982 **Sorry!** — DB-D3 / 2"
Written by Ian Davidson and Peter Vincent.
With Ronnie Corbett (Timothy), Barbara Lott (Mother), William Moore (Father).

27.12.1982 **Butterflies** — DB-D3 / 2"
Written by Carla Lane.

27.12.1982 **Smith And Jones** — DB-D3 / 2"
Written by Griff Rhys Jones and Mel Smith.
With Mel Smith (Mr Mather), Griff Rhys Jones (Trevor).

27.12.1982 **Open All Hours** — DB-D3 / 2"
Written by Roy Clarke.
With Ronnie Barker (Arkwright), David Jason (Granville), Lynda Baron (Nurse Gladys Emmanuel).

See also: BUTTERFLIES (BBC) / LAST OF THE SUMMER WINE (BBC) / THE LES DAWSON SHOW (BBC) / ONLY FOOLS AND HORSES.... (BBC) / YES MINISTER (BBC)

THE FUNNY SIDE OF...

A BBC Scotland production for BBC 2. Transmission details are for BBC 2. Duration: 60 minutes.

Main regular credit(s): Music by Ronan Breslin and Colin McGeoch; designed by Judi Ritchie; executive producer Toby Stevens; production manager Tracy McParland; studio direction by John Smith.

Main regular cast: Clive Anderson (Host).

	Holding / Source

22.12.2009 **Christmas** — DB / DBSW
Written by Clive Anderson, Dan Gaster, Paul Powell and Will Ing; research Graham Kibble-White, Holly Ritchie, David Macnicol and Jack Kibble-White; assistant producer Andrea Miller; produced by Jenny Macleod; directed by Ewan Torrance.
With Tony Blackburn, Les Dennis, Esther Rantzen, Diane-Louise Jordan, Mike Read.

A FUNNY THING... FOR NEW YEAR

A BBC production for BBC 1. Transmission details are for BBC 1.
Introduced by Ray Moore; produced and directed by John Longley.
Arthur Askey, Ted Ray, Tommy Trinder.

	Holding / Source
01.01.1974	J / 2"

THE FURTHER ADVENTURES OF BILLY THE FISH

A John Brown Publishing production for Channel 4. Transmission details are for Channel 4. Duration: 4 minutes.

Main regular credit(s): Based on a story by Chris Donald; series producer Philip Morrow; produced and directed by Tony Barnes.

Main regular cast: Harry Enfield (Voices).

	Holding / Source
25.12.1990 **Episode 1**	1" / 1"S
26.12.1990 **Episode 2**	1" / 1"S
27.12.1990 **Episode 3**	1" / 1"S

THE FURTHER ADVENTURES OF BILLY THE FISH

28.12.1990 **Episode 4**

THE GABRIEL ASSIGNMENT

A Thames Television production. Transmission details are for the Thames Television region. Duration: 8 minutes.

What if you were visited by an angel? Most of the people in the Christmas story were visited by Gabriel. This week, Theophilus, the young man to whom Luke dedicated his gospel, tracks the angel Gabriel through his assignments. Tonight, Zachary hears of the forthcoming birth of John the Baptist.

Main regular credit(s): Written by Jack Shepherd; arranged by Mavis Airey; produced and directed by Edward Joffe.
Main regular cast: Jack Shepherd (Presenter).

	VT Number	Holding / Source
22.12.1975	11888A	DB / 2"
23.12.1975	11888B	DB / 2"
25.12.1975	11888C	J / 2"
26.12.1975	11888D	DB / 2"
27.12.1975	11888E	J / 2"
28.12.1975	11888F	J / 2"

A GALA EVENING WITH HINGE AND BRACKET

A BBC Manchester production for BBC 2. Transmission details are for BBC 2. Duration varies - see below for details.

Main regular credit(s): Written by George Logan and Patrick Fyffe; produced by Peter Ridsdale Scott; directed by Hazel Lewthwaite.
Main regular performer(s): George Logan (Doctor Evadne Hinge), Patrick Fyffe (Dame Hilda Bracket).

	Holding / Source
26.12.1978 **A Gala Evening At The Royal Hall, Harrogate 1978**	DB-D3 / 2"

Duration: 45 minutes.
Designed by Kenneth Lawson; production team George Clarke and Paul Loosley.
With Corbet Woodall (Host).

	Holding / Source
22.12.1979 **A Gala Evening At The Royal Hall, Harrogate 1979**	DB-D3 / 2"

Duration: 45 minutes.
Designed by John Coleman.
With Jon Curle (Host).

See also: HINGE AND BRACKET'S NEW YEAR'S EVE PARTY (BBC)

GALA NIGHT WITH THE STARS

A BBC Scotland production for BBC 1 Scotland. Transmission details are for BBC 1 Scotland. Duration: 60 minutes.

	Holding / Source
31.12.1971	J / 2"

GAME FOR A LAUGH

An LWT production. made in association with Action Time / Little Joey Inc / Ralph Edwards Productions. Transmission details are for the Central region.
Main regular performer(s): Jeremy Beadle (Presenter).

SERIES 1
Transmission details are for the ATV/Central region. Duration: 40 minutes.
Main regular credit(s): Designed by Pip Gardner; associate producer Brian Wesley; produced by Alan Boyd; film sequences directed by John Longley.
Main regular performer(s): With Matthew Kelly (Presenter), Sarah Kennedy (Presenter), Henry Kelly (Presenter).

	VT Number	Holding / Source
25.12.1981	90376	D2 / 2"

Studio direction by Phil Bishop.

SERIES 2
Main regular credit(s): Designed by Pip Gardner; associate producers Keith Stewart and Brian Wesley; produced by Alan Boyd; directed by John Longley, Phil Bishop and Noel D. Greene.
Main regular performer(s): With Matthew Kelly (Presenter), Sarah Kennedy (Presenter), Henry Kelly (Presenter).

	VT Number	Holding / Source
25.12.1982 **Christmas Special**	90566	D2 / 2"

SERIES 3
Duration: 50 minutes.
Main regular credit(s): Series producer Alan Boyd; produced by Keith Stewart and Brian Wesley; directed by Phil Bishop, John Gorman and Tom Poole.
Main regular performer(s): With Matthew Kelly (Presenter), Sarah Kennedy (Presenter), Henry Kelly (Presenter).

	Holding / Source
31.12.1983 **Best Of Game For A Laugh**	D2 / 1"

THE GANG SHOW GALA

A BBC production for BBC 1. Transmission details are for BBC 1. Duration: 40 minutes.

Written by John Antrobus* and Eddie Braben*; television presentation by Michael Hurll; designed by Ian Rawnsley; produced by Ralph Reader; directed for television by Michael Hurll.

Peter Sellers, Dick Emery, Graham Stark, Cardew Robinson, Reg Dixon, David Lodge, Scout Gang Show 1970, Burt Rhodes and his Orchestra.

	Holding / Source
24.12.1970	J / 2"

THE GANG SHOW

A BBC production for BBC 1. Transmission details are for BBC 1. Duration: 50 minutes.

Lyrics by Ralph Reader; music directed by Burt Rhodes; music by Ralph Reader; television presentation by Michael Hurll; designed by Robert Corp Reader; produced by Ralph Reader.

The Scout Association.

	Holding / Source
24.12.1968	J /

THE GANG SHOW

A BBC production for BBC 1. Transmission details are for BBC 1. Duration: 50 minutes.

Written by Ralph Reader; lyrics by Ralph Reader; music directed by Burt Rhodes; music by Ralph Reader; television presentation by Michael Hurll; designed by Robert Corp Reader; produced by Ralph Reader.

The Scout Association.

	Holding / Source
24.12.1969	J / 2"

THE GANG SHOW

A BBC production for BBC 1. Transmission details are for BBC 1. Duration: 35 minutes.

Written by Ralph Reader; produced by Ralph Reader and Michael Hurll; produced for television by Brian Whitehouse.

Ralph Reader, Burt Rhodes and his Orchestra.

	Holding / Source
26.12.1971	

THE GANG SHOW

A BBC production for BBC 1. Transmission details are for BBC 1. Duration: 45 minutes.

Introduced by Ken Dodd; written by Ralph Reader; television presentation by Michael Hurll; produced by Ralph Reader.

Dick Emery, Brian Johnston, David Lodge, Graham Stark.

	Holding / Source
23.12.1972	DB-1" / 2"

GANGSTA GRANNY

A BBC production for BBC 1. Transmission details are for BBC 1. Duration: 70 minutes.

A bored boy discovers another side to his seemingly sweet old grandma. When she reveals her secret past, they embark on a series of adventures.

Adapted by David Walliams, Kevin Cecil and Andy Riley; based on a book by David Walliams; produced by Jo Sargent; directed by Matt Lipsey.

Julia McKenzie (Granny), Reece Buttery (Ben), David Walliams (Mike), Miranda Hart (Linda), Harish Patel (Raj), Rob Brydon (Mr Parker), Robbie Williams (Flavio Flavioli), Joanna Lumley (The Queen), Jocelyn Jee Esien (Kelly), India Ria Amarteifio (Florence).

	Holding / Source
26.12.2013	HD/DB / HDC

THE GARDEN PARTY

A BBC production for BBC 1. Transmission details are for BBC 1.

Transmission details are for BBC 1 Scotland.

	Holding / Source
26.12.1989 **Highlights**	DB / 1"

Highlights programme on BBC Scotland only.

GARY BARLOW'S BIG BEN BASH

A BBC production for BBC 1. Transmission details are for BBC 1. Duration varies - see below for details.

The singer rounds off the year with a live gig at he Central Hall in Westminster, performing Take That favourites.

Main regular credit(s): Executive producer Guy Freeman; produced by Cerrie Frost.

Main regular performer(s): Gary Barlow.

	Holding / Source
31.12.2013 **Part One**	HD/DB / Live
Duration: 40 minutes.	
01.01.2014 **Part Two**	HD/DB / Live
Duration: 20 minutes.	

GAVIN AND STACEY

A Baby Cow Productions production for BBC. Transmission details are for Various BBC Channels. Duration: 30 minutes.

Main regular credit(s): Written by James Corden and Ruth Jones.

Main regular cast: Mathew Horne (Gavin), Joanna Page (Stacey), Ruth Jones (Nessa), James Corden (Smithy), Alison Steadman (Pamela), Larry Lamb (Mick), Melanie Walters (Gwen), Rob Brydon (Uncle Bryn).

Transmission details are for BBC 1.

Holding / Source
24.12.2008 DB / DBSWF
Duration: 60 minutes.

Designed by Dave Ferris; associate producers James Corden and Ruth Jones; executive producers Cheryl Taylor and Henry Normal; head of production Kerry Waddell; produced by Ted Dowd and Gill Isles.

With Steffan Rhodri (Dave), Julia Davis (Dawn), Adrian Scarborough (Pete), Edna Doré (Edna), Robert Wilfort (Jason), Zakk Furness-Jones, Lewis Merchant, Cari Kiernan.

SERIES 3

A Baby Cow Manchester production for Baby Cow Productions. Transmission details are for BBC 1.

Main regular credit(s): Script supervisor Yasmin Rais; director of photography Doug Hallows; art director Gillian Miles; designed by Dave Ferris; associate producers James Corden and Ruth Jones; executive producers Henry Normal and Lindsay Hughes; head of production Kerry Waddell; production manager Lyndsay Robinson; produced by Ted Dowd; directed by Christine Gernon.

Holding / Source
25.12.2009 HD/DB / HD/DB

With Margaret John (Doris), Steffan Rhodri (Dave), Johnny Tudor (Marco), Ewan Kennedy (Neil the Baby), Oscar Hartland (Neil the Baby), Gwynfor Roberts.

GAWAIN AND THE GREEN KNIGHT

A Thames Television production. Transmission details are for the Central region. Duration: 79 minutes.

Written by David Rudkin; based on an original story by an unknown author; music by Walter Fabeck and The King's Consort; executive producer Ian Martin; produced and directed by John Michael Phillips.

Malcolm Storry [as Tommy Scarroll] (The Green Knight), Jason Durr (Sir Gawain), Valerie Gogan (The Lady), Malcolm Storry (The Red Lord), Marc Warren (Arthur), Martin Crocker (Knight), Patrick Moore (Knight), Stephen Tiller (Knight), Marie Francis (Guinevere), Jonathan Adam (Ferryman), Michael Povey (Blacksmith), Gethin Mills (Blacksmith's Son), Sally Mates (Woman In Black), Shay Gorman (Chamberlain), Arthur Kelly (Older Servant), Nigel Cairns (Younger Servant), John Lyons (Woodman), George Sweeney (Guide).

VT Number | Holding / Source
03.01.1991 | 52967 | 1" / C1S

To hide the identity of The Green Knight, the TV Times used the pseudonym Tommy Scarroll.

GENERATION FAME

A BBC production for BBC 1. Transmission details are for BBC 1. Duration: 60 minutes.

A celebrity version of The Generation Game.

Programme associates Jon Magnusson and Rob Colley; script supervisor Tony Grech; music by Dan McGrath; associate producer Rob Billington; production executive Claire Bridgland; executive producer Martin Scott; series producer Victoria Ashbourne; produced by Kevin Mundye; directed by Nikki Parsons.

Graham Norton (Host), Davina McCall, Andrew McCall, Rupert Grint, Chris Grint, Kelly Holmes, Pamela Thomson, James Fleet, Stanley Parkinson, Johnny Vegas, Engelbert Humperdinck, Harry Hill, Double-D-Force, Jean-Christophe Novelli, John Hicks, Bruno Tonioli, Vanessa Leigh Hicks.

Holding / Source
31.12.2005 **[pilot]** DB / DBSW

(BRUCE FORSYTH AND) THE GENERATION GAME

A BBC production for BBC 1. Transmission details are for BBC 1. Usual duration: 50 minutes.

"A lawn mower, a set of chef's knives, a basket of fruit, a set of towels, a cuddly toy!" The list seemed endless, but it wasn't. And pity the poor assistant floor manager picking each item up, and putting it on the conveyor belt.

It was, of course, the end of another show of The Generation Game. You may think the format of The Generation Game was evident in its title – different generations of a family competing to win prizes. But no, every quiz show uses that generic concept. If you want to make a new series of The Generation now, you would approach the show's format owners and pay them money for only one consideration – the right to use a conveyor belt to display the prizes. Indeed, the world of copyright is a funny world!

It was a gameshow that launched the Saturday evening careers of three high-profile entertainers – Bruce Forsyth (twice), Larry Grayson and Jim Davidson. All three were well-known entertainers in their own right, but The Gen Game rocketed them to superstar status.

In Brucie terms it was a quiet lull in his career (his Yorkshire TV 1969 series had quietly died) and Bruce was doing guest appearances on different LE shows. Then he was offered The Gen Game, and never looked back. For Larry Grayson it was a blatant poaching of an ITV star to come to the BBC, and Jim Davidson we will discuss in part 3 of this article.

The Gen Game saw members of different families compete through a series of challenges. They were marked and given points. The challenges were diverse – cake making, flower arranging, spelling, and in later rounds appearing in pantomime sketches or dancing with morris dancers. The range of guests from season to season were very diverse - Arthur Negus, Ralph Reader, Larry Ogles, Michael Connick and Josephine Knight were on a typical show. Non-celebrity guests would be represented by Ivor Spencer or Lieutenant Andrew Linsley and divers from HMS Daedalus; or The King's Squad, Royal Marines and Headington Quarry Handbell Ringers. Diverse indeed!

Launching in Autumn 1971, Bruce Forsyth was assisted by Anthea Redfern, later to become his wife. The series did many specials – May 1972 saw The Gen Game mingling with Miss United Kingdom, Christmas Day specials abounded with guests such as Joe Brown, Roy Castle, Leslie Crowther, Jimmy Edwards, Kenny Lynch, Cardew Robinson, Eric Sykes, Amanda Barrie, Melvyn Hayes, Madeline Smith and The Rupert Christmas Show all aided and arranged by Ronnie Hazlehurst and his Orchestra. Ronnie wrote the catchy theme tune as well.

The show weathered a few ups and downs along the way. In October 1974 Anthea was away from the screen and Jenny-Lee Wright was the stand-in hostess. In November 1976 there was a repeat of a 1973 edition due to Bruce's illness, introduced by Anthea Redfern and Arthur Weston. In October 1977 Jenny Lee-Wright returned, because Anthea was away having a baby! And in November 1977 an edition starring The Brother Lees was blacked out after 39 minutes due to industrial action.

When Bruce left to pursue other projects with ITV, the BBC quickly moved Larry Grayson and his new hostess, Isla St. Clair, into the job.

Main regular credit(s): Theme music by Ronnie Hazlehurst.

Main regular performer(s): Bruce Forsyth (Presenter), Anthea Redfern.

SERIES 1

Main regular performer(s): With Anthea Redfern (Hostess), Ronnie Hazlehurst and his Orchestra.

	Holding / Source
25.12.1971	J / 2"

Duration: 60 minutes.

Programme associates Denis Gifford and Tony Hawes; designed by Andy Dimond.

SERIES 2

Main regular credit(s): Programme associate Tony Hawes; music by Ronnie Hazlehurst; produced by Alan Tarrant and James Moir.

Main regular performer(s): With Anthea Redfern (Hostess).

	Production No	VT Number	Holding / Source
25.12.1972	1242/1041	VTC/6HT/82727	DB-D3 / 2"

Duration: 58 minutes.

Additional material by Olga Kersner; designed by Robin Tarsnane; production team Brian Whitehouse, Paul Hughes-Smith, John Norton and Helen Gartell; directed by Alan Tarrant and James Moir.

With Joe Brown, Roy Castle, Leslie Crowther, Jimmy Edwards, Kenny Lynch, Margaret Powell, Cardew Robinson, Eric Sykes, Amanda Barrie, Melvyn Hayes, Madeline Smith, The Rupert Christmas Show, Bob Blackman, Tomas Rilo-Valcarcel, Ronnie Hazlehurst and his Orchestra.

SERIES 3

Main regular credit(s): Programme associate Tony Hawes; music directed by Ronnie Hazlehurst; produced by Terry Henebery and James Moir.

Main regular performer(s): With Anthea Redfern (Hostess).

	Holding / Source
25.12.1973	DB-D3 / 2"

Duration: 60 minutes.

Designed by James Hatchard; directed by Terry Henebery and James Moir.

With Frankie Howerd, Fanny Cradock, Lynne Frederick.

SERIES 4

Main regular credit(s): Programme associate Tony Hawes; music directed by Ronnie Hazlehurst and his Orchestra; directed by Alan Boyd.

Main regular performer(s): With Anthea Redfern (Hostess).

	Holding / Source
25.12.1974	DB-D3 / 2"

Duration: 59 minutes.

Graphics by Mic Rolph; costume Bobi Bartlett; lighting by John Green; sound Laurie Taylor; designed by Andy Dimond; produced by James Moir.

With Jimmy Jewel, Raymond Baxter, Matt Monro, Barbara Mitchell, Terry Wogan, Henry Cooper, Jack Douglas, Bob Wilson, Bryn Williams, The Cherokees, Sam & Samantha.

British Christmas Television Guide   **(BRUCE FORSYTH AND) THE GENERATION GAME (continued)**

SERIES 5
Main regular credit(s):   Programme associate Tony Hawes; orchestra conducted by Ronnie Hazlehurst; designed by James Hatchard; produced by James Moir; directed by Alan Boyd.

Main regular performer(s):   With Anthea Redfern (Hostess).

	Holding / Source
25.12.1975	DB-D3 / 2"

SERIES 6
Main regular credit(s):   Programme associates Barry Cryer and Tony Hawes; orchestra conducted by Ronnie Hazlehurst; designed by Bob Cove; produced by Robin Nash; directed by Alan Boyd.

Main regular performer(s):   With Anthea Redfern (Hostess).

	Holding / Source
25.12.1976	DB-D3 / 2"

With Eddie Waring, Patrick Moore, Valerie Singleton, Marjorie Proops, Ed Stewart, Michael Parkinson.

SERIES 7
Main regular credit(s):   Programme associates Barry Cryer and Garry Chambers; orchestra conducted by Ronnie Hazlehurst; designed by Paul Trerise; executive producer Robin Nash; produced and directed by Alan Boyd.

Main regular performer(s):   With Anthea Redfern (Hostess).

	Holding / Source
25.12.1977	DB-D3 / 2"

With Mick McManus, Russell Harty, Mike Reid, Jimmy Tarbuck, Peter Gilmore, Lulu, Magnus Magnusson, David Vine, William Franklyn, Anna Dawson, Danny Street.

See also: (BRUCE FORSYTH'S) GENERATION GAME (BBC)

(LARRY GRAYSON'S) GENERATION GAME

A BBC production for BBC 1. Transmission details are for BBC 1. Duration varies - see below for details.

Main regular performer(s):   Larry Grayson (Host), Isla St. Clair (Hostess).

SERIES 8
Main regular credit(s):   Programme associate Tony Hawes; orchestra conducted by Ronnie Hazlehurst; executive producer Robin Nash; produced by Alan Boyd.

	Holding / Source
25.12.1978	DB-D3 / 2"

Duration: 61 minutes.
Designed by Tony Burroughs; directed by Marcus Plantin.

With Terry Wogan, Jon Pertwee, Gerald Harper, Iain Cuthbertson, Barbara Windsor, Eric Sykes, Mollie Sugden, Norman Collier, Esther Rantzen, Freddie Davies, Marti Caine, Roger de Courcey & Nookie Bear, Norman Vaughan, Babette, Ishaq Bux, Anne Stone, Jimmy Winterflood, Soraya.

SERIES 9
Main regular credit(s):   Programme associate Tony Hawes; orchestra conducted by Ronnie Hazlehurst; produced by Alan Boyd.

	Holding / Source
25.12.1979	DB-D3 / 2"

Duration: 60 minutes.
Designed by Bob Cove; produced by Alan Boyd; directed by Paul K. Jackson.

With Johnny Vyvyan, Engelbert Humperdinck, Peter Alliss, The Bachelors, Matt Monro, Vince Hill, Clodagh Rodgers, Alfred Marks, Keith Harris & Orville, Rod Hull and Emu, Percy Edwards.

SERIES 10
Duration: 55 minutes.
Main regular credit(s):   Programme associate Tony Hawes; orchestra conducted by Ronnie Hazlehurst; produced by Marcus Plantin.

	Holding / Source
25.12.1980	DB-D3 / 2"

Designed by John Anderson; directed by Keith Stewart.

With Robin Cousins, The Fortunes, Val Doonican, Carol Drinkwater, Stuart Hall, Noele Gordon, Vince Hill, Alfred Marks, Bernie Winters, Barbara Woodhouse, Wei Wei Wong, Rita Webb, George Chisholm.

SERIES 11
Duration: 55 minutes.
Main regular credit(s):   Programme associate Tony Hawes; orchestra conducted by Ronnie Hazlehurst; designed by Chris Hull; produced by Marcus Plantin; directed by Keith Stewart.

	Holding / Source
25.12.1981	DB-D3 / 2"

With Los Gauchos, Donny MacLeod, Cliff Michelmore, Judith Chalmers, Magnus Magnusson, Arthur Marshall, Lennie Bennett, Kenny Lynch, Anna Dawson, William Rushton.

(BRUCE FORSYTH'S) GENERATION GAME

A BBC production for BBC 1. Transmission details are for BBC 1. Duration varies - see below for details.

Game shows are often revived for fresh, new audiences. In the 1980s the trend continued with new versions of What's My Line? And Take Your Pick. The 1990s ushered in Celebrity Squares and a new version of The Generation Game.

In 1990 The Observer asked game show hosts who was the best at their trade – Bob Monkhouse, Tom O'Connor and others nominated "Nice to see you, to see you nice" Mr Bruce Forysth. Producer David Taylor, who had been a Production Assistant on the original Generation Game was given the job of bringing back the Saturday night favourite by his BBC bosses. To avoid too many similarities it was shown on Fridays in the end. Taylor saw The Observer poll and poached Forsyth from ITV where he was hosting You Bet! And Play Your Cards Right. Forsyth enjoyed being back at the BBC where he was able to do a wider range of shows including some variety specials.

Bruce Forsyth's Generation Game promised to be the same, but different. A modern set and some surprises in the prizes. The audience were introduced to the Brucie Bonus, quite different from the one in his other BBC1 game, Takeover Bid. The cuddly toys and conveyor belt were back and Anthea Redfern's replacement was bright but unassuming Rosemarie Ford who was a singer/dancer known to theatergoers from her lead role in Cats. The games were still as silly: cocktail-making, pork pie-stuffing and, yes, the plays were back. They really worked best as pantomime at Christmas, of course. Forsyth, who was aged 62 by now, hadn't lost his touch. Producer David Taylor said at the time "He's just as cheeky, cheerful and quick with the replies as ever. He does his own warm-ups with the studio audiences. In the trial runs we've done so far, they've been so funny, I wish we could show those too. There were no empty seats."

Series 1 began in typical fashion with a range of celebrity guests and specialist acts. Clive James, Ken Dodd mingled with the Royal Navy Training School and The Fabulous Singlettes. There was an 'Allo Allo' themed edition in October 1990. Five seasons were made, including Christmas specials every year and mini editions for Children in Need. After 1994 specials based around James Bond and Dick Whittington, the series came to an end on Christmas Eve 1994.

When the series returned in Autumn 1995, Bruce had moved on to fresh projects and a very different host had arrived. Previously hosts had come from a light entertainment/variety background, but the final BBC version of The Generation Game had a craft cockney comic as its leading man. Jim Davidson found fame on ATV's New Faces, and worked mainly for Thames TV as a comedian before becoming compere for the BBC snooker quiz show Big Break. Davidson was more risqué in his humour and enjoyed a career in the clubs telling altogether more blue jokes. Seven seasons followed, a record for any host in a single run. Initially Sally Meen was the hostess, but then Melanie Stace took over for five seasons. Stace is remembered as the most popular second-in command. Scandinavian Lea Kristensen took over for the final series. By the final season in 2002 the other Saturday night favourite 'Noel's House Party' had finished, so Mr Blobby switched series and became a regular on the Gen Game. Sadly, whilst ratings were still good, the Gen Game was struggling with the humourous material of its host, and Davidson was eventually asked to work on other BBC projects. The conveyor belt had finally run out of steam.

Main regular performer(s): Bruce Forsyth (Host), Rosemarie Ford (Hostess).

SERIES 12
Main regular credit(s): Produced by David Taylor; directed by Sylvie Boden.

Holding / Source

25.12.1990 DB / 1"
Duration: 65 minutes.

SERIES 13
Main regular credit(s): Produced by David Taylor; directed by John Gorman.

Holding / Source

25.12.1991 **Christmas Generation Game** DB / 1"S
Duration: 70 minutes.
With Leslie Grantham, Bruno Brookes, Frank Bruno, Bobby Davro, Bella Emberg, Mark Greenstreet, Gloria Hunniford, Kathy Tayler, Dennis Taylor.

SERIES 14
Main regular credit(s): Produced by David Taylor; directed by Bill Morton.

Holding / Source

25.12.1992 "Peter Pan" DB / D3S
Duration: 65 minutes.
With Jimmy Tarbuck, Bernie Clifton, Mollie Sugden.

SERIES 15
Main regular credit(s): Music directed by Don Hunt; theme music by Bruce Forsyth and Ian Wilson; consultant Bruce Forsyth; designed by Richard Morris; assistant producer Clive Grainger; production manager Simon Spencer; produced by David Taylor; directed by Bill Morton.

Holding / Source

24.12.1993 "Aladdin" DB / D3S
Duration: 65 minutes.
Programme associates Garry Chambers and Wally Malston; additional material by Eddie Braben; choreography by Jeff Thacker.
With Bob Holness, Little and Large, Bernie Clifton, Jules Andrews, Croydon Citadel Salvation Army.

SERIES 16
Main regular credit(s): Produced by David Taylor; directed by Bill Morton.

Holding / Source

24.12.1994 "Dick Whittington" DB / D3S
Duration: 65 minutes.
See also: (BRUCE FORSYTH AND) THE GENERATION GAME (BBC)

(JIM DAVIDSON'S) GENERATION GAME

A BBC production for BBC 1. Transmission details are for BBC 1.

Main regular performer(s): Jim Davidson (Presenter).

SERIES 17
Duration: 55 minutes.
Main regular credit(s): Produced and directed by Guy Freeman.
Main regular performer(s): With Sally Meen (Assistant).

	Holding / Source
23.12.1995 Christmas Special	DB / D3S

With Oz Clarke, The Ballet Rambert, Roy Wood Band, Kriss Akabusi, Roy Barraclough, Jim Bowen, Bella Emberg, Gloria Hunniford, Michael Keating, Vicki Michelle.

SERIES 18
Duration: 60 minutes.
Main regular credit(s): Produced by Jonathan Beazley; directed by John L. Spencer.
Main regular performer(s): With Melanie Stace (Hostess).

	Holding / Source
21.12.1996	DB / D3S

In the last in the present series of family game shows, contestants take part in a yuletide pantomime.
With Norman Collier, Windsor Davies, Bobby Davro, Stephen Lewis.

SERIES 21
Duration: 45 minutes.
Main regular credit(s): Produced by Sue Andrew; directed by Stuart Hall.
Main regular performer(s): With Melanie Stace (Hostess).

	Holding / Source
24.12.1999 **Christmas Generation Game**	DB / DBSW

With Rick Wakeman, Stephen Lewis, Lawrence Dallaglio, Kathy Staff, John Virgo, Rambert Dance Company.

01.01.2000 **New Year Generation Game**	DB / DBSW

With Barbara Windsor, Rio (Gladiator), Leslie Phillips, Rocky Taylor.

GENIUS (RADIO)

A BBC production for BBC Radio 4. Transmission details are for BBC Radio 4. Duration: 29 minutes.
Main regular credit(s): Created by Ali Crockatt and David Scott; produced by Simon Nicholls.
Main regular cast: Dave Gorman (Host).

	Holding / Source
22.12.2008	DAS /

With Lee Mack (Guest Genius).

GENTLEMEN'S RELISH

A BBC production for BBC 1. made in association with Principal Pictures / Stock Productions. Transmission details are for BBC 1.

Adapted by David Nobbs; based on a novel by Miles Gibson; executive producers Geoffrey Perkins, Mike Slee and Jim Reeve; produced by Sarah Boote and Martyn Auty; directed by Douglas Mackinnon.

Billy Connolly (Kingdom Swann), Sarah Lancashire (Violet Askey), Douglas Henshall (Cromwell Marsh), Katie Blake (Charlotte Crisp), Liz Ewing (Alice Hancock), Nick Stringer (Edward Shelburne), Emily Hillier (Ethel Spooner), Teresa Banham (Jane Davidson), John Warnaby (Gordon Simms), Simon Chandler (Mr Prestwick), Jamie Bradley (Stanley Gaunt), Dominic Mafham (Lord Thornycroft), Chris Middleton (Lanky Parsons), Tony Bluto (Market Stall Holder), Rebecca Johnson (Elder Rossetti), Emma Stansfield (Younger Rossetti), Andrew Johns (Perkins), Seana Montague (Cleopatra), Tony Maudsley, Trevor Martin, Oliver Meek, David Streames, Stephen Holland, Zoe Caryl.

	Holding / Source
01.01.2001	DB / V1SW
Duration: 90 minutes.	

GEORGE & MILDRED

A Thames Television production. Transmission details are for the ATV midlands region. Usual duration: 25 minutes.

In April 1976, the final episode of Man About the House brought the series to a close. Johnnie Mortimer and Brian Cooke had been asked already to create a sequel sitcom to continue the huge ratings. Thames Television, keen to secure the services of Richard O'Sullivan, gave him an option to star in "Robin's Nest". However, Mortimer and Cooke were also keen to explore the surprising hit of Man about the House – the landlord couple George and Mildred Roper.

Played by stalwart character actors Brian Murphy and Yootha Joyce, the British public loved the lazy, workshy, sexually-demotivated George, whose only interests were beer, darts and budgies. Mildred was warm, lively and full of unfulfilled passion. George would set up the jokes, and Mildred would deliver the punchline. George frequently looked intimidated by Mildred, but seemed to get his own way far too frequently, including his love for eating pickled onions in bed, which suggested that Mildred's bark was far worse than her bite!

In September 1976 the Ropers returned. Now they were homeless, having had their house purchased by the council for a new road development. They chose to settle in middle-class suburban London, in a road uncannily looking like a new housing estate only a mile from the London Teddington studios of Thames Television.

The famous jazz musician Johnny Dankworth created a catchy little number for the theme tune and the series burst onto the screen with life and vitality. Mildred was the ultimate social climber and wanted to join the Women's Institute. George hated snobbery and the writers Mortimer/Cooke were inspired by their choice of neighbours – the Fourmile family.

Jeffrey Fourmile – fellow social climber and snob; his wife Ann – warm and motherly and little Tristram: endearing, sweet intelligent and remarkably similar looking to Kaleidoscope's TV Memories column writer Adrian Petford!

The clash between Jeffrey and George allowed the comedy to flow freely, whilst Mildred and Ann could bond and become closer. The casting of Nicholas Bond-Owen as Tristram was inspired, because he brought innocence and a steady source of feed lines to keep the comedy coming.

The series quickly moved to a second and third series, including the honour of a Boxing Day 1977 special. The fourth series was moved forwards and shown straight after the third series, because advertisers were desperate to place product in the top ten rated show of the UK,

However, the final 'series 5 and 6' were actually a random and sporadic assembly of episodes made for different series and a short run of new production in 1979. Why? Well the series was experiencing enormous production problems due to Yootha Joyce having an alcohol problem.

The film version of George and Mildred in December 1979 was to be Joyce's last work. She was admitted to hospital in the summer of 1980. Yootha died of liver failure four days after her 53rd birthday on 24 August 1980. Brian Murphy was at her bedside. She was cremated at Golders Green Crematorium. The inquest into her death revealed that she had been drinking over half a bottle of brandy a day for ten years. She made her last television appearance as herself on Max on 14 January 1981, but she continued to play Mildred Roper until February 1981.

With the lead star unavailable any more the series finished. The series is available to watch again on DVD. Murphy went on to make The Incredible Mr Tanner, L for Lester and appear in Last of the Summer Wine for many years.

Main regular credit(s): Written by Johnnie Mortimer and Brian Cooke; produced and directed by Peter Frazer-Jones.

Main regular cast: Brian Murphy (George Roper), Yootha Joyce (Mildred Roper), Norman Eshley (Jeffrey Fourmile), Sheila Fearn (Ann Fourmile), Nicholas Bond-Owen (Tristram Fourmile).

SERIES 2

Main regular credit(s): Theme music by Roger Webb; designed by David Richens.

Holding / Source

26.12.1977 No Business Like Show Business D3 / 2"

When the Hampton Wick Players put on Cinderella, Mildred finally gets her chance to act—not in the title role, but as an Ugly Sister. "Type casting," says George. But her theatrical ambitions look in jeopardy—will she make it to her glamorous opening night in the Scouts' Hut?

With Reginald Marsh (Humphrey), Avril Elgar (Ethel), Roy Barraclough, Rosanne Wickes, Sue Bond, Derek Deadman, Mike Lewin.

Holding / Source

27.12.1978 On The Second Day Of Christmas D3 / 2"

Duration: 26 minutes.

This episode is set in that no-man's land between the indigestion of Christmas and the hangover of New Year's Day. Goodwill to all men doesn't apply between George and Jeffrey when a game of telly tennis gets out of hand.

Designed by David Ferris.

With Reginald Marsh (Humphrey), Avril Elgar (Ethel), Gretchen Franklin (Mother).

Holding / Source

25.12.1980 December 1979 Film C3 / C3

A CHIPS Productions Ltd production for Cinema Arts International. Duration: 89 minutes.

Mildred Roper is determined to celebrate her wedding anniversary in style. Her husband George, who had quite forgotten it, books at a table at the luxury restaurant where he once proposed to her. Unfortunately, over the years the restaurant has changed into a transport café — so Mildred decides they will spend a weekend at a plush London hotel — where George is mistaken for a professional assassin...

Written by Dick Sharples; music by Les Reed; executive producer Brian Lawrence; produced by Roy Skeggs; directed by Peter Frazer-Jones.

With Stratford Johns (Harry Pinto), David Barry (Elvis), Sue Bond (Marlene), Kenneth Cope (Harvey), Dudley Sutton (Jacko), Neil McCarthy (Eddie), Michael Angelis (Cafe Proprietor), Garfield Morgan (Bridges), Harry Fowler (Fisher), Caron Gardner (Bishop's lady), Vicky Michelle (Bishop's lady), Linda Frith (Angela), Bruce Montague, Hugh Walters, Johnny Wade, John Carlin, Suzanne Owens, Bridget Brice, Robin Parkinson, Roger Avon, Mimi De Braie, Joan Ware, Dennis Ramsden.

See also: THE DAVID NIXON SHOW / ROBIN'S NEST

GEORGE AND THE DRAGON

An ATV London production for ATV. Transmission details are for Various ITV Companies. Duration: 25 minutes.

Main regular credit(s): Written by Vince Powell and Harry Driver; theme music by Tom Springfield.

Main regular cast: Sid James (George Russell), Peggy Mount (Gabrielle Dragon), John Le Mesurier (Colonel Maynard), Keith Marsh (Ralph The Gardener).

SERIES 1

Transmission details are for the ABC midlands region.

Main regular credit(s): Designed by Richard Lake; produced by Alan Tarrant; directed by Shaun O'Riordan.

	VT Number	Holding / Source
24.12.1966	9286	DB-R1 / 40

With Yootha Joyce, Kim Smith, Jack Wild, Stephen Bullivent, Shelagh Fraser, Jeffrey Segal, Bob Hornery.

GET IT TOGETHER

A Granada production. Transmission details are for the ATV midlands region. Duration varies - see below for details.

SERIES 2

Main regular credit(s): Research Stephen Leahy; music directed by Mike Moran; designed by Taff Batley; produced by Muriel Young; directed by Nicholas Ferguson.

Main regular performer(s): With Roy North (Host), Linda Fletcher (Host).

	Production No	Holding / Source
27.12.1977 **Get It Together With The Bay City Rollers**	P904/14	DB / 2"

Duration: 26 minutes.
Postponed from 20.12.1977.
Bay City Rollers - It's A Game; Roy sings 'A Christmas Dream'; Bay City Rollers with Becky - La Belle Jeane; Linda sings 'Yes Sir I Can Boogie'; Bay City Rollers - You Made Me Believe In Magic; Roy & Linda sing 'Don't It Make My Brown Eyes Blue'; Bay City Rollers - Love Fever.
With The Bay City Rollers.

SERIES 3

Main regular credit(s): Designed by Chris Truelove; produced by Muriel Young; directed by Nicholas Ferguson.

Main regular performer(s): With Roy North (Host), Linda Fletcher (Host), Teri Scoble Dancers, Mike Moran and The Band.

	Production No	Holding / Source
26.12.1978 **Get It Together Christmas Special**	P904/41	DB / 2"

Duration: 33 minutes.
Roy sings 'Won't Change My Mind'; Mike Rose - Star In The Sky (Christmas song); Linda sings 'Hush'; The Pleasers - A Girl I Know; TSD's dance to 'Round And Round' by Daniel Boone; Val, Lynn & Victy - Let Your Love Flow; Roy Hill - I Like I Like I Like; Linda sings 'Sometimes When We Touch'; Mike Moran Band - Crocodile Rock; Showaddywaddy - Pretty Little Angel Eyes (Promo).
With The Pleasers, Mike Rose, Showaddywaddy, The Roy Hill Band, Val, Lynn and Victy.

SERIES 5

Main regular credit(s): Produced by Muriel Young; directed by Dave Warwick.

Main regular performer(s): With Roy North (Host), Linda Fletcher (Host), Mike Moran and The Band, TSD's.

	Production No	Holding / Source
26.12.1979 **Get It Together Christmas Bonanza**	P904/52	DB / 2"

Duration: 43 minutes.
With Child, Sally Oldfield, Chas & Dave, Blondie*, Dave Edmunds, Rockpile.

SERIES 6

Main regular credit(s): Choreography by Teri Scoble; designed by Ann Dabinett; produced by Muriel Young; directed by David Warwick.

Main regular performer(s): With Roy North (Host), Linda Fletcher (Host), Ollie Beak, Teri Scoble Dancers.

	Production No	Holding / Source
23.12.1980	P904/74	DB / 2"

Duration: 38 minutes.
Roy sings 'Rock Around The Clock'; Moondogs - Schoolgirl Crush; Val, Victi & Lynn - Snowbird; TSD's dance to Sweet People's 'Et Les Oiseaux Chantaient (...And The Birds Were Singing)'; Megg sings ' Mirrors'; Matchbox - Over The Rainbow; TSD's dance to 'Midnite Dynamos' by Matchbox; The Cheaters - Gonna Get Myself A Car; The Cheaters - I Wanna Be A Policeman; The Get It Together Team - A Christmas Dream/When A Child Is Born/Cradle Song 'medley'; Moondogs - Talking In The Canteen.
With The Cheaters, Matchbox, The Moondogs.

SERIES 7

Main regular credit(s): Designed by Chris Bradshaw; produced by Muriel Young; directed by Eugene Ferguson.

Main regular performer(s): With Roy North (Host), Megg Nicol, Ollie Beak, Teri Scoble Dancers.

	Production No	Holding / Source
22.12.1981	P904/91	DB / 2"

Duration: 36 minutes.
With Chas & Dave, The Tweets.

GET KNIGHTED

A Barron Knights Ltd production for Channel 4. Transmission details are for Channel 4. Duration: 50 minutes.

Produced by Butch Baker and Tony Avern; directed by Butch Baker and Tony Avern.

The Barron Knights.

	Holding / Source
01.01.1983	1" / 1"

GET SOME IN! British Christmas Television Guide

GET SOME IN!

A Thames Television production. Transmission details are for the ATV midlands region. Duration: 25 minutes.

Main regular credit(s): Written by John Esmonde and Bob Larbey; theme music by Alan Braden; produced by Michael Mills.

Main regular cast: Tony Selby (Corporal Marsh), Gerard Ryder (Matthew Lilley), Brian Pettifer (Bruce Leckie), David Janson (Ken Richardson).

	VT Number	Holding / Source
25.12.1975 "Home-Cooked Turkey"	12320	D3 / 2"

All is not happiness and light in C Flight of R.A.F. Skelton—four National Servicemen are doomed to spend Yuletide in camp. Christmas without cheer is bad enough when you are away from home for the first time, but Christmas with Corporal Marsh as a demonic Santa Claus is plain misery. The promise of a home-cooked turkey dinner from Alice Marsh seems like a miracle, but when you are a raw recruit, miracles are forbidden: "What are they? They are forbidden!"

Designed by Robin Parker; produced and directed by Robert Reed.

With Lori Wells (Alice Marsh), Tim Barrett (Padré), Madge Hindle (Min), Frankie Jordan (Mary Wanstead), Leonard Gregory (Cook), Mike Halsey (Dog handler).

GET UP AND GO!

A Yorkshire Television production. Transmission details are for the ATV/Central region. Duration: 20 minutes.

SERIES 1

Transmission details are for the ATV midlands region.

Main regular credit(s): Written by Rick Vanes and Shirley Isherwood; designed by Mike Joyce; produced by Lesley Rogers.

Main regular cast: With Beryl Reid (Host), Stephen Boxer (Host), David Claridge (Host).

	VT Number	Holding / Source
24.12.1981 **Christmas**	EA28	1" / 1"

While Mooncat, a visitor from Space, waits for Father Christmas to come, his hosts Beryl and Stephen find him plenty of things to do.

Directed by Len Lurcuck.

GETAWAY

A BBC production for BBC 2. Transmission details are for BBC 2. Duration: 55 minutes.

	Holding / Source
24.12.1974 **The Golden Girls Of Garie Beach**	C1 / C1

Most Australians will spend Christmas swimming, surfing, water skiing, or eating turkey and mince pies at a beach barbecue. This enthusiasm for an active life outdoors has produced more than their fair share of world champions in sport and recreation. What is the reason?

Edited by Brian Robins; produced by Tony Salmon; directed by Peter Cleaver.

With Ray Barrett (Presenter), Diana Fisher (Presenter).

GHOST IN THE WATER

A BBC Children's Department production for BBC 1. Transmission details are for BBC 1. Duration: 55 minutes.

Tess Willetts. Born 10 June 1968, Netherton, West Midlands. Abigail Parkes. Died 10 December 1860. Suicide by drowning. Gosty Hill Canal. What strange forces are drawing the two girls together?

Adapted by Geoffrey Case; based on a book by Edward Chitham; executive producer Paul Stone; produced and directed by Renny Rye.

Judith Allchurch (Tess), Ian Stevens (David), Jane Freeman (Mrs Willetts), Dave Mitty (Mr Willetts), Joanne James (Jean Willetts / Abigail Parkes), Hilary Mason (Nan), Paul Marks (Steve), Lynda Higginson (Tracy), Paul Copley (Mr Reed), Peter Brooks (Mr Milner), Neville Barber (Henry Parkes), Ysanne Churchman (Mrs Parkes), Angus Kennedy (David Caddick), Samantha Gamble (Susanna Caddick), Ralph Lawton (Coroner), Simon Orme (Wayne), Val Hastings (Miss Jones), Daniel D'Arcy (Count Dracula), Mark Danesi (Boy In Class), Johnny Thomas (Farm Labourer).

	Holding / Source
31.12.1982	C1 / C1

(CHRISTOPHER LEE'S) GHOST STORIES FOR CHRISTMAS

A BBC Scotland production for BBC 2. Transmission details are for BBC 2. Duration: 30 minutes.

Main regular credit(s): Narrated by Christopher Lee; based on stories by M. R. James; produced by Richard Downes; directed by Eleanor Yule.

	Holding / Source
23.12.2000 **The Stalls Of Barchester**	DB / DBSW
26.12.2000 **The Ash Tree**	DB / DBSW
29.12.2000 **Number 13**	DB / DBSW
31.12.2000 **A Warning To The Curious**	DB / DBSW

A GHOST STORY FOR CHRISTMAS

A BBC production for BBC 1. Transmission details are for BBC 1. Duration varies - see below for details.

Based on stories by M. R. James.

	Holding / Source
24.12.1971 **The Stalls Of Barchester**	DB-D3 / C1

Duration: 46 minutes.

Adapted by Lawrence Gordon Clark; designed by Keith Harris; produced and directed by Lawrence Gordon Clark.

With Robert Hardy (Archdeacon Haynes), Clive Swift (Doctor Black), Thelma Barlow (Letitia), Harold Bennett (Archdeacon Pulteney), Penny Service (Jane Lee), Will Leighton (Librarian), Martin Hoyle (Verger), Erik Chitty (Priest), David Pugh (John), Ambrose Coghill (Museum Curator), Havoc.

A GHOST STORY FOR CHRISTMAS

A GHOST STORY FOR CHRISTMAS (continued)

24.12.1972 A Warning To The Curious DB-D3 / C1
Duration: 50 minutes.
Adapted by Lawrence Gordon Clark; produced and directed by Lawrence Gordon Clark.
With Peter Vaughan (Mr Paxton), Clive Swift (Doctor Black), John Kearney (Ager Ghost), David Cargill (Boots), Gilly Fraser (Girl), Julian Herington (Archeologist), George Benson (Vicar), Roger Milner (Antique Shop Owner), David Pugh (Porter), Cyril Appleton (Labourer).

25.12.1973 Lost Hearts DB-D3 / C1
Duration: 35 minutes.
Dramatised by Robin Chapman; based on a story by M. R. James; script editor Frank Hatherley; produced by Rosemary Hill; directed by Lawrence Gordon Clark.
With Joseph O'Conor (Mr Abney), Susan Richards (Mrs Bunch), Simon Gipps-Kent (Stephen), James Mellor (Parkes), Christopher Davis (Boy), Michelle Foster (Girl), Roger Milner (Vicar).

23.12.1974 The Treasure Of Abbot Thomas DB-D3 / C1
Duration: 37 minutes.
Adapted by John Bowen; script editor Matthew Walters; music by Geoffrey Burgon; film editor Roger Waugh; designed by Stuart Walker; produced by Rosemary Hill; directed by Lawrence Gordon Clark.
With Michael Bryant (Reverend Justin Somerton), John Herrington (Abbot Thomas), Frank Mills (Mr Tyson), Virginia Balfour (Lady Dattering), Paul Lavers (Peter, Lord Dattering), Sheila Dunn (Mrs Tyson), Anne Blake (Local Lady), Peggy Aitchison (Landlady).
The closedown afterwards exists on DVCam, held by Kaleidoscope.

23.12.1975 The Ash Tree C1 / C1
Duration: 32 minutes.
Adapted by David Rudkin; designed by Allan Anson; produced by Rosemary Hill; directed by Lawrence Gordon Clark.
With Edward Petherbridge (Sir Richard Fell / Sir Matthew), Lucy Griffiths (Mrs Chiddock), Lalla Ward (Lady Augusta), David Pugh (Herdsman), Preston Lockwood (Doctor Croome), Cyril Appleton (Master Procathro), Barbara Ewing (Anne Mothersole), Clifford Kershaw (The Witchfinder), Oliver Maguire (William Beresford), Glynn Sweet (Young Cleric).
Terry Coles was the Production Assistant.

THE GHOSTS OF MOTLEY HALL

A Granada production. Transmission details are for the HTV region.

After success with the first series of Catweazle, writer Richard Carpenter and producer/director Quentin Lawrence joined forces a few years later to make a humorous programme for children called The Ghosts of Motley Hall. In 1976, Lawrence was looking for a series which could be filmed predominantly in a single set. Carpenter's new idea mostly adhered to this restriction and Granada designer Alan Price came up with a very impressive two-storey set of the main hall at Motley featuring a fireplace, a long balcony and staircases on two different sides. Borwick Hall in Carnforth, Lancashire was used for any exterior shots.

None of the main characters in the series were living and instead were a mixed collection of ghosts from Motley Hall's past who were the only remaining occupants of the hall which had otherwise been empty for twenty years.

The oldest was Bodkin, a fool by profession, played by former comedian Arthur English. Bodkin had died in the seventeenth century after being repeatedly thrown in the duck pond for the amusement of the then owner of Motley, Sir Richard Uproar.

Next came Matt, a young stable boy from the time of George III. Played by Sean Flanagan, he was the only one of the ghosts who could leave the house and roam the grounds, because he alone had not died in the house itself. As such he would often act as the eyes and ears of the others if events were afoot outside.

Nicholas Le Prevost played Sir Francis Uproar, known as Fanny. He had been something of a regency rake much taken with duelling, although that had been the cause of his demise when he attempted his twelfth such contest while drunk. Fanny was very well-meaning, but not particularly bright.

The most modern Uproar in the house was General Sir George Uproar, played with great gusto by Freddie Jones. He had met his end falling down the stairs early in the twentieth century and his military background meant that he thought he should be in charge. Although not as dim as Fanny he wasn't a particularly smart cookie either and most of the real thinking usually had to be done by Bodkin, Matt and The White Lady.

Something of a mystery, The White Lady was played by Sheila Steafel. The most conventional ghost, she felt it was her duty to haunt the place in a more traditional fashion ('I always do the stairs on Thursdays'). She had no memory of who she had been in life and how she came to be in Motley Hall and thus, despite a couple of red herrings, her true identity remained unknown.

Each of the spirits had a unique character, and consistency in their behaviour was further provided by the fact that every episode was penned by Richard Carpenter himself. The actors obviously relished the well-written scripts and delivered excellent performances throughout.

One further character, this time from the land of the living, also appeared from time-to-time. This was Mr Gudgin, an estate agent charged with selling Motley Hall. He is aware that the house is haunted and is terrified of the ghosts, though usually he can only see The White Lady.

To facilitate the ghostly goings on and various materialisations and de-materialisations, a second version of the set was built but painted completely in green to allow the actors to move about in a fashion identical to the those on the main set, but with the ability for them to be keyed in and out electronically using 'green screen' technology.

The episodes involved a mixture of interaction between the ghosts themselves and between them and a variety of one-off interlopers. Thieves with stolen televisions, a pair of ghost hunters and a television crew shooting a documentary all make memorable appearances as do a number of visiting ghosts such as the headless Old Gory who appears once every five years clanking around in his suit of armour, and Sir George's domineering sister Alexandra who had died in an unlikely croquet accident.

Sadly, this series would be the last time that Carpenter and Lawrence would work together as only two years later Quentin Lawrence died aged just 58.

Main regular credit(s):   Created by Richard Carpenter; written by Richard Carpenter; theme music by Wilfred Josephs; produced and directed by Quentin Lawrence.

Main regular cast: Freddie Jones (Sir George Uproar), Sheila Steafel (The White Lady), Arthur English (Bodkin), Nicholas Le Prevost (Sir Francis 'Fanny' Uproar), Sean Flanagan (Matt).

SERIES 2
Duration: 26 minutes.
Main regular credit(s):   Designed by Alan Price and Denis Parkin.

	Production No	Holding / Source
26.12.1976 The Christmas Spirit	P849/10	D2 / 2"

With Peter Sallis (Mr Gudgin / Old Gudgin), Lynette Davies, Matthew Ryan.

| THE GHOSTS OF MOTLEY HALL (continued) | | British Christmas Television Guide |

SERIES 3

	Production No	Holding / Source
26.12.1977 **Phantomime**	P849/20	D2 / 2"

Duration: 51 minutes.
Christmas Eve at Motley Hall.
Music by Wilfred Josephs and Derek Hilton; designed by Taff Batley and Alan Price.
With Yolande Palfrey (Elly), Fanny Rowe (Aunt Edith), Diana King (Aunt Ethel), Alfred Marks (Abdullah el Raschid ben Saladin).

A GIFT FOR GRACIE

A Yorkshire Television production. Transmission details are for the ATV midlands region. Duration: 52 minutes.

Take a set sweeping the entire length of Yorkshire Television's largest studio (7,650 square feet); add an all-star line up, two top writers and a director who has been connected with some of television's leading shows and the result can only be a variety spectacular with a capital S. The set is made up of three levels to look like the entrance hall and grand staircase of an 18th century mansion. It is here that Gracie's party takes place.

Music directed by Charles Smitton; designed by Geoffrey Martin; executive producer Jess Yates; produced and directed by Ian Fordyce.

Gracie Fields (Hostess), The Bachelors, Bruce Forsyth, Harry Secombe, Mike and Bernie Winters, Ted Ray, Les Dawson, Arthur Askey, Sandy Powell, Patricia Ruanna, Lionel Blair and his Dancers, The Mike Sammes Singers.

	Holding / Source
25.12.1970	J|a / 2"

Kaleidoscope hold an audio-only version.

THE GIFTIE

A TVS production for Channel 4. Transmission details are for Channel 4. Duration: 50 minutes.

Written by Wally K. Daly; graphics by John Austin; costume Lawrie Oxley; make-up Jan Musgrove; music by Jim Parker; edited by Ian Higginson; lighting director Robert Byde; sound Andrew Emsley; camera operated by Ron Dallinger; designed by Greg Lawson; executive producer John Kaye Cooper; produced by Humphrey Barclay; directed by David Askey.

Richard O'Sullivan (Paul), John Wells (Frank), Joanna Van Gyseghem (Faye), Janet Key (Margaret), Peter Geddis (Harold), Bryan Coleman (Major).

	VT Number	Holding / Source
31.12.1987	10619	1" / 1"

GILBERT O'SULLIVAN'S GREATEST HITS

A Yorkshire Television production. Transmission details are for the ATV midlands region. Duration: 40 minutes.

Music directed by Trevor Bastow; designed by Vic Symonds; produced and directed by Vernon Lawrence.

Gilbert O'Sullivan, The Thurnscoe Harmonic Male Voice Choir, Cross Hall Junior School, Morley.

	Holding / Source
26.12.1976	DB / 2"

GILBERT O'SULLIVAN--WELCOME TO MY SHOW

An LWT production. Transmission details are for the ATV midlands region. Duration: 50 minutes.

Music by Richard Holmes; designed by Bill McPherson; produced and directed by David Bell.

Gilbert O'Sullivan, The Johnnie Spence Orchestra.

	VT Number	Holding / Source
22.12.1973	9345	D2 / 2"

GIMME GIMME GIMME

A Tiger Aspect production for BBC 2. made in association with Hartswood Films. Transmission details are for BBC 2. Duration: 30 minutes.

Main regular credit(s): Written by Jonathan Harvey.
Main regular cast: Kathy Burke (Linda La Hughes), James Dreyfus (Tom Farrell).

SERIES 2
Transmission details are for BBC 2.
Main regular credit(s): Executive producer Jon Plowman; produced by Sue Vertue; directed by Liddy Oldroyd.

	Holding / Source
29.12.1999 **Millennium**	DB / DBSW

With Rowland Rivron, Melinda Messenger, Simon Shepherd.

THE GIRL

A BBC production for BBC 2. Transmission details are for BBC 2. Duration: 90 minutes.

An evening of Alfred Hitchcock-themed programmes begins with this dramatisation of the relationship between the director and Tippi Hedren. He chose the unknown fashion model to star in The Birds, and proceeded to mould her into the perfect "Hitchcock blonde" - but a dangerous obsession was developing.

Written by Gwyneth Hughes; produced by Amanda Jenks; directed by Julian Jarrold.

Toby Jones (Alfred Hitchcock), Sienna Miller (Tippi Hendren), Imelda Staunton (Alma Hitchcock), Penelope Wilton (Peggy Robertson), Carl Beukes (Jim Brown), Conrad Kemp (Evan Hunter), Angelina Ingpen (Melanie), Candice D'Arcy (Josephine Milton), Kate Tilley (Rita Riggs), Leon Clingman (Ray Berwick), Patrick Lyster (Bob Boyle), Aubrey Shelton (Maitre D').

	Holding / Source
26.12.2012	HD/DB / HDC

THE GIRL

GISELLE

An ATV production. Transmission details are for the ATV midlands region. Duration: 75 minutes.

Based on a book by Vernoy De Saint-Georges, Theophile Gautier and Jean Coralli; music by Adolphe Adam; designed by Henry Graveney; produced by Stanley Dorfman; directed by Stanley Dorfman and Rudolf Nureyev.

Rudolf Nureyev (Albrecht), Lynn Seymour (Giselle), Monica Mason (Myrtha, Queen of The Wilis), Youri Vamos (Hilarian), Gerd Larsen (Berthe), Hella Schonbrunt (Bathilde), Yvanka Lukateli (Zulme), Joyce Cuoco (Moyna), Jaroslav Dlask (Wilfrid), Werner Dittrich (Duke of Courland), Jurgen Wienert (Leader of The Hunt), Ballet of The Bavarian State Opera House.

	Holding / Source
30.12.1979	DB / 2"

GIVE MY HEAD PEACE

A BBC Northern Ireland production for BBC 1 Northern Ireland. Transmission details are for BBC 1 Northern Ireland. Duration: 30 minutes.

Main regular credit(s): Written by Tim McGarry, Damon Quinn and Michael McDowell.
Main regular cast: Tim McGarry (Da), Damon Quinn (Cal).

SERIES 2

		Holding / Source
18.12.1998	It'a A Horrible Life	DB / DBS

SERIES 3

Main regular credit(s): Produced and directed by Martin Shardlow.

		Holding / Source
17.12.1999	Wish You Weren't Here	DB / DBS

SERIES 4

Main regular credit(s): Produced by Colin Lewis; directed by David G. Croft.

		Holding / Source
21.12.2000	A Fairytale Of New York	DB / DBSW

SERIES 6

		Holding / Source
21.12.2001	A Christmas Carol	DB / DBSW

		Holding / Source
23.12.2005	It Was A Very Good Year	DB / DBSW
22.12.2006	The McGlinchey Code	DB / DBSW
28.12.2007	The Story Of Give My Head Peace	DB / DBSW
28.12.2007	The Last Farewell	DB / DBSW

GIVE US A BREAK

A BBC production for BBC 1. Transmission details are for BBC 1.

Micky Noades sees himself as a professional manager. Mo is his talented client, a snooker talent more than 'a bit warm'.

Main regular credit(s): Written by Geoff McQueen; opening theme sung by Joe Brown; music by Harry South; produced by Terence Williams.
Main regular cast: Robert Lindsay (Micky Noades), Paul McGann (Mo Morris), Shirin Taylor (Tina Morris).

		Holding / Source
31.12.1984	Hustle Bustle Toil And Muscle	C1 / C1

Duration: 95 minutes.

Micky invests in personal computers, while Tina leaves him. Mo is all loved-up. Micky and Mo head north to Liverpool to play a big-money match, giving Micky and Tina the opportunity to be reunited.

Directed by Christopher King.

With T. P. McKenna, Sara Sugarman, Tony Selby, Alexei Sayle, Ron Pember, Johnny Shannon, Victoria Burgoyne, Alan Ford, David Sibley, Peter Christian, George A. Cooper, Tony Osoba, Gilly Coman, David Swift, Valerie Lillie, Jim Dunk, Cheryl Leigh, Walter Sparrow, Ben Benison, Alan Cody, Tony Scoggo, John Whitehall, Robert Grosse, Muhammed Yermak Jr, Neil Patterson, Anthony Clark, Everton Wilson, Steve Harris, Trevor Harris.

GIVE US A CLUE

A Thames Television production. Transmission details are for the Central region. Duration: 25 minutes.

Main regular credit(s): Devised by Juliet Grimm and Vince Powell.
Main regular performer(s): Lionel Blair (Team Captain).

SERIES 3

Transmission details are for the ATV midlands region.
Main regular credit(s): Theme music by Alan Hawkshaw; produced and directed by David Clark.
Main regular performer(s): With Michael Aspel (Host), Una Stubbs (Team Captain).

		VT Number	Holding / Source
24.12.1980	Give Us A Clue For Christmas	23993	DB / 2"

With Jim Davidson, Kenny Everett, Alfred Marks, Mollie Sugden, Barbara Windsor, Julia McKenzie.

GIVE US A CLUE (continued)   British Christmas Television Guide

SERIES 4
Transmission details are for the ATV midlands region.
Main regular credit(s):   Produced by David Clark.
Main regular performer(s): With Michael Aspel (Host), Una Stubbs (Team Captain), Lionel Blair (Team Captain).

	Holding / Source
24.12.1981	DB / 2"

Directed by Robert Reed.
With Pat Coombs, Stacy Dorning, Joanna Van Gyseghem, Terry Scott, Joe Brown, Nicholas Lyndhurst.

SERIES 6
Main regular credit(s):   Designed by Harry Clark; produced and directed by David Clark.
Main regular performer(s): With Michael Parkinson (Host), Una Stubbs (Team Captain).

	Holding / Source
25.12.1984 **Christmas Special**	1" / 1"

With Lionel Blair (Team Captain), Julia McKenzie, Spike Milligan, Nicola Pagett, Wayne Sleep, Julie Walters, Bernie Winters.

01.01.1985 **New Year Special**	1" / 1"

Duration: 48 minutes.
With Lionel Blair (Team Captain), Julie Walters, Bernie Winters, Julia McKenzie, Bruce Forsyth, Nicola Pagett, Wayne Sleep.

GLADIATORS

An LWT production. Transmission details are for the Central region. Duration: 50 minutes.
Main regular credit(s):   Written by Colin Edmonds.

SERIES 2
Main regular credit(s):   Produced by Nigel Lythgoe; directed by Patricia Mordecai.
Main regular performer(s): With John Fashanu (Host), Ulrika Jonsson (Host), John Sachs (Commentator), Wolf (Gladiator), Jet (Gladiator).

	VT Number	Holding / Source
26.12.1993 **Battle Of The Gladiators**	92792	D2 / D2S

With Gary Mason, Vinny Jones.

SERIES 3
Main regular credit(s):   Executive producer John Kaye Cooper; produced by Nigel Lythgoe; directed by Patricia Mordecai.
Main regular performer(s): With John Fashanu (Host), Ulrika Jonsson (Host), John Sachs (Commentator).

	VT Number	Holding / Source
24.12.1994 **The Celebrity Challenge**	93018	D2 / D2S

With Mike Adamie (Co-Host), Martin Offiah, Barry McGuigan, Ellery Hanley, Eddie Kidd, Derek Redmond, Mark Bosnich.

31.12.1994 **The Fighting Forces Challenge**	93019	D2 / D2S

GLENCANNON

A Gross-Krasne production for ABC. made in association with Gross-Krasne, Inc. Transmission details are for the ATV midlands region. Duration: 25 minutes.
Main regular credit(s):   Based on the stories of Guy Gilpatric; executive producer Donald Hyde.
Main regular cast: Thomas Mitchell (Glencannon), Patrick Allen (Bosun Hughes), Charles Carson (Captain Ball), Barry Keegan (Montgomery), Georgie Wood (Cookie / Svenson).

	Holding / Source
22.12.1960 **The Christmas Story**	B3 / B3

Alt.Title(s):   *Souse Of The Border*
Written by Basil Dawson.
With Peter Collingwood (Sparks), Bill Nagy, Jennifer Wright, Peter Elliott, Roger Snowdon, Bill Edwards, John Bloomfield, Andy Ho.

Georgie Wood is occasionally listed as George Wood in the TV Times, it is not known whether this is also the case on screen.

GLOO JOO

An LWT production. Transmission details are for the ATV midlands region. Duration: 90 minutes.
This outrageous comedy about Britain's immigration laws won The London Evening Standard Comedy of the Year award.

It tells the story of Meadowlark Warner—black, British "through and through" and a target for deportation. To his utter amazement, Meadowlark suddenly finds himself forcibly removed from Brixton to Gatwick Airport, in imminent danger of being packed off on the next flight to Jamaica. Two immigration officials dealing with his case, however, have never encountered a deportee like Meadowlark - a feckless, charming rogue with a trick up every sleeve...

Written by Michael Hastings; music by George Fenton; designed by Rae George; executive producer Tony Wharmby; produced by Humphrey Barclay; directed by John Kaye Cooper.

Oscar James (Meadowlark Warner), Antony Brown (Raymond Borrall), Dave Hill (Gerry Radinski), Frances Tomelty (Irene O'Connor), Joan-Ann Maynard (Edna Walter), Edward Halsted (Elliott Brucknell), T-Bone Wilson (Livingstone).

	Holding / Source
29.12.1979	DB / 2"

GLOO JOO

THE GLORIES OF CHRISTMAS

A Yorkshire Television production. Transmission details are for the Yorkshire Television region. Duration: 50 minutes.

Two famous Christmas tales, Glories of Music and Charles Dickens World of Christmas, are adapted for television with the programme completed by a reading and re-enactment of the nativity.

Introduced by Richard Todd; script editor Andrew Kaveney; music directed by Peter Husband; designed by Howard Dawson; associate producers Peter Max-Wilson and Roger Cheveley; production associate Charles Gardiner; executive producer Jess Yates; produced and directed by Len Lurcuck.

Roy Barraclough (Innkeeper), John Bluthal (Fagin), Alan Browning (Mr Crummles), Dora Bryan (Mrs Gamp), Patrick Cargill (Wardle), Diana Coupland (Mrs Cratchit), Les Dawson (Mr Micawber), Arthur English (Policeman), Harry Fowler (Sam Weller), Gerald Harper (Jingle), Kathleen Harrison (Mrs Wardle), Melvyn Hayes (Bob Cratchit), James Hayter (Mr Pickwick), Gordon Honeycombe (David Copperfield), John Laurie (Scrooge), Alfred Marks (Mr Garderie), Penny Meredith (Mercy Pecksniff), Bob Monkhouse (Uriah Heep), Stephen Murray (Charles Dickens), Patrick Newell (Mr Bumble), Patricia Phoenix (Mrs Crummles), Patrick Troughton (Quilp), Freddie Trueman (Mr Carton), Gorden Kaye (Barnaby Rudge), Timothy Spall* (The Artful Dodger), Princess Grace of Monaco (Narrator of the Nativity), The Bachelors, Janet Baker, Margaret Barron, The Beverley Sisters, Igor Gridneff, Trevor Lawson, Kenneth McKellar, Ludmila Nova, Colin Prince, Rostal and Schaefer, Patricia Ruanna, Richard Tucker, Francis Van Dyke, Huddersfield Choral Society, Wheatsheaf Girls' Choir.

	VT Number	Holding / Source
25.12.1973	5342	DB / 2"

THE GLUMS

Alternative/Working Title(s): TAKE IT FROM HERE

An LWT production. Transmission details are for the ATV midlands region. Duration: 25 minutes.

Main regular credit(s): Written by Denis Norden and Frank Muir; produced by Simon Brett.

Main regular cast: Jimmy Edwards (Pa Glum), Ian Lavender (Ron), Patricia Brake (Eth), Michael Stainton, John Barron, Norman Bird.

Bruce Forsyth's Big Night mini-episodes:

Main regular credit(s): Designed by Colin Monk and Mike Oxley; directed by John Kaye Cooper.

	Holding / Source
24.12.1978	D2 / 2"

Main regular cast: With Michael Stainton (Ted, The Landlord).

	Production No	Holding / Source
23.12.1979 "The Christmas Party"	9L/90036	D2 / 2"

Designed by Colin Monk and Mike Oxley; directed by John Reardon.

See also: BRUCE FORSYTH'S BIG NIGHT

GOD ON... CHRISTMAS

A Granada production. Transmission details are for the Granada region. Duration: 48 minutes.

Produced and directed by John Muggleton.

The Lower Titmarsh-On-The-Heath Choral Society, David Alton M.P., Reverend Russ Parker, Reverend Dave Cave, Canon June Osborne.

	Production No	Holding / Source
23.12.1995	P8314/1	D3 / D3S

GOGGLES

An LWT production. Transmission details are for the Central region. Duration varies - see below for details.

	Holding / Source
19.12.1996 **The Goggles' Christmas Giggle**	D2 / D2S

Duration: 25 minutes.

Goggle Family Introducing Clips Of Percy The Park Keeper/the World's Greatest Magic Show/alice In Wonderland/willows In Winter/ Dennis/the World's Greatest Stunts. Family Invade A House And Prepare The Tree And Turkey For Christmas Day. Damage perform "Forever"

Produced and directed by John Morgan.

With Malcolm Jeffries (Presenter), Hilda Braid, Max Cane, Su Elliott, Leigh Foley, Paul Grunert, Melanie Martinez, Vaughan Sivelle, Damage.

GOGS

Commissioned by BBC 2. Transmission details are for BBC 2. Duration: 10 minutes.

Animated series. Animated saga telling the story of the Gogs, Stone-Age folk living before the invention of language and confronting the trials of life using a mixture of ingenuity and brute force. The mystery behind the construction of Stonehenge is resolved when Cramps builds baby a swing to keep him quiet.

Main regular credit(s): Executive producers Meirion Davies and Colin Rose; directed by Deiniol Morris and Michael Mort.

	Holding / Source
21.12.1996	DB-D3 /
23.12.1996	DB-D3 /
24.12.1996	DB-D3 /
25.12.1996	DB-D3 /
26.12.1996	DB-D3 /

GOING LIVE

A BBC Children's Department production for BBC 1. Transmission details are for BBC 1. Duration varies - see below for details.

SERIES 1
Duration: 162 minutes.
Main regular credit(s): Series editor Chris Bellinger.
Main regular cast: With Sarah Greene (Presenter), Phillip Schofield (Presenter), Simon Hickson, Trevor Neal.

	Holding / Source
26.12.1987	DB / 1"

SERIES 2
Duration: 162 minutes.
Main regular credit(s): Edited by Chris Bellinger.
Main regular cast: With Phillip Schofield (Presenter), Sarah Greene (Presenter), Trevor Neal, Simon Hickson, Peter Simon ('Double Dare').

	Holding / Source
24.12.1988	DB / 1"

SERIES 3
Duration: 192 minutes.
Main regular credit(s): Edited by Chris Bellinger.
Main regular cast: With Phillip Schofield (Presenter), Sarah Greene (Presenter), Trevor Neal, Simon Hickson, Peter Simon ('Double Dare').

	Holding / Source
23.12.1989	DB / 1"
30.12.1989 **Gone Live! : Philderella**	DB / 1"

Duration: 105 minutes.
Produced by David Mercer; directed by Peter Leslie.

With Phillip Schofield (Philderella), Sarah Greene (Sarahdonna), Trevor Neal (Ugly Sister Brother), Simon Hickson (Ugly Sister Brother), Gordon The Gopher (Bottoms), Helen Lederer (Narrator), Christopher Ryan (Manager), Vas Blackwood (Fairy Godfather), Big Fun (Band), Sydney Youngblood (Band), Phil Collins, Anneka Rice, Jason Donovan, Anne Charleston, Noel Edmonds, Ian Smith, Tony Robinson, Nigel Kennedy, Bill Giles, Michael Fish, Suzanne Charlton, Liz Kershaw, Bruno Brookes, Tessa Sanderson, Duncan Goodhew, John Leslie, Andy Crane, Lisa Stansfield, The London Boys, Ruby Turner, Curiosity Killed The Cat, Brother Beyond, Halo James, And Why Not?.

SERIES 4
Duration: 192 minutes.
Main regular credit(s): Series editor Chris Bellinger.
Main regular cast: With Phillip Schofield (Presenter), Sarah Greene (Presenter), Trevor Neal, Simon Hickson, Sophie Lawrence (Reporter), Jonathan Porrit, Peter Simon ('Double Dare').

	Holding / Source
22.12.1990	DB / 1"

With Cliff Richard, Jeffrey Holland, Su Pollard, Linda Robson, Pauline Quirke, Nick Conway, Victor McGuire.

29.12.1990 **Gone Live!: Scrooge - A Christmas Sarah**	DB / 1"

Duration: 110 minutes.
Written by Trev Neal and Simon Hickson; produced by David Mercer; directed by Peter Leslie.

With Sarah Greene (Sarah Scrooge), Phillip Schofield (Phil Scratchit), Trevor Neal (Narrator), Simon Hickson (Narrator), Peter Simon (Polcieman), Emma Forbes (Mrs Scratchit), Sonia (Charity Worker), Gordon The Gopher (Tiny Gordon), Rowland Rivron (Jacob Marley), Norman Lovett (Christmas Past), Susie Blake (Christmas Present), Normski (Christmas Future), Kate Lonergan, Danny John-Jules, Frank Bruno, Jakki Brambles, Hothouse Flowers, Twenty 4 Seven.

SERIES 5
Duration: 192 minutes.
Main regular credit(s): Edited by Chris Bellinger.
Main regular cast: With Phillip Schofield (Presenter), Sarah Greene (Presenter), Peter Simon ('Double Dare'), Nick Ball, James Hickish.

	Holding / Source
21.12.1991	DB / 1"

With Jason Donovan, Zandra Rhodes, Pet Shop Boys.

SERIES 6
Duration: 192 minutes.
Main regular credit(s): Edited by Chris Bellinger.
Main regular cast: With Phillip Schofield (Presenter), Sarah Greene (Presenter), Trevor Neal, Simon Hickson, Michael McNally (Reporter), Emma Freud (Reporter), Doctor Aric Sigman, Andi Peters (Reporter), Peter Simon ('Run The Risk'), Shane Richie ('Run The Risk').

	Holding / Source
19.12.1992	DB / D3S

With Take That, Linda Robson, Pauline Quirke, Lisa Stansfield.

Kristian Schmid was announced as a new presenter, but could not take part when his work visa was refused.

THE GOLDEN AGE OF MUSIC HALL

An ATV production. Transmission details are for the ATV midlands region. Duration: 20 minutes.
Written by Dan Douglas; produced and directed by Donald Shingler.
David Rees (Narrator), Hetty King, Ella Shields, Lily Morris, Charles Coburn Snr, Harold Manning, Wee Georgie Wood, Billy Russell.

	Holding / Source
26.12.1967	B1SEQ / 40

MACE hold film inserts for this programme. The material is logged against ATV Today as presumably it was made by the same team.

It was Midlands only and ran for 20 minutes in the ATV Today slot. The surviving film is mostly archive footage including Ella Shields, Charles Coburn and Lily Morris (who were all deceased by 1967). Wee George Wood, Hetty King, Billy Russell and Harold Manning appear in newly shot interviews. It runs 14 minutes so is most of the programme. The VT elements have long gone.

ATV Today also put together a complete studio programme for Christmas day that year which was presented by David Lloyd. Guests included Philip Harben and T.P. McKenna. Again information is from the schedules So like all VT material for that period it no longer exists. Source: MACE.

THE GOLDEN OLDIE PICTURE SHOW

A BBC production for BBC 1. Transmission details are for BBC 1.
Main regular performer(s): Dave Lee Travis (Host).

SERIES 1

		Holding / Source
23.12.1985	The Golden Oldie Christmas Show	DB / 1"

SERIES 2

		Holding / Source
22.12.1986	The Golden Oldie Christmas Show	DB / 1"
23.12.1987	The Golden Oldie Christmas Show	DB / 1"

With Freddie and The Dreamers, Tom Jones, Russ Conway, Jimi Hendrix, George Harrison, Slade, Jethro Tull.

THE GOLDEN RING

A BBC production for BBC 1. Transmission details are for BBC 1. Duration: 90 minutes.
Narrated by Humphrey Barclay; conducted by Georg Solti; associate producers John Drummond and Walter Klapper; produced and directed by Humphrey Barclay.
Birgit Nilsson (Brünnhilde), Wolfgang Winogassen (Siegfried), Gottlob Frick (Hagen), Dietrich Fisscher-Dieskau (Gunther), Claire Watson (Gutrune), The Vienna State Opera Chorus, The Vienna Philharmonic Orchestra.

	Holding / Source
26.12.1965	DB / 62

THE GOLDEN SEASWALLOW OF KNOKKE 1976

A BBC production for BBC 2. Transmission details are for BBC 2. Duration: 35 minutes.
Written by Austin Steele; music directed by Ronnie Hazlehurst; designed by Robin Tarsnane; produced by John Ammonds; directed by Alan Boyd.
Norman Wisdom, Rod Hull and Emu, Tony Fayne, The Francis Ray Orchestra, The Ladybirds.

	Holding / Source
29.12.1976	DB / 2"

THE GOLDEN SHOT

An ATV production. Transmission details are for the ATV midlands region. Duration varies - see below for details.

"Up… stop. Right… stop. Right a bit more… stop. Left a bit… stop. Down a bit… stop. Fire!"

If The Golden Shot has any long-standing legacy in British culture, it's probably formed of a phrase sounding something like that. This was a game show, at its peak the most watched one on British television. Its final edition was shown almost exactly 35 years ago – on 13 April 1975.

Its origin was a Swiss-German show – Der Goldener Schuss – devised by Werner and Hannes Schmidt which was a hit on German television. In 1967, Lew Grade bought the British rights to the programme for ATV and, apparently as a result of seeing him play the part of a game-show host on a Charlie Drake programme, decided that Canadian singer Jackie Rae was the ideal person to host it.

The premise of the show was incredibly simple, though technically quite complex for the time. Using a crossbow with a camera mounted on it looking straight down the bow's sight, contestants would attempt to score points by firing crossbow bolts at a series of targets, often involving apples in some way. The winner each week was given a chance to go for a prize which required them to shoot through a thread at the centre of a target. Hit the bullseye and break the thread – and they won the jackpot.

Although precise details would change over the years, the basic principles didn't. The opening round would consist of a minimum of four contestants – two selected from the studio audience and two viewers at home in touch with the studio by telephone. A blind-fold cameraman would operate the bow for this initial stage and the contestants, who were watching the crossbow sight on a TV screen, whether at home or in the studio, would instruct the cameraman how to move the bow, hence "Up bit… right a bit…" and so on, to try to hit a target. Those who succeeded became the contestants on the following week's show. From this point, the contestants would operate the crossbows themselves, either directly or – for one round – via a joystick, using a television monitor to line up the sight with the target, but either way, the camera on the bow let the viewers in on the action.

The programme started as a primetime Saturday evening show and while the critics weren't particularly fond of it, it was being watched by between eleven and thirteen million people and was regularly one of the twenty most-watched programmes of the week. However Jackie Rae was not the ideal host. At this point, it was a live show where things quite often went wrong, and Rae often looked ill at ease. Following an excellent appearance as a guest, Bob Monkhouse took over the reins and was instantly more at home, as perhaps he should have been – even then he already had quite a few game shows under his belt. A number of these had been for ABC Television and whether it was jealousy on their part at Bob working for ATV or just a coincidence, it was around the time of his arrival that ABC moved the programme to Sunday afternoons while the remainder of the network still watched on Saturdays.

Whether it was this or, as is often reported, a suggestion from Lew Grade's nephew Michael, soon that slot was the programme's home across the country, where it would remain for the rest of its life. While this would put an end to its regular appearances in the top twenty, it would still attract about ten million viewers, very impressive for a tea-time show on a Sunday.

Monkhouse would be with the programme until February 1972 at which point Norman Vaughan took over as host. Like Bob, Vaughan had previously compèred Sunday Night At The London Palladium but like Jackie Rae, Norman didn't always appear comfortable and in September 1973 he left the programme to be replaced by comedian Charlie Williams. Unfortunately while a gifted stand-up comedian, the programme was a step too far for Williams who only stayed with the programme for six months until it took its first break in over five years in March 1974.

Three months later, back came The Golden Shot, and back too came Bob Monkhouse. Bob had made a deal to try to make the show a success again and then leave on a high to present a new game show, Celebrity Squares, something he would be doing just three months after that final bolt was shot, 35 years ago.

Main regular credit(s):   Format by Hannes Schmid and Werner Schmid.

An ATV Birmingham production. Duration: 38 minutes.
Main regular performer(s):   With Bob Monkhouse (Host).

			Holding / Source
21.12.1969 "**The spirit of Christmas**"			NR|c / Live

Written by Wally Malston; music directed by Roger Webb; designed by Jill Oxley; produced and directed by John Pullen.
With Anne Aston (Golden Girl), Carol Dilworth (Golden Girl), Len Lowe (Punster), Freddie Davies, Karen Young.

An ATV Birmingham production.
Main regular performer(s):   With Bob Monkhouse (Host).

	Production No	VT Number	Holding / Source
19.12.1971 "Trip to Toyland"	4283		J|c / LivePAL

Duration: 43 minutes.
Written by Wally Malston; music directed by Johnny Patrick; designed by Don Davidson; produced and directed by Mike Lloyd.
With Anne Aston (Golden Girl), Ayshea Brough (Maid of the Month), John Baker (Bernie the Bolt), Blue Mink, Ted Rogers, Alan Randall.

26.12.1971 **Christmas Crackshots**	4307	4307/71	J|c / 2"

Duration: 48 minutes.
Written by Wally Malston; music directed by Johnny Patrick; designed by John Hickson; produced and directed by Mike Lloyd.
With Anne Aston (Golden Girl), Ayshea Brough (Golden Girl), Lesley Goldie (Golden Girl), Jenny Lee-Wright (Golden Girl), John Baker (Bernie the Bolt), Des O'Connor, Mary Hopkin, Severine, Alfie Bass, Jack Douglas, Stephen Lewis.
Recorded 14.12.71.

An ATV Birmingham production. Duration: 43 minutes.
Main regular credit(s):   Music directed by Johnny Patrick.
Main regular performer(s):   With Norman Vaughan (Host).

	Production No	VT Number	Holding / Source
24.12.1972	6259	6259/72	J / 2"

Norman and his star guests are prepared for anything today. For members of the staff of Birmingham Queen Elizabeth Hospital are the audience and contestants in this Christmas edition of the aimgame. But something is planned to happen that very few will be prepared for.
Written by Spike Mullins and Charles Hart; designed by Jay Clements; produced by Les Cocks; directed by Paul Stewart Laing.
With Anne Aston (Golden Girl), The New Seekers, Millicent Martin, Bobby Crush, Morris Parsons, Jack Douglas, Zena Clifton.
Recorded 12.12.72.

| British Christmas Television Guide | THE GOLDEN SHOT (continued) |

An ATV Birmingham production. Duration: 43 minutes.
Main regular credit(s): Written by Alec Myles and Les Lilley; music directed by Johnny Patrick.
Main regular performer(s): With Charlie Williams (Host), Anne Aston (Golden Girl).

        Holding / Source
23.12.1973   J / 2"

Jazzman George Chisholm appears with and without his trombone when he becomes the Golden Partner today in the show that's bang on target. Singer Joan Regan adds musical
charm to the proceedings, and Mrs. Mills matches the mood with some goodtime tunes on the old "Joanna". The Abraham Darby School Choir of 60 children are also in the show singing The Holy City.
Designed by Martin Davey; produced and directed by Dicky Leeman.
With Denise Distel (Maid Of The Month), Joan Regan, Mrs Mills, George Chisholm, The Abraham Darby School Choir.

Main regular credit(s): Programme associates Tony Hawes and Dennis Berson; music directed by Johnny Patrick; produced and directed by Dicky Leeman.
Main regular performer(s): With Bob Monkhouse (Host), Anne Aston (Golden Girl), Wei Wei Wong (Golden Girl).

	Production No	VT Number	Holding / Source
26.12.1974	9685	9685/74	J|c / 2"

Duration: 51 minutes.
In this special Christmas edition, shootalong with Bob and golden partner Michael Henry, and singalong with Max Bygraves, who wants to Dance in the Old Fashioned Way, and Crossroads' Noele Gordon, who dedicates her number To My Daughter.
Designed by Norman Smith and Jay Clements.
With Michael Henry, Max Bygraves, Noele Gordon, Tony Christie, Lionel Blair.
Recorded 01.12.74.

GOLLY GOES HOME FOR CHRISTMAS

An Associated-Rediffusion production. Transmission details are for Associated-Rediffusion. Duration: 14 minutes.
Illustrated by Neville Wortman.
Wally Whyton (Storyteller).

        Holding / Source
22.12.1959   NR / Live

THE GOOD LIFE

A BBC production for BBC 1. Transmission details are for BBC 1. Duration: 30 minutes.
Main regular credit(s): Written by John Esmonde and Bob Larbey; music by Burt Rhodes; designed by Paul Munting; produced and directed by John Howard Davies.
Main regular cast: Richard Briers (Tom Good), Felicity Kendal (Barbara Good), Penelope Keith (Margo Leadbetter), Paul Eddington (Jerry Leadbetter).

SERIES 4

        Holding / Source
26.12.1977 Silly, But It's Fun....   DB-D3 / 2"

Christmas is cancelled at the Leadbetters when the Christmas tree and entire order fails to arrive. The Goods host Christmas instead.
With David Battley.

The Good Life, Porridge, Dad's Army, Are You Being Served etc - all have had shorter versions made of most of their episodes because they were too close to or exceeded the 30 minute slot they were allocated. The original versions also exist, and are not going to be disposed of, it's just they are no longer deemed suitable for transmission without making other programmes run late, especially since multiple trails became compulsory... "Wind-Break War" was first shown in the edited version on 25/10/93 and has been shown only in that version since - the edit is in fact about 55 seconds long.

GOOD MORNING BRITAIN

A TV-am production. Transmission details are for TV-am.

	Holding / Source
24.12.1983	DB|n / Live
26.12.1983	DB|n / Live
25.12.1984	DB|n / Live

THE GOOD OLD DAYS

A BBC production for BBC 1. made in association with Stanley and Michael Joseph. Transmission details are for BBC 1. Usual duration: 50 minutes.

"My Lords, Ladies and Gentlemen, Boys and Girls, Madames and Messieurs… pray silence for the inimitable, the indescribable, the adorable…. Danny La Rue!"

Undoubtedly the advent of television killed music hall in Britain. Until the 1960s every town and city in the UK had a theatre that would attract good acts to top the bill, but mostly middle-of-the-road entertainers and poor cannon-fodder made up the majority of the evening. Touring from city to city an entertainer could use the same act for years without changes, but placed in front of a television camera an act could not be repeated and many artistes could not make the transfer to the cathode ray era.

The Good Old Days started in 1955 when music hall and variety theatre was still popular. By its finish in 1982, apart from The Royal Variety Performance, this single series represented the last acts of variety in its truest form. It is unsurprising that it was Jimmy Perry's favourite programme, since he began as a variety artist. First broadcast on 20th July 1953, The Good Old Days was the brainchild of Barney Colehan. He produced and directed every edition of the show. Inspired by the success of the 'Ridgeway's Late Joys' at the Players Theatre Club, London, many of the dancers and extras were recruited from this private members' club that ran fortnightly programmes of variety acts in the West End.

Originally shown live, it was later recorded as live at the Leeds City Varieties Theatre. For many years it was shown once per month, but then it started to go out in short runs and at special occasions such as Christmas or New Year.

The shows had an authentic atmosphere of Victorian/Edwardian music hall with sketches and songs performed by present-day acts in the style of original artistes. However these performers were genuine music-hall acts. Modern acts such as Tom O'Connor or Jim Davidson did not perform, but regulars included Roy Hudd, Billy Dainty and Danny La Rue.

The audience was always dressed in period costume, and consisted of members of the public mingled with some extras. They joined in the singing. The showman at the front, the man with the most, the compere's compere was the indefatigable, the inexhaustible, an uncomplicated man of sagacious wit, with a thousand lines of description, who could only be, of course…… Leonard Sachs. Sachs was a fine actor, a skill he used to entertain the audience with his long-winded introductions of the acts, and his gravel to bang on the desk for order in the audience.

As well as Colehan and Sachs, Bernard Herrmann was the Musical Director and leader of the orchestra throughout the entire run. Once BBC North opened, production moved up from London, which was a natural move, but the same team remained on the show for 29 years! Beat that!

A glance at some of the early billings reveals a history of UK variety acts now forgotten. In 1955 the BBC were showing The Hindley Taylor Olde Tyme Singers, The Ballet Montmarte and Albert Burdon and Company. A singer called Jill Summers would later become a stalwart of Coronation Street. Boxing Day 1969 saw Morecambe and Wise top the bill, meaning they appeared on both channels that year at Christmas! One of the few surviving early shows contains Nancy and Molly Munks, Hammond's Birds and Chong and Mana, but some acts are more familiar: Ray Alan and Lord Charles, Roy Castle and Frankie Vaughan.

By 1968 headline acts included comedians such as Tessie O'Shea, Don Maclean, David Nixon and Lennie Bennett. Rikki Fulton wanted to achieve success outside Scotland so he came down from Glasgow, and Doreen Hermitage And Teddy Green appeared. Hermitage would remain on the show as choreographer for many years afterwards.

The final live show (later shows were pre-recorded) was scheduled for New Year's Eve 1982 but was cancelled due to a technical fault and was replaced by a repeat. A documentary in 1983 marked the end of a piece of true variety history. As is fitting for this book, please join me now in a rousing chorus of 'Down at the Old Bull and Bush' which ended every show.

Main regular credit(s):   Devised by Barney Colehan; by arrangement with Stanley & Michael Joseph; produced by Barney Colehan.

A BBC production. Transmission details are for BBC/BBC1.

Holding / Source

30.12.1953 — J / Live
Duration: 60 minutes.
Music directed by Alyn Ainsworth.
With Leonard Sachs (Chairman), Margery Manners, Dick Henderson, Flack and Lucas, Pharos and Marina, G. H. Elliot, Jimmy James and Company.

31.12.1954 — J / Live
Duration: 45 minutes.
Music directed by Alyn Ainsworth.
With Leonard Sachs (Chairman), Bertha Willmott, Rex Jameson, Pharos and Marina, Granger Brothers, Harry Bailey, Tod Slaughter and Company.

26.12.1956 — J / Live
Duration: 60 minutes.
Music directed by Norman George.
With Bill Shine (Chairman), Margery Manners, Hylda Baker, Jimmy Gay, Lili Berdé, Mundy and Earl, The Marthys, Norman and Niki Grant, Humper and Dink.

26.12.1957 — J / Live
Duration: 45 minutes.
Music directed by Alyn Ainsworth.
With Leonard Sachs (Chairman), The Musketeers, The Allen Brothers and June, Billy McComb, The Dancing McKennas, Bill Waddington, Darly's Dogs, Laurie Lupino Lane and George Truzzi.

26.12.1958 — J / Live
Duration: 40 minutes.
Music directed by Alyn Ainsworth.
With Leonard Sachs (Chairman), Jimmy James, Bretton Woods, Dick Carlton, Arthur Worsley with Charlie Brown, Patricia Bredin, Libby Morris, The Jumpin' Jax.

26.12.1959 — R3 / 40
Duration: 60 minutes.
Music directed by Alyn Ainsworth.
With Leonard Sachs (Chairman), Morecambe and Wise, Betty Jumel, Cardew Robinson, Noberti, Smoothey and Layton, The Manton Brothers, Patricia Bredin.

26.12.1960 — J / 40
Duration: 45 minutes.
Music directed by Bernard Herrmann.
With Leonard Sachs (Chairman), Albert Burdon and Company, Elizabeth Larner, Ethel Revnell, The Trio Vitalites, The Two Pirates.

28.12.1961 — J / 40
Music directed by Billy Ternent.
With Leonard Sachs (Chairman), Mike and Bernie Winters, Dick Emery, Rosemary Squires, Jean and Peter Barbour, Judy Moxon, Derek Dene, Nick and Pat Lundon [as Nick and Patricia].

| British Christmas Television Guide | THE GOOD OLD DAYS (continued) |

25.12.1962   J / 40
Duration: 45 minutes.
Music directed by Bernard Herrmann.
With Leonard Sachs (Chairman), Max Wall, The Spencer Trio, Anna Sharkey, Pifar Shang, Don Smoothey, The Flying Comets.

24.12.1963   R1SEQ / 40
Music directed by Billy Ternent.
With Leonard Sachs (Chairman), Frankie Vaughan, Stan Stennett, The Clark Brothers, Albert Burdon and Company, Ray Alan and Lord Charles, Hammond's Birds, Margery Manners, Jimmy Edwards.
Only the Jimmy Edwards section survives.

26.12.1964   J / 40
Duration: 55 minutes.
Music directed by Bernard Herrmann.
With Leonard Sachs (Chairman), Des O'Connor, Patricia Bredin, Colin Welland, James Ellis, Marino, The Bowman-Hyde Singers, Les Najarros, Jack Douglas, Ross-Piquer, Jane Braham, Pauline Sansby, Tina Scholes, Pat Taylor.

26.12.1965   J / 40
Duration: 40 minutes.
Music directed by Bernard Herrmann.
With Leonard Sachs (Chairman), Sheila Burnett (Cinderella), Joan Sterndale Bennett (Fairy Godmother), Sheila Matthews (Prince Charming), John Heawood (Ugly Sister), Brian Blades (Ugly Sister), John Rutland (Buttons), Maureen Keetch (Carol Singer), Denis Martin (Major Domo), Jack Douglas, Jack Haig, The Clark Brothers, Freddy Davies, The Madcaps, Jean Lemoine.

30.12.1966   R1 / 40
Duration: 40 minutes.
Music directed by Bernard Herrmann.
With Leonard Sachs (Chairman), Davy Kaye, Leslie Crowther, Patricia Bredin, The Gaiety Playboys, Prassana Rao, The Curibars, Jack Alban.

29.12.1967   J / 40
Additional material by John Hewer and Mike Hall; music directed by Bernard Herrmann.
With Leonard Sachs (Chairman), Beryl Reid, John Hewer, Denis Martin, Tony Sympson, Davy Kaye, Anne Chivers, Gerald Campion, Kim Cordell, Les Rennos, Prassana Rao, Chantal and Dumont.

Main regular performer(s):   With Leonard Sachs (Chairman).

Holding / Source
26.12.1968   J / 62
Music directed by Bernard Herrmann.
With Billy Dainty, Len Lowe, Kim Cordell, Johnny Hackett, Freddie Sales, Joe Castor, Les Spectacles D'Animation, Jack Alban, The Taylor Twins.

Main regular performer(s):   With Leonard Sachs (Chairman).

Holding / Source
30.12.1969   J / 2"
Music directed by Billy Ternent.
With Jimmy Tarbuck, Barbara Windsor, Rita Morris, Jerry and Montigny, The Wychwoods, El Gran Picasso, Peter Baldwin, David Godsell, Peter Leslie, Mark Speight.

Main regular credit(s):   Music directed by Bernard Herrmann.
Main regular performer(s):   With Leonard Sachs (Chairman).

Holding / Source
25.12.1970   J / 2"
Duration: 50 minutes.
Choreography by Doreen Hermitage.
With Danny La Rue, June Bronhill, Neville King, Mac Lou, Carazini, Denis Martin, Godfrey Charles, Dudley Stevens, Jonathan Dennis, Michael Darbyshire, Deryk Parkin.

31.12.1970   J / Live
Duration: 65 minutes.
Choreography by Doreen Hermitage.
With Canon Edwin Young, Norman Wisdom, Tony Fayne, Denny Willis and Company, Kim Cordell, Eira Heath, Rita Morris, Jamie Phillips, Norman Collier, Paul Dutton, Chantel & Dumont, Doreen Hermitage, Jan Hunt, Lorraine Hart, Valerie Lloyd, Dudley Stevens, Deryk Parkin, Michael Darbyshire.

Main regular credit(s):   Music directed by Bernard Herrmann.
Main regular performer(s):   With Leonard Sachs (Chairman).

Holding / Source
25.12.1971   J / 2"
With Terry Scott, Lynda Gloria, Jack Douglas, John Inman, Philip Smith, George Truzzi, John Boulter, Johnny Hart, Julie Fisher, The Turkenders.

Main regular credit(s):   Music directed by Bernard Herrmann.
Main regular performer(s):   With Leonard Sachs (Chairman).

Holding / Source
25.12.1972 **The Good Old Days 1952-1973**   DB-D3 / 2"
Duration: 50 minutes.
With Ken Dodd, Neville King, Lyn Kennington, Alfredo, Louisa Jane White, The Trio Hoganas, Trevor Little.

THE GOOD OLD DAYS (continued) — British Christmas Television Guide

"A special edition marking the 150th programme of Old-Time Music-Hall from the stage of the Famous City Varieties Theatre, Leeds" so says Radio Times. As it happens this wouldn't be the 150th programme even if they count the one made in Sweden.

Main regular credit(s): Music directed by Bernard Herrmann; choreography by Doreen Hermitage.
Main regular performer(s): With Leonard Sachs (Chairman), Loraine Hart, Clifton Todd.

Holding / Source
26.12.1973   J / 2"
Duration: 60 minutes.
With Frankie Vaughan, Beryl Reid, Elaine Delmar, Syd Little and Eddie Large, The James Boys, The Villams, Jackie Toye, Dudley Stevens, Raewyn Blade, Deryk Parkin.

Main regular credit(s): Choreography by Doreen Hermitage.
Main regular performer(s): With Leonard Sachs (Chairman).

Holding / Source
26.12.1974   DB-D3 / 2"
Duration: 55 minutes.
Music directed by Bernard Herrmann.
With Edward Woodward, The King's Singers, Sheila Bernette, Wilma Reading, Ted Durante and Hilda, Brahma, The Orlandos, Jacquie Toye, Loraine Hart, Jenny Wren, Jacqui Leatherby, Clifton Todd, Dudley Stevens, Mike Fields.

A BBC Manchester production.
Main regular credit(s): Music directed by Bernard Herrmann; choreography by Doreen Hermitage.
Main regular performer(s): With Leonard Sachs (Chairman), Loraine Hart, Jenny Wren, Dudley Stevens.

Holding / Source
25.12.1975   DB-D3 / 2"
Duration: 50 minutes.
With Vera Lynn, Sheila Steafel, Windsor Davies and Don Estelle, Lyn Kennington, Davy Kaye, Ray C. Davis, Jacquie Toye, Clifton Todd, Norman Warwick.

A BBC Manchester production.
Main regular credit(s): Music directed by Bernard Herrmann; choreography by Doreen Hermitage.
Main regular performer(s): With Leonard Sachs (Chairman).

Holding / Source
28.12.1976   DB-D3 / 2"
Duration: 50 minutes.
Designed by Kenneth Lawson.
With Denis Martin, Danny La Rue, Loraine Hart, Duggie Brown, Lyn Kennington, David Ellen, Jenny Layland, Paul and Peta Page, Jenny Wren, Dudley Stevens, Jacquie Toye, Clifton Todd, Norman Warwick.

A BBC Manchester production.
Main regular credit(s): Music directed by Bernard Herrmann; choreography by Doreen Hermitage.
Main regular performer(s): With Leonard Sachs (Chairman).

Holding / Source
31.12.1977   DB-D3 / 2"
With Larry Grayson, Vince Hill, Billy Dainty, Janet Brown, Eira Heath, Chey-Fu-Dey, The Pompoff Thedy Family.

A BBC Manchester production.
Main regular credit(s): Music directed by Bernard Herrmann; choreography by Doreen Hermitage.
Main regular performer(s): With Leonard Sachs (Chairman), Jenny Till, Penny Rigden, Peter Sutherland.

Holding / Source
31.12.1978   DB-D3 / 2"
Duration: 55 minutes.
With Roy Castle, Dolores Gray, Robert White, Eira Heath, Russ Stevens, Perkano & Christina, Michel Arene and The Lido Can Can Girls, Deryk Parkin, Suzanne Roberts, David Machin, Pauline Antony, Norman Warwick.

A BBC Manchester production.

Holding / Source
31.12.1980   DB-D3-2" / 2"
Duration: 57 minutes.
Music directed by Bernard Herrmann; choreography by Doreen Hermitage; designed by Barry Roach; directed by Barney Colehan.
With Leonard Sachs (Chairman), Danny La Rue, Duggie Brown, Robert White, Keith Harris, Teresa Cahill, Bablu Mallik, Deryk Parkin, Jenny Till, Penny Rigden, Nicola Kimber, Lisa Westcott, Norman Warwick, Christopher Wren, Tony Bateman.
The 31/12/1982 edition was cancelled so a reversioned edit of this special was shown in its place, one minute removed.

THE GOOD OLD DAYS

A BBC Manchester production.

	Holding / Source
24.12.1981	DB-D3 / 2"

Music directed by Bernard Herrmann; choreography by Doreen Hermitage.

With Leonard Sachs (Chairman), John Inman, Barry Howard, Eira Heath, Jimmy Cricket, Ricardo Arancibia, Cosmotheka, Roy Castle, Penny Rigden, Nicola Kimber, Lisa Westcott, Debbie Goodman, Christopher Wren, Peter Sutherland, Chris Connah, Graham Richards.

A BBC Manchester production.
Main regular credit(s):   Music directed by Bernard Herrmann; choreography by Doreen Hermitage; directed by Barney Colehan.
Main regular performer(s): With Leonard Sachs (Chairman), Penny Rigden, Chris Connah, Graham Richards.

	Holding / Source
24.12.1983	DB-D3 / 2"

Duration: 60 minutes.

With Danny La Rue, Bernard Cribbins, Valerie Masterson, Robert White, Barry Cryer, The Clark Brothers, Gaetan Bloom, Doreen Hermitage, Deryk Parkin, Wendy Jones, Amanda Newman, Lisa Westcott, Peter Sutherland, Ray Mangion.

31.12.1983 **A Farewell Celebration Of The Good Old Days**	DB-D3 / 2"

Duration: 60 minutes.

With Eleanor McCready (Florrie Ford), Jenny Wren (Clarice Mayne), Dudley Stevens (Fred Barnes), Doreen Hermitage (Vesta Victoria), Sheila Mathews (Jessie Matthews), Jan Hunt (Marie Lloyd), Jenny Till (Vesta Tilley), Eira Heath, The Simmons Brothers, Richard Ross, Frankie Vaughan, Wendy Jones, Lisa Westcott, Julia Lewis, Deryk Parkin, Scott St Martyn.

GOODBYE 2000

A BBC production for BBC 1. Transmission details are for BBC 1. Duration: 60 minutes.

Executive producer Caroline Wright; produced by Kate Phillips.

Angus Deayton (Host).

	Holding / Source
31.12.1999	DB / DBSW

GOODBYE TO ALL THAT

A TVS production. Transmission details are for the TVS region. Duration: 70 minutes.

Fern Britton (Presenter), Fred Dinenage (Presenter), Bryan Murray, Matthew Kelly, Richard Branson, Jill Gascoine, Neil Buchanan, Harry Secombe, Peter Bowles, Stanley Baxter, Roy Walker, Ben Kingsley, George Baker.

	Holding / Source
31.12.1992	DB / 1"

No end credits.

THE GOODIES

Alternative/Working Title(s): NARROW YOUR MIND / SUPERCHAPS THREE

A BBC/LWT production for BBC 2/LWT. Duration varies - see below for details.

When this new comedy programme began its first series, even then its stars would have been familiar to viewers – and to radio listeners. Tim Brooke-Taylor had appeared with Marty Feldman, John Cleese and others in At Last The 1948 show; Graeme Garden had featured regularly in Twice A Fortnight – as had Bill Oddie; and all three had been regulars in the long-running radio series I'm Sorry, I'll Read That Again and had worked together in the spoof "University of the Air" comedy show Broaden Your Mind. This new programme was the first which was designed solely as a vehicle for the three of them – and it was, of course, The Goodies.

The series would mix visual and verbal humour and while a few of the gags were a little risqué, most of it was family-friendly fun and the legions of children who enjoyed it have meant that it has often been treated less seriously than its big rival at the time: Monty Python's Flying Circus.

Although the basic premise would be diluted as time passed, in the original series the three characters – named Tim, Graeme and Bill after the actors who played them – set up an agency to... to... "To do good to people," says Tim early in episode one. "How wet!" responds Bill, but that's pretty much what they did with adverts for their agency offering their services to do "Anything / Anytime".

This gave them carte blanche to do stories about pretty much whatever they wanted, from guarding the Crown Jewels to helping to advertise a bedtime drink and some toothpaste, to running a pirate radio station, making gender education films, battling a government made up of very large puppets of children's favourites, making silent movies, and demonstrating a variety of unusual martial arts.

Their adventures took them to Loch Ness, into space, down a Cornish clotted-cream mine, into the stomach of a dinosaur and around the centre of London while it was being menaced by a giant white kitten.

Although all three of the actors would work together to decide what the various episodes of each series would be about, the scripts were mostly written by Graeme and Bill, and as the series progressed they realised that the roles they were writing for the guest actors were getting all the best lines. So gradually these roles diminished in importance as did the whole agency idea and in its place most stories featured two of the trio trying to stop or sabotage some madcap scheme of the third.

While starting out in a small way on BBC 2, by the mid-1970s even these screenings were attracting audiences of 7 or 8 million while repeats on BBC 1 would regularly attract 11 or 12 million people. One such viewer was the unlucky Alex Mitchell who died while laughing at the episode "Kung Fu Kapers!" – a spoof of the then recent martial arts western series Kung Fu – in which Bill takes up the ancient Lancastrian martial art of Ecky Thump.

Musically the episodes were interesting too. As well as the theme song, a large number of songs were written by Bill Oddie and either Michael Gibbs or Dave MacRae and these were often used to accompany the sections of each episode which were made on location on film. Later, of course, Bill's musical talents would get wider exposure and various Goodies' singles would spent a total of 38 weeks in the charts between December 1974 and January 1976.

After their eighth series, which was shown in early 1980, the BBC temporarily put the programme on hold as their comedy budget had apparently been used up by the television adaptation of Douglas Adams' The Hitch Hiker's Guide To The Galaxy. The trio moved over to London Weekend for one final series.

Main regular cast: Tim Brooke-Taylor (Tim), Graeme Garden (Graeme), Bill Oddie (Bill).

SERIES 4

A BBC production for BBC 2. Transmission details are for BBC 2.

Main regular credit(s): Written by Graeme Garden, Bill Oddie and Tim Brooke-Taylor; music by Bill Oddie and Michael Gibbs; produced and directed by Jim Franklin.

Holding / Source

24.12.1973 The Goodies And The Beanstalk DB-D3 / 2"-C1

Duration: 44 minutes.

The Goodies barter their most valuable possession for some beans and get more than they bargained for.

Designed by John Stout.

With John Cleese, Eddie Waring, Alfie Bass, Corbet Woodall, Robert Bridges, Marcelle Samett, Toni Harris, Helli Louise, Marty Swift, Arthur Ellis.

A BBC production for BBC 2. Transmission details are for BBC 2.

Holding / Source

21.12.1975 Goodies Rule - O.K? DB-D3 / 2"-C1

Duration: 49 minutes.

Written by Graeme Garden and Bill Oddie; music by Bill Oddie and Dave MacRae; designed by John Stout; produced and directed by Jim Franklin.

With Michael Barratt, Terry Wogan, Tony Blackburn, Sue Lawley, Patrick Moore, Eddie Waring, Corbet Woodall, Norman Mitchell, Ronald Russell, Roland Macleod, Barry Cryer, Sheila Steafel.

SERIES 7

A BBC production for BBC 2. Transmission details are for BBC 2. Duration: 30 minutes.

Main regular credit(s): Written by Graeme Garden and Bill Oddie; music by Bill Oddie and Dave MacRae; produced by Jim Franklin; directed by Bob Spiers.

Holding / Source

22.12.1977 Earthanasia DB-D3 / 2"

Designed by John Stout.

With Jon Glover*.

SERIES 9

An LWT production. Transmission details are for the London Weekend Television region. Duration: 25 minutes.

Main regular credit(s): Written by Graeme Garden and Bill Oddie; executive producer David Bell; produced and directed by Bob Spiers.

Holding / Source

27.12.1981 Snow White 2 D2 / 2"-C1

Just when you thought it was safe to go back to the pantomime... The Goodies — Tim Brooke-Taylor, Graeme Garden and Bill Oddie — bring you Snow White 2.

Choreography by Ali Minto; designed by James Dillon.

With Richard Briers (Narrator), David Rappaport (Chief Dwarf), Annette Lyons (Snow White), Syd Wright, Kenny Baker, Peter Burroughs, George Claydon, Mike Cottrel, Malcolm Dixon, Mike Edmonds, Tony Friel, John Ghavan, Rusty Goffe, Jacki Barron, Caroline Dillon, Jane Faith, Carol Forbes, Jackie Hall, Nola Haynes, Chrissie Kendall, Chrissie Monk, Wanda Rokicki, Jane Winchester.

GOODNESS GRACIOUS ME

A BBC Birmingham production for BBC 2. Transmission details are for BBC 2. Duration varies - see below for details.

Main regular cast: Meera Syal, Sanjeev Bhaskar, Nina Wadia, Kulvinder Ghir.

SERIES 2

Main regular credit(s): Written by Sharat Sardana, Richard Pinto, Sanjeev Bhaskar and Meera Syal; designed by Gina Parr; executive producer Jon Plowman; produced by Anil Gupta; directed by Nick Wood.

Holding / Source
DB / DBS

23.12.1998 Christmas Special
Duration: 44 minutes.
Additional material by Anil Gupta and Sanjeev Kohli; music by Richard Webb; production managers Helen Grainger and Jez Nightingale.
With Fiona Allen, Dave Lamb, Sharat Sardana.

GOODWILL TO ALL MEN

A Thames Television production. Transmission details are for the Yorkshire Television region. Duration: 25 minutes.

In the seaside town of Deal, in Kent, the mining community is preparing for Christmas. But how will it be this year? The miners' strike is now in its ninth month and the programme shows the preparation for the celebration of the birth of Christ through the eyes of a miner and his family and through the eyes of the clergy for whom the strike has posed a moral dilemma.

Research Lesley Hilton; executive producer Catherine Freeman; produced by Nina Burr; directed by David Bellamy.

Holding / Source
24.12.1984   1" / 1"

THE GRAHAM NORTON SHOW

A So Television production for Various BBC Channels. Transmission details are for Various BBC Channels. Duration varies - see below for details.

Main regular credit(s): Theme music by Trellis; series producer Jon Magnusson; directed by Steve Smith.
Main regular performer(s): Graham Norton (Host).

SERIES 2

Transmission details are for BBC 2. Duration: 30 minutes.

Holding / Source
DB / DBSW

26.12.2007 The Graham Norton Christmas Show
With Lorraine Kelly, Barbara Windsor, Russell Brand, Christopher Biggins, The Feeling, Bob Stromberg.

SERIES 4

Transmission details are for BBC 2.
Main regular credit(s): Written by Rob Colley and Dan Gaster; script supervisor Lisa Anderson; designed by Chris Webster; executive producer Graham Stuart; head of production Rebecca Cotterill; production manager Catherine Strauss.

Holding / Source
DB / DBSW

30.12.2008 The Graham Norton Holiday Show
Duration: 60 minutes.
With Joe Swash, Michael McIntyre, Tim Minchin, Boyzone.

SERIES 6

Transmission details are for BBC 1.
Main regular credit(s): Written by Rob Colley, Kevin Day and Dan Gaster; script supervisor Lisa Anderson; titles by Jump Design; art director Andrea Simpson; designed by Chris Webster; assistant producers Russell Balkind, Liz Bunnell and Anna Coane; executive producer Graham Stuart; head of production Rebecca Cotterill; production manager Catherine Strauss.

Holding / Source
DB / DBSW

31.12.2009 New Year's Eve Show
Duration: 65 minutes.
With Sarah Jessica Parker, Dominic West, Joan Rivers, Sharleen Spiteri, JEdward.

SERIES 8

Transmission details are for BBC 1.
Main regular credit(s): Script supervisor Lisa Anderson; titles by Jump; art director Andrea Simpson; designed by Chris Webster; assistant producers Rina Dayalji, Pete Snell and Alan Thorpe; executive producer Graham Stuart; head of production Rebecca Cotterill; line producer Catherine Strauss.

Holding / Source
HD/DB / HDC

31.12.2010 The Graham Norton New Year's Eve Show
Duration: 60 minutes.
Written by Rob Colley and Dan Gaster.
With Louis Walsh, Alan Davies, Elizabeth McGovern, Eliza Doolittle.

SERIES 10

Transmission details are for BBC 1. Duration: 45 minutes.
Main regular credit(s): Written by Rob Colley, Dan Gaster and Jez Stevenson; designed by Chris Webster; executive producer Graham Stuart.

Holding / Source
HD/DB / HDC

23.12.2011 Christmas Special
With Gillian Anderson, Matt Smith, Russell Kane, Hilary Devey, Harry Judd, Dougie Poynter, The Military Wives Choir.

THE GRAHAM NORTON SHOW (continued)

	Holding / Source
31.12.2012 **New Year's Eve Special**	HD/DB / HDC

Duration: 65 minutes.

With Tom Cruise, Hugh Jackman, Billy Crystal, Paul Hollywood, Mary Berry, John Bishop, Pink.

	Holding / Source
31.12.2013 **New Year's Eve Special**	HD/DB / HDC

Duration: 60 minutes.

With Jackie Collins, John Cleese, Frank Skinner, Terry Jones, Michael Palin, Joan Collins, Michael Bublé.

GRANADA REPORTS

A Granada production. Transmission details are for the Granada region. Duration: 25 minutes.

	Production No	Holding / Source
31.12.1980	1/0917/0828	DB / Live
30.12.1982 **Christmas 1940**	1/0917/1320	DB / Live

GRANDPA IN MY POCKET

An Adastra Creative Ltd production for CBeebies. made in association with Finance Wales. Transmission details are for BBC 1. Duration: 15 minutes.

Main regular credit(s): Created by Mellie Buse and Jan Page; written by Mellie Buse and Jan Page; script supervisor Rhian Owen; music by Kate Edgar and Matthew Dilley; director of photography Dave Evans; art director Gerwyn Lloyd; designed by Ash Wilkinson and Phil Williams; executive producers Sarah Colclough and Angus Fletcher; produced by Mellie Buse and Jan Page; directed by Richard Bradley.

Main regular cast: James Bolam (Grandpa), Jay Ruckley (Jason).

	Holding / Source
26.12.2010	HD/DB / HD/DB

Alternative transmissions: CBeebies: 20.12.2010.

Shown previously on CBeebies.

GRANGE HILL

A BBC production for BBC 1. Transmission details are for BBC 1. Duration: 30 minutes.

Main regular credit(s): Devised by Phil Redmond.

SERIES 4

	Holding / Source
28.12.1981 **Christmas Special**	DB-D3 / C1

Duration: 24 minutes.

Written by Phil Redmond; based on an idea by Paul Manning; designed by Alan Anson; assistant producer Alan Mills; production manager Tony Ravenscraig; produced by Susi Hush; directed by Hugh David.

With Michael Cronin (Mr Baxter), Lucinda Gane (Miss Teri Mooney), Robert Hartley (Mr Keating), Gwyneth Powell (Mrs Bridget McClusky), James Wynn (Mr Graham Sutcliffe), Tommy Winward (Bus Driver), Rene Alperstein (Pamela Cartwright), George Armstrong (Alan Humphries), Lyndy Brill (Cathy Hargreaves), Todd Carty (Tucker Jenkins), Mark Eadie (Andrew Stanton), Vincent Hall (Michael Doyle), Michelle Herbert (Trisha Yates), Paul McCarthy (Tommy Watson), Robert Craig-Morgan (Justin Bennett), Terry Sue Patt (Benny Green), Neil Rogers (Robo), Linda Slater (Susi McMahon), Graham Fletcher Cook (Brookdale Boy), David Nunn (Brookdale Boy), Paul Manning (Brookdale Boy), Tony London (Grange Hill Boy), Miles Ross (Roger), Helen Titmus (Grange Hill Girl).

SERIES 8

Main regular credit(s): Script editor Anthony Minghella; assistant producer David Leonard; produced by Ben Rea.

	Holding / Source
27.12.1985 **Grange Hill For Christmas**	DB-D3 / 1"

Written by Phil Redmond; script editors Anthony Minghella and Norma Flint; production associate David Leonard; produced by Ronald Smedley; directed by John Smith.

With Michael Cronin (Mr Baxter), Michael Sheard (Mr Bronson), Gwyneth Powell (Mrs McClusky), Karen Ford (Miss Booth), George A. Cooper (Mr Griffiths), Nicholas Donnelly (Mr McKenzie), Simon Haywood (Mr Smart), Mike Savage (Mr Browning), Deirdre Costello (Mrs Donnington), Paula Ann Bland (Claire Scott), Mark Burdis (Stewpot Stewart), Mark Savage (Gripper Stebson), Erkan Mustafa (Roland Browning), Tim Polley (Banksie), Simone Nylander (Janet St. Clair), Lee Macdonald (Zammo McGuire), Alison Bettles (Fay Lucas), Melissa Wilks (Jackie Wright), Lisa York (Julie Marchant), John Holmes (Gonch), Bradley Sheppard (Hollo), Simone Hyams (Calley Donnington), Tina Mahon (Ronnie), Fleur Taylor (Imelda), Ruth Carraway (Helen), John Drummond (Trevor Cleaver), John Alford (Robbie Wright), Steve George (Vince Savage), Joann Kenny (Jane Bishop), Sandon Sorrel (Harriet The Donkey), Clair Kavanagh, Stephen Mullen, Mid-Herts Brass Ensemble.

THE GRANVILLE MELODRAMAS

An Associated-Rediffusion production. Transmission details are for Associated-Rediffusion. Duration: 25 minutes.

Adapted by Juan Cortez; produced by Maurice Browning; directed by Cyril Butcher.

	Holding / Source
20.12.1955 **Puss In Boots**	J / Live

Based on a play by J. R. Planche; music by Peter Moffatt and Ruth Pearl; choreography by Bert Stimmel; designed by Henry Federer.

With Helen Shingler (Ralph), Thane Bettany (Robin), Ian Scott (Richard), Hattie Jacques (Fairy Felina), John Bailey (Puss), Kenneth Gilbert (Baron Bagshot), Erik Chitty (King Pumpkin), Victoria Grayson (Princess Rosebud), Ian Scott (Kitchenstuff), George Cross (Ogre), Bert Stimmel (Harlequin), Mavis Traill (Columbine), Brian Todd, Frank Coda, Daphne Abbott.

GREAT BIG GROOVY HORSE

A BBC Children's Department production for BBC 2. Transmission details are for BBC 2. Duration: 50 minutes.

A rock musical romp through the legend of the wooden horse of Troy in a version specially written for BBC2.

Written by Simone Bloom and Arnold Shaw; music directed by Jonathan Cohen; choreography by Irving Davies; designed by Judy Porter; produced and directed by Paul Ciani.

Bernard Cribbins (The Storyteller), Paul Jones (Menelaus), Patricia Hodge, Richard Owens, Nigel Williams, Julie Covington, Richard Bartlett, Miquel Brown, Kim Goody, Michael Howe, Derek James, Julian Littman, Michael Staniforth, Caroline Villiers, Maynard Williams.

	VT Number	Holding / Source
25.12.1975	LCH2612S	DB-D3 / 2"

THE GREAT BRITISH POP MACHINE

A Zenith North production for Granada. made in association with Picture Music International. Transmission details are for the Granada region. Duration: 51 minutes.

Executive producer Andrea Wonfor; produced by Briony Cranstoun; directed by Gordon Elsbury.

Dawn French (Presenter), Jennifer Saunders (Presenter), Bros, Kim Wilde, Erasure, Bananarama, Eurythmics, Wet Wet Wet, Joe Elliott, Brother Beyond, Yazz.

	Holding / Source
25.12.1988	1" / 1"

THE GREATEST EVER CARRY ON FILMS

Commissioned by Channel 5. Transmission details are for Channel 5. Duration: 48 minutes.

The nation's favourite 'Carry On' films.

Produced and directed by Richard Mortimer.

	Holding / Source
27.12.2011	DB / DBSW

THE GREATEST MUSIC PARTY IN THE WORLD

A BBC production for BBC 1. Transmission details are for BBC 1. Duration: 90 minutes.

	Holding / Source
26.12.1995	DB-D3 / D3S

With David Bowie, Rod Stewart, Diana Ross, Soul II Soul, Lightning Seeds, Des'ree, Echobelly, Alanis Morissette, Alanah Myles, Curtis Stigers, Diana King.

| 27.12.1995 | DB-D3 / D3S |

With East 17, Eternal, Shaggy, Michelle Gayle, D:Ream, Boyzone, Ultimate Kaos, MN8.

THE GREATEST STORE IN THE WORLD

A BBC Children's Department production for BBC 1. Transmission details are for BBC 1. Duration: 75 minutes.

Written by Alex Shearer; produced by Gillian Gordon; directed by Jane Prowse.

Dervla Kirwan (Geraldine), Elizabeth Earl (Livvy), Holly Earl (Angeline), Peter Capaldi (Mr Whiskers), Ricky Tomlinson (Santa), Sean Hughes (Elf), Brian Blessed (Mr Scottley), Helen Schlesinger (Miss Greystone), Amanda Symonds (Woman Police Constable Mathley), Philip Wright (Mr Norris), Kelly Knatchbull (Scrooge), S Club 7.

	Holding / Source
24.12.1999	DB / V1SW

THE GREEN GREEN GRASS

A Shazam Productions production for BBC 1. Transmission details are for BBC 1. Duration varies - see below for details.

Main regular credit(s): Created by John Sullivan; music by Graham Jarvis.

Main regular cast: John Challis (Boycie), Sue Holderness (Marlene), Jack Doolan (Tyler), David Ross (Elgin).

SERIES 1

Main regular credit(s): Written by John Sullivan; script supervisor Ellie Gleave; executive producer Tim Hancock; produced by Gareth Gwenlan; directed by Tony Dow.

	Holding / Source
25.12.2005 **One Flew Over The Cuckoo Clock**	DB / DBSW

Duration: 50 minutes.

With Roy Heather (Sid), Roy Marsden (Danny Driscoll), Christopher Ryan (Tony Driscoll), Ivan Kaye (Bryan), Ella Kenion (Mrs Cakeworthy), Peter Heppelthwaite (Jed), Alan David (Llewellyn), Lisa Diveney (Beth), Sara Crowe, Liz Robertson, Roger Alborough, Matthew Marsh, Jamie Deeks, Fiona Bruce, Nick Ross.

SERIES 2

Main regular credit(s): Script supervisor Bernadette Darnell; associate producer Paul Alexander; executive producer Tim Hancock; series producer Gareth Gwenlan; produced by Julian Meers; directed by Dewi Humphreys.

Main regular cast: With Ivan Kaye (Bryan), Ella Kenion (Mrs Cakeworthy), Peter Heppelthwaite (Jed).

	Holding / Source
25.12.2006 **From Here To Paternity**	DB / DBSW

Duration: 45 minutes.

Written by John Sullivan.

With Alan David (Llewellyn), Lisa Diveney (Beth), Nigel Harrison, Sue Freeman, Neville Dean, Kevin Hoole, Paul Bown.

THE GREEN GREEN GRASS (continued)

SERIES 3
Main regular credit(s): Script associate Paul Alexander; script supervisor Bernadette Darnell; designed by David Hitchcock; executive producer John Sullivan; produced by Gareth Gwenlan and Henry Klejdys.

Main regular cast: With Ivan Kaye (Bryan), Ella Kenion (Mrs Cakeworthy), Peter Heppelthwaite (Jed).

Holding / Source

30.12.2007 **The Special Relationship** — HD/DB / HDC
Duration: 40 minutes.
Written by John Sullivan and Keith R. Lindsay; directed by Dewi Humphreys.
With Lisa Diveney (Beth), Alan David, Paul Bown, George Wendt.

See also: ONLY FOOLS AND HORSES.... (BBC)

GREEN WING

A Talkback production for Channel 4. Transmission details are for Channel 4.

Main regular credit(s): Created by Victoria Pile; devised by Victoria Pile; written by Robert Harley, James Henry, Gary Howe, Stuart Kenworthy, Oriane Messina, Victoria Pile, Richard Preddy and Fay Rusling; script supervisor Lesley Williamson; music by Trellis; executive producer Peter Fincham; produced by Victoria Pile.

Main regular cast: Sarah Alexander (Doctor Angela Hunter), Sally Bretton (Kim Alabaster), Oliver Chris (Boyce), Olivia Colman (Harriet Schulenburg), Michelle Gomez (Sue White), Tamsin Greig (Doctor Caroline Todd), Pippa Haywood (Joanna Clore), Mark Heap (Doctor Alan Statham), Katie Lyons (Naughty Rachel), Stephen Mangan (Doctor Guillaume Secretan), Lucinda Raikes (Karen Ball), Julian Rhind-Tutt (Doctor Macartney), Karl Theobald (Doctor Martin Dear).

SERIES 2
Main regular credit(s): Directed by Dominic Brigstocke and Tristram Shapeero.

Holding / Source

04.01.2007 **GREEN WING SPECIAL** — DB / DBSWF
Duration: 90 minutes.
With Robert Harley, Richard Freeman, Cavan Clerkin, Spencer McLaren, Simon Kunz, Yvonne D'Alpra, Derren Litten, Jeremy Sheffield.

THE GROVE FAMILY

A BBC production. Transmission details are for BBC. Duration varies - see below for details.

Main regular credit(s): Theme music by Eric Spear.

SERIES 1
Duration: 20 minutes.
Main regular credit(s): Written by Michael Pertwee and Roland Pertwee; produced by John Warrington.

Holding / Source

24.12.1954 **Christmas Eve** — J / Live
Directed by John Warrington.
With Edward Evans (Mr Grove), Ruth Dunning (Mrs Grove), Sheila Sweet (Pat), Peter Bryant (Jack), Margaret Downs (Daphne), Christopher Beeny (Lennie), Nancy Roberts (Gran), Spencer Hale, Petra Davies.

31.12.1954 **New Year's Eve** — J / Live
Directed by John Warrington.
With Edward Evans (Mr Grove), Ruth Dunning (Mrs Grove), Sheila Sweet (Pat), Peter Bryant (Jack), Margaret Downs (Daphne), Christopher Beeny (Lennie), Nancy Roberts (Gran), Jon Farrell, Viola Keats, Nan Braunton, Ian Fleming, Marjorie Manning, Marguerite Young, Philip Howard.

SERIES 2
Duration: 30 minutes.
Main regular credit(s): Written by Michael Pertwee and Roland Pertwee; produced by John Warrington.

Holding / Source

14.12.1955 **The Christmas Card** — J / Live
Directed by Richard West.
With Edward Evans (Mr Grove), Ruth Dunning (Mrs Grove), Margaret Downs (Daphne), Christopher Beeny (Lennie), Nancy Roberts (Gran), Nan Braunton (Miss Jones), Donald Finlay, Shirley Watson.

A feature film version entitled, "It's A Great Day", was released in 1956 by Grove/Butcher's Film Service. Directed by John Warrington, it starred Ruth Dunning, Edward Evans, Sidney James, Vera Day, Sheila Sweet, Peter Bryant, Nancy Roberts, Margaret Downs, Christopher Beeny, Victor Maddern, John Stuart and Marjorie Rhodes. 71 mins, B3.

THE GRUFFALO

An Orange Eyes Production production for Magic Light Pictures. made in association with Studio Soi. Transmission details are for BBC 1. Duration: 30 minutes.
Adapted by Julia Donaldson, Jakob Schuh and Max Lang; based on a book by Julia Donaldson and Axel Scheffler; music by René Aubry and Terry Davies; designed by Man Arenas; associate producer Daryl Shute; production manager Sabrina Schmid; co-produced by Carsten Bunte.
Helena Bonham Carter (Mother Squirrel), James Corden (Mouse), Tom Wilkinson (Fox), John Hurt (Owl), Rob Brydon (Snake), Robbie Coltrane (Gruffalo), Sam Lewis (First Little Squirrel), Phoebe Givron-Taylor (Second Little Squirrel).

Holding / Source

25.12.2009 — HD/DB / HD/DB
Animated film.

THE GRUFFALO'S CHILD

An Orange Eyes Production production for Magic Light Pictures. Transmission details are for BBC 1. Duration: 30 minutes.

Despite the Gruffalo's cautionary tales of the big, bad mouse, his brave daughter sets off in search of this scary creature.

Based on characters created by Julia Donaldson and Axel Scheffler; produced by Michael Rose and Martin Pope; directed by Johannes Welland and Uwe Heidschotter.

James Corden (Mouse), Tom Wilkinson (Fox), John Hurt (Owl), Robbie Coltrane (Gruffalo).

	Holding / Source
25.12.2011	HD/DB / HDC

Animated film.

THE GRUMBLEWEEDS RADIO SHOW

A Granada production. Transmission details are for the Central region. Usual duration: 25 minutes.

| Main regular credit(s): | Produced by John Hamp. |
| Main regular cast: | The Grumbleweeds. |

SERIES 1
| Main regular credit(s): | Designed by David Buxton; directed by David Liddiment. |
| Main regular cast: | With The Grumblegirls, Sally Wilde, Tracey Dixon, Mandy Montgomery. |

		Production No	Holding / Source
21.12.1984	**Christmas Special**	P1241/8	1" / 1"
28.12.1984	**New Year**	P1241/9	1" / 1"

SERIES 3
| Main regular credit(s): | Designed by David Buxton; directed by David Liddiment. |
| Main regular cast: | With Sally Wilde, The Grumblegirls, Tracey Dixon, Mandy Montgomery. |

		Production No	Holding / Source
27.12.1985	**Christmas Special**	P1241/24	1" / 1"

SERIES 4: The Grumbleweeds Show:
| Main regular credit(s): | Designed by David Buxton; directed by Dave Warwick and Noel D. Greene. |
| Main regular cast: | With The Grumblegirls, Tracey Dixon, Mandy Montgomery, Sally Wilde. |

	Holding / Source
28.12.1986	1" / 1"

GRUMPY GUIDE TO....

A BBC production for BBC 2. Transmission details are for BBC 2.

	Holding / Source
23.12.2009 **Christmas**	HD/DB / HDC

Duration: 60 minutes.

A chorus of celebrity Scrooges present their humorous grievances. There's John Thomson, who confuses his parents with anonymous Christmas cards, while Neil Morrissey would rather lock himself in the loo with a portable TV for the duration.

Produced and directed by Pip Banyard.

With Neil Morrissey, Ozzy Osbourne, Ronni Ancona, Al Murray, John Thomson.

A GUID NEW YEAR FROM GLASGOW

A Scottish Television production. Transmission details are for the Scottish Television region. Duration: 35 minutes.

Written by John Watson; produced by Rai Purdy; directed by Gordon Arnold, Lorne Freed and James Sutherland.

The Glasgow Phoenix Choir, The Inverscotia Singers, The Country Dancers, Mike and Bernie Winters, Desmond Lane, Jack House, Larry Marshall, Bobby McLeod and his Band, Jimmy Blair and his Orchestra.

	Holding / Source
31.12.1957	R1 / Live

H.M.S. PARADISE

A Rediffusion Television production. Transmission details are for the ATV midlands region. Duration: 25 minutes.

Main regular credit(s): Music by Malcolm Lockyer.

Main regular cast: With Frank Thornton (Commander Fairweather), Richard Caldicot (Captain Turvey), Robin Hunter (Lieutenant Pouter), Ronald Radd (Chief Petty Officer Banyard), Angus Lennie (Able Seaman Murdoch), Priscilla Morgan (Amanda).

	Holding / Source
##.##.#### **This Side Up - Use No Hooks**	J / 40

Alt.Title(s): *New Year's Eve*
Alternative transmissions: Rediffusion Television: 31.12.1964.
To help Able Seaman Murdoch get home for Hogmanay the island draft have to box exceedingly clever.
Written by Maurice Wiltshire; designed by Frank Gillman; produced by Sid Colin; directed by Ronald Marriott.
With No guest cast.

H.M.S. PINAFORE

An ATV production. Transmission details are for the ATV midlands region. Duration: 90 minutes.

Written by W. S. Gilbert and Arthur Sullivan; designed by Paul Dean Fortune; associate producer Peter Harris; produced and directed by John Sichel.

John Reed (Sir Joseph Porter), Michael Rayner (Captain Corcoran), Malcolm Williams (Ralph Rackstraw), John Ayldon (Dick Deadeye), Pamela Field (Josephine), Lyndsie Holland (Buttercup), Pauline Wales (Hebe), Jon Ellison (Bill Bobstay), John Broad (Bob Neckett), D'Oyly Carte Opera Company.

	Holding / Source
26.12.1973	DB / 2"

Opera.

HALE AND PACE

An LWT production. Transmission details are for the Central region. Duration varies - see below for details.

Main regular cast: Gareth Hale (Host), Norman Pace (Host).

Commissioned by Channel 4. Transmission details are for Channel 4.

	Holding / Source
20.12.1986 **The Hale And Pace Christmas Extravaganza**	D2 / 1"

Duration: 52 minutes.
Written by Geoff Atkinson, Hale and Pace and Kim Fuller; programme associate Sean Murphy; additional material by Terry Morrison; music directed by Ray Monk; designed by Alison Humphries; associate producer Kim Fuller; production manager Myra Hersh; produced by Marcus Plantin; directed by Vic Finch.
With Status Quo, Courtney Pine, Harry Enfield, Helen Atkinson Wood, Doon Mackichan, Jim Davidson, Tony Adams, Kit Hollerbach.

SERIES 6

Main regular credit(s): Script associate Richard Parker; music directed by Andy Street; choreography by Nicky Hinkley; designed by Robert Day.

	Holding / Source
26.12.1993 **The Business**	D2 / D2S

Duration: 51 minutes.
Written by Hale and Pace, Carson and Tomlinson, Lang and Greenall, Richard Parker, Laurie Rowley and Clive Whichelow; additional material by Les Anderson, David Kind, Caroline Marshall, Alistair Newton, Lee Russ and Ian Sainsbury; script editors Sean Carson, David Tomlinson and Laurie Rowley; designed by Robert Day, Margaret Howat and Alison Humphries; production managers Alan Sandbrook and Julia Weedon; produced by Alan Nixon and David G. Hillier; directed by David G. Hillier.
With Marilyn Cutts, Amanda Drewry, Maggie Henderson, Nigel Humphreys, Melanie Kilburn, Andy Linden, Sarah Milo, Anna Nicholas, Caroline Quentin, David Quilter, Andrew Sinclair.

	Holding / Source
29.12.1996 **Hale And Pace Down Under**	D2 / D2S

Duration: 51 minutes.
Written by Hale and Pace and Richard Parker; additional material by Bennett Aaron and Terry Morrison; script editor Richard Parker; music directed by Simon Webb; designed by Mike Oxley; executive producer Nigel Lythgoe; production managers Keith Lascelles and Peter Dudkin; produced by Mark Robson; directed by Nigel Lythgoe.
With Dieter Brummer, Merv Hughes [as Mervyn Hughes], Russell Gilbert, Jason Montgomery, Sandy Winton, Pete Beckett, Mick Mullins, Sonia Jones, Shaun Choolburra.

	Holding / Source
20.12.1998 **Ten Years Hard**	DB / D2S

Duration: 51 minutes.
Written by Hale and Pace; series script editors Laurie Rowley, Sean Carson and David Tomlinson; script editor Richard Parker; executive producer Humphrey Barclay; series producers Alan Nixon and David G. Hillier; produced by Mark Robson; series directors Vic Finch, Peter Orton and David G. Hillier; directed by Ian Hamilton.
A mixture of previously-used clips and new interviews/material with Hale and Pace.

HALLELUJAH IT'S CHRISTMAS!

A Thames Television production. Transmission details are for the Thames Television region. Duration: 25 minutes.

Devised by Roger Whittaker; written by Roger Whittaker; research Anthony Stancomb; produced by Mavis Airey and Margery Baker; directed by Margery Baker.
Roger Whittaker, Hollyfield School, Surbiton, Saffron.

	VT Number	Holding / Source
25.12.1975	12019	DB / 2"

HALLELUJAH IT'S CHRISTMAS! (continued)

HALLELUJAH!

A Yorkshire Television production. Transmission details are for the Central region. Duration: 25 minutes.

Main regular credit(s): Written by Dick Sharples; theme music by The James Shepherd Versatile Brass; conducted by Robert Hartley; produced and directed by Ronnie Baxter.

Main regular cast: Thora Hird (Captain Emily Ridley).

SERIES 2

Main regular credit(s): Graphics by Tony Sharpe.

Main regular cast: With Patsy Rowlands (Alice Meredith), David Daker (Brother Benjamin).

Holding / Source

21.12.1984 **A Goose for Mrs Scratchit**   1" / 1"

Costume Anne Weatherill; make-up Margaret Jackson; music by Alan Hawkshaw; lighting by Brian Hilton; sound Jim Andrew and Glyn Edwards; camera supervisors Doug Neale and Phil Knockton; designed by Peter Caldwell and Kirsten Dudley.

With Bryan Pringle, Joan Sims, Geoffrey Bayldon, Martin Pitman, Carly Roberts.

HANCOCK'S HALF HOUR

A BBC production. Transmission details are for BBC. Duration: 30 minutes.

Main regular credit(s): Written by Ray Galton and Alan Simpson; music by Wally Stott; produced and directed by Duncan Wood.

Main regular cast: Tony Hancock (Anthony Aloysius St John Hancock), Sidney James (Sidney Balmoral James).

SERIES 3

Main regular credit(s): Designed by George Djurkovic.

Holding / Source

23.12.1957 **Hancock's Forty-Three Minutes**   DB-R3 / Live

Duration: 44 minutes.

With John Gregson, The Keynotes, Max Geldray, John Vere, Dido The Chimp, John Vyvyan, Mario Fabrizi, Dawn White, The Glamazons, Sylvestri, Dennis Chinnery.

SERIES 4

Holding / Source

26.12.1958 **Ericson The Viking**   DB-R3 / R3

With John Vere, Pat Coombs, Laurie Webb, Ivor Raymonde, Mario Fabrizi, Anthony Shirvell, John Vyvyan, Arthur Mullard, Manville Tarrant, Alec Bregonzi, Philip Carr.

See also: HANCOCK'S HALF HOUR (RADIO) (BBC)

HANCOCK'S HALF HOUR (RADIO)

A BBC production for BBC Light Programme. Transmission details are for BBC Light Programme. Duration: 30 minutes.

Main regular credit(s): Written by Ray Galton and Alan Simpson.

Main regular cast: Tony Hancock (Himself).

SERIES 1

Holding / Source

21.12.1954 **Christmas at Aldershot**   J /

28.12.1954 **The Christmas Eve Party**   J /

SERIES 3

Holding / Source

21.12.1955 **The Trial of Father Christmas**   DA /

04.01.1956 **New Year Resolutions**   DASEQ /

SERIES 4

Holding / Source

23.12.1956 **Hancock's Happy Christmas**   DA /

Holding / Source

25.12.1958 **Bill And Father Christmas**   DA /

SERIES 6

Holding / Source

22.12.1959 **The Christmas Club**   DA /

See also: HANCOCK'S HALF HOUR (BBC)

THE HAPPENING

A Noel Gay Television production for BSB Galaxy. Transmission details are for BSB Galaxy. Duration: 90 minutes.

SERIES 2

Transmission details are for Sky One.

Holding / Source

22.12.1990   DV / 1"

With Bob Downe (Host), Alan Davies, Chris Lynam, Owen O'Neill, Cantabile, Brian Connolly's Sweet, Sound of The Supremes.

THE HAPPENING

British Christmas Television Guide | **THE HAPPENING (continued)**

The Xmas Show 18/12/90 Studio 9
This is a full timecoded recording of the edition of THE HAPPENING recorded on 1.12.90. The clock at the start states that it is show 2.14, its code is NGTV1186 and the production number PN00016620. There's a horizontal hold problem to begin with which eventually settles. Bob Downe hosts with guests including Alan Davies (a very early example of his stand up), Chris Lynam, Owen O'Neill, Cantabile, Brian Connolly's Sweet and the Sound of the Supremes.There is also 31mins timecoded copy of the rushes for a video insert used to open THE HAPPENING Xmas Show recorded on 1.12.90.

HAPPY CHRISTMAS

A TWW production. Transmission details are for Associated-Rediffusion. Duration: 25 minutes.
Music directed by Norman Whitehead; designed by Alan Pleass; produced and directed by Christopher Mercer.
Ivor Emmanuel, Pontcanna Children's Choir.

	Holding / Source
25.12.1959	J /

HAPPY CHRISTMAS - I LOVE YOU

A BBC production for BBC 1. Transmission details are for BBC 1. Duration: 40 minutes.

It is Christmas Eve. Bruce and Renee speak to us from the appropriate corners of their home and we discover that, after 23 years of marriage, they know absolutely nothing about each other.

Written by Carla Lane; produced by Fiona Finlay; directed by Guy Slater.

Michael Williams (Bruce Naylor), Gwen Taylor (Renee Naylor).

	Holding / Source
21.12.1989	DB / 1"

HAPPY EVER AFTER

A BBC production for BBC 1. Transmission details are for BBC 1. Duration: 30 minutes.

Main regular credit(s):   Theme music by Ronnie Hazlehurst.
Main regular cast: Terry Scott (Terry Fletcher), June Whitfield (June Fletcher).

SERIES 3
Main regular credit(s):   Written by John Chapman and Eric Merriman.
Main regular cast: With Beryl Cooke (Aunt Lucy).

	Holding / Source
23.12.1976 **Christmas Special**	DB-D3 / 2"

Designed by Richard Morris; executive producer Peter Whitmore; produced and directed by Ray Butt.
With Caroline Whitaker, Pippa Page, Tracy Plant, Kathleen Barnett, Simon Beal.

SERIES 4
Main regular credit(s):   Produced by Peter Whitmore.
Main regular cast: With Beryl Cooke (Aunt Lucy).

	Holding / Source
23.12.1977 **Christmas Special**	DB-D3 / 2"

Written by Eric Merriman and Christopher Bond; directed by Bill Wilson.
With Joyce Carey, Anthony Woodruff, Caroline Whitaker, Pippa Page.
See also: TERRY AND JUNE (BBC)

HAPPY NEW YEAR

A BBC Religious Department production for BBC 1. Transmission details are for BBC 1. Duration varies - see below for details.

	Holding / Source
31.12.1990	DB / 1"

Duration: 10 minutes.
With Archbishop Robert Runcie.

01.01.1994	D3 / LivePAL

Duration: 5 minutes.
With Archbishop Doctor George Carey.

A HAPPY NEW YEAR

A BBC Scotland production for BBC 1. Transmission details are for BBC 1. Duration: 49 minutes.
Join BBC Scotland to welcome 1981.
Music associate David Pringle; lighting by David Ogle; sound Ron Allen; designed by Campbell Gordon; produced and directed by Anne Somers.
Iain Cuthbertson, Peter Morrison, Anne Lorne Gillies, Alastair McDonald, Russell Hunter, Norman McLean, Silly Wizard, The Sandra Adams Dancers, The Jim Johnstone Scottish Country Dance Band, British Caledonian Pipe Band, Brian Fahey and The Scottish Radio Orchestra.

	Holding / Source
01.01.1981	

HAPPY SOUNDS

A Tyne Tees Television production. Transmission details are for the ATV midlands region. Duration: 25 minutes.

Designed by Eric Briers; produced by Christopher Palmer; directed by Tony Kysh.

Ray Fell (Presenter), Bryan Burdon (Presenter), Julie Rogers, The Ken Maddison Trio.

	Holding / Source
27.12.1971	DB / 2"

Alternative transmissions: Tyne Tees Television: 26.12.1971.
With Ray Fell, Julie Rogers.

HARK NOW HEAR THE ANGELS SING

A Thames Television production. Transmission details are for the Thames Television region. Duration: 25 minutes.

A journey in Christmas song along the banks of the mighty River Thames, sung by the choir of St. Richards with St. Andrews Church of England Primary School, Ham, Richmond, Surrey.

Orchestra conducted by Alan H. Dudenay; produced by Christopher Palmer.

Cindy Kent, John Fyffe, St Richards' Choir.

Holding / Source

24.12.1974

HARRY ENFIELD AND CHUMS

A Tiger Aspect production for BBC 1. Transmission details are for BBC 1. Usual duration: 30 minutes.

Main regular cast: Harry Enfield.

SERIES 1

Main regular credit(s):   Produced by Harry Thompson; directed by John Stroud.

	Holding / Source
16.12.1994	DB-D3 / D3S

Handy tips for Christmas presents.
With Leslie Ash, Rosemarie Ford, Paul Whitehouse, Kathy Burke.

Made in association with Pozzitive Television.

	Holding / Source
24.12.1997 **Harry Enfield And Christmas Chums**	DB-D3 / D3S

Duration: 40 minutes.

Back for a one-off special are the characters who last made their mark on the pubs and playgrounds of telly-watching land back in February. Say hello once more to Kevin the Self-Righteous Brothers, Modern Dad, Colombian footballer Julio Georgic, Cholmondley Warner and the Toddlers. But special welcome is reserved for new characters like Tim Nice-But-Dim's older sister, Tamara Nice-But-Dim and friend Tara Nice-But-Thin, whose lives are one long round of shopping and partying.

Produced and directed by Geoff Posner.

With Paul Whitehouse, Kathy Burke.

HARRY ENFIELD'S TELEVISION PROGRAMME

A Hat Trick production for BBC 2. Transmission details are for BBC 2.

Main regular cast: Harry Enfield.

	Holding / Source
24.12.1992 **Harry Enfield's Festive Television Programme**	DB-D3 / D3S

Duration: 40 minutes.

Produced by Geoffrey Perkins; directed by John Birkin and Metin Hüseyin.

With Martin Clunes, Gary Bleasdale, Kathy Burke, Paul Whitehouse, Selina Cadell, Joe McGann, Simon Bright, Steve Ismay, Leonard Kirby, Rocky Samrai, Derek Howard, David Barber, Victoria Avery, Rosemary Banks, Karen De Beaufort, Adele Silva, Carly Britnell, Laura James, Charlie Higson.

HARRY ENFIELD'S YULE LOG CHUMS

A Tiger Aspect production for BBC 1. Transmission details are for BBC 1. Duration: 38 minutes.

Executive producers Peter Bennett-Jones and Maureen McMunn; produced by Clive Tulloh; directed by Dewi Humphreys.

Harry Enfield, Brian Sewell, Kathy Burke, Paul Whitehouse, Jason Hughes.

	Holding / Source
28.12.1998	DB / DBSW

HARRY HILL

An Avalon Productions production for Channel 4. Transmission details are for Channel 4.

Main regular credit(s): Written by Harry Hill; script editor Stewart Lee; executive producers Richard Allen-Turner and Jon Thoday.
Main regular performer(s): Harry Hill.

SERIES 2
Duration: 25 minutes.
Main regular credit(s): Produced by Charlie Hanson; directed by Robin Nash.

Holding / Source
23.12.1998 Harry Hill's Christmas Sleigh Ride — DB / DBS

Music directed by John Collins; choreography by Jenny Arnold; titles by Andy Spence; puppetry by Mike Bayliss and Rebecca Nagan; art director Alex Evans; designed by Harry Banks; line producer Christopher Miles.

With Al Murray, Barrie Gosney, Burt Kwouk, Helen Patarot, Steve Bowditch, Sheila Dunn, Matt Bradstock, Ted Rogers, Acker Bilk, Angie O'Connell, Missy Mukit.

Holding / Source
23.12.1999 Harry Hill's Christmas Memory Lane Of Laughter — DB / DBS

Duration: 30 minutes.
Produced by Charlie Hanson; directed by Robin Nash.

With Burt Kwouk, Frank Skinner, Stewart Lee, Mark Thomas, Barry Cryer.

HARRY HILL'S TV BURP

An Avalon Productions production for ITV 1. Transmission details are for the Central region. Duration: 25 minutes.

Main regular credit(s): Written by Harry Hill.
Main regular cast: Harry Hill (Host).

Holding / Source
22.12.2001 [pilot] — DB / DBSW

Additional material by Andrew Collins, Paul Hawksbee and Iain Pattinson; research Jo Envori and Margaret Gordon; script supervisor Nikki Dowbiggin; costume Leah Archer; make-up Jane Walker; music by Steve Brown; edited by Mark Sangster; lighting director Rob Kitzmann [credited as Rob Kitzman]; titles by Be Animation; programme consultant Mark Tinkler; designed by Harry Banks; executive producers Richard Allen-Turner and Jon Thoday; head of production Lee Tucker; line producer Michele Lonergan; produced by Patricia McGowan; directed by Peter Orton.

With Bruce Jones, Simon Day, Alan Halsall, Barry Howard, Jennifer James, Sally Lindsay, Dave Thompson, Catherine Gee.

SERIES 6
Main regular credit(s): Music directed by Steve Brown; edited by Steve Nayler; lighting director Martin Kempton; titles by Be Animation; art director Nikki Startup; production designer Harry Banks; VT Producer Grant Philpott; executive producers Sally Debonnaire, Jon Thoday and Richard Allen-Turner; produced by Spencer Millman; directed by Peter Orton.

Holding / Source
30.12.2006 Christmas TV Burp — DB / DBSW

Programme associates Brenda Gilhooly, Paul Hawksbee, Daniel Maier and David Quantick; costume Leah Archer; make-up Vanessa White; production managers Gurjit Bilkhu and Francesca Milone.

With Jenny Éclair (Mrs Dolpin), Tony Audenshaw, Jonathan Kerrigan, Mark Jordon, Jennie McAlpine, Tricia Penrose, Wendi Peters, Glenn Ross.

SERIES 7
Main regular credit(s): Script supervisor Annie Gillott; music directed by Steve Brown; lighting director Martin Kempton; titles by Be Animation; art director Nikki Startup; designed by Harry Banks; VT Producer Grant Philpott; executive producers Jon Thoday and Richard Allen-Turner; head of production Bluey Richards; production manager Gurjit Bilkhu; produced by Spencer Millman; directed by Peter Orton.

Holding / Source
25.12.2007 Christmas TV Burp — DB / DBSW

Programme associates Brenda Gilhooly, Paul Hawksbee, Daniel Maier and David Quantick; make-up Vanessa White; edited by Steve Nayler.
With Shane MacGowan.

SERIES 8
Main regular credit(s): Programme associates Brenda Gilhooly, Paul Hawksbee, Daniel Maier and David Quantick; script supervisor Rebecca Havers; music directed by Steve Brown; designed by Harry Banks; associate producers James Johnson and Nikki Shaw; executive producers Jon Thoday and Richard Allen-Turner; head of production Bluey Richards; produced by Spencer Millman; directed by Peter Orton.

Holding / Source
26.12.2008 Harry Hill's TV Burp Review Of The Year — DB / DBSW

Programme associate Joe Burnside.
With Roland Rat, Ross Stone.

SERIES 10
Main regular credit(s): Research Laura Foskett and Claire Selim; script supervisor Annie Gillott; music directed by Steve Brown; titles by Be-Animation; art director Nikki Startup; designed by Harry Banks; associate producers James Johnson and Nikki Shaw; executive producers Jon Thoday and Richard Allen-Turner; head of production Bluey Richards; line producer Suzanne Knight; produced by Spencer Millman; directed by Peter Orton.

Holding / Source
26.12.2009 Review Of The Year — DB / DBSW

Programme associates Brenda Gilhooly, Paul Hawksbee, Daniel Maier, David Quantick, Madeleine Brettingham and Joe Burnside.
With Simon King, Steve Benham, Dave Thompson, Bob Wise.

THE HARRY SECOMBE SHOW

A BBC production for BBC 1. Transmission details are for BBC 1.

Main regular performer(s): Harry Secombe (Host).

Transmission details are for BBC 2.

	Holding / Source
25.12.1968	DB-R1 / 2"

Duration: 55 minutes.

Devised by Jimmy Grafton; written by Jimmy Grafton, Jeremy Lloyd and Gordon Clyde; music directed by Peter Knight; designed by Norman Vertigan; produced and directed by Terry Hughes.

With Ron Moody, Shani Wallis, Peggy Mount, Jack Wild, Lionel Bart, Myrna Rose, Barbara Speake Stage School, Corona Stage School, Frank and Peggy Spencer's Royston Ballroom Formation Team.

Including cast from film version of 'Oliver!'.

SERIES 4

Duration: 45 minutes.

Main regular credit(s): Programme associate Jimmy Grafton; orchestra directed by Peter Knight; designed by Peter Brachacki; produced and directed by Terry Hughes.

	Holding / Source
23.12.1972	DB-D3 / 2"

With Ann Howard, Harry Friedauer, The King's Singers.

HARTY'S CHRISTMAS PARTY

A BBC production for BBC 2. Transmission details are for BBC 2. Duration: 55 minutes.

Assistant producer George R. Clarke; executive producer Ian Squires; produced and directed by John Rooney.

Russell Harty (Presenter), Mike Harding, Ian Botham, Ivor Cutler, Brian Glover, Stuart Hall, Alex Higgins, Sue Lawley, Ken Livingstone, Edna O'Brien, Zandra Rhodes, Janet Street-Porter, Ned Sherrin, Freddie Trueman [as Fred Trueman].

	Holding / Source
24.12.1986	DB / 1"

HAUNTED

Alternative/Working Title(s): GHOST STORIES

A Granada production. Transmission details are for the ATV midlands region. Duration: 50 minutes.

Produced by Derek Granger.

	Production No	Holding / Source
23.12.1974 **The Ferryman**	P376/1	1" / C1

Alt.Title(s): *The Ferryman's Rest*

Adapted by Julian Bond; based on a story by Kingsley Amis; designed by Colin Rees; directed by John Irvin.

With Jeremy Brett (Sheridan Owen), Natasha Parry (Alex Owen), Geoffrey Chater (Miles Attingham), Lesley Dunlop (Jill Attingham), Andrew Bradford (George Partridge), Ray Mort (Fred Burge), Denise Buckley (TV Hostess), John Saunders (Bookshop Manager), Aimée Delamain (Woman in Bookshop), Elizabeth Tyrrell (Woman Journalist), John Quentin (Publisher), Bruce Boa (Man At Party), Anthony Wingate (Man At Party), Helen Rappaport (Girl At Party), Alick Hayes (Man in Estate Car), Kathy Proctor (Waitress).

	Production No	Holding / Source
30.12.1974 **Poor Girl**	FP376/2	1" / C1

Adapted by Robin Chapman; script associate Charles Sturridge; based on a story by Elizabeth Taylor; music by David Hartigan; production manager Roy Jackson; directed by Michael Apted.

With Lynne Miller (Florence Chasty), Stuart Wilson (Oliver Wilson), Angela Thorne (Louise Wilson), Matthew Pollock (Hilary Wilson), John Boxer (Corbett), Marjorie Sudell (Stoddard), Fidelma O'Dowda (Dawkins), Tommy Boyle (Williams), Desmond Perry (Mr Chasty), Joseph Berry (Vicar), Robert Swales (The Young Man), Helen Rappaport (The Young Woman).

HAUNTING HARMONY

A HTV production. made in association with Canadian Broadcasting Corporation / FUND for Pay Television / Ontario Film Development Corporation / Primedia Productions / Rogers Telefund / TV 60 Munich / ZDF Mainz. Transmission details are for the Central region. Duration: 50 minutes.

The story of a young Canadian boy, David, who is sent to an English cathedral school following his parents' separation. On arrival at the fictional Southminster Cathedral he makes an unusual schoolboy chum: unusual because he has been dead for 400 years. When David is selected to sing the solo at the Christmas service, he decides to call on the help of his ghostly friend.

Written by Fiona McHugh; script consultant Maureen Dorey; designed by Paul Laugier; production executive Derek McGillivray; executive producer Peter Murphy; produced by Jonathan Harris and Paul Sarony; directed by Alvin Rakoff.

Nathaniel Moreau (David Fabry), Jean Marc Perret (Huw Pritchard), Frank Middlemass (Priestly), Francesca Annis (Anna Fabry), Robert Jezek (Walter Fabry), Tim Wylton (Huw's Father), John Hallam (Staunton), Philip Neve (Watkins), Corinn Heliwell (Merryweather), Ben Langley (Dent), Michael Ford (McIntyre), Kitty Scopes (Tea Shop Owner), Marilyn Le Conte (Matron), Hayward Morse (Lawyer), Choir of Worcester Cathedral.

	Holding / Source
30.12.1993	1" / 1"S

HAVE A HARRY CHRISTMAS

A Yorkshire Television production. Transmission details are for the ATV midlands region. Duration: 52 minutes.

With cheery, chirpy, roly-poly ex-Goon Harry Secombe around, it's hard to visualise Christmas being anything other than happy. And that's what 'Have A Harry Christmas' is all about.

Written by Barry Cryer, Spike Mullins, Peter Vincent and Paul Robinson; music directed by Peter Knight; designed by Colin Pigott; produced and directed by Vernon Lawrence.

Harry Secombe (Host), Eric Porter, Pete Murray, David Hamilton, Tony Blackburn, Peter Brough & Archie Andrews, Terry Wogan, Catherine Howe, Gillian Lynne, Gayna Martine, Jane Darling, Clare Smalley, Heather Laurie, Jennifer Layland, Lorna Nathan, Barry Young, George May, Connel Miles, Roy Jones, Peppi Borza, Juan Sanchez, The Thurnscoe Harmonic Male Voice Choir.

	VT Number	Holding / Source
23.12.1977	2929	DB / 2"

With Tony Blackburn, Peter Murray, Terry Wogan, Eric Porter.

HAVE I GOT NEWS FOR YOU

A Hat Trick production for BBC. Transmission details are for Various BBC Channels. Usual duration: 29 minutes.

Main regular credit(s): Theme music by Big George; titles by Triffic Films.

Main regular performer(s): Ian Hislop (Team Captain).

SERIES 2

Transmission details are for BBC 2.

Main regular credit(s): Titles by Triffic Films; designed by Graeme Story and Hazel Lesniarek; executive producer Denise O'Donoghue; production manager Elaine Morris; produced by Harry Thompson; directed by John F. D. Northover.

Main regular performer(s): With Angus Deayton (Host), Paul Merton (Team Captain), Ian Hislop.

	Holding / Source
24.12.1991	1" / 1"

Duration: 44 minutes.
With Clive Anderson, Harry Enfield.

John F. D. Northover was credited as John Northover on episode 1 of this series.

SERIES 6

Transmission details are for BBC 2.

Main regular credit(s): Titles by Triffic Films; programme consultant Jimmy Mulville; designed by Jonathan Paul Green and Mikki Rain; associate producer Vincent Beasley; executive producer Mary Bell; production manager Carole De Caux; series producer Harry Thompson; produced by Colin Swash; directed by Ben Fuller.

Main regular performer(s): With Angus Deayton (Host), Paul Merton (Team Captain), Ian Hislop.

	Holding / Source
24.12.1993	D3 / D3S

With Bob Geldof, Griff Rhys Jones.

Unusually, in this programme Ian Hislop's team were seated to Angus Deayton's left and Paul Merson's to Angus's right, a reverse on the arrangement in pretty much every other edition.

SERIES 8

Transmission details are for BBC 2.

Main regular credit(s): Programme associates Mark Burton and John O'Farrell; graphics by Triffic Films; programme consultant Jimmy Mulville; designed by Jonathan Paul Green and Mikki Rain; executive producer Mary Bell; production manager Carole De Caux; series producer Harry Thompson; produced by Colin Swash; directed by John F. D. Northover.

Main regular performer(s): With Angus Deayton (Host), Paul Merton (Team Captain), Ian Hislop.

	Holding / Source
23.12.1994	D3 / D3S

With Kelvin Mackenzie, Alexei Sayle.

SERIES 12

Transmission details are for BBC 2.

Main regular credit(s): Programme associates Mark Burton, John O'Farrell and Robert Fraser Steele; graphics by Triffic Films; designed by Jonathan Paul Green and Mikki Rain; production manager Rick Wiseman; series producer Colin Swash; produced by Richard Wilson; directed by Paul Wheeler.

Main regular performer(s): With Angus Deayton (Host), Paul Merton (Team Captain), Ian Hislop.

	Holding / Source
20.12.1996 **Compilation & Outakes**	D3 / D3S

SERIES 22

Transmission details are for BBC 2.

Main regular credit(s): Graphics by Triffic Films; designed by Jonathan Paul Green and Mikki Rain; associate producers Darren Smith and Rachael Webb; head of production Laura Djanogly; production manager Charlotte Bevan; series producer Colin Swash; produced by Nick Martin; directed by Paul Wheeler.

	Holding / Source
31.12.2001 **Review Of The Year**	DB / DBSW

With James Naughtie, Andrew Marr, Jennie Bond, Dermot Murnaghan, Michael Crick, Clive Anderson, Keith Chegwin, Janet Street-Porter, Michael Grade, Gyles Brandreth, Richard Bacon, David Aaronovitch, Sara Cox, Boris Johnson, M.P., Francis Wheen, Andrew Mackinlay, Rosie Boycott, Will Self, Bill Bailey, Sean Lock, Jane Moore, Derek Draper, Rich Hall, Tracey Emin, Dom Joly, Shazia Mirza, John Humphrys.

HAVE I GOT NEWS FOR YOU (continued)

Transmission details are for BBC 1.

24.12.2008
Holding / Source: DB / DBSW

Presented by Alexander Armstrong; programme associates Mark Burton, Pete Sinclair and Colin Swash; script supervisor Jo Newey; designed by Jonathan Paul Green and Mikki Rain; assistant producers Jimmy Baker, Andy Rowan and Kate Stannard; executive producer Richard Wilson; head of production Laura Djanogly; production manager Julie Rose; series producer Nick Martin; produced by Paul McGettigan; directed by Lissa Evans.

With Frank Skinner, Noddy Holder, Brian Blessed*.

The extended version was shown two days later on 26.12.2008.

SERIES 40

Made in association with Ingenious Broadcasting. Transmission details are for BBC 1.

Main regular credit(s): Script supervisor Jo Newey; titles by Tim Searle; designed by Jonathan Paul Green and Mikki Rain; assistant producers James Pozzo, Ed Ryland and Luke Shiach; executive producer Richard Wilson; head of production Laura Djanogly; production manager Julie Rose; series producer Nick Martin; produced by Mark Barrett.

Main regular performer(s): With Paul Merton (Team Captain).

17.12.2010 Christmas Special
Holding / Source: HD/DB / HDC

Brought forward from 24.12.2010.

Presented by Alexander Armstrong; programme associates Mark Burton, Kevin Day, Ged Parsons, Giles Pilbrow, Pete Sinclair and Colin Swash; directed by Paul Wheeler.

With Micky Flanagan, Ross Noble.

24.12.2010 Seasonal Compilation
Holding / Source: HD/DB / HDC

Presented by Chris Addison, Alexander Armstrong, John Bishop, Jo Brand, Jeremy Clarkson, Martin Clunes, Benedict Cumberbatch, Bruce Forsyth, Miranda Hart, Damian Lewis, Lee Mack, John Prescott, Frank Skinner and Robert Webb; programme associates Mark Burton, Dave Cohen, Rob Colley, Kevin Day, Dan Gaster, Will Ing, Ged Parsons, Giles Pilbrow, Paul Powell, Shaun Pye, Pete Sinclair and Colin Swash; directed by Paul Wheeler and Lissa Evans.

With Penny Smith, David Threlfall, Clive Anderson, Claire Balding, Sally Bercow, James Blunt, Kevin Bridges, Marcus Brigstocke, Victoria Coren, Greg Davies, Andy Hamilton, Julia Hartley-Brewer, Richard Herring, Charlie Higson, Reginald D. Hunter, Ken Livingstone, Lembit Öpik, Jon Richardson, Nick Robinson, Janet Street-Porter.

"Have I Got A Little Bit More News For You" was the extended, 45-min re-edits with the swearing left in on BBC2, on the Saturday after.

SERIES 42

Transmission details are for BBC 1.

Main regular credit(s): Designed by Jonathan Paul Green and Mikki Rain; executive producer Richard Wilson; produced by Mark Barrett and Nick Martin; directed by Lissa Evans.

Main regular performer(s): With Paul Merton (Team Captain).

23.12.2011 Christmas Special
Holding / Source: HD/DB / HDC

Presented by Martin Clunes.

With Rebecca Front, David O'Doherty.

30.12.2011 Have I Got 2011 News For You
HD/DB / HDC

Compilation of highlights.

"Have I Got A Little Bit More News For You" was the extended, 45-min re-edits with the swearing left in.

SERIES 44

Main regular credit(s): Designed by Jonathan Paul Green and Mikki Rain; executive producer Richard Wilson; produced by Ben Wicks and Nick Martin.

Main regular performer(s): With Paul Merton (Team Captain).

21.12.2012 Christmas Special
Holding / Source: HD/DB / HDC

Programme associates Colin Swash, Ged Parsons, Dan Gaster, Kevin Day and Shaun Pye; directed by Paul Wheeler.

With Daniel Radcliffe (Presenter), Sara Cox, Andy Hamilton.

"Have I Got A Little Bit More News For You" was the extended, 45-min re-edits with the swearing left in.

SERIES 46

Performer(s): With Paul Merton (Team Captain).

20.12.2013 Have I Got News For You 2013
Holding / Source: HD/DB / HDC

A compilation of the popular news quiz that looks back at the big news stories of 2013. With team captains Paul Merton and Ian Hislop, and a variety of guest hosts and panellists.

Designed by Jonathan Paul Green and Mikki Rain; executive producers Richard Wilson and Pinki Chambers; series producers Jo Bunting and Nick Martin; produced by Ben Wicks and Jon Harvey; directed by Paul Wheeler and Lissa Evans.

HAVE YOURSELF A MERRY EIGHTIES CHRISTMAS

A BBC production for BBC 2. Transmission details are for BBC 2. Duration: 40 minutes.

A light-hearted tribute to Christmas singles of the 1980s. From Jona Lewie's Stop the Cavalry in 1980 right the way through to Do They Know It's Christmas by Band Aid 2, this is the story of the decade when everyone dreamed a seasonal smash. David Bowie and Bing Crosby formed an unlikely duo to bring Peace on Earth, Fatboy Slim could be seen singing an acappella version of Caravan Love. and the Pretenders, Bruce Springsteen and even Run DMC got caught up in the Christmas rush.

Produced and directed by Garry Hughes.

	Holding / Source
24.12.2002	DB / DBSW

HAY FEVER

A BBC production for BBC 2. Transmission details are for BBC 2. Duration: 95 minutes.

Written by Noël Coward; designed by Cecilia Brereton; produced and directed by Cedric Messina.

Penelope Keith (Judith Bliss), Paul Eddington (David Bliss), Patricia Hodge (Myra Arundel), Benjamin Whitrow (Richard Greatham), Joan Sims (Clara), Phoebe Nicholls (Sorel Bliss), Susan Wooldridge (Jackie Coryton), Michael Cochrane (Sandy Tyrell), Michael Siberry (Simon Bliss).

	Holding / Source
26.12.1984	DB / 1"

HE THAT SHOULD COME

A BBC production. Transmission details are for BBC. Duration: 60 minutes.

Written by Dorothy L. Sayers; music composed by Robert Chignell; music played by Ann Ross; settings by Stephen Bundy; play production by Douglas Allen.

Oliver Burt (Caspar), Geoffrey Dunn (Melchior), Glyn Lawson (Balthazar), Maurice Bannister (Merchant), Christopher Gill (Greek Gentleman), Willoughby Gray (Pharisee), Hugh Moxey (Centurion), Stanley Lemin (Landlord), Elizabeth Maude (Landlady), Joseph O'Conor (Joseph), Joanna Horder (Mary), Alan Wheatley (Jewish Gentleman), Andrew Leigh (First Shepherd), Leonard White (Second Shepherd), Frank Coburn (Third Shepherd), John Vere (Man), Evelyn Moore (Woman), Peter George (First Roman Soldier), Kenneth Cleveland (Second Roman Soldier), Anna Somerset (Maidservant).

	Holding / Source
24.12.1948	NR / Live

HEARTBEAT

A Yorkshire Television production. Transmission details are for the Central region. Usual duration: 50 minutes.

Main regular credit(s): Devised by Johnny Byrne; based on books by Peter Walker [credited as Nicholas Rhea]; executive producer Keith Richardson.

Main regular cast: Derek Fowlds (Oscar Blaketon), William Simons (Police Constable Alf Ventress), Mark Jordon (Police Constable Phil Bellamy (until series 23.12.2007)).

SERIES 4

Main regular credit(s): Produced by Martyn Auty.

Main regular cast: With Nick Berry (Police Constable Nick Rowan), Niamh Cusack (Doctor Kate Rowan), Tricia Penrose (Gina Ward), David Lonsdale (David Stockwell), Peter Firth (Doctor James Radcliffe), Karen Meagher (Inspector Murchison (11.9.1994 onwards)), Bill Maynard (Claude Jeremiah Greengrass).

		VT Number	Holding / Source
25.12.1994	A Winter's Tale	D200/16	B / BSF

Written by Brian Finch; directed by Tim Dowd.

With Stuart Golland (George Ward), Twiggy, Bruce Jones, Stacey Heywood, Richard Cadman, Sam Townend, Dean Gatiss, Eli Woods, Rosy Clayton.

SERIES 6

Main regular credit(s): Produced by Gerry Mill.

Main regular cast: With Nick Berry (Police Constable Nick Rowan), Tricia Penrose (Gina Ward), David Lonsdale (David Stockwell), Anne Stallybrass (Eileen), Peter Benson (Bernie Scripps), Juliette Gruber (Jo Rowan neé Weston), Kazia Pelka (Maggie Bolton), Bill Maynard (Claude Jeremiah Greengrass).

		VT Number	Holding / Source
25.12.1996	Charity Begins At Home	D211/16	DB / DBSF

Written by Jane Hollowood; directed by Tom Cotter.

With Stuart Golland (George Ward), Mary Healey, Biddy Hodson, John Michie.

SERIES 7

Main regular credit(s): Produced by Gerry Mill.

Main regular cast: With Nick Berry (Police Constable Nick Rowan), Juliette Gruber (Jo Rowan neé Weston), Tricia Penrose (Gina Ward), David Lonsdale (David Stockwell), Peter Benson (Bernie Scripps), Kazia Pelka (Maggie Bolton), Bill Maynard (Claude Jeremiah Greengrass), Jason Durr (Police Constable Mike Bradley (23.11.1997 onwards)), Anne Stallybrass (Eileen).

		VT Number	Holding / Source
21.12.1997	The Queens Message	D972/16	DB / DBSF

Written by Peter Gibbs; directed by John Anderson.

With Con O'Neill, Helen Ryan, Katharine Rogers, Chris Larner.

HEARTBEAT (continued)

SERIES 8

Duration: 75 minutes.

Main regular credit(s): Produced by Gerry Mill.

Main regular cast: With Jason Durr (Police Constable Mike Bradley), Bill Maynard (Claude Jeremiah Greengrass), David Lonsdale (David Stockwell), Peter Benson (Bernie Scripps), Arbel Jones (Auntie Mary), Tricia Penrose (Gina Ward), David Michaels (Doctor Neil Bolton), Kazia Pelka (Maggie Bolton), Philip Franks (Sergeant Raymond Craddock (22.2.1998 onwards))).

	VT Number	Holding / Source
24.12.1998 **Echoes Of The past**	D979/16	DB / DBSF

Written by Neil McKay; directed by Brian Farnham.

With Fiona Dolman (Jackie Lambert), Keeley Forsyth (Sue Driscoll), Phillippa Wilson, Caroline Langrishe, Roger Allam (Graham Hayes), Danny Seward (Stephen), Matyelok Gibbs (Miss Barker), Sheila Burrell (Mrs Hutton), Domini Winter (Choreographer).

SERIES 10

Main regular credit(s): Produced by Gerry Mill.

Main regular cast: With Bill Maynard (Claude Jeremiah Greengrass (until 14.01.2001)), Kazia Pelka (Maggie Bolton), Tricia Penrose (Gina Ward), David Lonsdale (David Stockwell), Peter Benson (Bernie Scripps), Jason Durr (Police Constable Mike Bradley), Philip Franks (Sergeant Raymond Craddock), Fiona Dolman (Jackie Bradley).

	VT Number	Holding / Source
24.12.2000 **Cold Turkey**	D994/08	DB / DBSWF

Written by Peter Gibbs; directed by Noreen Kershaw.

With David Beckett, Richard Walsh, Lorraine Sass, Jody Latham, Alwyne Taylor, Michael Begley (Chris Draycott), Emma Cleasby (Linda), Julie Corrigan (Wendy), Johnny Caesar (Drunk).

SERIES 14

Main regular credit(s): Music by Adrian Burch and David Whitaker; associate producer Mary Owen; produced by Archie Tait.

Main regular cast: With Jonathan Kerrigan (Police Constable Rob Walker), Geoffrey Hughes (Vernon Scripps), David Lonsdale (David Stockwell), Duncan Bell (Sergeant Dennis Merton), Peter Benson (Bernie Scripps), Sarah Tansey (Jenny Merton), Aislin McGuckin (Doctor Liz Merrick), Richard Lintern (Ben Norton), Tricia Penrose (Gina Ward).

	Holding / Source
26.12.2004 **In The Bleak Midwinter**	DB / DBSWF

Written by Johnny Byrne; directed by Gerry Mill.

With David Woodcock (Vicar), Sophie Ward (Doctor Trent), Vanessa Hehir (Rosie), Allan Corduner, Ram John Holder, Alan Price, Vicki Lee-Taylor, Jamie De Courcey, Ken Bones, Tim Carlton, Rachel Davies.

SERIES 16

A Granada Yorkshire production.

Main regular credit(s): Music by David Whitaker and Adrian Burch; associate producer Pat Brown; produced by Archie Tait.

Main regular cast: With Jonathan Kerrigan (Police Constable Rob Walker), David Lonsdale (David Stockwell), Tricia Penrose (Gina Ward).

	Holding / Source
18.12.2005 **Auld Acquaintance**	DB / DBSWF

Written by Peter Gibbs; script supervisor Christine Sharman; script editor Jonathan Critchley; directed by Roger Bamford.

With John Duttine (Sergeant George Miller), Gwen Taylor (Peggy Armstrong), Sophie Ward (Doctor Helen Trent), Steven Blakeley (Police Constable Geoff Younger), Vanessa Hehir (Rosie Cartwright), Peter Benson (Bernie Scripps), Todd Carty, Luke Adamson, Tom Georgeson, Lee Booth, Josh Jenkins.

SERIES 17

An ITV Productions production.

Main regular credit(s): Music by Adrian Burch and David Whitaker; associate producer Pat Brown; produced by Archie Tait.

Main regular cast: With David Lonsdale (David Stockwell), Jonathan Kerrigan (Police Constable Rob Walker), Peter Benson (Bernie Scripps), Lisa Kay (Carol Cassidy), Vanessa Hehir (Rosie Cartwright), Tricia Penrose (Gina Ward), Steven Blakeley (Police Constable Geoff Younger).

	Holding / Source
24.12.2006 **Hearts And Flowers**	DB / DBSWF

Written by Susan Wilkins; directed by Andrew Morgan.

With John Duttine (Sergeant George Miller), Clare Wille (Detective Sergeant Rachel Dawson), George Layton, Lindsey Coulson, Elizabeth Mansfield, Elizabeth Bennett, Garry Cooper, Claude Close.

31.12.2006 **Give Peace A Chance**	DB / DBSWF

Written by Jane Hollowood; script supervisor Christine Sharman; script editor Anna Gorst; directed by Jonas Grimas.

With Gwen Taylor (Peggy Armstrong), John Duttine (Sergeant George Miller), Clare Wille (Detective Sergeant Rachel Dawson), Pip Ripley, Jonathan Warde, Max Brown, Andrew Langtree, Roy Dotrice, James Quinn.

31.12.2006 **Dead Men Do Tell Tales**	DB / DBSWF

Written by Brian Finch; script supervisor Karen Wright; script editor Penny Brazier; directed by Judith Dine.

With Gwen Taylor (Peggy Armstrong), John Duttine (Sergeant George Miller), Paul Nicholas, Catherine Terris, Lisa Kay, Keiron Richardson, Carlton Dickinson, Beau Flood, Andrew Langtree, Gillian Bevan, Howard Grace, Letty Butler.

See also: THE ROYAL

HEARTBEAT CHRISTMAS ALBUM

A Granada Yorkshire production for ITV. Transmission details are for the Central region. Duration: 22 minutes.

What makes Christmas in Aidensfield so special? Is it the touching storylines, the sense of belonging or the people? HEARTBEAT CHRISTMAS ALBUM takes a nostalgic trip down memory lane with cast members old and new to find out what they think truly makes Christmas in Aidensfield. Traditionally, it snows in Aidensfield at Christmas, where you can find the villagers enjoying a drink in the Aidensfield Arms and guarantee Claude Greengrass is up to no good. HEARTBEAT CHRISTMAS ALBUM takes a look at the romances that began under the mistletoe, the Christmas parties and who's behind the Santa suit. Well known for the special guest appearances, Christmas is no different. In the 1999 Christmas special, Stag at Bay, Charlotte Church made her acting debut as Katie Kendall, a young girl whose parents had separated. With Katie going missing and deer being killed on Lord Ashfordly's grounds, Christmas is closing in. When Katie turns up and a goodwill gesture from Greengrass helps the police catch the poacher, the Christmas concert goes ahead as planned. Other well known faces that have appeared over the years include Twiggy Lawson and an early appearance by Bruce Jones, CORONATIONS STREET'S Les Battersby in 1994's A Winters Tale. It wouldn't be Christmas without Santa Claus and Greengrass, with some persuasion, will don the famous red suit to make it really feel like Christmas. HEARTBEAT CHRISTMAS ALBUM takes a look behind the scenes of this years Christmas special Auld Acquaintance with a guest appearance from TODD CARTY. Christmas in Aidensfield wouldn't be Christmas without drinks in the pub, a Christmas party at Lord Ashfordley's estate or a Christmas concert. A HEARTBEAT Christmas, no matter what happens will leave a festive feeling all round.

Executive producer Peter Gordon; produced by Jason Beresford.

Matthew Kelly (Narrator), Bill Maynard, Todd Carty, Nick Berry, Sophie Ward.

	Holding / Source
18.12.2005	DB / DBSWF

HEARTBURN HOTEL

A BBC production for BBC 1. Transmission details are for BBC 1. Duration: 30 minutes.

Main regular credit(s): Written by John Sullivan and Steve Glover; executive producer John Sullivan; produced by Gareth Gwenlan.

Main regular cast: Tim Healy (Harry Springer), Clive Russell (Duggie Strachan), Peter Gunn (Simon Thorpe), Kim Wall (Baker).

	Holding / Source
27.12.1998 **Christmas Special**	DB / D3S

Directed by Gareth Gwenlan.

With Kaleem Janjua, Adlyn Ross, Michael Jayston, Wale Ojo, Yomi A. Michaels, Sara Markland, Ifan Huw Dafydd, Stephen Aintree, Francesca Ryan, Karzan Krekar.

A HEAVENLY PEACE

A Thames Television production. Transmission details are for the Scottish Television region. Duration: 40 minutes.

Josef Mohr, parish priest of a village in Austria, hurriedly scribbled down some words for a hymn. The church organ had broken down and a new hymn was needed to help fill out the Christmas Eve service.

   This programme of Christmas music, recorded in Austria, tells the story of how the world's best loved carol Silent Night came to be written. From the riverside village near Saltzburg where the carol was composed to the mountains of the Tyrol, the programme traces the extraordinary way in which the carol was born and then spread around the world.

Written by Peter Hughes; produced and directed by Christopher Palmer.

Adele Leigh (Presenter), Rainer Singers, Wiltener Boys Choir of Innsbruck.

	VT Number	Holding / Source
25.12.1975	12280	DB / 2"

(P G WODEHOUSE'S) HEAVY WEATHER

A Cinema Verity production for BBC 1. made in association with Juniper Films / WGBH Boston. Transmission details are for BBC 1. Duration: 94 minutes.

Trouble is brewing at Blandings Castle, home to Clarence, Earl of Emsworth, his brother, his sisterand - most importantly of all - his prize pig.

Adapted by Douglas Livingstone; based on a book by P. G. Wodehouse; script supervisor Gillian Wood; music by Denis King; executive producers Rebecca Eaton, Michael Wills and Michael Wearing; co-produced by David Shanks; produced by Verity Lambert; directed by Jack Gold.

Peter O'Toole (Clarence, Earl of Emsworth), Richard Briers (The Hon Galahad Threepwood), Judy Parfitt (Lady Constance Keeble), Richard Johnson (Lord Tilbury), Sarah Badel (Lady Julia Fish), Roy Hudd (Beach), David Bamber (P. Frobisher Pilbeam), Samuel West ('Monty' Bodkin), Rebecca Lacey (Sue Brown), Bryan Pringle (Pirbright), Ronald Fraser (Sir Gregory Parsloe), Benjamin Soames (Ronnie Fish), Denyse Alexander (Miss Gutteridge), Anne Carroll (Barmaid), Matthew Byam-Shaw (Hugo Carmody), Charles Pemberton (Porter), James Horne (Voules), Tony Spooner (Sir Gregory's Pig Man).

	Holding / Source
24.12.1995	D3 / C1S

HELLO, CHRISTMAS PLAYMATES! (RADIO)

A BBC production for BBC Scottish Home Service. Transmission details are for BBC Scottish Home Service. Duration: 45 minutes.

Written by Bob Monkhouse and Denis Goodwin; play production by Bob Monkhouse and Denis Goodwin.

Arthur Askey (Host), David Nixon (The Melon), Petula Clark (The Mince Pie), Irene Handl (The Turkey), Pat Coombs (The Lemon), The Hedley Ward Trio (Nuts), BBC Variety Orchestra (Syrup), Leslie Bridgmont (Chef).

	Holding / Source
26.12.1955	DA|a /

HENRY'S CAT

A Bob Godfrey Films Ltd production for BBC 1. Transmission details are for BBC 1. Duration: 5 minutes.

Main regular credit(s): Music by Peter Shade; directed by Bob Godfrey.
Main regular cast: Bob Godfrey (Narrator).

SERIES 1
Main regular credit(s): Written by Bob Godfrey; music by Peter Shade; produced by Bob Godfrey.

Holding / Source
24.12.1984 Christmas Dinner — C1 / C1
Alternative transmissions: BBC 2: 25.12.1983.

SERIES 2
Main regular credit(s): Written by Bob Godfrey; music by Peter Shade; produced by Bob Godfrey.

Holding / Source
28.12.1984 New Year Resolution — C1 / C1

Duration: 10 minutes.
Main regular credit(s): Written by Bob Godfrey and Stan Hayward; produced by Mike Hayes.

Holding / Source
24.12.1992 Mystery Of The Missing Santa — C1 / C1

THE HERB ALPERT SHOW

An ATV production. Transmission details are for the ATV midlands region. Duration: 50 minutes.
Executive producer Bill Ward; produced and directed by Albert Locke.
Herb Alpert and The Tijuana Brass.

Holding / Source
24.12.1969 — DB-T3 / 2"

HERE COMES MUMFIE

An ITC production for ATV. Transmission details are for the ATV midlands region. Duration: 8 minutes.
Main regular credit(s): Based on stories by Katharine Tozer; produced by Mary Turner and John Read.

SERIES 1

Holding / Source
17.12.1975 An Unusual Christmas Cake — C1 / C1

HERE'S HARRY

A BBC production. Transmission details are for BBC. Duration: 30 minutes.
Main regular cast: Harry Worth (Himself).

SERIES 4
A BBC North production. Transmission details are for BBC. Duration: 25 minutes.
Main regular credit(s): Written by Vince Powell and Frank Roscoe; designed by Kenneth Lawson; produced and directed by John Ammonds.

Holding / Source
24.12.1962 The Pantomime — J /
With Reginald Marsh, Edwin Apps, Gordon Rollings, Doris Gambell, Joe Gladwin, Barbara Keogh, Pamela Manson, Tony Melody, Jack Woolgar, Douglas Clarke.
Caption illustrations by Bob Dunscombe.

SERIES 6
A BBC North production. Transmission details are for BBC.
Main regular credit(s): Written by Vince Powell and Frank Roscoe; designed by Kenneth Lawson; produced and directed by John Ammonds.

Holding / Source
20.12.1963 The Christmas Cards — J /
With Michael Brennan, Geoffrey Hibbert, Richard Caldicot, Doris Gambell, Roy Maxwell, Meg Johnson.

HEY PRESTO! CHRISTMAS MAGIC

A Thames Television production. Transmission details are for the ATV midlands region. Duration: 25 minutes.
Music directed by Don Hunt; designed by Colin Andrews and Jim Nicholson; produced and directed by Daphne Shadwell.
Ali Bongo (Presenter), Alan Shaxon and Anne, Terry Herbert, Kovari.

Holding / Source
29.12.1981 — DB / 2"

HI THERE 82!

A BBC Birmingham production for BBC 1. Transmission details are for BBC 1. Duration: 53 minutes.

New Year special.

Produced by Roy Norton; directed by Tony Wolfe.

Mike Murphy (Host), Hi-De-Hi! Team, Danny La Rue, Andy Williams, Norman Collier, Wall Street Crash, Kenny Ball and his Jazzmen.

Holding / Source
01.01.1982   DB-D3 / 2"

HI-DE-HI!

A BBC production for BBC 1. Transmission details are for BBC 1. Usual duration: 30 minutes.

You have been watching... Simon Cadell, Paul Shane, Ruth Madoc, Jeffrey Holland, Su Pollard, Felix Bowness and Leslie Dwyer. Perhaps the names may be unfamiliar but the faces and characters of this repertory theatre of comedy are instantly recognisable.

The writers Jimmy Perry and David Croft based all their sitcoms on personal experience, and created such hits as Dad's Army and It Ain't Half Hot Mum. So it is perhaps surprising that the famous comedy writers were not automatically guaranteed a series for every new idea they had. In 1977 after the disastrous science-fiction sitcom Come Back Mrs Noah, the BBC were reluctant to commission a new Perry/Croft sitcom. Had the magic run out? Were Perry and Croft good writers of war-based sitcoms or could they broaden their talents?

On New Year's Day 1980 the BBC1 audience saw the pilot to a new sitcom set at Maplin's Holiday Camp. Some of the faces would go on to become instant TV superstars – Simon Cadell as Jeffrey Fairbrother, the University academic; Ted Bovis the loveable rogue; Spike Dixon the new camp comic and potty chalet maid Peggy who wanted to become a yellowcoat. But who remembers Wilf Green aka Marty Storm, the Bill Haley impersonator? Like all TV pilots it set up a potential series but worked as a good stand-alone comedy full of gentle touches like Ted telling Spike he was auditioning for a part in Florizel Street, a new Granada TV soap opera. Florizel Street was the working title for Coronation Street.

A series was commissioned and each episode unravelled another adventure of the yellowcoats, led by Gladys Pugh who lusted after Jeffrey, and tried to stop Ted and all his fiddles. Each episode ended with the familiar You Have Been Watching caption - a tradition that began with Dad's Army and continued on every Perry/Croft sitcom afterwards. Perry admitted later that Croft had the ability to write witty gags but he preferred plotting the episodes and writing character dialogue.

After four seasons Simon Cadell left and was replaced by David Griffin as Squadron Leader Clive Dempster, DFC. Clive was a charming ladies man and initially pursued Gladys until he was forced to announce his engagement to her. Eventually he realised that he did love her and the series ended with their marriage.

Cadell was the first to leave, but others followed. Leslie Dwyer, the drunken punch and judy man Mr Partridge, died and the character 'left to visit a relative'. Barry Howard resigned and Yvonne Stuart-Hargreaves was forced to find a new partner - Julian Dalrymple-Sykes played by Ben Aris. The writing was on the wall when Perry/Croft decided to write You Rang M'Lord and even the addition of Kenneth Connor playing Sammy was not enough to save the series from cancellation. In true Perry/Croft style the series had a proper ending as Maplins was closed by Joe Maplin and it became self-catering chalets.

Such was the popularity of Paul Shane, Jeffrey Holland and Su Pollard that they returned as regulars in You Rang M'Lord? and Oh Doctor Beeching to continue the great Perry/Croft tradition of period-set sitcoms.

Main regular credit(s):	Written by Jimmy Perry and David Croft; theme music by Jimmy Perry.
Main regular cast:	Paul Shane (Ted Bovis), Ruth Madoc (Gladys Pugh), Jeffrey Holland (Spike Dixon), Felix Bowness (Fred Quilley), Su Pollard (Peggy Ollerenshaw), Nikki Kelly (Sylvia), Stan Ley (The Webb Twins), Bruce Ley (The Webb Twins), Chris Andrews (Gary).

SERIES 3

Main regular credit(s):	Produced by David Croft.
Main regular cast:	With Simon Cadell (Jeffrey Fairbrother), Leslie Dwyer (Mr Partridge), Diane Holland (Yvonne), Barry Howard (Barry), Rikki Howard (Betty), Susan Beagley (Tracey).

Holding / Source
26.12.1982 **Eruptions**   DB / 1"

Duration: 45 minutes.

Designed by Garry Freeman; directed by David Croft.

With Michael Redfern, Paul Toothill.

SERIES 5

Main regular credit(s):	Produced and directed by David Croft.
Main regular cast:	With David Griffin (Squadron Leader Clive Dempster, DFC (10.11.1984 onwards)), Barry Howard (Barry Stuart-Hargreaves), Leslie Dwyer (Mr Partridge), Linda Regan (Yellowcoat Girl), Laura Jackson (Yellowcoat Girl), Julie-Christian Young (Yellowcoat Girl).

Holding / Source
25.12.1984 **Raffles**   DB / 1"

Choreography by Kenn Oldfield; designed by Bernard Lloyd-Jones; production team Nikki Cockcroft, Roy Gould, Lindsey Chamier and Olwyn Silvester; production managers Martin Dennis and Susan Belbin.

With Ronnie Brody, Les Henry, Peggyann Clifford, Brenda Cowling, Geoffrey Leesley.

No Leslie Dwyer.

SERIES 6

Main regular credit(s):	Designed by Andrée Welstead Hornby; production team Bernadette Darnell, Roy Gould and Duncan Cooper; produced by David Croft.
Main regular cast:	With David Griffin (Squadron Leader Clive Dempster, DFC), Barry Howard (Barry Stuart-Hargreaves), Linda Regan (Yellowcoat Girl), Laura Jackson (Yellowcoat Girl), Julie-Christian Young (Yellowcoat Girl).

Holding / Source
25.12.1985 **The Great Cat Robbery**   DB / 1"

Duration: 58 minutes.

Production managers Robin Carr and Martin Dennis; directed by David Croft.

With John Rutland, Jeanne Mockford, Richard Speight, Lucy Gould.

HI-DE-HI! (continued)

SERIES 7

Main regular credit(s): Production team Valerie Letley, Laura Mackie, Janice Thomas and Sharon Porter; production manager Martin Dennis; produced by David Croft.

Main regular cast: With David Griffin (Squadron Leader Clive Dempster, DFC), Ben Aris (Julian Dalrymple-Sykes), Linda Regan (April), Kenneth Connor (Sammy), Laura Jackson (Dawn).

	Holding / Source
27.12.1986 **September Song**	DB / 1"

Duration: 45 minutes.
Choreography by Kenn Oldfield; designed by Chris Hull; directed by David Croft.
With Caroline Dennis, Toni Palmer, Billy Burdon [as Billy Burden].

SERIES 8

Main regular credit(s): Production team Valerie Letley, Judith Bantock, Francesca Gilpin and Yvonne O'Grady; executive producer David Croft; production manager Roy Gould.

Main regular cast: With David Griffin (Squadron Leader Clive Dempster, DFC), Ben Aris (Julian), Linda Regan (April), Kenneth Connor (Sammy), Laura Jackson (Dawn).

	Holding / Source
26.12.1987 **Tell It To The Marines**	DB / 1"

Duration: 45 minutes.
Designed by Andrée Welstead Hornby; produced and directed by David Croft.
With Brian Gwaspari, Perry Benson, Timothy Bateson, Michael Burns, Su Elliott.

HIGH LIVING

A Scottish Television production. Transmission details are for ITV Various. Usual duration: 25 minutes.

Main regular credit(s): Script editor Henry Hay; produced by Ian Dalgleish.

Transmission details are for the Scottish Television region.

	Holding / Source
25.12.1969	J / 40
24.12.1970	J / 2"

HIGH WATER

A Westward Television production. Transmission details are for the Westward Television region. Duration: 30 minutes.
Written by Nick Darke; produced and directed by Roger Gage.
Desmond Stokes, Ian Stirling.

	Holding / Source
22.12.1981	J /

HIGHWAY

Produced for Various ITV Companies by a variety of companies (see details below). Transmission details are for the Central region. Usual duration: 30 minutes.

Main regular credit(s): Executive producer Bill Ward.
Main regular cast: Harry Secombe (Presenter).

SERIES 2

Main regular credit(s): Executive producer Bill Ward.

23.12.1984 **Bethlehem (Dyfed)**
Duration: 50 minutes.
Bethlehem in Dyfed, West Wales.
Programme associate Ronnie Cass; directed by John Mead.
With Wendy Craig, Tim Healy, Roy Castle, Lorna Dallas, Evelyn Glennie, The Harpurs Hill School.

SERIES 3

	Holding / Source
22.12.1985 **Highway Christmas Special**	DB|n / 1"

SERIES 4

	Production No	Holding / Source
21.12.1986 **Christmas Special**	9C/51137	DB|n / 1"

An LWT production.

SERIES 5

	Production No	Holding / Source
27.12.1987 **Christmas Special**	HIY/01/032	1"|n / 1"

A HTV production. Duration: 45 minutes.
Programme associate Ronnie Cass; designed by Charles Bond; produced and directed by David Hammond-Williams.
With Roy Castle, Max Boyce, Helen Hessey-White, Richard Williams Singers, Brian Johnston.

| British Christmas Television Guide | HIGHWAY (continued) |

SERIES 7

	Holding / Source
24.12.1989 **Durham Cathedral**	1"|n / 1"

A Tyne Tees Television production.

Programme associate Ronnie Cass; associate producer Vin Arthey; produced and directed by John Reay.

With Jessye Norman, Thomas Allen, Very Reverend John R. Arnold, Right Reverend David Jenkins, Robert Hardy, Patricia Brake.

HIM AND HER

A Big Talk Productions production for BBC 3. made in association with Ingenious Broadcasting. Transmission details are for BBC 3. Duration: 30 minutes.

Main regular cast: Russell Tovey (Steve), Sarah Solemani (Becky).

SERIES 3

Main regular credit(s):   Written by Stefan Golaszewski; designed by John Stevenson; executive producer Matthew Justice; produced by Kenton Allen; directed by Richard Laxton.

	Holding / Source
23.12.2012	HD/DB / HD/DB

A surprise visitor turns up at the flat on Christmas Day - Steve's father Pete. The mood turns awkward, but later the pair share a special festive moment.

With Ricky Champ (Paul), Camille Coduri (Shelly), Christopher Fulford (Pete), Kerry Howard (Laura), Joe Wilkinson (Dan), Joanna Bacon (Janet), Louis Melton (Kieran).

HINGE AND BRACKET'S NEW YEAR'S EVE PARTY

Alternative/Working Title(s): A NEW YEAR'S EVE PARTY

A BBC Manchester production for BBC 2. Transmission details are for BBC 2. Duration: 50 minutes.

Written by George Logan and Patrick Fyffe; programme associate Gyles Brandreth; designed by Dugald Findlay; assistant producer Martin Hughes; produced by Peter Ridsdale Scott; directed by Mike Stephens.

George Logan (Doctor Evadne Hinge), Patrick Fyffe (Dame Hilda Bracket), Band of The Irish Guards, Stackton Chorus and Strings.

	Holding / Source
31.12.1981	DB-D3 / 2"

The opening credits do not mention Hinge and Bracket, the programme is billed as "A New Year's Eve Party".

See also: A GALA EVENING WITH HINGE AND BRACKET (BBC)

HOB Y DERI DANDO

A BBC Wales production. Transmission details are for BBC 1.

	Holding / Source
25.12.1964	J / 40

Duration: 45 minutes.

Introduced by Meredydd Evans; designed by Alan Taylor; produced by Meredydd Evans; directed by Ruth Price.

With Ryan Davies, Ivor Emmanuel, Margaret Williams, Olwen Jones, Eiri Jones, Caryl Owens, David Reynolds, Jim Howells, Justin Smith, Aled Hughes, Reg Edwards, Derek Boote, The Proclaimers.

Young people and their folk music. The 1968 editions had previously been shown on BBC 1 Wales and there are, almost certainly, further editions of this programme which were aired on BBC 1 Wales only.

HOGMANAY

A Scottish Television production. Transmission details are for the ATV midlands region. Duration: 40 minutes.

Music directed by Arthur Blake; designed by Pip Gardner; executive producer Liam Hood; produced and directed by Clarke Tait.

Andy Stewart (Host), Kenneth McKellar, Patricia Hay, Jimmy Blue and his Scottish Country Dance Band.

	Holding / Source
31.12.1975	J / 2"

HOGMANAY LIVE

A BBC Scotland production for BBC 1. Transmission details are for BBC 1. Duration: 50 minutes.

Produced and directed by John Smith.

Cathy MacDonald (Host), Wet Wet Wet, Bonnie Raitt, Midge Ure, Mary Black, Aly Bain, Phil Cunningham, Paul Brady, Archie Fisher, Wolfstone, The George Penman Jazzband, Na Seoid.

	Holding / Source
01.01.1994	DB-D3 / D3S

HOGMANAY LIVE

A BBC Scotland production for BBC 1. Transmission details are for BBC 1. Duration: 70 minutes.

Produced and directed by John Smith.

Hazel Irvine (Host), Cathy MacDonald (Host), Paul Coia, Nanci Griffith, Runrig, Mary And Frances Black, Capercaillie, Aly Bain, Phil Cunningham, Rab Noakes, Strathclyde Police Pipe Band.

	Holding / Source
01.01.1995	DB-D3 / D3S

HOGMANAY LIVE

A BBC Scotland production for BBC 1. Transmission details are for BBC 1. Duration: 50 minutes.
Executive producer Liz Scott; produced by Sarah Lawrence.
Gordon Kennedy (Host), Lorraine Kelly (Host), Gary Glitter, Big Country, Eddi Reader, Aly Bain, Phil Cunningham, Edwyn Collins.

	Holding / Source
01.01.1996	DB-D3 / LivePAL

HOGMANAY LIVE

A BBC Scotland production for BBC 1. Transmission details are for BBC 1. Duration: 50 minutes.
Carol Smillie (Host), Dougie Vipond (Host), Ainsley Harriott, Clive Anderson, Elaine Smith, Barry Norman, Jamie Theakston, Ally McCoist, Zoe Ball, Bill Paterson, Paul Young, Dougie MacLean, Aly Bain, Northbeat Reel Dancers, Capercaillie, Clarissa Dickson Wright, Gerard Kelly.

	Holding / Source
01.01.1998	DB-D3 / D3S

HOGMANAY PARTY

A Scottish Television production. Transmission details are for the ATV midlands region. Duration: 40 minutes.
Music directed by Arthur Blake; choreography by Denise Shaune; designed by Ron Franchetti; produced and directed by Douglas Moodie.
Jimmy Reid (Host), Bill Tennent (Host), Lulu, Eira Heath, Andy Stewart, Ian Wallace, Roddy McMillan, Ann Brand, Laura Brand, The Gaberlunzies, Sheena Houston.

	Holding / Source
31.12.1969	J / 2"

This was Scottish TV's first colour show from The Gateway studio.

HOGMANAY SHOW

A Scottish Television production. Transmission details are for the ATV midlands region. Duration: 40 minutes.
Designed by Pip Gardner; executive producer Liam Hood; directed by Clarke Tait.
Andy Stewart (Host), Calum Kennedy, Robin Hall, Jimmie McGregor, The Alexander Brothers, Allan Stewart, Billy Connolly.

	Holding / Source
31.12.1973	J / Live

THE HOGMANAY SHOW

A Scottish Television production. Transmission details are for the ATV midlands region. Duration: 45 minutes.
Designed by Archie McArthur; executive producer Liam Hood; produced and directed by Clarke Tait.
Andy Stewart (Host), Francie and Josie, Dana, Tommy Makem, Jimmy Shand, Linda Scott, The Jo Cook Dancers, Royal Scots Grays.

	Holding / Source
31.12.1970	J / 2"

Recorded in Edinburgh on the Sunday prior to New Year's Eve.

THE HOGMANAY SHOW

A Scottish Television production. Transmission details are for the ATV midlands region. Duration: 25 minutes.
Music directed by Arthur Blake; executive producer Clarke Tait; produced and directed by Archie McArthur.
Fulton Mackay (Host), Aneka, Kenneth McKellar.

	Holding / Source
31.12.1981	DV / Live

Recovered by Kaleidoscope.

THE HOGMANAY SHOW

A Scottish Television production. Transmission details are for the Central region. Duration: 35 minutes.
Designed by Paul Laugier; produced by Clarke Tait; directed by Haldane Duncan.
Peter Morrison (Host).

	Holding / Source
31.12.1982	J / Live

THE HOGMANAY SHOW

A Scottish Television production. Transmission details are for the Central region. Duration: 50 minutes.
Music directed by Arthur Blake; designed by Ken Smith; produced by Clarke Tait; directed by Chris Allen.
Andy Cameron (Host), Kenneth McKellar, Linda Esther Gray, The Corries, Hector Nicol, Kenny Smiles, Stutz Bear Cats, Gene Fitzpatrick.

	Holding / Source
31.12.1984	1" / Live

HOLBY CITY

A BBC production for BBC 1. made in association with BBC Worldwide. Transmission details are for BBC 1. Usual duration: 60 minutes.

Main regular credit(s): Created by Mal Young; theme music by Ken Freeman.

SERIES 2
Main regular credit(s): Executive producer Mal Young; produced by Yvon Grace.

Main regular cast: With Angela Griffin (Jasmine Hopkins), Michael French (Nick Jordan), George Irving (Anton Meyer), Clive Mantle (Mike Barratt (23.12.1999-onwards)), Thusitha Jayasundera (Tash Bandara), Jan Pearson (Kath Shaughnessy), Jeremy Edwards (Danny Shaughnessy), Dawn McDaniel (Kirstie Collins), Lisa Faulkner (Victoria Merrick).

Holding / Source

30.12.1999 Tidings Of Comfort And Joy — DB / DBSW

Written by Tony McHale; directed by Jamie Annett.

With Rebecca Wheatley (Amy), Martina Laird (Darleen Devern), Finbar Lynch, Ian Keith, Simon Quaterman, Neili Conroy, Ariyon Bakare, Steve Toussaint, Damien Goodwin, Louise Breckon-Richards, Michael Atkinson.

This episode tied in to the 'Casualty' story running simultaneously.

SERIES 3
Main regular credit(s): Executive producer Mal Young; series producer Stephen Garwood; produced by Sally Avens.

Main regular cast: With Laura Sadler (Sandy Harper), Jeremy Sheffield (Alex Adams), Dawn McDaniel (Kirstie Collins), Siobhan Redmond (Janice Taylor), Angela Griffin (Jasmine Hopkins), Clive Mantle (Mike Barratt), Thusitha Jayasundera (Tash Bandara), George Irving (Anton Meyer), Jan Pearson (Kath Shaughnessy), Jeremy Edwards (Danny Shaughnessy), Lisa Faulkner (Victoria Merrick (until 8.5.2001)), Anna Mountford (Keri McGrath).

Holding / Source

14.12.2000 A Christmas Carol: Episode 1 — DB / DBSW

Written by Peter Palliser; directed by Adrian Bean.

With Paul Shane, Kulvinder Ghir, Simon Williams, Julian Glover, Louie Ramsay, Sarah Flind.

21.12.2000 A Christmas Carol: Episode 2 — DB / DBSW

Written by Andrew Rattenbury; directed by Adrian Bean.

With Paul Shane, Kulvinder Ghir, Simon Williams, Marc Zuber, Tom Chadbon, Patricia Brake.

SERIES 4
Main regular credit(s): Executive producers Mal Young and Kathleen Hutchison; series producer Richard Stokes.

Main regular cast: With Thusitha Jayasundera (Tash Bandara (until 18.6.2002)), Jan Pearson (Kath Fox (nee Shaughnessy) (until 3.6.2003)), Jeremy Edwards (Danny Shaughnessy (until 15.04.2003)), Laura Sadler (Sandy Harper), Jeremy Sheffield (Alex Adams), Peter De Jersey (Steve Waring (until 6.5.2003)), Colette Brown (Samantha Kennedy (until 13.8.2002)), Dominic Jephcott (Alistair Taylor (until ?)), Tina Hobley (Chrissie Williams), Hugh Quarshie (Mr Ric Griffin), Martin Ledwith (Father Michael (27.11.2001-until ?)), Andrew Dunn (Simon Shaughnessy (11.12.2001-onwards), Luisa Bradshaw-White (Lisa Fox (31.12.2001?-onwards)), Mark Moraghan (Owen Davis (23.10.2001-onwards)), David Paisley (Ben Saunders (29.01.2002?-22.04.2003)), Miles Anderson (Terry Fox (?-31.12.2002)), Ian Aspinall (Mubbs Hussein (27.11.2001-onwards)), Verona Joseph (Jess Griffin (15.1.2002-onwards)), Denise Welch (Pam McGrath (11.6.2002-2.7.2002)), Denis Lawson (Tom Campbell-Gore (13.8.2002-29.7.2003)), Patricia Potter (Diane Lloyd (2.7.2002-onwards)), Siobhan Redmond (Janice Taylor (until 6.8.2002)), Rocky Marshall (Ed Keating (13.8.2002-), George Irving (Anton Meyer (until 20.08.2002)).

Holding / Source

23.12.2001 'Twas The Night... — DB / DBSW

Written by Jane Hollowood; produced by Richard Stokes; directed by Jim Goddard.

With Marvin Humes, Chris Thompson, James Quinn, Ray Emmet Brown.

SERIES 5
Main regular credit(s): Executive producers Kathleen Hutchison and Mal Young; series producer Richard Stokes.

Main regular cast: With Jan Pearson (Kath Fox), Jeremy Edwards (Danny Shaughnessy (until 15.04.2003)), Laura Sadler (Sandy Harper (until 2.9.2003)), Jeremy Sheffield (Alex Adams), Dawn McDaniel (Kirstie Collins), Peter De Jersey (Steve Waring (until 6.5.2003)), Tina Hobley (Chrissie Williams), Hugh Quarshie (Mr Ric Griffin), Martin Ledwith (Father Michael), Andrew Dunn (Simon Shaughnessy), Luisa Bradshaw-White (Lisa Fox), Mark Moraghan (Owen Davis), David Paisley (Ben Saunders (until 22.04.2003)), Miles Anderson (Terry Fox (until 31.12.2002)), Verona Joseph (Jess Griffin), Ian Aspinall (Mubbs Hussein), Patricia Potter (Diane Lloyd), Sharon Maughan (Tricia Williams (8.4.2003-onwards)), Denis Lawson (Tom Campbell-Gore), Rocky Marshall (Ed Keating), Kim Vithana (Rosie Sattar (13.5.2003-onwards)), Liam Garrigan (Nic Yorke (10.6.2003-onwards)), Art Malik (Zubin Khan (17.6.2003-onwards)), Rachel Leskovac (Kelly Yorke (1.7.2003-onwards)).

Holding / Source

26.12.2002 Sins Of The Father — DB / DBSW

Written by Andrew Holden; produced by Emma Turner; directed by James Erskine.

With Judy Loe (Jan Goddard), Leslie Phillips, Perri Snowdon, Jim Millea, Zoot Lynam, Colette O'Neil, Penelope McGhie, Delon Watson.

| HOLBY CITY (continued) | British Christmas Television Guide |

SERIES 6

Main regular credit(s): Associate producer Chris Ballantyne; executive producers Kathleen Hutchison and Mal Young.

Main regular cast: With Rocky Marshall (Ed Keating (until 18.5.2004?)), Kim Vithana (Rosie Sattar), Ian Aspinall (Mubbs Hussein), Luisa Bradshaw-White (Lisa Fox), Verona Joseph (Jess Griffin), Hugh Quarshie (Ric Griffin), Tina Hobley (Chrissie Williams), Denis Lawson (Tom Campbell-Gore (until 18.5.2004)), Art Malik (Zubin Khan), Patricia Potter (Diane Lloyd), Jan Pearson (Kath Fox), Sharon Maughan (Tricia Williams), Kelly Adams (Mickie Hendrie (16.3.2004 onwards)), Jaye Jacobs (Donna Jackson (16.3.2004 onwards)), Andrew Lewis (Paul Rose (13.1.2004-onwards)), Nitin Ganatra (Sami Sattar (27.1.2004-onwards)), Liam Garrigan (Nic Yorke (End of Oct 2003 I Think)), Rachel Leskovac (Kelly Yorke (End of Oct 2003 I Think)), Mark Moraghan (Owen Davis), Joseph Beattie (Robert Pullman (27.4.2004-)), Noah Huntley (William Curtis (4.5.2004-Onwards)), Amanda Mealing (Connie Beauchamp (01.06.2004-Onwards)), Deborah Poplett (Anna Chandler (29.06.2004-)), David Bedella (Carlos Fashola (03.08.2004 Onwards)).

Holding / Source

23.12.2003 In The Bleak Mid Winter — DB / DBSW

Written by Leslie Stewart; series producer Richard Stokes; produced by Emma Turner; directed by James Strong.

With Andrew Lewis, Nitin Chandra Ganatra, Ellie Haddington, Rowland Rivron, Rupert Ward Lewis, Dorothy Duffy, Sara Houghton, Victoria Pritchard.

SERIES 7

Main regular credit(s): Series producer Emma Turner.

Main regular cast: With Hugh Quarshie (Ric Griffin), Ian Aspinall (Mubbs Hussein (until 11.10.2005)), Luisa Bradshaw-White (Lisa Fox (until 13.9.2005)), Verona Joseph (Jess Griffin), Tina Hobley (Chrissie Williams), Patricia Potter (Diane Lloyd), Sharon Maughan (Tricia Williams), Kelly Adams (Mickie Hendrie), Jaye Jacobs (Donna Jackson), Mark Moraghan (Owen Davis), Noah Huntley (William Curtis (until 5.4.2005)), Amanda Mealing (Connie Beauchamp), David Bedella (Carlos Fashola), Deborah Poplett (Anna Chandler), Kim Vithana (Rosie Sattar (Until 11.1.2005)).

Holding / Source

21.12.2004 Elf And Happiness — DB / DBSW

Written by Julia Wall; script supervisor Ann Gallivan; series editor Johann Knobel; story editor Colin Steven; script editor Katy Harmer; music by Chantage; associate producer Lynn Grant; executive producers Kathleen Hutchison and Mal Young; produced by Roberto Troni; directed by Fraser MacDonald.

With Chinna Wodu (Sean Thompson), Albert Moses, Ursula Mohan, Leandra Lawrence, Nicholas Sidi, Samantha Beckinsale, Doreen Mantle, Paul Venables, Jamie Michie.

SERIES 8

Holding / Source

20.12.2005 The Long Goodbye — DB / DBSW

Written by Debbie O'Malley; script supervisor Jane Barton; series editor Gert Thomas; script editor Natasha Phillips; associate producer Simon Bird; executive producer Richard Stokes; series producer Emma Turner; produced by Johann Knobel; directed by Julie-Anne Robinson.

With Mark Moraghan (Owen Davis), Tina Hobley (Chrissie Williams), Kelly Adams (Mickie Hendrie), Paul Bradley (Elliot Hope), Amanda Mealing (Connie Beauchamp), Sharon D. Clarke (Lola Griffin), Sharon Maughan (Tricia Williams), Robert Powell (Mark Williams), Patricia Potter (Diane Lloyd), Georgina Terry, Rachel Hyde-Harvey, Stacey Roca, Alex McSweeney, Ron Moody, Victoria Williams, Jonty Stephens.

SERIES 10

Main regular credit(s): Executive producer Tony McHale; series producer Diana Kyle.

Holding / Source

27.12.2007 Elliot's Wonderful Life — DB / DBSWF

Written by Tony McHale; script supervisor Patricia Tookey Dickson; story producer Myar Craig-Brown; series editor Angus Towler; story editor Darren Guthrie; script editor Jane Wallbank; designed by Linda Conoboy; associate producer Katrine Dudley; directed by David Innes Edwards.

With Hugh Quarshie (Ric Griffin), Amanda Mealing (Connie Beauchamp), Alex Macqueen (Keith Green), Hari Dhillon (Michael Spence), Sharon D. Clarke (Lola Griffin), Rosie Marcel (Jac Naylor), Robert Powell (Mark Williams), Patsy Kensit (Faye Morton), Rakie Ayola (Kyla Tyson), Paul Bradley (Elliot Hope), Tom Chambers (Sam Strachan), Luke Roberts (Joseph Byrne), Tina Hobley (Chrissie Williams), Phoebe Thomas (Maria Kendall), Nadine Lewington (Maddy Young), Jaye Jacobs (Donna Jackson), Conor Mullen (Stuart McElroy), Sam Stockman (James Hope), Stella Gonet (Jayne Grayson), Holly Lucas, Andrew Lewis, Richard Briers, Gillian Bevan, Philip Whitchurch, Louise Bush, Elinor Colman, Jack O'Connor, Keeley Forsyth, Graeme Alexander, Amelia Donkor, Glynis Brooks, Paul McNeilly, Amanda Hurwitz, James Coombes, Anjel St Vincent, Wyn Moss, Lorren Bent, Anthony Adjekum, David Partridge.

SERIES 11

A BBC Productions production.

Main regular credit(s): Executive producer Tony McHale; series producer Diana Kyle.

Holding / Source

23.12.2008 Maria's Christmas Carol — DB / DBSWF

Written by Tony McHale; script supervisor Amy Rodriguez; story editor Darren Guthrie; script editor Yasmin Kalli; music by Darryl Way; designed by Linda Conoboy and Tracey Macario; produced by Myar Craig-Brown; directed by Bill MacLeod.

With Ayesha Antoine (Rachel Baptiste), Anna-Louise Plowman (Annalese Carson), Phoebe Thomas (Maria Kendall), Hari Dhillon (Michael Spence), Rosie Marcel (Jac Naylor), Robert Powell (Mark Williams), Paul Bradley (Elliot Hope), Tom Chambers (Sam Strachan), Luke Roberts (Joseph Byrne), Duncan Pow (Linden Cullen), Jaye Jacobs (Donna Jackson), Hugh Quarshie (Ric Griffin), Rebecca Grant (Daisha Anderson), Andrew Lewis (Paul Rose), Patsy Kensit (Faye Morton), Misha Crosby, Fiz Marcus, Charlie Roe, Fliss Walton, Karoline Jozwiak, Jonny Phillips, Ceri Mill, Victor Perez.

HOLBY CITY (continued)

SERIES 12
A BBC Productions production.
Main regular credit(s):   Series producer Diana Kyle.

Holding / Source

22.12.2009 Stand By Me   DB / DBSWF

The arrival of an old friend compels Linden to finally face up to his guilt over his wife's death. Michael enlists the help of Oliver and Maria to clear the wards of patients for Christmas.

Written by Tony McHale; senior script editor Michael Dawson; script supervisor Caroline Elliston; story producer Myar Craig-Brown; story editor Iona Vrolyk; script editor James Gillam-Smith; director of photography Alan Wright; art director Edd Cross; designed by Linda Conoboy and James Zafar; executive producer Tony McHale; directed by Jamie Annett.

With Amanda Mealing (Connie Beauchamp), Paul Bradley (Elliot Hope), Patsy Kensit Healy (Faye Byrne), Hugh Quarshie (Ric Griffin), Tina Hobley (Chrissie Williams), Luke Roberts (Joseph Byrne), Emma Catherwood (Penny Valentine), Hari Dhillon (Michael Spence), Duncan Pow (Linden Cullen), Rosie Marcel (Jac Naylor), James Anderson (Oliver Valentine), Robert Powell (Mark Williams), Rebecca Grant (Daisha Anderson), Phoebe Thomas (Maria Kendall), Charlotte Wakefield (Holly Cullen), Ginny Holder (Thandie Abebe-Griffin), Jaye Jacobs (Donna Jackson), Andrew Lewis, Ellie Darcey-Alden, Clara Salaman, Amy Shiels, Tianna Webster, Robyn Norwood, Lolita Chakrabarti, Fliss Walton, John Kavanagh, Karina Minhas, Glynis Brooks, Najan Ward.

29.12.2009 Resolutions   DB / DBSWF

Written by Chris Murray; senior script editor Michael Dawson; script supervisor Maggie Lewty; story producer Myar Craig-Brown; story editor Iona Vrolyk; script editor Kat Reynolds; director of photography Richard Mahoney; art director Spencer Robertson; designed by Linda Conoboy; executive producer Tony McHale; production manager Fiona Black; produced by Yasmin Kalli; directed by Dominic Keavey.

With Amanda Mealing (Connie Beauchamp), Paul Bradley (Elliot Hope), Hugh Quarshie (Ric Griffin), Hari Dhillon (Michael Spence), Duncan Pow (Linden Cullen), Rosie Marcel (Jac Naylor), Luke Roberts (Joseph Byrne), Emma Catherwood (Penny Valentine), James Anderson (Oliver Valentine), Robert Powell (Mark Williams), Rebecca Grant (Daisha Anderson), Patsy Kensit Healy (Faye Byrne), Tina Hobley (Chrissie Williams), Phoebe Thomas (Maria Kendall), Ginny Holder (Thandie Abebe-Griffin), Leslie Ash (Vanessa Lytton), Jaye Jacobs (Donna Jackson), Alan Morrissey, Riann Steele, Shelagh McLeod, Lisa Stevenson, Simon Nehan, Souad Faress.

SERIES 13
A BBC Productions production. Duration: 56 minutes.
Main regular credit(s):   Executive producer Belinda Campbell; consultant producer Justin Young; series producer Myar Craig-Brown; line producer Lynn Grant.

Holding / Source

21.12.2010 The Most Wonderful Time Of The Year   DB / DBSWF

Written by Tony McHale; senior script editor Michael Dawson; script supervisor Helene Oosthuizen; story editor Iona Vrolyk; script editor Emma Stuart; director of photography Richard Mahoney; art director Eleanor Rogers; designed by George Kyriakides and Dominic Roberts; production manager Kate Beeston; produced by Jane Wallbank; directed by Jamie Annett.

With Tina Hobley (Chrissie Williams), Olga Fedorí (Frieda Petrenko), Emma Catherwood (Penny Valentine), Hari Dhillon (Michael Spence), Bob Barrett (Sacha Levy), Robert Powell (Mark Williams), Guy Henry (Henrik Hanssen), La Charné Jolly (Elizabeth Tait), Jaye Jacobs (Donna Jackson), Amanda Mealing (Connie Beauchamp), Patsy Kensit (Faye), Edward MacLiam (Greg Douglas), James Anderson (Oliver Valentine), Rosie Marcel (Jac Naylor), Luke Roberts (Joseph Byrne), Barry Sloane, Ken Bones, Charlotte Randle, June Watson, Richard Lumsden, Susannah Corbett, Heather Craney.

SERIES 14

Holding / Source

27.12.2011 Wise Men   HD/DB / HDC

Elliot's Ukrainian Christmas trip takes an unexpected turn when he finds he has been invited there under false pretences. Sacha's determination to spread festive cheer looks likely to cost him dearly.

Written by Justin Young; produced by Sharon Bloom; directed by Rob Evans.

Holding / Source

24.12.2013 All I Want For Christmas Is You   HD/DB / HDC

Mary-Claire's refusal to forgive Edward puts him in a difficult position with Serena, Mr Thompson, meanwhile, is entertaining the troops in fine style.

Written by Julia Gilbert; produced by Anne Edyvean; directed by Jon Sen.

With Aden Gillett (Edward Campbell), Rosie Marcel (Jac Naylor), Bob Barrett (Sacha Levy), Carlyss Peer (Bonnie Wallis), Ben Hull (Mr Thompson), Niamh McGrady (Mary-Claire Carter), Camilla Arfwedson (Zosia March), June Watson (Margie Bennett), Nigel Betts (Noel Scanlon), Martin Brody (Sam Chandler), Laura Power (Nicky Bennett), Bronagh Taggart (Jess Chandler).

31.12.2013 Ring In The New   HD/DB / HDC

Zosia wins the battle of wills with Guy. Serena hits an all-time low.

Written by Julia Gilbert; produced by Anne Edyvean; directed by Jon Sen.

With Aden Gillett (Edward Campbell), Rosie Marcel (Jac Naylor), Bob Barrett (Sacha Levy), Carlyss Peer (Bonnie Wallis), Ben Hull (Mr Thompson), Niamh McGrady (Mary-Claire Carter), Camilla Arfwedson (Zosia March), June Watson (Margie Bennett), Nigel Betts (Noel Scanlon), Martin Brody (Sam Chandler), Laura Power (Nicky Bennett), Bronagh Taggart (Jess Chandler).

Since we like to be pedantic, the title of the series is now HOLBY CI+Y - given that we take the on-screen title as "gospel". Same applies to CASUAL+Y too :-)
See also: CASUALTY (BBC) / CASUALTY AT HOLBY CITY (BBC) / CASUALTY AT HOLBY CITY (BBC)

HOLIDAY ON ICE
A BBC production for BBC 1. Transmission details are for BBC 1.

Holding / Source

26.12.1972	J / 2"
26.12.1973	DB-D3 / 2"
25.12.1974	J / 2"
25.12.1976	DB-D3 / 2"
26.12.1977	DB-D3 / 2"

HOLIDAY ON ICE (continued)	British Christmas Television Guide

25.12.1978	DB-D3 / 2"
27.12.1981	DB-1" / 2"

2 studio recording tapes from November 1975 exist.

HOLIDAY QUIZ

A BBC production for BBC 1. Transmission details are for BBC 1.

Holding / Source

30.12.1988	DB / 1"

HOLIDAY STARTIME

An LWT production. Transmission details are for the ATV midlands region. Duration: 68 minutes.

For the next 75 minutes a galaxy composed of top television comedy stars and top musical performers join forces for your entertainment with Maggie Fitzgibbon as hostess. Join Arthur Lowe and Thora Hird in a classic comedy sketch. Then there's Peter Cook as E. L. Wisty, a park bench philosopher, and two wits from Jokers Wild : Ted Ray and Les Dawson.

Written by Peter Dulay, Barry Cryer and Peter Cook; music directed by Harry Rabinowitz; designed by Robert Macgowan; executive producer Terry Henebery; produced and directed by David Bell.

Maggie Fitzgibbon (Host), Peter Cook, Les Dawson, Thora Hird, Max Jaffa, Arthur Lowe, Vincent Price, Ted Ray, Reg Varney, The Bee Gees, Kenny Ball, Chris Barber, Acker Bilk, Hattie Jacques, Jimmy Hill.

Holding / Source

26.12.1970	DB / 62

HOLLYOAKS

Produced for Channel 4 by a variety of companies (see details below). Transmission details are for Channel 4. Usual duration: 25 minutes.

Main regular credit(s):   Created by Phil Redmond.

SERIES 1

A Mersey TV production. Transmission details are for Channel 4.

Main regular credit(s):   Executive producer Phil Redmond; produced by Phil Redmond.

Main regular cast: With Shebah Ronay (Natasha Andersen (until 18.3.96)), Anna Martland (Sarah Andersen), Alvin Stardust (Greg Andersen (only the first few weeks)), Charles Youlten (Tom Jenkins), Jeremy Edwards (Kurt Benson), Paul Leyshon (Ollie Benson), Kerrie Taylor (Lucy Benson), William Mellor (Jambo Bolton), Lisa Williamson (Dawn Cunningham), Liz Stooke (Angela Cunningham), Nick Pickard (Tony Hutchinson), Yasmin Bannerman (Maddie Parker), Brett O'Brien (Louise Taylor), Toby Sawyer (Bazz), Guy Parry (Joe), Julie Buckfield (Julie Matthews), Ian Puleston-Davies (Terry Williams), Terri Dwyer (Ruth Osbourne (8.1.96-onwards)).

Holding / Source

18.12.1995   "Louise Gets A Big Christmas Surprise. Wedding Bells Ring For The Cunninghams"   DB / V1S

Written by Phil Redmond; directed by Jo Hallows.

HOME COOKERY CLUB

A M. J. Locke & Associates production. Transmission details are for the Thames Television region. Duration: 5 minutes.

Holding / Source

19.11.1987   **Quick Christmas Cake**

04.11.1988   **Father's Christmas Cake**

HOME IS THE SAILOR

A BBC production. Transmission details are for BBC. Duration: 75 minutes.

Written by Arthur Macrae; play production by Michael Barry.

Brenda Bruce (Daisy), Charles Victor (Mr Parker), Richard Pearson (Sydney), Nan Munro (Mrs Slattery), Joan Newell (Ruby), Donald Morley (Mr Caldecott), Rose Alba (Andrée Courbois).

Holding / Source

25.12.1956	J /

HOME JAMES!

A Thames Television production. Transmission details are for the Central region.

Main regular credit(s):   Created by Geoff McQueen.

Main regular cast: Jim Davidson (Jim London), George Sewell (Robert Palmer), Harry Towb (Henry Compton).

SERIES 1

Main regular credit(s):   Written by Geoff McQueen; produced by Anthony Parker.

Holding / Source

21.12.1987   **It All Comes Out In The Wash**   1" / 1"

Duration: 40 minutes.

The guv'nor, Robert Palmer, calls on Jim when the boilers burst at the factory and flooding threatens to ruin the staff Christmas shindig. Jim puts out his 'East End feelers' and calls in a plumber 'par excellence' to the rescue. And this plumber turns out to be a rarity indeed. And so does the party!

Designed by Peter Joyce; directed by Anthony Parker.

With Vanessa Knox-Mawer (Sarah), Sherrie Hewson (Paula), Owen Whittaker (Terry), Cecilia-Marie Carreon (Connie), Linal Haft (Tonto), Suzanne Church (Emma), David Hatton (Sid), Geoffrey Hutchings (Wainright).

HOME JAMES!

HOME TO ROOST

A Yorkshire Television production. Transmission details are for the Central region.
Main regular credit(s): Written by Eric Chappell; music by Peter Knight.
Main regular cast: John Thaw (Henry Willows), Reece Dinsdale (Matthew Willows).

	Holding / Source
27.12.1987 **Family Ties**	1" / 1"

Duration: 53 minutes.
With Rebecca Lacey, Sherrie Hewson, Tim Barrett, Anthony Smee, Ian Tucker.

HONEY LANE

An ATV production. Transmission details are for the ATV midlands region.
Main regular credit(s): Created by Louis Marks; theme music by Derek Scott.
SERIES 1
Duration: 25 minutes.
Main regular credit(s): Produced by John Cooper.

	VT Number	Holding / Source
26.12.1968 **Episode 26**	8626/68	J / 40

Christmas Day in the market. For some, like Harry, Mike and Dave, it's a time for celebration. For Billy Bush, however, there are grim matters to attend to. Polly cooks Christmas dinner for Danny and Joe, but Danny has to go out on an errand which leads him into danger.
Written by Robert Holmes; directed by Paul Bernard.
With Ivor Salter (Harry Jolson), Ray Lonnen (Dave Sampson), Iain Gregory (Mike Sampson), Brian Rawlinson (Danny Jessel), John Barrett (Joey English), James Culliford (Alf Noble), Patricia Denys (Stella Noble), John J. Carney (Wally Knight), Pat Nye (Polly Jessel), John Bennett (Billy Bush), Marian Diamond (Ann Markham), Elspeth MacNaughton, Katy Gardiner.

HOOTS

A BBC Scotland production. Transmission details are for BBC Scotland. Duration: 28 minutes.
Executive producer Ewan Angus; series producer Alan Clements; produced by Fiona White; directed by Lyn Rowett.
Fred Macaulay (Host), Tim Brooke-Taylor, Gregor Fisher, Robbie Coltrane, Greg Hemphill, Rikki Fulton, Moira Anderson, Walter Carr, Bill Oddie, Graeme Garden, Les Dawson, Dawn French, Jennifer Saunders, Elaine Smith, Ron Bain, Tony Roper, Russ Abbot, Ford Kiernan, Brian Pettifer, Fulton Mackay, Gerard Kelly, Stanley Baxter, Iain McColl, Roddy McMillan, Chic Murray, Dorothy Paul, Will Fyffe, Lex McLean, Harry Gordon, Buff Hardie, George Donald, Duncan McCrae, Tommy Morgan, Steve Robertson, Derek Cameron, Mike Cameron, Tommy Lorne.

	Holding / Source
31.12.1999	DB / DBSW

HOOVES OF FIRE

A BBC Animation Unit production for BBC Children's Department. Transmission details are for BBC 1. Duration: 30 minutes.
Readings by Andy Riley; written by Richard Curtis and Kevin Cecil; music by Mark Knopfler; director of photography Fred Reed; art director Lee Wilton; executive producers Richard Curtis, Kevin Cahill, Colin Rose and Helen Nabarro; produced by Richard Goleszowski and Jacqueline White; directed by Richard Goleszowski.
Robbie Williams (Narrator).

	Holding / Source
25.12.1999	DB /

Animated film.
See also: LEGEND OF THE LOST TRIBE (BBC)

THE HOPE AND KEEN SCENE

A BBC production for BBC 1. Transmission details are for BBC 1. Duration: 25 minutes.
Main regular credit(s): Music by Ray Bishop; designed by John O'Hara; produced by Paul Ciani; film sequences directed by David Crichton.
Main regular cast: Albie Keen (Himself), Mike Hope (Himself), Jennifer Hill.

	Holding / Source
24.12.1974 **Christmas**	DB-D3 / 2"

Mike and Albie will be taking a light-hearted look at Christmas. You'll see Mike and Albie as Ugly Sisters, join them on a spy-packed adventure serial — and you'll meet the zany Whoopee Band. It's Christmas Crackers all right!
Written by John Morley, Barry Jones and Philip Griffin; directed by Paul Ciani.
With Bob Kerr's Whoopee Band.

| 31.12.1974 **New Year** | J / 2" |

Written by John Morley and Barry Jones; directed by Paul Ciani.
With Johnny Hart.

HORIZON CHRISTMAS SPECIAL

A BBC Science Features Department production for BBC 2. Transmission details are for BBC 2. Duration: 35 minutes.

	Holding / Source
25.12.1966 **Hand Me My Sword, Humphrey**	J / C1

Written by Richard Wade; edited by R. W. Reid; produced by Ramsay Short; directed by Peter R. Smith.
With Dudley Foster (Edward Hastings), Prunella Scales (Florence Hastings), William Burleigh (Humphrey), Deborah Watling (Sophy), Julie Samuel (Emma).

The BBC used to list it but the holdings, (which were some mute film sequences only) turned out to be from the One Hundred Years of Humphrey Hastings series that followed.

HORNE A'PLENTY

An ABC/Thames production for Various ITV Companies. Transmission details are for Various ITV Companies. Duration: 25 minutes.

Main regular cast: Kenneth Horne, Ken Parry.

SERIES 2
A Thames Television production. Transmission details are for the ATV midlands region.

Main regular credit(s): Produced by Barry Took; directed by Peter Frazer-Jones.

Holding / Source

25.12.1968 Christmas Horne A'Plenty   DBSEQ|n / 2"

Written by David Cumming, Michael Green, Johnnie Mortimer, Brian Cooke, Donald Webster, Geoff Rowley and Andy Baker; designed by Jim Nicholson.

With Graham Stark, Sheila Steafel, Alan Curtis, Ken Parry, Donald Webster, Rogers and Starr.

The surviving material is studio fooatge.

HORRIBLE HISTORIES

A Lion Television production for CBBC. Transmission details are for BBC Various. Duration: 30 minutes.

Main regular credit(s): Based on books by Terry Deary.

SERIES 2
Made in association with Citrus. Transmission details are for CBBC.

Main regular credit(s): Written by Mathew Baynton, Gerard Foster, Jon Holmes, Greg Jenner, Giles Pilbrow, Steve Punt and Laurence Rickard; script supervisors Anne Patterson and Rebecca Rycroft; music by Richie Webb; directors of photography Pete Edwards, John Sorapure and Shahana Meer; designed by Miranda Jones; assistant producer Greg Jenner; executive producers Alison Gregory and Richard Bradley; production managers Patsy Blades and Laura Steele-Perkins; series producer Caroline Norris; produced by Giles Pilbrow; directed by Dominic Brigstocke and Steve Connelly.

Main regular cast: With John Eccleston (Puppeteer), Jon Culshaw (Voices), Dave Lamb (Voices), Jess Robinson (Voices), Mathew Baynton, Simon Farnaby, Martha Howe-Douglas, Jim Howick, Laurence Rickard, Ben Willbond, Lawry Lewin, Alice Lowe, Katy Wix.

Holding / Source

17.12.2010 Horrible Christmas   HD/DB / HD/DB

Alternative transmissions: BBC 1: 24.12.2010.

Additional material by Lucy Clarke.

With David Baddiel.

First tx'd on BBC HD Channel and CBBC (simulcast).

HOT SEAT

An LWT production. Transmission details are for the London Weekend Television region.

Holding / Source

20.12.1970   J / 2"

Lord Soper, the Methodist Minister and President of the Methodist Conference, is best known for his sermons to the West London Mission at Kingsway Hall. Tonight he faces a very different type of audience; a group of young people from schools and youth organisations who ask questions on contemporary Christian values. Des Wilson, the New Zealand journalist who has campaigned for the homeless as director of Shelter, is in the chair.

Designed by Gordon Toms; executive producer Francis Coleman; produced by Malcolm Stewart; directed by David Coulter.

With Des Wilson (Interviewer), Cliff Richard, Lord Soper.

THE HOT SHOE SHOW

A BBC production for BBC 1. Transmission details are for BBC 1.

Main regular performer(s): Wayne Sleep.

SERIES 2
Main regular credit(s): Choreography by Anthony Van Laast; produced by Tom Gutteridge.

Holding / Source

23.12.1984   DB / 1"

Written by Nigel Crowle; song by Gerard Kenny, Jacqui McShee, Nicky Moore, Ray Shell and Carl Wayne; music directed by Allan Rogers; music by Howard Goodall, Gerard Kenny, Drey Shepperd, Scott English, David Mindel, Allan Rogers and Richard Stilgoe; choreography by Charles Augins, Christopher Bruce, Arlene Phillips, Wayne Sleep and Stewart Avon Arnold; designed by Dacre Punt; production manager Carmella Milne; directed by Tom Gutteridge and Ron Isted.

With Bonnie Langford, Cherry Gillespie, Stewart Avon Arnold, Stephen Beagley, Claud-Paul Henry, Andy Norman, Wendy Roe, Kim Rosato, Lizie Saunderson, Tim Spain, Oke Wambu, Finola Hughes, Hugh Craig, Daniel Chamberlain, Andre Winch.

HOTEL PARADISO

A BBC production. Transmission details are for BBC. Duration: 75 minutes.

Written by Georges Feydeau and Maurice Desvallieres; translated by Peter Glenville; play production by Rosemary Hill.

Cyril Shaps (Boniface), Geoffrey Bayldon (Martin), William Kendall (Cot), Joan Sanderson (Angélique), June Whitfield (Marcelle), Josephine Woodford (Victoire), Patrick Godfrey (Maxim), Julia McCarthy (Paquerette), Frances Guthrie (Violette), Patricia Pacy (Marguerite), Sandra Skerner (Pervenche), Robert Gillespie (Georges), Reginald Marsh (Inspector Bouchard), Peter Wyatt (Policeman).

Holding / Source

21.12.1962   J /

THE HOUND OF THE BASKERVILLES

A Tiger Aspect production for BBC 1. made in association with Canadian Broadcasting Corporation / Isle of Man Film Commission / WGBH Boston. Transmission details are for BBC 1. Duration: 99 minutes.

The mysterious death of Sir Charles Baskerville leads the detective duo to investigate an alleged family curse and forces of evil at work on Dartmoor.

Dramatised by Allan Cubitt; based on a book by Sir Arthur Conan Doyle; executive producers Allan Cubitt, Steve Christian, Rebecca Eaton, Gareth Neame, Sally Woodward Gentle and Greg Brenman; produced by Christopher Hall; directed by David Attwood.

Richard Roxburgh (Sherlock Holmes), Ian Hart (Doctor Watson), Richard E. Grant (Stapleton), Matt Day (Henry Baskerville), Neve McIntosh (Beryl Stapleton), John Nettles (Doctor Mortimer), Geraldine James (Mrs Mortimer), Peter Roberts (Sir Charles Baskerville), Ron Cook (Barrymore), Liza Tarbuck (Mrs Barrymore), Danny Webb (Inspector Lestrade), Paul Kynman (Selden), Jim Norton (Coroner), David McNeill (Hotel Porter), Richard Hawley (Clayton), Tom Freeman (Father Christmas), Malcolm Shields (Knight), Eddie Brittain (Hound), Casper Zafer (Warder), Stephan Bessant (Warder), John Maude (Perkins).

	Holding / Source
26.12.2002	DB / V1SW

HOUSEPARTY

A Southern Television production. Transmission details are for the Southern Television region.

	Holding / Source
31.12.1981 **Ep 2067**	DB-DV / 2"

With Sylvia Marshall, Avril Bell, Cherry Marshall, Ann Ladbury, Mary Morris, Lucy Morgan, Vivian Tidbury, Daphne Lee, Claire Kitchen, Marian Shuttleworth, Vida Adamoli, Sarah Litvinoff, Maggie Baldari, Lynne Inglis, Sister Immaculata, Karen Saxby, Anna Clements, Pauline Parrington, Mim Summers, Anne Scott, Sunny Stout, Judy Andreason.

All surviving shows circa 1980/1981. For the series "Southern Gold" and in particular the one featuring the ladies from Houseparty, one of the ladies had kept quite a few off air "Houseparty" programmes on VHS. They wanted to use a clip, as none of the 2 inch survived, so we used these VHSs. An engineer took the opportunity to dub off all the available programmes and these are what survive now on Digi at Wessex. They're mainly off air from Thames and some have the opening and ends clipped. Appearing though, in various combinations, are the regular ladies from Houseparty. e.g Mary Morris, Sylvia Marshall, Cherry Marshall, Ann Ladbury, Claire Kitchen, Marion Shuttleworth, Sister Immaculata etc.

Held at Wessex Archive.

HOW

Alternative/Working Title(s): KNOW HOW

A Southern Television production. Transmission details are for the Southern Television region. Duration: 25 minutes.

SERIES 14

Transmission details are for the Thames Television region.

Main regular credit(s):   Research Diane Campbell and Andy Prendergast; directed by George Egan.

Main regular cast: With Jack Hargreaves (Presenter), Jon Miller (Presenter), Marian Davies (Presenter), Fred Dinenage (Presenter).

	Holding / Source
27.12.1978 **Christmas How**	J / 2"

HOW NOT TO LIVE YOUR LIFE

A Brown Eyed Boy Production production for BBC 3. Transmission details are for BBC 3.

Main regular credit(s):   Written by Dan Clark.

Main regular cast: Dan Clark (Dom).

	Holding / Source
22.12.2011 **It's A Don-derful Life**	HD/DB / HD/DB

Commissioned by BBC Scotland. Duration: 60 minutes.

Script editor Drew Pearce; music by Ben Parker; designed by Iain McDonald; executive producer Kristian Smith; produced by Gary Reich and Dan Clark; directed by Sam Leifer.

With Laura Haddock (Samantha Parker), David Armand (Edward 'Eddie' Singh), Leila Hoffman (Mrs Treacher), Alex Carter (Blake), Julia Davis (Anne Yeaman), Sinead Moynihan (Abby Jones), Daniel Lawrence Taylor (Jason), Laura Fedorowycz (Louise), Oliver Maltman (Derek Yeaman), Tom Meeten (Graham Length), Fiona Mollison (Sam's Mum), Joanna Neary (Care Worker).

HOW ON EARTH?

An ABC production. Transmission details are for the Anglia region. Duration: 40 minutes.

Religious adviser Ian MacKenzie; produced and directed by Helen Standage.

Dean Edward Patey (Host), Noel Rawsthorne (Organist), The Bee Gees, The Crofters, Kenny Everett, Pete Lewis, The Settlers, Everyman's Theatre, Liverpool, Liverpool Cathedral Choir.

	Holding / Source
24.12.1967	J / 40

HOW WE USED TO LIVE

A Yorkshire Schools production for Yorkshire Television. Transmission details are for ATV/Central/Channel 4. Duration varies - see below for details.

SERIES 1: Victorians

Transmission details are for the ATV midlands region. Duration: 25 minutes.

	VT Number	Holding / Source
01.12.1968 **Festive Season**	4021	R1N / 2"

Introduced by Jimmy Hanley; produced by Peter Hunt; directed by Charles Leigh Bennett.

HOW WE USED TO LIVE (continued)

SERIES 3
Transmission details are for the ATV midlands region.
Main regular credit(s): Produced by Richard Handford.

	VT Number	Holding / Source
27.11.1978 **Christmas**	E462	1" / 2"

Duration: 21 minutes.
Written by Freda Kelsall; directed by Richard Handford.
With David Ross (Captain Selwyn), Jeannie Hammersleigh (Dora Selwyn), Charles Tomlinson (Humphrey Selwyn), Ashley Barker (Edmund Hughes), Joanne Whalley (Sarah Hughes), Haydn Conway (Matt Fairhurst), Alison Ambler (Annie Fairhurst), Tessa Worsley (Mrs Hughes), James Tomlinson (Doctor Hughes), Brenda Hall (Mrs Tandy).

SERIES 4
Transmission details are for the ATV midlands region.
Main regular credit(s): Music by Robert Hartley; produced by David H. Wilson.

	VT Number	Holding / Source
02.12.1981 **Peace On Earth**	E859	1" / 2"

Duration: 20 minutes.
Narrated by Redvers Kyle; written by Freda Kelsall; directed by Frank W. Smith.
With John Keyworth (Arthur Hodgkins), Diana Davies (Mabel Hodgkins), Julie Shipley (Patricia Hodgkins), Mark Uttley (Jimmy Hodgkins), Rachel Ambler (Avril Hodgkins), Christopher Ley Rose (Edward Hodgkins), Doreen Sloane (Mrs Maitland), Jay Benedict (Anton Podemski).

HUMPTY DUMPTY
A BBC production for BBC 1. Transmission details are for BBC 1. Duration: 90 minutes.
Adapted by David Cumming; based on a book by David Croft and Phil Park; music directed by Burt Rhodes; choreography by Roy Gunson; designed by Andy Dimond; produced and directed by Peter Whitmore.
Leslie Crowther (Humpty Dumpty), Reg Varney (Simple Simon), Ken Platt (The King Of Hearts), Lynda Baron (Tommy Tucker), Sally Smith (Mary Mary), Alan Curtis (Grimm), Kathleen West (The Queen Of Hearts), Max Latimer (The Ogre), Iris Sadler (Mother Goose), Kay Lyell (Priscilla The Goose), Barrie Duprés (The Knave), The Roy Gunson Dancers, The George Mitchell Singers.

	Holding / Source
25.12.1968	J /

A HUNDRED HUMAN CRIES
An ABC production. Transmission details are for the ABC midlands region. Duration: 40 minutes.
An anthology for New Year from Coventry Cathedral. The last hours of a day, the dying minutes of a year, moments in time, fractions of all our lives, another spent year for the historian to dissect. 1968 is to be the International Year for Human Rights: what will this New Year offer, what can we offer this New Year, how can we answer a hundred human cries?
Written by Trevor Preston; executive producer Ian MacKenzie; produced and directed by Helen Standage.
David Lepine, Michael Bryant, Earl Cameron, Colette O'Neil, Carolyn Hester, Paul Tortelier, John Williams, Nerine Barratt, Derek Garside, Victor Godfrey.

	Holding / Source
31.12.1967	J /

A HUNDRED YEARS OF HUMPHREY HASTINGS
Alternative/Working Title(s): LIFE WITH A PRACTICAL FATHER
A BBC production for BBC 2. Transmission details are for BBC 2. Duration: 30 minutes.
Main regular credit(s): Written by Richard Wade; produced by Ramsay Short; directed by Peter R. Smith.
Main regular cast: Dudley Foster (Humphrey Hastings).

	Holding / Source
21.12.1967 **1967 - A Very Cold Christmas**	J / 2"

With John Wentworth (Major Wilson / Grandfather), Deddie Davies, Louis Selwyn, Julie Samuel.

THE HUNTING OF THE SNARK
A Rediffusion Television production. Transmission details are for the Anglia region. Duration: 25 minutes.
Written by Lewis Carroll; drawings by John Ryan; music by Johnny Pearson; produced and directed by Diana Potter.
Michael Hordern (Reader).

	Holding / Source
23.12.1967	B3N|n / B3

Alternative transmissions: Associated-Rediffusion: 26.12.1967; Rediffusion Television: 26.12.1967.
See also: THE RIME OF THE ANCIENT MARINER

HUXLEY PIG
A Filmfair production for Central. Transmission details are for the Central region. Duration: 14 minutes.
Main regular credit(s): Written by Rodney Peppe; produced by Jo Pullen; directed by Martin Pullen.
Main regular cast: Martin Jarvis (Voices).

SERIES 2
Main regular credit(s): Executive producer David Yates.

	Holding / Source
18.12.1990 **Cinderella**	1" / C1

HUXLEY PIG

A HYMN FOR BRITAIN

A Southern Television production. Transmission details are for the Southern Television region. Duration: 25 minutes.

"A Hymn for Britain" together with spin-offs "A Carol for Christmas" and "A Song for Easter" were network Sunday evening shows where writers had the chance to compose new religious songs, as the names suggest. Viewers voted and over the weeks a winner was found, in each case. Some clips survive on the "Southern Gold 21 years" insert VHS.

Holding / Source

28.12.1967 J / 40

I CAN SEE IT ALL

Alternative/Working Title(s): THE GRAND ILLUSION
A BBC production for BBC 2. Transmission details are for BBC 2. Duration: 30 minutes.
Written by Richard Wade; designed by David Spode; produced by Ramsay Short; directed by David Maloney.
Dudley Foster (Humphrey Hastings), Elvi Hale (Constance Hastings), John Wentworth (Grandfather), Mary Merrall (Grandmother), Simon Turner (Edward Hastings), Carolyn Courage (Mary Hastings), Susan White (The Maid).

	Holding / Source
25.12.1971	J / 2"

I GOTTA SHOE

Alternative/Working Title(s): CINDY-ELLA
A BBC production for BBC 2. Transmission details are for BBC 2. Duration: 60 minutes.
Written by Caryl Brahms and Ned Sherrin; drawings by Tony Walton; music by Ron Grainer and Peter Knight; designed by Brian Tregidden; produced and directed by Ned Sherrin.
Cleo Laine, Elisabeth Welch, Cy Grant, George Browne, The Peter Knight Singers.

	Holding / Source
24.12.1966	J /

I HATE CHRISTMAS TOO!

A BBC production for BBC 1. Transmission details are for BBC 1. Duration: 4 minutes.
Written by Brian Sibley; executive producer Chris Loughlin; produced by Nick Stillwell.
Samuel West, Peter Capaldi.

	Holding / Source
25.12.1997	DB / DBS

I LOVE CHRISTMAS

A BBC production for BBC 2. Transmission details are for BBC 2. Duration: 90 minutes.
Produced by Will Bryant; directed by Andrew Nicholson.

	Holding / Source
24.12.2001	DB / DBSW

Celebrities recall how people celebrated the festive season in the 1970s and 1980s.

IAN BREAKWELL'S CHRISTMAS DIARY

An Annalogue Production production for Channel 4. Transmission details are for Channel 4. Duration: 8 minutes.
Main regular credit(s): Written by Ian Breakwell; produced and directed by Anna Ridley.
Main regular cast: Ian Breakwell.

		Holding / Source
22.12.1984	**One Million Turkeys**	1" / 1"
23.12.1984		1" / 1"
24.12.1984	**Victorian Values**	1" / 1"
25.12.1984	**1984**	1" / 1"
26.12.1984	**The Monarch Of Misrule**	1" / 1"

IDEAL

A Baby Cow Productions production for BBC 3. Transmission details are for BBC 3. Duration: 30 minutes.
Main regular credit(s): Written by Graham Duff; theme music by Candidate.
Main regular cast: Johnny Vegas (Moz).
Credits: Additional material by Tony Burgess; script editor Henry Normal; associate producers Graham Duff and Johnny Vegas; executive producers Kenton Allen and Henry Normal; produced by Ted Dowd; directed by Dan Zeff.
Cast: With Ben Crompton (Colin), Nicola Reynolds (Nicki).

	Holding / Source
27.12.2005 **An Ideal Witness**	DB / DBSWF

Script supervisor Mandy Mason.
With Natalie Gumede (China), Sinead Matthews (Jenny), Tom Goodman-Hill (Police Constable), Graham Duff (Brian), Ronny Jhutti (Kuldiq), Beatrice Kelley (Sheila), Seymour Leon Mace (Steve), David Sant (Cartoon Head), Sunetra Sarker (Sangita), Haruka Kuroda, Ryan Hope.

IF IT MOVES – IT'S RUDE!

A BBC production for BBC 1. Transmission details are for BBC 1. Duration: 50 minutes.
Written by Robert Vas; produced and directed by Robert Vas.
Kenneth More (Narrator), Jimmy Edwards, Arthur English, Bruce Forsyth, Pearl Hackney, Stanley Holloway, Alfred Marks, Des O'Connor, Harry Secombe, Sheila Van Damm.

	Holding / Source
26.12.1969	C1 / C1

IF MUSIC BE THE FOOD OF LOVE, MINE'S A JAM BUTTY (RADIO)

A BBC production for BBC Radio 4. Transmission details are for BBC Radio 4. Duration: 45 minutes.

Written by Lesley Whiteley and Julie Wilkinson; music by Tayo Akimbode; play production by Pauline Harris.

Sunetra Sarker (Beth), Russell Dixon (Michael), Kevin Knapman (Wayne), Eileen O'Brien (Sally / Aunt Val), Susan Twist (Vera), John Jardine (Peter), Amy Freston (Singer, 'Pie Jesu').

	Holding / Source
29.12.1999	DA /

YR IFANC A'R WYL

A BBC Wales production for BBC 1 Wales. Transmission details are for BBC 1 Wales. Duration: 50 minutes.

A school prepares for Christmas.

	Holding / Source
12.12.1976	J / 2"

I'M ALL RIGHT JACQUES

A BBC Scotland production for BBC 2. Transmission details are for BBC 2. Duration: 30 minutes.

Written by Pete McCarthy; produced and directed by Caroline Roberts.

Pete McCarthy.

	Holding / Source
21.12.1992	DB-D3 / D3S

Alternative transmissions: BBC Scotland: 09.12.1992.

I'M DREAMING OF A TV CHRISTMAS

A BBC production for BBC 2. Transmission details are for BBC 2. Duration: 54 minutes.

Executive producer Helen Bullough; produced by Martyn Smith and Annabelle Waller.

Phill Jupitus (Host), Ronnie Barker, Ronnie Corbett, Noel Edmonds, Jimmy Savile, Tony Blackburn.

	Holding / Source
24.12.2003	DB / DBSW

THE IMPORTANCE OF BEING EARNEST

A Terence Donovan Consolidated production for Channel 4. Transmission details are for Channel 4. Duration: 105 minutes.

Written by Oscar Wilde; produced by Terence Donovan; directed by Michael Lindsay-Hogg.

Wendy Hiller (Lady Bracknell), Gary Bond (John Worthing JP), Jeremy Clyde (Algernon Moncrieff), Gabrielle Drake (Gwendolen Fairfax), Ann Thornton (Cecily Cardew), Rosamund Greenwood (Miss Prism), Henry Moxon (Reverend Canon Chasuble DD), Alan Hay (Lane), Sydney Arnold (Merriman), David Matthews (Footman).

	Holding / Source
25.12.1986	1" / 1"

IN CONCERT

A BBC production for BBC 2. Transmission details are for BBC 2. Duration varies - see below for details.

	Holding / Source
24.12.1979	DB-D3 / 2"

A BBC Manchester production. Duration: 50 minutes.

From The Royal Exchange, Manchester.

Produced by Peter Ridsdale Scott; directed by Johnnie Stewart.

With Alan Price.

IN LOVING MEMORY

A Yorkshire Television production. Transmission details are for the ATV/Central region.

Oldshaw, 1929 - when you could have a night out at the Theatre Royal, a pint of ale in the interval, a hot pie on the way home - and still have change out of a shilling. You could also have an argument with a brewer's dray and end up as a client of Jeremiah Unsworth and Co., Undertakers and Monumental Masons....and be the subject of the most disastrous funeral in the long and noble history of undertaking.

Main regular credit(s): Created by Dick Sharples; written by Dick Sharples; produced and directed by Ronnie Baxter.

Main regular cast: Thora Hird (Ivy Unsworth), Christopher Beeny (Billy Henshaw).

SERIES 3

Transmission details are for the Central region.

		Production No	Holding / Source
24.12.1982	'God Rest Ye Merry Gentlemen'	L412	1" / 2"

Duration: 50 minutes.

Never heard the Undertakers' Glee Club? You can now as Ivy Unsworth and Billy Henshaw provide their special brand of Christmas cheer.

Designed by Andrew Sanderson.

With Liz Smith, Roger Brierley, Milton Johns, Lesley Dunlop, Davyd Harries, Johnny Allen.

IN SEARCH OF FATHER CHRISTMAS

A Central production. Transmission details are for the Central region. Duration: 35 minutes.

In the far north of Sweden lies a mountain where, it is said, Father Christmas lives. Stuart Room, an 11-year-old schoolboy from Birmingham, and - Professor Jan Oivind Svalui journey there in search of Santa.

Programme associate Sven Gosta Holst; music by Jugg; executive producer Lewis Rudd; produced and directed by Colin Nutley.

Stuart Room (Presenter), Professor Jan Oivind (Presenter).

	Holding / Source
23.12.1983	C1 / C1

IN SEARCH OF SANTA

A BBC production for BBC 2. Transmission details are for BBC 2. Duration: 40 minutes.

Executive producer Tony Moss; produced by Chris Oxley.

	Holding / Source
23.12.1995	DB-D3 / D3S

IN SICKNESS AND IN HEALTH

A BBC production for BBC 1. Transmission details are for BBC 1. Duration: 30 minutes.

| Main regular credit(s): | Written by Johnny Speight. |
| Main regular cast: | Warren Mitchell (Alf Garnett). |

SERIES 1

| Main regular credit(s): | Designed by Graham Lough; produced and directed by Roger Race. |
| Main regular cast: | With Dandy Nichols (Else). |

	Holding / Source
26.12.1985 "Rita At Christmas"	DB / 1"

With Una Stubbs (Rita), Arthur English (Arthur), Eamonn Walker (Winston), Arnold Diamond, Michael Osborne, Campbell Graham.

SERIES 2

| Main regular credit(s): | Produced by Roger Race; directed by Richard Boden. |
| Main regular cast: | With Una Stubbs (Rita), Arthur English (Arthur), Eamonn Walker (Winston), Carmel McSharry (Mrs Hollingbery). |

	Holding / Source
23.12.1986 "Caribbean Magic"	DB / 1"

Designed by Janine Killick.

With Eileen Kennally (Mrs Johnson), Ken Campbell (Mr Johnson), Alison Steadman, Renu Setna, Arnold Diamond, Scott Farrell, Edmund Kente, Jo Kendall, Richard Henry, Mark Vella.

SERIES 3

| Main regular credit(s): | Designed by Michael Trevor; produced by Roger Race; directed by Richard Boden. |
| Main regular cast: | With Eamonn Walker (Winston), Carmel McSharry (Mrs Hollingbery), Arthur English (Arthur). |

	Holding / Source
25.12.1987 "Hip Replacement"	DB / 1"

Christmas is a time to be with the family, but not for Alf. He is destined to spend Christmas in hospital, having his hip replaced.

With Eileen Kennally (Mrs Johnson), Ken Campbell (Fred Johnson), John Bird, Norman Rossington, Arnold Diamond, Maggie Jones, Brenda Cowling, Georgia Mitchell.

SERIES 5

| Main regular credit(s): | Produced by Richard Boden. |
| Main regular cast: | With Carmel McSharry (Mrs Hollingbery). |

	Holding / Source
25.12.1989 "Bread And Cheese"	DB / 1"

Directed by Richard Boden.

With Arthur English (Arthur), Ken Campbell (Fred Johnson), Tricia Kelly, Philip Fox, Tamara Steele.

| 30.12.1990 "Full Of Christmas Spirit" | DB / 1" |

Directed by Richard Boden.

With Arthur English (Arthur), Ken Campbell (Fred Johnson), Pat Coombs (Mrs Carey), Hugh Lloyd (Mr Carey), Tricia Kelly, Philip Stone, Harry Fowler.

See also: THE SPIRIT OF 66 WITH ALF GARNETT (BBC) / THE THOUGHTS OF CHAIRMAN ALF - AT CHRISTMAS - ON YER ACTUAL BOXING DAY / "TILL DEATH US DO PART" (BBC)

IN THE DARK WITH JULIAN CLARY

A Mai Production production for ITV. made in association with Fuji / Fundamental Films / Tilt Production. Transmission details are for the Central region. Duration: 25 minutes.

Produced by Lisa Clark; directed by Sue McMahon.

Julian Clary (Host).

	Holding / Source
23.12.1996	D2 / D2S

Game show in which three couples take on challenges in total darkness, while high-tech cameras follow the action.

IN THE HOUSE WITH CLEOPATRA AND FRIENDS

An Initial Film & TV production for ITV. Transmission details are for the Central region. Duration: 50 minutes.

Written by Roger Griffiths; produced by Catherine Whelton; directed by Royston Mayoh.

Cleopatra, Shane Richie, Jenny Eclair, Matthew Cottle, Steps, Another Level, Ultimate Kaos, Ian Wright, Wolf (Gladiator), Ace (Gladiator), John Inman, Sooty.

Holding / Source

25.12.1998   DB / DBS

IN THE SPIRIT

A Granada production for ITV/Channel 4. Transmission details are for ITV/Channel 4.

Natalie Cole, Reverend James Cleveland, Marion Williams, Dorothy Norwood, Southern California Community Choir.

Commissioned by Channel 4. Transmission details are for Channel 4.

Credits: Executive producer Norman Swallow; produced by Simon Albury; directed by Nicholas Ferguson.

Holding / Source

24.12.1982   1" / 1"

Duration: 50 minutes.

With Natalie Cole, Reverend James Cleveland, Marion Williams, Dorothy Norwood, Southern California Community Choir.

Repeat tx date.

THE INBETWEENERS

A Bwark Production production for E4. made in association with Young Films. Transmission details are for E4. Duration: 25 minutes.

Main regular credit(s):	Written by Damon Beesley and Iain Morris; script editor Robert Popper; designed by Richard Drew; head of production Leo Martin; produced by Christopher Young.
Main regular cast:	Simon Bird (Will), James Buckley (Jay), Blake Harrison (Neil), Joe Thomas (Simon).

SERIES 1

Main regular credit(s):	Script supervisor Angelica Pressello; executive producers Damon Beesley and Iain Morris; directed by Gordon Anderson.
Main regular cast:	With Henry Lloyd-Hughes (Mark Donovan).

Holding / Source

29.05.2008   **Xmas Party**   DB / DBSWF

Alternative transmissions: Channel 4: 10.12.2008.

Will takes his role as chairman of the Christmas prom committee seriously.

With Martin Trenaman (Mr Cooper), John Seaward (John), Emily Head (Carli), Greg Davies (Mr Gilbert), Ash Varrez, Amanda St John, Jo Maycock, Emily Atack, Ollie Holme, Transformer.

THE INCH MAN

A BBC production. Transmission details are for BBC. Duration: 30 minutes.

Main regular credit(s):	Written by Lester Powell.
Main regular cast:	Robert Ayres (Stephen Inch).

SERIES 2

Main regular credit(s):	Produced and directed by Douglas Moodie.
Main regular cast:	With Hamlyn Benson (George Packer, Manager of the Imperial Crescent Hotel), Joan Harben (Miss Bromsgrove, Receptionist), Faith Bailey (Cherry, Telephonist).

Holding / Source

29.12.1951   **I Hate Christmas**   NR / Live

With Edmund Willard, Olivia Burleigh, Peter Cresswell, John Kyle, Alvys Maben.

INSIDE STORY

An Anglia production. Transmission details are for the Central region. Duration: 50 minutes.

Main regular credit(s):	Written by Peter Ransley; produced by John Rosenberg; directed by Moira Armstrong.
Main regular cast:	Roy Marsden (John Bennet), Francesca Annis (Paula Croxley), Harry Andrews (Lord Glenross), Douglas Lambert (Walter Schiff), Alan MacNaughtan (Frank Ormsby), James Smith (Toby Greene), Tenniel Evans (David Clare), Michael Graham Cox (Alan Merton).

Holding / Source

05.10.1986   **Auld Lang Syne**   1" / 1"

With Ian Thompson (Jim Fowler), Lord Wilson of Rievaulx, Roger Brierley, Clare Clifford, Diana King, Chantelle Urquhart, Christopher Peters, Carol Gleeson.

INTO 71

A BBC production for BBC 1. Transmission details are for BBC 1. Duration: 55 minutes.

Music directed by John Cameron; choreography by Flick Colby; lighting by Clive Thomas; sound Richard Chamberlain; designed by Spencer Chapman; produced and directed by Stanley Dorfman.

Blue Mink, CCS, Georgie Fame, Elton John, Alexis Korner, Lulu, Pan's People, Alan Price, Labi Siffre, Cat Stevens, Sue and Sunny, Livingston Taylor, Peter Thorup, Traffic, The Who, The Barbara Moore Singers.

Holding / Source

31.12.1970   J / 2"

IT HAPPENED ONE CHRISTMAS

Alternative/Working Title(s): CHRISTMAS WEEK CLOSE

A Thames Television production. Transmission details are for the Thames Television region. Duration: 10 minutes.

Main regular credit(s): Research Pamela Moncur; designed by Jim Nicolson; produced and directed by Margery Baker.

Main regular cast: Gillian Reynolds (Presenter).

	VT Number	Holding / Source
19.12.1981	25897	DB / 2"

On 2 March, 1942, after the fall of Singapore to the Japanese, Freddy Bloom was sent to Changi Prison with more than 400 other women. She was to spend three Christmases in jail, and here she talks to Gillian Reynolds about her faith.

With Freddy Bloom.

20.12.1981	25898	DB / 2"

With Terry Waite.

21.12.1981	25899	DB / 2"

With Gary Armstrong.

22.12.1981	25900	DB / 2"

With Laurens Van Der Post.

23.12.1981	25901	DB / 2"

With Thora Hird.

IT MIGHT BE YOU

A BBC production for BBC 1. Transmission details are for BBC 1. Duration: 80 minutes.

Bob, Sue and Wendy never meant to buy a lottery ticket, and they certainly didn't mean to lose it when it could be the £25 million jackpot winner.

Written by Nigel Williams; produced by Kenith Trodd; directed by Christopher Morahan.

Douglas Hodge (Bob), Frances Barber (Wendy), Jim Carter (Wally 'Lottery' Whaley), Amanda Mealing (Sue), Alexander Scott (Ben), Freddie Jones (David), Julian Curry (Barrister), Vera Jakob (Sue's Grannie), Arthur Whybrow (George), Steve Sweeney (Bookseller), Ramsay Gilderdale (Nigel), Susie Brann (Janeybee), Rollo Weeks (Damon), Rishi Chopra (Aziz), Laita Ahmed (Aziz's Mother), Ross McCaul (Youth), Neil Maskell (Youth), Jake Wood (Policeman), Christopher Adamson (Shady), Ian Liston (Editor), Vanessa Knox-Mawer (Interviewer), Renu Setna (Aziz's Father), Caroline John (Barrister's Wife), Norman Mitchell (Norman), Helena McCarthy (Lady Caller), Bella Emberg (Lady Caller), Ruby Snape (Lady Caller), John Gill (Vicar), Laila Khan (Islamic Woman), Meneka Das (Islamic Woman), Jasu Pandya (Islamic Woman), Ahmed Khalil (Islamic Man), Raj Patel (Islamic Man), Badi Uzzaman (Islamic Man), John Scott Martin (Arthur), Nick Edmett (Barman), David Webb (Shopkeeper).

	Holding / Source
23.12.1995	DB-D3 / V1S

IT ONLY SEEMS LIKE YESTERDAY

A Granada production. Transmission details are for the Granada region. Duration: 50 minutes.

Produced by Peter Wildeblood; directed by Gordon Flemyng.

Patrick Campbell, David Battley, Kathleen Breck, Eleanor Bron, David Buck, Pamela Ann Davy, Jeremy Geidt, Gordon Gostelow, Barry Letts.

	Production No	Holding / Source
31.12.1965	420/7	J / 40

Alternative transmissions: Rediffusion Television: 30.12.1965.

Made under the same production code as SECOND CITY REPORTS, although its billing would suggest an altogether separate programme.
See also: SECOND CITY REPORTS

IT'LL BE ALRIGHT ON THE NIGHT

Alternative/Working Title(s): ALL RIGHT ON THER NIGHT

An LWT production. Transmission details are for the Central region. Duration: 50 minutes.

Main regular performer(s): With Denis Norden (Host).

	Holding / Source
25.12.1981 It'll Be Alright On The Night 3	D2 / 2"

Written by Denis Norden; designed by James Dillon; produced and directed by Paul Smith.

	Holding / Source
25.12.1987 It'll Be Alright On The Night 5	D2 / 1"

Written by Denis Norden; research Suzanne Gray and Mark Tinkler; designed by Mike Oxley; produced by Paul Lewis; directed by Terry Kinane.
With Cliff Richard, Anne Diamond, Jimmy Tarbuck, Cilla Black, Paul Nicholas.

	Holding / Source
25.12.1988 Ten Years Of It'll Be Alright On The Night	D2 / 1"

Written by Denis Norden; designed by Bill McPherson; produced by Paul Lewis; directed by Chris Fox.

	Holding / Source
24.12.2004 Alright On The Night 19	DB / DBSW

Main regular performer(s): With Griff Rhys Jones (Host).

	Holding / Source
25.12.2008 It'll Be Alright On The Night 24	DB / DBSW

With Vernon Kay, Sally James, Leigh Francis, Christopher Biggins.

	Holding / Source
28.12.2011 Brand New It'll Be Alright On The Night 1	DB / DBSW

Series producer Grant Philpott; directed by Ian Hamilton.

	Holding / Source
31.12.2011 Brand New It'll Be Alright On The Night 2	DB / DBSW

Series producer Grant Philpott; directed by Ian Hamilton.

IT'S A GRAND NIGHT FOR SINGING

A BBC Wales production for BBC 1 Wales. Transmission details are for BBC 1 Wales. Duration: 35 minutes.

	Holding / Source
29.12.1977	DB / 2"

Some film inserts also exist.

IT'S A HUDD HUDD WORLD

A Gambit Enterprises production for Anglia. Transmission details are for Channel 4. Duration: 25 minutes.
Executive producer Cecil Korer; produced and directed by Ron Downing.
Roy Hudd (Host), June Whitfield, Chris Emmett, Suzy Aitchison, Robert Howie, Kalli Greenwood.

	Holding / Source
31.12.1987	1" / 1"

IT'S A KNOCKOUT

A BBC production for BBC 1. Transmission details are for BBC 1. Duration varies - see below for details.

	Holding / Source
26.12.1970 It's A Christmas Knockout	J / 2"

	Holding / Source
27.12.1971 It's A Christmas Knockout	J / 2"

Duration: 50 minutes.
A special festive competition between teams from Great Britain, Holland, Belgium, Italy from the Aviemore Centre, Scotland. Great Britain represented by Blackpool, Holland by Aalten, Belgium by Tournal, Italy by Jesolo.
Designed by Stuart Furber; produced by Barney Colehan; directed by Ian Smith.
With David Vine (Commentator), Eddie Waring (Commentator), Genaro Olivieri (Referee).
(Joint production by the BBC - NCRV - RTB - RAD.

	Holding / Source
26.12.1972 It's A Christmas Knockout	J / 2"

	Holding / Source
26.12.1973 It's A Christmas Knockout	DB-D3 / 2"

	Holding / Source
23.12.1974 It's A Christmas Knockout	DB-D3 / 2"

Duration: 65 minutes.
Designed by Stuart Furber; produced by Barney Colehan; directed by Bill Taylor.
With Eddie Waring (Commentator), Stuart Hall (Commentator), June Pickering, Karen Apted.

	Holding / Source
30.12.1975 It's A Christmas Knockout	DB-D3 / 2"

	Holding / Source
26.12.1976 It's A Christmas Knockout	DB-D3 / 2"

	Holding / Source
26.12.1977 It's A Christmas Knockout	DB-D3 / 2"

	Holding / Source
26.12.1978 It's A Christmas Knockout	DB-D3 / 2"

	Holding / Source
24.12.1979 It's A Christmas Knockout	DB-D3 / 2"

	Holding / Source
27.12.1980 It's A Christmas Knockout	DB-D3 / 2"

	Holding / Source
02.01.1982 It's A Christmas Knockout	DB-D3 / 2"

A BBC Manchester for BBC/NCRV/RAI/RTB production. Duration: 60 minutes.
Designed by Stuart Furber; produced by Geoffrey Wilson; directed by Bill Taylor.
With Stuart Hall (Presenter), Michel Lemaire (Presenter), Dick Passchier (Presenter), Claudio Lippi (Presenter).

A BBC Manchester production. Duration: 50 minutes.

	Holding / Source
28.12.1984 **Christmas Knockout 1984**	DB / 1"

Designed by Stuart Furber; produced by Geoffrey Wilson; directed by Paul Walker.

With Stuart Hall (Host).

25.12.1988 **It's A Charity Knockout**	DB / 1"

Charity version of IT'S A KNOCKOUT with three teams from Australia, Great Britain and USA in a series of crazy games to raise money for Children in Need. Recorded at Walt Disney World, Florida.

Executive producer Alan Walsh; directed by John Rooney.

With Stuart Hall (Host).

A number of editions of Jeux Sans Frontières not kept by the BBC do survive in the archives of other European broadcasters.

IT'S A SQUARE WORLD

A BBC production for BBC 1. Transmission details are for BBC. Duration: 30 minutes.

Main regular credit(s):	Devised by Michael Bentine and John Law.
Main regular cast:	Michael Bentine (Various roles).

SERIES 6

Transmission details are for BBC. Duration: 25 minutes.

Main regular credit(s):	Written by Michael Bentine and John Law; music directed by Harry Rabinowitz; designed by George Djurkovic; produced and directed by Joe McGrath.
Main regular cast:	With Frank Thornton, Leon Thau, Joe Gibbons, Freddie Earlle, Clive Dunn.

	Holding / Source
26.12.1963	R3 /

With No guest cast.

IT'S A TERRIBLE WASTE OF AN EGG

A BBC production for BBC 2. Transmission details are for BBC 2. Duration: 30 minutes.

Written by Richard Wade; designed by Roger Murray Leach; produced by Ramsay Short; directed by Adrian Brown.

Dudley Foster (Humphrey Hastings), John Wentworth (Grandfather), Maggie Jones (Constance Hastings), Mary Merrall (Grandmother), Christopher Reynalds (Edward Hastings), Susan Payne (Mary Hastings).

	Holding / Source
25.12.1970	DB / 2"

An Edwardian After-Dinner Christmas Entertainment.

IT'S CHARLIE WILLIAMS

A Granada production. Transmission details are for the ATV midlands region. Duration: 35 minutes.

Main regular cast:	Charlie Williams (Host).

	Production No	Holding / Source
22.12.1972	2/459/1	DB / 2"

Music directed by Derek Hilton; designed by Roy Graham; produced by John Hamp; directed by Peter Walker.

With No guest cast.

IT'S CHRISTMAS

A Thames Television production. Transmission details are for the ATV midlands region. Duration: 9 minutes.

Carols sung by the children of St. Richard's with St. Andrew's School, Ham, Surrey.

Research Sue Dawson; produced and directed by Margery Baker.

Mildred Howes (Pianist), St Richards' Choir, St Andrews Choir.

	Holding / Source
26.12.1980 **In England**	DB / 2"

IT'S CHRISTMAS WITH JONATHAN ROSS

An Open Mike production for BBC 1. Transmission details are for BBC 1. Duration: 60 minutes.

With only three days to go until the big day, a host of well-known faces including Barbara Windsor, Ricky Gervais and Jools Holland join Jonathan in a celebration of all things festive. There's a look at some unusual seasonal practices around the world, and the public reveal how they feel about the holiday season. With music from Roy Wood and the Pogues, who perform Fairytale of New York with Katie Melua.

Produced by Kate Teckman; directed by Mick Thomas.

Jonathan Ross (Host), Ricky Gervais, Barbara Windsor, Jools Holland, Roy Wood, The Pogues, Katie Melua.

	Holding / Source
22.12.2005	DB / DBSW

IT'S CLIFF--AND FRIENDS

A BBC production for BBC 1. Transmission details are for BBC 1. Duration: 50 minutes.

Main regular performer(s):   Cliff Richard (Host).

	Holding / Source
27.12.1975	DB-D3 / 2"

Produced by Phil Bishop.

IT'S KEN GOODWIN

A Granada production. Transmission details are for the ATV midlands region. Duration: 38 minutes.

Music directed by Derek Hilton; designed by Colin Rees; produced by John Hamp; directed by Bill Podmore.

Ken Goodwin (Host), Elaine Delmar, The Black Abbots.

	Holding / Source
27.12.1971	DB / 2"

IT'S NICE TO REMEMBER

A BBC production for BBC 2. Transmission details are for BBC 2. Duration: 50 minutes.

Music directed by Peter Knight; designed by Brian Tregidden; produced and directed by Yvonne Littlewood.

Nana Mouskouri, The Athenians, Margot Fonteyn, Desmond Kelly, Michel Legrand.

	Holding / Source
26.12.1970	J / 2"

IT'S PAUL BURLING

An ITV Studios production for ITV 1. Transmission details are for the Central region. Duration: 43 minutes.

Written by Tom Jamieson, Nev Fountain, Nico Tatarowicz, John Camm, Will Maclean, Paul Powell, Fay Rusling, Marc Haynes, Carl Carter, Tony Cooke and Will Ing; script supervisors Hayley Boyd and Marilyn Kirby; script editor Paul Butler; music directed by John Collins; choreography by Nadia Sohawon; director of photography Martin Hawkins; art director Cath Pater-Lancucki [credited as Cath Pater]; designed by Mick Hurd; associate producer Katie Mavroleon; production executive Wendy Hutchinson; executive producers Lee Connolly and Saurabh Kakkar; production manager Polly Coupland; produced by Charlie Hanson; directed by Angie De Chastelai Smith.

Paul Burling (Various Roles), Jessica Robinson, Anthony Spargo, Eve Webster, Matthew Bazell.

	Holding / Source
22.12.2010	HD/DB / HDC

IT'S ROGER MELLIE - THE MAN ON THE TELLY

A John Brown Publishing production for Channel 4. Transmission details are for Channel 4. Duration: 5 minutes.

Main regular credit(s):   Produced and directed by Tony Barnes.

Main regular cast: Peter Cook (Voice of Roger Mellie), Harry Enfield (Other Voices).

	Holding / Source
30.12.1991	1" / 1"S
31.12.1991	1" / 1"S
01.01.1992	1" / 1"S
02.01.1992	1" / 1"S
03.01.1992	1" / 1"S

See also: ROGER MELLIE

IT'S TODAY

A BBC production for BBC 2. Transmission details are for BBC 2. Duration: 40 minutes.

Music directed by Phil Phillips; choreography by Judy Gridley; designed by Vic Meredith; produced and directed by Anne Gobey.

Helen Chappelle, Derek Griffiths, Katie Budd, Jean Gilbert, Vicky Silva.

	Holding / Source
26.12.1978	DB-D3 / 2"

IT'S YOUR NEW YEAR'S EVE PARTY

A BBC production for BBC 1. Transmission details are for BBC 1. Duration: 65 minutes.

Executive producer Beatrice Ballard; produced by Sam Donnelly.

Jonathan Ross (Host), Neil Morrissey, Ulrika Jonsson, Terry Wogan, Vic Reeves, Bob Mortimer, Mariah Carey, The Corrs, Ronan Keating.

	Holding / Source
31.12.2001	DB / DBSW

ITV PLAYHOUSE

Produced for ITV by a variety of companies (see details below). Transmission details are for the ATV midlands region. Duration varies - see below for details.

SERIES 5

	VT Number	Holding / Source
21.12.1980 **The Schoolmistress**	D509	1" / 2"

A Yorkshire Television production. Duration: 75 minutes.

An enchanting production of Pinero's delightful outrageous farce. Take one singing schoolmistress, two angry husbands, three pretty girls, add a sprig of mistletoe and a handful of fireworks to start with. Then mix in secret marriages, secret careers, secret parties, young love, old love, love triumphant and Christmas will never be the same again.

Written by Arthur Wing Pinero; designed by Roger Andrews; executive producer David Cunliffe; produced by Pat Sandys; directed by Douglas Argent.

With Eleanor Bron (Miss Dyott), Jane Carr (Peggy), Charles Gray (Admiral Rankling), Nigel Hawthorne (Vera Queckett), Daniel Abineri (Reginald Paulover), Pamela Cundell (Jane), Michael Deeks (Tyler), Sarah Prince (Gwendoline), Amanda Kirby (Ermyntrude), Rebecca Saire (Dinah), Bernard Spear (Otto Bernstein), Noël Dyson (Mrs Rankling), Rupert Frazer (Jack Mallory), Mark Rogers (Mr Saunders), Tony Hughes (Jaffray), Sam Kydd (Goff).

ITV TRAILS 1976/77

Produced for ITV by a variety of companies (see details below). Transmission details are for ITV.

	Holding / Source
##.##.#### **The Ghosts Of Motley Hall**	DV / 2"
##.##.#### **Sale Of The Century (specially-filmed)**	DV / 2"

With Nicholas Parsons.

Ex Phillips 1500.

IVOR THE INVISIBLE

A Screen Firsts production for Channel 4. Transmission details are for Channel 4. Duration: 26 minutes.

Written by Raymond Briggs; music by Nitin Sawhney; produced by Paul Madden; directed by Hilary Audus.

Albey Brookes (Voice), Jane Horrocks (Voice), Timothy Spall (Voice), Alison Steadman (Voice), Archie Panjabi (Voice), David Haig (Voice), Emma Tate (Voice), Tina Grace (Voice), Nina Miranda (Voice).

	Holding / Source
24.12.2001	DB / C1SW

JACK & THE BEANSTALK

A Wishbone production for LWT. Transmission details are for the Central region. Duration: 74 minutes.

A family pantomime for Christmas. with a star-studded cast of top comedians takingto the stage of the Old Vic in London for an affectionate and boisterous version of the traditional tale.

Written by Simon Nye; script supervisor Mary Gardner; music by Philip Pope; choreography by Nicky Hinkley; art director Jacqueline Abrahams; production designer Anne Tilby; production team Janina O'Connor and Louise Dancy; production associate Diana Crystal Honey; executive producer Humphrey Barclay; production manager Sarah McHarry; produced by Sarah Williams and Helen Pitcher; directed by John Henderson.

Paul Merton (Narrator), Neil Morrissey (Jack), Adrian Edmondson (Dame Dolly), Griff Rhys Jones (Baron Wasteland), Denise van Outen (Jill), Julie Walters (The Fairy Godmother), Morwenna Banks (Goldilocks), Julian Clary (Tima / First Henchman), Peter Serafinowicz (Second Henchman), Will Barton (The Harp), Vince Williams (Pat The Cow), John Willett (Pat The Cow).

	Holding / Source
25.12.1998	DB / DBS

JACK AND JILL

A BBC production. Transmission details are for BBC. Duration: 45 minutes.

Introduced by Brian Johnston; written by Emile Littler; lyrics by Hastings Mann; music directed by Jack Walker; music by Hastings Mann; choreography by Phyllis Blakston; television presentation by Berkeley Smith; produced by Emile Littler.

Arthur Bell (Landlord Of 'The Pail O' Water'), Tommy Jover (Dame Horner), Michael Bentine (Twist, The Crooked Man), Carol Decy (Jill), Hy Hazell (Jack), Charlie Chester (Cheerful Charlie), Moyra Fraser (The Wicked Witch), Kirby and Hayes (Johnnie Stout / Willie Green), Maureen Spooner (Mary, Mary, Quite Contrary), Jacqueline St. Clere (The Fairy Of The Magic Well), Harry Welchman (King Of Sylvania), The Baronas, Trio Gypsys, The Tiller Girls, The Terry Juveniles, The Normandy Singers.

	Holding / Source
24.12.1952	NR / Live

Excerpts from the stage of the London Casino.

JACK AND JO'S YO-HO-HO (RADIO)

An Open Mike production for BBC Radio 2. Transmission details are for BBC Radio 2.

Produced and directed by Mark Hill.

Jack Dee, Jo Brand, Jeremy Milnes, Mike Ingham, Allegra McEverly, Chris Moyles, David Tennant, Alesha Dixon, Jamie Cullum, Kian Egan, Mark Feehily, Harry Connick Jnr, Noddy Holder, Jon Culshaw, Debra Stephenson.

	Holding / Source
25.12.2009	DA /

JACK AND THE BEANSTALK

An Active Television production. Never intended for transmission.

Written by Simon Ellingham; choreography by John Cumberlidge; produced and directed by Ernest Maxin.

Jeremy Beadle (Jack), Bruno Brookes (Giant Blunderbore), Alistair Divall, Richard Franklin, Audrey Leybourne, Sammy Plank, Barry Craine, Misha and Larissa Kalinin, Sarah Miller, The Hanley Dancers and Babes, The Theatre Royal Orchestra.

	Holding / Source
##.##.####	DV /

Filmed at the Theatre Royal, Hanley, between Thursday 23rd December 1993-Saturday 15th January 1994.

JACK AND THE BEANSTALK

The companies who commissioned and produced this production are not known. Never intended for transmission.

Jeremy Beadle.

	Holding / Source
##.##.####	DV /

Filmed at the White Rock Theatre, Hastings, Sussex on 28th December 1988.

JACK AND THE BEANSTALK

A BBC production. Transmission details are for BBC.

Written by Barry Lupino and Arty Ash; lyrics by Barry Lupino and Arty Ash; television presentation by Campbell Logan; produced for the stage by Barry Lupino.

Barry Lupino (Dame Durden), Marjorie Sandford (Jack), Reg Kinman (Archie), Sybil Summers (Princess Beauty), Theo Hook (The King), Bert Thompson (Giant Blunderbore), The Famous Leopolds (Jessie The Cow), Frances Hughes (Fairy Lunar), Morton Clifford (Mother Shipton), The Grandison Juveniles, The Permanes, Six Mighty Atoms, Armour Boys, Eugene's Sensational Flying Ballet, The Iris Kirkwhite Dancers.

		Holding / Source
06.01.1947	**Part One**	NR / Live
07.01.1947	**Part Two**	NR / Live

Broadcast from the Grand Theatre, Croydon.

JACK AND THE BEANSTALK ON ICE

A BBC production for BBC 1. Transmission details are for BBC 1. Duration: 60 minutes.

Written by Stanley Lloyd; lyrics by Stanley Lloyd; music directed by Leslie Kerrigan; music by Malcolm Lockyer; choreography by Reg Park; television presentation by John Vernon; designed by Anthony Holland; produced and directed by Gerald Palmer.

Alan Weeks (Commentator), Reg Park, Linda Davis, Frances Waghorn, Bernard Ford, Diane Towler, Ted Deeley, Jeff and Franzisca, Charlie Cairoli & Company.

	Holding / Source
03.01.1971	J / 2"

Direct from the Empire Pool, Wembley.

JACK DEE LIVE IN LONDON

A BBC production for BBC 1. Transmission details are for BBC 1. Duration: 65 minutes.

Produced by Dave Morley; directed by Tom Poole.

Jack Dee.

	Holding / Source
30.12.1999	DB / DBSW

THE JACK DEE SHOW

An Open Mike production for Channel 4. Transmission details are for Channel 4.

Main regular credit(s): Written by Jack Dee; produced by Dave Morley.

Main regular cast: Jack Dee (Host).

SERIES 1

Main regular credit(s): Directed by Juliet May.

	Holding / Source
23.12.1992	1" / 1"S

Duration: 50 minutes.

With Tom Jones, The Amazing Jonathan.

JACK DEE'S SATURDAY NIGHT

An Open Mike production for Granada. Transmission details are for the Central region.

Main regular credit(s): Directed by Julia Knowles.

Main regular performer(s): Jack Dee (Host).

	VT Number	Holding / Source
21.12.1996 Jack Dee's Christmas Show	1/8288/0007	D3 / D3S

Duration: 38 minutes.

Written by Jack Dee; programme associate John Tiffney; script supervisor Manique Ratner; music associate Graham K. Smith; designed by James Dillon; associate producers Ivan Douglass and Addison Cresswell; executive producer Andy Harries; production manager Caitlin Samways; produced by Dave Morley.

With Lily Savage, The London Welsh Male Voice Choir, Pulp, Björk, Sandra Bowing, Greg Proops, The Amazing Jonathan.

JACK DEE'S SUNDAY SERVICE

An Open Mike production for Granada. Transmission details are for the Central region. Duration: 25 minutes.

Mostly JACK DEE stand-up comedy, with the occasional sketch.

Main regular credit(s): Written by Jack Dee, Richard Morton and Rob Colley; executive producers Addison Cresswell and Andy Harries; series producer Spencer Campbell; produced by Andy Davies; directed by Steve Smith.

Main regular cast: Jack Dee (Host), Rich Hall.

	VT Number	Holding / Source
21.12.1997	1/8288/0018	DB / DBSW

With Rich Hall.

JACK HARGREAVES - A YORKSHIRE CHILDHOOD

A Southern Television production. Transmission details are for the Tyne Tees region. Duration: 25 minutes.

A nostalgic return to his childhood home by the presenter of Out of Town.

Research Tim Edmunds; directed by Graham Hurley.

Jack Hargreaves (Presenter).

	Holding / Source
26.12.1980	C1 / C1

Held by Wessex Archive.

JACK HYLTON PRESENTS...

A Jack Hylton TV Productions production for Associated-Rediffusion. Transmission details are for Associated-Rediffusion. Duration varies - see below for details.

Main regular performer(s): Jack Hylton.

	Holding / Source
22.12.1955	J /

Duration: 50 minutes.

An hour of star studded variety. A grand Christmas programme of music, dancing and laughter bringing to you some of the great personalities of show business.

British Christmas Television Guide	JACK HYLTON PRESENTS... (continued)

20.12.1956 Humpty Dumpty   J /
Duration: 52 minutes.
An excerpt from the pantomime.
Orchestra directed by Van Damm; dance direction by Sheila Holt; television presentation by Kenneth Carter; directed for the stage by Richard Bird.
With Arthur Askey (Dame Clara Crumpett), George Betton (King Eggbert), Angela Anderson (Princess Sylvia), George Street (Plonk, The Chancellor), Lauri Lupino Lane (Umpah), George Truzzi (Jumpah), Anthea Askey (Humpty Dumpty), Maggie Fitzgibbon (Prince Valentine), Muriel Zillah (Malovena, The Witch).

21.12.1956 Christmas Greetings   J /
Duration: 25 minutes.
A half-hour of light-hearted, seasonal entertainment.
Produced and directed by Peter Croft.
With Dickie Henderson, Rosalina Neri, Phillipe Clay, The Peiro Brothers.

An umbrella title for occasional comedy and variety specials.

THE JACK JACKSON SHOW

An ATV production. Transmission details are for the ATV midlands region. Duration: 25 minutes.
Main regular credit(s):   Devised by Jack Jackson and Mark White.
Main regular performer(s): Jack Jackson (Host).

SERIES 1
An ITP production. Transmission details are for the ATV London region.
Main regular credit(s):   Written by Jack Jackson and Mark White.

                              Holding / Source
25.12.1955   J / Live
Designed by Richard Greenough; produced by Peter Glover.

JACK PARNELL AND THE BAND SHOW

An ATV production. Transmission details are for the Tyne Tees region. Duration: 40 minutes.
Written by Bryan Blackburn; music associate Derek Scott; designed by Gerry Roberts; produced by Alan Tarrant; directed by Dicky Leeman.
Jack Parnell and his Orchestra, The Polka Dots, Marti Caine, Trevor Chance.

                              Holding / Source
25.12.1975   J / 2"

JACKANORY

A BBC Children's Department production for BBC 1. Transmission details are for BBC 1. Duration: 15 minutes.

SERIES 1
Duration: 15 minutes.

Duration: 15 minutes.
Main regular credit(s):   Written by Alison Uttley; pictures by Margaret Tempest; graphics by James Matthews Joyce; production team Anna Home and Joanne Symons; associate producer Molly Cox; produced by Joy Whitby.
Main regular cast: With Wendy Hiller (Storyteller).

                              Holding / Source
24.12.1965 Little Grey Rabbit's Christmas   J / 62

Christmas Stories

Duration: 15 minutes.
Main regular credit(s):   Graphics by Hilary Hayton; production team Anna Home and Joanne Symons; associate producer Molly Cox; produced by Joy Whitby.
Main regular cast: With Brian Way (Storyteller).

                              Holding / Source
27.12.1965 **Presents**   J / 62
28.12.1965 **Lights**   J / 62
29.12.1965 **Glass**   J / 62
30.12.1965 **Bells**   J / 62
31.12.1965 **Time**   J / 62

SERIES 2
Duration: 15 minutes.
Credits: Programme editor Joy Whitby.

The Barrow Street Gang

Duration: 15 minutes.
Main regular credit(s):   Written by Noel Streatfeild; photographed by James Matthews Joyce; assistant producer Molly Cox.
Main regular cast: With Rodney Bewes (Storyteller).

                              Holding / Source
28.11.1966 Pretty Christmas   J / 62

JACKANORY (continued)

The Children Of Green Knowe

Duration: 15 minutes.
Main regular credit(s):   Written by Lucy M. Boston; film editor Terry Cornelius; assistant producer Anna Home.
Main regular cast: With Susannah York (Storyteller).

Date	Title	Holding / Source
19.12.1966	**Arrival At Green Knowe**	J / 62
20.12.1966	**Hide And Seek**	J / 62
21.12.1966	**Alexander's Flute**	J / 62
22.12.1966	**Green Noah**	J / 62
23.12.1966	**Christmas At Green Knowe**	J / 62

SERIES 3

Babar, The King Of The Elephants

Main regular credit(s):   Written by Jean de Brunhoff; pianist Jonathan Cohen; produced by David Coulter; directed by Joanne Symons.
Main regular cast: With Celia Johnson (Storyteller).

Date	Title	Holding / Source
20.10.1967	**Babar And Father Christmas**	J / 62

Traditional Christmas Stories

Main regular credit(s):   Produced by David Coulter.

Holding / Source

18.12.1967 The Selfish Giant J / 62
Written by Oscar Wilde; illustrated by Gertraud Reiner and Walter Reiner.
With Ronald Eyre (Storyteller).

19.12.1967 The Christmas Rocket J / 62
Written by Anne Molloy; drawings by Artur Marokvia.
With Anna Massey (Storyteller).

20.12.1967 The First Christmas In The New World J / 62
Research June A. Grimble.
With Glynn Christian (Storyteller).

21.12.1967 Baboushka J / 62
Written by David Coulter.
With Celia Johnson (Storyteller).

22.12.1967 The Little Juggler J / 62
Translated by Barbara Cooney; adapted by Barbara Cooney; illustrated by Barbara Cooney.
With Ted Ray (Storyteller).

24.12.1967 The Christmas Tale Of Sam Pig J / 62
Written by Alison Uttley.
With Dandy Nichols (Storyteller).
This was the only edition of Jackanory to receive its first broadcast on a weekend.

Pantomime

Main regular credit(s):   Written by Paul Ciani; music by Patrick Harvey; produced by Anna Home; directed by Paul Ciani.
Main regular cast: With Mike Hope (Storyteller), Alby Keen (Storyteller).

Date	Title	Holding / Source
25.12.1967	**The Splendid History Of Mother Goose And Her Golden Eggs**	J / 62
26.12.1967	**The Incredible Saga Of Sinbad The Sailor**	J / 62
27.12.1967	**The Fantastic, Fantabulous Story Of Jack And The Beanstalk**	J / 62
28.12.1967	**The Thrilling Adventures Of The Babes In The Wood**	J / 62
29.12.1967	**The Sensational De-light-ful Of Cinderella**	J / 62

SERIES 4

Christmas Stories

Main regular credit(s):   Produced by Anna Home; directed by Marilyn Fox and Susan Ball.

Holding / Source

23.12.1968 Babar And Father Christmas J / 62
Written by Jean de Brunhoff.
With Alan Bennett (Storyteller).

24.12.1968 The Little Juggler J / 62
With Ted Ray (Storyteller).

JACKANORY

| British Christmas Television Guide | JACKANORY (continued) |

	Holding / Source
25.12.1968 **The Minstrel And The Mountain**	J / 62
Written by Jane Yolen.	
With John Stride (Storyteller).	
27.12.1968 **The Selfish Giant**	J / 62
Written by Oscar Wilde.	
With Ronald Eyre (Storyteller).	

SERIES 5

	Holding / Source
24.12.1969 **The Minstrel And The Mountain**	J / 62

Written by Jane Yolen; pictures by Anne Rockwell; series producer Anna Home; directed by Marilyn Fox.
With John Stride (Storyteller).

SERIES 6

Castaway Christmas

Main regular credit(s):	Written by Margaret J. Baker; adapted by Denise Cremona; pictures by Mina Martinez; series producer Anna Home; directed by Angela Beeching.
Main regular cast:	With Michael Craig (Storyteller).

	Holding / Source
14.12.1970 **Floods Ahead**	J / 2"
15.12.1970 **Oliver To The Rescue**	J / 2"
16.12.1970 **The First Victory**	J / 2"
17.12.1970 **The Christmas Candle**	J / 2"
18.12.1970 **A Message Is Delivered**	J / 2"

More About Paddington

Credits:	Written by Michael Bond; pictures by Carol Jones; series producer Anna Home; produced by Daphne Jones; directed by Christine Secombe.
Cast:	With John Bird (Storyteller).

	Holding / Source
24.12.1970 **Paddington's Christmas**	J / 2"

SERIES 7

The Armourer's House

Main regular credit(s):	Written by Rosemary Sutcliff; adapted by Marilyn Fox; pictures by Sandra Archibald; executive producer Anna Home; directed by Marilyn Fox.
Main regular cast:	With Janina Faye (Storyteller).

	Holding / Source
24.12.1971 **Christmas**	J / 2"

SERIES 9

Credits: Executive producer Anna Home.

The Thirteen Days Of Christmas

Main regular credit(s):	Written by Jenny Overton; adapted by Janie Griffiths; music directed by Bruce Pullan; produced by Angela Beeching; directed by Janie Griffiths.
Main regular cast:	With Helen Mirren (Storyteller).

	Holding / Source
17.12.1973 **A Partridge In A Pear Tree**	J / 2"
18.12.1973 **Four Calling Birds**	J / 2"
19.12.1973 **Eight Maids A-Milking**	J / 2"
20.12.1973 **Eleven Drummers Drumming**	J / 2"
21.12.1973 **The Last Day Of Christmas**	J / 2"

	Holding / Source
24.12.1973 **The Tailor Of Gloucester**	J / 2"

Written by Beatrix Potter; adapted by Jeremy Swan; pictures by Beatrix Potter; produced by Daphne Jones; directed by Jeremy Swan.
With Eileen Atkins (Storyteller).

JACKANORY (continued)

The Long Winter

Main regular credit(s):	Written by Laura Ingalls Wilder; adapted by Angela Beeching; pictures by Graham McCallum.
Main regular cast:	With Eileen Atkins (Storyteller).

Holding / Source

25.01.1974 Christmas J / 2"
Directed by Angela Beeching.

SERIES 10

Credits: Executive producer Anna Home.

Wurzel Gummidge Again

Main regular credit(s):	Written by Barbara Euphan Todd; adapted by Roger Singleton-Turner; pictures by Jan Brychta; produced by Daphne Jones; directed by Roger Singleton-Turner.
Main regular cast:	With Geoffrey Bayldon (Storyteller).

Holding / Source

08.11.1974 The Christmas Party J / 2"

SERIES 11

Credits: Executive producer Anna Home.

Mrs Pepperpot's Year

Main regular credit(s):	Written by Alf Prøysen; translated by Marianne Helweg; adapted by Maralyn Corless; pictures by Graham Round; produced by Angela Beeching; directed by Jeremy Swan.
Main regular cast:	With Thora Hird (Storyteller).

Holding / Source

07.11.1975 Mrs Pepperpot's Christmas J / 2"

The stories broadcast w/c 10.05.1976 were repeats of William Rushton reading from Winnie-the-Pooh and The House at Pooh Corner.

SERIES 15

Credits: Executive producer Anna Home; produced by Angela Beeching.

Christmas Stories

Main regular credit(s):	Written by Rosemary Harris; directed by Michael Kerrigan.

Holding / Source

24.12.1979 The Black Lamb Of Bethlehem D3 / 2"
Pictures by Ann Strugnell.
With Sinead Cusack (Storyteller).

Other editions this week were repeats.

SERIES 16

Credits: Executive producer Anna Home; produced by Angela Beeching.

The Good Little Devil

Main regular credit(s):	Written by Ann Lawrence; adapted by Roger Singleton-Turner; pictures by Maggie Raynor; directed by Roger Singleton-Turner.
Main regular cast:	With Maurice Denham (Storyteller).

Holding / Source

31.10.1980 Christmas J / 2"

Main regular credit(s):	Directed by Jeremy Swan.

Holding / Source

23.12.1980 The Church Mice At Christmas D3 / 2"
Written by Graham Oakley.
With Cyril Luckham (Storyteller).

24.12.1980 The Tailor Of Gloucester D3 / 2"
Written by Beatrix Potter.
With Judi Dench (Storyteller).

SERIES 17

The Snow Queen

Main regular credit(s):	Written by Hans Christian Andersen; adapted by David Bell; illustrated by Annabel Spenceley; produced by Angela Beeching; directed by David Bell.
Main regular cast:	With Cheryl Campbell (Storyteller).

Holding / Source

24.12.1981 The Sixth And Seventh Stories D3 / 2"

JACKANORY (continued)

SERIES 18
Paul Gallico Stories

Main regular credit(s): Designed by Andrew Howe Davies; produced by Angela Beeching; directed by Nel Romano.
Main regular cast: With Jeremy Irons (Storyteller).

	Holding / Source
24.12.1982 **The Small Miracle - part 2**	1" / 1"

Pictures by Susan Broadley.

SERIES 20

	Holding / Source
24.12.1984 **Snowflake**	1" / 1"

Written by Paul Gallico; pictures by Steve Gilmore; designed by Andrew Howe Davies; produced by Angela Beeching; directed by Nel Romano.
With Jeremy Irons (Storyteller).

William – At Christmas

Main regular credit(s): Written by Richmal Crompton; adapted by Martin Jarvis; produced by Angela Beeching; directed by Christine Secombe.
Main regular cast: With Martin Jarvis (Storyteller).

	Holding / Source
27.12.1984 **William Starts The Holidays**	D3 / 1"
28.12.1984 **The Outlaws And Cousin Percy**	1" / 1"
02.01.1985 **William And The Snowman**	1" / 1"
03.01.1985 **William Plays Santa Claus**	1" / 1"
04.01.1985 **The Christmas Truce**	D3 / 1"

SERIES 25

Fred The Angel

Main regular credit(s): Written by Martin Waddell; illustrated by Linda Birch; executive producer Angela Beeching; directed by Nigel Douglas.
Main regular cast: With Christopher Timothy (Storyteller).

	Holding / Source
22.12.1989 **Sarah's Christmas**	1" / 1"

SERIES 30
Duration: 10 minutes.

The Twitches

Duration: 10 minutes.
Main regular credit(s): Written by Roy Apps; adapted by Philippa Langdale; produced by Nel Romano; directed by Philippa Langdale.
Main regular cast: With Niall Ashdown (Storyteller).

	Holding / Source
30.03.1995 **The Twitches At Chrissy-Mess**	D3S / D3S

SERIES 31
Transmission details are for BBC 2.

	Holding / Source
24.12.1995 **Jack And The Beanstalk**	D3S / D3S

A Tricorn Associates production.
Written by Adrian Mitchell; illustrated by Victor Ambrus; produced and directed by Elizabeth Bennett.
With Rik Mayall (Storyteller).

JACKANORY PLAYHOUSE

A BBC production for BBC 1. Transmission details are for BBC 1. Usual duration: 25 minutes.

SERIES 1
Main regular credit(s): Executive producer Anna Home.

	Holding / Source
22.12.1972 **The Coming Of The Kings**	J / 2"

Duration: 35 minutes.
A nativity play with a difference. A fortune-teller tells the innkeeper and his wife that three kings will visit them; but how do you recognise a king when you see one?
Written by Ted Hughes; designed by Paul Munting; directed by Daphne Jones.

With Brian Peck (Fortune-Teller), Harry Towb (Innkeeper), Alex Marshall (Innkeeper's Wife), Ferdy Mayne (Priest), Al Mancini (Businessman), Bill Pertwee (Police Inspector), Sebastian Graham-Jones (Minstrel), Barry Wilsher (Joseph), Suzannah Williams (Mary), Earl Cameron (First King), John Moore (Second King), David Thomas (Third King).

JACKANORY PLAYHOUSE (continued)

Holding / Source

28.12.1973 The Magician's Heart   DB-D3 / 2"
Duration: 35 minutes.
Adapted by David Wade; based on a book by E. Nesbit; designed by Christine Ruscoe; executive producer Anna Home; directed by Daphne Jones.
With Maurice Denham (The Magician), Dandy Nichols (Nurse), Richard Morant (Prince Fortunatus), Vivien Heilbron (Princess Aura), Beryl Cooke (Fairy Godmother), Elizabeth Power (White Fairy), Anthony Dawes (First Courtier), Peter Bennett (Second Courtier), John Bryning (Herald), Jonathan Prowse (Magician, Child), Ian Lindsay (King Of Bellamont), George Raistrick (Guard), Christopher Biggins (Prince Arbuthnot).

31.12.1973 The Long Nosed Princess   DB-D3 / 2"
Duration: 30 minutes.
Adapted by Veronica Cecil; based on a story by Priscilla Hallowell; designed by Christine Ruscoe; directed by Paul Stone.
With Joseph O'Conor (King Angus), Lorna Heilbron (Princess Felicity), Sheila Brownrigg (Lady Violet), Martin Jarvis (Prince Fustian), Joe Dunlop (Herald), Sally Stephens (Princess Lucinda), Leonard Fenton (King), Lewis Wilson (Farmer), Geoffrey Burridge (Prince Harry).

Holding / Source

22.12.1976 The Winter Warrior   DB-D3 / 2"
Written by Martin Booth; music by Mary Hemnant; designed by Charles Lawrence; executive producer Anna Home; directed by Daphne Jones.
With Ashley Knight (Eadwerd), James Laurenson (Theodric), Frances White (Godwin), Kenneth Gilbert (Eadwacer), Peter Sallis (Deor), Edward Kalinski (Aelfred), Peta Mason (Emma), Tom Chadbon (Sigehere).

SERIES 7
Main regular credit(s):   Produced by Angela Beeching.

Holding / Source

15.01.1979 The Christmas Cuckoo   DB-D3 / 2"

JAM AND JERUSALEM
Alternative/Working Title(s): CLATTERFORD
Produced for BBC 1 by a variety of companies (see details below). made in association with BBC America. Transmission details are for BBC 1.
Main regular credit(s):   Written by Jennifer Saunders; additional material by Abigail Wilson; theme music by Ray Davies.
Main regular cast: Sue Johnston (Sal Vine), Dawn French (Rosie), Maggie Steed (Eileen), Pauline McLynn (Tip), Sally Phillips (Tash), Jennifer Saunders (Caroline), Rosie Cavaliero (Kate Bales), Hazel John (Pauline).

SERIES 1
A Saunders & French production.
Main regular credit(s):   Script supervisor Lucy Crayford; music by Kate Rusby; assistant producer Nerys Evans; production executive Jez Nightingale; executive producer Jon Plowman; produced by Jo Sargent; directed by Steve Bendelack.
Main regular cast: With Doreen Mantle (Queenie), Suzy Aitchison (Susie), Ebony The Dog.

Holding / Source

30.12.2006   DB / DBSWF
Duration: 45 minutes.
Sal faces up to the fact that she must make a decision about her husband's ashes and worries about the festive season.
Music by Kate Rusby and John McCusker.
With Simon Farnaby (Spike), Robbie Richardson (Colin), Joanna Lumley, Nigel Lindsay, Patrick Barlow, David Mitchell, Salima Saxton, Thomas Assafuah, Elanor Grimes, Porky, Freya Edmondson, Jan Lammercraft.

JAMES AND THE GIANT PEACH
A BBC Children's Department production for BBC 1. Transmission details are for BBC 1. Duration: 50 minutes.
James Henry Trotter had been living with his terrible aunts for three whole years, and then one day, something rather peculiar happened....
Adapted by Trevor Preston; based on a book by Roald Dahl; music by Peter Howell; designed by Anna Ridley; produced by Anna Home; directed by Paul Stone.
Simon Bell (James), Anna Quayle (Aunt Spiker), Ann Beach (Aunt Sponge), Arthur Hewlett (Old Man), Andrew Sachs (Interviewer / First Naval Officer / Security Chief), Thorley Walters (Grasshopper), Pat Coombs (Spider), Kate Lock (Ladybird), Bernard Cribbins (Centipede), Hugh Lloyd (Earthworm), Christopher Owen (Silkworm / Second Naval Officer), Jo Kendall (Glow-Worm / American Woman), James Berwick (American General / Ship's Captain), Blain Fairman (First American / Fourth Naval Officer), Bernard Taylor (Second American / Third Naval Officer), Weston Gavin (Newscaster), Garry McDermott (Police Chief), Robert MacLeod (Fire Chief).

Holding / Source

28.12.1976   DB-D3 / 2"

JAMES GALWAY'S CHRISTMAS CAROL
A BBC production for BBC 1. Transmission details are for BBC 1. Duration: 55 minutes.
Executive producers Timothy Woolford and Michael Emmerson; produced and directed by Yvonne Littlewood.
James Galway, Royal Philharmonic Orchestra, The Ambrosian Singers, St Albans Cathedral Choir.

Holding / Source

21.12.1986   DB / 1"

JANET AND COMPANY

A Thames Television production. Transmission details are for the ATV/Central region. Duration: 25 minutes.

Britain's favourite female comedy impressionist Janet Brown presents a special Christmas show, introducing a top line-up of personalities from the world of stage, screen and politics including Margaret Thatcher, Barbara Woodhouse, Meg Mortimer and Hilda Ogden.

Main regular credit(s): Written by Eric Davidson, David Renwick and Laurie Rowley; music associate Don Hunt; theme music by Laurie Holloway; designed by Harry Clark; produced and directed by Keith Beckett.

Main regular cast: Janet Brown (Performer), Roy Kinnear, Frank Windsor, Rod Hull and Emu, Tina Martin, Michael Kilgarriff, Maurice Lane, Desmond and Marks.

Transmission details are for the ATV midlands region.

	Holding / Source
25.12.1980	D3 / 2"

Written by Eric Davidson, David Renwick and Laurie Rowley; theme music by Laurie Holloway; designed by Harry Clark.
With Roy Kinnear, Frank Windsor, Rod Hull and Emu, Tina Martin, Michael Kilgarriff, Maurice Lane, Desmond and Marks.

SERIES 1

Transmission details are for the ATV midlands region.

	Holding / Source
17.02.1981	D3 / 2"
With Tim Barrett.	
24.02.1981	D3 / 2"
With Ernest Clark.	
03.03.1981	D3 / 2"
With Joan Sanderson.	
10.03.1981	D3 / 2"
With David Jacobs.	
17.03.1981	D3 / 2"
With Roy Kinnear.	

SERIES 2

Transmission details are for the Central region.

Main regular credit(s): Written by Eric Davidson, Chris Miller and Clifford Henry; music directed by Don Hunt; designed by Harry Clark.

	Holding / Source
08.04.1982	D3 / 2"
With Terence Alexander.	
15.04.1982	D3 / 2"
With Michael Barrington, Tim Barrett, William Lindsay.	
22.04.1982	D3 / 2"
With Michael Lees.	
29.04.1982	D3 / 2"
With Derek Batey.	

The Falklands War interrupted proceedings and extended editions of TV Eye took over the slot.

30.06.1982	D3 / 2"
Postponed from 06.05.1982.	
07.07.1982	D3 / 2"
Postponed from 13.05.1982.	

JASPER CARROTT GOT THIS MOLE

Alternative/Working Title(s): I'VE GOT THIS MOLE

Commissioned by Central. Transmission details are for the Central region. Duration: 10 minutes.

Cartoon about Jasper Carrott's vain attempts to stop a mole digging up his garden.

Written by Jasper Carrott; animated by Les Gibbard; camera operated by Antony Pooley; executive producer John Starkey; produced and directed by Maurice Pooley.

Jasper Carrott (Narrator).

	Holding / Source
23.12.1984	C1 / C1

JAYNE TORVILL AND CHRISTOPHER DEAN SPECIAL

A Thames Television production. Transmission details are for the Central region. Duration: 50 minutes.

Music directed by Simon Reed; executive producer Bob Burrows; produced and directed by John Davis.

Jayne Torvill, Christopher Dean.

	Holding / Source
25.12.1984	1" / 1"

JAZZ 625

A BBC production for BBC 2. Transmission details are for BBC 2. Duration: 30 minutes.
Main regular credit(s): Produced and directed by Terry Henebery.
Main regular performer(s): Steve Race (Presenter).

	Holding / Source
26.12.1964 **Christmas Compilation**	R3 / R3

With Henry 'Red' Allen Jr, The Dave Brubeck Quartet, Erroll Garner, Coleman Hawkins Quintet, The Woody Herman Orchestra, The Newport All Stars, The Oscar Peterson Trio, Mel Tormé, Jimmy Witherspoon with The Ronnie Scott Quartet.

Includes footage from missing programmes.

JAZZ AT THE MILL

A BBC Birmingham production for BBC 2. Transmission details are for BBC 2. Duration: 35 minutes.
A tribute to Fats Waller.
Written by Reg Perrin; produced and directed by Reg Perrin.
Rick Jones (Presenter), George Chisholm and The Friends of Jazz, Salena Jones, Tommy Burton, Alan Haven Trio.

	Holding / Source
22.12.1973	J / 2"

JAZZ FROM MONTREUX

A BBC production for BBC 2. Transmission details are for BBC 2.

SERIES 1
Main regular credit(s): Introduced by Humphrey Lyttelton; television presentation by Don Sayer.

	Holding / Source
30.12.1977	DB-D3 / 2"

Duration: 50 minutes.
With Count Basie, Benny Carter, Ella Fitzgerald, Dizzy Gillespie, Milt Jackson, Charles Mingus.

SERIES 2

	Holding / Source
05.01.1979	DB-D3 / 2"

With The Buddy Rich Big Band, Mary Lou Williams, Xanadu All Stars, Miriam Makeba, The Bill Evans Trio, Kenny Burrell.

SERIES 3

	Holding / Source
11.12.1979 **From Newport To Montreux**	DB-D3 / 2"

A recording tape from August 1978 exists.

JAZZ SCENE

A BBC production for BBC 2. Transmission details are for BBC 2.

	Holding / Source
26.12.1969 **... At The Ronnie Scott Club**	DB / 2"

Duration: 55 minutes.
Introduced by Ronnie Scott; theme music by Francy Boland; designed by Paul Joel; produced and directed by Terry Henebery.
With The Clarke-Boland Big Band, Guitar Workshop, The Miles Davis Quintet, The Stéphane Grapelli-Teddy Wilson Quartet, Sarah Vaughan and her Trio, The Charlie Shavers Quartet, The Oscar Peterson Trio, The Gary Burton Quartet, The Stars of Faith, Buddy Rich and his Orchestra.
Preview of new series from Jazz Expo 69, compilation of previous programmes. COMPLETE PROGRAMME PLUS UNCUT RECORDING OF GUITAR WORKSHOP (BARNEY KESSEL, KENNY BURRELL, GRANT GREEN).

JEAN-MICHEL JARRE: DESTINATION DOCKLANDS

A Mike Mansfield Television production for Channel 4. made in association with Capital Radio. Transmission details are for Channel 4. Duration: 55 minutes.
Produced and directed by Mike Mansfield.
Jean Michel Jarre.

	Holding / Source
25.12.1988	1" / 1"

JEEVES LIVE (RADIO)

A BBC production for BBC Radio 4. Transmission details are for BBC Radio 4. Duration: 30 minutes.
Main regular credit(s): Written by P. G. Wodehouse; produced and directed by Rosalind Ayres.
Main regular cast: Martin Jarvis (Jeeves).

	Holding / Source
24.12.2007	DA /
31.12.2007 **Bertie Changes His Mind**	DA /

JEFFREY BERNARD IS UNWELL

An Independent Image production for BBC 2. Transmission details are for BBC 2. Duration: 123 minutes.

Based on the life and writings of the late Jeffrey Bernard, a womaniser, heavy drinker and Soho hellraiser.

Written by Keith Waterhouse; designed by John Gunter; produced by Paddy Wilson, Tom Kinninmont and Laurence Myers; directed for the stage by Ned Sherrin; directed by Tom Kinninmont.

Peter O'Toole (Jeffrey Bernard), Royce Mills, Timothy Ackroyd, Sarah Berger, Annabel Leventon.

	Holding / Source
23.12.1999	DB / DBSW

Recorded at London's Old Vic Theatre.

JELLABIES

Alternative/Working Title(s): JELLIKINS

A Winchester Television production for GMTV. made in association with Optical Image Broadcast. Transmission details are for GMTV. Duration varies - see below for details.

Main regular cast: Rik Mayall (Narrator).

	Holding / Source
##.##.#### 25 Mins Christmas Special	DB /

Duration: 25 minutes.

3D CGI animation.

JENNY ECLAIR: THE PLATINUM COLLECTION

An Avalon Productions production for Channel 5. Transmission details are for Channel 5. Duration: 70 minutes.

Written by Jenny Eclair and Pete Richens; executive producers Richard Allen-Turner and Jon Thoday; produced by Dean Nabarro and Sam Pinnell; directed by Peter Orton.

	Holding / Source
23.12.1998	DB / DBS

JESSYE NORMAN'S CHRISTMAS SYMPHONY

A Thames Television production. made in association with Filmscreen International Ltd. Transmission details are for the Thames Television region. Duration: 50 minutes.

The celebrated American singer Jessye Norman, whose range spans spirituals to grand opera, turns her attention to Christmas carols which she has known and loved since childhood. The carols are arranged in a symphony of four movements, incorporating old favourites like Silent Night and Hark the Herald Angels Sing and a new song Jessye's Carol which was specially written for her with music by Donald Fraser and words by Jane McCulloch. In the magnificent setting of Ely Cathedral, it is an occasion to which Jessye brings her own brand of special warmth, and, in her own words, you will `feel the joy'.

Music by Donald Fraser and Jane McCulloch; orchestra conducted by Robert de Cormier; executive producer Ian Martin; produced by Timothy Woolford; directed by John Michael Phillips.

Jessye Norman, Vocal Arts Chorus, American Boychoir, Ely Cathedral Choir, Bournemouth Symphony Orchestra.

	Holding / Source
22.12.1987	1" / 1"

JESUS

A BBC production for BBC 2. Transmission details are for BBC 2. Duration: 45 minutes.

Main regular credit(s): Lyrics by John McCarthy; music directed by Alyn Ainsworth; music by Claude-Henri Vic and Alan Roper; choreography by Douglas Squires, designed by J. Roger Lowe; produced and directed by Stewart Morris.

Main regular performer(s): Derek Francis (Narrator), The Young Generation.

	Holding / Source
25.12.1969	2"|n / 2"
##.##.#### Music Only Version, No Narration	DB / 2"

There are two versions, one 'music only' and the tx version, the BBC have the former on digibeta ex 2", the 2" tape of the tx version was sent to the NFA in 1992 without the BBC copying it for some reason.

THE JIM DAVIDSON SHOW

A Thames Television production. Transmission details are for the ATV/Central region. Duration: 25 minutes.

Main regular cast: Jim Davidson (Compere).

SERIES 2

Transmission details are for the ATV midlands region.

Main regular credit(s): Designed by Harry Clark; produced by John Ammonds; directed by Stuart Hall.

	Holding / Source
31.12.1979 The Jim Davidson Special	D3 / 2"

Written by John Junkin, Barry Cryer and Alex Shearer.

With The Dooleys, Ernest Clark, Rudolph Walker, Sabina Franklyn.

THE JIM DAVIDSON SHOW (continued)   British Christmas Television Guide

SERIES 3

Transmission details are for the ATV midlands region.

Main regular credit(s): Designed by Bill Palmer; produced and directed by Mark Stuart.

Holding / Source

23.12.1980 D3 / 2"

Seasonal laughs with joker Jim Davidson. Jim gets into trouble trying to photograph a cake and ends up as Tiny Tim in a Scrooge sketch.

Written by Dave Freeman, Bernie Sharp, Alex Shearer, Hugh Stuckey and Eddie Braben; music directed by Allan Rogers.

With Bob Todd, Tim Barrett, Hugh Paddick.

Transmission details are for the ATV/Central region.

Holding / Source

22.12.1981 D3 / 2"

A seasonal session of laughs with jovial jester Jim Davidson, assisted by Bob Todd. Pop Cockney duo Chas and Dave perform a medley and singing group The Midas Touch introduce Little Drummer Boy.

Written by Eric Davidson, Wally Malston, Bill Martin and Jackie Lynton; music directed by Harry Rabinowitz; choreography by Christopher Wren; designed by David Richens; produced by Mark Stuart; directed by Neville Green.

With Chas & Dave, The Midas Touch [as Midas Touch], Bob Todd, Jacoba, Irene Gorst.

Transmission details are for the ATV/Central region.

Holding / Source

29.12.1982 D3 / 2"

Duration: 50 minutes.

Written by David Renwick, Andrew Marshall, Andrea Solomons, John Revell, James Hendrie, Ian Brown and John Muir; designed by Martyn Hébert; produced and directed by Mark Stuart.

With Windsor Davies, Chas & Dave, Iris Williams, Derek Waring, Burt Kwouk, Stanley Unwin, Debbie Arnold, Jethro, The Brian Rogers Dancers.

JIM DAVIDSON'S SPECIAL

A Thames Television production. Transmission details are for the Central region. Duration varies - see below for details.

Main regular cast: Jim Davidson.

Holding / Source

24.12.1984 Falklands Special 1" / 1"

Duration: 50 minutes.

Produced by Robert Louis; directed by Stuart Hall.

With John Mills (Narrator), Jim's Band, Tricia Dusky, Vanessa Biddulph, Alison Richards, Sam Spencer-Lane, Sara Throssell.

24.12.1986 Jim Davidson In Germany 1" / 1"

Duration: 50 minutes.

Devised by Jim Davidson; written by Jim Davidson; music directed by Ray Monk; music played by Francis Hayward, Val McKenna, John 'Smudger' Smith and Peter Stroud; choreography by Nicky Hinkley; produced by Bob Louis; produced for the stage by Rick Price; directed by Stuart Hall.

With Richard Digance, Diane Solomon, Lindsey Cole, Mandy Hearnden, Samantha Spencer-Lane, Suzie Waring.

JIM'LL FIX IT

A BBC production for BBC 1. Transmission details are for BBC 1. Duration varies - see below for details.

Jimmy Savile fixes it for children to achieve their dreams.

Main regular performer(s): Jimmy Savile (Presenter).

Holding / Source

24.12.1975 Christmas Special DB-D3 / 2"

Duration: 45 minutes.

Designed by Gerry Scott; produced by Roger Ordish; outside broadcast director John Shrewsbury; directed by Stanley Appel.

With Lulu, Ron Moody.

Holding / Source

24.12.1976 Christmas Special DB-D3 / 2"

Duration: 45 minutes.

Lighting by John Dixon; sound Richard Chamberlain; designed by Paul Munting; produced by Roger Ordish; directed by David G. Hillier.

With John Inman, Rod Hull and Emu.

Holding / Source

26.12.1977 Christmas Special DB-D3 / 2"

Duration: 35 minutes.

Lighting by John Dixon; sound Peter Rose; designed by Ken Ledsham; produced by Roger Ordish; studio sequences directed by Phil Bishop.

With Val Doonican.

Holding / Source

26.12.1978 Boxing Day Special DB-D3 / 2"

Duration: 40 minutes.

Lighting by Jimmy Purdie; sound Alan Machin; designed by Barbara Gosnold; produced and directed by Roger Ordish.

With Frankie Vaughan, Doctor Magnus Pyke, Christopher Timothy, James Herriot, Don Maclean.

JIM'LL FIX IT

26.12.1979   Holding / Source: DB-D3 / 2"
Duration: 35 minutes.
Lighting by John Farr; sound John Holmes; designed by John Holland; produced by Roger Ordish; directed by Rick Gardner.
With Dollar, Roger de Courcey & Nookie Bear.

SERIES 7
Main regular credit(s): Produced by Roger Ordish.

26.12.1980 Boxing Day Special   Holding / Source: DB-D3 / 2"
Duration: 40 minutes.
Lighting by Peter Wesson; sound Richard Chamberlain; designed by Sheila Lawson; directed by Peter Campbell.
With B. A. Robertson, The Brother Lees, Bernie Clifton.

SERIES 8
Main regular credit(s): Produced by Roger Ordish.

25.12.1981   Holding / Source: DB-D3 / 2"
Duration: 40 minutes.
Lighting by Gerry Millerson; sound Richard Chamberlain; designed by Andy Dimond; directed by Peter Campbell.
With The Nigel Lythgoe Dancers.

SERIES 9
Main regular credit(s): Produced by Roger Ordish.

25.12.1982   Holding / Source: DB / 1"
Duration: 40 minutes.
Lighting by Peter Wesson; sound Richard Chamberlain; designed by Sally McKee; directed by Peter Campbell.
With Ken Dodd, Val Doonican.

SERIES 10
Main regular credit(s): Produced by Roger Ordish.

25.12.1983   Holding / Source: DB / 1"
Duration: 40 minutes.
Lighting by Peter Wesson; sound Richard Chamberlain; designed by John Stout; directed by Peter Campbell.

SERIES 11
Main regular credit(s): Theme music by Dave Mindel; produced by Roger Ordish.

24.12.1984   Holding / Source: DB / 1"
Duration: 40 minutes.
Lighting by Peter Wesson; sound Richard Chamberlain; designed by Gwen Evans; directed by Marcus Mortimer.
With Tommy Steele.

SERIES 12
Main regular credit(s): Produced by Roger Ordish.

24.12.1985   Holding / Source: DB / 1"
Duration: 45 minutes.
Lighting by Eric Wallis; sound Richard Chamberlain; designed by Bob Steer; directed by Michael Leggo.

SERIES 13
Main regular credit(s): Produced by Roger Ordish.

24.12.1986   Holding / Source: DB / 1"
Duration: 40 minutes.
Lighting by Eric Wallis; sound Peter Barville; designed by Ken Ledsham; directed by David Taylor.

SERIES 14
Main regular credit(s): Produced by Roger Ordish.

24.12.1987   Holding / Source: DB / 1"
Duration: 40 minutes.
Lighting by Chris Townsend; sound Bob Foley; designed by John Bristow; directed by Tony Newman.

JIM'LL FIX IT (continued)   British Christmas Television Guide

SERIES 16
Main regular credit(s):   Produced by Roger Ordish.

                                                                    Holding / Source
26.12.1989   DB / 1"
Duration: 45 minutes.
Directed by Peter Laskie.

SERIES 17
Main regular credit(s):   Produced by Roger Ordish.

                                                                    Holding / Source
26.12.1990 **Jim'll Fix It For Christmas**   DB / 1"
Duration: 45 minutes.
Directed by Peter Laskie.

                                                                    Holding / Source
28.12.1991 **Christmas Special**   DB / 1"
Duration: 40 minutes.
Produced by Roger Ordish; directed by Helen Gartell.
With Frank Bruno, Ruth Madoc.

                                                                    Holding / Source
28.12.1992   DB / D3S
Duration: 45 minutes.
Produced by Roger Ordish; directed by Helen Gartell.
With Take That, Roddy Piper.

JIM'LL FIX IT WITH SHANE RICHIE

A BBC production for BBC 1. Transmission details are for BBC 1. Duration: 30 minutes.
Executive producers Michelle Langer and Derek McLean.
Shane Richie (Presenter).

                                                                    Holding / Source
26.12.2011   HD/DB / HDC

JIMMY TARBUCK'S CHRISTMAS ALL STARS

An LWT production. Transmission details are for the Central region. Duration: 80 minutes.
Designed by Bill McPherson; produced by David Bell; directed by Alasdair MacMillan.
Jimmy Tarbuck (Host), Bruce Forsyth, Mike Yarwood, Max Bygraves, Cannon and Ball, Shakin' Stevens, Bonnie Tyler, Michael Barrymore, Jeremy Beadle, Henry Kelly, Matthew Kelly, Sarah Kennedy, Andy Williams, The Temptations, The Four Tops, Robert Wagner, Stefanie Powers, David Hasselhoff, Alyn Ainsworth Orchestra and Singers.

                                                                    Holding / Source
25.12.1983   DB / 1"

JO BRAND THROUGH THE CAKEHOLE

A Channel X production for Channel 4. Transmission details are for Channel 4. Duration: 25 minutes.
Main regular credit(s):   Executive producer Katie Lander.
Main regular cast: Jo Brand (Host).

                                                                    Holding / Source
30.12.1993 **(pilot)**   D3 / D3S
Duration: 30 minutes.
Produced and directed by Marcus Mortimer.

SERIES 1
Main regular credit(s):   Written by Jo Brand; produced by Geoff Atkinson; directed by Mike Adams.

                                                                    Holding / Source
23.12.1994 **Jo Brand Through The Christmas Cakehole**   D3 / D3S
With Martin Kemp, Gary Glitter.

JO BRAND'S CHRISTMAS LOG

A Vera production for Channel 4. Transmission details are for Channel 4. Duration: 55 minutes.
Written by Jo Brand; additional material by Kevin Day; executive producer Geoff Atkinson; produced by Elaine Morris; directed by Tony Keene.
Jo Brand, Elaine C. Smith, Edna Doré, Janine Duvitski.

                                                                    Holding / Source
28.12.1998   D3 / D3S

JOE

Produced for BBC 1 by a variety of companies (see details below). Transmission details are for BBC 1. Duration: 15 minutes.

Main regular credit(s): Written by Alison Prince; drawings by Joan Hickson; music by Laurie Steele; produced and directed by Diana Potter.

SERIES 1
A BBC production.

Main regular cast: With Lee Montague (Narrator).

	Holding / Source
26.12.1966 **Joe And The Dustcart**	R1 /

JOE 90

A Century 21 production for ITC. made in association with ITC. Transmission details are for the ATV midlands region. Duration: 25 minutes.

Main regular credit(s): Format by Gerry Anderson and Sylvia Anderson; based on characters created by Sylvia Anderson; script editor Tony Barwick; music by Barry Gray; executive producer Reg Hill; produced by David Lane.

Main regular cast: Len Jones (Voice of Joe McClaine), Rupert Davies (Voice of Professor Ian McClaine), Keith Alexander (Voice of Sam Loover), David Healy (Voice of Shane Weston).

	Holding / Source
22.12.1968 **The Unorthodox Shepherd**	DB / C3

Written by Tony Barwick; directed by Ken Turner.

With Gary Files, Martin King.

JOE AND MARY

An Anglia production. Transmission details are for the ATV midlands region. Duration: 50 minutes.

Just before Christmas, Joe and his wife Mary go to a town where Joe has a new job. But the town is full for the holiday season, and accomodation is almost impossible to find .. .

Written by Arden Winch; designed by Jane Martin; associate producer Robert Bell; executive producer John Woolf; produced by John Rosenberg; directed by Gareth Davies.

Bryan Marshall (Joe), Cathryn Harrison (Mary), Barrie Ingham (Frank Forrest), Gerry Haggerty (Garage Attendant), Jeffery Kissoon (Peter Gold), David Roper (Mervyn Ainsworth), Godfrey James (George), Frank Duncan (Watkins), Mary Healey (Beryl), Raymond Witch (Marsh), John Gill (Badger), Elizabeth Millbank (Jean Meadows), Harry Waters (Harry Meadows), Paddy O'Hagan (Doug), Jill Balcon (Della Forbes), John Bryans (Reggie).

	Holding / Source
19.12.1977	D2 / 2"

THE JOE PASQUALE SHOW

An LWT production. Transmission details are for the Central region. Duration: 42 minutes.

Written by Charlie Adams; script associate Alan Wightman; executive producer Nigel Lythgoe; produced by John Bartlett; directed by Paul Kirrage.

Joe Pasquale (Host), Sacha Distel, Eric Sykes, Norman Collier, Jim Bowen, Ray Tizzard, Serena Destouche, Alan Bodenham, Hughie O'Neill, Christine O'Neill, Fleur Golding, Rusty Goffe, Symond Lawes, Norman Vaughan, OTT.

	Holding / Source
28.12.1996	D2 / D2S

With Joe Pasquale.

JOE PASQUALE: RETURN OF THE LOVE MONKEY

A Talent TV Production production for ITV 1. made in association with 2 Entertain. Transmission details are for the Central region. Duration: 48 minutes.

Script associate John Moloney; script supervisor Denise Lonsdale; magical adviser Wayne Dobson; designed by Simon Kimmel; executive producers Robert Voice and Paul Hembury; produced and directed by John Kaye Cooper.

Joe Pasquale (Host), Peter Dickson (Voice Only).

	Holding / Source
27.12.2007	DB / DBSW

JOHN BISHOP'S BRITAIN

Produced for BBC 1 by a variety of companies (see details below). made in association with 3 Amigos Productions. Transmission details are for BBC 1. Duration: 30 minutes.

Main regular cast: John Bishop.

SERIES 2
An Objective Scotland production.

Main regular credit(s): VT directors Andrew Chaplin and Lucy Forbes; written by John Bishop; script supervisor Annie McDougall; theme music by Audioputty; designed by Dominic Tolfts; assistant producers Laura Clark, Rachael Jenkins and Charlotte Lewis; production executive Ruth Emerson; executive producers Karl Warner, Jim Reid, Lisa Thomas, Lee Hupfield and Andrew Newman; head of production Debi Roach; production manager Susi Hollins; series producer Jonno Richards; produced by Adam Copeland; directed by Paul Wheeler.

	Holding / Source
27.12.2011 **Christmas Special**	HD/DB / HDC

With Noddy Holder.

JOHN BISHOP'S CHRISTMAS SHOW

A BBC production for BBC 1. Transmission details are for BBC 1. Duration: 60 minutes.

rtiThe comedian hosts an evening of comedy and music from the Lyceum Theatre, London.

Produced by Cameron Banks.

John Bishop, Nina Conti, Jason Manford, Lee Nelson, David O'Doherty, Tim Vine.

	Holding / Source
23.12.2013	HD/DB / HDC

THE JOHN CURRY ICE SPECTACULAR

An LWT production. Transmission details are for the ATV midlands region. Duration: 60 minutes.

Music directed by Harry Rabinowitz; music associate Martin Goldstein; choreography by Norman Maen; designed by Roger Hall; produced and directed by Jon Scoffield.

John Curry (Host), Millicent Martin, Wayne Sleep, Peggy Fleming, Julia McKenzie, David Kernan, La Compagnie Andre Tahon, The Norman Maen Dancers.

	Production No	Holding / Source
25.12.1976	9L/09852	D2 / 2"

JOHN WELLS AND THE THREE WISE MEN

An Open Media production for Channel 4. Transmission details are for Channel 4. Duration: 35 minutes.

Written by John Wells; produced by Justin Scroggie and Kathy Ceaton; directed by Simon Holder.

John Wells.

	Holding / Source
25.12.1988	1" / 1"

THE JOHNNY VEGAS GAME SHOW

A BBC production for BBC Choice. made in association with Big Eye Film & Television. Transmission details are for BBC Choice. Duration: 43 minutes.

Devised by BBC and Big Eye Film & Television; written by Johnny Vegas; additional material by Mobashir Dar and Hugh Rycroft; titles by Moov; art director Sara Hawden; designed by Jonathan Paul Green [credited as Jonathan Green]; associate producer Johnny Vegas; production executive Andrew Wiltshire; executive producers Steve Lock, Lisa Clark and Myfanwy Moore; production manager Stan Matthews; produced by Mobashir Dar; directed by David G. Croft.

Johnny Vegas (Host).

	Holding / Source
22.12.2002 (pilot)	DB / DBSW

THE JOHNNY VEGAS TELEVISION SHOW

A Big Eye Productions production for Channel 4. Transmission details are for Channel 4. Duration: 40 minutes.

Written by Steven Lock and Michael Pennington; executive producer Mary Richmond; produced and directed by Steven Lock.

Johnny Vegas, Phil Hawkins (Club Secretary), Dave Knowles (Park Ranger), Adrian Manfred (Ice Cream Man).

	Holding / Source
27.12.1998	DB / DBS

JOKERS WILD

A Yorkshire Television production. Transmission details are for the ATV midlands region. Usual duration: 25 minutes.

Joke-telling competition.

Main regular credit(s):   Devised by Ray Cameron and Mike King.

Main regular performer(s): Barry Cryer (Chairman).

SERIES 6

Main regular credit(s):   Designed by Richard Jarvis, Malcolm Dawson and Tim Trout; produced and directed by David Millard.

	VT Number	Holding / Source
24.12.1973 Joker's Wild Christmas Special	2695	1" / 2"

Take one Barry Cryer, eight jokers, an audience in party mood and what have you got? Jokers Wilder!

With Barry Cryer, Les Dawson, Michael Aspel, Lennie Bennett, Clive Dunn, Jack Douglas, David Nixon, Alfred Marks, John Cleese, Mike Goddard, Norman Vaughan.

JONAH AND THE WHALE

A Scottish Television production. Transmission details are for the ATV midlands region. Duration: 60 minutes.

Jonah is a small-town prophet from Gittah Hepher in Palestine. It is ordained that he shall prophesy the destruction of Nineveh. He attempts to avoid this by travelling in the opposite direction to Nineveh but the ship in which he is travelling encounters a violent storm. Jonah is thrown overboard, swallowed by a whale and duly deposited at Nineveh.

Adapted by Ronald Mavor; based on a story by James Bridie; music by Arthur Blake; designed by Pip Gardner; executive producer Liam Hood; directed by Tina Wakerell.

Rodney Bewes (Jonah), Shirley Steedman (Euodias), Martin Cochrane (Bilshan), Mary Riggans (Eshtemoa), Paul Kermack (Sea Captain), Bryden Murdoch (Voice of the Whale), David Stewart (Josibiah), Stassia Stakis (Naaran), John Young (Shual), John Shedden (Sentry), Jan Wilson (Sophereth), Mary Ann Reid (Shiprah).

	Holding / Source
28.12.1975	J / 2"

JONATHAN CREEK

A BBC Light Entertainment production for BBC 1. Transmission details are for BBC 1. Duration varies - see below for details.
Main regular credit(s):   Written by David Renwick; theme music by Saint-Saens and Julian Stewart Lindsay.
Main regular cast: Alan Davies (Jonathan Creek).

	Holding / Source
24.12.1998 **Black Canary**	DB / V1SW

Duration: 90 minutes.
Script supervisor Janice Brackenridge; associate producer Jonathan Paul Llewellyn; executive producer David Renwick; produced by Verity Lambert; directed by Sandy Johnson.
With Caroline Quentin (Maddy Magellan), Rik Mayall, Stuart Milligan (Adam Klaus), Hannah Gordon, Kate Isitt, Francis Matthews, Murray Melvin, Suzanna Hamilton, Vincent Wong, Simone Huber, Tomas Lukes, Simon Roberts, Dave Haskell, John Hales, Corinne Laidlaw, Sanjeev Bhaskar, Nikki Jhutti.

SERIES 3
Main regular credit(s):   Produced by Verity Lambert.
Main regular cast: With Caroline Quentin (Maddy Magellan).

	Holding / Source
28.12.1999 **Miracle In Crooked Lane**	DB / V1SW

Duration: 50 minutes.
Directed by Richard Holthouse.
With Benjamin Whitrow, Dinah Sheridan, Nicholas Ball, Hetty Baynes, Tom Goodman-Hill, Emma Kennedy, Frances Low, Ben Craze, William Vanderpuye, Paul Fuller.

	Holding / Source
26.12.2001 **Satan's Chimney**	DB / V1SW

Duration: 120 minutes.
Script supervisor Caroline Thomas; music by Julian Stewart Lindsay; production executive Sarah Hitchcock; executive producer David Renwick; produced by Verity Lambert; directed by Sandy Johnson.
With Julia Sawalha (Carla Borrego), Stuart Milligan (Adam Klaus), Steven Berkoff, Mary Tamm, Bill Bailey, James Saxon, Jay Benedict, Lisa Stökke, Matt Rippy, Elliot A. Cowan, Raymond Griffiths, Penny Smith, Sonya Saul, Bill Ward, Marcus Knibbs, Lorraine Hilton, Nina Bhirangi.

A BBC Productions production.
Main regular cast: With Sheridan Smith (Joey Ross).

	Holding / Source
01.01.2009 **The Grinning Man**	HD/DB / HD/DB

Duration: 118 minutes.
Script supervisor Janice Brackenridge; music by Rick Wentworth; director of photography Geoff Harrison; art director Anthony Cartlidge; designed by John Asbridge; production executive Sarah Hitchcock; executive producer Pete Thornton; line producer Maria Cooper; produced by Nerys Evans; directed by David Renwick.
With Stuart Milligan (Adam Klaus), Andrew Havill (Newsreel Narrator), Jon Campling (Jacques Futrelle), Patrick Poletti (Eli Mencken), Eloise Rakic-Platt (Child Constance), Sarah Champion (Marcia), Sally Plumb (Housewife), Adam James (Alec), Naomi Bentley (Mina), Ciaran McMenamin (Glen), Nicholas Boulton (Lance Gessler), Jenna Harrison (Elodie), Judy Parfitt (Constance Gessler), Katherine Parkinson (Nicola), Jemma Walker (Candy Mountains), Kate Mullins (Puppini Sisters), Marcella Puppini (Puppini Sisters), Stephanie O'Brian (Puppini Sisters), Julia Ford (Delia Gunning), Deborah Maclaren (Ellen Ashley Adams), Nick Nevern (Lenny), Charlotte Comer (Young Constance), Graham Vanas (Maitre D').

THE JONATHAN ROSS SHOW

An ITV Productions production for ITV 1. Transmission details are for the Central region. Usual duration: 48 minutes.
Main regular performer(s):   Jonathan Ross (Host).

SERIES 1
Main regular credit(s):   Series producer Tom Barrett; directed by Chris Howe.

	Holding / Source
23.12.2011	HD/DB / HDC

Duration: 57 minutes.
With Jessica Brown-Findlay, Laura Carmichael, Michelle Dockery, Simon Bird, Joe Thomas, James Buckley, Blake Harrison, Tim Minchin, Il Volo, Tom Cruise.

SERIES 3
Main regular credit(s):   Series producer Tom Barrett; directed by Chris Howe.

	Holding / Source
22.12.2012	HD/DB / HDC

With Michael McIntyre, Sheridan Smith, Ellie Simmonds, Jonnie Peacock, Charlotte Church.

	Holding / Source
28.12.2013 **Christmas Special**	HD/DB / HDC

Duration: 57 minutes.
Series producer Tom Barrett; directed by Chris Howe.
With Sir David Attenborough, John Bishop, Ray Winstone, Jamie Oliver, Susan Boyle.

JOOLS' 12TH ANNUAL HOOTENANNY

A BBC production for BBC 2. Transmission details are for BBC 2. Duration: 135 minutes.

Produced by Alison Howe; directed by Janet Fraser Crook.

Jools Holland (Host), Jools Holland's Rhythm and Blues Orchestra, Eric Clapton, Franz Ferdinand, Amy Winehouse, Jamie Cullum, Basement Jaxx, Ian Hunter, Natasha Bedingfield, Paul Carrack, Mavis Staples, R.A.F. Halton.

	Holding / Source
31.12.2004	DB / DBSW

JOOLS' ANNUAL HOOTENANNY

A BBC production for BBC 2. Transmission details are for BBC 2. Duration varies - see below for details.

	Holding / Source
31.12.2005	DB / DBSW

A BBC production. Duration: 120 minutes.

Assistant producer Stephanie McWhinnie; associate producer Jools Holland; production executive Stephania Minici; executive producer Mark Cooper; produced by Alison Howe; directed by Janet Fraser Crook.

With Jools Holland (Host), Jools Holland's Rhythm and Blues Orchestra, Kaiser Chiefs, Goldfrapp, Irma Thomas, Corinne Stanley Rae, Robin Gibb, James Blunt, Ruby Turner, K. T. Tunstall, Marc Almond, Kate Rusby, Chris Difford, Pipes and Drums, 1st Battalion Scots Guards, Rory Bremner, Adrian Edmondson, Jennifer Saunders, Rowland Rivron.

31.12.2006	DB / DBSW

A BBC production. Duration: 120 minutes.

Assistant producer Stephanie McWhinnie; associate producer Jools Holland; production executive Stephania Minici; executive producer Mark Cooper; produced by Alison Howe; directed by Janet Fraser Crook.

With Jools Holland (Host), Adrian Edmondson, Jennifer Saunders, Lenny Henry, Dawn French, Alan Davies, Rowland Rivron, Alan Carr, Peter Kay, Paul Weller, The Zutons, Sam Brown, Sam Moore, Amy Winehouse, Lily Allen, Jools Holland's Rhythm and Blues Orchestra, Madeleine Peyroux, Marc Almond, Ray LaMontagne, The Kooks, James Morrison, Seasick Steve, The Pipes and Drums of The 1st Battalion Scots Guards.

31.12.2007 **Jools's Annual Hootenanny**	DB / DBSW

A BBC production. Duration: 130 minutes.

Designed by Simon Rogers; assistant producer Stephanie McWhinnie; associate producer Jools Holland; production executive Stephania Minici; executive producer Mark Cooper; produced by Alison Howe; directed by Janet Fraser Crook.

With Jools Holland (Host), Jools Holland's Rhythm and Blues Orchestra, Paul McCartney, Eddie Floyd, Mika, Kate Nash, Kylie Minogue, Kaiser Chiefs, Madness, Robbie Coltrane, Seasick Steve, Ruby Turner, Lulu, Duffy, Pipes and Drums, 1st Battalion Scots Guards.

31.12.2008 **Jools's Annual Hootenanny**	HD/DB / HDC

A BBC Productions production. Duration: 140 minutes.

Designed by Simon Rogers; associate producer Jools Holland; production executive Stephania Minici; executive producer Mark Cooper; production manager Gesa Schlotfeldt; produced by Alison Howe; directed by Janet Fraser Crook.

With Jools Holland (Host), Martha and The Vandellas, Dave Edmunds, Annie Lennox, Lily Allen, Dizzee Rascal, The Ting Tings, Duffy, Svang, Adele, Ruby Turner, Sam Sparro, Kelly Jones, Scots and Irish Guards Pipers, Jools Holland's Rhythm and Blues Orchestra.

31.12.2009	HD/DB / HDC

A BBC Productions production. Duration: 130 minutes.

Designed by Simon Rogers; associate producer Jools Holland; production executive Stephania Minici; executive producer Mark Cooper; production manager Gesa Schlotfeldt; produced by Alison Howe; directed by Janet Fraser Crook.

With Jools Holland (Host), Jools Holland's Rhythm and Blues Orchestra, Paolo Nutini, Florence and The Machine, Boy George, Rodrigo Y Gabriela, Ruby Turner, Paloma Faith, Kasabian, Tom Jones [as Sir Tom Jones], Kelly Jones, Dizzee Rascal, Shingai Shoniwa, Dave Edmunds, The Pipes and Drums of The 1st Battalion Scots Guards.

JOOLS' ELEVENTH ANNUAL HOOTENANNY

A BBC production for BBC 2. Transmission details are for BBC 2. Duration: 120 minutes.

Produced by Alison Howe; directed by Janet Fraser Crook.

Jools Holland (Host), Desmond Dekker, Lulu, Paul Rodgers, Shane MacGowan, Primal Scream, Texas, Candi Staton, Jools Holland's Rhythm and Blues Orchestra.

	Holding / Source
31.12.2003	DB / DBSW

JOOLS'S 19TH ANNUAL HOOTENANNY

A BBC Productions production for BBC 2. Transmission details are for BBC 2. Duration: 75 minutes.

Executive producer Mark Cooper; produced by Alison Howe; directed by Janet Fraser Crook.

Jools Holland (Host), Cyndi Lauper, Jessie J, Sandie Shaw, Aloe Blacc, James Morrison, The Vaccines, Betty Wright, Caro Emerald, Buddy Greco, Imelda May, Pokey LaFarge, South City Three, Charlie Musselwhite, Gregory Porter, Ruby Turner, Jools Holland's Rhythm and Blues Orchestra, Pipes & Drums of 1st Battalion Scots Guards.

	Holding / Source
31.12.2011	HD/DB / HDC

JOOLS'S ANNUAL HOOTENANNY

A BBC Productions production for BBC 2. Transmission details are for BBC 2. Duration varies - see below for details.

Main regular performer(s): Jools Holland.

	Holding / Source
31.12.2010	HD/DB / HDC

Duration: 135 minutes.

Designed by Simon Rogers; associate producer Jools Holland; production executive Stephania Minici; executive producer Mark Cooper; production manager Vicky Singer; produced by Alison Howe; directed by Janet Fraser Crook.

With Cee Lo Green, Jools Holland's Rhythm and Blues Orchestra, Wanda Jackson, Vampire Weekend, Toots Hibbert, Bellowhead, Alison Moyet, The Secret Sisters, Rico Rodriguez, Rumer, Plan B, Ruby Turner, Kylie Minogue, Roger Daltrey, Henry Dagg, The Pipes and Drums of The 1st Battalion Scots Guards.

31.12.2011	HD/DB / HDC

Duration: 135 minutes.

Produced by Alison Howe and Mark Cooper; directed by Janet Fraser Crook.

With Jessie J, Cyndi Lauper, Sandie Shaw, Aloe Blacc, James Morrison, The Vaccines, Betty Wright, Caro Emerald, Buddy Greco, Imelda May, Pokey LaFarge, South City Three, Ruby Turner, Jools Holland's Rhythm and Blues Orchestra, 1st Battalion Scots Guards.

31.12.2012	HD/DB / HDC

Duration: 90 minutes.

Produced by Alison Howe and Mark Cooper; directed by Janet Fraser Crook.

With Petula Clark, Emeli Sandé, Lianne La Havas, Paloma Faith, Ruby Turner, Bettye Lavette, Bobby Womack, Adam Ant, Jake Bugg, Roland Gift, Kevin Rowland, The Hives, The Dubliners, 1st Battalion Scots Guards.

31.12.2013	HD/DB / HDC

Duration: 120 minutes.

Executive producer Mark Cooper; produced by Alison Howe; directed by Janet Fraser Crook.

With Lisa Stansfield, Ray Davies, Jools Holland's Rhythm and Blues Orchestra, Rudimental, Ella Eyre, Emeli Sandé, Charlie Wilson, Laura Mvula, John Newman, Haim, Melanie C, The Proclaimers, Ruby Turner, The Lumineers, Lee Thompson, 1st Battalion Scots Guards.

JOOLS'S TENTH ANNUAL HOOTENANNY

A BBC production for BBC 2. Transmission details are for BBC 2. Duration: 130 minutes.

Produced by Alison Howe and Mark Cooper; directed by Janet Fraser Crook.

Jools Holland (Host), Jools Holland's Rhythm and Blues Orchestra, Jimmy Cliff, Tom Jones, Solomon Burke, Ms Dynamite, Pulp, Doves, Chrissie Hynde, Robert Plant, Jeff Beck, Chas & Dave, Vic Reeves, Scots and Irish Guards Pipers.

	Holding / Source
31.12.2002	DB / DBSW

JOSEPH AND THE AMAZING TECHNICOLOR DREAMCOAT

A Granada production. Transmission details are for the ATV midlands region. Duration: 35 minutes.

The Young Vic Company presents a rock musical version of the story from Genesis about Joseph and his coat of many colours.

Written by Tim Rice; lyrics by Tim Rice; music directed by Alan Doggett; music by Andrew Lloyd Webber; choreography by Christopher Bruce; designed by Peter Phillips; produced and directed by Peter Plummer.

Gary Bond (Joseph), Gavin Reed (Potiphar), Joan Heal (Potiphar's Wife), Riggs O'Hara (Baker), Andrew Robertson (Butler), Gordon (Pharaoh), Joanna Wake (Girl), Digby (Pharaoh's Slave), Michael Watkins (Pharaoh's Slave), Peter Reeves (Narrator), Barbara Courtney (Girl), Alison Groves (Girl), Alex McAvoy (Jacob), Julia McCarthy (Mrs Jacob), Paul Brooke (The Brothers), Riggs O'Hara (The Brothers), Mason Taylor (The Brothers), Richard Kane (The Brothers), Gavin Reed (The Brothers), Gordon (The Brothers), Ian Trigger (The Brothers), David Wynn (The Brothers), Ian Charleson (The Brothers), Jeremy James-Taylor (The Brothers), Andrew Robertson (The Brothers), Choir of Whitgift School, Croydon.

The Young Vic Company

	Holding / Source
24.12.1972 **[Parade]**	DB / 2"

JOSEPH AND THE AMAZING TECHNICOLOR DREAMCOAT

A Really Useful Films production for Channel 5. Transmission details are for Channel 5. Duration: 75 minutes.

Lyrics by Tim Rice; music by Andrew Lloyd Webber; executive producer Austin Shaw; produced by Andrew Lloyd Webber; directed by Steven Pimlott and David Mallett.

Donny Osmond (Joseph), Maria Friedman (Narrator), Richard Attenborough (Jacob), Ian McNeice (Potiphar), Joan Collins (Mrs Potiphar), Robert Torti (Pharaoh), Alex Jennings (Butler), Christopher Biggins (Baker).

	Holding / Source
21.12.2005	DB / DBSWF

"The Making of Joseph and the Amazing Technicolor Dreamcoat", 25mins, was shown prior.

JOURNEY OF A LIFETIME

An Associated British Pathe production for ABC. Transmission details are for the ABC midlands region. Duration: 15 minutes.

Main regular credit(s): Devised by Eric Fletcher; produced by Terry Ashwood.
Main regular cast: Anne Lawson, John Bonney.

SERIES 2
Main regular credit(s): Directed by Frederic Goode.

	Holding / Source
24.12.1961 A Child Is Born	C3 / C3

Written by Jean Scott Rogers; associate producer Lionel Hoare.
With Anne Lawson, John Bonney.

	Holding / Source
31.12.1961 The Innocents Of Bethlehem	C3 / C3

Written by Stewart Farrar.

THE JOURNEY

A Thames Television production. Transmission details are for the Central region. Duration: 25 minutes.
Using 16th-century Flemish paintings and contemporary graphic designs, The Journey tells the Christmas story.
Music by Tom Parker; executive producer Diana Potter; produced and directed by Richard Mervyn.
Robin Askwith (Narrator), Kim Goody (Carols), Gordon Neville (Carols).

	Holding / Source
24.12.1982	1" / 1"

JOY AT CHRISTMAS

A BBC production for BBC 1. Transmission details are for BBC 1. Duration: 20 minutes.
Arranged by Joy Webb; produced and directed by Raymond Short.
Joy Webb (Salvation Army's Joystrings), The Croydon Junior Singers.

	Holding / Source
26.12.1971	

JOY TO THE WORLD

A Granada production. Transmission details are for the Central region. Duration: 40 minutes.

David Pickering, 12-year-old Chorister of the Year, takes you on a magical tour of Christmas past and present. Baker Street, Coronation Street, a stable and Granada's Studio One (a new studio complex) are shared by famous faces, students of the Royal Northern College of Music and local children in this joyous celebration of Christmas.

Music directed by Joseph Ward; designed by James Weatherup; produced by June Howson; directed by Alan Grint.

Jean Alexander, Jeremy Brett, Johnny Briggs, David Burke, Kid Creole, Betty Driver, Jane Eaglen, Julie Goodyear, Don Henderson, David Pickering, Rosalie Williams, Royal Northern College of Music.

	Holding / Source
24.12.1984	1" / 1"

JOY TO THE WORLD

A BBC production for BBC 1. Transmission details are for BBC 1. Duration: 55 minutes.
Devised by Major Michael Parker; television presentation by Simon Betts; produced by Major Michael Parker.
Sarah Greene (Host), Jane Asher, Peter Bowles, Chris De Burgh, David Copperfield, Paul Daniels, Evelyn Glennie, Bonnie Langford, Benjamin Luxon, Suzi Quatro, Bertice Reading, Leo Sayer, Wayne Sleep, Robert Tear, London Oriana Choir, English Baroque Choir, London Brass, Waverley Singers, Haberdashers' Aske's Boys, English Baroque Orchestra.

	Holding / Source
23.12.1990	DB / 1"

JOY TO THE WORLD

A BBC production for BBC 1. Transmission details are for BBC 1. Duration: 60 minutes.
Television presentation by Simon Betts.
Sarah Brightman, Cliff Richard, Patricia Hodge, Siân Philips, Christopher Biggins, Grace Kennedy, Anthony Andrews, Fascinating Aida, Anthony Way, Gloria Hunniford, Nickolas Grace.

	Holding / Source
23.12.1995	DB-D3 / D3S

JOY TO THE WORLD

A BBC production for BBC 1. Transmission details are for BBC 1. Duration: 60 minutes.
A gala of carols, comedy, music and dance from the Royal Albert Hall.
Television presentation by Simon Betts.
Cliff Richard, Hannah Gordon, Diana Rigg, Peter Bowles, Gloria Hunniford, Chicken Shed Theatre Co.
A feast of Christmas cheer!

	Holding / Source
24.12.1997	DB-D3 / D3S

JOY TO THE WORLD

JOY TO THE WORLD: MUSIC FOR CHRISTMAS FROM LINCOLN CATHEDRAL

A Yorkshire Television production. Transmission details are for the ATV midlands region. Duration: 50 minutes.
Christmas music for everyone.
Music associates Robert Hartley and Simon Lindley; music arranged by Peter Knight; designed by Helena Walker; produced and directed by Terry Henebery.
Peter Barkworth, Sandra Browne, Wynford Evans, Cantabile, Peter Knight, The Halle Orchestra, The Halle Choir, Lincoln Cathedral Choir, Bishop of Lincoln, The Fanfare Trumpeters.

	Holding / Source
21.12.1980	1" / 2"

A JUBILEE OF MUSIC

A BBC production for BBC 1. Transmission details are for BBC 1. Duration: 75 minutes.
Written by Austin Steele; choreography by Nigel Lythgoe; designed by Jan Spoczynski; produced and directed by Stewart Morris.
Vera Lynn, Acker Bilk, Max Bygraves, Petula Clark, Ken Dodd, Val Doonican, Rolf Harris, Kathy Kirby, Lulu, Matt Monro, Cliff Richard, Helen Shapiro, Norman Wisdom, The Young Generation, Alyn Ainsworth and his Orchestra.

	Holding / Source
31.12.1976	DB-D3 / 2"

With Vera Lynn, Acker Bilk, Max Bygraves, Petula Clark, Ken Dodd, Val Doonican, Rolf Harris, Kathy Kirby, Lulu, Matt Monro, Cliff Richard, Helen Shapiro, Norman Wisdom, The Young Generation.

THE JUBILEE SHOW

An Associated-Rediffusion production. Transmission details are for the ATV midlands region. Usual duration: 27 minutes.

SERIES 1

	Holding / Source
31.12.1957	J /

Dances staged by Malcolm Goddard; settings by Henry Federer; directed by Peter Croft.
With Ian Wallace (Chairman), Dennis Lotis, Elizabeth Larner, Jimmy Thompson, Nicolette Roeg, Betty Driver, The George Mitchell Singers, The Jubilee Dancers, Van Phillips and his Orchestra.

SERIES 2

	Holding / Source
26.12.1958	J /

Duration: 50 minutes.
Script by Dominic Roche; orchestrations by Van Phillips and Alfred Ralston; choreography by Denny Bettis; settings by Henry Federer and Michael Wield; directed by Peter Croft.
With Ian Wallace (Chairman), Michael Holliday, Marion Ryan, Pamela Harrington, Denny Bettis, Denis Martin, Geoffrey Hibbert, Anthony Shaw, Dominic Roche, John Hewer, Nicolette Roeg, Dorothy Ward, Shaun Glenville, Van Phillips and his Orchestra, The George Mitchell Singers, The Jubilee Dancers.

JULIA JEKYLL AND HARRIET HYDE

A BBC production for BBC 1. Transmission details are for BBC 1. Duration: 15 minutes.
Main regular credit(s): Created by Jeremy Swan; executive producer Anna Home; produced by Jeremy Swan.
Main regular cast: Olivia Hallinan (Julia Jekyll), John Asquith (Harriet Hyde).

SERIES 2
Duration: 14 minutes.

	Holding / Source
19.12.1996 **Rocket Christmas**	DB / D3S

Which of the many Santas at the Christmas party is the real one?
Written by Jim Eldridge.
With Victoria Williams (Moira Jekyll), Bill Fellows (Jerry Jekyll), Simon Green (Memphis Rocket), Ann Emery (Mrs Rocket), Roger Hammond (Santa Claus).

THE JULIE ANDREWS HOUR

An ATV production. Transmission details are for the ATV midlands region. Duration: 50 minutes.
Main regular performer(s): Julie Andrews (Host).

	VT Number	Holding / Source
23.12.1972	6386	R1 / 2"

With a Smile and a Song, Julie opens the door to a world of fantasy, where film unfolds to mix magically with the settings in a glittering tribute to the musical delights of Walt Disney.
   Snow White, Pinocchio, Dumbo and Fantasia find new life through Julie and her guests. In a songful scene from Snow White, Julie introduces the voice of the cartoon princess Adriana Caselotti, who was chosen from hundreds of Hollywood hopefuls when the film was made 34 years ago.
   Teen-star of the Forties Donald O'Connor plays the toymaker to Julie's puppet Pinocchio with I've Got No Strings. But Donald really comes into his own as Donald—wait for it!—Duck, making the miserable most of his marriage to one of Cinderella's ugly sisters, played by Alice Ghostley.
Music directed by Nelson Riddle; choreography by Tony Charmoli; produced by Nick Vanoff; directed by Bill Davis.
With Young Americans, Donald O'Connor, Alice Ghostley.

| THE JULIE ANDREWS HOUR (continued) | British Christmas Television Guide |

	VT Number	Holding / Source
24.12.1973 Julie's Christmas Special: Merry Christmas With Love, Julie	7612	DB / 2"

The show starts when Julie takes a welcome break from rehearsing a seasonal programme and retires to her dressing room... In the blink of an eye she's in a world of fantasy with Santa Claus and the Sugar Plum Fairy, played by guests Peter Ustinov and Peggy Lee.

Written by Frank Waldman; music associate Derek Scott; designed by Brian Bartholomew; executive producer Blake Edwards; produced and directed by Jon Scoffield.

With Dougie Squires, The Second Generation, The Treorchy Male Voice Choir, Peter Ustinov, Peggy Lee, Jack Parnell and his Orchestra.

JULIE WALTERS AND FRIENDS

An LWT production. Transmission details are for the Central region. Duration: 50 minutes.

Written by Victoria Wood, Alan Bennett, Willy Russell and Alan Bleasdale; produced by Nicholas Barrett; directed by Alasdair MacMillan.

Julie Walters, Victoria Wood, Alan Bennett, Willy Russell, Alan Bleasdale.

	Holding / Source
29.12.1991	DB / 1"S

JUNIOR KICKSTART

A BBC production for BBC 1. Transmission details are for BBC 1.

Main regular cast: Peter Purves (Presenter).

	Holding / Source
29.12.1980	DB-D3 / 2"

SERIES 3

	Holding / Source
24.12.1984	DB / 1"
26.12.1984	DB / 1"
27.12.1984	DB / 1"
28.12.1984	DB / 1"

JUNIOR SHOWTIME

A Yorkshire Television production. Transmission details are for the ATV midlands region. Usual duration: 25 minutes.

SERIES 2

Main regular credit(s): Music by Bryan Rodwell; choreography by Jean Pearce and Minnie Thompson; designed by Ian McCrow; executive producer Jess Yates; directed by Burt Budin.

Main regular performer(s): With Bobby Bennett, Fred Barker, 'Mr Albert'.

	Holding / Source
24.12.1969	J / 2"
31.12.1969 Junior Showtime Pantomime	J / 2"

SERIES 3

Main regular credit(s): Script by Bert Gaunt; music associate Charles Smitton; executive producer Jess Yates.

Main regular performer(s): With Bobby Bennett (Host), Mark Curry (Host), Glyn Poole (Host).

	Holding / Source
24.12.1970 Christmas Party	J / 2"

Duration: 40 minutes.

Choreography by Jean Pearce, Minnie Thompson and Mary Leadbetter; designed by Mike Long; directed by David Millard.

With Billy Dainty, Beverly Hall, Craig Hall, The Tiddleywinks.

SERIES 4

Main regular credit(s): Executive producer Jess Yates; directed by David Millard.

Main regular performer(s): With Bobby Bennett (Host), Glyn Poole (Host), Kathryn Apanowicz (Host), Mark Curry (Host), Bonnie Langford (Host), Miss Marjorie (Host).

	Holding / Source
24.12.1971 Junior Showtime Christmas Pantomime	J / 2"

Duration: 45 minutes.

Written by Garry Chambers; designed by Richard Jarvis.

With Bobby Bennett (Baron Brain), Glyn Poole (Little Glyn), Marjorie Phillips (Miss Marjorie), Bonnie Langford (Baron's Daughter), Bev and Craig Hall (Wiggy And Ziggy), Sharon Banks (Fairy Fortune), Diane Mewse (Town Cryer), Joe Baker (Giant).

SERIES 7

Main regular credit(s): Dances staged by Jean Pearce; music directed by Tony Cervi; associate producer Peter Max-Wilson; executive producer Jess Yates; directed by Roger Cheveley.

	Holding / Source
24.12.1973	J / 2"

See also: BABES IN THE WOOD / CINDERELLA

JUNIOR SHOWTIME

JUNIOR SUPERSTARS

A BBC production for BBC 1. Transmission details are for BBC 1.

	Holding / Source
26.12.1981	DB-D3 / 2"

JUST GOOD FRIENDS

A BBC production for BBC 1. Transmission details are for BBC 1. Duration varies - see below for details.

Main regular credit(s): Written by John Sullivan; lyrics by John Sullivan; theme music by Ronnie Hazlehurst.

Main regular cast: Paul Nicholas (Vince Pinner / Singer theme tune), Jan Francis (Penny Warrender).

SERIES 2

Main regular credit(s): Produced and directed by Ray Butt.

	Holding / Source
25.12.1984	DB / 1"

Duration: 90 minutes.

Designed by David Hitchcock; production team Lesley Bywater, Caroline Andrews, Tony Dow and Kevin Mullery; production manager Sue Bysh.

With Sylvia Kay (Daphne Warrender), John Ringham (Norman Warrender), Ann Lynn (Rita Pinner), Shaun Curry (Les Pinner), James Lister, Paul James, Kate Saunders, Daniel Peacock, Lisa Jacobs, Howard Samuels, Lisa Anselmi, David Rhule, Douglas W. Iles, John Pennington, Eve Pearce, Stifyn Parri, Peter Blake, Steve Whyment, Kate Williams, Daphne Goddard, Debbi Blythe, Andrew Tourell, Erika Hoffman, Bill Wallis, Richenda Carey, Adrienne Burgess, Brian Jameson, Debbie Linden, Derek Newark, Royston Tickner, Colette Gleeson, David Neville.

"Frank and Selina's Christmas Time", 23.12.1984 BBC1, went behind-the-scenes making this special. With Frank Bough and Selina Scott. 35 mins 1".

SERIES 3

Main regular credit(s): Designed by David Hitchcock; production manager Evan King; produced by Ray Butt; directed by Sue Bysh.

	Holding / Source
25.12.1986 "The End"	DB / 1"

Duration: 35 minutes.

With Sylvia Kay (Daphne Warrender), John Ringham (Norman Warrender), Ann Lynn (Rita Pinner), Shaun Curry (Les Pinner), Adam French (Cliff Pinner), Charlotte Seely (Georgina), Bill Wallis, Martin Cochrane, Thomas Henty, Claude Le Saché, John Serret, Katherine Kath, Pamela Stirling, Hugh De Vernier.

JUST JIMMY

An ABC production. Transmission details are for the ABC midlands region. Duration: 25 minutes.

Main regular cast: Jimmy Clitheroe (Himself).

SERIES 1

Main regular credit(s): Designed by Peter Le Page; produced by Ronnie Taylor; directed by Ronnie Baxter.

Main regular cast: With Mollie Sugden, Danny Ross.

	Holding / Source
03.01.1965 **What A Pantomime!**	J / 40

Written by Ronnie Taylor.

With Mollie Sugden, Jameson Clark.

JUST PET

A BBC production for BBC 1. Transmission details are for BBC 1. Duration: 50 minutes.

Written by Dick Vosburgh and Bill Solly; designed by Brian Tregidden; produced and directed by Yvonne Littlewood.

Petula Clark (Host), Johnny Harris and his Orchestra, Frank Owens, The Breakaways, London Welsh Association Choir.

	Holding / Source
27.12.1969	J / 2"

JUST WHAT I ALWAYS WANTED

A BBC Religious Department production for BBC 1. Transmission details are for BBC 1. Duration: 5 minutes.

Written by John Wells; produced and directed by Chris Loughlin.

John Wells, Margot Boht (Auntie Flo).

	Holding / Source
25.12.1991	DB-D3 / D3S

JUST WILLIAM

An LWT production. Transmission details are for the ATV midlands region.

Main regular credit(s): Adapted by Keith Dewhurst; based on books by Richmal Crompton; theme music by Denis King; executive producer Stella Richman; produced and directed by John Davies.

Main regular cast: Adrian Dannatt (William Brown).

SERIES 2

	Production No	Holding / Source
25.12.1977 **William's Worst Christmas**	9D/11115	D2 / 2"

Duration: 50 minutes.

"If you ask me," said William, "it's the worst Christmas I've ever had. Look at what I did."

Designed by Colin Monk.

With Diana Fairfax (Mrs Brown), Hugh Cross (Mr Brown), Simon Chandler (Robert Brown), Stacy Dorning (Ethel Brown), Diana Dors (Mrs Bott), Bonnie Langford (Violet Elizabeth Bott), Michael McVey (Ginger), Craig McFarlane (Henry), Tim Rose (Douglas), John Stratton, Julian Orchard, Norman Space, Richard Hurndall, Lloyd Lamble, Peggy Ann Wood, Ronald Mayer, Ruth Kettlewell, Richard Goolden, Gillian Royale, Hilary Mason, Ann Curthoys, Georgina Melville, Graham Seed, Osmund Bullock, Patrick Harvey, Wally Goodman.

JUST WILLIAM

A CBBC production for BBC 1. Transmission details are for BBC 1. Duration: 30 minutes.

Main regular credit(s): Adapted by Simon Nye; based on a book by Richmal Crompton; script supervisor Caroline O'Reilly; music by Stephen Warbeck; director of photography Erik Wilson; consultant Martin Jarvis; art director Sarah Pasquali; designed by Gary Williamson; production executives Sam Moor and David Noble; executive producer Gina Cronk; line producer Rhian Griffiths; produced by John Chapman; title sequence directed by Huge Designs; directed by Paul Seed.

Main regular cast: Daniel Roche (William Brown), Martin Jarvis (Narrator).

	Holding / Source
28.12.2010 **The Sweet Little Girl In White**	HD/DB / HD/DB

With Caroline Quentin (Mrs Bott), Warren Clarke (Mr Bott), Rebecca Front (Mrs Brown), Daniel Ryan (Mr Brown), Isabella Blake-Thomas (Violet Elizabeth), Lily James (Ethel Brown), Harry Melling (Robert Brown), Jordan Grehs (Ginger), Edward Percy (Douglas), Robert Foster (Henry), Max Hiller, Bruce MacKinnon, Adam Gillen, Richard Southgate, Paul Thornley, Roy Hudd.

29.12.2010	HD/DB / HD/DB
30.12.2010 **The School Report**	HD/DB / HD/DB

With Roy Hudd (Bob Andrews), Warren Clarke, Caroline Quentin, Rebecca Front, Daniel Ryan, Judy Parfitt, Bruce MacKinnon, Lily James, Harry Melling, Jordan Grehs, Edward Percy, Robert Foster, Max Hiller, Isabella Blake-Thomas, Lottie Bell, Denis Lawson.

31.12.2010	HD/DB / HD/DB

K.9 AND COMPANY

Alternative/Working Title(s): SARAH AND K9

A BBC production for BBC 1. Transmission details are for BBC 1. Duration: 50 minutes.

Christmas at Moreton Harwood. All is peaceful. Or is it?

Written by Terence Dudley; script editors Eric Saward and Antony Root; theme music by Ian Levine and Fiachra Trench; music by Peter Howell; designed by Nigel Jones; production associate Angela Smith; production manager Robert Gabriel; produced by John Nathan-Turner; directed by John Black.

Elisabeth Sladen (Sarah Jane Smith), John Leeson (Voice of K-9), Bill Fraser (Commander Bill Pollock), Ian Sears (Brendan Richards), Colin Jeavons (George Tracey), Mary Wimbush (Aunt Lavinia), Linda Polan (Juno Baker), Sean Chapman (Peter Tracey), Gillian Martell (Lilly Gregson), Neville Barber (Howard Baker), John Quarmby (Henry Tobias), Nigel Gregory (Sergeant Wilson), Stephen Oxley (Police Constable Carter).

	Holding / Source
28.12.1981 **A Girl's Best Friend** [pilot]	DB-D3 / 2"

Alt.Title(s): *One Girl and her Dog*

See also: DOCTOR WHO (BBC) / THE SARAH JANE ADVENTURES (BBC)

KATE

A BBC Birmingham production for BBC 2. Transmission details are for BBC 2. Duration: 45 minutes.

Produced by Roy Ronnie; directed by Roy Norton.

Kate Bush, Peter Gabriel, Gary Hurst, Stewart Avon-Arnold.

	Holding / Source
28.12.1979	DB-D3 / 2"

KEEPING UP APPEARANCES

A BBC production for BBC 1. Transmission details are for BBC 1. Usual duration: 30 minutes.

Main regular credit(s):	Written by Roy Clarke; theme music by Nick Ingman; titles by Sid Sutton.
Main regular cast:	Patricia Routledge (Hyacinth Bucket (pronounced Bouquet)), Clive Swift (Richard Bucket), Josephine Tewson (Liz), Geoffrey Hughes (Onslow), Judy Cornwell (Daisy).

SERIES 2

Main regular credit(s):	Script editor Christopher Bond; designed by Tim Gleeson; produced and directed by Harold Snoad.
Main regular cast:	With Mary Millar (Rose).

	Holding / Source
25.12.1991 "The Father Christmas Suit"	DB / 1"S

Production manager Richard Beighton.

With David Griffin (Emmet Hawksworth), Tony Kemp, Mark Brackenbury, Annet Peters, Jeremy Gittins, Robert Packham.

SERIES 4

Main regular credit(s):	Script editor Christopher Bond; production manager Peter Laskie; produced and directed by Harold Snoad.
Main regular cast:	With Mary Millar (Rose), David Griffin (Emmet).

	Holding / Source
26.12.1993 "Cruise On The QE2"	DB / D3S

Duration: 58 minutes.

Designed by Derek Evans.

With David Janson, Alice MacDonald, Michael Cochrane, Bernard Holley, Barry Bethel [as Barry Bethell], Mark Brignal, Band of The Welch Fusiliers, Lyndsay Frost, Mark Joyce Showband, Lord Lichfield.

25.12.1994 "The New Kitchen"	DB / D3S

Duration: 48 minutes.

Designed by Derek Evans.

With Trevor Bannister, Jeremy Gittins, Andrew Bicknell, Caroline Strong, Preston Lockwood, George Webb.

SERIES 5

Main regular credit(s):	Production manager Peter Laskie; produced and directed by Harold Snoad.
Main regular cast:	With Mary Millar (Rose), David Griffin (Emmet).

	Holding / Source
25.12.1995 "The Pageant"	DB / D3S

Designed by Derek Evans and Sara Hawden.

With George Webb (Daddy), Jeremy Gittins, Marion Barron, Una Stubbs, Anna Dawson, John Evitts, Tony Stuart, Miranda Kingsley.

KEITH AND ORVILLE'S CHRISTMAS CIRCUS

A BBC Children's Department production for BBC 1. Transmission details are for BBC 1. Duration: 40 minutes.

Written by George Martin and Brian Marshall; music directed by Barry Francis; choreography by Irving Davies; designed by Alan Spalding; produced and directed by Paul Ciani.

Keith Harris & Orville, Dana, Eli Woods, Ronnie Brody, Los Martinos, Robbie Barnett, Circus Dancers.

	Holding / Source
24.12.1985	DB / 1"

See also: THE KEITH HARRIS SHOW (BBC)

THE KEITH BARRET SHOW

Produced for BBC 2 by a variety of companies (see details below). Transmission details are for BBC 2. Duration: 29 minutes.
Main regular cast: Rob Brydon (Keith Barret).

Holding / Source
20.12.2004 DB / DBSW
With Ulrika Jonsson, Lance Gerrard-Wright.

THE KEITH HARRIS SHOW

A BBC production for BBC 1. Transmission details are for BBC 1. Duration varies - see below for details.
Main regular performer(s): Keith Harris (Host), Bucks Fizz.

Holding / Source
31.12.1982 **[pilot]** DB / 2"
Duration: 30 minutes.
Written by George Martin; music directed by Ronnie Hazlehurst; choreography by Norman Maen; produced and directed by Paul Ciani.
With Bucks Fizz, Ray Dondy, Jacqui Scott, The Norman Maen Dancers.

Holding / Source
26.12.1983 **The Keith Harris Christmas Party** DB / 1"
Duration: 35 minutes.
Written by Wally Malston; music directed by Nigel Hess; lighting by Peter Wesson; sound Keith Gunn; designed by Barbara Gosnold; produced and directed by Paul Ciani.
With Shakin' Stevens, Stu Francis.

22.12.1984 **Keith Harris Christmas Show** DB / 1"
Duration: 35 minutes.
Script associate Wally Malston; music directed by Barry Francis; lighting by Eric Wallis; sound Len Shorey; designed by Malcolm Thornton; produced and directed by Stan Appel.
With Alvin Stardust, The Roly Polys, Ding Bats, Patrick Moore.

See also: KEITH AND ORVILLE'S CHRISTMAS CIRCUS (BBC)

KELLY

An Ulster Television production. Transmission details are for the Ulster Televison region.
Main regular performer(s): Gerry Kelly (Host).

Holding / Source
23.12.1994 **Christmas Special** 1" /
Christmas special shot in Romania, reporting on the Irish volunteers whose on-going commitment supports and cares for children in Romanian orphanages.

31.12.1994 **New Year Special** 1" /
Gerry Kelly hosts a New Year's party at home in Ardglass.
With Roy Walker, Christie Hennessy.

Holding / Source
31.12.2004 DB / DBSW
Gerry celebrates New Year's Eve with interviews and music.
With Brian Kennedy, Katie Melua, Michael Ball.

KEN DODD AND THE DIDDYMEN

A BBC North/Manchester production for BBC 1. Transmission details are for BBC 1. Duration: 10 minutes.
Main regular cast: Ken Dodd and The Diddy Men.

Holding / Source
21.12.1969 **Carol Singers** C1 / C1
Written by Bob Block; designed by Stuart Furber; produced by Stan Parkinson; directed by Ken Wrench.
With Sydney Arnold, Cyril Varley, Bryan Thanner.

KEN DODD AT THE LONDON PALLADIUM

A Thames Television production. Transmission details are for the Central region. Duration: 65 minutes.
Ken Dodd brings you a special show for Christmas from The London Palladium. He is joined by the 'Diddymen' and Roby Gasser and his performing seals, Adolph and Dixie.
Music directed by John Coleman; produced by John Fisher; directed by Paul Kirrage.
Ken Dodd (Host), The Brian Rogers Dancers, Roby Gasser, John Coleman and his Orchestra.

Holding / Source
25.12.1990 1" / 1"

THE KEN DODD SHOW

A BBC production for BBC 1. Transmission details are for BBC 1. Duration varies - see below for details.
Main regular performer(s): Ken Dodd (Host).

	Holding / Source
25.12.1965	R1 /

Duration: 60 minutes.
Written by Ken Dodd and Eddie Braben; orchestra directed by Ken Jones; choreography by Irving Davies; produced and directed by Michael Hurll.
With Sandie Shaw, Graham Stark, John Laurie, Neville King, Irving Davies, David Mahlowe, Patricia Hayes, The Irving Davies Dancers, The Michael Sammes Singers.
This is an uncut telerecording.

	Holding / Source
25.12.1966	J /

Duration: 45 minutes.
Written by Ken Dodd and Eddie Braben; orchestra directed by Bernard Herrmann; designed by John Burrowes; produced and directed by Michael Hurll.
With The Bachelors, Graham Stark, John Laurie, Patricia Hayes, Rita Webb, David Mahlowe, Roger Stevenson, The Diddymen, Penny Nairn, Wally Lamb, Jeanette Rossini, Jimmy Mac, The Lissa Gray Singers.

25.12.1967 **The Ken Dodd Christmas Show**   J /
Duration: 60 minutes.
Written by Ken Dodd and Eddie Braben; choreography by Sylvia Blake; designed by Norman Vertigan; produced and directed by Michael Hurll.
With The Seekers, Graham Stark, Patricia Hayes, John Laurie, Silvan, The Tiller Girls, Peter Knight and his Orchestra, The Michael Sammes Singers.

THE KEN DODD SHOW

A Thames Television production. Transmission details are for the ATV midlands region. Duration: 50 minutes.
Written by Ken Dodd, Frank Hughes and Norman Beedle; music directed by Alan Braden; designed by David Richens; produced and directed by Dennis Kirkland.
Ken Dodd (Host), Graham Stark, Hilda Fenemore, Talfryn Thomas, Jo Manning Wilson, Michael McClain, The Mike Sammes Singers.

	Holding / Source
28.12.1978	D3 / 2"

KEN DODD'S CHRISTMAS LAUGHTER SHOW

A BBC North West production. Transmission details are for BBC North West.
Ken Dodd.

	Holding / Source
13.12.1977	J / 2"

KEN DODD'S CHRISTMAS LAUGHTER SHOW

A BBC North West production. Transmission details are for BBC North West.
Ken Dodd.

	Holding / Source
18.12.1979	DB-1" / 2"

THE KEN DODD'S NEW YEAR'S EVE SPECIAL

A BBC production for BBC 1. Transmission details are for BBC 1. Duration: 50 minutes.
Written by Ken Dodd; choreography by Geoffrey Richer; produced and directed by Michael Hurll.
Ken Dodd, Rolf Harris, Ronnie Hazlehurst and his Orchestra, New Edition, Wilma Reading, Fivepenny Piece, Joan Rosaire, Goldie the Wonderhorse, Chris Emmett, The Diddymen.

	Holding / Source
31.12.1975	DB-D3 / 2"

KEN DODD'S OLD ENGLISH ROAST

A BBC production. Untransmitted.
Main regular performer(s): Ken Dodd.

	Holding / Source
##.##.####	DB-D3 / 2"

With Esther Rantzen.

| ##.##.#### | DB-D3 / 2" |

With Pete Murray.

THE KENNY EVERETT TELEVISION SHOW

A BBC production for BBC 1. Transmission details are for BBC 1. Duration: 30 minutes.
Main regular performer(s): Kenny Everett.

	Holding / Source
24.12.1981	DB-D3 / 2"

With The Police, David Frost, Billy Connolly, Bob Geldof.

THE KENNY EVERETT TELEVISION SHOW (continued)

SERIES 2
Main regular credit(s): Written by Ray Cameron, Barry Cryer and Kenny Everett; produced by Bill Wilson.

	Holding / Source
28.12.1982	DB / 1"

Directed by Bill Wilson.

	Holding / Source
27.12.1984	DB / 1"

Designed by Graham Lough and Richard McManan-Smith; directed by David Taylor.

With Culture Club, Lennie Bennett, Fiona Fullerton, Bonnie Langford, Lulu, Patrick Mower, Willy Rushton, Bernie Winters.

See also: KENNY EVERETT'S CHRISTMAS CAROL (BBC)

THE KENNY EVERETT VIDEO SHOW

A Thames Television production. Transmission details are for the ATV midlands region. Usual duration: 25 minutes.

Main regular performer(s): Kenny Everett, Hot Gossip.

SERIES 1
Main regular credit(s): Written by Barry Cryer, Ray Cameron and Kenny Everett; designed by Bill Laslett; associate producer Bridget Moore; produced and directed by David Mallet.

Main regular performer(s): With Arlene Phillips (Choreographer / Dancer), Hot Gossip (Regular Dance Troupe).

	Holding / Source
01.01.1979 **They Didn't Quite Make It In Time For Christmas Video Show**	D3 / 2"

Duration: 35 minutes.

With Rod Stewart, Leo Sayer, Dean Friedman.

Captain Kremen film made by Cosgrove Hall Productions.

SERIES 3
Main regular credit(s): Written by Barry Cryer, Ray Cameron and Kenny Everett; choreography by Arlene Phillips; designed by David Ferris and Rod Stratfold; associate producer Bridget Moore; produced and directed by David Mallet; film sequences directed by Cosgrove Hall Productions.

	Holding / Source
31.12.1979 **The "Will Kenny Everett Make It To 1980?" Show**	D3 / 2"

Duration: 50 minutes.
It's trembling suspense as zany Kenny Everett battles against overwhelming odds to make it into 1980.
Research Martin Robertson.

With Cliff Richard, The Boomtown Rats, David Bowie, Suzi Quatro, Bryan Ferry, The Greedies.

	Holding / Source
31.12.1980 **The Kenny Everett New Year's Daze Show**	D3 / 2"

Greet the New Year the Everett way-with Sid Snot and his newly-acquired family Clint, Enoch, Daphne and Mum. See Captain Kremmen in person with Anna Dawson as Carla. Also, there's the first game of Kenny's new American-style Star Quiz, which takes the country's top stars-and "completely humiliates them". Who's the first victim?

Written by Barry Cryer, Ray Cameron and Kenny Everett; music directed by Geoff Westley; music by Alan Hawkshaw; choreography by Arlene Phillips; designed by Peter Elliott; associate producer Bridget Moore; produced and directed by Royston Mayoh.

With David Essex, Christopher Biggins, Pat Ashton, Debbie Bishop, Tony London, Anna Dawson.

KENNY EVERETT'S CHRISTMAS CAROL

A BBC production for BBC 1. Transmission details are for BBC 1. Duration: 30 minutes.

Written by Barry Cryer and Neil Shand; designed by Nigel Curzon and Marjorie Pratt; produced and directed by John Bishop.

Kenny Everett, Michael Barrymore, Peter Cook, Spike Milligan, Willie Rushton, John Wells.

	Holding / Source
24.12.1985	DB / 1"

See also: THE KENNY EVERETT TELEVISION SHOW (BBC)

KICK OFF

A Granada production. Transmission details are for the Granada region. Duration: 25 minutes.

	Production No	Holding / Source
21.12.1979	P738/295	DB / 2"

Duration: 50 minutes.
Produced by P. Doherty; directed by Patricia Pearson.

With Elton Welsby (Host), Gerald Sinstadt (Host), Stan Boardman, Brian Hall, Charlie Williams, Davey Jones, Mick Miller, Frank Carson, Ray Clemence, Mike Harding, David Essex, Eric Morecambe, Ernie Wise, Ossie Ardiles, Pat Partidge, Malcolm Allison, The Harris Childrens Home, The Acrefield Bank Home For The Elderly, Andrew Sachs, Kenny Dalglish, Jimmy Frizzell, Peter Swales, Little and Large, Tom O'Connor, Bill Maynard, Freddie Starr, Bernard Manning, Derek Spence, Brian Green, Leonard Rossiter.

18.12.1981 **Christmas Panto**	P738/369	DB / 2"

Produced by P. Doherty; directed by Patricia Pearson.

With Bryan Robson (Aladdin), Joe Corrigan (Ugly Sister), Jim McDonaugh (Ugle Sister), Kenny Clements (Robinson Crusoe), Alan Bailey (Buttons), Eamon O'Keefe (Robin Hood), Gary Bailey (Peter Pan), Ian Rush (Dick Whittington), Elton Welsby (Presenter), Martin Tyler (Presenter), Denis Law (Presenter).

Football programme - only specials listed.

THE KIDS INTERNATIONAL SHOW

A BBC production for BBC 1. Transmission details are for BBC 1. Duration varies - see below for details.

	Holding / Source
24.12.1982	DB / 1"

Duration: 30 minutes.
Designed by John Anderson; produced and directed by Ernest Maxin.
With Charlie Smithers, Alyn Ainsworth and his Orchestra.

THE KING'S CHRISTMAS

A Yorkshire Television production. Transmission details are for the Central region. Duration: 25 minutes.
Music associate Howard Goodall; choreography by Domini Winter; designed by Colin Pigott; produced and directed by Vernon Lawrence.
The King's Singers.

	Holding / Source
25.12.1983	1" / 1"

THE KING'S COLLECTION

A Thames Television production. Transmission details are for the Thames Television region. Duration: 5 minutes.

	Holding / Source
21.12.1974	DB|n / 2"
22.12.1974	DB|n / 2"
##.##.####	DB|n / 2"
##.##.####	DB|n / 2"
##.##.####	DB|n / 2"
##.##.####	DB|n / 2"
##.##.####	DB|n / 2"

THE KING'S SINGERS SING CHRISTMAS

A BBC production for BBC 2. Transmission details are for BBC 2. Duration: 30 minutes.

Music for Christmas played and sung by two complementary groups of outstanding musicians. Part of a concert given in High Wycombe Parish Church in support of the RAF Benevolent Fund.

Orchestra conducted by Richard Hickox; lighting by Bert Robinson; sound Jeff Baker; produced and directed by Ken Griffin.
The King's Singers, The Richard Hickox Orchestra.

	Holding / Source
25.12.1978	DB-D3 / 2"

KIRI TE KANAWA AT CHRISTMAS

A BBC production for BBC 2. Transmission details are for BBC 2. Duration: 50 minutes.

A special programme of seasonal music both classical and contemporary from the Barbican Hall in London.
Orchestra conducted by Carl Davis; television presentation by Yvonne Littlewood.
Dame Kiri Te Kanawa, London Philharmonic Orchestra, Tallis Chamber Choir.

	Holding / Source
25.12.1985	DB / 1"

A KISS FOR CINDERELLA

A BBC production. Transmission details are for BBC. Duration: 90 minutes.

Written by J. M. Barrie; music by Christopher Whelen and The Pro Arte Orchestra; play production by Desmond Davis.

Jeannie Carson (Cinderella), Michael Aldridge (Mr Bodie), Kendrick Owen (Policeman), Walter Hudd (Storyteller), Tony Sympson (Elderly Gentleman), Violet Gould (Mrs Maloney), Gretchen Franklin (Marion), Harold Siddons (Man), Judy Stephens (Gladys), Susan Bown (Marie-Thérèse), Diane Gray (Delphine), Patricia Wilson (Gretchen), Mary Jones (Fairy Godmother), Raymond Rollett (Lord Mayor), Ralph Tovey (Lord Times), Max Latimer (Censor), Marjorie Gresley (Queen), Tony Sympson (Reverend Penguin), Mary McMillen (Maid), Beatrice Kane (Doctor Bodie), Henry Soskin (Danny), Virginia Stride (Nurse).

	Holding / Source
25.12.1959	J /

KISS ME KATE

A Carlton production for BBC 1. Transmission details are for BBC 1. Duration: 30 minutes.

Main regular credit(s):	Written by Chris Langham and John Morton; executive producers Geoffrey Perkins and John Bishop; produced by Nick Symons.
Main regular cast:	Caroline Quentin (Kate), Chris Langham (Douglas), Amanda Holden (Mel).

SERIES 3

Main regular credit(s):	Directed by Nick Wood.
Main regular cast:	With Darren Boyd, Elizabeth Renihan.

	Holding / Source
26.12.2000 Christmas Special	DB / DBSW

With Bill Nighy, Joan Walker, Tom Ellis, Darren Boyd, Katie Blake, Joanne Heywood, Ursula Holden-Gill, Elizabeth Renihan, Andrew Barclay, Peter Crebbin, Giancarla Pfleger, Samantha Clay, John Woodford.

KNOWING ME, KNOWING YOU... WITH ALAN PARTRIDGE

A Talkback production for BBC 2. Transmission details are for BBC 2.

Main regular credit(s): Written by Steve Coogan, Armando Iannucci and Patrick Marber; music directed by Steve Brown; produced by Armando Iannucci; directed by Dominic Brigstocke.

Main regular performer(s): Steve Coogan (Alan Partridge), Steve Brown (Glenn Ponder).

	Holding / Source
29.12.1995 **Knowing Me Knowing Yule... With Alan Partridge**	D3 / D3S

Duration: 40 minutes.
Lighting director Mike Sutcliffe; art director Jo Sutherland; production designer Dennis De Groot; production team Jim Imber and Darrin Nightingale; executive producer Peter Fincham; head of production Sally Debonnaire; production manager Alison MacPhail; produced by Armando Iannucci; directed by Dominic Brigstocke.
With Rebecca Front (Mary), Kevin Eldon (Fanny Thomas), David Schneider (Tony Hayers), Doon Mackichan (Liz Herron), Patrick Marber (Gordon Herron), Tom Binns, Carl Forgione, Alan Francis, Mick Hucknall.

THE KRANKIES KLUB

An LWT production. Transmission details are for the Central region. Duration varies - see below for details.

Main regular cast: The Krankies.

	Holding / Source
26.12.1982 **The Krankies Christmas Club**	D2 / 2"

Duration: 35 minutes.
Script associate Russel Lane; designed by Bryce Walmsley; produced by David Bell; directed by Alasdair MacMillan.
With Bananarama, Modern Romance, Ricky Patrick, The Gnaff Ensemble.

SERIES 1

Main regular credit(s): Script associate Russel Lane; music directed by Laurie Holloway; designed by Alison Humphries; produced and directed by Noel D. Greene.

Main regular cast: With Jimmy Cricket.

	Holding / Source
24.12.1983 **The Krankies At Christmas**	D2 / 2"

Duration: 35 minutes.
Written by Russel Lane; music by Laurie Holloway; designed by Alison Humphries.
With Bernie Winters, Melvyn Hayes, Jimmy Cricket, Sara Hollamby, Pepe and The Gang, The Flying Rollers, Barbara Dickson, Modern Romance, David Grant.

THE KRYPTON FACTOR

A Granada production. Transmission details are for the ATV/Central region. Duration: 25 minutes.

Main regular performer(s): Gordon Burns (Presenter).

SERIES 2

Transmission details are for the ATV midlands region.

Main regular credit(s): Music by Mike Moran.

	Production No	Holding / Source
29.12.1978 **Christmas Special**	P901/23	DB / 2"

Designed by Tim Farmer; produced by Jeremy Fox; directed by Patricia Pearson.
With Robin Knox-Johnston, Sir Ranulph Fiennes, Chris Bonington, Don Cameron.

SERIES 4

Transmission details are for the ATV midlands region.

Main regular credit(s): Graphics by Murray Cook; produced by Stephen Leahy.

	Production No	Holding / Source
22.12.1980 **Champion Of Champions**	P901/46	DB / 2"

Research Katie Woods and Alan Frank; directed by Charles Kitchen.
With Harry Evans, Ken Wilmhurst, Peter Richardson, Philip Bradley.

	Production No	Holding / Source
29.12.1980 **World Champions**	P901/47	DB / 2"

Research Katie Woods and Alan Frank; directed by Charles Kitchen.
With Lynn Davies, Jim Fox, Clare Francis, David Wilkie.

SERIES 5

Transmission details are for the ATV midlands region.

Main regular credit(s): Produced by Stephen Leahy.

	Production No	Holding / Source
22.12.1981 **Celebrity Special**	P901/65	DB / 2"

Designed by Roy Graham; directed by Mary McMurray.
With Naomi James, Andy Ripley, Beryl Burton, Richard Fox.

	Production No	Holding / Source
30.12.1981 **UK vs USA**	P901/66	DB / 2"

Designed by Roy Graham; directed by Mary McMurray.
With Clare Francis.

		Holding / Source
30.12.1982 **Special 1982**		1" / 1"

Designed by Paul Danson; produced by Nick Turnbull; directed by David Hillier.
With Geraldine Rees, Cindy Buxton, Charles Burton, Jonathan Adams.

SERIES 6
Transmission details are for the Central region.

	Production No	Holding / Source
30.12.1982 **Special 1982**	P901/84	DB / 1"

Research Thelma McGough; designed by Paul Danson; produced by Nick Turnbull; directed by David Hillier.
With Geraldine Rees, Cindy Buxton, Charles Burton, Jonathan Adams.

SERIES 7
Transmission details are for the Central region.

	Production No	Holding / Source
19.12.1983 **Celebrity**	P901/104	DB / 1"

Research Thelma McGough; designed by Paul Danson; produced by David Jenkins; directed by Brian Lenane.
With Peter Bird, Richard Crane, Liz Hobbs, Julie Tullis.

SERIES 8
Transmission details are for the Central region.

	Production No	Holding / Source
27.12.1984 **Olympic Special**	P901/122	DB / 1"

Research Thelma McGough; designed by Alison Hart; produced by David Jenkins; directed by Graham C. Williams.
With Tessa Sanderson, Andy Holmes, Neil Adams, June Croft.

SERIES 9
Transmission details are for the Central region.

	Production No	Holding / Source
26.12.1985 **Christmas Show**	P901/142	DB / 1"

SERIES 10
Transmission details are for the Central region.

	Production No	Holding / Source
23.12.1986	P901/159	DB / 1"

SERIES 13
Transmission details are for the Central region.

	Production No	Holding / Source
31.12.1989 **Sports Celebrities**	P901/210	DB / 1"

Research Brian Machin and Peter Kessler; designed by Stephen Fineren and Nick King; executive producer David Liddiment; produced by Rod Natkiel; directed by Jonathan Bullen.
With Wasim Akram, Bob Champion, Sally Jones, Steve Ovett, Steve Coogan.

SERIES 14
Transmission details are for the Central region.

	Production No	Holding / Source
26.12.1990 **Celebrity Special**	P901/224	DB / 1"

Produced by Kieran Roberts; directed by Sue McMahon.
With Jon Iles, Glenda McKay, Philip Middlemiss, Annie Miles, Gwyneth Strong.

THE KUMARS AT NO.42

A Hat Trick production for BBC. Transmission details are for BBC. Duration: 30 minutes.

Main regular performer(s): Sanjeev Bhaskar (Sanjeev), Meera Syal (Ummi), Indira Joshi (Mum), Vincent Ebrahim (Dad).

SERIES 1
Transmission details are for BBC 2.
Main regular credit(s): Written by Sanjeev Bhaskar, Richard Pinto and Sharat Sardana; executive producers Jimmy Mulville and Denise O'Donoghue; produced by Lissa Evans, Richard Pinto and Sharat Sardana; directed by Lissa Evans.

	Holding / Source
30.12.2001	DB / DBSW

With Gary Lineker, Mel B, Claire Sweeney, Belinda Carlisle.

THE KUMARS AT NO.42 (continued)   British Christmas Television Guide

SERIES 2
Transmission details are for BBC Choice.

Main regular credit(s): Written by Richard Pinto, Sharat Sardana and Sanjeev Bhaskar; executive producer Denise O'Donoghue; produced by Lissa Evans, Richard Pinto and Sharat Sardana; directed by Lissa Evans.

Holding / Source

29.12.2002 **Christmas Special**   DB / DBSW

With Trinny Woodall, Susannah Constantine, Darius Danesh, Mark Owen.

SERIES 5
Transmission details are for BBC 2.

Main regular credit(s): Written by Richard Pinto, Simon Blackwell, George Jeffrie, Bert Tyler-Moore and Sukbir Pannu; produced by Helen Williams; directed by Dominic Brigstocke.

Holding / Source

22.12.2003   DB / DBS

With Cliff Richard, Neil Morrissey.

26.12.2004 **Christmas Special**   DB / DBSW

Will Anne Robinson's saucy wink leave Sanjeev hot under the collar? And what will Phil Collins make of mischievous Granny's below-the-belt questions? Plus ex-Wizzard frontman Roy Wood with I Wish It Could Be Christmas Every Day.

With Phil Collins, Anne Robinson, Roy Wood.

LADIES AND GENTLEMEN... JO BRAND

A Vera production for Channel 4. Transmission details are for Channel 4. Duration: 25 minutes.
Written by Jo Brand and Mark Kelly; produced by Jon Rolph and Geoff Atkinson; directed by John L. Spencer.
Jo Brand.

	Holding / Source
22.12.1999	DB / DBS

LADY LUST

Alternative/Working Title(s): LADY LUST'S LOVELIES
A Granada production for Granada Sky Broadcasting. Transmission details are for Granada Sky Broadcasting. Duration: 8 minutes.

Main regular cast: Teresa May (Lady Lust).

SERIES 1
Main regular credit(s): Produced by Mike Wiseman.

	Production No	Holding / Source
20.12.1998	P2932/8	DB / DBS

In this episode we meet Nicola the 'Christmas Cracker'. Full of festive fun she dances for us and tells us about her career. We get a sneaky preview of next week's lovely, Ginny the 'Beach Babe'.

LAFFS AT THE BATHS

A Yorkshire Television production. Transmission details are for the Yorkshire Television region. Duration: 23 minutes.

Seven male comedians perform stand-up comedy routine in front of a live audience in a night-club setting at the Harrogate Baths.

Main regular credit(s): Produced by Arch Dyson; directed by David Reynolds.
Main regular cast: Rory Motion, Vladimir McTavish, Mike Milligan, Kevin Kopfstein, Danny Brown, Parrot, Alan Tyler.

	Holding / Source
21.12.1996	D3 / D3S
28.12.1996	D3 / D3S

LAPLAND

Commissioned by BBC 1. Transmission details are for BBC 1.

It's Christmas and hearts must be warmed. That's the rule. So prepare to have that vital organ not just warmed but barbecued as we join the tumultuous Lewis clan on a trip to, yes, Lapland, to visit the actual Santa Claus. They are a noisy, aggressive bunch, headed by widowed matriarch Eileen, who start arguing on the plane before the holiday has even begun. And the squabbles continue as they squash into a tour bus for horrible organised trips in festive hats led by a ghastly guide, Jingle Jill.

Written by Michael Wynne; produced by Rosemary McGowan; directed by Catherine Morshead.

Sue Johnston (Eileen), Julie Graham (Mandy), Stephen Graham (Pete), Elizabeth Berrington (Paula), William Ash (Ray), Emily Joyce (Miranda), Rufus Jones (Julian), Jane Ashton (Jingle Jill), Keith Barron (Maurice), Caspar Phillipson (Teppo), Fraser Ayres (Brian), Juha Leppajarvi (Bavval), Andrei Alen (Hans), Nigel Harris (Santa Claus), Ellis Murphy (Liam), Adam Scotland (Jack), Connor Dempsey (Ethan), Georgia Doyle (Melissa).

	Holding / Source
24.12.2011	HD/DB / HDC

LARK RISE TO CANDLEFORD

Alternative/Working Title(s): CANDLEFORD GREEN / LARK RISE, OVER TO CANDLEFORD
A BBC Productions production for BBC 1. Transmission details are for BBC 1.

Main regular credit(s): Based on books by Flora Thompson.

SERIES 2
Main regular credit(s): Script editor Marigold Joy; music by Julian Nott; consultant Carmel Maloney; designed by Martin Boddison; executive producers Bill Gallagher and Susan Hogg; produced by Ann Tricklebank.
Main regular cast: With Claudie Blakley (Emma Timmins), Brendan Coyle (Robert Timmins), John Dagleish (Alf Arless), Fergus Drysdale (Frank Timmins), Olivia Hallinan (Laura Timmins), Mark Heap (Thomas Brown), Sophie Miles (Sally Arless), Thomas Jones (Edmund Timmins), Sarah Lancashire (Adult Laura), Harry Miles (Archie Arless), Julia Sawalha (Dorcas Lane), Martha Murdoch (Ethel Timmins), Hope Yeomans (Lizzie Arless).

	Holding / Source
21.12.2008	HD/DB / HD/DB

Duration: 75 minutes.
Adapted by Bill Gallagher; script supervisor Amanda Lean; directed by Alan Grint.
With Linda Bassett (Queenie Turrill), Victoria Hamilton (Ruby Pratt), Karl Johnson (Twister Turrill), Matilda Ziegler (Pearl Pratt), Sandy McDade (Miss Ellison), Dawn French, Robert Pugh, Sheridan Smith.

THE LARKINS

Alternative/Working Title(s): LOOK IN WITH THE LARKINS
An ATV production. Duration varies - see below for details.
Main regular credit(s): Created by Fred Robinson.
Main regular cast: Peggy Mount (Ada Larkins), David Kossoff (Alf Larkins).

SERIES 1
An ATV Midlands production. Transmission details are for the ATV midlands region.
Main regular credit(s): Written by Fred Robinson; music by Jackie Brown; designed by Pembroke Duttson; produced and directed by Bill Ward.
Main regular cast: With Ronan O'Casey (Jeff Rogers), Ruth Trouncer (Joyce Rogers), Shaun O'Riordan (Eddie Larkins).

	VT Number	Holding / Source
26.12.1958 **Christmas With The Larkins**	267	R3 / LiveR1

Duration: 29 minutes.
With Hilary Bamberger (Myrtle Prout), Barbara Mitchell (Hetty Prout), George Roderick (Sam Prout), Norman Mitchell, John Barrard, Charles Lloyd Pack, Fred Robinson, Bill Beesley, Roy Hines, Malcolm Knight, Richard Jacques, 77th North London Scout Troop.

LARRY'S CHRISTMAS PARTY

An ATV production. Transmission details are for the ATV midlands region. Duration: 52 minutes.
Written by Peter Dulay, Bryan Blackburn and Bernie Sharp; script associate Peter Dulay; designed by Richard Lake; production manager Harry Bell; produced and directed by Colin Clews.
Larry Grayson (Host), Mike and Bernie Winters, Noele Gordon, Rod Hull and Emu, Heathmore, Lionel Blair and his Dancers, Jack Parnell and his Orchestra.

	VT Number	Holding / Source
22.12.1972	6188/72	J / 2"

LAST CHRISTMAS

A Tiger Aspect production for BBC 1. Transmission details are for BBC 1. Duration: 80 minutes.
Written by Tony Grounds; produced by David Snodin; directed by Adrian Shergold.
Phillip Dowling (Frank), Pauline Quirke (Gwen), Phil Daniels (Geoff), Ray Winstone (Neville), Ella Daniels (Judy), Mark Benton (Father Christmas), Matt Bardock (Bobby Moore), Ahsen Bhatti (Doctor), Donna Ewin (Donna), Suzanne Burden (Tessa), Tony Grounds (Mourner).

	Holding / Source
22.12.1999	DB / V1SW

THE LAST GOON SHOW OF ALL

A BBC production for BBC 1. Transmission details are for BBC 1. Duration: 40 minutes.
Written by Spike Milligan; produced and directed by Douglas Hespe.
Peter Sellers (Grytpye-Thynne, Bluebottle, Major Denis Bloodnok, Henry Crun), Harry Secombe (Neddy Seagoon), Spike Milligan (Eccles, Minnie Bannister, Moriarty), Max Geldray, The Ray Ellington Quartet, Andrew Timothy, The Wally Stott Orchestra.

	Holding / Source
26.12.1972	DB-D3 / 2"

LAST OF THE SUMMER WINE

A BBC production for BBC 1. Transmission details are for BBC 1. Usual duration: 30 minutes.

Take three men, retired and bored, place them in the picturesque Yorkshire countryside… and find inventive ways to create situation comedy. Pitch that idea to a modern TV executive and it would be rejected outright.

Even in 1972, the BBC were sceptical and commissioned a pilot originally. "Of funerals and fish" was broadcast on the 4th January 1973. The original cast of the Comedy Playhouse was Michael Bates as Cyril Blamire, Bill Owen as Compo Simmonite, Peter Sallis as Walter Clegg, John Comer as Sid, Jane Freeman as his wife Ivy and Kathy Staff as Nora Batty. Thirty series later when the series prematurely ended, the cast had seen many real-life deaths and changes, but in essence the spirit remained unchanged with Peter Sallis still there as Clegg.

The first significant cast change came in series three. Michael Bates was equally famous for his role in "It ain't half hot mum" and was juggling both sitcoms. However, he became terminally ill and in 1976 the producer of Last of the Summer Wine, Sydney Lotterby, made the decision to cast a new third lead – Brian Wilde as Foggy. Like Bates, Wilde's character was the instigator, the commander. Clegg was the observer, the commentator and Compo was the womaniser, the hero of every scheme.

The new line-up of Foggy, Compo and Clegg is indeed the most famous and best-loved combination. Sydney Lotterby, a straightforward sitcom director, left the series in 1980 and his successor Alan J W Bell was keen to broaden the appeal of the series when he began in 1981. Under Bell's new direction, the cast expanded significantly, the budgets improved with more location filming and the Holmfirth countryside/Ronnie Hazlehurst's music became the fourth and fifth leading members of the cast. Most of Bell's former career had been with Crackerjack, but he was a director who understood how to use film to increase the beauty of an area and his wider use of location filming created a picture-postcard landscape of Yorkshire that attracted tourists in their thousands.

The 1980s was the peak of Last of the Summer Wine's success. As well as filming new series annually, the Yorkshire tourist board promoted the series strongly, there were many Christmas specials and several Royal Variety performance appearances. However, mindfall of the cast's age and health, a plethora of new, popular, characters were carefully written into the new plots. In 1983, John Comer died, so Ivy carried on running the café with help from her nephew Crusher.

Buoyed by the success of the series, Brian Wilde left for a short period in 1986 and was replaced by Michael Aldridge as Seymour. This allowed the producer to cast Thora Hird as Edie, Seymour's sister; and after her departure from Coronation Street, Jean Alexander played Auntie Wainwright. Most of the Seymour years saw the storylines revolve around the love triangle of Pearl, Howard and Marina, whilst Seymour invented some new and frankly dangerous gadget that needed testing by Compo. Brian Wilde returned in 1990 and the next big cast change saw Bill Owen being replaced by Frank Thornton in 1999, when Owen died. In later years the series became a haven for older comedy actors and actresses – Brian Murphy, June Whitfield, Josephine Tewson, Trevor Bannister, Stephen Lewis, Mike Grady. The cast was also joined by Tom Owen, Bill's son, who played Tom.

In December 2008 the producer Bell said that the BBC had not yet commissioned a new series and that the BBC had said that no more series would be produced. The BBC denied these claims, saying that a decision had not yet been reached whether to commission another series or not. On 26th June 2009 a new series was commissioned. However, on 2nd June 2010, the BBC announced that it would not renew Last of the Summer Wine after its latest series was broadcast during the summer. The final episode of the show, "How Not to Cry at Weddings", was subsequently broadcast on 29th August 2010. It was the end of an era. Every single episode had been written by Roy Clarke, regarded by many as a comedy genius, and the man who gave us Potter, Keeping Up Appearances and Rosie. Available to view again on DVD, Last of the Summer Wine gives the older generation hope that life begins with retirement.

Main regular credit(s):   Written by Roy Clarke; theme music by Ronnie Hazlehurst.

SERIES 4

Main regular credit(s):   Music by Ronnie Hazlehurst; produced and directed by Sydney Lotterby.

Main regular cast: With Bill Owen (Compo), Peter Sallis (Clegg), Brian Wilde (Foggy).

Holding / Source

26.12.1978 Small Tune On A Penny Wassail   DB-D3 / 2"

Designed by Jan Spoczynski.

With Kathy Staff (Nora Batty), Jane Freeman (Ivy), John Comer (Sid), Joe Gladwin (Wally Batty), Teddy Turner, Larry Noble, Charles Booth, John Dunbar, Stuart Fell, Dodworth Colliery Band.

SERIES 5

Main regular credit(s):   Music by Ronnie Hazlehurst; produced by Sydney Lotterby.

Main regular cast: With Bill Owen (Compo), Peter Sallis (Clegg), Brian Wilde (Foggy).

Holding / Source

27.12.1979 And A Dewhurst Up A Fir Tree   DB-D3 / 2"

Designed by Shelagh Lawson, directed by Sydney Lotterby.

With Jane Freeman (Ivy), Kathy Staff (Nora), John Comer (Sid), Juliet Cooke.

SERIES 6

Main regular credit(s):   Music by Ronnie Hazlehurst; production manager Michael Cager; produced and directed by Alan J. W. Bell.

Main regular cast: With Bill Owen (Compo), Peter Sallis (Clegg), Brian Wilde (Foggy), John Comer (Sid), Jane Freeman (Ivy), Kathy Staff (Nora).

Holding / Source

25.12.1981 Whoops   DB-D3 / C1

Duration: 31 minutes.

Designed by Stephan Paczai and Valerie Warrender.

With Joe Gladwin (Wally), John Rutland, Paula Tilbrook, Arnold Peters, Gordon Faith, Holmfirth Choral Society.

SERIES 7

Main regular credit(s):   Music by Ronnie Hazlehurst; designed by Tim Gleeson; production manager Mandie Fletcher; produced and directed by Sydney Lotterby.

Main regular cast: With Bill Owen (Compo), Peter Sallis (Clegg), Brian Wilde (Foggy).

Holding / Source

25.12.1982 All Mod Conned   DB-D3 / 2"

Duration: 33 minutes.

With Kathy Staff (Nora Batty), Joe Gladwin (Wally), John Comer (Sid), Jane Freeman (Ivy), Gordon Salkilld, Frank Marlborough, Norman Robbins, David Hanson, Linda James, Stuart Fell.

LAST OF THE SUMMER WINE (continued)

SERIES 8

Main regular credit(s): Music by Ronnie Hazlehurst; produced and directed by Alan J. W. Bell.
Main regular cast: With Bill Owen (Compo), Peter Sallis (Clegg), Brian Wilde (Foggy).

Holding / Source

27.12.1983 Getting Sam Home DB-D3 / C1
Duration: 87 minutes.
Designed by Tim Gleeson; production manager Michael Cager.
With Joe Gladwin (Wally Batty), Kathy Staff (Nora Batty), John Comer (Sid), Jane Freeman (Ivy), David Williams, Lynda Baron, Olive Pendleton, Peter Russell, Jim Marsh, Johnny Leeze, Maxton G. Beesley [as Maxton Beesley], Muriel Rogers, Bill Croasdale, Ken Kitson, Christine Cox, Igor Gridneff, Anthony Benson, Randal Herley, Paula Randell, The Mike Sammes Singers.

30.12.1984 The Loxley Lozenge DB / 1"
Designed by Stephen Fawcett; production managers Peter R. Lovell, Evan King and Michael Cager.
With Gordon Wharmby (Wesley), Jane Freeman (Ivy), Kathy Staff (Nora), Joe Gladwin (Wally), Ashley Jackson.

SERIES 9

Main regular credit(s): Music by Ronnie Hazlehurst; produced and directed by Alan J. W. Bell.
Main regular cast: With Michael Aldridge (Seymour), Bill Owen (Compo), Peter Sallis (Clegg).

Holding / Source

01.01.1986 Uncle Of The Bride DB / C1
Duration: 84 minutes.
Designed by Roger Cann.
With Thora Hird (Edie), Kathy Staff (Nora Batty), Joe Gladwin (Wally), Jane Freeman (Ivy), Jonathan Linsley (Crusher), Gordon Wharmby (Wesley), Robert Fyfe (Howard), Jean Fergusson (Marina), Juliette Kaplan (Pearl), Mike Grady (Barry), Sarah Thomas (Glenda), Derek Ware, Rosemary Chamney, James Duggan, Brenda Halbrook, Albert Welch.

28.12.1986 Merry Christmas Father Christmas DB / 1"
Duration: 35 minutes.
Designed by Stephan Paczai.
With Jane Freeman (Ivy), Gordon Wharmby (Wesley), Robert Fyfe (Howard), Kathy Staff (Nora), Joe Gladwin (Wally), Sarah Thomas (Glenda), Mike Grady (Barry), Jonathan Linsley, Jean Fergusson, Juliette Kaplan.

27.12.1987 Big Day At Dream Acres DB / 1"
Duration: 33 minutes.
Designed by Stephan Paczai.
With Kathy Staff (Nora Batty), Robert Fyfe (Howard), Juliette Kaplan (Pearl), Jonathan Linsley (Milburn), Jane Freeman (Ivy), Thora Hird (Edie), Gordon Wharmby (Wesley), Ray McAnally, David Ellison, Joanne Good, Rachel Davies, Danny O'Dea, Tony Capstick.

SERIES 10

Main regular credit(s): Music by Ronnie Hazlehurst; produced and directed by Alan J. W. Bell.
Main regular cast: With Michael Aldridge (Seymour), Bill Owen (Compo), Peter Sallis (Clegg), Jane Freeman (Ivy), Kathy Staff (Nora), Gordon Wharmby (Wesley).

Holding / Source

24.12.1988 Crums DB / 1"
Duration: 60 minutes.
Designed by Stephan Paczai; production manager Andy Smith.
With Jean Alexander (Auntie Wainwright), Thora Hird (Edie), Mike Grady (Barry), Sarah Thomas (Glenda), Juliette Kaplan (Pearl), Robert Fyfe (Howard), Jean Fergusson (Marina), James Duggan, Danny O'Dea, Jim Bowen, Yvette Fielding, Jim Casey, Eli Woods, Ina Clough, Mary Wray, Len Fox, Denis Mawn, Barry Axup, The Barnsley College of Technology Band.

SERIES 11

Main regular credit(s): Music by Ronnie Hazlehurst; designed by Stephan Paczai; produced and directed by Alan J. W. Bell.
Main regular cast: With Michael Aldridge (Seymour), Bill Owen (Compo), Peter Sallis (Clegg), Thora Hird (Edie), Jane Freeman (Ivy), Robert Fyfe (Howard), Juliette Kaplan (Pearl).

Holding / Source

23.12.1989 What's Santa Brought For Nora Then? DB / 1"
Duration: 49 minutes.
Production manager Nick Jowitt.
With Jean Alexander (Auntie Wainwright), Sarah Thomas (Glenda), Jean Fergusson (Marina), Gordon Wharmby (Wesley), Mike Grady (Barry), Barry Axup, Charlie Dickinson, Len Fox, Anthony Havering, Mike Kelly, Joyce Kennedy, Denis Mawn, Jacqueline Naylor, James Thackwray.

SERIES 12

Main regular credit(s): Produced and directed by Alan J. W. Bell.
Main regular cast: With Brian Wilde (Foggy), Bill Owen (Compo), Peter Sallis (Clegg), Jean Alexander (Auntie Wainwright), Jane Freeman (Ivy), Thora Hird (Edie), Kathy Staff (Nora Batty), Jean Fergusson (Marina), Robert Fyfe (Howard), Juliette Kaplan (Pearl), Gordon Wharmby (Wesley).

Holding / Source

27.12.1990 Barry's Christmas DB / 1"S
With Kathy Staff (Nora Batty), Jane Freeman (Ivy), Thora Hird (Edie), Mike Grady (Barry), Gordon Wharmby (Wesley), Robert Fyfe (Howard), Jean Fergusson (Marina), Juliette Kaplan (Pearl), Sarah Thomas (Glenda), Danny O'Dea, James Duggan, Bernard Atha, Grace Mitchell, Peter Diamond.

LAST OF THE SUMMER WINE

British Christmas Television Guide LAST OF THE SUMMER WINE (continued)

SERIES 13
Main regular credit(s):	Produced and directed by Alan J. W. Bell.
Main regular cast:	With Bill Owen (Compo), Peter Sallis (Clegg), Brian Wilde (Foggy), Jean Alexander (Auntie Wainwright), Jane Freeman (Ivy), Thora Hird (Edie), Kathy Staff (Nora Batty), Jean Fergusson (Marina), Robert Fyfe (Howard), Juliette Kaplan (Pearl), Gordon Wharmby (Wesley).

Holding / Source
22.12.1991 Situations Vacant   DB / 1"S
With Thora Hird (Edie), Kathy Staff (Nora Batty), Jane Freeman (Ivy), Robert Fyfe (Howard), Sarah Thomas (Glenda), Juliette Kaplan (Pearl), Jean Fergusson (Marina), Gordon Wharmby (Wesley), Tom Owen, Danny O'Dea, Diana Brooks.

SERIES 14
Main regular credit(s):	Music by Ronnie Hazlehurst; director of photography Jonathan Keeping; designed by Richard Brackenbury and Linda Conoboy [credited as Linda Connoboy]; production managers Mark Mylod and Anne Throup; produced and directed by Alan J. W. Bell.
Main regular cast:	With Bill Owen (Compo), Peter Sallis (Clegg), Brian Wilde (Foggy), Jane Freeman (Ivy), Thora Hird (Edie), Kathy Staff (Nora Batty), Jean Fergusson (Marina), Robert Fyfe (Howard), Juliette Kaplan (Pearl), Danny O'Dea (Eli).

Holding / Source
26.12.1992 Stop That Castle!   DB / 1"S
Duration: 29 minutes.
With Jean Alexander (Auntie Wainwright), Stephen Lewis (Smiler), Gordon Wharmby (Wesley), Sarah Thomas (Glenda), Tony Simon, Tony Capstick, Ken Kitson, Stuart Hutchison, Len Fox, Denis Mawn.

SERIES 15
Main regular credit(s):	Music by Ronnie Hazlehurst; designed by Richard Brackenbury; produced and directed by Alan J. W. Bell.
Main regular cast:	With Bill Owen (Compo), Peter Sallis (Clegg), Brian Wilde (Foggy), Jane Freeman (Ivy), Kathy Staff (Nora Battey), Thora Hird (Edie), Sarah Thomas (Glenda), Juliette Kaplan (Pearl).

Holding / Source
19.12.1993 Aladdin Gets On Your Wick   DB-D3 / D3S
Designed by Richard Brackenbury and Pippa Howes.
With Jean Alexander (Auntie Wainwright), Jean Fergusson (Marina), Robert Fyfe (Howard), Stephen Lewis (Smiler), Gordon Wharmby (Wesley), Danny O'Dea (Eli), John Jardine, Benedict Wong.

27.12.1993 Welcome To Earth   DB-D3 / D3S
With Jean Fergusson (Marina), Gordon Wharmby (Wesley), Paul Bown, Robert Fyffe, Robin Banks.

SERIES 16
Main regular credit(s):	Produced and directed by Alan J. W. Bell.
Main regular cast:	With Bill Owen (Compo), Peter Sallis (Clegg), Brian Wilde (Foggy), Thora Hird (Edie), Jane Freeman (Ivy), Robert Fyfe (Howard), Juliette Kaplan (Pearl), Jean Alexander (Auntie), Jean Fergusson (Marina), Sarah Thomas (Glenda), Stephen Lewis (Smiler), Mike Grady (Barry), Gordon Wharmby (Wesley).

Holding / Source
01.01.1995 The Man Who Nearly Knew Pavarotti   DB-D3 / D3S
Duration: 58 minutes.
Designed by Richard Brackenbury.
With Danny O'Dea (Eli), Kathy Staff, Jane Freeman, Jean Alexander, Sarah Thomas, Juliette Kaplan, Tony Capstick, Richard Mapletoft, Thora Hird [as Dame Thora Hird], Stephen Lewis, Robert Fyfe, Norman Wisdom, Jean Fergusson, Ken Kitson, Gordon Wharmby.

SERIES 17
Main regular credit(s):	Produced and directed by Alan J. W. Bell.
Main regular cast:	With Bill Owen (Compo), Peter Sallis (Clegg), Brian Wilde (Foggy), Thora Hird (Edie), Jane Freeman (Ivy), Robert Fyfe (Howard), Juliette Kaplan (Pearl), Jean Alexander (Auntie), Jean Fergusson (Marina), Sarah Thomas (Glenda), Stephen Lewis (Smiler), Mike Grady (Barry), Gordon Wharmby (Wesley).

Holding / Source
24.12.1995 A Leg Up For Christmas   DB-D3 / D3S
Duration: 57 minutes.
With Danny O'Dea (Eli), Thora Hird, Matthew Kelly, Robert Fyfe, Kathy Staff, Anita Dobson, Jane Freeman, Jean Alexander, Stephen Lewis, Sarah Thomas, Juliette Kaplan, Jean Fergusson, James Casey, Gordon Wharmby, Eli Woods.

29.12.1996 Extra! Extra!   DB-D3 / D3S
Duration: 43 minutes.
With Danny O'Dea (Eli), Thora Hird, Kathy Staff, Jane Freeman, Mike Grady, Jean Alexander, Stephen Lewis, Robert Fyfe, Sarah Thomas, Juliette Kaplan, Norman Wisdom, Jean Fergusson, George Chakiris, Mark Jameson, Leon De St Croix, Lesley Staples, Denis Mawn, Tony Simon, Robin Banks, Gordon Wharmby.

LAST OF THE SUMMER WINE (continued)   British Christmas Television Guide

SERIES 19
Main regular credit(s):	Produced and directed by Alan J. W. Bell.
Main regular cast:	With Bill Owen (Compo), Frank Thornton (Truly), Peter Sallis (Clegg), Thora Hird (Edie), Jane Freeman (Ivy), Robert Fyfe (Howard), Juliette Kaplan (Pearl), Jean Alexander (Auntie), Jean Fergusson (Marina), Sarah Thomas (Glenda), Stephen Lewis (Smiler), Mike Grady (Barry), Gordon Wharmby (Wesley).

Holding / Source
28.12.1997 **There Goes The Groom**   DB / DBS
Duration: 60 minutes.
With Kathy Staff, Jane Freeman, Thora Hird, Jean Alexander, Jean Fergusson, Robert Fyfe, Juliette Kaplan, Sarah Thomas, Gordon Wharmby, Mike Grady, Stephen Lewis, Danny O'Dea, Michelle Whitehead, Kriss Akabusi, Allan O'Keefe, Tony Capstick, Ken Kitson, Lloyd Peters, Diana Flacks, Brenda Kempner, Muriel Lawford, Michele Whitehead.

SERIES 21
Main regular credit(s):	Produced and directed by Alan J. W. Bell.
Main regular cast:	With Peter Sallis (Clegg), Frank Thornton (Truly), Thora Hird (Edie), Jane Freeman (Ivy), Robert Fyfe (Howard), Juliette Kaplan (Pearl), Jean Alexander (Auntie), Stephen Lewis (Smiler), Jean Fergusson (Marina), Sarah Thomas (Glenda), Mike Grady (Barry), Gordon Wharmby (Wesley), Tom Owen (Tom).

Holding / Source
02.01.2000 **Last Post And Pigeon**   DB / DBSWF
Duration: 59 minutes.
With Bill Owen (Compo), Enn Reitel (Narrator), Kathy Staff, Jane Freeman, Thora Hird, Jean Alexander, Dora Bryan, Ray Cooney, Robert Fyfe, Jean Fergusson, Mike Grady, Juliette Kaplan, Stephen Lewis, Sarah Thomas, Gordon Wharmby, Keith Clifford, Eileen O'Brien, Hilary Sesta, Stephanie Roscoe, Gerard Hayling.
Followed by "Bill Owen: A Tribute", BBC1 45mins.

SERIES 22
Main regular credit(s):	Produced and directed by Alan J. W. Bell.
Main regular cast:	With Frank Thornton (Truly), Peter Sallis (Clegg), Thora Hird (Edie), Jane Freeman (Ivy), Robert Fyfe (Howard), Juliette Kaplan (Pearl), Jean Alexander (Auntie), Jean Fergusson (Marina), Sarah Thomas (Glenda), Stephen Lewis (Smiler), Mike Grady (Barry), Gordon Wharmby (Wesley), Tom Owen (Tom).

Holding / Source
30.12.2001 **Potts In Pole Position**   DB / DBSWF
Duration: 29 minutes.
With June Whitfield, Thora Hird, Warren Mitchell, Dora Bryan, Mike Grady, Jean Alexander, Stephen Lewis, Robert Fyfe, Sarah Thomas, Juliette Kaplan, Jean Fergusson, Keith Clifford, Gordon Wharmby, Tom Owen.

SERIES 23
Main regular credit(s):	Produced and directed by Alan J. W. Bell.
Main regular cast:	With Peter Sallis (Clegg), Frank Thornton (Truly), Thora Hird (Edie), Jane Freeman (Ivy), Robert Fyfe (Howard), Juliette Kaplan (Pearl), Jean Alexander (Auntie), Jean Fergusson (Marina), Sarah Thomas (Glenda), Stephen Lewis (Smiler), Mike Grady (Barry), Gordon Wharmby (Wesley), Tom Owen (Tom).

Holding / Source
29.12.2002 **A Musical Passing For A Miserable Muscroft**   DB / DBSWF
With Thora Hird, Jean Alexander, Burt Kwouk, Sarah Thomas, Jean Fergusson, Kathy Staff, Jane Freeman, Dora Bryan, Mike Grady, Stephen Lewis, Robert Fyfe, Juliette Kaplan, Norman Wisdom, Keith Clifford, Trevor Bannister, Tom Owen, Tony Capstick, Ken Kitson, Eric Potts, Megan James, Sean Robertshaw, Sylvia Hamer.

Holding / Source
21.12.2003 **A Short Blast Of Fred Astaire**   DB / V1SW
Duration: 29 minutes.
Produced and directed by Alan J. W. Bell.
With Peter Sallis (Clegg), Frank Thornton (Truly), Burt Kwouk, Kathy Staff, Brian Murphy, Mike Grady, Sarah Thomas, Dora Bryan, Jean Alexander, Stephen Lewis, Tom Owen, Lionel Blair, Robert Fyfe, Josephine Tewson, Juliette Kaplan, Keith Clifford, Damian Jackson.

SERIES 25
Main regular credit(s):	Produced and directed by Alan J. W. Bell.
Main regular cast:	With Peter Sallis (Clegg), Frank Thornton (Truly), Keith Clifford (Billy), Brian Murphy (Alvin), Mike Grady (Barry), Sarah Thomas (Glenda), Robert Fyfe (Howard), Juliette Kaplan (Pearl), Kathy Staff (Nora Batty), Jean Alexander (Auntie Wainwright), Stephen Lewis (Smiler), Jane Freeman (Ivy), Josephine Tewson (Miss Davenport), Tom Owen (Tom).

Holding / Source
19.12.2004 **Variations On A Theme Of The Widow Winstanley**   DB / DBSWF
With Dora Bryan, Ken Kitson, Norman Wisdom, Louis Emerick, Christopher Beeny, Betty Manessi, Jean Fergusson, Burt Kwouk.

LAST OF THE SUMMER WINE (continued)

SERIES 26
Main regular credit(s): Script supervisor Dionne Fletcher; production executive Sarah Hitchcock; produced and directed by Alan J. W. Bell.
Main regular cast: With Peter Sallis (Clegg), Keith Clifford (Billy), Brian Murphy (Alvin), Burt Kwouk (Entwistle), Jean Alexander (Auntie), Tom Owen (Tom), Kathy Staff (Nora), Jean Fergusson (Marina), Juliette Kaplan (Pearl), Robert Fyffe (Howard), Sarah Thomas (Glenda), Josephine Tewson (Miss Davenport), Stephen Lewis (Smiler), Mike Grady (Barry), Frank Thornton (Truly).

Holding / Source
18.12.2005 **Merry Entwistle And Jackson Day** — DB / DBSWF
Script supervisor Louise Johnson.
With Ken Kitson (First Policeman), Louis Emerick (Second Policeman), June Whitfield, Trevor Bannister.

SERIES 27
Main regular credit(s): Script supervisor Louise Johnson; production executive Sarah Hitchcock; produced and directed by Alan J. W. Bell.
Main regular cast: With Peter Sallis (Clegg), Frank Thornton (Truly), Keith Clifford (Billy), Kathy Staff (Nora), Brian Murphy (Alvin).

Holding / Source
28.12.2006 **A Tale Of Two Sweaters** — HD/DB / HD/DB

SERIES 30
A BBC Productions production.
Main regular credit(s): Script supervisor Sue Davies; music by Ronnie Hazlehurst; director of photography Pat O'Shea; designed by Steve Wright; associate producer Simone Dawson; production executive Sarah Hitchcock; production manager Ian Locker; produced and directed by Alan J. W. Bell.
Main regular cast: With Russ Abbot (Hobbo), Burt Kwouk (Entwistle), Brian Murphy (Alvin), Frank Thornton (Truly), June Whitfield (Nelly), Mike Grady (Barry), Robert Fyfe (Howard), Barbara Young (Stella), Sarah Thomas (Glenda), Juliette Kaplan (Pearl).

Holding / Source
31.12.2008 **I Was A Hitman For Primrose Dairies** — HD/DB / HD/DB
With Peter Sallis (Clegg), Trevor Bannister (Toby), Jean Alexander (Aunty Wainwright), Tom Owen (Tom), Christopher Beeny [as Chris Beeny] (Morton), Josephine Tewson (Miss Davenport), Jane Freeman (Ivy), Ken Kitson (Police Constable Cooper), Louis Emerick (Police Constable Walsh).
Dedicated to Kathy Staff 1928-2008.
See also: THE FUNNY SIDE OF CHRISTMAS (BBC)

THE LAST RESORT WITH JONATHAN ROSS
Produced for Channel 4 by a variety of companies (see details below). Transmission details are for Channel 4. Duration varies - see below for details.
Main regular performer(s): Jonathan Ross (Host).

SERIES 2
A The Callender Company production. made in association with Channel X. Duration: 40 minutes.
Main regular performer(s): With Steve Nieve (Musical Director), Kevin Armstrong (Band (Steve Nieve & The Playboys)), Steve Lawrence (Band (Steve Nieve & The Playboys)), Pete Thomas (Band (Steve Nieve & The Playboys)), John Benson (Announcer).

Holding / Source
25.12.1987 **The Least Embarrassing Of!** — 1" / 1"
Written by Ian Brown and Lise Mayer; research Graham K. Smith; costume Jo Dawn; lighting director Mike Sutcliffe; produced by Katie Lander; directed by Peter Orton.
With Jerry Hall, Barry Humphries, Les McKeown, Rex Roper, Steve Martin, Donny Osmond, Billy Bragg, Hank Wangford, Carrie Fisher, Peter Cook, Stevie Starr, Dawn French, Tom Jones, Mange-Tout, Katie Boyle, Brigitte Nielsen, Robbie Coltrane, Sting, Leslie Crowther, Bernard Manning, Lenny Henry, Eric Idle, Marie Helvin, Muriel Gray, The Beverley Sisters, Crispin Glover, Paul McCartney, Bald Eagle & Chaqita.

A Channel X production.

Holding / Source
24.12.1997 — D3 / D3S
With Helen Mirren, Tim Roth, Frank Skinner, Quentin Tarantino, Helen Goodman.

LAST TANGO IN HALIFAX
A BBC production for BBC 1. Transmission details are for BBC 1. Duration: 60 minutes.
Main regular credit(s): Written by Sally Wainwright.
Main regular cast: Derek Jacobi (Alan), Anne Reid (Celia), Sarah Lancashire (Caroline), Nicola Walker (Gillian).

SERIES 2
Main regular credit(s): Produced by Karen Lewis; directed by Jill Robertson.

Holding / Source
24.12.2013 — HD/DB / HDC
A surprise visitor makes Alan's day, while Caroline promises to keep Gillian's big secret. At Alan and Celia's wedding on Christmas Eve, Kate makes a gesture that stuns the assembled company.
With Tony Gardner (John), Louis Greatorex (Lawrence), Nina Sosanya (Kate), Paul Copley (Harry), Josh Bolt (Raff), Katherine Rose Morley (Ellie), Meriel Schofield (Beverley), Edward Ashley (William), Timothy West (Ted), Dean Andrews (Robbie), Rachel Leskovac (Cheryl), Felix Johnson (Angus), Ronni Ancona (Judith).

THE LAST TURKEY IN THE SHOP SHOW

A BBC production for BBC 2. Transmission details are for BBC 2. Duration: 35 minutes.

Written by Spike Milligan and Neil Shand; additional material by Chris Langham; designed by Paul Munting; produced by Sydney Lotterby; directed by Ray Butt.

Spike Milligan, John Bluthal, Julian Chagrin, Fanny Carby, Carmel Cryan, Carol Cleveland, Chris Langham, Rita Webb, Neil Shand, Johnny Vyvyan, Julia Breck, Ed Welch, Pop Art String Quartet, Jeremy Taylor.

	Holding / Source
23.12.1974	DB-D3 / 2"

THE (NOEL EDMONDS) LATE LATE BREAKFAST SHOW

A BBC production for BBC 1. Transmission details are for BBC 1. Duration: 50 minutes.

Main regular performer(s): Noel Edmonds (Host).

SERIES 3

Main regular credit(s): Produced and directed by Michael Hurll.

Main regular performer(s): With Mike Smith (Reporter).

	Holding / Source
25.12.1984 **The Noel Edmonds Live Live Christmas Breakfast Show**	DB / 1"

Duration: 89 minutes.

Research David Nicolson, Sarah Williams, Juliet Rix and Jane Prowse; designed by John Anderson; production team Vanessa Bollands, Jackie Tyler, Sue Hills, Donna Rolfe, Kevin Mullery and Caroline Carter; production manager Ed Bye; outside broadcast director Michael Leggo.

With Michael Fish, Kim Wilde, Howard Jones, The Thompson Twins, Johnny Morris, Tony Blackburn, Gerry Cottle, Strawberry Switchblade.

SERIES 4

	Holding / Source
25.12.1985 **The Noel Edmonds Live Live Christmas Breakfast Show**	DB / 1"

LATE LUNCH

A Princess Productions production for Channel 4. Transmission details are for Channel 4.

SERIES 2

Duration: 50 minutes.

	Holding / Source
23.12.1998	DB / DBS

See also: LIGHT LUNCH

LATE NIGHT LINE-UP

A BBC production for BBC 2. Transmission details are for BBC 2. Duration varies - see below for details.

	Holding / Source
24.12.1967 **Someone In The Lift**	J / 2"

Adapted by David Campton; based on a book by L. P. Hartley; designed by Colin Green; produced and directed by Ian Keill.

With Caroline Blakiston (Mummy), Antony Webb (Daddy), Bryan Mosley (Liftman), Billy Milton (Father Christmas), Gregory Scott (Peter's Voice).

12/09/64 – MATCH OF THE DAY (LOS6520X) – front: end of News (Sports news); "Line Up" (complete if very short programme!), Denis Tuohy announcing that from now on it will go out at the end of programmes and be known as "Late Night Line-Up" (genuine moment of broadcasting history!!!), he plugs tonight's edition featuring Fenella Fielding; '2' logo with announcement. End: 'Patchwork 2'/'Saturday' caption with announcement that footballer Dave McKay has broken his leg (ref. to Match Of The Day) (picture obscured), announcement 'BBC2'; start of music for…

LATE NIGHT STORY

A BBC production for BBC 2. Transmission details are for BBC 2. Duration: 20 minutes.

Horror stories read by a narrator.

Main regular credit(s): Produced and directed by Tony Harrison.

Main regular cast: Tom Baker (Narrator).

	Holding / Source
##.##.#### **Sredni Vashtar**	DB-D3 / 2"

Originally scheduled for 22.12.1978.
Written by Saki.

23.12.1978 **The Photograph**	DB-D3 / 2"

Written by Nigel Kneale.

25.12.1978 **The Emissary**	DB-D3 / 2"

Written by Ray Bradbury.

26.12.1978 **Nursery Tea**	DB-D3 / 2"

Written by Mary Danby.

28.12.1978 **The End Of The Party**	DB-D3 / 2"

Written by Graham Greene.

LATER WITH JOOLS HOLLAND

A BBC production for BBC 2. Transmission details are for BBC 2. Duration varies - see below for details.
Main regular performer(s):   Jools Holland (Presenter).

SERIES 2

	Holding / Source
01.01.1994 **Jools Holland's Hootenanny**	DB-D3 / D3S

Duration: 60 minutes.
Produced by Mark Cooper; directed by Janet Fraser Crook.
With Sting, Gypsy Kings, Sly and Robbie.

SERIES 4
Main regular credit(s):   Produced by Mark Cooper; directed by Janet Fraser Crook.

	Holding / Source
01.01.1995 **The Second Annual Jools' Hootenanny**	DB-D3 / D3S

Duration: 60 minutes.
With Blur, Steve Winwood, Shane MacGowan, The Popes.

SERIES 6
Main regular credit(s):   Produced by Mark Cooper; directed by Janet Fraser Crook.

	Holding / Source
01.01.1996 **The Third Annual Jools' Hootenanny**	DB-D3 / D3S

Duration: 75 minutes.
With Jools Holland's Rhythm and Blues Orchestra, Eric Clapton, Dr John, Alanis Morissette, Dick Dale, David McAlmont, Audioweb, The Mike Flower Pops, Supergrass.

SERIES 8
Main regular credit(s):   Produced by Mark Cooper; directed by Janet Fraser Crook.

	Holding / Source
01.01.1997 **Jools's Hootenanny**	DB-D3 / D3S

With Paul Weller, Jools Holland's Rhythm and Blues Orchestra, The Electra Strings, Elton John, Mick Hucknall, Lighthouse Family, Manic Street Preachers, 1st Battalion The Irish Guards.
See also: LATER... WITH JOOLS HOLLAND (BBC)

LATER... WITH JOOLS HOLLAND

A BBC production for BBC 2. Transmission details are for BBC 2. Duration varies - see below for details.
Main regular performer(s):   Jools Holland (Presenter).

SERIES 10
Main regular credit(s):   Produced by Mark Cooper; directed by Janet Fraser Crook.

	Holding / Source
31.12.1997 **Jools's Hootenanny**	D3 / DBS

Duration: 80 minutes.
With Jools Holland's Rhythm and Blues Orchestra, The Electra Strings, B. B. King, Shaun Ryder, Gabrielle, Jewel, Blur, Bentley Rhythm Ace, Fun Lovin Criminals, 1st Battalion The Welsh Guards.

SERIES 12
Main regular credit(s):   Produced by Mark Cooper; directed by Janet Fraser Crook.

	Holding / Source
31.12.1998 **Jools's Sixth Annual Hootenanny**	DB / DBSW

Duration: 80 minutes.
With The Corrs, Tom Jones, All Saints, Sharleen Spiteri, Paul Heaton, Jools Holland's Rhythm and Blues Orchestra, Catatonia, Gomez, Scots Guards, Richard Wilson, Tony Adams, Zoe Ball, Stephen Fry, Natasha Little.

SERIES 14
Main regular credit(s):   Produced by Mark Cooper; directed by Janet Fraser Crook.

	Holding / Source
30.12.1999 **Jools's Millennium Hootenanny**	DB / DBSW

Duration: 90 minutes.
With Bryan Ferry, Van Morrison, Chrissie Hynde, Skin, Jamiroquai, Travis, Lonnie Donegan, Jools Holland's Rhythm and Blues Orchestra.

SERIES 16
Main regular credit(s):   Produced by Mark Cooper; directed by Janet Fraser Crook.

	Holding / Source
31.12.2000 **Jools At The New Year Hootenanny**	DB / DBSW

Duration: 125 minutes.
With Lionel Richie, Coldplay, Kelly Jones, Roisin Murphy, Jools Holland's Rhythm and Blues Orchestra, Craig David, Joe Brown, 1st Battalion The Scots Guards.

LATER... WITH JOOLS HOLLAND (continued)

SERIES 18
Main regular credit(s):   Produced by Mark Cooper and Alison Howe; directed by Janet Fraser Crook.

	Holding / Source
31.12.2001 **Jools's Annual Hootenanny**	DB / DBSW

Duration: 90 minutes.

With Jools Holland's Rhythm and Blues Orchestra, Edwin Starr, Huey Morgan, Paul Heaton, John Cale, Marc Almond, Ronnie Wood, Slash, David Gray, Ash, Beverley Knight, 1st Battalion The Scots Guards.

See also: LATER WITH JOOLS HOLLAND (BBC)

LEAD BALLOON

An Open Mike production for Various BBC Channels. Transmission details are for Various BBC Channels.

Main regular credit(s):   Created by Jack Dee; produced and directed by Alex Hardcastle.

Main regular cast: Jack Dee (Rick Spleen), Sean Power (Marty), Raquel Cassidy (Mel), Antonia Campbell Hughes (Sam), Anna Crilly (Magda), Tony Gardner (Michael), Rasmus Hardiker (Ben).

SERIES 3
Commissioned by BBC 2. Transmission details are for BBC 2.

Main regular credit(s):   Written by Jack Dee and Pete Sinclair; script supervisor Caroline Elliston; designed by Gordon Whistance; associate producers Jack Dee and Pete Sinclair; executive producers Addison Cresswell and Andrew Beint; production manager Liz Seymour.

	Holding / Source
23.12.2008 **Nuts**	HD/DB / HD/DB

Duration: 40 minutes.

With John Biggins (Clive), William Poulter, Alex Lowe.

THE LEAGUE OF GENTLEMEN

A BBC production for BBC 2. Transmission details are for BBC 2. Duration varies - see below for details.

Main regular credit(s):   Written by Jeremy Dyson, Mark Gatiss, Steve Pemberton and Reece Shearsmith; music by Joby Talbot; executive producer Jon Plowman.

Main regular cast: Mark Gatiss, Steve Pemberton, Reece Shearsmith.

	Holding / Source
27.12.2000 **Christmas Special**	DB / DBSWF

Duration: 60 minutes.

Choreography by Pat Garrett; director of photography Rob Kitzmann; assistant director Carlene King; art directors Sarah Kane and Ruth Winn; production designer Grenville Horner; assistant producer Jeremy Dyson; production manager Alison Passey; produced by Jemma Rodgers; directed by Steve Bendelack.

With Freddie Jones, Liza Tarbuck, Andrew Melville, Frances Cox, Bay White, Rusty Goffe, Gerald Stadden, Jon Key, Judith Vause, New London Children's Choir, The Royston Vasey Line Dancers.

A LEAGUE OF THEIR OWN

A CPL (Celador) production for Sky One. Transmission details are for Sky One. Duration varies - see below for details.

Comedy sports panel show.

Main regular credit(s):   Executive producers Danielle Lux, Duncan Gray and Murray Boland.

Main regular performer(s):   James Corden (Referee).

SERIES 2
Main regular credit(s):   Written by Simon Bullivant, Kevin Day, Lee Stuart Evans, Phil Kerr, Shaun Pye, Christine Rose, Aiden Spackman, Fraser Steele, Martin Trenaman, Colin Swash, Dan Taylor and Mark Webster; script supervisor Rebecca Havers; music by Will Slater; art director Charlotte Pearson; associate producers Olly Bland, Mark Boutros, Ish Kalia, Aaron Morgan and Tommy Panays; production executive Sarah Sedazzari; executive producers Duncan Gray, Murray Boland, Danielle Lux and Jim Pullin; production managers Nancy Adair and Amber Rose Lambert; series producer David Taylor; co-produced by David Ricketts; produced by David Ricketts and Ben Wicks; directed by Claire Winyard.

Main regular performer(s):   With Andrew Flintoff MBE (Team Captain), Jamie Redknapp (Team Captain), John Bishop, Georgie Thompson.

	Holding / Source
23.12.2010	DB / DBSW

Duration: 48 minutes.

With Ricky Hatton, Ruth Jones, John Virgo, Frank Bruno, Tessa Sanderson.

SERIES 4
Main regular credit(s):   Music by Will Slater; designed by Andrew Gates; executive producers Duncan Gray, Danielle Lux, Murray Boland and Jim Pullin; series producer David Taylor; produced by David Ricketts, Tommy Panays, Kate Staples and Matt Wilkinson; directed by Steve Smith.

Main regular performer(s):   With Andrew Flintoff MBE (Team Captain), Jamie Redknapp (Team Captain), John Bishop, Georgie Thompson.

	Holding / Source
16.12.2011 **End Of Year Show**	DB / DBSW

Duration: 48 minutes.

Written by Shaun Pye, Fraser Steele, Simon Bullivant, Kevin Day and Aiden Spackman.

With Stacey Solomon, Gabby Logan, Geraint Thomas.

LEAVE HIM TO HEAVEN

A BBC production for BBC 2. Transmission details are for BBC 2. Duration: 65 minutes.

Written by Ken Lee; choreography by Patricia Adams; designed by Vic Meredith; play production by Robin Nash.

Brian Protheroe (Conway), Ken Shorter (Eddie), Paul Felber (Johnnie), Steven Pacey (Joe), Larry Dann (Morton), Colin Copperfield (Louis), Lesley Duff (Luanne), Sue Bond (Janeen), Nicky Croydon (Verona), Cindy Wells (Adele), Anita Dobson (Roxanne).

	Holding / Source
27.12.1979	DB-D3 / 2"

LEGEND OF THE LOST TRIBE

Commissioned by BBC Children's Department. Transmission details are for BBC 1. Duration: 30 minutes.

Robbie the Reindeer and pals search for a band of warriors.

Ardal O'Hanlon (Voice), Steve Coogan (Voice), Jane Horrocks (Voice), Harry Enfield (Voice), Alistair McGowan (Voice), Paul Whitehouse (Voice), David Attenborough (Voice), Rob Brydon (Voice), Ricky Gervais (Voice), Jeff Goldblum (Voice), Sean Hughes (Voice), Natalie Imbruglia (Voice).

	Holding / Source
25.12.2002	DB /

See also: CLOSE ENCOUNTERS OF THE HERD KIND (BBC) / HOOVES OF FIRE (BBC)

LEMON LA VIDA LOCA

A Thames Television production for ITV 2. Transmission details are for ITV 2.

Main regular cast: Leigh Francis (Keith Lemon).

Merry Keithmas!

Duration: 40 minutes.

	Holding / Source
22.12.2012	HD/DB / HDC

With Emily Atack.

| 22.12.2012 | HD/DB / HDC |

Keith Lemon and girlfriend Rosie jet off for a skiing break.

LEN GOODMAN'S PERFECT CHRISTMAS

A BBC production for BBC 1. Transmission details are for BBC 1. Duration: 60 minutes.

From presents to party games, good food to good company, the Strictly judge offers his own version of the ideal Christmas. He takes a twirl through the archives to relive an unforgettable moment for every step of the day.

Produced and directed by Delyth Lloyd.

Len Goodman (Presenter).

	Holding / Source
26.12.2013	HD/DB / HDC

LENA

An ATV production. Transmission details are for the ATV London region. Duration: 55 minutes.

Music associate Kenny Powell; conducted by Lennie Hayton; settings by Peter Roden; executive producer Ralph Harris; produced and directed by Jon Scoffield.

Lena Horne, The Jack Parnell Orchestra.

	Holding / Source
26.12.1965	R1 /

LENNIE AND JERRY

A BBC production. Transmission details are for BBC 1. Duration varies - see below for details.

Main regular performer(s): Lennie Bennett, Jerry Stevens.

Main regular credit(s): Produced and directed by Ernest Maxin.

	Holding / Source
30.12.1979	C1 POSEQ / 2"

Duration: 40 minutes.

Written by Dennis Berson, Barry Cryer, Neil Shand, Howard Imber and Peter Vincent; designed by Michael Young.

With Arthur Lowe, Hush, Iris Williams, Albert Pontefract, Alyn Ainsworth and his Orchestra.

LENNY - LIVE AND UNLEASHED

A Palace/Sleeping Partners Production production for BBC 1. made in association with British Sky Broadcasting / Telso International. Transmission details are for BBC 1. Duration: 95 minutes.

Written by Lenny Henry and Kim Fuller; additional material by Anne Caulfield, Geoff Atkinson and James Hendrie; script editor Kim Fuller; theme music by Steve Nieve; music by Dennis Bovell and Kim Fuller; director of photography Peter Sinclair; designed by Christopher Hobbs; associate producer Redmond Morris; executive producers Stephen Woolley and Nik Powell; production manager Ewa Radwanska; produced by Martyn Auty and Andy Harries; directed by Andy Harries.

Lenny Henry, Jeff Beck, Robbie Coltrane, Fred Dread Band.

	Holding / Source
27.12.1990	C1 / C1

LENNY HENRY IN PIECES

A Tiger Aspect production for BBC 1. Transmission details are for BBC 1. Duration: 30 minutes.
Main regular credit(s):   Executive producer Clive Tulloh; produced by Lucy Robinson.
Main regular cast: Lenny Henry (Host).

	Holding / Source
30.12.2000	DB /

Written by Martin Shea, Charles Peattie, Martin Trenaman, Matt Owen, Eamonn O'Neill, James O'Neill, Paul Henry, George Jeffrie, Lenny Henry and Mark Warren; executive producer Clive Tulloh; directed by Matt Lipsey.

29.12.2001	DB /

Director of photography John Sorapure; executive producer Clive Tulloh; directed by Ed Bye.
With Omid Djalili, Tony Gardner, Roger Griffiths, Gresby Nash.

THE LENNY THE LION SHOW

A BBC production. Transmission details are for BBC.
Main regular cast: Lenny The Lion.

	Holding / Source
27.12.1958	R1 /

Produced and directed by Johnny Downes.
With Sheila Buxton, Mink Devine and Barbara, Michael Balfour, Joe Greig, Judy Horn, Larry Parker.

THE LES DAWSON SHOW

A BBC production for BBC 1. Transmission details are for BBC 1. Duration varies - see below for details.
Main regular cast: Les Dawson.

	Holding / Source
28.12.1987	DB / 1"

Duration: 50 minutes.
Written by Les Dawson, Barry Cryer, David Nobbs, Paul Minett and Brian Leveson; script associate Barry Cryer; music directed by Alyn Ainsworth; choreography by Jeff Richer; designed by Martin Methven; produced and directed by John Bishop.
With Patrick Mower, Roy Barraclough, Toni Palmer, Graeme Garden, Brian Godfrey, Peter Goodwright, Johnny More, Mo Moreland, Jane Marie Osborne, The Roly Polys.

SERIES 5
Main regular credit(s):   Script editor Charlie Adams; music directed by John Coleman; choreography by Graham Fletcher; designed by John Anderson; produced and directed by Stewart Morris.

	Holding / Source
30.12.1989	DB / 1"

Duration: 40 minutes.
Written by Les Dawson, Charlie Adams, Paul Alexander and Gavin Osbon.
With Michael Ball, Marti Webb, John Williams, Stuart Anderson, Lia Malcolm, Michael Corder, Jay Jolley.
See also: THE FUNNY SIDE OF CHRISTMAS (BBC)

THE LES DENNIS LAUGHTER SHOW

A BBC production for BBC 1. Transmission details are for BBC 1. Duration: 30 minutes.
Main regular cast: Les Dennis.

SERIES 1
Main regular credit(s):   Script associate Geoff Atkinson; music directed by Ray Monk; choreography by Jeff Richer; produced and directed by Kevin Bishop.
Main regular cast: With Martin Daniels, Lisa Maxwell, Mark Walker, Jeff Richer Dancers.

	Holding / Source
23.12.1989 **The Les Dennis Christmas Laughter Show: White Christmas At The Holiday Inn**	DB / 1"

Duration: 35 minutes.
Written by Geoff Atkinson; designed by Roger Harris.
With Bella Emberg, Mac McDonald, Gary Lovini.

SERIES 2

	Holding / Source
22.12.1990 **The Les Dennis Christmas Laughter Show**	DB / 1"

Produced and directed by Geoff Miles.
With Lisa Maxwell.

A LIFE IN PIECES

A Talkback production for BBC 2. Transmission details are for BBC 2. Duration: 5 minutes.
Main regular credit(s):   Written by Peter Cook; script editor Rory McGrath; produced by Peter Fincham; directed by John Lloyd.
Main regular cast: Peter Cook (Sir Arthur Streeb-Greebling), Ludovic Kennedy (Interviewer).

	Holding / Source
26.12.1990 **Partridge In A Pear Three**	DB / 1"

A LIFE IN PIECES

27.12.1990	Turtle Doves	DB / 1"
28.12.1990	French Hens	DB / 1"
29.12.1990	Calling Birds	DB / 1"
30.12.1990	Gold Rings	DB / 1"
31.12.1990	Geese A-Laying	DB / 1"
01.01.1991	Swans A-Swimming	DB / 1"
02.01.1991	Maids A-Milking	DB / 1"
03.01.1991	Drummers Drumming	DB / 1"
04.01.1991	Pipers Piping	DB / 1"
05.01.1991	Ladies Dancing	DB / 1"
06.01.1991	Lords A-Leaping	DB / 1"

THE LIFE OF JOLLY

A BBC Scotland production for BBC 1 Scotland. Transmission details are for BBC 1 Scotland. Duration: 38 minutes.

Main regular credit(s): Series producer Philip Differ; produced by Ron Bain.

Main regular cast: Rikki Fulton (Reverend I. M. Jolly), Paul Coia, Juliet Cadzow, Mary Marquis, Gavin Mitchell, Cathy MacDonald, Donald McLeary, Simon Scott, Louise Goodall, Ally McLeod, John Stahl, Brian Cowan, Tommy Flanagan, Brian Reid, Ronnie Beharry, Stewart Mclean, Ginni Barlow, Steven McNicoll.

Holding / Source
31.12.1995   DB / D3S
31.12.1995   DB / D3S

LIFE WITH THE LYONS

Produced for BBC and ITV companies by a variety of companies (see details below). Duration: 25 minutes.

Main regular cast: Ben Lyon (Himself), Bebe Daniels (Herself), Barbara Lyon (Herself), Richard Lyon (Himself).

SERIES 3

An Associated-Rediffusion production. Transmission details are for the ATV midlands region.

Main regular credit(s): Written by Bob Ross, Bebe Daniels and Bob Block.

Holding / Source
24.12.1957   'Twas The Night Before   J /

All children between nine and 90 believe in Santa Claus, and Bebe sets out to prove this to the family.
Directed by John Phillips.
With Molly Weir (Aggie MacDonald), Doris Rogers (Florrie Wainwright), Norman Shelley, Leonard Monaghan, Skeeter Lyon.

LIFT OFF

A Granada production. Transmission details are for the ATV midlands region. Duration: 25 minutes.

Main regular performer(s): Ayshea Brough (Host).

SERIES 1

Main regular credit(s): Music directed by Derek Hilton; produced by Muriel Young; directed by Baz Taylor.
Main regular performer(s): With Graham Bonney (Host), Wally Whyton.

Holding / Source
24.12.1969   J / 2"

With Frankie Vaughan, The Love Affair, The Scaffold, John Walker, Ray Davies, Susan Maughan.

SERIES 2

Main regular credit(s): Music directed by Derek Hilton; choreography by Ken Martyne; designed by Eddie Buziak; produced by Muriel Young; directed by Mike Becker.
Main regular performer(s): With Wally Whyton (Co-Host), The Pattern, The Feet.

Holding / Source
23.12.1970   Christmas Show   J / 2"

Young Ayshea Brough has a co-host in this special Christmas show. It's Graham Bonney, who used to share the show with Ayshea last year. Singer Mike Leroy sings his own version
of Noel, and Cassidy, a boy/girl duo, sing their current release Place in My Heart.
With Graham Bonney, Mike Leroy, Marmalade, Cassidy.

SERIES 4

Main regular credit(s): Music directed by Derek Hilton; music arranged by Gerry Allison; choreography by Ken Martyne; designed by Eddie Buziak; produced by Muriel Young; directed by Dave Warwick.
Main regular performer(s): With Wally Whyton (Host), Ollie Beak, The Feet.

Holding / Source
24.12.1971   Christmas Lift Off   J / 2"

Alternative transmissions: Granada: 24.12.1971.
With Middle of The Road, Jack Wild, Kim Jones.

LIFT OFF WITH AYSHEA

A Granada production. Transmission details are for the ATV midlands region. Usual duration: 25 minutes.

Main regular performer(s): Ayshea Brough (Host).

SERIES 2

Main regular credit(s): Designed by Chris Wilkinson; produced by Muriel Young; directed by David Warwick.

Main regular performer(s): With Fred Barker, The Feet.

Holding / Source

24.12.1972 **Christmas Lift Off**   J / 2"

Duration: 35 minutes.

Ayshea Brough and her guests Lift Off for a special Christmas look at the music scene. With seasonal songs such as Snow Bird, an excerpt from the film Snow White, the whole cast presenting a musical montage-including God Rest Ye Merry Gentlemen-and The Feet dancing to Christmas Time, this is a party for everyone. Look out, too, for new numbers as yule time really gets off the ground and into ring-a-ding-ding orbit.

Music directed by Derek Hilton; music arranged by Gerry Allyson; choreography by Ken Martyne.

With The Sweet, New World, Ben Thomas, Miki Anthony, The Improvisers.

SERIES 4

Main regular credit(s): Designed by Steve Fineren; produced by Muriel Young; directed by David Warwick.

Main regular performer(s): With Fred Barker, Guy Lutman, The Feet.

Holding / Source

27.12.1973   J / 2"

With Slade, New World, All Night Rock Show.

See also: LIFT OFF

LIGHT LUNCH

A Princess Productions production for Channel 4. Transmission details are for Channel 4.

SERIES 2

Holding / Source

26.12.1997 **The Light Lunch Cardigan Christmas**   DB / DBS

See also: LATE LUNCH

THE LIGHT OF HEART

A BBC production. Transmission details are for BBC. Duration: 90 minutes.

Adapted by Desmond Davis; based on a play by Emlyn Williams; settings by James Bould; play production by Desmond Davis.

Gladys Henson (Mrs Banner), George Benson (Barty), Doris Hare (Fan), Edward Evans (Bevan), Donald Wolfit (Maddoc Thomas), Margaret Johnston (Cattrin), James Donald (Robert), Margery Fleeson (Mrs Lothian).

Holding / Source

26.12.1948 **First Performance**   NR / Live

THE LIGHT PRINCESS

A BBC production for BBC 2. Transmission details are for BBC 2. Duration: 70 minutes.

Written by Ian Keill; drawings by Errol Le Cain; animated by Mike Hibbert; music by Carl Davis; lighting by Derek Slee; sound Michael McCarthy; produced by Ian Keill; directed by Andrew Gosling.

Stacy Dorning (Princess), John Fortune (Prince), Irene Handl (Nanny), George A. Cooper (King), Gwen Taylor (Queen), Anna Quayle (Makemnoit), Terence Bayler (Lord Chamberlain), Annette Robertson (Maid), Tony Higginson (Bishop), Peter Bull (Voice of Fat Frog), Kenneth Williams (Voice of Thin Frog And The Cat), James Hayter (Voice of the Owl), John Wells (Voice of the Bee), David Kelly (Voice of the Oracle).

Holding / Source

24.12.1978   DB-D3 / 2"

THE LIKES OF SYKES

A Thames Television production. Transmission details are for the ATV midlands region. Duration: 50 minutes.

Festive fun and laughter when Eric has a dream.

Written by Eric Sykes; music directed by Peter Knight; choreography by Irving Davies; designed by Martyn Hébert; produced and directed by Paul Stewart Laing.

Eric Sykes, Diana Coupland, John Williams, Debbie Arnold, Hugh Burden, David Battley, Diane Holland, John Comer, Ricardo Montez.

Holding / Source

01.01.1980   DB / 2"

LILY SAVAGE'S BLANKETY BLANK

A Fremantle production for BBC 1. made in association with Wildflower Productions. Transmission details are for BBC 1. Duration: 30 minutes.

Main regular credit(s): Theme music by Ronnie Hazlehurst.

Main regular performer(s): Lily Savage (Host).

Holding / Source

26.12.1997 **[pilot]**   DB / DBS

Written by Charlie Adams and Dennis Berson; script supervisor Anthea Dudley; designed by Andy Walmsley; executive producers Brendan Murphy and Keith Stewart; production manager Paul Kelly; produced by Dean Jones; directed by Geoff Miles.

With Adrian Finighan (Voice Over), Ronan Keating, Christopher Cazenove, Gwen Taylor, Elizabeth Dawn, Gareth Hale, Carol Vorderman.

LINDISFARNE CHRISTMAS SHOW

A BBC Manchester production for BBC 2. Transmission details are for BBC 2. Duration: 45 minutes.
Produced and directed by Barry Bevins.
Lindisfarne.

	Holding / Source
27.12.1984	DB / 1"

LINGALONGAMAX

A Thames Television production. Transmission details are for the ATV midlands region. Duration: 25 minutes.
Main regular performer(s):   Max Bygraves (Host).

SERIES 1
Main regular credit(s):   Written by Eric Davidson; designed by Peter Le Page; produced and directed by Royston Mayoh.
Main regular performer(s):   With Geoff Love and his Orchestra, The Tony Mansell Singers, Bob Dixon.

	Holding / Source
25.12.1978	D3 / 2"

SERIES 3
Main regular credit(s):   Written by Eric Davidson; produced and directed by Royston Mayoh.
Main regular performer(s):   With Lorraine Chase, Bob Dixon, Geoff Love and his Orchestra, The Tony Mansell Singers.

	VT Number	Holding / Source
31.12.1979 **From Max With Love**	22109	D3 / 2"

Duration: 50 minutes.
Designed by Bill Palmer.
With Lorraine Chase, Bob Dixon, The Maggie Stredder Singers.

THE LITTLE AND LARGE "TELLYSHOW"

A Thames Television production. Transmission details are for the ATV midlands region. Duration: 25 minutes.
Main regular cast: Little and Large (Hosts).

	Holding / Source
20.12.1976 **[pilot]**	D3 / 2"

Written by Tony Hawes, Syd Little and Eddie Large; programme associate Tony Hawes; music by Sam Harding; designed by Anthony Cartledge; produced and directed by Royston Mayoh.
With Tom Shelley.

THE LITTLE AND LARGE SHOW

A BBC production for BBC 1. Transmission details are for BBC 1. Duration varies - see below for details.
Main regular performer(s):   Little and Large (Hosts).

Little and Large:
Duration: 45 minutes.

	Holding / Source
27.12.1977 **The Little and Largest Show On Earth**	DB-D3 / 2"

A BBC Manchester production.
Written by Mike Craig, Lawrie Kinsley, Ron McDonnell, David Renwick, Gavin Osbon, Tony Hawes, Syd Little and Eddie Large; choreography by Geoffrey Richer; produced and directed by Michael Hurll.
With Leo Sayer, Al Hakim, Marti Caine, Smokie, Geoff Richer's New Edition, Pierre Picton, The Inaros Sisters, Stromboli, Ronnie Hazlehurst and his Orchestra, The Maggie Stredder Singers.

SERIES 1: Little and Large:
Main regular credit(s):   Choreography by Geoffrey Richer; designed by Anna Ridley; produced and directed by Michael Hurll.
Main regular performer(s):   With Ronnie Hazlehurst and his Orchestra, Geoff Richer's Birds of A Feather, The Ladybirds.

	Holding / Source
23.12.1978 **The Little And Large Christmas Show**	DB-D3 / 2"

Duration: 40 minutes.
Written by Eddie Braben, Eric Davidson, Ron McDonnell and Terry Ravenscroft.
With Cliff Richard, Dana Gillespie, Berni Flint.

	Holding / Source
20.12.1980	DB-D3 / 2"

Duration: 50 minutes.
Written by Eric Davidson; additional material by David Newman, Peter Osborne and Bob Williams; choreography by Chris Power; designed by Martin Collins; produced and directed by Michael Hurll.
With Lena Zavaroni, Sheena Easton, Foxy Feeling, Ronnie Hazlehurst and his Orchestra.

THE LITTLE AND LARGE SHOW (continued)

Holding / Source

24.12.1981 **The Christmas Edition** DB-D3 / 2"
Duration: 30 minutes.
Designed by Andrew Howe Davies; produced and directed by John B. Hobbs.
With Madness, Lulu, Stutz Bear Cats, Ronnie Hazlehurst and his Orchestra.

SERIES 4
Main regular performer(s): With Ronnie Hazlehurst and his Orchestra.

Holding / Source

24.12.1983 DB / 1"
Duration: 40 minutes.
Written by Gavin Osbon, Wally Malston and Eric Merriman; designed by Paul Joel and Jim Clay; produced and directed by Bill Wilson.
With Joe Brown, Jimmy Cricket, Martin Daniels, Cleo Rocos, Chas & Dave.

LITTLE BIG TIME
A Southern Television production. Transmission details are for the ATV midlands region.
Main regular cast: Freddie and The Dreamers.
SERIES 5: Freddie's Joke Hall of Fame
Main regular cast: With Tony Robinson.

Holding / Source

26.12.1973 **Freddie's Christmas Joke Hall** J / 2"
Duration: 35 minutes.
Written by David McKellar; music by Bill Davies; designed by Gregory Lawson; produced and directed by Angus Wright.
With Freddie Garrity, June Ellis, Talfryn Thomas, Gordon Clyde, Patricia Brake, June Kidd, Pete Kidd, Frankie Holmes, Bob McBain, Pete Birrel.

LITTLE BLUE
A Yorkshire Television production. Transmission details are for the ATV midlands region. Duration: 8 minutes.

	VT Number	Holding / Source
04.12.1980 **The Christmas Play**	C262	B / 2"

Produced by Joy Whitby.

LITTLE BRITAIN
A BBC production for BBC 3. made in association with Pozzitive Television. Transmission details are for BBC. Duration: 30 minutes.
Character-based sketches satirising modern life written and performed by Matt Lucas and David Walliams.
Main regular credit(s):   Created by Matt Lucas and David Walliams; written by Matt Lucas and David Walliams; music by David Arnold.
Main regular cast: Matt Lucas, David Walliams, Tom Baker (Narrator, Voice Only).
SERIES 3
Transmission details are for BBC 1.
Main regular credit(s):   Additional material by Cecil and Riley; script supervisor Chrissie Bibby; script editor Richard Herring; consultant Myfanwy Moore; production executive Jez Nightingale; executive producer Jon Plowman; produced by Geoff Posner; directed by Declan Lowney.

Holding / Source

24.12.2005 DB / DBSWF
With Keith Alexander, Joanna Bacon, Sam Beazley, Su Bhoopongsa, Charubala Chokshi, Joann Condon, Rebecca Cooper, Cheryl Fergison, Richard Freeman, Steve Furst, Stirling Gallacher, Ruth Jones, Sody Singh Kahlon, Yuki Kushida, Joshua Lawton, Phoenix Lee, Janette Legge, Steven Lim, Diana May, Paul Putner, Kirris Riviere, Leelo Ross, Harmage Singh Kalirai [as Harmage Singh], Gordon Sterne, Indira Varma, Dean Whatton, Rob Brydon, Anthony Head, Imelda Staunton.

"Little Britain - a South Bank Show Special", tx:25.12.2005 on Central featured Matt Lucas, David Walliams, Barry Humphries, Elton John, Vic Reeves, Ronnie Corbett and Ken Russell. Produced and directed by Roz Edwards. 50 mins. LWT.

Transmission details are for BBC 3.

Holding / Source

26.12.2005 **Little Britain Night** DB / DBSW
With Rob Brydon.
Matt Lucas and David Walliams join Rob Brydon to introduce favourite episodes, discuss characters and take questions from a studio audience.

The BBC1 'repeats' were re-edited for a mainstream audience.
See also: LITTLE BRITAIN ABROAD (BBC)

LITTLE BRITAIN ABROAD
A BBC production for BBC 1. made in association with Little Britain Productions. Transmission details are for BBC 1. Duration: 30 minutes.
Main regular credit(s):   Written by Matt Lucas and David Walliams; additional material by Kevin Cecil and Andy Riley; script supervisor Chrissie Bibby; music by David Arnold; associate producer Jed Leventhall; production executive Jez Nightingale; executive producer Jon Plowman; produced by Geoff Posner; directed by Matt Lipsey and Geoff Posner.
Main regular cast: Matt Lucas (Various Roles), David Walliams (Various Roles), Tom Baker (Voice Only).

Holding / Source

25.12.2006 DB / DBSWF
With Steve Coogan, Ronnie Corbett, Morwenna Banks, Dawn French, Paul McKenna, Guido Adorni, Imogen Bain, Charubala Chokshi, Joann Condon, Steve Furst, Mandy Holliday, Vilma Hollingbery, Barbara Horne, Junix Inocian, Shirley Jaffe, Ruth Jones, Mac McDonald, Samantha Power, Paul Putner, Robert Rietty, Sally Rogers, Leelo Ross, Rolf Saxon, Ruby Turner, Vee Vimolmal, Yuki, Julia Davis, Anthony Head, Peter Kay.

LITTLE BRITAIN ABROAD

| British Christmas Television Guide | LITTLE BRITAIN ABROAD (continued) |

30.12.2006   DB / DBSWF

With Dawn French, Morwenna Banks, Steve Coogan, Guido Adorni, Imogen Bain, Charubala Chokshi, Joann Condon, Steve Furst, Mandy Holliday, Vilma Hollingbery, Barbara Horne, Junix Inocian, Shirley Jaffe, Ruth Jones, Mac McDonald, Samantha Power, Paul Putner, Robert Rietty [as Robert Rietti], Sally Rogers, Leelo Ross, Rolf Saxon, Ruby Turner, Vee Vimolmal, Yuki, Ronnie Corbett, Julia Davis, Anthony Head, Peter Kay, Paul McKenna.

See also: LITTLE BRITAIN (BBC)

LITTLE CRACKERS

Produced for Sky One by a variety of companies (see details below). Transmission details are for Sky One.

SERIES 1

Duration: 12 minutes.

Holding / Source

19.12.2010   **The Giddy Kipper**   HD/DB / DB

A Blue Door Adventures / Phil McIntyre Television production.

Introduced by Victoria Wood; written by Victoria Wood; script supervisor Jane Burrows; director of photography Tony Slater-Ling; assistant director Alex Rendell; production designer Pat Campbell; executive producers Lucy Ansbro and Lucy Lumsden; produced by Chris Thompson; directed by Victoria Wood.

With Briony Farr (Eunice), Samuel Roukin (Dad), Isabelle Walker (Marilyn), Hattie Atkinson (Sheila), Lorraine Ashbourne (Miss Meadowcroft), Sinéad Keenan (Mrs Whitefield), Joel Davies (Alistair), Andy Brady (Dancer), Claire Rogers (Dancer), Caroline Royce (Dancer).

19.12.2010   **Capturing Santa**   HD/DB / DB

A Sprout Pictures production.

Narrated by Chris O'Dowd; written by Chris O'Dowd and Nick Murphy; script supervisor Heather Storr; music by Jonathan Whitehead; director of photography Hubert Taczanowski; assistant director Joanna Crow; art director Chris Rosser; production designer Gary Williamson; associate producer Zoë Rocha; production executives Emily Martin and Rebecca Parkinson; executive producers Stephen Fry, Lucy Lumsden, Gina Carter and Charles Elton; production manager Ben Holt; line producer Charlotte Ashby; produced by Mike Elliott; directed by Peter Cattaneo.

With Chris O'Dowd (Santa), Robert Donnelly (Young Chris), Sharon Horgan (Mother), John O'Dowd (Father), Lucy Laverty (Sister 1), Eva Laverty (Sister 2), Jamie McIntyre (Padraic), Clive Swift (Real Father Christmas), Philomena McDonagh (Staff Member).

20.12.2010   **My First Nativity**   HD/DB / DB

A Tiger Aspect production.

Written by Catherine Tate; script supervisor Anne Patterson; music by Jane Watkins; director of photography Pete Rowe; assistant director Tom Dunbar; art director Natalie Valentine; production designer Jo Sutherland; production executive Philippa Catt; executive producers Lucy Lumsden and Sophie Clarke-Jervoise; head of production Toby Ward; line producer Rachel Alabaster; produced by Izzy Mant; directed by Catherine Tate.

With Madeleine Power (Young Catherine), Brid Brennan (Sister Mary Bernadette), Anita Dobson (Nan), Ellie Haddington (Nellie), Catherine Tate (Josephine), Niky Wardley (Angie).

20.12.2010   **Satan's Hoof**   HD/DB / DB

A Silver River Productions production.

Written by Julian Barratt; script supervisor Penelope Chong; music by Julian Barratt; director of photography Gavin Finney; assistant director Guy De Glanville; art director Natalie Valentine; production designer Jo Sutherland; executive producers Daisy Goodwin, Chris Sussman and Lucy Lumsden; head of production Samantha Lawrence; line producer Jo Hunter; produced by Pippa Brown; directed by Julian Barratt.

With Paul Conway (Julian), Megan Winnard (Emma), Cavan Clerkin (Step-Dad), Alex Sheldon (Nick), Perry Fitzpatrick (Gerard), Jessica Hynes (Dawn), Julian Barratt (Satan).

21.12.2010   **Bunce**   HD/DB / DB

A Sprout Pictures production.

Narrated by Stephen Fry; written by Stephen Fry; script supervisor Heather Storr; music by Jonathan Whitehead; director of photography Hubert Taczanowski; assistant director Joanna Crow; art director Chris Rosser; production designer Gary Williamson; associate producer Zoë Rocha; production executives Emily Martin and Rebecca Parkinson; executive producers Stephen Fry, Lucy Lumsden, Gina Carter and Charles Elton; production manager Ben Holt; line producer Charlotte Ashby; produced by Mike Elliott; directed by Peter Cattaneo.

With Stephen Fry (Headmaster), Daniel Roche (Fry), Milo Quinton (Bunce), Benjamin Dewhurst (Kirk), Christian Lees (Prestwick-Agutter), Jonah Lees (Prestwick-Agutter), Annette Badland (Mrs Chitterling).

21.12.2010   **Better Than Christmas**   HD/DB / DB

A Tiger Aspect production.

Written by Kathy Burke; script supervisor Anne Patterson; music by Daniel Pemberton; director of photography Pete Rowe; assistant director Tom Dunbar; art director Natalie Valentine; production designer Jo Sutherland; production executive Philippa Catt; executive producers Lucy Lumsden and Ben Cavey; head of production Toby Ward; line producer Rachel Alabaster; produced by Izzy Mant; directed by Tim Kirkby.

With Ami Metcalf (Young Cathy), Aimeé-Ffion Edwards (Mary), Sam Palladio (Joe Stummer), Kathy Burke (Nun).

22.12.2010   **Goodbye Fluff**   HD/DB / DB

A Renegade Pictures production.

Written by Jo Brand; script supervisor Jemma Field; script editor Chris Reddy; director of photography Lukas Strebel; assistant director Phil Booth; art director Tim Gibson; production designer Louise Corcoran; executive producers Lucy Lumsden and Lucy Robinson; head of production Maria Livesey; line producer Lorraine Goodman; produced by Alan Hayling and Jon Rowlands; directed by Mike Christie.

With Jo Brand (Herself), Dani Harmer (Young Jo), Kevin Doyle (Dick), Amelia Bullmore (Helen), Eddie Oyenden (Clive), Ailish O'Connor (Lesley), Jasmyn Banks (Susan), Jessica D'Souza (Kim), Elizabeth Berrington (Terry), Jason Watkins (Vince).

22.12.2010   **Car Park Babylon**   HD/DB / DB

A Sprout Pictures/Glassbox production.

Written by Bill Bailey and Joe Magee; script supervisor Heather Storr; director of photography Hubert Taczanowski; assistant director Richard Styles; art director Chris Rosser; production designer Gary Williamson; associate producer Zoë Rocha; production executives Emily Martin and Rebecca Parkinson; executive producers Gina Carter, Charles Elton, Kris Bailey, Stephen Fry and Lucy Lumsden; production manager Ben Holt; line producer Charlotte Ashby; produced by Mike Elliott; directed by Bill Bailey and Joe Magee.

With Bill Bailey (Bill), Chris Brassington (Joe), Lucy McCall (Mary), Henry Miller (Dean), Martin Hancock (Mr Fix It), Rich Fulcher (The Controller).

LITTLE CRACKERS (continued) British Christmas Television Guide

23.12.2010 **The Norris McWhirter Chronicles** HD/DB / DB
An Avalon/Fierce Tears Productions production.
Narrated by David Baddiel; written by David Baddiel; script supervisor Kendall Anderson-Mut; music sung by Jules Brookes; music by Erran Baron Cohen; director of photography Martin Hawkins; assistant director Ross Coughlin; art director Jacqueline Fey; production designer Dennis De Groot; executive producers Lucy Lumsden, Richard Allen-Turner, David Baddiel and Jon Thoday; head of production Bluey Richards; production manager Gurjit Kharbanda; produced by Charlie Hanson; directed by David Baddiel.

With Alistair McGowan (Norris McWhirter), John Thomson (DJ Geoff), Paul Jerricho (Headmaster), Lee Mack (Jez), Sebastian Applewhite (Young David), David Baddiel (Himself), Frank Skinner (Himself), Roy Arvatz (Schoolboy), Alexander Edwards (Schoolboy), Hadyn-Sky Bauzon (Schoolboy), Louis Demosthenous (Schoolboy).

23.12.2010 **The Kiss** HD/DB / DB
A Silver River Productions production.
Written by Julia Davis; additional material by Kevin Eldon; script supervisor Penelope Chong; director of photography Gavin Finney; assistant director Guy De Glanville; art director Natalie Valentine; production designer Jo Sutherland; executive producers Daisy Goodwin, Chris Sussman and Lucy Lumsden; head of production Samantha Lawrence; line producer Jo Hunter; produced by Pippa Brown; directed by Julia Davis; co-directed by Christine Gernon.

With Clementine Starling (Young Julia), Julia Davis (Susan Johnways), Kevin Eldon (Ron Johnways), Emily Atack (Charlie), Jason Brasier (Nigel), Jack de Carle (Jerry), Pierro Niel Mee (Matt Johnson), Toby Carter (Tom), Jamie Metcalfe (Steve), Melissa Suffield (Alison), Stuart Matthews (James).

24.12.2010 **Operation Big Hat** HD/DB / DB
A Tiger Aspect production.
Written by Emma Kilcoyne and Beth Kilcoyne; story by Dawn French; script supervisor Anne Patterson; music by Jane Watkins; director of photography Pete Rowe; assistant director Tom Dunbar; production designer Jo Sutherland; production executive Philippa Catt; executive producers Lucy Lumsden and Sophie Clarke-Jervoise; head of production Toby Ward; line producer Rachel Alabaster; produced by Izzy Mant; directed by Dewi Humphreys.

With Dawn French (Her Majesty the Queen Mother), Sarah Smart (Roma French), Tom Stuart (Denys French), Brooke Holmes (Young Dawn French), Jem Savin (Gary French), Patrick Barlow (Patrick), Sam Battersea (Peggy), Geraldine McNulty (Nora).

25.12.2010 **Uncle Santa** HD/DB / DB
A Renegade Pictures/Can Communicate production.
Written by Meera Syal; script supervisor Jemma Field; music by Jonathan Goldstein; director of photography David Raedeker; assistant director Steve Robinson; art director Tim Gibson; production designer Louise Corcoran; executive producers Jon Rowlands, David Wooster and Lucy Lumsden; head of production Maria Livesey; line producer Lorraine Goodman; produced by Lucy Robinson; directed by Peter Lydon.

With Narisa Padhiar (Young Meera), Ayesha Dharker (Mama), Sanjeev Bhaskar (Papa), Mark Williams (Father Christmas), Mark Roper (Bill), Bethany Randswalsh (Tracey), Madhav Sharma (Uncle Satnam), James Carcaterra (Policeman), Meera Syal (Herself), Adlyn Ross (Old Woman).

This edition was shot in 3D and was shown in that format on Sky 3D.

───────────────────────────────

SERIES 2
Duration: 12 minutes.

Holding / Source

18.12.2011 **My First Brassiere** HD/DB / HDC
A Lovely Day production.
Babs takes her first top-heavy steps.
Written by Matt Evans; designed by Anna Pritchard; executive producers Barbara Windsor, Lucy Lumsden, Saskia Schuster and Diederick Santer; produced by Dominic Treadwell-Collins; directed by Paul King.

With Barbara Windsor (Narrator / Shop Assistant), Samantha White (Barbara Windsor), Sally Hawkins (Mummy), Neil Jackson (Daddy), Lesley Joseph (Wardrobe Mistress), Clara Paget (Linda), Louisa Connolly-Burnham (Susan Butler), Tony Bignell (Bobby Sims), Eugene McCoy (Johnny Brandon), Ben Hull (Builder).

18.12.2011 **Daddy's Little Princess** HD/DB / HDC
A Tiger Aspect production.
A young Jack Whitehall asks for Barbie dolls for Christmas.
Written by Jack Whitehall and Freddy Syborn; script editor Simon Carlyle; music by Simon Lacey; designed by Jo Sutherland; executive producers Lucy Lumsden, Ben Cavey and Saskia Schuster; produced by Margot Gavan Duffy; directed by Juliet May.

With Jack Whitehall (Robin), Archie Lyndhurst (Young Jack), Robert Daws (Michael), Belinda Stewart-Wilson (Hilary), Anthony O'Donnell (Uncle Peter), Hilary Whitehall (Relation).

19.12.2011 **Barbra** HD/DB / HDC
A Sprout Pictures production.
A frail schoolgirl obsessed with Barbra Streisand has trouble turning male heads. Her idea of chat-up involves bopping a boy over the head with her breathalyser. But this is no ordinary schoolgirl; it's a teen Jane Horrocks. In this magical micro-comedy the 70s are lovingly re-created (with help from Leo Sayer and Middle of the Road) and there's a joyous twist in the tale.
Written by Nick Vivian; designed by Kem White; executive producers Lucy Lumsden, Stephen Fry, Gina Carter, Saskia Schuster and Zoe Rocha; produced by Mike Elliott; directed by Paul Norton Walker.

With Sophie Wright (Young Jane Horrocks), Jane Horrocks (Hairdresser), Katy Clayton (Tracy), Ciara Baxendale (Patsy), James Ainsworth (Andrew), Charlie Kenyon (Lad), Claire Greenaway (Margaret).

19.12.2011 **Your Face** HD/DB / HDC
A Blurred Vision production.
Harry Hill's flashbacks keep clashing with those of his younger self. Utterly daft, utterly fantastic, it's full of trademark low-fi effects that consistently ramp up the laughs.
Written by Harry Hill; produced by Charlie Leech; directed by Harry Hill.

With Harry Hill, Jude Wright (Harry Junior), Joshua Oakes-Rogers (Teen Harry), Hélène Patarot (May Sung), Sarah Gatenby-Howells (Young Sarah Ferguson), Bridget Christie (Air Hostess), Junior Simpson (Tribesman).

| British Christmas Television Guide | LITTLE CRACKERS (continued) |

20.12.2011 The Curious Incident Of The Dog In The Daytime HD/DB / HDC
A Sprout Pictures production.
Alan finds himself lumbered with his father's Alsatian after a messy run-in with the next-door neighbour's Sheltie. John Sessions makes a cameo playing a fabulously poker-faced canine
psychiatrist as Davies and dog bury their differences.
Written by Alan Davies and Oliver Lansley; executive producers Gina Carter and Zoe Rocha; produced by Mike Elliott; directed by Oliver Lansley.
With Alan Davies, John Sessions (Doctor Edward Cole), Benjamin Whitrow (Dad), Felicity Montagu (Mrs Peters), Ewan Bailey (Dog Instructor), Roger Ashton-Griffiths (First Magistrate), Iain McKee (Policeman), Mona Hammond (Neighbour).

20.12.2011 Shappi 4 Todd HD/DB / HDC
An Open Mike production.
Shappi Khorsandi's tale is about her ten-year-old self. The only thing she has in common with her schoolmates is a whopping crush on Tucker in Grange Hill, so it should be a dream come true when he opens the Christmas fayre. If only silly young Shappi hadn't told a little white lie.
Written by Shappi Khorsandi; script editor Andrew Collins; designed by Sarah Jenneson; executive producers Lucy Lumsden, Saskia Schuster, Addison Cresswell and Andrew Beint; produced by Katherine Lannon; directed by Chris Cottam.
With Shappi Khorsandi, Paradis Farahati (Young Shappi), Oliver Johnstone (Young Todd), Gwyneth Powell (Headmistress), Faraz Khokhar (Peyvand), Nadim Sawalha (Baba Aziz), Nathalie Armin (Maman), George Spittle-McGuire (Chris), Macauley Keeper (Joe Dilly), Nicole Davies (Lucy), Eliza Newman (Carol), Cicely Giddings (Art Teacher), Paul Bazely (Hadi), Viss Elliot Safavi (Party Guest), Peyvand Khorsandi (Party Guest), Amanda Lawrence (Mrs Oliver), Todd Carty.

21.12.2011 My First Ton HD/DB / HDC
A Baby Cow Productions production.
Written by John Bishop; executive producers Lucy Lumsden, Saskia Schuster and John Bishop; produced by Gill Isles; directed by John Bishop.
With John Bishop (Bobby), Sam Benjamin (Eddie), Gary Mavers (Ernie), Ray Quinn (Davey), Charlene Evans (Girl), Alistair Mann (Commentator Voice), Mummy Bishop (Voice, John's Mum).

21.12.2011 The Daltons HD/DB / HDC
A Lovely Day production.
Determined to go to her parents' gigs (as country act the Daltons), young Sheridan became, age seven, part of the act...
Written by Michael Wynne; designed by Anna Pritchard; executive producers Lucy Lumsden, Saskia Schuster and Diederick Santer; produced by Dominic Treadwell-Collins; directed by Paul King.
With Sheridan Smith (Marilyn Smith), Ralf Little (Colin Smith), Alan Davies (Comedian), Frankie Taylor (Young Sheridan), Annette Badland (Mrs Ramsbottom), Mark Flanagan (Julian Smith), Tom Rolinson (Damian Smith), Colin Smith, Marilyn Smith, Howard Johnson, Matt Ferguson, Clive Johns.

22.12.2011 My First Christmas Number One HD/DB / HDC
A Tiger Aspect production.
Sally Lindsay recalls her part when St Winifred's School Choir made a rather traumatic visit to the Top of the Pops studio to perform There's No One Quite like Grandma. An audience of teenagers was never going to be receptive to the sweetest song in pop.
Written by Sarah Hooper; music by Simon Lacey; designed by Jo Sutherland; executive producers Lucy Lumsden, Saskia Schuster and Sophie Clarke-Jervoise; produced by Margot Gavan Duffy; directed by Dewi Humphreys.
With Sally Lindsay (Miss Foley), Olivia Cosgrove (Young Sally), Owen Salthouse (Young Chris), Jennifer James (Mum), Kathryn Hunt (Gran), Julia Deakin (Sister Aquinas), Lee Boardman (Reg), Steve Furst (Frank).

22.12.2011 Papaji Saves Christmas HD/DB / HDC
A Sprout Pictures production.
It is 1975, and Christmas begins joyfully for the 12-year-old Sanjeev with his dad marking up his copy of Radio Times so he doesn't miss any current affairs. But terror rules the Bhaskar home when a mouse is discovered in the bathroom. It takes the visiting Papaji, Sanjeev's uncle and a man previously considered (with affection) to be both lazy and boring, to oust the rodent.
Written by Sanjeev Bhaskar; executive producers Gina Carter, Lucy Lumsden, Saskia Schuster and Zoe Rocha; produced by Mike Elliott; directed by Sanjeev Bhaskar.
With Sanjeev Bhaskar (Dad), Joshan Patel (Young Sanjeev), Seeta Indrani (Mum), Kaleem Janjua (Uncle Papaji), Nishi Malde (Sangeeta), Vincent Ebrahim (Uncle Arun), Harvey Virdi (Auntie Nimmi).

23.12.2011 I Was A Teenage Santa! HD/DB / HDC
A Baby Cow / Woolyback Productions production.
A young Johnny is obliged to play Santa at a grotty Christmas fair in 1983.
Written by Johnny Vegas; executive producers Lucy Lumsden, Saskia Schuster, Lindsay Hughes and Johnny Vegas; produced by Gill Isles; directed by Johnny Vegas.
With Johnny Vegas (Kevin), Thomas Mills (Young Johnny Vegas), Guy Hargreaves (Craig), Margaret Henshaw (Agnes), Joan Kempson (Hilda), Jeffrey Longmore (Jeff), Jacob Newby (Skate Boy), Aiden Kelly (Jumper Boy), Paige Walsh (New Toy Girl).

SERIES 3
Duration: 25 minutes.

Holding / Source

10.12.2012 Baby, Be Blonde HD/DB / HDC
A Tiger Aspect production.
Written by Tessa Gibbs; designed by Jo Sutherland; executive producers Lucy Lumsden, Sophie Clarke-Jervoise, Ben Cavey and Saskia Schuster; produced by Margot Gavan Duffy; directed by Joanna Lumley.
With Joanna Lumley (Features Commissioner), Ottilie Mackintosh (Jo), Daniel Ings (Dan), Chris Geere (Harry), Joanna Higson (Sarah), Elsie Bennett (Mel), Freddie Rogers (Nigel), Felicity Montagu (Mrs Phipps), Rufus Wright (Art Director), Daisy Tonge (Model), Jessica Dyas (Model), Roxanna Hollt (Model), Milanka Brooks (Model), Natalie Jayne Batten (Model).

11.12.2012 Rainy Days And Mondays HD/DB / HDC
A Tiger Aspect production.
Written by Rebecca Front and Jeremy Front; designed by Jim Holloway; executive producers Lucy Lumsden, Sophie Clarke-Jervoise, Ben Cavey and Saskia Schuster; produced by Jane Wallbank; directed by Christine Gernon.
With Rebecca Front (Miss Dyson), Samantha Spiro (Mum), Richard Lumsden (Dad), Selina Griffiths (Educational Pyschologist), Oliver Clymer (Jeremy), Imogen Front (Karen), Sadie Hasler (Teacher).

LITTLE CRACKERS (continued)

12.12.2012 Howler — HD/DB / HDC
A Baby Cow Productions production.
Written by Tommy Tiernan; designed by Jeffrey Sherriff; executive producers Lucy Lumsden, Saskia Schuster, Lindsay Hughes and Henry Normal; produced by Mobashir Dar; directed by Tommy Tiernan.
With Tommy Tiernan (Dad), Ronni Ancona (Ex-Wife), Stephane Cornicard (Psychiatrist), David Crow (Vet), Alfie Davis (Nigel), Marie Mullen (Mother), Jim Fowler (Detective).

13.12.2012 Nutcracker — HD/DB / HDC
A Merman / Bwark production.
Written by Caroline Quentin; designed by Heather Gibson; executive producers Lucy Lumsden, Saskia Schuster, Damon Beesley, Sharon Horgan and Simon Wilson; produced by Celia Mountford; directed by Caroline Quentin.
With Caroline Quentin (Mrs Bunnichevski), Alice Evans (Kitty), Rosalind Halstead (Mother), Seann Walsh (Jesus Of Nazareth), Elsie Salmon (King Mouse), Gabrielle Smith (Clara), Jessica Gunning (Matron).

17.12.2012 The Autograph — HD/DB / HDC
A Sprout Pictures production.
Written by Alison Steadman and Hils Barker; designed by Nick Palmer; executive producers Lucy Lumsden, Saskia Schuster, Zoe Rocha and Paul Jackson; produced by Adrian Bate; directed by Peter Cattaneo.
With Alison Steadman (Alison's Mum), Lauren McQueen (Alison), Francesca Dolan (Irene), Alexa Davies (Hilary), Jake Roche (Paul), Sam Coulson (John).

17.12.2012 The Awkward Age — HD/DB / HDC
A Pirate production.
Written by Dylan Moran; script editor Elaine Davidson; music directed by Dave Wallace; designed by Mike McLoughlin; executive producers Lucy Lumsden, Saskia Schuster, Annie Griffin and Dylan Moran; produced by Jenny Williams; directed by Ian Fitzgibbon.
With Dylan Moran (Father), Daniela Nardini (Mother), Keith Ramsay (Michael), Amber O'Grady (Daughter), Ian Fitzgibbon (Waiter).

18.12.2012 A Tender Christmas — HD/DB / HDC
A Left Bank Pictures / Invisible Man production.
Written by Jason Manford; music adviser Carly Paradis; designed by Simon Rogers; executive producers Saskia Schuster, Lucy Lumsden, Jenna Jones, Jason Manford and Andy Harries; produced by Lindsay Salt; directed by Mustapha Kseibati.
With Jason Manford (Dad / Nurse / Surgeon), Ellis Hollins (Young Jason), Ellie Hodgson (Judy), Evie O'Sullivan (Bulldog), Jason Manford (Spiderclown).

18.12.2012 The Ten Year Plan: Fringe To Hollywood — HD/DB / HDC
A Tiger Aspect production.
Written by Omid Djalili; designed by Jo Sutherland; executive producers Lucy Lumsden, Sophie Clarke-Jervoise, Ben Cavey and Saskia Schuster; produced by Margot Gavan Duffy; directed by Omid Djalili.
With Omid Djalili (Tobacconist), Ashley Kumar (Omid), Beattie Edmondson (Annabel), Harry Kershaw (Craig), Tim Downie (Polcie Constable Goodhand), Max Brophy (Rupert), Steve Brody (MC Comedy Club), Cara Jenkins (Claire).

19.12.2012 Boo! A Ghost Story — HD/DB / HDC
A Sprout Pictures production.
Written by Paul O'Grady; designed by Nick Palmer; executive producers Lucy Lumsden, Saskia Schuster, Zoe Rocha and Paul Jackson; produced by Adrian Bate; directed by Peter Cattaneo.
With Paul O'Grady (Lily Savage / Tramp), Robin Morrissey (Paul), Keith Rice (Paul's Friend), Alison Steadman (Paul's Mum), Paul O'Grady (Ghost).

19.12.2012 Of All The Trees — HD/DB / HDC
A Hillbilly Television production.
Written by Katy Brand; music by Jack C. Arnold; designed by Lisa Marie Hall; executive producers Lucy Lumsden, Saskia Schuster, Polly Leys and Kate Norrish; produced by Matthew Mulot; directed by Edward Dick.
With Katy Brand (Adult Katy), Hannah Norton (Young Katy), Rebecca Gethings (Mum), Oliver Maltman (Dad), Amelia Baldock (Little Sister), Wendy Craig (Grandma), Roger Sloman (Grandad).

20.12.2012 The Week Before Christmas — HD/DB / HDC
A Merman / Bwark production.
Written by Sharon Horgan; designed by Heather Gibson; executive producers Lucy Lumsden, Saskia Schuster, Damon Beesley, Sharon Horgan and Simon Wilson; produced by Clelia Mountford; directed by Sharon Horgan.
With Sharon Horgan (Sharon's Mum), Katherine Rose Morley (Young Sharon), Sam Keeley (James), Conleth Hill (Sharon's Dad), Cian Mulhall (Shane), Quaid Cleland (Mark), Aisling Loftus (Maria), Susie Power (Lorraine), Peter Harkness (Guarda).

20.12.2012 The Ten Year Plan: Fringe To Hollywood — HD/DB / HDC
A Little Comet production.
Written by Darren Boyd; music by Ian Masterson; designed by Louise Corcoran; executive producers Lucy Lumsden and Saskia Schuster; produced by Lucy Robinson; directed by Darren Boyd.
With Darren Boyd (Dad), Doon Mackichan (Mum), Tom Meeten (Rival Dancer), Barunka O'Shaugnessy (Rival Dancer), Theo Stevenson (Boy).

Each play was billed with the writer's name in the title (e.g. "Victoria Wood's Little Cracker") but this wasn't replicated on screen. The series was also billed as a comedy, but some segments were definitely more dramatic than comedic.

THE LITTLE MATCH GIRL

An ATV production. Transmission details are for the ATV midlands region. Duration: 30 minutes.

On a freezing Christmas Eve, a little girl is trying to sell matches—she darenot go home until she has done so or her father will beat her...

Dramatised by Jeremy Paul; based on a story by Hans Christian Andersen; designed by James Weatherup; produced and directed by Richard Bramall.

Lynsey Baxter (Little Match Girl), David Howe (Arthur), Annabelle Lanyon (Charlotte), Georgina Kean (Harriet), Anna Steele (Charlotte's Mother), Ivor Roberts (Charlotte's Father), Susan Field (Cook), Michael Hall (Butler), Norma Pitt (Richman), Paul Henry (Pieman), Maggie Ollerenshaw (Tart), Edwin Brown (Blindman), Golda Casimir (Old Washerwoman), Susan Richards (Grandmother), Dorothea Phillips (First Spinster), Marion Fiddick (Second Spinster).

	Holding / Source
24.12.1974	DB / 2"

THE LITTLE MATCH GIRL

THE LITTLE MATCHGIRL

A HTV production. made in association with Picture Base International. Transmission details are for the Central region. Duration: 75 minutes.

Christmas 1880, London: A poor matchgirl discovers in a flame a magical world.

Introduced by Michael Hordern; adapted by Jeremy Paul and Leslie Stewart; based on a story by Hans Christian Andersen; music by Keith Strachan; choreography by David Toguri; designed by Phil Williams; produced by Peter Jeffries; directed by Michael Custance.

Twiggy (Josie Roberts), Roger Daltrey (Jebb Macklin), Natalie Morse (The Matchgirl), Russell Lee Nash (Arthur), Jemma Price (Charlotte Fairbrother), Nicola Dawn (Liza Fairbrother), Paul Daneman (Mr Fairbrother), Jennie Linden (Mrs Fairbrother), Jimmy Jewel (Butler), Paddie O'Neil (Cook), Stratford Johns (Rich Man), Patricia Lawrence (Maud), Dorothea Phillips (Winifred), Robert Putt (Landlord), Pearl Hackney (Mrs Prothero), Fanny Carby (Washerwoman), John Rogan (Pie-Seller), Christina Avery (First Tart), Eithne Hannigan (Second Tart), Kelly George (First Urchin), Ian Hooper (Second Urchin).

	Holding / Source
28.12.1986	1" / 1"

THE LITTLE MERMAID

A BBC production for BBC 1. Transmission details are for BBC 1. Duration: 30 minutes.

Dramatised by Marilyn Fox; based on a story by Hans Andersen; song by Carol Hall; music by Joseph Horovitz; designed by Rochelle Selwyn; produced by Anna Home; directed by Marilyn Fox.

Penny Casdagli (Little Mermaid), Marion Diamond (First Sister), Karen Ford (Second Sister), Rosalind Knight (Grandmother), Malcolm Reynolds (Prince Ossian), Malcolm Terris (Captain), Louise Hall-Taylor (Princess Maria), Melinda Clancy (Lisa), Margery Mason (Sea Witch), Kathleen Byron (Queen), William Gossling (Herald), Nikki Heard (Dancer), Maurice Lane (Dancer), Gene Foad (Narrator).

	Holding / Source
26.12.1974	DB-D3 / 2"

THE LITTLE SWEEP

A Thames Television production for Channel 4. made in association with Canadian Broadcasting Corporation. Transmission details are for Channel 4. Duration: 50 minutes.

A short opera about an eight-year-old chimney sweep who is rescued from a life of Dickensian misery by a group of children and their governess.

Libretto by Eric Crozier; written by Benjamin Britten; adapted by Sydney Newman; executive producer Ian Martin; produced by Sydney Newman; directed by Basil Coleman.

Dennis Wicks (Balck Bob), Neill Archer (Clem), Jamie Adams (Sam), Susan Bullock (Rowan), Maureen Forrester (Miss Baggott), Elen ap Robert (Juliet), Cecilia Osmond (Sophie), Benjamin Child (Jonny), Matthew Kitteridge (Hughie), Tracey Garratty (Tina), Christopher Riches (Gay), Roderick Kennedy (Tom), Gerard O'Beirne (Alfred).

	Holding / Source
25.12.1989	1" / 1"S

LIVE FROM TWO

A Granada production. Transmission details are for the Granada region. Usual duration: 38 minutes.

Main regular credit(s): Series editor Steve Morrison.

Main regular performer(s): Shelley Rhodes (Presenter).

	Production No	Holding / Source
31.12.1980	P972/101	DB / 2"

A look back at 1980 and look ahead to 1981.

Research Max Graesser, David Wason, Susan Brookes and Marian Nelson; designed by Nick King; produced by Sue Woodford.

With Vanessa Redgrave, Lady Masham, Stephen Pile, Ray Gosling, Chris Dunkley, William Foggit, Ian Dury, Cantabile.

THE LIVER BIRDS

A BBC production for BBC 1. Transmission details are for BBC 1. Duration varies - see below for details.

Main regular credit(s): Created by Carla Lane and Myra Taylor; theme music by The Scaffold.

Main regular cast: Nerys Hughes (Sandra).

SERIES 6

Main regular credit(s): Written by Carla Lane; produced and directed by Douglas Argent.

Main regular cast: With Elizabeth Estensen (Carol), Mollie Sugden (Mrs Hutchinson), Michael Angelis (Lucian).

	Holding / Source
23.12.1975 **In Every Street**	DB-D3 / 2"

Duration: 40 minutes.

Designed by Tim Gleeson.

With Mollie Sugden (Mrs Hutchinson), Eileen Kennally (Mrs Boswell), Michael Angelis (Lucian), Jack Le White (Grandad), Hilda Barry, Herbert Ramskill, Ivan Beavis, Mollie Maureen, Roger Gale, Michael Bilton, Garry Cook.

SERIES 7

Main regular credit(s): Written by Carla Lane; produced and directed by Douglas Argent.

Main regular cast: With Elizabeth Estensen (Carol).

	Holding / Source
22.12.1976 **It Insists On Coming Once A Year**	DB-D3 / 2"

Duration: 40 minutes.

Designed by Ian Rawnsley.

With Eileen Kennally (Mrs Boswell), Ray Dunbobbin (Mr Boswell), Michael Angelis (Lucian), Jackie Fishel (Barbara), John Nettles (Paul), Jack Le White, John Alkin, Kenneth Waller, David Valla, John Scott Martin, Brian Godfrey, Maggie Flint, Nellie Griffiths, Iris Fry.

THE LIVER BIRDS (continued)

SERIES 8
Main regular credit(s): Written by Carla Lane; produced and directed by Roger Race.
Main regular cast: With Elizabeth Estensen (Carol), Mollie Sugden (Mrs Hutchinson), Carmel McSharry (Mrs Boswell), Michael Angelis (Lucian), Ray Dunbobbin (Mr Boswell).

	Holding / Source
23.12.1977 Open Your Eyes - And It Still Hasn't Gone	DB-D3 / 2"

Duration: 35 minutes.
Designed by Antony Thorpe.
With Tom Chadbon (Derek Paynton), Jack Le White (Grandad), William Moore, Jackie Fishel, Frank Vicary, Diana Harker, Dinah Handley, Betty Wernick, Lovette Edwards.

LIVERPOOL NATIVITY

A BBC production for BBC 3. Transmission details are for BBC 3. Duration: 60 minutes.

Devised by Andy King-Dabbs; written by Mark Davies Markham; script supervisors Michelle Arnold and Louise Johnson; developed by Mark Davies Markham; designed by Alex Craig; assistant producer Rachael Smith; associate producer Alison Havell; executive producer Sue Judd; directed for the stage by Noreen Kershaw; directed by Richard Valentine.

Jodie McNee (Mary), Kenny Thompson (Joseph), Geoffrey Hughes (Angel Gabriel), Jennifer Ellison (Angel), Cathy Tyson (Herodia), Stephen Fletcher (Max), Joe McGann (Magi), David Yip (Magi), Louis Emerick (Magi), Rachel Rae (Angel), Antonia Sheppard (Child Angel), Alfie Davies (Child Angel), Andrew Schofield (Shepherd), Leah Hackett (Shepherd), Paul Barber (Landlord), Nerys Hughes (Woman In Cafe), Gerry Marsden (Ferry Captain), Sense of Sound Choir, Shepherds Choir, Royal Liverpool Philharmonic Orchestra, Ferry Band, Herodia Band, Liverpool Walton Salvation Army Brass Band.

	Holding / Source
16.12.2007	DB / Live

Alternative transmissions: BBC 1: 23.12.2007.

LIVING WITH DINOSAURS

A Jim Henson Productions production for Channel 4. made in association with TVS Films. Transmission details are for Channel 4. Duration: 50 minutes.

Written by Anthony Minghella; produced by Duncan Kenworthy; directed by Paul Weiland.

Michael Maloney (Lee), Juliet Stevenson (Vicky), Gregory Chisholm (Dom), Patrick Malahide (Uncle Adrian).

	Holding / Source
30.12.1989	1" / C1

LONDON BRIDGE

A Carlton production. Transmission details are for the Central region. Duration: 25 minutes.
Main regular credit(s): Theme music by Craig Armstrong; executive producer Jane Tranter; produced by Matthew Bird.

SERIES 2
A Carlton production. Transmission details are for the Carlton region.
Main regular credit(s): Series editor Pippa Harris; script editor Liza Marshall; music by Paul O'Duffy; associate producer Alexei de Keyser.
Main regular cast: With Simone Lahbib (Mary O'Connor).

	Production No	Holding / Source
16.12.1996 "Oh! and a very merry Christmas to you too"	CAR/21950/0007	DB / DBS

Written by Kelly Marshall and Chris Murray; directed by Joanna Hogg.
With Sean Francis (Jed Kemp), Ayub Khan Din (Ravi Shah), Charles Simpson (Anthony Webster), Mandana Jones (Sam Haynes), Dawn McDaniel (Allie Walker), Rosalind March (Liz Kemp), Sally Edwards (Isobel Kemp), Glen Berry (Jarvis Jones), Oliver Haden (Nick Kemp), Billy Geraghty (Cliff Lewis), Amelia Curtis (Lucy Shepherd), Kemi Baruwa (Kim Symmons), Peter McNally (Sean Stephenson), Jo-Anne Stockham (Claire Turner), Jack Waters, Sarah Wellington, Heather Imani.

18.12.1996 "Topless shots"	CAR/21950/0008	DB / DBS

With Oliver Haden (Nick Kemp), Sally Edwards (Isobel Kemp), Charles Simpson (Anthony Webster), Dawn McDaniel (Allie Walker), Kemi Baruwa (Kim Symmons), Reginald Tsiboe (Dave Symmons), Rosalind March (Liz Kemp), Peter McNally (Sean Stephenson), Jo-Anne Stockham (Claire Turner), Debra Penny, Helena Little, Sarah Wellington, Heather Imani.

23.12.1996 "We're closing. Christmas Eve or no..."	CAR/21950/0009	DB / DBS

With Charles Simpson (Anthony Webster), Rosalind March (Liz Kemp), Kemi Baruwa (Kim Symmons), Sean Francis (Jed Kemp), Dawn McDaniel (Allie Walker), Ayub Khan Din (Ravi Shah), Amelia Curtis (Lucy Shepherd), Glen Berry (Jarvis Jones), Billy Geraghty (Cliff Lewis), Mandana Jones (Sam Haynes), Jo-Anne Stockham (Claire Turner), Andrew Hilton.

24.12.1996 "Christmas wouldn't be Christmas without that scratch on the record"	CAR/21950/0010	DB / DBS

With Oliver Haden (Nick Kemp), Mandana Jones (Sam Haynes), Ayub Khan Din (Ravi Shah), Charles Simpson (Anthony Webster), Rosalind March (Liz Kemp), Sean Francis (Jed Kemp), Billy Geraghty (Cliff Lewis), Sally Edwards (Isobel Kemp), Desmond Jordan.

30.12.1996 "Nick, you're the first person that i have been with since Tim"	CAR/21950/0011	DB / DBS

With Oliver Haden (Nick Kemp), Sean Francis (Jed Kemp), Billy Geraghty (Cliff Lewis), Rosalind March (Liz Kemp), Mandana Jones (Sam Haynes), Ayub Khan Din (Ravi Shah), Charles Simpson (Anthony Webster), Amelia Curtis (Lucy Shepherd), Kemi Baruwa (Kim Symmons), Glen Berry (Jarvis Jones), Peter McNally (Sean Stephenson), Nisha K. Nayar (Shaila), Jo-Anne Stockham (Claire Turner).

31.12.1996 "A post New Year's Eve party"	CAR/21950/0012	DB / DBS

With Oliver Haden (Nick Kemp), Glen Berry (Jarvis Jones), Reginald Tsiboe (Dave Symmons), Kemi Baruwa (Kim Symmons), Ellen Thomas (Diane Symmons), Rosalind March (Liz Kemp), Billy Geraghty (Cliff Lewis), Amelia Curtis (Lucy Shepherd), Charles Simpson (Anthony Webster), Ayub Khan Din (Ravi Shah), Mandana Jones (Sam Haynes), Sally Edwards (Isobel Kemp), Sean Francis (Jed Kemp), Nisha K. Nayar (Shaila).

LONDON NIGHT OUT

A Thames Television production. Transmission details are for the ATV/Central region. Duration: 52 minutes.

Main regular performer(s): Tom O'Connor (Host).

SERIES 2

Transmission details are for the ATV midlands region.

Main regular credit(s): Script consultant Dick Hills; music directed by Alan Braden; choreography by Irving Davies; produced by Paul Stewart Laing.

Main regular performer(s): With The Ladybirds, The Irving Davies Dancers.

	VT Number	Holding / Source
24.12.1979 London Night Out Christmas Special	22086	D3 / 2"

Duration: 75 minutes.

Written by Dick Hills, Pat Finan and Frank Hughes; music by Alan Braden; designed by Jan Chaney; directed by Paul Stewart Laing.

With Petula Clark, Topo Gigio, The Nolan Sisters, Dick Franco, The Irving Davies Dancers.

SERIES 3

Transmission details are for the ATV midlands region.

Main regular credit(s): Script consultant Dick Hills; music by Alan Braden; choreography by Arlene Phillips; designed by Alex Clarke; produced and directed by Paul Stewart Laing.

Main regular performer(s): With The Ladybirds, Hot Gossip.

	Holding / Source
24.12.1980 **Christmas Special**	D3 / 2"

Written by Dick Hills and Pat Finan.

With Cilla Black, Bernie Winters, Mark Ryan, The New Black Abbots, The Dymeks.

SERIES 4

Transmission details are for the ATV/Central region.

Main regular credit(s): Written by Dick Hills, Spike Mullins and Pat Finan; music directed by Alan Braden; choreography by Geoff Richer; designed by Martyn Hébert; produced and directed by David Clark.

Main regular performer(s): With The Ladybirds, The Geoff Richer Dancers.

	Holding / Source
24.12.1981 **Christmas Special**	D3 / 2"

With Rolf Harris, Basil Brush, Jenny Lee-Wright, Choir of Winchester Cathedral.

LONDON PLAYHOUSE

A Future Productions Ltd production for Associated-Rediffusion. Transmission details are for Associated-Rediffusion.

	Holding / Source
22.12.1955 **The Man Who Liked Christmas**	J / B3

Written by Reuben Ship; settings by John Clements; produced and directed by John Moxey.

With David Kossoff (Charlie Crockett), Hartley Power (Mr Ferguson), Lew Davidson (Homer Botts), Estelle Brody (Mrs Botts), Kit Terrington (Arthur Botts), Evelyn Moore (Mother), Sheila Mackenzie (Angela Botts), Sheldon Lawrence (Frank Wilson), Brenda Dunrich (Mayor's Wife), Macdonald Parke (Mayor), Launce Maraschal (Mr Thorncliff), Peter Mannering (Conservative), Douglas Storm (Liberal), John Marquand (Socialist), Anita Sharp Bolster (Spinster), Bill Nagy (George Peterson), Jack Cunningham (Minister), John McLaren (Reporter), Neil McCallum (Newsreel Cameraman), Maurice Lane, Vernon Morris, Paddy Edwards, Martin Wyldeck.

LONDON'S BURNING

An LWT production. Transmission details are for the Central region. Duration varies - see below for details.

Main regular credit(s): Devised by Jack Rosenthal.

SERIES 1

Main regular credit(s): Executive producer Linda Agran; produced by Paul Knight.

Main regular cast: With Glen Murphy (George Green), Rupert Baker (Malcolm), Eric Deacon (Gerry), James Marcus (Tate), Sean Blowers (Hallam), Gerard Horan (Charisma), Treva Etienne (Tony), Katharine Rogers (Josie), Gil Taper Myers (David), Richard Walsh (Sicknote), James Hazeldine (Bayleaf), Mark Arden (Vaseline).

	VT Number	Holding / Source
25.12.1988 **Ding Dong Merrily**	10844	1" / V1

Duration: 78 minutes.

Seasons greetings from Blue Watch as they prepare for extra work during the festive period. Unfortunately, some of them are soon to discover that the season of goodwill extends only so far. Features a short song from AMANDA DICKENSON (Jean) and SIMON BUTTERISS (Buttons), "I Love You".

Written by Tony Hoare; directed by Les Blair.

With Ross Boatman (Kevin), Kim Clifford (Sandra), Shirley Greenwood (Maggie), Yvonne Edgell (Nancy), Helen Blizard (Marion), Amanda Dickinson (Jean), Carole Harrison (Dorothy), Paddy Navin, Doug Fisher, Charles Simon, Hazel Bainbridge, Henry Goodman, Joseph Long, Dave Atkins, Toni Palmer, Isabelle Lucas, Ruddy L. Davis, Sandra Voe, Glenn Williams, David Warwick, Simon Butteriss, Richard Syms, Peter MacKriel, Alec Bregonzi, Arthur Smith, Caroline Webster, Paul Carter, Charles Collingwood, Brenda Peters, Garrie J. Lammin, Alan Cowan, Yvonne Riley, Denise Ryan, Fred Haggerty, Trevor Cooper, Mark Barratt, Sarah Sherborne.

THE LONG CHRISTMAS DINNER

A BBC production. Transmission details are for BBC. Duration: 30 minutes.

Written by Thornton Wilder; play production by Kevin Sheldon.

Barbara Kelly (Lucia), Guy Kingsley Poynter (Roderick), Natalie Lynn (Mother Bayard), Henry Worthington (Cousin Brandon), David Major (Charles), Helen Horton (Genevieve), Anne Lewis (Leonora), Gerry Metcalfe (Roderick (The Second)), Warren Stanhope (Sam), Daphne Dyer (Lucia (The Second)).

	Holding / Source
27.12.1949	NR / Live

THE LONG CHRISTMAS DINNER (continued)　　　　　　　　　　　　　　　　　　　　British Christmas Television Guide

LOOK - MIKE YARWOOD!

A BBC production for BBC 1. Transmission details are for BBC 1. Usual duration: 30 minutes.
Main regular performer(s):　Mike Yarwood (Various roles).

SERIES 3
Main regular credit(s):　　　Written by Eric Davidson; music directed by Alan Braden; produced and directed by James Moir.
Main regular performer(s):　With Peter Noone, Cheryl Kennedy, The Breakaways.

　　　Holding / Source
25.12.1973　**The Mike Yarwood Christmas Show**　　　　　　　　　　　　　　　　　　　DB-D3 / 2"
Designed by Ian Rawnsley; executive producer John Ammonds.
With Eddie Waring, Cheryl Kennedy, The Ladybirds.
Peter Noone and The Breakaways are not in this special.

　　　Holding / Source
25.12.1974　**The Mike Yarwood Christmas Show**　　　　　　　　　　　　　　　　　　　DB-D3 / 2"
Duration: 40 minutes.
Written by Eric Davidson; music directed by Alan Braden; designed by Ian Watson; produced and directed by John Ammonds.
With Max Bygraves, Jacqueline Stanbury, Larry Martyn, Sue Bond.

　　　Holding / Source
26.12.1975　**The Mike Yarwood Christmas Show**　　　　　　　　　　　　　　　　　　　DB-D3 / 2"
Duration: 45 minutes.
Written by Eric Davidson; music directed by Alan Braden; designed by Bryan Ellis; assistant producer Alan Boyd; produced and directed by John Ammonds.
With Lulu, Reflections, Margaret John, Royce Mills, Jacqueline Stanbury, The Ladybirds.

LOOK ALIVE

A Granada production. Transmission details are for the ATV midlands region. Duration: 25 minutes.
'Music Is What It's All About' All sorts of music, pop old and new, pop people, fashion ideas and books about the current scene. Every week Gordon will be looking into some music of the past.
Main regular credit(s):　　　Research David Wason; designed by Taff Batley; produced by Muriel Young; directed by Terry Steel.
Main regular performer(s):　Stephanie De Sykes (Host), Gordon Bennett (Host), Him and Us.

　　　　　　　　　　　　　　　　　　　　　　　　　　　　Production No　　　　　　　　　Holding / Source
23.12.1975　　　　　　　　　　　　　　　　　　　　　　　P856/11　　　　　　　　　　　　DB / 2"
Dana woos the weathermen with her new single It's Going to be a Cold, Cold Christmas, as Stephanie and Gordon swing you into the festive season.
With Dana, Sheer Elegance, New Edition, Teeside Fettlers.

LOOK AROUND

An ATV Midlands production. Transmission details are for the ATV midlands region. Duration varies - see below for details.

SERIES 2

　　　Holding / Source
15.12.1961　**Christmas**　　　　　　　　　　　　　　　　　　　　　　　　　　　　　　B1 / 40

SERIES 3

　　　Holding / Source
31.12.1963　**Retrospect 1963**　　　　　　　　　　　　　　　　　　　　　　　　　　　B1 / 40
Duration: 25 minutes.
Around 20 minutes survives.

LOOK WHO'S TALKING

A Border Television production. Transmission details are for border region. Usual duration: 25 minutes.
Main regular credit(s):　　　Produced by Derek Batey.
Main regular performer(s):　Derek Batey (Host).

SERIES 1

　　　Holding / Source
26.12.1973　**Ken Dodd Says Look Who's Talking**　　　　　　　　　　　　　　　　　　　DB|n / 2"
Duration: 50 minutes.
Alternative transmissions: ATV: 26.12.1973.
With Ken Dodd.
This edition was networked across the whole of ITV.

SERIES 4
Main regular credit(s):　　　Designed by John Henderson.

　　　Holding / Source
24.12.1974　　　　　　　　　　　　　　　　　　　　　　　　　　　　　　　　　　　　　B / 2"
Duration: 50 minutes.
Directed by Norman Fraser.

LOOK WHO'S TALKING

Derek Batey introduces clips from the earlier series.

Most of this season looks to have been shown around the ITV network on the same day as the Border transmissions, but with most regions taking it at lunchtime and only Border giving it an evening slot.

	Holding / Source
29.12.1977 **Look Who's Talking Special**	J / 2"

Duration: 40 minutes.

Christmas is a time for reminiscences in good company. Which is exactly what Derek Batey offers with a selection of highlights from his interviews with showbusiness stars.

Among those you meet on film are: Little and Large, Tom O'Connor, Noele Gordon, Dana, The Bachelors, Sandy Powell , Jimmy Jewel, Frank Carson, Alan Stewart, Peter Goodwright, Bobby Bennett and Edmund Hockridge.

Designed by John M. Henderson; produced by Derek Batey; directed by Norman Fraser.

With Norman Collier.

	Holding / Source
28.12.1979	J / 2"

Designed by Ian Reed; directed by Harry King.

With Vince Hill.

There are many further seasons of this programme which we have yet to research.

LOOK, STRANGER

A BBC Various production for BBC 2. Transmission details are for BBC 2. Duration: 25 minutes.

SERIES 2

	Holding / Source
22.12.1971 **Reindeer Man**	C1 / C1

Alt.Title(s): *Mikel Utsi - Reindeer Man (repeat title)*

For 800 years reindeer, which once flourished in the Highlands of Scotland, were not seen in this country. It toox MIKEL UTSI a - Laplander, to reintroduce them. In this week's programme he tells of the trials and tribulations of his efforts during the past 20 years.

Produced by Bridget Winter.

With Mikel Utsi.

The edition shown on 24.11.1971 was a repeat of Together They Made It On The Euston Road.

LOOKING FORWARD TO CHRISTMAS

An Anglia production. Transmission details are for the Anglia region. Duration: 5 minutes.

A carol by the choir of Dunstable Priory Church.

Dunstable Priory Church Choir.

	Holding / Source
24.12.1973	J / 2"

Closedown film.

LOOKS FAMILIAR

A Thames Television production. Transmission details are for the ATV midlands region. Duration: 25 minutes.

Main regular credit(s):	Devised by Denis Gifford.
Main regular performer(s):	Denis Norden (Presenter).

SERIES 4

Main regular credit(s):	Produced by David Clark; directed by Anthony Parker.

	Holding / Source
27.12.1974	D3 / 2"

Denis and his guests turn back the clock to Christmas in the Thirties and Forties, and later in the show Douglas Byng will explain the art of playing pantomime dames.

Directed by Daphne Shadwell.

With Margaret Lockwood, Tommy Trinder, Jack Douglas, Douglas Byng.

SERIES 8

Main regular credit(s):	Designed by Graham Guest; produced by David Clark; directed by Anthony Parker.

	Holding / Source
26.12.1978 **Boxing Day Special**	D3 / 2"

Duration: 35 minutes.

With Frankie Howerd, Beryl Reid, Alan Whicker.

LOST CHRISTMAS

A BBC production for BBC 1. Transmission details are for BBC 1.

Eddie Izzard stars in a modern fairy tale about an enigmatic man who wakes up on a Manchester street on Christmas Eve spouting obscure facts and acting strangely. He discovers he has the remarkable power to find the lost - whether it's a bracelet or a loved one. Central to the story is young lad Goose (Larry Mills) and through him we're introduced to four people who are apparently unconnected, yet who have all been touched by tragedy or guilt and whose lives are intertwined.

Written by John Hay and Dave Logan; produced by Elliot Jenkins; directed by John Hay.

Eddie Izzard (Anthony), Jason Flemyng (Frank), Geoffrey Palmer (Doctor Clarence), Christine Bottomley (Helen), Sorcha Cusack (Nan), Steven Mackintosh (Henry), Larry Mills (Goose), Connie Hyde (Linda), Brett Fancy (Paul), Adlyn Ross (Lal), Chloe Newsome (Alice), Jason Watkins (Noel Boble), Jessie Clayton (Gemma), Libbi Rubens (Milly).

	Holding / Source
18.12.2011	HD/DB / HDC

THE LOST INVITATION

An Associated-Rediffusion production. Transmission details are for Associated-Rediffusion.

	Holding / Source
21.12.1959	NR / Live

THE LOST WORLD

A BBC production for BBC 1. made in association with Arts & Entertainment Network / RTL. Transmission details are for BBC 1. Duration: 75 minutes.

Main regular credit(s): Adapted by Tony Mulholland and Adrian Hodges; based on a novel by Sir Arthur Conan Doyle; executive producers Kate Harwood, Jane Tranter and Delia Fine; co-produced by Tim Haines; produced by Christopher Hall; directed by Stuart Orme.

Main regular cast: Bob Hoskins (Challenger), James Fox (Summerlee), Tom Ward (Lord Roxton), Matthew Rhys (Edward Malone), Elaine Cassidy (Agnes Cluny), Peter Falk (Theo Kerr), Robert Hardy (Illingworth), Joanna Page (Gladys), Tim Healy (McArdie), Tessa Peake-Jones (Mrs Summerlee), Nathaniel Lees (Chief), Tamati Te Nohotu (Achille), Nicole Whippy (Maree), Inia Maxwell (Indian Leader), Tom Goodman-Hill (Arthur Hare), Malcolm Shields (Lead Ape), Paul Joseph (Ape 2), Jane Howie (Ape 3), Mason West (Ape 4), Julia Walshaw (Ape 5), Michael Bertenshaw (Reporter At Docks), Jasper Jacob (Stuttgart Man), David Quilter (Businessman 1), Terry Mortimer (Businessman 2), Brian Abbott (Reporter 1), Dominic Rowan (Reporter 2), Laurence Kennedy (Angry Man).

Commissioned by BBC.

		Holding / Source
25.12.2001	**Episode 1**	DB / C15W
26.12.2001	**Episode 2**	DB / C15W

LOVE THY NEIGHBOUR

A Thames Television production. Transmission details are for the ATV midlands region. Duration: 25 minutes.

Main regular credit(s): Created by Vince Powell and Harry Driver.

Main regular cast: Jack Smethurst (Eddie Booth), Rudolph Walker (Bill Reynolds), Nina Baden-Semper (Barbie Reynolds), Kate Williams (Joan Booth).

SERIES 4

	VT Number	Holding / Source
31.12.1973 "Working on New Year's Eve"	8653	D3 / 2"

Duration: 40 minutes.
With Keith Marsh (Jacko), Paul Luty (Nobby), Peter Jones, Tommy Godfrey, Tim Barrett, Harry Littlewood.

SERIES 8

Main regular cast: With Keith Marsh (Jacko), Tommy Godfrey (Arthur), Paul Luty (Nobby).

	VT Number	Holding / Source
25.12.1975 "Christmas spirit"	12276	D3 / 2"

The Booth household is busy preparing for Christmas. The Booth household, that is, minus Eddie, who is otherwise engaged with Christmas "spirit" which means Joan must cope alone. But when wayward Eddie returns to his usual verbal chastisement, his punishment is increased by his dreams of Christmas dinner in which he has pride of place as the main course!

Written by Sid Colin; designed by David Richens; produced and directed by Anthony Parker.

With Diana King.

LOVEJOY

A BBC production for BBC 1. made in association with Witzend. Transmission details are for BBC 1. Duration varies - see below for details.

Main regular credit(s): Created by Ian La Frenais; based on novels by Jonathan Gash; theme music by Denis King; music by Denis King.

Main regular cast: Ian McShane (Lovejoy), Dudley Sutton (Tinker Dill).

Made in association with Barrandov Film Studios / McShane Productions / Witzend.
Credits: Associate producer Tony Redston; executive producers Allan McKeown and Tony Charles; produced by Emma Hayter.
Cast: With Chris Jury (Eric), Phyllis Logan (Lady Jane Felsham).

	Holding / Source
26.12.1992 **The Prague Sun**	DB-D3 / C1S

Duration: 93 minutes.
Written by Dick Clement and Ian La Frenais; directed by Geoffrey Sax.

With Peter Vaughan, Dinah Sheridan, Leonie Mellinger, Donald Pleasence, Malgoscha Gebel, Brian McGrath, William Chubb, Irène Prador, Lloyd Maguire, Stanislav Zindulka, Rudolf Jelinek, Rosie Kerslake, Miranda Forbes, Katerina Bittmanova, Sona Vesela.

LOVEJOY (continued)

SERIES 5
Made in association with McShane Productions.
Main regular credit(s): Associate producer Paul Richmond; executive producers Allan McKeown and Tony Charles; produced by Jo Wright.
Main regular cast: With Chris Jury (Eric Catchpole (Until 10.10.1993)), Malcolm Tierney (Gimbert), Phyllis Logan (Lady Jane Felsham (Until 12.09.1993)), Caroline Langrishe (Charlotte (19.09.1993 onwards)), Diane Parish (Beth (26.09.1993 onwards)).

	Holding / Source
27.12.1993 **The Lost Colony**	DB-D3 / C1S

Duration: 95 minutes.
Written by Dick Clement and Ian La Frenais; directed by Geoffrey Sax.

With Maggie Ollerenshaw (Kate Henshaw), Ken Kercheval, Kate Vernon, Barbara Barrie, John Gielgud, Alex Van, Daniel Greene, Rick Walker, Hilary Mason, Barbara Young, Arthur Cox, Richard Syms, David Arlen, Philip Loch, Don Bland, David Fonteno, Crystal Grey, Pearl Jones, John Bennes, Ed Lillard, Margeurite Ayers, Tom Hull, Patricia Gray, Rand Courtney, Kate Finlayson, Don Tilley, Kenneth Sprunt, Pat Miller, Lucille McIntyre.

LOVING MISS HATTO

A BBC production for BBC 1. Transmission details are for BBC 1. Duration: 90 minutes.

In essence a love story, it tells of an "ordinary" married couple who harbour great ambitions but find themselves knocked back by life. However, when fate takes a hand, they end up orchestrating one of the greatest hoaxes in classical music, all from their modest bungalow in Hertfordshire.

Written by Victoria Wood; produced by Radford Neville; directed by Aisling Walsh.

Alfred Molina (Barrie), Francesca Annis (Joyce), Rory Kinnear (Young Barrie), Maimie McCoy (Young Joyce), Phoebe Nicholls (Mrs Hatto), Tony Turner (Mr Hatto), Sarah Woodward (Birdy), Eve Matheson (Pilks), Nell Wiliiams (Young Birdy), Zenobia Voegele-Downing (Young Pilks), Ned Dennehy (Philip), Nicholas Woodeson (Erich), Nicholas Rowe (James), Patrick Joseph Byrnes (Larry), Jane Brennan (Miss Guisely), Stephen Cromwell (Young Erich).

	Holding / Source
23.12.2012	HD/DB / HDC

LULU'S BIG SHOW

An Indigo Productions production for BBC 2. Transmission details are for BBC 2. Duration: 55 minutes.
Musical show recorded at the Tramway in Glasgow, hosted by Lulu and including some of her favourite hits.
Produced by Kim Turbeville; directed by Pedro Romhanyi and Gavin Taylor.
Lulu.

	Holding / Source
31.12.1993	DB-D3 / D3S

LUNCH BOX

An ATV production. Transmission details are for the ATV midlands region. Duration varies - see below for details.
Lunchtime magazine programme with band and both resident and guest singers.
Duration: 28 minutes.

	Holding / Source
25.12.1959 **Christmas Box**	J / Live

Duration: 50 minutes.
Settings by Nevil Dickin; produced by Jack Barton.
With Noele Gordon (Hostess), Jerry Allen and his TV Trio, Roy Edwards, Eula Parker, Boyer and Ravel, The Polka Dots.

26.12.1960	J / Live

Duration: 50 minutes.

25.12.1961 **Christmas Box**	J / Live

Duration: 47 minutes.

25.12.1962 **Christmas Box**	J / Live

Duration: 48 minutes.
Settings by Don Davidson; produced by John Pullen.
With Noele Gordon (Hostess), Eula Parker, Peter Elliott, Roy Edwards, Jerry Allen and his TV Trio and Orchestra, Alan Grahame, Lionel Rubin, Ken Ingarfield, Frank Ifield, Dorothy Ward, The Polka Dots.
Later this same day, Noele, Jerry Allan amd Lionel Rubin also appeared in GREETINGS FROM THE FORCES (q.v.).

25.12.1963 **Christmas Box**	J / Live

Duration: 48 minutes.
Settings by Elizabeth Dorrity; produced by John Pullen; directed by Brian Bell.
With Noele Gordon (Hostess), Eula Parker, Roy Edwards, Peter Elliott, Jerry Allen and his TV Trio, Lionel Rubin, Alan Grahame, Ken Ingarfield, The Jerry Allen Big Band.

27.12.1963 **An Old-Age Pensioners' Christmas Party**	J / Live

Settings by Elizabeth Dorrity; produced and directed by John Pullen.
With Noele Gordon (Hostess), Jerry Allen and his TV Trio, Eula Parker, Roy Edwards, Peter Elliott, Clarkson Rose.

M R JAMES AT CHRISTMAS (RADIO)

A BBC production for BBC Radio 4. Transmission details are for BBC Radio 4. Duration: 15 minutes.
Based on stories by M. R. James; produced and directed by Gemma Jenkins.
Derek Jacobi (M. R. James).

	Holding / Source
24.12.2007 **Oh, Whistle, And I'll Come To You, My Lad**	DA /

With Jamie Glover (Professor Parkins), Nicholas Boulton (Colonel Wilson), Rachel Atkins (Mrs Driver), Ben Onwukwe (Professor Rogers).

25.12.2007 **The Tractate Middoth**	DA /

With Joseph Millson (David Garrett), Joannah Tincey (Lucy), John Rowe (Mr Eldred), Sam Dale (M Thompson).

26.12.2007 **Lost Hearts**	DA /

With James D'Arcy (Stephen), Sophie Roberts (Jane), Jordan Clarke (Young Stephen), Peter Marinker (Mr Abney), Katy Cavanagh (Mrs Bunch).

27.12.2007 **The Rose Garden**	DA /

With Anton Lesser (George), Carolyn Pickles (Mary), Susan Jameson (Miss Wilkins), Ben Crowe (Jim), Simon Treves (Judge Nashe).

28.12.2007 **Number 13**	DA /

With Julian Rhind-Tutt (Doctor Anderson), Jan De Lokuwitz (Herr Lund), Simon Treves (Herr Scavenius), Ben Onwukwe (The Voice).

M. H. & 5P

A BBC Manchester production for BBC 2. Transmission details are for BBC 2. Duration varies - see below for details.
Main regular credit(s):   Written by Mike Harding; produced and directed by Barry Bevins.
Main regular performer(s): Mike Harding, Fivepenny Piece.

	Holding / Source
23.12.1978 **Christmas With Mike Harding And The Fivepenny Piece**	DB-D3 / 2"

Duration: 40 minutes.

M.R. JAMES' GHOST STORIES

Alternative/Working Title(s): CLASSIC GHOST STORIES
A BBC Children's Department production for BBC 2. Transmission details are for BBC 2. Duration: 15 minutes.
Narrated by Robert Powell; adapted by David Bell; based on novels by M. R. James; designed by Austin Ruddy; produced by Angela Beeching; directed by David Bell.

	Holding / Source
25.12.1986 **The Mezzotint**	DB / 1"

With Jeremy Roberts (Williams), Norman Bacon (Binks), Michael Richmond (Nisbet).

26.12.1986 **The Ash Tree**	DB / 1"

With Cameron Miller (Reverend Crome), Barry Summerford (Late Sir Mathew Fell), Arthur Nightingale (Sir Richard Fell).

28.12.1986 **Wailing Well**	DB / 1"
29.12.1986 **Oh, Whistle, And I'll Come To You, My Lad**	DB / 1"
30.12.1986 **The Rose Garden**	DB / 1"

With Ken Parry (Judge), Jakson Raab (Boy), Arthur Nightingale (Mr Anstruther).

M.R. JAMES GHOST WRITER

A BBC production for BBC 2. Transmission details are for BBC 2. Duration: 60 minutes.
Mark Gatiss explores the life of the devout Anglican bachelor whose supernatural tales still terrify readers more than a century after they were penned. To help reveal the writer's inspirations, Mark visits James's childhood home in Suffolk, Eton College, King's College, Cambridge and France.
Executive producer Michael Poole; produced by John Das.
Mark Gatiss (Presenter).

	Holding / Source
25.12.2013	HD/DB / HDC

MAD MOVIES

A Mitchell Monkhouse Eyeline production for Comex Films Ltd. made in association with De Lane Lea / Mitchell Monkhouse Associates. Transmission details are for the ABC midlands region.
Main regular credit(s):   Created by Bob Monkhouse; written by Bob Monkhouse; research Philip Jenkinson; music by Malcolm Mitchell; associate producer Raymond Rohauer; executive producer Henry Howard; directed by Jeff Inman.
Main regular cast: Bob Monkhouse (Presenter).

	Holding / Source
24.12.1966 **Christmas Mad Movies**	J /

An ABC production. Duration: 40 minutes.
Designed by Mike Perry; directed by Keith Beckett.

This one edition is not mentioned in any of Bob's paperwork so we think it might have actually been commissioned and made by ABC themselves rather than being an independent production. The TV listings magazines mention Charlie Chaplin, Abbott and Costello, Laurel and Hardy, Jerry Lewis, Jacques Tati and Michael Bentine which also suggests different fare to the usual.

The synopses included here are Bob's own. We have tried to work out the correct transmission dates for the episodes in these three series but at times it has come down to educated guesswork as the synopses in the ITV listings magazines are often vague. Where there are no tx dates it isn't that we think the edition remains unshown just that we really don't have a clue.

THE MAD O'HARAS

A BBC production. Transmission details are for BBC. Duration: 30 minutes.

Main regular credit(s): Adapted by Pamela Brown; based on a book by Patricia Lynch; produced and directed by Richard West.

Main regular cast: Jacqueline Ryan (Grania O'Hara).

	Holding / Source
18.11.1958 **Christmas At Kilvaragh**	J /

With Pauline Letts (Eily O'Hara), Gladys Young (Mrs O'Hara), Diana Lambert (Judy O'Hara), James Neylin (Phil O'Hara), John Hussey (Terry O'Hara), John Colin (Jer O'Hara), Sean Barrett, John Kelly, Neil McCarthy, Liam Gaffney, Shay Gorman, Dermot Kelly.

THE MAGIC CIRCLE CHRISTMAS BOX

A Thames Television production. Transmission details are for the Thames Television region. Duration: 40 minutes.

From King George's Hall, London, DAVID HAMILTON introduces this annual children's show featuring Magic Circle stars old and new. Were you given any conjuring tricks for Christmas? If so, look in this afternoon and see how the experts do them.

Main regular credit(s): Directed by Jim Pople.

Main regular performer(s): David Hamilton (Host).

	Holding / Source
01.01.1969	J /
07.01.1969	J /

With Michael Biley (Compere), The Leslie Soden Trio.

THE MAGIC FLUTE

A Southern Television production. Transmission details are for the ATV midlands region. Duration: 100 minutes.

Written by Amadeus Mozart; designed by David Hockney; produced and directed by Dave Heather.

Leo Gocke (Tamino), Felicity Lott (Pamina), Benjamin Luxon (Papgeno), Elizabeth Conquet (Papagena), May Sandoz (Queen of The Night), Thomas Thomaschke (Sarastro), Willard White (Speaker), John Fryatt (Monostatos), Teresa Cahill (First Lady), Patricia Parker (Second Lady), Fiona Kimm (Third Lady), Kate Flowers (First Genie), Lindsay John (Second Genie), Elizabeth Stokes (Third Genie), Richard Berkeley-Stokes (First Priest), Neil McKinnon (First Armed Man), John Rath (Second Priest / Second Armed Man), London Philharmonic Choir, The Glyndebourne Chorus.

	Holding / Source
30.12.1978	DB / 2"

English sub-titles by Spike Hughes.

THE MAGIC ROUNDABOUT

A BBC production for BBC 1. Transmission details are for BBC 1. Duration: 4 minutes.

Main regular credit(s): Created by Serge Danot; written by Eric Thompson; produced and directed by Ursula Eason.

Main regular cast: Eric Thompson (Narrator).

SERIES 1

	Holding / Source
22.12.1965 **Roundabout Christmas**	B1 / B1

SERIES 4

	Holding / Source
24.04.1974 **Letter To Father Christmas**	C1 / C1
19.12.1974 **Letter To Father Christmas**	C1 / C1

MAGICAL MYSTERY TOUR

An Apple Films production for BBC 1. Transmission details are for BBC 1. Duration: 50 minutes.

Devised by The Beatles; written by The Beatles; music by Paul McCartney, John Lennon, George Harrison and Ringo Starr; produced by Denis O'Dell; directed by The Beatles.

The Beatles (Themselves), Jan Carson (Stripper), George Claydon (Photographer), Ivor Cutler (Mr Bloodvessel), Shirley Evans (Accordionist), Nat Jackley (Rubber Man), Nichola (Little Girl), Jessie Robins (Ringo's Aunt), Derek Royle (Jolly Jimmy), Victor Spinetti (Army Sergeant), Mandy Weet (Hostess), Maggie Wright (Starlet), Bonzo Dog Doo Dah Band.

	Holding / Source
26.12.1967	C3 / C3

Apple hold the 35mm print.

MAGPIE

A Thames Television production. Transmission details are for the ATV midlands region. Duration: 25 minutes.

SERIES 1

	Holding / Source
31.12.1968	R1 / 2"

EXPLOSIONS/HELICOPTERS/XMAS/WATER-SKI FIREWALK

SERIES 3

Main regular credit(s):	Produced by Sue Turner.

Holding / Source

22.12.1970   J / 2"

Christmas is only three days away and Sue, Pete and Tony make their last appearance before flinging themselves into the festivities. Today they come up with some special Christmas surprises. Murgatroyd - one bird who won't end up on the table - has promised to make an eggstraordinary contribution to the fun.
Directed by Robert Reed, David Hodgson and Diana Potter.
With Susan Stranks (Presenter), Pete Brady (Presenter), Tony Bastable (Presenter).

SERIES 4

Main regular credit(s):	Produced by Sue Turner.
Main regular cast:	With Susan Stranks (Presenter), Tony Bastable (Presenter), Douglas Rae (Presenter).

Holding / Source

21.12.1971   J / 2"

Early Christmas presents and Magpie Christmas Appeal.
Directed by Diana Potter, John Russell and David Hodgson.

28.12.1971   J / 2"

A Georgian Christmas at Woburn Abbey.
Directed by John Russell.
With Duke of Bedford, Duchess of Bedford, Peter Fairley.

SERIES 7

Holding / Source

24.12.1974   J / 2"

SERIES 8

Main regular credit(s):	Produced by Tim Jones.
Main regular cast:	With Jenny Hanley (Presenter), Douglas Rae (Presenter), Mick Robertson (Presenter).

Holding / Source

23.12.1975   J / 2"

Christmas Day around Britain.
Directed by Audrey Starrett, Peter Yolland and Richard Mervyn.

SERIES 10

Main regular credit(s):	Produced by Tim Jones.
Main regular cast:	With Jenny Hanley, Tommy Boyd, Mick Robertson.

Holding / Source

23.12.1977   DB / 2"

SERIES 12

Main regular cast:	With Jenny Hanley, Mick Robertson, Tommy Boyd.

Holding / Source

28.12.1979   DB / 2"

Jenny, Mick and Tommy untie Christmas parcel of facts and fun.
Produced by Tim Jones; directed by Peter Yolland, Michael Kent and Ian Little-Smith.
With Jenny Hanley (Presenter), Mick Robertson (Presenter), Tommy Boyd (Presenter).

MAID MARIAN AND HER MERRY MEN

A BBC production for BBC 1. Transmission details are for BBC 1. Duration: 25 minutes.

Main regular credit(s):	Written by Tony Robinson; produced by Richard Callanan; directed by David Bell.
Main regular cast:	Kate Lonergan (Marian), Wayne Morris (Robin), Danny John-Jules (Barrington), Howard Lew Lewis (Rabies), Mike Edmonds (Little Ron), Forbes Collins (King John), Tony Robinson (Sheriff).

SERIES 3

Main regular credit(s):	Music by David Chilton and Nick Russell-Pavier; designed by Chris Robilliard, Robert Foster and Frederic Evard; production associate Alison Law; production manager Ken Robertson.
Main regular cast:	With Mark Billingham (Gary), David Lloyd (Graeme), Ramsay Gilderdale (Guy Of Gisborne).

Holding / Source

24.12.1993   **Maid Marian And Much The Mini-Mart Manager's Son**   DB-D3 / D3S

With Philip Wright (Much), Siobhan Fogarty (Rotten Rose), Hilary Mason (Gladys), Robin Chandler (Snooker), Josh Maguire, Wayne Fowkes.

MAIGRET

Alternative/Working Title(s): INSPECTOR MAIGRET / TALES OF INSPECTOR MAIGRET

A BBC production. made in association with Winwell Productions. Transmission details are for BBC. Duration: 55 minutes.

Main regular credit(s):   Based on novels by Georges Simenon; theme music by Ron Grainer.

Main regular cast: Rupert Davies (Chief Inspector Maigret), Ewen Solon (Lucas), Neville Jason (Lapointe), Victor Lucas (Torrance).

SERIES 2

Main regular credit(s):   Script editor Donald Bull; associate producer Bill Luckwell; executive producer Andrew Osborn.

Holding / Source

26.12.1961 **A Crime For Christmas** R1 /

Adapted by Margot Bennett; produced and directed by Campbell Logan.

With Carla Challoner, Helen Shingler, Heather Chasen, Howard Douglas, Christopher Steele, Alan Rolfe, Brian Hayes, George Coulouris, Esma Cannon, Jonathan Field, Barry Foster, Jenny Laird, Toke Townley, Joyce Donaldson.

Rupert Davies appeared as Maigret on stage in "Maigret And The Lady" in 1965.
See also: PLAY OF THE MONTH (BBC) / SUNDAY NIGHT THEATRE (BBC)

MAKE A DATE

A Yorkshire Television production. Transmission details are for the Central region. Duration: 25 minutes.

A light-hearted celebration of New Year's Days, past and present.

Designed by Robert Scott; produced by John Bartlett; directed by Terry Henebery.

Anne Diamond (Presenter), Nick Owen (Presenter), John Wells (Denis Thatcher), Sarah Brightman, Barbara Dickson, Andrew O'Connor, Jimmy Savile, The Stranglers.

Holding / Source

01.01.1988 **(pilot)** 1" / 1"

MAKING FACES

A BBC production for BBC 2. Transmission details are for BBC 2.

Main regular credit(s):   Written by Michael Frayn; produced and directed by Gareth Gwenlan.

Main regular cast: Eleanor Bron (Zoya), Tim Preece (Stuart).

Holding / Source

09.10.1975 **Packaging Industry Convention 1963 : A Christmas Box** J / 2"

Duration: 29 minutes.

With David Swift, Gwen Nelson, Paul Besterman, Aimée Delamain, Ruby Head, Nigel Greaves, Deborah Crosbie, Earl Rhodes, Ian Hoare, Claire McLellan, Denis Carey.

MAN ALIVE

A BBC production for BBC 2. Transmission details are for BBC 2. Duration varies - see below for details.

Main regular credit(s):   Programme editors Desmond Wilcox and Bill Morton.

Holding / Source

27.12.1968 **Panto** C1SEQ / 2"

Reporters Jim Douglas Henry, Jeremy James, John Percival, Desmond Wilcox and Harold Williamson; produced by Adam Clapham.

MAN DOWN

Commissioned by Channel 4. Transmission details are for Channel 4. Duration: 25 minutes.

Written by Greg Davies, Sian Harries and Stephen Morrison; music by Chris Egan and Bob Bradley; designed by Richard Drew; executive producers James Taylor, Richard Allen-Turner, Jon Thoday and Toby Stevens; series producer Spencer Millman; directed by Matt Lipsey.

Greg Davies (Dan), Rik Mayall (Dad), Roisin Conaty (Jo), Mike Wozniak (Brian), Gwyneth Powell (Mum).

Holding / Source

25.12.2013 **Christmas Special** HD/DB / HDC

A terrifying Yuletide tradition, visited upon him by his psychotic father, and Scrooge 3000 - a school play set in space - are but two of the Christmas challenges likely to keep the hapless Dan on a downward curve.

With Jeany Spark (Emma), Ashley Maguire (Shakira), Brian Murphy (Mr Field-Williams), Madeleine Harris (Karen), Daniel Jones (Alan), Alfie Davies (Dennis), George Bothamley (Maurice), George Hill (Tiny Toby 2.0), Chloe Symonds (Maureen), Kassius Carey-Johnson (Morgan), Angela Curran (Vicar).

MAN OF PARTS

A Scottish Television production. Transmission details are for the Scottish Television region. Duration: 25 minutes.

John Buchan-The First Lord Tweedsmuir - was born 100 years ago. Buchan was the Scottish author of unforgettable adventure stories such as The 39 Steps and Greenmantle, featuring the upperclass hero Richard Hannay. But Buchan wasn't just the writer of adventure yarns.

He was also a Governor-General of Canada, an M.P., and a man who, some say, might have stopped World War II with a special "peace plan" he devised with President Roosevelt. Buchan's also been called a vastly under-rated literary talent-the best writer since Robert Louis Stevenson. But his critics have labelled him a social climber, a snob, and a racist. So who was the real John Buchan? In the centenary year of his birth Scottish Television have produced a documentary analysing the man through his family, his friends, and his critics.

Sound Clive Wood and Gary Coleman; film editor Iain Mackenzie; executive producer Russell Galbraith; directed by Archie McArthur.

Jim Manson (Reporter).

The Life of John Buchan

Holding / Source

30.12.1975 J / C1

MAN OF PARTS

MAN OF THE DECADE

An ATV production. Transmission details are for the ATV midlands region. Duration: 52 minutes.

Screened on commercial televison in colour on the penultimate day of the 1960s, three eminent people were asked to choose the person felt to have been the man of the decade. Sociologist and anthropologist Dr Desmond Morris chose John Lennon, the broadcaster Alistair Cooke selected John F Kennedy, and the writer Mary McCarthy opted for Ho Chi Minh. Each made a 20 minute documentary to support their choice, the resulting one hour of material forming 'Man of the Decade'. The interview with John Lennon and Yoko Ono took place on 2nd December 1969 as they strolled through the grounds of Tittenhurst Park, their estate near Ascot in Berkshire. Topics discussed by Lennon include youth culture, Vietnam, peace, love, LSD, the establishment and Woodstock. He also personally selected the Beatles archive clips featured in this section of the programme.

Desmond Morris, John Lennon, Alistair Cooke, Mary McCarthy, Yoko Ono.

	Holding / Source
30.12.1969	DB|n / 2"

MAN ON THE MOON

A BBC production for BBC 2. Transmission details are for BBC 2. Duration: 105 minutes.

The story of Project Apollo, the US space programme, from the early days of the space race with the Soviet Union to the first moon landing 25 years ago in 1969. Featuring interviews with astronauts and ground staff, plus spectacular and rarely seen archive film.

Introduced by Neil Armstrong; executive producer Clare Paterson; produced by Jenny Abbott and Richard Bradley.

	Holding / Source
26.12.1994	DB-D3 / D3S

MANHUNT

An LWT production. Transmission details are for the ATV midlands region. Duration: 51 minutes.

Main regular credit(s):   Created by Rex Firkin; theme music by Ludwig Van Beethoven; executive producer Rex Firkin.

	Production No	Holding / Source
20.02.1970 **A Different Kind Of War**	9D/01184	D2 / 2"

It's Christmas Eve. Vincent takes Jimmy and Nina to shelter at a farmhouse. At once they realise they've walked into a bizarre and sinister situation...

Written by Jonathan Hales; story consultant Andrew Brown; designed by John Emery; directed by Rex Firkin.

With Alfred Lynch (Jimmy), Peter Barkworth (Vincent), Cyd Hayman (Nina), Moira Redmond, Julian Glover.

MANILOW'S CHRISTMAS MAGIC

A BBC Birmingham production for BBC 1. Transmission details are for BBC 1. Duration: 50 minutes.

Produced and directed by John G. Smith.

Barry Manilow (Host).

	Holding / Source
28.12.1984	DB / 1"

A MANY SPLINTERED THING

A Lucky Dog production for BBC 1. Transmission details are for BBC 1. Duration: 30 minutes.

Main regular credit(s):   Written by Geoff Deane.

Main regular cast: Alan Davies (Russel Boyd).

	Holding / Source
25.12.1998 [pilot]	DB / DBSW

The last thing you need as a married man is to wake up naked and hungover next to another woman. But when Russel meets Elly, somehow good intentions go out the window.

Music by Keith Miller; executive producer Danielle Lux; produced by Geoff Deane and Kenton Allen; directed by Paul Harrison.

With Kate Ashfield (Elly Rawsthorn), Victor McGuire (Luis Banks), Paul Trussell (Alistair Cranwell), Kate Isitt (Susanna Boyd), Steve Robling, Vanessa Feltz.

In 2001 Lucky Dog made a US pilot for the Paramount Channel.

MARKHEIM

A Scottish Television production. Transmission details are for the ATV midlands region. Duration: 25 minutes.

It is Christmas Day in 1870 in the shop of an antique dealer in Edinburgh. The dealer admits Markheim, a dissolute young man. An argument develops which has tragic consequences...
   Special music and sound effects are by Frank Spedding.

Adapted by Tom Wright; based on a story by Robert Louis Stevenson; music by Frank Spedding; designed by Peter Alexander; executive producer Liam Hood; directed by Tina Wakerell.

Derek Jacobi (Markheim), Julian Glover (The Stranger), Paul Curran (The Dealer), Sally Kinghorn (Maid), Willie Joss (Caller).

	Holding / Source
24.12.1974	DB / 2"

MARTHA JAC A SIANCO

A Boomerang production for S4C. Transmission details are for S4C. Duration: 100 minutes.

Executive producer Lona Llewelyn Davies.

	Holding / Source
25.12.2008	HD/DB / HD/DB

MARTI CAINE

A BBC production for BBC 2. Transmission details are for BBC 2. Duration varies - see below for details.

Main regular performer(s): Marti Caine (Host).

SERIES 4

Main regular credit(s): Music directed by Alyn Ainsworth; choreography by Geoffrey Richer; produced and directed by Brian Whitehouse.

Holding / Source

27.12.1982 — DB-D3 / 2"
Duration: 50 minutes.
Designed by Gary Pritchard.
With Bucks Fizz, Juan Martin, Gene Pitney, Geoff Richer's First Edition.

MARVIN HAMLISCH

A BBC production for BBC 2. Transmission details are for BBC 2. Duration: 60 minutes.

Orchestra conducted by Barry Griffiths; produced and directed by Stewart Morris.

Marvin Hamlisch, London Philharmonic Orchestra, Diane Langton, Marie Santell, Sandra Voris.

Holding / Source

30.12.1977 — DB-D3 / 2"

MARY HOPKIN IN THE LAND OF...

A BBC production for BBC 1. Transmission details are for BBC 1. Duration: 30 minutes.

Main regular credit(s): Written by Myles Rudge; based on an idea by Eric Merriman; music directed by Burt Rhodes; choreography by Gillian Lynne; designed by Roger Ford; produced and directed by Vernon Lawrence.

Main regular performer(s): Mary Hopkin, The Mike Sammes Singers.

Holding / Source

11.12.1970 **Pantomime** — J / 2"
With Charlie Chester, Lynda Baron, Valentine Dyall.

THE MASKS OF DEATH

A Tyburn production for Channel 4. Transmission details are for Channel 4. Duration: 75 minutes.

By 1913 — with war clouds gathering over Europe — Sherlock Holmes has retired to his beekeeping in Sussex. But during a brief stay at his Baker Street apartments the Home Secretary arrives, unannounced, and begs Holmes to undertake one final, vital mission .

Written by N. J. Crisp; based on a story by John Elder; based on characters created by Sir Arthur Conan Doyle; executive producer Kevin Francis; produced by Norman Priggen; directed by Roy Ward Baker.

Peter Cushing (Sherlock Holmes), John Mills (Doctor Watson), Anne Baxter (Irene Adler), Anton Diffring (Graf Udo Von Felseck), Ray Milland (Home Secretary), Russell Hunter (Alfred Coombs), Gordon Jackson (Alec MacDonald), Susan Penhaligon (Miss Derwent), Marcus Gilbert (Anton Von Felseck), Jenny Laird (Mrs Hudson), James Cossins (Frederick Baines), Eric Dodson (Lord Claremont), Georgina Coombs (Lady Claremont), James Head (Chauffeur), Dominic Murphy (Boot Boy).

Holding / Source

23.12.1984 — C1 / C1

THE MATING CALL

An Alan Landsburg production for Yorkshire Television. Transmission details are for Channel 4. Duration: 24 minutes.

Marty Ross, an American reporter for a New York magazine, works in London for the Metro-Press. He's an average American with average looks; height weight and below average results with girls With his friends Jonathan and Katie Grant to support him through his tangled emotions, Marty tries to trace the start of his below average successes Then Marty meets Joan, a friend of Katie's — exquisite, intelligent and attractive, everything a man could want in life. But can Marty keep her affections?

Written by Mort Lachman and Sy Rosen; designed by Richard Jarvis; executive producer Mort Lachman; directed by Joe McGrath.

Joe Regalbuto (Marty Ross), Marcia Strassman (Katie Grant), Ian Lavender (Jonathan Grant), Rikki Howard (Iris), June Chadwick (Joan Sims), Royston Farrell (Frank Sims).

Holding / Source

24.12.1984 — 1" / 1"

THE MATING SEASON

A Thames Television production. Transmission details are for the ATV midlands region. Duration: 75 minutes.

Written by Sam Cree; produced by William G. Stewart and Bill Roberton; directed by William G. Stewart and Bill Roberton.

Bruce Forsyth (Bruce Gillespie), Joy Stewart (Mrs Jamieson), Joyce Blair (Stella Morley), Bill Waddington (Fred Woods), Dorothy Dampier (Violet Harris), Sarah Maxwell (Helga Herdman), Linda Cunningham (Barbara Nixon), Rosalyn Elvin (Vanessa Morley), Keith Morris (Marvyn Gillespie), Brian Godfrey (Robin Gillespie).

Holding / Source

26.12.1976 — D3 / 2"

MAX

A Thames Television production. Transmission details are for the ATV midlands region. Duration varies - see below for details.

Main regular performer(s): Max Bygraves (Host).

	Holding / Source
27.12.1977 **Max's Holiday 'Hour'**	D3 / 2"

Duration: 50 minutes.
Written by Eric Davidson; music directed by Geoff Love; music by Norman Stevens; designed by Rod Stratfold; produced and directed by Mark Stuart.
With Lena Zavaroni, Jim Davidson, Sandra Dickinson, Charlie Cairoli, Margaret Powell, Sharon Hudson, The Tony Mansell Singers, The Nigel Lythgoe Dancers.

MAX BOYCE

A BBC Wales production for BBC 1. Transmission details are for BBC 1. Duration varies - see below for details.

Main regular credit(s): Written by Max Boyce.
Main regular performer(s): Max Boyce.

SERIES 1
Commissioned by BBC 1 Wales. Transmission details are for BBC 1 Wales.

	Holding / Source
25.12.1975 **Christmas Show**	DB / 2"

Duration: 50 minutes.
Designed by Michael Wright; produced and directed by David Richards.

	Holding / Source
21.12.1977	DB-D3 / 2"

Duration: 40 minutes.
Orchestra conducted by Benny Litchfield; designed by Phil Williams; produced and directed by David Richards.
With Neil Lewis, John Luce, Rob Allen, The Richard Williams Junior Singers.

	Holding / Source
27.12.1978 **Christmas Show**	DB-D3 / 2"

Duration: 40 minutes.

21.12.1981	DB / 1"

Duration: 35 minutes.

MAX BYGRAVES

An ATV production. Transmission details are for Associated-Rediffusion. Duration: 25 minutes.
A story of a child's joy and the grown-ups who tried to bring it to her. Max Bygraves invites viewers to share tears, laughter and - A Bonus for Christmas.
Written by Walter McDonnell; story by Christine Bygraves; produced by Bill Ward.
Max Bygraves.

	Holding / Source
24.12.1956	J /

THE MAX BYGRAVES CHRISTMAS SHOW

A Thames Television production. Transmission details are for the ATV midlands region. Duration: 50 minutes.
Written by Eric Davidson; music directed by Geoff Love; music associate Norman Stevens; choreography by Nigel Lythgoe, designed by Rod Stratfold, produced and directed by Mark Stuart.

Max Bygraves (Host), Sharon Hudson, Lena Zavaroni, Jim Davidson, Sandra Dickinson, Charlie Cairoli & Company, Margaret Powell, The Tony Mansell Singers, The Nigel Lythgoe Dancers.

	VT Number	Holding / Source
27.12.1977	18146	DB / 2"

MAX BYGRAVES SAYS... I WANNA TELL YOU A STORY

A BBC production for BBC 1. Transmission details are for BBC 1.
Main regular performer(s): Max Bygraves (Host).

	Holding / Source
31.12.1975	DB-D3 / 2"

Duration: 75 minutes.
Written by Eric Davidson; music directed by Peter Knight; choreography by Dougie Squires; designed by Robin Tarsnane; produced by Yvonne Littlewood and John Ammonds; directed by Yvonne Littlewood and John Ammonds.
With Dougie Squires Dancers, The Eddie Lester Singers.

Duration: 50 minutes.
Main regular credit(s): Written by Eric Davidson; music directed by Peter Knight; choreography by Dougie Squires; designed by Michael Young; produced by John Ammonds; directed by Stanley Appel.
Main regular performer(s): With Dougie Squires Dozen, The Eddie Lester Singers.

	Holding / Source
27.09.1976 **The 1920s**	DB-D3 / 2"

With Simon Beal.

MAX BYGRAVES SAYS... I WANNA TELL YOU A STORY (continued)

11.10.1976 **The 1930s**		DB-D3 / 2"
With No guest cast.		
08.11.1976 **The 1940s**		DB-D3 / 2"
With No guest cast.		
06.12.1976 **The 1950s**		DB-D3 / 2"
With Christopher Wilson.		
03.01.1977 **The 1960s**		DB-D3 / 2"
With Christopher Wilson.		
24.01.1977 **The 1970s**		DB-D3 / 2"
With No guest cast.		

MAX HEADROOM SHOW

A Chrysalis TV production for Channel 4. Transmission details are for Channel 4.

Main regular credit(s): Based on an idea by George Stove, Rocky Morton and Annabel Jankel.

SERIES 3

Main regular credit(s): Written by David Hansen and Paul Owen; produced by Heather Hampson; directed by David G. Hillier.

Holding / Source

26.12.1986 **Max Headroom's Giant Christmas Turkey**   DB|n / 1"
Duration: 40 minutes.

Live and direct from Max's own fireside — and Max knows you just won't be able to resist this huge fat bird. Yes, if it's got anything to do with Christmas, then Max will be reaching in and pulling it out of the parson's nose of his turkey — music, kids from all nations, choirs, and really wacky guests. Plus Max's new Christmas song.

Executive producer Peter Wagg; produced by Heather Hampson.

With Tina Turner, Dave Edmunds, Bob Geldof.

All NFTVA 1" holdings from this season are off-air recordings.

MAX WITH LOVE

A Thames Television production. Transmission details are for the ATV midlands region. Duration: 50 minutes.

Max Bygraves and Geoff Love mix music and comedy to swap their personal recollections of 1979. The classic showbusiness success story of the year is the rise of model Lorraine Chase to become a household name. After her series with Max, she returns for tonight's special show.

Written by Eric Davidson; designed by Bill Palmer; produced and directed by Royston Mayoh.

Max Bygraves, Lorraine Chase, Geoff Love, Twiggy, Bob Dixon, The Maggie Stredder Singers.

Holding / Source
31.12.1979   DB / 2"

MAX'S HOLIDAY HOUR

A Thames Television production. Transmission details are for the ATV midlands region. Duration: 52 minutes.

Max Bygraves in holiday mood takes a look at some of the things that make us laugh and warm our hearts at Christmas. Christmas carols, pantomime, comedy and popular songs make a light-hearted hour of seasonal goodwill.

Written by Eric Davidson; music directed by Geoff Love; music associate Norman Stevens; choreography by Nigel Lythgoe; designed by Rod Stratfold; produced and directed by Mark Stuart.

Max Bygraves, Jim Davidson, Sandra Dickinson, Lena Zavaroni, Sharon Hudson, Charlie Cairoli & Company, Margaret Powell, The Tony Mansell Singers, The Nigel Lythgoe Dancers.

	VT Number	Holding / Source
27.12.1977	18146	DB / 2"

MAY TO DECEMBER

A Cinema Verity production for BBC 1. Transmission details are for BBC 1.

Main regular credit(s): Created by Paul A. Mendelson; executive producer Verity Lambert.

Main regular cast: Anton Rodgers (Alec Callender).

SERIES 3

Main regular credit(s): Written by Paul A. Mendelson; produced by Sharon Bloom; directed by Paul Harrison.

Main regular cast: With Lesley Dunlop (Zoe Angell), Frances White (Miss Flood), Rebecca Lacey (Hilary), Paul Venables (Jamie).

Holding / Source

31.12.1990 **I'll See You In My Dreams**   DB / 1"
Duration: 55 minutes.

With Carolyn Pickles (Simone), Kate Williams (Zoe's Mum), Chrissie Cotterill (Debbie), Paul Raynor (Roy), Ronnie Stevens, Rupert Holliday Evans, Isabelle Lucas, Bernice Stegers, Tim Wylton, Eric Francis, Richard Cubison.

MCCALLUM

A Scottish Television production. Transmission details are for the Central region. Duration varies - see below for details.

Holding / Source

28.12.1995 **The Key To My Heart [pilot]** DB / V1S
Duration: 80 minutes.
McCallum is called in to investigate the death of a Vietnamese banker, whose body is washed ashore on the Isle of Dogs. It could be suicide - except for a bullet hole in the skull.
Written by Stuart Hepburn; script supervisor Elaine Matthews; script editor Nicole Cauverien; music by Daemion Barry; executive producer Robert Love; produced by Murray Ferguson; directed by Patrick Lau.
With John Hannah (Doctor Iain McCallum), Suzanna Hamilton (Joanna Sparks), Gerard Murphy (Detective Inspector Bracken), Zara Turner (Doctor Angela Moloney), James Saxon (Fuzzy Brightons), Richard O'Callaghan (Bobby Sykes), Alex Walkinshaw (Detective Constable Small), Richard Durden (Sir Paddy Penfold), Simon Slater, Cathryn Harrison, Gary Lammin, Patricia Garwood, Anita Parry, Miriam Leake, Bruce Barnden.

MCCOIST AND MCCAULEY

A BBC Scotland production for BBC 1 Scotland. Transmission details are for BBC 1 Scotland.
Main regular cast: Ally McCoist (Host), Fred Macaulay (Host).

SERIES 1

Transmission details are for BBC 1 Scotland.

Holding / Source

31.12.1997 DB / DBS

Transmission details are for BBC 1 Scotland.

Holding / Source

23.12.1999 DB / DBS

MEANWHILE BACK IN SUNDERLAND

A Tyne Tees Television production. Transmission details are for the ATV midlands region. Duration: 25 minutes.
The F.A. Cup Final at Wembley.
Executive producer Leslie Barrett; directed by Ken Stephinson and Jeremy Lack.

Holding / Source

27.12.1973 DB|n / 2"-C1

MEDITATION FOR CHRISTMAS NIGHT

A Thames Television production. Transmission details are for the Thames Television region. Duration: 8 minutes.
Written by C. P. Taylor; produced and directed by John Woods.

Holding / Source

26.12.1978 J / 2"

MEETING POINT

A BBC production. Transmission details are for BBC/BBC1. Usual duration: 25 minutes.

Holding / Source

16.12.1956 **Christians And Christmas** J /

14.12.1958 **The Christmas Child** J /
Duration: 40 minutes.
Written by D. G. Bridson; music by Matyas Seiber; produced and directed by D. G. Bridson.
With Wilfred Pickles (Joe), Isla Cameron (Mary), Marjorie Rhodes (Lizzie), Edric Connor (Statesman), John Sharp (Zachary), Frederick Wilson (Tom Shepherd), Fred Fairclough (Billy Spinner), Tom Harrison (Johnny Miner), Howieson Culff (Man of Law), John Harvey (Scientist), James McKechnie (Narrator).

20.12.1964 **The Coming Of Christ** J /

19.12.1965 "Notting Hill prepares for Christmas"

24.12.1967 **The House By The Stable** B1 / B1
Duration: 35 minutes.
Adapted by Richard Martin; based on a play by Charles Williams; produced by Vernon Sproxton; directed by Richard Martin.
With Emrys James (Bill Manly), Caroline Blakiston (Mandy Pride), Terry Wale (Jeremy Helm), Antony Webb (Gabriel Gabriel), Alan Bennion (Joseph), Annette Whiteley (Mary).

MEN BEHAVING BADLY

A Hartswood Films production for BBC/ITV. Duration varies - see below for details.

Main regular credit(s): Written by Simon Nye; theme music by Alan Lisk; produced by Beryl Vertue; directed by Martin Dennis.

Main regular cast: Martin Clunes (Gary Strang), Leslie Ash (Deborah), Caroline Quentin (Dorothy).

Commissioned by BBC 1. made in association with Pearson Television. Transmission details are for BBC 1.

	Holding / Source
25.12.1997 **Christmas Day**	DB-D3 / DBSW

Alt.Title(s): *Merry Christmas*
Duration: 45 minutes.
Script editor Elaine Cameron; director of photography John Rosenberg; art director Lindsay Brunnock; designed by Steve Groves; production manager Debbie Vertue; line producer Julian Scott.
With John Thomson (Ken), Ian Lindsay (George), Valerie Minifie (Anthea), Edna Doré, Lisa Lewis, Luke Strain, Ben McCosker, Matt Price.

SERIES 7

Commissioned by BBC 1. made in association with Pearson Television International. Transmission details are for BBC 1. Duration: 45 minutes.

Main regular credit(s): Script editor Elaine Cameron; director of photography John Rosenberg; art director Susie Ayton; designed by David Buckingham; line producers Chris Griffin and Debbie Vertue.

	Holding / Source
25.12.1998 **Performance**	DB / DBSW

With Ian Lindsay (George), Valerie Minifie (Anthea), John Thomson (Ken), Marcia Ashton, Ian Kelsey, Rory Tapsell.

26.12.1998 **Gary In Love**	DB / DBSW

With Amanda Drew, Lucy Speed, Peter Shea.

28.12.1998 **Delivery**	DB / DBSW

With Ian Lindsay (George), John Thomson (Ken), Valerie Minifie (Anthea), Dido Miles, Eileen Dunwoodie.

THE MERRY CHRISTMAS

An Associated-Rediffusion production. Transmission details are for Associated-Rediffusion. Duration: 40 minutes.

Book by Donald Cotton; adapted by Tom Twigge; based on a book by Charles Dickens; lyrics by Donald Cotton; music directed by Steve Race; music by Brian Burke; settings by Timothy O'Brien; produced by Douglas Hurn.

Hugh Griffith (Scrooge), John Gower (Night Watchman), Michael O'Halloran (Mr Topper), Norman Tyrrell (Bob Cratchit), Peter Reeves (Fred / Scrooge as a Young Man), Edmund Willard (Marley's Ghost), Martin Lawrence (Spirit of Christmas), George Murcell (Mr Fezziwig), Eira Heath (Belle), Irene Byatt (Mrs Cratchit), Barry Huband (Tiny Tim), Madi Hedd (Mrs Fred).

	Holding / Source
21.12.1955	J /

A MERRY MAX

An ATV production. Transmission details are for the ATV London region. Duration: 52 minutes.
Designed by Bill McPherson; produced and directed by Albert Locke.
Max Bygraves, Kenny Ball's Jazzmen, Piccola Pupa, The Two Tones, Anthony Bygraves, Burt Rhodes and his Orchestra.

	Holding / Source
25.12.1961	J /

A MERRY MORNING

A Yorkshire Television production. Transmission details are for the Anglia region. Duration: 25 minutes.
Executive producer Lawrie Higgins; produced by Burt Budin.
Leslie Crowther (Presenter), Bozo The Clown.

	Holding / Source
25.12.1969	J /

A MERRY MORNING

A Yorkshire Television production. Transmission details are for the Yorkshire Television region. Duration: 25 minutes.
Leslie Crowther is at Pinderfields Hospital, Wakefield, at a party for the youngsters in hospital at Christmas.
Executive producer Lawrie Higgins; produced by Burt Budin.
Leslie Crowther (Presenter), John Bouchier.

	Holding / Source
25.12.1970	J / 2"

A MERRY MORNING

A Yorkshire Television production. Transmission details are for the Yorkshire Television region. Duration: 25 minutes.
Executive producer Lawrie Higgins; directed by Andy Gullen.
John Alderton (Presenter), Daisy May and Saveen.

	Holding / Source
25.12.1971	J / 2"

A MERRY MORNING

A MERRY MORNING

A Yorkshire Television production. Transmission details are for the ATV midlands region. Duration: 25 minutes.
Music associates Tony Cervi and Geoff Myers; executive producer Lawrie Higgins; directed by Andy Gullen.
Leslie Crowther (Presenter), Alan Randall.

	Holding / Source
25.12.1972	J / 2"

A MERRY MORNING

A Yorkshire Television production. Transmission details are for the Yorkshire Television region. Duration: 25 minutes.
Executive producer Lawrie Higgins; produced by Burt Budin.
Leslie Crowther (Presenter), Ward Allen, Tony Cervi, Father Christmas.

	Holding / Source
25.12.1973	B / 2"

A MERRY MORNING

A Yorkshire Television production. Transmission details are for the ATV midlands region. Duration: 25 minutes.
Executive producer Lawrie Higgins; produced by Andy Gullen.
Leslie Crowther (Presenter), Keith Harris & Cuddles.

	Holding / Source
25.12.1974	B / 2"

A MERRY MORNING

A Yorkshire Television production. Transmission details are for the ATV midlands region. Duration: 52 minutes.
Music directed by Charles Smitton; executive producer Lawrie Higgins; produced and directed by Burt Budin.
Jimmy Tarbuck (Presenter), Larry Parker, Animal Kwackers.

	Holding / Source
25.12.1975	B / 2"

A MERRY MORNING

A Yorkshire Television production. Transmission details are for the Yorkshire Television region. Duration: 25 minutes.
Designed by Howard Dawson; executive producer Lawrie Higgins; produced and directed by Guy Caplin.
Jimmy Tarbuck (Presenter), Johnny Hart, Charles Smitton, Father Christmas.

	Holding / Source
25.12.1976	B / 2"

A MERRY MORNING

A Yorkshire Television production. Transmission details are for the ATV midlands region. Duration: 35 minutes.
Written by Lawrie Kinsley and Ron McDonnell; music directed by Robert Hartley [credited as Bob Hartley]; designed by Howard Dawson; executive producer Lawrie Higgins; produced and directed by Burt Budin.
Jimmy Tarbuck (Presenter), Tina Charles, Guy Kent, The Wurzels, Roger Stevenson.

	Holding / Source
25.12.1977	D / 2"

A MERRY MORNING

A Yorkshire Television production. Transmission details are for the ATV midlands region. Duration: 35 minutes.
Written by Lawrie Kinsley and Ron McDonnell; designed by Mike Long; executive producer Lawrie Higgins; produced and directed by Guy Caplin.
Jimmy Tarbuck (Presenter), Animal Kwackers, Mike Harding, Ward Allen.

	Holding / Source
25.12.1978	B / 2"

A MERRY MORNING

A Yorkshire Television production. Transmission details are for the Yorkshire Television region. Duration: 52 minutes.
Written by Lawrie Kinsley and Ron McDonnell; designed by Mike Long; executive producer Lawrie Higgins; produced and directed by Guy Caplin.
Jimmy Tarbuck (Presenter), Animal Kwackers, Ward Allen, Mike Harding.

	Holding / Source
25.12.1979	B / 2"

A MERRY MORNING

A Yorkshire Television production. Transmission details are for the Yorkshire Television region. Duration: 44 minutes.
Music directed by Robert Hartley; executive producer Lawrie Higgins; produced and directed by Burt Budin.
Don Maclean (Presenter), Guys & Dolls, The Chuckle Brothers, Father Christmas, Eddie Idris, Pepe and Friends.

	Holding / Source
25.12.1980	1" / 2"

THE MERRY WIDOW

A Scottish Television production. Transmission details are for the ATV midlands region. Duration: 90 minutes.

Written by Franz Lehar; orchestra conducted by Alexander Gibson; choreography by Virginia Mason; designed by John Stoddart; produced for television by Chris Allen; produced for the stage by Anthony Besch.

Catherine Wilson (Anna Glawari), Johnny Blanc (Count Danilo Danilovitch), William McCue (Baron Mirko Zeta), Patricia Hay (Valencienne), David Hillman (Camille De Rosillon), James Paterson (Vicomte Cascada), David Fieldsend (Raoul De St. Brioche), Peter Bodenham (Bogdanowitsch), Rosanne Brackenbridge (Sylviane), Arthur Jackson (Kromow), Lola Biagioni (Olga), David Scrivens (Pritschitsch), Linda Finnie (Praskowia), Graham Allum (Njegus), Scottish Philharmonic Orchestra, The Scottish Opera Chorus.

	Holding / Source
26.12.1976	J / 2"

MERRY WITH MEDWIN

An Associated-Rediffusion production. Transmission details are for Associated-Rediffusion. Duration: 50 minutes.

Written by Neville Phillips; music by Neville Phillips and Robb Stewart; designed by Frank Nerini; produced and directed by Peter Croft.

Michael Medwin, Shirley Bassey, Sidney James, Betty Marsden, Vince Eager, Silent Three, Stephanie Voss, Ron Moody, The George Mitchell Singers, Billy Ternent and his Orchestra, The Denny Bettis Dancers.

	Holding / Source
24.12.1959	J /

THE MESSAGE OF THE ANGELS

A BBC production for BBC 1. Transmission details are for BBC 1. Duration: 65 minutes.

Midnight mass.

Television presentation by Stewart Cross.

Reverend Don Lewis (Celebrant), Duncan Eyre (Organist / Choirmaster).

	Holding / Source
24.12.1974	J / 2"

METAL MICKEY

An LWT production. Transmission details are for the ATV/Central region. Duration: 25 minutes.

Main regular credit(s):   Created by Michael Dolenz; written by Colin Bostock-Smith; theme music by Phil Coulter; produced by Michael Dolenz.

Main regular cast: Metal Mickey (Himself), Michael Stainton (Father), Georgina Melville (Mother), Irene Handl (Granny), Ashley Knight (Ken), Lola Young (Janey), Gary Shail (Steve), Lucinda Bateson (Haley).

SERIES 3
Transmission details are for the ATV midlands region.

		VT Number	Holding / Source
19.12.1981	**Merry Christmas Mickey**		D2 / 2"

Designed by Rae George; directed by Michael Dolenz.

With Mark Farmer, Fred Bryant.

26.12.1981	**Pantomickey**	90399	D2 / 2"

Music by Nigel Hess; designed by Rae George; production manager Mike Hack; directed by Michael Dolenz.

With Cy Grant, Louise Nelson, Madeline Simpson, Ian Sheriden, Valerie Masters, Frank Holmes.

MICHAEL BALL

An Action Time production for Carlton. Transmission details are for the Central region.

Main regular performer(s):   Michael Ball (Host).

	Holding / Source
24.12.1995	D3 / D2S

Duration: 48 minutes.

Produced by Trish Kinane; directed by Gavin Taylor.

With Dusty Springfield, Gresley Male Voice Choir, Michael Bolton.

MICHAEL BENTINE'S POTTY TIME

A Thames Television production. Transmission details are for the ATV midlands region. Duration: 14 minutes.

Main regular credit(s):   Devised by Michael Bentine; written by Michael Bentine.

Main regular cast: Michael Bentine.

SERIES 1
Main regular credit(s):   Designed by John Plant; produced and directed by Leon Thau.

		VT Number	Holding / Source
24.12.1973	**Father Christmas**	8469	D3 / 2"

It's such a peaceful scene - Father Christmas floating from snowy rooftop to rooftop, delivering the presents. But surely in this modern day things must have changed? Quite so, say the Pottys. Today. they show Michael Bentine how Father Christmas manages in an age of overpopulation, computers and jet sleighs.

MICHAEL BUBLE: HOME FOR CHRISTMAS

An ITV Studios production for ITV 1. Transmission details are for the Central region. Duration: 66 minutes.
The crooner performs a selection of seasonal favourites from the comfort of his Canadian mountain chalet.
Produced by Christian Fletcher; directed by Simon Staffurth.
Michael Bublé (Host), Kelly Rowland, Gary Barlow, Dawn French.

	Holding / Source
18.12.2011	HD/DB / HDC

MICHAEL MCINTYRE'S COMEDY ROADSHOW

An Open Mike Manchester production for BBC 1. Transmission details are for BBC 1.

Main regular cast: Michael McIntyre (Host).

	Holding / Source
25.12.2011 **Michael McIntyre's Christmas Comedy Roadshow**	HD/DB / HDC

Duration: 60 minutes.
From London's Theatre Royal, Drury Lane.
Produced by Anthony Caveney; directed by Paul Wheeler.
With Jack Dee, Miranda Hart, James Corden, Rob Brydon, David Mitchell.

MICHAEL MCINTYRE'S SHOWTIME

Commissioned by BBC 1. Transmission details are for BBC 1. Duration: 60 minutes.
Stand-up comedy.
Produced by Anthony Caveney; directed by Paul Wheeler.
Michael McIntyre.

	Holding / Source
25.12.2013	HD/DB / HDC

MIDSOMER MURDERS

A Bentley Films production for ITV/ITV 1. made in association with Arts & Entertainment Network. Transmission details are for the Central region. Duration varies - see below for details.

Main regular credit(s): Based on the character created by Caroline Graham; theme music by Jim Parker; music by Jim Parker.

SERIES 3

Made in association with Arts & Entertainment Network.

Main regular credit(s): Script supervisor Carol Gardner; script editor Mariana Mejia; associate producer Ian Strachan; executive producers Brian True-May and Delia Fine.

Main regular cast: With Daniel Casey (Sergeant Troy), John Nettles (Detective Chief Inspector Barnaby), Jane Wymark (Joyce Barnaby).

	Holding / Source
31.12.1999 **Death Of A Stranger**	DB / V1S

Duration: 99 minutes.
Written by Douglas Livingstone; produced and directed by Peter Cregeen.

With Laura Howard (Cully Barnaby), Richard Johnson, Jennifer Hilary, Dominic Mafham, Diane Fletcher, James Bolam, Janet Dale, Sarah Winman, Jeanne Hepple, Peter Bayliss, Jane Wood, Fred Ridgeway, Tom Smith, Jonie Broom, Simon McBurney, Toby Jones, Patricia Valentine, Arlene Cockburn, David Maybrick, Shenagh Govan, Frank Mills, Eve Pearce, Grant Gillespie, Simon Greiff.

Cut on original transmission to allow for New Year celebrations.

SERIES 8

Duration: 100 minutes.
Main regular credit(s): Script editor Christopher Penfold; produced by Brian True-May.
Main regular cast: With John Hopkins (Sergeant Dan Scott), John Nettles (Detective Chief Inspector Barnaby), Jane Wymark (Joyce Barnaby).

	Holding / Source
25.12.2004 **Ghosts Of Christmas Past**	DB / V1SW

At a seasonal family get-together, a cracker riddle states two people will die before midnight on Boxing Day. A few hours later, family matriarch Lydia meets an untimely end - giving Barnaby the perfect reason to escape a boring Christmas with his in-laws.

Written by David Hoskins; script supervisor Vivianne Royal; consultant Betty Willingale; directed by Renny Rye.

With Laura Howard (Cully Barnaby), Barry Jackson (Doctor George Bullard), Haydn Gwynne, Margery Mason, Bruce Alexander, Mel Martin, Philip Quast, William Chubb, Alice Patten, Dominic Colenso, Rory Copus, Lydia Leonard, Kevin Doyle, Claire Carrie, Daphne Oxenford, John Burgess, Bryan Matheson, Harry Gostelow, Charles Millham, Christopher Sutton, Gemma Martin, Luke Foster, Tim Treloar, Laura Jeffree.

John Styles was the Magic Advisor.

MIDSOMER MURDERS (continued)

SERIES 13
A Bentley Productions production. Duration: 100 minutes.

Main regular credit(s): Series script editor Christopher Penfold; director of photography Colin Munn; designed by Paul Cowell; executive producer Brian True-May; consultant producer Betty Willingale; line producer Ian Strachan; produced by Brian True-May.

Main regular cast: With John Nettles (Detective Chief Inspector Barnaby), Jason Hughes (Detective Sergeant Ben Jones), Barry Jackson (Doctor Bullard), Kirsty Dillon (Woman Police Constable Gail Stephens), Jane Wymark (Joyce Barnaby).

Holding / Source
24.12.2008 Days Of Misrule   DB / V1SW

Barnaby and Jones are dragged away from a team building exercise to investigate an explosion at a haulage yard run by Territorial Army commander Matt Parkes and his son James. The young man is ruthless in business and wit.

Written by Elizabeth-Anne Wheal; directed by Renny Rye.

With Elspeth Rae (Layla Barkham), Joseph Millson (James Parkes), Alexandra Morris (Daisy), Judy Parfitt (Caroline Halsey), Tim Pigott-Smith (Matt Parkes), Nick Fletcher (C.S. John Cotton), Niamh Cusack (Penny Galsworthy), Gus Gallagher (Dale Mitchinson), Sidney Livingstone (Don Mitchinson), Tom Beard (Tim Galsworthy), Tony Ball (Ed Lovell), Alyson Spiro (Nina Barkham), Philip Martin Brown (George Barkham).

Main regular credit(s): Produced by Louise Sutton.

Main regular cast: With Neil Dudgeon (Detective Chief Inspector John Barnaby), Gwilym Lee (Detective Sergeant Charlie Nelson).

Holding / Source
24.12.2013 The Christmas Haunting   HD/DB / HDC

A Bentley Productions production. Duration: 100 minutes.

New detective Charlie Nelson moves to Midsomer at Christmas - and is soon plunged into a murder inquiry. The season of goodwill fails to extend to all men when a guest attending a ghost-hunting party in Morton Shallows is slain with an antique sword.

Written by Chris Murray; directed by Nick Laughland.

With Fiona Dolman (Sarah Barnaby), Tamzin Malleson (Kate Wilding), Mark Heap (Simon Fergus-Johnson), Nadia Cameron-Blakey (Tabby Fergus-Johnson), Hannah Tointon (Pippa Fergus-Johnson), Emily Joyce (Valerie Fergus-Johnson), James Murray (Ollie Tabori), Les Dennis (Brendan Pierce), Elizabeth Berrington (Libs Pearce), Susie Trayling (Mel Bridgeman), Jonah Russell (Conor Bridgeman), Perdita Avery (Felicity Hearn), Nikesh Patel (Dev Kardek), Paul Blair (Ross Clymer).

THE MIGHTY BOOSH

A Baby Cow Productions production for BBC 3. Transmission details are for BBC 3.

Main regular credit(s): Written by Julian Barratt and Noel Fielding; music by Julian Barratt.

Main regular cast: Julian Barratt, Noel Fielding.

Holding / Source
26.12.2007 The Mighty Boosh Live   DB / DBSWF

An Universal Studios production. Duration: 145 minutes.

Script supervisor Emma Ramsay; executive producer Helen Parker; produced by Celia Blaker; directed by Nick Morris.

With Matt Berry.

THE MIGHTY WURZELS IN THE HEART OF THE WEST

A HTV production. Transmission details are for the HTV region. Duration: 25 minutes.

Choreography by Flick Colby; designed by Ken Jones; produced and directed by Derek Clark.

The Wurzels, Ruby Flipper.

Holding / Source
24.12.1976   DB|n / 2"

The Wurzels perform some of their best-known songs in front of an audience, in a studio in Bristol designed to look like a pub. Included in the set are "I Am A Cider Drinker", "The Blackbird Song" and "I've Got A Brand New Combine Harvester". Interspersed with the studio footage are sequences featuring the band pursuing - in a style akin to that of Benny Hill - a young woman through various locations in Bristol.

THE MIKADO

A BBC production for BBC 1. Transmission details are for BBC 1. Duration: 65 minutes.

Opera.

Written by W. S. Gilbert and Arthur Sullivan; costume Odette Barrow; make-up Marion Richards; orchestra conducted by David Lloyd-Jones; choreography by Bob Stevenson; lighting by Dennis Channon; sound Alan Fogg and Adrian Stocks; designed by Richard Henry; produced by Cedric Messina; directed by Michael Hayes.

David Hillman (Nanki-Poo), Derek Hammond-Stroud (Ko-Ko), Heather Begg (Katisha), Ian Wallace (Pooh-Bah), Valerie Masterson (Yum-Yum), Philip Summerscales (Pish-Tush), Sara de Javelin (Peep-Bo), Janet Hughes (Pitti-Sing), Richard Angas (The Mikado), Ambrosian Opera Chorus, Royal Philharmonic Orchestra.

Holding / Source
28.12.1973   DB-D3 / 2"

MIKE AND BERNIE WINTERS' ALL-STAR CHRISTMAS COMEDY CARNIVAL

Alternative/Working Title(s): CHRISTMAS '71 COMPILATION PROGRAMME

Produced for ITV by a variety of companies (see details below). Transmission details are for the ATV midlands region. Duration: 130 minutes.

Holding / Source
25.12.1971 Presentation   J / 2"

Written by Mike and Bernie Winters, David Cumming, Derek Collyer, Wally Malston and Spike Mullins; music directed by Harry Rabinowitz; designed by Bryce Walmsley; produced and directed by Bryan Izzard.

With Mike and Bernie Winters (Hosts).

British Christmas Television Guide	MIKE AND BERNIE WINTERS' ALL-STAR CHRISTMAS COMEDY CARNIVAL (continued)

25.12.1971 **Doctor At Large** J / 2"
An LWT production.
Written by Oliver Fry and Jonathan Lynn; based on books by Richard Gordon; designed by Eric Shedden; executive producer Humphrey Barclay; directed by Alan Wallis.
With George Layton (Paul Collier), Geoffrey Davies (Dick Stuart-Clark), Richard O'Sullivan (Lawrence Bingham).

25.12.1971 **The Lovers** J|c / 2"
A Granada production.
Written by Jack Rosenthal; music by Derek Hilton; designed by Colin Pocock; produced and directed by Les Chatfield.
With Paula Wilcox (Beryl Bottomley), Richard Beckinsale (Geoffrey P. Scrimshaw), Joan Scott (Beryl's Mum).

25.12.1971 **... And Mother Makes Three** J / 2"
A Thames Television production.
Written by Richard Waring; theme music by Johnny Hawkesworth; designed by Bill Palmer; produced and directed by Peter Frazer-Jones.
With Wendy Craig (Sally Harrison), Robin Davies (Simon), David Parfitt (Peter), Valerie Lush (Auntie).

25.12.1971 **His And Hers** J / 2"
A Yorkshire Television production.
Written by Ken Hoare and Mike Sharland; designed by Chris George; produced and directed by Ian Davidson.
With Ronald Lewis (Rupert Sherwin), Barbara Murray (Kay Sherwin).

25.12.1971 **Please Sir!** J / 2"
An LWT production.
Written by John Esmonde and Bob Larbey; designed by Andrew Gardner; executive producer Mark Stuart; directed by Howard Ross.
With Deryck Guyler (Norman Potter), Noel Howlett (Mr Cromwell), Joan Sanderson (Miss Ewell), Richard Davies (Mr Price), Erik Chitty (Mr Smith).

25.12.1971 **Fenn Street Gang** J / 2"
An LWT production.
Written by Lew Schwarz; designed by David Catley; directed by Mark Stuart.
With Peter Cleall (Eric Duffy), Carol Hawkins (Sharon Eversleigh), David Barry (Frankie Abbott), Léon Vitali (Peter Craven), Liz Gebhardt (Maureen Bullock), Peter Denyer (Dennis Dunstable).

25.12.1971 **Girls About Town** J / 2"
An ATV production.
Written by Adele Rose; designed by Don Fisher; produced by Shaun O'Riordan; directed by John Scholz-Conway.
With Denise Coffey (Brenda), Julie Stevens (Rosemary), Robin Parkinson (George), Peter Baldwin (Harold), David Baron.

25.12.1971 **Dear Mother..... ..... Love Albert** J / 2"
A Yorkshire Television production.
Written by Rodney Bewes; designed by Mike Long; produced by Rodney Bewes; directed by David Mallett.
With Rodney Bewes (Albert Courtney).

25.12.1971 **Sez Les** J / 2"
A Yorkshire Television production.
Designed by Roger Cheveley; produced and directed by David Mallett.
With Les Dawson.

25.12.1971 **Lollipop Loves Mr. Mole** J / 2"
An ATV production.
Written by Jimmy Perry; designed by Paul Dean Fortune; produced by Shaun O'Riordan; directed by David Askey.
With Peggy Mount (Maggie Robinson), Hugh Lloyd (Reg Robinson), Pat Coombs (Violet Robinson), Rex Garner (Bruce Robinson).

25.12.1971 **Father, Dear Father** J / 2"
A Thames Television production.
Written by Johnnie Mortimer and Brian Cooke; designed by Harry Clark; produced and directed by William G. Stewart.
With Patrick Cargill (Patrick Glover), Natasha Pyne (Anna Glover), Ann Holloway (Karen Glover), Noël Dyson (Nanny).

##.##.#### **Other people taking part:**
With David Allister, Eamonn Andrews, John Baddeley, Lionel Blair, Joyce Carey, Esta Charkham, Nigel Chilvers, Dickie Davies, The Denys Palmer Dancers, Elaine Donnelly, Diana Dors, Sheridan Grant, Hughie Green, The Hanwell Brass Band, Anita Harris, Jimmy Hill, Gordon Honeycombe, Anna Karen, Stephen Lewis, Brian Moore, David Nixon, Anthony O'Keefe, Nosher Powell, Harry Shacklock, Trevor Lucas, Valerie Stanton, Sally Stephens, The Syd Lawrence Orchestra, Kent Walton, Marilyn Ward, Richard Warwick, Wei Wei Wong.

See also: ALL STAR COMEDY CARNIVAL

MIKE AND BERNIE'S SHOW

A Thames Television production. Transmission details are for the ATV midlands region. Duration varies - see below for details.
Main regular performer(s): Mike and Bernie Winters (Hosts).

Holding / Source

01.01.1973 **The Redman And Ross Story** J / 2"
Duration: 52 minutes.
Written by Ronnie Taylor; music directed by Ronnie Aldrich; music by Ronnie Taylor; choreography by Johnny Greenland; designed by Harry Clark; produced and directed by Peter Frazer-Jones.
With Peter Noone (Willie Topple), Sylvia Syms (Pauline Ross), Sheila White (Jenny Jones), Reginald Marsh (Barney Balham), Derek Francis (Gerard Prince), Mike Winters (Charlie Ross), Bernie Winters (Joe Redman), Ronnie Aldrich and his Orchestra.

MIKE THE KNIGHT

Commissioned by CBeebies. Transmission details are for CBeebies.
Animated adventure of the son of the King and his pet dragons.

Holding / Source

20.12.2011 **Santa's Little Helper** HD/DB / HDC
Duration: 15 minutes.
The Kingdom of Glendragon lies under a carpet of snow on the night before Christmas, and Mike, Evie and the dragons creep down the stairs for sneaky peek at their presents. But our knight in training has nothing waiting for him. Presuming that he's not on Santa's nice list, he sets out for the village in order to be extra helpful and win back the favour of the man in red.

MIKE YARWOOD IN PERSONS

A BBC production for BBC 1. Transmission details are for BBC 1. Duration varies - see below for details.
Main regular performer(s): Mike Yarwood (Various roles).

Holding / Source

27.12.1976 **Mike Yarwood Christmas Show** DB-D3 / 2"
Duration: 40 minutes.
Written by Eric Davidson and Neil Shand; music directed by Alan Braden; designed by Gary Pritchard; assistant producer Alan Boyd; produced and directed by John Ammonds.
With The New Seekers, Raymond Mason, Ballard Berkeley, Renée Roberts, Paula Scott, Michael Sharvell-Martin.

Holding / Source

25.12.1977 **Mike Yarwood Christmas Show** DB-D3 / 2"
Duration: 35 minutes.
Written by Eric Davidson and Neil Shand; music directed by Alan Braden; designed by Valerie Warrender; produced by James Moir; directed by Alan Boyd.
With Wings, Jenny Lee-Wright.

Holding / Source

25.12.1978 **The Mike Yarwood Christmas Show** DB-D3 / 2"
Duration: 45 minutes.
Written by Eric Merriman and Neil Shand; music directed by Alan Braden; designed by Gary Pritchard; produced by James Moir; directed by Alan Boyd.
With Abba, Janet Brown.

Holding / Source

25.12.1979 DB-D3 / 2"
Duration: 40 minutes.
Written by Eric Davidson and Neil Shand; music directed by Alan Braden; designed by Phil Roberson; produced by James Moir; directed by Stanley Appel.
With Janet Brown, Johnny Mathis.

25.12.1980 **The Mike Yarwood Christmas Show** DB-D3 / 2"
Duration: 40 minutes.
Written by Eric Davidson, Andy Hamilton and David Renwick; music directed by Alan Braden; designed by Vic Meredith; produced by James Moir; directed by Stanley Appel.
With Englebert Humperdinck.

Holding / Source

26.12.1981 **The Mike Yarwood Christmas Show** DB-D3 / 2"
Duration: 41 minutes.
Written by Eric Davidson, Neil Shand and David Renwick; music directed by Alan Braden; designed by Martin Collins; production team Lesley Langan, Mark Williams and Rowena Painter; production manager David Taylor; produced and directed by Peter Whitmore.
With Marti Caine, Bucks Fizz, Suzanne Danielle, Esther Rantzen, Philip Tan.

MIKE YARWOOD IN PERSONS

A Thames Television production. Transmission details are for the Central region. Duration varies - see below for details.
Main regular performer(s): Mike Yarwood (Various roles).

Holding / Source

21.12.1982 **The Mike Yarwood Christmas Show** D3 / 1"
Duration: 52 minutes.
Written by David Renwick, Barry Cryer, Eric Davidson and Eric Merriman; script associate Dick Hills; music directed by Alan Braden; choreography by Irving Davies; designed by Bill Palmer; produced and directed by Keith Beckett.
With Selina Scott, The Nolans, Claire Lutter, Petula Clark, Suzanne Danielle, The Irving Davies Dancers, Sharon Boone, Sandra Easby, Marie Gribbin, Debra Hemmings, Fiona Lewis, Gayna Martine, Christine Monk, Wanda Rokicki, Kathryn Sinclair, Clare Smalley, Pauline Thompson, The Maggie Stredder Singers.

Holding / Source

27.12.1983 **The Mike Yarwood Hour** D3 / 1"
Duration: 50 minutes.
Written by David Renwick; music directed by Alan Braden; music associate Bobby Heath; choreography by Brian Rogers and Molly Molloy; designed by Alex Clarke; produced by John Ammonds; directed by Robert Reed.
With Janet Brown, The Three Degrees, Suzanne Danielle.

MIKE YARWOOD IN PERSONS

	Holding / Source
26.12.1984 **The Mike Yarwood Show**	D3 / 1"

Duration: 50 minutes.
Written by Eddie Braben and Eric Merriman; additional material by Bill Naylor; script associate Eric Merriman; music directed by Alan Braden; designed by David Richens; produced and directed by David G. Hillier.
With Cliff Richard, Barbara New, Julie Wooldridge, The Ken Warwick Dancers, The Maggie Stredder Singers.

23.12.1985 **Mike Yarwood's Christmas Special**	D3 / 1"

Duration: 50 minutes.
Written by Eric Merriman and Eric Davidson; script associate Eric Merriman; music directed by Geoff Love; choreography by Ken Warwick; designed by Jane Krall; produced and directed by Philip Casson.
With Dudley Moore, Shirley Bassey, Anneka Rice.

22.12.1986 **The Yarwood Chat Show**	D3 / 1"

Duration: 50 minutes.
Written by John Junkin, Barry Cryer, William Rushton and Colin Edmonds; script associate John Junkin; music directed by Alan Braden; designed by Robert Ide; produced and directed by Keith Beckett.
With Kate Robbins, Five Star, Linda Nolan.

MILLIGAN IN...

A BBC production for BBC 2. Transmission details are for BBC 2. Duration: 30 minutes.
Main regular cast: Spike Milligan (Various roles).

	Holding / Source
24.12.1972 **Winter**	DB-D3 / 2"

Written by Spike Milligan; designed by Bryan Ellis; produced and directed by Roger Race.
With John Bluthal, Arthur Mullard, Fanny Carby, Alan Clare, Julia Breck, Sadie Corre, John Antrobus, Reuben Martin, Katie Allan, Karen Sirett.

MINDER

A Euston Films production for Thames/Central. Transmission details are for the ATV/Central region. Usual duration: 50 minutes.
Main regular credit(s):   Devised by Leon Griffiths; theme music by Gerard Kenny.
Main regular cast: George Cole (Arthur Daley), Glynn Edwards (Dave).
Commissioned by Thames Television. Transmission details are for the Central region.
Credits: Script executive Linda Agran; associate producer Ian Toynton; executive producer Verity Lambert; produced by Lloyd Shirley and George Taylor.
Cast: With Dennis Waterman (Terry McCann).

	Holding / Source
26.12.1983 **Minder's Christmas Bonus**	DB / C1

Written by Leon Griffiths; directed by Ian Toynton.
With George Baker, John Bardon, John Benfield, Anthony Chinn, Pamela Cundell, Anton Darby, Colin Edwynn, Derek Fowlds, Richard Griffiths, Brian Hall, Prentis Hancock, David Hargreaves, Russell Hunter, David Jackson, Roy Kinnear, George Layton, Phil McCall, Bridget McConnel, Lloyd McGuire, Clive Mantle, Jamila Massey, Adrian Mills, Warren O'Neill, Peter Postlethwaite, David Sibley, Gwyneth Strong, Royston Tickner, Anthony Valentine, Wanda Ventham, April Walker, Larrington Walker, Max Wall, Tony Westrope, Gary Whelan.

Commissioned by Thames Television. Transmission details are for the Central region.

	Holding / Source
26.12.1984 **Around The Corner**	DB / C1

Written by Tony Hoare; script executive Linda Agran; script editor Frances Heasman; associate producer Phillip Bowman; executive producer Lloyd Shirley; produced by George Taylor; directed by Roy Ward Baker.
With Patrick Malahide (Chisholm), Michael Povey (Detective Constable Jones), Brian Capron, Arthur Whybrow, Colin Farrell, Jeff Pirie, Michael Troughton, Joy Lemoine, Tony Caunter, Sidney Kean.

Commissioned by Thames Television. Transmission details are for the Yorkshire Television region.

	Holding / Source
01.01.1985 **Hypnotising Rita**	DB / C1

Alternative transmissions: Central: 22.07.1987.
Written by Alan Jones; directed by Terry Green.
With Renu Setna, Ray Burdis, Nicola Cowper, June Brown, Michael Redfern, Donald Sumpter, Tony Calvert, Vincent Allen, Margery Withers, Frank Williams, Sally Faulkner, Sheila Mathews, Charles Rae.

MINDER (continued)

Commissioned by Thames Television. Transmission details are for the Central region.
- Main regular credit(s): Executive producer Lloyd Shirley.
- Main regular cast: With Dennis Waterman (Terry McCann).

	VT Number	Holding / Source
25.12.1985 **Minder On The Orient Express**	61258	DB / C3

Duration: 100 minutes.

Written by Andrew Payne; script executive Linda Agran; music by Denis King; associate producer Simon Channing-Williams; produced by George Taylor; directed by Francis Megahy.

With Patrick Malahide (Chisholm), Michael Povey (Detective Constable Jones), Peter Childs (Rycott), Ralph Bates, Robert Beatty, Honor Blackman, James Coombes, Maurice Denham, Adam Faith, Amanda Pays, John Hartley, Alexandra Avery, Katharine Schofield, Arthur Whybrow, Karl Howman, Jesse Birdsall, Linal Haft, Jonathan Kydd, Linda Hayden, Frank Duncan, Dennis Edwards, Patrick Field, Michael Troughton, Milton Cadman, Garfield Morgan, David Beale, Richard Linford, Hans Meyer, Katja Kersten, James Faulkner, Virginia Wetherell, Ronald Lacey, Manning Redwood, Debbie Arnold, Roger Tallon, Helen Horton, John Serret, John Moreno, Colin Vancao, Daniel Rovai.

SERIES 7

Commissioned by Thames Television. Transmission details are for the Central region.
- Main regular credit(s): Story editor Joanna Willett; executive producer John Hambley; produced by George Taylor.
- Main regular cast: With Dennis Waterman (Terry McCann), Mark Farmer (Justin).

	VT Number	Holding / Source
26.12.1988 **An Officer And A Car Salesman**	47395	DB / C1

Duration: 73 minutes.

Written by Tony Hoare; directed by Roy Ward Baker.

With Patrick Malahide (Mr Chisholm), Peter Childs (Rycott), Michael Povey (Jones), Richard Briers, Diana Quick, Mark McManus, Simon Williams, Garfield Morgan, George Sweeney, Clive Swift, Al Ashton, John Judd, Nigel Miles Thomas, Gary Raynsford, Gordon Salkilld, Timothy Carlton, Iain Rattray, Jim Dunk, Bill Leadbitter, Martin Fisk, Sean Blowers.

A Thames Television production for Central. Transmission details are for the Central region.
- Credits: Associate producer Laura Julian; executive producer John Hambley; produced by Ian Toynton.
- Cast: With Gary Webster (Ray Daley).

	VT Number	Holding / Source
25.12.1991 **The Cruel Canal**	53573	DB / C1S

Written by Bernard Dempsey and Kevin Sperring; music by Alan Parker; directed by Keith Washington.

With Anthony O'Donnell, Emma Cunningham, Neil Phillips, Cathy Murphy, Trevor Cooper, Michael Goldie, Metin Marlow, Richard Heap.

MIRANDA

A BBC Productions production for BBC 2. Transmission details are for BBC 2. Duration: 30 minutes.
- Main regular credit(s): Created by Miranda Hart.
- Main regular cast: Miranda Hart (Miranda).

SERIES 2

- Main regular credit(s): Script supervisor Katie Wilkinson; script editor Jon Brown; director of photography Pete Rowe; art director Joanna King; designed by Harry Banks; associate producer Miranda Hart; production executive Sarah Hitchcock; executive producers Jo Sargent and Mark Freeland; production manager Sue Longstaff; produced by Emma Strain; directed by Juliet May.
- Main regular cast: With Patricia Hodge (Penny), Tom Ellis (Gary), Sarah Hadland (Stevie), James Holmes (Clive).

	Holding / Source
20.12.2010 **The Perfect Christmas**	HD/DB / HDC

Miranda plans a quiet holiday with her friends - and away from her parents - but as things become stressful, Christmas with her family starts to seem preferable.

Written by Miranda Hart, James Cary, Richard Hurst, Paul Powell, Paul Kerensa, Will Ing and Dan Gaster.

With Sally Phillips (Tilly), Tom Conti (Charles), Adam Rayner (Doctor Gail), Steve Speirs (Ray), Louisa Rix, Beth Chalmers, Annalisa Rossi, Mark Parsons.

SERIES 3

Commissioned by BBC 1. Transmission details are for BBC 1.
- Main regular credit(s): Written by Miranda Hart; produced by Emma Strain; directed by Juliet May.
- Main regular cast: With Patricia Hodge (Penny), Tom Ellis (Gary), Sarah Hadland (Stevie), James Holmes (Clive), Bo Poraj (Mike), Naomi Bentley (Rose).

	Holding / Source
26.12.2012 **It Was Panning**	HD/DB / HDC

Penny threatens to cancel Christmas unless Miranda sorts her life out. Step one is a detox, while step two involves trying to follow Stevie's example by getting a sensible, grown-up job. But can she cut it in the workplace?

MIRRORBALL

A BBC production for BBC 1. Transmission details are for BBC 1. Duration: 29 minutes.

Vivienne Keill is a West End singer and Jackie Riviera a seventies disco diva, both of whom have fallen on hard times. But then along comes an audition for Angela's Ashes - the Musical.

Written by Jennifer Saunders; script editor Ruby Wax; theme music by Hugh Cornwell; designed by Dennis De Groot; produced by Jon Plowman; directed by Adrian Edmondson.

Jennifer Saunders (Vivienne Keill), Joanna Lumley (Jackie Riviera), Julia Sawalha (Freda Keill), Jane Horrocks (Yitta Hilberstam), Harriet Thorpe (Cat Rogers), Tim Wylton (Brice Michaels), June Whitfield (Dora Vermouth), Matthew Francis (Theatre Producer), Sean Chapman (Mark), Alan Corser (Johnny), Andy Clarkson (Postman), Rupert Bates (Gordon), Nigel Ellacott (Jackie's Fan 1), Peter Robbins (Jackie's Fan 2), George Hall (Pianist), Bonnie Langford (Herself).

		Holding / Source
22.12.2000 [pilot]		DB / DBSW

MISFITS

A Clerkenwell Films production for E4. Transmission details are for E4. Duration: 48 minutes.

Main regular credit(s): Created by Howard Overman.

Main regular cast: Robert Sheehan (Nathan), Antonia Thomas (Alisha), Lauren Socha (Kelly), Iwan Rheon (Simon), Nathan Stewart-Jarrett (Curtis).

SERIES 2

Main regular credit(s): Script supervisor Marissa Cowell; script editor Matt Jarvis; music by Vince Pope; director of photography Christopher Ross; titles by Momoco; art director Debbie Burton; designed by Tom Bowyer; executive producers Murray Ferguson, Petra Fried and Howard Overman; line producer Adam Browne; produced by Kate Crowe.

	Holding / Source
19.12.2010 **Christmas Special**	DB / DBSWF

Written by Howard Overman; directed by Tom Harper.

With Ruth Negga (Nikki), Harry Hepple, Edward Hogg, Gwyneth Keyworth, Matthew McNulty, Rachel Rae.

MISS MARPLE (RADIO)

A BBC production for BBC Radio 4. Transmission details are for BBC Radio 4. Duration: 30 minutes.

Main regular cast: June Whitfield (Miss Marple).

SERIES 1: The Murder At The Vicarage

	Holding / Source
26.12.1993	DA /
27.12.1993	DA /
28.12.1993	DA /
29.12.1993	DA /
30.12.1993	DA /

SERIES 3: At Bertram's Hotel

Main regular credit(s): Adapted by Michael Bakewell; produced and directed by Enyd Williams.

Main regular cast: With Frederick Jaeger (Chief Inspector Davy), Siân Philips (Bess Sedgwick), Maurice Denham (Canon Pennyfather), Tracy Wiles (Elvira Blake), Jillie Meers (Miss Gorringe), Patrick Allen, John Hartley, Geoffrey Whitehead, Garard Green, David Timson, Gavin Muir, Margaret Courtenay, Geoffrey Bayldon, Preston Lockwood, Freddie Jones, Sarah Plowright, Jane Whittenshaw, David Collings, Zulema Dene, Alan Rowe, Ross Livingstone, Louisa Seddon, Tessa Worsley, Sandra James-Young, Patience Tomlinson, Andrew Branch.

	Holding / Source
25.12.1995	DA /
26.12.1995	DA /
27.12.1995	DA /
28.12.1995	DA /
29.12.1995	DA /

THE MIXER

An Almaro production for Yorkshire Television. made in association with Antenne 2 Productions / BetaFilm / Grego / ORF / Satel / ZDF Productions. Transmission details are for Carlton Select. Duration: 50 minutes.

Main regular credit(s): Based on characters created by Edgar Wallace; music by Gerhard Heinz; executive producers Gert Mechoff and Alexander Ollig; series producer Herbert Reuterrer; produced by John Frankau.

Main regular cast: Simon Williams (Sir Anthony Rose), Jeremy Clyde (Paul), Peter Jones (Inspector Bradley (eps 1,2,6,7,10,11,12)), Nicholas Frankau (Sergeant Sennet (eps 1,2,6,7,10,11,12)), Catherine Alric (Diane Delorme).

	Holding / Source
##.##.#### **The Mixer's Christmas Present**	DB / V1

Written by Philip Broadley; based on a story by Simon Booker; directed by Hermann Leitner and John Frankau.

With Kenneth Alan Taylor, John Laing, Lisa O'Connell, Rula Lenska, Jack May, Robert Whelan.

A Michael von Wolkenstein Presentation. This series was shown on the cable channel, Carlton Select, but precise dates are unavailable at this stage.

MOCK THE WEEK

An Angst Productions production for BBC 2. Transmission details are for BBC 2. Duration: 29 minutes.

Main regular credit(s): Presented by Dara Ó Briain; created by Dan Patterson and Mark Leveson; theme music by The Jam; titles by Moov.

SERIES 6

Main regular credit(s): Art director Norah Marshall; designed by Jonathan Paul Green; associate producers Adam Copeland, Róisín Doyle and Matt Nida; executive producer Jed Leventhall; consultant producer Mark Leveson; production manager Sarah McHarry; series producer Dan Patterson; produced by Ruth Wallace and Ewan Phillips; directed by Geraldine Dowd.

Main regular performer(s): With Hugh Dennis, Frankie Boyle, Russell Howard, Andy Parsons.

Holding / Source

23.12.2008 Christmas Special Clips / Highlights / Outtakes DB / DBSW

Script supervisor Patricia Morgan.

SERIES 7

Main regular credit(s): Script supervisor Patricia Morgan; art director Louisa Morris; designed by Jonathan Paul Green; associate producer Russell Balkind; executive producer Jed Leventhall; consultant producer Mark Leveson; production manager Sarah McHarry; series producer Dan Patterson; co-produced by Ben Wicks and Luke Shiach; produced by Ruth Wallace and Ewan Phillips; directed by Geraldine Dowd.

Main regular performer(s): With Hugh Dennis, Frankie Boyle, Russell Howard, Andy Parsons.

Holding / Source

22.12.2009 Christmas Special Clips / Highlights / Outtakes DB / DBSW

SERIES 9

Main regular credit(s): Script supervisor Patricia Morgan; designed by Jonathan Paul Green; associate producers Luke Goddard, Carrie Matthews and Niki Xenophontos; executive producer Jed Leventhall; consultant producer Mark Leveson; production manager Sarah McHarry; series producer Dan Patterson; produced by Ruth Wallace and Ewan Phillips.

Main regular performer(s): With Hugh Dennis, Andy Parsons.

Holding / Source

21.12.2010 Christmas Special Clips / Highlights / Outtakes DB / DBSW

SERIES 10

Main regular credit(s): Script supervisor Patricia Morgan; designed by Jonathan Paul Green; associate producers Judith Hay and Niki Xenophontos; executive producer Jed Leventhall; consultant producer Mark Leveson; production manager Sarah McHarry; series producer Dan Patterson; produced by Ewan Phillips; directed by Geraldine Dowd.

Main regular performer(s): With Hugh Dennis, Andy Parsons.

Holding / Source

20.12.2011 Christmas Special DB / DBSW

With Chris Addison, Miles Jupp, Holly Walsh, Ed Byrne, Adam Hills, Greg Davies, Stewart Francis, Milton Jones, Micky Flanagan, Ava Vidal, Nathan Catan, Carl Donnelly, Simon Evans, Andi Osho.

Holding / Source

27.12.2012 Christmas Special HD/DB / HDC

Duration: 60 minutes.

Designed by Jonathan Paul Green; executive producers Jed Leventhall, Gilly Hall, Pinki Chambers and Suzanne Gilfillan; series producer Dan Patterson; produced by Ewan Phillips and Ruth Wallace; directed by Geraldine Dowd.

With Hugh Dennis (Team Captain), Andy Parsons (Team Captain), Chris Addison, Ed Byrne, David Mitchell, Adam Hills, Jo Caulfield, Alun Cochrane, Greg Davies, Stewart Francis, Milton Jones, Ava Vidal, Carl Donnelly, Miles Jupp, Andi Osho, Gary Delaney, Josh Widdicombe, Chris Ramsey, Joe Wilkinson, Katherine Ryan.

31.12.2013 Christmas Special HD/DB / HDC

Designed by Jonathan Paul Green; executive producers Jed Leventhall and Pinki Chambers; series producer Dan Patterson; produced by Mark Leveson, Ewan Phillips and Ruth Wallace; directed by Geraldine Dowd.

With Hugh Dennis (Team Captain), Andy Parsons (Team Captain), Stewart Francis, Holly Walsh, Chris Addison, Ed Byrne, Seann Walsh, Milton Jones, Ava Vidal, Nathan Catan, Miles Jupp, Gary Delaney, Josh Widdicombe, Chris Ramsey, Katherine Ryan, Hal Cruttenden, Rob Beckett, Alistair McGowan, Romesh Ranganthan.

MONARCH OF THE GLEN

An Ecosse Films production for BBC Scotland. Transmission details are for BBC 1.

Main regular credit(s): Created by Michael Chaplin; based on novels by Compton Mackenzie; theme music by Simon Brint.

Main regular cast: Susan Hampshire (Molly), Alexander Morton (Golly), Dawn Steele (Lexie (until 03.10.2004)), Hamish Clark (Duncan (until 3.10.2004)).

Credits: Executive producers Robert Bernstein, Gaynor Holmes, Barbara McKissack and Douglas Rae.

Holding / Source

28.12.2003 Hogmanay Special DB / V1SW

Duration: 59 minutes.

Written by Michael Chaplin; directed by Robert Knights.

With Callum Williams, Robin Hooper, Antonia Bernath.

MONGRELS

Alternative/Working Title(s): THE UN-NATURAL WORLD / WE ARE MONGRELS
A BBC Productions production for BBC 3. Transmission details are for BBC 3. Duration: 30 minutes.

Main regular credit(s): Created by Adam Miller.

SERIES 2
Main regular credit(s): Script editor Paul Mayhew-Archer; designed by Simon Rogers; produced by Stephen McCrum; directed by Adam Miller.
Main regular cast: With Dan Tetsell (Marlon), Rufus Jones (Nelson), Lucy Montgomery (Destiny), Katy Brand (Kali), Paul Kaye (Vince), Tony Way (Gary).

Holding / Source
19.12.2011 "It's New Year's Day" HD/DB / HD/DB
No one can remember New Year's Eve...
Written by Jon Brown and Henry White; additional material by Dan Tetsell and Daniel Peak.
With Ruth Bratt (Koon-Yi), Nina Wadia (Nita), Lembit Öpik.
Adult puppet comedy. Puppets created by Talk To The Hand.

MOODY

A Yorkshire Television production. Transmission details are for the ATV midlands region. Duration: 25 minutes.
One man comedy show.
Music directed by Ronnie Aldrich; designed by Jane Martin; produced by Sid Colin; directed by John Frankau.
Ron Moody.

Holding / Source
24.12.1968 J / 2"

MOON JUNE

A BBC production for BBC 2. Transmission details are for BBC 2. Duration: 45 minutes.
Written by Brian Thompson; designed by Colin Green; produced by John Norton; directed by Chris Lovett.
June Barry (June), Roderick Smith (Don).

Holding / Source
24.12.1980 DB-D3 / 2"

THE MORECAMBE AND WISE SHOW

A BBC production for BBC Various. Transmission details are for BBC Various. Duration varies - see below for details.
Main regular performer(s): Morecambe and Wise (Hosts).

Commissioned by BBC 1. Transmission details are for BBC 1.

Holding / Source
25.12.1969 The Morecambe And Wise Christmas Show DB / 2"
Duration: 60 minutes.
Written by Eddie Braben; music directed by Peter Knight; designed by Bernard Lloyd-Jones; produced by John Ammonds.
With Fenella Fielding, Frankie Vaughan, Nina, Sacha Distel (xxx), The Pattersons, Kenny Ball and his Jazzmen, Alan Curtis, Diane Keen, Rex Rashley.

Transmission details are for BBC 1.
Main regular credit(s): Written by Eddie Braben; music directed by Peter Knight; produced by John Ammonds.

Holding / Source
25.12.1970 DB-1" / 2"
Duration: 60 minutes.
Designed by Bernard Lloyd-Jones.
With Peter Cushing, William Franklyn, Nina, Eric Porter, Edward Woodward, Kenny Ball and his Jazzmen, Ann Hamilton, Alan Curtis, Rex Rashley, George Day, John Higgins, Clinton Morris, Janet Webb.

SERIES 6
Commissioned by BBC 1. Transmission details are for BBC 1. Duration: 45 minutes.
Main regular credit(s): Written by Eddie Braben; orchestra directed by Peter Knight; produced and directed by John Ammonds.

Holding / Source
25.12.1971 The Morecambe & Wise Christmas Show DB-D3 / 2"
Dance direction by Ernest Maxin; designed by Bernard Lloyd-Jones.
With Shirley Bassey, Glenda Jackson, Francis Matthews, André Previn, Los Zafiros, Dick Emery, Frank Bough, Robert Dougall, Cliff Michelmore, Patrick Moore, Michael Parkinson, Eddie Waring, Ann Hamilton, Kenneth Hendel, Rex Rashley, Arthur Tolcher, Ken Alexis, The Mike Sammes Singers.

Commissioned by BBC 1. Transmission details are for BBC 1.

Holding / Source
25.12.1972 The Morecambe And Wise Christmas Show DB-1" / 2"
Duration: 67 minutes.
Written by Barry Cryer, John Junkin, Mike Craig and Lawrie Kinsley; additional material by Morecambe and Wise; orchestra directed by Peter Knight; dance direction by Ernest Maxin; designed by Victor Meredith; produced and directed by John Ammonds; film sequences directed by Ed Stuart.
With Glenda Jackson, Jack Jones, Vera Lynn, Pete Murray, Kenny Ball and his Jazzmen, Ann Hamilton, Janet Webb, Ian Carmichael, Fenella Fielding, Bruce Forsyth, Eric Porter, André Previn, Flora Robson, The Mike Sammes Singers.

THE MORECAMBE AND WISE SHOW (continued) British Christmas Television Guide

SERIES 7

Commissioned by BBC 1. Transmission details are for BBC 1.

Main regular credit(s):   Orchestra directed by Peter Knight; produced and directed by John Ammonds.

Holding / Source

25.12.1973 **The Morecambe And Wise Christmas Show**   DB-D3 / 2"

Duration: 63 minutes.

Written by Eddie Braben; additional material by Morecambe and Wise; dance direction by Ernest Maxin; designed by Victor Meredith.

With Vanessa Redgrave, Hannah Gordon, John Hanson, The New Seekers, Arthur Tolcher, Yehudi Menuhin, Rudolf Nureyev, Laurence Olivier, André Previn.

Commissioned by BBC 1. Transmission details are for BBC 1.

	Production No	VT Number	Holding / Source
25.12.1975	1245/1867	VTC/6HT/B02702	DB-D3 / 2"

Duration: 66 minutes.

Written by Eddie Braben; additional material by Morecambe and Wise; orchestra directed by Peter Knight; choreography by Flick Colby; designed by Victor Meredith; produced by Ernest Maxin.

With Diana Rigg, Des O'Connor, Gordon Jackson, Robin Day, Diane Solomon, Brenda Arnau, Ann Hamilton, Pan's People, Reg Turner, Debbie Ash, Fiona Gray.

Commissioned by BBC 1. Transmission details are for BBC 1.

Holding / Source

25.12.1976   DB-D3 / 2"

Duration: 65 minutes.

Written by Mike Craig, Barry Cryer, Lawrie Kinsley and Ron McDonnell; additional material by Morecambe and Wise; orchestra directed by Peter Knight; designed by Vic Meredith; produced and directed by Ernest Maxin.

With Elton John, Des O'Connor, John Thaw, Dennis Waterman, Angela Rippon, Kate O'Mara, Marian Montgomery, The Nolans, Gertan Klauber, Arthur Tolcher, The Peter Knight Orchestra.

25.12.1977   DB-D3 / 2"

Duration: 67 minutes.

Written by Eddie Braben; additional material by Morecambe and Wise; orchestra directed by Peter Knight; choreography by Ernest Maxin; designed by Victor Meredith; produced and directed by Ernest Maxin.

With Penelope Keith, Elton John, Angharad Rees, Francis Matthews, Arthur Lowe, John Le Mesurier, John Laurie, Richard Briers, Paul Eddington, James Hunt, Stella Starr, Michael Parkinson, Angela Rippon, Michael Aspel, Richard Baker, Frank Bough, Philip Jenkinson, Kenneth Kendall, Barry Norman, Eddie Waring, Richard Whitmore, Peter Woods, Sandra Dainty, Jenny Lee-Wright, Valerie Leon, The Mike Sammes Singers.

Commissioned by BBC 1. Transmission details are for BBC 1.

Holding / Source

30.12.1986 **Ernie Wise Introduces The Morecambe And Wise Classics**   DB / 1"

Duration: 60 minutes.

Written by Eddie Braben; television presentation by Robin Nash.

With Michael Aspel, Richard Baker, Shirley Bassey, Frank Bough, Ian Carmichael, Robert Dougall, Fenella Fielding, Glenda Jackson, Philip Jenkinson, Jack Jones, Penelope Keith, Cliff Michelmore, Marian Montgomery, Patrick Moore, Barry Norman, Michael Parkinson, André Previn, Eric Porter, Angela Rippon, Eddie Waring, Richard Whitmore, Peter Woods.

Eric Morecambe had passed away so Ernie Wise hosted this show alone.

See also: SHOW OF THE WEEK (BBC)

THE MORECAMBE AND WISE SHOW

A Thames Television production. Transmission details are for the ATV/Central region. Duration varies - see below for details.

Main regular performer(s): Morecambe and Wise (Hosts).

Transmission details are for the ATV midlands region.

Holding / Source

25.12.1978 **Eric And Ernie's Xmas Show**   D3 / 2"

Duration: 61 minutes.

Written by Barry Cryer and John Junkin; additional material by Morecambe and Wise; music directed by Peter Knight; designed by David Marshall; produced and directed by Keith Beckett.

With Leonard Rossiter, Nicholas Parsons, Frank Finlay, Sir Harold Wilson, Anna Dawson, Jenny Hanley, Jan Hunt, Frank Coda, Syd Lawrence and his Orchestra, Jillianne Foot, Denise Gyngell, Yvonne Dearman, Italia Conti Stage School, The Mike Sammes Singers, Eamonn Andrews.

25.12.1979 **Christmas With Eric And Ernie**   D3 / 2"

Duration: 56 minutes.

Programme associate Neil Shand; additional material by Eric Morecambe and Ernie Wise; music directed by Peter Knight; music by Keith Beckett; assistant director Keith Beckett; designed by Peter Le Page; produced and directed by John Ammonds.

With David Frost, Glenda Jackson, Des O'Connor, Arthur Tolcher, Janet Webb, Peter Knight and his Orchestra.

THE MORECAMBE AND WISE SHOW

THE MORECAMBE AND WISE SHOW (continued)

SERIES 1
Transmission details are for the ATV midlands region.

Main regular credit(s): Written by Eddie Braben; additional material by Morecambe and Wise; music directed by Peter Knight; choreography by Nigel Lythgoe; designed by Peter Le Page; produced and directed by John Ammonds.

	Holding / Source
25.12.1980 The Morecambe And Wise Christmas Show	D3 / 2"

Duration: 51 minutes.

Music associate Sam Harding; dance direction by Tudor Davies.

With Peter Barkworth, Peter Cushing, Jill Gascoine, Sir Alec Guinness, Peter Vaughan, Gemma Craven, Hannah Gordon, Glenda Jackson, Mick McManus.

SERIES 2
Transmission details are for the ATV midlands region.

Main regular credit(s): Written by Eddie Braben; music directed by Peter Knight; designed by Peter Le Page; produced and directed by John Ammonds.

	Holding / Source
23.12.1981 The Morecambe And Wise Christmas Show	D3 / 2"

Duration: 50 minutes.

Choreography by Nigel Lythgoe.

With Ralph Richardson, Robert Hardy, Suzannah York, Ian Ogilvy, Alvin Stardust, Suzanne Danielle, Steve Davis, Valerie Minifie.

SERIES 3
Transmission details are for the Central region.

Main regular credit(s): Written by Eddie Braben; designed by Peter Le Page; produced and directed by John Ammonds.

	Holding / Source
27.12.1982 The Morecambe And Wise Christmas Show	D3 / 2"

Duration: 50 minutes.

Music directed by Peter Knight; choreography by Lud.

With Robert Hardy, Rula Lenska, Richard Vernon, Diana Dors, Denis Healey, Glenda Jackson, Jimmy Young, Wall Street Crash, André Previn.

SERIES 4
Transmission details are for the Central region.

Main regular credit(s): Written by Eddie Braben; additional material by Eric Morecambe and Ernie Wise; designed by Peter Le Page; produced and directed by Mark Stuart.

	Holding / Source
27.12.1983 Eric And Ernie's Christmas Show	D3 / 1"

Duration: 50 minutes.

Additional material by Sid Green and Dick Hills; music directed by Harry Rabinowitz; choreography by Norman Maen.

With Gemma Craven, Nigel Hawthorne, Derek Jacobi, Felicity Kendal, Burt Kwouk, Patrick Mower, Nanette Newman, Peter Skellern, Tony Monopoly, Fulton Mackay, Jennie Linden.

MORRIS WITH MUSIC IN ULSTER

An Ulster Television production. Transmission details are for the Thames Television region. Duration: 50 minutes.

Johnny Morris hosts this family Christmas concert from the Ulster Hall, Belfast. The Ulster Orchestra, conducted by music director Bryden Thomson, is joined by baritone Jack Smith and choirs from three schools — Belfast Royal Academy, Grosvenor High School and Methodist College.

Music directed by Bryden Thomson; produced and directed by Alan Hailes.

Johnny Morris (Presenter), The Ulster Orchestra, Jack Smith.

	Holding / Source
24.12.1981	J / 2"

MOTHER GOOSE

A BBC production. Transmission details are for BBC. Duration: 90 minutes.

Written by Bertram Montague; play production by Richard Afton.

Frankie Howerd (Mother Goose), Harry Granley (The Goose), Joe Church (Johnny), Eddie Leslie (Mayor), Anne Daly (Colin), Wendy Cook (Jill), The Trio Sparkes (The Brokers Men), Rhoda Rogers (The Fairy), Leslie Adams (The Demon), Austen Gaffney (King Goose), Myrta Esteves (King Frog), Gillian Blair (Water Lily), Dave Jackley, Jack Daly, Sunny Rogers, Lee Young, The Dagenham Girl Pipers, Twelve Peggy O'Farrell Juveniles, The Television Toppers.

	Holding / Source
26.12.1959	J /

MOTHER GOOSE

A BBC production for BBC 1. Transmission details are for BBC 1. Duration: 95 minutes.

Adapted by John Law; based on a book by Emile Littler; lyrics by Hastings Mann; music by Hastings Mann; orchestra directed by Eric Rogers; choreography by Roy Gunson; designed by Colin Shaw; produced by David Croft; directed by Travers Thorneloe.

Norman Vaughan, Terry Scott, Jon Pertwee, Lauri Lupino Lane, Joanna Rigby, Anna Dawson, Kay Lyell, Susan Denny, Bernadette Milnes, The Lynton Boys, David Jason.

	Holding / Source
25.12.1965	R1 /

MOUNT PLEASANT

A Tiger Aspect production for Sky Living. Transmission details are for Sky Living. Duration: 48 minutes.

SERIES 2

Credits: Story producer Jane Wallbank; music by Jonathan Whitehead; designed by Christopher Walker; executive producers Sophie Clarke-Jervoise and Lucy Lumsden; produced by Howard Ella.

Cast: With Sally Lindsay (Lisa), Daniel Ryan (Dan), Paula Wilcox (Pauline), Sian Reeves (Bianca), Ainsley Howard (Denise), George Sampson (Gary), James Dreyfus (Reverend Roger), Angela Griffin (Shelley), Liza Tarbuck (Kate), Robson Green (Chris), David Bradley (Charlie).

		Holding / Source
23.12.2012	**Christmas Special**	HD/DB / HDC

In a festive episode, Lisa is missing her parents and Dan makes the mistake of buying the wrong gifts.

Written by Sarah Hooper; directed by Ian Barnes.

MOUSE AND MOLE AT CHRISTMAS

Commissioned by BBC 1. Transmission details are for BBC 1.

	Holding / Source
26.12.2013	HD/DB / HDC

Animated film.

MOVIELAND

A Thames Television production. Transmission details are for the Yorkshire Television region. Duration: 50 minutes.

Keith Fordyce visits the Movieland Exhibition at Whiteley's store in London to look at the exhibits and talk to some of the people who work in this fascinating miniature world. On show are Thunderbirds, James Bond's secret weapons, Lady Penelope's Rolls-Royce, puppets and models from television and films.

Produced by Jim Pople.

Keith Fordyce (Presenter).

	Holding / Source
22.12.1970	J / 2"

MR BROC

Commissioned by S4C. Transmission details are for S4C. Duration: 50 minutes.

	Holding / Source
26.12.1996	D3 / V1S

MR CHETHAM'S MUSIC SCHOOL

A BBC Manchester production for BBC 1. Transmission details are for BBC 1. Duration: 30 minutes.

Words and music in tune with Christmas spoken, sung and played by the boys and girls of this unique school — over 300 years old, now Britain's first national junior school for young musicians. Including We wish you a Merry Christmas; Twelve Days of Christmas; Torches. An outside broadcast from the Halls and Cloisters of the ancient Great House in Manchester.

Produced by Nick Hunter.

	Holding / Source
24.12.1973	J / 2"

MR DIGBY DARLING

A Yorkshire Television production. Transmission details are for the ATV midlands region. Duration: 25 minutes.

Main regular credit(s): Written by Ken Hoare and Mike Sharland; theme music by Bob Leaper.

Main regular cast: Sheila Hancock (Thelma Teesdale), Peter Jones (Roland Digby).

SERIES 2

Main regular credit(s): Designed by Roger Cheveley; produced and directed by Christopher Hodson.

		Holding / Source
22.12.1969	**Festive Spirit**	B / 2"

When the annual office party is cancelled because of Mr. Digby, even Thelma is likely to forget it's the season of goodwill...

With Peter Stephens, Janet Brown, Pat Coombs, Jean Wyn Scott, Mark Powell, John Cazabon.

MR MAJEIKA

A TVS production. Transmission details are for the Central region.

Main regular credit(s): Adapted by Jenny McDade; based on books by Humphey Carpenter; executive producer J. Nigel Pickard.

Main regular cast: Stanley Baxter (Mr Majeika).

SERIES 2

Main regular credit(s): Designed by John Newton Clarke; produced by John Price.

		VT Number	Holding / Source
25.12.1988	**Have Yourself A Wizard Little Christmas**	22890	1" / 1"

Duration: 50 minutes.

Adapted by Jenny McDade; directed by Michael Kerrigan.

With Roland Macleod, Ken Jones, Eve Ferret, Richard Murdoch, Andrew Read, Claire Sawyer, Simson Pearl, Fidelis Morgan, Hilda Fenemore, Robin Driscoll, Tony Haase, Sonia Graham.

MR MOON'S LAST CASE

A Yorkshire Television production. Transmission details are for the Central region. Duration: 35 minutes.
Based on a book by Brian Patten; produced by Joy Whitby and Anne Wood; directed by Doug Wilcox.
Alun Armstrong (Narrator), Stratford Johns (Mr Moon), Big Mick (Nameon), Cy Chadwick (Johnny), David Graham-Jones (Watch-Man), Tom Harrison (Watch-Man), Elizabeth Lawless (Receptionist), Roger Greenwood (Interviewer), Godfrey Byrn (Tobias), Pat Wallis (Landlady), Gerry Cowan (Mr O'Lovelife), David Ericsson (Verger), June Broughton (Miss Dawling), Sajjad Shah (Benjamin Platts).

	VT Number	Holding / Source
29.12.1983	C016	DB / C1

MR STINK

A BBC production for BBC 1. Transmission details are for BBC 1.
Lonely 12-year-old Chloe invites local tramp Mr Stink to hide out in her dysfunctional family's garden shed.
Adapted by David Walliams and Simon Nye; based on a book by David Walliams; produced by Jo Sargent; directed by Declan Lowney.
Hugh Bonneville (Mr Stink), Johnny Vegas (Dad), Sheridan Smith (Mum), David Walliams (Prime Minister), Nell Tiger Free (Chloe), Isabella Blake-Thomas (Annabelle), Harish Patel (Raj), Jemma Donovan (Pippa), Steve Pemberton (Sir Derek Dimble), Pudsey (The Duchess).

	Holding / Source
23.12.2012	HD/DB / HDC

Made in 3-D.

MR TOBY'S CHRISTMAS

An Associated-Rediffusion production. Transmission details are for the ATV midlands region. Duration: 25 minutes.
Main regular credit(s):   Written by Marc Miller; choreography by Ronnie Curran; designed by Barbara Bates; produced and directed by Marc Miller.
Main regular performer(s): Andrew Sachs (Mr Toby), Carol Dilworth (Sarah), Gareth Robinson (Jeremy), Raymond Mason (Sam Bundy), The Orpington Junior Singers, Ronnie Curran, Greta Hanby.

	VT Number	Holding / Source
21.12.1962	W1530/352	J / 40

With Will Stampe, Derek Royle.

28.12.1962	W1542/411	J / 40

With Johnny Lamonte.

04.01.1963		J / 40

MR WHITE GOES TO WESTMINSTER

A Hat Trick production for Channel 4. Transmission details are for Channel 4. Duration: 75 minutes.
Written by Guy Jenkin; script supervisor Janice Schumm; music by Matthew Scott; designed by Graeme Story; executive producer Denise O'Donoghue; produced by Colin Swash; directed by Guy Jenkin.
Bill Paterson (Ben White), Robert Duncan (Paul Madison), Celia Imrie (Victoria), Dervla Kirwan (Pam), Samantha Bond (Helen Nash), Andy Hamilton (Editor), Josephine Butler (Liz White), John Bowler (Peter Edworthy), Matilda Ziegler (Yvonne Freeman), Phil Nice (Minister), Helena McCarthy (Mrs Shipley), Benedict Sandiford (Edward), Terence Harvey (Newsreader), Adam Kotz (Don Nash).

	Holding / Source
30.12.1997	DB / C1SW

MR. AND MRS.

A Border Television production. Transmission details are for the ATV midlands region. Duration: 25 minutes.
Main regular performer(s): Derek Batey (Host).

	Holding / Source
24.12.1973 **Christmas Special**	J / 2"

It's a special edition of the husband and wife quiz game-and who knows what the contestants will find in their Christmas stockings, in addition to cash prizes and jackpots? The winners of the Mr. and Mrs. Christmas Card competition will be announced on today's show.
Designed by John Henderson; produced by Derek Batey; directed by Anna K. Moore.
With Marion MacDonald.

31.12.1973 **New Year Special**	J / 2"

Designed by John Henderson; produced by Derek Batey; directed by Anna K. Moore.

23.12.1974	J / 2"

Designed by John M. Henderson; produced by Derek Batey; directed by William Cartner.
With Marion MacDonald, Pete Murray, Mrs Pete Murray, Carlisle Cathedral Choristers.

24.12.1975 **Christmas Party**	J / 2"

Designed by John M. Henderson; produced by Derek Batey; directed by William Cartner.
With Marion MacDonald, Helen McArthur.

31.12.1975 **New Year Special**	J / 2"

A Hogmanay party.
Designed by John M. Henderson; produced by Derek Batey; directed by William Cartner.
With Marion MacDonald, Helen McArthur.

24.12.1977 **Celebrity Mr. And Mrs.**	J / 2"

Designed by John M. Henderson; produced by Derek Batey; directed by William Cartner.
With Sue Cuff (Hostess).

MR. AND MRS. (continued)

27.12.1979   J / 2"

Designed by Ian Reed; produced by Derek Batey; directed by William Cartner.

With Susan Cuff (Hostess), The Krankies.

Only specials are listed.

MR. BEAN

A Tiger Television/Tiger Aspect production for a variety of companies (see details below). Transmission details are for the Central region. Usual duration: 25 minutes.

Main regular credit(s):   Theme music by Howard Goodall.

Main regular cast: Rowan Atkinson (Mr Bean).

Holding / Source

01.01.1990 **Mr. Bean (pilot)**   D3 / 1"

A Tiger Television production for Thames Television.

Written by Richard Curtis, Rowan Atkinson and Ben Elton; music by Howard Goodall; designed by Gillian Miles; production executive Peter Bennett-Jones; produced and directed by John Howard Davies.

With Richard Briers, Paul Bown, Rudolph Walker, Roger Sloman, Howard Goodall.

29.12.1992 **Merry Christmas Mr Bean**   D3 / 1"S

A Tiger Television production for Thames Television. Duration: 27 minutes.

Written by Robin Driscoll, Richard Curtis and Rowan Atkinson; theme music by Choir of Southwark Cathedral; music by Howard Goodall; designed by Andrew Howe Davies; executive producer Peter Bennett-Jones; production manager Julian Meers; produced by Sue Vertue; directed by John Birkin.

With Matilda Ziegler, C. J. Allen, Owen Brenman, John Warner, Lee Barrett, Chris Sanders, Jonathan Stratt, Sylvia Young Stage School.

MR. PASTRY

A BBC production. Transmission details are for BBC. Duration varies - see below for details.

Main regular cast: Richard Hearne (Mr Pastry).

Holding / Source

23.12.1952 **Mr Pastry Takes A Holiday**   B3 / B3

Alt.Title(s):   *Mr Pastry Learns to Ski*

Duration: 15 minutes.

Written by Richard Hearne and J. C. Tobin; produced and directed by D. A. Smith.

With McDonald Hobley.

21.12.1958 **How Mr Pastry Joined The Circus**   B3 / B3

Written by Richard Hearne; produced and directed by Bill Parry Jones.

The two circus ones seem to have been filmed at the same location. "Holiday" and "Ski" both involve filming in Norway which you would think meant they were shot together - except that "Holiday" says it was first shown in 1952 on Infax. RT implies they are the same episode as the billing is almost identical for its showings on 23/12/52, 30/12/53 and 29/11/54. Kaleidoscope doesn't have immediate access to PasBs from pre-1955, but we wonder if there was more than one version of the "Holiday" episode - the BBC card files don't say these are repeats. "Holiday" however is repeated on 20/12/55 and it states on that PasB that it was previously shown on 29/11/54, not mentioning the other dates (and often films for children in this era e.g. "Watch With Mother" state all previous showings on the PasB). "Holiday" and "Ski" also have similar title cards, suggesting they are linked.

MR. PICKWICK

A Granada production. Transmission details are for the ATV midlands region. Duration: 78 minutes.

Written by Stanley Young; adapted by William Slater and Harry Kershaw; settings by Michael Grimes; produced by Derek Granger; directed by Claude Whatham.

Arthur Lowe (Mr Pickwick), Jack May (Tupman), Philip Grout (Snodgrass), Trevor Danby (Winkle), Susan Field (Mrs Bardell), James Bolam (Sam Weller), Patrick Newell (Mr Weller), Jean Conroy (Betsy Cluppins), Glen Slowther (Tommy Bardell), Gordon Rollings (Jingle), Betty Huntley-Wright (Mrs Leo Hunter), Roy Bunter (Joe), John Wentworth (Mr Wardle), Eileen Kennally (Rachel Wardle), Deborah Millington (Emily Wardle), Harriet Harper (Isabella Wardle), Jack Austin (Dodson), Martin Dobson (Fogg), Allen Sykes (Jackson), Roy Minton (Wicks), Roy Kinnear (Sergeant Buzfuz), Eric Longworth (Mr Perker), Jack Woolgar (Judge), Eric Sutton (Court Usher), Leslie Twelvetrees (Foreman of the Jury), Ray Gatenby (Sergeant Stubbins), Leslie Clark (Turnkey).

	Production No	Holding / Source
25.12.1963	P23/53	J / 40

THE MRS MERTON SHOW

A Granada production for BBC North. Transmission details are for BBC 2. Usual duration: 30 minutes.

Main regular performer(s): Caroline Aherne (Mrs Merton).

SERIES 2

Commissioned by BBC North. Transmission details are for BBC 2.

Main regular credit(s):   Written by Caroline Hook, Craig Cash, Henry Normal and Dave Gorman; script editor Henry Normal; designed by Paul Rowan; assistant producer Lisa Mayhew; executive producers Andy Harries and Clive Tulloh; produced by Peter Kessler; directed by Pati Marr.

Main regular performer(s):   With Caroline Hook (Mrs Merton), Hooky and The Boys (Resident Band).

	Production No	Holding / Source
24.12.1995	1/2127/13	D3 / D3SW

With Gary Rhodes, Johnny Briggs, Amanda Barrie, Glenys Kinnock.

THE MRS MERTON SHOW (continued)

SERIES 3
Commissioned by BBC North. Transmission details are for BBC 1.

Main regular credit(s): Written by Caroline Aherne, Craig Cash, Henry Normal and Dave Gorman; designed by Paul Rowan and Stephen Graham; assistant producer Lisa Mayhew; associate producers Caroline Aherne, Craig Cash and Henry Normal; executive producers Andy Harries and John Whiston; produced by Mark Gorton; directed by Pati Marr.

Main regular performer(s): With Caroline Aherne (Mrs Merton).

	Production No	Holding / Source
24.12.1996	1/2127/20	D3 / D3SW

With Noddy Holder, Clive James, Daniel O'Donnell.

27.12.1997	1/2127/21	D3 / D3SW

Duration: 29 minutes.
With Edwina Currie, Max Bygraves.

MRS MINIVER (RADIO)

A BBC production for BBC Radio 4. Transmission details are for BBC Radio 4.

	Holding / Source
22.11.2001 **Christmas Shopping**	DA /

MRS. BROWN'S BOYS

A BBC Productions production for BBC 1. made in association with BocPix / RTE. Transmission details are for BBC 1. Usual duration: 30 minutes.

Main regular credit(s): Written by Brendan O'Carroll.

Main regular cast: Brendan O'Carroll (Agnes Brown), Jennifer Gibney (Cathy Brown), Dermot O'Neill (Grandad Brown), Paddy Houlihan (Dermot Brown), Elish O'Carroll (Winnie McGoogan).

SERIES 2
Main regular credit(s): Script editor Paul Mayhew-Archer; designed by Iain McDonald; executive producers Justin Healy, Mark Freeland and Ewan Angus; produced by Stephen McCrum and Martin Delany; directed by Ben Kellett.

	Holding / Source
26.12.2011 **Mammy's Ass**	HD/DB / HDC

Agnes tries to arrange the perfect Christmas for her family.
With Susie Blake (Hillary Nicholson), Danny O'Carroll (Buster Brady), Rory Cowan (Rory Brown), Fiona O'Carroll (Maria Brown), Amanda Woods (Betty Brown), Pat 'Pepsi' Shields (Mark Brown), Emily Reagan (Barbara), Gary Hollywood (Dino Doyle), Fiona Gibney (Sharon McGoogan), Andy Wilkinson (Mr Foley), Martin Delany (Trevor Brown).

SERIES 3
Main regular credit(s): Script editor Paul Mayhew-Archer; designed by Iain McDonald; executive producers Justin Healy, Mark Freeland and Ewan Angus; produced by Stephen McCrum and Martin Delany; directed by Ben Kellett.

Main regular cast: With Susie Blake (Hillary Nicholson), Danny O'Carroll (Buster Brady), Rory Cowan (Rory Brown), Fiona O'Carroll (Maria Brown), Amanda Woods (Betty Brown), Emily Reagan (Barbara), Gary Hollywood (Dino Doyle), Martin Delany (Trevor Brown).

	Holding / Source
24.12.2012 **Mammy Christmas**	HD/DB / HDC

Agnes finds herself facing her busiest Christmas ever when the family descends and if that wasn't enough to raise her blood pressure, she's also staging a Nativity play.
With Conor Moloney (Father Damien), Jamie O'Carroll (Bono Brown).

26.12.2012 **The Virgin Mammy**	HD/DB / HDC

Agnes has finished the script for her Nativity play - but will her unorthodox version of the story gain Father Damien's approval? And will she really get to play the Virgin Mary?
With Pat 'Pepsi' Shields (Mark Brown), Conor Moloney (Father Damien), Derek Reddin (Doctor Flynn), Martin Delany (Trevor Brown), Jamie O'Carroll (Bono Brown), Mike Nolan (Mr Foley), Dean Donnelly (Shepherd), Evan Rogers (Shepherd), Mick Byrne (Shepherd), Marian O'Sullivan (Shepherd), Jim Davers (Shepherd), Peter Burke (Shepherd), Conor Gibney (King), Mark Sheridan (King), Felix Delany (Angel), Charlie Hollywood (Angel), Jack Hollywood (Angel).

SERIES 4
Main regular credit(s): Written by Brendan O'Carroll and Paul Mayhew-Archer; designed by Iain McDonald; executive producers Justin Healy, Mark Freeland and Ewan Angus; series producer Stephen McCrum; produced by James Farrell and Martin Delany; directed by Ben Kellett.

Main regular cast: With Pat 'Pepsi' Shields (Mark Brown), Amanda Woods (Betty Brown), Rory Cowan (Rory Brown), Conor Moloney (Father Damien), Fiona O'Carroll (Maria Brown), Fiona Gibney (Sharon McGoogan), Emily Regan (Barbara), Mark Dymond (Mick), Susie Blake (Hillary Nicholson), Gary Hollywood (Dino Doyle), Martin Delany (Trevor Brown).

	Holding / Source
25.12.2013 **Buckin' Mammy**	HD/DB / HDC

Duration: 35 minutes.
Agnes finds festive spirit lacking during a games night when her rules are disobeyed
With Jamie O'Carroll (Bono Brown), Caolan Byrne (Fitter), Conor Gibney (Fitter), Steven Wickham (Santa).

30.12.2013 **Who's A Pretty Mammy?**	HD/DB / HDC

Duration: 40 minutes.
With Jimmy Gibney (Father McBride).

THE MUCH LOVED MUSIC SHOW

A BBC production for BBC 2. Transmission details are for BBC 2.

		Holding / Source
23.12.1979	The Much Loved Music Christmas Show	DB-D3 / 2"
21.12.1980		DB-D3 / 2"
23.12.1982		DB-D3 / 2"

Duration: 50 minutes.
Produced and directed by John Vernon.
With Owain Arwel Hughes (Presenter), Janet Baker, BBC Concert Orchestra, Philharmonia Chorus.

MUFFIN THE MULE

A BBC production. Transmission details are for BBC.

Main regular credit(s): Puppetry by Ann Hogarth.
Main regular cast: With Annette Mills (Host).

		Holding / Source
26.12.1947	Children's Christmas Party	NR / Live
08.01.1950	Christmas Party	NR / Live
26.12.1950	Muffin The Mule presents his Pantomime	NR / Live
23.12.1951	"Muffin prepares for Christmas"	NR / Live
19.12.1954	Father Christmas Muffin	DB-D3 / B1
02.01.1955	Dick Muffington And His Cat	DB-D3 / B1

Many of the 1940s appearances listed here were not productions in themselves, merely parts of a longer umbrella programme entitled FOR THE CHILDREN. From December 1946, Annette Mills and Ann Hogarth appear with a variety of puppets in FOR THE CHILDREN, but it isn't until February 1947 that Muffin is mentioned by name. A Radio Times article accompanying the 09.02.1947 broadcast makes it clear that Muffin was one of a number of puppets which had already appeared in the series, but unsurprisingly it doesn't indicate on precisely which edition(s).

A number of titles were made for markets other than the BBC. Only episodes with transmission dates can reliably be treated as BBC episodes.

MULTI-COLOURED SWAP SHOP

A BBC production for BBC 1. Transmission details are for BBC 1. Duration: 180 minutes.

Main regular cast: Noel Edmonds (Presenter).

SERIES 1
Main regular credit(s): Produced and directed by Rosemary Gill.
Main regular cast: With John Craven (Presenter), Keith Chegwin (Presenter).

		Production No	VT Number	Holding / Source
27.12.1976	Swap Of The Pops	3346/1340	VTC/6HT/B14849/ED	DB-D3 / 2"

Alt.Title(s): *Son of Swap Shop*
With Abba, Showaddywaddy, Mud, Smokie, John Christie, White Rhino, Pussycat, Another Pussycat, The Wurzels, Doctor Hook, Britain's Only Quackologist.

SERIES 2
Main regular credit(s): Edited by Rosemary Gill.
Main regular cast: With John Craven (Presenter), Keith Chegwin (Presenter).

		Holding / Source
24.12.1977	Swap Of The Pops	2"|n / 2"

Duration: 90 minutes.
BBC1 1977 Xmas Pudding Symbol at start. Noel Edmonds presents the best bits from the first series of The Multi-Coloured Swap Shop. Various bits of chat between Edmonds, Craven and Chegwin plus Showaddywaddy, Barbara Dickson, Chegwin on go-cart, lion cubs at zoo, Concorde footage, Skateboarding, Suzie Quatro, Liverpool Express, Osibisa, Harry Secombe (Harry the Frog), Chegwin/Swaparama, Chegwin sings. Brief clip of unidentified pop group at end, followed by brief v.extract from World of Sport. Abba, Pash Paws sequence, Skiing, Trumptonshire type-puppets, ice-ckating, Smokie, Tina Charles, Bonnie Tyler, Obadia and Flo (animation), Status Quo, Leo Sayer, Georgio, Wings/Mull of Kintyre, chat about guests past and present, ends with "Super Group"; TotP slide, Xmas trail (v. brief fragment), bit of unidentified film at end.
Directed by Crispin Evans.

With Abba, Smokie, Wings, Bonnie Tyler, Carvells, Chopin, Chuck Berry, Cliff Richard, Giorgio, Heatwave, Harry Secombe, Leo Sayer, Wolfgang Mozart, Showaddywaddy, Status Quo, Tina Charles, Twiggy, Vivaldi, The Wurzels.

SERIES 3
Main regular credit(s): Series editor Rosemary Gill; produced by Crispin Evans.
Main regular cast: With John Craven (Presenter), Keith Chegwin (Presenter), Maggie Philbin (Presenter (From 14.10.1978 Onwards)).

	Holding / Source
23.12.1978	J / 2"

With John Salisse, Cliff Richard.

SERIES 4
Main regular credit(s): Series editor Rosemary Gill.

Holding / Source
22.12.1979   DVSEQ / 2"
Produced by Crispin Evans.
With Isla St. Clair, Peter Holden, Debbie Harry, Chris Stein.
24 mins with Debbie Harry. Christmas tree on set, Noel's birthday. Held by Kaleidoscope, ex-private collector, as a VHS off-air transferred to a HDD file.

SERIES 5
Main regular credit(s): Edited by Rosemary Gill; produced by Crispin Evans.
Main regular cast: With John Craven (Presenter), Keith Chegwin (Presenter), Maggie Philbin (Presenter).

Holding / Source
20.12.1980   C1SEQ / 2"
Fly to the other side of the world for a look round exotic Hong Kong. Try out DELIA SMITH'S special recipe. Go transatlantic for a New York Christmas and don't miss the story of the Haunted Bike with a star-studded cast - and there's a Sting in the tail!!
With Delia Smith.

27.12.1980   DB-D3 / 2"
Go to the pantomime the Swap Shop way when NOEL, JOHN and MAGGIE present their version of Cinderella — but has anyone told KEITH? Plus jokes, cartoons, prizes, swaps and the best in music. Ring in (after 9.30) on 01-811 8055.
With Terry Wogan.
The titles exist on C3.

THE MUPPET SHOW
An ATV production. Transmission details are for the ATV midlands region. Duration: 25 minutes.
Main regular performer(s): Jim Henson (Kermit / Rowlf / Waldorf), Frank Oz (Miss Piggy / Fozzie / Animal), Jerry Nelson (Floyd / Robin / Crazy Harry), Richard Hunt (Scooter / Statler / Sweetums), Dave Goelz (Gonzo / Bunsen / Honeydrew / Zoot), Louise Gold (Annie Sue).

SERIES 2
Main regular credit(s): Written by Jerry Juhl, Jim Henson, Don Hinkley, Chris Langham and Joseph A. Bailey; designed by Bryan Holgate and David Chandler; executive producer David Lazer; produced by Jim Henson; directed by Philip Casson.

Holding / Source
25.12.1977   1" / 2"
With Julie Andrews.

All material held by Jim Henson Associates in the USA. On the material released on DVD, there are no ATV idents and the end credits appear to be different to the original ones with the idents on the end being either "Muppet Holdings Co LLC" on some of the releases or "Jim Henson Productions" on some of the other releases. ITV now only hold the editions featuring Twigyy and Carol Burnett. Kaleidoscope do not know if the original ATV versions still exist in the USA.

MUPPETS TONIGHT!
A BBC production for BBC 1. Transmission details are for BBC 1.

Holding / Source
30.12.1996   DB / D3S
With Garth Brooks.
USA series.

MURIEL'S CHRISTMAS PARTY
An Associated-Rediffusion production. Transmission details are for Associated-Rediffusion. Duration: 12 minutes.
Directed by Tig Roe.
Janet Nicholls (Presenter), Muriel Young (Presenter).

Holding / Source
23.12.1959   NR / Live

MURRAY AND MARTIN'S CHRISTMAS F1 SPECIAL
A Mach 1 Productions production for LWT. Transmission details are for the London Weekend Television region. Duration: 48 minutes.
Highlights of the 1999 Formula 1 season.
Executive producer Gerard Lane; produced by Rupert Bush.
Murray Walker (Presenter).

Holding / Source
30.12.2000   DB / DBS

MUSIC AT NIGHT: THE CHRISTMAS TREE SUITE

A BBC Manchester production for BBC 1. Transmission details are for BBC 1. Duration: 4 minutes.

Written in 1874 for his grand-daughter Daniela von Bulow.

Main regular credit(s): Graphics by Linda Page; music by Franz Liszt; lighting by John Spicer; sound Paul Bush; designed by Chris Edwards; produced by Kenneth Corden; directed by Helen Morton.

Main regular performer(s): Rhondda Gillespie (Pianist).

On the Twelve Days of Christmas:

		Holding / Source
26.12.1979	1: An Old Christmas Song	DB-D3 / 2"
27.12.1979	2: O Holy Night	DB-D3 / 2"
28.12.1979	3: The Shepherds At The Manger (In Dulci Jubilo)	DB-D3 / 2"
29.12.1979	4: March Of The Three Wise Men (Adeste Fideles!)	DB-D3 / 2"
30.12.1979	5: Lighting The Candles On The Christmas Tree	DB-D3 / 2"
31.12.1979	6: Carillon	DB-D3 / 2"
01.01.1980	7: Slumber Song	DB-D3 / 2"
02.01.1980	8: Old Provencal Carol	DB-D3 / 2"
03.01.1980	9: Evening Bells	DB-D3 / 2"
04.01.1980	10: Once Upon A Time	DB-D3 / 2"
05.01.1980	11: In Hungarian Rhythm	DB-D3 / 2"
06.01.1980	12: In Polish Rhythm	DB-D3 / 2"

It's not a special, these were always 5 minute programmes that went out usually last thing at night – but they are compiled on a single tape, from the off, the broadcast engineers would just have had to wind through to the correct point to transmit each one.

MUSIC BY JEROME KERN

A BBC production for BBC 1. Transmission details are for BBC 1. Duration: 60 minutes.

Introduced by Arthur Schwartz; script associate Benny Green; music directed by Ronnie Hazlehurst; music by Jerome Kern; choreography by Gillian Gregory; designed by Stephen Brownsey; produced by Kenneth Corden; directed by Don Isted.

Dennis Wilson (Pianist), Don Lusher (Trombone), Julia McKenzie, Elizabeth Seal, Teddy Green, David Kernan, Christine Carlson, Jane Darling, Carolynn Hamilton, Harry Higham, Gerard Hunt, Bryan Payne, The Mike Sammes Singers.

	Holding / Source
30.12.1977	DB-D3 / 2"

MUSIC ROOM

An ATV production. Transmission details are for the ATV midlands region. Duration: 25 minutes.

Main regular credit(s): Designed by Rex Spencer; produced by Philip Grosset; directed by Dilys Howell.

Main regular performer(s): John Pearse (Host).

	VT Number	Holding / Source
22.12.1970	1897/70	DB / 2"

With Olivia Lyons, Peter Connah.

MUSIC TIME

A BBC Schools production for BBC 1 Schools. Transmission details are for BBC 1 Schools.

		Holding / Source
21.11.1977	A Christmas Journey Part One	DB / 2"
28.11.1977	A Christmas Journey Part Two	DB / 2"

A MUSICAL NATIVITY WITH JOHN RUTTER

A BBC production for BBC 2. Transmission details are for BBC 2. Duration: 60 minutes.

For many choristers, the name John Rutter is synonymous with Christmas. His music is so devotional and steeped in Christian doctrine that it's a surprise to learn he's an agnostic - or, as he describes himself here, a "bruised optimist in a very imperfect world". His gift for arrangement and tune shines out in an uplifting programme of personal favourites and his own compositions, from Nativity Carol, written at 16, to his latest work (he's now a sprightly 66). Rutter's excitement for the occasion is beautifully expressed not only in interview and in his playful, darting songs, but also in sparkly and moving versions of familiar works.

Music by John Rutter.

	Holding / Source
25.12.2011	HD/DB / HDC

MY ALMOST FAMOUS FAMILY

A CBBC production. Transmission details are for BBC 2. Duration: 30 minutes.

Main regular credit(s):	Script supervisor Annetta Laufer; script editor Hilary Frankland; music directed by Richard Webb; music by Tom Nichols; choreography by Lucie Pankhurst; director of photography Ian Liggett; designed by Anna Higginson; production executive Eamon Fitzpatrick; executive producer Steven Andrew; line producer Ian D. Tootle; produced by Paul McKenzie.
Main regular cast:	Andrew Clover (Gary), Rakie Ayola (Shalondra), Rachel Brady (Martha), Dominique Moore (Aretha), Naomi Battrick (Toyah), Angus Harrison (Hadley), Matt Morgan (Isaac), Emily Joyce (Jill), Alice Henley (Annabelle).

Holding / Source
HD/DB / HD/DB

21.11.2009 Christmas Time

Written by Holly Lyons; directed by Jonathan Gershfield.

With No guest cast.

MY DAD'S THE PRIME MINISTER

A BBC production for CBBC Channel. made in association with Deleste Productions Ltd. Transmission details are for BBC 1. Duration: 30 minutes.

Main regular credit(s):	Written by Ian Hislop and Nick Newman.
Main regular cast:	Robert Bathurst (Prime Minister), Joe Prospero (Dillon Phillips), Carla Mendonca (Clare Phillips), Emma Sackville (Sarah Phillips), Jasper Britton (Duncan Packer).

Holding / Source
DB / DBSWF

31.12.2004 Powerless

A BBC Drama Serials production.

Script supervisor Suzanne Baron; executive producer Sophie Clarke-Jervoise; produced by Matthew Francis; directed by Juliet May.

With Jane Bertish (Education Secretary), Rupert Vansittart (Chancellor), Martin Chamberlain (Trade And Industry Secretary), Neil McCaul (Foreign Secretary), Steve Toussaint (Transport Secretary), Amanda Holt (Health Secretary), Michael Fenton Stevens (Home Secretary), Marcia Warren (Granny Phillips), Paterson Joseph (Detective Gary McRyan), Dean Cook, John Sergeant, Caroline Gruber, Mark Perry, Bruce McGregor, Wil Ashcroft, Tony Britton, Ian Gelder, Ian Midlane, Kenny Ireland, Jeff Rawle.

MY FAMILY

A Rude Boy Productions production for BBC 1. made in association with Don Taffners Entertainment Ltd. Transmission details are for BBC 1. Usual duration: 30 minutes.

Main regular credit(s):	Created by Fred Barron.
Main regular cast:	Robert Lindsay (Ben Harper), Zoë Wanamaker (Susan Harper), Gabriel Thomson (Michael Harper).

SERIES 3

Main regular credit(s):	Script associate Paul Mayhew-Archer; music by Graham Jarvis; designed by Ian Fisher and Merle Downie; production team Sophie Hetherington, Sacha Grimsditch, Rebecca Rycroft and Rachel Stewart; executive producers Sophie Clarke-Jervoise, Fred Barron and Donald Taffner Jnr; production manager Tracy Garrett; produced by John Bartlett; directed by Dewi Humphreys.
Main regular cast:	With Kris Marshall (Nick Harper).

Holding / Source
DB / DBSW

25.12.2002 Ding Dong Merrily

Duration: 29 minutes.

Written by Ian Brown and James Hendrie; script supervisor Bernadette Darnell; associate producers Ian Brown, James Hendrie, Steve Armogida, Jim Armogida, Andrea Solomons and Angela Billington.

With Trevor Peacock, Peter Hugo Daly, Harry Peacock, Christine Ellerbeck.

SERIES 4

Main regular credit(s):	Script associate Paul Mayhew-Archer; script supervisor Bernadette Darnell; music by Graham Jarvis; designed by Ian Fisher and Merle Downie; production team Sophie Hetherington, Francesca Singler, Rebecca Rycroft and Rachel Stewart; associate producers James Hendrie, Ian Brown, Steve Armogida, Jim Armogida, Andrea Solomons and Angela Billington; executive producers Sophie Clarke-Jervoise, Fred Barron and Donald Taffner Jnr; production manager Tracy Garrett; produced by John Bartlett; directed by Dewi Humphreys.

Holding / Source
DB / DBSW

25.12.2003 Sixty Feet Under

Written by Ian Brown and James Hendrie.

With Siobhan Hayes (Abi), Keiron Self (Roger Bailey), Richard Whiteley, Patrick Godfrey, Amanda Walker, Robert Webb, Philip Brodie, Nigel Lindsay, Sydney Stevenson, Tony Marshall.

SERIES 5

Main regular credit(s):	Script associate Paul Mayhew-Archer; script supervisor Bernadette Darnell; music by Graham Jarvis; production team Sophie Hetherington, Rachel Stewart, Rebecca Rycroft, Jason Cunningham and Louise Wodehouse-Easton; assistant producer Angela Billington; associate producers Dave Cohen, Darin Henry, Paul McKenzie and Andrea Solomons; executive producers Sophie Clarke-Jervoise, Ian Brown, James Hendrie and Donald Taffner Jnr; production manager Paula Munro; produced by John Bartlett; directed by Dewi Humphreys.
Main regular cast:	With Siobhan Hayes (Abi).

Holding / Source
DB / DBSW

24.12.2004 Glad Tidings We Bring

Duration: 48 minutes.

Written by Andrea Solomons; associate producers Andrea Solomons and Darina Henry; produced by John Bartlett; directed by Dewi Humphreys.

With Kris Marshall (Nick), Keiron Self (Roger Bailey), Danny Webb, Rosemary Leach, Freddie Davies, Edna Doré, John Hodgkinson, Alex Dawson, Verity-Jane Dearsley, Michael Mears, Peter Heppelthwaite, Cressida Whyte, Laura Harling, Mathew Bose, Stephen Evans.

MY FAMILY (continued)

	Holding / Source
25.12.2005 **... And I'll Cry If I Want To**	DB / DBSW

Duration: 49 minutes.

Written by Brian Leveson and Paul Minett; programme associate Sophie Hetherington; script associates George Jeffrie, Tess Morris and Bert Tyler-Moore; script supervisor Patricia Morgan; music by Graham Jarvis; designed by Ian Fisher and Sandie Shepherd; assistant producer Angela Billington; associate producers Brian Leveson and Paul Minett; executive producers Micheal Jacob, Donald Taffner Jnr and Tom Leopold; produced by John Bartlett; directed by Dewi Humphreys.

With Daniela Denby-Ashe (Janey), Siobhan Hayes (Abi), Keiron Self (Roger Bailey), Rosemary Leach (Grace), Rhodri Mellir (Alfie), John Burgess, Neil Henry, Jim Johnson, Rosalind Adler, Dan Clark, Taylor Marshall.

SERIES 6

Main regular credit(s):   Programme associate Sophie Hetherington; script associates George Jeffrie, Tess Morris and Bert Tyler-Moore; script supervisor Patricia Morgan; music by Graham Jarvis; assistant producer Angela Billington; associate producers Brian Leveson and Paul Minett; executive producers Micheal Jacob, Donald Taffner Jnr and Tom Leopold; produced by John Bartlett; directed by Dewi Humphreys.

Main regular cast: With Siobhan Hayes (Abi), Keiron Self (Roger Bailey).

	Holding / Source
25.12.2006 **The Heart Of Christmas**	DB / DBSW

Duration: 50 minutes.

Written by Brian Leveson and Paul Minett; script supervisor Bernadette Darnell.

With Daniela Denby-Ashe, Rhodri Mellir, Tayler Marshall, Clive Russell, Mike Walling, Raymond Sawyer, Ed Coleman, Dominic Carter, Jack Brough, Roy Heather, Jenny Gleave, Jenna Harrison, Angela Clerkin, Chloe Billington.

Tess Morris is not a Script Associate on this edition.

	Holding / Source
26.12.2007 **Ho Ho No**	DB / DBSW

Duration: 57 minutes.

Written by Tom Anderson; script associates Ed Dyson and Amy Shindler; script supervisor Hayley Boyd; music by Graham Jarvis; designed by Sandie Shepherd; associate producers Brian Leveson and Paul Minett; executive producers Micheal Jacob, Tom Anderson and Donald Taffner Jnr; produced by John Bartlett; directed by Baz Taylor.

With Daniela Denby-Ashe (Janey), Gabriel Thomson (Michael), Siobhan Hayes (Abi), Keiron Self (Roger), Rhodri Meilir (Alfie), Tayler Marshall (Kenzo), John Challis, Paul Brooke, Niky Wardley, Amy Noble, Martin Herdman, Howard Lew Lewis, James Watson, Dan Cade.

SERIES 8

Main regular credit(s):   Music by Graham Jarvis; designed by Ian Fisher and Sandie Shepherd; executive producers Micheal Jacob, Tom Anderson and Donald Taffner Jnr; production manager Alex Bridcut; line producer J. Clive Hedges; produced by John Bartlett.

	Holding / Source
24.12.2008	DB / DBSW

Duration: 60 minutes.

Written by Brian Leveson and Paul Minett; script associates Ed Dyson, Amy Shindler and Robin Taylor; script supervisor Bernadette Darnell; associate producers Brian Leveson and Paul Minett; directed by Nic Phillips.

With Daniela Denby-Ashe (Janey), Rhodri Meilir (Alfie), Tayler Marshall (Kenzo), Keiron Self (Roger Bailey), Julian Clary, James Smith, Robin Sebastian, Terry Bird, Andy Bennett.

	Holding / Source
24.12.2009 **2039: A Christmas Oddity**	DB / DBSW

Duration: 60 minutes.

Written by Tom Anderson and David Cantor; script associates Ed Dyson, Amy Shindler and Robin Taylor; script supervisor Bernadette Darnell; music by Graham Jarvis; designed by Ian Fisher and Sandie Shepherd; associate producers Brian Leveson and Paul Minett; executive producers Micheal Jacob, Tom Anderson and Donald Taffner Jnr; production manager Paula Munro; produced by John Bartlett; directed by Ed Bye.

With Daniela Denby-Ashe (Janey), Keiron Self (Roger), Tayler Marshall (Kenzo), Nathaniel Parker, Mike Walling, Sally Bretton, Pascal Langdale.

	Holding / Source
24.12.2010 **Mary Christmas**	HD/DB / HDC

Duration: 60 minutes.

Written by Brian Leveson, Paul Minett and Darin Henry; script associates David Cantor, Ed Dyson, George Jeffrie, Amy Shindler, Robin Taylor and Bert Tyler-Moore; script supervisor Bernadette Darnell; music by Graham Jarvis; designed by Ian Fisher and Sandie Shepherd; executive producers Micheal Jacob, Simon Lupton, Tom Anderson and Donald Taffner Jnr; production manager Paula Munro; produced by John Bartlett; directed by Ed Bye.

With Daniela Denby-Ashe (Janey), Keiron Self (Roger), Tayler Marshall (Kenzo), Paul Bown, Nickolas Grace, Louisa Millwood-Haigh, Hannah Waddingham, Ben Uttley, Nathan Brine, Dolly Knott, Benjamin Greaves Neal, Phoebe Marshall, J. D. Kelleher, Ainsley Harriott, Rolf Harris.

MY HERO

A Big Bear Films production for BBC 1. Transmission details are for BBC 1. Duration: 30 minutes.

Main regular credit(s): Created by Paul Mendelson; music by Philip Pope.

SERIES 2

Main regular credit(s): Script supervisor Emma Thomas; titles by TSI Design; designed by James Dillon; associate producers Jed Leventhall and Barrie Westwell; executive producer Geoffrey Perkins; production manager Murray Peterson; produced by Marcus Mortimer and John Stroud; directed by John Stroud.

Main regular cast: With Hugh Dennis (Doctor Piers Crispin), Ardal O'Hanlon (George Sunday), Emily Joyce (Janet Dawkins), Lou Hirsch (Arnie), Tim Wylton (Stanley Dawkins), Lill Roughley (Ella Dawkins), Philip Whitchurch (Tyler).

Holding / Source

22.12.2000 **Christmas** — DB / DBSWF

Written by Paul Mayhew-Archer and Paul Mendelson.

With Hugh Lloyd (Santa), Karen Henthorn, Lexie Peel, Ryan Pope, Rebecca Clow, Nick Barnes, Holly Earl, Daniella Wilson, Parhys-Jai Cato, Andy Greenhalgh.

MY HUSBAND AND I

A Yorkshire Television production. Transmission details are for the Central region. Duration: 25 minutes.

Main regular credit(s): Written by Pam Valentine and Michael Ashton; theme music by Robert Hartley; produced and directed by Graham Wetherell.

Main regular cast: Mollie Sugden (Nora Powers), William Moore (George Powers), Deddie Davies (Bambi Bamber), Carol Hawkins (Tracy Cosgrove), John Horsley (Mr Mundy).

SERIES 1

Holding / Source

18.12.1987 **No Place Like Home** — 1" / 1"

Will Nora and George buy a villa in Spain? Or do they love Christmas in Yorkshire more?

Graphics by Geoff Brayley; costume John Fraser; make-up Di Lofthouse; lighting directors Peter Hardman and Chris Clayton; sound Keith Hargreaves; camera supervisor Norman Chadderton; designed by Alan Davis.

With Isabelle Lucas (Pearl), Jane Ashton (Henrietta), Roberta Tovey (Samantha), Natasha Gray (Anita), David John Pope (Luigi), William Key (Messenger), Philip Pentney*.

MY PARENTS ARE ALIENS

A Granada production. Transmission details are for the Central region. Duration: 25 minutes.

Main regular credit(s): Created by Andy Watts.

Main regular cast: Tony Gardner (Brian Johnson), Danielle McCormack (Melanie Barker), Alex Kew (Josh Barker), Charlotte Frances (Lucy Barker).

SERIES 2

Main regular credit(s): Executive producer Anne Brogan; produced by Bernard Krichefski.

Main regular cast: With Barbara Durkin (Sophie Johnson).

Holding / Source

11.12.2000 **First Christmas: Part One** — DB /

Written by Andy Watts; directed by David McKay.

With Isabella Melling (Wendy), Patrick Niknejad (Pete), Jordan Maxwell (Frankie), Keith Warwick (Trent), Marco Williamson, Kay Purcell.

18.12.2000 **First Christmas: Part Two** — DB /

Written by Andy Watts; directed by David McKay.

With Isabella Melling (Wendy), Keith Warwick (Trent), Patrick Niknejad (Pete), Jordan Maxwell (Frankie), Marco Williamson, Kay Purcell, Daniel O'Brien, Danny Robinson.

SERIES 6

A Granada Kids production for CITV.

Main regular credit(s): Assistant directors Carol Weller and Jo Harrison; associate producer Liz Noble; executive producers Anne Brogan and Andy Watts; produced by Bernard Krichefski.

Main regular cast: With Carla Mendonca (Sophie Johnson), Olisa Odele (CJ).

Holding / Source

25.12.2004 **The Naughty List** — DB /

Duration: 50 minutes.

Written by Joe Williams; directed by Ben Kellett.

With Jordan Maxwell (Frankie), Keith Warwick (Trent), Isabella Melling (Wendy), Patrick Niknejad (Pete), Daniel O'Brien, Beatrice Kelley, Raymond Bowers.

SERIES 8

A Granada Kids production for CITV.

Main regular credit(s): Executive producer Anne Brogan; produced by David Collier.

Main regular cast: With Carla Mendonca (Sophie), Daniel Feltham (Dan), Drew Carter-Cain (Guido), Jake Young (Eddie), Jessica Woods (Jaq), Katie Pearson (Becky).

Holding / Source

18.12.2006 **Winter Blunderland** — DB /

Written by Paul Rose; directed by Frank W. Smith.

With Gabriella Dixon (Blaise), Mark Chatterton, Paul Sullivan.

Only Mendonca and Gardner remained as regulars.

Y MYNDD GRUG

Commissioned by S4C. Transmission details are for S4C. Duration: 70 minutes.

Holding / Source

25.12.1997

D3 /

THE MYSTERIES

A Limehouse production for Channel 4. made in association with National Theatre Company. Transmission details are for Channel 4. Duration: 120 minutes.

Adapted by Tony Harrison; based on plays by Medieval English Mystery Plays; music by The Home Service; associate producer Joe McDonald; executive producer Al Burgess; produced by Bill Bryden and Derek Bailey; directed by Bill Bryden and Derek Bailey.

Brenda Blethyn, David Busby, Jim Carter, Edna Doré, Christopher Gilbert, Brian Glover, Howard Goorney, James Grant, Dave Hill, Karl Johnson, Phil Langham, Eve Matheson, Derek Newark, Robert Oates, Stephen Petcher, Trevor Ray, Jack Shepherd, Dinah Stabb, Robert Stephens, John Tams, Anthony Trent, Don Warrington.

Holding / Source

22.12.1985 **The Nativity**

1" / 1"

NAME THAT TUNE

A Thames Television production. Transmission details are for the Central region. Duration: 25 minutes.

	Holding / Source
26.12.1986 **Christmas Special**	1" / 1"

A special Christmas edition of the popular music quiz, with all the money won being donated to children's charities. Playing the game will be Angela Rippon and disc jockey Mike Read. Partnering Angela and Mike will be two contestants, both of whom have previously won cars on the show. They are Kay Bywater from Burton-on-Trent and Larry Walker from Leighton Buzzard.

Music directed by Alan Braden; music associate Ray Monk; designed by Alison Wratten; produced and directed by David Clark.

With Lionel Blair (Host), Maggie Moone, Angela Rippon, Mike Read, Alan Braden and his Orchestra.

30.12.1986 **New Year Special** — 1" / 1"

Music directed by Alan Braden; music associate Ray Monk; designed by Alison Wratten; produced and directed by David Clark.

With Lionel Blair (Host), Maggie Moone, Faith Brown, Joe Brown, Brian Day, Barbara Westerman, Alan Braden and his Orchestra.

THE NATION'S FAVOURITE CHRISTMAS SONG

A Shiver production for ITV 1. Transmission details are for the Central region. Duration: 75 minutes.

They arrive in early December like a heavy snowfall of nostalgia. Some of them set your teeth on edge with a surfeit of sleighbells, others melt all resistance and deliver just the right kind of sentimental glow. Now ITV asks the vital question: which of these festive hits do we love the most? As they count down through the likes of Greg Lake's I Believe in Father Christmas and Chris Rea's Driving Home for Christmas, we get to marvel at how well Bing Crosby and David Bowie dovetailed on Little Drummer Boy, while some Spice Girls, Cliff Richard and, naturally, Noddy Holder reminisce.

Executive producer Mark Robinson; produced by Kerry Allison.

Cliff Richard, Noddy Holder, Shane McGowan, Jona Lewie, Alexandra Burke.

	Holding / Source
22.12.2012	HD/DB / HDC

NATIONWIDE

A BBC production for BBC 1. Transmission details are for BBC 1. Duration varies - see below for details.

	Holding / Source
19.12.1977 **The Pantomime**	DBSEQ / 2"

Duration: 45 minutes.
Edited by John Gau.

21.12.1977 **Journey To Bethlehem** — DV|n / C1

Duration: 60 minutes.

While a million British children act out their Nativity plays, a thousand from East Sussex get to the heart of the story. Nationwide cameras join them on an educational cruise to Haifa aboard the SS Uganda, then overland to Jerusalem and on to Bethlehem itself to see the preparations for Christmas.

Edited by John Gau; film editor Mike Davidson; produced by Peter Bate.

With James Hogg (Reporter).

22.12.1977 **1977 Carol Competition Final** — DV|n / Live

Duration: 60 minutes.

School pupils throughout Britain entered for the 1977 Nationwide Christmas Carol Competition. Which of the last six will become the Nationwide Carol 1977?

With Valerie Singleton (Presenter), Noel Edmonds (Judge), Richard Stilgoe (Judge), Leslie East (Judge).

15.12.1980 **Christmas On Nationwide**	DV /
16.12.1980 **Christmas On Nationwide**	DV /
17.12.1980 **Christmas On Nationwide** Inserts only.	DBSEQ /
18.12.1980 **Christmas On Nationwide**	DV /
19.12.1980 **Christmas On Nationwide**	DV /
22.12.1980 **Christmas On Nationwide** Inserts only.	DBSEQ /
23.12.1980 **Christmas On Nationwide** Inserts only.	DBSEQ /

NATIVITY BLUES

A BBC Birmingham production for BBC 2. Transmission details are for BBC 2. Duration: 65 minutes.

There are two shopping days left till Chistmas and with the birth of his first baby, Hank Tater is not adapting too well to the joys of fatherhood and marriage.

Written by Wendy Macleod; music by Jeremy Sams; lighting by Dave Bushell; designed by Sally Engelbach; executive producer Brenda Reid; produced by Fiona Finlay; directed by Sue Dunderdale and Jeremy Ancock.

Alfred Molina (Hank), Julia Swift (Muriel), Anna Cropper (Francine), John Normington (Dick), Trudie Styler (Trudi).

	Holding / Source
01.01.1989	DB / 1"

THE NATIVITY

An Associated-Rediffusion production. Transmission details are for Associated-Rediffusion. Duration: 25 minutes.

Narrated by Robert Harris; dramatised by Martin Worth; costume Ernest Hewitt; music directed by John Churchill; choreography by Litz Pisk; produced and directed by Ian Fordyce.

Sheila Ballantine, Alan Edwards, Avril Elgar, Peter Gill, Ida Goldapple, John Gordon, George Hall, Christopher Hancock, Patricia Healey, Patrick Kavanagh, Rosalind Knight, Phyllida Law, James Maxwell, Morris Perry, Veronica Wells, Jerome Willis.

	Holding / Source
08.12.1959	J / 40

THE NATIVITY

A Rediffusion Television production. Transmission details are for the Rediffusion Television region. Duration: 20 minutes.

This programme tells the story of the birth of Jesus Christ as it was seen through the eyes of the 15th century Flemish painters and as it has been made familiar to us by the word of St. Matthew and St. Luke. Behind the story music of the period recorded in the Brampton Oratory, sets the mood of rejoicing we associate with the birth of our Saviour.

Music directed by Henry Washington; film camera Adrian Cooper; directed by Graham Young.

Cecil Lewis (Commentator).

	Holding / Source
25.12.1963	J /

In colour.

THE NATIVITY

A Red Planet Pictures production for BBC Wales. made in association with CBC / K Films / Kudos / Temple Street Productions. Transmission details are for BBC 1. Duration: 30 minutes.

Main regular credit(s): Written by Tony Jordan; script supervisor Non Eleri Hughes; music by Jonathan Goldsmith; director of photography Chris Seager; titles by Peter Anderson Studio; art director Tom Still; designed by Christina Moore; production executives Alison Barnett and Andrea Boyd; executive producers Bethan Jones, David Fortier, Ivan Schneeberg, Tony Jordan and Jane Featherstone; production manager Alex Jones; line producers Jules Hussey and Khadija Alami; produced by Ruth Kenley-Letts; directed by Coky Giedroyc.

Main regular cast: Andrew Buchan (Joseph), Tatiana Maslany (Mary), Obi Abili (Gaspar), Peter Capaldi (Balthasar), Al Weaver (Thomas), Jack Shepherd (Melchlor), Ruth Negga (Leah).

	Holding / Source
20.12.2010	HD/DB / HD/DB

With Claudie Blakley (Anna), Neil Dudgeon (Joachim), John Lynch (Gabriel), Gawn Grainger (Levi), Howard Samuels (Tax Collector), Rachid Berrrada, Frances Barber, Amine Naji, Colin Goodwin, Ken Bones.

21.12.2010   HD/DB / HD/DB

With John Lynch (Gabriel), Howard Samuels (Tax Collector), Claudie Blakley (Anna), Art Malik (Nicolaus), Vincent Regan (Herod), Neil Dudgeon (Joachim), David Sterne (Abimael), Younes Megri [as Younes Migri], Said Bey, Frances Barber, Rachid Berrrada.

22.12.2010   HD/DB / HD/DB

With Neil Dudgeon (Joachim), Art Malik (Nicolaus), Vincent Regan (Herod), Gawn Grainger (Levi), Claudie Blakley (Anna), David Sterne (Abimael), Ken Bones, Khadija Dahraiji, Said Tarchani, Nour Eddine Aberdine.

23.12.2010   HD/DB / HD/DB

With David Sterne (Abimael), Howard Samuels (Tax Collector), John Lynch (Gabriel), Vincent Regan (Herod), Ahamdane Lhabib, Helen Schlesinger, Matthew Deslippe, Sadie Shimmin.

NEAREST AND DEAREST

A Granada production. Transmission details are for the ATV midlands region. Usual duration: 25 minutes.

The Pledges are in a real pickle. Or, to be more precise, an antiquated North Country pickle factory. It is the setting for Nearest and Dearest. Jimmy is Eli Pledge, a bachelor playboy with a reputation for being a middle-aged Romeo. Hylda plays Nellie, his spinster sister and pillar of the local community.

The pair, hoping to benefit from their father's will, are stunned to learn that they will receive the princely sum of £9 17s. 6d. But a clause in the will lands that pickle-factory right into their unwilling hands. Nearest and Dearest is the story of the Pledges and their problem pickle factory.

Main regular credit(s): Devised by Vince Powell and Harry Driver; music by Derek Hilton.

Main regular cast: Hylda Baker (Nellie Pledge), Jimmy Jewel (Eli Pledge), Joe Gladwin (Stan), Madge Hindle (Lily), Edward Malin (Walter).

SERIES 3

Main regular credit(s): Produced by Peter Eckersley.

	Production No	Holding / Source
26.12.1969 **The Ghost Of Picklers Past**	P584/17	DB / 2"

Duration: 42 minutes.

Boxing Day at Pledge's Purer Pickles. The factory is quiet. The last consignment of special gift-wrapped gherkins for Christmas has long gone. Nellie and Eli find time to spend a few peaceful hours with the family. It is a small family circle these days and the Pledges are left with Lily and Walter, affectionately known by Eli at least as the Christmas Fairy and King Rat. But is it a good idea to hold a seance to try to get in touch with old Joshua Pledge who has been dead these two years? Is Lily really a medium? Can the ghosts of picklers long departed really roam the factory? Is dad trying to get in touch with Nellie from that great pickle factory in the sky? And, for that matter, what was that noise? It couldn't be the sound of phantom clog-steps, could it?

Written by Tom Brennand and Roy Bottomley; designed by Eric Deakins; directed by Bill Podmore.

With Freddie Rayner (Grenville), Windsor Davies (Vicar).

This series was shown in monochrome on ITV.

NEAREST AND DEAREST (continued)

SERIES 5

Main regular credit(s): Designed by Eric Deakins; produced and directed by Bill Podmore.

	Production No	Holding / Source
24.12.1970 **Compliments Of The Season**	P584/31	D2 / 62

Christmas... the time for the loved ones to be gathered together in one place. But when you don't want them, and you can't get rid of them, you might find that there is not quite enough goodwill - or indeed anything else - to go round.

Written by John Stevenson; script editor Lew Schwarz; designed by Eric Deakins.

With Freddie Rayner (Grenville).

SERIES 7

Main regular credit(s): Designed by Eric Deakins; produced and directed by Bill Podmore.

	Production No	Holding / Source
21.12.1972 **Cindernellie**	P584/47	D2 / 2"

The festive season is upon us... and for the stalwarts of Pledge's Purer Pickles, there's high drama and low farce 'mid the tinsel and the turkey when Eli becomes an impresario. He tries to double the picklers' Christmas party money by sinking it into a pantomime production.

"Sinking" seems the right word when the cast walks out and Nellie has to take over the part of Cinderella. She tells Eli : "If there's no money, them picklers will have your ear 'ole for an ashtray."

And it's as well that Christmas comes but once a year—for Nellie can't remember the script .

Written by John Stevenson; designed by Eric Deakins.

With Freddie Rayner (Grenville), Harry Littlewood (Landlord), John Barrie, Deirdre Costello, Charles Pemberton.

NETWORK

A BBC production for BBC 2. Transmission details are for BBC 2. Duration: 30 minutes.

	Holding / Source
21.12.1974 **The Corries In Concert**	J / 2"

A BBC Scotland production.

Designed by Jim Longmuir; executive producer Iain MacFadyen; produced and directed by Bob Hird.

With The Corries, Roy Williamson, Ronnie Browne.

NEVER MIND THE BUZZCOCKS

A Talkback production for BBC 2. Transmission details are for BBC 2. Usual duration: 30 minutes.

SERIES 2

Main regular credit(s): Produced by Jim Pullin; directed by Steve Bendelack.

Main regular performer(s): With Mark Lamarr (Host), Sean Hughes (Team Captain), Phill Jupitus (Team Captain).

	Holding / Source
29.12.1997 **Merry Mind The Buzzcocks**	D3 / D3S

Duration: 40 minutes.

With Jonathan Ross, Boy George, Noddy Holder, Louise Wener, Peter Felstead, Stuart Tosh.

SERIES 4

Main regular credit(s): Programme associate Warren Prentice; research Lamees Nuseibeh and Samantha Taylor; script supervisor Emma Ramsay; theme music by Vitamin; titles by Tarantula; consultants Jonathan Ruffle and Jeremy Simmonds; production designer Cath Pater-Lancucki; associate producers Simon Bullivant and Bill Matthews; executive producer Peter Fincham; head of production Sally Debonnaire; production manager Tamzin Fry; co-produced by Harry Thompson; produced by Richard Wilson; directed by Paul Wheeler.

Main regular performer(s): With Mark Lamarr (Host), Sean Hughes (Team Captain), Phill Jupitus (Team Captain).

	Holding / Source
27.12.1998 **Merry Mind The Buzzcocks (Christmas Special)**	DB / DBSW

Duration: 40 minutes.

With Boy George, Noddy Holder, Jonathan Ross, Louise Werner.

SERIES 6

Main regular credit(s): Research Sarah Bloomfield, Lamees Nuseibeh and David Scott; script supervisor Emma Ramsay; theme music by Vitamin; titles by Tarantula; consultants Bill Matthews and Jonathan Ruffle; production designer Cath Pater-Lancucki; assistant producer Warren Prentice; associate producer Jeremy Simmonds; executive producer Peter Fincham; head of production Sally Debonnaire; production manager Tamzin Fry; produced by Richard Wilson; directed by Paul Wheeler.

Main regular performer(s): With Mark Lamarr (Host), Phill Jupitus (Team Captain), Sean Hughes (Team Captain).

	Holding / Source
29.12.1999	DB / DBSW

Duration: 39 minutes.

Additional material by Simon Bullivant, Jim Pullin, Pete Sinclair and Robert Fraser Steele.

With Goldie, Martine McCutcheon, Les McKeown, Frank Skinner, Bill Bailey, Rick Wakeman, Flat Eric, Gordon The Gopher, Keith Harris & Orville, Pinky and Perky, Sweep.

NEVER MIND THE BUZZCOCKS (continued)

SERIES 7
Main regular credit(s): Additional material by Simon Bullivant, Jim Pullin, Pete Sinclair and Robert Fraser Steele; research David Scott, Anne Beaver and Liz Fay; script supervisor Emma Ramsay; theme music by Vitamin; titles by Tarantula; consultant Jonathan Ruffle; associate producers Sarah Bloomfield, Lamees Nuseibeh and Jeremy Simmonds; executive producer Peter Fincham; head of production Joanna Beresford; production manager Tamzin Fry; co-produced by Warren Prentice; produced by Richard Wilson.

Main regular performer(s): With Mark Lamarr (Host), Phill Jupitus (Team Captain), Sean Hughes (Team Captain).

Holding / Source
28.12.2000 Christmas Special — DB / DBSW
Duration: 38 minutes.
Production designers Cath Pater-Lancucki and Ravinder Takher; directed by Paul Wheeler.
With Rich Hall, Lorraine Kelly, Dave Hill, Tony Wright, Anne Robinson, Bob Ramsey, Joan O'Neill.

SERIES 9
Main regular credit(s): Produced by Warren Prentice and Simon Bullivant; directed by John Spencer.
Main regular performer(s): With Mark Lamarr (Host), Phill Jupitus (Team Captain), Sean Hughes (Team Captain).

Holding / Source
30.12.2001 Christmas Special — DB / DBSW
With Myleene Klass, Belinda Carlisle, Fish, Johnny Vegas.

SERIES 11
Main regular credit(s): Produced by Simon Bullivant and Warren Prentice; directed by Paul Wheeler.
Main regular performer(s): With Mark Lamarr (Host), Phill Jupitus (Team Captain), Bill Bailey (Team Captain).

Holding / Source
29.12.2002 Christmas Show — DB / DBSW
With Peter Stringfellow, Coolio, Geoffrey Hayes, Kelly Llorenna.

SERIES 13
Main regular credit(s): Produced by Richard Wilson and Warren Prentice; directed by Paul Wheeler.
Main regular performer(s): With Mark Lamarr (Host), Phill Jupitus (Team Captain), Bill Bailey (Team Captain).

Holding / Source
28.12.2003 Christmas Show — DB / DBSW
With Gloria Hunniford, D. J. Sammy, Alison Goldfrapp, Sabrina Washington, Ray Beavis, Henry McGee.

SERIES 15
Main regular credit(s): Produced by Steve Doherty; directed by Paul Wheeler.
Main regular performer(s): With Mark Lamarr (Host), Bill Bailey (Team Captain), Phill Jupitus (Team Captain).

Holding / Source
20.12.2004 — DB / DBSW
With Noddy Holder, David Oliver, Siobhan Fahey, Jackie Clune.

SERIES 17
Main regular credit(s): Script supervisor Cat Johnson; consultant Jonathan Ruffle; associate producer Isabel Forte; production executive Beatrice Gay; executive producer Richard Wilson; series producer Warren Prentice; produced by Mark Lamarr and Lucy Clarke.
Main regular performer(s): With Mark Lamarr (Host), Bill Bailey (Team Captain), Phill Jupitus (Team Captain).

Holding / Source
20.12.2005 — DB / DBSW
Duration: 40 minutes.
Additional material by Pete Sinclair, Kevin Day, Shaun Pye, Martin Trenaman, Fraser Steele and Jake Yapp; directed by Phil Chilvers.
With Tony Christie, Kate Garraway, David Grant, Aled Jones, Sheila Ferguson, Roy Johnson, General Levy, Mistress.

SERIES 19
Main regular credit(s): Script editor Jane Bell; theme music by Richard Blair Oliphant; assistant producer Tom Crew; production executive Beatrice Gay; executive producer Jim Pullin; series producer Warren Prentice; produced by Lucy Clarke; directed by Ian Lorimer.
Main regular performer(s): With Simon Amstell (Host), Bill Bailey (Team Captain), Phill Jupitus (Team Captain).

Holding / Source
24.12.2006 — DB / DBSW
Duration: 45 minutes.
Additional material by Fraser Steele, Shaun Pye, Kevin Day, Martin Treneman and Pete Sinclair.
With David Gest, Dan Gillespie Sells, Jenni Falconer, Danny Jones, Derek B, Mary Joe, Strings, The Ukulele Orchestra of Great Britain.

NEVER MIND THE BUZZCOCKS (continued)

SERIES 23

A Talkback Thames production.

Main regular credit(s): Script supervisor Alice Osborne; script editor Adam Copeland; theme music by Vitamin, Richard Blair Oliphant and David Blair Oliphant; titles by Skaramoosh; designed by Cath Pater-Lancucki and Ravinder Takher; assistant producer Mark Boutros; executive producer Jim Pullin; head of production Beatrice Gay; production manager Sarah Chaloner; produced by Stu Mather; directed by Ian Lorimer.

Main regular performer(s): With Phill Jupitus (Team Captain), Noel Fielding (Team Captain).

	Holding / Source
26.12.2009 **Where Are They Now?**	DB / DBSW

Written by Stu Mather, Shaun Pye and Dan Swimer; additional material by Lloyd Langford, Aiden Spackman, Kevin Day, Fraser Steele and Martin Trenaman.

With Matthew Crosby (Narrator).

Highlights and out-takes from last series with new interviews from guest hosts.

SERIES 25

Main regular credit(s): Designed by Cath Pater-Lancucki and Dominic Tolfts; executive producers Jim Pullin and Ruby Kuraishe; produced by James Longman and Arron Ferster; directed by Ian Lorimer.

Main regular performer(s): With Phill Jupitus (Team Captain), Noel Fielding (Team Captain).

	Holding / Source
29.12.2011 **Christmas Special**	DB / DBSW

With John Barrowman (Presenter), Jason Derulo, Joe Wilkinson, Jason Manford, Helen Skelton.

	Holding / Source
22.12.2012 **Christmas Special**	HD/DB / HDC

Series producer Andy Price; directed by Nick Harris.

With Bob Mortimer (Presenter), Phill Jupitus (Captain), Noel Fielding (Captain), D. J. Fresh, Melanie Chisholm [as Mel C], Russell Tovey, Joey Page.

23.12.2013 **Christmas Special**	HD/DB / HDC

Produced by Andy Price; directed by Nick Harris.

With Johnny Vegas (Presenter), Phill Jupitus (Team Captain), Noel Fielding (Team Captain), Jessica Hynes, Brian McFadden, D. J. Locksmith, Sara Pascoe.

NEVER MIND THE QUALITY, FEEL THE WIDTH

An ABC/Thames production. Duration: 25 minutes.

Main regular credit(s): Created by Vince Powell and Harry Driver.

Main regular cast: John Bluthal (Manny Cohen), Joe Lynch (Patrick Kelly).

A Thames Television production. Transmission details are for the ATV midlands region.

	VT Number	Holding / Source
26.12.1968 **I'm Dreaming Of A Kosher Christmas**	1475	D3 / 62

Christmas. When two Father Christmases, looking remarkably like the partners in a certain tailoring firm, are found in a convent, the local constabulary wishes to question them on one or two points. Does the Law believe in Santa Claus? If not the festive duo could be spending the holiday period behind the wrong type of bars.

Written by Vince Powell and Harry Driver; music by Bob Miller; designed by Norman Garwood; produced and directed by Ronnie Baxter.

NEVER THE TWAIN

Alternative/Working Title(s): BETWIXT AND BETWEEN

A Thames Television production. Transmission details are for the ATV/Central region. Duration: 25 minutes.

Main regular credit(s): Created by Johnnie Mortimer and Brian Cooke.

Main regular cast: Donald Sinden (Simon Peel), Windsor Davies (Oliver Smallbridge).

SERIES 9

Transmission details are for the Central region.

Main regular credit(s): Designed by Suzanne Fishwick; produced by Anthony Parker; directed by Nick Hurran.

	Holding / Source
28.12.1989 **A Winter's Tale**	1" / 1"

Written by Vince Powell.

With Zara Nutley (Aunt Eleanor), Derek Deadman (Ringo), Gordon Gostelow, Daniel John, Jasper Jacob.

THE NEW LONDON PALLADIUM SHOW

An ATV production. Transmission details are for the ABC midlands region.

Main regular credit(s): Written by Marty Feldman and Barry Took; designed by Bill McPherson; executive producer Val Parnell; produced and directed by Colin Clews.

Main regular performer(s): Jimmy Tarbuck (Compere), The Palladium Dancers, Jack Parnell and his Orchestra.

	Holding / Source
26.12.1965 **The Palladium's Christmas Special**	J / 40

Duration: 75 minutes.

Dance direction by Ross Taylor; designed by Eric Shedden.

With Frankie Vaughan, Eddie Calvert, Ray Fell, Jim Dale, Michael Allport.

See also: (VAL PARNELL'S) SUNDAY NIGHT AT THE LONDON PALLADIUM

NEW LOOK

An ATV production. Transmission details are for the ATV midlands region. Duration: 50 minutes.

Main regular credit(s): Devised by Brian Tesler; written by Jimmy Grafton, Alan Fell and Jeremy Lloyd; dance direction by Lionel Blair; produced and directed by Brian Tesler.

Main regular performer(s): Roy Castle, Joe Baker, Jack Douglas, Ronnie Stevens, Gillian Moran, Joyce Blair, Stephanie Voss, The Vernons Girls, Jack Parnell and his Orchestra.

	Production No	VT Number	Holding / Source
25.12.1958 **Christmas Edition**	8215	T/R 435	R1N / R1

Designed by Richard Lake.

With Bruce Forsyth.

Recorded 25.11.1958.

THE NEW STATESMAN

Produced for BBC/ITV by a variety of companies (see details below). Usual duration: 25 minutes.

Main regular credit(s): Written by Laurence Marks and Maurice Gran; music by Alan Hawkshaw.

Main regular cast: Rik Mayall (Alan B'Stard), Michael Troughton (Piers Fletcher-Dervish), Marsha Fitzalan (Sarah B'Stard).

SERIES 4

A Yorkshire Television production. Transmission details are for the Central region.

Main regular credit(s): Script supervisor Janet Mullins; executive producers Michael Pilsworth and John Bartlett; produced by Bernard McKenna; directed by Graeme Harper.

	Holding / Source
26.12.1992 **The Irresistible Rise Of Alan B'Stard**	B / 1"

With Terence Alexander (Sir Greville), Benjamin Whitrow (Paddy O'Rourke), John Warnaby (Political Editor), Vincent Grass (Claude Chagrin), Sandy Walsh (Newsreader).

Transmission details are for BBC 1.

	Holding / Source
30.12.1994 **A B'Stard Exposed**	DB-D3 / D3S

An Alomo production for BBC 1. Duration: 30 minutes.

Produced by Claire Hinson; directed by Marcus Mortimer.

With Brian Walden (Interviewer), Geoffrey McGivern, Phoebe Schofield, Sara Markland.

NEW YEAR LIVE

A BBC production for BBC 1. Transmission details are for BBC 1. Duration: 35 minutes.

The chimes of Big Ben and fireworks.

Executive producer Claire Popplewell; produced by Catherine Stirk.

Gabby Logan (Presenter).

	Holding / Source
31.12.2012	HD/DB / HDC

NEW YEAR LIVE

A BBC production for BBC 1. Transmission details are for BBC 1. Duration: 25 minutes.

Chimes and fireworks.

Executive producer Claire Popplewell; produced by Victoria Simpson.

Jake Humphrey (Presenter).

	Holding / Source
31.12.2011	HD/DB / HDC

NEW YEAR LIVE 2010

A BBC Productions production for BBC 1. Transmission details are for BBC 1. Duration: 30 minutes.

Executive producer Claire Popplewell.

	Holding / Source
31.12.2010	HD/DB / Live

No on-screen credits.

NEW YEAR PIECES

A Freeway Films production for Channel 4. Transmission details are for Channel 4. Duration: 50 minutes.

Written by John McGrath; music by Rick Lloyd and Robert Handleigh; produced and directed by John McGrath.

David Hayman, Maureen Beattie, Hope Augustus, Dorothy Paul, Elaine C. Smith, Catherine-Anne MacPhee, Simon MacKenzie, The Flat Sharps, Norman MacCaig, Adrian Mitchell, Adrian Henri, Liz Lochhead.

	Holding / Source
31.12.1987	1" / 1"

THE NEW YEAR SHOW

A Scottish Television production. Transmission details are for the Central region. Duration: 40 minutes.

Designed by Marius van der Werff; produced by David Bell; directed by Anne Mason.

Jack McLaughlin (Host), Russ Abbot, Lena Zavaroni, Sydney Devine, Andy Cameron, Allan Stewart, Peter Morrison, The Alexander Brothers, John Carmichael's Scottish Country Dance Band, The New Year Dancers.

	Holding / Source
31.12.1985	1" / 1"

NEW YEAR'S EVE AT THE GOLDEN GARTER

A Granada production. Transmission details are for the ATV midlands region. Duration: 35 minutes.

Research John Stirling; music directed by Derek Hilton; designed by Tim Farmer; produced by John Hamp; directed by Dave Warwick.

Bernard Manning (Host), Freddie Garrity, Frank Carson, The New Faces, Shep's Banjo Boys, Vince Hill, The Ukrainian Cossack Brotherhood, Anita Harris, George Best*, Peter Adamson*, Jim Bowen*, Mike Burton*, Colin Crompton*, Julie Goodyear*, Barbara Knox*.

	Holding / Source
31.12.1973	DB / 2"

NEW YEAR'S EVE FIREWORKS

A BBC production for BBC 1. Transmission details are for BBC 1. Duration: 15 minutes.

Fireworks and the chimes of Big Ben.

Executive producer Phil Dolling; produced by Victoria Simpson.

	Holding / Source
31.12.2013	HD/DB / Live

NEW YEAR'S EVE WITH JONATHAN ROSS

An Open Mike production for BBC 1. Transmission details are for BBC 1. Duration: 56 minutes.

Series producer Suzi Aplin; directed by Mick Thomas.

Jonathan Ross (Host), Louis Theroux, Tara Palmer-Tomkinson, Dale Winton, Alan Titchmarsh, Badly Drawn Boy, Sophie Ellis-Bextor, Damon Gough, The Cheeky Girls, Harry Hill, Edwin Starr.

	Holding / Source
31.12.2002	DB / DBSW

THE NEWCOMERS

A BBC Birmingham production for BBC 1. Transmission details are for BBC 1. Usual duration: 24 minutes.

Main regular credit(s): Devised by Colin Morris; theme music by John Barry.

Holding / Source

20.12.1966 Episode 127 J /

The Angleton boutique opens Its doors; the Coopers anticipate a dismal Christmas, and Eunice indulges in a mild deception.

Written by Bob Stuart; story by John Cresswell; produced by Ronald Travers; directed by Gerry Mill.

With Jeremy Bulloch (Philip Cooper), Alan Browning (Ellis Cooper), Maggie Fitzgibbon (Vivienne Cooper), Gerald Cross (Arnold Tripp), John Sharp (Augustus Tripp), Maggie McGrath (Ethel Louella Heppenstahl), Gladys Henson (Gran Hamilton), Eileen Way (Mrs. Brassett), Patrick Connor (Peter Connolly), Helen Cotterill (Betty Lloyd), Anthony Verner (Sydney Huxley), John Harvey (Mr. Waller), Stanley Meadows (Detective Thomson), Gordon Griffin (Naylor), Tony Steedman (Arthur Huntley), David Knight (James Neal), Naomi Chance (Amelia Huntley), Michael Collins (Jeff Langley), Sally Lahee (Eunice Huntley), Michael Johnson (Terry), Jonathan Dennis (Ian Creighton), Colin Bell (Archie Lean), Dorothea Phillips (Mrs. Hartley), Howard Douglas (Alfred Dodge).

23.12.1966 Episode 128 J /

Maria Cooper returns for the Christmas holidays: Sydney investigates a haunted house: and Arnold receives unpleasant news.

Written by Bob Stuart; story by John Cresswell; produced by Ronald Travers; directed by Gerry Mill.

With Gladys Henson (Gran Hamilton), Alan Browning (Ellis Cooper), Raymond Hunt (Lance Cooper), Susan Bills (Maisie Claw), Maggie Fitzgibbon (Vivienne Cooper), Judy Geeson (Maria Cooper), David Griffin (Roddy Vaughan), Thomas Heathcote (Frank Claw), Patrick Connor (Peter Connolly), Vanda Godsell (Mrs Heenan), Michael Collins (Jeff Langley), Sally Lahee (Eunice Huntley), Jeremy Bulloch (Philip Cooper), Gerald Cross (Arnold Tripp), Anthony Verner (Sydney Huxley), Naomi Chance (Amelia Huntley), David Knight (James Neal), Maggie McGrath (Ethel Louella Heppenstahl), Derek Ware (Stillman).

25.12.1968 Episode 337 J /

Christmas Day in Angleton: Vivienne goes to see Toby Smith; the Kerrs entertain their friends; Sydney has a solution to Turner's accommodation problem.

Written by Christopher Bond; story by John Cresswell; script editor Christopher Bond; produced by Bill Sellars; directed by Mary Ridge.

With Raymond Hunt (Lance Cooper), Gladys Henson (Gran Hamilton), Maggie Fitzgibbon (Vivienne Cooper), Neil Hallett (Charels Turner), Robin Bailey (Andrew Kerr), Heather Chasen (Caroline Kerr), Maggie Don (Kirsty Kerr), Sally-Jane Spencer (Margot Kerr), Robert Brown (Bert Harker), David Janson (Jimmy Harker), Wendy Richard (Joyce Harker), June Bland (Vera Harker), Michael Redfern (Rufus Pargeter), Gerald Cross (Arnold Tripp), Campbell Singer (Henry Burroughs), Michael Collins (Jeff Langley), Sandra Payne (Janet Cooper), Jeremy Bulloch (Philip Cooper), Anthony Verner (Sydney Huxley), Vanda Godsell (Mrs Heenan), Billy Russell (Toby Smith), Bert Brownbill (Harry Patch), Jean Ainslie (Matron), Naomi Chance (Amelia Huntley), Adrian Reynolds (Ray Blackwell), Julian Herington (Head Waiter).

THE NEWCOMERS (continued)

26.12.1968 **Episode 338** J /

Boxing Day brings a surprise visitor to the Kerrs; Turner makes plans to entertain the Cooper family; Burroughs finds Mrs. Crabtree too much under the influence of the Christmas spirit.

Written by Christopher Bond; story by John Cresswell; script editor Christopher Bond; produced by Bill Sellars; directed by Mary Ridge.

With Raymond Hunt (Lance Cooper), Gladys Henson (Gran Hamilton), Maggie Fitzgibbon (Vivienne Cooper), Neil Hallett (Charels Turner), Robin Bailey (Andrew Kerr), Heather Chasen (Caroline Kerr), Maggie Don (Kirsty Kerr), Sally-Jane Spencer (Margot Kerr), Robert Brown (Bert Harker), David Janson (Jimmy Harker), Wendy Richard (Joyce Harker), June Bland (Vera Harker), Michael Redfern (Rufus Pargeter), Gerald Cross (Arnold Tripp), Campbell Singer (Henry Burroughs), Michael Collins (Jeff Langley), Sandra Payne (Janet Cooper), Jeremy Bulloch (Philip Cooper), Anthony Verner (Sydney Huxley), Vanda Godsell (Mrs Heenan), Billy Russell (Toby Smith), Bert Brownbill (Harry Patch), Jean Ainslie (Matron), Naomi Chance (Amelia Huntley), Adrian Reynolds (Ray Blackwell), Julian Herington (Head Waiter).

An extract from an edition tx'd 1969 exists on "Talkback" tx'd 1969.

NEWMAN AND BADDIEL IN PIECES

An Avalon Productions production for BBC 2. Transmission details are for BBC 2. Duration varies - see below for details.

Main regular credit(s):   Written by Robert Newman and David Baddiel.

Main regular credit(s):   Theme music by The Sundays; titles by Paul Baguley; designed by Harry Banks; produced by Harry Thompson; directed by Babara Jones.

Main regular performer(s):   With Robert Newman, David Baddiel.

	Holding / Source
20.12.1993 **Christmas In Pieces**	DB-D3 / D3S

Duration: 31 minutes.

With Finola Geraghty, Alison Goldie, Denys Graham, Simon Greenall, Sue Lawley, Mike Potter.

	Holding / Source
29.12.1994 **Newman and Baddiel Live and In Pieces**	D3 / D3S

Duration: 59 minutes.

Executive producer Joanna Beresford; produced by Richard Allen-Turner and Jon Thoday; directed by Steve Bendelack.

With Sean Lock.

NEXT OF KIN

A BBC production for BBC 1. Transmission details are for BBC 1. Duration: 30 minutes.

Main regular cast: Penelope Keith (Maggie Prentice), William Gaunt (Andrew Prentice).

SERIES 1

Main regular credit(s):   Written by Jan Etherington and Gavin Petrie; produced and directed by Gareth Gwenlan.

	Holding / Source
21.12.1995 "The Nativity Play"	DB-D3 / D3S

Maggie gets a job, Jake stars in a Nativity play and Andrew is flattered by the attentions of another woman.

With Ann Gosling (Georgia), Matthew Clarke (Philip), Jamie Lucraft (Jake), Tracie Bennett (Liz), Mark Powley (Tom), Wanda Ventham (Rosie), Timothy Carlton (Hugh), Jeremy Swift (Ant), Diana Berriman (Barbara), Diana Magness (Roxanne), Sally Giles (Sandra), Amanda Fawsett (Trish), Lara Bruce (Laura), Luke Sheppard (Steven), Lloyd Moss (David).

NEXT YEAR - TONIGHT!

A Scottish Television production. Transmission details are for the ATV midlands region. Duration: 50 minutes.

Written by Dick Vosburgh and Garry Chambers; designed by Pip Gardner; executive producer Bryan Izzard; directed by Paul Kimberley.

Andy Stewart, Moira Anderson, Kenneth McKellar, Mike Reid, The Alexander Brothers, Jimmy Blue and his Band, Janet Brown, Alex Norton, Bill Paterson, John Bett, Ian Sutherland.

	Holding / Source
31.12.1977	J / 2"

NICE TO SEE YOU!

A Thames Television production. Transmission details are for the ATV midlands region. Duration: 52 minutes.

Written by Dick Hills and Barry Cryer; additional material by Eric Merriman, Garry Chambers, Andrew Marshall, David Renwick and Bruce Forsyth; music directed by Peter Knight; designed by Alex Clarke; produced and directed by Keith Beckett.

Bruce Forsyth (Host), Harry H. Corbett, Faith Brown, Marti Webb, Lionel Blair, Katie Randall, Alison Bell, Andre Reid, Jane Leeves, Karen Alexander.

	VT Number	Holding / Source
21.12.1981	24748	DB-1" / 2"

With Harry H. Corbett, Faith Brown, Marti Webb, Lionel Blair.

NICE WORK

A BBC production for BBC 1. Transmission details are for BBC 1. Duration: 30 minutes.

Main regular credit(s):   Written by Anthony Couch; theme music by Ronnie Hazlehurst; titles by Richard Markell; designed by Phil Roberson; production manager Evan King; produced and directed by Bernard Thompson.

Main regular cast: Edward Woodward (Edwin), Hilary Tindall (Monica), John Comer (Mr Blundell), Aubrey Woods (Frank Lazenby), Russell Lewis (Robert).

	Holding / Source
22.12.1980 **And Unto Us - And Them - A Child Is Born**	DB-D3 / 2"

With Christopher Godwin (Granville Walker), Amanda Kemp (Alice), Albert Moses, Robert Lee.

NICE WORK

A NIGHT AT CHAS N DAVE'S

A Thames Television production. Transmission details are for the Central region. Duration: 50 minutes.

Written by Bryan Blackburn; music directed by Alan Braden; music associate Ray Monk; designed by Alex Clarke; produced and directed by Dennis Kirkland.

Chas & Dave, Aiden J. Harvey, Allan Stewart, Bob Todd, Cambridge Heath Band [as Cambridge Heath Band Of The Salvation Army], Dennis Waterman, Jim Davidson, Roger de Courcey & Nookie Bear, Roy Skelton, Tim Healy, Ronnie Le Drew [as Zippy & George], Tony Hall [as Zippy & George].

	Holding / Source
29.12.1986	1" / 1"

NIGHT FEVER

A Grundy production for Channel 5. Transmission details are for Channel 5.

Main regular performer(s): Suggs (Presenter).

SERIES 2

			Holding / Source
25.12.1997	**Abba Special**		DB / DBS

SERIES 3

		VT Number	Holding / Source
25.12.1998		108323	DB / DBS

SERIES 4

		VT Number	Holding / Source
31.12.1999	**Party**	115371	DB / DBS

SERIES 5

		VT Number	Holding / Source
31.12.2000	**New Year's Eve 1**	124666	DB / DBS
31.12.2000	**New Year's Eve 2**	124667	DB / DBS

SERIES 6

		VT Number	Holding / Source
22.12.2001	**Panto Fever**	128494	DB / DBSW

NIGHT OF 100 STARS

An LWT production. Transmission details are for the ATV midlands region. Duration: 145 minutes.

Written by Ken Hoare, Garry Chambers, Colin Bostock-Smith, Eric Merriman and Sid Green; dances staged by Robert Nesbitt; choreography by Irving Davies and Brian Rogers; designed by Bill McPherson; produced by David Bell and Richard Drewett; directed by Alan Boyd.

Terry Wogan (Host), Marti Webb, Susannah York, Bruce Forsyth, Ron Moody, Wayne Sleep, Honor Blackman, Edward Fox, Mary Malcolm, Dickie Henderson, Alfie Bass, Ian Lavender, Charles West, Stella Moray, Jess Conrad, Rosamund Shelley, John Diedrich, Caroline Villiers, Cannon and Ball, Berni Flint, Dave Wolfe, Jimmy Cricket, Hinge & Bracket, Dudley Stevens, Bernard Cribbins, Denis Quilley, Jill Gascoine, Peter Cook, David Essex, David Frost, William Rushton, Kenneth Cope, Lance Percival, Lulu, Robert Powell, Twiggy, Jean Marsh, Albert Finney, Christopher Lee, Sean Connery, James Mason, Susan George, Vera Lynn, Paul Schofield, Jessie Matthews, Margaret Lockwood, Stewart Granger, Joan Greenwood, Dulcie Gray, Michael Denison, Anna Neagle, Anthony Steel, Claire Bloom, Donald Sinden, Phyllis Calvert, Norman Wisdom, Richard Todd, Kenneth More, Dinah Sheridan, Diana Dors, Bryan Forbes, Nigel Patrick, Shirley Anne Field, Tom Courtenay, Jack Wild, Mark Lester, Oliver Reed, Simon Ward, Jenny Agutter, Graham Chapman, Hazel O'Connor, Phil Daniels, Petricia Rock, Julia McKenzie, Millicent Martin, Leslie Mitchell, Sylvia Peters, Barbara Kelly, Eamonn Andrews, Ruth Dunning, Edward Evans, Christopher Beeny, Peggy Mount, Harry Fowler, Bill Fraser, Dai Francis, John Boulter, Margaret Savage, George Mitchell, Hughie Green, David Jacobs, Alan Freeman, Don Lang, Pete Murray, Josephine Douglas, Bernie Winters, Joe Brown, Marty Wilde, Showaddywaddy, Elvi Hale, Annette Crosbie, Raymond Francis, Eric Lander, James Ellis, Terence Edmond, Joe Brady, Frank Windsor, Nyree Dawn Porter, Carol Drinkwater, Christopher Timothy, Susan Penhaligon, James Aubrey, Deborah Grant, Frank Finlay, Andrew Cruickshank, Bill Simpson, Rula Lenska, Charlotte Cornwell, Jack Hedley, Hans Meyer, Christopher Neame, Joan Benham, David Langton, Ian Ogilvy, Rachel Gurney, Simon Williams, Patsy Smart, Jenny Tomasin, Gordon Jackson, Dennis Waterman, George Cole, Lewis Collins, Martin Shaw, Derek Nimmo, George Layton, Geoffrey Davies, Ernest Clark, Jacqui Ann Carr, Carol Hawkins, Peter Cleall, Peter Denyer, Liz Gebhardt, Reg Varney, Anna Karen, Bob Grant, Doris Hare, Stephen Lewis, Richard O'Sullivan, Paula Wilcox, Tessa Wyatt, John Le Mesurier, Bill Pertwee, Arnold Ridley, Frank Williams, Ron Tarr, Alyn Ainsworth and his Orchestra.

	Holding / Source
21.12.1980	D2 / 2"

NIGHT TRAIN TO MURDER

A Thames Television production. Transmission details are for the Central region. Duration: 70 minutes.

Written by Eric Morecambe, Ernie Wise and Joe McGrath; from an idea by Rod McLaren and Jack Hobbs; designed by Peter Le Page; executive producer Philip Jones; produced and directed by Joe McGrath.

Eric Morecambe (Himself), Ernie Wise (Himself), Fulton Mackay (McKay), Lysette Anthony (Kathy), Kenneth Haigh (Various Roles), Pamela Salem (Zelda), Margaret Courtenay (Dame Flora), Leonard Maguire (Voice of Great Uncle Robert), Richard Vernon (Uncle Felix), Edward Judd (Manzini), Roger Brierley (Rivers), Ben Aris (Theatre Manager), Tony Boncza (Joe), Frank Coda (Stage Manager), Big Mike Crane (Big Jim), Robert Longden (Vicar), Penny Meredith (Mrs Manzini), Tim Stern (Tiny Big Jim), Zoe Nicholas (Soubrette), Michelle Tascher (Soubretta), Alan Shaxon (Card Dealer), Charles Jameson (Policeman).

	Holding / Source
03.01.1985	D3 / 1"

NIGHTINGALES

An Alomo/SelecTV production for Channel 4. Transmission details are for Channel 4. Duration: 25 minutes.

Main regular credit(s): Closing theme sung by Robert Lindsay; music by Clever Music.
Main regular cast: Robert Lindsay (Carter), David Threlfall (Bell), James Ellis (Sarge).

SERIES 2
Main regular credit(s): Written by Paul Makin; executive producer Laurence Marks; produced by Rosie Bunting; directed by Tony Dow.

Holding / Source
30.12.1992 **Silent Night** 1" / 1"S
With Lia Williams.

THE NIXON LINE

A BBC production for BBC 1. Transmission details are for BBC 1.

Main regular credit(s): Written by George Martin; music by Burt Rhodes; produced and directed by Kenneth Carter.
Main regular performer(s): David Nixon (Host), Basil Brush (Host).

SERIES 1
Main regular credit(s): Additional material by Ian Messiter; designed by Andrew Dimond.

Holding / Source
27.12.1967 **The Nixon Line Special** J / 40
Duration: 30 minutes.
With Trisha Noble.

NO BANANAS

A BBC production for BBC 1. Transmission details are for BBC 1. Duration: 50 minutes.

Main regular credit(s): Produced by Peter Norris.
Main regular cast: Stephanie Beacham (Dorothea Grant), Alison Steadman (Evelyn Hamilton), Tom Bell (Thomas Slater), Dorian Healy (Tom Slater), Linda Bassett (Ellen Slater), Michael Byrne (Edward Grant), Edna Doré (Granma Slater), Michael Elwyn (Arthur Hamilton), Rachel Power (Mary Hamilton), Dominic Rowan (Harry Slater), Rachel Pickup (Kaye Bentley), Gregor Truter (Frank Slater), Paul Willams (Clifford Slater), Tim Matthews (William Hamilton), Paloma Baeza (Rose Grant), Eileen O'Brien (Mrs Dovey), Chris Crooks (Dovey), Elaine Donnelly (Ivy Collins), Christopher Driscoll (Reg Collins), Peter McNamara (DS Howard).

Holding / Source
26.05.1996 **Christmas** DB-D3 / C1S
Written by Ginnie Hole; directed by Roger Bamford.
With Ryan Davenport (Geoffrey Slater), Keeley Gainey (Moira Barnes), James Weber Brown (Toby), Emily Mortimer (Una), Johanna Hargreaves, Sariel Heseltine, Meryl Hampton, Peter Lovstrom, Brooke Kinsella, Lee Wilson, Bohdan Poraj, Rupert Holliday Evans, Hazel Ellerby, Tom Ward.

NO PLACE LIKE HOME

Alternative/Working Title(s): A GREAT LIFE / HOME SWEET HOME
A BBC production for BBC 1. Transmission details are for BBC 1. Duration: 30 minutes.

Main regular credit(s): Written by Jon Watkins.
Main regular cast: William Gaunt (Arthur Crabtree).

SERIES 2
Main regular credit(s): Written by Jon Watkins; produced and directed by Robin Nash.
Main regular cast: With Patricia Garwood (Beryl Crabtree), Martin Clunes (Nigel Crabtree), Dee Sadler (Tracy Crabtree), Stephen Watson (Paul Crabtree), Beverley Adams (Lorraine Codd), Marcia Warren (Vera Botting), Michael Sharvell-Martin (Trevor Botting), Daniel Hill (Raymond Codd).

Holding / Source
26.12.1984 DB / 1"
With Leonard Maguire, James Grout, Toni Palmer, Sophie Huggins, Erica Lynley.

SERIES 5
Main regular credit(s): Written by Jon Watkins [credited as John E. Watkins]; produced and directed by Robin Nash.
Main regular cast: With Patricia Garwood (Beryl Crabtree), Martin Clunes (Nigel Crabtree), Dee Sadler (Tracy Crabtree), Beverley Adams (Lorraine Codd), Michael Sharvell-Martin (Trevor Botting), Ann Penfold (Vera Botting), Andrew Charleson (Nigel Crabtree).

Holding / Source
22.12.1987 "The Hero" DB / 1"

NOAH AND NELLY IN SKYLARK

A Bob Godfrey Films Ltd production for BBC 1. Transmission details are for BBC 1. Duration: 4 minutes.

Main regular credit(s): Written by Grange Calveley; drawings by Bob Godfrey; produced and directed by Bob Godfrey.
Main regular cast: Richard Briers (Narrator), Peter Hawkins (Narrator).

Holding / Source
30.12.1976 **During A Seasonal Time** C3 / C3
All prints held by Bob Godfrey estate, not the BBC.

NODDY

A Cosgrove Hall production for Thames Television. Transmission details are for the ATV midlands region. Duration: 14 minutes.

Main regular credit(s):   Produced by Brian Cosgrove; directed by Mark Hall.

SERIES 2

	Holding / Source
22.12.1975 **Noddy Meets Father Christmas**	C1|n / C1

It is a cold winter's day in Toyland as the milkman arrives at Noddy's house. He's very excited because Father Christmas is coming, but the postman isn't impressed because he never gets thanked for delivering the post. Big Ears visits Noddy to tell him to hurry up and get ready to drive Father Christmas round Toyland.

Written by Ruth Boswell.

NOEL'S CHRISTMAS PRESENTS

A BBC production for BBC 1. Transmission details are for BBC 1. Duration varies - see below for details.

Main regular performer(s): Noel Edmonds (Host).

	Holding / Source
25.12.1989	DB / 1"

Duration: 59 minutes.

Written by Paul Minett, Martin Booth and Brian Leveson; produced by Michael Leggo; directed by Bill Morton.

25.12.1990 — DB / 1"

Duration: 60 minutes.

Produced and directed by Michael Leggo.

With Frank Bruno, David Essex, Arthur Bostrom.

25.12.1991 — DB / 1"

Duration: 62 minutes.

Produced by Michael Leggo; directed by Bill Morton.

With Les Dawson, John Nettles, Michael Ball.

25.12.1994 — DB / D3S

Duration: 59 minutes.

Music directed by Ernie Dunstall; choreography by Jeff Thacker; designed by Robert Steer; assistant producer Emma Cornish; executive producer Michael Leggo; production managers Ben Kellett and Mark Mylod; produced and directed by Guy Freeman.

With Alan Shaxon, Richard Ashcroft, Royal Scottish National Orchestra.

25.12.1997 — DB / DBS

Duration: 59 minutes.

Produced by Guy Freeman; directed by Ben Kellett.

With George Lucas.

25.12.1998 — DB / DBSW

Duration: 59 minutes.

Produced by Graham Owens; directed by Andrew Nicholson.

NOEL'S HOUSE PARTY

A BBC production for BBC 1. Transmission details are for BBC 1. Duration: 50 minutes.

Main regular performer(s): Noel Edmonds (Host).

SERIES 2

Main regular credit(s):   Produced and directed by Michael Leggo.

	Holding / Source
26.12.1992	DB / D3S

With Gotcha (Tony Blackburn).

SERIES 3

Main regular credit(s):   Script associate Charlie Adams; designed by Bob Steer; executive producer Michael Leggo; produced by Jon Beazley; directed by Guy Freeman.

	Holding / Source
01.01.1994 **Noel's 'New Year' House Party**	DB / D3S

With Gotcha (Jonathan Morris).

SERIES 7

Made in association with Unique Television.

Main regular credit(s):   Script associate Charlie Adams; music by Steve Brown, Ernie Dunstall and Stephen Green; designed by Robert Steer; executive producer Michael Leggo; production managers Francis Gilson and Norman Lockhart; produced by John McHugh; location sequences directed by Andrew Nicholson.

	Holding / Source
20.12.1997 **Noel's Christmas House Party**	DB / D3S

Written by Charlie Adams, Adam Bostock-Smith, Garry Chambers, Rob Colley, Richard Easter, Kevin Gill and Parsons and Naylor; additional material by Noel Edmonds; assistant producer Ryan Wallis; production manager Francis Gilson; location sequences directed by Ben Kellett and Andrew Nicholson; directed by Penny Ewing.

With Anthea Turner, Martine McCutcheon, Henry Cooper, Ant & Dec, Robin Askwith, Graham Cole, Andrew Paul, Mr Blobby, Robbie Barnett, The Chuckle Brothers, Barry Killerby, The Roy Wood Big Band.

NOT GOING OUT

An Avalon Productions production for BBC 1. Transmission details are for BBC 1. Duration: 30 minutes.

Main regular credit(s): Created by Andrew Collins and Lee Mack.
Main regular cast: Lee Mack (Lee).

SERIES 2

Main regular credit(s): Written by Andrew Collins and Lee Mack; script supervisor Kendall Anderson-Müt; music directed by Steve Brown; art director Jo Sutherland; designed by James Dillon; executive producers Richard Allen-Turner, Lee Mack and Jon Thoday; production manager Lay-Ee Quah; produced by Charlie Hanson; directed by Alex Hardcastle.
Main regular cast: With Sally Bretton (Lucy), Tim Vine (Tim Adams).

Holding / Source
21.12.2007 **Murder At Christmas**   DB / DBSW
Additional material by Simon Evans and Paul Kerensa.
With Miranda Hart (Barbara), Katy Wix (Daisy), Timothy West (Geoffrey), Deborah Grant (Wendy).

SERIES 3

Main regular credit(s): Script supervisor Kendall Anderson-Müt; music directed by Steve Brown; theme music by Alex Hardcastle; director of photography Peter Thornton; art director Neil Barnes; designed by James Dillon; executive producers Jon Thoday, Richard Allen-Turner and Lee Mack; line producer Chris Iliffe; produced by Jamie Rix; directed by Nick Wood.
Main regular cast: With Sally Bretton (Lucy), Miranda Hart (Barbara), Tim Vine (Tim Adams).

Holding / Source
23.12.2009 **Absent Father Christmas**   HD/DB / HDC
Written by Daniel Peak and Lee Mack; additional material by Simon Evans, Paul Kerensa, Dave Cohen, Simon Griffiths, David Isaac, Milton Jones and Liam Woodman.
With Katy Wix (Daisy), Bobby Ball (Frank), Thomas Gater.

SERIES 6

Holding / Source
24.12.2013 **The House**   HD/DB / HDC
Duration: 45 minutes.
Keen to impress for Christmas, Lee invites Lucy's parents to join them and Daisy at his dear dead aunt's cozy old country house.
Written by Lee Mack and Daniel Peak; produced by Jamie Rix; directed by Ed Bye.
With Sally Bretton (Lucy), Katy Wix (Daisy), Deborah Grant (Wendy), Geoffrey Whitehead (Geoffrey), Bobby Ball (Frank), Jane Lowe (Carol), Trixiebelle Harrowell (Molly).

NOT ONLY... BUT ALSO

A BBC production for BBC 2. Transmission details are for BBC 2. Duration varies - see below for details.
Main regular cast: Peter Cook (Various Roles), Dudley Moore (Various Roles).

Holding / Source
26.12.1966   R1 / 40
Duration: 50 minutes.
Written by Dudley Moore and Peter Cook; music by Dudley Moore and Dennis Wilson; orchestra conducted by Harry Rabinowitz; designed by Robert Macgowan; produced and directed by John Street.
With John Lennon ('Dan'), Sandra Fehr, John Stamp, Peter Wainwright, Marian Montgomery, The Dudley Moore Trio.

Holding / Source
24.12.1974 **The Best of Not Only...But Also**   R1 / 2"
Duration: 40 minutes.
Written by Peter Cook and Dudley Moore; produced and directed by James Gilbert; film sequences directed by Michael Mills.
With David Bird.

NOTHIN' BUT THE BLUES

A Granada production. Transmission details are for the Granada region. Duration: 29 minutes.
Main regular credit(s): Produced by John Hamp; directed by Philip Casson.
Main regular performer(s): Joe Turner [as Big Joe Turner], Sippie Wallaces, Roosevelt Sykes, Sleepy John Estes, Little Brother Montgomery, Jank Rachell, Robert Pete Williams.

	Production No	Holding / Source
27.12.1966	P541/1	R1|n / 40

NOYE'S FLUDDE

A BBC production for BBC 1. Transmission details are for BBC 1. Duration: 50 minutes.

The Chester miracle play. The old Chester play tells the story of Noah and the Ark, the animals, Noah's children and his wife, who was so very unco-operative — until the flood came. This play was one of the group of 'miracle' plays done by the Guilds of Chester in the Middle Ages. They were performed by the ordinary people, craftsmen and tradesmen in the local towns — each Guild performing one of the plays on the back of a cart.

Music by Benjamin Britten; conducted by Steuart Bedford; lighting by Tommy Thomas; sound Graham Haines; produced by Colin Graham; directed by Walter Todds.

Owen Brannigan (Noye), Sheila Rex (Mrs Noye), Norman Lumsden (The Voice of God), Andrew Phillips (Sem), Richard Cooper (Ham), Marcus Creed (Jaffet), Pauline Barrett (Mrs Sem), Margaret Perry (Mrs Ham), Francesca Lucy (Mrs Jaffet), David Sturgeon (The Raven), Amanda Gooding (The Dove), Glynis Bennett (Mrs Noye's Gossips), Patsie Cameron (Mrs Noye's Gossips), Sharon Cooper (Mrs Noye's Gossips), Nicolette Thomson (Mrs Noye's Gossips), Martin Behling (Property Man), Brian Eade (Property Man), John Hallas (Property Man), Grant Peters (Property Man), Richard Townshend (Property Man), The English Opera Group Players.

Holding / Source

26.12.1971

NUMBER 13

A BBC production for BBC 4. Transmission details are for BBC 4. Duration: 40 minutes.

Adapted by Justin Hopper; based on a story by M. R. James; script supervisor Shirin Smith; music by Matt Dunkley; production executive Gordon Ronald; executive producer Richard Fell; produced by Sue Smith; directed by Pier Wilkie.

Greg Wise (Anderson), Paul Freeman (Harrington), David Burke (Gunton), Tom Burke (Jenkins), Charlotte Comer (Alice), Anton Saunders (Hotel Porter).

Holding / Source

22.12.2006   DB / DBSWF

THE O ZONE

A BBC production for BBC 2. Transmission details are for BBC 2. Duration varies - see below for details.

SERIES 1

	Holding / Source
24.12.1989	DB / 1"

ODD MAN IN

A BBC production for BBC 1. Transmission details are for BBC 1. Duration: 90 minutes.

Adapted by Robin Maugham; based on a play by Claude Magnier; designed by Stanley Moore; produced and directed by Wallace Douglas.

Ian Carmichael (Mervyn Browne), Elspet Gray (Jane Maxwell), Brian Rix (George Maxwell).

	Holding / Source
29.12.1969	J / 2"

ODD ONE IN

A Zeppotron production for ITV 1. Transmission details are for the Central region. Duration: 40 minutes.

Main regular performer(s): Bradley Walsh (Host), Peter André (Home Team), Jason Manford (Home Team).

SERIES 2

Main regular credit(s): Written by Les Keen; programme associates Charlie Bennett, Simon Craig [credited as Simon J. K. Craig], Dominic English and Aiden Spackman; script supervisor Michelle Arnold; music by Jess Bailey and Graeme Perkins; art director Catherine Land; decor by Cath Pater-Lancucki; assistant producers Fran Davies, Henry Imbert and Jonny Lusk; production executive Jo Kay; executive producers Peter Holmes and Neil Webster; head of production Debra Blenkinsop; production manager Nadia Afiari; series producer Andrew Robertson; produced by Nina Clement and Paul Hupfield; directed by Richard Valentine.

	Holding / Source
18.12.2011 **Christmas Special**	HD/DB / HDC

With Carol Vorderman, Mark Watson.

ODDBODS

A Talent TV Production production for BBC 1. Transmission details are for BBC 1. Duration: 20 minutes.

Main regular credit(s): Written by Gareth Hale, Norman Pace and Richard Parker; executive producers John Kaye Cooper, Gareth Hale and Norman Pace; produced and directed by Peter Orton.

Main regular cast: Gareth Hale (Nobby), Norman Pace (Ginge), David Hamilton (Radio Voice Only).

	Holding / Source
28.12.1998 **Power Cut**	DB / DBSW

OF THE NATIVITE OF OURE LORDE

A BBC production for BBC 1. Transmission details are for BBC 1.

Olive Gregg (Reader).

	Holding / Source
26.12.1968	J /

Extracts from St. Bonaventura's 'Life of Jesus'.

OFF THE RECORD

A BBC production. Transmission details are for BBC. Usual duration: 30 minutes.

Main regular credit(s): Conducted by Stanley Black; produced by James Gilbert.

Main regular performer(s): Jack Payne (Host), The Concert Orchestra, The George Mitchell Singers.

SERIES 1

Main regular credit(s): Produced and directed by Francis Essex.

	Holding / Source
26.12.1955	J / Live

Duration: 45 minutes.

With Alma Cogan, Ruby Murray, Jimmy Young, Eddie Calvert, Ronnie Hilton, The Johnston Brothers, Don Lang with The Mairants-Langhorn Big Six, Cyril Stapleton, Julie Dawn.

SERIES 2

Main regular credit(s): Produced and directed by Bill Cotton [credited as Bill Cotton, Jnr.].

	Holding / Source
24.12.1956	J / Live

With Anne Shelton, Alma Cogan, Lonnie Donegan and his Skiffle Group, Jill Day, Stanley Black, Tommy Steele.

SERIES 3

Main regular credit(s): Produced and directed by James Gilbert.

	Holding / Source
27.12.1957	J / Live

With Dany Dauberson, Johnny Duncan and his Blue Grass Boys, Edmund Hockridge, Cleo Laine, Jimmy Shand and his Band, The Stargazers, Johnny Dankworth and his Orchestra.

THE OFFICE

A BBC production. Transmission details are for Various BBC Channels.

Main regular credit(s): Written by Ricky Gervais and Stephen Merchant; produced by Ash Atalla; directed by Ricky Gervais and Stephen Merchant.

Main regular cast: Ricky Gervais (David Brent), Martin Freeman (Tim Canterbury), Mackenzie Crook (Gareth Keenan), Lucy Davis (Dawn Tinsley).

SERIES 3: Christmas Specials

Transmission details are for BBC 1. Duration: 52 minutes.

Main regular credit(s): Script supervisor Emma John; assistant director Steve Roberts; art director Alex Merchant; production designer Alex Craig; production executive Sarah Hitchcock; executive producers Jon Plowman and Anil Gupta; production manager Paul Williams.

Main regular cast: With Patrick Baladi (Neil Godwin), Elizabeth Berrington (Anne), Ralph Ineson (Chris 'Finchy' Finch), Joel Beckett (Lee), Ewen Macintosh (Keith), Steve Brody (Peter The Agent), Howard Saddler (Oliver), Ben Bradshaw (Ben), Jamie Deeks (Jamie), Julie Fernandez (Brenda), Martha Howe-Douglas (Mel), Rachel Isaac (Trudy), Emma Manton (Emma), Jane Lucas (Sheila), Alexander Perkins (Ralph), Philip Pickard (Philip), Paul Ferguson, Howard Brown, Mike McClean, Greg Burns.

Holding / Source

26.12.2003 **Episode 1**   DB / DBSWF

With Howard Brown, Greg Burns, Alec Christie, Paul Ferguson, Mike McClean, Sandy McDade, Robert Purdy, Kellie Shirley, Dan Renton Skinner, Ash Varrez, Ben Forster.

27.12.2003 **Episode 2**   DB / DBSWF

With Sandy Hendrickse, Rebecca Charles, Alec Christie, Joann Condon, Julia Davis, Cally Lawrence, Sandy McDade, David Schaal, Ben Forster.

OH BOY!

An ATV production. Transmission details are for the ATV midlands region. Duration: 25 minutes.

SERIES 2

Main regular credit(s): Music directed by Keith Strachan; choreography by Carole Todd; designed by Jill Oxley; produced by Richard Leyland and Paul Smith; directed by Paul Smith.

Main regular performer(s): With Joe Brown and his Bruvvers, The Oh Boy! Boogie Band, The Oh Boy! Cats and Kittens.

Holding / Source

25.12.1979 **Christmas Oh Boy!**   DB / 2"

With Billy Hartman, Freddie 'Fingers' Lee, Alvin Stardust, Shakin' Stevens, Rachel Sweet, Tim Witnall, Fumble.

OH NO IT'S SELWYN FROGGITT

A Yorkshire Television production. Transmission details are for the ATV midlands region. Duration: 25 minutes.

Main regular credit(s): Created by Roy Clarke.

Main regular cast: Bill Maynard (Selwyn Froggitt), Robert Keegan (Maurice Froggitt), Richard Davies (Clive), Bill Dean (Jack), Harold Goodwin (Harry), Ray Mort (Ray), Megs Jenkins (Mum).

SERIES 3

Main regular credit(s): Designed by Roy Coldrick; produced and directed by Ronnie Baxter.

Main regular cast: With Lynda Baron (Vera Froggitt).

Holding / Source

27.12.1977 **On The Feast Of Selwyn**   1" / 2"

"If you can help somebody as you pass along, you'll never walk alone," says Selwyn. A pensioner he invited home for the day could make him change his mind.

Written by Mike Craig, Lawrie Kinsley and Ron McDonnell; music by John Clough and Peter Husband.

With Joe Gladwin (Mr Ramshaw).

OH NO! IT'S THE CHEEKY MONK

A BBC Wales production for BBC 1 Wales. Transmission details are for BBC 1. Duration: 30 minutes.

Main regular credit(s): Written by Wally Malston, Garry Chambers and Eric Merriman; produced and directed by John Hefin.

Main regular cast: Laurence Naismith (Father Humphrys), Felix Aylmer (Father Llewellyn).

Holding / Source

14.12.1972 **A Cheeky Christmas**   DB-D3 / C1

Unused material exists on C1.

Kaleidoscope are not aware that BBC Wales had telerecording facilities. These were recorded down the line at TV Centre (Primarily to make sales copies for export to Patagonia).

OH YES I AM... OH NO YOU'RE NOT!

A BBC Arts production for BBC 1. Transmission details are for BBC 1. Duration: 55 minutes.

Assistant producer Denise Smith; produced and directed by Sandra Gregory.

Prunella Scales (Commentator), Terry Scott, John Inman, Windsor Davies, Melvyn Hayes, George Lacy, Simon Barry, Alan Vicars, Nat Jackley, Reverend Richard Ames, Arthur Askey, Cyril Fletcher, John Morley.

Holding / Source

24.12.1982   C1 / C1

OH! MR TOAD

A Cosgrove Hall production for Thames Television. Transmission details are for the Central region.

Main regular credit(s): Animated by Paul Berry, Sue Pugh and Loyd Price; music by Keith Hopwood and Malcolm Rowe; produced by Mark Hall and Brian Cosgrove.

Holding / Source
29.12.1989 **A Tale Of Two Toads**   1" / C1
Duration: 50 minutes.
River-Banker and Wild-Wooder, the Chief Weasel has a new secret weapon - Toad himself.
Written by Brian Trueman; directed by Jackie Cockle.
With David Jason (Toad), Michael Hordern (Badger), Richard Pearson (Mole), Peter Sallis (Rat).

OLD BEAR STORIES

An Optomen TV/Ealing Animation production for Carlton. Transmission details are for the Central region. Duration varies - see below for details.

Main regular credit(s): Based on stories by Jane Hissey.
Main regular cast: Anton Rodgers (Narrator).

SERIES 1

Holding / Source
27.12.1993 **Christmas Special: The Perfect Presents**   D2 / C1S
Duration: 30 minutes.
Old Bear and his friends recall old adventures.

SERIES 4

Holding / Source
17.12.1997 **Christmas Special: Little Bear And The Christmas Star**   D2 / C1S
Duration: 25 minutes.

THE OLD GREY WHISTLE TEST

A BBC production for BBC 2. Transmission details are for BBC 2. Duration varies - see below for details.

SERIES 2

Duration: 30 minutes.
Main regular credit(s): Produced by Michael Appleton; directed by Colin Strong.

Holding / Source
26.12.1972 **Pick Of The Year**   DB-D3 / 2"
With Alice Cooper, David Bowie, The Beach Boys, Vinegar Joe, Curtis Mayfield, Mick Jagger, Poco, Roxy Music, Stevie Wonder, Jerry Lee Lewis, Kris Kristofferson, Rita Coolidge.
The 75 minute 'insert' tape is in fact a slightly longer edit of the complete programme. If the extra material is otherwise missing, Kaleidoscope does not know.

SERIES 3

Duration: 45 minutes.
Main regular credit(s): Produced by Michael Appleton; directed by Colin Strong.
Main regular performer(s): With Bob Harris (Presenter).

Holding / Source
31.12.1973 **Pick Of The Year**   DB-D3 / 2"
With Pink Floyd, Freddie King, The Everly Brothers, Steppenwolf, Jim Croce, Bill Withers, Rick Wakeman, Roberta Flack, Roger Daltrey, Ry Cooder, Humble Pie, Smokey Robinson and The Miracles, Terry Reid, Edgar Winter Band.
Iincludes Rick Wakeman track from 16/01/73 which doesn't otherwise exist.

SERIES 4

Duration: 40 minutes.
Main regular credit(s): Produced by Michael Appleton.
Main regular performer(s): With Bob Harris (Presenter).

Holding / Source
24.12.1974 **Elton John Christmas Concert Live From Hammersmith Odeon**   DB-D3 / 2"
Duration: 55 minutes.
Concert recorded live at the Hammersmith Odeon. TX'D FOOTAGE: "Bennie & the Jets" (dur 5m39s/23m00s in) "Lucy in the Sky with Diamonds" (dur 5m28s/30m58s in) "I Saw Her Standing There" (dur 2m45s/37m19s in) "Don't Let the Sun Go Down On Me" (dur 5m27s/40m41s in) "Honky Cat" (dur 6m20s/46m46s in) "Saturday Night's Alright For Fighting" (dur 7m43s/53m42s in) "Crocodile Rock" (dur 3m35s/63m57s in) "The Bitch Is Back" (dur 3m27s/68m21s in) "Your Song" (dur 3m49s/72m58s in) Two bunny girls present Elton with cake (77m12s- 77m34s); Rod STEWART & Gary GLITTER come on stage & hug Elton (77m34s-78m34s) "White Christmas".
Produced by Michael Appleton; directed by Tom Corcoran.
With Elton John, Gary Glitter.
Also different edit and extra material held.

31.12.1974 **Rock 'Til Two / OGWT 73-74**   DB-D3 / 2"
Highlights from last season.
With Bad Company, Leo Sayer, Ace.

THE OLD GREY WHISTLE TEST (continued)	British Christmas Television Guide

SERIES 5

Holding / Source

24.12.1975 **Queen's Christmas Concert**　　　　　　　　　　　　　　　　　　　　DB-D3 / Live
With Queen.

31.12.1975 **Pick Of The Year**　　　　　　　　　　　　　　　　　　　　　　　　DB-D3 / 2"
With Johnny Winter, Alvin Lee, Rush, Supertramp, Bonnie Raitt, Little Feat, The Ronettes, Joni Mitchell, Janis Ian, Bad Company, Smokey Robinson and The Miracles, Stackridge, John Lennon, Van Morrison, Joe Walsh, Yes.

SERIES 6

Main regular credit(s):　　　Produced by Michael Appleton.
Main regular performer(s):　　With Bob Harris (Presenter).

Holding / Source

24.12.1976 **Rod's Christmas Concert**　　　　　　　　　　　　　　　　　　　　　DB-D3 / 2"
Duration: 60 minutes.
Live from the stage at Olympia, London. A simultaneous stereo broadcast with Radio 1. To obtain the best effect viewers with stereo Radio 1 should turn off Tv sound and position their loudspeakers on either side of the screen but close enough to relate stereo image to picture size. Stereo headphones provide a suitable alternative.
Directed by Tom Corcoran.
With The Rod Stewart Group.

31.12.1976 **Pick Of The Year**　　　　　　　　　　　　　　　　　　　　　　　　DB-D3 / 2"

SERIES 7

Main regular credit(s):　　　Produced by Michael Appleton; directed by Tom Corcoran.
Main regular performer(s):　　With Bob Harris (Presenter).

Holding / Source

24.12.1977 **The Kinks' Christmas Concert**　　　　　　　　　　　　　　　　　　　DB-D3 / 2"
Duration: 60 minutes.
With The Kinks.

31.12.1977 **Pick Of The Year**　　　　　　　　　　　　　　　　　　　　　　　　DB-D3 / 2"
Duration: 85 minutes.
With Bob Dylan, Led Zeppelin, Fleetwood Mac, Jackson Browne, Linda Ronstadt, Eric Clapton, Elton John, Buddy Hollly And The Crickets.

SERIES 8

Main regular credit(s):　　　Produced by Michael Appleton; directed by Tom Corcoran.

Holding / Source

24.12.1978 **10cc in Concert**　　　　　　　　　　　　　　　　　　　　　　　　　DB-D3 / 2"
Introduced by Anne Nightingale.
With 10cc.

30.12.1978 **Pick Of The Year Part 1**　　　　　　　　　　　　　　　　　　　　　DB-D3 / 2"

31.12.1978 **Pick Of The Year Part 2**　　　　　　　　　　　　　　　　　　　　　DB-D3 / 2"

SERIES 9

Holding / Source

31.12.1979　　　　　　　　　　　　　　　　　　　　　　　　　　　　　　　　　DB-D3 / Live
BBC cataloguing:
(NB: Preceded by BBC2 logo V/O by announcer 59.44-59.59)
CONCERT: finale of unnamed track (0.31-0.47) HARRIS intro band (-1.30) band perf "Dreaming" (-4.37) "Slow Motion" (-7.52) "Shayla" (-11.52) into "Union City Blue" (-15.13) "Atomic" (-21.01) into "Eat To The Beat" (-21.20) into "Picture This" (-24.08) "Pretty Baby" (-28.48) "Heart of Glass" (-34.43) "Hanging On The Telephone" (-37.17) drum solo, pipers onto stage & perform "Sunday Girl" (-38.26) band takes over "Sunday Girl" (-40.22) (Titles over X Offender 39.17-39.51).
With Blondie.
The complete audio recording of this OGWT gig was issued on the 'Blondie At The BBC' CD/DVD.
It included these tracks before the TV broadcast began.

'Denis'/'The Hardest Part'/'Die Young Stay Pretty'/'Accidents Never Happen'/'Victor'/'Living In The Real World'/'Seven Rooms Of Gloom' (Four Tops cover)/'Eat To The Beat'/'X Offender' (it was during this last track when it went live on the radio and shortly afterwards on BBC2).

The BBC2 broadcast ended with 'Sunday Girl' but the concert carried on with 'I Feel Good' (James Brown cover) and a fantastic version of 'One Way Or Another' which Debbie Harry starts swearing about how high the Apollo stage is.

SERIES 10

Holding / Source

24.12.1980　　　　　　　　　　　　　　　　　　　　　　　　　　　　　　　　　DB-D3 / 2"
With Ian Dury and The Blockheads.

SERIES 11

Main regular credit(s):　　　Produced by Michael Appleton.

Holding / Source

24.12.1981 **Toyah In Concert**　　　　　　　　　　　　　　　　　　　　　　　　DB-D3 / 2"
With Toyah.

THE OLD GREY WHISTLE TEST

| British Christmas Television Guide | THE OLD GREY WHISTLE TEST (continued) |

| 31.12.1981 **Pick Of The Year** | DB-D3 / 2" |

SERIES 12
Main regular credit(s):   Produced by Michael Appleton; directed by Tom Corcoran.

Holding / Source

24.12.1982 **Elton John In Concert**   DB-D3 / 2"
With Elton John.

31.12.1982 **Pick Of The Year**   DB-D3 / 2"
Duration: 95 minutes.
With Anne Nightingale (Presenter), David Hepworth (Presenter), Altered Images, Japan, The Thompson Twins, King Crimson, Spandau Ballet, The Damned, The Doors, Gang of Four, Ry Cooder.

See also: WHISTLE TEST (BBC)

OLD HARRY'S GAME (RADIO)

A BBC production for BBC Radio 4. Transmission details are for BBC Radio 4. Duration: 28 minutes.
Main regular credit(s):   Written by Andy Hamilton; produced and directed by Paul Mayhew-Archer.
Main regular cast: Andy Hamilton (Satan), Jimmy Mulville (Thomas Quentin Crimp).

Holding / Source

31.12.2002 **The Roll Of The Dice**   DA /
01.01.2003 **Knocking On Heaven's Door**   DA /

THE OLD MAN OF LOCHNAGAR

A Verronmead Productions production for Channel 4. made in association with Whirligig Theatre. Transmission details are for Channel 4. Duration: 65 minutes.
Adapted by David Wood; based on a book by HRH The Prince of Wales; produced by Maureen Harter; directed by Dave Heather.
Iain Laughlan (The Old Man), Mary-Ann Coburn (Grouse / Queen of the Gorms), Percy Copley (Giant Gormless / Lagopus Scoticus), Teresa Gallagher (Aggie), Lesley Halliday (Maggie), Alec Westwood (Hamish), Katrina Ramsay (Nagar Maid / Gorm), Edward Brittain (Gorm), Alan Morley (Gorm).

Holding / Source

26.12.1987   1" / 1"

OMNIBUS

A BBC production for BBC 1. Transmission details are for BBC 1. Duration varies - see below for details.

Holding / Source

24.12.1973 **Gershwin's Porgy**   C1 / C1
Duration: 75 minutes.
'George Gershwin died in 1937, but I don't have to believe it if I don't want to ' wrote novelist John O'Hara. This music documentary is about Gershwin and his great operatic masterpiece, and marks the 75th anniversary year of Gershwin's birth. It includes some of his best-known, best-loved compositions as well as scenes from Porgy and Bess and a few surprises.
Written by Kenneth Corden; lighting by Ken Macgregor; sound Alan Edmonds; designed by Kenneth Sharp; produced by Kenneth Corden; directed by Rodney Greenberg.
With George Goodman (Porgy), Vivian Martin (Bess), Clive Farel (Sportling Life), Isabelle Lucas (Serena), Dorothy Ross (Clara), George Webb (Jake), Keefe West (Crown), Aubrey Morris (Ira Gershwin), David Knight (DuBose Heyward), Arthur Schwartz (Himself), Craig Sheppard, Royal Philharmonic Orchestra.

ON CHRISTMAS NIGHT

A BBC Productions Manchester production for BBC 1. Transmission details are for BBC 1. Duration: 4 minutes.
SERIES 1
Main regular credit(s):   Executive producer Tommy Nagra; produced by David Waters.

Holding / Source

26.12.2008 **Luke 2: 8-16**   DB / DBSW
Readings by Gabrielle Drake and Robert Hardy.

25.12.2009 **Matthew 1: 18-25**   DB / DBSW
Readings by Julie Fernandez.

25.12.2010   DB / DBSW

25.12.2011   DB / DBSW
Executive producer Tommy Nagra; produced by David Waters.

SERIES 2

Holding / Source

25.12.2012   HD/DB / HDC
The story of Christmas from Luke's gospel.
With Rachel Morris (Reader).

25.12.2013   HD/DB / HDC
No credits on-screen.

ON THE BUSES

An LWT production. Transmission details are for the ATV midlands region. Usual duration: 25 minutes.

By late 1969, Frank Muir, the Head of Light Entertainment at LWT, was desperately looking for some new shows, and the writers Ronnie Wolfe and Ronnie Chesney walked into his office at five o'clock one Friday afternoon. Frank skimmed through the format, dashed off to have a quick word with Cyril Bennett, the Programme Controller, and at twenty-past five came back to tell them they had a contract. It was pretty surprising, considering that only the previous week this same show had been rejected by the BBC!

This new show was to be called "On The Buses". The show would be done with two different set-ups – the bus garage, and the home. This would give rise to all the situations that could happen at work, and the domestic side which would incorporate family life and all the conflicts arising from that situation.

So, with the approval of the idea by London Weekend Television, Wolfe and Chesney wrote the first script and several storylines. Then came the agonising game of chance called casting. Frank asked for a short list of suggestions for the lead. The writers had made up their minds that they definitely wanted Reg Varney as Stan, the bus-driver, so they went in with the following list: (1) Ronnie Barker, (2) Reg Varney, (3) Bernard Cribbins.

The writers had found by experience that when you showed a TV executive a list of names, it was a bit like choosing from the wine list. They're a bit suspicious of the first, and usually plump for the second. Somehow they feel it's safe and not too expensive. Or maybe, with the first name, they feel the agent will push too hard for the fee?

The rest of the cast was found in a bizarre way. The part of The Inspector was offered to a very fine actor – Dudley Foster, who tragically died before the show began. Stephen Lewis was the next choice. He was chosen because he had recently worked in a Stratford East production of "MRS.WILSON'S DIARY". The TV director Stuart Allen, who had a great talent for choosing actors for specific roles, had directed the TV version of this show and suggested Stephen for the part. In that same play was Bob Grant, who was invited to play the part of Jack the Conductor. Doris Hare was everybody's favourite to play the part of Mum. There was no arguing, heart-searching or agonising over that piece of casting – that was easy. Except that Doris was in Mexico for a couple of months with her husband, a Professor of Medicine, who was attending a seminar. So she was not available. Cicely Courtneidge was booked for the first series on the understanding that if the show continued, she would be replaced by Doris.

The hardest part to cast was Olive, Stan's very plain and unattractive sister. Not many actresses wish to take on a role like that. The writers thought of Anna Karen. In real life, Anna is a very attractive lady; she started her career as a stripper. She worked the night clubs, billed as "Anna Karen, the Swedish Sex Bomb", alongside the very young Barbara Windsor. But more recently, by donning an unattractive wig, wearing heavy 'bottle-top' glasses, blacking out a few teeth and using padding, she had specialised in playing plain looking, worn-out, washed-out, whining characters. This is what the producer wanted, so the writers arranged for her to meet Stuart Allen and told her to arrive at the London Weekend Studio looking the part of Olive. But it wasn't 'Olive' that walked in! Anna, being all woman, glided in dressed to kill - beautifully made up with false eyelashes, eye-liner, mascara, the lot! We knew she would never get the part looking so attractive, so the writers dragged her out to the car park, pushed her into the back of Wolfe's car, and asked her to take it all off. And now – when Anna is asked how she was cast, she tells the following story. "The writers wanted me to take off all my make-up. They pushed me into the back of the car and said "Take everything off". I misunderstood – they got lucky – and I got the part". For the part of Olive's husband, Arthur, we found just the right actor, Michael Robbins, who played the role to perfection.

This show was crude and vulgar, and very working class. The critics panned it. The viewing figures were huge – it grew to 16 million - and it soon climbed to the top of the ratings. Forty years later it is still playing on ITV's digital channels and spawned three hit films.

Main regular credit(s): Created by Ronald Wolfe and Ronald Chesney.

SERIES 4

Main regular credit(s): Written by Ronald Wolfe and Ronald Chesney; designed by Alan Hunter-Craig; produced and directed by Stuart Allen.

Main regular cast: With Reg Varney (Stan Butler), Bob Grant (Jack Harper), Stephen Lewis (Inspector Cyril Blake), Doris Hare (Mum), Michael Robbins (Arthur Rudge), Anna Karen (Olive Rudge).

	Production No	Holding / Source
25.12.1970 **Christmas Duty**	9L/00502	DB / 62

With Ursula Mohan, Eunice Black, Roger Avon.

SERIES 5

Main regular credit(s): Designed by Alan Hunter-Craig; produced and directed by Derrick Goodwin.

Main regular cast: With Reg Varney (Stan Butler), Bob Grant (Jack Harper), Stephen Lewis (Inspector Cyril Blake), Doris Hare (Mum), Michael Robbins (Arthur Rudge), Anna Karen (Olive Rudge).

	Production No	Holding / Source
26.12.1971 **Boxing Day Social**	9L/00764	DB / 2"

The Boxing Day Social at the depot.

Written by Ronald Wolfe and Ronald Chesney; designed by Alan Hunter-Craig.

With Helen Fraser (Linda Rudge), Gillian Lind (Mrs Rudge), Janice Hoy (Beryl), Kenneth Waller (Busman M.C.).

ONCE UPON A BANK HOLIDAY

An Associated-Rediffusion production. Transmission details are for Associated-Rediffusion. Duration: 15 minutes.

A musical gambol that has nothing to do with Christmas with John Gower, Edmund Donlevy, Viki Emra, Ann Lancaster. Ann Lancaster is now appearing in 'The Famous Five' at the Princes Theatre.

Music directed by Andrew Fenner; music composed by Christopher Hodder-Williams; settings by John Clements; produced and directed by William Freshman.

John Gower, Edmund Donlevy, Viki Emra, Ann Lancaster.

	Holding / Source
26.12.1955	J /

ONCE UPON A CHRISTMAS

An Associated-Rediffusion production. Transmission details are for Associated-Rediffusion. Duration: 25 minutes.

A musical Christmas card. Even if you only have a few pennies in your pocket, a tune to dance to, and a dream in your heart, you may find your wishes coming true.

Written by Peter Ling; designed by Gregory Lawson; produced and directed by Prudence Nesbitt.

Mavis Traill, Tony Bateman, James Bree, Hope Jackman, Pauline Innes, Lennie Mayne.

	Holding / Source
25.12.1959	J /

ONE FOOT IN THE GRAVE

A BBC production for BBC 1. Transmission details are for BBC 1. Duration varies - see below for details.

Main regular credit(s): Written by David Renwick; theme music by Eric Idle.
Main regular cast: Richard Wilson (Victor Meldrew), Annette Crosbie (Margaret Meldrew).

SERIES 2
Main regular credit(s): Incidental music by Ed Welch; produced by Susan Belbin.

Holding / Source
27.12.1990 **Who's Listening** — DB-D3 / 1"
Duration: 59 minutes.
Designed by Chris Hull and John Asbridge; production manager Duncan Cooper; directed by Susan Belbin.
With Doreen Mantle (Mrs Warboys), Janine Duvitski (Pippa), Angus Deayton (Patrick), Cathy Shipton, Geoffrey Chater, Chase Marks, Bob Appleby, Enn Reitel.

SERIES 3
Main regular credit(s): Incidental music by Ed Welch; production manager Murray Peterson; produced and directed by Susan Belbin.

Holding / Source
30.12.1991 **The Man In The Long Black Coat** — DB-D3 / 1"
Duration: 48 minutes.
Designed by John Bristow.
With Angus Deayton (Patrick), Janine Duvitski (Pippa), Owen Brenman (Nick Swainey), Cecily Hobbs, Michael Robbins, Eric Idle.

In their respective episodes Eric Idle, John Du Prez and John Challis are voice-only artists.

Credits: Incidental music by Ed Welch; director of photography John Rhodes; assistant director Angela De Chastelai Smith; designed by Nick Somerville; produced and directed by Susan Belbin.

Holding / Source
26.12.1993 **One Foot In The Algarve** — DB-D3 / C1S
Duration: 92 minutes.
With Doreen Mantle (Mrs Warboys), Peter Cook, Joan Sims, Edward De Souza, Louis Mahoney, Eamonn Walker, Louise Duprey, Craig Ferguson, Anna Nicholas, Benjamin Falcáo, Margarida Rodrigues, Augusto Portela, Eduardo Viana, José Gomes, Jorge Parente, André Maia, Jorge Sequerra, João D'Avila, Maria D'Aires, Luis Zagalo, Lidia Franco, João Lagarto.
Purely from what's shown on-screen, this is just a TV film called "One Foot In The Algarve" – at no point does the title "One Foot In The Grave" appear.

SERIES 5
Main regular credit(s): Incidental music by Ed Welch; produced and directed by Susan Belbin.

Holding / Source
25.12.1994 **The Man Who Blew Away** — DB-D3 / D3S
Duration: 40 minutes.
Designed by Laurence Williams; production manager Nick Wood.
With Janine Duvitski (Pippa), Angus Deayton (Patrick), Brian Murphy, Daniel Smith, Ryan O'Leary.

Holding / Source
25.12.1995 **The Wisdom Of The Witch** — DB-D3 / D3S
Duration: 60 minutes.
Music by Ed Welch; art director Steve Wright; designed by John Asbridge; production associate Jonathan Paul Llewellyn; production manager Lesley Bywater; produced and directed by Susan Belbin.
With Angus Deayton (Patrick), Janine Duvitski (Pippa), Phil Daniels, Rachel Bell, Joanne Engelsman, Bruce Byron, Peter McNally, Peter Terry, Virginie Gilchrist, Tony Sibbald, Boris.
Christine Gernon was the Production Assistant.

Holding / Source
26.12.1996 **Starbound** — DB-D3 / D3S
Duration: 59 minutes.
Incidental music by Ed Welch; assistant director Paul Hastings; designed by John Asbridge and Linda Conoboy; production associate Lesley Bywater.
With Doreen Mantle (Mrs Warboys), Angus Deayton (Patrick), Janine Duvitski (Pippa), Owen Brenman (Nick Swainey), Ray Winstone, Lucy Davis, Roli Okorodudu, Elizabeth Chambers, Rula Lenska.
Eric Idle's theme song is not used on this special.

Holding / Source
25.12.1997 **Endgame** — DB / DBS
Duration: 68 minutes.
Script supervisor Jane Houston; incidental music by Ed Welch; assistant director Paul Leather; art director Sarah Milton; production designer Linda Conoboy; production manager Jenny Penrose; produced by Esta Charkham; directed by Christine Gernon.
With Owen Brenman (Nick Swainey), Tim Brooke-Taylor, Marian McLoughlin, Usha Patel, Norman Eshley, Ian Redford, Robin Davies, Christopher Robbie, Regina Freedman, Arif Hussein, Matthew Whittle, Ian Swann, Alisdair Ross, Nicholas Moore, Coral Lorne.

ONE FOR THE POT

A BBC production for BBC 1. Transmission details are for BBC 1. Duration: 90 minutes.

Written by Ray Cooney and Tony Hilton; television presentation by Eric Fawcett; designed by Rhoda Gray.

Sheila Mercier (Amy Hardcastle), Derek Royle (Jennifer Bowater-Smith), Leo Franklyn (Jugg), Rex Garner (Jonathan Hardcastle), Helen Jessop (Cynthia Hardcastle), Stefan Gryff (Max Weill), Dennis Ramsden (Arnold Piper), Basil Lord (Charlie Barnet), Brian Rix (Hickory Wood), Diane Appleby (Winnie), John Newbury (Guest), William Leeson (Guest).

	Holding / Source
26.12.1966	J /

ONE HOUR WITH JONATHAN ROSS

A Channel X production for Channel 4. Transmission details are for Channel 4. Duration: 50 minutes.

Main regular performer(s): Jonathan Ross (Host).

SERIES 1

Main regular credit(s): Series producer Katie Lander; produced by Alan Marke and Jonathan Ross; directed by Peter Orton.

	Holding / Source
24.12.1989 **Christmas Special**	1" / 1"S

ONE MAN'S LAUDER

An ATV production. Transmission details are for the ATV midlands region. Duration: 70 minutes.

Jimmy Logan pays a special tribute to Scotland's greatest entertainer-Sir Harry Lauder. Lauder was born in poverty in 1870 and rose to become one of the highest paid music hall artists in the world.

Written by Jimmy Logan; music by Laurie Holloway; designed by Bryan Holgate; produced and directed by Jon Scoffield.

Jimmy Logan (Sir Harry Lauder).

	Holding / Source
31.12.1980	DB / 2"

THE ONE O'CLOCK GANG

A Scottish Television production. Transmission details are for the Scottish Television region. Duration varies - see below for details.

	Holding / Source
31.12.1964	DA SO / Live

Duration: 27 minutes.
Hogmanay edition.

THE ONE RONNIE

A Little Britain Productions production for BBC 1. Transmission details are for BBC 1. Duration: 50 minutes.

Written by Matt Lucas, David Walliams, The Dawson Brothers, Ben Elton, John Finnemore, Robert A. Gray, Jason Hazeley, Joel Morris and Richard Law; additional material by Paul Davighi, Simon Evans, Milton Jones and Alan Stafford; script supervisors Helen Dobson and Sarah Leggett; music by Brint and Wallace; director of photography Pete Rowe; art director Carolyn Wilson; designed by Harry Banks; production executive Sarah Hitchcock; executive producers Jed Leventhall, Matt Lucas, David Walliams and Mark Freeland; line producer Francis Gilson; produced by Gareth Edwards; directed by Geoff Posner.

Ronnie Corbett (Various Roles), Alan Dedicoat (Opening Voice Over), Lionel Blair, Richard Wilson, Rob Brydon, Charlotte Church, James Corden, Jon Culshaw, Harry Enfield, Jocelyn Jee Esien, Miranda Hart, Robert Lindsay, Matt Lucas, Catherine Tate, David Walliams.

	Holding / Source
25.12.2010	HD/DB / HD/DB

ONEUPMANSHIP

Alternative/Working Title(s): GAMESMANSHIP, LIFEMANSHIP AND ONEUPMANSHIP

A BBC production for BBC 2. made in association with Open Road Films Ltd. Transmission details are for BBC 2.

Main regular credit(s): Adapted by Barry Took; based on books by Stephen Potter.

	Holding / Source
19.12.1974 **Christmas Oneupmanship**	DB-D3 / 2"

Alt.Title(s): *The Sadist's Guide to Yule*
Duration: 31 minutes.
Music directed by Peter Noyce; music by The Lichfield Choristers and Peter Noyce; designed by Keith Cheetham; produced and directed by Bernard Thompson.
With Richard Briers (David), Peter Jones, Frederick Jaeger, Donald Gee, John Quayle, Jean Harvey, Anita Carey, Vera Jakob.

ONLY FOOLS AND HORSES....

Alternative/Working Title(s): READIES

A BBC production for BBC 1. Transmission details are for BBC 1. Duration varies - see below for details.

Main regular credit(s): Written by John Sullivan; lyrics by John Sullivan; theme music by John Sullivan and Ronnie Hazlehurst.

Main regular cast: David Jason (Derek 'Del Boy' Trotter), Nicholas Lyndhurst (Rodney Trotter).

SERIES 1
Main regular credit(s): Music by Ronnie Hazlehurst; produced by Ray Butt; directed by Martin Shardlow.
Main regular cast: With Lennard Pearce (Grandad).

Holding / Source
28.12.1981 **Christmas Crackers** — DB-D3 / 2"
Duration: 35 minutes.
Produced by Bernard Thompson.
With Desmond McNamara, Nora Connolly.

SERIES 2
Duration: 30 minutes.
Main regular credit(s): Produced and directed by Ray Butt.
Main regular cast: With Lennard Pearce (Grandad).

Holding / Source
30.12.1982 **Diamonds Are For Heather** — DB-D3 / 2"
Designed by Don Giles.
With John Moreno, Rosalind Lloyd, Roger Brierley, Daniel Jones, Dev Sagoo.

SERIES 3
Duration: 30 minutes.
Main regular credit(s): Produced and directed by Ray Butt.
Main regular cast: With Lennard Pearce (Grandad).

Holding / Source
25.12.1983 **Thicker Than Water** — DB-D3 / 2"
With Michèle Winstanley (Karen, Barmaid), Peter Woodthorpe.

SERIES 4
Main regular credit(s): Produced by Ray Butt; directed by Susan Belbin.
Main regular cast: With Buster Merryfield (Uncle Albert).

Holding / Source
25.12.1985 **To Hull And Back** — DB-D3 / C1
Duration: 95 minutes.
With Kenneth MacDonald (Mike), John Challis (Boycie), Roger Lloyd Pack (Trigger), Paul Barber (Denzil), Jim Broadbent (Slater), Christopher Mitchell (Hoskins), Roy Heather (Sid), Jane Thompson, Kim Clifford, Johnny Wade, Annie Leake, Tony Anholt, Mark Burdis, Jeff Stevenson, Rachel Bell, Alan Hulse, Joe Belcher, Johnnie Allen, David Fleeshman, Philip Bond, Lorence Ferdinand.

Main regular cast: With Buster Merryfield (Uncle Albert), Roger Lloyd Pack (Trigger).

Holding / Source
25.12.1986 **A Royal Flush** — DB-D3 / 1"
Duration: 75 minutes.
Designed by Mark Sevant; production managers Tony Dow and Olivia Bazalgette; produced and directed by Ray Butt.
With Roy Heather (Sid), Diane Langton (June), Paul McDowell, Sarah Duncan, Andy Readman, Robert Vahey, Geoffrey Wilkinson, Alan Cody, Christina Michaels, Robin Herford, Richenda Carey, Gordon Salkilld, Jack Hedley, Peter Tuddenham, Arnold Peters, Ifor Gwynne-Davies, Kate Williams, Daphne Goddard, Stephen Riddle, Roger Davidson, Kent Opera.

25.12.1987 **The Frog's Legacy** — DB-D3 / 1"
Duration: 60 minutes.
Designed by Paul Trerise; production managers Sue Longstaff and Lesley Bywater; produced and directed by Ray Butt.
With Kenneth MacDonald (Mike), John Challis (Boycie), Sue Holderness (Marlene), Joan Sims (Auntie Reen), Adam Hussein, Mark Colleano, Gerry Cowper, Angus Mackay, Duncan Faber, Angela Moran.

25.12.1988 **Dates** — DB-D3 / 1"
Duration: 80 minutes.
Designed by Graham Lough; production managers Adrian Pegg and Gill Anderson; produced by Gareth Gwenlan; directed by Tony Dow.
With Tessa Peake-Jones (Raquel), John Challis (Boycie), Kenneth MacDonald (Mike), Sue Holderness (Marlene), Roy Heather (Sid), Patrick Murray (Micky Pearce), Steven Woodcock (Jevon), Paul Beringer, Andrée Bernard, Martin Cochrane, Nicholas Courtney, Maggie Norris, Chris Stanton, Jean Warren, Tony Marshall.

ONLY FOOLS AND HORSES.... (continued)

Christmas Specials

Main regular credit(s): Produced by Gareth Gwenlan; directed by Tony Dow.

Main regular cast: With Buster Merryfield (Uncle Albert), Gwyneth Strong (Cassandra Trotter), Tessa Peake-Jones (Raquel), Denis Lill (Alan Parry), Patrick Murray (Mickey Pearce).

Holding / Source

25.12.1989 The Jolly Boys' Outing DB-D3 / 1"

Duration: 85 minutes.

Closing theme by Chas 'n' Dave; designed by John Anderson; production manager Adrian Pegg.

With Paul Barber (Denzil), John Challis (Boycie), Roy Heather (Sid), Sue Holderness (Marlene), Kenneth MacDonald (Mike), Steven Woodcock (Jevon), Wanda Ventham (Pamela), Steve Alder, Del Baker, Brigid Erin Bates [as Bridget Erin Bates], Robin Driscoll, Roy Evans, Dawn Funnell, Lee Gibson, Gail Harrison, Daniel Hill, Rosalind Knight, Katharine Page, Jake Wood, Daniel LeCoutre.

25.12.1990 Rodney Come Home DB-D3 / 1"

Duration: 72 minutes.

Theme music by Joan Armatrading.

With Paula Ann Bland, Jean Harrington, Philip Blaine, Tony Marshall.

Christmas Specials

Main regular credit(s): Executive producer John Sullivan; produced by Gareth Gwenlan; directed by Tony Dow.

Main regular cast: With Buster Merryfield (Uncle Albert), Gwyneth Strong (Cassandra), Tessa Peake-Jones (Raquel), Roger Lloyd Pack (Trigger), John Challis (Boycie), Kenneth MacDonald (Mike Fisher), Sue Holderness (Marlene), Paul Barber (Denzil), Patrick Murray (Mickey Pearce).

Holding / Source

24.12.1991 Miami Twice: The American Dream DB-D3 / 1"S

Duration: 50 minutes.

Designed by Richard McManan-Smith; production manager Angela De Chastelai Smith.

With Roy Heather (Sid), Denis Lill (Alan), Wanda Ventham (Pamela), Treva Etienne, Richard Branson*.

25.12.1991 Miami Twice: Oh, To Be In England DB-D3 / C1S

Duration: 90 minutes.

Theme music by The Gutter Brothers; designed by Richard McManan-Smith; production manager Sue Longstaff.

With Denis Lill (Alan), Roy Heather (Sid), Jeff Gillen, Willis Knickerbocker, Renee Sweeney, Antoni Corone, Tom Kouchalakos [as Tom G. Kouchalakos], Raphael Gomez, Dave Corey, Jay Amor, Treva Etienne, Joshua Rosen, Grant Stevens, Robert Escobar, Roger Pretto, Mario Ernesto Sanchez, Alfredo Alvarez Calderon, John Archie Peak, Rob Stuart Fuller, Dee Dee Deering, D. L. Blakely, Damian Chuck, Jackie Davis, Janice Tesh, Barry Gibb.

25.12.1992 Mother Nature's Son DB-D3 / 1"S

Duration: 64 minutes.

Music by Clever Music.

With Denis Lill (Alan), Wanda Ventham (Pamela), Robert Glenister, Robert Liddement, Tony Marshall.

25.12.1993 Fatal Extraction DB-D3 / 1"S

Duration: 83 minutes.

Music by Clever Music.

With Roy Heather (Sid), Andrew Charleson, Mel Martin, Jamie Smith, Bryan Brittain, Linford Brown, Lyn Langridge, Nick Maloney, Derek Martin, Lorraine Parsloe, Kitty Scopes.

SERIES 8

Main regular credit(s): Music by Graham Jarvis; associate producer Sue Longstaff; executive producer John Sullivan; produced by Gareth Gwenlan; directed by Tony Dow.

Main regular cast: With Buster Merryfield (Uncle Albert), Gwyneth Strong (Cassandra), Tessa Peake-Jones (Raquel), John Challis (Boycie), Roger Lloyd Pack (Trigger), Kenneth MacDonald (Mike), Sue Holderness (Marlene), Paul Barber (Denzil), Jamie Smith (Damian).

Holding / Source

25.12.1996 Heroes And Villains DB / D3S

Duration: 59 minutes.

Designed by Donal Woods.

With Roy Heather (Sid), Douglas Hodge, Angela Bruce, Steve Weston, Scott Marshall, Dan Clark, Fuman Dar, Sheree Murphy, Bay White, Robin Meredith, Richard Hicks.

27.12.1996 Modern Men DB / D3S

Duration: 59 minutes.

Designed by Donal Woods.

With Patrick Murray (Mickey Pearce), Roy Heather (Sid), Bhasker Patel, Phil Cornwell, Beverley Hills, Corrine Britton, James Oliver, Lorraine Ashley.

29.12.1996 Time On Our Hands DB / D3S

Duration: 58 minutes.

With Patrick Murray (Mickey Pearce), Michael Jayston, Ann Lynn, Seymour Matthews.

| | British Christmas Television Guide | ONLY FOOLS AND HORSES.... (continued) |

SERIES 9

Main regular credit(s): Music by Graham Jarvis; designed by David Hitchcock; associate producer Gail Evans; production executive Sarah Hitchcock; executive producer John Sullivan; produced by Gareth Gwenlan; directed by Tony Dow.

Main regular cast: With Gwyneth Strong (Cassandra), Tessa Peake-Jones (Raquel), Roy Heather (Sid), Roger Lloyd Pack (Trigger), John Challis (Boyce), Paul Barber (Denzil), Sue Holderness (Marlene), Patrick Murray (Mickey Pearce), Benjamin Smith (Damian Trotter).

                                                                                                                                                        Holding / Source

25.12.2001 **If They Could See Us Now.....!**   DB / V1SW
Duration: 71 minutes.
With Jonathan Ross, Kim Wall, Colum Convey, Joan Hodges, Paul Strike, Jessica Willcocks, Conrad Nelson, Richard Braine.

25.12.2002 **Strangers On The Shore**   DB / V1SW
Duration: 73 minutes.
With James Ellis, Nabil Elouahabi, Fabienne Alousque, Martin Friend, Tamara Hinchco, Nasser Memarzia, David Olufemi, Charles Rhodes, Connie Pollard.

25.12.2003 **Sleepless In Peckham...!**   DB / V1SW
Duration: 73 minutes.
With Peter Blythe, Jay Kilbey, Louise Mantle, Pauline Whitaker [as Pauline Whittaker], Alan Nichol, Norman Langton, Dave Merrett, Tony Plant.

specials not made as official episodes:

                                                                                                                                                         Holding / Source

24.12.1985 **[Breakfast Time] White Mice**   DB / 1"
Duration: 5 minutes.
With Lynn Faulds-Wood.

See also: THE FUNNY SIDE OF CHRISTMAS (BBC) / THE GREEN GREEN GRASS (BBC) / ROCK AND CHIPS (BBC)

THE ONLY WAY IS ESSEX

A Lime Pictures production for ITV 2. Transmission details are for ITV 2.

                                                     Holding / Source

20.12.2011 **The Only Way Is EsseXmas**   HD/DB / HDC
Duration: 48 minutes.
'Tis the season of excess and TV doesn't get more indulgent than this ridiculously addictive reality show. Among the pressing questions fans will want answered in this festive special are: will Mark put in an appearance after his lachrymose farewell? (The club promoter boldly resolved to make his way in the real world only to pop up instantly on I'm a Celebrity...) And will his sis Jess and Joey be pulling each other's crackers after that surprise smooch?

ONLY WHEN I LAUGH

A Yorkshire Television production. Transmission details are for the ATV/Central region.

Main regular credit(s): Written by Eric Chappell; music by Ken Jones; produced and directed by Vernon Lawrence.

Main regular cast: James Bolam (Roy Figgis), Peter Bowles (Glover), Christopher Strauli (Norman Binns), Richard Wilson (Gordon Thorpe).

SERIES 3

Transmission details are for the ATV midlands region.

Main regular credit(s): Designed by Colin Pigott.

Main regular cast: With Derrick Branche (Gupte).

                                                                          VT Number   Holding / Source

24.12.1981 **Away For Christmas**   L290   DB / 2"
Duration: 24 minutes.
Christmas comes to the hospital ward and the patients decide to make the best of it. Out come the decorations and the mistletoe. When, unfortunately, a new patient is admitted everyone gets an unexpected chance to exercise the festive spirit.
Designed by Colin Pigott.
With Oliver Pye, Alexandra Brook, Jane Shackell, Susan Sheridan, Marian Davies, Kay Garner, Lee Gibson, Sue Glover.

OPEN RHODES

A BBC production for BBC 2. Transmission details are for BBC 2.
Gary Rhodes (Chef).

                                        Holding / Source

24.12.1997 **Christmas Open Rhodes**   DB-D3 / D3S
Duration: 30 minutes.
Chef Gary Rhodes visits the Caribbean island of Grenada to track down the origins of Christmas spices such as nutmeg, cloves and cinnamon. He also cooks alternatives to traditional festive fare, including peppered beef with sweet potato, satays of chicken, pork and exotic vegetables with peanut sauce, plus tropical fruit salad with rum-and-nutmeg syrup.
Executive producer Fiona Pitcher; produced by Gabrielle Jackson.

OPERATION GOOD GUYS

A Fugitive production for BBC 2. Transmission details are for BBC 2. Duration: 30 minutes.

Main regular credit(s): Created by Dominic Anciano and Ray Burdis; executive producers Jim Beach and Geoffrey Perkins.

SERIES 3

                                        Holding / Source

27.07.2000 **That's Entertainment**   DB /

OPPORTUNITY KNOCKS

Produced for ITV by a variety of companies (see details below). Usual duration: 40 minutes.

Talent show. The format involved inviting back each week's winner onto the next show, but in the main that act won't be listed on their subsequent appearance because publicity and listings were produced too far in advance to carry it. At various points in its life the programme's title carried an exclamation mark in TVTimes, but this certainly wasn't always reflected in the on-screen titles.

Main regular performer(s): Hughie Green (Host).

SERIES 3

An ABC production. Transmission details are for the ABC midlands region.

Main regular credit(s): Orchestra conducted by Bob Sharples; produced by Peter Dulay.

Main regular performer(s): With Nicky Allen (Hostess), The ABC Television Showband.

	Holding / Source
25.12.1965	J /

The first thirteen editions were networked, but the remainder were shown only by ABC, TWW, WWN, STV and Grampian (the latter two showing it the day after the others).

SERIES 4

An ABC production. Transmission details are for the ABC midlands region.

Main regular credit(s): Orchestra conducted by Bob Sharples.

Main regular performer(s): With The ABC Television Showband.

	Holding / Source
24.12.1966 **Gala Opportunity Knocks!**	J /

With Freddie Starr and The Delmonts, The Silverstone Set.

This series was seen more widely than the previous one, although - the Gala final aside - it was still unseen in London. Curiously, for a programme relying on interaction with the home audience, it was spread even further across the week with ABC's original screening on Saturday and further regional screenings on the following Sunday, Monday and Wednesday.

SERIES 5

An ABC production. Transmission details are for the ABC midlands region. Duration: 40 minutes.

Main regular credit(s): Programme associates Doris Barry and Vic Hallums; produced by Milo Lewis; directed by Roy Mayoh.

Main regular performer(s): With The ABC Television Showband.

	Holding / Source
23.12.1967 **Gala Opportunity Knocks!**	J /

Orchestra conducted by Bob Sharples; designed by Gordon Livesey.

With Ukranian Krylati Dancers, Mina Hall & Bill Dixon, Les Dawson, Joe Ruggles, Kathy, Allun Davies, The Jimmy Crawford Four, Jean Evans, Nazareth House Ceili Band, Graham F. Shach, Yvonne Marsh, Ken Wood, Doncaster Wheatsheaf Girls Choir.

SERIES 8

A Thames Television production. Transmission details are for the ATV midlands region. Duration: 40 minutes.

Main regular credit(s): Programme associates Doris Barry and Vic Hallums; associate producer Len Marten; produced and directed by Robert Fleming.

	Holding / Source
25.12.1968 **Gala Opportunity Knocks!**	J / 40

A Yuletide party.

Designed by Bernard Spencer.

With Monica Rose, Freddie Davies, Mary Hopkin, Bobby Bennett, Deano, Katie Engledew, Richard Langford, Ieuan Thomas, The Homin Ukranian Male Voice Choir, Barbara Spence Stage School, Hammersmith County School For Girls Choir, St Clement's Dane Grammar School For Boys Choir, Bob Sharples and his Orchestra.

SERIES 9

A Thames Television production. Transmission details are for the ATV midlands region.

Main regular credit(s): Programme associates Doris Barry and Vic Hallums; associate producer Len Marten; produced and directed by Robert Fleming.

Main regular performer(s): With Bob Sharples and his Orchestra.

	Holding / Source
22.12.1969 **All Winners Special**	J / 2"

Designed by Bill Palmer.

With Frank Carson, The Val de Neen Dancers, Anna McGoldrick, Karl Prinz, The Orange Blossom Sound, Erik Hansen.

SERIES 12

A Thames Television production. Transmission details are for the ATV midlands region.

Main regular credit(s): Programme associates Doris Barry and Len Marten; associate producer Len Marten; produced and directed by Royston Mayoh.

Main regular performer(s): With Bob Sharples and his Orchestra.

	Holding / Source
20.12.1971 **All Winners Show**	DB / 2"

Duration: 40 minutes.

Designed by David Ferris.

With Bob Sharples and his Orchestra.

SERIES 13

A Thames Television production. Transmission details are for the ATV midlands region.
Main regular credit(s): Programme associate Doris Barry; associate producer Len Marten.
Main regular performer(s): With Bob Sharples and his Orchestra.

Holding / Source
J / 2"

25.12.1972 Opportunity Knocks! Christmas Special
Duration: 35 minutes.
Designed by Michael Minas; produced and directed by Royston Mayoh.
With Yvonne Marsh, Ronnie Collis, The John Miles Set, Tony Holland.

SERIES 14

A Thames Television production. Transmission details are for the ATV midlands region.
Main regular credit(s): Programme associate Doris Barry; associate producer Len Marten; produced by Keith Beckett.
Main regular performer(s): With Bob Sharples and his Orchestra.

Holding / Source
J / 2"

24.12.1973 Christmas Variety Award Show
There's a unique Christmas gift corning the way of one of the winning acts from this series of Opportunity Knocks! It could be Peters and Lee. It could be singing miners Millican and Nesbitt. It could be 14-year-old vocalist Michael Ward. One of these acts will take home the silver dish awarded annually by the Variety Club to the act which has polled the highest average number of votes in the series. Also appearing are other artists you nave asked to see again. There is pianist Clara Evelyn; impressionist Tommy Tucker Kelly; Richard and Lara Jarmaine with their magic speciality act; Celli, who won the show's competition to appear as a princess in this year's Palladium pantomime, and singing Scotsman Stuart Gillies. Hughie Green introduces the show, backing is by Bob Sharpies and his Music, and last year's Award holder Bobby Crush hands it back for presentation to the new winner by a surprise guest star.
Designed by Norman Garwood; directed by Keith Beckett.
With Michael Ward, Clara Evelyn, Tommy Tucker Kelly, Richard & Lara Jarmaine, Calli, Stuart Gillies, Bobby Crush, Peters and Lee, Millican and Nesbitt.

SERIES 15

A Thames Television production. Transmission details are for the ATV midlands region.
Main regular credit(s): Programme associates Len Marten and Doris Barry; produced by Keith Beckett.
Main regular performer(s): With Bob Sharples and his Orchestra.

Holding / Source
J / 2"

23.12.1974 Songwriter's Show
Designed by Rod Stratfold; directed by Bruce Gowers.
With Jim and Ady, Calli, Stuart Gillies, Cool Breeze, Salt and Pepper, Canticle, Frankie McBride.
The songs were "Who made Mariana Cry?" by Arthur Bryant, "Troubadour" by John D. Bryant, "The Green Mistletoe" by Albert Lansfield, "A Quiet Man by John and Judith Shrive, "When the Summer's Gone" by Lance Wynsor, "Do It Some More" by Vic Lezal and "Shut the Gate" by Perry Vale and Al Perton.

The number of different designers working on this series seems extraordinarily high. There were 17 working on this series of 39 programmes and 13 on the next 26-edition series. Was the job such a prize that it was only fair to share it around? Or so horrible that spreading the load widely was the only way to handle it? Or maybe it was Thames' equivalent of the naughty step...

SERIES 16

A Thames Television production. Transmission details are for the ATV midlands region. Duration: 40 minutes.
Main regular credit(s): Programme associates Len Marten and Doris Barry; produced and directed by Keith Beckett.
Main regular performer(s): With Bob Sharples and his Orchestra.

Holding / Source
DD / 2"

22.12.1975 The Opportunity Knocks Songwriters Show
Designed by Bill Laslett.
With Tammy Jones, Lena Zavaroni.

SERIES 17

A Thames Television production. Transmission details are for the ATV midlands region. Duration: 40 minutes.
Main regular credit(s): Programme associates Len Marten and Doris Barry; produced and directed by Keith Beckett.
Main regular performer(s): With Bob Sharples and his Orchestra.

Holding / Source
J / 2"

27.12.1976 Christmas Opportunity Knocks: Songwriters' Show
Designed by John Plant; executive producer Jack Andrews.
With Iris Williams, Mahogany, Lips, The Cawson Mill Boys, The Barrytones, The Brothers, Roy Marsden.

SERIES 18

A Thames Television production. Transmission details are for the ATV midlands region.
Main regular credit(s): Programme associates Len Marten and Doris Barry; produced by Peter Dulay.
Main regular performer(s): With Bob Sharples and his Orchestra.

Holding / Source
J / 2"

26.12.1977 Songwriters' Show
Designed by Michael Minas; directed by Ronald Fouracre.

ORIGAMI

A Yorkshire Television production. Transmission details are for the Yorkshire Television region. Duration: 15 minutes.

Paper magic.

Main regular cast: Robert Harbin (Presenter).

SERIES 5

Main regular credit(s): Designed by Howard Dawson; executive producer Jess Yates; directed by David Millard.

Main regular cast: With Anita (Assistant).

	VT Number	Holding / Source
26.11.1970 **Japanese Parcel / Frog / Christmas Tree / Cross**	3366	1" / 2"

ATV transmissions commenced on 07.04.70.

ORION

A BBC production for BBC 2. Transmission details are for BBC 2. Duration: 55 minutes.

Written by Ken Howard, Alan Blaikley and Melvyn Bragg; lyrics by Ken Howard and Alan Blaikley; music by Ken Howard and Alan Blaikley; choreography by Nita Howard; designed by Rochelle Selwyn; executive producer Anna Home; produced and directed by Jeremy Swan.

Richard Barnes (Hoan), Leueen Willoughby (Mrs Hoan), Richard Kates (David), Julia Lewis (Carol), Jeremy Truelove (Bruce), Anthony O'Keefe (Chris), Eric Roberts (Le Verne), Philippa Boulter (Angie), Julian Littman (Joe), Pepsi Maycock (Geraldine), Paul Burton (Bob), Marlene Mackey (Catrina), Diana Martin (Louise), David Morris (Philippe), Mungo Hugh Farmer (Baby), Simon Gipps-Kent (Space Child).

	Holding / Source
26.12.1977	DB-D3 / 2"

ORPHEUS IN THE UNDERGROUND

A BBC production for BBC 2. Transmission details are for BBC 2. Duration: 30 minutes.

Lyrics by John Wells; music directed by Carl Davis; music by Carl Davis; choreography by Gillian Gregory.

Julian Littman (Orpheus), Joanna Carlin (Eurydice), Christine Carlson (Dancer), Jane Darling (Dancer), Gerry Hunt (Dancer), Maurice Lane (Dancer), Melanie Parr (Dancer), Bryan Payne (Dancer), Con Chambers (Commuter), John Dair (Commuter), Gail Galih (Commuter), Loretta Lee (Commuter), Elsa Smith (Commuter), Jules Walter (Commuter), George Fenton (Guitar), The Ambrosian Singers, The Gabrieli String Quartet.

	Holding / Source
27.12.1977	

ORPHEUS IN THE UNDERWORLD

A Brent Walker production for BBC 2. Transmission details are for BBC 2. Duration: 120 minutes.

Translated by Alexander Paris and Christopher Renshaw; based on material by Jacques Offenbach; designed by John Stoll; executive producer George Walker; produced by Judith De Paul; directed by Derek Bailey.

Denis Quilley (Jupiter / Napoleon III), Christopher Gable (Mercury), Lillian Watson (Eurydice), Alexander Oliver (Orpheus), Emile Belcourt (Pluto), Honor Blackman (Juno / Empress Eugenie), Elizabeth Gale (Cupid), Isobel Buchanan (Diana), Felicity Palmer (Venus), Pauline Tinsley (Public Opinion), Bernard Dickerson (John Styx), John Fryatt (Mars), BBC Concert Orchestra.

	Holding / Source
29.12.1983	D3 / 2"

ORSON WELLES' GREAT MYSTERIES

An Anglia production. made in association with 20th Century Fox. Transmission details are for the Anglia region. Duration: 25 minutes.

Story supervisor Donald Wilson; script editor John Rosenberg; theme music by John Barry and Paul Lewis; music by John Barry; executive producer Alan P. Sloan; produced by John Jacobs.

Transmission details are for the Anglia region.

	Holding / Source
26.11.1975 **Compliments Of The Season**	D2 / 2"

Dramatised by Donald Wilson; based on a story by O. Henry; directed by Philip Saville.

With Eli Wallach (Fuzzy), Hildegard Neil (Lady), Ed Bishop (Millionaire), Preston Lockwood (Butler), Ann Queensberry (Nanny), Billy Hamon (Peters), Philip Jackson (Carson), Nicola Teggin (The Child), Freddie Lees (Smith), Andrew Bradford (A Man), Jenifer Guy (A Young Woman), Michael Brennan (Publican), Ernest Bale (Piano Player).

Recorded 16.08.73.

THE OSMONDS

A BBC production for BBC 1. Transmission details are for BBC 1. Duration: 30 minutes.

Main regular credit(s): Research Michael Wale; designed by Bob Macgowan and Don Taylor; assistant producer Stanley Appel.

Main regular performer(s): The Osmonds, Noel Edmonds.

	Holding / Source
23.12.1974 **Compilation**	DB-D3 / 2"

Music directed by H. B. Barnum; produced by Robin Nash and James Moir; directed by Robin Nash and James Moir.

THE OTHER 'ARF

Alternative/Working Title(s): NOTHING IN COMMON
An ATV production for ATV/Central. made in association with Witzend. Transmission details are for the ATV/Central region. Duration: 25 minutes.
Main regular cast: Lorraine Chase (Lorraine Watts), John Standing (Charles Latimer).

SERIES 1
An ATV production. Transmission details are for the ATV midlands region.
Main regular credit(s): Written by Trevor Howard; script editors Dick Clement and Ian La Frenais; designed by Michael Perry; executive producer Allan McKeown; produced by John Kaye Cooper and Tony Charles; directed by John Kaye Cooper.
Main regular cast: With John Cater (George Watts).

	VT Number	Holding / Source
04.01.1981 **Away From It All**	5870/81	DB / 2"

With Allister Bain, Clifton Jones, T-Bone Wilson.

THE OTHER HALF

A BBC Entertainment production for BBC 1. Transmission details are for BBC 1. Duration: 40 minutes.
Main regular performer(s): Dale Winton (Presenter).
Credits: Produced by Andy Rowe; directed by Simon Staffurth.

	Holding / Source
27.12.1999 **Celebrity Special**	DB / DBS

Main regular credit(s): Produced by Andy Rowe; directed by Simon Staffurth.

	Holding / Source
30.12.2000 **Celebrity Special**	DB / DBSW

Duration: 40 minutes.
Produced by Andy Rowe; directed by Simon Staffurth.
With Sally Gunnell, Bradley Walsh, Linda Robson, Shaun Williamson, Anna Ryder-Richardson, Andy Kane.

OTHER MAN'S FARM

An ABC production. Transmission details are for the ABC north region.

	Holding / Source
24.12.1961 **Christmas On The Other Man's Farm**	J /

Duration: 40 minutes.
OTHER MAN'S FARM visits Mr. and Mrs. James Heyes, at Moenborough Hall Farm, Rainford, Lancashire, for a Christmas Eve party.
Introduced by Tim Brinton; produced by Geoffrey Gilbert; directed by Joe McGrath.
With Terry Lightfoot and his New Orleans Jazzmen, Clinton Ford, Carole Simpson.

THE OTHER SIDE OF ALF

A BBC production for BBC 2. Transmission details are for BBC 2. Duration: 55 minutes.
Produced by Michael Appleton; directed by Tom Corcoran.
Alison Moyet, John Altman Big Band.

	Holding / Source
22.12.1985	DB / 1"

THE OTHER SIDE OF CHRISTMAS

A Thames Television production. Transmission details are for the Central region. Duration: 90 minutes.
Anneka Rice hosts a live family Christmas morning show from the Arena in London's Docklands.
Research David Horbury, Pete Travis and Claire Walding; executive producer Simon Buxton; produced by Jane Clarke; outside broadcast director Melanie Eriksen.
Michael Aspel, Bill Waddington, Nick Owen, Anneka Rice, David Bellamy, Thelma Barlow, Helen Worth.

	Holding / Source
25.12.1989	DB / 1"

THE OTHER SIDE OF GERRY SADOWITZ

A Big Star in a Wee Picture production for Channel 4. Transmission details are for Channel 4. Duration: 14 minutes.
Main regular credit(s): Produced by Stuart Cosgrove; directed by Don Coutts.
Main regular performer(s): Gerry Sadowitz.

	Holding / Source
23.12.1990	1" / 1"
24.12.1990	1" / 1"
26.12.1990	1" / 1"

| THE OTHER SIDE OF LONDON | British Christmas Television Guide |

THE OTHER SIDE OF LONDON

A Bright Thoughts Company production for Channel 4. Transmission details are for Channel 4. Duration: 50 minutes.

Two women from the East End have a shopping outing to the West End — they are persuaded to join a vintage bus tour with Ron Moody as their guide and have the journey of a
lifetime finding out the real story of events and places on various well-known locations.

Written by Ron Moody and Ronnie Cass; lyrics by Ron Moody; music directed by Burt Rhodes; music by Ron Moody; produced by Neil Anthony; directed by Bryan Izzard.

Vivienne Martin, Jan Ravens.

	Holding / Source
31.12.1983	1" / 1"

OUR HOUSE

A Foster TV Productions production for ABC. Transmission details are for the ABC midlands region.

Main regular credit(s):   Created by Norman Hudis; produced by Ernest Maxin.

SERIES 2

Duration: 40 minutes.

Main regular credit(s):   Music by Norman Percival.

	Holding / Source
23.12.1961 **Complications Of The Season**	J / 40

Our House get busy with their preparations for Christmas, and take this opportunity of wishing all their friends the Complications of the Season.

Written by Brad Ashton and Bob Block.

With Hattie Jacques (Georgina Ruddy), Bernard Bresslaw (William Singer), Hylda Baker (Henrietta), Frederick Peisley (Herbert Keene), Leigh Madison (Marcia Hatton), Eugenie Cavanagh (Marina), Harry Korris, Johnny Vyvyan.

OUR MAN FROM ST. MARK'S

A Rediffusion Television production. Transmission details are for the ATV midlands region. Duration: 25 minutes.

Main regular credit(s):   Devised by James Kelly and Peter Miller; written by James Kelly and Peter Miller; produced by Eric Maschwitz.

Main regular cast: Donald Sinden (The Venerable Stephen Young), Joan Hickson (Mrs Peace).

	Production No	VT Number	Holding / Source
27.12.1966 **There Are More Things...**	SS 4/25	W4039/966	J / 40

Mrs. Treadwell has heard a voice commanding her to dig beneath the floor of the Cathedral. Her vision, if vision it was, leads to some surprising results...

Directed by Richard Doubleday.

With Clive Morton (The Bishop), Richard Hurndall (The Dean), Ruth Porcher (Mrs Treadwell), John McKelvey (Foreman), Caber.

Telerecording Number: TR16/17/71

OUR SHOW

An LWT production. Transmission details are for the London Weekend Television region. Duration varies - see below for details.

Saturday morning series.

	Production No	Holding / Source
23.12.1977	9L/99130	J / 2"

Duration: 70 minutes.

OUT AND ABOUT WITH ROBIN AND JIMMIE

A BBC Scotland production for BBC 1. Transmission details are for BBC 1. Duration: 30 minutes.

Designed by David McKenzie; produced and directed by Ian Christie.

Robin Hall, Jimmie McGregor, John Shearer, The McLean Sisters, The Wombles.

	Holding / Source
23.12.1974	J / 2"

Repeat tx date.

OUT WITH THE OLD, IN WITH THE NEW

Produced for Various ITV Companies by a variety of companies (see details below). Transmission details are for the Thames Television region.

	Production No	Holding / Source
31.12.1978 **Some Wonderful Scottish Girls**	3715	DB / Live

A Scottish Television production. Duration: 42 minutes.

Written by Philip Parsons, Peter Bain, Robert Gould, Wally McKinley and Sid Colin; music directed by Richard Holmes; choreography by Nita Howard; designed by Pip Gardner; executive producer Bryan Izzard; directed by Jim McCann.

With Ian Ogilvy (Host), Tony Currie (Voice Only), Janet Brown, Rikki Fulton, Anne Lorne Gillies, Marie Gordon Price, Eve Graham, Aimi MacDonald, Lulu, Una McLean, Colette O'Neil, Beryl Reid, Annie Ross, Johnny Vyvyan, Molly Weir.

	Holding / Source
31.12.1978 **Welcome To The Hogmanay Ceilidh**	J / Live

A Grampian Television production.

With Johnny Beattie, Alasdair Gillies, Hebbie Gray Band, Isobel James Dancers.

See also: WELCOME TO THE CEILIDH

OUT WITH THE OLD, IN WITH THE NEW

OUTNUMBERED

A Hat Trick production for BBC 1. Transmission details are for BBC 1. Duration varies - see below for details.

Main regular credit(s): Written by Guy Jenkin and Andy Hamilton; music by Philip Pope; designed by Graeme Story; executive producer Jimmy Mulville; produced by Andy Hamilton and Guy Jenkin; directed by Andy Hamilton and Guy Jenkin.

Main regular cast: Hugh Dennis (Dad), Claire Skinner (Mum), Tyger Drew-Honey (Jake), Daniel Roche (Ben), Ramona Marquez (Karen).

Holding / Source
27.12.2009 Christmas Special — DB / DBSWF
Duration: 40 minutes.

Boxing Day iin the Brockman household. Santa has visited but, unfortunately, so has a burglar. Sharp seven-year-old Karen, forever preoccupied with the little things in life is obsessing about a missing hamster, while destructive Ben has fun with a mechanical hand. Eldest son Jake is, meanwhile, helping mum to find a wandering aged relative.

Script supervisor Sarah Garner; director of photography Martin Hawkins; art director Margaret Spohrer; head of production Laura Djanogly; co-produced by Pat Lees.

With David Ryall (Grandad), Hattie Morahan, Felicity Montagu, Jake D'Arcy, Sophie Stanton, Anthony Parker.

Holding / Source
24.12.2011 Christmas Special — HD/DB / HDC
Duration: 40 minutes.

The Brockman household is probably the only one that can match EastEnders when it comes to ghastly family Christmas Days. So, after a dreadfully stressed few months -"Your sister, your dad, the job thing, the bedding infestation, Karen's silly letter... and the over-reaction of social services," lists Pete helpfully - they've decided to get Christmas done and dusted by 8.30am and fly off to the Canary Islands for a break.

With David Ryall (Grandad), Daisy Haggard (Charlene), Sam Kelly (Ron), Alice O'Connell (Doctor Hughes), Hattie Morahan (Jane), Okezie Morro (Jason), Kitty Martin (Maggie).

SERIES 4

Holding / Source
24.12.2012 Christmas Special — HD/DB / HDC
Duration: 40 minutes.

Last year the Brockmans decided to go away for Christmas: this year they're throwing a party at the heart of their community. But the bosom of the neighbourhood is not as pillowy and restful as they might like. The guests include Norris, who has opinions; Ray, who used to be a weatherman and doesn't seem to have coped well afterwards; and Jane, whose romantic life is unmanageable. Gran turns up for a surprise visit, Karen is online most of the time and at the window, there's the gentle, then insistent, tap-tap of a winter virus. There's only so much spirit-lifting a gathering of neighbours can be expected to do. For everything else, there's Ben and his party games. Christmas Swingball, anyone?

With Rosalind Ayres (Gran), Hattie Morahan (Jane), Mark Heap (Norris), Sanjeev Bhaskar (Ray), Sarah Woodward (Mary), Susannah Doyle (Tatiana), Bob Cryer (Police Constable Dixon).

OUTSIDE EDGE

A Central production for Central->Carlton UK. Transmission details are for the Central region.

Main regular credit(s): Based on a play by Richard Harris.

Main regular cast: Brenda Blethyn (Miriam Dervish), Robert Daws (Roger Dervish), Josie Lawrence (Maggie Costello), Timothy Spall (Kevin Costello), Denis Lill (Dennis Broadley).

SERIES 3

Commissioned by Carlton UK.

Main regular credit(s): Music by Fiachra Trench; art director David Allen; executive producer Paul Spencer; produced by Paula Burdon; directed by Nick Hurran.

Main regular cast: With Michael Jayston (Bob Willis), Nigel Pegram (Nigel).

Holding / Source
25.12.1995 Corfu - OK? Fair Enough — D2 / D2S
Duration: 51 minutes.

Designed by David Chandler; associate producer Nicolas Brown.

With Christopher Lang (Alex Harrington), May Boak (Nigel's Mum), Tracy Brabin, Hilary Crane, Amanda Waring, Dimitri Andreas, George Savvides, Andreas Constantinou.

THE P. D. JAMES' SERIALS

Produced for Anglia by a variety of companies (see details below). Transmission details are for the Central region. Duration varies - see below for details.

Main regular credit(s): Based on novels by P. D. James; theme music by Richard Harvey.

Main regular cast: Roy Marsden (Adam Dalgliesh).

An Anglia Television Films production.

	Holding / Source
02.01.1993 **Unnatural Causes**	DB-1" / V1S

Duration: 104 minutes.

Adapted by Peter Buckman; script editor Anna Dickie; music by Richard Harvey; director of photography Richard Crafter; art director Davina Tuckey; production designer Spencer Chapman; associate producer Elizabeth Hare; executive in charge of production David Fitzgerald; executive producer Brenda Reid; produced by Hilary Bevan Jones; directed by John Davies.

With Simon Chandler (Digby Seton), Kenneth Colley (Inspector Reckless), Mel Martin (Deborah Riscoe), Bill Nighy (Oliver Latham), James Cossins (Justin Bryce), Nicholas Jones (Luker), Anne Lambton (Sylvia Kedge), Marjie Lawrence (Celia Calthrop), Roger Alborough (Superintendent Maitland), Arthur Blake (Maurice Seton), Lucy Briers (Liz Marley), David Conville (Max Gurney), Erin Geraghty (TV Presenter), Oliver Haden (Charles Beech), Edward Peel (Detective Chief Superintendent Charlie Breen), Rosemary Williams (Writeron TV), Jerome Willis (Pathologist).

PADDINGTON

A Filmfair production for BBC 1. Transmission details are for BBC 1. Duration: 4 minutes.

Main regular credit(s): Written by Michael Bond; music by Herbert Chappell; produced and directed by Ivor Wood.

Main regular cast: Michael Hordern (Narrator).

SERIES 2

	Holding / Source
04.05.1976 **Paddington And The Christmas Shopping**	C1 / C1

	Holding / Source
29.12.1976 **Christmas**	C1 / C1

Duration: 5 minutes.

See also: PADDINGTON BEAR

PADDINGTON BEAR

A Filmfair production for Central. Transmission details are for the Central region. Duration: 20 minutes.

Main regular credit(s): Written by Michael Bond; executive producer Bruce Johnson; produced by Kay Wright.

Main regular cast: John Standing (Voice of Mr Brown), B. J. Ward (Voice of Mrs Brown), Georgia Brown (Voice of Mrs Bird), Charlie Adler (Voice of Paddington Bear).

	Holding / Source
14.12.1990 **The Ghost Of Christmas Pudding**	1" / C1

See also: PADDINGTON (BBC)

PADDY'S 2011 SHOW AND TELLY

Commissioned by ITV 1. Transmission details are for the Central region. Duration: 48 minutes.

Paddy McGuinness hosts as four pairs of celebrities answer questions about the year's TV, with one team getting the chance to win up to £20,000 for the charity of their choice.

Produced by Harriet Jaine; directed by Liz Clare.

Paddy McGuinness (Host).

	Holding / Source
29.12.2011	HD/DB / HDC

PADDY'S 2012 SHOW AND TELLY

Commissioned by ITV 1. Transmission details are for the Central region. Duration: 48 minutes.

Take Me Out host Paddy McGuinness presides over the squabbling as three celebrity pairs do battle to prove they watched the most TV in 2012 and the chance to win £20,000 for charity.

Produced by Rose Hanson; directed by Elizabeth Clare.

Paddy McGuinness (Host), Nicholas Owen, Denise van Outen, Nicky Byrne, Kate Garraway, Antony Cotton, Chris Fountain.

	Holding / Source
22.12.2012	HD/DB / HDC

PALACE HILL

A Central production. Transmission details are for the Central region. Duration: 25 minutes.

Main regular credit(s): Written by Peter Corey and Bob Hescott; executive producer Lewis Rudd; produced by Sue Nott.

SERIES 1

Main regular credit(s): Directed by Glyn Edwards.

	Holding / Source
21.12.1988 **Where Carol Singers Dare**	1" / 1"

Written by Bob Hescott; script associate Peter Corey; music directed by Colin Campbell; music by Tim Whitnall; choreography by David Morgan-Young; designed by Ian Doubleday.

With Julian Aubrey, Alison Hammond, Keeley Coxon, Richard De Sousa, Mark Dexter, Alison Dury, Ladene Hall, Oliver Hawker, James Hooton, Amanda Loy-Ellis, Katie McReynolds, Johann Myers, Steven Ryde, Julie Schatzberger, Tracie Stanley, Paul Stark, Philip Wombwell.

| PALACE HILL (continued) | British Christmas Television Guide |

PALLAS

A Noel Gay Television production for Channel 4. Transmission details are for Channel 4. Duration: 10 minutes.

Main regular credit(s): Written by Charlie Bell and Eric Pilkington; produced and directed by Geoff Atkinson.

Main regular cast: Richard E. Grant (Narrator), Jon Glover, Enn Reitel, Kate Robbins, Jim Broadbent, Joanna Brookes, Roger Blake.

Date	Episode	Holding / Source
24.12.1991	Episode 1	1" / 1"S
24.12.1991	Episode 2	1" / 1"S
24.12.1991	Episode 3	1" / 1"S
26.12.1991	Episode 4	1" / 1"S
26.12.1991	Episode 5	1" / 1"S
26.12.1991	Episode 6	1" / 1"S
27.12.1991	Episode 7	1" / 1"S
27.12.1991	Episode 8	1" / 1"S
27.12.1991	Episode 9	1" / 1"S
27.12.1991	Episode 10	1" / 1"S

See also: PALLAS 2

PALLAS 2

A Noel Gay Television production for Channel 4. Transmission details are for Channel 4. Duration: 20 minutes.

Main regular credit(s): Written by Charlie Bell and Eric Pilkington; produced and directed by Geoff Atkinson.

Main regular cast: Richard E. Grant (Narrator), Enn Reitel, Steve Nallon, Jon Glover, Kate Robbins.

Date	Episode	Holding / Source
22.12.1992	Episode 1	1" / 1"S
23.12.1992	Episode 2	1" / 1"S
24.12.1992	Episode 3	1" / 1"S

See also: PALLAS

PAM AYRES' CANADIAN CHRISTMAS

An LWT production. Transmission details are for the ATV midlands region. Duration: 50 minutes.

Produced and directed by Alan Ravenscroft.

Pam Ayres (Host), Peter Skellern.

Holding / Source

23.12.1979   D2 / 2"

PAM AYRES' HONGKONG CHRISTMAS

An LWT production. Transmission details are for the ATV midlands region. Duration: 50 minutes.

Produced and directed by Alan Ravenscroft.

Pam Ayres (Host).

Holding / Source

23.12.1978   D2 / 2"

See also: PAM AYRES' CANADIAN CHRISTMAS

PANTO!

An ITV Studios production for ITV 1. Transmission details are for the Central region. Duration: 75 minutes.

Lewis Loud, is Morecambe FM's cheeky DJ, who is about to make his stage debut as Jack the Lad in Dick Whittington, alongside soap star Tamsin, with whom he is smitten. When Lewis's ex-wife delivers his son to the stage door, he tries to take his fatherly duties seriously despite the chaos and ego clashes provided by veteran actor Johnny, ambitious actress-producer Di and accident-prone 1990s chart star Chesney Hawkes.

Written by John Bishop and Jonathan Harvey; produced by John Rushton; directed by Christine Gernon.

John Bishop (Lewis Loud), Sheridan Smith (Tamsin), Samantha Spiro (Di), Kenneth Cranham (Jerry), Mark Benton (Francis), Michael Cochrane (Johnny), Ami Metcalf (Chantelle), Daniel Bishop (Paul), Dean Whatton (Greg), John Macmillan (Finlay), Kaye Wragg (Gina), Trevor Dwyer-Lynch (Tony), Lisa Jackson (Deborah), Chesney Hawkes (Himself).

Holding / Source

27.12.2012   HD/DB / HDC

PANTOMANIA: DICK WHITTINGTON

A BBC production. Transmission details are for BBC. Duration: 60 minutes.

Written by Eric Sykes; music by Alan Bristow; orchestra conducted by George Clouston; choreography by Leslie Roberts; produced by John Street; directed by Eric Sykes.

Jean Kent, Sylvia Peters, Billy Cotton, Frankie Howerd, Hattie Jacques, Sam Kydd, David Attenborough, Roger Avon, Fred Emney, Edward Evans, Bill Greenslade, Peter Haigh, John Hall, Philip Harben, The Max Jaffa Trio, Jacqueline Mackenzie, Mary Malcolm, Spike Milligan, Freddie Mills, Robert Raglan, Nancy Roberts, Bruce Seton, Eric Sykes, Jimmy Wheeler, The Mitchell Singers.

Holding / Source

25.12.1956   J /

PANTOMANIA: DICK WHITTINGTON

PANTOMANIA: IT WAS NEVER LIKE THIS

A BBC production. Transmission details are for BBC. Duration: 60 minutes.

Written by Eric Sykes; play production by Ernest Maxin.

Sylvia Peters (Cinderella), Jill Day (Prince Charming), Mary Malcolm (Dandini), Jeanne Heal (Fairy Godmother), Jack Payne (Jack Payne), Peter Dimmock, McDonald Hobley, Freddie Mills, Bruce Seton, Brian Johnston, Victor Silvester, Raymond Baxter, Peter West, The George Mitchell Choir, The Show Dancers.

Holding / Source

24.12.1955 J /

PANTOMANIA: THE BABES IN THE WOOD

A BBC production. Transmission details are for BBC. Duration: 60 minutes.

Written by Brad Ashton, S. C. Green, Dick Vosburgh and R. M. Hills; produced and directed by Graeme Muir.

Eamonn Andrews, Isobel Barnett, The Beverley Sisters, Derek Bond, Kenneth Connor, Sam Costa, Peter Dimmock, Charlie Drake, Peter Haigh, Tony Hancock, Derek Hart, Benny Hill, Sidney James, Lenny The Lion, Terry Hall, Alex Macintosh, Bill Maynard, Jean Metcalfe, Cliff Michelmore, Pete Murray, Jack Payne, Sylvia Peters, Ted Ray, Geoffrey Johnson Smith, Peter West, Huw Wheldon, Frankie Vaughan, The George Mitchell Choir.

Holding / Source

25.12.1957 J /

PANTOMIME PARTY

A BBC production. Transmission details are for BBC. Duration: 60 minutes.

Orchestra conducted by Alyn Ainsworth; produced by Derek Burrell-Davis and Barney Colehan; directed by Derek Burrell-Davis and Barney Colehan.

Frank Gibson, Stan Stennett, Morecambe and Wise, Freddie Sales, June Bishop, Mary Millar, Ken Roberts, Phyllis Holden, The Zio Angels, Josef Locke, Syd Perkin, Edna Duffield, George Begley, Madge Larney, Joan Finnigan, Northern Variety Orchestra.

Holding / Source

23.12.1953 J /

From the Mecca Locarno Ballroom, Leeds.

PANTO-TIME!

A BBC Children's Department production for BBC 1. Transmission details are for BBC 1. Duration: 15 minutes.

Main regular credit(s):   Written by Brian Cant; music directed by Richard Brown; music by Tony McVey and Martin Frith; executive producer Cynthia Felgate; produced and directed by Sharon Miller.

Holding / Source

23.12.1986 **Aladdin** DB / 1"

With Brian Cant (Photographer / Abanaza), Matthew Devitt (Aladdin), Brian Jameson (Widow Twankey / Genie of the Lamp), Ben Thomas (Emperor / Genie of the Ring), Tracy Brabin (Princess).

30.12.1986 **Mother Goose** DB / 1"

With Brian Cant (Mrs Nosey Parker / Mother Goose), Matthew Devitt (Billy), Tracy Brabin (Fairy / Mary Mary), Ben Thomas (Demon / Colin), Brian Jameson (Squire / King Ganda), Robin Stevens (Priscilla Goose).

06.01.1987 **Jack And The Beanstalk** DB / 1"

With Brian Cant (Jack), Matthew Devitt (Dame Durden / Daisy), Ben Thomas (Merchant / Ogre / Daisy), Delia Morgan (Mrs Ogre / Daisy).

PAPERPLAY

A Thames Television production. Transmission details are for the ATV midlands region. Duration: 15 minutes.

A series of programmes that shows you how to create lots of lovely and useful things from scrap paper. Launched the careers of Itsy and Bitsy, the loveable puppets.

Main regular credit(s):   Devised by Susan Stranks.

SERIES 4

Main regular credit(s):   Designed by Sylva Nadolny; produced and directed by Charles Warren.

Main regular cast: With Susan Stranks (Presenter).

Holding / Source

23.12.1975 **Paperplay Christmas Special** DB|n / 2"

Snow has fallen in the Paperplay garden and Sue finds a snowman. She also discovers hanging Christmas decorations which Itsy and Bitsy have made. They show her how to make some from different shapes of cardboard, string, glue and glitter.

Itsy and Bitsy by Norman Beardsley.

PARDON THE EXPRESSION

A Granada production. Transmission details are for the ATV midlands region. Usual duration: 26 minutes.

Main regular cast: Arthur Lowe (Leonard Swindley).

SERIES 2

Main regular credit(s):   Executive producer H. V. Kershaw; produced by Derek Granger.

Main regular cast: With Robert Dorning (Walter Hunt).

Holding / Source

##.##.#### **Christmas Special** DB-R1 / Live

Originally scheduled for 03.01.1966.

Written by Vince Powell and Harry Driver; designed by Michael Grimes; directed by Michael Cox.

With Betty Driver (The Honourable Mrs Wentworth Brewster), Charles Victor, Donal Donnelly, Carmel Cryan, Martin Cook, Nita Valerie, Trevor Peacock, Allan O'Keefe, Malcolm Douglas, Jessie Robins, Elsie Woodhouse, Veronica Howard, Diana Flacks.

Script - The Presentation by Jack Rosenthal. Note says 'Not to be transmitted'. This may be a script for the pilot?

PARDON THE EXPRESSION (continued)

See also: CORONATION STREET

PARKIN'S PATCH

A Yorkshire Television production. Transmission details are for the ATV midlands region. Duration: 25 minutes.

Main regular credit(s): Devised by Elwyn Jones; script editor Nick McCarty; produced by Terence Williams.

Main regular cast: John Flanagan (Police Constable Moss Parkin), Heather Page (Beth Parkin), Gareth Thomas (Detective Constable Ron Radley).

	VT Number	Holding / Source
03.01.1970 **The Manchester Passenger**	1322	B / 2"

Alternative transmissions: Granada: 02.01.1970; LWT: 27.12.1969; Southern Television: 02.01.1970; Yorkshire Television: 02.01.1970.
Written by Tony Marsh; designed by Gordon Livesey; directed by Raymond Menmuir.
With Robert Urquhart (Superintendent), Wallas Eaton, Anthony Sagar, John Golightly, Malcolm Rogers.
Gareth Thomas does not appear in this episode.

Some of the videotapes were found to be damaged upon transfer.

PARKINSON

A BBC production for BBC 1. Transmission details are for BBC 1. Duration varies - see below for details.

Main regular performer(s): Michael Parkinson (Host).

SERIES 2

Duration: 60 minutes.

Main regular credit(s): Produced by Richard Drewett.

Main regular performer(s): With The Harry Stoneham Five.

	Holding / Source
23.12.1972	DB-D3 / 2"

With Bing Crosby.

SERIES 4

Main regular credit(s): Music by Harry Stoneham; produced by Roger Ordish.

	Holding / Source
25.12.1974 **A Christmas Look At Morecambe And Wise**	DB-1" / 2"

Duration: 55 minutes.
Orchestra directed by Peter Knight; directed by Colin Strong.
With André Previn, Glenda Jackson, Morecambe and Wise, Shirley Bassey, Peter Cushing, Tom Jones, Frank Bough, Ian Carmichael, Robert Dougall, Fenella Fielding, Cliff Michelmore, Eric Porter, Flora Robson, Eddie Waring, Ann Hamilton, Arthur Tolcher, Janet Webb.
Not a Parkinson show at all really, a compilation of highlights from Morecambe and Wise, linked by Michael Parkinson.

SERIES 5

	Holding / Source
25.12.1975	DB-D3 / 2"

With Bob Hope.

SERIES 6

Main regular credit(s): Music by Harry Stoneham; produced by Richard Drewett.

	Production No	VT Number	Holding / Source
25.12.1976 **The Parkinson Magic Show**	1246/1015	VTC/6HT/B13871	DB-D3 / 2"

Duration: 69 minutes.
Music by Harry Stoneham; consultant Ali Bongo; designed by Richard Morris; produced by John Fisher; directed by Colin Strong.
With Fred Kaps, Ricky Jay, Richiardi Junior.

	Production No	VT Number	Holding / Source
27.12.1976 **The Parkinson Music Show**	1246/1022	VTC/6HT/b14800	DB-D3 / 2"

Alt.Title(s): *Parkinson's Music*
Duration: 60 minutes.
Directed by Colin Strong.
With Bing Crosby, Sammy Davis Junior, Oscar Peterson, Dudley Moore, Elton John, Jack Jones, Michel Le Grand, Andy Williams, Fred Astaire, Blossom Dearie, Duke Ellington, Glynis Johns, Buddy Rich, Harry Stoneham.

SERIES 7

Main regular credit(s): Music by Harry Stoneham; produced by John Fisher; directed by David G. Hillier.

	Holding / Source
26.12.1977 **Parkinson and the Comedians**	DB-D3 / 2"

Duration: 70 minutes.
With Les Dawson, Harry Secombe, Rod Hull, Ray Ellington Quartet with Val Masters, Alfred Marks, Rita Hunter, George Burns, Max Wall, Jack Benny, Max Bygraves, Billy Connolly, Peter Cook, Joyce Grenfell, Bob Hope, Frankie Howerd, Bernard Manning.

PARKINSON

SERIES 8

Main regular credit(s):   Produced by John Fisher.

	Production No	VT Number	Holding / Source
25.12.1978 **Parkinson At The Pantomime**	1248/1236	LLVA/336N/2	DB-D3 / 2"

Duration: 65 minutes.

Programme associate Tony Hawes; designed by Paul Joel; production team Donald Clive, Graham Lindsay, Eve Lucas, Marie O'Shaunessy and Sita Williams; directed by Ian Hamilton.

With Arthur Askey, Charlie Cairoli, Les Dawson, Roy Barraclough, Patrick Moore, Little and Large, Lauri Lupino Lane, Stan Stennett, Fenella Fielding, Pat Kirkwood, George Truzzi, Jimmy Buchanan, Barbara Newman, Claude Zola, Humpty Dumpty, The Harry Stoneham Showband.

SERIES 9

	Holding / Source
25.12.1979 **Parkinson At Christmas**	DB-D3 / 2"

Produced by John Fisher; directed by Bruce Milliard.

With George Melly, Professor Percy Press, Commissioner Bramwell-Booth, Paul Phoenix, Peter Cook, Dame Edna Everage, Tommy Cooper.

SERIES 10

	Holding / Source
25.12.1980	DB-D3 / 2"

With Penelope Keith, James Galway, Ben Vereen.

SERIES 11: The Michael Parkinson Show

Duration: 60 minutes.

Main regular credit(s):   Music by Harry Stoneham; designed by Humphrey Jaeger; executive producer John Fisher.

	Holding / Source
25.12.1981 **Parkinson On Comedy**	DB-D3 / 2"

With Cannon and Ball, Dave Allen, John Cleese, Frankie Howerd, Rowan Atkinson, Mike Harding, Ronnie Barker, Michael Bentine, Mel Brooks, Roy Castle, James Casey, Eli Woods, Billy Connolly, Tommy Cooper, Jim Davidson, Ken Dodd, Bob Hope, Tom Lehrer, Arthur Marshall, Spike Milligan, Harry Secombe, Jimmy Tarbuck, Tommy Trinder, Kenneth Williams.

PARKINSON

A BBC production for BBC 1. Transmission details are for BBC 1.

Main regular credit(s):   Produced by Beatrice Ballard.

Main regular performer(s):   Michael Parkinson (Host).

SERIES 6

Main regular credit(s):   Directed by Stuart McDonald.

	Holding / Source
24.12.2001 **Parkinson At Christmas**	DB / DBS

With Lenny Henry, Robbie Williams, Dame Edna Everage, Geri Halliwell, Charlotte Church.

SERIES 8

Main regular credit(s):   Script supervisor Belinda Langford; music directed by Laurie Holloway; titles by Bernard Heyes Design; programme consultant Chris Greenwood; designed by Simon Kimmel; assistant producers Steven Lappin, George Morton and Sophie Newth; associate producer Cam Donnolly; executive producer Beatrice Ballard; production manager Robert High; produced by Danny Dignan; title sequence directed by Bernard Hayes Design; directed by Stuart McDonald.

	Holding / Source
24.12.2002 **Parkinson At Christmas**	DB / DBS

Duration: 45 minutes.

Directed by Stuart McDonald.

With Martine McCutcheon, Alistair Macgowan, Nigel Havers, Tom Jones, Barry Humphries, Benjamin Zephaniah, Mica Paris, Marc Paul, London Community Gospel Choir.

PARKINSON

A Granada production for ITV 1. Transmission details are for the Central region. Usual duration: 55 minutes.

Kaleidoscope believes that the Mike Parkinson who produces the show is Michael P's son - not Parky under another name - so we've changed the credit accordingly. MP Junior definitely works in TV, that much we do know.

Props Buyer for the series is Bobby Warans. Bob Richardson says, "Bobby Warans is a legend. He left the BBC to set up "G & T Prop Services Ltd" and is in great demand. He's far more than a prop buyer. On "Parkinson" Bobby will probably have decorated the "star" dressing rooms. He'll know the guests' favourite wines, and which hand-made chocolates they prefer. He'll also know their favourite colours and foods. He may have even arranged the finger buffet for hospitality (and it won't be Twiglets and warm beer - there'll be a lot of Harrod's labels around)."

"His Christmas card list is probably more impressive than the (other) Queen's. He's a close personal friend of many major international stars and is on first name terms with more divas than you can name. Bobby never boasts of his connections; he's incredibly professional in everything he does but you'll NEVER hear him name-dropping. He's also extremely discrete, so if Joan Collins has a little cry over some personal problem, she'll sob on Bobby's shoulder and he won't tell a soul.

"I worked on many shows which Bobby serviced. He bought all the prizes for "Big Break" and hundreds of other game shows and negotiated great "sale or return" deals for producers. The drinks at hospitality were often provided by Bobby, as were bowls of fruit and fresh flowers in the Green Room. There's no end to his talents and he's rarely unable to come up with the goods. I did a Jasper Carrott series with him and the show featured a sketch about Michael Fagin's visit to the Queen's bedroom which included half a dozen stuffed corgis. When I asked Bobby where he got them at short notice, he told me that he had "a little man in the East End who runs them up for me." They were real corgis, and apparently Bobby's "little man" had a large storage unit full of chest freezers containing dead animals which were stuffed to order...just one of the many bizarre contacts in Bobby's little black book.

"Prop buying apparently pays well. Bobby wears a brand new Gianni Versace silk shirt every day, made to his own specification (with a distinctive mandarin-style collar). He never wears the same shirt twice. After a single outing, they are cleaned, pressed and put away in his vast wardrobe. He's an absolutely unique character."

Main regular credit(s): Music by Laurie Holloway; executive producer Mark Wells; produced by Steven Lappin and Mike Parkinson; directed by Stuart McDonald.

Main regular performer(s): Michael Parkinson (Host).

SERIES 1

Main regular credit(s): Series producer Chris Greenwood.

Holding / Source
25.12.2004 — DB / DBSW
Duration: 57 minutes.
With Rod Stewart, Lily Savage, Barbara Windsor, Joe Pasquale.

SERIES 3

Main regular credit(s): Script supervisor Belinda Langford; assistant producers Lisa Douglas, Róisín Doyle, Sadie Fraser and Amy Hitchcock; head of production Leah Milton; series producer Chris Greenwood.

Holding / Source
24.12.2005 — DB / DBSW
With Joan Rivers, Martine McCutcheon, Cilla Black, Bryn Terfel.

SERIES 5

An ITV Productions production.

Main regular credit(s): Script supervisor Belinda Langford; music directed by Laurie Holloway; assistant producers Róisín Doyle, Sadie Fraser, Sarah Graham and Erin Reimer; head of production Leah Milton.

Holding / Source
23.12.2006 — DB / DBSW
With Judi Dench, Lenny Henry, Katherine Jenkins, Froncysylite Male Voice Choir.

SERIES 7

An ITV Productions production.

Main regular credit(s): Script supervisor Belinda Langford; music directed by Laurie Holloway; designed by Simon Kimmel; assistant producers Róisín Doyle, Sarah Graham and Erin Reimer; head of production Leah Milton.

Holding / Source
22.12.2007 **The Final Show [compilation of personal highlights]** — DB / DBSW
Duration: 55 minutes.
With Muhammad Ali, Fred Astaire, Richard Burton, Orson Welles, Billy Connolly, Lauren Bacall, Jack Benny, Elton John, Ricky Hatton, David Beckham, Cate Blanchett, Miss Piggy, Madonna, Renée Zellweger, Sandra Bullock, Sharon Stone, Meg Ryan, Paul Anka.

A PARTY FOR CHRISTMAS

A BBC production. Transmission details are for BBC. Duration: 90 minutes.

Written by N. C. Hunter; play production by Eric Fawcett.

Nora Nicholson (Alice Matheson), Carol Marsh (Caroline Firbanks), Anthony Parker (Stephen Firbanks), Agnes Lauchlan (Elinor Firbanks), Dorothea Alexander (Maid), Richard Johnson (Michael Firbanks), Wendy Williams (Pamela Sutton), Hugh Dempster (Robert Firbanks), Charles Victor (Fred Matheson), Peter Bartlett (Anthony Davidson).

Holding / Source
25.12.1954 — J / Live

PATRICK KIELTY LIVE

A BBC Northern Ireland production for BBC 1 Northern Ireland. Transmission details are for BBC 1 Northern Ireland.

Main regular performer(s): Patrick Kielty (Host).

Holding / Source
20.12.1996 **Patrick Kielty's Christmas Tale** — DB / D3S

THE PAUL DANIELS MAGIC SHOW

A Granada production. Transmission details are for the ATV midlands region. Duration: 50 minutes.
Music directed by Derek Hilton and Mike Moran; choreography by Fred Peters; designed by Tim Farmer; produced by Rod Taylor; directed by Nicholas Ferguson.
Paul Daniels (Host).

	Holding / Source
31.12.1977	DB / 2"

THE PAUL DANIELS MAGIC SHOW

A BBC production for BBC 1. Transmission details are for BBC 1. Duration varies - see below for details.
Main regular performer(s): Paul Daniels (Presenter).

	Holding / Source
22.12.1979	DB-D3 / 2"

Duration: 45 minutes.
Programme associate Ali Bongo; music by Ken Jones; choreography by Norman Maen; designed by Graeme Story; produced by John Fisher; directed by John Hughes.
With Jeffrey Atkins, Duo Brumbach, Bablu Mallick, Wong Mow Ting.

	Holding / Source
25.12.1980	DB-D3 / 2"

Duration: 50 minutes.
Programme associate Ali Bongo; music by Ken Jones; designed by Graeme Story; produced by John Fisher; directed by John Hughes.
With Harry Blackstone, Lilly Yokoi, Compagnie Philippe Genty, Michael McGiveney.

	Holding / Source
25.12.1981 **Paul Daniels' Magical Christmas**	DB-D3 / 2"

Duration: 40 minutes.
Programme associate Ali Bongo; music directed by Ken Jones; designed by Bob Cove; produced by James Moir; directed by Bill Wilson.
With Tux, Les Samurai, Pierre Brahma.

	Holding / Source
25.12.1982 **The Paul Daniels Magic Christmas Show**	DB / 1"

Duration: 55 minutes.
Music directed by Ken Jones; magical advisers Ali Bongo and Billy McComb; designed by Richard Morris; produced by John Fisher; directed by John Bishop.
With Kenneth Williams, Floella Benjamin, Lorraine Chase, Billy Dainty, Jill Gascoine, Lucinda Green, Rolf Harris, Nerys Hughes, Barbara Kelly, Patrick Moore, Tim Rice, Barry Took, Compagnie Philippe Genty, Luisa, The Rios, The Trocaderos, Glen Bexfield, Debbie McGee.

	Holding / Source
26.12.1983 **The Paul Daniels Magic Christmas Show**	DB / 1"

Duration: 50 minutes.
Music directed by Ken Jones; lighting by Dickie Higham; sound Laurie Taylor; designed by John Stout; production associate Ali Bongo; produced by John Fisher; directed by John Bishop.
With The Pendragons, The Five Star Endresz Family, Professor Al Carthy, Debbie McGee, Amanda Newman, Nicky Ellen, Rosemary Lane.

	Holding / Source
25.12.1984 **The Paul Daniels Magic Christmas Show**	DB / 1"

Duration: 50 minutes.
Programme associate Ali Bongo; music directed by Ken Jones; lighting by Bert Postlethwaite; sound Malcolm Johnson; designed by Tony Burrough; produced by John Fisher; directed by Geoff Miles.
With George Carl, Kris Kremo, The Olympiads, Robert Maxwell, Debbie McGee.

	Holding / Source
26.12.1985 "Snow White and the Seven Dwarves"	DB / 1"

Duration: 50 minutes.
Programme associate Ali Bongo; music directed by Ken Jones; lighting by Bill Millar; sound Malcolm Johnson; designed by Oliver Bayldon; produced by John Fisher; directed by Geoff Miles.
With Debbie McGee (Snow White), The Jazzy Jumpers, Fenella Fielding, Lance Burton, Sooty, Matthew Corbett, Zhou Shurong, Kate Bellamy, The Brian Rogers Dancers.

	Holding / Source
26.12.1987 **The Paul Daniels Magic Christmas Show**	DB / 1"

Duration: 50 minutes.
Programme associate Ali Bongo; music directed by Ken Jones; lighting by Bill Millar; sound Tony Philpott; designed by Don Giles; produced by John Fisher; directed by Kevin Bishop.
With René Levand, Philippe Genty, The Brave Seamen, Debbie McGee.

THE PAUL DANIELS MAGIC SHOW (continued)   British Christmas Television Guide

                                                                                   Holding / Source
26.12.1989   DB / 1"
Duration: 50 minutes.
Programme associate Ali Bongo; music directed by Ray Monk; produced and directed by Geoff Miles.
With Little and Large, Anne Charleston, Ian Smith, Kenny Raskin, Debbie McGee.

                                                                                   Holding / Source
24.12.1990   DB / 1"
Duration: 50 minutes.
Produced and directed by Geoff Miles.
With The Great Bosconi, Peter Hartly, Chester Baker, Sakura, Debbie McGee.

                                                                                   Holding / Source
28.12.1991   DB / 1"
Duration: 45 minutes.
Produced and directed by Geoff Miles.
With Band of The Life Guards, Debbie McGee.

                                                                                   Holding / Source
28.12.1993 **The Paul Daniels Christmas Magic Show**   DB / D3S
Duration: 50 minutes.
Produced and directed by Geoff Miles.
With Debbie McGee.

An end of series party tape exists on DVD.

PAUL O'GRADY LIVE

An Olga TV production for ITV 1. Transmission details are for the Central region. Duration: 48 minutes.

Main regular performer(s): Paul O'Grady (Host).

SERIES 1
Main regular credit(s):   VT directors James Abram and Mike Agnew; archive producer Alex Brassett-Harknett; research Michael Spencer; script supervisor Alison McGregor; music by Gary Crockett, Dominic Glover and Jay Glover; art director Ros Cumberland; designed by Peter Bingemann; assistant producer Nadia Dyer; executive producers Robert Gray and Paul O'Grady; consultant producer Lisa Clark; production manager Harriet Dormer; series producer Seamus Murphy-Mitchell; directed by Steve Smith.
Main regular performer(s): With Jon Briggs (Voice Only), Andy Collins (Studio Host).

                                                                                   Holding / Source
24.12.2010 **Paul O'Grady's Christmas**   HD/DB / HDC
Additional material by Christine Rose, Christian Manley, Colin Edmonds, Lee Stuart Evans and The Dawson Brothers; music directed by Paul Moran; produced by Natalie Walker and Chris Weller.
With Bette Midler, David Haye, Danny Miller, Cilla Black, The Soldiers.

PAUL O'GRADY: FOR THE LOVE OF DOGS

An ITV Studios production for ITV 1. Transmission details are for the Central region. Duration: 48 minutes.

A surprise autumn hit, this series attracted five million viewers. The format couldn't be simpler: Paul O'Grady goes to Battersea Dogs and Cats Home to tell the stories of abandoned and mistreated dogs. Although Paul brings humour to many of the situations, he's clearly touched by the plight of the animals.

Main regular cast: Paul O'Grady (Presenter).

SERIES 1
Credits: Series producer Alan Boyle; series director Jill Worsley.

                                                                                   Holding / Source
25.12.2012 **Christmas Special**   HD/DB / HDC
Paul returns to drive home the message that a dog is not just for Christmas. Among the four-legged waifs he meets are a stressed-out husky, a terrier with a dodgy hip and a litter of lurcher puppies.

SERIES 2
                                                                                   Holding / Source
25.12.2013 **Christmas Special**   HD/DB / HDC
The comedian helps out at Battersea Dogs & Cats Home over the festive period, having much fun with the 12 pups of Christmas and meeting a three-legged friend.
Produced and directed by Lucy Bing.

PAUL ZENON'S TRICKY CHRISTMAS

A Channel X production for Channel 4. Transmission details are for Channel 4. Duration: 55 minutes.
Streetwise magician Paul Zenon taking to the streets of London, Blackpool and Dublin.
Produced by Jim Reid; directed by Peter Orton.
Paul Zenon.

                                                                                   Holding / Source
30.12.1999   DB / DBS

PAUL ZENON'S TRICKY CHRISTMAS

PEBBLE MILL

A BBC Birmingham production for BBC 1. Transmission details are for BBC 1. Duration varies - see below for details.
SERIES 1

	Holding / Source
24.12.1974 **Pebble Mill Christmas**	J / Live

Duration: 25 minutes.
A Victorian family Christmas.
Edited by Terry Dobson.
With Bob Langley (Presenter), Donny MacLeod (Presenter), David Seymour (Presenter), Marian Foster (Presenter), Ken Hutchings (Presenter), Roy Hudd.

SERIES 2

	Holding / Source
24.12.1975 **Pebble Mill Christmas**	J / Live

Duration: 65 minutes.
With Bob Langley (Presenter), Don Maclean (Presenter), David Seymour (Presenter), Marian Foster (Presenter), Roy Hudd, Stan Boardman, The Haworth Brass Band.

SERIES 3

	Holding / Source
23.12.1976 **Pebble Mill Christmas**	J / Live

Duration: 50 minutes.
Final of the Pebble Mill Christmas Card competition.
Edited by Terry Dobson.
With Bob Langley (Presenter), David Seymour (Presenter), Donny MacLeod (Presenter), Jan Leeming (Presenter), Marian Foster (Presenter).

24.12.1976 **Pebble Mill Christmas Special**　　　　　　　　　　　　　　　　　　　　DB-D3-2" / LivePAL
Duration: 59 minutes.
Edited by Terry Dobson.
With Donny MacLeod (Presenter), Jan Leeming (Presenter), Bob Langley (Presenter), David Seymour (Presenter), Marian Foster (Presenter), David Nixon, Roger de Courcey & Nookie Bear, Dick Chipperfield, Acker Bilk, Peter Seabrook, Pip Tips, 30 Marching Santa Clauses.

SERIES 4
Duration: 50 minutes.

	Holding / Source
23.12.1977 **Pebble Mill Christmas Special**	DB-2" / LivePAL

Features on Boxing Day edition of 'Holiday on Ice' ice dancing show, and automatons.
With Donny MacLeod (Presenter), Jan Leeming (Presenter), Marian Foster (Presenter), David Seymour (Presenter), Michael Smith*, The Brighouse and Rastrick Brass Band*, Bill Stewart*, Paul Daniels*, Peter Seabrook.

See also: PEBBLE MILL AT ONE (BBC)

PEBBLE MILL AT ONE

A BBC Birmingham production for BBC 1. Transmission details are for BBC 1. Duration varies - see below for details.
SERIES 2
Duration: 45 minutes.
Main regular credit(s):　　　Edited by Terry Dobson.

	Holding / Source
21.12.1973	DB-D3-2"SEQ / LivePAL

With Marian Foster (Presenter), David Seymour (Presenter), Donny MacLeod (Presenter), Keith Best (Weatherman), Patrick Troughton, Bernard Wilkie, Arthur Negus.
No opening.

SERIES 3
Duration: 45 minutes.

	Holding / Source
21.12.1979	DB-2" / LivePAL

With Isla St. Clair, Jack Douglas, Peter Seabrook.

SERIES 5
Duration: 45 minutes.
Main regular credit(s):　　　Edited by Peter Hercombe.

	Holding / Source
23.12.1981 **Christmas Special**	DB / 2"

With Richard Baker, K-9, Cast of Hi-De-Hi.

SERIES 7

	Holding / Source
23.12.1983 **Christmas Special**	

Duration: 50 minutes.

PEBBLE MILL AT ONE (continued)

SERIES 8
Duration: 45 minutes.

Holding / Source

21.12.1984 **Christmas Special**
With Paul Coia (Presenter), Marian Foster (Presenter), Bob Langley (Presenter).

SERIES 9
Main regular credit(s): Edited by Peter Hercombe.

Holding / Source

23.12.1985 **Christmas Special**
Duration: 40 minutes.
With Magnus Magnusson (Presenter), Paul Coia (Presenter), Marian Foster (Presenter), Josephine Buchan (Presenter), Keith Harris & Orville, Black Lace, Willie Rushton.

Editions would occasionally be scheduled in slightly earlier or, more likely, later timeslots. These would generally be billed under the name PEBBLE MILL, but in all other respects these programmes were no different to any others. After a while someone must have become fed up with this and for a few years it was billed as PEBBLE MILL for a number of years. When it returned it did so as PEBBLE MILL.
See also: PEBBLE MILL (BBC)

PEEP SHOW

Alternative/Working Title(s): P.O.V.
An Objective Productions production for Channel 4. Transmission details are for Channel 4. Usual duration: 24 minutes.

Main regular credit(s): Created by Andrew O'Connor, Jesse Armstrong and Sam Bain; written by Jesse Armstrong and Sam Bain.
Main regular cast: David Mitchell (Mark Corrigan), Robert Webb (Jeremy Usborne).

SERIES 7
Main regular credit(s): Additional material by David Mitchell and Robert Webb; script supervisor Victoria Peacock; script editors Iain Morris and Robert Popper; music by Daniel Pemberton; director of photography Ben Wheeler; assistant director Andy Lumsden; art director Mo Holden; production designer Jeff Sherriff; production executive Jenny Hay; executive producers Andrew Newman, Jesse Armstrong and Sam Bain; line producer Debbie Pisani; produced by Phil Clarke; directed by Becky Martin.

Holding / Source

24.12.2010 "Christmas Day"   HD/DB / HD/DB
Written by Jesse Armstrong and Sam Bain; additional material by David Mitchell and Robert Webb.
With Matt King (Super Hans), Isy Suttie (Dobby), Eliza Bennett (Sarah), Lynn Farleigh (Pam Corrigan), Clive Merrison (Dan Corrigan).

29.12.2010 "New Year's Eve"   HD/DB / HD/DB
Additional material by David Mitchell and Robert Webb.
With Camilla Marie Beeput (Zahra), Olivia Colman (Sophie), Matt King (Super Hans), Isy Suttie (Dobby), Paterson Joseph (Alan Johnson), Sophie Winkleman (Big Suze), Jim Howick (Gerrard), Neil Fitzmaurice, Jake Harders, Kanako Nakano, Richard Sandling.

The episode titles are those contained in "Peep Show: The Scripts and More" by Armstrong and Bain – they do not appear on screen.

PEEP SHOW & TELL

An Objective Productions production for Channel 4. Transmission details are for Channel 4. Duration: 50 minutes.

Narrated by Sharon Horgan; associate producer Zanna Hall; production executive Jenny Hay; executive producer Andrew Newman; head of production Debi Roach; production manager Lucy Miller; produced and directed by Michael Forte.

Andrew O'Connor, Sam Bain, Jesse Armstrong, Robert Webb, David Mitchell, Graham Linehan, Arthur Mathews, Lucy Mangan, Jo Whiley, Iain Morris, Andrew Newman, Robert Popper, Phil Clarke, Anna Kipps, Joel Mackaay, Ben Caldwell, Alex Liang, Hannah Randle, Laura McKeown, Taylor Kirklin, Olivia Colman, Paterson Joseph, Matt King, Grace Dent, Vera Filatova, Izzy Mant, Isy Suttie, Becky Martin, James Lindsay, Melinda Lewis, Sean McKeown, Chris Murphy, Doron Zaresky.

Holding / Source

24.12.2010   HD/DB / DB

PEGGY

Alternative/Working Title(s): PEGGY LEE
A Thames Television production. Transmission details are for the ATV midlands region. Duration: 50 minutes.
Script associate Dick Vosburgh; music associate Don Hunt; designed by Peter Le Page; produced by David Clark; directed by Royston Mayoh.
Peggy Lee, Charles Aznavour, Peter Moore and his Orchestra.

Holding / Source

27.12.1977   DB / 2"

THE PENTANGLE

A BBC production for BBC 2. Transmission details are for BBC 2. Duration: 20 minutes.
Songs from a country church.
Produced and directed by Steve Roberts.
The Pentangle.

Holding / Source

25.12.1970   J / 2"

THE PEOPLE'S NATIVITY

A BBC Religious Department production for BBC 1. Transmission details are for BBC 1. Duration: 4 minutes.

A unique reading of the Christmas story from a star-studded cast.

Tom Jones, Barbara Windsor, Alan Titchmarsh, Desmond Lynam.

Holding / Source

25.12.1998   DB / DBS

A PERFECT DAY FOR CHRISTMAS

A BBC production for BBC 1. Transmission details are for BBC 1. Duration: 9 minutes.

BBC's promotional video, which is being shown several times over the holiday season. The single topped the chart following Children in Need.

Holding / Source

24.12.1997   DB-D3 / D3S

PERRY COMO'S OLDE ENGLISH CHRISTMAS

A BBC production for BBC 2. Transmission details are for BBC 2. Duration: 60 minutes.

Written by Eric Merriman; music directed by Nick Perito; choreography by Gillian Lynne; designed by Tony Abbott; produced and directed by Yvonne Littlewood.

Perry Como, Petula Clark, Leo Sayer, John Curry, Gemma Craven, Choir of St Paul's Cathedral, The Gillian Lynne Dancers, The Tony Mansell Singers.

Holding / Source

23.12.1977   DB-D3 / 2"

PETER ANDRE: MY LIFE AT CHRISTMAS

Commissioned by ITV 2. Transmission details are for ITV 2. Duration: 48 minutes.

Main regular cast: Peter André.

SERIES 5

Holding / Source

23.12.2013   HD/DB / HDC

The singer finds he has little time to enjoy a festive break, with home improvements on his to-do list before the arrival of Emily's baby.

PETER COOK A POSTHUMOUROUS TRIBUTE

A BBC production for BBC 2. Transmission details are for BBC 2. Duration: 62 minutes.

Executive producer Beatrice Ballard; produced by Sam Donnelly; directed for the stage by Terry Jones; directed for television by John Spencer.

David Frost (Host), Peter Cook (Subject of Documentary), Terry Jones, Michael Palin, Harry Enfield, Adrian Edmondson, Griff Rhys Jones, Angus Deayton, Clive Anderson, David Baddiel, Jon Culshaw, Rik Mayall, Josie Lawrence, Neil Innes, Greg Proops, Jimmy Carr, Dom Joly.

Holding / Source

28.12.2002   DB / DBSW

THE PETER SERAFINOWICZ SHOW

An Objective Productions production for BBC 2. Transmission details are for BBC 2. Duration: 30 minutes.

Main regular credit(s):   Written by Peter Serafinowicz, James Serafinowicz, Robert Popper, The Dawson Brothers, Jason Hazeley, Joel Morris and Dan Maier; script supervisor Anne Patterson; script editor David Quantick; music by Matt Berry; designed by Jeffrey Sherriff; production executive Jenny Hay; executive producers Phil Clarke and Andrew O'Connor; head of production Debi Roach; produced by James Serafinowicz.

Main regular cast: Peter Serafinowicz (Host).

Made in association with Hey Hey Hey.

Holding / Source

23.12.2008   The Peter Serafinowicz Christmas Show   DB / DBSW

Written by Peter Serafinowicz and James Serafinowicz; additional material by The Dawson Brothers, Nick Tanner, David Armand, Camm & Maclean, Robert Popper and Ben Farrell; script editor David Walliams; series producer Ben Farrell; directed by Becky Martin.

With David Armand, Paul Putner, Belinda Stewart-Wilson, Tony Bignell, Elsie Kelly.

A 40-minute extended version was shown on Christmas Eve.

THE PETERS AND LEE STORY

An ATV production. Transmission details are for the ATV midlands region. Duration: 50 minutes.

Written by Bryan Blackburn; music associate Alan Bence; designed by Bryan Holgate; produced by Colin Clews; directed by Peter Harris.

Lennie Peters (Host), Dianne Lee (Host), Mike and Bernie Winters, Aiden J. Harvey, Cleo Laine, John Dankworth, Jack Parnell and his Orchestra, The Maggie Stredder Singers.

Holding / Source

27.12.1975   J / 2"

PETS

A Fit 2 Fill Productions production for Channel 4. Transmission details are for Channel 4.

Main regular credit(s):	Written by Andrew Barclay and Brian West; music by Stacey Smith; produced by Andrew Barclay and Brian West; directed by Mike Stephens.
Main regular cast:	Ian Angus Wilkie (Hamish), Andrew Barclay (Trevor), Petros Emanual (JP), Sally Elsden (Davina).

SERIES 1

Holding / Source

05.05.2001 **Christmas**   DB /

Adult puppet sitcom.

PETTICOAT LANE

A BBC production for BBC 2. Transmission details are for BBC 2. Duration: 60 minutes.

Notebook in hand, Henry Mayhew, the Victorian author, wandered through the foggy streets of London. This new work commissioned for television is based on the characters he met as he recorded the sights and sounds of the East End — the Cockneys and the costermongers, the Queen's Own Ratcatcher, and motley gangs of artful dodgers in this musical portrait of London at Christmas.

Written by Cicely Herbert; lyrics by Cicely Herbert; costume Ann Beverley; make-up Jean Steward; music by Jim Parker; orchestra conducted by Robin Stapleton; lighting by Bert Postlethwaite; sound Ray Angel; designed by John Stout; executive producer Herbert Chappell; produced and directed by Peter Butler.

Sheila Hancock, Dennis Waterman, Freddie Jones, Cheryl Kennedy, Alfred Marks, Children's Choir, Pimlico School.

Holding / Source

24.12.1978   DB-D3 / 2"

PETULA

An ATV production. Transmission details are for the ATV midlands region. Duration: 50 minutes.

The tables have at last been turned on David Frost! It happens as Petula Clark puts the master interviewer himself in the hot seat and actually interviews him. But David proves more slippery, than any of his own "victims".

  It's all in fun of course, as part of Pet's own Christmas spectacular that sees David in an even more unfamiliar role -as Romeo to her Juliet. When it comes to sweeping a girl off her feet, Romeo has nothing on Dean Martin. In a sequence specially filmed in Hollywood, Dean takes his hostess for a real musical ride-with a song medley on horseback. Also on the bill with the Everly Brothers is the fabulous Peggy Lee, making her first trip to Britain for nine years specially for the show.

Written by Herb Sargent, Bob Ellison, Dick Vosburgh and Barry Cryer; music associate Kenny Powell; choreography by Paddy Stone; designed by Bill McPherson; produced by Gary Smith, Dwight Hemion and Les Cocks; directed by Dwight Hemion and John Pullen.

Petula Clark (Host), The Everly Brothers, David Frost, Dean Martin, Peggy Lee, The Paddy Stone Dancers, The Mike Sammes Singers, Jack Parnell and his Orchestra.

Holding / Source

26.12.1970   DB / 2"

PETULA

A Yorkshire Television production. Transmission details are for the Central region. Duration: 50 minutes.

Music directed by Kenny Clayton; designed by Colin Pigott; produced and directed by Vernon Lawrence.

Petula Clark, Paul Jones, Barry Took, Billy Eckstine, John Amis, Keith Barrow, Isla Blair, Eleanor Bron, Annetta Hoffnung, Brian Kay, Humphrey Lyttelton.

Holding / Source

31.12.1983   1" / 1"

PETULA AND FRIENDS

A BBC production for BBC 1. Transmission details are for BBC 1. Duration: 50 minutes.

Written by Barry Took and Ronnie Cass; costume Peter Shepherd; lighting by Ritchie Richardson; sound Hugh Barker; designed by Lesley Joan Bremness; produced and directed by Yvonne Littlewood.

Petula Clark, Warren Mitchell, Rolf Harris, Manitas De Plata, Johnny Harris and his Orchestra, Frank Owens*.

Holding / Source

27.12.1971   J / 2"

PETULA SINGS CHRISTMAS

A BBC production for BBC 1. Transmission details are for BBC 1. Duration: 45 minutes.

Programme associate Eric Merriman; choreography by Norman Maen; designed by Don Taylor; produced and directed by Yvonne Littlewood.

Petula Clark (Host), Frankie Howerd, The Norman Maen Dancers, The Peter Knight Orchestra, The Peter Knight Singers.

Holding / Source

21.12.1974   DB / 2"

PHILLIP SCHOFIELD'S NIGHT BEFORE CHRISTMAS

An ITV Productions production for ITV 1. Transmission details are for the Central region. Duration: 55 minutes.

Written by Adam Bostock-Smith; associate producers Bethan Mackenzie and Caroline Roseman; executive producer Mark Wells; produced by Mat Hodgson and Cillian De Buitléar; directed by Mat Hodgson and Chris Power.

Phillip Schofield (Presenter), Prince Charles, Peter André, Army Big Band, Elizabeth Emanuel, Katherine Jenkins, Leona Lewis, London Oratory School Schola, Kelly Osbourne, Ozzy Osbourne, Sharon Osbourne, Joe Pasquale, Katie Price, Gary Rhodes, St Petersburg Ballet Theatre, Chris Tarrant, Westlife.

Holding / Source

24.12.2006   DB / DBSW

PHILLIP SCHOFIELD'S NIGHT BEFORE CHRISTMAS

PICK OF 80

A BBC production for BBC 1. Transmission details are for BBC 1. Duration: 60 minutes.

Barry Took looks back on the year's television with highlights from some of the programmes which have achieved popularity, esteem and even notoriety.

VT editor Pete Bird; produced by Sue Mallinson.

Barry Took (Presenter), Penelope Keith, Kate Nelligan, Larry Hagman, Angela Rippon, Russell Harty, Pamela Stephenson, Rowan Atkinson, Griff Rhys Jones, Mel Smith, Stephanie Turner, Cheryl Campbell, Sue Peacock, Neil Innes, Paul Daniels, Michael Parkinson, Billy Connolly, Barbara Woodhouse, John Duttine, Dame Alicia Markova, John Cleese, Sarah Badel, Wendy Craig, Bob Hoskins, Tom Baker, Ronnie Barker, Ronnie Corbett, James Burke, Earl Mountbatten, Trevor Eve, Jack Galloway.

	Holding / Source
31.12.1980	DB-D3 / 2"

PICK OF THE YEAR

A BBC production for BBC 2. Transmission details are for BBC 2.

Edited by Rowan Ayers; produced and directed by Betty White.

Kenneth Williams, Max Robertson, Fanny Cradock, Dudley Moore, Marty Feldman, Robert Erkskine, Sheila Hancock, Ernie Wise, Marius Goring, Robert Robinson, James Cameron, Drusilla Beyfus, Benny Green, Joan Bakewell, Robert Morley.

	Holding / Source
31.12.1968	J / 2"

PICTURE BOX

A Granada production. Transmission details are for the ATV midlands region. Duration: 15 minutes.

A Granada production. Transmission details are for the ATV midlands region.

		Production No	Holding / Source
02.12.1975	Christmas Story	P543/230	DB / 2"
29.11.1977	Christmas Story	P543/280	DB / 2"
30.11.1978	Christmas Story	P543/317	DB / 2"
01.12.1980	Christmas Story	P543/368	DB / 2"
30.11.1981	Christmas Story	P543/396	DB / 2"
21.11.1983	The Christmas Messager - Part 1	P543/451	DB / 2"
28.11.1983	The Christmas Messenger - Part 2	P543/452	DB / 2"
26.11.1984	Christmas Story	P543/480	DB / 1"
17.11.1986	The Christmas Messenger - Part 1	P543/535	DB / 1"
24.11.1986	The Christmas Messenger - Part 2	P543/536	DB / 1"

PIED PIPER

Alternative/Working Title(s): CROSSING TO FREEDOM

A Granada Films production for Granada. Transmission details are for the Central region. Duration: 100 minutes.

In the summer of 1940, retired solicitor John Howard has to cut short his fishing holiday in France as the Germans begin their advance. On his journey home to England, Mr Howard finds himself a reluctant chaperone to a growing number of children whose lives have been put in danger by the onset of war.

Adapted by Jerome Kass; based on a book by Nevil Shute; music by Carl Davis; director of photography Ken Morgan; designed by Stephen Fineren; executive producers Michael Cox and Stan Margulies; production manager Don Bell; produced by Craig McNeil; directed by Norman Stone.

Peter O'Toole (John Howard), Mare Winningham (Nicole), Susan Wooldridge (Mrs Cavanagh), Michael Kitchen (Major Diessen), Alastair Haley (Ronnie), Clare Drummond (Sheila).

	Production No	Holding / Source
24.12.1989	P1463	C1 / C1

PINGU

A Trickfilmstudio/Hit Entertainment production for BBC 1. Transmission details are for BBC 1. Duration: 4 minutes.

SERIES 4

		Holding / Source
26.12.1993	Pingu's Family Celebrate Christmas	D3 / D3S

Polish series dubbed into English.

PINKY AND PERKY

A BBC North production for BBC. Transmission details are for BBC.

Main regular cast:	Pinky and Perky (Hosts), Jan Dalibor (Puppeteer), Vlasta Dalibor (Puppeteer).
Duration: 15 minutes.	
Main regular credit(s):	Written by Robert Gray; lyrics by Norman Newell and Alyn Ainsworth; theme music by Norman Newell and Alyn Ainsworth; designed by Stuart Furber; produced and directed by Stan Parkinson.
Main regular cast:	With Jimmy Thompson (Host).

		Holding / Source
20.12.1964	Robinson Riding Hood And His Magic Lamp	DB-R1 /
25.12.1964	Christmas Pig-Tale	J /

PINKY AND PERKY

A Thames Television production. Transmission details are for the ATV midlands region. Duration: 14 minutes.

Main regular cast: Pinky and Perky (Hosts), Jan Dalibor (Puppeteer), Vlasta Dalibor (Puppeteer).

SERIES 1

Main regular credit(s): Written by Don Nicholl; designed by Bill Palmer; produced and directed by Diana Potter.

Holding / Source

21.12.1970 **Guide To Greetings** J / 2"

Greetings from Pinky and Perky - and not just the Christmas variety. The precocious piglets will send a Get Well card to Horace Hare who snuffles his way through A Cold in My Nose. Beakel Paul presents his own special Christmas greeting and Pinky and Perky sing Snowy White Snow and Jingle Bells.

PINNY'S HOUSE

A Smallfilms production for Barn Productions. Transmission details are for BBC 1. Duration: 4 minutes.

Main regular credit(s): Written by Peter Firmin; drawings by Peter Firmin; music by Ar Log; produced and directed by Oliver Postgate.

Main regular cast: Matilda Thorpe (Reader).

Holding / Source

12.12.1986 **Pinny And The Holly Tree** DB-1" / C1

THE PIRATES OF THE PIRATES OF PENZANCE

A Westward Television production. Transmission details are for the London Weekend Television region. Duration: 35 minutes.

Written by Robin O'Connor; lyrics by W. S. Gilbert and Arthur Sullivan; music by W. S. Gilbert and Arthur Sullivan; produced and directed by Roger Gage.

Spike Milligan (Many Parts), Ian Wallace (Almost As Many Parts), Vivienne Ross (Helen Lenoir), John Reed (The Major General), Helen Walker (Mabel), Cynthia Morey (Ruth), Ed Welch (Mr Horner), Stuart Hutchison (Boatman).

Holding / Source

26.12.1980 C1 / C1

PLAGUE AND THE MOONFLOWER

An Ecosse Films production for BBC 2. made in association with CTVC. Transmission details are for BBC 2.

Written by Ralph Steadman; lyrics by Ralph Steadman; music by Richard Harvey; executive producer Avril MacRory; produced by Douglas Rae; directed by Robin Lough.

Ben Kingsley (Narrator), Sir Michael Hordern (Colonial Gentleman), Eileen Page (Colonial Lady), Graham Peskett (Tea-Room Violinist), Keith Wyncoll (The Plague Demon), Ian Holm (Voice of the Plague Demon), Penelope Wilton (Voice of Margaret Mee).

Holding / Source

31.12.1994 D3 / D3S

PLAIN MURDER

A BBC production for BBC 2. Transmission details are for BBC 2. Duration: 100 minutes.

London, 1929... a foggy November day .. and the grim spectre of unemployment threatens three young men from the Universal Advertising Agency . .. until Morris comes up with the perfect solution: Murder!

Dramatised by Richard Harris; based on a book by C. S. Forester; script editor Cicely Cawthorne; music by Ron Grainer; designed by Barrie Dobbins; produced by Richard Beynon; directed by Julian Amyes.

Michael Sheard (Harrison), Chris Fairbank (Oldroyd), Paul Angelis (Morris), Jeffrey Perry (Reddy), Rosalyn Elvin (Mary Morris), Clarissa Young (Molly Morris), Daniel Peacock (Shepherd), Clive Wouters (Clarence), Vicky Williams (Maud), Maryann Turner (Mrs Harrison), Michael Lees (Campbell), Royston Tickner (Police Inspector), Donald MacIver (Lewis), Peter Symonds (Howlett), J. J. Johnson (Johnny Morris), Hugh Moxey (Reddy's Father), Philip Wilde (Lamb), Fiona Gray (Doris Campbell).

Holding / Source

28.12.1978 DB-D3 / 2"

PLANS FOR A PARTY

An Associated-Rediffusion production. Transmission details are for Associated-Rediffusion.

Holding / Source

09.12.1960 NR / Live
16.12.1960 NR / Live
23.12.1960 NR / Live
30.12.1960 NR / Live

PLATFORMS AT CHRISTMAS

A BBC Manchester production for BBC 1. Transmission details are for BBC 1. Duration: 40 minutes.

TV documentary tracing the history of the Christmas song, charting its beginnings in traditional carols sung around the fire, to its peak in the mid-1970s with songs from glam-rockers Slade and Wizzard.

Produced and directed by Len Brown.

Holding / Source

21.12.2000 DB / DBSW

PLAY AWAY

A BBC production for BBC 2. Transmission details are for BBC 2. Usual duration: 20 minutes.

SERIES 5

Main regular credit(s): Presented by Brian Cant, Toni Arthur, Jonathan Cohen, Spike Healey and Alan Rushton; music directed by Jonathan Cohen; executive producer Cynthia Felgate; produced by Ann Reay.

	Production No	VT Number	Holding / Source
25.12.1975 **Christmas Day Play Away**	3355/3570	VTC/6HT/B03042	DB-D3 / 2"

Duration: 35 minutes.
Written by Brian Cant, Peter Charlton and Julia Donaldson; designed by Tony Snoaden; directed by Peter Charlton.
With Derek Griffiths, Lionel Morton, Stephen Henderson.

SERIES 6

	Holding / Source
25.12.1976 **Christmas Special**	DB|n / 2"

With Chloe Ashcroft, Derek Griffiths, Lionel Morton, Jeff Crampton, Stephen Henderson.

SERIES 7

Main regular credit(s): Presented by Brian Cant; executive producer Cynthia Felgate; produced by Ann Reay; directed by Peter Charlton.

	Holding / Source
24.12.1977 **Special: Thrice Welcome Christmas**	J / 2"

Duration: 30 minutes.
Written by Dave Arthur.
With Toni Arthur, Dave Arthur, Christopher Ball, Dolly Collins, Barry Dransfield, Twineham Handbell Ringers.

	Holding / Source
31.12.1977 **Away Day: Bringing In The Corn**	J / 2"

Duration: 30 minutes.
Written by Peter Charlton.
With Tony Robinson, Jonathan Cohen, Spike Heatley, Alan Rushton, Bob Falloon.

SERIES 8

Main regular credit(s): Presented by Brian Cant and Jonathan Cohen.

	Holding / Source
23.12.1978 **Christmas Is Coming**	J / 2"

With Julie Stevens, Tony Robinson, Anita Dobson.

SERIES 9

Main regular credit(s): Presented by Brian Cant; music directed by Jonathan Cohen; produced by Ann Reay.
Main regular cast: With Paul Carmichael (Musician), Jeff Crampton (Musician), John Hayman (Musician), Dave Roach (Musician).

	Holding / Source
22.12.1979 **Carol Concert**	DB-D3 / 2"

A PLAY FOR SUNDAY

An ATV production. Transmission details are for the ATV midlands region. Duration varies - see below for details.

	Holding / Source
26.12.1971 **The Crib**	J / 2"

Duration: 35 minutes.
Kate and Mary spend Christmas in the maternity ward of a hospital. Their circumstances differ but perhaps they share a common need.
Written by David Butler; designed by Jay Clements; produced by John Cooper; directed by Richard Bramall.
With Janet Key (Kate Lewis), Jenny Twigge (Mary Parker), Ray Lonnen (Charles Lewis), Emma Chapman (Staff Nurse McBain), Eve Pearce (Sister Harris).

PLAY FOR TODAY

A BBC production for BBC 1. Transmission details are for BBC 1. Duration varies - see below for details.

SERIES 4

	Holding / Source
13.12.1973 **Jingle Bells**	J / 2"

Duration: 75 minutes.
Written by Arthur Hopcraft; produced by Graeme McDonald; directed by Claude Whatham.
With Colin Farrell (Ralph), Brenda Bruce (Madge), John Barrie (Edwin), Jenifer Armitage (Brenda), Daphne Oxenford (Mrs Johnson), Peter Needham (Harry), Erin Geraghty (Angela), Robert Lister (Bill), Jane Collins (Doreen), Mike Savage (Ted), Jane Knowles (Mavis), Brian Stirner (Colin), Victor Langley (Vicar), John Dunbar (Old Man in Club), Tina Charles (Singer), Danny Street (Singer), Nat Jackley (Landlord), Carol Macready (Landlord's Wife), Anthony Mather (Anthony), Ian Hutchinson (Ian), Richard Millington (Kevin), Janine Graham (Sharon), Lynn Murphy (Baby Lynn).

PLAY FOR TODAY (continued)

SERIES 5

Holding / Source

01.05.1975 **The Saturday Party**
DB-D3 / 2"

Duration: 75 minutes.

The invitations are out for Richard and Jane Elkinson's annual Christmas party. Only trouble is stockbroker Richard is out of a job...

Written by Brian Clark; script editor Richard Broke; sound Chick Anthony; designed by Daphne Shortman; produced by Mark Shivas; directed by Barry Davis.

With Peter Barkworth (Richard Elkinson), Sheila Gish (Jane Elkinson), Jan Waters (Sarah), Judi Bowker (Emma Elkinson), John Welsh (Philip Hucknell), Paul Williamson (Jeremy), Jean Rimmer (Dorothy Adams), Don Henderson (Jack Adams), Robin Davies (Simon Elkinson), Will Stampe (Ted Jones), Julie May (Annie Jones), Myles Hoyle (Gerald), Pamela Moiseiwitsch (Celia), William Simons (Martin), John Scott (Major Hardy), Jonathan Coy (James Firnley), Joshua Le Touzel (David Elkinson), Sylvestra Le Touzel (Paula), Daphne Oxenford (Esther Hucknell).

See also: PLAY FOR TODAY - The Country Party.

SERIES 8

Holding / Source

03.01.1978 **Scully's New Year's Eve**
DB-D3 / 2"

A BBC Birmingham production. Duration: 75 minutes.

Scully's mother is having a New Year's Eve party, unaware that her son has invi- ted most of his friends along. Surprises are in store...

Written by Alan Bleasdale; script editor Michael Wearing; produced by David Rose; directed by Michael Simpson.

With Andrew Schofield (Franny Scully), Jane Freeman (Mrs Scully), Avis Bunnage (Florrie), John Junkin (Jack), Stan Stennett (Ms Scully), Kate Binchy (Marie), Arthur Kelly (Barney), Janine Duvitski (Vera), Paul Kelly (Tony), Angela Curran (Rita), Gil Brailey (Carol), Mick Miller (Joey), Ray Kingsley (Mooey), Roger Phillips (Henry), John Anderson (Harry), Daisy Bell (Mrs Riley), Spencer Gurley (Darryl), Jimmy Coleman (First Gatecrasher), Bill Rourke (Second Gatecrasher).

See also: RUMPOLE OF THE BAILEY

PLAY OF THE MONTH

A BBC production for BBC 1. Transmission details are for BBC 1. Duration varies - see below for details.

Holding / Source

24.12.1968 **Waters Of The Moon**
J /

Duration: 90 minutes.

Written by N. C. Hunter; designed by Fanny Taylor; produced by Cedric Messina; directed by Herbert Wise.

With Margaret Leighton (Helen Lancaster), Athene Seyler (Mrs Whyte), Vivien Merchant (Evelyn Daly), Kathleen Harrison (Mrs Ashworth), Michael Gwynn (Julius Winterhalter), Roland Culver (Colonel Selby), Cavan Kendall (John Daly), Joan Heath (Mrs Daly), Wendy Allnutt (Tonetta Landi), Jack Gwillim (Robert Lancaster).

See also: MAIGRET (BBC)

PLAY OF THE WEEK

Produced for ITV by a variety of companies (see details below). Transmission details are for the ATV midlands region. Usual duration: 83 minutes.

VT Number   Holding / Source

19.12.1956 **The White Carnation**
J / Live

An Associated-Rediffusion production.

A card trick; a man with a white carnation; a gust of wind... When the door slams behind John Greenwood after his Christmas Eve party, events take a curious and rather frightening turn. Why? Viewers with a taste for mystery and humour will enjoy R. C. Sheriff's unusual play. On no account miss the exciting and unexpected opening.

Written by R. C. Sheriff; settings by Fredric Pusey; produced and directed by Cyril Coke.

With Walter Fitzgerald (John Greenwood), Ann Walford (Lydia Truscott), Terence Alexander (Sir Horace Duncan), Winifred Shotter (Lady Mary Greenwood), Maurice Hedley (Sir George Wallace), Andrea Troubridge (Lady Wallace), Roger Ostime (Major Howard), Anarose Carrigan (Sally), John Fabian (Tony Dale), Avril Leslie (Cynthia), Stratford Johns (Police Constable Thompson), Neil Wilson (Sergeant Phillips), Charles Lloyd Pack (Mr Gurney), Jack Stewart (Doctor McGregor), Harold Scott (Mr Pendlebury), Amy Dalby (Mrs Carter).

22.12.1959 **Deep And Crisp And Even**
J / 40

An Associated-Rediffusion production. Duration: 75 minutes.

Written by Paul Jones; directed by Tania Lieven.

With Gladys Henson (Alice Martin), Leslie Dwyer (Billy Williams), Liz Fraser (Dora), Robert Desmond (Harry), John Stratton (Cyril Williams), Sheila Shand Gibbs (Beryl Williams), Paul Eddington (Vincent), Geoffrey Lumsden (Mr Fletcher), Richard Waring (Adrian), Charles Brodie (First Artist), Anthony Parker (Second Artist), Beaufoy Milton (A Pawnbroker), Jos Tregoningo (A Little Man), Margaret Flint (Vera), Edward Evans (Detective Sergeant Hurley), Paul Jones (The Commentator).

21.12.1964 **Deep And Crisp And Stolen**
R1|n / 40

A Rediffusion Television production. Duration: 80 minutes.

Written by Dave Freeman; story editor William Woods; music by Sydney Amos; designed by John Emery; executive producer Antony Kearey; directed by Ronald Marriott.

With Raymond Francis (Detective Chief Superintendent Tom Lockhart / Percy Turner), Dennis Price (William), Maggie Fitzgibbon (Leonie), Robert Dorning (Manager), Joan Hickson (Mrs Caley), Dennis Lotis (Bryant), George Moon (Ted), Arthur Mullard (Police Constable Muldoon), Grant Taylor (Bluey), Muriel Young (Woman Police Sergeant Saunders), Frances Guthrie (Miss Burton), Tony Quinn (Dooley), Jack Cunningham (First Landlord), John Quayle (Space Pilot), Margaret Nolan (Space Hostess), James Copeland (Security Man, Tom), Jack Lynn (Security Sergeant), Lewis Wilson (Packard), Nancy Nevinson (Cleaning Woman), Lionel Hamilton (Security Officer Potts), Peter Fraser (Police Constable Lomax), Clifford Earl (Detective Sergeant Brown), Nancy Roberts (Cleo), Michael Corcoran (Second Landlord), Joe Wadham (Police Constable Harry), Keith Peacock (Police Constable Fred), Buster Noble (Australian), Patrick Allen, Gerald Flood, Keith Fordyce, Jimmy Hanley, Sam Kydd, Cathy McGowan, Michael Miles, Laurie West.

See also: NO HIDING PLACE

| British Christmas Television Guide | PLAY OF THE WEEK (continued) |

| 28.12.1964 **The Rise And Fall Of Nellie Brown** | D6762 | DB-4W / 40 |

An Anglia production. Duration: 70 minutes.

Written by Robert Gould; lyrics by Robert Gould; music by Dolores Claman and Norman Kay; magical adviser David Berglas; designed by Robert Fuest; produced and directed by John Jacobs.

With Ron Moody (Jasper Waxo), Elisabeth Welch (Lillabelle Astor), Millie (Selina Brown), Kenny Lynch (Hector), Bryan Mosley (Dave), George Betton (Ticket Clerk), Harry Baird (Mr Johnson), Louise Nelson (Selina's Mother), Tommy Godfrey (Mr Hallan), Patsy Smart (Miss Pike), Virginia Clay (Mrs Mac), Avril Fane (Miss Pendleton), David Perry (Mr Jerome), The Cliff Adams Singers.

PLAY SCHOOL

A BBC production for BBC 2. Transmission details are for BBC 2. Duration varies - see below for details.

Main regular credit(s): Created by Joy Whitby.

Holding / Source

25.12.1967 Useful Box Day
J / 62

Duration: 25 minutes.

And all the bells on earth shall ring, On Christmas Day, on Christmas Day, And all the bells on earth shall ring, On Christmas Day in the morning. A star, a stable, a manger, a baby. The Christmas story re-told by Roy Castle.

Presented by Carole Ward and Brian Cant; written by David Turnbull; produced by Molly Cox; directed by David Turnbull.

With Roy Castle (Story Chair).

25.12.1968 Pets Day
J / 2"

Duration: 20 minutes.

The Christmas story.

Presented by Julie Stevens and Brian Cant; written by Peter Ridsdale Scott; produced by Cynthia Felgate; directed by Peter Ridsdale Scott.

25.12.1969 Christmas Day
J / 2"

Duration: 20 minutes.

Story: The Little Drummer Boy.

Presented by Carol Chell and Johnny Ball; written by Peter Wiltshire; illustrated by Ezra Jack Keats; series producer Cynthia Felgate; directed by Peter Wiltshire.

With Jonathan Cohen (Pianist).

24.12.1970 Ideas Day
DB / 2"

Duration: 20 minutes.

Story: The Twelve Days of Christmas.

Presented by Julie Stevens and Brian Cant.

25.12.1970 Science Day
J / 2"

Duration: 20 minutes.

Story: The Christmas Story.

Presented by Julie Stevens and Brian Cant; written by Anne Gobey; designed by Diana Bates; series producer Cynthia Felgate; directed by Anne Gobey.

With Paul Reade (Pianist).

20.12.1971
J / 2"

Duration: 25 minutes.

Story: The Christmas Tree.

Presented by Carol Chell and Derek Griffiths; written by Anne Gobey; story by Nancy Quayle; designed by Kassy Baker; executive producer Cynthia Felgate; produced by Peter Ridsdale Scott; directed by Anne Gobey.

With Paul Reade (Pianist).

24.12.1971
DB / 2"

Duration: 25 minutes.

Story: The Little Drummer Boy.

Presented by Derek Griffiths and Carol Chell; written by Anne Gobey; illustrated by Ezra Jack Keats; lyrics by Henry Onorati, Harry Simeone and Katherine Davis; music by Katherine Davis, Henry Onorati and Harry Simeone; designed by Kassy Baker; executive producer Cynthia Felgate; produced by Peter Ridsdale Scott; directed by Anne Gobey.

With Paul Reade (Pianist).

25.12.1971 The Christmas Story
DB / 2"

Duration: 25 minutes.

Presented by Carol Chell and Derek Griffiths; written by Anne Gobey; designed by Kassy Baker; executive producer Cynthia Felgate; produced by Peter Ridsdale Scott; directed by Anne Gobey.

With Paul Reade (Pianist).

No end credits.

27.12.1971
J / 2"

Duration: 25 minutes.

Story: King John's Christmas.

Presented by Miranda Connell and Lionel Morton; written by Christine Secombe; story by A. A. Milne; designed by Rosalind Inglis; executive producer Cynthia Felgate; produced by Peter Ridsdale Scott; directed by Christine Secombe.

With Peter Gosling (Pianist).

18.12.1972
J / 2"

Duration: 25 minutes.

Story: Grannie's Christmas surprise.

Presented by Chloe Ashcroft and Johnny Ball; story by L. Pitt; designed by Christine Castle; executive producer Cynthia Felgate; produced by Peter Wiltshire; directed by Richard Greening.

With John Horler (Pianist).

PLAY SCHOOL (continued)

25.12.1972 — DB / 2"
Duration: 25 minutes.
Story: The Christmas Story.
Presented by Miranda Connell and Rick Jones; written by Christine Secombe; designed by Barbara Gosnold; executive producer Cynthia Felgate; produced by Peter Ridsdale Scott; directed by Christine Secombe.
With William Blezard (Pianist).

26.12.1972 — J / 2"
Duration: 25 minutes.
Story: Good King Wencelas.
Presented by Miranda Connell and Rick Jones; written by Christine Secombe; designed by Barbara Gosnold; executive producer Cynthia Felgate; produced by Peter Ridsdale Scott; directed by Christine Secombe.
With William Blezard (Pianist).

24.12.1973 — J / 2"
Duration: 25 minutes.
Story: The Twelve Days of Christmas.
Presented by Carol Chell and Johnny Ball; written by Carole Ward; illustrated by Jack Kent; designed by Andrée Welstead Hornby; executive producer Cynthia Felgate; directed by Carole Ward.
With Peter Gosling (Pianist), Dave Moses (Percussionist).

25.12.1973 — DB / 2"
Duration: 25 minutes.
Story: The Christmas Story.
Presented by Carol Chell, Johnny Ball and Lionel Morton; written by Carole Ward; designed by Andrée Welstead Hornby; executive producer Cynthia Felgate; directed by Carole Ward.
With Peter Gosling (Pianist), Dave Moses (Percussionist).

26.12.1973 — DB / 2"
Duration: 25 minutes.
A Boxing Day outing to a village in Gloucestershire.
Presented by Carol Chell, Johnny Ball and Lionel Morton; written by Carole Ward; designed by Andrée Welstead Hornby; executive producer Cynthia Felgate; directed by Carole Ward.
With Peter Gosling (Pianist), Dave Moses (Percussionist).

23.12.1974 — DB / 2"
Story: The Silver Christmas Tree.
Presented by Derek Griffiths and Chloe Ashcroft; written by Barbara Deehan; story by Pat Hutchins; illustrated by Pat Hutchins; designed by Ken Ledsham; executive producer Cynthia Felgate; produced by Anne Gobey; directed by Barbara Deehan.
With Paul Reade (Pianist), Alan Grahame (Percussionist).

25.12.1974 — DB / 2"
Duration: 30 minutes.
Story: Christmas in the stable.
Presented by Chloe Ashcroft and Derek Griffiths; written by Barbara Deehan; story by Astrid Lindgren; illustrated by Harald Wiberg; designed by Ken Ledsham; executive producer Cynthia Felgate; produced by Anne Gobey; directed by Barbara Deehan.
With Paul Reade (Pianist), Alan Grahame (Percussionist).

24.12.1975 — DB / 2"
Duration: 25 minutes.
Story: The Christmas Spiders.
Presented by Chloe Ashcroft and Johnny Ball; written by Avril Price; illustrated by Hilary Hayton; designed by Richard McManan-Smith; executive producer Cynthia Felgate; produced by Anne Gobey; directed by Avril Price.
With Paul Reade (Pianist), Johnny Dean (Drummer).

25.12.1975 — DB / 2"
Duration: 25 minutes.
Story: The Story of Christmas.
Presented by Chloe Ashcroft and Johnny Ball; written by Avril Price; designed by Richard McManan-Smith; executive producer Cynthia Felgate; produced by Anne Gobey; directed by Avril Price.
With Paul Reade (Pianist), Johnny Dean (Drummer).

23.12.1977 — DB / 2"
Duration: 25 minutes.
The presenters visit Chalgrove Parish Church in Oxfordshire, and help the children prepare and perform a nativity play.
Presented by Chloe Ashcroft, David Hargreaves, Sarah Long and Delia Morgan; written by Christine Secombe; designed by Jim Clay; executive producer Cynthia Felgate; produced by Anne Gobey; directed by Christine Secombe.
With Paul Reade (Pianist), Alan Grahame (Percussionist), Jonathan Cohen (Musician).

19.12.1978 — J / 2"
Duration: 25 minutes.
Story: The Silver Christmas Tree.
Presented by Bruce Allan and Floella Benjamin; story by Pat Hutchins; illustrated by Pat Hutchins; designed by Jo Day; series producer Anne Gobey; produced by Peter Wiltshire; directed by Martin Fisher.
With Richard Brown (Pianist), Martin Frith (Woodwind).

20.12.1978 — J / 2"

Duration: 25 minutes.

Story: The Farm Animals' Christmas.

Presented by Floella Benjamin and Bruce Allan; written by Martin Fisher; story by Ted Moult; designed by Jo Day; series producer Anne Gobey; produced by Peter Wiltshire; directed by Martin Fisher.

With Ted Moult (Storyteller), Richard Brown (Pianist), Martin Frith (Woodwind).

26.12.1978 — DB / 2"

Duration: 25 minutes.

Story: The Pantomime.

Presented by Sarah Long, Don Spencer, Chloe Ashcroft, Carol Chell, Brian Cant, Derek Griffiths and Peter Baldwin; written by Albert Barber; story by Wilma Horsbrugh; graphics by Laurence Henry; designed by George Kyriakides; executive producer Cynthia Felgate; produced by Anne Gobey; directed by Albert Barber.

With Paul Reade (Pianist), Alan Grahame (Percussionist).

19.12.1979 — DB / 2"

Duration: 25 minutes.

Story: Christmas Spiders.

Presented by Chloe Ashcroft and Johnny Ball; written by Martin Fisher; story by Avril Price; illustrated by Hilary Hayton; designed by Patrick Tottle; executive producer Cynthia Felgate; produced by Anne Gobey; directed by Martin Fisher.

With William Blezard (Pianist).

20.12.1979 — DB / 2"

Duration: 25 minutes.

Story: The Mail Coach. Traditional Christmas at Bonsall, Derbyshire.

Presented by Chloe Ashcroft, Johnny Ball and Carol Leader; written by Martin Fisher; designed by Patrick Tottle; executive producer Cynthia Felgate; produced by Anne Gobey; directed by Martin Fisher.

With Ted Moult (Guest Presenter), William Blezard (Pianist).

24.12.1979 — DB / 2"

Duration: 25 minutes.

Story: The Little Shepherd Boy.

Presented by Sarah Long, Stuart McGugan and Elizabeth Millbank; written by Nick Wilson; story by Peggy Blakeley; illustrated by Bunshu Iguchi; designed by Patrick Tottle; executive producer Cynthia Felgate; produced by Anne Gobey; directed by Nick Wilson.

With Peter Pettinger (Pianist), Alan Grahame (Percussionist).

25.12.1979 — DB / 2"

Duration: 25 minutes.

Story: The Little Drummer Boy.

Presented by Sarah Long and Stuart McGugan; written by Nick Wilson; story by Ezra Jack Keats; lyrics by Katherine Davis, Henry Onorati and Harry Simeone; music by Katherine Davis, Henry Onorati and Harry Simeone; designed by Patrick Tottle; executive producer Cynthia Felgate; produced by Anne Gobey; directed by Nick Wilson.

With Peter Pettinger (Pianist), Alan Grahame (Percussionist), Nola Rae.

23.12.1980 — DB / 2"

Duration: 25 minutes.

Story: Mr Bits and Pieces Christmas Sack.

Presented by Carol Chell and Fred Harris; written by Peter Wiltshire; story by Frances Lindsay; graphics by Joanna Isles; designed by Mary Greaves; executive producer Cynthia Felgate; directed by Peter Wiltshire.

With Sam Kydd (Guest Storyteller), Paul Reade (Pianist), Alan Grahame (Percussionist)

25.12.1980 — DB / 2"

Duration: 25 minutes.

Story: The Shepherds on the Hill.

Presented by Carol Chell, Fred Harris and Carol Leader; written by Peter Wiltshire; graphics by Joanna Isles; photographed by Barry Boxall; designed by Mary Greaves; executive producer Cynthia Felgate; directed by Peter Wiltshire.

With Paul Reade (Pianist), Alan Grahame (Percussionist).

24.12.1981 — DB / 2"

Duration: 25 minutes.

Story: Christmas Spiders.

Presented by Carol Leader and Ben Thomas; written by John M. A. Lane; graphics by Joanna Isles; designed by Paul Trerise; executive producer Cynthia Felgate; produced and directed by John M. A. Lane.

With William Blezard (Pianist), Brian Brocklehurst (Double-Bass).

25.12.1981 — DB / 2"

Duration: 25 minutes.

Story: The Christmas Story.

Presented by Carol Leader and Ben Thomas; written by John M. A. Lane; graphics by Joanna Isles; designed by Paul Trerise; executive producer Cynthia Felgate; produced and directed by John M. A. Lane.

With William Blezard (Pianist), Brian Brocklehurst (Double-Bass).

21.12.1982 — DB / 2"

Duration: 25 minutes.

Story: King John's Christmas.

Presented by Elizabeth Millbank and Johnny Ball; written by John M. A. Lane; story by A. A. Milne; graphics by Joanna Isles; designed by Gary Brachacka; executive producer Cynthia Felgate; produced by John M. A. Lane; directed by Evelyn Skinner.

With Peter Pettinger (Pianist).

| PLAY SCHOOL (continued) | British Christmas Television Guide |

22.12.1982   DB / 2"
Duration: 25 minutes.
Story: The Silver Christmas Tree.
Presented by Elizabeth Millbank and Johnny Ball; written by John M. A. Lane; story by Pat Hutchins; graphics by Joanna Isles; designed by Gary Brachacka; executive producer Cynthia Felgate; produced by John M. A. Lane; directed by Evelyn Skinner.
With Peter Pettinger (Pianist).

24.12.1982   DB / 2"
Duration: 25 minutes.
Story: The Friendly Beast.
Presented by Elizabeth Millbank and Johnny Ball; written by John M. A. Lane; illustrated by Tomie De Paola; graphics by Joanna Isles; designed by Gary Brachacka; executive producer Cynthia Felgate; produced by John M. A. Lane; directed by Evelyn Skinner.
With Peter Pettinger (Pianist).

Duration: 20 minutes.

Holding / Source

19.12.1983 It's Monday   DB / 1"
Story: The Cobweb Christmas Tree.
Presented by Elizabeth Millbank and Brian Jameson; story by Shirley Climo; illustrated by Joe Lasker; graphics by Tom Brookes; music directed by Philip Colman; edited by Cynthia Felgate; series producer Anne Gobey; produced by Christine Hewitt; directed by Roy Milani.
With Dave Moses (Bass Guitarist), Martin Frith (Woodwind).

20.12.1983 It's Tuesday   DB / 1"
Story: Old Toby Keeps Warm.
Presented by Elizabeth Millbank, Fred Harris and Wayne Jackman; story by Margaret Joy; graphics by Tom Brookes; music directed by Philip Colman; edited by Cynthia Felgate; series producer Anne Gobey; produced by Christine Hewitt; directed by Roy Milani.
With Dave Moses (Bass Guitarist), Martin Frith (Woodwind).

21.12.1983 It's Wednesday   DB / 1"
Story: Wake Up, Bear... It's Christmas
Presented by Elizabeth Millbank and Iain Lauchlan; story by Stephen Gammell; graphics by Tom Brookes; music directed by Philip Colman; edited by Cynthia Felgate; series producer Anne Gobey; produced and directed by Christine Hewitt.
With Dave Moses (Bass Guitarist), Martin Frith (Woodwind).

22.12.1983 It's Thursday   DB / 1"
Story: Mog's Christmas.
Presented by Carol Chell and Brian Jameson; story by Judith Kerr; graphics by Tom Brookes; music directed by Philip Colman; edited by Cynthia Felgate; series producer Anne Gobey; produced and directed by Christine Hewitt.
With Dave Moses (Bass Guitarist), Martin Frith (Woodwind).

23.12.1983 It's Friday   DB / 1"
Story: The Story of Christmas.
Presented by Floella Benjamin, Carol Chell and Iain Lauchlan; graphics by Tom Brookes; music directed by Philip Colman; edited by Cynthia Felgate; series producer Anne Gobey; produced by Christine Hewitt; directed by Roy Milani.
With Dave Moses (Bass Guitarist), Martin Frith (Woodwind).

18.12.1984 It's Tuesday   DB / 1"
Christmas preparations.
Presented by Ben Thomas; story by Allison Stewart; music directed by Jonathan Cohen; edited by Cynthia Felgate; photographed by John Jefford; series producer Anne Gobey; directed by John M. A. Lane.
With Kate Copstick.

19.12.1984 It's Wednesday   DB / 1"
Story: Collecting a Christmas tree.
Presented by Ben Thomas; story by John M. A. Lane; music directed by Jonathan Cohen; edited by Cynthia Felgate; photographed by John Jefford; series producer Anne Gobey; directed by John M. A. Lane.
With Kate Copstick.

20.12.1984 It's Thursday   DB / 1"
A selection of decorations. Story: Baboushka.
Presented by Ben Thomas; story by Arthur Scholey; music directed by Jonathan Cohen; edited by Cynthia Felgate; photographed by John Jefford; series producer Anne Gobey; directed by Greg Childs.
With Kate Copstick.

21.12.1984 It's Friday   DB / 1"
Story: Len the Alien's Christmas.
Presented by Ben Thomas; story by Penny Casgaldi; music directed by Jonathan Cohen; edited by Cynthia Felgate; photographed by John Jefford; series producer Anne Gobey; directed by Greg Childs.
With Chloe Ashcroft, Kate Copstick, Brian Jameson.

24.12.1984 It's Christmas Eve   DB / 1"
Story: Santa's Crash-Bang Christmas.
Presented by Carol Chell; story by Stephen Kroll; illustrated by Tomie De Paola; graphics by Tom Brooks and Joanna Isles; music directed by Richard Brown; edited by Cynthia Felgate; designed by John Asbridge; series producer Anne Gobey; directed by Sharon Miller.
With Martin Frith (Woodwind), Peter Howland (Percussion), Ben Bazell.

PLAY SCHOOL

| British Christmas Television Guide | PLAY SCHOOL (continued) |

25.12.1984 It's Christmas Day DB / 1"
Story: The Nativity Story.
Presented by Carol Chell; graphics by Tom Brooks and Joanna Isles; music directed by Richard Brown; edited by Cynthia Felgate; designed by John Asbridge; series producer Anne Gobey; directed by Sharon Miller.
With Martin Frith (Woodwind), Peter Howland (Percussion), Brian Jameson.

26.12.1984 Pantomime: Cinderella DB / 1"
Written by Brian Cant; graphics by Tom Brooks and Joanna Isles; music directed by Richard Brown; edited by Cynthia Felgate; designed by John Asbridge; series producer Anne Gobey; directed by Sharon Miller.
With Martin Frith (Woodwind), Peter Howland (Percussion), Brian Cant, Carol Chell, Carol Leader, Brian Jameson, Wayne Jackman.

27.12.1984 It's Thursday DB / 1"
Story: The Night After Christmas.
Presented by Carol Chell; story by James Stevenson; graphics by Tom Brooks and Joanna Isles; music directed by Richard Brown; edited by Cynthia Felgate; designed by John Asbridge; series producer Anne Gobey; directed by Sharon Miller.
With Martin Frith (Woodwind), Peter Howland (Percussion), Fraser Wilson.

17.12.1985 DB / 1"
Story: A Christmas Crib for Mrs Richards.
Presented by Jane Hardy; story by Jean McKenzie; graphics by Joanna Isles; music directed by Richard Brown; edited by Cynthia Felgate; film editor Chris Gilders; series producer Barbara Roddam; directed by Sheila Fraser.
With Tony McVey (Percussion), Martin Frith (Woodwind), Wayne Jackman.

20.12.1985 DB / 1"
Story: The Little Green Tree.
Presented by Jane Hardy; story by Sonya Dann; graphics by Joanna Isles; music directed by Richard Brown; edited by Cynthia Felgate; film editor Chris Gilders; series producer Barbara Roddam; directed by Sheila Fraser.
With Tony McVey (Percussion), Martin Frith (Woodwind), Wayne Jackman.

23.12.1985 DB / 1"
Story: Angelina's Christmas.
Presented by Wayne Jackman; story by Katharine Holabird; illustrated by Helen Craig; graphics by Oliver Elmes and Joanna Isles; music directed by Jonathan Cohen; edited by Cynthia Felgate; series producer Barbara Roddam; directed by Greg Childs.
With Will Hill (Musician), Phil Todd (Musician), Carol Chell.

24.12.1985 DB / 1"
Story: A Close Shave for Father Christmas.
Presented by Wayne Jackman; story by Wayne Jackman; graphics by Oliver Elmes and Joanna Isles; music directed by Jonathan Cohen; edited by Cynthia Felgate; series producer Barbara Roddam; directed by Greg Childs.
With Will Hill (Musician), Phil Todd (Musician), Floella Benjamin.

25.12.1985 It's Christmas Day! DB / 1"
Story: The Nativity.
Presented by Wayne Jackman; graphics by Oliver Elmes and Joanna Isles; music directed by Jonathan Cohen; edited by Cynthia Felgate; series producer Barbara Roddam; directed by Greg Childs.
With Will Hill (Musician), Phil Todd (Musician), Carol Chell, Iain Lauchlan, Jonathan Cohen.

26.12.1985 A Magix Box For Boxing Day! DB / 1"
Duration: 25 minutes.
Story: The Nutcracker, based on the ballet.
Presented by Wayne Jackman; story by Wayne Jackman; graphics by Oliver Elmes and Joanna Isles; music directed by Jonathan Cohen; edited by Cynthia Felgate; series producer Barbara Roddam; directed by Greg Childs.
With Will Hill (Musician), Phil Todd (Musician), Carol Chell, Jonathan Cohen, Karen Paisey.

27.12.1985 DB / 1"
Story: Chestnuts at the Frost Fair.
Presented by Wayne Jackman; story by Wayne Jackman; graphics by Oliver Elmes and Joanna Isles; music directed by Jonathan Cohen; edited by Cynthia Felgate; series producer Barbara Roddam; directed by Greg Childs.
With Will Hill (Musician), Phil Todd (Musician), Floella Benjamin, Iain Lauchlan.

22.12.1986 DB / 1"
Story: The Christmas Tree Decorations Rehearse Their Song.
Presented by Stuart Bradley and Elizabeth Watts; story by Donald Austen; graphics by Oliver Elmes and Joanna Cheese; music directed by Michael Omer; edited by Cynthia Felgate; series associate producer Barbara Roddam; produced and directed by Christine Hewitt.

23.12.1986 DB / 1"
Story: The Nativity Play.
Presented by Stuart Bradley and Elizabeth Watts; story by Nick Butterworth and Mick Inkpen; graphics by Oliver Elmes and Joanna Cheese; music directed by Michael Omer; edited by Cynthia Felgate; series associate producer Barbara Roddam; produced and directed by Christine Hewitt.

24.12.1986 DB / 1"
Story: Crumble, the Christmas Cat.
Presented by Stuart Bradley and Elizabeth Watts; story by Catherine Stock; graphics by Oliver Elmes and Joanna Cheese; music directed by Michael Omer; edited by Cynthia Felgate; series associate producer Barbara Roddam; produced and directed by Christine Hewitt.

25.12.1986 DB / 1"
Story: The Nativity
Presented by Stuart Bradley and Elizabeth Watts; graphics by Oliver Elmes and Joanna Cheese; music directed by Michael Omer; edited by Cynthia Felgate; series associate producer Barbara Roddam; produced and directed by Christine Hewitt.

PLAY SCHOOL (continued)

26.12.1986   DB / 1"
Story: Another mince pie.
Presented by Stuart Bradley and Elizabeth Watts; story by H. E. Todd; graphics by Oliver Elmes and Joanna Cheese; music directed by Michael Omer; edited by Cynthia Felgate; series associate producer Barbara Roddam; produced and directed by Christine Hewitt.
With Nicola Katrak.

21.12.1987   DB / 1"
Story: The Cobweb Christmas.
Presented by Elizabeth Watts and Robert Kitson; story by Shirley Climo; illustrated by Joe Lasker; music directed by Jonathan Cohen; series producer Christine Hewitt; produced and directed by Sheila Fraser.

22.12.1987   DB / 1"
Story: Mog's Christmas.
Presented by Elizabeth Watts and Robert Kitson; story by Judith Kerr; music directed by Jonathan Cohen; series producer Christine Hewitt; produced and directed by Sheila Fraser.

23.12.1987   DB / 1"
Story: Peterkin Meets a Star.
Presented by Elizabeth Watts, Fred Harris and Robert Kitson; story by Emilie Boon; music directed by Jonathan Cohen; series producer Christine Hewitt; produced and directed by Sheila Fraser.

24.12.1987   DB / 1"
Story: The Nativity.
Presented by Elizabeth Watts; music directed by Jonathan Cohen; series producer Christine Hewitt; produced and directed by Sheila Fraser.
With St Paul's Roman Catholic First School, Thames Ditton.

25.12.1987   DB / 1"
Presented by Elizabeth Watts, Fred Harris and Floella Benjamin; music directed by Jonathan Cohen; series producer Christine Hewitt; produced and directed by Sheila Fraser.

More details in Paul R Jackson's book.

PLAYDAYS

A BBC production for BBC 1. Transmission details are for BBC 1.

Holding / Source

Date	Title	
25.12.1989	The Christmas Tree Stop	DB / 1"
26.12.1989	The Christmas Tree Stop	DB / 1"
27.12.1989	The Christmas Tree Stop	DB / 1"
28.12.1989	The Christmas Tree Stop	DB / 1"
29.12.1989	The Christmas Tree Stop	DB / 1"
17.12.1990	The Christmas Tree Stop	DB / 1"
18.12.1990	The Christmas Tree Stop	DB / 1"
19.12.1990	The Christmas Tree Stop	DB / 1"
20.12.1990	The Christmas Tree Stop	DB / 1"
21.12.1990	The Christmas Tree Stop	DB / 1"
25.12.1991	The Christmas Tree Stop	DB / 1"
23.12.1994	The Tent Stop - A Christmas Book	DB / 1"

PLEASE SIR!

An LWT production. Transmission details are for the ATV midlands region. Usual duration: 25 minutes.

Main regular credit(s): Created by John Esmonde and Bob Larbey; theme music by Sam Fonteyn.

Main regular cast: Deryck Guyler (Mr Norman Potter), Noel Howlett (Mr Maurice Cromwell), Joan Sanderson (Miss Doris Ewell), Richard Davies (Mr Price), Erik Chitty (Mr Smith).

Holding / Source

25.12.1976   **1971 Film**   C3 / C3
A London Weekend International Productions / Leslie Grade production for London Weekend International. Duration: 100 minutes.
Music by Mike Vickers and Cilla Black; executive producers Leslie Grade and Richard Bates; produced and directed by Andrew Mitchell.
With John Alderton (Bernard Hedges), Peter Cleall (Eric Duffy), Liz Gebhardt (Maureen Bullock), David Barry (Frankie Abbott), Malcolm McFee (Peter Craven), Peter Denyer (Dennis Dunstable), Carol Hawkins (Sharon Eversleigh), Jill Kerman (Penny Wheeler), Barbara Mitchell (Mrs Abbott), Brinsley Forde (Wesley), Peter Bayliss (Mr Dunstable), Patsy Rowlands, Norman Bird, Jack Smethurst, Eve Pearce, Daphne Heard, Todd Carty, Aziz Resham, Nicky Locise, Brenda Cowling, Richard Everett, Hayden Evans, Frederick Beauman, Graham Angell, Gregory Scott, Jenny Irvine, George Georgiou.
The film introduced Bernard Hedges to his future wife, Penny.

PLEASE SIR! (continued)

SERIES 3

Main regular credit(s): Written by John Esmonde and Bob Larbey; music by Sam Fonteyn; produced by Mark Stuart.

Main regular cast: With John Alderton (Bernard Hedges), Peter Cleall (Eric Duffy), Penny Spencer (Sharon Eversleigh), Jill Kerman (Penny Wheeler), Erik Chitty (Mr Smith), Liz Gebhardt (Maureen Bullock), David Barry (Frankie Abbott), Malcolm McFee (Peter Craven), Peter Denyer (Dennis Dunstable).

		Production No	Holding / Source
13.12.1970	**Peace In Our Time**	9L/00593	DB / 62

Directed by Mark Stuart.
With David Howe.

27.12.1970	**And Everyone Came Too**	9L/00722	DB / 62

Duration: 26 minutes.
Directed by Mark Stuart.

With Bert Palmer, Lindsay Campbell, Susan Richards, Jeffrey Gardiner.

See also: THE FENN STREET GANG

PLUM'S PLOTS AND PLANS

A BBC Manchester production for BBC 1. Transmission details are for BBC 1. Duration: 25 minutes.

Main regular credit(s): Written by Peter Robinson; based on characters created by Kay King; designed by Paul Montague; executive producer Anna Home; directed by Jeremy Swan.

Main regular cast: Arthur Howard (Cornelius Plum), Aubrey Woods (Major Huffin), William Hootkins (Doctor Pretzel).

		Holding / Source
23.12.1977	**In Search Of Santa**	2"|n / 2"

With Suzanne Tan, Pik Sen Lim.

POBOL Y CYM

A BBC Wales production for BBC Wales/S4C. Transmission details are for BBC 1 Wales/S4C. Duration varies - see below for details.

Main regular credit(s): Created by William Gwyn; music by Endaf Emlyn.

SERIES 1

A BBC Wales production. Transmission details are for BBC 1 Wales. Duration: 30 minutes.

Main regular credit(s): Produced by Myrfen Owen, Pennant Roberts and Gwyn Hughes Jones.

		Holding / Source
24.12.1974	**Episode 11**	B / 2"

POEMS AND PINTS

A BBC production for BBC 2. Transmission details are for BBC 2. Usual duration: 14 minutes.

	Holding / Source
21.12.1972	DB-D3 / 2"
22.12.1972	DB-D3 / 2"

	Holding / Source
25.12.1975	DB-D3 / 2"

Duration: 25 minutes.
Produced by Jack Williams; directed by Hywel Williams
With Max Boyce, Ryan Davies, Mari Griffiths, Philip Madoc.

POET AND PHEASANT

A BBC Birmingham production for BBC. Transmission details are for BBC. Duration: 60 minutes.

Written by Willis Hall; play production by Peter Dews.

Frank Pettingell (Frank Higgins), Geoffrey Bayldon (Tom Walters), Marion Dawson (Maud Higgins), Michael Bates (Mr Migglewood), John Sharp (Herbert Jackson), Michael Robbins (Eddie Fossgill), Ann Saker (Sally Higgins), Frank Atkinson (Joe Thropjoy), Betty Alberge (Mrs Throttle), Philip Garston-Jones (Mr Cartwright).

	Holding / Source
22.12.1959	J /

POINTLESS CELEBRITIES

A Remarkable Television production for BBC. Transmission details are for BBC. Duration varies - see below for details.

Can you find a pointless answer?

Main regular credit(s): Presented by Alexander Armstrong.

Main regular performer(s): Richard Osman (Co-Host).

Transmission details are for BBC 2.

	Holding / Source
22.12.2010 **(pilot)**	HD/DB / HDC

Duration: 40 minutes.

Research Rachel Armitage, Oliver Breckon, Rose Dawson, Carl Earl-Ocran, Rebecca Greenwood, Chris Hale, Julia Hobbs, Alex Kessie, Liam Nugent, Benjamin Polya and Helen Price; script supervisor Maria Trevers; graphics by Saint; music by Marc Sylvan; designed by Dominic Tolfts; assistant producers Nazia Butt, Paul Hepplewhite and Terri Marzoli; production executive Hana Canter; executive producers Pam Cavannagh, Tom Blakeson and David Flynn; production manager Tara Ali; series producer Michelle Woods; produced by Tom Cuckson; directed by Nick Harris.

With Richard Osman, Deborah Meaden, Theo Paphitis, Bill Turnbull, Sian Williams, Ginny Buckley, Rav Wilding, Tim Lovejoy, Simon Rimmer.

This was actually a standard edition of the main POINTLESS series.

	Holding / Source
21.12.2013 **Christmas Special**	HD/DB / HDC

Duration: 50 minutes.

With The Chuckle Brothers, Keith Harris & Orville, Linda Lusardi, Sam Kane, Roy Wood, Father Christmas.

POIROT (RADIO)

A BBC production for BBC Radio 4. Transmission details are for BBC Radio 4. Duration varies - see below for details.

Main regular credit(s): Based on stories by Agatha Christie.

	Holding / Source
24.12.1986 **Hercule Poirot's Christmas**	DA /
24.12.1987 **The Murder Of Roger Ackroyd**	DA /

Murder On The Orient Express

Duration: 30 minutes.

Main regular credit(s): Adapted by Michael Bakewell; produced and directed by Enyd Williams.

Main regular cast: With Michael Haslam (Pianist), André Maranne (Monsieur Bouc).

	Holding / Source
28.12.1992	DA /

With Siân Phillips (Princess Dragomiroff), Sylvia Syms (Mrs Hubbard), Francesca Annis (Miss Debenham), Desmond Llewelyn (Masterman), Frank Windsor (Pierre Michel), David Thorpe (Count Andrenyi), Siriol Jenkins (Countess Andrenyi), Peter Polycarpou (Doctor Constantine), Frank Coda (Foscarelli), Kate Binchy (Miss Ohlsson), James Telfer (MacQueen), John Church (Hardman), Stephen Hodson (Colonel Arbuthnot), Joss Ackland, Kevork Malikyan, Vic Tablian.

29.12.1992   DA /

With James Telfer (MacQueen), Peter Polycarpou (Doctor Constantine), Frank Windsor (Pierre Michel), Desmond Llewelyn (Masterman), Sylvia Syms (Mrs Hubbard).

30.12.1992   DA /

With Kate Binchy (Miss Ohlsson), Frank Windsor (Pierre Michel), Siân Phillips (Princess Dragomiroff), David Thorpe (Count Andrenyi), Siriol Jenkins (Countess Andrenyi), Stephen Hodson (Colonel Arbuthnot), John Church (Hardman).

31.12.1992   DA /

With Peter Polycarpou (Doctor Constantine), Frank Coda (Foscarelli), Francesca Annis (Miss Debenham), Sylvia Syms (Mrs Hubbard), David Thorpe (Count Andrenyi), Siriol Jenkins (Countess Andrenyi), Kate Binchy (Miss Ohlsson), Linda Polan.

01.01.1993   DA /

With Siriol Jenkins (Countess Andrenyi), David Thorpe (Count Andrenyi), Peter Polycarpou (Doctor Constantine), Siân Phillips (Princess Dragomiroff), Stephen Hodson (Colonel Arbuthnot), Francesca Annis (Miss Debenham), Frank Coda (Foscarelli), Kate Binchy (Miss Ohlsson), Desmond Llewelyn (Masterman), Frank Windsor (Pierre Michel), John Church (Hardman), Sylvia Syms (Mrs Hubbard), James Telfer (MacQueen), Linda Polan.

Murder In Mesopotamia

	Holding / Source
26.12.1994	DA /
27.12.1994	DA /
28.12.1994	DA /
29.12.1994	DA /
30.12.1994	DA /

	Holding / Source
24.12.2004 **The Adventure Of The Christmas Pudding**	DA /

POP GOES NEW YEAR

A Granada production. Transmission details are for the Central region. Duration: 44 minutes.

Tracey Ullman and Boy George with Culture Club are two of the stars in Pop Goes New Year, second in the explosive pop music series made by Granada Television of England.

Culture Club, whose hit single Karma Chameleon won them the prestigious Grammy Award from the National Academy of Arts and Sciences in the USA, sing two numbers from their hit album Colours: Mr Man and Victims - their most recent single realised at the time of recording Pop Goes New Year.

Tracey Ullman flew to Manchester from London, where she was appearing on stage at the Royal Court Theatre, specially to record the programme. She sings Shattered, from her album You Broke My Heart In 17 Places.

Main regular credit(s): Designed by Paul Danson; produced by Stephen Leahy; directed by David Liddiment.
Main regular performer(s): Culture Club, Nick Heyward, Eurythmics, Tracey Ullman, Heaven 17, The Style Council, Limahl, Rick Springfield.

	Production No	Holding / Source
31.12.1983	P1252	1" / 1"
29.12.1984 **Re-edit**	P1252	1" / 1"

Duration: 25 minutes.

POP QUEST

A Yorkshire Television production. Transmission details are for the ATV midlands region. Duration: 25 minutes.

SERIES 3

Main regular credit(s): Designed by Gordon Livesey; produced and directed by Ian Bolt.
Main regular performer(s): With Mike Read (Presenter), Megg Nicol (Presenter).

	Holding / Source
##.##.#### **Christmas Special**	NR / 2"

Originally scheduled for 27.12.1978.
With Sally James (Co-Host), Les Gray, Tim Rice, Jonathan King, Paul Gambaccini, Graham Dene, Chris Hill, Phil Easton, Jimmy Pursey.
Planned special that was never made because YTV were on strike Christmas 1978.

POP QUIZ

A BBC production for BBC 1. Transmission details are for BBC 1.

Main regular credit(s): Theme music by Howard Massey.
Main regular performer(s): Mike Read (Presenter).

SERIES 1
Duration: 30 minutes.
Main regular credit(s): Designed by Roger Cann; assistant producer Jill Sinclair; produced by Frances Whitaker; directed by John Burrowes.

	Holding / Source
29.12.1981	DB / 2"

With David Grant, Rick Parfitt, Cliff Richard, Barry Gibb, Midge Ure, Paula Yates.

SERIES 2
Duration: 30 minutes.
Main regular credit(s): Designed by Ian Rawnsley; assistant producers Jill Sinclair and Hilary Briegel; produced by Frances Whitaker; directed by Phil Chilvers [credited as Philip Chilvers].

	Holding / Source
28.12.1982	DB / 2"

With David Essex, Mari Wilson, Leo Sayer, Hank Marvin, Captain Sensible, John Taylor.

SERIES 3
Duration: 30 minutes.
Main regular credit(s): Designed by George Kyriakides; assistant producer Jill Sinclair; produced by Frances Whitaker; directed by Phil Chilvers [credited as Philip Chilvers].

	Holding / Source
24.12.1983	DB / 2"

With Roger Taylor, Limahl, Midge Ure, Dave Edmunds, Mari Wilson, Leee John.

SERIES 4
Duration: 30 minutes.
Main regular credit(s): Designed by Pia Graham; assistant producer John Wooler; executive producer Michael Appleton; produced by Jon Plowman; directed by Phil Chilvers [credited as Philip Chilvers].

	Holding / Source
24.12.1984	DB / 1"

With Noddy Holder, Toyah, Meat Loaf, Roger Taylor, Nasher, Green.

28.12.1984	DB / 1"

With Noddy Holder, Meat Loaf, Toyah, Roger Taylor, Nasher, Green.

PORRIDGE

A BBC production for BBC 1. Transmission details are for BBC 1. Duration varies - see below for details.

Main regular credit(s): Written by Dick Clement and Ian La Frenais; music by Max Harris; produced and directed by Sydney Lotterby.

Main regular cast: Ronnie Barker (Norman Stanley Wintson Fletcher), Richard Beckinsale (Lenny Godber (except pilot)), Fulton Mackay (Mr Mackay), Brian Wilde (Mr Henry Barrowclough).

SERIES 2

		Holding / Source
24.12.1975 **No Way Out**		DB-D3 / 2"

Duration: 41 minutes.
Designed by Tim Gleeson.

With Peter Vaughan (Harry Grout), Graham Crowden, Carol Hawkins, Sam Kelly (Warren), Christopher Biggins (Lukewarm), Elisabeth Day.

| 24.12.1976 **The Desperate Hours** | | DB-D3 / 2" |

Duration: 44 minutes.
Designed by Tim Gleeson.

With Dudley Sutton, Sam Kelly (Warren), Tony Osoba (McLaren), Ken Wynne, Michael Redfern, Michael Barrington (Governor), Jane Wenham.

POSH AND BECK'S BIG IMPRESSION

A BBC production for BBC 1. Transmission details are for BBC 1. Duration: 45 minutes.

Produced by Alison MacPhail; directed by Tony Dow.

Alistair McGowan (Becks), Ronni Ancona (Posh), Damian Lewis.

	Holding / Source
25.12.2003	DB / DBSW

POSTMAN PAT

A BBC production for BBC 1. Transmission details are for BBC 1. Duration: 20 minutes.

Main regular credit(s): Written by John Cunliffe; theme music by Bryan Daly and Ken Barrie; produced and directed by Ivor Wood.

SERIES 3

Main regular cast: With Ken Barrie (Narrator).

	Holding / Source
25.12.1991 **Postman Pat Takes The Bus**	DB-D3 / C1

SERIES 4

Transmission details are for CBBC.

	Holding / Source
24.12.2004 **Postman Pat's Magic Christmas**	DB / DB

SERIES 6

Transmission details are for CBBC.

	Holding / Source
24.12.2006 **Postman Pat's Christmas Eve**	DB / DB

PRINCE OF PEACE

A Tyne Tees Television production. Transmission details are for the Anglia region. Duration: 25 minutes.

Earlier this year the Sinfonia Chorus was formed to sing with the Northern Sinfonia Orchestra. The Chorus, of 40 voices, is made up of people from all walks of life and from all parts of North-East England. Tonight the Chorus sing a programme of traditional carols under chorus-master Alan Fearon. Bible readings are given by Maxwell Deas.

Designed by Eric Briers; executive producer Maxwell Deas; produced and directed by Lewis Williams.

The Sinfonia Chorus.

	Holding / Source
23.12.1973	

THE PRINCE'S TRUST GALA CONCERT

A BBC production for BBC 1. Transmission details are for BBC 1. Duration: 88 minutes.

Recorded earlier this month at the London Arena in Docklands, and is hosted from the top of London's Telecom Tower.

Produced by Chris Cowey; directed by Gavin Taylor.

Mark Goodier (Host), Jonathan Ross (Host), Richard Jobson (Host), Toby Anstis (Host), Cliff Richard, Kylie Minogue, Helen Lederer, Paul Young, Phil Collins, Vic Reeves, Bob Mortimer, Tracey Ullman, Graham Fellows, Meat Loaf, Dave Stewart, Luther Vandross, Joe Cocker, Andrew Roachford, Tommy Cockles, Sophie Hawkins.

	Holding / Source
26.12.1994	DB / D3S

THE PRINCESS AND THE PEA

Alternative/Working Title(s): THE REAL PRINCESS

A BBC production. Transmission details are for BBC. Duration: 50 minutes.

Adapted by E. J. Bell; based on a story by Hans Andersen; lyrics by E. J. Bell; music by Lawrence Leonard; play production by Kevin Sheldon.

Richard Vernon (The King), Edith Macarthur (The Queen), Jonathan Tait (The Prince), Aubrey Woods (The Lord Chamberlain), Karal Gardner (Miranda, The Lord Chamberlain's Daughter), Blake Butler (The Butler), Edgar Driver (The Town Crier), Julie Webb (The False Princess), Samantha Eggar (The Real Princess), Acker Bilk (Minstrel), François Landry, Valerie Bell, Linda Gardner.

	Holding / Source
26.12.1961	R1 /

PRINT EARLY FOR CHRISTMAS

A BBC production. Transmission details are for BBC. Duration: 9 minutes.

	Holding / Source
18.12.1950 [Newsreel]	DB / B1

No on-screen credits.

PRIVATE EYE TV

A BBC production for BBC 2. Transmission details are for BBC 2. Duration: 51 minutes.

Compiled by Barry Took; music by Ken Jones; designed by Peter Brachacki; produced and directed by Dennis Main Wilson.

John Bird, Eleanor Bron, Spike Milligan, William Rushton, John Wells, Christopher Booker, Barry Fantoni, Paul Foot, Richard Ingrams.

	Holding / Source
28.12.1971	DB-D3 / 2"

THE PRIVATE LIVES

A BBC production for BBC 1. Transmission details are for BBC 1. Duration: 30 minutes.

	Holding / Source
24.12.1969 The Robin	DB / C1

A PRIZE PERFORMANCE

A BBC Manchester production for BBC 2. Transmission details are for BBC 2. Duration: 55 minutes.

When Dame Hilda Bracket is invited as guest speaker to The Cheltenham Ladies' College Speech Day, Dr Hinge assumes it is because she is a distinguished 'old girl'. However, on closer
inspection, the history of Hilda's schooldays seems to elude the inquisitive doctor.

Written by Gyles Brandreth; designed by Paul Montague; produced and directed by Mike Stephens.

Patrick Fyffe (Doctor Evadne Hinge), George Logan (Dame Hilda Bracket), Myrtle Devenish, Leslie Fry, Dennis Jennings.

	Holding / Source
25.12.1985	DB / 1"

PROMOTED TO GLORY

A Thames Television production for ITV 1. Transmission details are for the Central region. Duration: 100 minutes.

Written by Rob Heyland; executive producer Chris Parr; produced by Kenith Trodd; directed by Richard Spence.

Ken Stott (Mike), Lesley Manville (Captain Annie Walsh), Kevin Whately (Major Nigel Hurst), Adrian Scarborough (Arnold), Sally Hawkins (Lisa), Joe Renton (Colin), Tanya Moodie (Olem), Jacqueline Tong (Bizzy), James Floet (Michael Prendergast), Stephanie Turner (Brigadier Angela Octraras), Souad Faress (Psychiatrist), Tanya Wiles (Mike'S Mother), James Hayes (Phonetician), Charlie Eva (Young Mike).

	Holding / Source
21.12.2003	DB / V1SW

A PROPER PANTOMIME

A Granada production. Transmission details are for the Granada region. Duration: 39 minutes.

Is Simon as simple as he appears? Does the Giant really prefer to eat Jack rather than turkey? Is the Prince as charming all the year round? Does Cinderella really take size fours? These questions may be answered during this light-hearted romp through panto-land by Duggie Brown, his parrot, and an all-star cast. Then again they may not be! But there'll still be plenty of music, magic and mirth to brighten your Christmas.

Written by Duggie Brown and Jimmy Marshall; music directed by Derek Hilton; designed by Roy Graham; produced by John Hamp; directed by Peter Walker.

Duggie Brown (Duggie), Max Wall (Chinese Policeman), Tsai Chin (Aladdin), Frank Carson (Long John Silver / Captain Hook), Zoe Spinks (Pretty Witch), Freddie Davis (Prince Charming), Isabel Duncan (Principal Boy), Danny Ross (Ugly Brother), Peter Warren (Ugly Brother 2), Bob Todd (Baron Hardup), Lynne Carol (Ugly Witch), Bruce Watt (Jack), Jackie Garrity (Jill), Russ Abbot (Abanazer), The Black Abbots (Disco Group), Liz Fraser (Olive).

	Production No	Holding / Source
29.12.1972	P761	DB / 2"

PRUDENCE KITTEN

A BBC production. Transmission details are for BBC.

	Holding / Source
23.12.1960	R1 /

PUB QUIZ

A BBC Wales production. Transmission details are for BBC Wales.

	Holding / Source
24.12.2004 **Pub Quiz Christmas Special**	DB /

PUBLIC EYE

An ABC/Thames production. Duration: 50 minutes.

Main regular credit(s): Created by Anthony Marriott and Roger Marshall; theme music by Robert Earley.

Main regular cast: Alfred Burke (Frank Marker).

SERIES 6

A Thames Television production. Transmission details are for the ATV midlands region.

Main regular credit(s): Story editor Michael Chapman; produced by Robert Love.

	VT Number	Holding / Source
20.12.1972 **Horse And Carriage**	6550	D3 / 2"

Written by Richard Harris; designed by Graham Guest; directed by Bill Bain.

With Pat Heywood, Tony Melody, Michael Bates, Anne Carroll, John Normington, Penny Spencer, John Flint, Roy Barraclough, Freddie Foot, Oscar Peck, Tony Selby.

PUDDLE LANE

A Yorkshire Television production. Transmission details are for the Central region. Duration: 18 minutes.

SERIES 3

Main regular credit(s): Executive producer Chris Jelley; produced by Michael Harris; directed by John Allen.

Main regular cast: With Neil Innes (The Magician), Kate Lee (Aunty Flo), Richard Robinson (Puppeteer).

	VT Number	Holding / Source
21.12.1987 **Christmas Special**	E110/09	1" / 1"

Written by Sheila McCullagh.

PUNCHLINES

An LWT production. Transmission details are for the ATV/Central region. Duration varies - see below for details.

Main regular performer(s): Lennie Bennett (Host).

SERIES 3

Transmission details are for the Central region. Duration: 25 minutes.

Main regular credit(s): Additional material by Garry Chambers; associate producer Dennis Berson; executive producer Alan Boyd; produced by Keith Stewart; directed by Noel D. Greene.

	Holding / Source
24.12.1982	D2 / 1"

SERIES 4

Transmission details are for the Central region. Duration: 28 minutes.

Main regular credit(s): Designed by Steve Groves; executive producer Alan Boyd; produced and directed by Noel D. Greene.

	Holding / Source
24.12.1983	D2 / 1"

With Christopher Biggins, Faith Brown, Bob Carolgees, Diana Dors, Pearly Gates, David Hamilton, Barbara Kelly, Mike Reid, Wincey Willis, Gary Wilmot.

SERIES 5

Transmission details are for the Central region.

Main regular credit(s): Written by Howard Imber; additional material by Garry Chambers; executive producer Alan Boyd; produced by Noel D. Greene; directed by Vic Finch.

	Holding / Source
22.12.1984 **Christmas Show**	D2 / 1"

Duration: 30 minutes.

Celebrities disguised as Santas play in tonight's Christmas game.

With Patti Boulaye, Freddie Davies, Faith Brown, Jayne Irving, Dave Lee Travis, Kenny Lynch, Bernard Manning, Mike Reid, Isla St. Clair, June Whitfield.

PUSS IN BOOTS

A BBC production. Transmission details are for BBC. Duration: 90 minutes.

Adapted by John Law; based on a book by Emile Littler; lyrics by Hastings Mann; music by Hastings Mann, Lance Mulcahy and John Law; play production by Harry Carlisle.

David Nixon (King), Reg Varney (Jolly, The Jester), Tommy Fields (Queen), John McHugh (Crispin, The Shoemaker), George Truzzi (Bubble), Lauri Lupino Lane (Squeak), David Davenport (Blackheart, The Wizard), Patricia Cree (Puss), Sylvia Norman (Colin), Bunty Turner (Princess), Judy Whalley (Fairy), Tommy Shaw (Principal Dancer), The Tommy Shaw Dancers, Woolf Phillips and his Orchestra.

	Holding / Source
25.12.1962	J /

PUZZLE PARTY

A Tyne Tees Television production. Transmission details are for the ATV midlands region. Duration: 25 minutes.
Main regular credit(s):　　Graphics by Ross Breckon; designed by Tim Trout; produced by Anne Wood; directed by Lewis Williams.
Main regular performer(s):　Gyles Brandreth (Presenter).

Holding / Source

27.12.1977　**Christmas Show**　　　　　　　　　　　　　　　　　　　　　　　　　　　　　　　　　　　DB / 2"
With Bonnie Langford.
Recorded on 12.10.1977.

THE PYRAMID GAME

An LWT production. made in association with Bob Stewart Productions / Philip Hindin. Transmission details are for the ATV midlands region. Duration: 25 minutes.
Main regular performer(s):　Steve Jones (Presenter).

SERIES 2
Main regular credit(s):　　Designed by Bill McPherson; associate producer Garry Chambers; produced by Alasdair MacMillan; directed by David MacMahon.

Holding / Source

26.12.1982　　　D2 / 2"
With Wendy Richard, Harry Fowler.

QI

A talkbackThames production for BBC. Transmission details are for BBC Various. Duration: 29 minutes.

Main regular credit(s): Created by John Lloyd; theme music by Howard Goodall; production designer Jonathan Paul Green.

Main regular performer(s): Stephen Fry (QI Master), Alan Davies.

SERIES A

Transmission details are for BBC 4.

Main regular credit(s): Script supervisor Alice Osborne; associate producers Alf Lawrie and John Mitchinson; production executive Beatrice Gay; executive producers Phil Clark and Phil Clarke; production manager Sarah Chaloner; produced by John Lloyd.

	Holding / Source
—.—.—— "Advent"	DB / DBSW

Alternative transmissions: BBC 2: 23.12.2003.
With Phill Jupitus, Sean Lock, John Sessions.

SERIES D

Transmission details are for BBC 4.

Main regular credit(s): Script supervisor Alison McGregor; associate producers Justin Pollard and Helen Younger; executive producers Lorraine Heggessey and Katie Taylor; head of production Beatrice Gay; production manager Sarah Chaloner; produced by John Lloyd.

	Holding / Source
15.12.2006 **December**	DB / DBSW

With Jo Brand, Rich Hall, Dara Ó Briain.

SERIES I

Transmission details are for BBC 2.

Main regular credit(s): Designed by Jonathan Paul Green; executive producers David Morley and Ruby Kuraishe; produced by Piers Fletcher and John Lloyd; directed by Ian Lorimer.

Main regular performer(s): With Alan Davies (Regular Panellist).

	Holding / Source
29.12.2011 **Ice**	HD/DB / HDC

With Ross Noble, Sean Lock, Brian Blessed.

Longer editions, entitled QI XL, were shown on BBC 2, usually the day after the original broadcast of the standard edition.

	Holding / Source
24.12.2013 **Kris Kringle**	HD/DB / HDC

Duration: 45 minutes.

Script editor James Harkin; designed by Jonathan Paul Green; executive producer Ruby Kuraishe; series producer John Lloyd; produced by Piers Fletcher; directed by Ian Lorimer.

With Alan Davies (Panellist), Jo Brand, Phill Jupitus, Brendan O'Carroll.

The XL edition was broadcast before the standard edition.

Titles in quotation marks are official but appear to have been retro-fitted. Titles without were billed on original transmission. None of them appear on-screen.

QUEEN OF HEARTS

An ATV production. Transmission details are for the ATV midlands region. Duration: 75 minutes.

The Queen of Hearts, she made some tarts All on a Summer's Day. The Knave of Hearts, he stole those tarts... And this being pantomime, you can be sure that the Queen sets out with plenty of guile and custard pies to stop him getting quite away. Changing from one sumptuous costume to another--12 in all and each more gorgeous than the last- -Danny La Rue glitters his way through this lively romp as the Queen of Hearts, while Peggy Mount plays the villainous Queen of Spades.

Written by Bryan Blackburn; music directed by Derek New; choreography by Tommy Shaw; designed by Berkley Sutcliffe; produced and directed by Alan Tarrant.

Danny La Rue (Queen of Hearts), Peggy Mount (Queen of Spades), Mike Goddard (Knave of Hearts), Alan Haynes (Queen Mother), Colette Gleeson (Princess Miranda), David Ellen (Mr Mix, Major Domo), Tony Adams (Prince Damian), Jenny Layland (Fairy Good Heart), Terry Hall and Lenny The Lion, The Tommy Shaw Dancers, The Derek New Singers, Vera Legg School of Dancing.

	Holding / Source
25.12.1973	J / 2"

THE QUEEN'S CHRISTMAS MESSAGE

A BBC production for BBC 1. Transmission details are for BBC 1. Duration varies - see below for details.

Main regular cast: Queen Elizabeth II.

	Holding / Source
25.12.1957	R3 /

In previous years these were radio only, since 1932.

25.12.1958	R3 /
25.12.1959	DA /

No TV message in 1959, just a sound programme, though it was also broadcast on TV.

25.12.1960	R3 /
25.12.1961	R3 /
25.12.1962	R3 /
25.12.1963	DA /

No TV message in 1963, just a sound programme, though it was also broadcast on TV.

THE QUEEN'S CHRISTMAS MESSAGE (continued)

Date	Format
25.12.1964	R3 /
25.12.1965	R3 /
25.12.1966	R3 /
25.12.1967	DB / 2"
25.12.1968	DB / 2"
25.12.1970	DB / 2"
25.12.1971	DB / 2"
25.12.1972	DB / 2"
25.12.1973	DB / 2"

Produced and directed by Richard Cawston.

Date	Format
25.12.1974	DB / 2"
25.12.1975	DB / 2"
25.12.1976	DB / 2"
25.12.1977	DB / 2"
25.12.1978	DB / 2"

Duration: 20 minutes.
Produced and directed by Richard Cawston.

Date	Format
25.12.1979	DB / 2"
25.12.1980	DB / 2"
25.12.1981	DB / 2"
25.12.1982	DB / 2"
25.12.1983	DB / 1"
25.12.1984	DB / 1"
25.12.1985	DB / 1"
25.12.1986	DB / 1"
25.12.1987	DB / 1"
25.12.1988	DB / 1"
25.12.1989	DB / 1"
25.12.1990	DB / 1"
25.12.1991	DB / 1"
25.12.1992	DB-D3 / D3S
25.12.1993	DB-D3 / D3S
25.12.1994	DB-D3 / D3S

No on-screen credits.

Date	Format
25.12.1995	DB-D3 / D3S
25.12.1996	DB-D3 / D3S
25.12.1997	DB-D3 / D3S
25.12.1998	DB-D3 / D3S
25.12.1999	DB / DBS
25.12.2000	DB / DBS
25.12.2001	DB / DBS
25.12.2002	DB / DBSW
25.12.2003	DB / DBSW
25.12.2004	DB / DBSW
25.12.2005	DB / DBSW
25.12.2006	DB / DBSW
25.12.2007	DB / DBSW
25.12.2008	DB / DBSW
25.12.2009	DB / DBSW
25.12.2010	HD/DB / HDC
25.12.2011	HD/DB / HDC

Duration: 10 minutes.

Date	Format
25.12.2012	HD/DB / HDC
25.12.2013	HD/DB / HDC

No broadcast in 1969 – "Royal Family" documentary instead.

A QUESTION OF POP

A BBC production for BBC 1. Transmission details are for BBC 1.
Main regular performer(s):   Jamie Theakston (Host).
SERIES 2
Main regular credit(s):   Produced by Pam Cavannagh; directed by Joanna Ball.
Main regular performer(s):   With Noddy Holder (Team Captain).

	Holding / Source
28.12.2000	DB / DBSW

Duration: 28 minutes.
With Natalie Cassidy, Chris Moyles, Patrick Kielty, Gail Porter, Brett Adams, Carol Decker.

A QUESTION OF SPORT

A BBC Manchester production for BBC 1. Transmission details are for BBC 1. Duration: 30 minutes.
SERIES 2
Main regular performer(s):   With David Vine (Presenter), Henry Cooper (Team Captain), Cliff Morgan (Team Captain).

	Holding / Source
24.12.1970	J / 2"

	Holding / Source
29.12.1983	DB-D3 / 1"

With Henry Cooper (Team Captain), Cliff Morgan (Team Captain), Max Boyce, Georgie Fame, Lennie Bennett, Anita Harris.

SERIES 15

	Holding / Source
31.12.1984 **New Year Special**	DB-D3 / 1"

SERIES 16

	Holding / Source
24.12.1985	DB-D3 / 1"

SERIES 19

	Holding / Source
26.12.1988	DB-D3 / 1"

SERIES 27
Main regular credit(s):   Executive producer Mike Adley.
Main regular performer(s):   With David Coleman (Questionmaster), Ally McCoist (Captain), John Parrott (Captain).

	Holding / Source
24.12.1996 **Christmas Special**	DB / D3S

SERIES 31
Main regular credit(s):   Produced by Carl Doran.

	Holding / Source
29.12.2000 **Christmas Special**	DB / DBS

SERIES 33

	Holding / Source
27.12.2002 **Christmas Special**	DB / DBS

SERIES 34

	Holding / Source
29.12.2003 **End Of Year Special**	DB / DBS

QUICK ON THE DRAW

A Thames Television production. Transmission details are for the ATV midlands region. Duration: 25 minutes.
Main regular credit(s):   Devised by Denis Gifford.
Main regular credit(s):   Produced by David Clark; directed by Daphne Shadwell.
Main regular performer(s):   With Bob Monkhouse (Host).

	Holding / Source
27.12.1974 **Quick On The Christmas Draw**	DB / 2"

In this special Christmas edition of the popular cartoon panel game, Bob Monkhouse keeps a line on a panel of rousing revellers. Keep with it to the end — there's a surprise guest who'll also be 'Quick on the Christmas Draw'.
With Leslie Crowther, William Rushton, Bill Tidy, Bob Godfrey*.

All editions featured three cartoonists who take part in all of the rounds. Most shows also featured a surprise guest from the world of cartooning who the celebrities had to identify. This latter guest was not billed in the TV Times and so we are unable to list him/her unless we have access to other sources for this information. Where known, we list the surprise guest last in the programme's cast list.

QUIZ OF THE YEAR

A BBC production for BBC 1. Transmission details are for BBC 1. Duration: 35 minutes.

Produced by Anthony Smith; directed by Peter Chafer.

Ned Sherrin (Quizmaster), Miriam Margolyes (Sketch Actor), Malcolm Ingram (Sketch Actor), Richard Ingrams, William Rushton, John Wells, Linda Blandford, Mary Kenny, Neil Shand.

Holding / Source

25.12.1968　　J /

QUIZ OF THE YEAR

A BBC production for BBC 1. Transmission details are for BBC 1. Duration: 30 minutes.

Produced by Michael Bukht and Anthony Smith; directed by Anthony Smith and Michael Bukht.

Ned Sherrin (Quizmaster), Douglas Fisher (Special Contributor), Richard Ingrams, William Rushton, John Wells, Malcolm Muggeridge, Patrick Campbell, Bernard Levin.

Holding / Source

27.12.1969　　J / 2"

RAB C. NESBITT

A BBC Scotland production for BBC 2. Transmission details are for BBC 2. Duration varies - see below for details.
Main regular credit(s):   Written by Ian Pattison; produced and directed by Colin Gilbert.
Main regular cast: Gregor Fisher (Rab C. Nesbitt).

	Holding / Source
31.12.1989 **Rab C. Nesbitt's Seasonal Greet**	DB / 1"

Duration: 45 minutes.
Alternative transmissions: BBC 1 Scotland: 21.12.1988.
Music by David McNiven.
With Elaine C. Smith (Mary Nesbitt), Tony Roper (Jamesie Cotter), Andrew Fairlie (Gash), Brian Pettifer (Andra), Eric Cullen, Andy Gray, Alex Norton, Charlie Sim, Mary Riggans, Gerard Kelly, Iain Cuthbertson, Rikki Fulton, Jonathan Watson, David McNiven, Gerry Sadowitz, Robert McGowan, Peter Capaldi, Viv Lumsden, Andy Cameron, Russell Hunter, Susan Gilmore, Elaine Collins.

SERIES 3
Main regular credit(s):   Music by David McNiven; titles by Sandi Anderson; designed by Alan Wright; production managers David Mack and Charles Marks.
Main regular cast: With Elaine C. Smith (Mary Nesbitt), Tony Roper (Jamesie Cotter).

	Holding / Source
31.12.1992 **Home**	DB-D3 / D3S

Duration: 50 minutes.
With Barbara Rafferty (Ella Cotter), Iain McColl (Dodie), Brian Pettifer (Andra), Sean Scanlan, Sara Corper, Roger Sloman, Lilla Scott, Tom Smith, Bill Barclay, Garry Stewart, Sandra McNeeley, Ivan Heng, Anne Christie, Roddie Patrizio.
BBC 1 in Wales, BBC 2 in England.

SERIES 4
Main regular credit(s):   Music by David McNiven; titles by Sandi Anderson; designed by Alan Wright; production manager Charles Marks.

	Holding / Source
29.12.1994 **More**	DB-D3 / D3S

Duration: 50 minutes.

	Holding / Source
23.12.2008 **Clean**	DB / DBSW

A the Comedy Unit production. Duration: 44 minutes.
Script supervisor Gillian Ewing; theme music by David McNiven; designed by Graham Rose; associate producer Ian Pattison; production executive Susan Haynes; executive producer Rab Christie; production manager Elaine Campbell.
With Elaine C. Smith (Mary Nesbitt), Tony Roper (Jamesie Cotter), Andrew Fairlie (Gash Nesbitt), Brian Pettifer (Andra), Barbara Rafferty (Ella Cotter), Gary Lewis, Kathleen McDermott, Julie Austin, Marj Hogarth, Susan Calman, George Drennan, Jordan Young, Debbie Welsh, Susheel Kumar, Artair Donald, Raymond Mearns.

	Holding / Source
02.01.2014 **Rab In Hoodie**	HD/DB / HDC

A the Comedy Unit production. Duration: 45 minutes.
Times for Rab seem harder than ever, so he turns to a very English inspiration: Robin Hood. But Rab will be robbing from the rich to give to the scum!
Music by David McNiven; designed by Tom Sayer; executive producers Rab Christie and Kristian Smith.
With Elaine C. Smith (Mary Nesbitt), Tony Roper (Jamesie Cotter), Barbara Rafferty (Ella Cotter), Brian Pettifer (Andra), Anna Devitt (Peaches), Billy Mack (Chief Inspector Cromer), Jane McCarry (Sergeant Heenan), Sally Reid (Jeanette), Callum Cuthbertson (Gleason), Louise Poise (Scarlett Mack), Mark Prendergast (Building Society Manager), Helen Mackay (Siobhan), Fiona Wood (Jenny Gilmour), Ron Bain (Elderly Man), Lewis Macleod (Coach Passenger), James Kirk (Museum Attendant), Tom Urie (Minstrel).

RADIO TIMES TRAILS

A BBC production for BBC 1. Transmission details are for BBC 1.

	Holding / Source
19.12.1966	DB-R1 / 40
19.12.1976	DB / 2"
31.12.1980	DV / 2"
17.12.1989	DV / 1"

THE RAG TRADE

Produced for BBC/LWT by a variety of companies (see details below). Duration varies - see below for details.

By the start of the sixties, Ronnie Wolfe and Ronnie Chesney had been writing for BBC radio for a number of years and had several radio shows behind them. This was at a time when almost everybody working in radio was trying to get into television. The general consensus was that radio was becoming old hat; telly people were trendy and that's where the action was.

From their experiences working in factories the two Ronnies always felt there was a good television show to be made out of working in a factory. Ronald Chesney's family had also worked in the textile business and he also had a business share in a clothing factory, so together Wolfe & Chesney thrashed out an idea about a series with a factory background allied to the clothing and fashion industry. They finally settled on a small dressmaking factory.

The series became an instantaneous winner. Wolfe & Chesney think the show, featuring real working people in real working conditions, must have been something of a breakthrough. It is still fondly remembered, as many years later, an article in "The Listener" about "The Rag Trade" ventured that 'it was the funniest comedy of all time".

Full of confidence, the writers took the idea to one of the commercial TV companies – Associated Rediffusion. They thought it was good. Rediffusion didn't. Their reaction was "millions of people spend all day working in a factory; they want to come home, relax and forget it. They'll never switch on to watch a series about factory life." Then they remembered that Frank Muir and Denis Norden, the brilliant writing team that penned so many great sitcoms, had been appointed comedy advisors to the BBC, so Wolfe & Chesney made a quick trip down to the Television Centre at White City where they were based. Being successful writers, they were immediately able to realise the format's potential.. Happily, they both loved the idea; commissioned some scripts, and then the casting started.

Miriam Karlin played the part of the Shop Steward, Paddy. But why Paddy? Well, the script was first sent to Alfred Marks asking if he'd play the part of the Boss, and, as an added inducement to his saying Yes, the part of the Shop Steward was offered to Alfred's wife, Paddy O'Neill. They both turned it down. The script was then sent to Miriam, but the typist forgot to change the name. Miriam didn't query it; she thought it rather amusing that a nice Jewish actress should be named Paddy.

Peter Jones and Reg Varney were soon cast without too many problems. Peter was a fine actor and a known commodity, and perfect for the part of Mr. Fenner - indecisive, untrustworthy, and just slightly dishonest. Ronald Chesney had worked with Reg in variety theatre and knew his worth as an actor and a comic.

For the other smaller parts, the producer, Dennis Main Wilson, didn't hold auditions. He just booked actors who were successfully appearing in shows at that moment. There was Ann Beach who was appearing in Billy Liar; Esma Cannon from Sailor Beware; and Toni Palmer from Fings Ain't Wot They Used to Be. How did the producer manage to get these talented actresses into the show to play such small parts, with maybe only two or three lines? It was easy. He lied. He promised that each week one of them would have the entire show written around them. They would virtually be the star for that week. But of course, it never happened and in the second or third series, quite disheartened and disgruntled, they left.

For the first few episodes, Barbara was put in a low-cut blouse showing lots of cleavage, a very tight miniskirt, and her hair piled up in what was known as the beehive style. But Barbara wasn't happy; she complained to the writers, "Ron, I'm fed up with this outfit. It's like a uniform. Can't you fix it that I wear something different? Have my hair done another way?" Ronnie Wolfe said "Look, you're playing a comedy character and you don't have many lines. You want to be noticed? Stay with that one outfit throughout the series". Then he added, "Think of Chaplin. He always wore the same clothes - the bowler hat, the baggy trousers, the cane. This sort of uniform seems to work for comedy characters". Barbara thought for a minute, then said "O.K. Ron, you could be right. I'll stay with it. Tits, Bum and Beehive!" Barbara did stay with it, and that get-up became her trademark – helped her into films, and started her carrying on in many a 'Carry On'!

After three successful seasons for the BBC, Wolfe & Chesney moved on to write 'Meet the Wife' and 'On The Buses'. Interested in a remake, the BBC commissioned a new pilot in 1975 with Tony Robinson in the Reg Varney role as Anthony. The BBC decided against going further so LWT picked up the idea and did two popular seasons in 1977-78. Two seasons of the BBC original and all the LWT remake is available to watch again on commercial DVD.

Main regular credit(s): Written by Ronald Wolfe and Ronald Chesney.

Main regular cast: Peter Jones (Mr Fenner), Miriam Karlin (Paddy).

SERIES 4

An LWT production. Transmission details are for the ATV midlands region. Duration: 25 minutes.

Main regular credit(s): Theme music by Lynsey De Paul; designed by David Catley.

Main regular cast: With Christopher Beeny (Tony), Anna Karen (Olive), Gillian Taylforth (Lyn), Deddie Davies (Mabel), Lucita Lijertwood (Jojo), Diane Langton (Kathy).

	VT Number	Holding / Source
24.12.1977 **Christmas Rush**	99076	D2 / 2"

Fenner Fashions is in a festive flap on the last working day before Christmas. Paddy's doing Mr. Fenner's shopping and Mabel's getting the bird. Tony's attempts to get Lyn under the mistletoe go disastrously wrong when Mrs. Fenner appears on the scene.

Produced and directed by Stuart Allen.

With Rowena Cooper (Mrs Fenner).

RAGDOLLY ANNA

A Yorkshire Television production. Transmission details are for the Central region. Duration: 14 minutes.

Main regular cast: Pat Coombs (Narrator).

SERIES 1

	Holding / Source
##.##.#### **Christmas Tape**	B / 1"

SERIES 2

Main regular credit(s): Designed by Judith Lang; produced by Jane Taylor; directed by John Allen.

	Holding / Source
09.01.1986 **Ragdolly Anna's Christmas**	1" / 1"

THE RAGGED CHILD

A BBC production for BBC 2. Transmission details are for BBC 2. Duration: 125 minutes.

Introduced by H.R.H. Prince Edward; written by Jeremy James Taylor and Frank Whately; music directed by David Nield; music by David Nield; produced by Julia Matheson; directed for television by David Buckton; directed by Jeremy James Taylor and Frank Whately.

Jonny Lee Miller (Joe Cooper), Victoria Hayes (Annie Cooper), Charles Edwards (Earl Of Shaftesbury), Jason Denvir (John Giles), David Bliss (Leary), John Killoran (Patterer), Neil Rutherford (Sweeper), Scott Ransome (Rob Roy McGregor).

National Youth Music Theatre:

	Holding / Source
24.12.1988	DB / 1"

THE RAGGY DOLLS

A Yorkshire Television/Orchid Productions production for Yorkshire Television. Transmission details are for the Central region. Duration: 8 minutes.

Main regular credit(s): Based on books by Melvyn Jacobson; music by Neil Innes.
Main regular cast: Neil Innes (Voices).

SERIES 2
A Yorkshire Television production.

Main regular credit(s): Adapted by Joy Whitby and Neil Innes; animated by John Marsden; produced and directed by Joy Whitby.

	VT Number	Holding / Source
18.12.1986 **Christmas Dolls**	C020/11	C1 / C1

Animated by Roy Evans.

RAGTIME - LATE JOYS

A Westward Television production. Transmission details are for the ATV London region. Duration: 30 minutes.

Presented by The Player's Theatre, London.

Devised by Reginald Woolley; choreography by Buddy Bradley; designed by Guy Baskin; produced and directed by John Bartlett.

Julia Sutton, Lisa Shane, Roy Sone, John Griffin, Ed Graham, Harry Haythorne, Geoffrey Brawn, Ronnie Lanchbury.

	Holding / Source
26.12.1965	J /

RAINBOW

A Thames Television production. Transmission details are for the ATV midlands region. Usual duration: 15 minutes.

Main regular credit(s): Created by Pamela Lonsdale.

SERIES 1
Main regular credit(s): Produced by Pamela Lonsdale.
Main regular cast: With David Cook (David), John Leeson, Roy Skelton, Telltale.

	VT Number	Holding / Source
18.12.1972 **Christmas Music**	6601	D3 / 2"

Written by John Kershaw; directed by Darrol Blake.

19.12.1972 **Christmas Tree**	6600	D3 / 2"

Written by John Kershaw; directed by Darrol Blake.
With Gwen Watford.

20.12.1972 **Christmas Decorations**	6599	2"|n / 2"

Written by John Kershaw; directed by Darrol Blake.

21.12.1972 **Christmas Food**	6598	D3 / 2"

Written by John Kershaw; directed by Darrol Blake.
With Jumoke Debayo.

22.12.1972 **Christmas Post**	6602	D3 / 2"

Written by John Kershaw; music by Telltale; edited by John Kershaw; associate producer Ruth Boswell; film sequences directed by Julian Cooper; directed by Darrol Blake.

Puppets by Violet Philpott. "Sally & Jake" / "Curly & Straight" by Stop Frame Animations Limited.

SERIES 3
Main regular credit(s): Produced by Pamela Lonsdale.
Main regular cast: With Geoffrey Hayes (Geoffrey), Stanley Bates (Bungle), Roy Skelton (Puppet Voices).

	Holding / Source
18.12.1973 **Christmas Decorations**	D3 / 2"
21.12.1973 **Christmas Post**	D3 / 2"
24.12.1973 **Christmas Music**	D3 / 2"

Written by John Kershaw; directed by Darrol Blake and Alan Horrox.
With Charmian Dore, Julian Littman, Karl Johnson.

25.12.1973 **Christmas Games**	D3 / 2"

Written by John Kershaw; directed by Darrol Blake and Alan Horrox.
With Charmian Dore, Julian Littman, Karl Johnson.

26.12.1973 **Christmas Party**	D3 / 2"

Geoffrey, Bungle and their friends invite you to a Boxing Day party. Geoffrey makes some paper hats and everyone joins in with party songs and games.
Written by John Kershaw; directed by Darrol Blake and Alan Horrox.
With Charmian Dore, Julian Littman, Karl Johnson.

Animations by Mark Hall and Brian Cosgrove. "Sally & Jake" / "Curley & Straight" by Stop Frame Animations Limited.

RAINBOW (continued)

SERIES 6
Main regular credit(s): Produced by Ruth Boswell.
Main regular cast: With Geoffrey Hayes (Geoffrey), Stanley Bates (Bungle), Roy Skelton, Jane Tucker, Rod Burton, Matthew Corbett.

	VT Number	Holding / Source
22.12.1975 **Christmas Decorations**	11562	D3 / 2"

Directed by Daphne Shadwell and Dennis Kirkland.
With Gwen Watford.

23.12.1975 **Christmas Post**	11563	D3 / 2"

Directed by Daphne Shadwell and Dennis Kirkland.

24.12.1975 **Christmas Present Wrapping**	11564	D3 / 2"

Christmas Eve.
Directed by Daphne Shadwell and Dennis Kirkland.

25.12.1975 **Christmas Music**	11565	D3 / 2"

Directed by Daphne Shadwell and Dennis Kirkland.

26.12.1975 **Christmas Party**	11566	D3 / 2"

Directed by Daphne Shadwell and Dennis Kirkland.
With Ali Bongo.

SERIES 10
Main regular credit(s): Animated by Brian Cosgrove and Mark Hall; produced by Charles Warren.
Main regular cast: With Geoffrey Hayes, Stanley Bates, Jane Tucker, Rod Burton, Roger Walker, Roy Skelton, Valerie Heberden (Puppeteer), Ronnie Le Drew (Puppeteer), Geoffrey Hayes, Stanley Bates, Jane Tucker, Rod Burton, Roger Walker, Roy Skelton.

	Holding / Source
17.12.1979 **Rainbow Christmas Show**	D3 / 2"

Duration: 25 minutes.
Written by John Kershaw; directed by Audrey Starrett.

SERIES 11
Main regular credit(s): Music by Rod Burton, Jane Tucker and Freddy Marks; executive producer Charles Warren; produced by Joe Boyer.
Main regular cast: With Ronnie Le Drew (Puppeteer), John Thirtle (Puppeteer), Geoffrey Hayes, Stanley Bates, Jane Tucker, Rod Burton, Freddy Marks, Roy Skelton.

	Holding / Source
26.12.1980 **Rainbow Christmas Show**	D3 / 2"

In this special pantomime, Geoffrey plays a wizard who uses magic to banish Rod, Jane
and Freddy to the ice forest. Can Sir Bungle and the Good Fairies—George and Lollipop —rescue them, and save Zippy from the wizard, too?
Written by John Kershaw; directed by John Woods.

Lines and Shapes by Brian Cosgrove and Mark Hall.

RAISED BY WOLVES
A Big Talk Productions production for Channel 4. Transmission details are for Channel 4. Duration: 24 minutes.

Comedy set on a Wolverhampton council estate, following the fortunes of a single mother and her six children.

Written by Caitlin Moran and Caroline Moran; costume Kat Willis; make-up Juliet Jackson; edited by Nigel Williams; director of photography Laurie Rose; titles by Yianni Papanicolaou; assistant director Lee Trevor; art director Andrea Coathupe; production designer David Butterworth; post production supervisor Alistair Hopkins; executive producers Matthew Justice, Kenton Allen and Caroline Leddy; head of production Rhian Griffiths; production supervised by Benjamin Richards; line producer Samantha Milnes; produced by Caroline Norris; directed by Ian Fitzgibbon.

Philip Jackson (Grampy), Rebekah Staton (Della Garry), Helen Monks (Germaine Garry), Alexa Davies (Aretha Garry), Molly Risker (Yoko Garry), Kaine Zajaz (Lee Rind), Lucie Brown (Mariah Garry), Caden-Ellis Wall (Wyatt Garry), Violet Maple (Cher Garry), Daisy Maple (Cher Garry).

	Holding / Source
23.12.2013 (pilot)	HD/DB / HDC

RAZZAMATAZZ
A Tyne Tees Television production. Transmission details are for the Central region. Duration varies - see below for details.

	Holding / Source
01.01.1982 **New Year Special 1981**	1" / 2"

Duration: 20 minutes.
Produced by Malcolm Gerrie; directed by Gavin Taylor.

With Alastair Pirrie (Presenter), Lyn Spencer (Presenter), Abba, Shakin' Stevens, Bad Manners, Shock, Brendan Healey, Chris Gittins, Richard Burgess, John Walters, Alan Hilary.

SERIES 3
Duration: 20 minutes.
Main regular credit(s): Designed by Peter Bingeman; produced and directed by Royston Mayoh.
Main regular performer(s): With Alastair Pirrie (Presenter), Suzanne Dando (Presenter), John Harker (DJ).

	Holding / Source
31.12.1982 **Special**	1" / 1"

With Melba Moore, Bucks Fizz, Little and Large, Eurythmics, Jermaine Jackson, Ted Rogers, Gyles Brandreth, Slade, Showaddywaddy.

British Christmas Television Guide — RAZZAMATAZZ (continued)

SERIES 5

Main regular credit(s):   Series editor Alastair Pirrie; produced and directed by Royston Mayoh.

Main regular performer(s):   With Alastair Pirrie (Presenter), Lisa Stansfield (Co-Presenter), Paul Gough (DJ).

	Holding / Source
20.12.1983 **Christmas Special**	1" / 1"

Duration: 26 minutes.

Designed by Peter Bingeman.

With Eurythmics ("Love Is A Stranger"), Blancmange ("That's Love That It Is"), Eddy Grant ("Electric Avenue"), Spandau Ballet ("Gold"), Adam Ant ("Puss In Boots"), The Police ("Every Breath You Take"), Modern Romance, The Belle Stars, Junior, Musical Youth, Kajagoogoo, Bob Geldof, David Grant, Bananarama, Limahl, Roman Holliday.

Main regular performer(s):   With Alastair Pirrie (Presenter).

	Holding / Source
23.12.1985 **Christmas Special**	1" / 1"

Duration: 52 minutes.

Series editor Alastair Pirrie; designed by Peter Bingeman; produced and directed by Royston Mayoh.

With David 'Kid' Jensen (Co-Presenter), Phil Lynott ("Nineteen"), Madness ("The Sweetest Girl"), Lloyd Cole and The Commotions ("Cut Me Down"), Feargal Sharkey ("You Little Thief"), Slade ("Do You Believe In Miracles ?"), Jennifer Rush ("Ring Of Ice"), Fine Young Cannibals ("Suspicious Minds"), John Parr, John Harker.

Main regular credit(s):   Produced by Alastair Pirrie; directed by Royston Mayoh.

Main regular performer(s):   With David 'Kid' Jensen (Presenter).

	Holding / Source
17.12.1986 **Christmas Special**	1" / 1"

Duration: 25 minutes.

With Patsy Kensit (Co-Presenter), The Housemartins ("Happy Hour"), Berlin (-"No More Words"), INXS (-- "Listen Like Thieves"), Nu Shooz ("I Can't Wait"), Feargal Sharkey ("You Little Thief").

02.01.1987 **New Year Special**	1" / 1"

Duration: 52 minutes.

With Spandau Ballet ("How Many Lies"), Go West ("True Colours"), Gary Moore ("Over The Hills and Far Away"), Jaki Graham ("Step Right Up"), Eighth Wonder ("Will You Remember"), Siouxsie and The Banshees ("Wheels On Fire"), Dead Or Alive ("Something In My House").

A READING AT CHRISTMAS

A Tyne Tees Television production. Transmission details are for the Yorkshire Television region. Duration: 4 minutes.

	Holding / Source
26.12.1970 **Howard's End**	J / 2"

Written by E. M. Forster.

With Linda Thorson (Reader).

READY STEADY GO!

An Associated-Rediffusion production. Transmission details are for the Rediffusion Television region. Duration varies - see below for details.

	Holding / Source
31.12.1964 **THE NEW YEAR STARTS HERE**	J / 40

Duration: 75 minutes.

Produced and directed by Peter Croft.

With Keith Fordyce (Presenter), Cathy McGowan (Presenter), The Animals, The Dave Clark Five, Freddie and The Dreamers, The Kinks, Kenny Lynch, Manfred Mann, Susan Maughan, Sandie Shaw, Dusty Springfield.

31.12.1965 **THE NEW YEAR STARTS HERE**	J / 40

Duration: 55 minutes.

The most exciting New Year's Eve Party in Britain is at Television House, London, where the stars go to dance to the music of the top popstars. At home or at your own party, switch on--it's there to add to your fun.

Edited by Vicki Wickham; executive producer Elkan Allan; produced by Francis Hitching; directed by Robert Fleming.

With Keith Fordyce (Presenter), Cathy McGowan (Presenter), The Animals, Chris Andrews, Dave Berry, The Dave Clark Five, Tom Jones, The Kinks, Kenny Lynch, Lulu.

Copyright on this series is owned by Dave Clark (ex-Dave Clark Five). Only a few editions exist in his hands, which we have shown in this listing, except a Motown Special where we cannot identify a tx date. There are also several clips including The Who and The Walker Brothers, allegedly from June 1966.

The editions shown between 02.04.65 and 28.05.65 inclusive were broadcast under the title READY STEADY GOES LIVE!

THE REG VARNEY REVUE

An LWT production. Transmission details are for the ATV midlands region.

Main regular credit(s): Written by Dick Vosburgh, Wally Malston, Garry Chambers and David Cumming; music directed by Harry Rabinowitz; designed by Bob McGowan; produced and directed by Bryan Izzard.

Main regular performer(s): Reg Varney (Host), The Ladybirds.

	Production No	Holding / Source
23.12.1972 **The Reg Varney Christmas Revue**	9L/00988	D2 / 2"

Duration: 52 minutes.

Bus-hoppers, teeny-boppers, Scottiboppers, Dotti-boppers — this is your show. The irrepressible Reg presents a revue to keep you giggling and toe-tapping right through the holiday. What could be more seasonable than a panto? And who else could play the Dame but Reg himself? And who better to keep the whole thing swinging than guests Kenneth McKellar, Dorothy Squires and superstars The Osmonds?

Music associate Sam Harding; choreography by Malcolm Clare.

With The Osmonds, Kenneth McKellar, Dorothy Squires, Olivia Newton-John, George Chisholm, Pat Coombs, Elizabeth Counsell, David Lodge, Frank Thornton.

THE REGIMENT

A BBC production for BBC 1. Transmission details are for BBC 1. Duration: 50 minutes.

Main regular credit(s): Created by Jack Gerson and Nick McCarty.

Main regular cast: Christopher Cazenove (Lieutenant, later Captain, Richard Gaunt), Denis Lill (Captain, later Major, Fred Slingsby), Shirley Dixon (Maud La Vereker), Frederick Treves (Colonel Cranleigh-Osborne), James Bate (Corporal Bright), Virginia Balfour (Mrs Cranleigh-Osborne), Michael Brennan (RSM Bright), Bernard Brown (Captain, later Major, Rupert Saunders), Wendy Allnutt (Charlotte Gaunt).

SERIES 1

Main regular credit(s): Story editor Geoffrey Tetlow; produced by Royston Morley.

Main regular cast: With John Hallam (Lieutenant James Willoughby), Wendy Williams (Honourable Alice Gaunt), Maria Aitken (Dorothy Saunders).

	Holding / Source
22.05.1972 **Christmas At The Cape**	DB-D3 / 2"

Written by Richard Daniel; directed by Viktors Ritelis.

With Richard Cornish, Eric Dodson, John Cunningham, Norman Eshley, Maria O'Brien, David Steele, Joy Harington.

REJOICE

A Southern Television production. Transmission details are for the Scottish Television region. Duration: 50 minutes.

	Holding / Source
21.12.1975	J / 2"

A programme celebrating Christmas, through pictures and music. The nativity pictures are from the National Gallery.

Music associate Jonathan Burton; orchestra conducted by Simon Rattle; sound Cyril Vine; designed by Greg Lawson; produced and directed by Dave Heather.

With Lillian Watson, David Hurley, Benjamin Luxon, Swingle II, Winchester Cathedral Choir, Bournemouth Symphony Orchestra.

RELEASE

A BBC production for BBC 2. Transmission details are for BBC 2. Duration: 45 minutes.

SERIES 1

	Holding / Source
30.12.1967 "End of year special"	C1SEQ / C1

Programme editor Lorna Pegram; produced by Colin Nears.

With Robert Hughes, Peter Lewis, William Mann, Alexander Walker, Irving Wardle.

What has 1967 meant? Will it be remembered for the start of something big? Or without much character? What will be significant in 1968?

In this and subsequent editions, Hughes would report on Art; Lewis on Plays; Mann on Music; Walker on Films; Wardle on Books. No-one reported on Television.

NB: Throughout this series directing credits, where given, generally relate to one of the main features within the programme rather than the main programme itself. Often only inserts survive, not complete shows.

RENTAGHOST

A BBC production for BBC 1. Transmission details are for BBC 1.

Main regular credit(s): Created by Bob Block; written by Bob Block.

SERIES 4

Main regular credit(s): Music by Jonathan Cohen; produced by Jeremy Swan.

Main regular cast: With Anthony Jackson (Fred Mumford), Michael Darbyshire (Hubert Davenport), Michael Staniforth (Timothy Claypole), Edward Brayshaw (Mr Meaker).

	Holding / Source
19.12.1979 **Rentasanta**	DB-D3 / 2"

Duration: 40 minutes.

Postponed from 21.12.1978. Alternative transmissions: BBC Wales: 16.12.1979.

Music directed by Roy Civil; choreography by Nita Howard; designed by Carol Golder; directed by Jeremy Swan.

With Christopher Biggins (Adam Painting), Ann Emery (Ethel Meaker), John Dawson (Mr Mumford), Betty Alberge (Mrs Mumford), Jane Egan, William Perry, Roland A. Wollens, Geoffrey Russell, Geoffrey Leesley, Roy Stewart.

All BBC programmes were pulled on 21.12.1978 due to a strike.

| British Christmas Television Guide | RENTAGHOST (continued) |

SERIES 7
Duration: 30 minutes.
Main regular credit(s): Music by Jonathan Cohen; produced by Jeremy Swan.
Main regular cast: With Michael Staniforth (Timothy Claypole), Edward Brayshaw (Harold Meaker), Sue Nicholls (Nadia Popov), Pantomime Horse (Themselves).

	Holding / Source
21.12.1982 **It's Pantomime Time**	DB-D3 / 2"

Designed by Martin Collins; directed by Jeremy Swan.

With Molly Weir (Hazel The McWitch, McPuss), Hal Dyer (Rose Perkins, Cinderella), Jeffrey Segal (Arthur Perkins, Humpty Dumpty), Christopher Biggins (Adam Painting, Jack's Mother), Paddie O'Neil (Queen Matilda, Fairy Godmother).

THE RETURN OF THE ANTELOPE

A Granada production. Transmission details are for the Central region.

Main regular cast: Gail Harrison (Brelca), John Quentin (Fistram), John Branwell (Spelbush), Alan Bowyer (Gerald Garstanton), Derek Farr (William Garstanton), Fiona McArthur (Milly).

SERIES 2

	Production No	Holding / Source
21.12.1986 **The Antelope Christmas**	P1260/27	1" / 1"

Duration: 50 minutes.
Written by Willis Hall; produced and directed by Eugene Ferguson.

With Lila Kaye, Al Gillyon, Jeremy Hodson, Claudia Gambold, Ter Bayliss, Rosalind Knight, Roy Barraclough, Julie Shipley, Paul Elsam, Alan Starkey, Terry Cundall, Gillian Kerrod, Rosie Dynevor, Tony Kennedy, Allyson Lee, Martin Pitman, Jane Bird, Stephen Bird, Iain Cuthbertson, Aubrey Morris, Christine Moore, Paul Chapman, Donald Bisset, Samantha Ferguson, Peter Martin, John De Frates, Robert James, Donald Eccles, Madge Hindle, Tony Haygarth, Sheila Steafel, John Keyworth, Ruth Holden, Dickie Arnold, Susan Robson, Stephanie Cole, Jazzer Jeyes, Bill Lund.

REV.

A Big Talk Productions production for BBC 2. made in association with Ingenious Broadcasting. Transmission details are for BBC 2. Duration: 30 minutes.
Main regular credit(s): Created by James Wood, Tom Holland and Tom Hollander.
Main regular cast: Tom Hollander (The Reverent Adam Smallbone).

	Holding / Source
20.12.2011 **Christmas Special**	HD/DB / HDC

It's Christmas at St Saviour's and someone has stolen the Three Wise Men's camels from the Nativity display. Vicar Adam Smallbone refuses to be downhearted — maybe the missing beasts can be replaced by cows? "A Wise Man crossing the desert on a cow?" blusters outraged parishioner Adoha. That's Adam, a man for whom there are never problems, there are only solutions. But even his legendary compassion and good nature are stretched by a truly testing Christmas. He loses a friend, he is head-butted by another, supposed, mate and his father-in-law arrives unexpectedly. Worse, Midnight Mass is disrupted by drunks and Adam melts down in a spectacular, funny/sad, Adam-type way.

Written by James Wood and Sam Bain; produced by Hannah Pescod; directed by Peter Cattaneo.

With Olivia Colman (Alex Smallbone), Jimmy Akingbola (Mick), Steve Evets (Colin Lambert), Miles Jupp (Nigel McCall), Lucy Liemann (Ellie Patman), Simon McBurney (Archdeacon Robert), Ellen Thomas (Adoha Onyeka), Geoffrey Palmer (Martin), Severn Brand (Courtney), Katie Males (Lisa), Eliza Newman (Chloe), Ben Willbond (Steve Warnick).

REVIEW OF THE YEAR

A BBC production for BBC 1. Transmission details are for BBC 1.

	Holding / Source
31.12.1991	DD / D3S
29.12.1994	DB / D3S
30.12.1997	DB / D3S

REX THE RUNT

An Aardman Animations production for BBC 2. Transmission details are for BBC 2. Duration: 10 minutes.

Claymation series featuring the adventures of Rex the Runt and his canine friends, Bad Bob, Wendy and Vince.

SERIES 1

Main regular credit(s): Executive producers Colin Rose, David Sproxton and Peter Lord; production manager Fred De Bradeny; produced by Jacqueline White; directed by Richard Goleszowski.
Main regular cast: With Andrew Franks (Voice of Rex), Kevin Wrench (Voice of Bad Bob), Dave Lewis (Voices), Doug Wort (Voices).

		Holding / Source
21.12.1998	**Stinky's Search For A Star**	DB / DBS
21.12.1998	**Holiday In Vince**	DB / DBSW
22.12.1998	**Too Many Dogs**	DB / DBS
22.12.1998	**Easter Island**	DB / DBS
23.12.1998	**The City Shrinkers**	DB / DBS
23.12.1998	**1 :Adventures On Telly**	DB / DBS
24.12.1998	**2 :Adventures On Telly**	DB / DBS
25.12.1998	**3 :Adventures On Telly**	DB / DBS
27.12.1998	**The Trials Of Wendy**	DB / DBS
30.12.1998	**Under The Duvet**	DB / DBS

REX THE RUNT (continued)

31.12.1998	**Johnny Saveloy's Undoing**	DB / DBS

Written by David Freedman and Alan Gilbey.

With Bob Monkhouse (Voice of Johnny Saveloy), Stanley Unwin (Voice of Mr Wangle), Sarah Walden (Voice of Nurse).

31.12.1998	**Bob's International Hiccup Centre**	DB / DBS
01.01.1999	**Carbonara**	DB / DBS

RICH HALL: HELL NO I AIN'T HAPPY

An Open Mike production for BBC 2. Transmission details are for BBC 2. Duration: 60 minutes.

Written by Rich Hall; script supervisor Tricia Canavan; designed by Colin Pigott; executive producers Addison Cresswell, Joe Norris, Helen Parker and Andrew Beint; production manager Liz Seymour; produced by Anthony Caveney; directed by Paul Wheeler.

Rich Hall, Otis Lee Crenshaw and The Honky Tonk A**Holes, Rob Childs, David Lindsay, Mark Hewitt, Nigel Portman-Smith.

	Holding / Source
30.12.2010	DB / DBSW

RICHARD BURTON'S CHRISTMAS STORY

A HTV Wales production. Transmission details are for the Central region. Duration: 50 minutes.

Written by Richard Burton; produced by Richard Meyrick; directed by Alan Clayton.

Dewi Thomas (Richie), Hefin Rees (Trevor), Dafydd Hywel (Mad Dan), Catherine Treganna (Cis), Dorien Thomas (Elfed), Sue Jones-Davies (Mrs Tabor), Gwyn Parry (Mr Bowen), Daniel Collier Roberts (Billy Terror), Emlyn Williams (Granpa Evans).

	Holding / Source
24.12.1991	1" / C1

RICHARD HAMMOND MEETS EVEL KNIEVEL

A Visual Voodoo Films production for BBC 2. Transmission details are for BBC 2. Duration: 60 minutes.

Associate producer Rebecca Mills; executive producers Ben Gale and Tony Moss; head of production Gemma Addison; produced by Ben Devlin; directed by Nigel Simpkiss.

Richard Hammond (Host), Evel Knievel.

	Holding / Source
23.12.2007	DB / DBSW

RICHARD LITTLEJOHN LIVE AND UNCUT

Alternative/Working Title(s): LITTLEJOHN TAKES ON THE WORLD

An LWT production. made in association with NPC Productions. Transmission details are for the London Weekend Television region. Duration varies - see below for details.

Main regular performer(s): Richard Littlejohn (Presenter).

	Holding / Source
23.12.1994 **Richard Littlejohn's Christmas Offensive**	DB /

Duration: 95 minutes.

Fireworks are guaranteed when Richard Littlejohn returns to welcome in the festive season with a line-up of celebrities and entertainment.

Produced by Ambreen Hameed; directed by Michael Toppin.

RICHARD WHITTINGTON ESQUIRE

A Rediffusion Television production. Transmission details are for the ATV midlands region. Duration: 72 minutes.

Written by Sid Colin; based on an idea by Tommy Steele; lyrics by Tommy Steele; music by Tommy Steele; produced and directed by Joan Kemp-Welch.

Tommy Steele (Richard Whittington), Sally Smith (Alice), Bill Fraser (Trollop), Bernard Bresslaw (Brown), Michael Finlayson (Baron), Barbara Lewis (Old Woman), Dickie Owen (Bragg), Jeanne Craig (Cat), Jeanine Garrard (Maid), Tom Gill (Fitzwarren), Marian Davies (Nurse), Kim Grant (Town Crier), Tom Kyffin (Landlord), Norman Allen (Sweeper), Tony Bateman (King of Metrodoro), Desmond Newling (Guard), The Michael Sammes Singers, Diana Simpson, Michael Younger, Pamela Rowe, Susan Harwich, Jan Colet, Heather Beckers, Richard Garner, Marie Betts, Bill Hayden, Linda Bywaters, Tony Manning, Jean Clarke, John McDonald, Janece Graham, Tommy Merrifield, Patsy Spencer.

	Holding / Source
25.12.1964	J|a /

Kaleidoscope hold a complete audio-only copy.

THE RIDDLERS

A Yorkshire Television production. Transmission details are for the Central region.

SERIES 4

		VT Number	Holding / Source
25.03.1993	**The Riddlers' Christmas**	C088/05	B / 1"

THE RIFF RAFF ELEMENT

A BBC production for BBC 1. Transmission details are for BBC 1. Duration: 50 minutes.

Main regular credit(s): Written by Debbie Horsfield; produced by Liz Trubridge.

Main regular cast: Richard Hope (Mortimer), Nicholas Farrell (Boyd), Pippa Guard (Pheonix), Ronald Pickup (Roger), Celia Imrie (Joanna), Trevor Peacock (Acky), Ashley Wright (Nathan), Mossie Smith (Pet), Jayne Ashbourne (Carmen), Cal MacAninch (Declan), Stewart Pile (Oliver), Kate Binchy (Dearbhla), Brenda Bruce (Granny Grogan), Greg Wise (Alister), Lionel Guyett (Father Casper).

SERIES 1

Holding / Source

02.04.1993 **"Two Days Before Christmas"**   DB-D3 / V1S
Directed by Simon Cellan Jones.
With George Costigan (Vincent), Con O'Neill, Nicholas Fry.

09.04.1993 "New Year's Eve"   DB-D3 / V1S
Directed by Simon Cellan Jones.
With Dicken Ashworth (Nelson), Jackie Fielding, Malcolm Farquhar, Muriel Barker.

THE RIME OF THE ANCIENT MARINER

A Centre for Educational Television Overseas production for Argo Records. Transmission details are for the Scottish Television region. Duration: 29 minutes.
Written by Samuel Taylor Coleridge; drawings by John Ryan; produced by Bernard Queenan; directed by Harley Usill, John Ryan and Bernard Queenan.
Richard Burton (Narrator), John Neville (Other Voices), Robert Hardy (Other Voices).

Holding / Source

31.12.1967   B1 / B3

Held by Kaleidoscope. (c) 1967.
See also: THE HUNTING OF THE SNARK

RING A BELL

An ABC production. Transmission details are for the ABC midlands region. Duration: 20 minutes.

26.12.1965 **No 13 Christmas Every Day**

As schoolchildren on Tyneside perform at their Assembly, re-creating events from history and legend. Out walking on Boxing Day, a group of children make a wonderful discovery. What they find out is often forgotten by grown-ups, but it is important and exciting news for all of us.

Devised by James Madden; programme associate Allen Sharp; produced by Ben Churchill; directed by David Wickes.
With Children of Heworth Modern School, County Durham.

RING IN THE NEW

A BBC Scotland production for BBC 1. Transmission details are for BBC 1.
Designed by Jim Longmuir; produced and directed by Iain MacFadyen.
Moira Anderson, Bill Simpson, The Corries, George Chisholm, John Grieve, Stuart Henry, Bernadette, Ted Darling, Alasdair Gillies, The Brian Sievwright Dancers, Pipe Major Jimmy Pryde Royal Scots Greys, BBC Scottish Radio Orchestra.

Holding / Source

01.01.1970   J / Live

RING IN THE NEW

A Scottish Television production. Transmission details are for the ATV midlands region. Duration: 52 minutes.
Written by Kenneth Little; music directed by Arthur Blake; choreography by Nita Howard; designed by Geoff Nixon; executive producer Liam Hood; directed by Ted Williamson.
Vince Hill, Bill Simpson, Allan Stewart, Eve Graham, Elaine Simmons, Bill McCue, The STV Dancers, The STV Singers.

Holding / Source

31.12.1974   J / 2"

RING IN THE NEW

A Grampian Television production. Transmission details are for the Scottish Television region. Duration: 50 minutes.
Designed by Eric Mollart; produced and directed by Mike Bevan.
Bill McCue, Marie Gordon Price, Hebbie Gray, Juniper Green, Jim McCloud, Helen McArthur, The Davis Hamilton Dancers, Blackburn and District Pipe Band, Alex Sutherland and his Band.

Holding / Source

01.01.1976   J / 2"

Scottish Television would show the New Year programme made by Grampian on the afternoon of New Year's Day. Grampian did likewise with the STV version.

RING OUT THE BELLS

An ATV production. Transmission details are for the ATV London region. Duration: 52 minutes.
Written by Marilyn Keith and Alan Bergman; music associate Kenny Powell; choreography by Lionel Blair; settings by Tom Lingwood; produced and directed by Bill Ward.
Jo Stafford, Harry Secombe, The Polka Dots, Lionel Blair and his Dancers, The George Mitchell Singers, Amy and Tim Weston, Corona Stage School, Choir of Westminster Abbey, Sir William McKie, Jack Parnell and his Orchestra.

Holding / Source

24.12.1961   J /

RING OUT THE OLD

A BBC Scotland production for BBC 1 Scotland. Transmission details are for BBC 1 Scotland. Duration varies - see below for details.
Hogmanay show.

	Holding / Source
31.12.1970	J / 2"
Duration: 25 minutes.	
01.01.1971	J / 2"
Duration: 40 minutes.	

RINGS ON THEIR FINGERS

A BBC production for BBC 1. Transmission details are for BBC 1. Duration: 30 minutes.

Main regular credit(s):   Written by Richard Waring.

SERIES 1

Main regular credit(s):   Theme music by Frank Barber; music by Jack Point; produced and directed by Harold Snoad.

Main regular cast: With Martin Jarvis (Oliver Pryde), Diane Keen (Sandy Pryde).

	Holding / Source
23.12.1978 **Merry Christmas**	DB-D3 / 2"

Designed by Tony Snoaden.
With Barbara Lott (Mrs Bennett), Keith Marsh (Mr Pryde), John Harvey, Margaret Courtenay, Blake Butler.

RISING DAMP

A Yorkshire Television production. Transmission details are for the ATV midlands region. Duration: 25 minutes.
Comedy set in a seedy house where Rigsby rents rooms.

Main regular credit(s):   Written by Eric Chappell; music by Dennis Wilson.

Main regular cast: Leonard Rossiter (Rupert Rigsby), Don Warrington (Philip Smith), Frances de la Tour (Ruth Jones).

SERIES 2

Main regular credit(s):   Designed by Colin Pigott; executive producer Duncan Wood; produced by Ronnie Baxter.

Main regular cast: With Richard Beckinsale (Alan).

	Holding / Source
26.12.1975 **For The Man Who Has Everything**	DB / 2"

It's party time and everyone's made arrangements for celebrating. Rigsby himself fancies his chances of joining in the Christmas spirit.
Directed by Ronnie Baxter.
With Helen Fraser, Gay Rose (Brenda), Larry Martyn, Elizabeth Adare.

RISING STARS

A BBC production for BBC 1. Transmission details are for BBC 1.

Main regular performer(s):   Lennie Bennett (Presenter).

SERIES 1

	Holding / Source
27.12.1979 **Grand Final**	DB-D3 / 2"

SERIES 2

	Holding / Source
30.12.1980 **Final**	DB-D3 / 2"

THE RITZ

A BBC Birmingham production for BBC 2. Transmission details are for BBC 2. Duration varies - see below for details.

Main regular credit(s):   Written by John Godber; script editor Fiona Finlay; music by Irving Berlin, Peter Skellern, Ronnie Hazlehurst and Peter Grahame; produced by Chris Parr; directed by Martin Shardlow and John Godber.

Main regular cast: Richard James Lewis (Eric), Paul Rider (Chike), Andrew Dunn (Skodge), Andrew Livingston (Kenny), Richard Ridings (Mad Mick), Julia Ford (Carol), Mark Addy (Tony), Martin Ronan (Gary).

	Holding / Source
31.12.1987 **The Continental**	DB / 1"

Duration: 61 minutes.
Designed by Ian Ashurst.
With Lloyd Williams (Beef), Andrew Searle (Beef), Frank Bruno, Jane Clifford, Lachelle Carl, Chris Walker, Stuart McQuarrie, Wendy Schoemann, Jessica Taylor, Ingrid Wells, David Urquhart.

THE RIVALS OF SHERLOCK HOLMES

A Thames Television production. Transmission details are for the ATV midlands region. Duration varies - see below for details.
Theme music by Robert Sharples; consultant Hugh Greene.

SERIES 1
Main regular credit(s):   Story editor George Markstein; executive producer Lloyd Shirley.

	VT Number	Holding / Source
13.12.1971 **The Case Of Laker, Absconded**	4822	D3 / 2"

Duration: 49 minutes.
Dramatised by Philip Mackie; based on a story by Arthur Morrison; designed by Mike Hall; produced by Robert Love; directed by Jonathan Alwyn.

With Peter Barkworth (Martin Hewitt), Ronald Hines (Jonathan Pryde), Jane Lapotaire (Emily Shaw), Arthur Pentelow (Inspector Plummer), Tim Hardy (Sam Gunter), Charles Lloyd Pack (Mr Neal), Anthony Sharp (Mr Lister), James Ottaway (Parsloe), Michael Lynch (Mr Merston), Leslie Dwyer (Lost Property Man), Toke Townley (Lost Property Assistant), John Kidd (Estate Agent), Malcolm McFee (Travel Clerk), Michael Cashman (Henry Stevens), Joe Dunlop (Wilkins), Barry Ashton (Buller's Bank Clerk), Lynette Erving (Maid), Roger Cartland (Charles Laker), Brian Godfrey (Peach), Wally Thomas (Bank Porter), Peter Sugden (Fake Bank Porter).

THE ROAD AND THE MILES OF MAX BOYCE

A BBC production for BBC 1. Transmission details are for BBC 1. Duration: 30 minutes.
Written by Max Boyce; produced and directed by Jack Williams.
Max Boyce, Our Lady of Fatima Primary School, Bridgeton, Llandeilo County Primary School, Dyfed.

	Holding / Source
26.12.1979	DB-D3 / 2"

ROARING JELLY'S CHRISTMAS TRIFLE

A BBC Scotland production for BBC 1 Scotland. Transmission details are for BBC 1 Scotland.

	Holding / Source
21.12.1979	DB / 2"

THE ROB BRYDON SHOW

Produced for BBC 2 by a variety of companies (see details below). made in association with Talkback Thames. Transmission details are for BBC 2. Duration: 30 minutes.

Main regular performer(s):   Rob Brydon (Host).

SERIES 1
An Arbie production.
Main regular credit(s):   Script supervisor Hayley Ayers; series editor Dave Morley; theme music by Lawrence Oakley and Piers Moth; assistant director Isabel Forte; art director Catherine Land; designed by Dominic Tolfts; associate producer Kate Edmunds; executive producers Ruby Kuraishe and Miles Ross; head of production Beatrice Gay; production manager Emma Hind; series producer James Longman; directed by Steve Smith.

	Holding / Source
30.12.2010	DB / DBSW

Written by Rob Brydon, Paul Hawksbee and Andy Milligan.
With Justin Edwards, Jo Brand, Jack Dee, Alice Cooper, Bryn Terfel, The Hypnotic Brass Ensemble, The London Welsh Male Voice Choir, Wren Shepherd.

SERIES 2
A Talkback Thames production. made in association with Small Man.
Main regular credit(s):   Script supervisor Laura Vallis; series editor Dave Morley; theme music by Lawrence Oakley and Piers Moth; art director Lucy Fyfe; designed by Dominic Tolfts; associate producers Toby Brack and Emily Howe; executive producers Ruby Kuraishe and Miles Ross; head of production Beatrice Gay; production manager Gemma Whitford; series producer James Longman; directed by Tim Van Someren.

	Holding / Source
19.12.2011 **Christmas Show**	DB / DBSW

With Charlie Baker, Rhys Darby, Noel Fielding, Sarah Harding, Angelos Epithemiou, Alejandro Toledo, Magic Tombolinis.

ROBBIE WILLIAMS: FOR ONE NIGHT ONLY

A BBC production for BBC 1. Transmission details are for BBC 1. Duration: 50 minutes.
Produced by Lee Lodge; directed by Chris Cowey.
Robbie Williams.

	Holding / Source
25.12.1998	DB / DBSW

ROBERT MAYOR CAROL CONCERT

A BBC production for BBC 1. Transmission details are for BBC 1. Duration: 50 minutes.
For 50 years Sir Robert Mayer has been associated with concerts for children. In honour of his services to music, the annual Carol Concert was this year given by The Academy of the BBC. Concert Master Peter Mountain conducted by The Prime Minister Rt Hon Edward Heath, MP. As well as traditional Christmas carols, in which the audience is led by the BBC Singers, Mr Heath conducts Rossini's Overture to the fairytale Cinderella,' and is joined by Richard Baker as narrator in John Dankworth's setting of ' Tom Sawyer's Saturday.'
Directed by Roy Tipping.
Sir Robert Mayer, Edward Heath, The Academy of the BBC, Richard Baker.

	Holding / Source
24.12.1973	J / 2"

ROBERT'S ROBOTS

A Thames Television production. Transmission details are for the ATV midlands region. Duration: 25 minutes.

Main regular credit(s):	Written by Bob Block.
Main regular cast:	John Clive (Robert Sommerby), Nigel Pegram (Eric), Brian Coburn (Katie).

SERIES 2

Main regular credit(s):	Designed by Darrell Lass; produced and directed by Vic Hughes.
Main regular cast:	With Doris Rogers (Aunt Millie), Leon Lissek (Marken), David Pugh (Plummer).

	VT Number	Holding / Source
23.12.1974 **Santa Claus-Trophobia**	10259	D3 / 2"

Robert Sommerby's latest invention, a computerised self-playing electronic organ, has a musical effect on Katie. And the robots go to a Christmas party, but Desiree insists on kissing
everyone under the mistletoe - including Santa's reindeer.

Music by John Clive.

With William Lawford (Robot George), April Olrich (Desiree).

ROBIN HOOD

A BBC production for BBC 1. Transmission details are for BBC 1. Duration: 95 minutes.

Adapted by Austin Steele; based on a book by John Morley; music directed by Burt Rhodes; choreography by Sheila O'Neill; designed by Reg Allen and Keith Cheetham; produced and directed by Peter Whitmore.

Terry Scott (The Bad Robber), Hugh Lloyd (The Good Robber), Freddie Davies (Samuel Tweet), Anita Harris (Robin Hood), Billy Dainty (Nurse Trumpet), Dana (Maid Marion), Alan Curtis (Sir Robert), Denise Dove (A Babe), Stephen Black (A Babe), Ritchie Stewart (Friar Tuck), Trevor Adams (Will Scarlet), Sheila O'Neill Dancers, The Bowles Bevan Singers.

	Holding / Source
25.12.1973	DB-D3 / 2"

ROBIN HOOD

A Tiger Aspect production for BBC 1. made in association with BBC America / Plain Vanilla Ltd. Transmission details are for BBC 1.

Main regular credit(s):	Created by Dominic Minghella and Foz Allan; music by Andy Price; executive producers Greg Brenman, Foz Allan and Dominic Minghella.
Main regular cast:	Jonas Armstrong (Robin Hood), Gordon Kennedy (Little John), Sam Troughton (Much), Joe Armstrong (Allan A Dale).

SERIES 2

Main regular credit(s):	Script editors Jenny White and Melissa Gallant; designed by Stephen Campbell; head of production Frith Tiplady; series producer Nick Pitt; produced by Jane Hudson.
Main regular cast:	With Richard Armitage (Guy of Gisborne), Anjali Jay (Djaq), Lucy Griffiths (Marian), Harry Lloyd (Will Scarlet), Keith Allen (Sheriff of Nottingham).

	Holding / Source
29.12.2007 **A Good Day To Die / We Are Robin Hood**	HD/DB / HD/DB

Duration: 90 minutes.

Written by Dominic Minghella; script supervisor Dora Simko; directed by David Evans.

With Agost Zord, Paul Usher, Gabor Nagypal, Bela Gados, Abhin Galeya, Mark Smith, Nadim Sawalha, Konnie Huq, Joseph Kennedy, Steven Waddington, Barna Illyés.

"We Are Robin Hood" the episode title for the 13th episode was billed in the Radio Times, but did not appear on-screen.

ROBIN'S NEST

A Thames Television production. Transmission details are for the ATV midlands region. Usual duration: 25 minutes.

Main regular credit(s):	Devised by Johnnie Mortimer and Brian Cooke; theme music by Richard O'Sullivan and Brian Bennett; produced and directed by Peter Frazer-Jones.
Main regular cast:	Richard O'Sullivan (Robin Tripp), Tessa Wyatt (Vicky Nicholls/Tripp), Tony Britton (James Nicholls).

SERIES 5

Main regular credit(s):	Designed by Mike Hall.
Main regular cast:	With David Kelly (Albert Riddle).

	Holding / Source
25.12.1979 **Christmas At Robin's Nest**	D3 / 2"

Written by George Layton.

With No guest cast.

SERIES 6

Main regular cast:	With David Kelly (Albert Riddle).

	Holding / Source
24.12.1980 **Christmas At Robin's Nest: No Room At The Inn**	D3 / 2"

Written by Johnnie Mortimer and Brian Cooke; designed by Tony Borer.

With Barbara Murray (Marion Nicholls), Louis Mansi (Pedro), Paul McDowell (Doctor), Yvette Harris (Nurse).

See also: GEORGE & MILDRED

ROBINSON CRUSOE

A BBC production for BBC 1. Transmission details are for BBC 1. Duration: 120 minutes.

Adapted by Eddie Leslie and Len Lowe; based on a book by Harry Bright; orchestra directed by Eric Tann; choreography by Tommy Shaw; produced by Travers Thorneloe and Bryan Sears; directed by Travers Thorneloe and Bryan Sears.

Norman Wisdom, Marion Grimaldi, Eddie Leslie, Billy Whittaker, Patricia Stark, Len Lowe, Betty Wheeler, Terry Kendall, David Fallon, Harold Holness, The George Mitchell Singers.

	Holding / Source
25.12.1964	J /

ROBINSON CRUSOE

A BBC production for BBC 1. Transmission details are for BBC 1. Duration: 90 minutes.

Based on a book by Phil Park; music directed by Burt Rhodes; choreography by Roy Gunson; produced and directed by Terry Hughes.

Ken Dodd (Billy Crusoe), Lyn Kennington (Robinson Crusoe), Peter Glaze (Bosun's Mate), Arthur Mullard (Bosun), Stanley Platts (Will Atkins), Billy Whittaker (Mrs Crusoe), Liz Edmiston (Polly Perkins), David Davenport (Davy Jones), Holly Doone (Spirit of The Sea), Arch Taylor (Cannibal King), Ken McGregor (Man Friday), George Barnes (Umpire), Ken Dodd's Diddymen, The Maljohns, The Roy Gunson Dancers, The Bowles Bevan Singers.

	Holding / Source
25.12.1970	J / 2"

ROBSON AND JEROME CHRISTMAS SPECIAL

A Central production. Transmission details are for the Central region. Duration: 25 minutes.

Produced by Peter Bigg; directed by Norman Stone.

Robson & Jerome.

	Holding / Source
25.12.1995	D2 / D2S

ROCK AND CHIPS

Alternative/Working Title(s): SEX, DRUGS & ROCK 'N' CHIPS

A BBC Productions production for BBC 1. made in association with Shazam Productions. Transmission details are for BBC 1. Duration varies - see below for details.

Main regular credit(s): Written by John Sullivan; director of photography John Sorapure; designed by David Hitchcock; production executive Sarah Hitchcock; executive producers Mark Freeland and John Sullivan; produced by Gareth Gwenlan; directed by Dewi Humphreys.

Main regular cast: Nicholas Lyndhurst (Freddie Robdal), Kellie Bright (Joan Trotter), James Buckley (Del Trotter), Phil Daniels (Ted Trotter), Shaun Dingwall (Reg Trotter), Stephen Lloyd (Boycie), Lewis Osborne (Trigger), Ashley Gerlach (Denzil), Lee Long (Jumbo Mills), Jonathan Readwin (Albie Littlewood), Paul Putner (Gerald 'Jelly' Kelly), Robert Daws (Ernie Rayner), Billy Seymour (Raymond), Bobby Bragg (Don), Alison Pargeter (Val).

	Holding / Source
29.12.2010 **Five Gold Rings**	HD/DB / HD/DB

Duration: 60 minutes.

Script supervisor Valerie Letley; art director Debbie Burton; line producer Paula Munro.

With Calum Macnab (Roy Slater), Katie Griffiths (Glenda), Paula Wilcox (Vi Trotter), Mel Smith (Detective Inspector Thomas), Tom Brooke (Detective Constable Stanton), Joan Hodges (Gwen), Dave Lamb (Sergeant Foster), Emma Cook, Kacey Ainsworth, Giles New, Nigel Douglas, Chandeep Uppal, Daniel Cerqueira, Sophie Ash.

See also: ONLY FOOLS AND HORSES.... (BBC)

THE ROCK AND GOAL YEARS

A Granada production. Transmission details are for the Granada region. Duration: 25 minutes.

SERIES 1

Main regular credit(s): Produced and directed by John Moulson.

Main regular performer(s): With John Moulson (Commentator).

	Production No	Holding / Source
05.12.1995 **A Christmas Special**	P2290/10	DB / D3S

Christmas special mixture of football and pop music. Looks at various games played in atrocious wintery conditions and most played with an orange ball. Liverpool v Derby Jan '73, 1 - 1 scorers Davies and Toshack. Mari Wilson performs Christmas version of 'Just What I Always Wanted'. Denis Law introduces mystery footballers dressed in pantomime costumes - Bryan Robson, Ian Rush, Joe Corrigan and Jim McDonagh. Burnley v Fulham Feb '80, 2 - 1 scorers Leighton James, Burke and Tony Gail. Showaddywaddy sing 'Hey Mr Christmas'. John McGinlay scores for Bolton. Comments of a match from Colin Crompton. Stan Boardman reads bogus football results. Mike Yarwood impersonates Brian Clough. Brief shots Jimmy Tarbuck and Bernard Manning. Dexy's Midnight Runners perform 'Merry Christmas Everybody'. Stoke v Oldham Jan '79. Two goals scored by Irvine of Stoke but match abandoned by referee because of poor playing conditions (score 2 - 0). David Essex sings 'A Winters Tale'. Match between Sheffield Wednesday and Arsenal at Hillsborough delayed at half time due to fans throwing snowballs at goalkeeper Pat Jennings. Compilation of violent incidents between players. Shakin' Stevens sings 'Blue Christmas'. Jimmy Armfield conducts 'choir' of footballers singing 'O Come All Ye Faithful' and 'We Wish You A Merry Christmas'. Grounds begin to install undersoil heating. Intv Martin Edwards chairman Man United. Man United v Arsenal Dec'79, 3 -0 scorers Gordon McQueen, Joe Jordan and Sammy McIlroy. The Nolans sing 'Have Yourself A Very Merry Christmas'. Coventry v Everton Dec '78 game played on pitch half cleared of snow. Scorers Wallace,Thompson, Hunt, Lyons and Latchford. Spoof commercial for 'The Very Best of Hugh Johns' record. Oldham v Blackburn Rovers Dec'81, 0 - 3 scorers Garner, Stonehouse and Bell.

With Mike Yarwood, The Nolans, Dexy's Midnight Runners, Mari Wilson, Denis Law, Bryan Robson, Ian Rush, Joe Corrigan, Jim McDonaugh, Showaddywaddy, Colin Crompton, Stan Boardman, David Essex, Shakin' Stevens, Jimmy Armfield, Martin Edwards.

THE ROCK GOSPEL SHOW

A BBC production for BBC 1. Transmission details are for BBC 1.

SERIES 1

Main regular performer(s): With Sheila Walsh.

	Holding / Source
24.12.1984 **Christmas Special**	DB / 1"

With Sal Solo, Alvin Stardust and The Church of God in Christ Choir, Cliff Richard.

26.12.1984 **From America**	DB / 1"

With Amy Grant, Steve Taylor, Petra, The Mighty Clouds of Joy, The Rez Band.

SERIES 2

	Holding / Source
29.12.1985	DB / 1"

With Paul Jones, Fiona Hendley.

ROCK NATIVITY

A Scottish Television production. Transmission details are for the ATV midlands region. Duration: 50 minutes.

Stage musical about the birth of Christ.

Written by David Wood; music by Tony Hatch and Jackie Trent; designed by Pip Gardner; produced and directed by David Bell.

Helen Chappelle (Mary), Michael Scholes (Joseph), Dicken Ashworth (Herod), Andy Forray (Evangelist), Philip Hatton (Gabriel), David Sebastian Bach (Wise Man), Carl Andrews (Wise Man), Les Saxon (Wise Man), Mike Wade (Shepherd), John Newton (Shepherd), Jim Cassidy (Shepherd), Anni Domingo, Margot Gordon, Barbara Sexton, Jay Smith, Mandi Wilson.

	Holding / Source
26.12.1976	J / 2"

ROD HULL AND EMU SING A CHRISTMAS SONG

A BBC Manchester production for BBC 1. Transmission details are for BBC 1. Duration: 29 minutes.

Written by Rod Hull; music directed by Bernard Herrmann; designed by Mel Bibby; produced by Hazel Lewthwaite; directed by Geoff Wilson.

Rod Hull and Emu, Tom Chatto (Theatre Manager), Rolf Harris, Children of New Mills, Derbyshire.

	Production No	VT Number	Holding / Source
25.12.1976	02746/3089	/TC/6HT/BH809/MMF	DB-D3 / 2"

ROD STEWART'S CHRISTMAS

An ITV Studios production for ITV 1. Transmission details are for the Central region. Duration: 52 minutes.

The rock star is in his beloved Scotland, amid the stunning surroundings of Stirling Castle, to perform a selection of his favourite songs for the season. The show includes duets with Michael Buble and Kylie Minogue, and award-winning classical violinist Nicola Benedetti also takes to the stage. Rod also talks about life at home with his family and explains what Christmas means to him.

Produced by Sally Wood; directed by Julia Knowles.

Rod Stewart, Nicola Benedetti, Kylie Minogue, Michael Bublé.

	Holding / Source
08.12.2012	HD/DB / HDC

ROGER MELLIE

A John Brown Publishing production for Channel 4. Transmission details are for Channel 4. Duration: 5 minutes.

Main regular credit(s):   Produced and directed by Miles Ross.

Main regular cast: Peter Cook (Voice of Mellie), Harry Enfield (Other Voices).

	Holding / Source
29.12.1992	C1 / C1S
30.12.1992	C1 / C1S
31.12.1992	C1 / C1S
01.01.1993	C1 / C1S

See also: IT'S ROGER MELLIE - THE MAN ON THE TELLY

ROGUE MALE (RADIO)

A BBC production for BBC Radio 4. Transmission details are for BBC Radio 4. Duration: 90 minutes.

Adapted by Frederick Bradnum; based on a book by Geoffrey Household; produced and directed by Graham Gauld.

Simon Cadell (Sir Ben), David Goudge (Major Quive-Smith), Ian Michie (Karl), Christopher Scott (Colonel), Geoffrey Whitehead (Police Chief), David Rose (Fisher), Philip Sully (Vaner), Leslie Heritage (Saul), Ian Targett (Peale), Jonathan Scott (Tom), Ysanne Churchman (Mrs Whelkes), Manning Wilson (Patachon), Susan Sheridan (Barmaid), Joan Matheson (Mrs Erksine).

	Holding / Source
26.12.1989	DA /

In Stereo.

ROLAND RAT: THE SERIES

A BBC production for BBC 1. Transmission details are for BBC 1.
Main regular credit(s): Produced by Marcus Mortimer.
Main regular performer(s): Roland Rat (Presenter).

	Holding / Source
25.12.1986 **Christmas Special**	DB / 1"

ROLAND'S WINTER WONDERLAND

A TV-am production. Transmission details are for the Central region. Duration: 24 minutes.
Main regular credit(s): Directed by Tony Orsten.
Main regular performer(s): Roland Rat, Kevin the Gerbil.

	Holding / Source
19.12.1983	1" / 1"
20.12.1983	1" / 1"
21.12.1983	1" / 1"
27.12.1983	1" / 1"
29.12.1983	1" / 1"
02.01.1984	1" / 1"
03.01.1984	1" / 1"
04.01.1984	1" / 1"
06.01.1984	1" / 1"

ROLAND'S YULETIDE BINGE

A BBC production for BBC 1. Transmission details are for BBC 1. Duration: 25 minutes.
Executive producer Michael Hurll; produced by Stanley Appel; directed by Tony Newman.
Roland Rat (Host), Russell Grant, Frankie Howerd, Jan Leeming, Ian McCaskill, Beryl Reid, Valerie Singleton, Jeannette Charles, James Saxon, Barbara Speake Stage School.

	Holding / Source
25.12.1985	DB / 1"

ROLF AT CHRISTMAS

A BBC production for BBC 1. Transmission details are for BBC 1. Duration: 35 minutes.
Rolf and 200 young guests bring you a selection of Christmas songs from the historic city of Chester.
Written by Tony Hawes; music directed by Barry Booth; designed by Marjorie Pratt; produced by Jim Moir; directed by Brian Penders.
Rolf Harris (Host), Keith Harris, Darts, Overleigh Middle School.

	Holding / Source
20.12.1980	DB-D3 / 2"

THE ROLF HARRIS SHOW

A BBC production for BBC 1. Transmission details are for BBC 1. Duration varies - see below for details.
Main regular performer(s): Rolf Harris (Host).

SERIES 3
Main regular credit(s): Choreography by Douglas Squires; produced and directed by Stewart Morris.
Main regular performer(s): With Alyn Ainsworth and his Orchestra, The Young Generation.

	Holding / Source
31.12.1969	J / 2"

Duration: 45 minutes.
Written by Mike Kinsley and Lawrie Kinsley; music directed by Alyn Ainsworth; designed by J. Roger Lowe; produced and directed by Stewart Morris.
With The Young Generation, Dusty Springfield, Joe Benjamin.

SERIES 4
Made in association with ZDF. Duration: 50 minutes.
Main regular credit(s): Written by Eric Merriman; associate producer Klaus Weising; produced and directed by Stewart Morris.
Main regular performer(s): With The Young Generation, Alyn Ainsworth and his Orchestra.

	Holding / Source
26.12.1970	R1 / 2"

With Franco Carelli, Dana Valery.

ROLF!

A Billy March Productions production for Carlton UK. Transmission details are for the Central region. Duration: 50 minutes.
Executive producers Jan Kennedy and John Bishop; produced by John Bartlett; directed by Pati Marr.
Rolf Harris (Host), Dannii Minogue, Kathy Staff, June Whitfield, Wallis Bychanon, Jamiroquai, Bradley Walsh.

	Holding / Source
23.12.1996	D2 / D2S

ROLL BACK THE CARPET AND DANCE

An ATV production. Transmission details are for the ATV London region. Duration: 25 minutes.

Designed by Philip Hickie; produced and directed by Dinah Thetford.

Cyril Stapleton and His Orchestra, June Marlow, The Raindrops, Harry Smith-Hampshire, Doreen Casey.

	Holding / Source
25.12.1960	J /

THE ROMAN INVASION OF RAMSBOTTOM

A Granada production. Transmission details are for the ATV midlands region. Duration: 50 minutes.

Musical play for the whole family performed by members of The Children's Music Theatre. Thirty-five boys and girls sing and dance this page of history which may be missing from the pages of your history books. A Roman road-building scheme hits trouble just outside Mancunium, the Roman name for Manchester, in 79 A.D.

Written by Jeremy James-Taylor; lyrics by Jeremy James-Taylor; music by David Nield; designed by Jane Martin; produced by Diana Bramwell; directed by Mary McMurray.

Simon Martindale (Agricola), Jason Denvir (Conkus Maximus), Jeremy Allanson (Gracie Trotter), Gary Davis (Acrimonius), Timothy Walter (Parsimonius), Richard Pead (Accrington Stanley).

The Children's Music Theatre

	Production No	Holding / Source
26.12.1980	P1026	DB / 2"

ROMAN ROAD

A Zenith Entertainment production for ITV 1. Transmission details are for the Central region. Duration: 85 minutes.

Written by Kirkham Jackson; script supervisor Ruth Atkinson; script editor Alex Jones; music by Charlie Dore and Julian Littman; executive producer Ivan Rendall; produced by Adrian Bate; directed by Paul Seed.

Alan Davies (Vince), John Gordon Sinclair (Matt Bancroft), Anna Wing (Lady In Wheelchair), James Larkin (Paul), Anna Chancellor (Maddy Bancroft), Holly, Rosey and Daisy McDermott (Ella), Anna Wilson-Jones (Jenny), Rupert Vansittart (Farmer), Paul Humpoletz (Barman), Simon Green (Christian), Matt Hickey (Drug Dealer).

	Holding / Source
31.12.2004	DB / V1SW

ROMARK

A BBC Manchester production for BBC 1. Transmission details are for BBC 1. Duration: 30 minutes.

Designed by Kenneth Lawson; produced by Peter Ridsdale Scott; directed by Peggy Walker.

Romark.

	Holding / Source
30.12.1973	DB-D3 / 2"

ROME, SWEET HOME

An ITC production for ATV. Transmission details are for the ATV London region. Duration: 25 minutes.

Created by Irving Taylor and Jack Harvey; written by Irving Taylor and Jack Harvey; associate producer John Pellatt; produced and directed by Hal Stanley.

Lois Maxwell (Megadorus), Peggy Mount (Lippia), Susan Baker (Faith), Jennifer Baker (Hope), Hughie Green (Braggius), Kip King (Philoxenus), Del Moore (Cashio), Peter Brace (Spartacus), Murray Kash (Lambus), Melvyn Hayes (Pentamus), Aubrey Morris (Tailor), Paul Whitsun-Jones (Flavius), Kevin Scott (First slave), Ivor Salter (Second slave), Vic Wise (Connivus), Keith Marsh (Demosthenes), Vicky Smith (First girl), Monica Lewis (Second girl), Pat Finch (Third girl), Tommy Reeves (Chariot driver), John Scripps (Chariot driver).

	Holding / Source
25.12.1966	C3N / C3

Alternative transmissions: ATV Midlands: 24.06.1970; Southern Television: 09.04.1970; Tyne Tees Television: 26.03.1967.

THE RONN LUCAS SHOW

A Thames Television production. Transmission details are for the Central region.

Main regular performer(s): Ronn Lucas (Host).

SERIES 3

Main regular credit(s): Written by Nigel Crowle; produced by Sean Murphy; directed by Paul Kirrage.

Main regular performer(s): With The John Coleman Orchestra.

	Holding / Source
25.12.1990 Who's In Charge Here?	1" / 1"

RONNIE CORBETT TICKLES YOUR FANCY

A Scottish Television production. Transmission details are for the Scottish Television region. Duration: 50 minutes.

Hogmanay special in which Ronnie Corbett reveals his favourite moments from a century of Scottish comedy, featuring vintage performances from comics including Harry Lauder, Stanley Baxter and Rory Bremner.

Ronnie Corbett.

	Holding / Source
31.12.1999	DB / DBS

RONNIE CORBETT'S SATURDAY SPECIAL

A BBC production for BBC 1. Transmission details are for BBC 1. Duration: 45 minutes.

Main regular credit(s): Written by Eddie Braben; script associate David Renwick; choreography by Geoffrey Richer; designed by David Myerscough-Jones; produced and directed by Michael Hurll.

Main regular cast: Ronnie Corbett (Host), Ronnie Hazlehurst and his Orchestra, New Edition.

Holding / Source

01.01.1977 DB-D3 / 2"
Lyrics by Dick Vosburgh.
With Peters and Lee, Rod Hull and Emu, Dana, Bernie Clifton.

ROOBARB

A Roobarb Enterprises production for BBC 1. Transmission details are for BBC 1. Duration: 4 minutes.

Main regular credit(s): Created by Grange Calveley; written by Grange Calveley; theme music by Johnny Hawkesworth; produced and directed by Bob Godfrey.

Main regular cast: Richard Briers (Narrator).

Holding / Source

24.12.1974 **When It Was Christmas** C1 / C1

ROOBARB & CUSTARD TOO.

A Roobarb Productions production for Channel 5. made in association with A&B Films / Celador International. Transmission details are for Channel 5. Duration: 7 minutes.

Main regular credit(s): Narrated by Richard Briers; created by Grange Calveley; written by Grange Calveley; drawings by Grange Calveley; script editor Nick Wilson; theme music by Johnny Hawkesworth; music by Jon Atkinson; executive producers Bernadette O'Riordan and Adam Sharp; produced by Gerard O'Rourke; directed by Jason Tammemägi.

Holding / Source

##.##.#### **When Mouse Arrived For Christmas** DB /
Produced under license from Grange Calveley and Green Dog Films Ltd.

ROOM ON THE BROOM

Commissioned by BBC 1. Transmission details are for BBC 1. Duration: 25 minutes.

Gruffalo creators Julia Donaldson and Axel Scheffler have a knack for dreaming up characters who are likeable without being goody-goody. In this lovely animation, it's a kindly, inept witch, who's joined on her broomstick by a raggletaggle menagerie -and her protective cat.

Written by Julia Donaldson and Axel Scheffler; produced by Martin Pope and Michael Rose; directed by Max Lang and Jan Lachauer.

Gillian Anderson (Voice), Rob Brydon (Voice), Martin Clunes (Voice), David Walliams (Voice), Sally Hawkins (Voices).

Holding / Source

25.12.2012 HD/DB / HDC

RORY BREMNER - WHO ELSE?

A Vera production for Channel 4. Transmission details are for Channel 4. Duration varies - see below for details.

Main regular cast: Rory Bremner (Various roles), John Bird, John Fortune, Steve Bell.

SERIES 1
Duration: 40 minutes.
Main regular cast: With Steve Bell.

Holding / Source

01.01.1994 **Rory Bremner's Christmas Special** D3 / D3S

SERIES 2
Main regular credit(s): Produced by Geoff Atkinson and Elaine Morris.

Holding / Source

30.12.1994 **Rory Bremner's Christmas Turkey** D3 / D3S
Duration: 50 minutes.
Directed by Steve Connelly and Juliet May.
With Annette Crosbie, Sheila Hancock.

SERIES 3
Main regular credit(s): Directed by Steve Connelly and David Crean.

Holding / Source

29.12.1995 **Rory Bremner, Apparently** D3 / D3S
Duration: 50 minutes.
Produced by Elaine Morris.

SERIES 5
Main regular credit(s): Written by Rory Bremner and John Langdon; produced by Geoff Atkinson and Elaine Morris; directed by Steve Smith.

Holding / Source

29.12.1996 **Two Fat Rorys** D3 / D3S
Duration: 25 minutes.

RORY BREMNER - WHO ELSE? (continued)

Holding / Source
D3 / D3S

30.12.1997 **And Finally... Rory Bremner**
Duration: 50 minutes.
Written by Geoff Atkinson, David Tyler, Debbie Barham, Rory Bremner, Sean Hardie, John Fortune and John Langdon; executive producer Geoff Atkinson; produced by David Tyler and Sean Hardie; directed by John Birkin.

Holding / Source
D3 / D3S

31.12.1998 **The Greatest Rory Ever Told**
Duration: 50 minutes.
Produced by Jon Magnusson; directed by Geraldine Dowd and Henry Murray.

RORY BREMNER... AND THE MORNING AFTER THE YEAR BEFORE

A Kudos Film & Television production for Channel 4. Transmission details are for Channel 4. Duration: 60 minutes.
Written by Rory Bremner and John Langdon; produced by Geoff Atkinson; directed by Phil Chilvers and David G. Hillier.
Rory Bremner (Various Roles).

Holding / Source
D3 / D3S

01.01.1993

A ROSE FOR WINTER

A BBC Birmingham production for BBC 2. Transmission details are for BBC 2. Duration varies - see below for details.
Main regular credit(s):   Written by Laurie Lee; music by Julian Bream; produced and directed by John King.
Main regular cast: John Wild (The Young Laurie Lee), Cordelia Roche (His Wife, Cathy), Laurie Lee (Narrator).

	Production No	VT Number	Holding / Source
23.12.1989	50/NBM/L536S	HR64620	DB / 1"

Duration: 51 minutes.
With Stanley Cheesewright, Robert Sanguinetti, Philip Valverdr, Tony Pike, Peter Gomez, D. A. Connor, John Dalmedo, Antonio Jimenez Rodriguez, Juan Perez Dominguez, Francisco Quiros Martin, Encarnacion Novo Rivas, Jose Guerrero, Jose Alamino Guerrero.

| 24.12.1989 | 50/NBM/L548X/71X | HR58466 | DB / 1" |

Duration: 59 minutes.
With Adora Rodriquez, Jeronomio Martin, Jose A. Rodriguez, Isidro Carrascosa Jeronimo, Antonio Ratco Jeronimo, Jose Novo Rivas, Manuel Villoslada, Valentino Mateo Jeronimo, Josefina Cortes Rodriguez, Belen Montoro Jimenez, Monica Sanchez Palagios, Carmen Saez Rodriguez, Jose Vidal Pazos.

ROSEMARY AND THYME

A Carnival Films production for ITV 1. Transmission details are for the Central region. Duration varies - see below for details.
Main regular credit(s):   Theme music by John Williams; music by Christopher Gunning; produced by Brian Eastman.
Main regular cast: Felicity Kendal (Rosemary Boxer), Pam Ferris (Laura Thyme).

SERIES 3
Main regular credit(s):   Story consultant Peter Lovesey; associate producer Peter Hider.

Holding / Source
DB / V1SW

23.12.2005 **The Cup Of Silence**
Duration: 75 minutes.
Written by Stephen Gallagher; script supervisor Marissa Cowell; directed by Brian Farnham.
With Robert Portal, Dorian MacDonald, Clive Francis, Helen Grace, Philip Brook, Brian Shelley, Robin Parkinson, Niky Wardley, Francine Morgan, Eluned Jones, Grant Ibbs, Joe Dunlop, Dick Brannick, Rod Culbertson, Peter Vollebregt, Laura Checkley, Joanna Dunn.

Billed as a seven-part series (plus the Christmas special), its broadcast was curtailed with two episodes still unseen although these were released on DVD. They were eventually shown in the second half of 2007.
Sponsored by Lindemans.

ROTTEN APPLES

A MVP production for Channel 4. Transmission details are for Channel 4. Duration: 50 minutes.
Written by Niall Leonard; produced by Alan Janes; directed by Niall Leonard.
Ian McElhinney (Detective Inspector Spallen), B. J. Hogg (Dan Maguire), Des McAleer (Chief Inspector Blakey), Aiden Hamilton (Detective Constable Brian McCaul), Lynda Steadman (Mrs Maguire), Toby E. Byrne (Detective Sergeant Dargan), Mark Aiken (Police Constable Perry), Frank Brennan (Police Constable Tyler), Ingrid Craigie (First Nun), Lollie May (Second Nun), Adele Silva (Aine Maguire).

Holding / Source
1" / 1"

26.12.1989

THE ROY CASTLE SHOW

A BBC production for BBC 1. Transmission details are for BBC 1. Duration varies - see below for details.
Main regular performer(s): Roy Castle (Host).
Transmission details are for BBC 2.

Holding / Source
J /

26.12.1964 **Roy Castle's Show**
Duration: 45 minutes.
Written by Dick Hills and Sid Green; orchestra conducted by Harry Rabinowitz; designed by Martin Johnson; produced and directed by Dennis Main Wilson.
With Bernard Cribbins, Paddy Stone, The Don Riddell Four, The Paddy Stone Dancers.

THE ROY CASTLE SHOW

A ROYAL CONCERT OF CAROLS

A Granada production. Transmission details are for the Central region. Duration: 41 minutes.

Research Helen McMurray; orchestra conducted by Charles Farncombe; designed by Taff Batley; produced by Stephen Leahy; directed by David Liddiment.

Robert Powell (Presenter), Marti Webb, Peter Donohoe, Rod Argent, Simon Lindley, Richard Fullbrook, Charles Fullbrook, William Lockhart.

	Holding / Source
25.12.1983	1" / 1"

ROYAL INSTITUTION CHRISTMAS LECTURES

A BBC production for BBC 2. Transmission details are for BBC 2.

	Production No	VT Number	Holding / Source
03.01.1973 **Ripples In The Ether 4: Pictures With And Without Wires**	06251/8376	VTC/6HT/82868	DB-D3 / 2"

Duration: 59 minutes.
Produced and directed by Alan Sleath.
With Geoffrey Gouriet (Speaker).

THE ROYAL

A Yorkshire Television production. Transmission details are for the Central region. Duration: 48 minutes.

Main regular credit(s):	Theme music by Michael Starke.

SERIES 3

Main regular credit(s):	Executive producer Keith Richardson; produced by Ken Horn.
Main regular cast:	With Amy Robbins (Doctor Jill Weatherill), Andy Wear (Alun Morris), Polly Maberly (Doctor Lucy Klein), Denis Lill (Mr Rose), Anna Madeley (Samantha Beaumont), Paul Fox (Doctor Jeff Goodwin), John Axon (Mr Harper), Ian Carmichael (T. J. Middleditch), Julian Ovenden (Doctor David Cheriton), Robert Daws (Doctor Gordon Ormerod), Wendy Craig (Matron), Michael Starke (Ken Hopkirk), Michelle Hardwick (Lizzie Kennoway), Linda Armstrong (Sister Brigid), Zoie Kennedy (Staff Nurse Meryl Taylor).

	Holding / Source
21.12.2003 **Famous For A Day**	DB / DBSWF

There's snow on the ground in Elsinby and Christmas is coming. For the staff of The Royal, the festive season is proving to be as eventful as ever. Dr Gordon Ormerod and Staff Nurse Meryl Taylor are faced with a battle against time when they are called out to help a young boy who has fallen through the ice on a frozen lake. On their arrival at the scene they are horrified to discover that Peter Thomas has been trapped below the surface for over twenty minutes. The emergency services eventually manage to break the ice and drag his lifeless body from the water. Dr Ormerod desperately tries to resuscitate Peter but disaster strikes on the way back to the hospital when the ambulance becomes stuck in a snowdrift. With time of the essence they eventually manage to dig out the stranded vehicle and on their arrival back at The Royal the medical team continue their attempts to revive Peter. But as the minutes tick by, Dr Ormerod begins to accept that their efforts are futile. Matron prepares Peter's parents for the worst, whilst back in the operation theatre Dr Ormerod and Dr Jill Weatherill reluctantly agree to stop any further attempts at resuscitation and begin to remove Peter's breathing tube. But the young lad appears to have a guardian angel hovering over him and there is a sigh of relief when he suddenly starts to cough and calls out for his parents. Meanwhile, Dr Jeffrey Goodwin is faced with a few problems of his own when Ray Piper is brought in to the hospital with a huge bump on his head. Dr Goodwin and Mr Rose can barely contain their amusement when Ray explains that his injures are the result of being hit on the head by a frozen turkey which was thrown by his wife. Alun is taken aback when he opens a cupboard door to find an elderly gentleman sitting inside. Matron and Student Nurse Samantha Beaumont try to find out the man's identity and are surprised to learn that he is Ray's father, Ernest. On hearing that her grandfather has been admitted to hospital, Suzanne Piper arrives to see him. She is furious to discover that her mother has grown tired of looking after Ernest and dumped him at the hospital. Suzanne rushes off to confront her mother and it's not long before another member of the Piper clan is admitted to casualty - Mrs Norma Piper! There is excitement in the air when a film crew from Tyne Tees Television arrives at The Royal to film a special Christmas item for their evening news programme. Desperate for his fifteen minutes of fame Mr Harper decides to join the hospital choir. After a tuneless singing display in rehearsals, Mr Middleditch tells Mr Harper that he can't be in the choir as he has a much more important job for him. And the troublesome official is less than impressed to discover that he will have to appear on camera dressed as Father Christmas. As the moment of transmission draws closer, Lizzie is star struck when veteran television presenter Lennie Lemarr arrives. But as the cameras roll, trouble is just around the corner. Guest star for the Christmas episode is SIMON BATES who plays television presenter Lennie Lemarr.

Written by Jane Hollowood; directed by Tim Dowd.

With William Simons (Police Constable Ventress), Daniel Ryan, Bernard Wrigley, Keith Marsh, Catherine Breeze, Steve Huison, Rebecca Atkinson, Smug Roberts, Jonathan Essex, Carl Cleka, Simon Bates.

See also: HEARTBEAT

THE ROYLE FAMILY

A Granada production for BBC Manchester. Transmission details are for BBC 1. Usual duration: 30 minutes.

Main regular cast:	Ricky Tomlinson (Jim Royle), Sue Johnston (Barbara Royle), Caroline Aherne (Denise Royle/Best), Craig Cash (Dave Best).

SERIES 2

Main regular credit(s):	Written by Caroline Aherne and Craig Cash; additional material by Ricky Tomlinson; theme music by Oasis; designed by James Dillon; associate producers Caroline Aherne and Craig Cash; executive producer Andy Harries; head of production Susy Liddell; production manager John Rushton; produced by Kenton Allen; directed by Steve Bendelack.
Main regular cast:	With Ralf Little (Antony Royle), Liz Smith (Nana aka Norma Speakman).

	Holding / Source
25.12.1999	DB / V1SW
Duration: 40 minutes.	

SERIES 3

Main regular credit(s):	Written by Caroline Aherne and Craig Cash; executive producer Andy Harries; produced by Kenton Allen and Caroline Aherne; directed by Caroline Aherne.
Main regular cast:	With Ralf Little (Antony Royle), Liz Smith (Nana), Matthew Hughes (Baby David), James Hughes (Baby David).

	Holding / Source
25.12.2000 **The Royle Family At Christmas**	DB / V1SW

With Andrew Whyment, Sheridan Smith, Sharon Duce, John Henshaw.

THE ROYLE FAMILY (continued)   British Christmas Television Guide

Holding / Source
25.12.2008   **The New Sofa**   HD/DB / HD/DB

A Jellylegs Productions Ltd production for Granada. Duration: 60 minutes.

Written by Caroline Aherne, Craig Cash and Phil Mealey; script supervisor Mo Johnstone; designed by Margaret Coombes; executive producers Caroline Aherne, Craig Cash, Phil Mealey, Rebecca Papworth and Saurabh Kakkar; production manager Dominique Molloy; produced by John Rushton; directed by Caroline Aherne.

With Tom Courtenay, Geoffrey Hughes, Helen Fraser.

Holding / Source
25.12.2009   **The Golden Egg Cup**   HD/DB / HD/DB

A Jellylegs Productions Ltd production for Granada. Duration: 60 minutes.

Written by Caroline Aherne, Craig Cash and Phil Mealey; script supervisor Mo Johnstone; director of photography Jeremy Hiles; art director Chris Kay; designed by Margaret Coombes; executive producers Caroline Aherne, Craig Cash, Phil Mealey, Jon Rolph and Saurabh Kakkar; production manager Dominique Molloy; produced by John Rushton; directed by Caroline Aherne.

With Ralf Little (Anthony), Jessica Hynes (Cheryl), Peter Martin.

Holding / Source
25.12.2010   **Joe's Crackers**   HD/DB / HD/DB

A Jellylegs Productions Ltd production for Granada. Duration: 60 minutes.

Written by Caroline Aherne, Craig Cash and Phil Mealey; script supervisor Mo Johnstone; director of photography Jeremy Hiles; art director Chris Kay; designed by Margaret Coombes; executive producers Caroline Aherne, Craig Cash, Phil Mealey, Kristian Smith, Saurabh Kakkar and Lucy Ansbro; production manager Dominique Molloy; produced by John Rushton; directed by Caroline Aherne.

With Joanne Froggatt (Saskia), Jessica Hynes (Cheryl), Ralf Little (Anthony), Peter Martin (Joe Carrol).

Holding / Source
25.12.2012   **Barbara's Old Ring**   HD/DB / HDC

A Jellylegs Productions Ltd production for Granada. Duration: 60 minutes.

Written by Caroline Aherne, Craig Cash and Phil Mealey; produced by Lucy Ansbro; directed by Caroline Aherne.

With Peter Martin (Joe Carrol), Mary Healey (Philomena), Sheila Vaughan (Doreen), Denice Hope (Brenda), Menyee Lai (Ling Su), Marie Mitchell (Betty), Steve Money (Petula), Iris Sharples (Elsie), Lorraine Bruce (Carol).

RPM

A BBC West production for BBC 1 West. Transmission details are for BBC 1 West. Duration: 30 minutes.

SERIES 1: Rock

Holding / Source
21.12.1979   DB-D3 / 2"

THE RUBY IN THE SMOKE

A BBC production for BBC 1. made in association with WGBH Boston. Transmission details are for BBC 1. Duration: 95 minutes.

Adapted by Adrian Hodges; based on a book by Philip Pullman; music by Martin Phipps; executive producers Sally Woodward Gentle and Rebecca Eaton; produced by Kate Bartlett; directed by Brian Percival.

Billie Piper (Sally Lockhart), Julie Walters (Mrs Holland), J. J. Feild (Frederick Garland), David Harewood (Matthew Bedwell / Reverend Nicolas Bedwell), Don Gilet (Henry Hopkins), Robert Glenister (Samuel Selby), Hayley Atwell (Rosa Garland), Elliot Cowan (Van Eeden), Matt Smith (Jim Taylor), Sian Thomas (Mrs Rees), Kay Lyon (Ellen), Robert Putt (Porter), Trevor Cooper (Mr Higgs), Dominic Coleman (Jeremiah Blyth), Miles Anderson (Major Marchbanks), Tilly Vosburgh (Mrs Thorpe), Chloe Walker (Adelaide), Ramon Tikaram (Maharajah), Matthew Cureton (Young Marchbanks), Tom Davey (Young Lockhart), Martin Jarvis (Voice of Captain Lockhart), Tony Maudsley (Mr Berry), Pik Sen Lim (Madame Sheng), Julia Joyce (Young Sally Lockhart), Tom Wu (Perak), Billy Seymour (Paddy).

Holding / Source
27.12.2006   HD/DB / HDC

RUM PUNCH

An Associated-Rediffusion production. Transmission details are for Associated-Rediffusion. Duration: 50 minutes.

Written by Bill Owen and Peter Ling; dance direction by Jack Billings; associate producer Robert Tronson; produced and directed by Michael Westmore.

Bill Owen, John Blythe, Hannah Watt, Cherry Lind, Clive Dunn, Toni Le Pore, Rohan de Saram, Gordon Needham, Benny Lee, Peter Reeves, Janet Ball, Corinne Grey, Eunice Jebbett, Gilda Russell, Marigold Russell, Rosemary Stewart, The Visionaires, The Visionettes, Peter and Quedita, Steve Race and his Concert Orchestra.

Holding / Source
26.12.1955   J /

RUMOURS OF ANGELS

A BBC production for BBC 1. Transmission details are for BBC 1. Duration: 4 minutes.

Written by Tony Robinson; produced by Graham Judd; directed by Tristram Powell.

Thora Hird (Storyteller).

Holding / Source
25.12.1999   DB / DBSW

RUMPOLE OF THE BAILEY

A Thames Television production. Transmission details are for the Central region. Duration varies - see below for details.

Main regular credit(s): Written by John Mortimer; theme music by Joseph Horovitz.

Main regular cast: Leo McKern (Horace Rumpole), Julian Curry (Claude Erskine-Brown), Jonathan Coy (Henry).

Transmission details are for the ATV midlands region.

Credits: Executive producer John Frankau; produced by Jacqueline Davis.

Cast: With Peggy Thorpe-Bates (Hilda Rumpole).

	VT Number	Holding / Source
30.12.1980 **Rumpole's Return**	23624	D3 / 2"

Duration: 100 minutes.

Will Horace Rumpole, one time Old Bailey hack lawyer, be content to ripen like an orange in his retirement in Miami, or will a surprise letter from a lady barrister tempt him back to his life of crime? Is She Who Must Be Obeyed right to suspect Rumpole of turning to "sex"?

Designed by Philip Blowers; directed by John Glenister.

With Peter Bowles (Guthrie Featherstone), Patricia Hodge (Phyllida Erskine-Brown), Richard Murdoch (Uncle Tom), Bill Fraser (Judge Bullingham), Maureen Darbyshire (Dianne), Albert Welling, Robin Halstead, Carl Andrews, Shelagh Stephenson, John Price, Grafton Radcliffe, Ken Rahgers, Patsy Smart, Deborah Fallender, Ian Gelder, Dick Sterling, Phil Marquis, Maxine Johnson, Christine Page, Jorge Gill, Gordon Salkilld, James Smith, Leonard Maguire, Derek Benfield, Alan Lake, John Alkin, Robert Hartley, John Humphry, Roger Booth, Gerald Cross, Trevor Bowen, Peter Hughes, Moray Watson.

See also: PLAY FOR TODAY (BBC)

RUNAROUND

A Southern Television production. Transmission details are for the ATV midlands region. Duration: 25 minutes.

Main regular credit(s): Devised by Meril Heatter and Bob Quigley; theme music by Jugg Music.

SERIES 1

Main regular credit(s): Designed by Greg Lawson; produced and directed by Colin Nutley.

Main regular performer(s): With Mike Reid (Host).

	Holding / Source
26.12.1975 **A Christmas Runaround**	J / 2"

With The Wombles, Roy Castle, Winchester Cathedral Choir.

SERIES 4

Main regular credit(s): Designed by Greg Lawson; produced and directed by Colin Nutley.

Main regular performer(s): With Mike Reid (Host).

	Holding / Source
27.12.1976 **Christmas Runaround**	J / 2"

With Barbara Windsor, Murray Head.

SERIES 6

Main regular credit(s): Designed by Greg Lawson; produced and directed by Greg Lanning.

Main regular performer(s): With Stan Boardman (Host).

	Holding / Source
28.12.1977 **Christmas Runaround**	J / 2"

Special circus edition.

	VT Number	Holding / Source
24.12.1979 **A Christmas Runaround**	3969	DB / 2"

Research Jude Hackett; designed by Greg Lawson; executive producer Lewis Rudd; produced and directed by Colin Nutley.

With Mike Reid (Host), Barbara Dickson, Pipes & Drums of 1st Battalion Irish Guards And Cormack, Russell Brandon, Lynn Harrison, Anthony Willson, Jude Hackett*.

SERIES 11

Main regular credit(s): Designed by Greg Lawson; executive producer Lewis Rudd; produced by John Coxall.

Main regular performer(s): With Mike Reid (Host).

	VT Number	Holding / Source
24.12.1980 **Runaround Christmas Special: Runaround On Ice**	5149	2" / 2"

A Christmas Runaround promises to be a chilly affair. Not only do 10 young contestants don skates to chase prizes on an ice-rink built in the studio, but Mike comes face to face with an eskimo in an igloo, some penguins, and a pair of reindeer. There's also a display of ice pantomime costumes, plus guest pop group Madness.

Directed by John Coxall.

With Big Daddy, Madness, Frankie Au, John L. Neal.

RUPERT

Produced for Various ITV Companies by a variety of companies (see details below). Transmission details are for the Central region.

Main regular credit(s): Based on characters created by Mary Tourtel.

SERIES 4

Commissioned by Scottish Television.

	Holding / Source
04.01.1996 **Rupert's Christmas Adventure**	DB / V1

THE RUSS ABBOT SHOW

A BBC production for BBC 1. Transmission details are for BBC 1. Duration varies - see below for details.

Main regular cast: Russ Abbot (Various roles).

SERIES 1
Main regular credit(s): Music directed by Alyn Ainsworth; produced and directed by John Bishop.

Holding / Source
23.12.1986 Christmas Show   DB / 1"
Duration: 40 minutes.
Written by Barry Cryer, Dick Vosburgh, Paul Minett, Brian Leveson, Russel Lane and Bobby Crush; script associate Barry Cryer; choreography by Domini Winter; designed by Gary Williamson.
With Les Dennis, Bella Emberg, Maggie Moone, Tom Bright, Suzy Aitchison, Paul Shearer.

SERIES 3
Main regular credit(s): Script associates Barry Cryer and Peter Vincent; music directed by Alyn Ainsworth; theme music by Steve Brown and Gary Roberts; produced and directed by John Bishop.

Holding / Source
25.12.1988 The Russ Abbot Christmas Show   DB / 1"
Duration: 43 minutes.
Written by Paul Alexander, Barry Cryer, Paul Minett, Brian Leveson, Peter Robinson, Peter Vincent and Dick Vosburgh; lyrics by Paul Minett and Brian Leveson; music by Alyn Ainsworth; choreography by Phil Winston; designed by Dacre Punt; production manager Garrie Mallen.
With Les Dennis, Bernard Cribbins, Tom Bright, Bella Emberg, Sherrie Hewson, George Malpas, John Nettleton, Stuart St. Paul.

SERIES 4
Main regular credit(s): Script associate Barry Cryer; choreography by Tudor Davies; produced and directed by John Bishop.

Holding / Source
25.12.1989 The Russ Abbot Christmas Show   DB / 1"
Duration: 40 minutes.
Designed by David Hitchcock and Bob Cove.
With Les Dennis, Bella Emberg, Sherrie Hewson, Tom Bright, Michael Stainton.

SERIES 5
Main regular credit(s): Produced by John Bishop; directed by Peter Laskie.
Main regular cast: With Les Dennis, Bella Emberg, Lisa Maxwell, Tom Bright, Sherrie Hewson.

Holding / Source
26.12.1990 The Russ Abbot Christmas Show   DB / 1"
Duration: 40 minutes.
With Barry Craine.

THE RUSS ABBOT SHOW

A Granada production. Transmission details are for the Central region.
Main regular cast: Russ Abbot (Various roles).

Holding / Source
26.12.1996 The Russ Abbot Christmas Special   D2 / D2S
Duration: 37 minutes.
Christmas special of the comedy sketch programme including parodies of The X Files and Pride and Prejudice.
Produced by Mark Gorton; directed by Tony Prescott.
With Bella Emberg, Peter Gunn, Siobhan Finneran, Gary Lovini, Angela Douglas, Les Dennis.

RUSS ABBOT'S SATURDAY MADHOUSE

An LWT production. Transmission details are for the ATV/Central region. Duration varies - see below for details.
Main regular cast: Russ Abbot (Various roles).

SERIES 1
Transmission details are for the ATV midlands region.
Main regular credit(s): Music directed by Alyn Ainsworth; designed by Pip Gardner; produced and directed by John Kaye Cooper.

Holding / Source
26.12.1981 Russ Abbot's Christmas Madhouse   D2 / 2"
Duration: 40 minutes.
Written by Russel Lane, Howard Imber, Geoff Rowley and Bernard Wilkie; script associate Russel Lane; lyrics by Colin Bostock-Smith, Paul Minett and Brian Leveson; music by Colin Bostock-Smith, Paul Minett and Brian Leveson; associate producer Bruce McClure; production manager Brian Penny.
With Dustin Gee, Patti Gold, Michael Barrymore, Susie Blake, Jeffrey Holland, Bella Emberg, Alyn Ainsworth and his Orchestra.

SERIES 2

Transmission details are for the Central region.
Main regular cast: With Dustin Gee.

	Holding / Source
31.12.1982 **Russ Abbot's Hogmanay Madhouse**	D2 / 2"

Alt.Title(s): *Russ Abbot's Scottish Madhouse*
Duration: 39 minutes.
Written by Colin Bostock-Smith, Russel Lane, Paul Minett, Brian Leveson and Geoff Rowley; script associate Russel Lane; music by Alyn Ainsworth; designed by Pip Gardner; produced and directed by John Kaye Cooper.
With Michael Barrymore, Susie Blake, Les Dennis, Bella Emberg, Dustin Gee, Sherrie Hewson, Jeffrey Holland, Jan Mark.

SERIES 5

Transmission details are for the Central region.
Main regular credit(s): Designed by Pip Gardner; associate producer Russel Lane; produced and directed by David Bell.

	Holding / Source
22.12.1984 **Russ Abbot's Christmas Madhouse**	D2 / 1"

Duration: 49 minutes.
Music directed by Alyn Ainsworth.
With Dustin Gee, Jeffrey Holland, Susie Blake, Les Dennis, Sherrie Hewson, Bella Emberg, Bill Pridden.

RUSSELL BRAND'S PONDERLAND

A Vanity Projects production for Channel 4. Transmission details are for Channel 4. Duration: 25 minutes.
Main regular cast: Russell Brand (Host).

SERIES 2

Main regular credit(s): Written by Russell Brand; script supervisor Rebecca Havers; theme music by Jason Tarver and Ben Vella; programme consultant Matt Morgan; designed by Rudi Thackray; associate producer Nik Linnen; executive producer John Linnen; production manager Amber Rose Lambert; produced by Jack Bayles; directed by Toby Baker.

	Holding / Source
21.12.2008 **Russell Brand's Christmas Ponderland**	DB / DBSW

Written by Russell Brand, Jack Bayles and Gareth Roy.

RUSSELL HARTY

An LWT production. Transmission details are for the London Weekend Television region.
Main regular performer(s): Russell Harty (Presenter).

SERIES 1

	Production No	Holding / Source
20.12.1974	9L/09492	D2 / 2"

With Roger Moore, Fleur Coles, ITN Newscasters carol singing.

SERIES 2

	Production No	Holding / Source
26.12.1975 **Russell Harty Goes Upstairs Downstairs**	9L/02911	D2 / 2"

Duration: 25 minutes.
You either like him or loathe him... his style of questioning either engages or enrages you... either way, tune in tonight with controversial "chat show" personality Russell Harty and find out the truth about 165 Eaton Place and those people downstairs of upstairs.
   See what you think of Mrs. Bridges' mince pies... hear what Hudson really thinks of Rose, Frederick and Ruby... and if you've ever wondered what Ruby was really like, listen into some of the secrets of that superior scullery...
Written by Nicholas Barrett; produced by Nicholas Barrett; directed by Mike Mansfield.

RUSSELL HARTY

A BBC Manchester production for BBC 2. Transmission details are for BBC 2. Duration varies - see below for details.
Main regular performer(s): Russell Harty (Presenter).

SERIES 7

Duration: 32 minutes.
Main regular credit(s): Executive producer Ken Stephinson.

	Holding / Source
15.12.1981	DB / 1"

Designed by Humphrey Jaeger; assistant producer Chris Riley; produced by Tom Gutteridge; studio sequences directed by Ron Isted.
With Kenny Everett, Penelope Keith, Choristers And Vicars Choral Of St Pauls Cathedral.

SERIES 8

	Holding / Source
21.12.1982 **Russell Harty's Christmas Party**	DB / 1"

Duration: 35 minutes.
Music directed by Laurie Holloway; produced and directed by Tom Gutteridge.
With Shaw Taylor, Peter Moore, Nicholas Parsons, Sandra Dickinson, Peter Davison, Sarah Kennedy, Matthew Kelly, Esther Rantzen, St Paul's Cathedral Choir, Shelley Winters, James Burke, Hazel Fletcher, Rosalind Runcie.

RUSSELL HARTY (continued)

See also: RUSSELL HARTY AT HOME (BBC)

RUSSELL HARTY AT HOME

A BBC production for BBC 2. Transmission details are for BBC 2. Duration: 50 minutes.

Produced by Ken Stephinson; directed by Alan Walsh.

Russell Harty (Presenter), Cilla Black, The Cambridge Buskers, Dame Edna Everage, Madge Hindle, Arthur Marshall, Edna O'Brien, The Great Soprendo, John Tovey, Giggleswick and Settle Brass Band, Keasden Carol Singers, Kirkby Lonsdale Handbell Ringers.

	Holding / Source
24.12.1981	DB-D3 / 2"

See also: RUSSELL HARTY (BBC)

RUSSELL HARTY PLUS

An LWT production. Transmission details are for the London Weekend Television region. Duration varies - see below for details.

Main regular performer(s): Russell Harty (Presenter).

SERIES 1

Main regular credit(s): Executive producer Geoffrey Hughes; produced by Michael Lindsay-Hogg; directed by Bruce Gowers.

	Production No	Holding / Source
23.12.1972 The Best Of Russell Harty Christmas Special	9L/09160	D2 / 2"

Duration: 52 minutes.

With Carol Channing, Amy Spencer, David Frost, Rita Hunter, Spike Milligan, Margaret Powell, Johnny Weismuller, Elaine Stritch, Little Richard, Roger Moore, Tony McCabe.

Tony McCabe is a man who jumps on eggs without breaking them.

RUSSELL HOWARD LIVE: DINGLEDODIES

An Avalon Productions production for BBC 3. Transmission details are for BBC 3. Duration: 60 minutes.

Written by Russell Howard; script supervisor Rebecca Havers; designed by Dennis De Groot; executive producers Richard Allen-Turner, James Taylor and Jon Thoday; head of production Bluey Richards; production manager Lay-Ee Quah; directed by Peter Orton.

Russell Howard.

	Holding / Source
16.12.2010	HD/DB / HDC

Alternative transmissions: BBC 2: 21.12.2010.

RUSSELL HOWARD'S GOOD NEWS

An Avalon Productions production for BBC 3. Transmission details are for BBC 3. Duration: 30 minutes.

Main regular cast: Russell Howard.

SERIES 1

Main regular credit(s): Written by Russell Howard; script supervisor Annie Griffiths; titles by Blac Ionica; art director Neil Barnes; designed by James Dillon; production team Emma Sinclair; assistant producer David Howarth; executive producers Karl Warner, Richard Allen-Turner, James Taylor and Jon Thoday; head of production Bluey Richards; production manager Lay-Ee Quah; series producer Robyn O'Brien; produced by Mark Iddon; directed by Peter Orton.

	Holding / Source
17.12.2009 Russell Howard's Good News Xmas Special	HD/DB / HDC

Programme associates Dan Atkinson, Karl Minns and Steve Williams.

"Russell Howard's Good News Extra" was broadcast on the Saturday evening afterwards, 45 minutes in length.

* Acts marked with the asterisk appeared only on the longer extended Saturday evening shows.

RUTH JONES'S CHRISTMAS CRACKER

A Tidy Productions production for BBC Wales. Transmission details are for BBC 2. Duration: 40 minutes.

Jones's cosy, retro talk show works well at Christmas. Not all seasonal programmes are festive, and not all chat shows are actually chatty, but this is both.

Executive producer David Peet; produced by Tony Followell.

Ruth Jones (Host), James Corden, Lulu, Manic Street Preachers, Micky Flanagan.

	Holding / Source
21.12.2011	HD/DB / HDC

THE RUTH RENDELL MYSTERIES

Produced for TVS/Meridian by a variety of companies (see details below). Transmission details are for the Central region. Duration varies - see below for details.

Main regular credit(s):   Based on books by Ruth Rendell; developed by John Davies.

	VT Number	Holding / Source
23.12.1988 **No Crying He Makes**	12982	1" / 1"

A TVS production. Duration: 100 minutes.

Adapted by Paula Milne; script executive Corinne Cartier; music by Brian Bennett; designed by Christine Ruscoe; executive producer Graham Benson; produced by Neil Zeiger; directed by Mary McMurray.

With George Baker (Detective Chief Inspector Wexford), Christopher Ravenscroft (Detective Inspector Burden), Louie Ramsay (Dora Wexford), Jane Horrocks (Pippa Bond), Clive Wood (Tony Jasper), Christine Kavanagh (Leila Jasper), Jonathan Lacey (Trevor Bond), Alison Rose (Susan Raines), Dorothy Vernon (Mrs Carter), Meera Syal (Matron), Ann Penfold (Jean Burden), Charon Bourke (Sylvia Wexford), Emma Smith (Pat Burden), Noah Huntley (John Burden), Natasha Williams (Julie), Ashley Barker (Pete Jasper), Ken Kitson (Detective Sergeant Martin), Sasha Mitchell (Woman Police Constable Carla), Colin Campbell (Sergeant Willoughby), Kenneth Midwood (Mr Henderson), Julia Lang (Mrs Henderson), Richard Haddon-Haines (Mr Hunter), Karen Archer (Mrs Hunter), Shirley-Anne Selby (Mandy), Barbara Marten (Katharine Freeman), Ian Bleasdale (Mr Franklin), Karen Gledhill (Mrs Franklin), Rosalind Thomas (Senior Nursing Officer), Tom Knight (Man In Police Station), Peggy Ann Wood (Woman In Newsagents).

	VT Number	Holding / Source
17.12.1989 **The Veiled One**	22719	1" / C1

A TVS production. Duration: 100 minutes.

Adapted by Trevor Preston; script executive Corinne Cartier; music by Richard Blackford; executive producer Graham Benson; produced by Neil Zeiger; directed by Mary McMurray.

With George Baker (Chief Inspector Wexford), Christopher Ravenscroft (Detective Inspector Ravenscroft), Louie Ramsay (Dora Wexford), Paola Dionisotti (Dorothy Sanders), Camille Coduri (Lesley Arbel), Ian Fitzgibbon (Clifford Sanders), Hugh Lloyd (Ralph Robson), Simon Chandler (Reese), Deborah Poplett (Sheila Wexford), Tony Vogel (Roy Carroll), David Fleeshman (Serge Olson), Arthur Hewlett (Archie Greaves), Philip Bretherton (John Whillon), Susie Lindeman (Nina Jago), Paula Jacobs (Dila Jago), Teohna Williams (Nicola Resnick), Gillian Eaton (Sandra Dale), Ann Windsor (Ms Moore), Phil Atkinson (Leary), Sally Toft (Woman Police Constable).

	VT Number	Holding / Source
24.12.1990 **Put On By Cunning**	22715	1" / V1

A TVS production. Duration: 100 minutes.

Adapted by Trevor Preston; script executive Corinne Cartier; music by Brian Bennett; executive producer Graham Benson; produced by Neil Zeiger; directed by Sandy Johnson.

With George Baker (Detective Chief Inspector Wexford), Christopher Ravenscroft (Detective Inspector Burden), Louie Ramsay (Dora Wexford), Diane Keen (Jenny Burden), Rossano Brazzi (Sir Manuel Carmargue), Beryl Reid (Mrs Mountnessing), Janet Maw (Dinah Sternhold), Cherie Lunghi (Natalie Arno), Malcolm Raeburn (Ted Hicks), Philip Locke (Kenneth Ames), Charon Bourke (Sylvia Fairfax), Sally Home (Mrs Murray-Burgess), Helena McCarthy (Mary Woodhouse), Michael Bilton (Philip Cory), Malcolm Tierney (Ivan Zoffany), Amanda Boxer (Jane Zoffany), Vincenzo Nicoli (John Cooper), Amy Werba (Therese Leremy), Angus MacInnes (Dobrowski), Tim Meats (Rector), Bob Sessions (Tom Sessamy), Valerie Colgan (Edith Sessamy), Beth Porter (Davina Ilbert), Nathan Dambuza (Mr Haq), Myra McFadyen (Muriel Hicks), Eileen Maciejewska (Mavis Roland), David Stoll (Coroner), Peter Penry Jones (Mr Browning), Ian Talbot (Mr Rochford), Carmen Gomez (Mrs Romero), Sheri Foxcroft (Receptionist), Ruth Trouncer (Magistrate), Stephen Solloway (Flautist).

	VT Number	Holding / Source
26.12.1991 **Achilles Heel**	22911	1" / V1

A Blue Heaven Productions production for TVS. Duration: 100 minutes.

Adapted by Guy Hibbert; script executive Corinne Cartier; music by Brian Bennett; executive producer Graham Benson; produced by Neil Zeiger; directed by Sandy Johnson.

With George Baker (Detective Chief Inspector Wexford), Christopher Ravenscroft (Detective Inspector Burden), Louie Ramsay (Dora Wexford), Diane Keen (Jenny Burden), Stephen Dillane (Philip Blackstock), Norman Eshley (Jon Walsh), Saira Todd (Lucy Rieux), Julia Lane (Anna), Kim Darclay (Iris Blaoketook), Andre Oumansky (Ange), Anna Way (Mrs Penn), Robert Hands (Police Constable Stevens), Charlotte Howard (Linda Blackstock), Kate O'Connell (Jane Conway), Preston Lockwood (Auden), Richard Strange (Howard, Photographer), Philip McGough (Davies, Forensic Scientist), Sadie Shimmin (Cleaner).

	VT Number	Holding / Source
27.12.1992 **Talking To Strange Men**	23668	1" / V1

A Blue Heaven Productions production for Meridian. Duration: 100 minutes.

Executive producers Graham Benson and Colin Rogers; produced by Neil Zeiger; directed by John Gorrie.

With John Duttine (John Creevey), Mel Martin (Jennifer Creevey), Robert Jones (Charles Mabledene), Nicholas Haley (Mungo Cameron), Alistair Haley (Patrick Crawshaw), Jonathan Bancroft (Nigel Hobhouse), Justin Chadwick (Gavin), Ralph Brown (Peter Mullin), Sara Griffiths (Penelope), Trevor Cooper (Detective Chief Inspector Fordwych), Abigail McKern (Detective Constable Susan Aubrey), Adrian Ross-Magenty (Angus Cameron), Elspeth Charlton (Doctor Lucy Cameron), Keeley Hawes (Sarah Mabledene), Miles Anderson (Mark Simms), Richard Williams (Graham O'Neill), Corrin Helliwell (Les), Josephine Clarke (Sharon), Harmage Singh Kalirai (Sikh), Basil Moss (Doctor Fergus Cameron), Susan Tracy (Gloria Mabledene), Geoffrey Greenhill (Vic).

	Production No	Holding / Source
01.01.1996 **Heartstones**	MER/194006/T01	D2 / V1S

A Blue Heaven Productions production for Meridian. Duration: 99 minutes.

Adapted by Guy Meredith; executive producers Colin Rogers and Graham Benson; produced by Neil Zeiger; directed by Piers Haggard.

With Anthony Andrews (Luke), Emily Mortimer (Elvira), Daisy Haggard (Spinny), Alan MacNaughtan (The Dean), Helena Michell (Mary), Jack Galloway (Anthony Lewis), Roger Hammond (Doctor Trewynne), Elspet Gray (Mrs Crossland), Leon Lissek (Professor Cyprian), Elizabeth Mickery (Doctor Sayles), Jeannie Crowther (Rosemary), Richard Cubison (Doctor Bulmer), Ursula Mohan (Mrs Cyprian), Antony Higginson (Doctor Walsh), Gresby Nash (Daniel), Marian Diamond (Doctor Jamieson), Danny Dyer (Tom), Idris Elba (Pest Controller), Gilbert Wynne (Coroner), Pamela Ruddock (Invigilator), Geoff Dodsworth (Uncle Sam), Dot Latham (Dean's Wife), Wayne Ings (Policeman).

Made as a two-part serial and then edited together. Each episode ran for 51 minutes.

RUTLAND WEEKEND TELEVISION

A BBC Various production for BBC 2. Transmission details are for BBC 2. Duration: 29 minutes.

Main regular credit(s): Written by Eric Idle; music by Neil Innes; produced by Ian Keill.

Main regular cast: Eric Idle.

Holding / Source

26.12.1975 **Christmas With Rutland Weekend Television** DB-D3 / 2"

Music by Neil Innes; designed by Geoff Powell and Humphrey Jaeger; directed by Andrew Gosling.
With Lyn Ashley, Carinthia West, David Battley, Jeannette Charles, Fatso, Neil Innes, Derek Ware, Henry Woolf, George Harrison.

RYAN AND RONNIE

Alternative/Working Title(s): RYAN A RONNIE

A BBC Wales production for BBC 1. Transmission details are for BBC 1. Duration: 30 minutes.

Main regular performer(s): Ryan Davies, Ronnie Williams.

Welsh language surviving editions:

Transmission details are for BBC 1 Wales. Duration: 25 minutes.

Holding / Source

25.12.1972 DB / 2"

RYAN DAVIES

A BBC Wales production for BBC 1 Wales. Transmission details are for BBC 1 Wales. Duration: 40 minutes.
Ryan Davies.

Holding / Source

25.12.1974 DB / 2"

Held at BBC Wales.

SAINT NICOLAS CANTATA OPUS 42

A Thames Television production. Transmission details are for the Thames Television region. Duration: 55 minutes.
Written by Benjamin Britten; lyrics by Eric Crozier; orchestra conducted by Russell Burgess; lighting by Bill Lee and Les Furlonger; sound Bill Sutton and Arthur Duff; designed by Vic Symonds; associate producer John Woods; executive producer Francis Coleman; produced and directed by Margery Baker.
Ian Partridge (Tenor), Wandsworth School Choir, St Alban's Girls' Choir, Orchestra Nova of London.

	VT Number	Holding / Source
22.12.1976	15344	DB / 2"

Won the Prix Italia for a music programme.

SALE OF THE CENTURY

An Anglia production. Transmission details are for ITV Various. Duration: 25 minutes.
Main regular credit(s): Music by Peter Fenn.
Main regular performer(s): Nicholas Parsons (Presenter).

SERIES 1
Transmission details are for the Anglia region.
Main regular credit(s): Designed by James Weatherup; produced and directed by Peter Joy.
Main regular performer(s): With Peter Fenn (Organist).

	Holding / Source
22.12.1972 **Christmas Special**	J / 2"

Alternative transmissions: LWT: 23.12.1972.
With Carol Dilworth (Hostess), Jennifer Cresswell (Hostess), Peter Marshall (Hostess), Thora Hird, Kenneth Connor, William Rushton.

SERIES 2
Transmission details are for the ATV midlands region.

	Holding / Source
22.12.1973	J / 2"

Sale of The Century brings you the chance of the year... to see two top quiz-masters quizzed! Nicholas Parsons fires his questions at Hughie Green, Alan Taylor of Mr. and Mrs., and comedian Norman Vaughan. All the goods won by this celebrity trio will be donated to various charities. Jennifer and Canasta display the prize -Christmas presents", John Benson describes them while Peter Fenn provides music to match the festive mood.
Music by Peter Fenn; designed by James Weatherup; produced and directed by Peter Joy.
With Jennifer Cresswell (Hostess), John Benson (Commentator), Hughie Green, Norman Vaughan, Alan Taylor, Canasta.

SERIES 4
Transmission details are for the ATV midlands region.
Main regular credit(s): Designed by Peter Farman; produced and directed by Bill Perry.

	Holding / Source
25.12.1976 **Christmas Sale Of The Century**	J / 2"

The Fire, Police and Nursing services take part in this special Christmas show. The fireman comes from Scotland, the policeman from West Yorkshire and the nurse from the south of England.
 As usual, Nicholas Parsons has questions valued at £1, £3 and £5 and it will he up to one of the contestants to try and out-buzz the other two.
With Angela Daniels (Hostess), Linda Hooks (Hostess), John Benson (Commentator).

SERIES 5
Transmission details are for the ATV midlands region.
Main regular credit(s): Designed by Peter Farman; produced and directed by Bill Perry.

	Holding / Source
25.12.1977 **Christmas Sale Of The Century**	J / 2"

With John Benson (Commentator), Sneh Gupta, Tina Robinson.

SERIES 6
Transmission details are for the ATV midlands region.
Main regular credit(s): Designed by Peter Farman; produced and directed by Bill Perry.
Main regular performer(s): With John Benson (Commentator).

	Holding / Source
26.12.1978 **Christmas Special**	J / 2"

With Eunice Denny (Hostess), Christine Owen (Hostess), Sophie Batchelor (Hostess), Carol Greenwood (Hostess), Laura Beaumont (Hostess).

SERIES 8
Transmission details are for the ATV midlands region.
Main regular credit(s): Designed by Peter Farman; produced and directed by Bill Perry.

	Holding / Source
22.12.1979 **Christmas Sale Of The Century**	J / 2"

With Christine Owen (Hostess), John Benson (Commentator), Sophie Batchelor (Hostess), Eunice Denny (Hostess), Laura Beaumont (Hostess), Carol Greenwood.

SALLY AND JAKE

A Cosgrove Hall production for Thames Television. Transmission details are for the ATV midlands region. Duration: 10 minutes.

SERIES 1

Main regular credit(s): Music by Malcolm Rowe; produced by Mark Hall and Brian Cosgrove.

Main regular cast: With Mike Savage (Narrator), Keith Hopwood (Singer).

Holding / Source

25.12.1973 **Sally And Jake's Christmas Adventure**   C1 / C1

There are plenty of surprises for Sally and Jake on Christmas Day. Surprises in the show, and from Harry and Mum.

Written by John Kershaw; directed by Bridget Appleby.

SANDI'S CHRISTMAS CRACKER

Commissioned by Sky Arts 1. Transmission details are for Sky Arts 1. Duration: 100 minutes.

Written by Dillie Keane.

Sandi Toksvig (Host), Ronnie Corbett (Co-Host), Frances Ruffelle (Vocalist), Arthur Smith (Scrooge), Sue Perkins (Cratchits), London Gay Men's Chorus.

Holding / Source

22.12.2009   HD/DB / Live

A SANTA FOR CHRISTMAS

An ATV production. Transmission details are for the ATV midlands region. Duration: 75 minutes.

Written by Sid Colin and Jimmy Grafton; music by Kenny Powell; dance direction by Eleanor Fazan; designed by Tom Lingwood and Tony Waller; executive producer Bill Ward; produced and directed by Brian Tesler.

Dickie Henderson, Tommy Cooper, Joyce Blair, Joan Savage, The Eleanor Fazan Dancers, Jack Parnell and his Orchestra, Anthea Askey, Arthur Haynes, Arthur Askey, Terry-Thomas, Avril Angers, Leslie Mitchell, Donald Gray, Diana Decker, William Hartnell, Geoffrey Sumner, Paddie O'Neil, Robin Bailey, Michael Miles, Hughie Green, David Jacobs, Irene Handl, Pat Coombs, Freddie Mills, Jack Solomons, Alfred Marks, Bill Owen, Danny Green, Len Harvey, Eric Boon, Kid Lewis, Billy Wells [as Bombardier Billy Wells], Dave Crowley, Val Parnell, Norman Wisdom, Johnnie Ray, Shani Wallis, Joan Regan, Rosemary Miller, Jill Browne, Charles Tingwell, Glyn Owen, Frederick Bartman.

Holding / Source

26.12.1957   J /

SARA AND HOPPITY

A P.P. Productions production for Roberta Leigh. Transmission details are for Associated-Rediffusion. Duration: 13 minutes.

Main regular credit(s): Written by Roberta Leigh; lyrics by Roberta Leigh; music by Roberta Leigh; produced by Roberta Leigh; directed by Arthur Provis.

Holding / Source

11.12.1962 **Sara And Father Christmas**   J / B3

18.12.1962 **Father Christmas And The Presents**   J / B3

THE SARAH JANE ADVENTURES

A BBC Wales production for BBC Children's Department. Transmission details are for CBBC.

Main regular credit(s): Created by Russell T. Davies; theme music by Murray Gold; production executive Julie Scott.

Main regular cast: Elisabeth Sladen (Sarah Jane Smith), Tommy Knight (Luke Smith).

Transmission details are for BBC 1.

Holding / Source

01.01.2007 **Invasion Of The Bane**   DB / DBSWF

Duration: 60 minutes.

Doctor Who's former assistant Sarah Jane Smith is now working as an investigative journalist. She joins forces with her 13-year-old neighbour Maria to fight evil alien forces at work in Britain. Their first case sees the duo come up against the Scheming Ms Wormwood.

Written by Russell T. Davies and Gareth Roberts; script editor Simon Winstone; music by Sam Watts; executive producers Julie Gardner, Russell T. Davies and Phil Collinson; produced by Susie Liggat; directed by Colin Teague.

With John Leeson (Voice of K.9), Yasmin Paige (Maria Jackson), Samantha Bond (Mrs Wormwood), Porsha Lawrence-Mavour, Jamie Davis, Joseph Millson, Juliet Cowan, Rungano Nyoni, Philip North, Alexander Armstrong, Sydney White, Olivia Hill, Konnie Huq, Gethin Jones.

See also: DOCTOR WHO (BBC) / K.9 AND COMPANY (BBC)

THE SARAH MILLICAN TELEVISION PROGRAMME

Commissioned by BBC 2. Transmission details are for BBC 2. Duration: 30 minutes.

Sarah Millican (Presenter).

SERIES 1

Credits: Executive producer Graham Stuart; produced by Paul McGettigan.

Holding / Source

23.12.2012 **The Sarah Millican Christmas Television Programme**   HD/DB / HDC

With Hugh Bonneville, Shane Richie.

THE SATURDAY BANANA

A Southern Television production. Transmission details are for the Southern Television region.

Main regular credit(s): Designed by Greg Lawson; produced by Anthony Howard; directed by Dave Heather and John Coxall.
Main regular cast: Bill Oddie (Presenter), Susan Tully (Presenter), Bill Gamon (Presenter).

SERIES 1

Holding / Source
23.12.1978 **Christmas Edition** J / 2"

THE SATURDAY NIGHT ARMISTICE

A BBC production for BBC 2. Transmission details are for BBC 2. Duration varies - see below for details.

Main regular cast: Armando Iannucci (Presenter), Peter Baynham (Presenter), David Schneider (Presenter).

Holding / Source
22.12.1995 **The Saturday Night Armistice Party Bucket** DB-D3 / D3S
Duration: 40 minutes.
Written by Armando Iannucci, Peter Baynham, David Schneider, Kevin Cecil, Sarah Smith, Graham Linehan, Arthur Mathews and Andy Riley; theme music by Jonathan Whitehead; theme sung by Johnny More; music by Jonathan Whitehead; assistant producer Susie Gautier-Smith; produced by Sarah Smith; directed by Steve Bendelack, Dominic Brigstocke, Andy De Emmony and John Kilby.
With Jean Beaton, Tim Berrington, Dave Charnley, Chris Dee, Gandini Juggling Project, Griffin Roddy O'Loughlin Dancers, Jonny Hackman, Mo Moreland, Sarah Parish, The Perez Boys [as The Perez Children], Jonathan Whitehead, The Jeremy Hanley Fan Club.
This edition was a compilation of highlights of the preceding series together with new seasonal material shot at the Putney Exchange shopping centre. The credits for this edition include those relating to the repeated material.
See also: THE FRIDAY NIGHT ARMISTICE (BBC)

SATURDAY NIGHT AT THE MILL

A BBC Birmingham production for BBC 1. Transmission details are for BBC 1. Duration varies - see below for details.

SERIES 1
Duration: 45 minutes.
Main regular credit(s): Produced by Roy Ronnie; directed by Roy Norton.
Main regular performer(s): With Bob Langley (Host), Donny MacLeod (Host), Kenny Ball and his Jazzmen.

Holding / Source
18.12.1976 **Back For Christmas** DB-D3 / 2"
With Frankie Howerd, Moira Anderson, Billy Dainty, Pam Ayres, Paul Melba.

SERIES 2
Main regular credit(s): Designed by David Crozier; assistant producer John Hughes; produced by Roy Ronnie; directed by Roy Norton.
Main regular performer(s): With Bob Langley (Host), Donny MacLeod (Host), Kenny Ball and his Jazzmen.

Holding / Source
28.12.1977 **If It's Wednesday It Must Be Saturday At The Mill** DB-D3 / 2"
Duration: 40 minutes.
With Ron Moody, Charlie Cairoli.

SERIES 3
Duration: 50 minutes.
Main regular credit(s): Produced by Roy Ronnie; directed by Roy Norton.
Main regular performer(s): With Bob Langley (Host), Tony Lewis (Host), Kenny Ball and his Jazzmen.

Holding / Source
26.12.1978 **Boxing Night At The Mill** DB-D3 / LivePAL
With Norman Wisdom, Libby Morris.
Four audition tapes dated Feb - Mar 78 exist on D3 ex-2".

SERIES 4
Main regular credit(s): Produced by Roy Ronnie; directed by Roy Norton.
Main regular performer(s): With Bob Langley (Host), Tony Lewis (Host), Kenny Ball and his Jazzmen.

Holding / Source
26.12.1979 **Boxing Night At The Mill** DB-D3 / 2"
Duration: 40 minutes.
With Les Dawson, Dana.

SERIES 5
Main regular credit(s): Produced by Roy Ronnie; directed by Roy Norton.
Main regular performer(s): With Bob Langley (Host), Kenny Ball and his Jazzmen.

Holding / Source
26.12.1980 **Boxing Night At The Mill** DB-D3 / 2"
Duration: 60 minutes.
With Ken Dodd, Susan Hampshire, Peter Davison, Wall Street Crash.

SATURDAY NIGHT THEATRE

Produced for ITV by a variety of companies (see details below). Transmission details are for the ATV midlands region. Usual duration: 53 minutes.

	Production No	Holding / Source
26.12.1970 **The Policeman And The Cook**	23043	D2 / 62

An Anglia production.

Victorian London, midnight, mist swirling through the darkened streets, and a terrifying cry. The classic ingredients of the classic murder story. But, as the young policeman who goes to investigate soon discovers, this is no ordinary case. He finds himself involved beyond the call of duty with a mysterious group of suspects and a crime that leads to more than murder...

Dramatised by Peter Van Greenaway; based on a story by Wilkie Collins; script editor John Rosenberg; designed by Eileen Diss; produced by John Jacobs; directed by Alan Gibson.

With Michael Crawford (Constable Gough), Gwen Ffrangcon-Davies (Miss Mybus), Felicity Gibson (Priscilla Smith), Reginald Marsh (Inspector Pennycuick), Pauline Delany (Mrs Crosscapel), William Lucas (Sergeant Gribble), John Normington (Mr Cramber), Callum Mill (Doctor Macleish), Pamela Moiseiwitsch (Mrs Jane Zebedee), Tim Curry (Crosscapel), Jill Richards (Betsy).

Advanced LWT press information suggested that John Hale and William Trevor would also be writing for the Wicked Women thread.

SATURDAY SCENE

An LWT production. Transmission details are for the London Weekend Television region.

SERIES 2

Main regular cast: With Sally James (Host).

	Holding / Source
27.12.1975 **Christmas Saturday Scene**	J / 2"

With Kenny.

	Holding / Source
28.12.1975 **Christmas Sunday Scene**	J / 2"

With Sally James (Presenter), Kenny.

(VAL PARNELL'S) SATURDAY SPECTACULAR

An ATV production. Transmission details are for the ATV London region. Usual duration: 50 minutes.

	Production No	VT Number	Holding / Source
26.12.1959 **This Particular Show**	2339	1195	DB-R1 / 40

The last explosion of stars in the old year.

Choreography by Malcolm Clare; designed by Peter Roden; produced and directed by Alan Tarrant.

With Tommy Steele, Morecambe and Wise, The Malcolm Clare Dancers, Jack Parnell and his Orchestra.

Recorded 01.12.1959.

	Production No	VT Number	Holding / Source
24.12.1960 **A Christmas Card From The Stars**	5425	3099	R1 / 40

Written by Richard Waring; orchestra conducted by Ron Goodwin, Tony Osborne, Bob Sharples and Cyril Stapleton; settings by Anthony Waller; produced by Francis Essex.

With Eve Boswell, Joyce and Lionel Blair, Tony Britton, Alma Cogan, Diane Hart, Michael Holliday, Rosalind Iden, David Jacobs, George Moon, Vera Lynn, Kenneth MacLeod, Des O'Connor, Wilfred Pickles, Jackie Rae, Brian Rix, Marion Ryan, Janette Scott, John Slater, Bert Weedon, Donald Wolfit, The Cyril Stapleton Show Band.

Recorded 18.12.1960.

Val Parnell's name was dropped from the title of the later programmes, and those were billed as SATURDAY SPECTACULAR. When other regions took the show on another weekday, as happened regularly during the programme's first year or so, it was billed there as VAL PARNELL'S SPECTACULAR.

After the end of the series in 1961, ATV London continued to broadcast a number of similar variety specials in the same slot, with names in the style of "The So-and-So Show". On occasion, contemporary reviewers would still refer to these as SATURDAY SPECTACULAR but ATV's own contemporary paperwork shows that the final production made under the title was the one broadcast on 18.03.1961.

For the majority of the surviving editions there is little contemporary paperwork, and what we have seen rarely notes whether the episode was recorded. For a period, ABC Television only broadcast alternate editions, and those which they missed were shown a few days later by ATV midlands, so these must have been telerecorded to allow that to happen. However plenty of editions survive which did not need to be recorded for this purpose while, conversely, a few which must have been recorded to allow the later broadcast are lost. With that in mind, it is probable that a number of other programmes in the series, which no longer survive, were also recorded but, unless we have specific evidence which confirms this, we have assumed that they were never telerecorded or, in the case of later shows, taped.

THE SATURDAY STARSHIP

A Central production. Transmission details are for the Central region. Duration: 60 minutes.

Main regular credit(s): Programme associate Peter Matthews; production team Pat Harris, Kathleen Darby, Jill Fraser and Simon Massey; produced by Graham Mole; directed by Mike Connor.

Main regular cast: Bonnie Langford (Presenter), Tommy Boyd (Presenter).

	Holding / Source
22.12.1984	D2 / 1"

With Nigel Roberts.

SAVE THE CHILDREN WITH MICHAEL CRAWFORD

A John Kaye Cooper Productions production for ITV. Transmission details are for the Central region. Duration: 55 minutes.
Associate producer Jackie Tyler; executive producer Robert MacKintosh; produced and directed by John Kaye Cooper.
Michael Crawford (Presenter), Michael Ball, David Essex, Anita Harris, Bonnie Langford, Julia McKenzie, Claire Moore, Paul Nicholas, Elaine Paige, Frances Ruffelle, Lon Satton, Colm Wilkinson, Royal Philharmonic Orchestra, London Philharmonic Orchestra, The London Symphony Orchestra, The Wren Orchestra, Alyn Ainsworth and his Orchestra.

	Holding / Source
25.12.1988	1" / 1"

SCHOOLGIRL CHUMS

A BBC production for BBC 2. Transmission details are for BBC 2. Duration: 62 minutes.
Written by Peter Glidewell; music by Carl Davis; designed by Ian Rawnsley; produced and directed by Ian Keill.
Lalla Ward (Miss Devine), Martin Benson (Count Slansky), Barry Jackson (Colonel Dayne / 'The Chauffeur'), Barbara Bolton (Miss Prosser), Charlotte Long (Alison), Patsy Kensit (Hilary), Katie Locker (Jennifer), Debbie Norris (Maud), Gary Russell (Stephen), Jimmy Mac (Gardener), Jean Reeve (Games Mistress).

	Holding / Source
19.12.1982	DB-1" / C1

See also: ST. URSULA'S IN DANGER! (BBC)

SCOOP

A BBC Bristol production for BBC 2. Transmission details are for BBC 2.
Main regular credit(s):   Produced by Colin Godman; studio sequences directed by Mike Derby.
Main regular performer(s): Barry Norman (Presenter), Diane Harron, Derek Jameson, Miles Kington, Alan Whicker.

SERIES 2
Main regular performer(s): With Richard Stilgoe.

	Holding / Source
28.12.1983 **Scoop Of The Year**	DB-D3 /

SCOTCH AND WRY

A BBC Scotland production for BBC 1 Scotland. Transmission details are for BBC 1 Scotland. Duration varies - see below for details.

Christmas Specials:
Main regular cast: With Rikki Fulton, Claire Nielson.

	Holding / Source
31.12.1980	DB / 2"

Duration: 45 minutes.
Produced and directed by Gordon Menzies.
With Gregor Fisher, Tony Roper, Maureen Beattie, Andrea Miller.

31.12.1982	DB / 2"

Duration: 40 minutes.
Alternative transmissions: BBC 1: 01.01.1983.
Written by Guy Jenkin, Laurie Rowley, Niall Clark, Mick Deasy, Neil MacVicar and Rikki Fulton; script editor Colin Gilbert; produced by Gordon Menzies; directed by Rod Natkiel.
With Gregor Fisher, Miriam Margolyes, Phyllis Logan, Pat Doyle, Pookiesnackenburger, Tony Roper.

31.12.1983	DB / 1"

Duration: 50 minutes.
Produced and directed by Gordon Menzies.
With Gregor Fisher, Tony Roper, Steven Pinder, Sheila Grier.

31.12.1984	DB / 1"

Duration: 50 minutes.
Produced and directed by Gordon Menzies.
With Gregor Fisher, Tony Roper, Judy Sweeney.

31.12.1985	DB / 1"

Duration: 50 minutes.
Produced and directed by Gordon Menzies.
With Gregor Fisher, Tony Roper, Annette Staines.

31.12.1986	DB / 1"

Duration: 50 minutes.
Produced and directed by Gordon Menzies.
With Gregor Fisher, Tony Roper, Annette Staines, Juliet Cadzow.

31.12.1987	DB / 1"

Duration: 50 minutes.
Produced and directed by Gordon Menzies.
With Gregor Fisher, Tony Roper, Judy Sweeney, Juliet Cadzow.

31.12.1988	DB / 1"

Duration: 60 minutes.
Produced and directed by Gordon Menzies.
With Gregor Fisher, Tony Roper, Judy Sweeney.

SCOTCH AND WRY (continued)

31.12.1989   DB / 1"
Duration: 40 minutes.
Produced by Gordon Menzies; directed by Brian Jobson.
With John Bett, Tony Roper, John Hannibal, Julie Miller, Eric Cullen.

31.12.1990   DB / 1"
Duration: 55 minutes.
Produced by Philip Differ; directed by Ron Bain.
With John Bett, Tony Roper.

31.12.1991   DB-D3 / 1"
Duration: 40 minutes.
Produced by Philip Differ; directed by Ron Bain.
With John Bett, Tony Roper.

31.12.1992   DB-D3 / 1"
Duration: 40 minutes.
Produced by Tony Roper; directed by Ron Bain.
With John Bett, Grant Smeaton.

Main regular credit(s):	Written by Bob Black.
Main regular cast:	With Rikki Fulton (Reverend I M Jolly).

		Holding / Source
31.12.1993	'Tis The Season To Be Jolly	B / D3
31.12.1994	Jolly - A Man For All Seasons	B / D3S
31.12.1995	The Life Of Jolly	DB-D3 / D3S
31.12.1996	Ricky Fulton's Scotch And Wry	DB-D3 / D3S
31.12.1998	Rev I M Jolly	DB-D3 / D3S
31.12.1999	It's A Jolly Life	DB-D3 / D3S

Duration: 30 minutes.
Produced and directed by Ron Bain.

THE SCOTCHED EARTH SHOW

A BBC Scotland production for BBC 1 Scotland. Transmission details are for BBC 1 Scotland. Duration: 50 minutes.

Written by Stephen Mulrine; designed by Helen Rae; produced and directed by Gordon Menzies.

Rikki Fulton, Russell Hunter, Robert Trotter, Eileen McCallum, Claire Nielson, Mary Ann Reid, The McCalmans.

Holding / Source
01.01.1977   J / 2"

SCOTLAND ON SHOW

A Scottish Television production. Transmission details are for the ATV London region. Duration: 52 minutes.

A programme to celebrate Hogmanay.

Written by S.C. Green, R. M. Hills, Eric Merriman and John Taylor; orchestra conducted by George Keenan; designed by Peter Alexander; produced by Francis Essex; directed by Bryan Izzard and James Sutherland.

Kenneth McKellar, Rikki Fulton, Jimmy Logan, Jack Milroy, Sheila Paton, Marillyn Gray, Ethel Scott, Kara Wilson, Bill Tennent, C. R. M. Brookes, The Alexander Brothers, Jimmy Blair's Band, The Norman Maen Dancers, The Allan Water Dance Group, The Kay Gordon Singers, The Linn Choir.

Holding / Source
31.12.1965   J /

SCOTT

A BBC production for BBC 1. Transmission details are for BBC 1. Duration: 30 minutes.

Main regular credit(s):	Designed by Peter Brachacki; produced and directed by Michael Hurll.
Main regular performer(s):	Scott Walker, Peter Knight and his Orchestra, The Breakaways.

Holding / Source
30.12.1968   J /
With Blossom Dearie, Salena Jones.

SCOTT ON...

A BBC production for BBC 2. Transmission details are for BBC 2. Duration: 45 minutes.

Main regular cast: Terry Scott.

Holding / Source

02.11.1969   **Christmas**   DB-R1 / 2"
Alt.Title(s): *Xmas*
Written by Bryan Blackburn; music associate Art Day; music arranged by Burt Rhodes; choreography by Bob Stevenson; designed by Malcolm Goulding; produced and directed by Kenneth Carter.
With June Whitfield, Peter Butterworth, The Rita Williams Singers, Robin Hunter, George Moon, Henry McGee, Elizabeth Chambers, Patrick O'Dwyer, Jeffrey Chandler, Rosemary Page, Tudor Davies, Wendy Martin, Bob Howe, Sheila Falconer, Connel Miles, Isobel Hurll, Jerry Manley.

Shown as part of SHOW OF THE WEEK.

SCOTT ON...

British Christmas Television Guide **SCOTTISH BAND SPECTACULAR**

SCOTTISH BAND SPECTACULAR
A BBC Scotland production for BBC 1 Scotland. Transmission details are for BBC 1 Scotland.

	Holding / Source
21.12.1979	DB / 2"

SCREEN ONE
Produced for BBC 1 by a variety of companies (see details below). Transmission details are for BBC 1. Duration varies - see below for details.

Holding / Source

27.12.1989 Ball-Trap On The Côte Sauvage DB / C1
Duration: 85 minutes.
Written by Andrew Davies; music by Richard Hartley; designed by John Bone; production associate Chris Cherry; produced by Sue Birtwistle; directed by Jack Gold.
With Jack Shepherd (Joe Marriot), Zoë Wanamaker (Sarah Marriot), Jamie Groves (Tom Marriot), Katerina Hadjimatheou (Lisa Marriot), Miranda Richardson (Early Bird), Michael Kitchen (Smiley Face), Peter Howitt (Topless), Erika Hoffman (Mrs Topless), Dave Atkins (Fatty Granada), Terry Sue Patt (Young Fitness), Timothy Kightley (Prat), Edward Holmes (James), Amy Melhuish (Chloe), Victoria Shalet (Anna), Linal Haft (Mr In-The-Trade), Jane Wood (Mrs In-The-Trade), Annie Hayes (Mrs Prat), Nicholas Barnes (Paul), Victoria Hasted (Hilary), Louis Emerick (Fitness), Liz Whiting (Mrs Fitness), Sarah Smart (Nadine), Donna Smart (Linette), Elspeth Charlton (Sad French Wife), Daniel André Pageon (Jealous Husband), Paula Tinker (Adulterous Wife), Jean-Michel Dagory (Adulterous Husband), Dariane Lorian (Amandine Girl), Eric Lafitte (Club Toto Lout), Valerie Marion (Club Toto Girl).

Holding / Source

01.01.1991 Happy Feet DB / C1
Duration: 90 minutes.
Written by Mike Bradwell; music by Errollyn Wallen and Stephen Warbeck; associate producer Daphne Spink; executive producer Richard Broke; produced by Ann Scott; directed by Mike Bradwell.
With Phyllis Logan (Dora), Derrick O'Connor (Clifford), Natalie Forbes (Mrs Ross), Marjie Lawrence (Mrs Jackson), Stephen Hancock (Mr Jackson), Diana Rayworth (Mrs O'Nolan), Meryl Hampton (Mrs Irving), Jeannie Crowther (Mrs Roux), Veronica Roberts (Mrs Galt), Eric Allan (Mr Galt), David Newborn (Terry), John Naylor (John), Sarah-Jane Nicoll (Stephanie), Alison Mitchell (Anne), Barbara Wheeler (Lorna), Julie Westmoreland (Patricia), Rebecca Simms (Christine), Stephanie Burton (Marilyn), Marie Rawlings (Jackie), Catherine Winn (Heather), Chris Jury (Festival Steward), Heather Chasen (Madam Ptzinski), Fred Pearson (Mayor), Mandy More (Sandra), Gillian Raine (Hilda Pybus), Joan Linder (Phyllis Pybus), Robin Plant (Beach Photographer), Fergus Connor (Beach Photographer), Jim Broadbent (Grocer), Claire Lewis (Assistant), Mark Long (George), Ruth Perry (Katrina), Arlene Atkin (Pybus Dancer), Ruth Holden (Teacher), Linda Jane Holmes (Teacher), Deddie Davies (Landlady), John Tindle (Barker), Richard Zajdlic (Bingo Caller), Joseph Peters (Policeman), Barbara Dryhurst (Waitress), Brian McNeill (Bus Driver).

Holding / Source

01.01.1992 Adam Bede DB / C1S
Duration: 105 minutes.
Adapted by Maggie Wadey; based on a book by George Eliot; produced by Peter Goodchild; directed by Giles Foster.
With Iain Glen (Adam Bede), Patsy Kensit (Hetty Sorrel), Susannah Harker (Dinah Morris), James Wilby (Arthur Donnithorne), Julia McKenzie (Mrs Poyser), Robert Stephens (Reverend Irwine), Jean Marsh (Lisbeth Bede), Freddie Jones (Squire), Patsy Byrne (Sarah Stone), Paul Brooke (Martin Poyser), Michael Robbins (Thias Bede), Jonathan Coy (Pym), George Innes (John Olding), Alan Cox (Seth Bede), Tacita Haffenden (Totty Poyser), Edward Jewesbury (Judge).

Holding / Source

20.12.1992 The Hummingbird Tree DB-D3 / C1
Duration: 80 minutes.
Adapted by Jonathan Falla; based on a book by Ian McDonald; produced by Gub Neal; directed by Noella Smith.
With Patrick Bergin (Stephen Holmes), Susan Wooldridge (Marjorie Holmes), Tom Beasley (Alan Holmes), Desha Penco (Jaillin), Sunily Y Ramjitsingh (Kaiser), Clive Wood (Tom Ross), Niall Buggy (Priest).

Holding / Source

15.02.1997 Gobble DB-D3 / C1SW
A Hat Trick production. Duration: 73 minutes.
Postponed from 21.12.1996.
It's Christmas Day, and the family is just tucking into roast turkey when father keels over, clutching his stomach in agony. He's the latest victim of what the press soon learns to call "mad turkey disease" - a deadly virus that strikes at one of our most cherished traditions. This drama is a satirical variation on the theme of BSE and allied food scares. It stars Kevin Whately as the hapless government official who is commissioned to find out the truth - braving the wrath of animal rights activists and paranoid turkey barons along the way.
Written by Nick Newman and Ian Hislop; executive producers Mary Bell and David M. Thompson; produced by Grainne Marmion; directed by Jimmy Mulville.
With Kevin Whately (Colin Worsfold), Keith Barron (Arthur Hedley), Jack Dee (Pathologist), Peter Egan (Peter Villiers), Warren Mitchell (Waterboard Chairman), Pippa Guard (Claire Worsfold), Nicholas Jones (George Cranley), Geoffrey McGivern (Geoffrey Lester), Matthew Delamere (Ben Worsfold), Jake Wood (Androcles), Caroline Trowbridge (Maureen), Morgan Jones (Spike), Selina Cadell (Treasury Boss), Jonathan Coy (Hans Gluck), Michael Thomas (Montague), Stephen Frost (Gun Shop Assistant), Cas Harkins (Journalist), Melissa Wilson (Journalist), Tom Hollander (Pipsqueak), Jason O'Mara (Regional Newspaper Journalist), Sara Mair Thomas (Scientist), Mark Spalding (Policeman), Suzy Aitchison (Newsreader), Hugo Chandor (Newsreader), Richard Whitmore (Celebrity Newspaper), Paul Broughton (Security Man), Alan Igbon (Security Man), Michael Fenton Stevens (Gordon The Gobbler), Philip Rowlands (Beardie), Howard Lew Lewis (Fat Bloke).
The end titles were transmitted in 4x3 mode.

SCREEN TEST

A BBC Manchester production for BBC 1. Transmission details are for BBC 1. Duration varies - see below for details.

SERIES 2
Duration: 24 minutes.
Main regular credit(s): Designed by Peter Mavius; produced by John Buttery; directed by John C. Miller.
Main regular cast: With Michael Rodd (Chairman).

	Holding / Source
24.12.1971	J / 2"

With H. Robinson Cleaver.

	Production No	VT Number	Holding / Source
23.12.1974 **Christmas Special (Unedited Version)**	02744/5102	VTC/6HT/94673	DB-D3 / 2"

Duration: 30 minutes.
Designed by Peter Mavius; produced by John Buttery; directed by David Brown.
With Michael Rodd (Chairman).
The original running length is indicated here, but the studio recording runs to 60 mins.

SERIES 21
Main regular credit(s): Designed by Barry Roach; produced by Tony Harrison; directed by Judy Merry.
Main regular cast: With Mark Curry (Chairman).

	Holding / Source
20.12.1984 **Christmas Special**	DB / 1"

Duration: 20 minutes.
Mark Curry introduces a friendly test of observation between the Screen Test champions of 1989 and a guest team representing Grange Hill. They will be answering questions about clips from The Christmas Story. 101 Dalmatians and Pluto's Christmas Tree.

SCREEN TWO

A BBC Films and Various Other Companies production for BBC 2. Transmission details are for BBC 2. Duration varies - see below for details.

SERIES 10

	Holding / Source
30.12.1993 **The Railway Station Man**	DB-D3 / C3S

Duration: 100 minutes.
Painter Helen Cuffe has fled to Donegal with her young son Jack after the killing of her husband in Northern Ireland. She lives in isolation until she meets a mysterious, disabled American, who is obsessed with restoring an abandoned railway station. Romance blossoms. but then a group of so-called freedom fighters decides to store arms in the railway station — and enlists the help of Helen's son.

Adapted by Shelagh Delaney; based on a book by Jennifer Johnston; produced by Andrée Molyneux and Roger Randall-Cutler; directed by Michael Whyte.

With Julie Christie (Helen Cuffe), Donald Sutherland (Roger Hawthorne), John Lynch (Damian Sweeney), Frank McCusker (Jack Cuffe), Mark Tandy (Manus Dempsey), Niall Cusack (Father Quinlan).

SERIES 12

	Holding / Source
26.12.1994 **Midnight Movie**	DB-D3 / C1SSW

A Whistling Gypsy production. Duration: 96 minutes.

Henry, a quiet bachelor, is drawn to Amber by a powerful sexual attraction. He is invited to a dinner party after which the guests watch the midnight movie on television. Amber's mother stars in the movie, which stirs many passionate, long forgotten memories in Henry. Midnight Movie is a tribute to the emotional power of memory and also a celebration of the art of cinema.

Adapted by Dennis Potter; based on a book by Rosalind Ashe; associate producer Alison Barnett; executive producers Mark Shivas and Ruth Caleb; produced by Dennis Potter; directed by Renny Rye.

With Jim Carter (Henry Harris), Louise Germaine (Amber Boyce / Mandy Mason), Brian Dennehy (James Boyce), Colin Salmon (Bob Maclean), Steven Mackintosh (Bertie), Anna Cropper (Mrs Morrey), David Curtiz (Vic), Stephen Greif (Johnny), Lucinda Ann Galloway (Anne Maclean), John Cater (Old Man), Gerard Horan (Policeman), Anthony Pedley (Inspector), Michael Gardiner (Sergeant), Michael Poole (Doctor), Robert Putt (Cabbie), Georgine Anderson (Old Lady), Melanie Ramsay (Bertie's Girlfriend), Geoffrey Larder (Detective), Mark Frost (Barney), Kelly Moorhouse (Child), Joshua O'Brien (Child), Pietra Pittman (Child), Amelia Whiston-Dew (Child).

SERIES 14

	Holding / Source
24.12.1995 **The Hawk**	DB-D3 / C1SSW

An Initial Production/BBC Enterprises/Screen Partners production for BBC Films. Duration: 83 minutes.

Written by Peter Ransley; script supervisor Libbie Barr; script editor Asmaa Pirzada; music by Nick Bicat; associate producer Joanna Gueritz; production executive Geoffrey Paget; executive producers Mark Shivas, Eric Fellner, Larry Kirstein and Kent Walwin; produced by Ann Wingate and Eileen Quinn; directed by David Hayman.

With Helen Mirren (Annie Marsh), George Costigan (Stephen Marsh), Rosemary Leach (Mrs Marsh), Melanie Hill (Norma), Owen Teale (Ken Marsh), Clive Russell (Chief Inspector Daybury), David Harewood (Sergeant Streete), Pooky Quesnel (Woman Police Constable Clarke), Caroline Paterson (Jan), John Duttine (John), Nadim Sawalha (Bahnu), Daryl Webster (Woman Driver), Thomas Taplin (Boy In Car), Joshua Taplin (Boy In Car), Marie Hamer (Jackie Marsh), Christopher Madin (Matthew Marsh), Helen Ryan (Mrs Crowther), Joyce Falconer (Woman In Capri), Jayne Mackenzie (Eileen), Sean Flanagan (Harry), Rachel Moores (Susan), Margery Mason (Greengrocer), Sydney Cole (Weighbridge Operator), Frazer James (Crane Operator).

The sound was recorded using Dolby Spectral Sound.

British Christmas Television Guide SCREEN TWO (continued)

26.12.1995 **The Hour Of The Pig** DB-D3 / C1SW
A Ciby Production/British Screen/European Co-Prod. Fund production for BBC Films. Duration: 108 minutes.
Written by Leslie Megahey; script editors Elinor Day and Jane Tranter; music by Alexandre Desplat; executive producers Claudine Sainderichin and Michael Wearing; produced by David M. Thompson; directed by Leslie Megahey.

With Colin Firth (Richard Courtois), Ian Holm (Albertus), Donald Pleasence (Pincheon), Amina Annabi (Samira), Nicol Williamson (Seigneur Jehan D'Auferre), Michael Gough (Magistrate Boniface), Harriet Walter (Jeannine), Lysette Anthony (Filette D'Auferre), Michael Cronin, Jim Carter, Elizabeth Spriggs.

31.12.1995 **Return Of The Native** DB-D3 / C1S
Duration: 100 minutes.
Adapted by Robert W. Lenski; based on a book by Thomas Hardy; produced by Nick Gillott; directed by Jack Gold.

With Catherine Zeta Jones (Eustacia Vye), Clive Owen (Damon Wildeve), Joan Plowright (Mrs Yeobright), Ray Stevenson (Clym Yeobright), Claire Skinner (Thomasin Yeobright), Paul Rogers (Captain Vye), Celia Imrie (Susan Nunsuch), Steven Mackintosh (Diggory Venn), Richard Avery (Humphrey), Peter Wight (Timothy), Jeremy Peters (Sam), Gregg Saunders (Charley), John Boswall (Granfer Cantle), William Waghorn (Christian Cantle), Matthew Owens (Johnny), Britta Smith (Olly Dowden), John Breslin (Vicar), Daniel Newman (Mummer).

SERIES 16

Holding / Source
31.12.1996 **Burn Your Phone** DB-D3 / C1S
A Sarah Radclyffe Films/Sundial Films production. Duration: 30 minutes.
Written by Andrew Wallace; script editor Tracey Scoffield; music by Simon Boswell; assistant director Paul Dale; executive producers George Faber and Sarah Radclyffe; produced by Dixie Linder; directed by Alan Cumming.

With Alan Cumming (Andy Wallace), Jason Isaacs (The Killer), Burt Caesar (Caller), Trevor Cooper (Caller), Ian Dunn (Caller), Beverley Hills (Caller), Anthony Jackson (Caller).

SERIES 18

Holding / Source
28.12.1997 **Mothertime** DB-D3 / C1S
Duration: 90 minutes.
Adapted by Matthew Jacobs; based on a book by Gillian White; produced by Josh Golding; directed by Matthew Jacobs.

With Kate Maberly (Vanessa), Gina McKee (Caroline), Anthony Andrews (Robin), Imogen Stubbs (Suzie), Zohren Weiss (Dominic), Rosy De Wolf (Amber), Megan De Wolf (Sacha), Felix Bell (Lot), Ian Reddington (Bart), Faith Brook (Isobel), Sheila Allen (Eileen), Rosalind Bennett (Ruby), Stephanie Fayerman (Mrs Guerney), Georgie Glen (Sister Louise), Sarah-Marie Maltha (Ilse), Kevin Dyer (Park Supervisor), Fenella Shepherd (Assistant).

01.01.1998 **Small Faces** DB-D3 / C1SW
A Skyline Production production for BBC Scotland/BBC Films. Duration: 105 minutes.
Written by Billy Mackinnon and Gillies Mackinnon; music by John Keane; executive producers Eddie Dick, Mark Shivas and Andrea Calderwood; produced by Billy Mackinnon and Steve Clark-Hall; directed by Gillies Mackinnon.

With Iain Robertson (Lex Maclean), Joseph McFadden (Alan Maclean), J. S. Duffy (Bobby Maclean), Laura Fraser (Joanne Macgowan), Garry Sweeney (Charlie Sloan), Clare Higgins (Lorna), Kevin McKidd (Malky), Mark McConnochie (Gorbals), Steven Singleton (Welch), David Walker (Fabio), Ian McElhinney (Uncle Andrew), Paul Doonan (Jake), Colin Semple (Dowd), Colin McCredie (Doug), Debbie Welsh (Rebecca), Eilidh McCormick (Alice), Elizabeth McGregor (Mrs MacGowan), Andy Gray (Tactless Man), Louise O'Kane (Polly), Lisa McIntosh (Patty), Kirsty Mitchell (Maggie), Sheila Greer-Smith (Assistant), Karen McColl (Helen), Karyn Murphy (Maria), Alastair Galbraith (Minors MC), Carmen Pieraccini (Jeannie), Rab Christie (Talker), Allan Atkins (Boy With Scar), Tom Gallacher (Davie), Joanne Reilly (Barbara), Liz Lochhead (Librarian), John Murtagh (Teacher), Matt Costello (Shuggy), Tom Logan (Tutor), Bobby Hodgens (V5 Band Member), Malky McKay (V5 Band Member), Ross Miller (V5 Band Member), Scott Laing (V5 Band Member), Paul Woodside (V5 Band Member), Ross Laing (V5 Band Member).
In association with the Glasgow Film Fund.

SEAN HUGHES IS THIRTY SOMEHOW

A My World Productions production for Channel 4, made in association with Tiger Aspect. Transmission details are for Channel 4. Duration: 51 minutes.

Written by Sean Hughes; costume Pennie Robertson; make-up Sally Hennen; music by Stefan Girardet; edited by Perry Widdowson; lighting director Rob Kitzmann; titles by Nick Edwards; designed by Harry Banks; production team James Reekie, Polly Sheldon and Kristian Dench; executive producer Charles Brand; production manager Nick Mortimer; produced by Sylvie Boden and Jamie Rix; directed by Sylvie Boden.
Sean Hughes (Performer).

Holding / Source
22.12.1995 D3 / D3S

SEARCH

A BBC Bristol production for BBC 1. Transmission details are for BBC 1. Duration: 25 minutes.
SERIES 2
Main regular credit(s): Presented by John Craven.

Holding / Source
22.12.1971 **The Spirit Of Christmas** C1SEQ / 2"
Christmas is a time for happiness and giving. Today JOHN CRAVEN examines the origins of the great mid-winter festival and asks a group of children in the studio what 'they think of Christmas and what it means to them.
Produced by David Turnbull; directed by David Hawkins.

SEARCH

SEARCH (continued)

SERIES 5

Main regular credit(s): Presented by John Craven; produced by David Turnbull.

	Holding / Source
02.01.1974 **Happy Viewing To You**	DB / 2"

A BBC Bristol production.

John Craven pres children's discussion prog. This week he hosts a discussion on children's views on christmas & new year programmes. Excerpts from Morcambe and Wise; Goodies (and Beanstalk); The Happiest Millionaire; Casino Royale (films); Blue Peter Pantomime (John, Pete, Lesley, Val, Athur Askey); Xmas Record Breakers - Roy as Father Chrismas); Mr Chatem's(sp?) Music School.

Directed by Jill Roach.

Film inserts mainly.

A SEASON FOR MIRACLES

A Scottish Television production. Transmission details are for the Scottish Television region. Duration: 50 minutes.

Written by Edward Boyd; executive producer Liam Hood; directed by Clarke Tait.

Roddy McMillan, Fulton Mackay, Callum Mill, Morag Hood, John Cairney.

	Holding / Source
23.12.1972	J / 2"

SEASON'S GREETINGS

A BBC production for BBC 2. Transmission details are for BBC 2. Duration: 110 minutes.

Written by Alan Ayckbourn; script editor Stuart Griffiths; music by Jim Parker; produced by Shaun Sutton; directed by Michael Simpson.

Nicky Henson (Neville), Barbara Flynn (Belinda), Anna Massey (Rachel), Geoffrey Palmer (Bernard), Shaun Scott (Clive), Bridget Turner (Phyllis), Peter Vaughan (Harvey), Michael Cashman (Eddie), Lesley Dunlop (Pattie).

	Holding / Source
24.12.1986	DB / 1"

Adam Tandy remembers: "Seasons Greetings" was the first BBC production I worked on as a proper behind the scenes person, having trailed for a month on other programmes. It really was an epic of its day and one of the last studio Play of the Months. The set was three storeys high with camera cranes and platforms to capture the upstairs action, and floating fourth walls on the ground floor to allow deep cross-shooting through the set. Television Centre's TC1 was actually the only electronic studio in Europe large enough to hold it. I think we used 8 cameras in all. Even the outside rehearsal technical run seemed to be the most complicated thing I'd ever been involved in.

Michael Simpson camera rehearsed the first 30 minutes of the play as a single sequence for the best part of a day and a half, and managed to get the first 20 minutes in the can in the evening of day 2. In one take. We had a four day schedule and it ran into five days eventually. It was a very pressured working environment for everyone, and I remember on one occasion when we failed to get a scene completed by suppertime on the third or fourth day Barbara Flynn burst into tears of frustration as the lights were turned off around her. There were no over-runs without union agreement in those days.

Michael Simpson is one of my all-time heroes. Drama studio multi-camera is a dying art, but Simpson just had the knack. He obviously felt he wanted to capture the fluid wit of Ayckbourn by recording as-live if possible, but it was a hugely ambitious attempt with such a big set, even one as carefully designed as theirs and with a properly rehearsed cast and a camera crew as experienced as Ron Green's (Crew 7).

They just bit off more than they could chew, but as someone who had just come from several years in proper theatre I found this sort of approach entirely appropriate. We all started with these long flowing scenes and huge bundles of camera cards. As the days wore on, the style became more and more piecemeal, grabbing scenes where they could, until unnecessary reverses into rooms with floaters in began to be dropped and complicated camera scripting and action was simplified. But the cast loved him, he never flapped or shouted, and obviously got the best out of everyone in the studio as a result. I think that warmth came over in the finished play.

He came up to visit his good lady wife on location for Last of the Summer Wine when I worked on it a couple of years later and I found him to be just as charming when "off-duty", so to speak.

SEASON'S GREETINGS (RADIO)

A BBC production for BBC World Service. Transmission details are for BBC Radio 4. Duration: 90 minutes.

Adapted by Richard Wigmore; based on a play by Alan Ayckbourn; play production by Gordon House.

Peter Vaughan (Harvey), Ronald Herdman (Bernard), Maggie McCarthy (Belinda), Heather Bell (Pattie), Nicky Henson (Neville), Robin Summers (Eddie), Jennifer Piercey (Rachel), Susan Uebel (Phyllis), Guy Holden (Clive).

	Holding / Source
28.12.1985	DA /

In Stereo.

SEASON'S GREETINGS (RADIO)

A BBC production for BBC Radio 4. Transmission details are for BBC Radio 4. Duration: 90 minutes.

Adapted by Vanessa Rosenthal; based on a play by Alan Ayckbourn; play production by Polly Thomas.

Geoffrey Palmer (Harvey), Frances Barber (Belinda), Bill Nighy (Neville), John Sessions (Bernard), Sophie Thompson (Phyllis), Lia Williams (Rachel), Phil Daniels (Eddie), Ruth Lass (Pattie), Andrew Lincoln (Clive).

	Holding / Source
26.12.1999	DA /

SECOMBE AND FRIENDS

An ATV production. Transmission details are for the ABC midlands region. Duration: 50 minutes.
Main regular performer(s): Harry Secombe.

	VT Number	Holding / Source
24.12.1967	8643	J / 40

Written by Jimmy Grafton; programme associate Jimmy Grafton; additional material by Jeremy Lloyd; designed by Eric Shedden; produced and directed by Jon Scoffield.
With Alfred Marks, Peter Maxwell, Nina and Frederick, Joan Turner, Norman Vaughan, Tom Jones, Jack Parnell and his Orchestra, The Lionel Blair Dancers, The Mike Sammes Singers.

SECOMBE AT CHRISTMAS

A Yorkshire Television production. Transmission details are for the Central region. Duration: 52 minutes.

The unforgettable voice of Harry Secombe can be heard in this programme for all the family, as Harry sings christmas carols and songs to celebrate the festive season. Harry Secombe, Gemma Craven and Chris Gable sing "Have Yourself A Merry Little Christmas"; Harry, Chris and Ray C. Davis perform "Dance of the Goblins"; Gemma sings "Wexford Carol"; a Dickensian medley; Gemma and Chris sing "Run Run Run Cinderella"; Harry sings "Keep Love Alive" and "Peter and the Wolf"; Chris sings "The Happiest Christmas"; the choirs sing a medley of traditional christmas carols; Harry, Gemma and Chris close with "We Went To A Marvellous Party".

Written by Myles Rudge; music by Peter Knight; designed by Colin Pigott; produced and directed by Vernon Lawrence.
Harry Secombe (Host), Rosemarie Ford, Gemma Craven, Christopher Gable, Ray C. Davis, Choir of Leeds Parish Church & Malsis School.

	Holding / Source
26.12.1982	1" / 1"

SECOMBE WITH MUSIC

A Yorkshire Television production. Transmission details are for the ATV midlands region. Duration: 50 minutes.

Harry and his famous friends mix up a sparkling cocktail of comedy and music to banish those post-Christmas blues. Pop, jazz, opera, sketches, reminiscences — all this and more in a happy party at which you are guest of honour.

Written by Alistair Beaton, Jimmy Grafton, Russell Davies, Sonny Hayes, Vernon Lawrence and Nick Bicat; designed by Colin Pigott; produced and directed by Vernon Lawrence.
Harry Secombe (Host), Cleo Laine, Dennis Waterman, Cantabile, Mitch Dalton, Richard Wilson, Ray C. Davis, Shirley Cheriton, Peter Knight and his Orchestra, Ronnie Cass.

	Holding / Source
27.12.1981	1" / 2"

SECOND CITY FIRSTS

A BBC Birmingham production for BBC 2. Transmission details are for BBC 2. Usual duration: 30 minutes.
SERIES 3
Main regular credit(s): Produced by Barry Hanson.

	Holding / Source
16.12.1974 **The Festive Poacher**	J / 2"

Written by Ian Taylor; script editor William Smethurst; directed by Tara Prem.
With Liz Smith (Mrs Murphy), Bernard Wrigley (Tommy), Susan Tracy (Christine).

SECOND CITY REPORTS

A Granada production. Transmission details are for the ATV midlands region. Duration varies - see below for details.
Main regular credits(s): Written by Michael Frayn, John Bird and Ian Davidson; produced by Bernard Sahlins; directed by David Cunliffe.
Main regular cast: David Battley, Kathleen Breck, Eleanor Bron, David Buck, Pamela Ann Davy, Jeremy Geidt, Gordon Gostelow, Barry Letts.

	Holding / Source
31.12.1965 **It Only Seems Like Yesterday**	DB-4W / 40

Duration: 43 minutes.
With No guest cast.
See also: IT ONLY SEEMS LIKE YESTERDAY

SECOND THOUGHTS (RADIO)

A BBC production for BBC Radio 4. Transmission details are for BBC Radio 4. Duration: 35 minutes.
Main regular credit(s): Written by Jan Etherington and Gavin Petrie.
Main regular cast: James Bolam (Bill), Lynda Bellingham (Faith), Mark Denham (Joe).

	Holding / Source
25.12.1992	DA /

With Julia Sawalha (Hannah).
In Stereo.

SECRET ARMY

Alternative/Working Title(s): LIFE-LINE

A BBC production for BBC 1. made in association with BRT (Belgium). Transmission details are for BBC 1. Duration varies - see below for details.

Main regular credit(s): Theme music by Robert Farnon; titles by Alan Jeapes; produced by Gerard Glaister.

Main regular cast: Bernard Hepton (Albert Foiret), Angela Richards (Monique), Clifford Rose (Ludwig Kessler).

SERIES 2
Duration: 53 minutes.
Main regular credit(s): Script editor John Brason.
Main regular cast: With Michael Culver (Brandt).

Holding / Source

29.11.1978 **Guests At God's Table**   DB-D3 / 2"

Approaching Christmas, Lifeline receives list of demands from a group of orphaned children who have a hidden Group Captain. The man is drifting in and out of consciousness. Albert is worried that it might be a German trap, but the man is handed over to Lifeline disguised as a St Nicolas dummy in a pram. Meanwhile, Brandt's sympathy with senior officers starting to plot against Hitler leads to Kessler confronting him, but concealing his knowledge of Brandt's indirect involvement.

Written by John Brason; designed by Marjorie Pratt; directed by Terence Dudley.

With Stephen Yardley (Max), Juliet Hammond-Hill (Natalie), John D. Collins (Inspector Delon), John Line, Keith Jayne, Rachelle Beasly, John Nani, Natasha Green, Michael Remick, Mark Taylor, Stephen Phillips, Bill Rourke.

THE SECRET LIFE OF BOB MONKHOUSE

Alternative/Working Title(s): SERIOUSLY FUNNY

A BBC Productions production for BBC 4. Transmission details are for BBC 4. Duration: 90 minutes.

Archive producer Rory Sheehan; written by Andy Humphries; programme consultants Chris Perry, Rory Clark and Alexandra Briscoe; designed by Frank Centurion; assistant producer Willy Norton; production executive Stan Matthews; executive producers Caroline Wright and Karen Steyn; production manager Jill Hallowell; produced and directed by Andy Humphries.

Julian Rhind-Tutt (Narrator), Bob Monkhouse (Subject Of Documentary), Michael Grade*, Christopher Perry*, David Hamilton*, Anne Aston*, Abigail Williams*, Denis Norden*, Lenny Henry*, Colin Edmonds*, Peter Prichard*, Dabber Davies*, Barry Cryer*, Mike Winters*, William G. Stewart*, Dave Ismay*, Joe Pasquale*, Gail Renard*.

Holding / Source

03.01.2011   DB / DBSW

SEE A WEDNESDAY

A BBC Scotland production for BBC 1 Scotland. Transmission details are for BBC 1 Scotland. Duration: 50 minutes.

Holding / Source

31.12.1970   J / 2"

SEE HEAR!

A BBC production for BBC 1. Transmission details are for BBC 1.

Holding / Source

22.12.1985 **Christmas Special With A 'Soap Opera' For The Deaf**   DB / 1"

Written by Dorothy Miles; series producer Charles Pascoe; produced by Eddie Montague.

With Maggie Woolley, Clive Mason, John Lee, Sarah Scott, Terry Ruane, Dorothy Miles, Issy Schlisselman.

20.12.1987 **A Christmas Carol**   DB / 1"

Duration: 30 minutes.
Based on a story by Charles Dickens.

With Doug Alker, Maureen Denmark, Craig Flynn, John Lee, Clive Mason, Dorothy Miles, Heathlands School.

SEE HOW THEY RUN

A Theatre of Comedy production for TVS. Transmission details are for Channel 4. Duration: 75 minutes.

Into a country vicarage in wartime England sneaks an escaped prisoner of war to disguise himself as a clergyman. Into the same vicarage strolls an old friend of the vicar's scatterbrained wife — and he, too, soon exchanges khaki for clerical garb in his pursuit of a good night out. Enter a real-life bishop, a totally bemused visiting preacher and the thoroughly sloshed village busybody...

Adapted by Ray Cooney; based on a play by Philip King; executive producer Michael Blakstad; produced by Martin Schute; directed by Les Chatfield and Ray Cooney.

Liza Goddard (Penelope Toop), Michael Denison (Bishop of Lax), Maureen Lipman (Miss Skillon), Derek Nimmo (Reverend Arthur Humphrey), Christopher Timothy (Lieutenant Corporal Clive Winton), Peter Blake (Intruder), Bill Pertwee (Sergeant Towers), Carol Hawkins (Ida), Royce Mills (Reverend Lionel Toop), Steven Mackintosh (Willie Briggs), Ray Cooney (Police Sergeant), Anthony Verner (Ticket Collector), James Charles (Soldier), Marc Raymond (Soldier), Alan Stone (Soldier).

Holding / Source

25.12.1984   1" / 1"

SEEING CHRISTMAS STARS

An ABC production. Transmission details are for the ABC north region. Duration: 14 minutes.

Relax, look and listen as we capture the festive feeling with the recorded voices of Harry Belafonte, Ella Fitzgerald, Mel Torme, Lionel Blair and the music of the Modern Jazz Quartet.

Directed by Joe McGrath.

The Modern Jazz Quartet.

	Holding / Source
24.12.1961	J /

A SERVICE OF CAROLS AND LESSONS

A Tyne Tees Television production. Transmission details are for the ATV midlands region. Duration: 50 minutes.

Executive producer Maxwell Deas; produced and directed by Roy Lomas.

Very Reverend C. C. Wolters (Conductor), John Robertson (Reader), Christine Smith (Reader), Hilary Spence (Reader), Nigel Brown (Reader), Cathedral Church of St Nicholas Choir, Newcastle Upon Tyne, Cappella Novocastriensis, The Settlers.

	Holding / Source
24.12.1972	J / 2"

SETTLERS AT CITY HALL

A Tyne Tees Television production. Transmission details are for the Scottish Television region. Duration: 25 minutes.

From City Hall, Newcastle Upon Tyne.

Produced and directed by Lewis Williams.

The Settlers.

	Holding / Source
23.12.1975	J / 2"

THE SEX GAME

A Thames Television production. Transmission details are for the ATV midlands region. Duration: 50 minutes.

Associate producer John Kershaw; produced by Joan Kemp-Welch.

		VT Number	Holding / Source
25.12.1968	Hippy, Hippy, Who Cares?	2155	J / 62

A man can make a million out of turkeys, but he may not be very good with birds. The background of this Christmas comedy is a slogan-seeking London advertising agency. Julia Foster plays Perdita, a young secretary who is persuaded to step out.

Written by Fay Weldon; designed by Peter Le Page; directed by Voytek.

With Julia Foster (Perdita Watson), Valerie Gearon (Rachel Wells), Frederick Jaeger (Sir Charles Edey), Renée Houston (Polly), Julian Orchard (Lucas Krell), Norman Mitchell (Salt), Julie May (Mrs Salt), John Gill (Ted), Donald Sumpter (Eddie), Ann Way (Housemaid).

Ways And Means, The Secretary, Floods Of Flowers, Success Story, Heir Apparently and Trial Run were given production numbers and were not made. Despite its title, it seems that Thames' early publicity was calling this a series of "romantic plays" and named the writers as Fay Weldon, Nigel Balchin, Barbara Cartland, Leo Lehman, Shona MacKay and Margaret Drabble.

SEXTON BLAKE

Commissioned and produced by a variety of companies (see details below). Transmission details are for the ATV midlands region. Duration: 25 minutes.

Main regular credit(s): Produced by Ronald Marriott.

Main regular cast: Laurence Payne (Sexton Blake), Roger Foss (Tinker).

SERIES 1

A Rediffusion Television production.

The Vanishing Snowman

	Production No	Holding / Source
25.12.1967	CHI/50/15	J|c / 40

Alt.Title(s): *The Disappearing Man*

Written by David Edwards; re-written by Derry Quinn; directed by Michael Currer-Briggs.

With Bryan Pringle (Henry Brown), Hilary Mason (Mrs Abbot), Zuleika Robson (Wendy), Julia McCarthy (Lady Trevana), Derek Francis (Sir Gerald Trevana), Royston Tickner (Stanley Mears), Helen Lindsay (Diana Grant), Nicola Pagett (Patricia), John Woodnutt (Detective Sergeant Lace), Peter Macann (Jack), Lee Menzies (Peter), Dorothea Phillips (Mrs Bardell).

Recorded 15.12.1967.

SEZ LES

A Yorkshire Television production. Transmission details are for the ATV midlands region. Duration varies - see below for details.

Main regular cast: Les Dawson.

		VT Number	Holding / Source
26.12.1973	That's Christmas - Sez Les!	2692	1" / 2"

Duration: 51 minutes.

Written by Les Dawson, Barry Cryer, Peter Vincent, John Hudson and Alec Gerrard; script editor David Nobbs; music directed by Johnny Pearson; choreography by Irving Davies; designed by Andrew Drummond and Robert Macgowan; executive producer John Duncan; produced by Bill Hitchcock; directed by David Mallet.

With David Essex, Lynsey De Paul, Slade, The Kessler Twins, Roy Barraclough, Gorden Kaye, Jack Douglas, Clive Dunn, Ronnie Carroll, Eli Woods, Syd Lawrence and his Orchestra, The Irving Davies Dancers.

SEZ LES (continued)

	Holding / Source
21.12.1974 **Les Dawson's Christmas Box**	DB / 2"

Duration: 52 minutes.

Written by Barry Cryer and David Nobbs; additional material by Les Dawson, Alec Gerrard and Eric Idle; music directed by Peter Husband; music arranged by John McCarthy; choreography by Dougie Squires; designed by Robert Macgowan; produced and directed by Vernon Lawrence.

With The Second Generation, Roy Barraclough, Wanda Ventham, John Cleese, Kenny Ball and his Jazzmen, Gilbert O'Sullivan, Denise Bryer.

26.12.1975 **Les Dawson's Christmas Box** DB / 2"

Duration: 52 minutes.

Written by Barry Cryer, David Nobbs, Peter Robinson and Les Dawson; music directed by Peter Husband; music arranged by Kenny Clayton, Peter Husband and Christopher Bowers-Broadbent; designed by Colin Pigott; produced and directed by Vernon Lawrence.

With Roy Barraclough, The King's Singers, Julian Orchard, Kenny Ball and his Jazzmen, Nina, Roy Alon, Bert Palmer, Susie Baker, Felix Bowness, Simon Clarke.

SHAMELESS

A Company Pictures production for Channel 4. Transmission details are for Channel 4. Duration varies - see below for details.

Main regular credit(s):   Created by Paul Abbott; theme music by Johnny Marr.

The Christmas Special

	Holding / Source
23.12.2004 "The contaminated meat"	DB / DBSWF

Duration: 75 minutes.

Written by Paul Abbott; script supervisor Jane Houston; script editor John Griffin; music by Murray Gold; executive producers George Faber, Charles Pattinson, Paul Abbott and Matt Jones; produced by Matt Jones; directed by Jonny Campbell.

With Anne-Marie Duff (Fiona), David Threlfall (Frank), James McAvoy (Steve), Jody Latham (Lip), Gerard Kearns (Ian), Dean Lennox Kelly (Key), Maxine Peake (Veronica), Jack Deam (Marty), Marjorie Yates (Carol), Rebecca Ryan (Debbie), Maggie O'Neill (Sheila), Elliott Tittensor (Carl), Joseph Furnace (Liam), Rebecca Atkinson (Karen), Chris Bisson (Kash), Kelli Hollis (Yvonne), Shireen Shah, Pam Shaw, Anthony Flanagan, Warren Donnelly, Lindsey Dawson, Alice Barry, Neil Bell, Paul Brennen, Neil Maskell, June Broughton.

"The Royal Television Society Huw Wheldon Lecture", tx:19.9.2005 BBC 2. 40 mins. Paul Abbott condemned modern TV drama. Produced by Mary Sackville-West, directed by Amanda Crayden.

SHAPING UP

A HTV Wales production. Transmission details are for the HTV West region. Duration: 25 minutes.

Jack Dixon is made redundant. His wife persuades him to invest his redundancy money in a health studio.

Written by Ronald Wolfe and Ronald Chesney; executive producer Peter Elias Jones; produced and directed by Bryan Izzard.

Ruth Madoc (Shirley Dixon), Gareth Hunt (Jack Dixon), Elizabeth Morgan (Gwyneth), Lesley Guinn (Annabel), Peter Greenwell (Freddy), Guinevere John (Mrs Price Jones).

	Holding / Source
22.12.1988 **[pilot]**	1" / 1"

Lizzie Webb was the Exercise Consultant.

SHARI'S SHOW

An LWT production. Transmission details are for the Anglia region. Duration: 25 minutes.

Main regular credit(s):   Written by Jeremy Tarcher and Shari Lewis; designed by Martin Johnson; produced by Philip Casson.

Main regular performer(s):   Shari Lewis (Host).

	Holding / Source
26.12.1970	J /

Boxing Day with Shari Lewis and her friends is lust like the one in your home — if you have a talking Lamb Chop, a wise-cracking Charley Horse and a singing Hush Puppy. If you don't be sure to see this full-scale family musical comedy. Shari and her puppets are joined by six young English entertainers in sketches. singing and dancing.

Music associate Sam Harding; choreography by David Toguri; designed by Martin Johnson; produced and directed by Philip Casson.

With No guest cast.

THE SHELL SEEKERS

A Marian Rees Associates production for Central Films. Transmission details are for the Central region. Duration: 75 minutes.

Adapted by John Pielmeier; based on a book by Rosamunde Pilcher; directed by Waris Hussein.

Angela Lansbury (Penelope), Anna Carteret (Nancy), Patricia Hodge (Olivia), Sam Wanamaker (Richard), Christopher Bowen (Noel), Denis Quilley (Cosmo), Michael Gough (Roy Brookner), Tracey Childs (Young Penelope), Mark Lewis Jones (Danus), Irene Ward (Dolly), Sophie Ward (Antonia).

	Holding / Source
21.12.1989	C1 / C1

SHELLEY

A Thames Television production. Transmission details are for the ATV/Central region. Duration: 25 minutes.

Main regular credit(s):   Created by Peter Tilbury; theme music by Ron Grainer; produced and directed by Anthony Parker.
Main regular cast: Hywel Bennett (James Shelley).

SERIES 3
Transmission details are for the ATV midlands region.
Main regular credit(s):   Written by Peter Tilbury; designed by Jan Chaney.
Main regular cast: With Belinda Sinclair (Fran).

	VT Number	Holding / Source
22.12.1980 **Christmas With Shelley**	23901	D3 / 2"

Duration: 24 minutes.
With Josephine Tewson (Mrs Hawkins), James Richardson (Geoff), Matthew Firth (Matthew), Madoline Thomas (Mrs Ratcliffe).

SERIES 7
Transmission details are for the Central region.
Main regular credit(s):   Designed by David Richens.

	VT Number	Holding / Source
26.12.1989 **Cold Turkey**	49299	1" / 1"

Written by Andy Hamilton and Guy Jenkin.
With Stephen Hoye (Phil), Andrew Castell (Graham), John Cater, Andrew Dennis, Matthew Ashforde.

SERIES 8
Transmission details are for the Central region.
Main regular credit(s):   Designed by David Richens.
Main regular cast: With David Ryall (Ted).

	VT Number	Holding / Source
01.01.1991 **Forward To The Past**	52773	1" / 1"S

Written by Barry Pilton.
With James Grout, Matthew Scurfield, John Woodnutt, Dawn Perllman, Paul Valentine.

SHERLOCK HOLMES (RADIO)

A BBC Birmingham production for BBC Radio 4. Transmission details are for BBC Radio 4. Duration: 30 minutes.
Based on stories by Sir Arthur Conan Doyle.
Barry Foster (Sherlock Holmes), David Buck (Doctor Watson).

	Holding / Source
23.07.1978 **The Blue Carbuncle**	J /

Adapted by Bill Morrison; produced and directed by Peter Novis.
With Peter Symonds, Jack Holloway, David Strong, Martin Friend, Ralph Lawton, Jonathan Scott, Elizabeth Reville, Hilda Schroder.
In Stereo.

(SIR ARTHUR CONAN DOYLE'S) SHERLOCK HOLMES

A BBC production for BBC 1. Transmission details are for BBC 1. Duration: 50 minutes.

Main regular credit(s):   Based on stories by Sir Arthur Conan Doyle; music by Alan Fogg; produced by William Sterling.
Main regular cast: Peter Cushing (Sherlock Holmes), Nigel Stock (Doctor Watson).

	Holding / Source
23.12.1968 **The Blue Carbuncle**	DB-D3 / 2"

Adapted by Stanley Miller; script editor Donald Tosh; designed by Ian Watson; directed by Bill Bain.

With Madge Ryan (Lady Morcar), James Beck (James Ryder), Diana Chappell (Catherine Cusack), Neil Fitzpatrick (John Horner), Richard Butler (Mr Baker), Ernest Hare (Windigate), Frank Middlemass (Peterson), Grace Arnold (Mrs Hudson), Clyde Pollitt (Police Sergeant), Michael Robbins (Breckinridge), Edna Doré (Mrs Oakshott).

18/06/68 - SPORTSVIEW (LOS2994A) - front: end of end credits for "Lulu's Back in Town"; trailer for "The Stanley Baxter Show" (Sherlock Holmes sketch); clock with announcement and plug for "24 Hours".

SHERLOCK HOLMES AND THE CASE OF THE SILK STOCKING

A Tiger Aspect production for BBC 1. made in association with Canadian Broadcasting Corporation / WGBH Boston. Transmission details are for BBC 1. Duration: 100 minutes.

Written by Allan Cubitt; based on characters created by Sir Arthur Conan Doyle; script executive Hilary Norrish; script supervisor Karen Jones; music by Adrian Johnston; executive producers Allan Cubitt, Rebecca Eaton, Gareth Neame and Greg Brenman; produced by Elinor Day; directed by Simon Cellan Jones.

Rupert Everett (Sherlock Holmes), Nicholas Palliser (Doctor Dunwoody), Neil Dudgeon (Lestrade), Ian Hart (Doctor Watson), Anne Carroll (Mrs Hudson), Tamsin Egerton (Miranda Helhoughton), Perdita Weeks (Roberta Massingham), Jennifer Moule (Georgina Massingham), Eleanor David (Mary Pentney), John Cunningham (Bates), Michael Fassbender (Charles Allen), Jonathan Hyde (George Pentney), Gina Beck (Maid), Helen McCrory (Mrs Vandeleur), Andy Wisher (Constable), Julian Wadham (Hugo Massingham), Penny Downie (Judith Massingham), Stewart Bevan (Proprietor), Anthony Cozens (Young Constable), Guy Henry (Mr Bilney), Rachel Hurd-Wood (Imogen Helhoughton), Christine Kavanagh (Lady Helhoughton), Roger Monk (Workman), Jonathan Emmett (Policeman), Max Harvey (Master of Ceremonies).

	Holding / Source
26.12.2004	DB / V1SW

SHE'S DONE IT AGAIN!

A BBC production for BBC 1. Transmission details are for BBC 1. Duration: 90 minutes.

Who put the cheese sandwich and the pornographic book in the Bishop's briefcase? What drives the Rector to eat lemon meringue pie off the beautiful blonde's chest?... Why is the professor's daughter dragging a heavy gas cylinder from bedroom to bedroom? When will the tax inspector spot which quin is the phoney?

Written by Michael Pertwee; settings by Rhoda Gray; directed by Wallace Douglas.

Peter Bland (Freddy Gimble), Leo Franklyn (Pop), Margaret Nolan (Sylvia), Robert Dorning (Rodney Percival), Brian Rix (Hubert Porter), Sheila Hammond (Mary Porter), Leon Greene ('Whisper' Grogan), Derek Royle (Professor Hogg), Hazel Douglas (Ada Hogg), Elaine Baillie (Faith), Anthony Sharp (The Bishop).

	Holding / Source
26.12.1971	J / 2"

A BBC outside broadcast, recorded at the Wimbledon Theatre.

SHE'S GOTTA HAVE IT

A Talkback production for Channel 4. Transmission details are for Channel 4. Duration: 50 minutes.

	Holding / Source
15.12.1999 Christmas Special	DB / DBS

The current series concludes with this hour-long special in which Arabella Weir takes two best friends, a mother and daughter and a married couple on the shopping spree of a lifetime to buy an outfit for the millennium. Plus seasonal baubles on a budget, and how accessorising can transform a little black dress into different party outfits.

Series producer Orla Doherty; produced by Joanna Bartholomew.

With Arabella Weir (Presenter), Amanda Platt.

SHINE ON HARVEY MOON

A Witzend production for ATV/Central/Meridian. Transmission details are for the Central region.

Main regular credit(s):   Devised by Laurence Marks and Maurice Gran; executive producer Allan McKeown; produced by Tony Charles.

Main regular cast: Elizabeth Spriggs (Nan), Maggie Steed (Rita Moon), Linda Robson (Maggie Moon), Lee Whitlock (Stanley Moon), Nigel Planer (Lou Lewis).

SERIES 1

A Witzend production for ATV. Duration: 25 minutes.

Main regular credit(s):   Written by Laurence Marks and Maurice Gran; script editors Dick Clement and Ian La Frenais; theme music by Jack Parnell and his Orchestra; music by David Lindup; directed by Baz Taylor.

Main regular cast: With Kenneth Cranham (Harvey Moon).

	Production No	VT Number	Holding / Source
12.02.1982 A Christmas Truce	9036	9036/81	DB / 2"

Designed by Stanley Mills and Jeff Tessler.

With Fiona Victory (Harriet Wright), Cliff Kelly (Nobby), Bunny May, Emma Whitlock, Tricia Thorns.

SHIRLEY BASSEY

A BBC production for BBC 1. Transmission details are for BBC 1. Duration varies - see below for details.

Main regular performer(s): Shirley Bassey.

	Holding / Source
26.12.1972	DB-D3 / 2"

Duration: 45 minutes.

Choreography by Nigel Lythgoe; designed by Kenneth Sharp; produced and directed by Stewart Morris.

With Segment, Alyn Ainsworth and his Orchestra.

01.01.1974 At The Royal Albert Hall	DB-D3 / 2"

Duration: 45 minutes.

Produced and directed by Johnnie Stewart.

28.12.1974 Shirley	DB-D3 / 2"

Duration: 50 minutes.

Choreography by Nigel Lythgoe; designed by Keith Harris and John O'Hara; produced and directed by Stewart Morris.

With Neil Diamond.

27.12.1975	DB-D3 / 2"

Duration: 45 minutes.

Orchestra conducted by Arthur Greenslade; choreography by Nigel Lythgoe; designed by Tony Abbott; produced and directed by Stewart Morris.

With No guest cast.

SERIES 1

Main regular credit(s):   Produced by Stewart Morris.

	Holding / Source
23.12.1977	DB-D3 / 2"

SHIRLEY BASSEY: VIVA DIVA!

A Mike Mansfield Television production for BBC 1. Transmission details are for BBC 1. Duration: 50 minutes.

Shirley Bassey sings a selection of show stopping songs, with the help of a large orchestra, the cast of the hit West End stage musical Chicago and a million pounds' worth of diamonds.

Produced and directed by Mike Mansfield.

Shirley Bassey.

	Holding / Source
31.12.1998	DB / DBS

SHOESTRING

A BBC Serials production for BBC 1. Transmission details are for BBC 1. Usual duration: 52 minutes.

Main regular credit(s): Created by Richard Harris and Robert Banks Stewart; graphics by Sid Sutton; music by George Fenton; produced by Robert Banks Stewart.

Main regular cast: Trevor Eve (Eddie Shoestring), Michael Medwin (Don Satchley), Doran Godwin (Erica Bayliss), Liz Crowther (Sonia).

SERIES 2

	Holding / Source
21.12.1980 **The Dangerous Game**	DB / C1

When Santa gets his toys off the back of a lorry Eddie's Christmas becomes less than merry...

Written by Chris Boucher; photographed by Ken Westbury; film editor Jon Gregory; designed by Humphrey Jaeger; directed by Ben Bolt.

With Michael Elphick, Alan Cox, Julia Vidler, Burt Kwouk, Celia Imrie, Leslie French, Maurice Colbourne, Nick Stringer, Rachel Bell, Tariq Yunus, Eric Richard, Constantin De Goguel, Thomas Bolt, Ros Simmons, Philip Rowlands, Jo Ross, Norman Tipton, Aaron Shirley, Russell Wootton, Rebecca Lalonde, Katherine Potter.

SHOOTING STARS

Produced for BBC 2 by a variety of companies (see details below). Transmission details are for BBC 2. Usual duration: 30 minutes.

Main regular credit(s): Created by Vic Reeves and Bob Mortimer; theme music by Peter Baikie.

Main regular performer(s): Vic Reeves (Host), Bob Mortimer (Host), Ulrika Jonsson (Team Captain), Matt Lucas (George Dawes).

SERIES 1

A Channel X production.

Main regular credit(s): Produced by Alan Marke; directed by Mark Mylod.

Main regular performer(s): With Mark Lamarr (Team Captain), Matt Lucas (George Dawes), Ulrika Jonsson.

	Holding / Source
29.12.1995 **Xmas Shooting Stars**	D3 / D3S

Duration: 40 minutes.

Directed by David G. Croft.

With Anna Friel, Clive Mantle, Neil Morrissey, Alvin Stardust, Edwyn Collins, George Dawes.

SERIES 2

A Channel X production.

Main regular credit(s): Produced by Alan Marke; directed by Mark Mylod.

Main regular performer(s): With Mark Lamarr (Team Captain), Matt Lucas (George Dawes), Ulrika Jonsson.

	Holding / Source
27.12.1996	D3 / D3S

Duration: 40 minutes.

With Ewen Bremner, Jarvis Cocker, Emma Forbes, Ian Kelsey, Denise van Outen, Charlie Higson.

SERIES 3

A Channel X production.

Main regular credit(s): Produced by Alan Marke; directed by Mark Mylod.

Main regular performer(s): With Mark Lamarr (Team Captain), Matt Lucas (George Dawes).

	Holding / Source
22.12.1997 **Christmas Special**	D3 / D3S

With Lorraine Kelly, Melvyn Hayes, Mark Owen, Louise Nurding.

SERIES 5

A Channel X production. Transmission details are for BBC Choice.

Main regular credit(s): Produced by Lisa Clark; directed by Richard Valentine.

Main regular performer(s): With Will Self (Team Captain), Johnny Vegas (Team Member), Graham Skidmore (Narrator).

	Holding / Source
22.12.2002 **Christmas Special**	DB / DBSW

Duration: 45 minutes.

With Robin Gibb, Hugh Laurie, Anthea Turner, Stephen Fry.

| SHOOTING STARS (continued) | British Christmas Television Guide |

	Holding / Source
30.12.2008 **All New Shooting Stars**	DB / DBSW

A Pett Productions production.
Alternative transmissions: BBC Choice: 30.12.2008.
Written by Vic Reeves and Bob Mortimer; script supervisor Jenni Cator; music by Peter Baikie and Dan McGrath; assistant producer Alex Moody; executive producer Katie Taylor; head of production Anne Cafferky; produced by Lisa Clark; directed by Ian Trill.
With Jack Dee (Guest Team Captain), Dizzee Rascal, Peter Jones, Kate Garraway, Christine Walkden, Stuart Kale.
No Mark Lamarr.

A Pett Productions production.

	Holding / Source
30.12.2010	HD/DB / HDC

Written by Vic Reeves and Bob Mortimer; script supervisor Hayley Boyd; music by Dan McGrath and John Phillips; titles by Half Man Half Pixel; designed by Jane Tomblin; assistant producer Alex Moody; executive producer Ruby Kuraishe; head of production Erika Leonard; series producer Lisa Clark; location sequences directed by Ben Wheatley; studio sequences directed by Ian Trill.
With Jack Dee (Team Captain), Angelos Epithemiou, Ronnie Wood, Thandie Newton, Joanna Page, Ricky Tomlinson.

THE SHOP OF GHOSTS

A Tyne Tees Television production. Transmission details are for the Tyne Tees region. Duration: 11 minutes.
Richard Todd reads G. K. Chesterton's fanciful story for Christmas.
Written by G. K. Chesterton; produced by Maxwell Deas; directed by Lisle Willis.
Richard Todd (Narrator).

	Production No	VT Number	Holding / Source
02.01.1977	SG 76/45/1	206	DB / 2"

SHOUT!

A BBC production for BBC 1. Transmission details are for BBC 1. Duration: 50 minutes.
Music for Christmas. From gospel to pop, from the cotton fields to the recording studios - a unique collection of songs for and about the real Christmas.
Lighting by Eric Wallis; sound Len Shorey; designed by James Grant; produced and directed by Jim Murray.
Gary Byrd, COGIC Choir, Chris Corcoran, The Housemartins, St Philip's Choir, Lon Satton, Sal Solo, Alvin Stardust, Rebecca Storm, Marti Webb.

	Holding / Source
21.12.1986	DB / 1"

A SHOW FOR HOGMANAY

A Scottish Television production. Transmission details are for the ATV midlands region. Duration varies - see below for details.
Main regular performer(s): Norman Wisdom.

	Holding / Source
31.12.1966	J /

Duration: 65 minutes.
Music arranged by Peter Knight, Allan Cameron and Pat McCann; produced and directed by Bryan Izzard.
With Jimmy Logan, Rikki Fulton, The Alexander Brothers, Una McLean, Roy Castle, The Bachelors, Ivor Emmanuel, The Peiro Brothers, The Fred Peters Dancers, The Kay Gordon Singers, Massed Pipes & Drums, 4/5th Batt. Royal Scots Fusiliers, 6/7th Battalion The Cameronians (Scottish Rifles), 5/6th Battalion Highland Light Infantry, 1st Battalion The Glasgow Highlanders, The George Keenan Orchestra.

31.12.1966	J / 40

Produced and directed by Bryan Izzard.
With Rikki Fulton, Jimmy Logan, The Alexander Brothers, Una McLean, Roy Castle, The Bachelors, Ivor Emmanuel, The Piero Brothers, The Fred Peters Dancers, The Kay Gordon Singers.

31.12.1967	J /

Duration: 50 minutes.
Written by John Cairney; orchestra conducted by Richard Holmes; choreography by Bruce McClure; settings by Ron Franchetti; produced and directed by Clarke Tait.
With Bill Tennent (Compere), Frankie Vaughan, Eamonn Andrews, Dave Allen, The Alexander Brothers, Margaret Savage, The Islanders, The Bruce McClure Dancers.

31.12.1968	J / 2"

SHOW OF THE WEEK

A BBC production for BBC 2. Transmission details are for BBC 2. Duration varies - see below for details.
Mantovani and his Concert Orchestra
Main regular performer(s): With Mantovani and his Concert Orchestra.

	Holding / Source
24.12.1969	J / 2"

Duration: 50 minutes.
Choreography by Ralph Tobert; designed by David Chandler; produced and directed by John Street.
With Lena Martell, Mike Redway, The Mike Sammes Singers, Derek Hardwick, Nina Chalmers, Celia Hetherington, Lesley North, Rosemary Page.
See also: THE MORECAMBE AND WISE SHOW (BBC)

SHOW OF THE WEEK

SILENT NIGHT

Alternative/Working Title(s): HARRY'S CHRISTMAS
An Initial Film & TV production for Channel 4. Transmission details are for Channel 4. Duration: 25 minutes.
Written by Steven Berkoff; directed by Bob Baldwin.
Steven Berkoff (Harry).

	Holding / Source
24.12.1991	1" / C1S

In stereo.

THE SILENT WORLD OF MARCEL MARCEAU

A BBC Birmingham production for BBC 2. Transmission details are for BBC 2. Duration: 55 minutes.

Mime is the oldest of the performing arts. The legendary Marcel Marceau not only revived this ancient skill but has made of it a new and brilliantly original art form. He talks to Donny MacLeod about his technique, his philosophy and the debt he owes to the greats of the silent screen. The programme includes film extracts and specially recorded performances of his work.

Lighting by Barry Hill; designed by Ian Ashurst; executive producer Jonathan Fulford; produced by Jim Dumighan.
Donny MacLeod (Interviewer), Marcel Marceau.

	Holding / Source
27.12.1981	DB-D3 / 2"

SIMENON'S MAIGRET (RADIO)

A BBC production for BBC Radio 4. Transmission details are for BBC Radio 4. Duration varies - see below for details.
Main regular credit(s):   Based on books by Georges Simenon.

	Holding / Source
21.12.1997 **Maigret's Christmas**	DA /

Adapted by John Petherbridge; produced and directed by Andy Jordan.
With Barry Foster (Maigret).

In Stereo.

SING A SONG FOR CHRISTMAS

A Southern Television production. Transmission details are for the ATV midlands region. Duration: 25 minutes.
Main regular credit(s):   Music directed by Nigel Brooks; designed by Gregory Lawson; produced and directed by Bob Leng.
Main regular performer(s):   Fred Dinenage (Host).

	VT Number	Holding / Source
##.##.#### **Heat 1**	6485	DB / 2"
Rx: 20.10.1973		
23.12.1973 **Christchurch County Junior School v King Edward VI School, Southampton (Heat 2)**	6486	DB / 2"
Rx: 21.11.1973		
30.12.1973 **Finals Night**	6504	DB / 2"
Rx: 5.11.1973		

Incomplete listing. "Sing a Song for Christmas" - 2 Heats and a Final exist. Not sure who owns the rights but transferred from 2 inch to Digibeta and they're at the Wessex Archive.

SING A SONG OF CHRISTMAS

A Thames Television production. Transmission details are for the Thames Television region. Duration: 40 minutes.

Children from a selection of London schools sing carols old and new. The juniors of Bevington School sing two carols written by themselves and the boys of St. Mark's, Fulham, sing carols composed for the school, more than 100 years ago. Folk singing is by the boys and girls of Archbishop Temple's School and the girls of Burlington Girls' Grammar
School.

Written by Roger Mansfield; produced by George Sawford.
David Hamilton (Narrator), Bevington School, St. Mark's, Fulham, Archbishop Temple School, Burlington Girls Grammar School.

	Holding / Source
25.12.1970	J / 2"

SING ALL YE FAITHFUL

A BBC production for BBC 2. Transmission details are for BBC 2. Duration varies - see below for details.

	Holding / Source
25.12.1976	J / 2"

Duration: 45 minutes.
A presentation of popular carols sung in Devonshire settings In true folk-song fashion, the news of Bethlehem is spread.
Organist George F. Budden; produced and directed by Douglas Hespe.
With Andrew Cruickshank (Narrator), The Faraway Folk, Choir of Holy Trinity Buckfastleigh, Benedictine Community of Buckfast Abbey.

25.12.1977	J / 2"

Duration: 45 minutes.
Produced and directed by Douglas Hespe.
With Andrew Cruickshank (Narrator), Cantanti Camerati, Choirs of St Catherine's School, Twickenham, Choir of St Mary's College, The Chorale.

SING CHOIRS OF ANGELS

A Thames Television production. Transmission details are for the ATV midlands region. Duration: 35 minutes.

The Settlers link up with the choir of St. Richards with St. Andrews Church of England Primary School, Ham, Surrey, for a programme of carols. Together they sing in the school church and also go out into the district to bring you carols against backgrounds including from beside the River Thames. The children themselves have drawn pictures of winter and the Nativity to illustrate the carols, which include Silent Night, See Amid the Winter Snow and In the Bleak Mid-Winter.

Produced and directed by Christopher Palmer.

The Settlers, Choir of St Richards, St Andrews Church of England Primary School, Ham, Surrey.

Holding / Source
24.12.1973   DB / 2"

THE SINGING KETTLE NEWS

A Scottish Television Enterprises production. Transmission details are for the Central region. Duration: 8 minutes.

A group of youngsters work on a newspaper in the village of Kettle.

SERIES 3

Holding / Source
15.12.1998   DB / DBSW

Santa is on hand to grant festive wishes.

SIR GAWAIN AND THE GREEN KNIGHT (RADIO)

A BBC production for BBC Radio 4. Transmission details are for BBC Radio 4. Duration: 45 minutes.

Translated by Simon Armitage; based on a story by an unknown author; music by Gary Yershon; play production by Susan Roberts.

Ian McKellen (Narrator), Samuel West (Sir Gawain), David Fleeshman (The Green Knight / Sir Bertilak), Deborah McAndrew (Bertilak's Wife), Conrad Nelson (Arthur / Servant).

Holding / Source
21.12.2006   DA /

SIR JIMMY SAVILE AT THE BBC :HOW'S ABOUT THAT THEN?

A BBC production for BBC 2. Transmission details are for BBC 2. Duration: 60 minutes.

A tribute to the former DJ, TV entertainer and charity fundraiser, who died last October. Includes rarely seen footage of his Saturday night variety show Clunk Click, which ran for two series in the 1970s before being replaced by Jim'll Fix it.

Executive producer Mark Cooper; produced by Dawn Payne.

Jimmy Savile (Subject Of Tribute).

Holding / Source
28.12.2011   HD/DB / HDC

SIXPENNY CORNER

An Associated-Rediffusion production. Transmission details are for Associated-Rediffusion. Duration: 15 minutes.

Main regular credit(s):   Devised by Jonquil Antony and Hazel Adair.

Main regular cast: Patricia Dainton (Sally Norton), Howard Pays (Bill Norton), Betty Bowden (Mrs Doris Sharpe), Robert Webber (Mr Norton), Stuart Saunders (Uncle Fred), Olive Milbourne (Aunt Mabel).

Holding / Source
26.12.1955 **Episode 67**   J /

Bill and Sally Norton found themselves involved in the usual last-minute problems before Christmas. In today's episode we see just how they fared in the holiday season.

Written by Hazel Adair and Jonquil Antony; produced by John Lemont; directed by Ronald Marriott.

With Robert Desmond (Stan Norton), Shirley Mitchell (Yvonne Sharpe), O'Donovan Shiell (Doctor O'Shea), Walter Horsbrugh (Mr Sharpe), Christine Pollen (Grete Edler), Edward Malin (Mr Muldoon), Seymour Green (M. Louis Delorme), Gladys Spencer (Mrs Vince), Vi Stevens (Rosie Chubb), Anne Warren (Joanie Chubb), Joan Ingram (Stella), John Charlesworth (Eddy Perkins), Anthony Lang (Mike Perkins), Elizabeth Fraser (Julie Perkins), Gay McGregor (Nurse).

Transmitted in the London region only, this daytime serial was the first daily (weekdays) and daytime soap in the UK. It only ran as a daytime serial for its first 76 episodes after which it took an early evening slot, which it kept for the remaining 105 episodes.

SKY AT DRURY LANE

A BBC production for BBC 2. Transmission details are for BBC 2.

Sky.

Holding / Source
24.12.1983   DB / 1"

THE SKY AT NIGHT

A BBC production for BBC 1. Transmission details are for BBC 1. Duration varies - see below for details.

Transmission details are for BBC.

20.12.1961   **A Telescope For Christmas**

| British Christmas Television Guide | THE SKY AT NIGHT (continued) |

Transmission details are for BBC 1.

Holding / Source

24.12.1969 **Special: 1969 – Year Of Space**
Duration: 30 minutes.

13.12.1981 **The Star Of Bethlehem** DB / 2"

15.11.1987 **A Telescope For Christmas?** DB / 1"

05.12.1999 **A Telescope For Christmas** DB / DBS

From 2004, extended editions of most episodes have been broadcast on BBC 4 later in the same week.

SKY STAR SEARCH

A Reg Grundy Productions production for Sky Television. Transmission details are for Sky One. Duration: 25 minutes.

SERIES 3

Holding / Source

24.12.1989 **Sky Christmas Star Search** UM|n / 1"

In its earliest days it was billed as STAR SEARCH, we are unsure whether this difference was carried across to the on-screen title.

THE SKY'S THE LIMIT

A Yorkshire Television production. Transmission details are for the ATV midlands region. Duration: 25 minutes.

Main regular credit(s):   Format by Vic Hallums.
Main regular performer(s): Hughie Green (Host).

SERIES 2
Main regular credit(s):   Research Vic Hallums; designed by Howard Dawson; produced by Peter Holmans; directed by Royston Mayoh.
Main regular performer(s): With Monica Rose (Hostess), Kate Wyeth (Hostess), Audrey Graham (Hostess).

	VT Number	Holding / Source
24.12.1971	2392	1"|n / 2"

Hughie announces the result of the Christmas Personality Contest. Your musical requests are sung by Audrey Graham, accompanied on the organ by Jackie Brown. The questions and answers are verified by Encyclopaedia Britannica.
With Jackie Brown.

SLEEPING BEAUTY ON ICE

An ATV production. Transmission details are for the ATV midlands region. Duration: 50 minutes.

Music, romance, slapstick and surprise in the best tradition of Christmas panto - plus the breathtaking beauty of skating with skill. Today, ITV cameras bring you an hour of Sleeping Beauty, this year's ice spectacular at Wembley.

Two British skaters head an international cast of more than 80 skaters. Lovely Patricia Pauley, three times a British amateur champion, plays the hapless princess; Martin Minshull, three times World and five times British Professional Champion, is her prince.

Music directed by Leslie Kerrigan; choreography by Reg Park; designed by Anthony Holland; produced by Gerald Palmer; directed by Colin Clews.

Shaw Taylor (Narrator), Martin Minshull (Prince), Patricia Pauley (Princess), Reg Park (Carabosse), Jo Ann McGowan (Lilac Fairy), Liz Dixon (Fairy of Happiness), Jock McConnell (King), Tony Guy (Queen), Carrie and Joop (Royal Dancers), The Dick Taverner Singers.

Holding / Source

24.12.1972 DB / 2"

THE SLEEPING BEAUTY

A BBC production. Transmission details are for BBC. Duration: 60 minutes.

Written by Rex Tucker; music by John Hotchkis; play production by Rex Tucker.

Josephine Griffin (Perianne), Joseph Wise (Dominic), Richard Wordsworth (King), Olive Gregg (Queen), Ann Hanslip (Princess), William Russell (Prince), Patricia Fryer (Ice Fairy), Stella Riley (Flame Fairy), Edna Petrie (Fairy of Ancient Days), Kynaston Reeves (Butler), Enid Lorimer (Nurse), Michael Lewin (Page), Hilda Barry (Old Woman), Brenda Bennett (Lady Katherine), Balbina (Lady Isobel), Colin Douglas (Guard), Alan Edwards (Town Crier), Maria Hanson, Dennis Ramsden, Nigel Arkwright, Garth Adams, Peter Macarte.

Holding / Source

26.12.1955 R3 /

THE SLEEPING BEAUTY

An Anglia production. made in association with WGBH Boston. Transmission details are for the Central region. Duration: 50 minutes.

Written by Tom Gutteridge; music by Tchaikowsky; orchestra conducted by Bramwell Tovey; choreography by Lar Lubovitch; executive producers Colin Ewing and Greg Harney; produced by Bernice Olenick; directed by Tom Gutteridge.

Robin Cousins (Prince Florimund), Rosalynn Sumners (Princess Aurora), Nathan Birch (King Florestan), Catherine Foulkes (Queen Guinevere), Shaun McGill (Carabosse, The Evil Fairy), Patricia Dodd (Hippoluya, The Good Fairy), Stephen Pickavance (Archbishop), Rainer Schonborn (Lord Chamberlain), Karen Barber (Fairy), Tammy Crowson (Fairy), Shelley Winters (Fairy), William Fauver (Fairy), James Robb Freeman (Fairy), Kelly Johnson (Fairy), Lee Ann Miller (Fairy), Jonathan Thomas (Fairy), The London Symphony Orchestra.

Holding / Source

26.12.1987 1" / 1"

SLEEPING BEAUTY: UNCOVERED

A BBC Children's Department production for BBC 1. Transmission details are for BBC 1. Duration: 50 minutes.

Written by Ben Ward and Richard Webb.

Fearne Cotton (Sleeping Beauty), Ortis (Evil Warlock), Angellica Bell (Queen), Simon Thomas (King), Kirsten O'Brien (Good Fairy), Dick and Dom (Panto Horse), Barney Harwood (Prince), Simon Grant (Prince's Father), Steve Wilson (Prince's Mother), Matt Baker (Hector), Mark Speight (Princess Trevor), Reggie Yates (Postman).

	Holding / Source
22.12.2003	DB / DBSW

Alternative transmissions: CBBC: 25.12.2003.

THE SLOW NORRIS

A HTV production. Transmission details are for the Central region. Duration: 8 minutes.

Main regular cast:	Nick Ryan (Slow Norris), Gary Martin (Ben Beetle / Walter Worm), Buddie Maddicott (Allie), Daniel Del Guidice (?).

SERIES 3

Main regular credit(s):	Written by Jeanne Willis; music by John Du Prez; produced by Bob Harvey; directed by Dan Maddicott.

	Holding / Source
15.12.1997 "Allie's Christmas Present"	D3 / D3S

SMACK THE PONY

Alternative/Working Title(s): SPOT THE PONY

A Talkback production for Channel 4. Transmission details are for Channel 4. Duration varies - see below for details.

Main regular credit(s):	Theme sung by Jackie Clune.
Main regular cast:	Fiona Allen, Doon Mackichan, Sally Phillips.

Duration: 24 minutes.

Main regular credit(s):	Written by Sally Phillips, Doon Mackichan, Fiona Allen, Victoria Pile, Georgia Pritchett, Robert Harley and Fay Rusling & Oriane Messina; script supervisor Lesley Williamson; music by Jonathan Whitehead; assistant director Duncan Gaudin; art director Cissy Cook; production designer Jonathan Paul Green; assistant producer Phil Secretan; production executive Penelope Chong; executive producer Peter Fincham; line producer Caroline Wyard; produced and directed by Victoria Pile.
Main regular cast:	With Sarah Alexander (Special Guest), Darren Boyd, Cavan Clerkin, Kevin Eldon.

	Holding / Source
26.12.2002	DB / DBSW

Additional material by Kevin Cecil & Andy Riley, Melanie Finn & Christian Azzola, David Garrett, Stuart Kenworthy, Paul Powell and Richard Preddy & Gary Howe; choreography by Zoe Uffindell and Cydney Uffindell; production team Simon Bailey, Keith Warwick, Ronnie Roe, Sam Brooke-Taylor [credited as Sam Brooketaylor], Jo Ellis and Tom Howard.

SMITH AND GOODY

A Thames Television production. Transmission details are for the ATV midlands region. Duration: 25 minutes.

Main regular credit(s):	Written by Mel Smith and Bob Goody; designed by Jane Krall; executive producer John Hambley; produced and directed by Roger Gale.
Main regular cast:	Mel Smith, Bob Goody.

	VT Number	Holding / Source
30.12.1980 **... On Ice**	23978	D3 / 2"

A holiday extravaganza to set you laughing all the way to next year, as Smith and Goody discover the wonderful world of presents, party games, pantomimes— and nuts, which brings us back to Mel and Bob.

Music by Peter Brewis.

THE SMOKING ROOM

A BBC production for BBC 3. Transmission details are for BBC 3. Duration: 30 minutes.

Main regular credit(s):	Written by Brian Dooley; theme music by Robert Smith; executive producers Sophie Clarke-Jervoise and Michael Jacob; produced by Peter Thornton; directed by Gareth Carrivick.
Main regular cast:	Robert Webb (Robin), Fraser Ayres (Clint), Nadine Marshall (Sally), Debbie Chazen (Annie), Selina Griffiths (Janet), Paula Wilcox (Lilian), Jeremy Swift (Barry), Leslie Schofield (Len), Siobhan Redmond (Sharon).

	Holding / Source
20.12.2004 **Christmas Special**	DB / DBSWF

A charity variety show on Christmas Eve.

THE SNOWMAN AND THE SNOWDOG

Commissioned by Channel 4. Transmission details are for Channel 4. Duration: 25 minutes.

A gentle story of friendship and loss. A young boy - who looks remarkably like James in the original - moves into his new home with his mother and, one winter's day, discovers the Snowman's hat and scarf in a box secreted under the floorboards in his bedroom. As the first snowflakes fall, he rushes out into the garden to build the exact same figure - but with a Snowdog at its side.

Produced by Camilla Deakin and Ruth Fielding; directed by Hilary Audus.

	Holding / Source
24.12.2012	HD/DB / HDC

Animated sequel to 'The Snowman'.
See also: THE SNOWMAN

THE SNOWMAN

A Snowman Enterprises production for Channel 4. Transmission details are for Channel 4. Duration: 25 minutes.

Christmas Eve and snow is falling. A boy rushes out to build a snowman. And, when everyone's asleep, the snowman comes alive.

Introduced by David Bowie; written by Raymond Briggs; music by Howard Blake; executive producer Iain Harvey; produced by John Coates; directed by Dianne Jackson.

Mel Smith (Voice of Father Christmas).

	Holding / Source
26.12.1982	DB / 1"S

Special flying sequence animated by Stephen Weston and Robin White. Animation by Hilary Audus and Joanne Fryer.
See also: THE SNOWMAN AND THE SNOWDOG

SO GRAHAM NORTON

A So Television production for Channel 4. Transmission details are for Channel 4. Duration: 25 minutes.

Main regular performer(s): Graham Norton (Host).

SERIES 1
An United Film & TV Productions production.
Main regular credit(s): Executive producer Graham Stuart; produced by Peter Kessler; directed by Steve Smith.

	Holding / Source
24.12.1998 **Snow Graham Norton**	DB / DBS

SERIES 3
Main regular credit(s): Executive producer Graham Stuart; produced by Jon Magnusson.

	Holding / Source
24.12.1999 **Snow Graham Norton**	DB / DBS

With Goldie, Valerie Singleton.

SERIES 4
Main regular credit(s): Written by Jon Magnusson and Graham Norton; directed by Ian Denyer.

	Holding / Source
22.12.2000 **Snow Graham Norton**	DB / DBS

With Carrie Fisher, Nigella Lawson, Roger Moore.

SERIES 5
Main regular credit(s): Written by Graham Norton; directed by Jon Magnusson.

	Holding / Source
21.12.2001 **Snow Graham Norton**	DB / DBS

With Martine McCutcheon, Alison Moyet, Kate Beckinsale, S Club 7.

	Holding / Source
28.12.2003 **Snow Graham Norton: The Hollywood And The Ivy**	DB / DBS

SO THIS IS CHRISTMAS

A twofour production production for Channel 4. Transmission details are for Channel 4. Duration: 48 minutes.

Comedians relive memories, both good and bad, of Christmases past, as they explore the gulf between our idealistic Yuletide fantasies and the sometimes crushing disappointment of reality.

Music by Ian Masterson; designed by Charlotte Pearson; executive producer Andrew Mackenzie-Betty; produced by Sean Doherty and Michael Forte; directed by Mike Christie.

Mark Dolan (Presenter), Katy Wix, Anna Crilly, Isy Suttie, Rhys Thomas, Charlie Baker, Daniel Sloss, Martin Trenaman, Holly Walsh, Stefan Abingdon, Ashley Horne, Andrew Wakely, Andi Osho, Celia Pacquola, Nick Helm, Matt Forde, Andrew Maxwell, Tony Law, Roisin Conaty, Elis James, Sarah Kendall, Milton Jones, Ben Clark, Matthew Crosby, Tom Parry.

	Holding / Source
25.12.2011	HD/DB / HDC

SOB SISTERS

A Central production. Transmission details are for the Central region. Duration: 25 minutes.

Main regular credit(s): Written by Andrew Marshall; music by Dave Cooke; produced by Christopher Walker.
Main regular cast: Gwen Taylor (Liz), Polly Adams (Dorothy), Freddie Jones (Leo), Philip Bird (Charlie), Beryl Cooke (Edna).

	VT Number	Holding / Source
07.07.1989 **We Need A Little Christmas**	3635/89	1" / 1"

Designed by Ian Doubleday and Ann Croot-Hawkins; directed by Ray Butt.
With Jason Rose, Bhasker, Bert Tyler-Moore, Andrew Searle.

SOFTLY SOFTLY

A BBC production for BBC 1. Transmission details are for BBC 1. Duration: 50 minutes.

Main regular credit(s): Format by Elwyn Jones.

SERIES 4
Main regular credit(s): Script editor Arnold Yarrow; produced by Leonard Lewis.

	Production No	VT Number	Holding / Source
27.12.1968 **On Christmas Day In The Morning**	22/1/8/1174	VTM/6LT/49100	DB-R1 / 62

Duration: 49 minutes.

Written by Alan Plater; music by Anthony Isaac; designed by Barry Newbery; directed by Henri Safran.

With Howell Evans (Detective Constable Morgan), Norman Bowler (Detective Sergeant Hawkins), Frank Windsor (Detective Chief Inspector Wattt), Stratford Johns (Detective Chief Superintendent Charles Barlow), Michael Hawkins, Joan Crane, Glyn Houston, Gillian Royale, Susan Tebbs, John Boxer, Bay White, Kenneth Gilbert, John Challis, Angus Mackay.

SERIES 5
Main regular credit(s): Script editor Arnold Yarrow; produced by Leonard Lewis.

	Production No	VT Number	Holding / Source
01.01.1970 **Any Other Night**	2249/4014	VTC/6HT/55214	DB-D3 / 2"

And here's a hand, my trusty frien', And gie's a hand o' thine. And we'll tak' a richt guid willie waught. For auld lang syne

Written by Robert Barr; designed by Ian Rawnsley; directed by Peter Cregeen.

With Stratford Johns (Detective Chief Superintendent Charles Barlow), Norman Bowler (Detective Inspector Hawkins), Walter Gotell (Chief Constable Cullen), David Lloyd Meredith (Sergeant Evans), David Allister (Sergeant Jackson), Terence Rigby (Police Constable Snow), Basil Dignam, Michael Hall, Nicholas Brent, Tony Caunter, Michael Francis, Peter Lund, Victor Maddern, Douglas Livingstone, Kenton Moore, Peter Lawrence.

Series Titles becomes Softly Softly: Task Force as of 20.11.69

Unmade episode: 'Safe Conduct' by Brian Wright.

See also: Z CARS (BBC)

SOLID GOLD TOP 20

A Granada production. Transmission details are for the Tyne Tees region. Duration: 25 minutes.

A rundown of the best selling singles over the last twenty years, with videos, archive film, and concert clips of the groups and artists.

Research Trish Kinane; designed by Tim Farmer; executive producer John Hamp; produced by Stephen Leahy; directed by David Liddiment.

Jimmy Pursey (Presenter).

	Holding / Source
28.12.1979	1"|n / 2"

Digi of this GRA216176 is not the finished programe, just inserts- videos for Blondie, Village People, 'Grease' etc. 1" contains whole show.

SOME MOTHERS DO 'AVE 'EM

A BBC production for BBC 1. Transmission details are for BBC 1. Duration varies - see below for details.

Main regular credit(s): Written by Raymond Allen; based on stories by Michael Crawford; theme music by Ronnie Hazlehurst.

Main regular cast: Michael Crawford (Frank Spencer), Michele Dotrice (Betty Spencer).

SERIES 2
Main regular credit(s): Produced and directed by Michael Mills.

	Holding / Source
25.12.1974 **Jessica's First Christmas**	DB-D3 / 2"

Duration: 52 minutes.

Frank wants to be in the Nativity Play. Eventually he gets his chance, as an angel, with disastrous results.

Costume Jim Acheson; make-up Ann Briggs; lighting by Derek Slee; sound John Lloyd; designed by Bryan Ellis.

With Emma Ware (Jessica), Cyril Luckham (Father O'Hara), Bryan Pringle (Jackson), Brian Hayes (Hudson), Bartlett Mullins (King Herod), Alan Bowerman (First Shepherd), Ian Milton (Second Shepherd), Tony Bateman (First Wise Man), Peter MacKriel (Second Wise Man), Marjorie Hogan (Miss Murphy), Bruce Callender, Reginald Thomason, Havoc.

John B. Hobbs was the Production Assistant.

	Holding / Source
25.12.1975	DB-D3 / 2"

Duration: 44 minutes.

Frank loses his job as a Christmas elf, causes chaos on his driving test and becomes the star of a BBC DIY show.

Script associate Michael Mills; costume Nicholas Rocker; make-up Judy Cain; lighting by Derek Slee; sound John Lloyd; designed by Rochelle Selwyn.

With Hazel Bainbridge (Mrs Perkins), George Sewell (Wheeler), Alrich Riley (Rude Boy), Chris Leonard (Rude Boy), Campbell Singer (Finney), David Jacobs (TV Interviewer), Michael Angrave (Cameraman), Wendy Gilmore (Linda), Richard Latham (Neville), David Woodcock (Clapper Boy), Peter Jeffrey (Hayes), Marc Boyle (Action).

John B. Hobbs was the Production Assistant.

SERIES 3
Main regular credit(s): Produced and directed by Sydney Lotterby.

	Holding / Source
25.12.1978 **"Learning To Fly"**	DB-D3 / 2"

Duration: 46 minutes.

Frank plans to emigrate to Australia, so he needs to know how to fly. All does not go well in the air....

Costume Dinah Collin; make-up Gillian Thomas; lighting by Jimmy Purdie; sound Richard Chamberlain; designed by Andrew Howe Davies.

With Jessica Forte (Jessica Spencer), Frederick Jaeger, Dick Bentley, Tenniel Evans, Tony Steedman, Christopher Biggins, Linda Beckett, Alexander Moss.

| British Christmas Television Guide | SOMETHING ELSE |

SOMETHING ELSE
A Community Programmes Unit Production production for BBC 2. Transmission details are for BBC 2. Duration varies - see below for details.
Magazine programme for teenagers.
SERIES 2

Holding / Source

01.01.1982 Just The Music [compilation]   DB-D3 / 2"
Duration: 50 minutes.
With Adam and The Ants, The Specials, The Clash, Dexy's Midnight Runners, The Jam, Joy Division, Linx, Siouxsie and The Banshees, Talisman.

SON OF MOTHER GOOSE (RADIO)
A BBC production for BBC Light Programme. Transmission details are for BBC Light Programme. Duration: 45 minutes.
Written by Terry Nation and John Junkin; produced and directed by Alastair Scott-Johnston.
Frankie Howerd (Host), Robin Boyle (Announcer), Ronnie Hilton, Gilbert Harding, Shani Wallis, Stanley Unwin, Billy Ternent and his Orchestra.

Holding / Source

26.12.1957   J /

SON OF SANTA (RADIO)
A BBC production for BBC Radio 4. Transmission details are for BBC Radio 4. Duration: 30 minutes.
Written by Nev Fountain; play production by Maria Esposito.
Ron Moody (Santa Claus), James Fleet (Son), Lynda Bellingham (Holly Berry / Secretary), Dave Lamb (Elf), Ronni Ancona (Elf).

Holding / Source

20.12.1999   DA /

THE SONG AND THE STORY
A BBC production for BBC 1. Transmission details are for BBC 1.
Main regular cast: Isla St. Clair (Presenter).

Holding / Source

26.12.1982 **Sing A Song Of Christmas**   C1 / C1
Duration: 25 minutes.
Written by David Turnbull; music by Rick Kemp; produced and directed by David Turnbull.

SONG BY SONG BY NOËL COWARD
A Yorkshire Television production. Transmission details are for the ATV midlands region. Duration: 65 minutes.
Written by Caryl Brahms, Peter Greenwell and Neil Shand; lyrics by Noël Coward; music directed by Peter Knight; music by Noël Coward and Cole Porter.
Ned Sherrin (Host), Cleo Laine, Gemma Craven, David Kernan, Ian Carmichael.

Holding / Source

28.12.1980   DB / 2"

A SONG FOR CHRISTMAS
A BBC Birmingham production for BBC 1. Transmission details are for BBC 1. Duration: 45 minutes.
Edited by Peter Hercombe.
Paul Coia (Host), Josephine Buchan (Host), Peter Skellern (Chairman of Judges), Cliff Richard.

Holding / Source

24.12.1985   DB / 1"

A SONG FOR CHRISTMAS
A BBC Birmingham production for BBC 1. Transmission details are for BBC 1. Duration: 25 minutes.
Main regular credit(s):   Produced by David Weir; directed by Mark Kershaw.
Main regular performer(s):   Phillip Schofield (Host).

Holding / Source

22.12.1986   DB / 1"
With Aled Jones.

23.12.1986   DB / 1"
With Chris De Burgh.

24.12.1986   DB / 1"
With Elaine Paige, Peter Skellern.

A SONG FOR CHRISTMAS
A BBC Birmingham production for BBC 1. Transmission details are for BBC 1. Duration: 55 minutes.
Produced by David Weir; directed by Mark Kershaw.
Phillip Schofield (Host), Peter Skellern (Chairman), Aled Jones (Panel), Chris De Burgh.

Holding / Source

23.12.1988   DB / 1"

A SONG FOR CHRISTMAS

| SONGS OF PRAISE (INCOMPLETE LISTING) | British Christmas Television Guide |

SONGS OF PRAISE (INCOMPLETE LISTING)

A BBC production for BBC 1. Transmission details are for BBC 1. Usual duration: 40 minutes.

	Holding / Source
24.12.1995	DB / D3S

Edited by Helen Alexander; produced by Bart Gavigan.
With Cliff Richard.

SOOTY

A BBC North production for BBC. Transmission details are for BBC. Duration varies - see below for details.

Main regular credit(s):   Written by Harry Corbett.
Main regular cast: Harry Corbett (Himself).

	Holding / Source
06.11.1955 **Sooty's Christmas Pudding**	R3 /
27.12.1960 **Sooty's Christmas Party**	R1 /
17.12.1961 **Sooty's Christmas Pantomime**	R1 /
27.12.1962 **Sweep's Christmas Adventure**	R1 / 40

Produced by Trevor Hill; directed by Barney Colehan.

| 12.12.1965 **Sooty's Panto Rehearsal** | J / |

Duration: 10 minutes.
Produced and directed by Trevor Hill.

| 24.12.1967 **The Carol Singers** | J / |

Duration: 10 minutes.
Designed by Paul Montague; produced and directed by Trevor Hill.

| 25.12.1967 **Christmas Shopping** | J / |

Duration: 10 minutes.
Produced and directed by Trevor Hill.
See also: THE SOOTY SHOW

SOOTY & CO

A Sooty Films production for Granada. Transmission details are for the Central region. Duration: 18 minutes.

Main regular cast: Sooty.

SERIES 4

	Production No	Holding / Source
16.12.1996 **An Izzy Wizzy Xmas**	1/8239/0051	DB / DBSW

With Neil Buchanan, Shane Ritchie, William Roache.

SERIES 5

	Production No	Holding / Source
15.12.1997 **Christmas Special**	1/8239/0074	DB / DBSW

SOOTY HEIGHTS

A Sooty Films production for Granada. Transmission details are for the Central region. Duration: 18 minutes.

Main regular cast: Liana Bridges (Host), Richard Cadell (Host), Brian Sandford (Puppeteer), Craig Almond (Puppeteer), Crispin Lowrey (Puppeteer), Brenda Longman (Voice of Soo), Rob Rackstraw (Voices of Butch and Ramsbottom).

SERIES 7

	Production No	Holding / Source
20.12.1999 **A Christmas Carrot**	1/8239/0096	DB / DBSW

THE SOOTY SHOW

A Thames Television production. Transmission details are for the ATV midlands region. Usual duration: 25 minutes.

Main regular credit(s):   Devised by Harry Corbett.

SERIES 1

Main regular credit(s):   Produced by Daphne Shadwell; directed by Alan Braden.
Main regular cast: With Harry Corbett (Host).

	Holding / Source
24.12.1968 **Sooty's Christmas Show**	J / 40

Duration: 33 minutes.

SERIES 2

Main regular cast: With Harry Corbett (Host).

	Holding / Source
23.12.1969 **Sooty's Christmas Party**	J / 2"

THE SOOTY SHOW

THE SOOTY SHOW (continued)

SERIES 6
Main regular credit(s): Music by Alan Braden; designed by Nevil Dickin; produced by Daphne Shadwell; directed by Ronald Marriott.
Main regular cast: With Harry Corbett.

Date	Title		Holding / Source
23.12.1971	Sooty's Christmas Show		DB / 2"

Duration: 45 minutes.
With Clive Dunn, Gerry Marsden.

SERIES 11
Main regular credit(s): Designed by Colin Andrews; produced and directed by Dennis Kirkland.
Main regular cast: With Harry Corbett (Host).

Date	Title	VT Number	Holding / Source
25.12.1974	Sooty's Christmas Party	9985	D3 / 2"

With Freddie Davies, Charmian Dore, Matthew Corbett, Karl Johnson, Gerry Marsden, Julian Littman.

SERIES 12
Main regular credit(s): Written by Harry Corbett and Matthew Corbett; music by Sooty-Braden Show Band; designed by Frank Gillman; produced and directed by Charles Warren.
Main regular cast: With Harry Corbett (Host), Matthew Corbett (Host).

Date	Title	VT Number	Holding / Source
24.12.1975	Christmas Special Show	11960	D3 / 2"

Come and join Sooty, Sweep and Soo at their Christmas party and help Sweep to sing Good King Wenceslas. Also have fun watching the gang play forfeits and Billy Dainty as Widow Twanky being taught how to count up to nine by children from the audience.
With Billy Dainty.

SERIES 17
Main regular credit(s): Music directed by Ted Brennan; designed by Jan Chaney; produced by Charles Warren; directed by John Stroud.
Main regular cast: With Matthew Corbett (Presenter), The Cap and Bells Puppet Theatre.

Date	Title	VT Number	Holding / Source
26.12.1980	Christmas Show	22927	D3 / 2"

Matthew Corbett presides over all sorts of seasonal puppet pranks — including an exploding Christmas pudding. Butch and Maggie Mouse add to the antics when they drop in on Sooty, Sweep and Soo. Sooty also welcomes a guest appearance of The Cap and Bells Puppet Theatre, which performs a story about Tommy Rot, who doesn't like Christmas until a meeting with Father Christmas makes him change his mind.
With The Cap and Bells Puppet Theatre.

SERIES 18
Main regular credit(s): Written by Matthew Corbett; music directed by Ted Brennan; designed by John Plant; produced by Charles Warren; directed by John Woods.
Main regular cast: With Matthew Corbett (Host), Marjorie Corbett (Puppeteer), Lawrence T. Doyle (Puppeteer), Ronnie Le Drew (Puppeteer), Peter Jago (Puppeteer), Richard Lockwood (Puppeteer).

Date	Title	VT Number	Holding / Source
21.12.1981	Christmas Show	24692	D3 / 2"

SERIES 21
Main regular credit(s): Written by Matthew Corbett; produced by Charles Warren; directed by Nick Bigsby.
Main regular cast: With Matthew Corbett (Host), Brenda Longman (Voice).

Date	Title		Holding / Source
26.12.1985	Sooty's Christmas Special		D3 / 1"

SERIES 25
Main regular credit(s): Written by Matthew Corbett; executive producer Charles Warren; produced and directed by Stan Woodward.
Main regular cast: With Matthew Corbett (Presenter), Brenda Longman (Soo's Voice).

Date	Title		Holding / Source
26.12.1988	The Sooty Christmas Show		D3 / 1"

With Roger Walker, Suzy Aitchison.
See also: SOOTY (BBC)

SORRY ABOUT LAST NIGHT

A BBC production for BBC 1. Transmission details are for BBC 1. Duration: 50 minutes.
Written by Alexei Sayle; produced by Jacinta Peel; directed by Metin Hüseyin.

Alexei Sayle (Andy Carolides), Siobhan Redmond (Julie Cordova), Alun Armstrong (Mickey), Steve Wright (DJ), Joe Melia (Andy's Father), Victor McGuire (Michael), Richard Ridings (Greg), Nabil Shaban (Lawyer), Anthony Barclay (First Arab), Simon Smith (Hot Dog Seller), Brinley Jenkins (Old Welshman), David Nellist (Doorman), Carlton Dixon (Dancer), Candida Rundle (Bartender), Charlie Caine (Mark), Peter Baikie (Scotsman), Anna Gilbert (Policewoman), Suzzanna Carney (Arab Woman), Eddie Osei (Second Arab), Danny Worters (Boy Driver), Matthew Evans (Second Boy), Sakinah Fraser (Girl).

Date		Holding / Source
27.12.1995		DB-D3 / V1S

THE SOUND OF PETULA

A BBC production for BBC 1. Transmission details are for BBC 1. Duration: 45 minutes.

Programme associate Eric Merriman; music directed by Peter Knight; designed by Don Taylor; produced and directed by Yvonne Littlewood.

Petula Clark (Host), Anthony Newley, The Mike Sammes Singers, Wandsworth School Choir, City of London Band, The Irving Davies Dancers.

	Holding / Source
26.12.1972	DBSEQ / 2"

Held in the John Henshall Collection, which is archived by Kaleidoscope.

SOUNDS FUN

A BBC Scotland production for BBC 1 Scotland. Transmission details are for BBC 1 Scotland. Duration: 45 minutes.

A holiday concert.

	Holding / Source
28.12.1977	J / 2"

SOUNDS OF CHRISTMAS

A BBC production for BBC 2. Transmission details are for BBC 2. Duration: 50 minutes.

Carols from a Choir and the audience, which came into existence nearly 50 years ago at Goldsmiths College in London.

Introduced by Richard Baker; music directed by Brian Wright; lighting by Alan Roberts; sound Vic Godrich; produced and directed by Ken Griffin.

The Goldsmiths Choral Union.

	Holding / Source
25.12.1978	DB-D3 / 2"

SOUNDS OF SUMMER

A Tyne Tees Television production. Transmission details are for the Anglia region. Duration: 40 minutes.

	Holding / Source
25.12.1967	J /

Produced and directed by Christopher Palmer.

With James Lloyd, Louanne Richards, Jane Kells, Wendy Lampard, Barrie Wilkinson, Jan Colet.

THE SOUTH BANK SHOW

Commissioned and produced by a variety of companies (see details below). Usual duration: 52 minutes.

Main regular cast: Melvyn Bragg (Host).

SERIES 15
An LWT production. Transmission details are for the ATV/Central region.

	Production No	Holding / Source
22.12.1991 **Kiri Te Kanawa At Christmas**	9A/80586	D2 / D2S

SERIES 17
An LWT production. Transmission details are for the ATV/Central region.

	Production No	Holding / Source
24.12.1993 **Cliff Richard**	9A/80679	D2 / D2S

With Cliff Richard.

SERIES 28
An LWT production. Transmission details are for the ATV/Central region.

	Production No	Holding / Source
25.12.2005 **Little Britain**	9A/81614	DB / DBSW

SOUTHERN TV CONTINUITY

A Southern Television production. Transmission details are for the Southern Television region.

	Holding / Source
25.12.1981 **ITN News**	DV / Live

Duration: 6 minutes.

With Alastair Stewart (Newscaster).

Followed by the weather forecast.

Held at Wessex Archive.

SPENDER

A Big Boy Productions production for BBC 1. made in association with Initial Film and Television (Series 3 only) / TriSquare Production (29.12.1993 ONLY). Transmission details are for BBC 1.

Main regular credit(s): Created by Jimmy Nail and Ian La Frenais.
Main regular cast: Jimmy Nail (Spender).

Holding / Source

29.12.1993 **The French Collection** D3 / V1S
Duration: 95 minutes.
Written by Jimmy Nail; produced by Steve Lanning and Jen Samson; directed by Matt Forrest.
With Peter Guinness (Detective Chief Superintendent Gillespie), Sammy Johnson (Stick), Lynn Harrison (Kate), Dawn Winlow (Laura), Laure Killing (Janet Thornton), Tom Bell, Jean François Balmer, Phillipe Smolikowski, Jerome Meadows, Michel Julienne, Anne Schofield.

SPICE GIRLS' STORY: VIVA FOREVER!

Commissioned by ITV 1. Transmission details are for the Central region. Duration: 75 minutes.

With the Spice Girls, the bestselling all-female group ever, in the London West End spotlight with a musical featuring all their hits, a look back at the story of the five performers who took "girl power" around the world. As well as hearing from the creative team behind Viva Forever! - which is written by Jennifer Saunders and produced by Mamma Mia's Judy Craymer - there are exclusive interviews with all of the women, as they reflect on their lives both before and after fame.
Executive producers Judy Craymer and Clive Tulloh; directed by Suzannah Wander.
Geri Halliwell, Melanie Chisholm, Victoria Beckham, Emma Bunton, Mel B.

Holding / Source

24.12.2012 HD/DB / HDC

SPIKE MILLIGAN'S SAD/HAPPY ENDING STORY OF THE BALD TWIT LION

A BBC production for BBC 2. Transmission details are for BBC 2. Duration: 30 minutes.
Written by Spike Milligan; drawings by Carol Barker; animated by Colin Whitaker; music by Malcolm Williamson; designed by Paul Munting; produced and directed by Francis Coleman.
Spike Milligan (Narrator).

Holding / Source

26.12.1967 HD-R1 / 2"

THE SPINNERS

A BBC Manchester production for BBC 1. Transmission details are for BBC 1. Duration varies - see below for details.
Main regular performer(s): The Spinners.

Holding / Source

24.12.1969 **The Spinners At The Phil** J / 2"
Duration: 35 minutes.
Produced and directed by Nick Hunter.

Holding / Source

20.12.1971 **The Spinners At The Phil** DB-D3|n / 2"
Produced and directed by Nick Hunter.

Holding / Source

22.12.1972 **The Spinners At Christmas** J / 2"
Duration: 35 minutes.
With Bill Brown (Double-Bass).

SERIES 3
Main regular credit(s): Produced and directed by Barry Bevins.

Holding / Source

21.12.1973 **At Christmas** J / 2"
Duration: 35 minutes.

SERIES 4

Holding / Source

23.12.1974 **The Spinners At Christmas** J / 2"
Duration: 30 minutes.
Lighting by John Crowther; sound Alan Fox; produced and directed by Nick Hunter.
With John McCormick.

23.12.1976 **The Spinners At Christmas** DB-D3 / 2"

25.12.1978 **At Christmas** DB-D3 / 2"
Duration: 30 minutes.
A Dickensian street within York Museum provides a Christmas card setting for Tony, Mick, Cliff and Hughie.
Lighting by John Crowther; sound Alan Fox; produced and directed by Barry Bevins.

25.12.1979 **At Christmas** DB-D3 / 2"

THE SPINNERS (continued)

21.12.1980 At Christmas — DB-D3 / 2"
Duration: 30 minutes.
Tony, Mick, Cliff and Hughie celebrate Christmas with the people of Yorkshire when they take their Christmas show to Bradford's famous Alhambra Theatre.
Music directed by John McCormick; lighting by John Crowther; sound Eddie Magrath; produced and directed by Barry Bevins.

THE SPIRIT OF 66 WITH ALF GARNETT

A BBC production for BBC 1. Transmission details are for BBC 1. Duration: 60 minutes.
Executive producer Tony Moss; produced and directed by Tina Jenkins.
Warren Mitchell (Alf Garnett), Norman Wisdom, Tony Blair, Kenneth Wolstenholme, Pelé, Geoff Hurst, Jack Charlton, Nobby Stiles, Gordon Banks, Bobby Charlton, Barbara Castle.

Holding / Source
29.12.1996 — DB-D3 / D3S

See also: IN SICKNESS AND IN HEALTH (BBC) / "TILL DEATH US DO PART" (BBC)

SPIRIT OF CHRISTMAS

A BBC Scotland production for BBC 1 Scotland. Transmission details are for BBC 1 Scotland. Duration: 60 minutes.
Produced and directed by David Martin.
Fulton Mackay (Host), Rikki Fulton, Hannah Gordon, Russell Hunter, Margo McDonald, Mary Marquis, Jimmy Reid, James Hunter, Graham Ross, Agnes Hoey, Susan Geddes.

Holding / Source
22.12.1985 — DB / 1"

THE SPIRIT OF CHRISTMAS

A BBC Scotland production for BBC 2. Transmission details are for BBC 2. Duration: 40 minutes.
Produced and directed by David Martin.
Selina Scott (Host), Kirsty Wark, Joanna Lumley, Paul Coia, Ronnie Corbett, Clement Freud, Bill Owen, Wendy Craig, Beryl Reid.

Holding / Source
23.12.1990 — DB / 1"

THE SPIRIT OF CHRISTMAS

A Grampian Television production. Transmission details are for the Central region. Duration: 50 minutes.
David Rintoul (Host), Vivien Heilbron (Host).

Holding / Source
23.12.1994 — D3 / D3S
Alternative transmissions: Grampian Television: 18.12.1994.
A choir of 1000 singers join special guests for songs and poems to celebrate the 200th anniversary of Union Street in Aberdeen.

SPITTING IMAGE

A Central production. made in association with Spitting Image Productions. Transmission details are for the Central region. Usual duration: 25 minutes.
Main regular credit(s):   Created by Roger Law and Peter Fluck.

SERIES 5
Main regular credit(s):   Script associate Paul Mayhew-Archer; music by Philip Pope; produced by Geoffrey Perkins.

Holding / Source
27.12.1987 Christmas Show Special — 1" / 1"
An unmistletoeable Christmas cracker of a pudding stuffed with stockings - full of festive yuletide cheer, holly, ivy, Perry Como, etc etc...
You get the idea.
Written by Ian Hislop, Nick Newman, Rob Grant, Doug Naylor, John Docherty, Moray Hunter and Geoff Atkinson; script editor Paul Mayhew-Archer; designed by Ken Ryan; executive producer John Lloyd; directed by Peter Harris.
With Anthony Asbury, Kevin Bradshaw, Simon Buckley, Richard Coombs, Alistair Fullarton, Nigel Plaskitt, Jon Glover, Kate Robbins, Harry Enfield, Enn Reitel, Chris Barrie, Steve Nallon.

SERIES 16
A Spitting Image Productions production.
Main regular credit(s):   Produced by Bill Dare; directed by Steve Bendelack and Andy De Emmony.

Holding / Source
26.12.1993 The Panto: Cinderella Goose And The Seven Beanstalks In Boots In The Wood — D2 / D2S
Written by Mark Burton, John O'Farrell, Stuart Silver and Pete Sinclair; programme associate Angela Littlejohn; script consultant Bryan Blackburn; music by Steve Brown; art director Jo Graysmark; designed by Charlotte Watts; executive producers Joanna Beresford and Roger Law; production manager Pat Lees; directed by Andy De Emmony.
With Roger Blake (Impressionist), Brian Bowles (Impressionist), Alistair McGowan (Impressionist), Kate Robbins (Impressionist), Steve Steen (Impressionist), Simon Buckley, Philip Eason, Barnaby Harrison, Mark Jefferis, Robin Kingsland, Steve Nallon, Nigel Plaskitt, John Thirtle, Patrick Comerford, Brian Herring, Sal Yusuf, Orlando Bishop, Jeremy Stockwell.
Filmed at the Hackney Empire.

SPITTING IMAGE (continued)

SERIES 18

A Spitting Image Productions production.

	Holding / Source
01.01.1995 **Ye Olde Spitting Image**	D2 / D2S

Puppets created by Luck and Flaw, based on an original lunch with Martin Lambie Nairn.

SPLASH O.K.

A BBC production for BBC 2. Transmission details are for BBC 2. Duration: 35 minutes.

Devised by David Proudfoot; written by Jack Gerson; lyrics by Clifford Hanley; music by Iain Sutherland; choreography by David Ellen; produced by David Hanley; directed by David Proudfoot.

Gerard Slevin Jr (Andrew Rivet II), Jameson Clark (Councillor Barton), David Hanley Jr (Archie), Elaine Boyle (Sally), Andrew Byatt (Hughie), Phil McCall (Grovel), Bernadette Reilly (Lil), John Young (Mr Mutrie), James Copeland (Donny Rivet), Joan Fitzpatrick (Meg Rivet), Jan Wilson (Jeannie Logan), James Cosmo (Hamish MacPherson), Willy Joss (Doctor Sharp), Gerard Slevin Sr (Specialist), Edmond Sully (First Gentleman), John Lancaster (Second Gentleman), Shenah Douglas (Maid), Eric Wightman (Wee Worker), Stuart Brown (Big Worker), Jean Faulds (Nurse).

	Holding / Source
27.12.1968	C1N PO / C1

SPOT THE TUNE

A Granada production. Transmission details are for the ATV midlands region. Duration: 25 minutes.

SERIES 2

	Holding / Source
25.12.1957	NR / Live

Music directed by Peter Knight; directed by Philip Jones.

With Marion Ryan, Ken Platt, Margaret Lockwood, Petula Clark, Thora Hird, Ted Heath, Ronald Shiner, Tony Wright.

SERIES 5

	Holding / Source
26.12.1960	J / 40

Designed by Bernard Carey; produced by Mark White; directed by Philip Casson.

With Ted Ray, Marion Ryan, Frances Youles, Alyn Ainsworth and his Orchestra, Michael Medwin, Irene Handl, Richard Thorp, Jill Browne, Alfie Bass, Bill Fraser.

SPY!

A Hat Trick production for Sky One. Transmission details are for Sky One.

Main regular credit(s):	Created by Simeon Goulden; written by Simeon Goulden.
Main regular cast:	Darren Boyd (Tim), Robert Lindsay (The Examiner), Jude Wright (Marcus).

SERIES 2

Main regular credit(s):	Music by Oli Julian; executive producers Jimmy Mulville, Helen Williams and Lucy Lumsden; produced by Charlie Leech and Simeon Goulden; directed by John Henderson.
Main regular cast:	With Miles Jupp (Owen), Dolly Wells (Judith), Mark Heap (Philip).

	Holding / Source
26.12.2012 **Codename: Show Stopper**	HD/DB / HDC

Duration: 48 minutes.

Portis is furious when he finds out about Tim's feelings for Caitlin.

With Matthew Baynton (Chris), Hebekah Staton (Caitlin), Ed Coleman (Moritz), Terence Maynard (Portis), Joseph H. King (Goldstein), Alfie Abel (Oliver), Mia Clifford (Mia), Maurice Cole (Arthur), Neil Edmond (Mr Harris), Tatum Duprey (Sadie), Lindsay Duncan (The Director), Kerron Darby (Gang Man), Frieda Thiel (Gang Girl), Duncan James (Self).

SQUIRE DODD'S CHRISTMAS SPECIAL

Alternative/Working Title(s): KEN DODD'S CHRISTMAS FEAST

A BBC North West production. Transmission details are for BBC North West.

Ken Dodd.

	Holding / Source
19.12.1978	J / 2"

A 2" spool is listed at the BBC, but it was logged as missing in 2003. It may have disappeared any time since 1978.

ST. URSULA'S IN DANGER!

A BBC production for BBC 2. Transmission details are for BBC 2. Duration: 65 minutes.

Written by Peter Glidewell; music by Carl Davis; produced and directed by Ian Keill.

Charlotte Long (Alison Dayne), Frederick Jaeger (Mr Forson), Doreen Mantle (Miss Cowley), Barbara Bolton (Miss Prosser), Robert Dorning (Major Farquhar), Brenda Cowling (Mrs Trimble), Katie Locker (Jennifer), Sally Pickering (Sally), Biddy Hodson (Kitty), Sophie Brew (Verity), Rupert Graves (Teddy), Tom Mennard ('The Surveyor'), Mike Edmonds (The Gypsy).

	Holding / Source
20.12.1983	C1 / C1

See also: SCHOOLGIRL CHUMS (BBC)

STAINLESS STEEL AND THE STAR SPIES

A Euston Films production for Thames Television. Transmission details are for the Central region. Duration: 50 minutes.
Written by Gray Jolliffe; executive producer Verity Lambert; produced by Ray Corbett; directed by Anthony Simmons.
Deryck Guyler (Vicar), Anna Karen (Mum), Debbie Farrington (Young Girl), Charles Pemberton (Dad), Fabia Drake (Miss Ruby).

	Holding / Source
01.01.1981	C1 / C1

STAND BY YOUR BEDOUIN!

A BBC production for BBC 1. Transmission details are for BBC 1. Duration: 90 minutes.
The adventures of Fred Florence — British agent. Caught up in a revolution, he brings hilarious chaos to friend and foe alike.
Written by Ray Cooney and Tony Hilton; designed by Rhoda Gray; produced and directed by Wallace Douglas.
Brian Rix (Fred Florence), Leo Franklyn (Stan Charrington), Helen Jessop (Lady Tracy Spence), Derek Royle (Hamid), Sheila Mercier (Eloise), Peter Bland (Hubert Wooley), Anna Dawson (Farina), Bill Treacher (Colonel Wazir), Stefan Gryff (Captain Abu), Gary Warren (Arab Boy), Michael Cronin (Captain Sareed El Dur), John Shorter (Sir John Spence), Michael Franks (Arab Soldier).

	Holding / Source
23.12.1970	J / 2"

STAND UP PERRIER

An Angel Eye (Scotland) production for Channel 4. Transmission details are for Channel 4.
Main regular credit(s):   Directed by James Harding.

	Holding / Source
27.12.1999	DB / DBS

Duration: 45 minutes.
Produced by Richard Osborne.
With Julian Barratt, Noel Fielding, Ross Noble, Simon Munnery, Terry Alderton, Ben 'n' Arn, Al Murray.

STANLEY BAXTER IN PERSON

A Watchmaker Productions production for Carlton. Transmission details are for the Central region. Duration: 50 minutes.
Executive producers Elaine Bedell and Richard Drewett; produced by Karen Steyn.
Stanley Baxter, Clive James, Billy Connolly, Robbie Coltrane, Stephen Fry.

	Holding / Source
31.12.1998	DB / DBS

STANLEY BAXTER IN REEL TERMS

A Mentorn Films production for LWT. Transmission details are for Channel 4. Duration: 50 minutes.
Written by Ken Hoare; additional material by Russel Lane, Paul Minett, Brian Leveson and Jim Pullin; produced by Henry Eagles; directed by Tom Gutteridge.
Stanley Baxter, Dawn French.

	Holding / Source
26.12.1996	D3 / D3S

THE STANLEY BAXTER PICTURE SHOW

An LWT production. Transmission details are for the ATV midlands region. Duration varies - see below for details.
Main regular performer(s):   Stanley Baxter (Various roles).

		Production No	Holding / Source
21.12.1973	The Stanley Baxter Big Picture Show	9L/09277	D2 / 2"

Duration: 52 minutes.
Written by Ken Hoare; music directed by Harry Rabinowitz; choreography by Norman Maen; designed by Bill McPherson; produced and directed by David Bell.
With The Norman Maen Dancers, Liza Mimammi, George Hornby.

		Production No	Holding / Source
26.12.1976	Stanley Baxter's Christmas Box	9L/09831	D2 / 2"

Duration: 51 minutes.
Written by Ken Hoare, Barry Cryer, Iain McIntyre, Neil Shand and Stanley Baxter; lyrics by Paul Horner; music directed by Harry Rabinowitz; music by Paul Horner; choreography by Norman Maen; designed by Bill McPherson; produced by Humphrey Barclay; directed by Bruce Gowers.
With Miriam Margolyes, Moray Watson, The Norman Maen Dancers, The Tony Mansell Singers.

THE STANLEY BAXTER SERIES

Produced for LWT/BBC by a variety of companies (see details below). Transmission details are for the ATV midlands region. Duration varies - see below for details.
Main regular cast: Stanley Baxter (Various roles).
An LWT production. Transmission details are for the Central region.

		Production No	Holding / Source
24.12.1982	The Stanley Baxter Hour	90412	D2 / 2"

Duration: 51 minutes.
Written by Ken Hoare; additional material by Alec Mitchell, Russel Lane, Paul Minett and Brian Leveson; choreography by Bruce McClure; designed by Bill McPherson; associate producer Bruce McClure; production manager Brian Penny; produced by David Bell; directed by John Kaye Cooper.
With Cass Allen, Susie Blake, Denise Coffey, Roland Curram, Harriet Reynolds, Kara Wilson, Peggy O'Farrell Children, Tony Aitken, Jennifer Croxton, Ken Halliwell, Ronald Markham, Mavis Pugh, Diana Rayworth, Earl Rhodes, Hugh Ross, Holly Watson, Dino Shafeek, Alan Woodhouse, Alyn Ainsworth and his Orchestra.

	Holding / Source
27.12.1985 Stanley Baxter's Christmas Hamper	DB / 1"

Duration: 50 minutes.
Written by Ken Hoare; additional material by Stanley Baxter, Simon Brett, Denise Coffey, Brian Leveson and Peter Vincent; produced and directed by John Bishop.

29.12.1986 Stanley Baxter's Picture Annual	DB / 1"

Duration: 55 minutes.
Written by Brian Leveson, Ken Hoare, Paul Minett, Russel Lane and Gary Denis; additional material by Paul Minett, Brian Leveson, Russel Lane and Gary Denis; script associate Ken Hoare; music directed by Alyn Ainsworth; music by Alyn Ainsworth; choreography by Norman Maen; designed by Graham Lough; production manager Jenny Leah; produced and directed by John Bishop.

With Lesley Collier, Pat Ashton, Rory Bremner, Sherrie Hewson, Robert James, Nick Maloney, Sarah Payne, Harriet Reynolds, Llewellyn Rees, Michael Stainton, Brendan Stapleton, Troy Harewood, Leigh Miles, Grant Santino, Philip Broomhead, Roy Rowlands, Stuart Myers, Leslie Weekes, Peter Whitaker, The Norman Maen Dancers.

STANLEY BAXTER: NOW AND THEN

An ITV Productions production for ITV 1. Transmission details are for the Central region. Duration: 48 minutes.

Written by Paul Minett and Brian Leveson; music by Paul Thomson; production team Simon Hedges and Silvi Subba; associate producer Catherine Coleman; production executive Wendy Hutchinson; executive producer Rachel Ashdown; production manager Ruth Glaser; produced by Tony Nicholson; directed by Alasdair MacMillan and Jane Littlewood.

Stanley Baxter (Host), Julia McKenzie (Narrator), Celia Imrie, Michael Grade, Victoria Wood, Rob Brydon, Eddie Izzard.

	Holding / Source
25.12.2008	DB / DBSW

STAR GAMES

A Thames Television production. made in association with Trans World International. Transmission details are for the ATV midlands region.

Main regular credit(s):   Production team John Scholz-Conway and Vincent Stafford; executive producer Brian Venner; produced and directed by Dave Rogers.
Main regular performer(s): With Michael Aspel (Host).

	Holding / Source
26.12.1978 Christmas Star Games	DB / 2"

Duration: 50 minutes.
With Gerald Sinstadt (Football Commentator), Alan Pascoe, Linda Thorson, Jack Shepherd, Jackie Pallo, Roger de Courcey, Nigel Havers, Liza Goddard, Colin Baker, Tom Adams, Julian Holloway, Robin Askwith.

See also: STAR GAMES

STAR GAMES

A Thames Television production. made in association with Trans World International. Transmission details are for the ATV midlands region. Duration: 50 minutes.

Main regular credit(s):   Production team John Scholz-Conway and Peter Tabern; executive producer Brian Venner; produced and directed by Dave Rogers.
Main regular performer(s): Michael Aspel (Host), Jenny Hanley (Host), Alan Pascoe (Commentator), Gerald Sinstadt (Commentator).

	Holding / Source
25.12.1979 The Grand Final - Comedy V. TV Presenters	D3 / 2"

With Bill Oddie, Jeremy Bulloch, David Janson, Micky Dolenz, Robert Lindsay, Liza Goddard, Linda Hayden, Robin Askwith, Alfred Marks, Brough Scott, Peter Taylor, William Woollard, Tommy Boyd, Ray Moore, Sandra Harris, Diana Harron, Jimmy Savile, Doctor Magnus Pyke.

STAR IN THE SKY

Alternative/Working Title(s): CHRISTMAS WEEK CLOSE / IT HAPPENED ONE CHRISTMAS
A Thames Television production. Transmission details are for the Thames Television region. Duration: 10 minutes.
Closedown songs sung by Richmond schools.
Research Pamela Moncur; designed by Jim Nicholson; produced and directed by Margery Baker.
Alan Dudeney (Conductor), St Richard's with St Andrew's School Choir, Richmond.

	VT Number	Holding / Source
26.12.1981	25902	DB / 2"

STAR OVER BETHLEMEN

A BBC production for BBC 2. Transmission details are for BBC 2. Duration: 60 minutes.
Written by Christopher Fry; associate producer Noble Wilson; produced by Brian Large and John Vernon; directed by Brian Large* and John Vernon*.
Judi Dench, Tom Fleming.

	Holding / Source
24.12.1977	J / 2"

Failed transfer from 2", tape junked.

STAR TRADERS: THE CHRISTMAS CHALLENGE

Commissioned by ITV 1. Transmission details are for the Central region. Duration: 48 minutes.
Series producer Rachel Watson; directed by Paul Kirrage.
Myleene Klass (Host), Kyran Bracken (Host).

	Holding / Source
22.12.2007	DB / DBSW

STARBURST

An ATV/Central production. Transmission details are for the ATV/Central region. Duration: 50 minutes.

SERIES 3
An ATV production. Transmission details are for the ATV midlands region.
Main regular credit(s): Script associate Ronnie Cass.
Main regular performer(s): With Jack Parnell and his Orchestra.

	Holding / Source
22.12.1981	DB / 2"

Choreography by Norman Maen; designed by Richard Plumb; produced and directed by Peter Harris.
With Petula Clark and The Von Trapp Family, Ron Moody, Jim Bowen, Wall Street Crash, The Brother Lees, David Berglas, Sarah Payne, Hilary Macnamara, Harry Rabinowitz, The Harry Rabinowitz Orchestra, The Norman Maen Dancers.

STARS AND GARTERS

An Associated-Rediffusion production. Transmission details are for the ATV midlands region. Usual duration: 25 minutes.
Main regular performer(s): The Alan Braden Band and Quartet.

SERIES 2
Main regular performer(s): With Ray Martine (Compere).

	Holding / Source
26.12.1963	J|a / 40

Settings by Michael Yates; directed by John P. Hamilton and Daphne Shadwell.
With Kathy Kirby, Vince Hill, Debbie Lee, Al Saxon, Lynnette Rae, Roy Glen, Wally Whyton, The Alan Braden Quartet.

SERIES 3
Main regular credit(s): Programme editor Barry Cawtheray; music directed by Peter Knight; designed by Michael Yates; directed by Rollo Gamble.
Main regular performer(s): With Ray Martine (Compere).

	Holding / Source
25.12.1964	J / 40

Duration: 40 minutes.
With Susan Maughan, Kim Cordell, Johnny Sheldon, Lee Martin, Tommy Wright, Dixie Lee, Sulky Gowers, Celia Hunt, Steve Perry, The Square Pegs, Bud Flanagan, Joan Turner.

STARS AND THEIR LIVES

A Hanrahan Media production for Carlton UK. Transmission details are for the Central region. Duration: 25 minutes.
Main regular performer(s): Carol Vorderman (Presenter).

	Holding / Source
26.12.1999	DB / DBS

SERIES 3
Main regular credit(s): Executive producer Mark Wells; produced by Will Hanrahan.

	Holding / Source
31.12.2002	DB / DBSW

With Jennifer James.

STARS AT CHRISTMAS WITH SONGS OF CHRISTMAS

A Yorkshire Television production. Transmission details are for the ATV midlands region. Duration: 51 minutes.
Bob Monkhouse and the stars bring you seasonal greetings and songs of Christmas.
Music associate Nigel Brooks; designed by Howard Dawson; production associate Peter Max-Wilson; produced and directed by Len Lurcuck.
Bob Monkhouse (Host), The Beverley Sisters, Michael Gallois, Anita Harris, Frank Ifield, Arthur Lowe, Julie Rogers, Leila Khalil Utshant, The Piano Chorale, The Nigel Brooks Singers, Pueri Cantores of Westminster.

	VT Number	Holding / Source
24.12.1972	Y/2245/0137	J / 2"

See also: STARS ON SUNDAY

STARS IN THE WEST

A Westward Television production. Transmission details are for the Westward Television region. Duration: 25 minutes.

SERIES 3

	Holding / Source
17.12.1964 **Theatre Royal, Drury Lane**	J /

Presented by John Pett; written by John Pett; directed by John Bartlett.
With Laurence Harvey, Elizabeth Laner, Harry Welchman, Cardew Robinson, William Boulter, George Hoare.

STARS IN THEIR EYES

A Granada production for ITV 1. Transmission details are for the Central region.

	Production No	Holding / Source
28.12.1991 **Christmas Special**	1/1663/0013	DB / 1"

STARS IN THEIR EYES

STARS IN THEIR EYES (continued)

Date	Title	Production No	Holding / Source
01.01.1994	New Year Special	1/1663/0032	DB / D3S
24.12.1994	Christmas Special	1/1663/0044	DB / D3S
23.12.1995	Christmas Special	1/1663/0055	DB / D3S
26.12.2000	Christmas Special	1/1663/0150	DB / DBSW
25.12.2001	Christmas Special	1/1663/0165	DB / DBSW
28.12.2002	Christmas Special	1/1663/0185	DB / DBSW

Produced by Rachel Ashdown.
With Matthew Kelly (Host), Caprice, Frank Skinner, Kim Wilde, Boy George, Tracy Shaw.

Date	Title	Production No	Holding / Source
18.12.2004	Christmas Special	1/1663/0217	DB / DBSW
24.12.2005	Celebrity Duets	1/1663/0250	DB / DBSW
23.12.2006	Celebrity Special	1/1663/0251	DB / DBSW

Written by Richard Easter; produced by Simon Staffurth; directed by Simon Marsh.
With Cat Deeley (Host), Paul Burrell, Tom Lister, Phina Oruche, Jayne Tunnicliffe, Mark Radcliffe.

STARS ON SUNDAY

A Yorkshire Television production. Transmission details are for the ATV midlands region. Duration varies - see below for details.

SERIES 4
Main regular credit(s): Executive producer Jess Yates.

Date	Title	Holding / Source
26.12.1971	Stars On Christmas Sunday	J / 2"

Duration: 25 minutes.
Music associates Walter Bradley, Bev Jones, Joe Makar, George Thompson, Trevor Walmsley and Geoffrey Whitham; designed by Howard Dawson; directed by Len Lurcuck.
With Petula Clark, The Beverley Sisters, Beryl Reid, The Poole Family, Shirley Bassey, Hughie Green, Bobby Bennett, Stars On Sunday Choir, Grimethorpe Colliery Band, Hammond Sauce Works Junior Band, Band of Yorkshire Imperial Metals, Stars On Sunday Singers.

SERIES 15
Main regular credit(s): Music adviser Robert Hartley; music directed by Peter Husband; designed by Howard Dawson; produced by Peter Max-Wilson; directed by Lesley Smith.

Date	Title	Holding / Source
25.12.1977	Stars On Christmas Day	J / 2"

Duration: 35 minutes.
Introduced by Moira Anderson.
With Moira Anderson (Host), Bing Crosby, Don Estelle, Gracie Fields, John Mills, Valerie Monese, Mary O'Hara, Harry Secombe, Opus VII, The Northern Singers.
See also: STARS AT CHRISTMAS WITH SONGS OF CHRISTMAS

STEPPIN' OUT WITH KATHERINE JENKINS

An ITV Studios production for ITV 1. Transmission details are for the Central region. Duration: 54 minutes.
A cabaret show.
Katherine Jenkins, Mark Benton, Il Divo, Stooshe, André Rieu, The Overtones, Tom Chambers, Only Boys Aloud, Kev Orkian.

Date	Holding / Source
02.12.2012	HD/DB / HDC

STEPTOE AND SON

A BBC production for BBC 1. Transmission details are for BBC 1. Duration varies - see below for details.

Main regular credit(s): Written by Ray Galton and Alan Simpson; theme music by Ron Grainer; produced by Duncan Wood.

Main regular cast: Harry H. Corbett (Harold Steptoe), Wilfrid Brambell (Albert Steptoe).

SERIES 7

Main regular credit(s): Music by Dennis Wilson.

Holding / Source

24.12.1973 A Christmas Party — DB-D3 / 2"

Alt.Title(s): *The Party*

Duration: 43 minutes.

Albert is busy making preparations for Christmas—and so is Harold. But his plans don't include his father. He's determined to go away— the further the better. Like Majorca. He has his plane tickets, his hotel reservations, his spending money. There is only one more little thing to do. Tell Albert...

Costume Rupert Jarvis; make-up Joan Barrett; lighting by Ritchie Richardson; sound John Lloyd; designed by David Chandler; produced and directed by Graeme Muir.

With Frank Thornton, Arnold Diamond, Mary Barclay, Valerie Bell, Peter Hughes, Peter Thornton, Jenny Cox, Sue Walker, Shirley Hafey.

Studio recording exists on digibeta ex 2".

SERIES 8

Main regular credit(s): Music by Dennis Wilson; produced and directed by Douglas Argent.

Holding / Source

26.12.1974 A Christmas Holiday — DB-D3 / 2"

Alt.Title(s): *A Perfect Christmas*

Duration: 43 minutes.

Designed by Paul Allen.

With Leon Eagles.

There is also a longer edit for the 1974 Christmas special.

STEWPOT

An LWT production. Transmission details are for the Anglia region.

Main regular credit(s): Programme associate David Block; designed by Bryce Walmsley; produced by Keith Beckett.

Main regular performer(s): Ed Stewart (Host).

SERIES 2

Main regular credit(s): Programme associate David Block; designed by Bryce Walmsley; directed by Keith Beckett.

Holding / Source

26.12.1970 — J / 2"

Duration: 38 minutes.

This is Stewart's recipe for post- Christmas gluttony : a programme of music, dancing, comedy and film clips with food for the theme. It is a Boxing Day feast in which The Scaffold sing jellied Eels and a special lyric to their celebrated Thank you very much, Pickettywitch prove themselves gourmets, ballerina Carol Grant dances The Sugar Plum Fairy, Charlie Cairoli shows you how to make a trifle, and Gordon Banks of Stoke City shows charity footballer Stewart how to save a goal despite over-indulgence at the table. And what is Roger Whittaker doing? "That's a good question," says producer Keith Beckett. "I wish I knew."

With The Scaffold, Roger Whittaker, Pickettywitch, Carol Grant, Charlie Cairoli, Gordon Banks.

STICKY MOMENTS WITH JULIAN CLARY

A Wonderdog Productions production for Channel 4. Transmission details are for Channel 4. Duration: 40 minutes.

Main regular credit(s): Conceived by Julian Clary and Paul Merton; written by Julian Clary and Paul Merton; produced by Toni Yardley; directed by John Henderson.

Main regular performer(s): Julian Clary (Host).

Holding / Source

31.12.1989 Sticky New Year With Julian Clary — 1" / 1"S

STILL GAME

A the Comedy Unit production for BBC Scotland. made in association with Effingee Productions. Transmission details are for Various BBC Channels. Duration: 30 minutes.

Main regular credit(s): Written by Greg Hemphill and Ford Kiernan; directed by Michael Hines.

Main regular cast: Gavin Mitchell (Boabby), Ford Kiernan (Jack Jarvis), Greg Hemphill (Victor McDade), Paul Riley (Winston Ingram), Mark Cox (Tam Mullen), Sanjeev Kohli (Navid), Jane McCarry (Isa Drennan).

SERIES 4

Transmission details are for BBC 2.

Main regular credit(s): Script supervisor Liz Sherry; titles by Anemotion; art director Floraidh Mackenzie; designed by Graham Rose; production executive April Chamberlain; executive producers Ewan Angus, Colin Gilbert, Ford Kiernan and Greg Hemphill; production manager Angela Murray; produced by Michael Hines.

Holding / Source

28.12.2005 Cold Turkey — DB / DBSWF

With James Martin (Eric), Jake D'Arcy (Pete), Lynne McCallum (Peggy), Shamshad Ahktar (Meena), Kate Donnelly, Doreen McGillivray, Annette Staines, Mark Young, Sandy Nelson, Michael Mackenzie, Alexander West, Katherine Connolly, Eliza Langland.

| British Christmas Television Guide | STILL GAME (continued) |

SERIES 6
An Effingee Productions Ltd production for the Comedy Unit. Transmission details are for BBC 2.

Main regular credit(s): Script supervisor Liz Sherry; director of photography Phil Dawson; titles by Anemotion; art director Nicki McCallum; designed by Graham Rose; executive producers Ewan Angus, Ford Kiernan and Greg Hemphill; production manager Pam Roberts; produced by Angela Murray.

Holding / Source
01.01.2007 **Hogmanay Special**   DB / DBSWF

An Effingee Productions Ltd production.
Alternative transmissions: BBC 2 Scotland: 31.12.2006.
With Grant Thomson, Tony Martin, Gary French, Jennifer Black, Ronnie Letham, Callum Cuthbertson.
No Gavin Mitchell.

SERIES 7
An Effingee Productions Ltd production for the Comedy Unit. Transmission details are for BBC 2 Scotland.

Main regular credit(s): Script supervisor Liz Sherry; executive producers Ewan Angus, Ford Kiernan and Greg Hemphill; produced by Angela Murray.
Main regular cast: With James Martin (Eric).

Holding / Source
31.12.2007 **Hogmanay Special**   DB / DBSWF

Alternative transmissions: BBC 2: 02.01.2008.
Designed by Iain MacDonald.
With Shamshad Ahktar (Meena), John Buick, Ashok Srivastava, Karen Power, Michele Gallagher, Hamish Wilson, Adrianne Boyd, Lewis Howden, Iain Agnew, Ian Barrie.

STILL OPEN ALL HOURS
A BBC production for BBC 1. Transmission details are for BBC 1. Duration: 30 minutes.
Written by Roy Clarke.
David Jason (Granville).

Holding / Source
26.12.2013 **(pilot)**   HD/DB / HDC

Granville has inherited the emporium from his Uncle Arkwright and runs it with his son Leroy. But some things never change: Nurse Gladys Emmanuel and the Black Widow are still regulars.
Produced by Gareth Edwards; directed by Dewi Humphreys.
With Lynda Baron (Gladys Emmanuel), Stephanie Cole (Mrs Featherstone), Maggie Ollerenshaw (Mavis), Johnny Vegas (Wet Eric), Mark Williams (Planter's Salesman), James Baxter (Leroy), Brigit Forsyth (Madge), Kulvinder Ghir (Cyril), Sally Lindsay (Mrs Agnew), Nina Wadia (Mrs Hussein), Barry Elliot (Mr Marshall), Kathryn Hunt (Vera), Misha Timmins (Cindy), Cathy Breeze (Mrs Hemstock), Sally Womersley (Mrs Travis), Emily Fleeshman (Hayley), Nadine Mulkerrin (Ashley).

STINGRAY
An AP Films production for ITC, made in association with ATV. Transmission details are for the ATV midlands region. Duration: 25 minutes.

Main regular credit(s): Theme music by Barry Gray and Gary Miller; music by Barry Gray; associate producer Reg Hill; produced by Gerry Anderson.
Main regular cast: Don Mason (Voice of Captain Troy Tempest and others), Robert Easton (Voice of Lieutenant George Phones Sheridan and others), Ray Barrett (Voice of Commander Sam Shore and others), Lois Maxwell (Voice of Lieutenant Atlanta Shore), David Graham (Various Voices).

Holding / Source
22.12.1964 **A Christmas To Remember**   DB / C3

A small orphaned boy, spending Christmas with Troy Tempest and Atlanta, becomes unexpectedly involved in a strange mystery—and for the Stingray crew it becomes a Christmas never to be forgotten.
Written by Dennis Spooner; directed by Alan Pattillo.
With Sylvia Anderson (Voice of Barry Byrne).

A STOCKING FULL OF STARS
A BBC production for BBC 1. Transmission details are for BBC 1. Duration varies - see below for details.

Holding / Source
25.12.1972   R1N / 2"
Duration: 120 minutes.
Designed by Philip Lindley; executive producer Philip Lewis; produced and directed by Ian Smith.
With Mike Aspel (Host), Roy Castle (Host), Bruce Forsyth, The Generation Game, Basil Brush, Blue Peter, Charlie Cairoli, The Goodies, Animal Magic, Top of The Pops, Top Soccer Stars, Vision On, The Geoff Sanders Quartet.

25.12.1973   DB-D3 / 2"
Duration: 120 minutes.
Designed by Louise Vanson; executive producer Philip Lewis; produced and directed by Ian Smith.
With Michael Aspel (Host), Hope and Keen, Blue Peter, Roy Castle, Charlie Cairoli, The Goodies, The Osmonds, Top Soccer Stars, Vision On, The Bert Hayes Quartet, Joe Baker.

25.12.1974   DB-D3 / 2"
Duration: 60 minutes.
Designed by Andrew Davies; produced and directed by Ian Smith.
With Michael Aspel (Host), Rolf Harris, Blue Peter, Basil Brush, Vision On, Showaddywaddy, Michael Crawford, The Bert Hayles Sextet.

A STORY FOR CHRISTMAS

A BBC production for BBC 1. Transmission details are for BBC 1. Duration varies - see below for details.

	Holding / Source
24.12.1970 **The Gift Of The Magi**	J / 2"

Duration: 10 minutes.
Written by O. Henry; produced and directed by Will Wyatt.
With John Slater (Storyteller).

	Holding / Source
22.12.1974 **The Visitor's Book**	J / 2"

Duration: 10 minutes.
Written by A. J. Alan; produced and directed by Frances Whitaker.
With John Slater (Storyteller).

THE STORY OF ARE YOU BEING SERVED?

A BBC Productions production for BBC 2. Transmission details are for BBC 2. Duration: 60 minutes.

Research Henrietta Baidoo; associate producer James Norton; production executive Stan Matthews; executive producer Caroline Wright; production manager Nathalie McCarty; produced and directed by Samantha Peters.

Alexander Armstrong (Narrator), Frank Thornton, Mollie Sugden, Trevor Bannister, Mike Berry, Nicholas Smith, Jeremy Lloyd, David Croft, Sarah Hayes, Richard Russell, James Insell, John Howard Davies, Robin Carr, Jo Austin, Alan Yentob, Doremy Vernon, Georgina Andrews, Leslie Parker, Willy Norton, Wendy Richard, John Inman, Michael Knowles, Deanne Turner, Nigel Curzon, Russell T. Davies, Andy Beckett.

	Holding / Source
01.01.2010	HD/DB / HDC

See also: "ARE YOU BEING SERVED?" (BBC)

THE STORY OF DOCTOR WHO

A BBC production for BBC 1. Transmission details are for BBC 1. Duration: 59 minutes.

Programme consultant Kevin Davies; production executive Jez Nightingale; executive producer Caroline Wright; produced and directed by Clare Finnett.

Verity Lambert, Peter Purves, Carole Ann Ford, Peter Davison, Colin Baker, Tom Baker, Roger Murray-Leach, Nicola Bryant, Philip Hinchcliffe, Barry Letts, Terrance Dicks, Sophie Aldred, Sylvester McCoy, Frazer Hines, Louise Jameson, Elisabeth Sladen, Brian Hodgson, Anneke Wills, Nicholas Courtney, Graham Cole, Nicholas Evans, John Scott Martin, Jon Culshaw.

	Holding / Source
30.12.2003	DB / DBSW

See also: DOCTOR WHO (BBC)

STORYTIME

A BBC production for BBC 1. Transmission details are for BBC 1.

SERIES 3

	Holding / Source
23.11.1992 **Christmas Bear**	DB / D3S

STRICTLY COME DANCING

A BBC production for BBC 1. Transmission details are for BBC 1. Duration varies - see below for details.
Main regular credit(s): Created by Fenia Vardanis; theme music by Dan McGrath and Josh Phillips.

	Holding / Source
24.12.2005 **Strictly Come Dancing Christmas Special**	DB / DBSW

Duration: 65 minutes.
Written by Bruce Forsyth, Rob Colley and Adam Bostock-Smith; script supervisors Helen Dobson and Belinda Marsh; music by Laurie Holloway; production executive Claire Bridgland; executive producer Karen Smith; series producer Sam Donnelly; series director Alex Rudzinski.
With Bruce Forsyth (Host), Tess Daly (Hostess), Alan Dedicoat (Voice Over), Darren Gough, Colin Jackson, Evander Holyfield, Rachel Hunter, James Martin, Zoë Ball, Tony Christie.

SERIES 5

Main regular credit(s): Written by Bruce Forsyth and Rob Colley; script supervisors Tony Grech and Belinda Marsh; designed by Patrick Doherty; assistant producers Cally Haycox, Claire Callaghan, Claire Knowles and Jay Miller; executive producers Simon Shaw, Martin Scott and Sam Donnelly; series producer Michele Burgess; produced by Sam Donnelly; series director Nikki Parsons.

Main regular performer(s): With Bruce Forsyth (Host), Tess Daly (Host), Alan Dedicoat (Voice Over), Penny Lancaster Stewart, Stephanie Beacham, Matt Di Angelo, Kenny Logan, Gabby Logan, Gethin Jones, Alesha Dixon, John Barnes, Kate Garraway, Willie Thorne, Brian Capron, Dominic Littlewood, Kelly Brook, Letitia Dean.

	Holding / Source
25.12.2007	HD/DB / HDC

Duration: 60 minutes.
With Darren Gough, Mark Ramprakash.

	Holding / Source
28.12.2007 **The Strictly Come Dancing Story**	DB / DBSW

Duration: 60 minutes.
Executive producer Caroline Wright; produced by Jeff Simpson.
With Bruce Forsyth, Tess Daly.

STRICTLY COME DANCING

British Christmas Television Guide   **STRICTLY COME DANCING (continued)**

SERIES 6
A BBC Productions production.
Main regular credit(s): Written by Rob Colley and Bruce Forsyth; associate producers Nina Hytner, Jay Miller and Luis Pulido; production executive Claire Bridgland; executive producers Sam Donnelly and Martin Scott; series producer Clodagh O'Donoghue; series director Nikki Parsons.
Main regular performer(s): With Bruce Forsyth (Host), Tess Daly (Host), Alan Dedicoat (Voice Over), Rachel Stevens, Jodie Kidd, Austin Healey, Gary Rhodes, Jessie Wallace, Cherie Lunghi [as Cherie Lunghie], Don Warrington, Lisa Snowdon, Andrew Castle, Heather Small, Mark Foster, Christine Bleakeley, John Sergeant, Tom Chambers, Gillian Taylforth, Phil Daniels.

Holding / Source
25.12.2008 **Strictly Come Dancing Christmas Special**   HD/DB / HDC
Duration: 60 minutes.
Script supervisors Tony Grech and Belinda Marsh; designed by Patrick Doherty; assistant producers Lee English, Cally Haycox, Luis Pulido and Piers Shorrock; production manager Simi Gupta; produced and directed by Ben Archard.
With Rachel Stevens, Kelly Brook, Alesha Dixon, Jill Halfpenny, Lisa Snowdon, Tom Chambers.

All live except first show. A shorter Results Show was broadcast on the Sunday evening. It was not live but pre-recorded on the Saturday night.

Holding / Source
25.12.2009 **Strictly Come Dancing Christmas Special**   HD/DB / HDC
A BBC Productions production. Duration: 60 minutes.
Written by Rob Colley and Bruce Forsyth; script supervisors Tony Grech and Belinda Marsh; music directed by David Arch; series consultant Phil Parsons; art director Kat Berry; designed by Patrick Doherty; assistant producers Nick Jones, Rosie Franks, Francesco Palmer and Luis Pulido; production executive Claire Bridgland; executive producer Sam Donnelly; production manager Jane Atkinson; series producer Liz Foley; series director Nikki Parsons.
With Bruce Forsyth (Host), Tess Daly (Host), Alesha Dixon (Judge), Len Goodman (Judge), Craig Revel Horwood (Judge), Bruno Tonioli (Judge), Ricky Whittle, Austin Healey, Rachel Stevens, Gethin Jones, Ali Bastian, Chris Hollins.

Holding / Source
25.12.2010   HD/DB / HDC
A BBC Productions production. Duration: 60 minutes.
Written by Rob Colley and Bruce Forsyth; script supervisor Belinda Marsh; music directed by David Arch; series consultant Phil Parsons; art director Lizzie Chambers; designed by Patrick Doherty; assistant producers Louisa Booth, Nykki Parker, Rosie Franks, Nicola Barber and Laetitia Nneke; VT Producer Laura Bugden; production executive Claire Bridgland; executive producer Moira Ross; production manager Kirsty Reid; series producers Ed Booth and Liz Trott; line producer Jane Ashford; produced and directed by Ben Archard; series director Nikki Parsons.
With Bruce Forsyth (Host), Tess Daly (Host), Alan Dedicoat (Voiceover), Alesha Dixon (Judge), Len Goodman (Judge), Craig Revel Horwood (Judge), Bruno Tonioli (Judge), John Barrowman, Vince Cable M.P., Fern Britton, Ronni Ancona, June Brown.

A BBC Productions production.

Holding / Source
25.12.2011   HD/DB / HDC
Duration: 60 minutes.
Written by Rob Colley, Bruce Forsyth and Kevin Day; script supervisors Belinda Marsh and Annie McDougall; series editor Clodagh O'Donoghue; music consultant Mark Campbell; music directed by David Arch; art director Lizzie Chambers; designed by Patrick Doherty; assistant producers Caitlin Cowdry, Kim Winston, Nicola Benham and Tom Bezemer; VT Producer Ben Stevens; production executive Claire Bridgland; executive producer Moira Ross; production manager Kate Jones; series producer Ed Booth; line producer Kirsty Bysouth; produced and directed by Robin Lee-Perrella; series director Nikki Parsons.
With Bruce Forsyth (Host), Tess Daly (Host), Alan Dedicoat (Voiceover), Alesha Dixon (Judge), Len Goodman (Judge), Craig Revel Horwood (Judge), Bruno Tonioli (Judge), Russell Grant (Christmas Tree Fairy), Charlie Brooks, Su Pollard, Barry McGuigan, Simon Webbe, Debra Stephenson, Shakin' Stevens.

Holding / Source
25.12.2012 **Christmas Special**   HD/DB / HDC
Duration: 75 minutes.
With Bruce Forsyth (Host), Tess Daly (Host), Alan Dedicoat (Voiceover), Len Goodman (Judge), Craig Revel Horwood (Judge), Bruno Tonioli (Judge), Darcey Bussell (Judge), Sheila Hancock, Katy Brand, Helen Skelton, Bobby Ball, Fabrice Muamba, Rod Stewart.

Holding / Source
25.12.2013 **Christmas Special**   HD/DB / HDC
Duration: 75 minutes.
With Bruce Forsyth (Host), Tess Daly (Host), Alan Dedicoat (Voiceover), Len Goodman (Judge), Craig Revel Horwood (Judge), Bruno Tonioli (Judge), Darcey Bussell (Judge), Rochelle Humes, Rufus Hound, Matt Goss, Ricky Norwood, Elaine Paige, Sara Cox, Jack Topping.
See also: STRICTLY COME DANCING CHRISTMAS SPECIAL (BBC)

STRICTLY COME DANCING CHRISTMAS SPECIAL

A BBC production for BBC 1. Transmission details are for BBC 1. Duration varies - see below for details.
Main regular credit(s): Written by Rob Colley and Bruce Forsyth; theme music by Dan McGrath and Josh Phillips; executive producer Martin Scott; series producer Sam Donnelly; series director Nikki Parsons.
Main regular performer(s): Bruce Forsyth (Host), Tess Daly (Host), Alan Dedicoat (Voice Over), Mark Ramprakash, Matt Dawson, Louisa Lytton, Emma Bunton, Colin Jackson, Zoë Ball, Marti Pellow.

Holding / Source
25.12.2006 **Preview**   DB / DBSW
Duration: 10 minutes.
25.12.2006 **Special**   DB / DBSW
Duration: 60 minutes.

STRICTLY COME DANCING CHRISTMAS SPECIAL

STRICTLY COME DANCING CHRISTMAS SPECIAL (continued)

See also: STRICTLY COME DANCING (BBC)

STRIKE IT LUCKY

A Thames Television production for Thames/Central. Transmission details are for the Central region. Duration varies - see below for details.

Main regular performer(s): Michael Barrymore (Host).

	Holding / Source
25.12.1989 **Christmas Special**	1" / 1"

A Thames Television production. Duration: 40 minutes.
Associate producer David Mason; produced by Maurice Leonard; directed by John Birkin.
With Frank Bruno.

25.12.1990 **Christmas Special**	1" / 1"

Duration: 40 minutes.
The contestants were all children.
Produced by Maurice Leonard; directed by John Birkin.

29.12.1994 **Christmas Special**	DB / D2S

A Thames Television production for Central. Duration: 45 minutes.
Produced by Maurice Leonard.

THE STRIP SHOW

A Spitting Image Productions production for Channel 4. Transmission details are for Channel 4. Duration: 30 minutes.
Written by Hunt Emerson and Sky Robert-Thompson; produced and directed by Giles Pilbrow.
Ronni Ancona, Alistair McGowan, Rebecca Front, Enn Reitel.

	Holding / Source
29.12.1995	D2 / D2S

SUMMER'S CHRISTMAS

A BBC production. Transmission details are for BBC. Duration: 45 minutes.
Written by Anne Allen; play production by Julian Amyes.
Mary Hinton (Mrs Tuftnell), Rosamund Greenwood (Miriam Tuftnell), John Stratton (Eric), Geoffrey Matthews (Johnny O'Brien), Mary Steele (Jane O'Brien), Jerold Wells (Harry Summer), Lane Meddick (Steve Robertson), June Cunningham (Mona).

	Holding / Source
27.12.1957	J /

THE SUNDAY GANG

A BBC production for BBC 1. Transmission details are for BBC 1.

SERIES 4

Main regular cast: With John Dryden (Presenter), Tina Heath (Presenter), Jill Shakespeare (Presenter), Glen Stuart (Presenter).

	Holding / Source
24.12.1978 **Christmas Special**	DB-D3 / 2"

(VAL PARNELL'S) SUNDAY NIGHT AT THE LONDON PALLADIUM

An ATV production. Transmission details are for ITV. Usual duration: 52 minutes.

Live from the London Palladium the British viewing public had a taste of all the greatest stars between 1955 and 1974. Lew Grade, the master negotiator of ATV Television made regular trips to the USA signing up major artistes to come and perform every week.

It began on the 25th September 1955 when ITV was in its infancy. The first host, Tommy Trinder, was supported by the George Carden Dancers and the London Palladium Orchestra. Given various names over the years including the London Palladium Girls, the Pamela Devis Dancers and the Tiller Girls, these girls would give showbiz glamour support to many hosts including Bob Monkhouse, Jim Dale, Ted Rogers, Dickie Henderson, Jimmy Tarbuck and most famously Bruce Forsyth. Bruce was by the far the most successful host for the series. Its biggest audience was in January 1960 with Bruce in an edition featuring Cliff Richard watched by over twenty million people.

The orchestras, directed at different times by Eric Rogers and Jack Parnell always played live, speeding up when a show over-ran or slowing down to make sure that a show finished on time!

After the Tiller girls and the less known acts in the first part was the game show, Beat the Clock. People had to arrange words stuck to a magnetic board "into a well known phrase or saying" in thirty seconds. Could the contestants cope with the pressure as the second hand moved around the large clock face?

The second section of the show was reserved for star names. In the early days Trinder introduced many well-known acts including Gracie Fields, Eartha Kitt, Lonnie Donegan, Shirley Bassey and Howard Keel. In later years there were visits from Judy Garland, Bob Hope, Vic Damone, Cliff Richard and the Shadows and Ella Fitzgerald. Comedy interludes were provided by Frankie Howerd, Arthur Askey, Bernard Bresslaw, Morecambe and Wise and Tommy Cooper amongst others.

The show always ended with a large revolving stage where the glamour girls, the compere and that night's guests stood on it as it slowly turned clockwise to the familiar theme tune of the show.

Despite the huge plethora of famous guest stars, the series is best remembered for an edition made during the 1961 strike by the acting union Equity, who refused to allow its performers to appear that week. Bruce Forsyth and Norman Wisdom had signed contracts before the dispute began so they performed the entire show themselves, improvising quickly to fill fifty minutes of live chaos.

Rebranded as The New Palladium Show, and filmed in colour for export to US audiences, the series was abruptly cancelled by Lord Grade in 1967. Regretting his mistake, it returned briefly in 1973. Beginning in October 1973 with live transmissions, after four weeks the IRA mainland bombing campaign led to a severe curtailment of all live television. The 25th November 1973 edition was not live, instead being constructed of previous recordings of Pamela Giselle, Larry Grayson and Paul Anka. The 6th January 1974 episode was cancelled due to a bomb scare close by and was never shown, despite a rushed edit being created from previous inserts. The end of the 1974 run saw the shows being recorded earlier the same day to prevent this happening again.

The few surviving editions have now been released on DVD to be enjoyed again, except for the 28th October 1973 edition featuring Petula Clark, Rudolph Nureyev, Merle Park, Bryn Phillips and Desmond & Marks which was unclearable.

SERIES 1
Transmission details are for the ATV London region.
Main regular performer(s): With The London Palladium Girls [as George Carden's London Palladium Girls], The London Palladium Orchestra.

Holding / Source

18.12.1955 **Cinderella**   J / Live
Duration: 75 minutes.
Brought forward from 25.12.1955.
Orchestra directed by Eric Rogers; choreography by George Carden; directed by Bill Lyon-Shaw.

With Max Bygraves (Buttons), Richard Hearne (Baron), Adele Dixon (Prince Charming), Bartlett & Ross (The Ugly Sisters), Barbara Leigh (Cinderella), Zoe Gail (Dandini).

This edition was entirely given over to a pantomime. Bygraves, Hearne and Dixon had all appeared in Cinderella when it was presented as The London Palladium's panto in the winter of 1953/54, and it seems that it was hoped that Julie Andrews, who then took the title role, would reprise it here. Some ATV publicity seemed to suggest that this would be the case with the programme being earmarked for Christmas Day. We are unsure whether Andrews' absence is connected to its broadcast being brought forward to a less prestigous date.

25.12.1955   J / Live
Directed by Bill Ward.

With Tommy Trinder (Host), Vic Damone, Pier Angeli, Max Wall, Alma Cogan, Bob Hope, Jewel and Warriss, Billy Cotton, Manci Crompton, Zoe Gail, Bert Bernard.

01.01.1956 **Mother Goose**   J / Live
Duration: 65 minutes.
Book by Basil Thomas, orchestra directed by Eric Rogers, directed by Bill Ward.

With Max Bygraves (Sammy), Richard Hearne (Mother Goose), Hy Hazell (Colin), Harry Cranley (The Goose), Sid Millward and his Nitwits, Pauline Grant, The George Carden Dancers, The London Palladium Orchestra.

This edition contained no variety elements as such and instead featured a potted version of the pantomime "Mother Goose" which had been at the Palladium in the winter of 1954/55.

See also: THE NEW LONDON PALLADIUM SHOW

THE SUNDAY NIGHT PLAY

A BBC production. Transmission details are for BBC. Duration varies - see below for details.

Holding / Source

25.12.1960 **Tuppence In The Gods**   R1 /
Duration: 90 minutes.
Written by Michael Voysey; music by James Turner; play production by Chloe Gibson.

With Fay Compton (Mrs Sarah Victoria Marryot), Frederick Bartman (Walter Murray), Vivienne Martin (Fanny Marryot), Patsy Rowlands (Daisy Peacock), Tony Sympson (Gus Elen), Robert Hewitt (Albert Vaughan), Ray Brooks (Alfie), Dandy Nichols (Rosie Pennyfeather), Hugh Lloyd (Herbert Pennyfeather), Alice Bowes (Cleaner), Bryan Hulme (George), Robert Bernal (Beggar), Peter Digby Smith (Beggar), Nelson Evans (Beggar), Hilda Campbell-Russell (Barmaid), Chris Carlsen (Dan Leno), Howard Lamb (Cabbie), James Belchamber (Business Man), Sherry Brind (Connie Meadows), Ivor Dean (Lester), The George Mitchell Singers.

SUNDAY NIGHT THEATRE

A BBC production. Transmission details are for BBC. Usual duration: 90 minutes.

Holding / Source

24.12.1950 A Soldier For Christmas NR / Live
Duration: 105 minutes.
Written by Reginald Beckwith; settings by James Bould; play production by Douglas Allen.
With Jimmy Holland (First Carol Singer), Jimmy Holland (Child), Roger Field (Second Carol Singer), Keith Faulkner (Third Carol Singer), Evelyn Moore (Postwoman), Heather Thatcher (Mrs Ferguson), Rachel Gurney (Phoebe Ferguson), Joan Harben (Brenda Nicholls), Anthony Forwood (Ronald Vines), Esmé Church (Mrs Jones), Noel Howlett (Mr Ferguson), Robert Beatty (Private William Mackenzie), Jessie Evans (Milly Smith), Susan Richmond (Lady Doubeny), Frances Waring (Mrs Jarvis), Janet Cottam (Child).

28.12.1952 Markheim NR / Live
Duration: 30 minutes.
Adapted by Winston Clewes; based on a story by Robert Louis Stevenson; designed by Stephen Taylor; play production by Christian Simpson and Tony Richardson.
With Douglas Wilmer (Markheim), Erik Chitty (Dealer), Robin Bailey (Man), Josée Richard (Maid), Harry Brunning (Jovial Gentleman), Arthur Edmonds (Carol Singer), Michael Gulbenkian (Carol Singer), Derek Hodgson (Carol Singer), James Perkins (Carol Singer), Jack Vincent (Carol Singer).

20.12.1953 Amahl And The Night Visitors J / Live
Duration: 50 minutes.
Written by Gian Carlo Menotti; music by Gian Carlo Menotti; play production by Christian Simpson.
With Charles Vignoles (Amahl), Gladys Whitred (His Mother), John Lewis (King Kaspar), John Cameron (King Melchior), Scott Joynt (King Balthasar), Edric Connor (Page), Josephine Gordon (Dancer).

25.12.1955 Bird In Hand J / Live
Written by John Drinkwater; play production by Douglas Allen.
With Terry-Thomas (Cyril Beverley), Jacqueline Mackenzie (Joan Greenleaf), Beatrice Varley (Alice Greenleaf), Herbert Lomas (Thomas Greenleaf), Eric Lander (Gerald Arnwood), Charles Victor (Mr Blanquet), William Mervyn (Ambrose Godolphin, Q.C.), Robert Speaight (Sir Robert Arnwood), Edward Higgins, Brian Moorehead, Dudley Buttrum, Alice Esmie-Bell, Ronald Clarke, Dudley Williams.

"The Baikie Charivari" by James Bridie was planned as a production for August 1950.
See also: MAIGRET (BBC)

SUNDAY NIGHT THEATRE

Produced for ITV by a variety of companies (see details below). Transmission details are for the ATV midlands region. Usual duration: 50 minutes.

Production No VT Number Holding / Source

26.12.1971 Who Killed Santa Claus D2 / 2"
An Anglia production. Duration: 70 minutes.
Postponed from 26.12.1971.
It is Christmas Eve. In her beautiful Chelsea home, lovely television star Barbara Love awaits the guests for her Christmas party. Inside the house all is warmth and gaiety - but someone is planning a murder. Has he been invited to the party, or is he a stranger?
Written by Terence Feely; edited by John Rosenberg; designed by Marilyn Taylor; produced and directed by John Jacobs.
With Barbara Murray (Barbara Love), Robert Hardy (Christopher Moore), Carolyn Seymour (Connie Bell), Lyndon Brook (Paul Reston), Peter Bowles (Jack Campbell-Barnes), John Franklyn-Robbins (Donald Lewis), Noel Davis (Ray Lacey), Len Jones (Dave Ogden).
WKSC wasn't transmitted at 22:20, as originally scheduled, on 26/12/1971, it was replaced by live Boxing, but according to all the papers it was transmitted earlier in the evening (19:55) - replacing the film that's listed in TVT.

23.12.1973 Visitors 7372 7372/73 T1 / 2"
An ATV production.
Sylvia, widowed during the war, has always seemed a source of strength to her daughter, Jan, and her younger sister, Lydia, whom she brought up after the death of their mother. So Jan and Lydia are puzzled by the strange letters Sylvia sends them. A trip to Sylvia's cottage reveals the presence of Yvonne, a young girl Sylvia has taken in for Christmas.
Written by Ellen Dryden; designed by Michael Bailey; produced by Nicholas Palmer; directed by Don Taylor.
With Kathleen Byron (Sylvia), Moira Redmond (Lydia), Jennie Linden (Jan), Gabrielle Lloyd (Yvonne).

SUNDAY PREMIERE

A BBC production for BBC 1. Transmission details are for BBC 1. Duration varies - see below for details.
SERIES 2

Holding / Source

06.09.1987 The Happy Valley DB / C1
Duration: 90 minutes.
Written by David Reid; music by Geoffrey Burgon; consultant Juanita Carberry; produced by Cedric Messina; directed by Ross Devenish.
With Denholm Elliott (Sir Henry 'Jock' Delves Broughton), Holly Aird (Juanita Carberry), Amanda Hillwood (Lady Diana Delves Broughton), Richard Heffer (Assistant Superintendent Poppy), Kathryn Pogson (June Carberry), Michael Byrne (John Carberry), Cathryn Harrison (Helen Tapsell), Peter Sands (Lord Erroll), Mawa Makonido (Waiganjo), Ka Vundla (Gatimu), Roshan Seth (Defence Solicitor), Fiona Walker (Miss Tanner), Frank Lazarus (Doctor), Jon Cartwright (Constable), Abdullah Sunado (Witchdoctor), Oliver Rowe (Ian Eatwell), Jane Wellman (Yacht Party Guest), Michael Stround (Yacht Party Guest), Diana Kent (Christmas Party Guest), Julian Cope (Christmas Party Guest), Gordon Mellor (Christmas Party Guest), Guy Williams (Christmas Party Guest), Ian Collier (Hotel Guest), Stuart McGugan (Hotel Guest), Boni Wanda (Broughton's Gardener), Zembi Okendo (Woman In Court), Graham Crowden (Chief Justice's Voice), Mark Wynter (Vocalist).

SUNDAY PREMIERE

SUNDAY STORY

A BBC production. Transmission details are for BBC/BBC1. Duration: 5 minutes.

SERIES 4
Transmission details are for BBC 1.

Three Stories for Christmas

Main regular credit(s):   Produced by John Elphinstone-Fyffe.

	Holding / Source
20.12.1964 **Once For Yes, Twice For No**	J /

Alternative transmissions: BBC 1: 20.12.1964.
Written by Richard Wade.

27.12.1964 **Bombed Out**	J /

Alternative transmissions: BBC 1: 27.12.1964.
Written by Richard Wade.

SUPERGRAN

A Tyne Tees Television production. Transmission details are for the Central region.

Main regular credit(s):   Adapted by Jenny McDade; based on books by Forrest Wilson; theme music by Billy Connolly and Phil Coulter.

Main regular cast: Gudrun Ure (Supergran).

	Holding / Source
24.12.1986 **Supergran And The World's Worst Circus**	1" / C1

Duration: 52 minutes.
Produced by Graham Williams; directed by Gerald Blake.

With Iain Cuthbertson (The Scunner Campbell), Bill Shine (Inventor Black), Alan Snell (Muscles), Brian Lewis (Dustin), Michael Graham (Willie), Samantha Duffy (Edison), Hedley Dodd (Ben), Paul Shane, Rikki Fulton, Anna Dawson, Eli Woods.

SUPERSONIC

An LWT production. Transmission details are for ITV. Duration varies - see below for details.

Main regular credit(s):   Produced and directed by Mike Mansfield.

SERIES 1
Transmission details are for the London Weekend Television region.

Main regular credit(s):   Programme associate Susie Deyong.

	Production No	Holding / Source
27.12.1975 **Christmas Special**	9C/09701	D2 / 2"

Duration: 51 minutes.
Designed by Bryce Walmsley.

With Alvin Stardust, Gary Glitter, Marc Bolan, Roxy Music, Slade, Mud, Leo Sayer, Linda Lewis, The Sweet, David Essex, The Bay City Rollers, Justin Hayward, John Lodge.

SERIES 2
Transmission details are for the London Weekend Television region.

	Production No	Holding / Source
25.12.1976	9C/09899	D2 / 2"

Duration: 35 minutes.
Programme associate Susie Deyong; designed by Bryce Walmsley.

With Russell Harty (Host), Joanna Lumley (Host), Marc Bolan ("New York City"), Marc Bolan ("The Soul Of My Suit"), Marc Bolan and T Rex ("I Love To Boogie"), Tina Charles ("Doctor Love"), Tina Charles ("Dance Little Lady Dance"), Gary Glitter (Hits Medley), The Glitter Band, T. Rex.

Entries marked thus - ° - look to have been recorded - possibly for inclusion in another edition - but not included in the final edit.

SUPERSONIC

A Mike Mansfield Television production for Channel 4. Transmission details are for Channel 4. Duration: 50 minutes.

Production assistant Hilary Stewart; produced and directed by Mike Mansfield.

Modern Romance (Good Friday), John Cougar (Tumblin' Down), Soft Cell (Down In The Subway), Limahl (Only For Love), Status Quo (Margarita Time), Shakin' Stevens & Bonnie Tyler (A Rockin' Good Way), Marilyn (Calling Your Name), Meat Loaf (All Revved Up), Elton John (Crystal.), Adam Ant (Strip.).

	Holding / Source
27.12.1983	1" / 1"

SUPERTED

A Siriol Animation production for S4C. Transmission details are for BBC 1. Duration: 4 minutes.

The magical bear and his friend Spottyman undertake adventures.

Main regular credit(s):   Directed by Dave Edwards.

SERIES 2
Main regular credit(s):   Written by Robin Lyons; music by Chris Stuart and Mike Townend; produced by Mike Young.

Main regular cast: With Derek Griffiths (Voices), Peter Hawkins (Voices), Melvyn Hayes (Voices), Roy Kinnear (Voices), Jon Pertwee (Voices), Victor Spinetti (Voices), Sheila Steafel (Voices).

	Holding / Source
20.12.1984 **SuperTed Meets Father Christmas**	1" / 1"

SURPRISE SURPRISE

An LWT production. Transmission details are for the Central region. Usual duration: 51 minutes.

Main regular performer(s): Cilla Black (Presenter).

SERIES 2

Main regular credit(s):   Executive producer Alan Boyd.

	VT Number	Holding / Source
23.12.1984	91075	D2 / 1"

Programme associate Vince Powell; music by Alyn Ainsworth; produced by Bob Merrilees and Brian Wesley; directed by Phil Bishop, John Gorman and Tom Poole.

With Christopher Biggins.

| 22.12.1985 | 91294 | D2 / 1" |

SERIES 3

	VT Number	Holding / Source
28.12.1986	91437	D2 / 1"

SERIES 4

	VT Number	Holding / Source
27.12.1987 **Christmas Surprise Surprise**	91745	D2 / 1"

Music directed by Alyn Ainsworth; designed by Colin Pigott; produced by David Bell and Brian Wesley; film sequences directed by Ted Ayling and Sue McMahon; directed by John Gorman.

With Bob Carolgees, Gordon Burns.

SURVIVAL SPECIAL

An Anglia production. Transmission details are for the Tyne Tees region.

	Holding / Source
26.12.1980 **Penguin Christmas**	C1 / C1

Duration: 50 minutes.

The remote Falkland Islands in the South Atlantic were occupied by Britain just over 150 years ago. Now, they are claimed by the Argentines. But this programme is not about the sovereignty issue. It's about the rights of the original inhabitants—the wildlife, especially penguins. Cindy Buxton filmed a vast colony of more than five million birds on one small island.

Written by Colin Willock; produced and directed by Colin Willock.

With David Niven (Narrator).

THE SWEEPSTAKES GAME

An LWT production. Transmission details are for the ATV midlands region. Usual duration: 25 minutes.

Main regular credit(s):   Programme associate Neil Shand; programme consultant Tito Burns; produced and directed by Bruce Gowers.

Main regular performer(s): Bernard Braden (Host).

	Production No	Holding / Source
24.12.1976 **Holiday Sweepstakes Game**	9L/09849	D2 / 2"

Research Paul Flattery; designed by Bryce Walmsley.

With Faith Brown, Janet Brown, Peter Goodwright, Kristine, Johnny More, Little and Large.

SWINGIN' CHRISTMAS

A BBC Productions production for BBC 2. Transmission details are for BBC 2. Duration: 85 minutes.

Format by China Parker and Victoria Jones; script supervisor Claire Mathias; designed by Chris Webster; executive producer Oliver Macfarlane; production manager Alison Brodie; produced by Helen Mansfield; directed by Ian Russell.

Michael Parkinson (Presenter), John Wilson Orchestra, Seth MacFarlane, Anna-Jane Casey, Curtis Stigers.

	Holding / Source
25.12.2010	HD/DB / HDC

THE SYD LAWRENCE BAND SHOW

A Yorkshire Television production. Transmission details are for the Yorkshire Television region. Duration: 25 minutes.

Music directed by Syd Lawrence; designed by Ian McCrow; produced by John Duncan; directed by David Mallet.

Syd Lawrence and his Orchestra, Kevin Kent, The Skylarks, Les Dawson.

	Holding / Source
31.12.1970 **(pilot)**	DB / 62

SYKES

A BBC production for BBC 1. Transmission details are for BBC 1. Duration: 30 minutes.

Main regular cast: Eric Sykes (Eric), Hattie Jacques (Hattie).

SERIES 13

Transmission details are for BBC 1.

Main regular credit(s):   Written by Eric Sykes; music by Ken Jones; produced and directed by Roger Race.

Main regular cast: With Deryck Guyler (Corky).

Holding / Source

12.12.1975 Christmas Party   DB-D3 / 2"

Postponed from 21.11.1975.

Designed by Steve Brownsey.

With Sheila Steafel, Annie Leake, Jeremy Gagan, Wendy Stone, Nicholas Drake.

SERIES 15

Transmission details are for BBC 1.

Main regular credit(s):   Written by Eric Sykes; music by Ken Jones; designed by Antony Thorpe; produced by Roger Race.

Main regular cast: With Deryck Guyler (Corky).

Holding / Source

22.12.1977 Christmas Party   DB-D3 / 2"

Eric and Hattie spend Christmas Day at Corky's.

Music by The Ken Jones Trio; directed by Roger Race.

With Sylvia Peters, Jimmy Edwards, Joy Harington.

"The South Bank Show: Eric Sykes", LWT, 50 mins. Tx:18.09.2005. Directed and produced by Aurora Gunn. With Ken Dodd, Michael Palin and Jimmy Tarbuck.

T. BAG'S CHRISTMAS DING DONG

A Thames Television production. Transmission details are for the Central region. Duration: 25 minutes.

Written by Lee Pressman and Grant Cathro; produced by Charles Warren; directed by Glyn Edwards.

Georgina Hale (T-Bag), Glenda Jackson (Vanity Bag), John Hasler (T-Shirt), Peter Woodthorpe (Count Pumpernickel), James Saxon (Archduke Fritz), Megan Kelly (Maria).

	Holding / Source
26.12.1990	1" / 1"

T. BAG'S CHRISTMAS TURKEY

A Thames Television production. Transmission details are for the Central region. Duration: 25 minutes.

Written by Lee Pressman and Grant Cathro; produced by Charles Warren; directed by Glyn Edwards.

Georgina Hale (T-Bag), John Hasler (T-Shirt), Peggy Mount (Mumsie), John Cater (King Wenceslas), Sebastian Abineri (Papa Pepe Pepperoni), Laurence Bouvard (Marguerita Pepperoni).

	Holding / Source
26.12.1991	1" / 1"

T.BAG'S CHRISTMAS CAROL

A Thames Television production. Transmission details are for the Central region. Duration: 25 minutes.

Written by Lee Pressman and Grant Cathro; produced by Charles Warren; directed by Leon Thau.

Elizabeth Estensen (T. Bag), John Hasler (T. Shirt), Kellie Bright (Sally), Gillian Martell (Emily Scrumptious), John Clive (Giles Pickens).

	Holding / Source
26.12.1989	1" / 1"

T.T.V

A BBC production for BBC 1. Transmission details are for BBC 1.

Main regular cast: Marcus Kimber (Storyteller).

	Holding / Source
19.12.1985 Christmas Kerfuffle	DB / 1"

T•F•I• FRIDAY

A Ginger Productions production for Channel 4. Transmission details are for Channel 4.

Main regular performer(s): Chris Evans (Presenter).

SERIES 2

Main regular performer(s): With Will Macdonald (Host), Andrew the Barman (Host).

	Holding / Source
20.12.1996	D3 / D3S

With Danny Baker, Black Grape, James Dean Bradfield, Grimethorpe Colliery Band, Leo, Richard Madeley & Judy Finnigan, Sleeper.

All editions t/x'd from 20.09.96 until 29.11.96 had extra material in the late night repeats.

TAGGART

A Scottish Television production. Transmission details are for the Central region. Duration varies - see below for details.

Main regular credit(s): Created by Glenn Chandler; theme music by Mike Moran.

	Holding / Source
31.12.1987 Cold Blood	1" / C1

Duration: 75 minutes.

Written by Glenn Chandler; script associate Murray Ferguson; music by Mike Moran; produced by Robert Love; directed by Haldane Duncan.

With Mark McManus (Detective Chief Inspector Jim Taggart), James Macpherson (Detective Sergeant Jardine), Iain Anders (Superintendent McVitie), Harriet Buchan (Jean Taggart), Diane Keen (Ruth Wilson), Freddie Boardley (Ricki Keenan), Leonard O'Malley (Donny McGregor), Mona Bruce (Mrs McVitie), Patricia Ross (Sergeant Laura Campbell), Robert Robertson (Doctor Andrews), Joan Scott (Mrs Keenan), Margo Gunn (Geraldine Keenan), Anne Smith ('Aqua' Assistant), Lloret Mackenna (Mrs Franchetti), Choy Ling Man (Lin Chang), Nicholas Coppin (Norman Brownlow), John Williamson (Basketball Coach), Paul Morrow (Cafe Owner), Kenneth Lindsay (Cafe Assistant), Forbes Masson (Hotel Manager), Bill Henderson (Gordon Roe), Billy McElhaney (Customer In Gym), Bill Barclay (Tattoo Artist), Hilary Maclean (Protestor).

	Holding / Source
30.12.1988 Double Jeopardy	DB-1" / C1

Duration: 75 minutes.

Written by Glenn Chandler; music by Mike Moran; designed by Geoff Nixon; associate producer Waltraud Pusl; executive producer Robert Love; produced by Peter Barber-Fleming; directed by Jim McCann.

With Mark McManus (Jim Taggart), James Macpherson (Mike Jardine), Iain Anders (Superintendent McVitie), Harriet Buchan (Jean Taggart), James Laurenson (Maurice Bain), Sheila Ruskin (Pam Fleming), Valerie Gogan (Carol Bain), Rose McBain (Rowena Bain), Herbert Trattnigg (Ulrich Geissler), Claus Elssmann (Bernhard Geissler), Alec Heggie (Frank Sweeney), Barbara Rafferty (Agnes Sweeney), John Shedden (Ernest Atkin), Robert Robertson (Doctor Andrews), Sarah Collier (Professor Joan Thompson), Leon Sinden (Judge), Vari Sylvester (Prosecuting Counsel), Peter Finlay (Defence Counsel), John Mitchell (Minister), Wilma Duncan (Woman At Funeral), Jonathan Battersby (Jason Hammond), Bridget Biagi (Marti Hammond), Leigh Gardner (Cocktail Waitress), Jill Lennon (Cafe Waitress), Laurie Ventry (Scottish Doctor), Ernest Blake (German Doctor), Valerie Edmond (Hotel Receptionist), Eric P. Caspar (Superintendent Bauer), Wolfgang Jorg (Gunter), Erika Wackernagel (Ingeborg), Edi Bierling (Brewery Representative).

TAGGART (continued)

Holding / Source

01.01.1990 Love Knot — DB-1" / C1

Duration: 75 minutes.

Written by Glenn Chandler; music by Mike Moran; associate producer Murray Ferguson; executive producer Robert Love; produced and directed by Peter Barber-Fleming.

With Mark McManus (Jim Taggart), James Macpherson (Mike Jardine), Iain Anders (Superintendent McVitie), Harriet Buchan (Jean Taggart), Jenny Runacre (Countess Von Aschenberg), David Robb (Jack MacFarlane), John Michie (Robby Meiklejohn), Nicholas McArdle (C. I. Fraser), Shauna Baird (Susan Bryant), Ewan Bremner (Jason), Hugh Ross (Richard Smiley), Robert Robertson (Doctor Andrews), Stewart Porter (Ken Stirton), Peter Mullan (Peter Lewis), Freddie Earlle (McPhee), Elspeth MacNaughton (Mrs Macbeth), Laurie Ventry (Stranger), Lewis Howden (Police Constable Craig), Ann-Louise Ross (Post Woman), Douglas Henshall (Motor Cyclist), Mandy Matthews (Schoolgirl), Rachel Boyd (Schoolgirl), Peter Quilliam Cane (Back Packer), John Batty (Highland Police Constable).

Holding / Source

31.12.1990 Rogues' Gallery — DB-1" / C1

Duration: 75 minutes.

Written by Stuart Hepburn; music by Mike Moran; produced by Robert Love; directed by Alan Macmillan.

With Mark McManus (Detective Chief Inspector Jim Taggart), James Macpherson (Detective Sergeant Jardine), Iain Anders (Superintendent McVitie), Harriet Buchan (Jean Taggart), Edita Brychta (Valerie Sinclair), Jack Galloway (Neil Gallagher), Ross Dunsmore (Scott Kerr), Peter Mullan (Peter Latimer), Blythe Duff (Jackie Reid), Robert Robertson (Doctor Andrews), Bill Murdoch (Jack Greig), Vincent Marzello (Enzo Fabrizzi), Julie Ann Gilchrist (Tracy Smeaton), Vivienne Brown (Sheila Ross), Andrew Gillan (David Ross), Eilidh Fraser (Sheenagh Patience), Allan Sharpe (Frank McGovern), David Arneil (Danny Ferguson), Iain Glass (Ian McKenzie), David McGowan (Tommy Wilson), George Drennan (Joe Harvey), Joe Brady (Norrie Walker), Kenneth Orr (Police Mechanic), Janet Michael (Baglady), Diana Olsson (Woman With Poodle), Nell Brennan (Art Critic), Joey Cooper (McGovern's Heavy), Harry Glass (Builder), David Heller (Desk Sergeant), Liz Kristiansen (TV Newscaster).

Holding / Source

01.01.1992 Violent Delights — DB-1" / C1

Duration: 75 minutes.

Written by Glenn Chandler; music by Mike Moran; associate producer Dennis Mulligan; produced by Robert Love; directed by Alan Macmillan.

With Mark McManus (Detective Chief Inspector Jim Taggart), James Macpherson (Detective Sergeant Mike Jardine), Iain Anders (Superintendent McVitie), Harriet Buchan (Jean Taggart), Robert Robertson (Doctor Andrews), Blythe Duff (Jackie Reid), Tom Smith (Philip Dempster), Florence Guerin (Francoise Campbell), Jason Hetherington (Ian McLaughlin), John Dougall (Andy Collins), Paul Hickey (Tony Jacovelli), Natalie Robb (Sheila McIntosh), Ronald Fraser (Angus Collins), Gordon Cameron (Billy Kavan), Alastair Cording (Mick Dawson), Robert McBain (Keith Dempster), Sheila Donald (Aunt Hettie), Ronald Aitken (Peter Campbell), Sandy Neilson (Headmaster), Anna Hepburn (Mary Meiklejohn), Victoria Nairn (Marilyn Telfer), Hugh Larkin (Alec Telfer), Graham Macgregor (Funeral Driver), Simon Sharkey (Funeral Singer), Nicola Auld (Hospital Sister), Leonard McLure (Taxi Driver), James A. Tennant (Minister).

Holding / Source

01.01.1993 Fatal Inheritance — DB-1" / C1

Duration: 75 minutes.

Written by Glenn Chandler; music by Mike Moran; associate producer Dennis Mulligan; produced by Robert Love; directed by Alan Macmillan.

With Mark McManus (Jim Taggart), James Macpherson (Mike Jardine), Blythe Duff (Jackie Reid), Iain Anders (Superintendent McVitie), Robert Robertson (Doctor Andrews), Harriet Buchan (Jean Taggart), Hannah Gordon (Doctor Janet Napier), Francis Matthews (Doctor Gerald Napier), Caroline Hunnisett (Belinda Napier), Scott Cleverdon (Jeremy Napier), Meg Johnson (Mrs Jeffrey), Jamie Roberts (John Helliwell), Jill Melford (Mrs Drake), Henry Ian Cusick (Ian Gowrie), Ian Briggs (Gilbert Vance), Angela Chadfield (Doctor Daniels), Pamela Kelly (Nurse Clark), Sharon Mackenzie (Doctor's Receptionist), Sharon Erskine (Housekeeper), Sheila Duffy (TV Reporter), Lloret Mackenna (Caroline Kemp).

Holding / Source

01.01.1994 Forbidden Fruit — DB-1" / C1SW

Duration: 100 minutes.

Written by Glenn Chandler; music by Mike Moran; produced by Robert Love; directed by Mike Vardy.

With Mark McManus (Jim Taggart), James Macpherson (Mike Jardine), Blythe Duff (Jackie Reid), Iain Anders (Superintendent McVitie), Harriet Buchan (Jean Taggart), Neil Duncan (Peter Livingstone), Tony Doyle (Doctor Colin Millar), Maureen O'Brien (Ruth Millar), Hilary Maclean (Cathy Adams), Paul Goodwin (Martin Adams), Phyllida Law (Joan Mathieson), Gray O'Brien (Detective Constable Rob Gibson), Liam Brennan (Ian Mathieson), John Stahl (Tom Fleming), Sharon Small (Michelle Gibson), Marissa Benlloch (Marta Livingstone), Mary Boyle (Agnes Moore), Bob Docherty (Ernie Watts), Kevin Rooney (Jackson), Lawrie McNicol (Reverend Ken Morton), Robin Thomson (Doctor Rossi), Paul Hegarty (Detective Chief Inspector McQuiston), Paul Stanfield (Roy Moore), Ali Walton (Hospital Doctor), Gary Bakewell (Constable), Sophie Turner (Claire Lennox), Gregor Powrie (Canadian Son).

SERIES 38

A STV Productions production. Duration: 48 minutes.

Main regular credit(s): Script editor Denise Paul; music by Paul Stirling Taylor; director of photography Grant Cameron; designed by Marius van der Werff; executive producer Eric Coulter; produced by Graeme Gordon.

Main regular cast: With Blythe Duff (Detective Sergeant Jackie Reid), Alex Norton (Detective Chief Inspector Matt Burke), John Michie (Detective Inspector Robbie Ross), Colin McCredie (Detective Constable Stuart Fraser).

Holding / Source

24.12.2009 Fact And Fiction — DB / V1SW

Written by Ian Madden; directed by Ian Madden.

With Finlay Robertson, Kim Thomson, Jimmy Yuill, Mairi Morrison, Susan Coyle, Alan McHugh, Scott Hoatson, Charlene Boyd, Rob Drummond, Inga Stewart, Puja Panchkoty, Mike Edwards.

Episode 100.

TAKE IT AWAY

A BBC production. Transmission details are for BBC. Duration: 75 minutes.

Written by Moss Mindelbaum; play production by Adrian Waller.

Harry Green (Victor Levison), Gareth Wigan (Eric Abelson), Brian Oulton (John Dignity), Harriette Johns (Margot Dignity), Willoughby Goddard (Bishop Dignity), Toke Townley (Tich Dignity), Roland Green (Sammy Dignity), Frank Royde (Matthew Abelson), Danny Green (Butcher Dignity), Alfie Bass (Split Sargent), Rowena Gregory (Philippa Levison), Sidney Keith (Detective), Richard Caldicot (Andrew Bull), Donald Bisset (Sneider), Charles Lamb (Jelenek).

	Holding / Source
26.12.1955	J /

TAKE ME OUT

A Thames Television production for ITV 1. Transmission details are for the Central region.

Paddy McGuinness (Presenter).

	Holding / Source
15.12.2012 **Celebrity Christmas Special**	HD/DB / HDC

Duration: 58 minutes.

Executive producers Suzy Lamb and Mel Balac; series producer Ed Arrens.

With Joe Swash, Matt Johnson, Leigh Francis [as Keith Lemon].

TAKE ONE SWANN

A Thames Television production. Transmission details are for the Thames Television region. Duration: 25 minutes.

Join Donald Swann at home with some of his many musical friends including Nadia Cattouse and Andreas Toumazis, as they prepare for Christmas Day. Donald's interest in people and music covers most of the world, and they will be singing songs and carols from Russia, Australia, Cyprus, Germany, Honduras and England. Four of these carols will be performed for the first time on British television.

Arranged by Helen Best; produced by Marjorie Ruse; directed by John Rhodes.

Donald Swann (Host), Nadia Cattouse, Andreas Toumazis, Catherine Martin, Heather Kay, Ginny Broadbent, Brian Kay.

	Holding / Source
24.12.1970	J / 2"

TAKE THAT AT EARLS COURT

An Anglia production. Transmission details are for the Central region. Duration: 55 minutes.

Main regular performer(s): Take That.

	Holding / Source
25.12.1995	DB /
26.12.1995	DB /

TAKE THE HIGH ROAD

Alternative/Working Title(s): HIGH ROAD - LOW ROAD

A Scottish Television production. Transmission details are for the Scottish Television region.

Main regular credit(s):   Created by Don Houghton.

SERIES 9

Main regular credit(s):   Executive producer Robert Love; produced by Brian Mahoney.

	Holding / Source
31.12.1987 **HIGH ROAD TO HOGMANAY**	1" / 1"

Duration: 35 minutes.

Written by Peter May; music by John Carmichael; directed by Fiona Cumming.

With Ian Stewart, John Stahl, Jeannie Fisher, Marjorie Thomson, Alec Monteath, Iain Agnew, Mary Riggans, Teri Lally, James Macdonald, Stuart Bishop, Robert Trotter, John Young, Muriel Romanes, Eileen McCallum, Kenneth Watson, Jan Waters, Michael Browning, Joan Alcorn, Lesley Fitzsimons, Frank Wylie, Paul Kermack, Michael Elder, Derek Lord, Jay Smith, Steven Brown, Caroline Ashley, Andrew Devlin, Elspeth MacNaughton, Gordon MacArthur, Primrose Milligan, Marjorie Dalziel, Angus Fitchet.

TAKE TWO

A BBC production for BBC 1. Transmission details are for BBC 1.

SERIES 2

Main regular cast: With Lucie Skeaping (Host).

	Holding / Source
27.12.1983	DB / 1"

SERIES 3

Main regular cast: With Josephine Buchan (Host).

	Holding / Source
29.12.1984	DB / 1"

With Renny Rye, Mike Read, Floella Benjamin, Gary Wilmot.

TAKE TWO (continued)   British Christmas Television Guide

SERIES 4
Main regular cast: With Josephine Buchan (Host).

                                                                         Holding / Source
26.12.1985   DB / 1"
With Mark Curry, Les Dawson, Debbie Greenwood, Lenny Henry, John Craven, Sue Lawley, Noel Edmonds.

SERIES 5
Main regular cast: With Phillip Schofield (Host).

                                                                         Holding / Source
26.12.1986   DB / 1"
Duration: 45 minutes.
Produced by Phil Chilvers [credited as Philip Chilvers].

SERIES 9
Main regular cast: With Phillip Schofield (Host).

                                                                         Holding / Source
21.12.1990   DB / 1"
With Tony Robinson.

SERIES 10
Main regular cast: With Sarah Greene (Host).

                                                                         Holding / Source
20.12.1991 **Quiz And Game Shows / Behind The Scenes On 100%**   DB / 1"

SERIES 12
Main regular cast: With Andi Peters (Host).

                                                                         Holding / Source
17.12.1993 **Preview Of Christmas TV And Films / Grange Hill In Germany**   DB / D3S

SERIES 13
Main regular cast: With Juliet Morris (Host).

                                                                         Holding / Source
20.12.1994 **Enough Variety In Pop Music Entertainment / Behind The Scenes On London's Burning**   DB / D3S

TAKE YOUR PICK

Produced for Associated Rediffusion/Rediffusion Television by a variety of companies (see details below). Transmission details are for Associated Rediffusion/Rediffusion Television. Duration: 25 minutes.
Main regular performer(s): Michael Miles (Host).

SERIES 2
An Arlington Television and Radio production. Transmission details are for Associated-Rediffusion.
Main regular credit(s):   Announcer Bob Danvers-Walker; organist Harold Smart; directed by Audrey Starrett.

                                                                         Holding / Source
21.12.1956 **Christmas Special**   J / FNK
Tonight is a special Christmas programme in which the tables are turned and those who win prizes have the opportunity of giving them away to hospitals, old age pensioners and children's homes.

SERIES 5
An Arlington Television and Radio production. Transmission details are for Associated-Rediffusion.
Main regular credits(s):   Announcer Bob Danvers-Walker; organist Harold Smart; on the gong Alec Dane; directed by Audrey Starrett.

                                                                         Holding / Source
25.12.1959   J / FNK
Special Christmas Day edition of his popular quiz programme. The audience and all the competitors are old age pensioners, so why not join in the fun.
With Elisabeth Kingdon (Hostess), Shaun Glenville, Billy Danvers.

SERIES 11
A Michael Miles Television production. Transmission details are for the Rediffusion Television region.
Main regular credit(s):   Announcer Bob Danvers-Walker; organist Harold Smart; on the gong Alec Dane; directed by Audrey Starrett.
Main regular performer(s): With Jane Murray (Hostess).

                                                                         Holding / Source
24.12.1965   J / FNK

TAKE YOUR PICK

| British Christmas Television Guide | TAKE YOUR PICK (continued) |

SERIES 12
A Michael Miles Television production. Transmission details are for the Rediffusion Television region.
Main regular credit(s):　Announcer Bob Danvers-Walker; organist Harold Smart; on the gong Alec Dane; directed by Audrey Starrett.
Main regular performer(s): With Jane Murray (Hostess).

　　　　　　　　　　　　　　　　　　　　　　　　　　　　　　　　　　　　Holding / Source
23.12.1966　**Christmas Special**　　　　　　　　　　　　　　　　　　　　J / FNK
Old age pensioners special.

SERIES 13
A Michael Miles Television production. Transmission details are for the Rediffusion Television region.
Main regular credit(s):　Announcer Bob Danvers-Walker; organist Harold Smart; on the gong Alec Dane; produced by Michael Miles; directed by Audrey Starrett.

　　　　　　　　　　　　　　　　　　　　　　　　　　　　　　　　　　　　Holding / Source
22.12.1967　**Christmas Edition**　　　　　　　　　　　　　　　　　　　　J / FNK
It was noted, in TV Times, that programmes were recorded and that a number of contestants who went on the show did not make it into the finished programme. Whether this method of production was employed throughout the programme's life is not clear, but it would probably mean that for much of the time the show would have had to be telerecorded on film.

TALENTSPOTTING

A World production for Channel 4. Transmission details are for Channel 4. Duration: 50 minutes.
Executive producer Tony Garnett.

　　　　　　　　　　　　　　　　　　　　　　　　　　　　　　　　　　　　Holding / Source
01.09.1996　**Christmas**　　　　　　　　　　　　　　　　　　　　　　　　C1 / C1
Written by Jez Butterworth and Tom Butterworth; produced by Roger Brown; directed by Marc Munden.
With Hans Matheson (Manny), Jason Durr (Martin), Henry Goodman (Pinter), Sean Gallagher (Sean).

TALES FROM DICKENS

A Towers of London Productions production for ABC. Transmission details are for the ABC midlands region. Duration: 25 minutes.
Based on stories by Charles Dickens; production supervised by Frank Sherwin Green; produced by Harry Alan Towers.
Fredric March (Host).

　　　　　　　　　　　　　　　　　　　　　　　　　　　　　　　　　　　　Holding / Source
25.12.1960　**Christmas At Dingley Dell**　　　　　　　　　　　　　　　　B3 / B3
Adapted by Michael Dyne; directed by Ross Mackenzie.
With John Salew (Mr Pickwick), Jack Watling (Mr Snodgrass), John Hewer (Mr Tupman), Richard Briers (Mr Winkle), Gerald William Mervyn (Mr Wardle), Ambrosine Phillpotts (Aunt Rachael Wardle), Karal Gardner (Miss Emily Wardle), Pamela Binns (Miss Isabel Wardle), Nancy Roberts (Old Mrs Wardle), Ken Parry [as Kenneth Parry] (Fat Boy), James Donald (Mr Jingle), John Sherlock (Sam Weller), Nan Marriott Watson (Innkeeper's Wife), Humphrey Heathcote (Innkeeper), Pat Goddferey (First Servant), Ronald Howe (Second Servant).

27.12.1959　**A Christmas Carol**　　　　　　　　　　　　　　　　　　　　B3 / B3
Adapted by Michael Dyne; directed by Robert Lynn.
With Basil Rathbone (Scrooge), Alexander Gauge (Ghost of Christmas Present), Walter Hudd (Ghost of Christmas Past), Michael McCarthy (Ghost of Christmas Future), Howard Williams (Scrooge (when young)), Kaplan Kaye (Scrooge (as a boy)), Toke Townley (Bob Cratchit), Mary Jones (Mrs Cratchit), Mark Mileham (Tiny Tim), Brian McDermott (Fred Scrooge), Wilfred Fletcher (Jacob Marley), Gabriel Toyne (Fezziwig), Rita Webb (Charwoman), Sydney Arnold (Old Joe).

A number of the episodes broadcast in June and July 1962 were listed by the TV Times as repeats; we have been unable to locate any earlier transmissions. The Stage reported on 19.02.59 that seven plays were taken from 'David Copperfield', four from 'The Pickwick Papers' and one each from 'A Christmas Carol' and a story called 'The Runaways'. According to the same journal on 16.04.59 the number of episodes had risen to 39, though on 14.01.1960 it noted that the series had been sold to a U.S. network, which necessited the production of a further 13 episodes to bring the total to 26. A screening of an as yet unknown episode on Channel Television in early 1974 made that region's top ten. See: ARMCHAIR THEATRE - Young David.

TALES FROM THE THOUSAND AND ONE NIGHTS

A BBC production for BBC 1. Transmission details are for BBC 1. Duration: 115 minutes.
Translated by Sir Richard Burton; adapted by Victor Pemberton; music by Norman Kay; designed by Stuart Walker; produced by Cedric Messina; directed by Michael Hayes.
Frank Finlay, Anne Cunningham, Stratford Johns, Paul Hardwick, Patrick Troughton, Norman Beaton, Anne-Marie Marriott, Tony Allef, Ishia Bennison, Emily Bolton, Ishaq Bux, Ava Cadell, Lyndom Gregory, Emma Jacobs, Neville Jason, Bernard Kay, Leon Lissek, Eva Louise, Andrew Manson, Linda Polan, Raad Rawi, David Rappaport, Cengiz Saner, Shireen Shah.

　　　　　　　　　　　　　　　　　　　　　　　　　　　　　　　　　　　　Holding / Source
30.12.1981　　　　　　　　　　　　　　　　　　　　　　　　　　　　　　DB-D3 / 2"

TALES OF THE UNEXPECTED

An Anglia production. Transmission details are for the ATV/Central region. Duration: 25 minutes.
SERIES 3
Transmission details are for the ATV midlands region.
Main regular credit(s):　Executive producer John Woolf; produced by John Rosenberg.

　　　　　　　　　　　　　　　　　　　　　　　　　　　　　　　　　　　　Holding / Source
19.12.1980　**The Party**　　　　　　　　　　　　　　　　　　　　　　　　1" / 2"
Robert Morley and Joyce Redman get together for The Party, the annual Christmas staff do at a toy firm. But even the best-laid party plans can come to grief ...
Adapted by Chaim Bermant; based on a story by Doug Martin; directed by Giles Foster.
With Robert Morley (Henry Knox), Joyce Redman (Linda Knox), Raymond Francis (Mr Peckham), Leonard Preston (Leighton), Amanda Redman (Pat), Olivier Pierre (Leclerc), Michael Nagel (Noel), Janthea Williams (Sue).

TALKABOUT

A BBC Schools production for BBC 1 Schools. Transmission details are for BBC 1.

For 5-7 year olds. Stories to stimulate oral development.

SERIES 1

Duration: 18 minutes.

Main regular credit(s): Produced by Moyra Gambleton.

Main regular cast: With Jill Shilling (Presenter).

Holding / Source

27.11.1979 **Mog's Christmas**   DB / 2"

Story by Judith Kerr.

TALKING TURKEY

A Seventh Art Production production for Channel 4. Transmission details are for Channel 4. Duration: 40 minutes.

An alternative to Christmas lunch in which cynics Warren Mitchell and Nina Myskow dispense with festive spirit and lay into the pro-Christmas lobby.

Produced by Michael Whiteley; directed by Phil Grabsky.

Barry Took (Host), Warren Mitchell, Nina Myskow, Helen Lederer, John Noakes, Johnny Speight, Frank Sidebottom.

Holding / Source

25.12.1990   1" / 1"

TALL, DARK AND HANDSOME

A Winning Format production for Channel 4. Transmission details are for Channel 4. Duration: 50 minutes.

Executive producer Malcolm Frederick; produced and directed by Phil Bishop.

Blacka and Bello, Janet Kay.

Holding / Source

29.12.1992   1" / 1"S

TAN AR Y COMIN

Commissioned by S4C. Transmission details are for S4C. Duration: 105 minutes.

Based on a book by T. Llew Jones.

Edward Woodward (Tim Boswel), Meredith Edwards, Gweirydd Gwyndaf.

Holding / Source

24.12.2000   DB /

This is a repeat transmission date.

THE TARBUCK FOLLIES

A BBC production for BBC 1. Transmission details are for BBC 1. Duration: 45 minutes.

Written by Eric Davidson, Bryan Blackburn and Bill Solly; music directed by Ronnie Hazlehurst; choreography by Lionel Blair; designed by Dick Coles; produced and directed by Michael Hurll.

Jimmy Tarbuck (Host), Clodagh Rodgers, Liz Fraser, Valerie Leon, Talfryn Thomas, Daphne Oxenford, Three's A Crowd, Gypsie Kemp, The Tarbuck Girls, The Lionel Blair Dancers.

Holding / Source

01.01.1973   J / 2"

TARBY AND FRIENDS

An LWT production. Transmission details are for the Central region. Duration varies - see below for details.

Main regular credit(s): Written by Wally Malston, Garry Chambers, Colin Edmonds, Alan Wightman and Russel Lane; produced by David Bell; directed by Alasdair MacMillan.

Main regular performer(s): Jimmy Tarbuck (Host).

SERIES 1

Main regular credit(s): Designed by Bill McPherson.

Main regular performer(s): With The Brian Rogers Dancers, Alyn Ainsworth and his Orchestra.

Holding / Source

22.12.1984 **Tarby And Christmas Friends**   D2 / 1"

Duration: 50 minutes.

With Millicent Martin, The Moody Blues, Les Dennis, Dustin Gee, David Brenner.

29.12.1984 **Tarby And New Year Friends**   D2 / 1"

Duration: 50 minutes.

With Michael Aspel, Cilla Black, Foster Brooks, Gloria Hunniford, Michael Parkinson, Gary Wilmot.

TAXI!

A BBC production for BBC 1. Transmission details are for BBC. Duration: 45 minutes.

Main regular cast: Sidney James (Sid Stone).

SERIES 2

Transmission details are for BBC 1.

Main regular credit(s): Theme music by Bunny Lewis and Harry Robinson; music by Bill McGuffie; film sequences directed by Douglas Argent.

Main regular cast: With Ray Brooks (Terry Mills).

Holding / Source

30.05.1964 **Christmas In May** J /

Produced by Harry Carlisle; studio sequences directed by Harry Carlisle.

With Jack Bligh (Jonty), Diane Aubrey (Sandra), Michael Gover, David Cole, Eric Dodson, Sidonie Bond, Edith Saville, Damaris Hayman, George Tovey, Harry Littlewood, Douglas Ives, Joyce Parry, Glyn Houston, Jennifer Wilson.

T-BAG'S CHRISTMAS CRACKER

A Thames Television production. Transmission details are for the Central region. Duration: 25 minutes.

Written by Lee Pressman and Grant Cathro; designed by John Plant; executive producer Charles Warren; produced and directed by Leon Thau.

Elizabeth Estensen (T-Bag), John Hasler (T-Shirt), James Hillier-Brook (Edward), Veronica Clifford (Mrs Jolly), John Blythe (Santa).

Holding / Source

27.12.1988 1" / 1"

TEA AND BISCUITS WITH MAGGIE PRITCHARD

A BBC Wales production for BBC 2 Wales Digital. Transmission details are for BBC 2 Wales Digital. Duration: 10 minutes.

Main regular credit(s): Written by Paul Warlow; produced and directed by Gareth Gwenlan.

Main regular cast: Margaret John (Maggie).

Transmission details are for BBC 2 Wales.

Holding / Source

22.12.2004 **Christmas Present** DB / DBSW

TEA BREAK

A Thames Television production. Transmission details are for the Thames Television region. Duration: 25 minutes.

Holding / Source

23.12.1971 J / 2"

Produced by Meg Trace; directed by George Sawford.

With Michael Parkinson (Presenter), Mary Parkinson (Presenter).

TEACHERS

A Tiger Aspect production for Channel 4. Transmission details are for Channel 4. Duration: 55 minutes.

Main regular credit(s): Created by Tim Loane.

Main regular cast: Lloyd McGuire (Bob), Ursula Holden-Gill (Carol), Gillian Bevan (Clare).

SERIES 2

Main regular credit(s): Executive producer Greg Brenman; produced by Rhonda Smith.

Main regular cast: With Shaun Evans (JP), Navin Chowdhry (Kurt), Adrian Bower (Brian), Andrew Lincoln (Simon), Raquel Cassidy (Susan), Nina Sosanya (Jenny), Simon Chandler (Geoff), Niamh Elstone (Molly), Anna Hollar (Marcella), Bob Mason (Stephen), Zoe Tolford (Maggie), Ellen Thomas (Liz), Daniel Bliss (Danny), Kelly Brennan (Tanya), James Corden (Jeremy), Nadine Egal (Katy), Peter England (Arnie), Ashley Madekwe (Bev), Keir Mills (Teddy), Lucy Shore (Hayley).

Holding / Source

15.05.2002 "The Christmas party" DB / V1SW

Written by Richard Stoneman; directed by Reza Moradi.

With James Lance.

SERIES 4

Main regular credit(s): Assistant producer Liz Lewin; executive producer Jane Fallon; produced by Rhonda Smith.

Main regular cast: With Daon Broni (Damien), Mathew Horne (Ben), Vicky Hall (Lindsay), Tamzin Malleson (Penny), Lee Williams (Ewan), Ellen Thomas (Liz).

Holding / Source

21.12.2004 "The Christmas party" DB / V1SW

Written by Ed Roe; script supervisor Dorothy Friend; directed by Iain B. MacDonald.

With Gillian Bevan (Clare), Ursula Holden-Gill (Carol), Lloyd McGuire (Bob), Jonas Armstrong (Anthony), Su Bhoopongsa (Ping), Jason Boyd (Grint), Alison Belbin, Brent Ford, Rosie Gunn, Ellena Ibal, Sandy McDare, Sarah Milligan, Nishil Patel, Harry Snale, Nicholas Ward.

TED AND RALPH

A BBC production for BBC 2. Transmission details are for BBC 2. Duration: 65 minutes.

Created by Arthur Mathews and Graham Linehan; written by Paul Whitehouse; script supervisor Alison Grist; associate producer Henrietta Hope; executive producers Paul Whitehouse, Charlie Higson and Geoffrey Perkins; produced by Paul Schlesinger; directed by Christine Gernon.

Paul Whitehouse (Ralph), Charlie Higson (Ted), Richard Wilson, Simon Day, Fiona Allen, Richard Griffiths, John Thomson, Arabella Weir, Kathy Burke, Miranda Richardson, Mark Williams, Colin McFarlane, Maria McErlane, Paul Bigley, Gina Bellman, Saskia Wickham, Eryl Maynard, Andrew Livingston, Donna Ewin, Louise Brill, Angela Lee, Simon Roberts, Ollie Peel.

	Holding / Source
27.12.1998	DB / DBSW

See also: THE FAST SHOW (BBC)

TED VILES TV

A Princess Productions production for Channel 4. Transmission details are for Channel 4. Duration: 50 minutes.

Written by Sean Cullen; executive producers Sebastian Scott and Sharon Ali; produced by Nicholas Steinberg; directed by Julia Knowles.

Sean Cullen (Ted Viles), Andy Kane, Penny Smith, Tom Adams.

	Holding / Source
22.12.1998	DB / DBS

TEETIME AND CLAUDIA

A Yorkshire Television production. Transmission details are for the Central region. Duration: 8 minutes.

SERIES 2
Duration: 8 minutes.
Main regular credit(s): Written by Simon Purcell; drawings by Digby Turpin; produced and directed by Joy Whitby.
Main regular cast: With Gerry Cowan (Voices), Tessa Worsley (Voices).

		VT Number	Holding / Source
29.12.1983	Merry Crispness	C008/01	1" / 1"

THE TELEGOONS

A Grosvenor Films production for BBC. Transmission details are for BBC. Duration: 15 minutes.

Main regular credit(s): Written by Spike Milligan; adapted by Maurice Wiltshire; produced and directed by Tony Young.
Main regular cast: Peter Sellers (Voices), Harry Secombe (Voices), Spike Milligan (Voices).

SERIES 1
Transmission details are for BBC.

		Holding / Source
21.12.1963	The International Christmas Pudding	B1 / B1

TELETUBBIES

A Ragdoll production for BBC 2. Transmission details are for BBC 2.
Main regular credit(s): Created by Anne Wood and Andy Davenport.

		Holding / Source
22.12.1997	Christmas Tree	DB-D3 / D3S
23.12.1997	Christmas Tree	DB-D3 / D3S
24.12.1997	Crackers	DB-D3 / D3S
25.12.1997	Christmas Tree	DB-D3 / D3S

See also: BIG HUG:THE STORY OF TELETUBBIES (BBC)

TELEVISION CHRISTMAS PARTY

A BBC production. Transmission details are for BBC. Duration varies - see below for details.

	Holding / Source
25.12.1951	NR / Live

Duration: 90 minutes.
Produced and directed by Walton Anderson.

With Leslie Mitchell (Host), Jerry Desmonde (Host), Terry-Thomas, Norman Wisdom, Ethel Revnell, Jewel and Warriss, Vic Oliver, Rawicz and Landauer, Anne Ziegler, Webster Booth, Petula Clark, The Twelve Toppers, Eric Robinson and his Orchestra.

25.12.1952	Television's Second Christmas Party	NR / Live

Duration: 105 minutes.
Produced by Bryan Sears and Bill Lyon-Shaw; directed by Bryan Sears and Bill Lyon-Shaw.

With McDonald Hobley (Host), Norman Wisdom, Ethel Revnell, Arthur Askey, Betty Driver, Tommy Cooper, John Slater, Frankie Howerd, Petula Clark, Eamonn Andrews, Joe Stuthard, Eric Robinson and his Orchestra.

25.12.1953	NR / Live

Duration: 105 minutes.
Produced and directed by Bill Lyon-Shaw.

With McDonald Hobley (Host), Leslie Mitchell (Host), Terry-Thomas, Norman Wisdom, Arthur Askey, John Slater, Max Bygraves, The Beverley Sisters, Shirley Abicair, Chan Canasta, Julie Andrews, Eric Robinson and his Orchestra.

25.12.1954   NR / Live
Duration: 100 minutes.
Written by McDonald Hobley; produced and directed by Bill Lyon-Shaw.
With McDonald Hobley (Host), Leslie Mitchell (Host), Arthur Askey, Richard Murdoch, David Nixon, Bob Monkhouse, Denis Goodwin, Wilfred Pickles, Kenneth Horne, Petula Clark, Tommy Cooper, Eve Boswell, Harry Secombe, Harry Corbett, Sooty.

TELEVISION PARTY OF THE YEAR

An Indigo Productions production for Carlton. Transmission details are for the Central region. Duration: 48 minutes.

Executive producer Kim Turbeville.

Gaby Roslin (Host), Gabby Logan (Host).

    Holding / Source
21.12.2002   DB / DBSW

TELEVISION PLAYHOUSE

Produced for ITV by a variety of companies (see details below). Transmission details are for the ATV midlands region. Usual duration: 50 minutes.

SERIES 1
Transmission details are for the ATV midlands region.

	Production No	Holding / Source
11.09.1959 **The Silk Purse**	P24/28	J /

Alt.Title(s): *One Of Us / The Backbone*
A Granada production.
Anne has married in secret. On Christmas Day she brings her husband home to meet her parents for the first time - and the cross-examination begins. It does not take long for her family to decide that Anne has made a poor match. but their attempts to upset her happiness backfire in a surprising way. Cast in order of appearance.
Written by Clive Exton; designed by Paul Bernard; produced and directed by Henry Kaplan.
With Donald Pleasence (Robert Robertson), Gillian Lind (Doris Robertson), Sylvia Kay (Anne Marshall), Peter Fraser (Peter Marshall).

18.12.1959   **The Christmas Card**   R1N /
A H. M. Tennent Ltd production for ATV.
Written by Richard Harris; produced and directed by Peter Potter.
With Joan Hickson (Mrs Hinson), Daphne Anderson (Elizabeth Hinson), Maureen Pryor (Mrs Woodall), Tom Criddle (Len Hinson), Thomas Heathcote (Bert Woodall), Barbara Lott (Lil), George Tovey (Fred), Matthew Vaughan (A Postman), William Patenall (A Temporary Postman), Patricia Wilson (Susan), Charles Hill (Cartwright), Geoffrey Goldsmith (Harry), Winifred Braemar (Woman in Bar).

22.12.1960   **The Two Wise Virgins Of Hove**   D829   DB-4W / 40
An Anglia production.
Written by Robin Maugham; designed by Reece Pemberton; produced and directed by George More O'Ferrall.
With Margaret Rutherford (Emily Blagdon), Martita Hunt (Mabel Roach), Malou Pantera (Lina), Joan Young (Mrs Dent), Joseph Cuby (Adil), Hamlyn Benson (Boutros), P. G. Stephens (Father Michael), John van Eyssen (Professor Craig).

28.12.1961   **Winner Takes The Lady**   P24/61   J / 40
A Granada production.
Adapted by Denis Webb; based on a play by Harold Brighouse; produced and directed by John Moxey.
With Daniel Massey (Laurence Enderby), Alison Leggatt (Constance Enderby), Richard Pearson (Jonas Enderby), William Kendall (Mr Smith), John Forrest (Dick Carrington), April Wilding (Barbara Weir), Irene Hamilton (Dolores), John Miller (Simmons).

SERIES 2
Transmission details are for the ATV midlands region.

	Production No	Holding / Source
01.02.1963 **East Of Christmas**	DRA 5/1	J / 40

An Associated-Rediffusion production.
Written by Peter Yeldham; produced and directed by Mark Lawton.
With Guy Doleman (Cliff Bennett), Carl Bernard (Clarry Ford), Thomas Gallagher (Tom Norton), Anthony Chinn (Jimmy Hana), Edric Connor (Steamboat), Arthur Lee (Jacko).

TELEVISION'S GREATEST CHRISTMAS HITS

A BBC production for BBC 1. Transmission details are for BBC 1. Duration: 60 minutes.
Includes Stanley Baxter delivering the Queen's speech and 'There is Nothing like a Dame' with Morecambe and Wise and a chorus line of newsreaders and presenters.
Produced and directed by Bill Wilson.
Phillip Schofield (Presenter).

    Holding / Source
21.12.1992   DB-D3 / D3S
Highlights from the 20 highest-audience Christmas programmes.

TELL THE TRUTH

An LWT production for Channel 4. Transmission details are for Channel 4. Duration: 25 minutes.

Main regular performer(s): Graeme Garden (Chairman).

SERIES 2
Main regular credit(s):   Executive producer Alan Boyd; produced by Brian Wesley; directed by John Gorman.

Holding / Source
01.01.1984   D2 / 1"
With Beverley Anderson, Lynda Bellingham, Nigel Rees, William Rushton.

TELLY ADDICTS

A BBC Birmingham production for BBC 1. Transmission details are for BBC 1. Usual duration: 25 minutes.

Main regular credit(s):   Theme music by George Fenton.

Main regular performer(s): Noel Edmonds (Host).

SERIES 1
Main regular credit(s):   Directed by Juliet May.

Holding / Source
24.12.1985 **The Pain Family v TV Personalities**   DB / 1"
Additional material by Laurie Rowley; assistant producer Louis Robinson; produced by John King and Juliet May; directed by John King and Juliet May.
With Nina Myskow, Michael Grade, Barry Took, Larry Grayson, Alistair Burnett, Pamela Armstrong, John Humphrys, Julia Sommerville, The Pain Family.

SERIES 2
Main regular credit(s):   Directed by John Smith.

Holding / Source
23.12.1986   DB / 1"
With Nina Myskow, Barry Took, Larry Grayson, Michael Grade.

SERIES 3
Main regular credit(s):   Directed by Annette Martin.

Holding / Source
26.12.1987   DB / 1"

SERIES 4
Main regular credit(s):   Executive producer John King; produced by Richard Lewis and Tim Manning; directed by Nick Hurran.

Holding / Source
23.12.1988 **Christmas Telly Addicts**   DB / 1"
With Michael Grade's All Stars, Bill Cotton's Brigade, Terry Wogan, Margaret Ford, Tim Rice, Michael Grade, Ernie Wise, Leslie Grantham, Bill Cotton.

SERIES 5
Main regular credit(s):   Directed by Nick Hurran.

Holding / Source
24.12.1989   DB / 1"
With Graeme Garden, Frank Carson, Liza Goddard, Jessica Martin, Chris Tarrant, Jim Bowen, Barry Cryer, George Layton.

SERIES 6
Main regular credit(s):   Designed by Andrew N. Gagg; executive producer John King; produced by Richard L. Lewis; directed by Nick Hurran.

Holding / Source
29.12.1990   DB / 1"
With Leslie Crowther, Tony Hart, Jenny Powell, John Craven, Jenny Hanley, Andi Peters, Brian Cant, Cheryl Baker.

SERIES 7
Main regular credit(s):   Produced by Richard L. Lewis; directed by Nick Hurran.

Holding / Source
26.12.1991   DB / 1"
With Les Dawson, Carmen Silvera, Mike Reid, Suzanne Charlton, Matthew Kelly, Sarah Kennedy, Bob Holness, Geoffrey Durham.

SERIES 8
Main regular credit(s):   Produced by Richard L. Lewis; directed by Graham Wetherell.

Holding / Source
28.12.1992 **Christmas Special**   DB / D3S
With Pauline Quirke, Linda Robson, Michael Ball, Keith Barron, Michelle Collins, Rosemarie Ford, Geoffrey Hughes, Danny Baker.

British Christmas Television Guide — TELLY ADDICTS (continued)

SERIES 9
Main regular credit(s): Written by Charlie Adams and John Machin; programme associate Louis Robinson; designed by Andrew N. Gagg; assistant producer Robert Davies; executive producer John King; produced by Richard L. Lewis; directed by Graham Wetherell.

Holding / Source

29.12.1993 Christmas Special DB / D3S
With Frank Carson, Gwen Taylor, Diane Bull, Philippa Forrester, Craig Charles, Gary Olsen, Jonathon Morris, Felix Bowness.

SERIES 10
Duration: 30 minutes.
Main regular credit(s): Produced by Richard Lewis; directed by Graham Wetherell.

Holding / Source

28.12.1994 Christmas Special DB / D3S
With Thora Hird, Brian Blessed, Sean Maguire, Lynda Baron, Frazer Hines, Diane Keen.

SERIES 12
Main regular credit(s): Produced by Richard L. Lewis; directed by Graham Wetherell.

Holding / Source

28.12.1995 Christmas Special: Blue Peter v Are You Being Served? DB / D3S
Duration: 30 minutes.
With Valerie Singleton, John Noakes, Peter Duncan, Janet Ellis, Wendy Richard, John Inman, Frank Thornton, Nicholas Smith.

SERIES 13
Main regular credit(s): Produced and directed by Richard L. Lewis.

Holding / Source

23.12.1996 Christmas Special Eastenders v Emmerdale DB / D3S
With Lisa Riley, Howard Antony, Brian Croucher, Deepak Verma, Syan Blake, Paula Tilbrook, Tonicha Jeronimo, Paul Loughran, Charles Collingwood.

SERIES 14
Main regular credit(s): Produced by Helen Lott; directed by Sue Robinson.

Holding / Source

29.12.1997 Christmas Special DB / DBS
With Angela Griffin, Tracy Shaw, Buster Merryfield, Claudia Winkleman, Shane Richie, Declan Donnelly, Anthony McPartlin.

TEMPO

An ABC production. Transmission details are for the ABC midlands region. Duration: 25 minutes.

SERIES 1
Duration: 45 minutes.
Main regular performer(s): With Jonathan Miller, Peter Cook, Dudley Moore, Alan Bennett.

Holding / Source

24.12.1961 Isaac Stern / The Art Of The Cartoon Film / A Portrait Of Christ J /
Introduced by Clive Goodwin; written by Dick Williams and John Whiting; programme editor Kenneth Tynan; designed by Voytek; produced and directed by Reginald Collin.
With Isaac Stern, Leonard Rose, Eugene Istomin, Dick Williams, John Whiting, Voytek.

SERIES 4

Holding / Source

15.12.1963 Two Tales For Christmas: A Meadow Prospect Christmas / The Dream J /
Introduced by Leonard Maguire; written by Gwyn Thomas and Anton Chekhov; produced and directed by Reginald Collin.
With Paul Rogers.

22.12.1963 Carols Mean Christmas DB-4W|n / 40
Have you ever tried to sing a carol really well? At Oxford is one of the most remarkable groups of young singers to be found in Britain. It is the creation of LaszJo Heltay, Merton College's Director of Music. Heltay has made this choir an honoured representative of British music in Europe as well as in Britain. How then, do they prepare a carol? The creative process is really a collaboration between the conductor and the choir. In the ancient hall of Merton College, Tempo watches the vital work of rehearsal taking place.
Introduced by David Mahlowe; written by Louis Marks; conducted by Laszlo Heltay; produced and directed by Reginald Collin.
With The Collegium Musicum Oxoniense.

TEN YEARS OF WHAT?

A BBC production for BBC 2. Transmission details are for BBC 2. Duration: 145 minutes.
Produced and directed by Jeremy Murray-Brown.
Jimmy Savile (Presenter), Sir Francis Chichester, Cardinal Heenan, Yehudi Menuhin, Malcolm Muggeridge, Enoch Powell M.P., Mary Quant, Arthur Schlesinger Jr, Thomas Barman, James Mossman, John Peel, The Archbishop of Canterbury, David Sheppard, The Bonzo Dog Doo-Dah Band, Robert Dougall.

Holding / Source

28.12.1969 B1SEQ / 2"
Various 16mm and 35mm colour film sequences exists, plus VT insert rushes (Bonzos, Jimmy Saville etc as per Bob Pratt tapes).

TENKO

A BBC production for BBC 1. Transmission details are for BBC 1. Duration varies - see below for details.

Main regular credit(s): Created by Lavinia Warner.

                                        Holding / Source

26.12.1985 **Tenko Reunion**   DB / 1"

Duration: 110 minutes.

Five years after their release from internment, the women return to Singapore for a reunion, unaware of the intrigue that is to involve them in treachery and murder.

Written by Jill Hyem; based on a story by Jill Hyem, Anne Valery and Lavinia Warner; music by James Harpham; produced by Ken Riddington; directed by Michael Owen Morris.

With Ann Bell (Marion Jefferson), Veronica Roberts (Dorothy Bennett), Elizabeth Mickery (Maggie Carter), Cindy Shelley (Alice Courtenay), Bernard Gallagher (Mr Courtenay), Stephanie Cole (Doctor Beatrice Mason), Preston Lockwood (Stephen Wentworth), Emily Bolton (Christina Campbell), Swee Hoe Lim (Lau Peng), Claire Oberman (Kate Norris), Elizabeth Chambers (Dominica), Patricia Lawrence (Sister Ulrica), Damien Thomas (Jake Haulter), P. Sivakumar (Raffles Receptionist), Christian Rodska (Duncan Fraser), Robert Lang (Teddy Forster-Brown), Jamaludin Jalil (Policeman), Lim Kay Tong (Leader), Kim Kay Siu (Soldier), Jimmy Tan Gek Hua (Soldier).

"Television Writer: Tenko", tx: 26.5.1982. 25 mins BBC 1 made for BBC Schools: General Studies. Anne Valery and Jill Hyem describe the writing process. Produced by Richard Callanan, directed by Laurie Stanley.

THE TENNESSEE ERNIE FORD SHOW

An ATV production. Transmission details are for the ATV midlands region. Duration: 50 minutes.

Written by Sheldon Keller and Digby Wolfe; dances staged by Irving Davies; music associate Derek Scott; designed by Henry Graveney; produced by Digby Wolfe and Bob Wynn; directed by Albert Locke.

Ernie Ford (Host), Davy Jones, Harry Secombe, Terry-Thomas, Norman Wisdom, The Ambrosian Singers, The Irving Davies Dancers, The Mike Sammes Singers, Jack Parnell and his Orchestra.

                                        Holding / Source

31.12.1969   R1SEQ / 2"

TERRAHAWKS

An Anderson-Burr Pictures production for LWT. Transmission details are for the Central region. Duration: 25 minutes.

Main regular credit(s): Created by Gerry Anderson; theme music by Richard Harvey; associate producer Bob Bell; produced by Gerry Anderson and Christopher Burr.

Main regular cast: Jeremy Hitchen (Voice of Doctor Tiger Ninestein), Anne Ridler (Voice of Captain Kate Kestrel), Denise Bryer (Voice of Captain Mary Falconer), Windsor Davies (Voice of Sergeant Major Zero), Ben Stevens (Voice of Space Sergeant 101 & Hudson).

SERIES 1

                                        Holding / Source

24.12.1983 **A Christmas Miracle**   C1 / C1

Written by Tony Barwick [credited as Kate Noweestein]; directed by Tony Lenny.

The Terrahawks characters also presented some Childrens ITV links from 1.10.1984-31.10.1984.

TERRY AND JUNE

A BBC production for BBC 1. Transmission details are for BBC 1. Duration: 30 minutes.

Main regular credit(s): Created by John Kane.

Main regular cast: Terry Scott (Terry), June Whitfield (June).

SERIES 2

Main regular credit(s): Produced and directed by Peter Whitmore.

                                        Holding / Source

23.12.1980 **Christmas Show**   DB-D3 / 2"

Written by John Kane; designed by Barrie Dobbins; production manager David Taylor.

With Tim Barrett (Malcolm), Rosemary Frankau (Beattie), Patsy Smart, Daphne Oxenford, Tommy Barnett, Gerry Dolan, Vincent Pakosz, Christopher Poole.

SERIES 3

                                        Holding / Source

28.12.1981 **Christmas**   DB-D3 / 2"

Written by John Kane; designed by Tom Yardley-Jones; production manager Lisa Braun; produced and directed by Peter Whitmore.

With Tim Barrett (Malcolm), Rosemary Frankau (Beattie), Jessica Turner, Kit Thatcher.

This season was released on DVD as two separate series.

SERIES 4

Main regular credit(s): Production manager Bruce Millar; produced by Peter Whitmore.

                                        Holding / Source

24.12.1982 **Christmas With Terry And June**   DB-D3 / 2"

Written by John Kane; designed by Gloria Clayton; directed by Peter Whitmore.

With Reginald Marsh (Sir Dennis Hodge), Tim Barrett (Malcolm), Rosemary Frankau (Beattie), Joanna Henderson.

TERRY AND JUNE (continued)

SERIES 7

Main regular credit(s):   Produced by Robin Nash.

	Holding / Source

24.12.1985 Pantomania — DB / 1"

Written by John Kane; designed by George Kyriakides; production manager Richard Boden; directed by Martin Shardlow.

With Reginald Marsh (Sir Dennis Hodge), John Quayle (Malcolm), Rosemary Frankau (Beattie), John Warner, Joanna Henderson, Michael Sharvell-Martin, Paul Kidd, June Kidd, Roy Heather, Stan Young, Tony McHale, Patricia Varley, Jean Challis, Gracie Cole.

See also: HAPPY EVER AFTER (BBC)

TERRY IN PANTOLAND

A BBC production for BBC 1. Transmission details are for BBC 1. Duration: 35 minutes.

Programme associate Jeff Thacker; series producer Peter Weil; produced by Jon Plowman; directed by John Burrowes.

Terry Wogan (Prince Wogan), Christopher Biggins, Bernard Cribbins, Jim Davidson, Roy Hudd, Little and Large, Barbara Windsor.

Holding / Source

21.12.1989 [Wogan] — DB / 1"

See also: WOGAN (BBC)

TERRY WAITE

A BBC News and Current Affairs production for BBC 1. Transmission details are for BBC 1. Duration: 32 minutes.

Michael Buerk (Interviewer), Terry Waite (Interviewee).

Holding / Source

22.12.1991 — DB / 1"

This programme was not billed in the Radio Times. No on-screen credits.

THE TESTIMONY OF TALIESIN JONES

A Frontier Pictures production for ITV 1. made in association with IAC Film / Snake River. Transmission details are for the HTV Wales region. Duration: 60 minutes.

Adapted by Maureen Tilyou; based on a novel by Rhidian Brook; script supervisor Pam Humphries; music by Mark Thomas; designed by Hayden Pearce; executive producers Peter Edwards, Helena Mackenzie and Michael Ryan; production manager Tilly Cresswell; produced by Beth Goddard, Dominic Berger and Kevin Marcy; directed by Martin Duffy.

Jonathan Pryce (Da), Ian Bannen (Billy), Griff Rhys Jones (Caesar), Geraldine James (Mum), Matthew Rhys (Jonathan).

Holding / Source

26.12.2001 — DB / V1SW

THANK YOU 1980, AND GOODBYE...

A BBC production for BBC 1. Transmission details are for BBC 1. Duration: 65 minutes.

With two teams of special guests and a studio audience to look back on some of the events of the past 12 months. With some film of the year to jog the memory, they examine the proposition that all was not gloom in 1980.

Production team Virginia Ashcombe, Peter Bate and Valerie Turner; produced by David Harrison; studio sequences directed by Bruce Todd.

David Dimbleby (Presenter), Peter Ustinov, John Mortimer.

Holding / Source

29.12.1980 (panorama Special) — DB-D3 / 2"

THANK YOUR LUCKY STARS

An ABC production. Transmission details are for the ABC midlands region.

SERIES 2

Main regular performer(s): With Brian Matthew (Host).

Holding / Source

23.12.1961 Christmas Lucky Stars — J /

Duration: 35 minutes.

Designed by Robert Fuest; produced and directed by Philip Jones.

With The Beverly Sisters, Ronnie Hilton, The Springfields, Elaine & Derek, Zack Laurence, Lonnie Donegan, Jimmy Savile, David Lisbon.

SERIES 3

Duration: 35 minutes.

Holding / Source

25.12.1965 Christmas Lucky Stars — J / 40

Introduced by Jim Dale; designed by Tony Borer; directed by Keith Beckett.

With Frankie Vaughan, The Barron Knights, Ray Fell, The Ivy League, Ruby Murray, Jane Bartlett, Thelma Bignall, Linda Hotchkin, Barbara Von Der Hyde.

Editions from 29.06.63 to 21.09.63 and 03.07.65 to 25.09.65 billed as LUCKY STARS SUMMER SPIN and from 04.07.64 to 26.09.64 as LUCKY STARS - SUMMER SPIN.

Holding / Source

31.12.1966 Lucky Stars New Year Special — J / 40

With Paul Jones, Russ Conway, Adam Faith, Sandie Shaw, Max Bygraves, Frankie Vaughan and The V Men.

'THANKS A MILLION'

A Central production. Transmission details are for the Central region. Duration: 25 minutes.
Associate producer Kathy Nelson; produced and directed by Bob Cousins.
Leslie Crowther, Bob Warman, Jim Bowen, Jimmy Cricket, Michael Elphick, John Caine, Andy Craig, Bob Hall, Bill Tidy.

Holding / Source
22.12.1988 **(pilot)**   1" / 1"

THAT WAS THE WEEK THAT WAS

A BBC production. Transmission details are for BBC. Duration: 50 minutes.

Main regular credit(s):	Produced and directed by Ned Sherrin.
Main regular cast:	David Frost (Presenter), Millicent Martin (Presenter), Kenneth Cope (Presenter), David Kernan (Presenter), Bernard Levin (Presenter), Lance Percival (Presenter), William Rushton (Presenter).

SERIES 1
Transmission details are for BBC.

Main regular credit(s):	Drawings by Timothy Birdsall; music by Ron Grainer, Johnny Dankworth and Dave Lee.
Main regular cast:	With David Frost.

Holding / Source
29.12.1962 **That Was The Year That Was**   R1 /

Written by Christopher Booker, Caryl Brahms, Peter Lewis, Peter Dobereiner, Keith Waterhouse and Willis Hall; designed by Malcolm Middleton.
With Roy Kinnear, Timothy Birdsall.

29.12.62 - SATURDAY SPORT (LOS7606K) - front: end of weather forecast (wobbly picture - caption shown 'There is a fault - do not adjust your set'!); UK logo with announcement "This is BBC Television". End: 'UK' logo with announcement 'This is BBC Television'; start of "That Was the Week That Was" titles, obscured after a couple of seconds, recording cuts.

SERIES 2
Transmission details are for BBC 1.

Main regular credit(s):	Music by David Harding.
Main regular cast:	With Roy Kinnear (Presenter), Al Mancini (Presenter).

Holding / Source
21.12.1963 **Dick Whittington And His Fascist Hyena**   R3 /

Written by Christopher Booker, Caryl Brahms, David Frost, Herbert Kretzmer, Dave Lee, Bill Oddie, Peter Lewis, Peter Dobereiner, David Nathan, Dennis Potter, Keith Waterhouse and Willis Hall; based on an idea by Hugh Carlton Greene; designed by Michael Young.
With Robert Lang.

28.12.1963 **That Was The Year That Was**   R1 /
Designed by Michael Young.

That Was The Week That Was - Goodbye TW3 (Production Tape) containing unbroadcast material in audio form is held by Kaleidoscope.

THAT'S MY BOY

A Yorkshire Television production. Transmission details are for the Central region. Duration: 26 minutes.

Main regular credit(s):	Written by Pam Valentine and Michael Ashton; music by Dennis Wilson; produced by Graeme Muir.
Main regular cast:	Mollie Sugden (Ida Willis), Jennifer Lonsdale (Angie Price), Christopher Blake (Robert 'Shane' Price).

SERIES 2

Main regular credit(s):	Designed by Tony Jones; directed by Graeme Muir.

Holding / Source
23.12.1983 **Cold Turkey**   1" / 2"

Wilfred invites himself for Christmas, and offers to bring the turkey. He arrives with a live turkey called Cuddles. Who can do the deadly deed? What will Charles Barber, Robert's boss, eat for Christmas dinner?
Graphics by Ed Bailey; costume Maggie Hall; make-up Gill Rogerson; lighting by Walter Hanlon; sound Ron Parker; camera supervisor Dave Ramsey.
With Harold Goodwin (Wilfred Willis), Clare Richards (Mrs Price), Anthony Howard (Charles Barber).

SERIES 3

Main regular credit(s):	Designed by Tony Jones.

Holding / Source
28.12.1984 **Little Donkey**   1" / 1"
Directed by Graeme Muir.
With Harold Goodwin (Wilfred Willis), David English, Ann Coombs.

THAT'S SHOWBUSINESS

A BBC production for BBC 1. Transmission details are for BBC 1. Duration: 30 minutes.
Main regular performer(s): Mike Smith (Host).

SERIES 1
Main regular performer(s): With Gloria Hunniford, Kenny Everett.

Holding / Source
30.12.1989   DB / 1"

SERIES 2
Main regular credit(s): Produced and directed by Peter Hamilton.
Main regular performer(s): With Gloria Hunniford, Kenny Everett.

	Holding / Source
31.12.1990	DB / 1"

With Barbara Windsor, Wendy Richard, Barry Cryer, Bryan Murray, Gloria Hunniford, Kenny Everett.

SERIES 3
Main regular performer(s): With Gloria Hunniford, Kenny Everett.

	Holding / Source
31.12.1991	DB / 1"

With Wendy Richard, Mike Reid, Anen Charleson, Ian Smith.

SERIES 4

	Holding / Source
31.12.1992 New Year's Eve Show	DB / 1"

Produced by Nick Vaughan-Barratt; directed by John Rooney.
With Lesley Joseph, Keith Barron.

SERIES 5

	Holding / Source
20.12.1993	DB / D3S

With Nigel Havers, Keith Barron, Michelle Collins, Cathy Shipton.

SERIES 6

	Holding / Source
22.12.1994 100th edition	DB / D3S

SERIES 7

	Holding / Source
29.12.1995 Movies Special	DB / D3S

Produced by Graham B. Owens; directed by John Rooney.
With Bryan Mosley, Paul O'Grady, Denise Welch, Bruce Samazan.

THAT'S WHAT I CALL TELEVISION
An Unique Television production for ITV 1. Transmission details are for the Central region. Duration: 48 minutes.

Main regular credit(s): Devised by Mike Brosnan; script supervisor Corinne Davies; music by Yellow Boat Music; designed by Simon Kimmel; associate producers Lissa Blomley and Simon Marks; executive producers Chris Bellinger and David Sankey; series producer Fiona Clark; directed by Simon Staffurth.
Main regular performer(s): Fern Britton (Host).

	Holding / Source
26.12.2007 That's What I Call Christmas Television	DB / DBSW

Written by Ivor Baddiel and Peter Vincent; designed by Simon Kimmel; associate producers Madeline Addy, Lissa Blomley and Simon Marks.
With Ronnie Corbett (Host), John Noakes, Paul Nicholas, Jan Francis, Valerie Singleton, Tony Blackburn, David 'Kid' Jensen, Emma Ware, Peter Purves.

THEATRE '60'
An ATV production. Transmission details are for the ABC midlands region. Duration: 50 minutes.

	Holding / Source
31.12.1960 Boy On The Telephone	R1 / 40

Peter's Christmas present is to be a surprise for his family- but will it arrive from Australia in time, and can he keep his secret?
Written by Michael Noonan; designed by Vic Symonds; produced and directed by Christopher Morahan.

With Dorothy Allison (Lois Jerrard), Susan Richards (Gran), J. Leslie Frith (Grandad), Sean Scully (Peter Jerrard), David Langton (Cliff Jerrard), Elsie Arnold (Postmistress), Meadows White (Newsagent), Rosemarie Anderson (Sally Jerrard), Ivor Danvers (Roger), Phyllida Law (Flight clerk), Anthony Sheppard (Male clerk), Kenneth J. Warren (Ossie), Henry McGee (Jack Bowden), Julia Nelson (Hilda Bowden .), Winifred Hindle (Grandma Harrison), Mischa de la Motte (Howard), Norman Mitchell (Man at the telephone), Marie Sheringham (Telephone operator).

THEATRE BOX

A Thames Television production. Transmission details are for the ATV midlands region. Duration: 25 minutes.

Executive producer Pamela Lonsdale; produced by Sue Birtwistle.

	VT Number	Holding / Source
24.12.1981 **You Must Believe All This**	24694	D3 / 2"

A play for children set in Victorian times, about four youngsters who find themselves at loggerheads with the grown-ups. At their brother's christening they are ridiculed and humiliated by their parents, the vicar and their teachers. Sent to bed in disgrace, for being too truthful, they escape to the attic where they decide to write a magazine to educate the grown-ups.

Written by Adrian Mitchell; music by Nick Bicat and Andrew Dickson; designed by Robin Parker; directed by Richard Bramall.

With Patrick Malahide (Charles Dickens), Joanna Van Gyseghem (Mrs Rainbird), Roger Sloman (Doctor Snead), Ralph Nossek (Reverend White), Donald Gee (Mr Rainbird), Sonia Graham (Miss Grimmer), Joyce Grant (Drowvey), Alasdair Cameron (Robin), Alex Lowe (William), Sandra Osborn (Alice), Zoe Loftin (Nettie), Mark Farmer (Joe), Yolande Palfrey (Peggy).

THEODORE

An Associated-Rediffusion production. Transmission details are for Associated-Rediffusion.

Main regular credit(s): Produced and directed by William Freshman.

Main regular cast: Larry Parker.

	Holding / Source
20.12.1957 "Christmas comes but once a year"	NR / Live

THERE GOES 1980

A Granada production. Transmission details are for the ATV midlands region. Duration: 50 minutes.

For many of us, it's been a year of recession and depression but for the artists appearing in tonight's variety spectacular, it's been a very good year. There Goes 1980 features a bevy of the year's showbusiness award winners.

Music directed by Derek Hilton; designed by Tim Farmer; executive producer John Hamp; directed by David Liddiment.

Roy Walker (Host), Faith Brown, Johnny Logan, The Rockin' Berries, Victoria Wood, Jean Munroe-Martyn [as Jean Munro-Martin], Liquid Gold, Wall Street Crash, Liverpool Ladies Barbershop Chorus, Terry Seabrooke, Ray Fell, Sue Berger, Geoff Richer's First Edition.

	Holding / Source
30.12.1980	DB / 2"

THERE'S ALWAYS HOPE

An ATV production. Transmission details are for the ATV midlands region. Duration: 25 minutes.

Orchestra conducted by Peter Knight; designed by Tom Lingwood; produced and directed by Bill Ward.

Bob Hope, Yana, The Jack Parnell Orchestra.

	Holding / Source
24.12.1962	J /

THERE'S SOMETHING ABOUT MARY (AND JOSEPH)

A BBC production for BBC 1. Transmission details are for BBC 1. Duration: 4 minutes.

Executive producer Chris Loughlin; produced by Jonathan Mayo.

Adam Hart-Davis (Host), Laurence Llewellyn-Bowen (Host).

	Holding / Source
26.12.2002	DB /

THERE'S SOMETHING WRONG IN PARADISE

A Granada production. Transmission details are for the Central region. Duration: 80 minutes.

A magical musical set on the mythical Caribbean island of Zyllha. Kid Creole and his Coconuts are shipwrecked on the island and anxious to get back home to New York, but Zyllha is ruled by President Nignat, who believes in racial purity. He is incensed by the Kid's mixed-race group winning his island's music festival. The president wants the Kid off the island. Guerillas want the kid's support. When he discovers his old girlfriend, Gina Gina, is running a pirate radio station and finds his true love Mimi, the scene is set for adventure.

Written by Mustapha Matura; music directed by Richie Close; music by Richie Close and Kid Creole and The Coconuts; choreography by Anthony Van Laast; designed by James Weatherup; produced by Steve Morrison; directed by David Liddiment.

August Darnell (Kid Creole), Karen Black (Gina Gina), Oscar James (President Nignat), Peter Straker (Major Po Paul), Pauline Black (Mimi), Sugar Coated Andy Hernandez (Coati Mundi), Adriana Kaegi (The Coconuts), Cheryl Poirer (The Coconuts), Taryn Hagey (The Coconuts), The Three Degrees (Jim Jam Trio), Ruddy L. Davis (Lorry Driver), Donald Eccles (The Duke), Tommy Eytle (Judge), Alfred Fagon (Judge), Joseph Iles (Judge), Paul Medford (Teenager), Vivienne Mckone (Teenager), Philip Bliss (Teenager), Count Prince Miller (Announcer), Barbara Yu Ling (Madame OO), Bryan Strachan (Veronica).

	Production No	Holding / Source
22.12.1984	P1223/1	DB / 2"

THEY THINK IT'S ALL OVER

A Talkback production for BBC 1. Transmission details are for BBC 1. Duration varies - see below for details.

SERIES 1
Main regular credit(s): Produced by Harry Thompson; directed by Steve Smith.

Main regular performer(s): With Nick Hancock (Host), Lee Hurst (Team Captain), David Gower (Team Captain), Gary Lineker (Team Captain), Rory McGrath (Team Member).

Holding / Source
28.12.1995   D3 / D3S
Duration: 40 minutes.
With Mel Smith, Allan Lamb.

SERIES 2
Main regular credit(s): Produced by Harry Thompson.

Main regular performer(s): With Nick Hancock (Host), Lee Hurst (Team Captain), David Gower (Team Captain), Gary Lineker (Team Captain), Rory McGrath (Team Member).

Holding / Source
23.12.1996   D3 / D3S
Duration: 40 minutes.
Directed by Ian Lorimer.
With Steve Backley, David Baddiel.

SERIES 4
Main regular credit(s): Produced by Harry Thompson; directed by Ian Lorimer.

Main regular performer(s): With Nick Hancock (Host), Lee Hurst (Team Captain), David Gower (Team Captain), Gary Lineker (Team Captain), Rory McGrath (Team Member).

Holding / Source
25.12.1997   D3 / D3S
Duration: 35 minutes.
With Matthew Corbett, Sooty, Graeme Le Saux, Martin Bell, Mad Maurice, Fred Zeppelin, Lyndsey McKenzie.

SERIES 5
Main regular credit(s): Produced by Harry Thompson; directed by Ian Lorimer.

Main regular performer(s): With Nick Hancock (Host), David Gower (Team Captain), Gary Lineker (Team Captain), Rory McGrath (Team Member).

Holding / Source
25.12.1998   DB / DBS
Duration: 33 minutes.
With Colin Montgomerie, Phil Cornwell, Jonathan Ross.

THE THICK OF IT

A BBC production for Various BBC Channels. Transmission details are for Various BBC Channels.

Main regular credit(s): Devised by Armando Iannucci.

Commissioned by BBC 4. made in association with BBC America. Transmission details are for BBC 4.

Holding / Source
02.01.2007   Christmas Special - Rise Of The Nutters   DB / DBSWF
Duration: 60 minutes.
Alternative transmissions: BBC 2: 07.07.2007.
Written by Jesse Armstrong, Simon Blackwell, Armando Iannucci and Tony Roche; additional material by Ian Martin and The Cast; script supervisor Suzanne Baron; assistant producer Natalie Bailey; production executive Jez Nightingale; executive producer Jon Plowman; series producer Armando Iannucci; produced by Adam Tandy; directed by Armando Iannucci.

With Peter Capaldi (Malcolm Tucker), Chris Addison (Oliver Reeder), Joanna Scanlan (Terri Coverley), James Smith (Glenn Cullen), Justin Edwards (Ben Swain), Paul Higgins (Jamie), Alex Macqueen (Julius Nicholson), Roger Allam, Vincent Franklin, Olivia Poulet, Will Smith, Lucinda Raikes, David Dawson.

There was a film version, "In the Loop".

THE THIEF

A Thames Television production. Transmission details are for the Central region. Duration: 50 minutes.

Written by Jan Needle; designed by David Marshall; executive producer Alan Horrox; produced by Sheila Kinany; directed by Neville Green.

Martino Lazzeri (Kevin), Nicholas Delve (Buzz), Vanessa Halsey (Jenn), Kerryann White (Tracey), Janette Legge (Kevin's Mum), Holly De Jong (Miss Smith), Rudolph Walker (Paddy), Dean Winters (Jack), Ozzie Stevens (Alan), Martin Phillips (Bob), Michael Burns (Tim), Carl Proctor (Detective), Kairen Kemp (Librarian).

Holding / Source
28.12.1988   1" / 1"

THE THIN BLUE LINE

A Tiger Aspect production for BBC 1. Transmission details are for BBC 1. Usual duration: 30 minutes.

Main regular credit(s): Written by Ben Elton; music by Howard Goodall; executive producer Peter Bennett-Jones; produced by Ben Elton and Geoffrey Perkins; directed by John Birkin.

Main regular cast: Rowan Atkinson (Inspector Raymond Fowler), Mina Anwar (Police Constable Maggie Habib), James Dreyfus (Police Constable Kevin Goody), Serena Evans (Sergeant Patricia Dawkins), David Haig (Detective Inspector Derek Grim), Rudolph Walker (Police Constable Frank Gladstone).

SERIES 1

Duration: 29 minutes.

Main regular credit(s): Designed by James Dillon; production manager Rachel Salter; line producer Marcus Mortimer.

Main regular cast: With Kevin Allen (Detective Constable Kray).

Holding / Source

26.12.1995 **Yuletide Spirit**   D3 / D3S

Fowler plans to play the lead role in the annual am dram panto.

With Ben Elton (Homeless Man), Jacqueline Defferary (Homeless Woman), Joy Brook, Geoffrey Chater, Cherith Mellor, Phil Nice, Jake Wood.

THIRTEEN THOUSAND AND EIGHTY-THREE POUNDS

A Thames Television production. Transmission details are for the ATV midlands region. Duration: 25 minutes.

Written by Fay Weldon; music by Paul Samwell-Smith; designed by Tony Borer; produced and directed by Nicholas Ferguson.

Elizabeth Crowther (Esther), Howard Trevor (Danny), James Hayter (Postmaster), Marjie Lawrence (Marion), Harry Baird (Danny's Stepfather), Anne Blake (Journalist), James Bree (Pastrycook), Clifford Earl (Mr Hope), Hugh Manning (Waiter), Brian Oulton (Mr Sale), Jennifer Wilson (Danny's Mother).

Holding / Source

24.12.1968   J /

THIRTY MINUTE THEATRE

A BBC production for BBC 2. Transmission details are for BBC 2. Usual duration: 30 minutes.

SERIES 1

Holding / Source

23.12.1965 **Family Christmas**   J /

Celia is the beautiful and scatterbrain black sheep of the family. This year she goes too far. and reveals just how fragile the spirit of Christmas can be.

Adapted by Jonquil Antony; based on a book by Jean Stubbs; music by Dudley Simpson; designed by Daphne Shortman; produced by Harry Moore; directed by Mary Ridge.

With Madge Ryan (Janet Harford), David Langton (Julian Harford), John Gregson (Paul Harford), Elizabeth Sellars (Celia), Calvin Lockhart (Mark).

THIS IS CHRISTMAS EVE

A Yorkshire Television production. Transmission details are for the London Weekend Television region. Duration: 55 minutes.

Fiona Armstrong (Presenter), Lesley Garrett, Thomas Allen, Kathryn Tickell, Doctor David Hope.

Holding / Source

24.12.1995   D3 / D3

THIS IS YOUR LIFE

Produced for BBC/ITV by a variety of companies (see details below). Usual duration: 25 minutes.

Main regular credit(s): Devised by Ralph Edwards.

SERIES 15

A Thames Television production. Transmission details are for the ATV midlands region.

Main regular credit(s): Programme consultants Tom Brennand and Roy Bottomley; produced by Jack Crawshaw; directed by Robert Reed.

Main regular performer(s): With Eamonn Andrews (Presenter).

Holding / Source

25.12.1974 **Arthur Askey**   D3 / 2"

Duration: 30 minutes.

Programme associate Martin Robertson.

With Arthur Askey.

SERIES 16

A Thames Television production. Transmission details are for the ATV midlands region.

Main regular credit(s): Programme associate Kay Bird; programme consultants Tom Brennand and Roy Bottomley; produced by Jack Crawshaw; directed by Royston Mayoh.

Main regular performer(s): With Eamonn Andrews (Presenter).

Holding / Source

24.12.1975 **Gladys Mills**   D3 / 2"

Christmas Eve... and as families and friends all over the world get together, Eamonn prepares to spring a surprise summoning up a lifetime of Christmases past. A very special Christmas present for a very special guest...

With Gladys Mills.

British Christmas Television Guide		THIS IS YOUR LIFE (continued)

SERIES 19
A Thames Television production. Transmission details are for the ATV midlands region.
Main regular credit(s): Programme associate Kay Bird; programme consultants Tom Brennand and Roy Bottomley; produced by Jack Crawshaw; directed by Terry Yarwood and Royston Mayoh.
Main regular performer(s): With Eamonn Andrews (Presenter).

		VT Number	Holding / Source
25.12.1978	**Muhammed Ali**	20168	D3 / 2"

Duration: 35 minutes.
With Muhammad Ali.

SERIES 20
A Thames Television production. Transmission details are for the ATV midlands region.
Main regular credit(s): Programme associate Maurice Leonard; programme consultants Tom Brennand and Roy Bottomley; produced by Jack Crawshaw; directed by Terry Yarwood and Tony Parker.
Main regular performer(s): With Eamonn Andrews (Presenter).

		VT Number	Holding / Source
25.12.1979	**Eric Sykes**	21954	D3 / 2"

Duration: 40 minutes.
With Eric Sykes.

SERIES 21
A Thames Television production. Transmission details are for the ATV midlands region.
Main regular credit(s): Written by Tom Brennand and Roy Bottomley; programme associate Maurice Leonard; programme consultants Tom Brennand and Roy Bottomley; produced by Jack Crawshaw; directed by Stuart Hall and Terry Yarwood.
Main regular performer(s): With Eamonn Andrews (Presenter).

		Holding / Source
25.12.1980	**Joan Wells**	D3 / 2"

With Joan Wells.

SERIES 22
A Thames Television production. Transmission details are for the ATV/Central region.
Main regular credit(s): Written by Tom Brennand and Roy Bottomley; programme associate Maurice Leonard; programme consultants Tom Brennand and Roy Bottomley; produced by Jack Crawshaw; directed by Terry Yarwood and Paul Stewart Laing.
Main regular performer(s): With Eamonn Andrews (Presenter).

		VT Number	Holding / Source
25.12.1981	**Kiri Te Kanawa**	24992	D3 / 2"

With Kiri Te Kanawa.

SERIES 25
A Thames Television production. Transmission details are for the Central region.
Main regular performer(s): With Eamonn Andrews (Presenter).

		VT Number	Holding / Source
26.12.1984	**Millicent Martin**	32171	1" / 1"

With Millicent Martin.

SERIES 26
A Thames Television production. Transmission details are for the Central region.
Main regular credit(s): Programme consultant Roy Bottomley; associate producer Brian Klein; produced by Malcolm Morris; directed by Michael D. Kent and Terry Yarwood.
Main regular performer(s): With Eamonn Andrews (Presenter).

		Holding / Source
26.12.1985	**Joyce Carey**	1" / 1"

With Joyce Carey.

SERIES 31: 1
A Thames Television production. Transmission details are for the Central region.
Main regular performer(s): With Michael Aspel (Presenter).

		Holding / Source
26.12.1990	**Ernie Wise**	1" / 1"

With Ernie Wise.

SERIES 32: 2
A Thames Television production. Transmission details are for the Central region.
Main regular performer(s): With Michael Aspel (Presenter).

		VT Number	Holding / Source
25.12.1991	**David Berglas**	55089	1" / 1"

With David Berglas.

THIS IS YOUR LIFE

THIS IS YOUR LIFE (continued)

SERIES 38
A Thames Television production for BBC 1. made in association with Ralph Edwards Productions / T.I.Y.L. Productions. Transmission details are for BBC 1. Duration: 29 minutes.

Main regular credit(s): Programme associate Joe Steeples; associate producer Liz Rawlings; executive producer John Longley; series producer Jack Crawshaw; produced by Sue Green.

Main regular performer(s): With Michael Aspel (Presenter).

Date	Title	Production No	VT Number	Holding / Source
22.12.1997	Trevor Bannister	60/ICEA139S/01	THS/62307	D3 / D3S

Alt.Title(s): *Stair*

Written by Ian Brown; production manager Dawn Gray; directed by John Gorman and Steve Docherty.

With Trevor Bannister, Kathy Staff, Pamela Bannister, Christopher Biggins, Henry McGee, Anna Dawson, Willie Thorne, Wayne Sleep, Wendy Richard, Mollie Sugden, Frank Thornton, John Inman, Bill Pearson, Peggy Mount, Tim Wylton, Bryan Pringle, Tony Randall, Jack Klugman, Peter Ellis, Lynda Baron, Ray Cooney.

THIS IS... TOM JONES

An ATV production. Transmission details are for the ATV midlands region. Duration: 52 minutes.

Main regular performer(s): Tom Jones (Host).

SERIES 2
Main regular credit(s): Written by Tom Waldman, Frank Waldman, Ronnie Cass and Donald Ross; music associates Kenny Powell and Art Day; produced by Jon Scoffield.

Main regular performer(s): With The Mike Sammes Singers, The Norman Maen Dancers, Sue & Sonny.

Date	Holding / Source
25.12.1969	DB / 2"

Ella Fitzgerald, rated the Queen of Jazz, the High Priestess of Scat and probably the best-loved female vocalist in the business, is Tom's Christmas present to viewers. For ballet lovers, Rudolf Nureyev and Merle Park dance the pas-de-deux from the Nutcracker Suite.

Designed by Brian Bartholomew; directed by Philip Casson.

With Judy Collins, David Frye, Millicent Martin, The Treorchy Male Voice Choir, The Mike Sammes Singers, Ella Fitzgerald, Rudolf Nureyev, Merle Park.

All footage held by Tom Jones.

THIS OFFICE LIFE

Alternative/Working Title(s): OFFICE LIFE

A BBC production for BBC 1. Transmission details are for BBC 1. Duration: 80 minutes.

Written by Keith Waterhouse; music by Trevor Jones; designed by John Asbridge; production associate Andrew Gosling; production managers Jacmel Dent and Enid Musson; produced and directed by Ian Keill.

Dinsdale Landen (Clement Gryce), Jenny Agutter (Pam Fawce), Roy Kinnear (Commissionaire), Bryan Pringle (Commissionaire), Geoffrey Bayldon (Norman Ferrier), Rosemary Leach (Widow Rashman), John Quayle (Pendlebury), Terence Bayler (Henderson), Norman Bird (Ron Seeds), John Savident (Copeland), Diana Bishop (Ms Lucas), Lionel Taylor (Grant-Peignton), Madhav Sharma (Hakim), Ewan Hooper (Hatch), Karen Seacombe (Thelma), Murray Melvin (Reporter), Antony Higginson (Eric), Nigel Bellairs (Albion Player), Anne Haydn (Albion Player), Alan Mason (Albion Player), Alexandra Davies (British Albion employee), Fiona Sloman (British Albion employee), Jane Wenden (British Albion employee), Lee Richards (British Albion employee), Eric Kent (British Albion employee), Stephen Calcutt (British Albion employee), Elizabeth Stone (British Albion employee), Bunny Losh (British Albion employee), Judith Cox (British Albion employee), Gordon Johnstone (British Albion employee), David Bartlett (British Albion employee), Carol Vaughan (British Albion employee), Hubert Tucker (British Albion employee).

Date	Holding / Source
30.12.1984	C1 / C1

THIS WAS THE FUTURE

A BBC production. Transmission details are for BBC. Duration: 55 minutes.

A film which recalls some of the highlights from twenty-one years of Television programmes — entertainment, sport, and personalities from all walks of life, together with glimpses from the record of history between 1936 and this New Year's Eve.

Edited by Geoffrey Baines; produced and directed by Geoffrey Baines.

Robert Donat (Storyteller).

Date	Holding / Source
31.12.1957	B3 / B3

THIS WEEK

A Thames Television production. Transmission details are for the Central region. Usual duration: 25 minutes.

SERIES 1

Date	Title	Holding / Source
31.12.1968	**1968: A Year Of This Week**	J /

SERIES 3

Date	Title	VT Number	Holding / Source
##.##.####	**Review Of The Year 1970**	60718	1" / C1

SERIES 5

Date	Title	VT Number	Holding / Source
01.01.1973	**Review Of The Year 1972**	7039	DB / 2"

THIS WEEK

SERIES 8

	VT Number	Holding / Source
01.01.1976 **Review Of The Year 1975**	12646	DB / 2"

Duration: 50 minutes.
Research Mike Maddison; produced by David Elstein.
With Jonathan Dimbleby (Reporter).

SERIES 10

	VT Number	Holding / Source
29.12.1977 **Review Of The Year 1977**	18301	DB / 2"

Duration: 40 minutes.
Produced by David Elstein; directed by Ken Craig, Norman Fenton, Ian Stuttard, Peter Tiffin and Judy Lever.
With Jonathan Dimbleby (Presenter).

SERIES 18

	VT Number	Holding / Source
17.12.1992 **That Was This Week That Was**	57742	DB / 1"

THOMAS THE TANK ENGINE AND FRIENDS

A Central production. Transmission details are for the Central region.

Main regular credit(s): Based on stories by Reverend W. Awdry.

SERIES 1
Duration: 8 minutes.
Main regular credit(s): Executive producer Britt Allcroft; directed by David Mitton.
Main regular cast: With Ringo Starr (Storyteller).

	Holding / Source
25.12.1984 **Dirty Objects / Thomas's Christmas Party**	D2 / C1

SERIES 2
Main regular credit(s): Executive producer Britt Allcroft; directed by David Mitton.
Main regular cast: With Ringo Starr (Storyteller).

	Holding / Source
17.12.1986 **Woolly Bear / Thomas And The Missing Christmas Tree**	D2 / C1

THE THOMPSON FAMILY

A BBC production. Transmission details are for BBC. Duration: 30 minutes.

Main regular credit(s): Written by Noel Streatfeild; produced and directed by Dorothea Brooking.

SERIES 1
Main regular credit(s): Film sequences directed by Leonard Newson.
Main regular cast: With John Paul (John Thompson), Marion Jennings (Elizabeth Thompson), Diana Beevers (Susan), Nigel Lambert (Andrew), Sandra Michaels (Caroline).

	Holding / Source
21.12.1957 **That Christmas Feeling**	J /

With Charles Carson (Mr Thompson, Snr), Cavan Kendall (Guy James), Douglas Storm, Edna Morris, Roger Kemp.

THOSE KIDS

An ABC production. Transmission details are for the ABC midlands region. Duration: 25 minutes.

Main regular credit(s): Written by Patricia Latham; produced by Patricia Latham; directed by Vivian Milroy.
Main regular cast: Peter Butterworth (Mr Oddy), George Howell (Henry), Lynn Grant (Maisie), David Higson (Mike), Shandra Walden (Sally).
Main regular cast: With Peter Soule (Al).

	Holding / Source
15.12.1956 **Christmas Edition**	J /

With No guest cast.

22.12.1956 **Christmas Edition**	J /

Those Kids arc determined that Mr. Oddy should have a good Christmas - with hectic results!
With No guest cast.

THOSE WONDERFUL TV TIMES   British Christmas Television Guide

THOSE WONDERFUL TV TIMES

A Tyne Tees Television production. Transmission details are for the Tyne Tees region.

Main regular credit(s):   Devised by John Johnson.

SERIES 2

Main regular credit(s):   Programme associates Malcolm Frazer and Cy Young; designed by Eric Briers; produced by Tony Sandford; directed by Lisle Willis.

Main regular performer(s):   With Barry Cryer (Host).

	VT Number	Holding / Source
27.12.1977 **Those Wonderful TV Times Christmas Show**	TV77/40/01	DB / 2"

Duration: 35 minutes.

Designed by Eric Briers; executive producer Tony Sandford; directed by Lisle Willis.

With Aimi MacDonald, Nerys Hughes, Jack Douglas, Patrick Mower, Lance Percival, Willie Rushton, George Chisholm.

THE THOUGHTS OF CHAIRMAN ALF - AT CHRISTMAS - ON YER ACTUAL BOXING DAY

An ATV production. Transmission details are for the ATV midlands region. Duration: 25 minutes.

It is time the nation heard again from Alf Garnett. Tonight — in the first of an occasional series — he makes his debut as a solo television performer to give the thoughts of Chairman Alf on Christmas and national affairs.

Written by Johnny Speight; designed by Jeff Tessler; produced and directed by William G. Stewart.

Warren Mitchell (Alf Garnett).

	Holding / Source
26.12.1980	DB / 2"

See also: IN SICKNESS AND IN HEALTH (BBC) / "TILL DEATH US DO PART" (BBC)

THE THREE HOSTAGES

A BBC production for BBC 1. Transmission details are for BBC 1. Duration: 85 minutes.

Adapted by John Prebble; based on a book by John Buchan; script editor Richard Broke; designed by Don Taylor; produced by Mark Shivas; directed by Clive Donner.

Barry Foster (Richard Hannay), Diana Quick (Mary Hannay), John Castle (Dominick Medina), Peter Blythe (Sandy Arbuthnot), Hilary Mason (Mes Medina), Constance Chapman (Madame Breda), David Markham (Greenslade), Donald Pickering (McGillivray), John Shrapnel (Gaudian), John Quarmby (Newhover), Richard Cornish (Archie Roylance), Philip Sayer (Turpin), Stuart Mungall (Angus), James Copeland (Kennedy), Pat Gorman (Odell), Maurice Quick (Fletcher), Andrew Bradford (Abel), Margo Cunningham (Shopwoman), Arthur Cox (Salvation Army Captain), Pat Starr (Salvation Army Singer), William Relton (Lord Mercot), Bobbie Brown (Adela Victor), Saul Eden Smith (David Warcliff), Noel Davis (First Club Member), John Harvey (Secone Club Member).

	Holding / Source
27.12.1977	C1 / C1

The Three Hostages, by John Buchan, was dramatised in two 60m episodes as the BBC Radio 4 Classic Serial, beginning 3pm, 7 Sep 2003.

THE THREE KISSES

A BBC production for BBC 1. Transmission details are for BBC 1. Duration: 65 minutes.

Adapted by Ben Steed; based on a book by Jerome K. Jerome; designed by Steve Brownsey; executive producer Anna Home; produced and directed by John Prowse.

Richard Murdoch (Professor Christopher Littlecherry), Damian Earle (Jimmy Arlington), Julia Schopflin (Jane Arlington), Ian Hogg (Mr Arlington), Lynn Farleigh (Mrs Arlington), Ian Gelder (Arthur Raffleton), Natalie Ogle (Malvina), Margaret D'Arcy (Mrs Muldoon), Amanda Bell (Lucy), Frank Jarvis (Mr Marigold), John Rapley (Mr Calthorpe), Beth Harris (Mrs Calthorpe), Jill Gascoine (Mrs Marigold), John Crocker (Vicar), Janet Dale (Miss Hawthorne), George Bezani (Rufus).

	Holding / Source
28.12.1978	DB-D3 / C1

THREE MEN IN A BOAT

A BBC production for BBC 2. Transmission details are for BBC 2. Duration: 65 minutes.

Adapted by Tom Stoppard; based on a book by Jerome K. Jerome; music by David Fanshawe; designed by Martin Collins; produced by Rosemary Hill; directed by Stephen Frears.

Tim Curry (Jerome), Stephen Moore (George), Michael Palin (Harris), Bill Stewart (First Porter), Michael Elphick (Second Porter), John Blain (Traffic Supervisor), George Innes (Train Driver), Russell Dixon (Harris' Cousin), Mary McLeod (Pathetic Woman), Clifford Kershaw (Irate Man), Alan Collins (Desolate Man), Eileen Helsby (Woman With Baby), Herbert Tucker (First Lock Keeper), Harry Markham (Second Lock Keeper), Tony Rohr (Blackmailer), Frank Mills (Old River Hand), John Dicks (Launch Owner), Anne Zelda (Fashionable Girl), William Russell (Doctor), Hugh Thomas (Chemist), George Camiller (Shelley), Alan Lawrance (Riverman), John Harding (First Scholar), John Burrows (Second Scholar).

	Holding / Source
31.12.1975	C1 / C1

THREE NON-BLONDES

A BBC production for BBC 3. Transmission details are for BBC 3. Duration: 30 minutes.

Main regular performer(s):   Tameka Empson (Various roles), Ninia Benjamin (Various roles), Jocelyn Jee Esien (Various roles).

SERIES 2

Main regular credit(s):   Produced by Kara Lockett; directed by John F. D. Northover.

	Holding / Source
21.12.2003 **Christmas Special**	DB / DBSWF

Produced by Monica Alonso.

THREE NON-BLONDES

THE THREE PRINCES

A BBC production. Transmission details are for BBC. Duration: 60 minutes.

Written by Rex Tucker; play production by Shaun Sutton.

Ann Sears (Princess Yasmin), Barry Letts (Prince of the Isles of Nowhere), Paul Whitsun-Jones (Prince of the Yellow Moon), Laurence Hardy (The Caliph), Roger Delgado (Prince of the Rising Sun), Patrick Cargill (Carpet Dealer), Lionel Ngakane (Janissary), Lisa Peake (Shalima, Slave Girl), Peter Russell (Egyptian), David Rayner (Persian), Bobby Naidoo (Indian), David Waller (Mongolian), Wilfred Grove (Syrian), Geoffrey Biddeau (African), John Woodnutt (The Vizier), Philip Rose (Moon Prince Guard), Ralph Truman (Irfeet Kafur), Nigel Arkwright (Doctor), Frank Singuineau (Sun Prince Attendant), Stanley Jack (Sun Prince Guard), Gwen Watford (Voice of Scheherazade).

	Holding / Source
26.12.1959	J /

THE THREE PRINCES

A BBC production for BBC 2. Transmission details are for BBC 2. Duration: 60 minutes.

Written by Rex Tucker; music by James Conistein; designed by Jeremy Davies; produced by Ronald Travers; directed by Mark Cullingham.

Timothy Dalton (Ahmed), Isla Blair (Princess Yasmin), Gordon Gostelow (The Carpet Dealer), Peter Jeffrey (The Sun Prince), Roy Kinnear (The Moon Prince), Kenneth Mackintosh (The Caliph), Cleo Laine (Voice of Scheherazade), Neil Fitzpatrick (Janissary), Frank Wylie (Egyptian), Roderick Horn (Persian), Frederick Pyne (Indian), William Hobbs (Chinese), Oliver Cotton (Tibetan), Lousie Breslin (Shalima), William Hoyland (Vizier), Roy Pearce (Soldier), Gavin Richards (Kafur), Roger Kemp (Doctor), Marc Gebhard (Ali).

	VT Number	Holding / Source
26.12.1968 [The Christmas Play]	VTC/6HT/48854	J / 2"

THE THREE SISTERS

A Thames Television production. Transmission details are for the ATV midlands region. Duration: 175 minutes.

Written by Anton Chekhov; designed by David Marshall; executive producer John Frankau; produced and directed by Trevor Nunn.

Janet Dale (Olga), Emily Richard (Irina), Suzanne Bertish (Masha), Roger Rees (Tusenbach), Griffith Jones (Chebutikin), Bob Peck (Soliony), Rose Hill (Anfisa), Clyde Pollitt (Ferrapont), Hilary Townley (The Maid), Edward Petherbridge (Vershinin), Timothy Spall (Andrei), Patrick Godfrey (Kulighin), Susan Tracy (Natasha), Teddy Kempner (Fedotik), Roderick Horn (Rode), Richard Springate (The Musician).

The Royal Shakespeare Company in...

	Holding / Source
29.12.1981	D3 / 2"

THROUGH THE LOOKING GLASS AND WHAT ALICE FOUND THERE (RADIO)

A BBC production for BBC Radio 4. Transmission details are for BBC Radio 4. Duration: 140 minutes.

Adapted by John Wells; based on a book by Lewis Carroll; music by Carl Davis; play production by Ian Cotterell.

Polly James (Alice), Ann Beach (White Queen), David Garth (White King), Robert Bowman (Tweedledee), Leslie Fyson (Tweedledum), June Tobin (Tiger Lily), Tessa Worsley (Rose), Patricia Routledge (Red Queen), Alan Thompson (Guard), Alec Bregonzi (Gnat), Jane Leonard (Fawn), Danny Schiller (Humpty-Dumpty), David Learner (Haigha), John Wells (Hatta), Simon Hewitt (Unicorn), Ronald Herdman (Lion), John Church (Red Knight), Michael Aldridge (White Knight), Spike Milligan (Wasp), Trevor Nichols (Beak).

	Holding / Source
25.12.1985	DA /

In Stereo.

THUNDERBIRDS

Alternative/Working Title(s): INTERNATIONAL RESCUE

An AP Films production for ITC, made in association with ATV. Transmission details are for the ATV midlands region.

Main regular credit(s): Created by Gerry Anderson and Sylvia Anderson; theme music by Barry Gray.

Main regular cast: Ray Barrett (Voice of Alan Tracy / John Tracy / The Hood / guest voices), Peter Dyneley (Voice of Jeff Tracy), David Graham (Voice of Brains / Aloysius Parker / guest voices), Sylvia Anderson (Voice of Lady Penelope), Christine Finn (Voice of Tin-Tin Kyrano), David Holliday (Voice of Virgil Tracy), Shane Rimmer (Voice of Scott Tracy), Matt Zimmerman (Voice of Alan Tracy / guest voices).

SERIES 2
Duration: 24 minutes.
Main regular credit(s): Designed by Keith Wilson and John Lageu; associate producer John Read; executive producer Gerry Anderson; produced by Reg Hill.

	Holding / Source
26.12.1966 **Give Or Take A Million 1**	DB / C3

Alternative transmissions: ATV London: 25.12.1966; Granada: 25.01.1967.

Stand by for a special Christmas adventure... Thunderbirds are go...

Written by Alan Pattillo; directed by Desmond Saunders.

With Jeremy Wilkin (Virgil Tracy), Charles Tingwell.

| 27.12.1966 **Give Or Take A Million 2** | DB / C3 |

Alternative transmissions: ATV London: 25.12.1966; Granada: 25.01.1967.

These editions were shown as single 50-minute episodes by ATV London. In the Granada region they were shown in two 25-minute segments either side of the early evening news. They survive in their 50-minute form.

TICH AND QUACKERS

A BBC North production for BBC 1. Transmission details are for BBC 1.

Main regular credit(s):   Written by Ray Alan; produced and directed by Stan Parkinson.
Main regular cast: Ray Alan (Voices / Host).

SERIES 3
Duration: 15 minutes.
Main regular credit(s):   Designed by Stuart Furber.

		Holding / Source
14.04.1968 **Merry Christmas, April Fool**		J /

With Derek Dene.

TICKLE ON THE TUM

A Granada production. Transmission details are for the Central region.

Main regular cast: Ralph McTell (Presenter).

SERIES 3
Duration: 8 minutes.
Main regular credit(s):   Drawings by Valerie Pye; designed by Ann Dabinett; executive producer Stephen Leahy; produced by Martyn Day and Diana Bramwell; directed by Peter Plummer.

	Production No	Holding / Source
15.12.1986 **The Christmas Goose**	P1226/47	1" / 1"

Written by Rick Vanes.
With Jacqueline Reddin, John Wells.

24.12.1986 **Christmas Special**	P1226/90	1" / 1"

"TILL DEATH US DO PART"

Alternative/Working Title(s): KING DAD

A BBC production for BBC 1. Transmission details are for BBC 1. Usual duration: 30 minutes.

The quotation marks in the title came and went at different points during the various series.

Unfunny, racist, sexist and homophobic are just a few of the accusations made against the seminal work of Johnny Speight, "Till Death Us Do Part", since its first broadcast in 1965.

Indeed for a piece of television to be this attacked would normally result in it being buried under a pile of concrete like a traitor within the ranks of the mafia. Quietly forgotten about by history. However, forty five years later, the legend of Alf Garnett remains as iconic as it did in the swinging sixties.

"Till Death" remains for many to be the perfect stereotypical sitcom that produced perfect unstereotypical jokes. It was controversial, it was always discussed the day after at work, it wasn't always funny, but it did make people think, and question the nature of sixties society.

On the 22nd November 1965 the BBC's Comedy Playhouse strand introduced us to Alf and Else Ramsey, and their daughter Rita and husband Mike. Three of the actors would remain with the series – Warren Mitchell as Alf, Una Stubbs are Rita and Tony Booth as Mike. The role of Else was played by Gretchen Franklin (Ethel from Eastenders) and was re-cast and given to Dandy Nicols.

The pilot opened with Alf checking the chimes of Big Ben and proclaiming he had proof that Big Ben was inaccurate. Intermingled with discussions about politics and the role of women came a semblance of plot – Rita and Mike looking for their own home, only eight weeks after they were married.

Johnny Speight, the writer, originally wanted Peter Sellers or Lionel Jeffries to play Alf Ramsey, who lived at 10 Percy Road, Canning Town, but neither Sellers or Jeffries were firmly approached. With time running out Warren Mitchell was cast as Alf. The production of the pilot was indicative of the mayhem of making the series that would follow later in years. Speight proclaimed that Alf Ramsey was a bigot, and the audience would laugh at his prejudices, but critics were not convinced, arguing that the character was so foul-mouthed that any satirical impression was lost. On the first run through Warren Mitchell rubbished the script and a rewrite was ordered. Mitchell got his way and Speight altered some lines. In future years Speight would deliver scripts sometimes only hours before the first rehearsal with a clause in his BBC contract stating that not a single line could be altered. Indeed as the series progressed, Speight drank more and more alcohol and became harder and harder to work with, becoming a parody of Alf Garnett in so many ways.

Tom Sloan, the Head of Light Entertainment, was not impressed by the pilot. He objected to its rants against God, the Royal Family, the church and the state saying that it was very unbritish, but it got very good audiences and press reaction was very favourable. People found the sitcom funny. It was commissioned for a series by Michael Peacock, the Controller of BBC1.

With the World Cup due in 1966 the name of Alf Ramsey was changed to Alf Garnett to avoid any confusion with the famous footballer. The producer Dennis Main Wilson envisaged the show to a traditional sitcom about a family discussing topical issues, but the issues raised by Alf Garnett were not typical sitcom territory. Sid Abbott in Bless This House never talked about the faults of the Prime Minister! The first three series followed a semblance of structure with a comedic purpose to be achieved. But when the series was revived in 1972, plot seemed superfluous and Speight's writing became more and more based around four people sitting in an armchair discussing life.

The early monochrome seasons were actually funny. Audiences loved them, the clean-up TV campaigner Mary Whitehouse hated them. Tom Sloan was delighted when the opportunity came to cancel the series in 1968. The unpredictable nature of Johnny Speight to work with had made production difficult and the pressure from Mary Whitehouse was beginning to undermine the reputation of the BBC. When Mary Whitehouse described the show as being "dirty, blasphemous and full of bad language" she was being complimentary! Those were its good points!

Main regular credit(s):   Written by Johnny Speight; produced by Dennis Main Wilson.
Main regular cast: Warren Mitchell (Alf Garnett), Anthony Booth (Mike), Una Stubbs (Rita).

SERIES 2
Main regular credit(s):   Music by Dennis Wilson.
Main regular cast: With Dandy Nichols (Else Garnett).

	Holding / Source
26.12.1966 **Peace And Goodwill**	DB-D3-R1 / 40

Designed by Paul Allen; directed by Dennis Main Wilson.
With John Junkin, Billy Milton.

| British Christmas Television Guide | "TILL DEATH US DO PART" (continued) |

Holding / Source
26.12.1972 **Cast of 'Jesus Christ Superstar'**   DB-D3 / 2"
Duration: 43 minutes.
Designed by Gloria Clayton; directed by Dennis Main Wilson.
With Bill Maynard, Derek Griffiths, Brian Leeson, Sally Riggs, Will Stampe, Paul Nicholas, Dana Gillespie, Maureen Lane, Carolyn Moody.
Insert tape still on D3 ex 2".

SERIES 7
Main regular credit(s):   Directed by Dennis Main Wilson.
Main regular cast: With Alfie Bass (Bert), Patricia Hayes (Min).

Holding / Source
17.12.1975 **Unemployed**   DB-D3 / 2"
With Pat Coombs (Ethel Carey), Joan Sims (Gran), Hugh Lloyd, Richard Speight.

See also: IN SICKNESS AND IN HEALTH (BBC) / THE SPIRIT OF 66 WITH ALF GARNETT (BBC) / THE THOUGHTS OF CHAIRMAN ALF - AT CHRISTMAS - ON YER ACTUAL BOXING DAY

THE TIM VINE CHRISTMAS PRESENT

A Grundy production for Channel 5. Transmission details are for Channel 5. Duration: 50 minutes.
Written by Tim Vine; produced by Robin Greene and Richard Hearsey; directed by Phil Chilvers.
Tim Vine, Steve Brody, Tom Butcher, Sarah Greene, John Archer, Seeta Indrani, Sophie Lawrence, Shaun Williamson.

Holding / Source
24.12.1997   DB-D3 / D3S

TIME FOR BAXTER

A BBC Scotland production for BBC 1. Transmission details are for BBC 1 Scotland. Duration: 45 minutes.
Written by Ken Hoare; choreography by Bruce McClure; designed by Helen Rae; produced and directed by David Bell.
Stanley Baxter (Various roles), Clodagh Rodgers.

Holding / Source
31.12.1971   DB-D3 / 2"
Alternative transmissions: BBC 1: 01.01.1972.

TIME FOR MURDER

A Granada production. Transmission details are for the Central region. Duration: 50 minutes.
Executive producer Michael Cox; produced by Pieter Rogers.

	Production No	Holding / Source
14.12.1985 **The Thirteenth Day Of Christmas**	P1283/5	1" / 1"

Written by Gordon Honeycombe; music by Paul Lewis; designed by Michael Grimes; directed by Patrick Lau.
With Patrick Allen (Gilbert Smith), Elizabeth Spriggs (Evelyn Smith), John Wheatley (Richard Smith), Joan Moon (Juliet Smith), James Bree (Bill Norton), Rhoda Lewis (Meg Norton).

TIME GENTLEMEN PLEASE

An Avalon Productions production for Sky One. Transmission details are for Sky One. Usual duration: 23 minutes.
Main regular credit(s):   Script supervisor Kendall Anderson Mut; script editor Stewart Lee; music by Grand Western.
Main regular cast: Al Murray (Guv), Phil Daniels (Terry Brook), Jason Freeman (Steve Crosby), Roy Heather (Pops), Andrew Mackay (The Professor), Janine Buckley (Lesley), Jeff Rudom (Leslie).

SERIES 1
Main regular cast: With Julia Sawalha (Janet Wilson).

Holding / Source
25.12.2000 **Bar Humbug**   DB /
Duration: 24 minutes.
Written by Richard Herring and Al Murray; art director Joanna King; designed by Harry Banks; executive in charge of production Mark Freeland; executive producers Richard Allen-Turner, Richard Herring, Al Murray and Jon Thoday; production manager Carla McGilchrist; series producer Phil Bowker; produced and directed by Richard Boden.
With Rebecca Front (Vicky Jackson), Marc Bannerman (Greg Thomson), Richard Herring (Mike the Postie), Edna Doré, Jenny Éclair, Alex Lowe, Stewart Weybridge, The Mediæval Bæbes [as The Medieval Babes], Toby Farkes, Dax O'Callaghan.

01.01.2001 **New Year's Steve**   DB /
Written by Richard Herring and Al Murray; art director Joanna King; designed by Harry Banks; executive in charge of production Mark Freeland; executive producers Richard Allen-Turner, Richard Herring, Al Murray and Jon Thoday; production manager Carla McGilchrist; series producer Phil Bowker; produced and directed by Richard Boden.
With Marc Bannerman (Greg Thomson), Frank Skinner, Dave Johns, Russell Mabey, Lloyd Martin.

Holding / Source
25.12.2001 **It's A Wonderful Pint**   DB /
Written by Richard Herring and Al Murray; art director Margaret Spohrer; designed by Harry Banks; executive producers Mark Freeland, Richard Allen-Turner, Richard Herring, Al Murray and Jon Thoday; produced and directed by Richard Boden.
With Rebecca Front (Vicky Jackson), Marc Bannerman (Greg Thomson), Barrie Gosney (Uncle Barrie), Greg Fleet, Mike Gunn, Dave Thompson, Ian Drysdale, Karl Hansen.

TIME GENTLEMEN PLEASE (continued)   British Christmas Television Guide

TIME SHIFT

A BBC production for BBC 4. Transmission details are for BBC 4. Duration varies - see below for details.

	Holding / Source
29.12.2003 **Missing Believed Wiped**	DB / DBSW

A BBC Bristol production. Duration: 38 minutes.

Documentary on the hunt for 'lost' British television programmes and the work of the National Film and Television Archive in the search. The programme includes an item on the recent discovery in Australia of a previously lost episode of THE COMPLETE AND UTTER HISTORY OF BRITAIN.

Research Elaine Sinclair; theme music by Studio 53; assistant producer Alison Fellowes; production executive David Postlethwaite; executive producer Michael Poole; production manager Marie Coyne; series producer Tom Ware; produced and directed by Jo Haywood.

With Veronika Hyks (Narrator), John Cleese, Terry Jones, Christine Slattery, Dick Fiddy, Professor John Ellis, Steve Bryant, Neil Ingoe, Tim Disney.

A TIME TO BE BORN

A BBC production. Transmission details are for BBC. Duration: 50 minutes.

A play for Christmas Eve.

Written by P. D. Cummins; music by Herbert Murrill; produced and directed by Dorothea Brooking.

John Le Mesurier (Joseph), Hazel Penwarden (Mary), Julian Somers (Landlord), Pixie Murphy (Servant Girl), Eugene Leahy (Old Shepherd), Nancy Roberts (Wife), Martin Starkie (Son), Anthony Snell (Son), Jeremy Spenser (Son), Oliver Burt (King), Robin Cull (King), Frank Singuineau (King), Juliet Wood (Angel), Sally Judd (Angel), Stephen Alexander (Voice of the Angel).

	Holding / Source
24.12.1951	NR / Live

TIMESLIP - THE BLOCK

A The Callender Company production for Yorkshire Television. Transmission details are for the Central region. Duration: 25 minutes.

Adapted by Jim Hawkins; based on a story by Robert Holmes; associate producer Carol Williams; produced by Colin Callender; directed by Willi Paterson.

John Taylor (The Hacker), Jeff Harding (Greg), Virginia Hey (Jenny), Liza Ross (Candy), Manning Redwood (Lee), Blain Fairman (Billy).

	VT Number	Holding / Source
28.12.1985 (pilot)	D040	1" / C1

TIMMY TIME

An Aardman Animations production for CBeebies. Transmission details are for CBeebies.

Animated adventure of a young sheep at school.

	Holding / Source
18.12.2011 **Timmy's Christmas Surprise**	HD/DB / HDC

Duration: 25 minutes.

Aardman Animations have pulled out all the stops for this bumper-length adventure for Timmy and friends. It's richly detailed, utterly charming and all achieved without anyone Saying more than "hoot hoot". Timmy wakes up on Christmas Eve dreaming of a smart new scooter, but a blizzard descends and the baby animals have to sleep overnight at nursery.

TIMMY TOWERS

Commissioned by ITV. Transmission details are for the Central region. Duration: 25 minutes.

Timmy Mallett (Timmy).

	Holding / Source
15.12.1998 **Christmas Special**	DB / DBS

Timmy awakes to find his presents haven't arrived, while the Abominable No Man sets out to ruin everybody's Christmas.

With Rodger Bremble, Sophie Lawrence, Mark Speight, Rod Hull and Emu.

THE TINGHA AND TUCKER CLUB

An ATV production. Transmission details are for the ATV midlands region. Usual duration: 13 minutes.

Main regular cast: Jean Morton (Presenter).

	Holding / Source
25.12.1968 **Christmas Day With Tingha And Tucker**	J /

Duration: 25 minutes.

Fly with us on a magic carpet to the land of make-believe and meet a wicked magician, a genie of the lamp, a talking elephant and Prince Origami with his magic fan.

Designed by Rex Spencer; produced by Jean Morton; directed by John Pullen.

21.01.1970 **Tucker Whittington**	J / 2"

19.07.62 - 21.10.70 Incomplete Listing

TISWAS

Produced for ATV/Central by a variety of companies (see details below). Transmission details are for the ATV/Central region. Duration varies - see below for details.

SERIES 8

Transmission details are for the ATV/Central region.

	Holding / Source
26.12.1981	J / Live

Duration: 75 minutes.

Produced by Glyn Edwards; directed by Bob Cousins.

With Sally James, Gordon Astley, Fogwell Flax, Den Hegarty, Terry Coates, The Phantom Flan Flinger.

TISWAS

TITCH

A Hutchins Film Company production for Yorkshire Television. Transmission details are for the Central region.

SERIES 1

		Holding / Source
12.12.1997	The Christmas Tree	D3 / D3S

SERIES 2

		Holding / Source
14.12.1998	The Christmas Tree	D3 / D3S

TITIPU

Alternative/Working Title(s): THE MIKADO

A BBC production for BBC 2. Transmission details are for BBC 2. Duration: 90 minutes.

Adapted by Alan Melville; based on a play by W.S. Gilbert and Arthur Sullivan; costume Mary Woods; make-up Toni Chapman; music directed by Harry Rabinowitz; choreography by Irving Davies; designed by Mel Cornish; produced and directed by David Croft.

Harry Worth (Ko-Ko), Richard Wattis (Pooh-Bah), Hattie Jacques (Katisha), Cyril Ritchard (The Mikado), Mary Millar (Yum-Yum), Valentine Palmer (Nanki-Poo), Julian Orchard (Lord Chamberlain), Patricia Bredin (Pitti-Sing), Geraldene Merrow (Peep-Bo), John Inman (Gatekeeper).

	Holding / Source
26.12.1967	J / 2"

Based on the opera, "The Mikado".

TITTYBANGBANG

A Pett Productions production for BBC 3. Transmission details are for BBC 3. Duration: 30 minutes.

Main regular credit(s): Created by Jill Parker; head of production Anne Cafferky; produced by Lisa Clark.

SERIES 2

Main regular credit(s): Written by Jill Parker; additional material by Lucy Montgomery and Steve Burge; script supervisor Emma John; assistant producer Alex Moody; directed by Angie De Chastelai Smith.

Main regular cast: With Lisa Clark, Lucy Montgomery, Debbie Chazen.

		Holding / Source
25.12.2006	Chrissytittybangbang	DB / DBSWF

SERIES 3

Main regular credit(s): Script supervisor Marzenna Hiles; music by Dan McGrath and Josh Phillips; designed by Jane Tomblin; directed by Robert Mortimer.

Main regular cast: With Lucy Montgomery, Debbie Chazen, Lisa Clark.

		Holding / Source
26.12.2007	Chrissytittybangbang	DB / DBSWF

Written by Robert Mortimer, Jill Parker and Steve Burge; additional material by David Cadji-Newby and Nico Tatarowicz.

With Steven O'Donnell, Tony Way, Shelley Longworth, Lorraine Cheshire, Stephen Aintree, Steve Burge, Steve Oram, Rhys Thomas, Di Botcher, Esther Coles, Iain Lee, Colin Edwin, Javone Prince.

TO BE OR NOT TO BE... IN SHAKESPEARE

Commissioned by More4. Transmission details are for More4. Duration: 55 minutes.

Ian McKellen.

	Holding / Source
25.12.2008	DB /

TO ME... TO YOU

A BBC production for BBC 1. Transmission details are for BBC 1.

SERIES 2

		Holding / Source
23.12.1997	Christmas Special	DB-D3 / D3S

With Emma Lee, Peter Simon, Richard Bacon, Kirsten O'Brien.

SERIES 3

		Holding / Source
25.12.1998	Christmas Special	DB-D3 / D3S

TO RUSSIA WITH ELTON

An ATV production. Transmission details are for the ATV midlands region. Duration: 75 minutes.

A musical extravaganza that is part pop happening, part voyage into the unknown — and total entertainment. Like some pre-Revolutionary Tsar, Elton John claimed Leningrad and Moscow as his own during a concert tour of the U.S.S.R. in May, 1979. This film shows exactly what it is like being on a concert tour, capturing the flavour of the concerts themselves and the times in between—the anxieties, the strain, the tension, the moments when frenzy is overtaken by hysteria.

Edited by Michael Nunn; sound Clive Winter; camera operated by Harvey Harrison; produced by Allan McKeown and Ian La Frenais; directed by Dick Clement.

Dudley Moore (Commentator), Elton John.

	Holding / Source
21.12.1980	C1 / C1

TO RUSSIA WITH ELTON (continued)   British Christmas Television Guide

TO THE MANOR BORN

A BBC production for BBC 1. Transmission details are for BBC 1. Duration: 30 minutes.

Main regular credit(s):	Written by Peter Spence; theme music by Ronnie Hazlehurst; music by Ronnie Hazlehurst; produced and directed by Gareth Gwenlan.
Main regular cast:	Penelope Keith (Audrey Fforbes-Hamilton), Peter Bowles (Richard DeVere), Angela Thorne (Margery Frobisher).

SERIES 1

Main regular credit(s):	Script associate Christopher Bond; designed by Ian Rawnsley.
Main regular cast:	With John Rudling (Brabinger).

                                                                                                Holding / Source

25.12.1979 "The Christmas Crib"   DB-D3 / 2"

With Michael Bilton (Ned), Daphne Heard (Mrs Polouvicka), Gerald Sim (The Rector).

John Rudling is not in this episode.

TOBIAS AND THE ANGEL

A Scottish Television production. Transmission details are for the ATV midlands region. Duration: 50 minutes.

The family of Tobit in Nineveh has fallen on hard times. The son of the house, Tobias, is sent on a journey to faraway Rages to collect an old debt. He is accompanied by a strange and wonderful porter, Azarias. Many strange things happen during the journey showing that Javeh moves in mysterious ways, his miracles to perform.

Adapted by Ronald Mavor; based on a play by James Bridie; music by Herbert Chappell; designed by Geoff Nixon; executive producer Liam Hood; directed by Tina Wakerell.

John Alderton (Azarias), Wilfrid Brambell (Tobit), Madeleine Christie (Anna), Chris Harris (Tobias), Ian Ireland (Bandit), Callum Mill (Raguel), Christine McKenna (Sara), Gerry Slevin (Asmoday), Victor (Toby The Dog).

                                       Holding / Source

23.12.1973   J / 2"

TODAY

A Thames Television production. Transmission details are for the Thames Television region. Duration varies - see below for details.

                                                                                             VT Number   Holding / Source

24.12.1971   **Today... Is Christmas Eve**   J / Live

Duration: 25 minutes.

Who guards the Crown Jewels over Christmas? What are the perils of last-minute Christmas shopping? Christmas customs are changing, but does the meaning remain the same? These are some of the questions in this special Christmas Eve edition of Today.

Programme editor Simon Buxton; produced by Marjory Ruse; directed by Robert Fleming.

With Eamonn Andrews (Presenter).

21.12.1973   **Christmas Special**   8748   DB / C1

Duration: 30 minutes.

No end credits.

20.12.1976   **Christmas Special**   15824   DB / Live

Duration: 40 minutes.

Production team Anne Burrow, Frank Hayes, Susan Kyle, Lois Lorant, Martin Lucas, Pauline Pogorelske, Gordon Stevens, Gill Southcott, Diana Wallis and Christine Whitehead; executive producer Tom Steel; produced by Mike Housego; film sequences directed by Vincent Stafford; outside broadcast director Mike Dormer; directed by Tony Bulley.

With Eamonn Andrews (Presenter), Nina Baden-Semper, Mike Reid.

Regional news programme.

TODAY IS HOGMANAY

A Scottish Television production. Transmission details are for the Scottish Television region. Duration: 25 minutes.

                                       Holding / Source

31.12.1965   J / 40

TODAY IS HOGMANAY

A Scottish Television production. Transmission details are for the Scottish Television region. Duration: 24 minutes.

                                       Holding / Source

31.12.1965   J /

TOFFEE IN HIS POCKET

A STV Productions production for Scottish Television. Transmission details are for the Scottish Television region. Duration: 22 minutes.

A celebration of Chic Murray, including footage of Chic from THE CALUM KENNEDY SHOW (1983).

Narrated by Derek Munn; edited by Eric McIntyre; associate producer Angela Morton; executive producer Paul Murray; produced by Kim Kinnie; directed by Paul Hineman.

Alex Norton, Andy Cameron, Robert Love, Billy Sloan, Dorothy Paul, Johnny Beattie, Dean Park, Haldane Duncan [as Hal Duncan], Des McLean, Anna Di Mascio.

                                       Holding / Source

31.12.2008   DB / DBSW

TOM BARNADO

Alternative/Working Title(s): FATHER OF NOBODY'S CHILDREN
A BBC production. Transmission details are for BBC. Duration: 90 minutes.
Adapted by Arthur Swinson; based on a book by Norman Wymer; play production by Harold Clayton.

Thomas Hare (Tom Barnardo), John Gorrie (Henry Vincent), Mary Quinn (Mary Bilton), Mollie Hare (Mrs Foldes), Peter Eveleigh (Alec Bilton), Diane Grey (Florrie Bilton), Edwin Brown (Arthur Bilton), Ian Sadler (Doctor Garvey), Henry Davies (Peter Haughton), Beatrice Varley (Mrs Dent), Redmond Phillips (Reverend Hudson Taylor), Carl Lanchbury (Jack), Peter Whitmarsh (Jim Jarvis), Donald McCollum (Collins), Percy Marmont (Lord Shaftesbury), Edith Saville (Lady Shaftesbury), Maurice Hedley (Doctor Thompson), Graham Stuart (Sir John Mason), Roger Maxwell (Colonel Fairweather), Maurice Bennis (Boy), Dudley Grapes (Ginger), Bernard Spear (Dick), Dorothy Gordon (Miss Foster), Beckett Bould (Mr Dyce), Keith Crane (Billy Fetter), Robin Ranson (Peter Derrick), Anthony Lyons (Pincher), Gordon Whiting (Fred Calder), Jessica Dunning (Mary Calder), Martin Cox (Shorty), Jacky Martin (Blackie), Leonard Monaghan (Carrots).

	Holding / Source
23.12.1958	R1 /

TOM JONES

A BBC production for BBC 1. Transmission details are for BBC 1. Duration: 45 minutes.
Main regular performer(s): Tom Jones.

	Holding / Source
31.12.1971	DB-D3 / 2"

Written by Ronnie Cass; orchestra directed by Johnnie Spence; designed by Victor Meredith; produced and directed by Stewart Morris.
With The Treorchy Male Voice Choir, The Blossoms.

28.12.1972	DB-D3 / 2"

Designed by J. Roger Lowe; produced and directed by Stewart Morris.
With Johnnie Spence and his Orchestra.

TOM JONES, A BOY FROM PONTY

A BBC Wales production for BBC 1 Wales. Transmission details are for BBC 1 Wales. Duration: 59 minutes.
Tom Jones, Noel Edmonds, Jools Holland, Robbie Williams, Brian Mulroney, Jerry Lewis, Cerys Matthews, Wyclef Jean, Kelly Jones, Mark Woodward.

	Holding / Source
22.12.2005	DB / DBSW

TOM TOM

A BBC West production for BBC 1. Transmission details are for BBC 1.

SERIES 5
Main regular cast: With Norman Tozer (Presenter), Jan Leeming (Presenter), John Earle (Presenter).

	Holding / Source
31.12.1969 **Special**	J /

TOMMY COOPER

Alternative/Working Title(s): COOP
An LWT production. Transmission details are for the ATV midlands region. Duration: 25 minutes.
Main regular credit(s): Script editor Dick Vosburgh; associate producer Miff Ferrie; produced by Bill Hitchcock; directed by Bill Turner.
Main regular cast: Tommy Cooper (Host), Clovissa Newcombe, Peter Reeves, Bob Sharples and his Orchestra.

	Production No	Holding / Source
26.12.1969	9L/00391	DB / 2"

Designed by Cephas Howard.

TOMMY COOPER

A Thames Television production. Transmission details are for the ATV midlands region. Duration: 52 minutes.
Main regular performer(s): Tommy Cooper.

	Holding / Source
28.12.1976 **Tommy Cooper's Guest Night**	D3 / 2"

Written by Dick Hills, Barry Cryer, Spike Mullins and Eddie Bayliss; music directed by Ronnie Aldrich; music associate Sam Harding; choreography by Lionel Blair; designed by Colin Andrews; produced and directed by William G. Stewart.
With Arthur Askey, The Three Degrees, Los Zafiros, Lionel Blair, Harry Littlewood, William Shearer, William Lawford, Stan Van.

THE TOMMY COOPER HOUR

A Thames Television production. Transmission details are for the ATV midlands region. Duration: 52 minutes.
Main regular cast: Tommy Cooper (Host).

	VT Number	Holding / Source
25.12.1973 **Tommy Cooper's Christmas**	8556	D3 / 2"

Christmas may never be the same again after Tommy Cooper has given the season of goodwill his own personal touch. If you have never cooked a duck egg omelette, played snooker with a sand-wedge or ridden an ostrich, Tommy will demonstrate the correct way to do it.
Written by Johnnie Mortimer and Brian Cooke; music directed by Ronnie Aldrich; designed by Darrell Lass; produced and directed by Peter Frazer-Jones.
With Sacha Distel, Clodagh Rodgers, Allan Cuthbertson, Michael Segal, Verne Morgan, Dany Clare, Dorian Healy, The Mike Sammes Singers, Three's A Crowd, Roger Stevenson [as Roger Stevenson and Daisy The Duck], Joe Davis.

THE TOMMY COOPER HOUR (continued)

25.12.1974	9853	DB / 2"

Duration: 51 minutes.
Written by Dick Hills; music directed by Ronnie Aldrich; designed by John Plant and Alex Macintyre; produced and directed by Royston Mayoh.
With André Tahon, Dana, Vic Damone, Allan Cuthbertson, Tommy Godfrey, Glyn Houston, Damaris Hayman, Annette Potts, The Tony Mansell Singers.

THE TOMMY STEELE SHOW

An ATV production. Transmission details are for the ATV London region. Duration: 50 minutes.
Written by Sid Green and Dick Hills; choreography by Pamela Devis; designed by Tom Lingwood; produced and directed by Alan Tarrant.
Tommy Steele, Bernard Cribbins, Peggy Mount, April Olrich, Graham Crowden, Dick Bentley, Anton Diffring, The Cliff Adams Singers, The Pamela Devis Dancers, Jack Parnell and his Orchestra.

	Holding / Source
25.12.1960	J|a /

Kaleidoscope hold the full audio.

THE TOMMY STEELE SHOW

An ATV production. Transmission details are for the ATV midlands region. Duration: 52 minutes.
Written by Eric Merriman and Francis Essex; story by Tommy Steele; music by Tommy Steele; choreography by Pamela Devis; designed by Tom Lingwood; produced and directed by Francis Essex.
Tommy Steele (Quincy), Elaine Millar (Mary), Harry Brunning (Toy Mender), John Frawley (Ted), Pat Coombs (Grizelda), Ronnie Brody (Jack), Keith Smith (Puffer), Peter Hawkins (Topper), Una Stubbs (Rebecca), Hugh Paddick (Jim Cracker), Alan Baulch (Sentry), Henry McGee (Snowman), The Michael Sammes Singers, The Pamela Devis Dancers, Peggy O'Farrell Children, Jack Parnell and his Orchestra.

Quincy's Quest

	VT Number	Holding / Source
23.12.1962	3101	R1N /

TOMMY'S TOY SHOP

An Ulster Television production. Transmission details are for the Ulster Televison region. Duration: 25 minutes.

	Holding / Source
26.12.1968	J /

TOMORROW'S WORLD

A BBC production for BBC 1. Transmission details are for BBC 1. Duration: 30 minutes.
Main regular credit(s):   Edited by Peter Bale.

	Holding / Source
24.12.1970 **Christmas Special**	C1SEQ / 2"

Edited by Lawrence Wade; produced by Brian Johnson, John Weiley and Andrew Wiseman.
With Raymond Baxter (Presenter), Graham Hill, James Burke, John Parry, Jimmy Savile, William Woollard.
Film inserts only.

24.12.1971 **Yesterday's World**	HD/DB / C1

Research David Gale; edited by Lawrence Wade; designed by Gary Pritchard; produced by Andrew Wiseman; directed by Richard Loncraine.
With Raymond Baxter (Host), Jimmy Young (Voice Only), James Burke, Michael Rodd, Hugh Griffith, Nerys Hughes, Clement Freud.

	Holding / Source
20.12.1990 **Christmas Quiz**	DB / 1"

Edited by Diana Purvis; produced by Jane Aldous and Rob Bayly.
With Julian Clary, Toyah Willcox, David Bellamy, Peter Shilton, Judith Hann, Howard Stableford, Peter Macann, Kate Bellingham.

23.12.1992 **Christmas Quiz**	DB / D3S

Produced by Jane Aldous.
With Howard Stableford (Host), Judith Hann (Presenter), Carmen Pryce (Presenter), Ian MacCaskill, Josie Lawrence, Wayne Dobson, Mike McShane.

TONIGHT (WITH TREVOR MCDONALD)

A Granada production. Transmission details are for ITV 1.

SERIES 5

	Production No	Holding / Source
08.12.2003 **Mistletoe And Crime**	1/2803/0303	DB / DBS

SERIES 6

	Production No	Holding / Source
10.12.2004 **Christmas In Debt**	1/2803/0388	DB / DBS

SERIES 7

	Production No	Holding / Source
16.12.2005 **Twelve Tales Of Christmas**	1/2803/0481	DB / DBS

TONIGHT (WITH TREVOR MCDONALD)

British Christmas Television Guide		TONIGHT (WITH TREVOR MCDONALD) (continued)

SERIES 8

		Production No	Holding / Source
18.12.2006	Cut Price Christmas	1/2803/0562	DB / DBS

SERIES 9

		Production No	Holding / Source
07.12.2007	A Merry Cheaper Christmas	1/2803/0640	DB / DBS

SERIES 10

		Production No	Holding / Source
05.12.2008	The 12 Crimes Of Christmas	1/2803/0724	DB / DBS

SERIES 11

		Production No	Holding / Source
11.12.2009	Christmas For A Pound	1/2803/0794	DB / DBS

SERIES 12

		Production No	Holding / Source
16.12.2010	Christmas Or Bust	1/2803/0846	DB / DBS

TONIGHT WITH DANNY LA RUE

An ATV production. Transmission details are for the ATV midlands region. Duration: 50 minutes.

Adding a touch of camp to Christmas, and a more than generous measure of mirth and glamour, Danny invites you to spend an evening with him and his guests, including the diminutive but dynamic Arthur Askey.

Written by Bryan Blackburn; music associate Derek Scott; choreography by Tommy Shaw; designed by Roger Allan; produced and directed by Colin Clews.

Danny La Rue (Host), Arthur Askey, Johnny Hart, Mike Goddard, Terry Wogan, Derek Hobson, Clifford Davis, Tony Hatch, Mickey Most, Jimmy Hunt, The Tommy Shaw Dancers, Jack Parnell and his Orchestra.

	VT Number	Holding / Source
26.12.1974	9419/74	DB / 2"

TONIGHT WITH DAVE ALLEN

An ATV production. Transmission details are for the ABC midlands region.

Main regular performer(s): Dave Allen (Host).

SERIES 1

Transmission details are for the ABC midlands region. Duration: 35 minutes.

		Holding / Source
23.12.1967	Christmas Special	J /

Written by Eric Merriman; research Max Monsarrat; designed by Richard Lake; produced by Colin Clews; directed by Colin Clews and Anthony Flanagan.

TONS OF MONEY

A BBC production. Transmission details are for BBC. Duration: 90 minutes.

Written by Will Evans and Valentine; play production by Graeme Muir.

Frankie Howerd (Aubrey Henry Maitland Allington), Eleanor Summerfield (Louise Allington), Jack Melford (Sprules), Rosemary Davis (Simpson), Joan Young (Miss Benita Mullett), Lee Young (Giles), George Benson (James Chesterman), Barbara Shotter (Jean Everard), Bill Fraser (Henery), Roland Green (George Maitland).

	Holding / Source
26.12.1954	J / Live

THE TONY FERRINO PHENEMENON

A Pozzitive Television production for BBC 2. Transmission details are for BBC 2. Duration: 50 minutes.

A programme of song and dance starring Steve Coogan as Portuguese entertainer Tony Ferrino.

Written by Steve Coogan; produced by David Tyler and Geoff Posner; directed by Geoff Posner.

Steve Coogan (Tony Ferrino), Mick Hucknall, Kim Wilde, Gary Wilmot.

	Holding / Source
01.01.1997	DB-D3 / D3S

TOP NUMBERS

An ABC production. Transmission details are for the ABC midlands region. Duration varies - see below for details.

Main regular credit(s): Dance direction by David Gardiner; settings by Rex Spencer.

SERIES 3

Duration: 25 minutes.

		Holding / Source
28.12.1958	Top Numbers Of 1958	J /

TOP OF THE POPS

A BBC production for BBC 1. Transmission details are for BBC 1. Duration varies - see below for details.

A BBC Manchester production.

Holding / Source

24.12.1964 Top Of The Pops '64 J /

Duration: 60 minutes.

Produced and directed by Johnnie Stewart.

With Jimmy Savile (DJ), David Jacobs (DJ), Pete Murray (DJ), Alan Freeman (DJ), Billy J. Kramer and The Dakotas, Cilla Black, The Go-Jo's, Herman's Hermits, Manfred Mann, Peter & Gordon, Roy Orbison*, Sandie Shaw, The Animals, The Beatles, The Four Pennies, The Honeycombs, The Kinks, The Searchers, The Supremes.

(25/12/64 "Christmas Night with the Stars sequence exists with The Barron Knights.)

25.12.1965 Top Of The Pops '65 DB-4WSEQ / 40

Duration: 75 minutes.

Designed by Geoff Kirkland; produced and directed by Johnnie Stewart.

With Jimmy Savile (DJ), Alan Freeman (DJ), Pete Murray (DJ), David Jacobs (DJ), The Beatles*, Elvis Presley*, Georgie Fame and The Blue Flames, Jackie Trent, Ken Dodd, Sandie Shaw, Sonny and Cher, The Byrds, The Hollies, The Kinks, The Moody Blues, The Righteous Brothers, The Rolling Stones, The Seekers, The Walker Brothers, Tom Jones, Unit 4 + 2.

VT inserts (not BBC made) – Beatles "We Can Work It Out" (different version) & "Day Tripper".

Duration: 25 minutes.

Holding / Source

26.12.1966 Top Of The Pops '66 Part 1 J|a /

Duration: 45 minutes.

Produced and directed by Johnnie Stewart.

With Jimmy Savile (DJ), Pete Murray (DJ), Nancy Sinatra*, Dusty Springfield, The Overlanders, Frank Sinatra*, Manfred Mann, The Beatles, The Rolling Stones, The Small Faces, The Spencer Davis Group, The Walker Brothers.

27.12.1966 Top Of The Pops '66 Part 2 J|a /

Produced and directed by Johnnie Stewart.

With Alan Freeman (DJ), Simon Dee (DJ), Chris Farlowe, The Kinks, Georgie Fame and The Blue Flames, Jim Reeves*, The Go-Jo's, The Beatles*, The Four Tops, The Small Faces, The Troggs, Tom Jones.

26.12.1967 Top Of The Pops '67 Part 2 DB-R3 /

Duration: 60 minutes.

Orchestra directed by Johnny Pearson; designed by J. Roger Lowe; produced and directed by Johnnie Stewart; film sequences directed by Peter Clifton and Dereck Barrell-Davis.

With Jimmy Savile (DJ), Pete Murray (DJ), Alan Freeman (DJ), Long John Baldry, The Bee Gees, The Monkees*, The Rolling Stones, Dave Dee, Beaky, Dozy, Mick & Titch, Lulu, Scott Mackenzie*, The Go-Jo's, Cliff Richard, Procol Harum, The Beatles, Engelbert Humperdinck, The Ladybirds.

Complete edition on telerecording plus trailer.

25.12.1968 Top Of The Pops '68 Part 1 J|a /

Duration: 45 minutes.

Produced and directed by Johnnie Stewart.

With Jimmy Savile (DJ), Pete Murray (DJ), The Beach Boys, Des O'Connor, Esther & Abi Ofarim, Gary Pucket and The Union Gap*, Georgie Fame, Manfred Mann, The Beatles*, The Love Affair, The Rolling Stones*, The Scaffold.

26.12.1968 Top Of The Pops '68 Part 2 J|a /

Duration: 40 minutes.

Produced and directed by Johnnie Stewart.

With Stuart Henry (DJ), Alan Freeman (DJ), Louis Armstrong*, Herb Alpert*, The Go-Jo's, Joe Cocker, Mary Hopkin, The Beatles*, The Bee Gees, The Equals, Tommy James and The Shondells*.

25.12.1969 Top Of The Pops '69 Part 1 J|a / 2"

Duration: 45 minutes.

Produced and directed by Mel Cornish.

With Jimmy Savile (DJ), Pete Murray (DJ), Blue Mink, Clodagh Rodgers, The Creedence Clearwater Revival*, Fleetwood Mac*, Marmalade, Peter Sarstedt, The Rolling Stones, The Beatles*, The Scaffold, Thunderclap Newman, Zager and Evans*.

Some uncut studio material is held by a private collector but the BBC don't have a copy. The complete soundtrack ex private collector is held by us. One VT item – The Tremeloes or Marmalade, we are not sure, was re-used in "Pop Go the Sixties" on 31/12/69 which exists.

26.12.1969 Top Of The Pops '69 Part 2 J / 2"

Duration: 40 minutes.

Produced and directed by Mel Cornish.

With Alan Freeman (DJ), Tony Blackburn (DJ), Amen Corner*, Lou Christie, Bobbie Gentry, The Dave Clark Five, Desmond Dekker and The Israelites, Herman's Hermits, Marvin Gaye*, Mary Hopkin, Rolf Harris, The Beatles*, Tommy Roe, Archies*.

31.12.1969 Pop Go The Sixties DB-1" / 2"

Duration: 75 minutes.

Introduced by Jimmy Savile and Elfie Von Kalckreuth; music directed by Johnny Harris; music associate Jack Goddard; designed by C. Ian Rawnsley; associate producer Klaus Weising; produced and directed by Johnnie Stewart.

With The Bachelors, The Who, Kenny Ball and his Jazzmen, The Beatles*, Cilla Black, Adam Faith, The Hollies, The Kinks, Lulu, Cliff Richard, The Rolling Stones, The Shadows, Helen Shapiro, Sandie Shaw, Dusty Springfield, The Tremeloes, Tom Jones, The Ascott Dancers, Horst Jankowski*, The Johnny Harris Orchestra.

With ZDF.

A BetaSP tape, ex-2" was found in 2007, but has since been lost. A DVD survives. Amongst other things it contained:

Sequences from TOTP '69 PT.1 (25/12/69): Title sequence / Saville-Murray link to... / Lily The Pink - The Scaffold (final chorus only) / Murray and dancers link to... / Goodnight Midnight - Clodagh Rodgers (ends abruptly but virtually complete) / Honky Tonk Women - Rolling Stones (starts / ends abruptly) / Dancer link to Something In The Air - Thunderclap Newman / Studio chatter and outro / end titles

Duration: 45 minutes.

Holding / Source

25.12.1970 Top Of The Pop Christmas '70 Part 1 J|a / 2"

Orchestra directed by Johnny Pearson; choreography by Flick Colby; designed by Valerie Warrender; produced and directed by Brian Whitehouse.

With Jimmy Savile (DJ), Tony Blackburn (DJ), The Creedence Clearwater Revival*, The First Edition, Desmond Dekker, Edison Lighthouse, Elvis Presley*, England World Cup Squad 1986, Kenny Rogers, Lee Marvin*, Marmalade, Matthew's Southern Comfort, Mr Bloe, Pickettywitch, Simon & Garfunkel*, Smokey Robinson and The Miracles*.

26.12.1970 Top Of The Pop Christmas '70 Part 2 J|a / 2"

Orchestra directed by Johnny Pearson; choreography by Flick Colby; designed by Valerie Warrender; produced and directed by Brian Whitehouse.

With Tony Blackburn (DJ), Jimmy Savile (DJ), Christie, Dana, Dave Edmunds, Freda Payne*, Free*, Hotlegs, Jimmy Ruffin, McGuinness Flint*, Mungo Jerry, Pan's People, The Jimi Hendrix Experience*, The Kinks.

31.12.1970 Pop Into '71 J / 2"

Duration: 55 minutes.

Produced and directed by Brian Whitehouse.

With Alexis Korner and Peter Thorup and BBC Orchestra, Lulu, The Barbara Moore Singers, Blue Mink, Cat Stevens and Friends, Fleetwood Mac, Labi Siffre, The BBC Orchestra, Sue & Sonny, Elton John, The Top of The Pops Orchestra, Alan Price & Georgie Fame, Alexis Korner and Peter Thorup With CCS, Livingston Taylor, The Who.

Short clip exists. (Made 1970) Film inserts – Canned Heat "In My Chair", Canned Heat "Sugar Bee Tin Tin "Is That the Way?", Frijid Pink "House of the Rising Sun", Ronnie Hawkins "Down in the Alley" (all untransmitted items). The Who - Naked Eye exists on dv as a very rare colour performance.

25.12.1971 Christmas 1971 Part 1 C1SEQ|a / 2"

Music directed by Johnny Pearson; choreography by Flick Colby; produced and directed by Johnnie Stewart.

With Jimmy Savile (DJ), Pan's People, Clive Dunn, Dave and Ansil Collins, Dave Edmunds, Dawn, Gilbert O'Sullivan, Middle of The Road, Mungo Jerry, Procol Harum, T-Rex, The Mixtures, The Supremes.

Film insert – CCS "Tap Turns on the Water"; plus complete soundtrack ex private collector.

27.12.1971 Christmas 1971 Part 2 DB-D3 / 2"

Music associate Derek Warne; orchestra directed by Johnny Pearson; choreography by Flick Colby; designed by Ian Rawnsley; produced and directed by Johnnie Stewart.

With Tony Blackburn (DJ), T-Rex, The Tams, Benny Hill*, Slade, Pan's People, The Rolling Stones, Ashton, Gardner & Dyke, The New Seekers, Rod Stewart and The Faces, The Ladybirds.

25.12.1972 Christmas 1972 Part 1 J|a / 2"

Duration: 50 minutes.

Orchestra directed by Johnny Pearson; choreography by Flick Colby; designed by Ian Rawnsley; produced and directed by Johnnie Stewart.

With Jimmy Savile (DJ), Ed Stewart (DJ), Pan's People, David Bowie, Don Maclean, Elton John, Gilbert O'Sullivan, Hawkwind*, David Cassidy*, Little Jimmy Osmond*, Rod Stewart, The Royal Scots Dragoon Guards*, Slade, The Move, T-Rex, The New Seekers, Lynsey De Paul, The Ladybirds.

Complete soundtrack held ex private collector; VT clip exists on programme "Thanks for the Frying Pan".

28.12.1972 Christmas 1972 Part 2 DB-D3 / 2"

Drawings by Rolf Harris; music associate Derek Warne; orchestra directed by Johnny Pearson; choreography by Flick Colby; designed by Ian Rawnsley; produced and directed by Johnnie Stewart; film sequences directed by Tom Taylor.

With Noel Edmonds (DJ), Tony Blackburn (DJ), Gary Glitter, Donny Osmond*, Alice Cooper, Lieutenant Pigeon, Roberta Flack, Slade, Benny Hill*, Chicory Tip, Pan's People, The Osmonds, Chuck Berry, Michael Jackson, T-Rex, Ringo Starr*, The Ladybirds.

25.12.1973 Christmas 1973 DB-D3 / 2"

Music directed by Johnny Pearson; music associate Derek Warne; choreography by Flick Colby; designed by Steve Brownsey; production team Bruce Milliard, Maurice Gallagher, Rick Gardner, Ann R. Mann and Valerie Wilson; produced and directed by Robin Nash; film sequences directed by Paul Smith.

With Noel Edmonds (DJ), Tony Blackburn (DJ), Donny Osmond*, Suzi Quatro, The Simon Park Orchestra, Little Jimmy Osmond*, The Sweet, Dawn With Tony Orlando, Pan's People, Gary Glitter, David Cassidy*, 10cc, Peters and Lee, Wizzard, Slade.

The BBC have the original studio recordings, because the tx tape was damaged, as well as the tx edit. There is also a spool logged as 'dub of 1" spools from JCA' which is probably a dub of a studio spool as it is 75 mins. but the broadcast version was actually 44'30". When it was repeated in 1991 the tx was 44'42, but that might be accounted for by the "Perfect Christmas" generic titles.

27.12.1973 10 Years Of Pop Music DB-D3 / 2"

Orchestra directed by Johnny Pearson; choreography by Flick Colby; designed by Steve Brownsey; produced by Robin Nash and Bruce Milliard; directed by Robin Nash and Bruce Milliard.

With Jimmy Savile (DJ), The Kinks*, Wizzard, The Dave Clark Five, Billy J. Kramer and The Dakotas, The Supremes, The Beatles*, The Bachelors, The Who*, The Righteous Brothers, Sonny and Cher, Jonathan King, Sandie Shaw, Scott Mackenzie, Procol Harum, The Tremeloes, Dave Dee, Beaky, Dozy, Mick & Titch, Joe Cocker, Status Quo, Alan Price, The Crazy World of Arthur Brown, Julie Driscoll, Brian Auger and The Trinity, The Move, Marmalade, Free, Pan's People, The Rolling Stones, Rod Stewart and The Faces, David Bowie.

"Ten Years of Pop Music 1964-1974" – complete programme on VT, insert tape featuring various archive clips.

25.12.1974 Christmas 1974 Part 1 DB-D3 / 2"

Music directed by Johnny Pearson; music associate Derek Warne; choreography by Flick Colby; designed by Paul Allen; produced and directed by Robin Nash.

With Jimmy Savile [as Jimmy Savile, OBE] (DJ), Tony Blackburn (DJ), Abba, Charles Aznavour, Ken Boothe, David Essex, The Osmonds*, Pan's People, Paper Lace, Slade, Sweet Sensation, Mud, The Three Degrees, The Ladybirds.

27.12.1974 Christmas 1974 Part 2 DB-D3 / 2"

Music directed by Johnny Pearson; music associate Derek Warne; choreography by Flick Colby; designed by Paul Allen; produced and directed by Brian Whitehouse.

With Dave Lee Travis (DJ), Noel Edmonds (DJ), The Rubettes, John Denver*, Alvin Stardust, George Macrae, Stephanie De Sykes, Sparks, Gary Glitter, Sylvia, Queen, Ray Stevens, Suzi Quatro, Carl Douglas, Terry Jacks, Mud, The Ladybirds.

TOP OF THE POPS (continued)

Complete programme on VT plus studio recordings (inc clips of earlier, missing editions).

23.12.1975 Christmas 1975 Part 1   DB-D3 / 2"
Duration: 50 minutes.
Music directed by Johnny Pearson; music associate Derek Warne; choreography by Flick Colby; designed by John Stout; produced by Robin Nash; directed by Stanley Appel.
With Dave Lee Travis (DJ), Jimmy Savile (DJ), Hot Chocolate, Steve Harley and Cockney Rebel, Billy Connolly, Status Quo, Pan's People, The Sweet, Rod Stewart*, Mud, The Bay City Rollers, Queen*, The Ladybirds.

25.12.1975 Christmas 1975 Part 2   DB-D3 / 2"
Music directed by Johnny Pearson and Derek Warne; choreography by Flick Colby; designed by John Stout; produced and directed by Robin Nash.
With Noel Edmonds (DJ), Tony Blackburn (DJ), The Osmonds (DJs), Mud, Pilot, Johnny Nash, Windsor Davies & Don Estelle, Pan's People, Ralph McTell, The Tymes, Tammy Wynette, The Bay City Rollers, Guys & Dolls, Telly Savalas, 10cc, David Essex.

25.12.1976 Christmas 1976 Part 1   DB-D3 / 2"
Duration: 50 minutes.
Music directed by Johnny Pearson; music associate Derek Warne; choreography by Flick Colby; designed by Robert Berk; produced by Johnnie Stewart; directed by Phil Bishop.
With Noel Edmonds (DJ), Dave Lee Travis (DJ), Slik, Elton John & Kiki Dee*, Legs & Co., J. J. Barrie, Laurel and Hardy*, Tina Charles, The Wurzels, Cliff Richard, Abba, Pussycat, Demis Roussos, Queen*.

26.12.1976 Christmas 1976 Part 2   DB-D3 / 2"
Music directed by Johnny Pearson; music associate Derek Warne; choreography by Flick Colby; designed by Robert Berk; produced by Johnnie Stewart; directed by Phil Bishop.
With Tony Blackburn (DJ), Jimmy Savile (DJ), Brotherhood of Man, Dr Hook*, Billy Ocean, Sailor, Legs & Co., The Real Thing, Abba*, Rod Stewart, Our Kid, Johnny Mathis*, Chicago*, Showaddywaddy.

25.12.1977 Top Of The Pops '77 Part 1   DB-D3 / 2"
Research Nick Maingay; music directed by Johnny Pearson; music associate Derek Warne; choreography by Flick Colby; designed by Graeme Thomson; produced by Robin Nash; directed by Stanley Appel.
With David 'Kid' Jensen (DJ), Noel Edmonds (DJ), Showaddywaddy, Deniece Williams, The Brighouse and Rastrick Brass Band, Legs & Co., Manhattan Transfer, Hot Chocolate, David Soul*, Abba*, Space*, Kenny Rogers*, Baccara, Wings*, Johnny Mathis*, The Ladybirds.

26.12.1977 Top Of The Pops '77 Part 2   DB-D3 / 2"
Research Nick Maingay; music directed by Johnny Pearson; music associate Derek Warne; choreography by Flick Colby; designed by Graeme Thomson; produced by Robin Nash; directed by David G. Hillier.
With Tony Blackburn (DJ), Dave Lee Travis (DJ), Boney M, Rod Stewart, Heatwave, David Soul, Julie Covington*, Floaters, Legs & Co., Queen*, Abba*, Brotherhood of Man, Billy Ocean, Joe Tex*, The Jacksons*, Elvis Presley*, Showaddywaddy, Labelle*, The Ladybirds.

25.12.1978 Christmas 1978   DB-D3 / 2"
Duration: 60 minutes.
Music directed by Johnny Pearson; music associate Derek Warne; choreography by Flick Colby; executive producer Robin Nash; produced and directed by David G. Hillier.
With Noel Edmonds (DJ), Darts, Rose Royce*, Boney M, Legs & Co., Wings*, Brotherhood of Man, Father Abraham and The Smurfs*, The Bee Gees*, Brian & Michael, The Brighouse and Rastrick Brass Band, Kate Bush*, Showaddywaddy, Abba*, John Travolta and Olivia Newton-John*, James Galway*.

25.12.1979 Christmas 1979 Part 1   DB-D3 / 2"
Duration: 60 minutes.
Music directed by Johnny Pearson; music associate Derek Warne; choreography by Flick Colby; designed by Humphrey Jaeger; executive producer Robin Nash; produced and directed by Phil Bishop; film sequences directed by Grant Watkins.
With David 'Kid' Jensen (DJ), Peter Powell (DJ), Boney M, Janet Kay, CCS, Ian Dury and The Blockheads, Gary Numan, Roxy Music, Legs & Co., The Buggles, B. A. Robertson, M, Elvis Costello and The Attractions, Lena Martell, Squeeze, Dr Hook, Blondie, Tubeway Army, Cliff Richard, The Maggie Stredder Singers.

27.12.1979 Christmas 1979 Part 2   DB-D3 / 2"
Music directed by Johnny Pearson; music associate Derek Warne; choreography by Flick Colby; designed by Humphrey Jaeger; executive producer Robin Nash; produced and directed by Phil Bishop.
With Mike Read (DJ), Dave Lee Travis (DJ), CCS, The Boomtown Rats*, Abba*, The Police*, The Village People*, Legs & Co., Art Garfunkel*, Queen*, Squeeze, Blondie*, Pink Floyd*, The Maggie Stredder Singers.

25.12.1980 Christmas 1980   DB-D3 / 2"
Duration: 60 minutes.
Music directed by Johnny Pearson; music associate Derek Warne; choreography by Flick Colby; designed by Andy Dimond; executive producer Michael Hurll; produced and directed by Stanley Appel.
With Peter Powell (DJ), Jimmy Savile (DJ), The Nolans, Blondie*, Dexy's Midnight Runners, Paul McCartney*, Liquid Gold, David Bowie*, Marti Webb, The Police*, Fern Kinney, Johnny Logan, Abba*, Legs & Co., Leo Sayer, Sheena Easton, Pink Floyd*, St Winifred's School Choir.

01.01.1981 Hits Of The Year   DB-D3 / 2"
Music directed by Johnny Pearson; music associate Derek Warne; choreography by Flick Colby; designed by Andy Dimond; executive producer Michael Hurll; production manager Gordon Elsbury; produced and directed by Brian Whitehouse.
With Dave Lee Travis (DJ), Tommy Vance (DJ), Status Quo, The Boomtown Rats*, Ottowan*, Madness, The Jam, Billy Preston and Syreeta, Legs & Co., UB40, Kelly Marie, Hot Chocolate, Stevie Wonder*, Abba*, The Pretenders.

24.12.1981 Christmas Eve 1981   DB-D3 / 2"
Dance direction by Flick Colby; designed by Phil Lindley; assistant producer Gordon Elsbury; production manager Tony Newman; produced and directed by Michael Hurll.
With David 'Kid' Jensen (DJ), Adam and The Ants*, Abba*, Wizzard, Elvis Costello, Bucks Fizz, Zoo, Altered Images, Dollar, The Human League.

	TOP OF THE POPS (continued)

25.12.1981 Christmas 1981 DB-D3 / 2"

Duration: 60 minutes.

Dance direction by Flick Colby; designed by Phil Lindley; produced by Michael Hurll and Gordon Elsbury; directed by Gordon Elsbury and Michael Hurll.

With Radio 1 DJ's, The Teardrop Explodes, Ultravox, Kim Wilde, The Human League, Godley & Creme, Kirsty MacColl, Dave Stewart and Colin Blunstone, Linx, The Beat, Spandau Ballet, Toyah, Zoo, Altered Images, Depeche Mode, OMD, Shakin' Stevens, The Top of The Pops Studio.

31.12.1981 Number Ones Of 81 DB-D3 / 2"

Designed by Gordon Elsbury; executive producer Michael Hurll; produced by Gordon Elsbury; directed by Gordon Elsbury and Michael Hurll.

With Mike Read (DJ), Shakin' Stevens*, Adam and The Ants*, John Lennon*, Roxy Music*, Aneka, The Police*, The Specials, Joe Dolce Music Theatre*, Julio Igelisias*, Bucks Fizz, Dave Stewart and Barbara Gaskin*, Michael Jackson*, Smokey Robinson*, Soft Cell, The Human League*, Queen and David Bowie*.

25.12.1982 Christmas 1982 DB / 1"

Duration: 60 minutes.

Dance direction by Flick Colby; designed by Jo Day; executive producer Michael Hurll; production manager Michael Leggo; directed by Gordon Elsbury.

With Radio 1 DJ's, Spandau Ballet, Shakin' Stevens, The Human League*, Kraftwerk, The Jam, Tight Fit*, Goombay Dance Band*, Bucks Fizz, Paul McCartney and Stevie Wonder*, Madness*, Adam Ant*, Renee & Renato*, Captain Sensible, Culture Club, Irene Cara*, Survivor*, Nicole, Eddy Grant*, Soft Cell, Haircut 100, Musical Youth, Cliff Richard, Zoo.

25.12.1983 Christmas 1983 DB / 1"

Duration: 60 minutes.

Designed by Paul Trerise; production manager Tony Newman; produced and directed by Michael Hurll.

With Simon Bates (DJ), Janice Long (DJ), Mike Smith (DJ), Andy Peebles (DJ), Adrian John (DJ), Gary Davies (DJ), Freeez, Shakin' Stevens, Men At Work*, Bonnie Tyler*, Eurythmics, Irene Cara*, Adam Ant, Duran Duran*, Bucks Fizz, Lionel Richie*, Heaven 17, David Bowie*, UB40, Billy Joel*, The Flying Pickets, K.C. and The Sunshine Band.

29.12.1983 Review Of 1983 DB / 1"

Designed by Paul Trerise; production manager Tony Newman; produced and directed by Michael Hurll.

With Richard Skinner (DJ), Tommy Vance (DJ), Culture Club, Jo Boxers, Spandau Ballet, Howard Jones, Mike Oldfield*, The Thompson Twins, Tracey Ullman*, The Cure, Phil Collins*, The Belle Stars, Paul Young*, Siouxsie and The Banshees, Rod Stewart*, The Style Council, Paul McCartney and Michael Jackson*.

25.12.1984 Christmas Special 1984 DB / 1"

Duration: 60 minutes.

Designed by Richard Dupré; production team Hilary Bennett, Sue Lester, Gilly Archer and Carmella Milne; production manager Tony Newman; produced and directed by Michael Hurll.

With Frankie Goes To Hollywood, Howard Jones, Duran Duran, Nik Kershaw, Culture Club, The Thompson Twins, Jim Diamond, Wham*, Paul Young, George Michael*, Band Aid*.

27.12.1984 Review Of 1984 DB / 1"

Designed by Richard Dupré; production manager John Birkin; produced and directed by Michael Hurll.

With Lenny Henry (DJ), Neil, Spandau Ballet, Ultravox, Slade, Chaka Khan*, Shakin' Stevens, Bronski Beat, Paul McCartney*, Bananarama, Lionel Richie*, Black Lace, The Flying Pickets, Joe Fagin, Stevie Wonder*, Ray Parker Jnr*.

25.12.1985 Christmas 1985 DB / 1"

Duration: 60 minutes.

Designed by Kathy Atty; produced and directed by Michael Hurll.

With Gary Davies (DJ), Jonathan King (DJ), Janice Long (DJ), Dixie Peach (DJ), John Peel (DJ), Steve Wright (DJ), Foreigner*, King, Sister Sledge*, Colonel Abrams*, Phyllis Nelson, Midge Ure*, Alison Moyet, Eurythmics*, Paul Hardcastle*, Dead Or Alive, Philip Bailey and Phil Collins*, David Bowie and Mick Jagger*, Baltimora, The Crowd*, USA For Africa*, Band Aid*, Billy Ocean, UB40 and Chrissie Hynde*, Feargal Sharkey, Madonna*, Tears For Fears*, George Michael*, Paul Young, Elaine Paige and Barbara Dickson*, Jennifer Rush*, Wham*, Whitney Houston*, Frankie Goes To Hollywood*.

25.12.1986 Christmas 1986 DB / 1"

Alt.Title(s): *Top Of The Pops Christmas Party*

Duration: 60 minutes.

Designed by John Bristow; produced and directed by Michael Hurll.

With Peter Powell (DJ), Gary Davies (DJ), Janice Long (DJ), Simon Bates (DJ), Billy Ocean, Doctor and The Medics, Boris Gardiner, Simply Red, Pet Shop Boys, Chris De Burgh, The Communards*, A-Ha*, Europe*, Cliff Richard and The Young Ones*, Spitting Image Puppets*, Diana Ross*, Berlin*, Nick Berry*, Falco*, George Michael*, Madonna*, The Housemartins, Jackie Wilson*, Wham*.

25.12.1987 Christmas 1987 DB / 1"

Duration: 55 minutes.

Designed by Barry Read; produced and directed by Michael Hurll.

With Mike Smith (DJ), Gary Davies (DJ), The Bee Gees ('You Win Again'), Rick Astley ('Never Gonna Give You Up'), Pet Shop Boys ('It's A Sin'), T'Pau ('China In Your Hand'), Whitney Houston ('I Wanna Dance With Somebody'), Johnny Hates Jazz ('Turn Back The Clock'), Pet Shop Boys ('Always On My Mind'), Spagna ('Call Me'), Jackie Wilson*, Ben E. King*, M/A/R/R/S*, Starship*, The Firm*, Ferry Aid*, Steve Silk Hurley*, George Michael and Aretha Franklin*, Madonna*.

Untx'd film inserts (1972?) – Holland-Dozier "Why Can't We Be Lovers?", Bread "Everything I Own", The Bee Gees "My World" (sound does not match pictures?), Buffy Sainte-Marie "I'm Gonna Be A Country Girl Again".

Duration: 30 minutes.

Holding / Source

25.12.1988 Christmas 1988 DB / 1"

Duration: 60 minutes.

Designed by May Eakin; produced and directed by Brian Whitehouse.

With Anthea Turner (DJ), Bruno Brookes (DJ), Gary Davies (DJ), S'Xpress, Pet Shop Boys, Belinda Carlisle*, Tiffany*, Kylie Minogue*, Whitney Houston*, Enya, Aswad, Fairground Attraction, Climie Fisher*, Rick Astley*, Bobby MacFerrin*, Brother Beyond*, Yazz and The Plastic Population, The Timelords, Bros*, Glenn Medeiros*, Phil Collins, Robin Beck, Wet Wet Wet, The Hollies, Cliff Richard.

| TOP OF THE POPS (continued) | British Christmas Television Guide |

25.12.1989 **Christmas 1989** DB / 1"
Duration: 60 minutes.
Designed by Adele Marolf; produced and directed by Stanley Appel.
With Jakki Brambles (DJ), Bruno Brookes (DJ), Gary Davies (DJ), Erasure, Alice Cooper*, Kylie Minogue and Jason Donovan*, Mike and The Mechanics, Marc Almond and Gene Pitney, Michael Ball*, Michael Jackson*, Simple Minds*, Madonna*, Jason Donovan, Simply Red*, The Bangles*, Natalie Cole*, Various Artists*, Kylie Minogue*, Cliff Richard*, Prince*, Soul II Soul*, Bros, The London Boys, The Beautiful South, Jive Bunny and The Master Mixers*, Sonia, Lil' Louis*, Richard Marx*, Black Box, Milli Vanilli*, Technotronic Featuring Felly*, Lisa Stansfield, Phil Collins*, Linda Ronstadt and Aaron Neville*, New Kids On The Block*, Band Aid II*.

25.12.1990 **Christmas 1990** DB / 1"
Duration: 60 minutes.
Produced and directed by Paul Ciani.
With Mark Goodier (Host), Anthea Turner (Host).

25.12.1991 **Christmas 1991** DB / 1"
Duration: 60 minutes.
Produced by Stanley Appel; directed by Arch Dyson.

25.12.1992 **Christmas 1992** DB / D3
Duration: 60 minutes.
Produced by Stanley Appel; directed by Arch Dyson.

25.12.1993 **Christmas 1993** DB / D3
Duration: 60 minutes.
Produced and directed by Stanley Appel.

25.12.1994 **Christmas 1994** DB / D3
Duration: 60 minutes.
Designed by Simon Kimmel; production team Nigel Caaro and Rory Sheehan; produced by Ric Blaxill; directed by Claire Winyard.
With Take That (DJs), D:Ream [as D-Ream], Doop, Tony Di Bart, Stiltskin, Wet Wet Wet, All 4 One, Let Loose, Whigfield, Pato Banton, Eternal, East 17.

25.12.1995 **Christmas 1995** DB / D3
Duration: 60 minutes.
Produced by Ric Blaxill; directed by Claire Winyard.

25.12.1996 **Christmas 1996** DB / D3S
Duration: 65 minutes.
Produced by Ric Blaxill; directed by Anne Gilchrist.
With The Spice Girls (DJs).

24.12.1997 **Spice Girls On Top Of The Pops** DB / DBS
Produced and directed by Chris Cowey.
With The Spice Girls (DJs).

25.12.1997 **Christmas 1997** DB / D3S
Duration: 60 minutes.
Produced by Chris Cowey; directed by Phil Chilvers.

25.12.1998 **Christmas 1998** DB / D3S
Duration: 60 minutes.
Theme music by Bad Man Bad and Led Zeppelin; titles by Chris Jennings; designed by Miranda Jones; production team Sandra Palormi, Charlotte Ross and Haydn Davies; assistant producer Lee Lodge; executive producer Trevor Dann; produced and directed by Chris Cowey.
With Kate Thornton (DJ), Jamie Theakston (DJ), Jayne Middlemiss (DJ), The Spice Girls, Tamperer & Maya, Denise & Johnny, Robbie Williams, Stardust*, B*Witched, Mousse T Vs Hot 'n' Juicy, All Saints, Fat Les, LeAnn Rimes, Boyzone, Celine Dion, Jane McDonald, Cher.

25.12.1999 DB / DBS
Duration: 120 minutes.
Executive producer Trevor Dann; series producer Chris Cowey; directed by Chris Cowey.

24.12.2000 **Tweenies Special** DB / DBSW
Duration: 25 minutes.

25.12.2000 **Christmas 2000** DB / DBSW
Duration: 60 minutes.

25.12.2001 DB / DBSW

25.12.2002 **Christmas 2002** DB / DBSW
Duration: 60 minutes.

25.12.2003 **All New Christmas 2003** DB / DBSW

25.12.2004 **Christmas 2004** DB / DBSW

25.12.2005 **Christmas 2005** DB / DBSW
Duration: 60 minutes.

Holding / Source

25.12.2006 **Christmas 2006** DB / DBSW
Duration: 60 minutes.

25.12.2007 **Christmas Special** DB / DBSW
Duration: 60 minutes.

25.12.2008 **Christmas** DB / DBSW
Duration: 60 minutes.

TOP OF THE POPS

British Christmas Television Guide	TOP OF THE POPS (continued)

31.12.2008 New Year's Eve Special DB / DBSW
Duration: 65 minutes.
Script supervisor Sandra Palormi; designed by Miranda Jones; production executive Stephania Minici; executive producer Mark Cooper; production manager Joanne Housden; produced by Sally Wood; directed by Phil Heyes.
With Reggie Yates (DJ), Fearne Cotton (DJ), Girls Aloud, Coldplay, Gabriella Cilmi, Kaiser Chiefs, Sam Sparro, The Pussycat Dolls, McFly, Adele, Keane, Duffy, The Last Shadow Puppets, Take That, Leona Lewis, The cast of Mamma Mia!, Alexandra Burke.

25.12.2009 Top Of The Pops Christmas HD/DB / HDC
A BBC Productions production. Duration: 60 minutes.
Script supervisor Sandra Palormi; designed by Markus Blee; assistant producer Arianna Maniscalco; production executive Stephania Minici; executive producer Mark Cooper; production manager Vicky Singer; produced by Sally Wood; directed by Phil Heyes.
With Fearne Cotton (DJ), Reggie Yates (DJ), Alexandra Burke, Dizzee Rascal, The Saturdays, Muse, La Roux, Sugababes, JLS, Florence and The Machine, Diversity, Kasabian, Shakira, Robbie Williams.

31.12.2009 Top Of The Pops New Year's Eve HD/DB / HDC
A BBC Productions production. Duration: 60 minutes.
Script supervisor Sandra Palormi; designed by Markus Blee; assistant producer Arianna Maniscalco; production executive Stephania Minici; executive producer Mark Cooper; production manager Vicky Singer; produced by Sally Wood; directed by Phil Heyes.
With Fearne Cotton (DJ), Reggie Yates (DJ), Robbie Williams, Shakira, JLS, Calvin Harris, N-Dubz, Alexandra Burke, Muse, Sugababes, Florence and The Machine, Dizzee Rascal, Joe McElderry.

25.12.2010 Christmas HD/DB / HDC
Duration: 60 minutes.
Script supervisor Sandra Palormi; designed by Jonathan Paul Green; assistant producer Holly Murray; production executive Stephania Minici; executive producer Mark Cooper; production manager Gesa Schlotfeldt; produced by Sally Wood; directed by Phil Heyes.
With Fearne Cotton (DJ), Reggie Yates (DJ), Cee Lo Green, Ellie Goulding, Jason Derulo, Olly Murs, Eliza Doolittle, Scouting For Girls, Take That, Tinie Tempah, JLS, Plan B, Coldplay.

25.12.2011 Christmas HD/DB / HDC
Duration: 60 minutes.
Script supervisor Sandra Palormi; designed by Chris Webster; assistant producer Caroline Cullen; production executive Stephania Minici; executive producer Mark Cooper; production manager Joanne Housden; produced by Stephanie McWhinnie; directed by Julian Smith.
With Reggie Yates (DJ), Fearne Cotton (DJ), Example, Professor Green featuring Emeli Sandé, Will Young, Olly Murs, Nicki Minaj*, Bruno Mars*, Adele*, Jennifer Lopez Featuring Pitbull*, LMFAO*, Lady GaGa*, Tinchy Stryder And Dappy*, Ed Sheeran, The Wanted, Jessie J, Noah and The Whale, Maroon 5 Featuring Christina Aguilera*, Rihanna Featuring Calvin Harris*, Pixie Lott, The Vaccines, Rizzle Kicks, Little Mix, Gareth Malone With The Military Wives*.

25.12.2012 Christmas HD/DB / HDC
Duration: 60 minutes.
Executive producer Mark Cooper; produced by Stephanie McWhinnie.
With Fearne Cotton (DJ), Reggie Yates (DJ), Robbie Williams, Girls Aloud, Emeli Sandé, Rita Ora, Wiley and The Rudimental, Sam and The Womp, Carly Rae Jepsen.

31.12.2012 New Year's Eve Special HD/DB / HDC
Duration: 60 minutes.
Executive producer Mark Cooper; produced by Stephanie McWhinnie.
With Fearne Cotton (DJ), Reggie Yates (DJ), Tinie Tempah, Robbie Williams, Rita Ora, Girls Aloud, The Script, Tulisa Contostavlos, Calvin Harris, Ellie Goulding, Rizzle Kicks, Stooshe, The Maccabees.

25.12.2013 Christmas HD/DB / HDC
Duration: 60 minutes.
Executive producer Mark Cooper; produced by Stephanie McWhinnie; directed by Julian Smith.

01.12.2013 New Year HD/DB / HDC
Duration: 60 minutes.
Executive producer Mark Cooper; produced by Stephanie McWhinnie; directed by Julian Smith.
With Little Mix, James Arthur, The Vamps, London Grammar, John Newman.

Acts marked with an asterisk indicate they were not live in the studio. Kaleidoscope's "Top Pop" book provides full information on every show.

TOP OF THE YEAR

A BBC production for BBC 1. Transmission details are for BBC 1. Duration varies - see below for details.

Holding / Source

31.12.1971 "The Variety Club Awards for 1971" R1 / 2"
Duration: 120 minutes.
Introduced by Michael Aspel; music directed by Ronnie Hazlehurst; designed by Ken Sharp; executive producer Philip Lewis; produced by Ian Smith and Michael Hurll.
With Bernard Delfont (Chief Barker), Frankie Howerd, Canon David Edwards.

31.12.1972 "The Variety Club Awards for 1972" DB-1" / 2"
Duration: 105 minutes.
Introduced by Michael Aspel; music directed by Burt Rhodes; designed by Bernard Lloyd-Jones; executive producer Philip Lewis; produced by Ian Smith, Alan Tarrant and James Moir; directed by Ian Smith, Alan Tarrant and James Moir.
With Bruce Forsyth, Clodagh Rodgers, Neville King, Reverend Austen Williams.

31.12.1973 "The Variety Club Awards for 1973" J / 2"
Duration: 95 minutes.
Introduced by Michael Aspel; music directed by Burt Rhodes; designed by Eric Walmsley; executive producer Philip Lewis; produced by Ken Griffin and Terry Henebery; directed by Brian Whitehouse.
With Canon David Edwards.

TOP OF THE YEAR (continued)

The titles for the edition t/x'd 31.12.73 exist on D3.

31.12.1974 "The Variety Club Awards for 1974" DB-D3 / 2"
Duration: 71 minutes.
Introduced by Michael Aspel; music directed by Burt Rhodes; produced and directed by Ken Griffin.
With Bernard Delfont, Claire Bloom, Tom Courtney, Jean Marsh, Ronnie Barker, Susannah York, Michael Crawford.

TOPPER'S TALES

A Yorkshire Television production. Transmission details are for the ATV midlands region. Duration: 8 minutes.

SERIES 1
Main regular credit(s): Drawings by Peter Parr; music by Peter Husband; produced and directed by Joy Whitby.
Main regular cast: With Julian Orchard (Narrator).

	VT Number	Holding / Source
09.11.1978 Honey For Christmas	C154	C1 / C1

SERIES 2
Main regular credit(s): Written by Julian Orchard; drawings by Peter Parr; produced and directed by Joy Whitby.
Main regular cast: With Julian Orchard (Narrator).

	VT Number	Holding / Source
20.12.1979 Father Christmas	C160	C1 / C1

TORCHY THE BATTERY BOY

Produced for ABC by a variety of companies (see details below). Transmission details are for the ABC midlands region. Duration: 15 minutes.

Main regular cast: Kenneth Connor (Voices), Olwen Griffiths (Voices), Jill Raymond (Voices), Patricia Somerset (Voices).

SERIES 2
An Associated British Pathe production for Roberta Leigh.
Main regular credit(s): Written by Roberta Leigh; lyrics by Roberta Leigh; music by Roberta Leigh and Barry Gray; produced by Roberta Leigh; directed by Vivian Milroy.

	Holding / Source
24.04.1960 Flopsy Makes A Christmas Pudding	B3 / B3

Alternative transmissions: Associated-Rediffusion: 20.12.1960.

Shown as part of SMALL TIME in London and some other regions.

TORVILL & DEAN WITH THE RUSSIAN ALL-STARS

A Central production. Transmission details are for the Central region. Duration: 50 minutes.

A contemporary ice spectacular from Nottingham Ice Rink, combining the artistry of Jayne Torvill and Christopher Dean with the excitement of the Russian Olympic skating stars.

Produced by Paula Burdon; directed by Nigel Lythgoe.

Torvill & Dean.

	Holding / Source
25.12.1990	1" / 1"

TOTS TV

A Ragdoll production for Central. Transmission details are for the Central region. Duration: 20 minutes.

Main regular cast: Jane Pardoe (Host).

SERIES 4

	Holding / Source
18.12.1996 Christmas Decorations	D2 / C1S

TOTTIE - THE STORY OF A DOLL'S HOUSE

A Smallfilms production for BBC 1. made in association with Goldcrest Films & Television Ltd. Transmission details are for BBC 1.

	Holding / Source
09.02.1984 Emily And Charlotte's Christmas Present Is Another Beautiful Doll	C1 / C1

A TOUCH OF FROST

An Excelsior Films production for Yorkshire Television. Transmission details are for the Central region. Duration varies - see below for details.

Main regular cast: David Jason (Detective Inspector Jack Frost), Bruce Alexander (Superintendent Mullett).

SERIES 7: Line Of Fire
Duration: 76 minutes.

Main regular credit(s): Written by Michael Russell; based on characters created by R. D. Wingfield; executive producers David Jason, David Reynolds, Richard Bates and Philip Burley; produced by Lars Macfarlane; directed by Robert Knights.

Main regular cast: With Lindy Whiteford (Shirley Fisher), Paul Jesson (Detective Sergeant Dorridge), Christopher Hollis (Detective Inspector Newcombe), Nicky Henson (Detective Sergeant Finlay), Beth Goddard (Helen Fox), Ben Caplan (Sam Goodwin), Georgia Mackenzie (Police Constable Susan Kavanagh), Trevor Byfield (George English), James McKenna (Sergeant Brady), Daniel Caltagirone (Ray English), Martina Laird (Miriam Madikane), Amanda Haberland (Tracy Cockroft), Emma Cooke (Sally Wainwright), Tara Moran (Anne Moore), David Spinx (Dick Rycroft), Lesley Nicol (Mrs Cockroft), Katie Williamson (Female Detective), Ryan Leigh (Keith), James Telfer (Menzies Hamilton), Paula Mason (Canteen Lady), Heather Pheonix (Bank Cashier), Andrew Norris (Barman), Joan Campion (Mrs Lampkin), Arthur White (Ernie Trigg).

		VT Number	Holding / Source
25.12.1999	**Episode 1**	L672/01	DB / V1SSW

With David Gooderson (Pathologist), Sally Knyvette, Bernard Holley, Graeme Hawley, Christine Brennan, Ali Bastian, Sarah Niles, Michael Simkins, Ian Embleton, Osmund Bullock, Jack Chissick.

01.01.2000	**Episode 2**	L672/02	DB / V1SSW

With Andrew Reece, Richard Stone, Adrian Schiller, Nicholas Hutchinson, Christopher Brennan.

A TOUCH OF THE CASANOVAS

Alternative/Working Title(s): CASANOVA

A Thames Television production. Transmission details are for the ATV midlands region. Duration: 36 minutes.

It's the lad himself, Frankie Howerd, as Francisco, body servant ("No, no... wait a minute...") to the great lover Giacomo Casanova. Casanova is having a spot of bother with the Doge of Venice, and proposes a change of identities with Francisco to keep out of the clutches of the Doge's police. Only then does Francisco discover that being Casanova is not always a bed of roses...

Written by Sid Collin and Hugh Stuckey; designed by John Wood; produced and directed by Michael Mills.

Frankie Howerd (Fransisco), Stuart Damon (Casanova), Patsy Rowlands (Clementina), Madeline Smith (Teresa), Marguerite Hardiman (Isabella), Leon Greene (Captain of the Guard), John Cater (Bartoldi), Roger Brierley (Count Pelligrini), Patricia Haines (Countess Pelligrini), Cyril Appleton (Count Malatesta), Gregory Powell (Doge's Guard), Billy Horrigan (Doge's Guard), Terry Maidment (Doge's Guard).

	VT Number	Holding / Source
31.12.1975	11809	D3 / 2"

THE TOYS THAT MADE CHRISTMAS

A BBC production for BBC 2. Transmission details are for BBC 2. Duration: 90 minutes.

Fed up with seeing games consoles and iPods unwrapped? Hankering for the days when toys were toys? Then watch this for a sharp pang of die-cast nostalgia. It's a portrait of old-school desirables such as Matchbox cars, Spirograph sets and Subbuteo. One contributor tells how his mother ("a game gal") started a gasket factory in her garden to help the war effort; to keep her workers' children happy she gave them bits of felt and place mats to play with, and right there was born the joy of Fuzzy Felt.

Executive producer Caroline Wright; produced by Suzannah Wander.

Robert Webb (Narrator).

	Holding / Source
25.12.2011	HD/DB / HDC

THE TRACTATE MIDDOTH

A BBC production for BBC 2. Transmission details are for BBC 2. Duration: 35 minutes.

When John Eldred goes in search of a special book at a university library, a young student who tries to help is drawn into a family feud over a will - with terrifying consequences.

Adapted by Mark Gatiss; based on a story by M. R. James; produced by Susie Liggat; directed by Mark Gatiss.

Sacha Dhawan (Garrett), John Castle (John Eldred), Louise Jameson (Mrs Simpson), Una Stubbs (Miss Chambers), David Ryall (Rant), Eleanor Bron (Mrs Goundry), Nicholas Burns (George Earle), Roy Barraclough (Hodgson), Charlie Clemmow (Anne Simpson), Matthew Foster (Labourer).

	Holding / Source
25.12.2013	HD/DB / HDC

TRAVELLERS' TALES

A BBC production. Transmission details are for BBC/BBC1. Duration: 25 minutes.

SERIES 1

	Holding / Source
28.12.1956 **Laplanders And Reindeer**	B3 / B3

TREASURE HUNT

A Westward Television production. Transmission details are for the Westward Television region. Duration: 25 minutes.

SERIES 14

	Holding / Source
26.12.1975 **Christmas Treasure Hunt**	J / 2"

TREE HOUSE FAMILY

An ATV production. Transmission details are for the ATV London region. Duration: 20 minutes.

Main regular credit(s): Designed by Rex Spencer; produced by Jean Morton; directed by John Pullen.
Main regular cast: Jean Morton (Host), The Tree House Family.
Main regular credit(s): Religious adviser Reverend Phillip Cliff.

	Holding / Source
31.12.1967 **The Three Wise Men**	J / 40

TRESARN

A BBC Wales production for BBC 1 Wales. Transmission details are for BBC 1 Wales. Duration: 30 minutes.

	Holding / Source
22.12.1971	J / 2"

TRIGGER HAPPY TV

An Absolutely production for Channel 4. Transmission details are for Channel 4. Duration: 25 minutes.

Main regular cast: Dom Joly (Presenter).

	Holding / Source
21.12.2001	DB / DBSW
24.12.2001	DB / DBSW

TRIPLE BILL

A BBC Manchester production for BBC 2. Transmission details are for BBC 2. Duration: 50 minutes.

Produced and directed by Mike Stephens.

Dave Shannon (Presenter), Ralph McTell, Therapy, The McClamans.

	Holding / Source
23.12.1982	DB-D3 / 2"

TROLLIED

A Roughcut production for Sky One. Transmission details are for Sky One. Duration varies - see below for details.

SERIES 2

Credits: Story producer Alexander Smith; designed by Julian Fullalove; executive producers Ash Atalla, Lucy Lumsden and Jon Mountague; series producer Nick Goding; produced by Rachel Salter; directed by Jonathan Gershfield.

Cast: With Jason Watkins (Gavin), Rita May (Margaret), Carl Rice (Colin), Beverley Rudd (Lisa), Lorraine Cheshire (Sue), Faye McKeever (Linda), Dominic Coleman (Neville), Victor McGuire (Ian), Jane Horrocks (Julie), Mark Addy (Andy), Nick Blood (Kieran), Chanel Cresswell (Katie), Joel Fry (Leighton), Jo Enright (Sharon).

	Holding / Source
24.12.2012 **Christmas Special**	HD/DB / HDC

Duration: 48 minutes.

Wigan, following the theft of essential supplies by a rival Valco store. Gavin leads a rescue attempt in an HGV and encounters some surprises. Viewers would be best advised to save their gasps, though, for the staff party, in which Lisa takes dirty dancing to a whole new level of filth, while Colin offers up a karaoke rendition of Wham's Last Christmas filled with raw emotion.

Written by Paul Doolan, Chris Hayward and Nat Saunders.

With Joe Shire (Customer), Leona Walker (Customer), David Ryall (Vic), Rebecca Jade Hammond (Customer), Warren Clarke (Barry Hound), Ian Botham (Self).

SERIES 3

Credits: Designed by Julian Fullalove and Gary Brown; executive producers Ash Atalla and Jon Mountague; series producer Nick Goding; produced by Alexander Smith; directed by Paul Harrison.

Cast: With Jason Watkins (Gavin), Rita May (Margaret), Carl Rice (Colin), Beverley Rudd (Lisa), Lorraine Cheshire (Sue), Faye McKeever (Linda), Dominic Coleman (Neville), Victor McGuire (Ian), Jane Horrocks (Julie), Joel Fry (Leighton), Adeel Akhtar (Ray), Danny Kirrane (Dave).

	Holding / Source
24.12.2013 **Christmas Special**	HD/DB / HDC

Duration: 48 minutes.

Gavin invites Julie for dinner.

Written by Paul Doolan and Abigail Wilson.

With David Calder (Santa), Owen Brady (Morris), Selina Griffiths (Helen), Paul Thornley (Mike), Oliver Woollford (Bully Scout), Kate Adams (Customer), Tim Prior (Customer), Frank Rozelaar-Green (Customer), Geri Halliwell (Self).

THE TROUBLESHOOTERS

A BBC production for BBC 1. Transmission details are for BBC 1. Usual duration: 50 minutes.

Main regular credit(s): Created by John Elliot; theme music by Tom Springfield.

SERIES 3

Main regular credit(s): Produced by Peter Graham Scott.

Holding / Source

22.12.1967 Rest You Merry   J /

Written by Eve Martell; designed by John Hurst; directed by Peter Cregeen.

With Ray Barrett (Peter Thornton), Geoffrey Keen (Brian Stead), Philip Latham (Willy Izard), Isobel Black (Eileen O'Rourke), Edward De Souza (Charles Grandmercy), Harry Towb (Calwin McQuitty), Wanda Ventham (Moira), Gerard Heinz (Doctor Freimann), Julian Battersby (Ken Roach), James Fitzgerald (Mike McCormick), Dermot Tuohy (Charlie Woods), Rio Fanning (Harry Cobbett), Edward Malin (Dan).

SERIES 6

Main regular credit(s): Associate producer Michael Glynn; produced by Anthony Read.

Main regular cast: With Geoffrey Keen (Brian Stead), Ray Barrett (Peter Thornton), Philip Latham (Willy Izard), John Carson (James Langley).

Holding / Source

03.01.1972 Whatever Became Of The Year 2000?   R1 / 2"

Written by John Elliot; directed by Cyril Coke.

With Dawn Addams, James Villiers, Ralph Arliss, Tania Robinson, Robin Stewart.

In text, the title was always billed as two words, but on screen the second word was split across two lines.

THE TRUTH ABOUT CHRISTMAS

A BBC Birmingham production for BBC 1. Transmission details are for BBC 1. Duration: 30 minutes.

Carols, songs, poems and original opinions.

Conducted by Roy Currie; produced by Mike Dornan; directed by John S. W. Taylor.

Richard Stilgoe (Presenter), Broom Leys Junior School, Wollescote Primary School, Peter's Hill School, Stourbridge.

Holding / Source

14.12.1988   DB / 1"

Alternative transmissions: BBC 1 Midlands: 18.12.1984.

This is the network date. It was shown previously only in the Midlands.

TRY FOR TEN

A TWW production. Transmission details are for the TWW (General) region. Duration: 30 minutes.

Holding / Source

25.12.1962   J /

THE TUBE

A Tyne Tees Television production for Channel 4. Transmission details are for Channel 4. Duration varies - see below for details.

Friday November 5 1982... the launch of Channel 4. 'Countdown' came first and its flagship pop music extravaganza 'The Tube' burst on to screens later. The first edition saw Toy Dolls sing She Goes To Finos, Heaven 17 perform Height Of The Fighting / Who Will Stop The Rain? Let Me Go, and The Jam did Ghost ,A Town Called Malice, This Is The Modern World, In The Crowd, The Great Depression, Move On Up and Precious/Leading Into War. All live.

Jools Holland was co-presenter with the now deceased Paula Yates - together their irreverent chemistry made 'The Tube' unique. Jools says they succeeded at the audition, because they were not clichéd and cute TV presenters.

Creator/Producers Malcolm Gerrie and Andrea Wonfor looked at the perspex tunnel entrance to their office at Tyne Tees TV and it inspired the programme's title.

Former producers Chris Cowey and Chris Phipps were part of a production team of music fans who launched Wet, Wet, Wet, Cameo, Frankie Goes to Hollywood, The Housemartins and Fine Young Cannibals, to name a few unknowns who got their first break on 'The Tube'.

For every unknown, there was a giant act. Tina Turner's renaissance began on The Tube in 1983, Madonna made her debut in the UK in 1984 and Paul Young sang on two consecutive live appearances that boosted his profile internationally. Paul Young says now that Gavin Taylor and the camera team made it more of a club gig than the formulaic Top of the Pops concept.

It was a live and frenetic programme to work on. The Big Tube in August 1985 was billed and trailed on TV, but cancelled at the last minute. Specials such as Eurotube in July 1986 pushed the boundaries of expectation. Live from Wembley Stadium, groups such as Pet Shop Boys, Zodiac Mindwarp, The Smiths, Arcadia, Yello and Rod Stewart performed for a Tyne Tees TV show that had a tiny budget but a massive influence.

Comedy was a new form of rock 'n' roll showcased by 'The Tube' - Vic Reeves remembers his TV debut on the Tube's spoof of 'Celebrity Squares'. Alongside Vic there was French and Saunders, Rik Mayall, Robbie Coltrane and a whole cutting-edge crew. One such spoof was The Laughing Prisoner in 1987. Poking fun at The Prisoner it featured Stephen Fry, Stanley Unwin, Siouxsie & The Banshees performing "Passengers, XTC performing "The Man Who Sailed Around His Soul" with Magnum, Jools Holland, Hugh Laurie and Terence Alexander. Showcasing local talent, John Peel introduced Welsh bands Anhrefn, Y Cyrff and Datblygu performing "Casserole". Lots of clips from the original Prisoner programmes starring Patrick McGoohan were interspersed into this bizarre occasion!

In 1999, Tyne Tees re-booted the formula. Chris Moyles and Donna Air hosted a major live three-hour broadcast. The one-off special saw a re-birth of The Tube. Acts included The Artist Formerly Known As Prince, Belle and Sebastian, Underworld, Robbie Williams, Travis, Skunk Anansie and Paul McCartney. Comedy came from Adam Bloom, The Pod and Matt Lucas.

Attempts to release the first series on DVD were stuck in copyright hell but a highlights DVD has since come out. The Tube was eclectic and ground-breaking and will never be seen again.

As creator, Andrea Wonfor says, 'The Tube - more an attitude than a TV programme'.

Main regular credit(s): Format by Andrea Wonfor.

SERIES 1
Duration: 78 minutes.

Main regular credit(s): Written by Tube Department; theme music by Jeff Beck and Jan Hammer; designed by Peter Bingeman, Eric Briers, Jane Coleman and Tim Trout; associate producers Jeff Brown and Lesley Oakden; film sequences directed by Peter Carr and Geoff Wonfor.

Main regular performer(s): With Jools Holland (Host), Paula Yates (Host, Except Number 11).

Holding / Source

24.12.1982 Christmas Eve — 1" / 1"

Christmas Eve - live in Studio Five.

Produced by Paul Corley and Malcolm Gerrie; directed by Malcolm Dickinson and Gavin Taylor.

With Mark Miwurdz (Host), Gary James (Host), Michael Cremona (Host), Nick Laird-Clowes (Host), Muriel Gray (Host), Foffo Spearjig, Brian Johnson, Beatles Ladies, Old Mother Eilly, Paul Shriek, The Bouncing Czechs, Alf, Sylvie and The Sapphires, Depeche Mode, Imagination, Gary Newman.

SERIES 5
Duration: 79 minutes.

Main regular credit(s): Executive producer Malcolm Gerrie; series producer John Gwynne.

Holding / Source

25.12.1986 Eric Clapton And Friends — 1" / 1"

Produced by Ken Schofield; directed by Gavin Taylor.

With Eric Clapton, Phil Collins.

Commissioned by Sky One.

Holding / Source

01.01.2000 Apocalypse Tube — DB / DBSW

Duration: 180 minutes.

Alternative transmissions: Sky One: 20.11.1999.

Directed by Geoff Wonfor.

With Donna Air (Presenter), Chris Moyles (Presenter), Jon Carter (DJ), Nick Warren (DJ), Seb Fontaine (DJ), Lottie (DJ), Carl Cox (DJ), The Artist Formerly Known As Prince, Robbie Williams, Belle and Sebastian, Underworld, Travis, Beverley Knight, Skunk Ananse, Paul McCartney, Adam Bloom, Henry Phillips, The Pod, Matt Lucas.

##.##.#### The Inner Tube — DB / DBSW

Duration: 24 minutes.

Originally scheduled for 07.01.2000.

Produced by Sheilagh Matheson and Liz Treadway; directed by Geoff Wonfor.

With Chris Moyles (Presenter), Donna Air (Presenter), Paul McCartney, The Artist Formerly Known As Prince, Robbie Williams.

Behind the scenes programme.

THE TURN OF THE SCREW

An Associated-Rediffusion production. Transmission details are for Associated-Rediffusion. Duration: 100 minutes.

Opera. The story of the opera is taken from Henry James famous ghost novel which tells of the conflict between the governess of two children, and the ghosts of a former governess and manservant who try to get possession of their souls.

Libretto by Myfanwy Piper; written by Benjamin Britten; orchestra conducted by Charles Mackerras; designed by John Piper; produced by Michael Yates; directed by Peter Morley.

Raymond Nilsson (The Prologue), Jennifer Vyvyan (The Governess), Tom Bevan (Miles), Janette Miller (Flora), Judith Pierce (Mrs Grose, The Housekeeper), Arda Mandikian (Miss Jessel, Former Governess), The English Opera Group Orchestra.

		Holding / Source
25.12.1959	Act I	DB-R3|n / 2"
28.12.1959	Act II	DB-R3|n / 2"

Also on digital formats: WAV(audio master), LTO5 (master) and MP4 (viewing copy).

THE TURN OF THE SCREW

A Martin Pope Productions production for Meridian. Transmission details are for the Central region. Duration: 94 minutes.

Adapted by Nick Dear; based on a book by Henry James; executive producers Michele Buck and Tim Vaughan; produced by Martin Pope; directed by Ben Bolt.

Pam Ferris (Mrs Grose), Jodhi May (Miss, The Governess), Colin Firth (Master), Grace Robinson (Flora), Caroline Pegg (Miss Jessell), Jenny Howe (Cook), Jason Salkey (Quint), Joe Sowerbutts (Miles).

	Holding / Source
26.12.1999	DB / V1SW

THE TURN OF THE SCREW

A BBC Productions production for BBC 1. Transmission details are for BBC 1. Duration: 90 minutes.

Adapted by Sandy Welch; based on a book by Henry James; script supervisor Elaine Matthews; script editor Claire Bennett; music by John Lunn; director of photography Tony Miller; consultant Gordon Ronald; art director Pilar Foy; designed by Stevie Herbert; executive producer Jessica Pope; line producer Chris Ballantyne; produced by Colin Wratten; directed by Tim Fywell.

Michelle Dockery (Ann), Eva Sayer (Flora), Josef Lindsay (Miles), Dan Stevens (Doctor Fisher), Mark Umbers (Master), Corin Redgrave (Professor), Wendy Albiston (Baines), Nicola Walker (Carla), Sue Johnston (Sarah Grose), Sarah Buckland (Diane), Edward MacLiam (Peter Quint), Katie Lightfoot (Emily Jessel), Nellie Burroughes (Abused Maid), Peter Bygott (Ann's Father), Honor Cargill-Martin (Young Ann), Cameron Stewart (Police Inspector).

	Holding / Source
30.12.2009	HD/DB / HD/DB

TURN OF THE YEAR

Alternative/Working Title(s): ALL THAT GLITTERS

An ATV production. Transmission details are for the ATV midlands region. Duration: 25 minutes.

Programme associate Jonathan Wright Miller.

		Production No	VT Number	Holding / Source
13.12.1970	The Christmas Present	2402	2402/70	J / 2"

Written by Andrew Davies; designed by Stanley Mills; directed by Pembroke Duttson.

With Louis Selwyn (Brian), Freddy Foote (Gary), Bill Matthews (Nightwatchman).

| 20.12.1970 | The Six-Horse Accumulator | 2403 | 2403/70/PAL | J / 2" |

It is the last betting day before Christmas, and Henry Selby, a battered old ex-demolition worker, goes into the corner betting shop to find that his first horse in a six-horse accumulator has won. How will Henry, who's been kicked around all his life, cope with the prospect of winning a lot of money?

Written by Stuart Douglass; designed by Trevor Paterson; directed by Victor Rudolf.

With Jack Woolgar (Henry Selby), Harry Landis (Jim Blake), Nikolas Simmonds (Layabout).

TV TIMES CHRISTMAS EXTRA: MEET THE STARS (ADVERTISEMENT)

A Lintas production for TV Times. Transmission details are for the ATV midlands region. Duration: 3 minutes.

Sidney James (Presenter).

	Holding / Source
##.##.####	C1|n / C1

1970 advertising film for the TV Times.

TWELVE DAYS TO CHRISTMAS

An Associated-Rediffusion production. Transmission details are for Associated-Rediffusion. Duration: 25 minutes.

Music by Ron Grainer; conducted by Billy Ternent; settings by Frederick Gray; produced by Eric Fawcett.

Edrich Connor, C. Denier Warren, Thomas Round, Hugh Sinclair, Doreen Lane, Dennis Bowen, Viera, Léon Goossens, A Group of Twelve, The Bert Stimmel Dancers.

		Holding / Source
12.12.1955	... or Someone Had To Start It!	J /

TWELVE-FIVE SPECIAL

A BBC production. Transmission details are for BBC. Duration: 40 minutes.

Join the New Year celebrations in the restaurant overlooking the runway at London Airport.

Written by Trevor Peacock; produced by Jack Good, Dennis Main Wilson and Dennis Monger; directed by Jack Good, Dennis Main Wilson and Dennis Monger.

Josephine Douglas, Pete Murray, Freddie Mills, Don Lang and his Frantic Five, The Jazz Couriers, Tubby Hayes, Ronnie Scott, Wee Willie Harris.

	Holding / Source
01.01.1958	J /

TWENTY YEARS OF WESTWARD TELEVISION

A Westward Television production. Transmission details are for the Westward Television region. Duration: 31 minutes.

Roger Shaw (Presenter).

	Holding / Source
20.12.1981	DB / 2"

TWICE KNIGHTLY

A Barron Knights Ltd production for Channel 4. Transmission details are for Channel 4. Duration: 50 minutes.

Produced by Butch Baker; directed by Terry Steel.

The Barron Knights.

	Holding / Source
25.12.1983	1" / 1"

TWO DOORS DOWN

A BBC production for BBC 1. Transmission details are for BBC 1. Duration: 60 minutes.

One-off TV adaptation of Radio 4's sitcom about the Bohemian residents of a road in Belfast. Family, friends and neighbours descend on Beth and Eric, ruining their Hogmanay.

Written by Simon Carlyle; produced by Justin Davies; directed by Catherine Morshead.

Alex Norton (Eric), Arabella Weir (Beth), Daniela Nardini (Caroline), Greg McHugh (Tony), Doon Mackichan (Cathy), Jonathan Watson (Colin), Kevin Guthrie (Ian), Sharon Rooney (Sophie), Jefferson Hall (Henning), Zoe Harrison (Nina), James Young (Angus), Jasmin Riggins (Ashley), James Allenby-Kirk (Gordy), Connor Curren (Maitland).

	Holding / Source
31.12.2013	HD/DB / HDC

TWO FAT LADIES

A BBC production for BBC 2. Transmission details are for BBC 2.

Jennifer Paterson (Chef), Clarissa Dickson Wright (Chef).

	Holding / Source
24.12.1997 **Christmas**	DB-D3 / D3S

Duration: 30 minutes.

In this yuletide tour, chefs Jennifer Paterson and Clarissa Dickson Wright visit Winchester. where they prepare a feast for the cathedral's choirboys. For their meal, they select a goose from Walsgrove farm, which they stuff with pate and prunes and serve with Swedish red cabbage, before ending with a Christmas pudding ice-cream bombe.

Executive producer Peter Gillbe; produced by Patricia Llewellyn.

THE TWO OF US

An LWT production. Transmission details are for the Central region.

Main regular credit(s):	Written by Alex Shearer.
Main regular cast:	Nicholas Lyndhurst (Ashley), Janet Dibley (Elaine).

SERIES 3

Main regular credit(s):	Designed by Gordon Melhuish; executive producer Marcus Plantin; produced by Robin Carr.
Main regular cast:	With Tenniel Evans (Perce).

	Holding / Source
23.12.1988 **Wedded Miss**	D2 / 1"

Duration: 51 minutes.

After three years of persuasion, Elaine finally agrees to marry Ashley. They discuss their honeymoon and opt for a skiing trip to Switzerland. But all the best laid plans...

Directed by Robin Carr.

With Jennifer Piercey (Mrs Philips), Paul McDowell (Mr Philips), Mark Jax (Gordon), Francesca Hall (Karen), Elizabeth Morgan, Richard Denning.

TWO PINTS OF LAGER AND A PACKET OF CRISPS

A BBC production for BBC Choice/BBC 3. Transmission details are for BBC 3. Duration varies - see below for details.

Main regular credit(s): Created by Susan Nickson; theme music by Christian Henson.
Main regular cast: Will Mellor (Gaz), Natalie Casey (Donna).

SERIES 4
Commissioned by BBC 3.

Main regular credit(s): Script supervisor Dale Byrne; script editor Paul Mayhew-Archer; music by Christian Henson; designed by Harry Banks; associate producer Susan Nickson; production executive Sarah Hitchcock; executive producers Sophie Clarke-Jervoise and Michael Jacob; produced by Stephen McCrum; directed by Gareth Carrivick.
Main regular cast: With Ralf Little (Jonny), Kathryn Drysdale (Louise), Sheridan Smith (Janet).

Holding / Source

21.12.2003 **The Musical: When Janet Met Johnny** DB / DBSW
Duration: 28 minutes.
Alternative transmissions: BBC 2: 10.05.2004.
Written by Susan Nickson; music by Simon Brint.
With No guest cast.

THE TWO RONNIES SKETCHBOOK

A BBC production for BBC 1. Transmission details are for BBC 1.

Main regular credit(s): Programme associate Danny Dignan; script associate Ged Parsons; script supervisor Teresa Powick; theme music by Ronnie Hazlehurst; assistant producer Liz Trott; production executive Katie Lecompte; executive producers Beatrice Ballard and Kevin Bishop; produced by Sam Donnelly; directed by Stuart McDonald.
Main regular cast: Ronnie Barker (Various roles), Ronnie Corbett (Various roles).

Holding / Source

25.12.2005 **The Two Ronnies Christmas Sketchbook** DB / DBSW
Duration: 65 minutes.
Written by Ronnie Barker [credited as Gerard Wiley], Bryan Blackburn, David McKellar, Spike Mullins, Colin Pearson, David Renwick and Peter Vincent; additional material by Ged Parsons.
With Katie Melua.

A tribute programme on 4.10.2005 featured contributions from Peter Hall, David Frost, Sydney Lotterby, Ian La Frenais, Dick Clement, Michael Parkinson, Lynda Baron, David Jason, Christopher Biggins, Leslie Phillips and Ronnie Corbett amongst others. Narrated by Jonathan Ross. BBC1.
See also: THE TWO RONNIES (BBC)

THE TWO RONNIES

A BBC production for BBC 1. Transmission details are for BBC 1. Duration varies - see below for details.

Main regular performer(s): Ronnie Corbett (Various roles), Ronnie Barker (Various roles).

SERIES 2
Main regular credit(s): Orchestra directed by Ronnie Hazlehurst; produced and directed by Terry Hughes.
Main regular performer(s): With Georgie Fame [as Price and Fame], Alan Price [as Price and Fame].

Holding / Source

26.12.1973 **The Two Ronnies Old Fashioned Christmas Mystery** DB-D3 / 2"
Duration: 58 minutes.
Written by Gerald Wiley; additional dialogue by David Nobbs, Peter Vincent, Spike Mullins and Dick Vosburgh; music by Ronnie Hazlehurst, Alan Braden and Ronnie Cass; choreography by Gillian Lynne; designed by Martin Collins.
With Cheryl Kennedy, Gabrielle Drake, Tux and his Flying Kitchen, Barrie Gosney, Lesley Hand, Sally James, Barbara New, John Rutland, April Walker, The Fred Tomlinson Singers.
Serial: Done To Death.

SERIES 6
Duration: 45 minutes.
Main regular credit(s): Script associate Ian Davidson; music directed by Ronnie Hazlehurst; produced and directed by Peter Whitmore.
Main regular performer(s): With The Nolan Sisters.

Holding / Source

26.12.1977 DB-D3 / 2"
Written by Spike Mullins, Gerald Wiley, Dave Dutton, Ted Kavanagh, David P. Lancaster, Tom Magee-Englefield, John Sullivan and Alan Wightman; designed by Nigel Curzon and Humphrey Jaeger.
With Kate O'Mara, Rowena Cooper, Penny Irving, The Aldershot Brass Ensemble.
Serial: Stop You're Killing Me.

SERIES 8
Duration: 45 minutes.
Main regular credit(s): Script associate Ian Davidson; music directed by Ronnie Hazlehurst; executive producer Michael Hurll; produced and directed by K. Paul Jackson.

Holding / Source

26.12.1980 DB-D3 / 2"
Written by David Newman, Peter Osborne, David Nobbs, David Renwick and Gerald Wiley; choreography by Ralph Tobert; designed by Andy Dimond.
With Barbara Dickson, Diana Dors, Michael Cochrane, Anthony Dawes, Michael Nightingale, Barbara Shelley, Rowena Cooper, Barbara New.
Serial: The Worm That Turned.

THE TWO RONNIES (continued)

SERIES 9
Main regular credit(s): Script associate Ian Davidson; music directed by Ronnie Hazlehurst; executive producer Michael Hurll; produced and directed by Paul Jackson.

25.12.1981
Holding / Source: DB-D3 / 2"
Duration: 50 minutes.
Written by Bryan Blackburn, David Nobbs, Peter Vincent, Peter Robinson, David Renwick and Gerald Wiley; choreography by Irving Davies; designed by Graeme Story.
With Sheena Easton, Chas & Dave, Jenny Logan, Liz Whiting, Derek Fincham, Ling Tai, Arnold Lee, Rowena Cooper, The Irving Davies Dancers.
Serial: Band Of Slaves.

25.12.1982
Holding / Source: DB / 1"
Duration: 45 minutes.
Written by Barry Cryer, Ian Davidson, David Nobbs, David Renwick, Peter Robinson, John Sullivan, Peter Vincent and Gerald Wiley; script associate Ian Davidson; designed by Jan Spoczynski; produced by Paul Jackson; film sequences directed by Marcus Plantin.
With David Essex, Debbi Blythe, Alec Bregonzi, Brigit Forsyth, Peter Hughes, Tracy Rispoli, Michael Redfern, Kenneth Sedd, Derek Ware, The Lordship Ringers, The Fred Tomlinson Singers.

SERIES 10
Duration: 50 minutes.
Main regular credit(s): Script associate Ian Davidson; music directed by Ronnie Hazlehurst; executive producer Michael Hurll; produced and directed by Marcus Plantin.

25.12.1983 **The Adventures Of Archie**
Holding / Source: DB / 1"
Written by Ian Davidson, David Newman, David Renwick and Peter Vincent; designed by Andrew Howe Davies.
With Elton John, Alec Bregonzi, Stuart Fell, Carol Hawkins, Ann Michelle, Ron Pember, Gerrie Raymond, Michael Redfern, John Rutland, Ken Wilson, The Fred Tomlinson Singers.

25.12.1984 **The Ballad Of Snivelling And Grudge**
Holding / Source: DB / 1"
Duration: 60 minutes.
Written by Gerald Wiley, Mike Radford, David Renwick, Peter Robinson, Laurie Rowley and Peter Vincent; script associate Ian Davidson; music directed by Ronnie Hazlehurst; choreography by Chris Power; designed by Andrew Howe Davies and James Grant; production manager John Birkin; produced and directed by Marcus Plantin.
With Elaine Paige, Patrick Troughton, Peter Wyngarde, Michael Cantwell, Daryl Debeau, John Owens, Ron Pember, Gerrie Raymond, John Rutland, Derek Ware, The Fred Tomlinson Singers, His Majesties Sagbutts and Cornetts.

SERIES 12
Duration: 50 minutes.
Main regular credit(s): Script associate Ian Davidson; music directed by Ronnie Hazlehurst; choreography by Jeff Thacker; produced by Michael Hurll; directed by Marcus Mortimer.

25.12.1985 **Little Big Shot**
Holding / Source: DB / 1"
Written by Bryan Blackburn, Robert A. Gray, Colin Pearson, David Renwick, Laurie Rowley and Gerald Wiley; designed by James Grant.
With Phil Collins, Janet Mahoney, Elizabeth Anson, John Blythe, Howard Lew Lewis, Paul McDowell, Gerrie Raymond.

25.12.1987 **Pinocchio II: Killer Doll**
Holding / Source: DB / 1"
Duration: 50 minutes.
Written by Colin Bostock-Smith, Bryan Blackburn, Spike Mullins, Colin Pearson, Laurie Rowley, David Renwick and Gerald Wiley; script associate Ian Davidson; music directed by Ronnie Hazlehurst; choreography by Jeff Thacker; designed by James Grant; produced and directed by Marcus Mortimer.
With Lynda Baron, Elton John, Maria Charles, Sandra Dickinson, Frank Finlay, Alfred Marks, Denis Quilley.

A BBC Productions production for BBC 2. Transmission details are for BBC 2.

23.12.2010 **The Studio Recordings**
Holding / Source: DB / 1"
Duration: 30 minutes.
Unedited takes from the classic comedy show, featuring both famous and more obscure sketches from programmes recorded in 1979 and 1980.
Archive producer Rory Sheehan; assistant producer Chris Bower; production executive Stan Matthews; executive producer Caroline Wright; production manager Jill Hallowell; produced and directed by Elaine Shepherd.

See also: THE TWO RONNIES SKETCHBOOK (BBC)

TWO TRACK MIND

A Tempest Films production for Channel 4. Transmission details are for Channel 4. Duration: 40 minutes.

Who is she — pop star or housewife? Is Kay really Karen or is Karen really Kay? This fast-paced musical drama takes the viewer on a mysterious journey. With six original songs.

Story by Vicky Pile; lyrics by Vicky Pile; music by Mike Moran; produced by Jacky Stoller; directed by Barrie Gavin.

Sue Jones-Davies (Karen/Kay), Jane Carr, Dermot Crowley.

	Holding / Source
22.12.1984	1" / 1"

TWO'S COMPANY

An LWT production. Duration: 25 minutes.

Main regular credit(s):　　Created by Bill MacIlwraith; theme music by Sammy Cahn and Denis King.

Main regular cast:　　Elaine Stritch (Dorothy McNab), Donald Sinden (Robert).

SERIES 2

Transmission details are for the ATV midlands region.

Main regular credit(s):　　Written by Bill MacIlwraith; designed by Michael Yates; produced by Humphrey Barclay; directed by John Reardon.

	Production No	Holding / Source
25.12.1976 **A Loving Christmas**	9L/09866	D2 / 2"

With Derek Waring (Nigel), Geraldine Newman, John Bay.

UNDER THE GREENWOOD TREE

An Ecosse Films production for ITV 1. made in association with BBC America / Ingenious Television LLP / WGBH Boston. Transmission details are for the Central region. Duration: 95 minutes.

Based on a book by Thomas Hardy and Ashley Pharoah; script supervisor Janice Brackenridge; music by John Lunn and Jim Williams; production executive Nicole Finnan; executive producers Matthew Arlidge, Douglas Rae and Robert Bernstein; produced by Jeremy Gwilt; directed by Nick Laughland.

Keeley Hawes (Fancy Day), James Murray (Dick Dewy), Terence Mortimer (Robert Penny), Richard Leaf (Thomas Leaf), Tony Haygarth (Reuben Dewy), Jane Wheldon (Mary Dewy), Sian Brooke (Susan Dewy), Ellie Thackeray (Bessy Dewy), Liam DeGruchy (Charley Dewy), John Axon (Elias Spinks), Steve Pemberton (Mr Shinar), Ben Miles (Parson Maybold), Alethea Steven (Anne Roebuck), Tom Georgeson (Geoffrey Day), Sean Arnold (Farmer), Robert Wilkinson (Gabriel).

	Holding / Source
26.12.2005	DB / V1SW

THE UNFORGETTABLE...

A North One Television production for ITV 1. Transmission details are for the Central region. Duration varies - see below for details.

SERIES 2

Main regular credit(s):   Executive producer John Quinn; series producer Karen Steyn.

	Holding / Source
27.12.2011 **Ernie Wise**	HD/DB / HDC

Duration: 48 minutes.
Archive producer John Greathead; programme consultant Sarah Stockton; consultant Chris Perry; production associates Verna Jaffe and Amanda Smith; production manager Tracy Manser.
With Martin Glyn Murray (Narrator), Ernie Wise.

01.01.2012 **John Thaw**	HD/DB / HDC

Duration: 48 minutes.
Produced and directed by Verity Maidlow.
With John Thaw, Sheila Hancock.

UNIVERSITY CHALLENGE

A Granada production for Granada/BBC 2.
Commissioned by Granada. Transmission details are for the Granada region.
Main regular performer(s): With Bamber Gascoigne (Presenter).

	Production No	Holding / Source
27.12.1967 **Christmas Edition: St. Hilda's College, Oxford V University Of Sussex**		J / 40

Produced by Douglas Terry; directed by Peter Mullings.
With St Hilda's College, University of Sussex.

28.12.1979 **University Challenge International**	1/0540/0996	DB / 2"

Bamber Gascoigne hosts a battle of wits between some of this country's brightest young minds and those from across the Atlantic. In this special edition of the fast-moving university quiz British champions, Sidney Sussex College, Cambridge, face Davidson College of North Carolina, winners of the American version of the programme.
Research Jaine Gambie; produced by Douglas Terry; directed by Peter Mullings.

31.12.1980	1/0540/2011	DB / 2"

Christmas University Challenge
Commissioned by BBC 2. Transmission details are for BBC 2. Duration: 30 minutes.
Main regular credit(s):   Produced by Irene Daniels, directed by Tracey Rooney.

	Production No	Holding / Source
19.12.2011 **York v Manchester**	1/2086/0689	DB / DBSW
With Steve Richards.		
20.12.2011 **Durham v Edinburgh**	1/2086/0690	DB / DBSW
With Minette Walters, Lord David Steel.		
21.12.2011 **Magdalen, Oxford v UCL**	1/2086/0691	DB / DBSW
22.12.2011 **Warwick v Sheffield**	1/2086/0692	DB / DBSW
24.12.2011 **Trinity, Cambridge v St Andrews**	1/2086/0693	DB / DBSW
With John Lloyd, Hazel Irvine.		
25.12.2011 **Edinburgh v Warwick**	1/2086/0694	DB / DBSW
26.12.2011 **Magdalen, Oxford v Trinity, Cambridge**	1/2086/0695	DB / DBSW
27.12.2011 **Warwick v Trinity,Cambridge**	1/2086/0696	DB / DBSW

Christmas University Challenge
Commissioned by BBC 2. Transmission details are for BBC 2. Duration: 30 minutes.
Main regular credit(s):   Produced by Irene Daniels; directed by Tracey Rooney.

	Production No	Holding / Source
17.12.2012 **Bristol v Leeds**	1/2086/0734	DB / DBSW
With Alistair McGowan, Jay Rayner.		
18.12.2012 **Newcastle v Loughborough**	1/2086/0735	DB / DBSW
19.12.2012 **New College v LSE**	1/2086/0736	DB / DBSW

UNIVERSITY CHALLENGE (continued)

Date	Match	Ref	Holding
20.12.2012	**Liverpool v Cardiff**	1/2086/0737	DB / DBSW
21.12.2012	**Newnham, Cambridge v Nottingham**	1/2086/0738	DB / DBSW
31.12.2012	**Exeter v Glasgow**	1/2086/0739	DB / DBSW
01.01.2013	**Birmingham v UEA**	1/2086/0740	DB / DBSW
02.01.2013	**Semi-Final: New College v Liverpool**	1/2086/0741	DB / DBSW
03.01.2013	**Semi-Final: Glasgow v East Anglia**	1/2086/0742	DB / DBSW
04.01.2013	**Final: New College v East Anglia**	1/2086/0743	DB / DBSW

Christmas University Challenge
Main regular credit(s): Produced by Irene Daniels; directed by Tracey Rooney.

Holding / Source

20.12.2013 — HD/DB / HDC
21.12.2013 — HD/DB / HDC
23.12.2013 — HD/DB / HDC
26.12.2013 — HD/DB / HDC
With Andrew Graham-Dixon, Helen Castor.

27.12.2013 — HD/DB / HDC
With Paul Lewis, Suzy Klein, Rowan Pelling, Richard Lochhead M.S.P..

30.12.2013 — HD/DB / HDC
31.12.2013 — HD/DB / HDC
With Rory Bremner, Susan Hill.

01.01.2014 — HD/DB / HDC
02.01.2014 — HD/DB / HDC
03.01.2014 — HD/DB / HDC

THE UNTOLD TOMMY COOPER

A Gogglebox production for Channel 4. Transmission details are for Channel 4. Duration: 78 minutes.
Produced and directed by Andy Humphries.
Tommy Cooper, Damien Hirst, Johnny Vegas, Ozzy Osbourne.

Holding / Source

28.12.2011 — DB / DBSWF

UP POMPEII!

A BBC/LWT production. Transmission details are for BBC 1/Central. Duration varies - see below for details.
Main regular credit(s): Created by Talbot Rothwell and Sid Colin; theme music by Alan Braden.
Main regular cast: Frankie Howerd (Lurcio), Kerry Gardner (Nausius), Jeanne Mockford (Senna), Elizabeth Larner (Ammonia).
An LWT production. Transmission details are for the Central region.

Holding / Source

14.12.1991 **Further Up Pompeii** — DB / D2S
Duration: 50 minutes.
Written by Brian Leveson and Paul Minett; executive producer Robin Carr; produced by Paul Lewis; directed by Ian Hamilton.
With Joanna Dickens (Colossa), Elizabeth Anson (Petunia), John Bardon (Villainus Brutus), Russell Gold (Noxius), Peter Geeves (Ambiguous), Roy Evans (Typhus), Tim Killick (Gluteus Maximus), Gary Rice (Umbilicus), Barry James (Claudius), Ben Aris (Flatus).

UP SUNDAY

A BBC production for BBC 2. Transmission details are for BBC 2. Duration varies - see below for details.
SERIES 2
Duration: 25 minutes.
Main regular credit(s): Produced by Ian Keill.

Holding / Source

24.12.1972 — DBSEQ / 2"
Directed by Max Donnellan.
With James Cameron, Kenny Everett, William Rushton, John Wells.
Inserts Only

SERIES 4
Duration: 25 minutes.
Main regular credit(s): Animated by Bob Gale; produced by Ian Keill.

Holding / Source

23.12.1973 **Up Christmas** — J|a / 2"
Directed by Ian Keill.
With Clive James, John Wells, John Fortune, William Rushton, James Cameron.

UP SUNDAY

THE UPPER HAND

A Central production. made in association with Columbia Pictures Television. Transmission details are for the Central region. Duration varies - see below for details.

Main regular credit(s): Created by Martin Cohan and Blake Hunter.

Main regular cast: Joe McGann (Charlie Burrows), Diana Weston (Caroline Wheatley), Honor Blackman (Laura West), Kellie Bright (Joanna Burrows), William Puttock (Tom Wheatley).

SERIES 1
Main regular credit(s): Music by Debbie Wiseman; produced by Christopher Walker.

	Holding / Source
27.12.1990 **Requiem**	D2 / 1"

Duration: 26 minutes.

A festive edition of the role-reversal sitcom. Caroline and Laura fear that Charlie owes the Mafia some money when they discover that he has been working in a pizza parlour to earn extra money to pay off a certain Mr Lipari.

Written by Paul Robinson Hunter, Robert Sternin and Prudence Fraser; story by Blake Hunter and Martin Cohan; directed by Martin Dennis.

With No guest cast.

UPSTAIRS DOWNSTAIRS

Alternative/Working Title(s): 165 EATON SQUARE / 75 EATON SQUARE / BELOW STAIRS / THE SERVANTS' HALL / TWO LITTLE MAIDS IN TOWN

An LWT production. made in association with Sagitta. Transmission details are for the ATV midlands region. Duration: 50 minutes.

This series joins a fashionable household in Eaton Place in 1903, to follow the trials of those in service and the human dramas being played out above stairs.

Main regular credit(s): Script editor Alfred Shaughnessy; theme music by Alexander Faris; executive producer Rex Firkin; produced by John Hawkesworth.

Main regular cast: Gordon Jackson (Hudson), Jean Marsh (Rose), Angela Baddeley (Mrs Bridges), David Langton (Richard Bellamy), Simon Williams (James Bellamy), Christopher Beeny (Edward).

SERIES 2
Main regular cast: With Jenny Tomasin (Ruby), Rachel Gurney (Lady Marjorie Bellamy), Nicola Pagett (Elizabeth Bellamy), John Alderton (Thomas Watkins), Pauline Collins (Sarah), Patsy Smart (Miss Roberts).

	Production No	Holding / Source
11.11.1972 **Whom God Hath Joined...**	9D/01505	DB / 2"

Written by Jeremy Paul; directed by Bill Bain.

With Nicola Pagett (Elizabeth Kirbridge), John Alderton (Thoams Watkins), Ian Ogilvy (Lawrence), Raymond Huntley (Sir Geoffrey Dillon), Patsy Smart (Miss Roberts), Bryan Coleman.

SERIES 3
Main regular cast: With Meg Wynn Owen (Hazel Forrest), Jenny Tomasin (Ruby).

	Production No	Holding / Source
22.12.1973 **Goodwill To All Men**	9D/01608	DB / 2"

Georgina comes to stay and persuades the new maid, Daisy, to visit her parents on Christmas Day. It is a shocking experience for both of them.

Written by Deborah Mortimer; designed by John Clements; directed by Christopher Hodson.

With Jacqueline Tong (Daisy), Lesley Anne Down (Georgina Worsley), Cathleen Nesbitt (Lady Southwold), Jennifer McEvoy (Mrs Peel), Dan Gillan (Bill).

"Russell Harty Goes Upstairs Downstairs", tx: 26.12.75. Written and produced by Nicholas Barrett, directed by Mike Mansfield. 25 mins LWT. D2 ex-2".
   There was a further LWT documentary, "Upstairs Downstairs Remembered", with numerous interviews and extracts made in 1996. Produced by Richard Marson. 25mins LWT. An extended overseas version exists.
   Kaleidoscope Publishing issues "Inside Updown - The Inside Story of Upstairs, Downstairs", written by Richard Marson. www.kaleidoscopepublishing.co.uk

---

UPSTAIRS DOWNSTAIRS

A BBC Wales production for BBC 1. made in association with Masterpiece. Transmission details are for BBC 1. Duration: 60 minutes.

SERIES 1
Main regular credit(s): Created by Heidi Thomas; written by Heidi Thomas; based on an idea by Jean Marsh, Eileen Atkins, John Hawkesworth and John Whitney; script supervisor Llinos Wyn Jones; script editor Elizabeth Kilgarriff; theme music by Alexander Faris; music by Daniel Pemberton; director of photography Adam Suschitzky; titles by Tom Hingston Studio; art director David Hindle; designed by Eve Stewart; associate producer Catrin Lewis Defis; production executive Julie Scott; executive producers Rebecca Eaton, Kate Harwood, Heidi Thomas and Piers Wenger; production manager Sam Baker; line producer Debbi Slater; produced by Nikki Wilson; directed by Euros Lyn.

Main regular cast: With Keeley Hawes (Lady Agnes Holland), Jean Marsh (Rose Buck), Ed Stoppard (Sir Hallam Holland), Claire Foy (Lady Porsie), Eileen Atkins (Maud, Lady Holland), Anne Reid (Mrs Thackeray), Art Malik (Mr Amanjit), Adrian Scarborough (Mr Pritchard), Anthony Calf (Anthony Eden), Neil Jackson (Harry Spargo), Ellie Kendrick (Ivy Morris).

	Holding / Source
26.12.2010 **The Fledgling**	HD/DB / HD/DB

With Blake Ritson, Nico Mirallegro, Emma Clifford, Edward Baker-Duly, Caroline O'Neill, Sadie Shimmin, Jack Bannell.

	Holding / Source
27.12.2010 **The Ladybird**	HD/DB / HD/DB

With Helen Bradbury, Sarah Crowden, Ian Barritt, Alexia James.

	Holding / Source
28.12.2010 **The Cuckoo**	HD/DB / HD/DB

With Blake Ritson, Alexia James, Christopher Harper, Richard Teverson, Edward Baker-Duly, Jemma Churchill, Emily Bowker, Sarah Gordy.

THE VAL DOONICAN MUSIC SHOW

A BBC production for BBC 1. Transmission details are for BBC 1. Duration varies - see below for details.
Main regular performer(s): Val Doonican (Host).

	Holding / Source
26.12.1976	DB / 2"

Duration: 50 minutes.
Written by Bryan Blackburn; music directed by Peter Knight; music associate Roger Richards; choreography by David Toguri; designed by Lesley Bremness; produced and directed by Yvonne Littlewood.
With Nana Mouskouri, James Galway, Terry Wogan, Arthur Askey, Henry Cooper, Tony Blackburn, Pete Murray, Janet Brown, Cliff Michelmore, The Eddie Lester Singers.

SERIES 1
Duration: 45 minutes.
Main regular credit(s): Written by Val Doonican, Spike Mullins and Ronnie Taylor; music directed by Ronnie Hazlehurst; music associate Roger Richards; designed by Martin Collins; produced and directed by Yvonne Littlewood.
Main regular performer(s): With The Mansells.

	Holding / Source
31.12.1977 **Val Doonican's Old Year Music Show**	DB-D3 / 2"

Designed by Ian Watson.
With John Inman, Chet Atkins, The King's Singers, Mary O'Hara.

SERIES 2
Main regular credit(s): Written by Chris Miller and Val Doonican; music directed by Ronnie Hazlehurst; music associate Roger Richards; designed by Jan Spoczynski; produced and directed by Yvonne Littlewood.

	Holding / Source
27.12.1978 **Val Doonican's Christmas In The Country**	DB-D3 / 2"

Duration: 50 minutes.
Designed by Martin Collins.
With Kelly Monteith, Stéphane Grapelli, Janie Fricke, Laurie Holloway, The Diz Disley Trio, The Nigel Lythgoe Dancers, The Tony Hayes Singers.

SERIES 3
Duration: 45 minutes.
Main regular credit(s): Written by Barry Took and Val Doonican; music directed by Ronnie Hazlehurst; music associate Roger Richards; designed by Roger Murray Leach; produced and directed by Yvonne Littlewood.

	Holding / Source
24.12.1979 **Val's Christmas Music Show**	DB / 2"

With Twiggy, Jane Freeman, Roy Castle, Magnus Magnusson, The Cambridge Buskers, Bill Owen, Peter Sallis, Brian Wilde.

SERIES 5
Duration: 45 minutes.
Main regular credit(s): Music directed by Ronnie Hazlehurst; music associate Roger Richards; designed by Martin Collins; produced and directed by Yvonne Littlewood.
Main regular performer(s): With The Saturday Singers.

	Holding / Source
28.12.1981 **Val Sings Bing**	DB-D3 / 2"

Written by Benny Green and Val Doonican; designed by Jan Spoczynski.
With Vic Damone, Marti Webb, Dickie Henderson, Rosemarie Ford.

SERIES 9
Duration: 45 minutes.
Main regular credit(s): Music directed by Ronnie Hazlehurst; music associate Roger Richards; produced and directed by Yvonne Littlewood.
Main regular performer(s): With Miriam Stockley, Val Stokes, Vicki Brown, Nick Curtis, Ken Barrie, Danny Street.

	Holding / Source
24.12.1986 **Christmas Eve With Val Doonican**	DB / 1"

Written by Chris Miller and Val Doonican; designed by John Anderson.
With Dennis Taylor, Evelyn Glennie.

24.12.1987 **Christmas Eve With Val Doonican**	DB / 1"

Duration: 50 minutes.
Written by Chris Miller and Val Doonican; designed by John Asbridge; production manager Janet Bone.
With Val Stokes (Singer), Danny Street (Singer), Ken Barrie (Singer), Tracey Miller (Singer), Mary Carewe (Singer), Nick Curtis (Singer), Howard Keel, Sky, Michala Petri, Jane Asher, St Philip's Choir.

24.12.1988 **Christmas Eve With Val Doonican**	DB / 1"

Duration: 40 minutes.
Written by Chris Miller and Val Doonican; designed by Ian Ashurst.
With Elaine Paige, Gorden Kaye, Brian Kay.

THE VAL DOONICAN SHOW

A BBC production for BBC 1. Transmission details are for BBC 1. Duration varies - see below for details.

Main regular performer(s): Val Doonican (Host).

SERIES 2
Duration: 45 minutes.
Main regular credit(s): Written by David Cumming and Val Doonican; orchestra conducted by Ken Thorne; dance direction by Jo Cook; designed by Roger Andrews; produced and directed by John Ammonds.
Main regular performer(s): With The Gojos, The Adam Singers.

	Holding / Source
24.12.1966	J /

With Frank Ifield, Millicent Martin, Ray Alan.

SERIES 3
Duration: 45 minutes.
Main regular credit(s): Written by Austin Steele, John Law and Val Doonican; orchestra conducted by Ken Thorne; dance direction by Jo Cook; designed by Brian Tregidden; produced and directed by John Ammonds.
Main regular performer(s): With The Gojos, The Adam Singers.

	Holding / Source
23.12.1967	J /

With Derek Nimmo, Ray Alan.

THE VAL DOONICAN SHOW

An ATV production. Transmission details are for the ATV midlands region. Duration: 52 minutes.

Main regular performer(s): Val Doonican (Host).

SERIES 1

	VT Number	Holding / Source
25.12.1970	2598/70	R1 / 2"

Val is at home for Christmas.
Written by Bryan Blackburn, David Cumming and Wally Malston; music directed by Kenny Woodman; designed by Michael Bailey; produced by Les Cocks; directed by Ian Fordyce.
With Sandie Shaw, Ronnie Corbett, Michael Flanders and Donald Swann, Stéphane Grapelli, The Mike Sammes Singers, The Jack Parnell Orchestra.

	VT Number	Holding / Source
24.12.1971	4184	R1 / 2"

Duration: 40 minutes.
Doonican at his festive best.
Written by Bryan Blackburn and Ronnie Taylor; music directed by Kenny Woodman; music associate Derek Scott; designed by Ray White; associate producer Les Cocks; produced and directed by John Robins.
With Harry H. Corbett, Friday Brown, Marian Davies, Lois Lane, Sylvia McNeill.

	VT Number	Holding / Source
26.12.1972	4185	R1 / 2"

Written by David Cumming and Ronnie Taylor; designed by Ray White; produced and directed by Keith Beckett.
With Terry Wogan, Georgie Fame, Charlie Drake, Alan Price, Tonia Bern-Campbell, Kenny Woodman and his Orchestra.

SERIES 6
Duration: 25 minutes.
Main regular credit(s): Written by Roy Tuvey and Maurice Sellar; music associate Roger Richards; designed by Lewis Logan; produced and directed by Keith Beckett.
Main regular performer(s): With Paul Melba, Kenny Woodman and his Orchestra, Fabric.

	Holding / Source
24.12.1974	J / 2"

With Jimmy Kennedy.

VAL DOONICAN'S CHRISTMAS PARTY

A BBC production for BBC 1. Transmission details are for BBC 1. Duration: 45 minutes.
Produced and directed by Yvonne Littlewood.
Val Doonican (Host), Howard Keel, The Nolan Sisters, Sky, Wall Street Crash, Tracey Miller, Val Stokes, Miriam Stockley.

	Holding / Source
24.12.1983	DB-D3 / 2"

VAL DOONICAN'S CHRISTMAS PARTY

A BBC production for BBC 1. Transmission details are for BBC 1. Duration: 50 minutes.

Written by Chris Miller and Val Doonican; music directed by Ronnie Hazlehurst; music associate Roger Richards; designed by John Anderson; produced and directed by Yvonne Littlewood.

Val Doonican (Host), Pat Boone, James Galway, Janet Brown, Stockton's Wing.

	Holding / Source
24.12.1985	DB / 1"

VAL PARNELL'S STAR TIME

Alternative/Working Title(s): VARIETY STAR TIME

An ATV production. Transmission details are for the ATV midlands region. Duration: 53 minutes.

SERIES 1

	Production No	Holding / Source
01.01.1957 Val Parnell's New Year Star Time	2641	J / Live

An ITP production.

Designed by Richard Lake; produced and directed by Albert Locke.

With Pat Boone, Jack Parnell and his Orchestra, Daisy May and Company with Saveen, The George Carden Dancers.

It isn't entirely clear why THE JEWEL AND WARRISS SCRAPBOOK (q.v.) is not billed as part of VAL PARNELL'S STARTIME but THE JEWEL AND WARRISS SHOW is, given that the people behind each show appear to be near enough identical.

SERIES 3

	Production No	Holding / Source
21.12.1960	5434	J / Live

Designed by Richard Lake; produced by Colin Clews.

With Alma Cogan (Host), The Dallas Boys, Norman Vaughan, Cyril Stapleton and His Orchestra.

SERIES 4

	Production No	VT Number	Holding / Source
25.12.1963 Christmas Startime	2851	6062	J / 40

Alt.Title(s):   *The Richard Hearne Show*

Music by Jack Parnell; orchestra conducted by Jack Parnell; designed by Peter Roden; produced by Francis Essex.

With Richard Hearne, Bruce Forsyth, David Nixon, Charlie Cairoli & Company, Bernard Braden, Barbara Kelly, Pearl Carr and Teddy Johnson, Mr Acker Bilk and his Paramount Jazz Band, The Pirellis, Sheila Pugh, Christina Davies, Elizabeth Edmiston.

Some early episodes billed as VARIETY STAR TIME.
See also: ALL KINDS OF MUSIC

VAL SINGS AND RINGS IN THE NEW

A BBC production for BBC 1. Transmission details are for BBC 1. Duration: 45 minutes.

Written by Spike Mullins and Val Doonican; music directed by Ronnie Hazlehurst; designed by Roger Cann; produced and directed by Yvonne Littlewood.

Val Doonican (Presenter), James Galway, Stutz Bear Cats, Sylvia, Tracey Miller, Val Stokes, Lindsay John, Nick Curtis, Danny Street, Ken Barrie.

	Holding / Source
01.01.1983	DB-D3 / 2"

VAL'S SPECIAL YEARS OF CHRISTMAS

A BBC production for BBC 1. Transmission details are for BBC 1. Duration: 45 minutes.

Written by Charles Chilton and Val Doonican; costume Laura Ergis; music directed by Ronnie Hazlehurst; music associate Roger Richards; lighting by Ken Macgregor; sound Larry Goodson; designed by Kenneth Sharp; produced and directed by Yvonne Littlewood.

Val Doonican (Host), Gilbert O'Sullivan, Gemma Craven, Roy Hudd, Boys Choir, St Paul's Cathedral, Tracey Miller, Val Stokes, Vicky Silva, Lee Gibson, Penny Lister, Lavinia Rodgers.

	Holding / Source
24.12.1980	DB-D3 / 2"

A VARIETY OF REG VARNEY

An LWT production. Transmission details are for the ATV midlands region. Duration: 53 minutes.

A long time before Reg Varney became a family favourite as Stan in On the Buses, he was known as a top-rated variety performer. Tonight he proves it. In this show, he recreates some of his finest hours in the variety theatre in sketches ranging from the "nervous boy at the audition" to a special version of Dick Whittington set in the Wild West, plus many new sketches.

Music directed by Harry Rabinowitz; orchestra conducted by Harry Rabinowitz; choreography by Malcolm Clare; designed by Bryce Walmsley; produced and directed by Bryan Izzard.

Reg Varney (Host), Pat Coombs, Frank Thornton, The Malcolm Clare Dancers, The Ladybirds, Richard Barnes, Margaret Burton, Cheryl Kennedy, David Lodge, Stéphane Grapelli.

	VT Number	Holding / Source
25.12.1971	0784	D2 / 2"

THE VERA LYNN SHOW

A BBC production for BBC 2. Transmission details are for BBC 2. Duration: 50 minutes.
Choreography by Nigel Lythgoe; designed by Brian Tregidden and Valerie Warrender; produced and directed by Terry Hughes.
Vera Lynn, Charles Aznavour, The King's Singers, Shari Lewis, Roger Webb, The Young Generation, Alyn Ainsworth and his Orchestra.

	Holding / Source
27.12.1973	DB-D3 / 2"

VERA LYNN SINGS

A Thames Television production. Transmission details are for the ATV midlands region. Duration: 35 minutes.
Music directed by Geoff Love; designed by Peter Le Page; produced and directed by Keith Beckett.
Vera Lynn (Host), Gillian Shearing.

	Holding / Source
26.12.1977	DB / 2"

A VERY JLS CHRISTMAS

Commissioned by Sky One. Transmission details are for Sky One. Duration: 75 minutes.
JLS.

	Holding / Source
23.12.2012	HD/DB / HDC

THE VICAR OF DIBLEY

A Tiger Aspect production for BBC 1. Transmission details are for BBC 1. Duration varies - see below for details.

Main regular credit(s):	Theme music by Howard Goodall and Christ Church Choir, Oxford.
Main regular cast:	Dawn French (Geraldine Granger), Gary Waldhorn (David Horton), James Fleet (Hugo Horton), Emma Chambers (Alice Tinker/Horton), John Bluthal (Frank Pickle), Trevor Peacock (Jim Trott), Roger Lloyd Pack (Owen Newitt).

	Holding / Source
25.12.1996 **The Christmas Lunch Incident**	DB-D3 / D3S

Geraldine agrees to attend three slap-up lunches.
Written by Richard Curtis and Paul Mayhew-Archer; produced by Sue Vertue and Jon Plowman; directed by Dewi Humphreys.
With Peter Capaldi, Orla Brady, Carol Macready, Mel Giedroyc.

SERIES 3

Main regular credit(s):	Written by Paul Mayhew-Archer and Richard Curtis; script supervisor Bernadette Darnell; script editor Emma Freud; art director Chris Thompson; designed by Andrew Howe Davies; executive producers Richard Curtis and Peter Bennett-Jones; production manager Rachel Salter; produced by Jon Plowman and Sue Vertue; directed by Dewi Humphreys.

	Holding / Source
26.12.1997 **Engagement**	DB / DBS

Duration: 38 minutes.
With Edward Halsted.

SERIES 4

Main regular credit(s):	Written by Richard Curtis and Paul Mayhew-Archer; script editor Emma Freud; music by Howard Goodall; executive producers Richard Curtis and Peter Bennett-Jones; produced by Margot Gavan Duffy and Jon Plowman; directed by Gareth Carrivick.

	Holding / Source
24.12.1999 **Autumn**	DB / DBSW

Duration: 40 minutes.
With Clive Mantle (Simon Horton).

25.12.1999 **Winter**	DB / DBSW

Duration: 40 minutes.
With Charles Pemberton, Linda Beckett.

27.12.1999 **Spring**	DB / DBSW

Duration: 39 minutes.
With Richard Griffiths, Nina Wadia, Les Pearson, Melissa Phelps, Sean Bean.

01.01.2000 **Summer**	DB / DBSW

Duration: 39 minutes.
With Roger Sloman, Jeremy Paxman, Edward Halsted, Stewart Wright, Guillaume Tobo, Martyn Lewis.

| British Christmas Television Guide | THE VICAR OF DIBLEY (continued) |

SERIES 5

Main regular credit(s): Written by Richard Curtis and Paul Mayhew-Archer; script editor Emma Freud; costume Rebecca Hale; make-up Jan Sewell; lighting director Martin Kempton; art director Nic Pallace; designed by Andrew Howe Davies; executive producers Richard Curtis, Peter Bennett-Jones and Jon Plowman; produced by Philippa Catt; directed by Martin Dennis.

Holding / Source

25.12.2004 Merry Christmas — DB / DBSW
Duration: 55 minutes.
Geraldine's tenth anniversary as Vicar in the village. How will the occasion be celebrated?
Script supervisor Valerie Letley.
With Simon McBurney (Choirmaster), Justin Pierre (Rachel's boyfriend), Rachel Hunter (Herself).

01.01.2005 Happy New Year — DB / DBSW
Duration: 40 minutes.
Geraldine tries speed dating for her 40th birthday, as she longs for a boyfriend. And the village writes to Tony Blair about world poverty.
With Miranda Hart, Nathalie Cox, Cristian Solimeno.
The end credits were replaced by pictures of the cast wearing white armbands symbolising the fight against Third World poverty.

SERIES 6
Duration: 60 minutes.
Main regular credit(s): Written by Richard Curtis and Paul Mayhew-Archer; script supervisor Penelope Chong; script editor Emma Freud; choreography by Nicky Hinkley; director of photography John Sorapure; art director Les McCallum; designed by Andrew Howe Davies; executive producers Peter Bennett-Jones, Richard Curtis and Jon Plowman; production manager Holly Bowcott; line producer Jo Hunter; produced by Sophie Clarke-Jervoise; directed by Ed Bye.
Main regular cast: With Richard Armitage (Harry Kennedy), Keeley Hawes (Rosie Kennedy).

Holding / Source

25.12.2006 The Handsome Stranger — DB / DBSW
With Nicholas Blane.

01.01.2007 The Vicar In White — DB / DBSW
With Peter Cartwright, Marlene Sidaway, Hugh Bonneville.

VICIOUS

Alternative/Working Title(s): VICIOUS OLD QUEENS
A Brown Eyed Boy Production production for ITV 1. made in association with Kudos. Transmission details are for the Central region. Duration: 25 minutes.
Written by Gary Janetti; designed by Harry Banks; executive producers Jane Featherstone and Gary Janetti; produced by Gary Reich; directed by Ed Bye.
Derek Jacobi (Stuart Bixby), Ian McKellen (Freddie Thornhill), Frances de la Tour (Violet Crosby).

Holding / Source

27.12.2013 Christmas Special — HD/DB / HDC
Freddie and Stuart invite friends round for a Christmas Day celebration.
With Iwan Rheon (Ash Weston), Marcia Warren (Penelope), Philip Voss (Mason).

VICTORIA WOOD AS SEEN ON TV

A BBC production for BBC 2. Transmission details are for BBC 2. Duration varies - see below for details.
Main regular credit(s): Written by Victoria Wood; music by Victoria Wood; produced by Geoff Posner.
Main regular cast: Victoria Wood.

Holding / Source

18.12.1987 As Seen On TV Special — DB-D3 / 1"
Duration: 40 minutes.
Music directed by David Firman; designed by Andrew Howe Davies; directed by Geoff Posner.
With Julie Walters, Maggie Steed, Celia Imrie, Duncan Preston, Susie Blake, Kay Adshead, Georgia Allen, Nicholas Barnes, David Bexon, Jim Broadbent, Bryan Burdon, Graham Callan, Christopher Connah, Rowena Cooper, Deborah Grant, Mary Hammond, Paul Heiney, Kenny Ireland, Meg Johnson, Sam Kelly, Terence Longdon, Lill Roughley, Chris Sanders, Sandra Voe, Sue Wallace, Ian Wallace, Clive Walton.

VICTORIA WOOD WITH ALL THE TRIMMINGS

A Good Fun / Ovation Entertainments production for BBC 1. Transmission details are for BBC 1. Duration: 52 minutes.
Written by Victoria Wood; music by Victoria Wood and David Firman; choreography by Kim Gavin; director of photography Alastair Meux; designed by Grenville Horner; associate producers David Harvey and Lucy Ansbro; executive producers Jon Plowman and Phil McIntyre; production manager Alison Passey; produced by Jemma Rodgers and Victoria Wood; directed by John Birkin.
Victoria Wood, Geraldine McEwan, Betty Boothroyd, Helen Coker, Andrew Dunn, Richard E. Grant, Shobna Gulati, H from Steps, Charlie Hicks, Adrian Hood, Philip Jackson, Derek Jacobi, Robert Lindsay, Bob Monkhouse, Deborah Moore, Roger Moore, Michael Parkinson, Billie Piper, Pete Postlethwaite, Anne Reid, Alan Rickman, Paul Rider, Angela Rippon, Amy Robbins, Emma Robbins, Kate Robbins, Ted Robbins, Delia Smith, Kathy Staff, Joe Starrs, Imelda Staunton, Alan Titchmarsh, Julie Walters, Jim Watson, Honeysuckle Weeks, Penelope Wilton, Anna Wing, Bernard Wrigley, Caroline Aherne, Susie Blake, James Bolam, June Brown, Richenda Carey, Craig Cash, Roger Cooke, Lindsay Duncan, Hannah Gordon, Nichola Holt, Celia Imrie, Hugh Laurie, Bill Paterson, Maxine Peake.

Holding / Source

25.12.2000 — DB / DBSWF
A Christmas special with Wood and her TV family spoofing the ghosts of Christmas programming past.

VICTORIA WOOD: LIVE IN YOUR OWN HOME

A BBC production for BBC 1. Transmission details are for BBC 1. Duration: 79 minutes.

Written by Victoria Wood; produced and directed by Geoff Posner.

Victoria Wood.

	Holding / Source
25.12.1994	DB / D3S

VICTORIA WOOD: WHAT LARKS!

A Blue Door Adventures production for BBC 1. made in association with Phil McIntyre Television. Transmission details are for BBC 1. Duration: 45 minutes.

Written by Victoria Wood; produced and directed by Victoria Wood.

Victoria Wood.

	Holding / Source
30.12.2009	HD/DB / HD/DB

Out-takes, unseen footage and interviews behind the scenes of 'Victoria Wood's Mid Life Crisis'. No end credits on-screen.
See also: VICTORIA WOOD'S MID LIFE CHRISTMAS (BBC)

VICTORIA WOOD'S MID LIFE CHRISTMAS

A Blue Door Adventures production for BBC 1. made in association with Phil McIntyre Television. Transmission details are for BBC 1. Duration: 60 minutes.

Written by Victoria Wood; script supervisors Chrissy Bibby, Jane Burrows and Mo Johnstone; choreography by Sammy Murray; director of photography John Rhodes; designed by Malcolm Thornton and James Dillon; executive producers Lucy Ansbro, Phil McIntyre and Victoria Wood; line producer Richard Moat; produced by John Rushton; directed by Tony Dow.

Victoria Wood, Julie Walters, Anton Du Beke, Delia Smith, Jayne Torvill, Christopher Dean, Lorraine Ashbourne, Emily Atack, Neil Bell, Dorothy Atkinson, Naomi Bentley, Gina Bramhill, Peta Cornish, Gabriel Churchill, Bob Cryer, Jennie Dale, Henry Durham, Steve Elias, Lauren Hood, Sinéad Keenan, Richard Lintern, Sylvestra Le Touzel, Tony Maudsley, Nika McGuigan, Stephen Mear, Wendy Nottingham, Isobel Powley, Daniel Ryan, Abdul Salis, Reece Shearsmith, Julian Stolzenberg, Harriet Thorpe, Jason Watkins, Marcia Warren.

	Holding / Source
24.12.2009	HD/DB / HD/DB

See also: VICTORIA WOOD: WHAT LARKS! (BBC)

A VICTORIAN CHRISTMAS

An Antelope South Productions production for Meridian. Transmission details are for the London Weekend Television region. Duration: 100 minutes.

Special Christmas programme showing how Victorians might have celebrated the festive season, featuring ballads, poems, prose and carols, set in Osborne House on the Isle of Wight and St Mildreds Church, Whippingham.

Produced by Kenneth Corden; directed by Sue Judd.

Robert Hardy, Dorothy Tutin, Magdalen College Choir.

	Holding / Source
23.12.1995	D2 / D2S

A VIEW FROM A HILL

A BBC production for BBC 4. Transmission details are for BBC 4. Duration: 40 minutes.

Adapted by Peter Harness; based on an idea by Alison Willett; based on a story by M. R. James; script supervisor Frances Mable; music by Andy Price and Harry Escott; associate producer Sue Smith; production executive Howard Kingston; executive producers Phillippa Giles and Richard Fell; produced by Pier Wilkie; directed by Luke Watson.

Mark Letheren (Doctor Fanshawe), Pip Torrens (Squire Richards), David Burke (Patten), Simon Linnell (Baxter).

	Holding / Source
23.12.2005	DB / V1SW

"M R James: The Corner of the Retina", tx:23.12.2005, explored the work of M.R. James. Narrated by Anthony Howell, Michael Poole was the Executive Producer, directed by Pete Lawrence for BBC Bristol. 30 mins. DB.

VIEWPOINT

A BBC production for BBC 1. Transmission details are for BBC 1.

	Holding / Source
23.12.1969 Exiles At Christmas	DB / 2"

VISION ON

A BBC production for BBC 1. Transmission details are for BBC 1.

SERIES 1

	Holding / Source
23.12.1964 A Christmas Tree	J /

An untransmitted insert exists on T3.
A foreign version of the edition tx'd 04.05.76 exists on D3.

A VISIT FROM ST NICHOLAS

A BBC production for BBC 2. Transmission details are for BBC 2. Duration: 5 minutes.

A poem for Christmas by Clement Clarke Moore. Spoken by children, and with illustrations from schools in Cropredy and Gunnersbury.

Written by Clement Clarke Moore.

	Holding / Source
24.12.1976	J / 2"

A VISIT TO MY COUSIN

Alternative/Working Title(s): A VISIT TO A COUSIN

A Tyne Tees Television production. Transmission details are for the Tyne Tees region. Duration: 25 minutes.

This play about a teenager's involvement in the break-up of family relationships was the winning entry in Tyne Tees Television's Young Playwright of the Year Competition.

Introduced by Hannah Gordon; written by Bryan Johnson; designed by Ashley Wilkinson; produced by Margaret Bottomley; directed by Tony Kysh.

Gavin Kitchen (Paul), Anne Orwin (Melody), Michael Wardle (Mick), Peggy Gosschalk (Auntie Doris), Barbara Peirson (Chrissie), Steven Tyler (Steve).

	Holding / Source
28.12.1979	DB / 2"

The TV Times ommitted to say who the writer was! :-)

British Christmas Television Guide

WAITING FOR GOD

A BBC production for BBC 1. Transmission details are for BBC 1. Duration: 30 minutes.

Main regular credit(s): Written by Michael Aitkens; theme music by The Nash Ensemble.

Main regular cast: Graham Crowden (Tom Ballard), Stephanie Cole (Diana Trent).

SERIES 3

Main regular credit(s): Produced and directed by Gareth Gwenlan.

Main regular cast: With Daniel Hill (Harvey Bains), Janine Duvitski (Jane).

	Holding / Source
23.12.1992	DB-D3 / 1"S

Duration: 49 minutes.

Production managers Peter Laskie and Simon Spencer.

With Dawn Hope (Jenny), Andrew Tourell (Geoffrey), Sandra Payne (Marion), Michael Bilton (Basil), Lucy Aston (Sarah), Mark McKenna, Katherine Toy, Jamie Ripman, Mark Charnock, Sue Scott-Davison, Danny Swanson, Chico Andrade, Daryl Kwan, Charlotte Grimes, Martha Mackintosh.

SERIES 4

Main regular credit(s): Designed by Roger Harris; production manager Johanna Kennedy; produced and directed by Gareth Gwenlan.

Main regular cast: With Daniel Hill (Harvey Bains), Janine Duvitski (Jane Edwards), Andrew Tourell (Geoffrey), Sandra Payne (Marion).

	Holding / Source
23.12.1993	DB / D3S

With Lucy Aston (Sarah), Paddy Ward (Jamie Edwards), Deddie Davies, Phyllida Hewat, Lucy Edelstein.

THE WAKEFIELD SHEPHERDS' PLAY

A BBC Schools production. Transmission details are for BBC Schools. Duration: 30 minutes.

Translated by Ronald Eyre; music by John Alldis; designed by Stuart Walker; produced and directed by Ronald Eyre.

Timothy Bateson (Mak), Barbara Hicks (Mak's Wife), Dudley Foster (First Shepherd), Neil McCarthy (Second Shepherd), Michael Williams (Third Shepherd), John Alldis (The Angel), Freda Dowie (Mary), Fred Rawlings (Joseph).

	Holding / Source
28.11.1961	R1 /

WALKING WITH DINOSAURS SPECIAL

A BBC production for BBC 1. Transmission details are for BBC 1. Duration varies - see below for details.

	Holding / Source
30.12.2002 **The Giant Claw**	DB /

Duration: 30 minutes.

Executive producer Adam Kemp; directed by Tim Haines.

With Nigel Marven (Host).

01.01.2003 **Land Of The Giants**	DB /

Duration: 30 minutes.

Executive producer Tim Haines; produced by Jasper James.

With Nigel Marven (Host).

WALLACE AND GROMIT

Commissioned and produced by a variety of companies (see details below). Duration varies - see below for details.

Created by Nick Park.

Peter Sallis (Voice of Wallace).

An Aardman Animations production for BBC 1. Transmission details are for BBC 1.

	Holding / Source
26.12.1993 **The Wrong Trousers**	DB / C1S

Duration: 30 minutes.

Written by Nick Park and Bob Baker; additional material by Brian Sibley; music by Julian Nott; executive producers Colin Rose, Peter Salmon, Peter Lord and David Sproxton; production manager Peter Thornton; produced by Christopher Moll; directed by Nick Park.

Made in association with BBC Bristol, Wallace & grimit Ltd, Lionheart Television and Children's International BBC.

24.12.1995 **A Close Shave**	DB / C1S

Duration: 30 minutes.

Written by Bob Baker and Nick Park; music by Julian Nott; consultant Peter Thornton; executive producers Colin Rose, Peter Lord and David Sproxton; produced by Carla Shelley and Michael Rose; directed by Nick Park.

With Anne Reid (Voice of Wendolene Ramsbottom).

Made in association with BBC Bristol, Wallace & grimit Ltd, Lionheart Television and Children's International BBC.

25.12.2008 **A Matter Of Loaf And Death**	DB / HD/DB

Duration: 30 minutes.

Written by Nick Park and Bob Baker; music by Julian Nott; consultants Mark Burton and Richard Goleszowski; designed by Phil Lewis; executive producers Peter Lord, David Sproxton and Miles Bullough; head of production Jacqueline White; production manager Richard 'Becky' Beck; produced by Steve Pegram; directed by Nick Park.

With Sally Lindsay (Voice of Piella Bakewell), Melissa Collier (Voice of Fluffles), Sarah Laborde (Buke O Lite Singer).

See also: CREATURE COMFORTS / WALLACE AND GROMIT'S CRACKING CONTRAPTIONS (BBC)

WALLACE AND GROMIT'S CRACKING CONTRAPTIONS

An Aardman Animations production for BBC 1. made in association with Wallace and Gromit Ltd. Transmission details are for BBC 1. Duration: 2 minutes.

Main regular credit(s):	Devised by Nick Park; written by Nick Park, Loyd Price, Christopher Sadler, Seamus Malone and Merlin Crossingham; music by Julian Nott; associate producers Sean Clarke and Carla Shelley; executive producers Peter Lord and David Sproxton [credited as Dave Sproxton]; produced by Nick Park; directed by Christopher Sadler and Loyd Price.
Main regular cast:	Peter Sallis (Voice of Wallace).

		Holding / Source
24.12.2002	**The Christmas Cardomatic**	DB /
23.12.2002	**The Snowmanotron**	DB /

Two episodes remain untransmitted.

See also: WALLACE AND GROMIT

THE WARD

A Granada production. Transmission details are for the Central region. Duration: 25 minutes.

SERIES 3

		Production No	Holding / Source
16.12.1997	"The real Santa?"	1/1519/110	D2 / D2S

Big Bob is an appalling ward Santa, then a second Santa arrives claiming to be the real one.

Written by Joe Turner.

With Gregg Baines (Greg), Brigit Forsyth (Sylvia Dickinson), Trevor Cooper (Big Bob), Anthony Lewis (Scott), Rita May (Mags), Phillip King (Nick), Victoria Finney (Julie), Sharon Muircroft (Fiona).

See also: CHILDREN'S WARD

A WARNING TO THE FURIOUS (RADIO)

A BBC production for BBC Radio 4. Transmission details are for BBC Radio 4. Duration: 45 minutes.

Written by Robin Brooks; play production by Fiona McAlpine.

Lucy Robinson (Karen), Catherine Shepherd (Zara), Carl Prekopp (Guy), Gerard McDermott (Bob), Andrew Wincott (Bookshop Man).

	Holding / Source
28.12.2007	DA /

See also: A GHOST STORY FOR CHRISTMAS (BBC)

WATCH

A BBC production for BBC 1. Transmission details are for BBC 1. Duration: 17 minutes.

		Holding / Source
22.11.1977	**The Nativity 1**	DB-D3 / 2"
29.11.1977	**The Nativity 2**	DB-D3 / 2"
28.11.1995	**Festivals And Celebrations: Christmas And The Nativity**	DB / D3S

This listing includes all surviving editions, drama and non-drama.

WATCHING

A Granada production. Transmission details are for the Central region. Usual duration: 25 minutes.

Main regular credit(s):	Written by Jim Hitchmough; lyrics by Charles Hart; theme music by Charles Hart.
Main regular cast:	Paul Bown (Malcolm Stoneway), Liza Tarbuck (Pamela Wilson/Lynch (from series 4 onwards)), Emma Wray (Brenda Wilson).

SERIES 1

Main regular credit(s):	Produced by David Liddiment; directed by Les Chatfield.
Main regular cast:	With Al T. Kossy (Harold).

		Production No	Holding / Source
27.12.1987	**Seasoning**	1/1368/0008	1" / 1"

Duration: 26 minutes.

With Patsy Byrne (Mrs Stoneway), Philip Fox (Sidney Clough), Bill Moores (Cedric), Michael Stark.

SERIES 3

Main regular credit(s):	Music by Richie Close; designed by Tim Farmer; executive producer David Liddiment; produced and directed by Les Chatfield.
Main regular cast:	With John Bowler (David Lynch).

		Production No	Holding / Source
24.12.1988	**Twitching**	1/1368/0016	1" / 1"

Duration: 52 minutes.

With Patsy Byrne (Mrs Stoneway), Ken Morley, Richard Ridings, Nick Maloney, Simon Wallis, Tommy Boyle.

SERIES 5

Main regular credit(s): Executive producer David Liddiment; produced and directed by Les Chatfield.
Main regular cast: With John Bowler (David Lynch).

	Production No	Holding / Source
25.12.1991 **Slipping**	1/1368/0042	D2 / 1"S

Duration: 50 minutes.
With Al T. Kossy (Harold), Bill Moores (Cedric), Charlotte Beeley (Sarah Lynch), Georgina Beeley (Sarah Lynch), Elizabeth Morton, Noreen Kershaw, Josh Moran, Neil Rowland, Neil Anthony, Andrew Hilton.

SERIES 6

Main regular credit(s): Produced and directed by David Liddiment.

	Production No	Holding / Source
01.01.1993 **Reverting**	1/1368/0049	D2 / D2S

With Patsy Byrne, John Bowler, Elizabeth Morton, Noreen Kershaw, Richard Good, Andrew Hilton, Al T. Kossy, Bill Moores.

WATERS OF THE MOON

A BBC production for BBC 1. Transmission details are for BBC 1. Duration: 100 minutes.

Written by N. C. Hunter; designed by Geoff Powell; produced by Cedric Messina; directed by Piers Haggard.

Penelope Keith (Helen Lancaster), Virginia McKenna (Mrs Whyte), Ronald Pickup (Julius Winterhalter), Joan Sims (Mrs Ashworth), Richard Vernon (Colonel Selby), Lesley Dunlop (Evelyn Daly), Geoffrey Palmer (Robert Lancaster), Dilys Laye (Mrs Daly), Phoebe Nicholls (Tonetta Landi), Dean Allen (John Daly).

	Holding / Source
30.12.1983	DB-D3 / 2"

WAY UPSTREAM

A BBC production for BBC 1. Transmission details are for BBC 1. Duration: 100 minutes.

Adapted by Terry Johnson; based on a play by Alan Ayckbourn; designed by Geoff Powell; produced by Andrée Molyneux; directed by Terry Johnson.

Barrie Rutter (Keith), Marion Bailey (June), Nick Dunning (Alistair), Joanne Pearce (Emma), Stuart Wilson (Vince), Lizzy McInnerny (Fleur), Veronica Clifford (Mrs Hatfield).

	Holding / Source
01.01.1988	DB-1" / C1

WAYNE AND SHUSTER IN LONDON

A BBC production. Transmission details are for BBC. Duration: 45 minutes.

Written by Johnny Wayne; orchestra conducted by Harry Rabinowitz; choreography by Alfred Rodrigues; designed by Tony Abbott; produced and directed by James Gilbert.

Wayne and Shuster, Sheila O'Neill, Annie Ross, The Cliff Adams Singers, Marianne Stone, Donald Sutherland, Pamela Conway, Donald Ewer.

	Holding / Source
22.12.1962	J /

WE SIX KINGS

A Yorkshire Television production. Transmission details are for the ATV midlands region. Duration: 25 minutes.

Designed by Colin Pigott; produced and directed by Vernon Lawrence.

The King's Singers

Christmas Special from Bramham Park

	Holding / Source
27.12.1976	DB / 2"

WE SIX KINGS

A Yorkshire Television production. Transmission details are for the ATV midlands region. Duration: 25 minutes.

A programme of songs from Nostell Priory, Yorkshire. The music ranges from carols to a comedy song.

Written by Barry Took; music directed by Howard Goodall; designed by Colin Pigott; produced and directed by Vernon Lawrence.

The King's Singers, Bill Ives, Anthony Holt, Jeremy Jackman, Alastair Hume, Simon Carrington, Brian Kay, William Rushton.

Christmas Special from Nostell Priory

	Holding / Source
25.12.1981	1" / 2"

WE WISH THEM A MERRY CHRISTMAS

An ATV production. Transmission details are for the ATV midlands region. Duration: 25 minutes.

Come and meet some of the many people who have to work on Christmas Day so that others can enjoy themselves. With the aid of film, we hope to take you and them to some of the places they would like to be if they were not working. Film by the ATV Midlands Film Unit.

Produced by Raymond Joss; directed by David Scott.

Leslie Dunn (Presenter), Judith Jackson (Presenter).

	Holding / Source
25.12.1963	J /

THE WEAKEST LINK

A BBC production. Transmission details are for BBC. Duration varies - see below for details.

Main regular credit(s): Devised by Fintan Coyle and Cathy Dunning; music by Paul Farrer; designed by Patrick Doherty.

Main regular performer(s): Anne Robinson (Host), Jon Briggs (Voice Over).

Transmission details are for BBC 2. Duration: 30 minutes.

	Holding / Source
24.12.2000	DB / DBSW

Produced by Phil Parsons; directed by James Ditchfield.

With Adam Woodyatt, Alice Beer, Nicholas Parsons, Vanessa Feltz, Simon Biagi, Sue Perkins, Charlotte Hudson, Mel Giedroyc, Louis Theroux.

28.12.2001 **Headliners**	DB / DBSW

Produced by Dee Todd; directed by James Ditchfield.

With Edwina Currie, Neil Hamilton, Darius, Nick Leeson, Eddie Edwards, Kim Cotton, Cindy Jackson, Kara Noble, Tom Naylor.

31.12.2002 **Entertainers**	DB / DBSW

Produced by Dee Todd, Jo Street and Alexandra McLeod; directed by Ian Hamilton.

With Graham Phillips, Philip Partridge, Jimmy Tamley, Leslie Gibson, Steve Harris, Jodie Moore, Michelle Wickison, John Catherall, Lesley Guinness.

Transmission details are for BBC 1. Duration: 45 minutes.

	Holding / Source
24.12.2001 **TV Presenters**	DB / DBSW

Produced by Eileen Herlihy; directed by James Ditchfield.

With Shauna Lowry, Andi Peters, Lowri Turner, Keith Chegwin, Quentin Willson, Lorraine Kelly, Jane Moore, Keith Duffy, Neil Fox.

24.12.2002 **Pantomime Special**	DB / DBSW

Produced by Dee Todd; directed by Mick Thomas.

With Wayne Sleep, Christopher Biggins, Bobby Davro, Carol Harrison, Malandra Burrows, Malcolm Dixon, Russ Kane, Caroline Buckley, Juliet Horne.

24.12.2004 **Pantomime Special**	DB / DBSW

Duration: 49 minutes.

Produced by Andy Rowe; directed by Ivan Youlden.

With Lucy Benjamin, Peter Duncan, Ruth Madoc, Alvin Stardust, Joe Pasquale, Britt Ekland, Shane Lynch, Nigel Ellacott, Helen Noble.

10.12.2005 **Pantomime Special**	DB / DBSW

Duration: 49 minutes.

Produced by Alexandra McLeod; directed by Mick Thomas.

With Anne Diamond, James Gaddas, Christopher Biggins, Dani Harmer, Danny La Rue, Stacey Cadman, Amanda Barrie, Warwick Davis, Jeff Brazier, Basil Brush.

27.12.2008 **Strictly Come Dancing**	DB / DBSW

A BBC Productions production. Duration: 60 minutes.

Executive producer Martin Scott; produced by Lamees Nuseibeh; directed by Ivan Youlden.

With Mark Ramprakash, Craig Revel Horwood, Mark Foster, Arlene Phillips, Anton Du Beke, Brendan Cole, Heather Small, Camilla Dallerup, Kristina Hanof.

Only celebrity editions are listed.

THE WEDNESDAY PLAY

A BBC production for BBC 1. Transmission details are for BBC 1. Duration varies - see below for details.

SERIES 2

	Holding / Source
22.12.1965 **The Coming Out Party**	R1 /

Duration: 60 minutes.

Tonight's play is a simple tale set in that part of London known as Notting Dale where the author himself grew up and still lives. It is almost Christmas, and a little boy begins a search—a sad search which leads him into trouble. But on the way there is a glorious knees-up comedy which should put us all in a Christmas spirit.
 Carols sung by Alan Sojka and fellow pupils of Christopher Wren School and Isaac Newton School.

Written by James O'Connor; lyrics by Nemone Lethbridge; theme music by Paul Jones and Mike Vickers; music by Stanley Myers; designed by Michael Wield; produced by James MacTaggart; directed by Kenneth Loach.

With Toni Palmer (Rosie), George Sewell (Ricketts), Dennis Golding (Scimpy), Jayne Muir (Sister Bridget), Wally Patch (Grandad), Will Stampe (Scrap Merchant), Carol White (The Princess), Hilda Barry (Granma), Alec Ross (Police Constable Nicholls), Julie May (Wendy), Penelope Parry (Prison Officer), Edwin Brown (Police Sergeant), Alister Williamson (Inspector Brisby), Tommy Godfrey (Jimmy The Gent), Rita Webb (Floss), Andrea Lawrence (Sandra), Griffith Davies (Pretty Boy), George Tovey (Tug Wilson), Dickie Owen (Big Al), Aubrey Richards (Governor), Ted Peel (Harry), Fanny Carby (Liz Kelly), Alec Coleman (Snuffy), Eunice Black (Audrey), Howell Evans (Prison Gatekeeper), Ray Barron (Fidgetty Joe), Frank Jarvis (Odd Ears), Bernard Stone (Jack The Butcher), Winifred Sabine (Customer), Tommy Fulbrook (Tommy), Dermot McDowell (Customer), Heather Barbour (Salvation Army Girl), Patrick O'Connell (Nobby), John Formosa (Boy), Tommy Gent (Boy), Barry Payne (Boy), Trevor Roger (Boy), Roy Thomas (Boy), Alan Sojka (Carol Singer).

22.12.65 - OBITUARY: RICHARD DIMBLEBY 1913-1965 (LCA6877J) - front: [leader, then line-up]; end credits of "The Wednesday Play" (directed by Kenneth Loach); caption 'BBC1 Newsflash', announcement; complete news flash about the death of Richard Dimbleby; globe with announcement that tribute to Dimbleby follows shortly, silent globe for a long time, announcement. End: globe, plug for extra News bulletin after the next programme at approximately 11.35pm, followed by prayers with the Bishop of London, anouncement that "Viewpoint" has been postponed, ident; first few seconds of "Joan Baez in Concert Part 1".

Philip Broadley submitted a script entitled "Our Pleasant Vices" but it was never made.

WEEKEND

A Granada production. Transmission details are for the Granada region. Duration: 50 minutes.

SERIES 1

Main regular credit(s): Produced by Trish Kinane.

	Holding / Source
23.12.1983	1" / 1"

With Paul Jones (Presenter), Bill Tidy (Presenter), Boy George, Limahl, Billy Connolly, Alexei Sayle.

WELCOME 1977

A BBC Scotland production for BBC 1. Transmission details are for BBC 1. Duration: 75 minutes.

Additional material by Ronnie Cass, Edward Boyd [credited as Eddie Boyd] and Dick Sharples; designed by Jim Longmuir; executive producer Iain MacFadyen; produced by Brian Hulme, Ian Christie, Anne Somers and John Scholz-Conway.

Faith Brown, Elizabeth Estensen, Anne Lorne Gillies, Peter Halliday, Joe Lynch, Peter Morrison, Alastair McDonald, Roddy McMillan, Jimmy Savile, Andy Stewart, Danny Street, Brian Fahey and The Scottish Radio Orchestra, The British Caledonian Airways (Renfrew) Pipe Band, Members of the Royal Scottish Country Dance Society, Billy Anderson's Band.

	Holding / Source
31.12.1976	J / 2"

"With New Year greetings from BBC stars, Kojak, Starsky and Hutch and Petula Clark and from the Armed Services worldwide."

WELCOME '69

A BBC production for BBC 1. Transmission details are for BBC 1.

Designed by Tim Harvey; produced and directed by Iain MacFadyen.

Jimmy Logan, Stuart Henry, Chic Murray, George Chisholm, John Grieve, The Corries, Marmalade, Dixie Ingram, Grant Frazer, The New Faces, Alex Welsh and his Band, City of Glasgow Police Pipe Band, BBC Scottish Radio Orchestra.

	Holding / Source
01.01.1969	J /

THE WELCOME OF WALES

A BBC Wales production for BBC 1 Wales. Transmission details are for BBC 1 Wales. Duration: 25 minutes.

A Christmas programme of music.

	Holding / Source
24.12.1974	C1 / C1

Held at BBC Wales.

WELCOME TO THE CEILIDH

A Grampian Television production. Transmission details are for the ATV midlands region. Duration: 25 minutes.

Main regular credit(s): Music associate Alex Sutherland; designed by Eric Mollart; produced and directed by Mike Bevan.

Main regular performer(s): Johnny Beattie, Johnny Beattie, Stuart Anderson, Margaret & Donnie MacLeod, Isla St. Clair, Isla St. Clair, Grant Frazer, Louise Kelly, Stuart Anderson, Davis-Hamilton Dancers, Hebbie Gray Band.

SERIES 1

	Holding / Source
24.12.1976	J / 2"

SERIES 2

		Holding / Source
23.12.1977	Welcome To The Christmas Ceilidh	J / 2"
31.12.1977	Welcome To The Hogmanay Ceilidh	J / 2"

Duration: 50 minutes.

SERIES 3

		Holding / Source
22.12.1978	Welcome To The Christmas Ceilidh	J / 2"

See also: OUT WITH THE OLD, IN WITH THE NEW

THE WELL DRESSED MAN

An ATV production. Transmission details are for the ATV midlands region. Duration: 25 minutes.

Written by S. C. Green and R. M. Hills; settings by Bill McPherson; produced by Alan Tarrant.

Shaw Taylor, James Laver, Marjorie Proops, Teddy Watson, John Taylor, Arthur Haynes.

	Holding / Source
26.12.1962	

A light-hearted survey.

WESTWARD CHRISTMAS PANTOMIME

A Westward Television production. Transmission details are for the Westward Television region. Duration: 25 minutes.

Written by John Bartlett; lyrics by Terry Roper and John Bartlett; music by Terry Roper and John Bartlett; designed by David Drewery; produced and directed by John Bartlett.

Kenneth MacLeod (Story Teller), Stuart Hutchison (Ebenezer Scrooge), Judi Spiers (Rag Doll), Roger Shaw (Station Announcer), Peter Forde (Tweedledum), Chris Fear (Tweedledee), Lawrie Quayle (Old King Cole), Frank Wintle (Lion), Gary Lovejoy (Bear), Brian Pedley (Gorilla), Bob Crampton (Beefeater), David Rodgers (Knave of Hearts), John Miller (Trophy), Ted Tuckerman (Trophy), David Young (Trophy), Ian Stirling (Effie Catious), Clive Gunnell (Gunnelver The Giant).

	VT Number	Holding / Source
24.12.1981	DP/4964/Ed	DB / 2"
Recorded 23.12.1981		

WHAT A CARRY ON?

A British Film Corporation production for Carlton. Transmission details are for the Central region. Duration: 48 minutes.

Executive producers John Hough and John Bishop; produced by Chris Skinner.

Peter Rogers (Presenter), Joan Sims, Barbara Windsor, Leslie Phillips, June Whitfield, Jim Dale.

	Holding / Source
29.12.1998	DB / DBS

WHAT DO YOU KNOW ABOUT CHRISTMAS?

A Southern Television production. Transmission details are for the Scottish Television region. Duration: 8 minutes.

Christmas for the young is an enchanted time full of coloured lights and brightly wrapped presents, great things to eat and drink, singing and staying up late... very much like a birthday party for everyone.

But do people still pause to reflect on whose birthday they are really celebrating? Father Cashman and some young children from his parish discuss the true meaning of Christmas.

Produced and directed by Stephen Wade.

Father Anthony Cashman.

	Holding / Source
21.12.1975	J / 2"

WHAT THE DICKENS

A HTV production for Channel 4. made in association with Tempest Films. Transmission details are for Channel 4. Duration: 70 minutes.

Written by Heathcote Williams; designed by John Reid; executive producer Derek Clark; produced by Jacky Stoller; directed by Joe McGrath.

Ben Cross (Charles Dickens), Kenneth Haigh (William Macready), Kenneth Cranham (Topping), Dinsdale Landen (John Dickens), Maggie Wilkinson (Mrs Macready), Mary Healey (Cook), Michael Elwyn (Albany Fonblanque), Valerie Whittington (Georgina Hogarth), Victoria Plucknett (Catherine Dickens), James Carter (Thackeray), Neil Cunningham (Thomas Carlyle), Eva Lohman (Jane Carlyle), Rosie Marcel (Mamie Dickens), James Holland (Charley Dickens), James Griffiths (John Pritt Harley), Jill Melford (Lady Blessington), Roddy Maude-Roxby (Count D'Orsay), David Horovitch (Sergeant Thomas Talfourd QC).

	Holding / Source
28.12.1983	1" / 2"

WHAT THE WORLD SAYS

A Granada production. Transmission details are for the Granada region. Duration: 25 minutes.

	Production No	Holding / Source
23.12.1981	P1141/8901	DB / 2"

WHATEVER HAPPENED TO CHRISTMAS?

An ATV production. Transmission details are for the ATV midlands region. Duration: 52 minutes.

Bruce Forsyth, as Santa Claus, brings Christmas goodies.

Written by Sid Green and Dick Hills; music associate Colin Keyes; choreography by Norman Maen; designed by Eric Shedden; produced and directed by Jon Scoffield.

Bruce Forsyth, Cliff Richard, Anita Harris, Bill Oddie, Arthur Mullard, Ronnie Brodie, Pat Coombs, Robert Lee, Jimmy Tarbuck, Ronnie Carroll, Mick McManus, Rita Webb, Peggy O'Farrell Children, Jack Parnell and his Orchestra, The Mike Sammes Singers.

	Holding / Source
24.12.1968	J /

WHATEVER HAPPENED TO THE LIKELY LADS?

A BBC production for BBC 1. Transmission details are for BBC 1. Duration varies - see below for details.

Main regular credit(s): Written by Dick Clement and Ian La Frenais; theme music by Mike Hugg and Ian La Frenais.

Main regular cast: James Bolam (Terry Collier), Rodney Bewes (Bob Ferris).

SERIES 2

Main regular credit(s): Music by Ronnie Hazlehurst; produced and directed by Bernard Thompson.

Main regular cast: With Brigit Forsyth (Thelma Ferris).

	Holding / Source
24.12.1974 The Likely Lads: A Special Christmas Edition	DB-D3 / 2"

Duration: 44 minutes.
Designed by Tim Gleeson.
With Brigit Forsyth (Thelma Ferris), Norman Mitchell (Jack), Joanna Ross, John Crocker, Lilian Verner, John White, Betty Bowden.

WHATEVER HAPPENED TO THE LIKELY LADS?

British Christmas Television Guide **WHATEVER HAPPENED TO THE LIKELY LADS? (continued)**

Clement and La Frenais appeared on "Real Time", BBC2, tx:28.3.1974 talking about the series. Produced and directed by Philip Speight. 45 mins. It does not exist.

WHAT'S MY LINE?

A BBC production. Transmission details are for BBC. Usual duration: 30 minutes.

Main regular credit(s): Devised by Mark Goodson and Bill Todman.

SERIES 1
Transmission details are for BBC.
Main regular credit(s): Television presentation by T. Leslie Jackson.

	Holding / Source
24.12.1951	J / Live

Duration: 45 minutes.
With Eamonn Andrews (Chairman), Lesley Storm, Jimmy Edwards, Elizabeth Allan, Gilbert Harding, Anona Winn, Jack Train, Joy Adamson, Richard Dimbleby.

SERIES 14
Transmission details are for BBC 2.
Main regular credit(s): Produced by Ernest Maxin.
Main regular performer(s): With David Jacobs (Chairman), Isobel Barnett, Kenneth Williams, William Franklyn, Nanette Newman.

	Holding / Source
25.12.1973	DB-D3-2" / 2"

Designed by Paul Montague.
With Marty Feldman*.
Recorded 19.12.73.

WHAT'S MY LINE?

A Thames Television production. Transmission details are for the Central region. Duration: 25 minutes.

	Holding / Source
24.12.1984 **Christmas Special**	DB / 1"

Research Sue Green; designed by Graham Probst; produced by Maurice Leonard; directed by Stuart Hall.
With Eamonn Andrews (Chairman), Ernie Wise, George Gale, Barbara Kelly, Jilly Cooper, Patrick Mower.

26.12.1988 **Christmas Special**	1" / 1"

Associate producer John Graham; produced by Maurice Leonard; directed by Brian Klein.
With Angela Rippon (Host), Jilly Cooper, Adrian Mills, Gabrielle Drake, Nino Firetto.

Incomplete listing.

WHEEL OF FORTUNE

A Southern Television production. Transmission details are for the Thames Television region. Duration: 25 minutes.

Welcome to another edition of a light-hearted quiz game, when contestants have to make the big decision-money or the wheel? Why not join them tonight and see what they decide to do? There's no script, and people from the studio audience are the stars of the show, often providing more laughs than some highly-paid funny men. The contestants are tempted by Michael's offer to buy their number. If they can resist, they spin the "Wheel of Fortune" for a major prize - or a booby!

Main regular credit(s): Designed by Greg Lawson; produced by Michael Miles.
Main regular performer(s): Michael Miles (Question-Master), Bob Danvers-Walker (Announcer).

SERIES 1
Main regular credit(s): Organist Harold Smart.

	Holding / Source
19.12.1969	J / 2"

A special edition of a light-hearted quiz game before a Christmas audience of old age pensioners.
Directed by Dave Heather.

WHEEL OF FORTUNE

A Scottish Television production. Transmission details are for the Central region. Duration: 25 minutes.
Main regular performer(s): Nicky Campbell (Presenter).

	Holding / Source
22.12.1988 **Christmas Special**	1" / 1"

Executive producer Sandy Ross; produced by Stephen Leahy; directed by Anne Mason.
With Angela Ekaette (Hostess), Jon Iles, Sue Jenkins, Brian Regan.

29.12.1988 **Celebrity Special**	1" / 1"

Executive producer Sandy Ross; produced by Stephen Leahy; directed by Anne Mason.
With Angela Ekaette (Hostess), Linda Lusardi, Cheryl Baker, Duncan Goodhew.

27.12.1990 **Christmas Special**	1" / 1"

With Carol Smillie (Hostess), Steve Hamilton (Voice Only), Bobby Davro, Anthea Turner, Carol Vorderman.

WHEELTAPPERS AND SHUNTERS SOCIAL CLUB

Alternative/Working Title(s): THE ENTERTAINERS

A Granada production. Transmission details are for the ATV midlands region. Duration varies - see below for details.

Main regular performer(s):　Colin Crompton (Host).

SERIES 2

Main regular credit(s):　　Research John Stirling; music directed by Derek Hilton; designed by Tim Farmer; produced by John Hamp; directed by Dave Warwick.

Main regular performer(s):　With The Derek Hilton Bandsmen.

	Production No	Holding / Source
31.12.1974 New Year's Eve At The Wheeltappers & Shunters Social Club	P788/16	DB / 2"

Duration: 50 minutes.

With Matt Monro, Charlie Williams, Freddie Garrity, Frank Carson, Design, Kristine.

SERIES 4

Main regular credit(s):　　Music directed by Derek Hilton; designed by Tim Farmer; produced by John Hamp; directed by Nicholas Ferguson.

Main regular performer(s):　With Bernard Manning (Compere).

	Production No	Holding / Source
31.12.1975 New Year's Eve At The Wheeltappers & Shunters Social Club	P788/31	DB / 2"

Duration: 39 minutes.

With Mike Harding, Charlie Williams, Dougie Brown, Russ Conway, Peter Gordeno and his Dancers.

WHEN JOSEPH MET MARIA

A BBC Productions production for BBC 1. Transmission details are for BBC 1. Duration: 60 minutes.

Written by Rob Colley; script supervisors Tony Grech and Maria Faley; theme music by Dan McGrath and Josh Phillips; designed by Chris Webster; associate producer Michael Canning; executive producer Martin Scott; series producer Kate Maddigan; produced by Kate Maddigan; film sequences directed by Holly Flynn; directed by Nikki Parsons.

Graham Norton (Host), Connie Fisher, Lee Mead, Denise van Outen, John Barrowman, Andrew Lloyd Webber.

	Holding / Source
24.12.2007	DB / DBSW

WHEN SANTA RODE THE PRAIRIE

A BBC production for BBC 2. Transmission details are for BBC 2. Duration: 50 minutes.

Written by William Rushton; music by Roy Civil and William Rushton; choreography by Jo Cook; designed by Judy Steele; produced by Anna Home; directed by Jeremy Swan.

Nigel Rhodes (Charlie Flagstaff), Abigail Brown (Tilly Flagstaff), William Rushton (Santa), Ed Devereaux (Lucifer Q. Millhouse), Gordon Gostelow (Old Hawkspit), Tim Stern (Tiny Earp), Malcolm Rennie (Beastly Bill Bracken), Pamela Charles (Aunt Mildred), Sue Nicholls (Aunt Martha), Marc Urquhart (Big Chief Loping Goat), Roy Evans (Apache), Victor Spinetti (United States Cavalry Trooper), Lance Aston (Apache), Martin Baker (Apache), Peter Height (Apache), Bryan Payne (Apache), Larry Ryan (Apache), Mark White (Apache).

	Holding / Source
23.12.1976	DB-D3 / 2"

WHEN THE ANGELS... AND THE WISE MEN AND THE SHEPHERDS GREW UP

A BBC production for BBC 2. Transmission details are for BBC 2. Duration: 45 minutes.

... they became engineers and PhDs, milkmen and comptometer operators, marketing executives and train drivers. Kenneth More tells a story from the tiny stage where it began at Christmas 18 years ago. On that stage in the school hall at Uxendon Manor some 65 children took the curtain call at the end of their nativity play, and television viewers all over the country saw them on Christmas Eve. Now, those children come together again for the first time since then, as the audience for this year's play. But what has happened to them since they were the angels and the wise men and the shepherds of 18 years ago? Their triumphs and failures since that Christmas Eve, make up this Christmas Day story.

Directed by Sandra Wainwright.

Kenneth More (Presenter).

	Holding / Source
25.12.1974	C1 / C1

WHEN THE CAMERAS CAME TO BRUM

A BBC Birmingham production for BBC 1 Midlands. Transmission details are for BBC 1. Duration: 30 minutes.

Produced and directed by Derek Smith.

Cliff Richard.

	Holding / Source
31.12.1973	J / C1

WHEN WE ARE MARRIED

A BBC production for BBC 2. Transmission details are for BBC 2. Duration: 120 minutes.

Written by J. B. Priestley; music by Jim Parker; designed by Tony Burrough; produced by Shaun Sutton; directed by Barry Davis.

Patricia Routledge (Maria Helliwell), Peter Vaughan (Alderman Helliwell), Prunella Scales (Annie Parker), Timothy West (Councillor Parker), Rosemary Leach (Clara Soppitt), Bernard Cribbins (Herbert Soppitt), Joss Ackland (Henry Ormonroyd), Tessa Peake-Jones (Nancy Holmes), Liz Smith (Mrs Northrop), Sue Devaney (Ruby Birtle), Patsy Rowlands (Lottie Grady), Patrick Pearson (Gerald Forbes), Gawn Grainger (Fred Dyson), Roger Brierley (Reverend Clement Mercer), Colin Douglas (Mayor).

Holding / Source
26.12.1987   DB / 1"

WHERE THE HEART IS

Commissioned and produced by a variety of companies (see details below). Transmission details are for the Central region.

Main regular credit(s):   Created by Ashley Pharoah and Vicky Featherstone; theme music by Paddy McAloon.

SERIES 7

A Meridian production for ITV 1.

Main regular credit(s):   Executive producers Michele Buck, Damien Timmer and Rebecca Keane; produced by Ian Hopkins.

Main regular cast: With Lesley Dunlop (Anna Kirkwall), Philip Middlemiss (David Buckley), Keith Barron (Alan Boothe), Samantha Giles (Sally Boothe), Andrew Paul (Billy Boothe), Kerrie Taylor (Beth Enright), Christian Cooke (Luke Kirkwall), Danny Seward (Joe Beresford), Tom Chadbon (Doctor Kenworthy), Holly Grainger (Megan Boothe), Katy Clayton (Samantha Boothe), Kelly Wenham (Jess Buckley), Julian Lewis Jones (Tom Beresford), Adam Paul Harvey (Nathan Boothe), Katie Riddoch (Molly Beresford), Luke de Woolfson (Russell Naylor).

Holding / Source
23.12.2003 **Archangel**   DB / V1SW

Duration: 75 minutes.

Written by John Johnson; directed by Moira Armstrong.

With Dennis Waterman, Georgia Taylor, Kieran Bew, Brodie Bass, Pauline Jefferson.

WHERE THE RAINBOW ENDS

An ATV London production. Transmission details are for the ATV London region. Duration: 50 minutes.

Conducted by Leighton Lucas; produced and directed by Arthur Lane.

Anton Dolin, Violetta Elvin, Valentine Dyall, Alfred Marks, Winifred Shotter, London Philharmonic Orchestra.

Holding / Source
24.12.1955   J /

WHICKER

A Yorkshire Television production. Transmission details are for the ATV midlands region. Usual duration: 25 minutes.

Main regular credit(s):   Presented by Alan Whicker; written by Alan Whicker.

	VT Number	Holding / Source
##.##.#### **Ecuador: A Right Royal Fiesta**	6016	1" / C1

Alternative transmissions: Yorkshire Television: 26.12.1968.

This was listed in the TV Times as an edition of 'The Reporters'.

WHICKER'S CHRISTMAS

A Yorkshire Television production. Transmission details are for the ATV midlands region. Duration: 25 minutes.

... and recalls a Christmas standing on the Equator (which was freezing), shopping for Christmas fare (which was unspeakable) and choosing the ideal Christmas present (which was a human head), Christmas in Ecuador is like Christmas nowhere else, as television's most treasured journalist reveals in a lighthearted report. Presented by Alan Whicker; written by Alan Whicker; executive producer Tony Essex; produced and directed by Michael Blakstad.

Holding / Source
26.12.1970 **Alan Whicker Introduces His Card From "Shangri La"...**   C1 / C1

A WHISTLE AND A FUNNY HAT

A Rediffusion Television production. Transmission details are for the Anglia region. Duration: 50 minutes.

Written by J. C. A. Whitewood; designed by John Emery; executive producer Peter Willes; directed by Marc Miller.

Martin Jarvis (David Bryant), Patrick Mower (Bill Carstairs), Lois Daine (Julie Bryant), Aimée Delamain (Miss Davidson), Michael McKevitt (Colin Smythe), John Shepherd (Tommy Smith), Dave Carter (Jack), Stanley Stewart (Frank), Tom Minnikin (Porter), Peter Street (Clerk), Michael Harding (Waiter).

Holding / Source
27.12.1967   J / 40

WHISTLE AND I'LL COME TO YOU

Alternative/Working Title(s): D

Commissioned by BBC 2. Transmission details are for BBC 2. Duration: 55 minutes.

Adapted by Neil Cross; based on a story by M. R. James; produced by Claire Armspach; directed by Andy De Emmony.

Holding / Source
24.12.2010   HD/DB / HD/DB

WHISTLE TEST

A BBC production for BBC 2. Transmission details are for BBC 2.

		Holding / Source
31.12.1984	**84 Whistle Test 85**	DB / 1"
	With Nik Kershaw, Big Country.	
31.12.1985	**85 Whistle Test 86 + Pick Of The Year**	DB / 1"
	With Madness, King.	
31.12.1986	**86 Whistle Test 87**	DB / 1"
	With Kim Wilde.	
31.12.1987	**87 Whistle Test 88**	DB / 1"
	With Gary Glitter.	

See also: THE OLD GREY WHISTLE TEST (BBC)

THE WHITE HEATHER CLUB

A BBC production. Transmission details are for BBC. Duration: 25 minutes.

	Holding / Source
31.12.1962	J /

Transmission details are for BBC 2.

	Holding / Source
31.12.1993	DB-D3 / D3S

A BBC Scotland production. Duration: 30 minutes.
Produced by May Miller; directed by Jane Rogerson.
Tribute to Andy Stewart who had died in 1993. Featured clips from surviving shows, reunties original cast and unseen footage from the very first episode. This is the network tx date. Shown earlier on BBC Scotland.

WHITE LIGHT

A Thames Television production. Transmission details are for the Thames Television region. Duration: 25 minutes.
James Maw (Presenter).

		Holding / Source
22.12.1981	**Christmas Concert**	DB / 2"

James Maw introduces all the bands from the current series.
Associate producer Lesley Burgess; produced by Roger Gale; directed by Roger Thomas.

THE WHITE ROOM

An Initial Film & TV production for Channel 4. Transmission details are for Channel 4. Duration: 50 minutes.

A blank canvas against which music can speak for itself.

Main regular performer(s): Mark Radcliffe (Presenter).

SERIES 2

Main regular credit(s):   Produced by Chris Cowey.

	Holding / Source
31.12.1995	D3 / D3S

With Oasis, David Bowie, P M Dawn, Chris Farlowe, Eternal, Pulp.

WHO DARES, WINS...

Produced for Channel 4 by a variety of companies (see details below). Transmission details are for Channel 4.

SERIES 2

Duration: 40 minutes.
Main regular credit(s):   Written by Colin Bostock-Smith, Andy Hamilton, Guy Jenkin, Tony Sarchet, Rory McGrath and Jimmy Mulville; produced by Denise O'Donoghue and Andy Hamilton; directed by John Stroud.
Main regular cast: With Philip Pope, Julia Hills, Rory McGrath, Jimmy Mulville, Tony Robinson.

		Holding / Source
21.12.1985	**A Season Ticket to Swansea City**	1" / 1"

With Martin Jarvis, Rosalind Ayres, Michael Fenton Stevens.

SERIES 3

A Who Dares Wins production. Duration: 40 minutes.
Main regular credit(s):   Written by Colin Bostock-Smith, Andy Hamilton, Guy Jenkin, Rory McGrath, Jimmy Mulville and Tony Sarchet; produced by Andy Hamilton and Denise O'Donoghue; directed by John Stroud.
Main regular cast: With Julia Hills, Tony Robinson, Rory McGrath, Jimmy Mulville, Philip Pope.

	Holding / Source
20.12.1986	1" / 1"

See also: COME DANCING WITH JOOLS HOLLAND

WHO DO YOU DO?

An LWT production. Transmission details are for the ATV midlands region. Duration: 25 minutes.

Main regular credit(s): Devised by Jon Scoffield.

SERIES 4

Transmission details are for the London Weekend Television region.

Main regular credit(s): Devised by Jon Scoffield; written by Barry Cryer, Dick Vosburgh, Wally Malston and Garry Chambers; music directed by Sam Harding; theme music by Sam Harding; produced and directed by Jon Scoffield.

Main regular cast: With Freddie Starr.

	Production No	Holding / Source
29.12.1974 **Christmas Edition**	9L/09511	D2 / 2"

Designed by Gordon Melhuish.

With Johnny More, Alan Clive, Peter Goodwright, Aiden J. Harvey, Janet Brown, Paula Scott, Mike Goddard, Jeannette Charles.

	Production No	Holding / Source
26.12.1975 **A Special Who Do You Do?**	9L/09516	D2 / 2"

Duration: 40 minutes.

There's never been a pantomime like it —can you imagine Cinderella with Cilla Black in the title role, W. C. Fields as Baron Horace, Arthur Askey as the Stepmother, 'Hortense' Cagney and 'Hermione' Bogart as the Ugly Sisters, Marlene Dietrich as the Principal Boy, all to a commentary by Eddie Waring? And that's only some of the action as the Who Do You Do gang get together for a gala edition.

Additional material by Peter Vincent; designed by Gordon Melhuish.

With Brother Lees, Faith Brown, Janet Brown, David Copperfield, Ray Fell, Peter Goodwright, Kristine, Little and Large, Len Lowe, Peter Reeves, Roy Starr, Jerry Stevens, Dailey and Wayne, Paul Melba, Roger Kitter.

WHO-DUN-IT

An ATV production. Transmission details are for the ATV midlands region. Duration: 50 minutes.

Created by Lewis Greifer; produced by Jack Williams.

	Production No	VT Number	Holding / Source
07.10.1969 **Crime At The Panto**	352	352/69	R1 / 62

Written by Lewis Greifer; directed by Peter Moffatt.

With Amanda Reiss (Cynthia Park), Eleanor Summerfield (Sylvie La-Coste), Derek Francis (Dorian Pettifer), Patricia Michael (Angela Warren), Tony Bateman (Andy Andrews), Polly Adams (Delphine Minniver), Jane Stonehouse (Usherette), Nicholas Pennell (Doctor Freddy Hamilton), Mischa de la Motte (Commissionaire), Effie Morrison (Mrs Acott), Jane Lowe (Phillipa Best), Preston Lockwood (Jack Steel), John Woodnutt (Detective Inspector Herd), John Cazabon (Mr Frazzel), Alexander Donald (Sergeant).

WHODUNNIT?

A Thames Television production. Transmission details are for the ATV midlands region. Duration varies - see below for details.

Main regular credit(s): Devised by Jeremy Lloyd and Lance Percival.

Credits: Written by Lance Percival and Jeremy Lloyd; designed by David Ferris; produced by Malcolm Morris; directed by Robert Reed.

Performer(s): With Jon Pertwee (Host).

	VT Number	Holding / Source
26.12.1974 **A Piece Of Cake**	9999	D3 / 2"

In this special Christmas edition of the popular Whodunnit? quiz, Alexander Anderson, who recently inherited a fortune, drops dead in the middle of his speech after the annual family dinner on Christmas Eve. There are six suspects — but which has the best motive? An added mystery is the brief appearance of two famous male stars. Who are they?

Designed by Roy Stannard.

With William Russell (Captain Alexander Anderson), Nicola Pagett (Marjorie Tempest), Michael Loos (James Anderson), Lesley Nunnerley (Betty Anderson), Ronald Hines (Doctor Eric Brooks), Valerie Holliman (Jane Anderson), Harold Kasket (Mr Louis), Barrie Gosney (Waiter), Eamonn Andrews (Waiter), Hughie Green (Drunk Customer), Patrick Mower, Wendy Craig, Derek Nimmo, Leslie Crowther.

WHOSE BABY?

A Thames Television production. Transmission details are for the ATV/Central region. Duration: 25 minutes.

Main regular credit(s): Devised by Eamonn Andrews.

SERIES 6

Transmission details are for the Thames Television region.

Main regular credit(s): Script associate Garry Chambers; research David Mason and Miriam O'Callaghan; graphics by Ian Kestle; designed by Jan Chaney; produced by Brian Klein; directed by Michael D. Kent.

Main regular performer(s): With Bernie Winters (Host), Sara Hollamby (Babysitter).

	VT Number	Holding / Source
31.12.1984	32467	DB / 1"

With Kenneth Williams, Nanette Newman, Roy Kinnear.

SERIES 7

Main regular credit(s): Produced by Maurice Leonard; directed by Robert Reed.

Main regular performer(s): With Bernie Winters (Host), Sara Hollamby (Babysitter).

	VT Number	Holding / Source
24.12.1985	34479	DB / 1"

WHOSE BODY? (RADIO)

A BBC Birmingham production for BBC Radio 4. Transmission details are for BBC Radio 4. Duration: 90 minutes.

Adapted by Michelene Wandor; based on a book by Dorothy L. Sayers; produced and directed by Vanessa Whitburn.

Gary Bond (Lord Peter Wimsey), John Cater (Bunter), Peter Rowland (Mr Parker), Michael Graham Cox (Sir Julian Freke), Veda Warwick (Duchess of Denver), Kim Durham (Mr Thipps / Doctor Grimbold / Waiter), Terry Molloy (John P. Milligan / Inspector Snugg / Gerald, Duke of Denver), Christopher Benjamin (Mr Crimplesham / Foreman / Sexton), Geoff Serle (Sir Reuben Levy / Graves / Coroner), Tim Brierley (Freddie Arbuthnot / Cummings), Charlotte Martin (Gladys Horrocks / Lady Levy), Alex Jones (Mr Piggott).

	Holding / Source
26.12.1987	DA /

WHOSE LINE IS IT ANYWAY?

A Hat Trick production for Channel 4. Transmission details are for Channel 4.

Main regular credit(s): Devised by Dan Patterson and Mark Leveson; theme music by Philip Pope.

Main regular cast: Clive Anderson (Host).

SERIES 2

Main regular credit(s): Music by Richard Vranch; designed by Pip Gardner and Graeme Story; executive producer Denise O'Donoghue; produced by Dan Patterson; directed by Chris Bould.

	Holding / Source
29.12.1989 **Christmas Special**	1" / 1"

Duration: 40 minutes.

With Josie Lawrence, Greg Proops, Paul Merton, Sandi Toksvig, Tony Slattery, Mike McShane.

THE WIDE WORLD OF ENTERTAINMENT

A BBC production for BBC 2. Transmission details are for BBC 2.

	Holding / Source
25.12.1978 **Buffalo Bill**	DB-D3 / 2"

Surviving editions only.

WIFE BEGINS AT 40

A BBC production for BBC 1. Transmission details are for BBC 1. Duration: 90 minutes.

Written by Arne Sultan, Earl Barrett and Ray Cooney; designed by Dinah Walker; produced and directed by Harold Snoad.

Liza Goddard (Linda Harper), Ray Cooney (George Harper), John Quayle (Roger Dixon), John Horsley (Bernard Harper), Tricia George (Betty Dixon), Grant Piro (Leonard Harper).

	Holding / Source
28.12.1988	DB / 1"

WILD AT HEART

A Company Pictures production for ITV 1. Transmission details are for the Central region.

Main regular credit(s): Created by Ashley Pharoah; music by Norwell and Green; executive producers Charles Pattinson, George Faber and Ashley Pharoah.

Main regular cast: Stephen Tompkinson (Danny Trevanion).

SERIES 7

	Holding / Source
30.12.2012	HD/DB / HDC

Duration: 100 minutes.

In the very last episode, Alice has returned, but there are tensions between her and Danny. When Cassidy the three-legged cheetah and his new mate are stolen by poachers, Du Plessis tries to persuade the family to go in search of the animals, hoping their return will pull everyone together - but a trip to the doctor brings him devastating news. Amid all this, Rosie is keen to marry fiance Dylan.

Written by Chris Murray and Ashley Pharoah; produced by Adam Frielander; directed by Nick Laughland.

With Deon Stewardson (Anders Du Plessis), Dawn Steele (Alice Trevanion), Olivia Scott-Taylor (Olivia Adams), Nomsa Xaba (Nomsa), Tarryn Faye Brummage (Charlotte), Hayley Mills (Caroline), Thapelo Mokoena (Fatani), Nick Boraine (Dylan), Liam Weatherall (Bobby), Colin Moss (Martin), Danny Keogh (Piet Stillman), Moshidi Motshegwa (Doctor Macmillan), Thato Molamu (Di), Joe Mafela (Vicar).

WILD THINGS

A BBC Films production for BBC 2. Transmission details are for BBC 2. Duration: 80 minutes.

Christmas at an eerie seaside hotel. Laura and Will are taken there to meet Jane, their future stepmother. She is glamorous and mysterious. But after an alarming discovery, their fascination turns to terror - and an
all-out battle begins.

Written by David Pirie; music by Richard Hartley; produced by David M. Thompson; directed by Rob Walker.

Karen Young (Jane), Stuart Wilson (Andrew), Willow Grylls (Laura), Ben Robb (Will), Donald Churchill (Brig Buchanan), Janet Henfrey (Sophie Buchanan), Tusse Silberg (Sarah), Joanna Joseph (Felicity Buchanan), Aaron Swartz (Mal Redfern), Hester MacGregor (Philippa), Duncan Faber (Head Porter), Tim Potter (Hotel Manager), Penelope Freeman (Receptionist), Janet Palmer (Receptionist), Jeremy Blake (Waiter), Robin Hooper (Chat-Show Host), Arbel Jones (TV Pundit).

	Holding / Source
30.12.1988	C1 / C1

WILDE ABOUT CHRISTMAS

A Granada Satellite Productions production for Granada Sky Broadcasting. Transmission details are for Granada Breeze. Duration: 23 minutes.

	Production No	Holding / Source
03.11.2000	1/3439/0001	DB / DBS
10.11.2000	1/3439/0002	DB / DBS
17.11.2000	1/3439/0003	DB / DBS
24.11.2000	1/3439/0004	DB / DBS
01.12.2000	1/3439/0005	DB / DBS
08.12.2000	1/3439/0006	DB / DBS
15.12.2000	1/3439/0007	DB / DBS
22.12.2000	1/3439/0008	DB / DBS
29.12.2000	1/3439/0009	DB / DBS

WILDLIFE SPECTACULAR

A BBC Bristol production for BBC 1. Transmission details are for BBC 1. Duration: 65 minutes.

Whales, lions, monkeys, elephants; a million flamingos; grizzly bears fishing; driver ants on the rampage; kingfishers, hippos and crocodiles underwater; the largest herd of animals in existence two and a half million fur seals; humming birds in ultraslow motion; the amazing angler fish in action; beautiful plankton, cheetahs and birds of paradise. Remarkable pictures of dragons on land and in the sea, penguins by the thousand, the incredible technique of the black heron and intimate pictures of chimpanzees in the wild.

Introduced by Peter Cushing and Doctor David Bellamy; produced and directed by Richard Brock.

Johnny Morris, HRH The Duke of Edinburgh, Kenneth Allsop, Jeffrey Boswall, Robert Dougall, Adam Faith, Joyce Grenfell, Rolf Harris, Spike Milligan, Eric Morecambe, Eva Reuber-Staier, Peter Scott, Harry Secombe, Tony Soper.

Holding / Source

26.12.1971

WILL ANY GENTLEMAN?

A BBC production. Transmission details are for BBC. Duration: 90 minutes.

Written by Vernon Sylvaine; produced by Mary Evans; directed by Wallace Douglas.

Jeanne Cook (Dancer), Larry Noble (Albert Boyle), Peter Mercier (Mendoza), Jacqueline Jones (Angel), Brian Rix (Henry Stirling), Leo Franklyn (Doctor Smith), Hazel Douglas (Beryl), Sheila Mercier (Florence Stirling), Basil Lord (Charley Stirling), Stuart Sherwin (Detective Inspector Martin), Terry Scott (Stanley Jackson), Helen Jessop (Honey), Fabia Drake (Mrs Whittle).

Holding / Source

26.12.1961
J /

WILLIE THE SQUOSE

A BBC production. Transmission details are for BBC. Duration: 60 minutes.

Narrated by Robert Wilson; written by Ted Allan; adapted by Ted Allan and Alvin Rakoff; harmonica Tommy Reilly; assistant producer Barry Learoyd; play production by Alvin Rakoff.

Bill Nagy (Joe), Lou Jacobi (Pete), Mark Daly (Humphrey), Amy Dalby (Henrietta), Ronan O'Casey (Richard), Tucker McGuire (Mrs Smith), Gordon Tanner (Mr Smith), Sheila Mackenzie (Lucille), Larry Cross (Mr Itchel).

Holding / Source

21.12.1954
J /

WILLO THE WISP

A BBC production for BBC 1. Transmission details are for BBC 1. Duration: 4 minutes.

Main regular credit(s): Written by Nicholas Spargo; music by Tony Kinsey; produced and directed by Nicholas Spargo.

Main regular cast: Kenneth Williams (Narrator).

Holding / Source

24.12.1981 **Christmas Box**
C3 / C3

THE WILLOWS IN WINTER

A TV Cartoons Ltd production for Carlton. made in association with Henson International Television. Transmission details are for the Central region. Duration: 70 minutes.

Feature-length animated sequel to THE WIND IN THE WILLOWS. Winter has come to the riverbank. When the intrepid Mole falls through the ice and is swept away by the river, his friends turn to Toad to help search for him using his new aeroplane.

Adapted by Ted Walker; based on a story by William Horwood; based on characters created by Kenneth Grahame; music by Colin Towns; art director Loraine Marshall; executive producers Jonathan Peel, Peter Orton and Michael Forte; produced by John Coates; directed by Dave Unwin.

Vanessa Redgrave (Narrator), Alan Bennett (Mole), Michael Palin (Rat), Michael Gambon (Badger), Rik Mayall (Toad), Enn Reitel (Otter), David Sinclair (Gaoler/Clerk), Mark Lockyer (Chief Weasel), Ronnie Fraser (Chief Judge), Windsor Davies (Commissioner Of Police), Mike Grady (Pilot), Adrian Scarborough (Nephew Mole), Zoot Lynam (Portly), Peter Cellier (Prendergast), Simon Williams (Bishop), Bill Oddie (Sweep), Jemima Ffyne (Alexandra), Jordan Hollywood (Emma), Tom Stourton (Edward).

Holding / Source

26.12.1996
D3 / D3S

See also: THE WIND IN THE WILLOWS

A WINCHESTER CHRISTMAS

A Southern Television production. Transmission details are for the ATV midlands region. Duration: 50 minutes.

Music by John Fiddy; produced by Angus Wright and Dave Heather; directed by Angus Wright and Dave Heather.

Dana, Choir of Winchester Cathedral, Anthony Quayle, Mel Martin, Bishop of Washington D.C., Bishop of Winchester, Martin Neary.

	VT Number	Holding / Source
30.12.1979 **[Come Sunday]**	3776	DB / 2"

Sold to EuroArts, Germany

VTR 3776 R/T 29:34/ 26:50 Protection copy at Wessex Archive. This is now on Digibeta

THE WIND IN THE WILLOWS

A Cosgrove Hall production for Thames Television. Transmission details are for the Central region. Duration: 25 minutes.

Main regular credit(s): Produced by Brian Cosgrove and Mark Hall.

	Holding / Source
27.12.1983 **The Wind In The Willows**	C1 / C1

Duration: 75 minutes.

Adapted by Rosemary Anne Sisson; based on a book by Kenneth Grahame; music by Keith Hopwood and Malcolm Rowe; edited by John McManus; executive producer John Hambley; directed by Mark Hall.

With Ian Carmichael (Rat), Richard Pearson (Mole), Michael Hordern (Badger), David Jason (Toad), Jonathan Cecil (Reggie), Beryl Reid (Magistrate), Una Stubbs (Jailer's Daughter), Allan Bardsley, Edward Kelsey, Brian Trueman.

SERIES 2

Main regular credit(s): Based on characters created by Kenneth Grahame; music by Keith Hopwood and Malcolm Rowe.

Main regular cast: With Ian Carmichael (Narrator), Michael Hordern (Badger), Richard Pearson (Mole), Peter Sallis (Rat), David Jason (Toad).

	Holding / Source
24.12.1984 **A Yuletide Entertainment**	C1 / C1

Written by Brian Trueman; directed by Chris Taylor.

No guest voices.

SERIES 3

Duration: 25 minutes.

Main regular credit(s): Written by Brian Trueman; music by Malcolm Rowe, Keith Hopwood and Ralph McTell; directed by Jackie Cockle.

Main regular cast: With Michael Hordern (Badger), Richard Pearson (Mole), Peter Sallis (Rat), David Jason (Toad), Ian Carmichael (Narrator).

	Holding / Source
24.12.1985 **Winter Sports**	C1 / C1

SERIES 4

	Holding / Source
30.12.1986 **Paperchase**	C1 / C1

SERIES 5

	Holding / Source
31.12.1987 **Auld Lang Syne**	C1 / C1

THE WIND IN THE WILLOWS

A TV Cartoons Ltd production for Carlton. made in association with Henson International Television. Transmission details are for the Central region. Duration: 75 minutes.

Animated version of the classic river bank adventure featuring Mole, Rat, Toad and Badger as they defeat the animals of the Wild Wood amd reclaim Toad's ancestral home from the Weasels.

Adapted by Ted Walker; based on a book by Kenneth Grahame; art director Loraine Marshall; executive producer Jonathan Peel; produced by John Coates; directed by Dave Unwin.

Alan Bennett (Mole), Michael Palin (Rat), Michael Gambon (Badger), Rik Mayall (Toad), Vanessa Redgrave (Narrator / Grandmother), James Villiers (Magistrate), Emma Chambers (Gaoler's Daughter), Judy Cornwell (Barge Woman), Barry Foster (Boatman), Enn Reitel (Other Voices), David Sinclair (Other Voices), Mark Lockyer (Other Voices).

	Holding / Source
25.12.1995	D3 / D3S

See also: THE WILLOWS IN WINTER

WINDMILL

A BBC production for BBC 2. Transmission details are for BBC 2. Duration: 60 minutes.

Main regular cast: Chris Serle (Presenter).

SERIES 1

	Holding / Source
22.12.1985 **Christmas**	DB / 1"

With John Craven.

WINE FOR CHRISTMAS

A Thames Television production. Transmission details are for the Yorkshire Television region. Duration: 50 minutes.

Ken Butler is in a wine cellar deep below the City of London with Iain Crawford and several other vinophiles. Butler, best known to viewers for his descriptions of horses for courses, is finding out about wines for courses, Christmas dinner and the festive parties. Vintners discuss how wine buying can be fitted into various family budgets. Keep a notebook at hand because this bibulous band is giving recipes for wine-based party drinks: cold fruit-embellisheddrinks, hot and cold punch, sherry punch, and mulled red wine.

Directed by Bob Service.

Ken Butler (Presenter), Iain Crawford (Presenter).

	Holding / Source
21.12.1970	J / 2"

WINNER TAKES ALL

A Yorkshire Television production. Transmission details are for the ATV midlands region. Usual duration: 25 minutes.

Main regular credit(s): Devised by Geoffrey Wheeler; executive producer Lawrie Higgins; produced and directed by Guy Caplin.

Main regular performer(s): Jimmy Tarbuck (Host), Geoffrey Wheeler (Voice Only).

Transmission details are for the ATV midlands region.

	VT Number	Holding / Source
23.12.1977 **All Star Winner Takes All**	2947	1" / 2"

Duration: 26 minutes.
Designed by Gordon Livesey.
With Honor Blackman, Diana Dors, Edward Woodward, Danny La Rue.

| 30.12.1978 **All Star Winner Takes All** | | 1" / 2" |

Designed by Ray Coldrick.
With Moira Anderson, Henry Cooper, Anita Harris, Dickie Henderson.

Only celebrity editions are listed.

A WINTER JOURNEY

Alternative/Working Title(s): TESS OF THE D'URBERVILLES

A Westward Television production. Transmission details are for the ATV midlands region. Duration: 25 minutes.

Based on Thomas Hardy's novel Tess of the d'Urhervilles, this special documentary traces a young woman's one day walking journey through Dorset as she seeks information about her husband, who left her on their wedding night.

Adapted by David Middlemiss; based on a book by Thomas Hardy; produced and directed by Clive Gunnell.

Sue Knight (Tess), Tony Church (Reader), Sally Mates (Reader).

	Holding / Source
28.12.1976	J / C1

WINTON'S WONDERLAND

A BBC production for BBC 1. Transmission details are for BBC 1. Duration: 50 minutes.

Main regular credit(s): Directed by Geoff Miles.

Main regular performer(s): Dale Winton (Host).

	Holding / Source
19.12.1998	DB / DBSW

Duration: 45 minutes.
Produced by John Beazley.
With Jimmy Nail, Jimmy Tarbuck, Barbara Windsor.

| 24.12.1999 | DB / DBSW |

Produced by Helen Tumbridge.
With Anne Robinson, David Seaman, Culture Club, Steps.

| 23.12.2000 | DB / DBSW |

Produced by Helen Tumbridge.
With Martine McCutcheon, Bob Monkhouse, June Whitfield, Billie Piper [as Billie], Clem Curtis, The Foundations.

WITH A FIDDLE AND A FLUTE

An Ulster Television production. Transmission details are for the Ulster Televison region.

Main regular credit(s): Music associate Tommy James; produced by John Scholz-Conway.

Main regular performer(s): Frank Carson, Teresa Duffy, Gertie Wine, Peter Tomelty.

	Holding / Source
25.12.1961	J / 40

Duration: 50 minutes.

WITHIN THESE WALLS

An LWT production. Usual duration: 51 minutes.

Main regular credit(s): Format by Mike Firman, Len Downs and Patrick Radcliffe.

SERIES 3

Transmission details are for the ATV midlands region.

Main regular credit(s): Theme music by Denis King; series consultant David Butler; executive producer Rex Firkin; produced by Jack Williams.

Main regular cast: With Googie Withers (Governor Faye Boswell), Jerome Willis (Deputy Governor Charles Radley), Mona Bruce (Chief Officer Mrs Armitage), Beth Harris (Miss Clarke), Denys Hawthorne (Doctor Mayes), Elaine Wells (Prison Officer Spencer).

	Production No	Holding / Source
20.12.1975 **On The Second Day Of Christmas**	9D/01812	D2 / 2"

Christmas comes to Stone Park Prison, with decorations, a concert party, and dinner served to the prisoners by the officers. "All the decorations! It's like putting rouge on a skeleton. I wish Christmas could last all year," exclaims Mrs. Armitage.

Written by David Butler; designed by Bryan Bagge; directed by Christopher Hodson.

With Sonia Graham (Miss Parrish), Floella Benjamin, Toni Palmer, Annie Hayes, Hazel Clyne, Diane Fletcher, Pamela Moiseiwitsch, Diana Rayworth, Betty Romaine, Raymond Adamson, Crispin Gillbard, Suzan Cameron, Patricia Maynard, Richard Aylen.

SERIES 4

Transmission details are for the ATV midlands region.

Main regular credit(s): Theme music by Denis King; series consultant David Butler; produced by Jack Williams.

Main regular cast: With Katharine Blake (Governor Helen Forrester), Jerome Willis (Deputy Governor Charles Radley), Elaine Wells (Prison Officer Spencer), Sonia Graham (Governor Martha Parrish), Denys Hawthorne (Doctor Mayes), Mona Bruce (Chief Officer Mrs Armitage), Beth Harris (Miss Clarke).

	Production No	Holding / Source
24.12.1976 **Silent Night**	9D/01976	D2 / 2"

Christmas is celebrated in Stone Park with the usual concerts and special meals. For a while, the inmates experience snatches of happiness. Rut when it is over, the weary routine of prison
life seems even harder to bear.

Written by David Butler; designed by John Emery; directed by Philip Casson.

With Miranda Forbes (Officer Parsons), Hazel Clyne (Marian Collins), Hilary Labow, Natalie Kent, Betty Romaine, Jenny Galloway, Lesley Daine, Tony Steedman, Suzan Cameron, Charles Morgan, Ann Gabrielle.

WIZADORA

A Meridian production. Transmission details are for the Central region. Duration: 8 minutes.

SERIES 6

	Holding / Source
16.12.1997 **Wizadora's Christmas Carol 1**	DB / D2S
18.12.1997 **Wizadora's Christmas Carol 2**	DB / D2S

WIZBIT

A BBC production for BBC 1. Transmission details are for BBC 1.

SERIES 3

	Holding / Source
27.01.1988 **The Christmas That Nearly Never Was 1**	DB / 1"
03.02.1988 **The Christmas That Nearly Never Was 2**	DB / 1"

WODEHOUSE PLAYHOUSE

A BBC production. Transmission details are for BBC.

Based on stories by P. G. Wodehouse.

SERIES 3

Commissioned by BBC 2. Transmission details are for BBC 2. Duration: 35 minutes.

Main regular credit(s): Adapted by David Climie; produced and directed by Gareth Gwenlan.

	Holding / Source
05.12.1978 **Big Business**	DB-D3 / 2"

Designed by Paul Munting.

With John Alderton (Reginald Mulliner), Maggie Henderson (Amanda Biffen), Derek Francis (Sir Jethro Mott), Gerald Sim (Vicar), Terence Conoley (Jarvis), Damaris Hayman (Miss Frisby), Norman Mitchell (Police Constable Popjoy), David Rowlands (Lord Knubble).

WOGAN

A BBC production for BBC 1. Transmission details are for BBC 1. Duration varies - see below for details.

Main regular performer(s): Terry Wogan (Host).

SERIES 4

Duration: 50 minutes.

Main regular credit(s): Programme associate Chris Greenwood; designed by David Buckingham.

	Holding / Source
25.12.1984 **Christmas Show**	DB / 1"

Produced by Geoff Posner; directed by Kevin Bishop.

With Freddie Starr, Kiri Te Kanawa, Elton John, Victoria Principal.

WOGAN

WOGAN (continued)

SERIES 5
Duration: 40 minutes.

	Holding / Source
20.12.1985 **Wogan's Christmas Box**	DB / 1"

With Paul Daniels, Judi Dench, Les Dawson, Aled Jones.

25.12.1985 **Dynasty Special**	DB / 1"

Research Irene Levin; series producer Frances Whitaker; produced by Jon Plowman.

17.11.1986	DB / 1"

With George Benson, Jeremy Cherfas, Father Christmas, Malcolm Jamieson, Dudley Moore.

19.12.1986 **Wogan's Christmas Box**	DB / 1"

The programme seems to have consisted of highlights of BBC Christmas programmes to come.
With Gillian Taylforth, Peter Dean, Julie Walters.

24.12.1986 "Dallas special"	DB / 1"

With Linda Gray, Larry Hagman.

31.12.1986	DB / 1"

Series producer Frances Whitaker; produced by Peter Estall; directed by Tony Newman.
With June Brown, Alan Coren, Samantha Fox, Spitting Image Puppets, Allo Allo Cast.

21.12.1988 **Wogan In Pantoland**	DB / 1"

Duration: 35 minutes.
Programme associate Jeff Thacker; series producer Peter Weil; produced by Jon Plowman; directed by John Burrowes.
With Christopher Biggins [as Chris Biggins], Bernard Cribbins, Jim Davidson, Roy Hudd, Little and Large, Barbara Windsor.

27.12.1989 **Wogan's Christmas Fancy Dress**	DB / 1"

With John Cole, Brian Glover, Linda Lusardi, Julia McKenzie, Colin Moynihan, Leslie Nielson, Jon Pertwee, Gary Wilmot.

20.12.1991	DB / 1"

Trails for Christmas programmes.
Executive producer Peter Estall; produced by Natalie Elsey.
With Letitia Dean, Ross Kemp, Pauline Collins & John Alderton, Patsy Kensit, Chicken Shed Theatre Co, The Inspirational Choir.

See also: TERRY IN PANTOLAND (BBC)

WOLVES, WITCHES AND GIANTS

A Honeycomb Animation production for Carlton UK. Transmission details are for the Central region. Duration: 15 minutes.

SERIES 2

	Holding / Source
09.12.1996 **Cinderella 1**	D3 / C1
16.12.1996 **Cinderella 2**	D3 / C1

THE WOMAN IN BLACK

A Central production. made in association with Capglobe Ltd. Transmission details are for the Central region. Duration: 102 minutes.

Young solicitor Arthur Kidd is sent to Crythin Gifford, a small coastal town, to tie up the estate of a Mrs Drablow. Despite warnings from the locals, he goes to the Drablow house and encounters the ghostly Woman in Black.

Adapted by Nigel Kneale; based on the book by Susan Hill; executive producer Ted Childs; produced by Chris Burt; directed by Herbert Wise.

Adrian Rawlins (Arthur Kidd), Bernard Hepton (Sam Toovey), David Daker (Josiah Freeton), Pauline Moran (Woman in Black), David Ryall (Sweetman), Clare Holman (Stella Kidd), John Cater (Arnold Pepperell), John Franklyn-Robbins (Reverend Guest), Fiona Walker (Mrs Toovey), William Simons (John Keckwick), Robin Weaver (Bessie), Caroline John (Bessie's Mother), Joseph Upton (Eddie Kidd), Steven Mackintosh (Rolfe), Andrew Nyman (Jackie), Robert Hamilton (Mr Girdler), Trevor Cooper (Farmer), Alison King (Gypsy Woman), Peter Guinness (Stall Holder), Timothy Block (Lorry Man), Albie Woodington (Fireman), Mary Lawlor (Gypsy Child), Clare Thomson (Gypsy Child).

	Holding / Source
24.12.1989	DB / C1

THE WOMBLES

A Filmfair production for a variety of companies (see details below).

Commissioned by Central. Transmission details are for the Central region.
Main regular credit(s):   Music by Mike Batt.

	Holding / Source
20.12.1991 **The Wandering Wombles**	C1 / C1

Commissioned by Carlton. made in association with Cinar. Transmission details are for the Central region.

	Holding / Source
06.04.1999 **Womble Winterland**	DB / C1
07.01.2000 **New Year! New You!**	DB / C1

THE WOODEN OVERCOAT (RADIO)

A BBC production for BBC Radio 4. Transmission details are for BBC Radio 4. Duration: 60 minutes.

Adapted by Mark Gatiss; based on a book by Pamela Branch; play production by Kate McAll.

David Tennant (Peter), Julia Davis (Fan), David Benson (Rex), Alan David (Beesum), Graham Crowden (Colonel Quincey), David Ryall (Creaker), John Castle (Flush), Tom Allen (Benji Cann), Barbara Kirby (Mrs Barratt), Katherine Jakeways (Lilli).

	Holding / Source
22.12.2007	DA /

A WORCESTER CAROL

A BBC Birmingham production for BBC 1. Transmission details are for BBC 1. Duration: 30 minutes.

Main regular credit(s): Produced and directed by Edmund Marshall.

Main regular performer(s): Choir of Worcester Cathedral, Christopher Robinson, Harry Bramma.

	Holding / Source
17.12.1973	J / 2"
22.12.1974	J / 2"

THE WORD

A Planet 24 production for Channel 4. Transmission details are for Channel 4. Duration: 52 minutes.

Main regular performer(s): Terry Christian (Host), Dani Behr (Host).

SERIES 1

A 24 Hour Productions production.

	Holding / Source
21.12.1990	1" / 1"

With Steve Coogan, Wilf Lunn, Janice Long, Omar, Dean Sullivan, Jacqui Stallone, The Stranglers, Martin Thomson.

SERIES 3

	Holding / Source
18.12.1992	D3 / D3S

With Dolph Lundgren, Nigel Benn, Jesus Jones, Nu Colors.

SERIES 4

Main regular credit(s): Edited by Paul Ross.

	Holding / Source
24.12.1993 **Christmas Special (compilation)**	D3 / D3S

The wildest, weirdest and wackiest moments from this year's show.

With Mark Lamarr, Huffty.

SERIES 5

Main regular credit(s): Edited by Duncan Grey.

	Holding / Source
23.12.1994	D3 / D3S

Gossip, music and celebrity interviews.

With Alex Langdon, Michelle Gayle, The Wombles, Corrosion of Conformity.

WORDS AND PICTURES

A BBC production for BBC 1. Transmission details are for BBC 1.

	Holding / Source
28.11.1977 **Christmas Tree Fairy**	DB / 2"

	Holding / Source
29.11.1982 **Sam's Christmas Tree**	DB-D3 / 2"

Transmission details are for BBC 2.

	Holding / Source
28.11.1990 **A Bear For Christmas**	DB / 1"

Transmission details are for BBC 2.

	Holding / Source
27.11.1996 **Father Christmas' Feet**	DB / D3S

THE WORKS

A Red Rooster Films production for S4C. Transmission details are for Channel 4. Duration: 70 minutes.

Written by Kerry Crabbe; produced by Linda James; directed by Stephen Bayly.

Glenn Sherwood (Davey Williams), Dafydd Hywel (Sam), Iola Gregory (Miss Puw), Brinley Jenkins (Mr Frazer), Glan Davies (Harry), Alun A. P. Brinley (Basil), Catrin Llwyd (Miss Price), Olly Williams (Mr Morgan), Kevin Staples (Alun Rose).

	Holding / Source
26.12.1986	1" / 1"

WORLD OF SPORT

Produced for ITV by a variety of companies (see details below). Transmission details are for ITV.

	Holding / Source
24.12.1977	DBSEQ / 2"

With Eric Morecambe.

THE WORLD TONIGHT

A Granada production. Transmission details are for the Granada region. Duration: 25 minutes.

		Production No	Holding / Source
21.12.1965	Christmas 1965	P487/40	R1 /
23.12.1965	Peace On Earth	P487/27	R1 /

What is the mood of America at war?

Executive producer Tim Hewat; produced by John Macdonald.

With Bill Biery (Reporter In New York), Jane Nicholls, Stewart Wilensky, Al Wertheimer.

THE WORST CHRISTMAS OF MY LIFE

A Hat Trick production for BBC 1. Transmission details are for BBC 1. Duration: 30 minutes.

Christmas starts badly for accident-prone Howard before becoming much, much worse. With the inevitability of passing seasons it's only a matter of time before Howard found himself naked, on his boss's front door step, in front of some very surprised carol singers.

Main regular credit(s): Written by Mark Bussell and Justin Sbresni; script supervisor Janice Brackenridge; music by Nina Humphreys; executive producers Margo Stylianides and Simon Wilson; head of production Jessica Sharkey; produced by Mark Bussell and Justin Sbresni; directed by Mark Bussell and Justin Sbresni.

Main regular cast: Ben Miller (Howard Steel), Sarah Alexander (Mel Steel), Alison Steadman (Angela), Geoffrey Whitehead (Dick), Janine Duvitski (Eve), Ronald Pickup (Fraser), Kim Wall (Mitch).

		Holding / Source
19.12.2006	23rd December	DB / DBSWF

With Sian Thomas (Nicola), Michael Bertenshaw, Philip Bird, Jody Halse, Sarah-Jayne Steed, Luing Andrews.

21.12.2006	Christmas Eve	DB / DBSWF

With Selina Cadell, Paul Brooke, Paul Mari, Geoffrey McGivern.

22.12.2006	Christmas Day	DB / DBSWF

With James Puddephatt, Michael Cochrane, Carmen Du Sautoy, Oliver Milburn.

WORZEL GUMMIDGE

A Southern Television production. Transmission details are for the HTV region.

Main regular credit(s): Written by Keith Waterhouse and Willis Hall; produced and directed by James Hill.

Main regular cast: Jon Pertwee (Worzel Gummidge).

SERIES 3

Main regular credit(s): Designed by Hazel Peiser; executive producer Lewis Rudd.

		Holding / Source
27.12.1980	A Cup O' Tea An' A Slice O' Cake	C1 / C1

Duration: 50 minutes.

All-singing, all-dancing Worzel Gummidge special which examines the important role that scarecrows play in helping Santa Claus find his way back to the North Pole on Christmas morning. The programme also explains what happens when one particular scarecrow - in this case, Worzel Gummidge - literally deserts his post.

Music by Denis King; choreography by Geraldine Stephenson.

With Una Stubbs (Aunt Sally), Megs Jenkins (Mrs Braithwaite), Geoffrey Bayldon (The Crowman), Barbara Windsor (Saucy Nancy), Charlotte Coleman (Sue), Jeremy Austin (John), Mike Berry (Mr Peters), Norman Mitchell (Police Constable Parsons), Thorley Walters (Colonel Bloodstock), Billy Connolly (Bogle McNeep), Bill Maynard (Sergeant Beetroot), Frank Marlborough (Atkins), Laurence Harrington (Cyril), Michael Ripper (Mr Shepherd), Bill Pertwee (Lorry Driver), Wayne Norman (Pickles Bramble).

WOULD I LIE TO YOU?

A Zeppotron production for BBC 1. Transmission details are for BBC 1. Duration: 30 minutes.

SERIES 7

Performer(s): With Rob Brydon (Host), Lee Mack (Team Captain), David Mitchell (Team Captain).

		Holding / Source
23.12.2013	Would I Lie To You At Christmas?	HD/DB / HDC

Executive producers Peter Holmes and Ruth Phillips; series producer Rachel Ablett.

With Miranda Hart, Miles Jupp, Stephen Mangan, Barry Cryer.

WYCLIFFE

Produced for HTV by a variety of companies (see details below). Transmission details are for the Central region. Duration varies - see below for details.

Main regular credit(s): Based on characters created by W. J. Burley.

Main regular cast: Jack Shepherd (Detective Superintendent Charles Wycliffe).

Holding / Source

27.12.1997 **Dance Of The Scorpions**   DB / V1SW

An United Film & TV Productions production. Duration: 79 minutes.

Written by Arthur McKenzie; script supervisor Elaine Matthews; script editor Barbara Cox; director of photography John Walker; art director Hayden Matthews; designed by Andrew Purcell; associate producer Keith Webber; executive producer Michele Buck; produced by Michael Bartley; directed by Paul Harrison.

With Jimmy Yuill (Detective Inspector Kersey), Helen Masters (Detective Inspector Lane), Tim Wylton (Franks), Lynn Farleigh (Helen Wycliffe), Michael Attwell (Detective Chief Constable Stevens), Rory Wilton, Leslie Grantham, Stevan Rimkus, Lesley Duff, Fine Time Fontayne, Jane Slavin, Rachel Shelley, Philip Glenister, Marc Warren, Daniel Moynihan, Celia Breckon [as Celia Breckan], Timothy Carlton, Dugald Bruce-Lochart, Heidi Monsen, Fiona England, Terry Arnold, Leonard Preston, Bill Cashmore, Ron Mills, Jane Galloway, Simon Cook, Tim Faraday.

Y SIOE FAWR FACH

A BBC Wales production for BBC 1 Wales. Transmission details are for BBC 1 Wales. Duration: 40 minutes.

Puppet pantomine.

	Holding / Source
25.12.1976	J / 2"

THE YEAR WE WON THE ASHES

A Mentorn production for Channel 4. Transmission details are for Channel 4. Duration: 105 minutes.

Executive producer Sam Collyns; produced and directed by Olly Lambert.

Mark Nicholas (Presenter).

	Holding / Source
31.12.2005	DB / DBSW

THE YEOMEN OF THE GUARD

An ATV production. Transmission details are for the ATV midlands region. Duration: 100 minutes.

Written by W.S. Gilbert and Arthur Sullivan; designed by Bryan Holgate; produced and directed by Stanley Dorfman.

Tommy Steele (Jack Point), Terry Jenkins (Colonel Fairfax), Tom McDonnell (Sir Richard Cholmondley), Dennis Wicks (Wilfred Shadbolt), Paul Hudson (Sergeant Meryll), David Fieldsend (Leonard Meryll), Laureen Livingstone (Elsie Maynard), Della Jones (Phoebe Meryll), Hilary Western (Dame Carruthers / Anne Collinskate), New World Philharmonic Orchestra, English National Opera.

	Holding / Source
23.12.1978	1" / 2"

YES MINISTER

A BBC production for BBC 2. Transmission details are for BBC 2.

Main regular credit(s): Written by Anthony Jay and Jonathan Lynn; drawings by Gerald Scarfe; theme music by Ronnie Hazlehurst.

Main regular cast: Paul Eddington (Jim Hacker, M.P.), Nigel Hawthorne (Sir Humphrey Appleby), Derek Fowlds (Bernard Woolley).

	Holding / Source
17.12.1984 **Party Games**	DB-D3 / 2"

Duration: 60 minutes.

Designed by Rochelle Selwyn; production manager Brian Jones.

With John Nettleton (Sir Arnold Robinson), Diana Hoddinott (Annie), James Grout, Peter Jeffrey, Philip Stone, André Maranne, Ludovic Kennedy, Anthony Pedley, David Warwick, Laura Calland, Roger Davidson, David Howey, Bernard Losh, Roger Ostime, John Pennington, Martyn Read, Rex Robinson.

See also: THE FUNNY SIDE OF CHRISTMAS (BBC)

YOU ARE HERE

A Big Talk Productions production for Channel 4. Transmission details are for Channel 4. Duration: 40 minutes.

Dark comedy set in a remote English village named Here. The small community is outraged when a local bigwig plans to sell off the village.

Written by Mark Freeland, Matt Lucas, David Walliams and Robert Popper; additional material by Keith Allen, Sally Phillips, John Thomson, Paul Kaye and Jon Ronson; produced by Nira Park; directed by John Birkin.

Keith Allen (Ken), Sally Phillips (Lara), Matt Lucas (Pat Magnet), David Walliams (Murray Moffat), Nigel Planer (Sheldon Cohen), Kate Robbins (Rita Cohen), John Thomson (Peter Keggie), Alfie Owen-Allen (Peter's Son), Paul Putner (Martin Moffat), Paul Kaye (Detective Inspector Lindsay De Paul), Eddie Marsan (Nigel Pubis), Peter Serafinowicz (Doctor Phillip Phillips), Ricky Grover (The Man).

	Holding / Source
30.12.1998 **Whatever Happened To Baby Jo?**	DB / DBSWF

YOU HAVE BEEN WATCHING... DAVID CROFT

Alternative/Working Title(s): THE MAN WHO MADE DAD'S ARMY

A BBC production for BBC 2. Transmission details are for BBC 2. Duration: 60 minutes.

David Croft died in September, aged 89.

Executive producer Caroline Wright; produced by Alexandra Briscoe.

David Croft (Subject Of Tribute).

	Holding / Source
27.12.2011	HD/DB / HDC

YOU RANG, M'LORD?

A BBC production for BBC 1. Transmission details are for BBC 1. Duration varies - see below for details.

Main regular credit(s):	Written by Jimmy Perry and David Croft; theme music by Jimmy Perry, Roy Moore, Bob Monkhouse and Paul Shane; produced by David Croft.
Main regular cast:	Paul Shane (Alf Stokes), Jeffrey Holland (Jim Twelvetrees), Su Pollard (Ivy Teesdale (aka Stokes)), Donald Hewlett (Lord George Meldrum), Michael Knowles (The Honourable Teddy), Bill Pertwee (Police Constable Wilson), Brenda Cowling (Mrs Blanche Lipton), Perry Benson (Henry Livingstone).

Made in association with Seven Network, Australia.

Holding / Source
29.12.1988 — DB / 1"

Duration: 49 minutes.

A new hour-long comedy performed in front of an audience, in which Lord Meldrum takes on a new butler who in turn engages his daughter as parlour-maid.

Designed by David Buckingham and Paul Cross; directed by David Croft.

With Mavis Pugh (Lady Lavender), Susie Brann (Poppy), Catherine Rabett (Cissy), Barbara New (Mabel), Angela Scoular (Lady Agatha), Sarah Mortimer, Ken Morley, Alf Pearson, John D. Collins, Karen Westwood, Cameron Stewart, Bob Appleby, Yvonne Marsh.

THE YOUNG VISITERS

A James Hill production for Channel 4. Transmission details are for Channel 4. Duration: 85 minutes.

Adapted by James Hill; based on a book by Daisy Ashford; music by John Cameron; produced and directed by James Hill.

Tracey Ullmann (Ethel Monticue), Alec McCowen (J. M. Barrie), Carina Radford (Daisy Ashford), Kenny Ireland (Alfred Salteena), John Harding (Bernard Clark), Bryan Pringle (Minnit The Butler), Colin McCormack (Horace The Footman), Anthony Milner (Edward Procurio), John Bett (Earl of Clincham), John Standing (Prince of Wales), Leonard Maguire (Archbishop of Canterbury), Kate Percival (Lady Herring), Annette Badland (Bessie Top).

Holding / Source
25.12.1984 — C1 / C1

THE YOUNG VISITERS

A BBC production for BBC 1. made in association with Deleste Productions Ltd. Transmission details are for BBC 1. Duration: 90 minutes.

Adapted by Patrick Barlow; based on a book by Daisy Ashford; executive producers Ian Gordon, Jim Broadbent, Pippa Harris and Laura Mackie; produced by Christopher Hall; directed by David Yates.

Jim Broadbent (Alfred Salteena), Hugh Laurie (Lord Bernard Clark), Lyndsey Marshall (Ethel Monticue), Bill Nighy (Earl of Clincham), Geoffrey Palmer (Minnit), Simon Russell-Beale (Prince of Wales), Sophie Thompson (Bessie Topp), Sally Hawkins (Rosalind), Richenda Carey (Lady Gay Finchling), Anne Reid (Angelique Monticue), Tom Burke (Horace), Guy Henry (Mr Domonic), Patrick Barlow (Archbishop of Canterbury), Janine Duvitski (Queen Victoria), Anabel Barnston (Daisy Ashford), Jenny Adams-Barbaro (Singer), Adam Godley (Procurio), Gaye Brown (Hotel Manageress), Roger Frost (Hotel Porter), Richard Beale (Man On Train), James Warrior (Station Master), Shaughan Seymour (Lifeguard), Alan Bennett (Narrator).

Holding / Source
26.12.2003 — DB / V1SW

YOU'RE ONLY HUMAN WITH JEFF GREEN

A Watchmaker Productions production for Carlton. Transmission details are for the Central region. Duration: 25 minutes.

Written by Jeff Green; executive producer Elaine Bedell; produced by Helen Morris and Andy Rowe.

Jeff Green, Rhona Cameron.

Holding / Source
27.12.1998 — DB / DBS

YOU'RE ONLY YOUNG TWICE

A Yorkshire Television production. Transmission details are for the ATV midlands region. Duration: 25 minutes.

Main regular credit(s):	Written by Pam Valentine and Michael Ashton; music by Dennis Wilson; produced and directed by Graeme Muir.
Main regular cast:	Peggy Mount (Flora Petty), Pat Coombs (Cissie Lupin), Lally Bowers (Dolly Love), Diana King (Mildred Fanshaw), Charmian May (Miss Milton).

SERIES 3

Main regular cast:	With Johnny Wade (Roger), Georgina Moon (Finchy).

Holding / Source
24.12.1979 Christmas At Paradise Lodge — B / 2"
23.12.1980 Twas The Night Before Christmas — B / 2"

A seasonal visit to Paradise Lodge, that hilarious home for ladies in retirement.

Designed by Roy Coldrick.

With Georgina Moon (Miss Finch), Johnny Wade (Roger), Glynn Edwards (Burgular), Raymond Bowers (Policeman).

YULETIDE FESTIVAL OF CAROLS AND MUSIC

An ABC production. Transmission details are for the ABC north region.

Holding / Source
25.12.1960 — J /
24.12.1961 — R1N /

Duration: 40 minutes.

Outside broadcast director David Southwood.

With Ronald Woan (Choirmaster), Mair Jones (Harp), Noel Rawsthorne (Organist).

Z CARS

Alternative/Working Title(s): CRIME PATROL

A BBC production for BBC 1. Transmission details are for BBC. Duration varies - see below for details.

Main regular credit(s): Format by Troy Kennedy Martin; theme music by Bridget Fry and Fritz Spiegl.

SERIES 3
Duration: 50 minutes.
Main regular credit(s): Produced by David E. Rose.

	Production No	VT Number	Holding / Source
25.12.1963 "It Never Rains...."	22/63/0586	35/T/20169	DB-R1|t / R3

A disagreement amongst thieves leads to the uncovering of a fraud involving illegal petrol that is finally stopped by Barlow and Watt on Christmas Eve.

Written by John Hopkins; script associate John Gould; film camera Charles Lagus; designed by Stanley Morris; directed by Terence Williams; casebook material C. N. Lindsay.

With James Ellis (Police Constable Lynch), Colin Welland (Police Constable Graham), Robert Keegan (Sergeant Blackitt), Stratford Johns (Detective Chief Inspector Charles Barlow), Terence Edmond (Police Constable Ian Sweet), Michael Forrest (Detective Constable Hicks), Frank Windsor (Detective Sergeant John Watt), Brian Blessed (Police Constable Smith), Joseph Brady (Police Constable Weir), Kate Brown (Shirley Burscough), Gwen Cherrell (Mary Watt), Norman Rossington (Ted Drysdale), Jon Rollason (Len Drysdale), Sheila Grant (Jenny Drysdale), John Woodvine (Andy Nolan), Joe Greig (Trevor Upton), Robert McBain (Mr Reardon), Jean Marlow (Mrs Reardon), Bud Ralston (Mr Bellew), Derek Benfield (Mr Healey), Anthony Hall (Publican), John Dawson (Mr Stringer), Margaret Ward (Mrs Stringer), Carole Lorimer (Helen Stringer), The Swinging Blue Jeans (The Beat Group).

Also telerecorded on 16/TU/20169.

	Production No	VT Number	Holding / Source
01.01.1964 " ...And A Happy New Year"	22/63/0588	16/TU/20927	HD-R1 / LiveR1

Duration: 48 minutes.

New Year's Eve. A vicious mugger is exposed when he keeps a membership card from the mugged man's wallet, and a burglar falls down a manhole, drunk off duty.

Written by John Hopkins; film camera Kenneth Westbury; fight arranger Derek Ware; designed by Frederick Knapman; directed by Christopher Morahan; casebook material William Prendergast.

With James Ellis (Police Constable Lynch), Colin Welland (Police Constable Graham), Michael Forrest (Detective Constable Hicks), Stratford Johns (Detective Chief Inspector Charles Barlow), Robert Keegan (Sergeant Blackitt), Terence Edmond (Police Constable Ian Sweet), Kate Allitt (Pamela Earnshaw), Jeffrey Ashby (Bonny Lucas), Leon Eagles (Greenhalgh), Edwin Brown (Satterthwaite), Katherine Story (Penelope Warren), Laidlaw Dalling (Doctor), Ann Rushbrooke (Nurse), John Rapley (Edward Rowen), Arthur Mayne (William Kenny), David Webb (Alexander Gibson), Peter Lawrence (Paisley), Stan Jay (Spooner), Lionel Stevens (Harper), Terry Bale (Norris), Julian Brooks (Regular in Pub), Geoffrey Hibbert (Denton), John Scott Martin (Preece), Billy Moss*.

SERIES 4
Duration: 50 minutes.
Main regular credit(s): Produced by David E. Rose.

	Production No	VT Number	Holding / Source
30.12.1964 **First Foot**	21/1/4/2177	35/4T/25221	R3|t / R3

Written by Alan Plater; directed by Paul Bernard.

With Brian Blessed (Police Constable Smith), Joseph Brady (Police Constable Smith), James Ellis (Detective Constable Lynch), Frank Windsor (Detective Sergeant John Watt), Robert Keegan (Sergeant Blackitt), Carole Schofield (Muriel Parr), Lynne Furlong (Woman Police Constable Stacey), Geoffrey Whitehead (Police Constable Baker), Colin Welland (Police Constable Graham), Kenneth Goodlet, Joyce Adcock, Glynn Edwards, Jennifer Wilson, John Landry, Nicholas Evans, Sandra Bryant, Michael Golden, Anthony Baird, Yootha Joyce, Petra Markham, Trevor Rhone, Barbara Everest, Jolyon Booth.

SERIES 6
Duration: 25 minutes.

Family Affair

Duration: 25 minutes.

	Production No	VT Number	Holding / Source
25.12.1967 **Episode 1**	23/1/7/9337	VTM/4T/42352	J / 40

Written by Geoffrey Tetlow; produced by Ronald Travers; directed by Paddy Russell.

With James Ellis (Sergeant Bert Lynch), Joseph Brady (Police Constable Weir), Stephen Yardley (Police Constable May), David Daker (Police Constable Culshaw), John Slater (Detective Sergeant Stone), Bernard Holley (Police Constable Newcombe), Jennie Goossens (Radio Girl), Pauline Taylor (Woman Police Constable Parkin), Joss Ackland (Detective Inspector Todd), Doreen Aris, Thelma Whiteley, Maureen Norman, Bryan Thanner, David Hammonds.

	Production No	VT Number	Holding / Source
26.12.1967 **Episode 2**	23/1/7/9338	VTM/4T/42415	J / 40

Written by Geoffrey Tetlow; produced by Ronald Travers; directed by Paddy Russell.

With David Daker (Police Constable Culshaw), John Slater (Detective Sergeant Stone), Stephen Yardley (Police Constable May), James Ellis (Sergeant Bert Lynch), Joseph Brady (Police Constable Weir), John Wreford (Police Constable Jackson), Jennie Goossens (Radio Girl), Bernard Holley (Police Constable Newcombe), Doreen Aris, Bryan Thanner, David Hammonds, Thelma Whiteley, Ann Lancaster, Joan Francis.

Should Auld Acquaintance

Duration: 25 minutes.

	Production No	VT Number	Holding / Source
01.01.1968 **Episode 1**	23/1/7/9333	VTM/4T/42773	J / 40

Written by Donald Ford and Derek Ford; produced by Ronald Travers; directed by Tristan de Vere Cole.

With Joss Ackland (Detective Inspector Todd), Bernard Holley (Police Constable Newcombe), James Ellis (Sergeant Bert Lynch), Joseph Brady (Police Constable Weir), Stephen Yardley (Police Constable May), John Wreford (Police Constable Jackson), Pauline Taylor (Woman Police Constable Parkin), Patrick Connell, Derrick Gilbert, Clare Jenkins, Michael Turner, Gerald Taylor, Colin Warman, Ray Mort.

Z CARS (continued)

	Production No	VT Number	Holding / Source
02.01.1968 **Episode 2**	23/1/7/9334	VTM/4T/42784	J / 40

Written by Donald Ford and Derek Ford; produced by Ronald Travers; directed by Tristan de Vere Cole.

With Joss Ackland (Detective Inspector Todd), Bernard Holley (Police Constable Newcombe), James Ellis (Sergeant Bert Lynch), Joseph Brady (Police Constable Weir), Stephen Yardley (Police Constable May), Pauline Taylor (Woman Police Constable Parkin), Derrick Gilbert, Clare Jenkins, Toke Townley, Kenneth Watson, Douglas Cummings, Michael Turner, Ray Mort, Pat Rossiter, Martin Carrigan, Richard Hampton, Julian Wilson, Darrell Scott, Stephanie Cole.

Blame It On Father Christmas

Duration: 25 minutes.

	Production No	VT Number	Holding / Source
23.12.1968 **Episode 1**	23/1/8/3164	VTM/6/LT/48537	J / 62

Written by David Ellis; produced by Richard Beynon; directed by Tristan de Vere Cole.

With John Woodvine (Detective Inspector Witty), John Slater (Detective Sergeant Stone), James Ellis (Sergeant Bert Lynch), Paul Angelis (Police Constable Bannerman), Ron Davies (Police Constable Roach), Bernard Holley (Police Constable Newcombe), Pauline Taylor (Woman Police Constable Parkin), Joe Gladwin, Diana Payan, Jonathan Greene, John Arnatt, Barbara Ashcroft.

	Production No	VT Number	Holding / Source
24.12.1968 **Episode 2**	23/1/8/3165	VTM/6LT/48536	J / 62

Written by David Ellis; produced by Richard Beynon; directed by Tristan de Vere Cole.

With John Woodvine (Detective Chief Inspector Witty), John Slater (Detective Sergeant Stone), James Ellis (Sergeant Bert Lynch), Paul Angelis (Police Constable Bannerman), Ron Davies (Police Constable Roach), Bernard Holley (Police Constable Newcombe), Pauline Taylor (Woman Police Constable Parkin), Joe Gladwin, Kate Lansbury, Jonathan Cohen, Sharon Campbell, Anthony Peplow.

For Auld Lang Syne

Duration: 25 minutes.

	Production No	VT Number	Holding / Source
30.12.1968 **Episode 1**	23/1/8/3180	VTM/6LT/48953	J / 62

Written by Allan Prior; produced by Richard Beynon; directed by Derek Martinus.

With John Slater (Detective Sergeant Stone), James Ellis (Sergeant Bert Lynch), Paul Angelis (Police Constable Bannerman), Ron Davies (Police Constable Roach), Bernard Holley (Police Constable Newcombe), Archie Duncan, Alex MacAvoy, Dermot MacDowell, Ben Edwards, Jack Watson, Rosalind Elliot, John Wright, Gerald Cowen.

	Production No	VT Number	Holding / Source
31.12.1968 **Episode 2**	23/1/8/3180	VTM/6LT/48954	J / 62

Written by Allan Prior; produced by Richard Beynon; directed by Derek Martinus.

With John Woodvine (Detective Inspector Witty), John Slater (Detective Sergeant Stone), James Ellis (Sergeant Bert Lynch), Bernard Holley (Police Constable Newcombe), Paul Angelis (Police Constable Bannerman), Ron Davies (Police Constable Roach), Archie Duncan, Alex MacAvoy, Jack Watson, Rosalind Elliot, John Scott Martin, Joanna Anin.

The Best Day Of The Year

Duration: 25 minutes.

	Production No	VT Number	Holding / Source
22.12.1969 **Episode 1**	23/1/9/9024	VTM/6LT/55154	J / 62

Written by Allan Prior; produced by Ron Craddock; directed by Hugh David.

With Paul Angelis (Police Constable Bannerman), James Ellis (Sergeant Bert Lynch), Douglas Fielding (Police Constable Quilley), Derek Waring (Detective Inspector Goss), John Slater (Detective Sergeant Stone), Bernard Holley (Police Cosntable Newcombe), John White, Roy Pattison, Karin MacCarthy, John Bindon, Joe Gladwin, Patrick Harvey, John Rolfe.

	Production No	VT Number	Holding / Source
23.12.1969 **Episode 2**	23/1/9/9025	VTM/6LT/55155	J / 62

Written by Allan Prior; produced by Ron Craddock; directed by Hugh David.

With Douglas Fielding (Police Constable Quilley), James Ellis (Sergeant Bert Lynch), John Slater (Detective Sergeant Stone), Paul Angelis (Police Constable Bannerman), Bernard Holley (Police Constable Newcombe), Derek Waring (Detective Inspector Goss), John White, John Bindon, Joe Darrall, Jeff Becker-Jones, Joe Gladwin.

Christmas Is Coming

Duration: 25 minutes.

	Production No	VT Number	Holding / Source
21.12.1970 **Episode 1**	23/4/0/9118	VTC/6HT/63304/E	J / 2"

Written by Bill Barron; produced by Ron Craddock; directed by Noel Lidiard-White.

With Derek Waring (Detective Inspector Goss), James Ellis (Sergeant Bert Lynch), Douglas Fielding (Police Constable Quilley), June Watson (Woman Police Constable Cameron), Barry Lowe (Police Constable Horrocks), John Swindells (Police Constable Bowman), Michael Forrest, Frank Mills, Jean Trend, Trisha Mortimer.

	Production No	VT Number	Holding / Source
22.12.1970 **Episode 2**	23/4/0/9119	VTC/6HT/63305/ED	J / 2"

Written by Bill Barron; produced by Ron Craddock; directed by Noel Lidiard-White.

With Derek Waring (Detective Inspector Goss), James Ellis (Sergeant Bert Lynch), Douglas Fielding (Police Constable Quilley), June Watson (Woman Police Constable Cameron), Barry Lowe (Police Constable Horrocks), John Swindells (Police Constable Bowman), Michael Forrest, Frank Mills, Jean Trend, Trisha Mortimer.

Duration: 25 minutes.

	Production No	VT Number	Holding / Source
29.12.1970 **Let Nothing You Dismay**	23/4/0/9120	VTC/6HT/63441/ED	J / 2"

Written by Leslie Duxbury; produced by Ron Craddock; directed by Raymond Menmuir.

With Derek Waring (Detective Inspector Goss), James Ellis (Sergeant Bert Lynch), Bernard Holley (Police Constable Newcombe), Douglas Fielding (Police Constable Quilley), Ian Cullen (Police Constable Skinner), Jennie Goossens (BD Girl), Dermot Kelly, Jack Watson, Royston Tickner, Valerie Lush, Eric Francis, Maryann Turner, Virginia Clay.

See also: SOFTLY SOFTLY (BBC)

Z CARS

ZZZAP!

A Media Merchants production for Meridian. Transmission details are for the Central region. Duration: 14 minutes.

Main regular credit(s):   Executive producer Richard Morss.
Main regular cast: Richard Waites (Cuthbert Lilly).

SERIES 4

		Holding / Source
29.11.1996	**Christmas Annuals**	D3 / D3S
06.12.1996	**Christmas Annuals**	D3 / D3S
13.12.1996	**Christmas Annuals**	D3 / D3S
20.12.1996	**Christmas Annuals**	D3 / D3S

		Holding / Source
16.12.1997	**Christmas Annual**	D3 / D3S

HOLDING AND SOURCE FORMAT CODES AND DESCRIPTIONS

1"	625 line PAL colour 1" videotape.
1"S	625 line PAL colour 1" videotape - transmitted in stereo.
2"	625 line PAL colour 2" videotape.
2"-C1	625 line PAL colour 2" videotape from 16mm colour film.
40	405 line monochrome 2" videotape.
62	625 line monochrome 2" videotape.
B	Betacam SP videotape.
B1	16mm monochrome film.
B1N	16mm monochrome negative film.
B3	35mm monochrome film.
B-R1	Betacam SP videotape taken from 16mm monochrome telerecording.
BS	Betacam SP videotape, recorded in stereo.
BSF	Betacam SP 625 line colour videotape which has been filmised - transmitted in stereo.
C1	16mm colour film.
C15W	16mm colour film - transmitted in dolby 5.1 and widescreen.
C1S	16mm colour film - transmitted in stereo sound.
C1SSW	16mm colour film - transmitted in stereo surround widescreen.
C1SW	16mm colour film - transmitted in stereo sound and widescreen.
C3	35mm colour film.
C3S	35mm colour film - transmitted in stereo.
C3SW	35mm colour film - transmitted in stereo widescreen.
D2	D2 digital videotape.
D2S	D2 digital videotape - transmitted in stereo.
D3	D3 digital videotape.
D3S	D3 digital colour videotape - transmitted in stereo sound.
D3SW	D3 digital colour videotape - transmitted in stereo widescreen.
D5H-DB/DB	D5 digital videotape high definition 1080 line master taken from 625 line Digital Betacam with 625 line Digital Betacam backup copy for use on standard definition transmissions.
DA	Digital Audio.
DAS	Digital Audio - Stereo.
DB	Digital Betacam videotape.
DB-1"	Digital Betacam videotape taken from 625 line PAL colour 1" videotape.
DB-2"	Digital Betacam videotape taken from 625 line PAL colour 2" videotape.
DB-4W	Digital Betacam videotape copy of converted 405 to 625 line monochrome videotape.
DB-D3	Digital Betacam copy of a D3 digital videotape.
DB-D3-2"	Digital Betacam copy of a D3 dub of a 625 line PAL colour 2" videotape.
DB-D3-R1	Digital Betacam copy of a D3 digital videotape transfer of a 16mm monochrome telerecording.
DB-DV	Digital Betacam copy of a 625 line PAL domestic format videotape including VHS, Betamax and Philips 1500.
DB-NT	Digital Betacam videotape taken from 525 line NTSC colour videotape.
DB-R1	Digital Betacam videotape taken from 16mm monochrome film recording.
DB-R3	Digital Betacam videotape taken from 35mm monochrome film recording.
DBS	Digital Betacam 625 line colour videotape - transmitted in stereo.
DBSF	Digital Betacam 625 line colour videotape which has been filmised - transmitted in stereo.
DBSW	Digital Betacam 625 line colour videotape - transmitted in stereo widescreen.
DBSWF	Digital Betacam 625 line colour videotape which has been filmised - transmitted in stereo widescreen.
DB-T3	Digital Betacam videotape taken from 35mm colour film telerecorded from 625 line colour videotape.
DV	625 line PAL domestic format videotape including VHS, Betamax and Philips 1500.
FNK	The format on which it is held, or on which it was recorded, is not known.
HD/DB	High Definition master with 625 line Digital Betacam backup copy for use on standard definition transmissions.
HD-B3	High Definition videotape from 35mm monochrome film (reverse anamorphic).
HDC	HD-CAM or HD-CAM SR high definition master.
HD-R1	High Definition videotape taken from 16mm monochrome film telerecording (reverse anamorphic)
J	Does not exist.
Live	Live transmission.
LivePAL	Live transmission - recorded onto 625 line PAL colour videotape off air.
LiveR1	Live transmission - telerecorded onto 16mm monochrome film off air.
MII	MII videotape.
NR	Not Recorded.
NT	525 line NTSC colour videotape.
R1	16mm monochrome film telerecorded from 405/625 line videotape or a live transmission.

HOLDING AND SOURCE FORMAT CODES AND DESCRIPTIONS

R3	35mm monochrome film telerecorded from 405/625 line videotape or a live broadcast.
T1	16mm colour film telerecorded from 625 line colour videotape.
UM	625 line U-Matic videotape copy.
V1	16mm colour film - edited on videotape.
V1S	16mm colour film - edited on videotape - transmitted in stereo.
V1SSW	16mm colour film - edited on videotape - transmitted in stereo surround widescreen.
V1SW	16mm colour film - edited on videotape/computer - transmitted in stereo widescreen.

ADDITIONAL FORMAT CODES

|a - Held on Domestic Audio
|c - Held as Script
|m - Holding Monochrome
|n - Held at NFTVA
|p - Holding Private
|t - Holding Telesnap
N - Only survives as film negative
PO - Picture only (no sound survives)
SEQ - Although the complete programme is missing, some sequences survive
SO - Sound only (no picture survives)

www.ingramcontent.com/pod-product-compliance
Lightning Source LLC
Chambersburg PA
CBHW081421300426
44108CB00016BA/2274